S0-ARP-709

Social Justice in a Diverse Society

Rita C. Manning
René Trujillo
San Jose State University

Mayfield Publishing Company
Mountain View, California
London • Toronto

Copyright © 1996 by Mayfield Publishing Company

All rights reserved. No portion of this book may be reproduced in any form or by any means without written
permission of the publisher.

Library of Congress Cataloging-in-Publication Data

Social justice in a diverse society : [compiled by] Rita
Manning & René Trujillo
    p.   cm.
  ISBN 1-55934-411-3
  1. Social justice.   2. Civil rights — United States.
  3. United States — Social conditions — 1980 –
  I. Manning, Rita C.   II. Trujillo, René.
JC575.S58   1996
303.3'72 — dc20   95-34562
                                 CIP

Manufactured in the United States of America
10 9 8 7 6 5 4 3 2 1

Mayfield Publishing Company
1280 Villa Street
Mountain View, California 94041

Sponsoring editor, James Bull; *production editor,* Merlyn
Holmes; *copyeditor,* Linda Purrington; *text designer,*
Wendy LaChance; *cover image,* © José Ortega; *cover
designer,* Donna Davis; *manufacturing manager,* Amy
Folden. The text was set in 10/12 Minion by ColorType
and printed on 45# Glatfelter Restorecote by R. R. Don-
nelley & Sons Co.

 Printed on acid-free, recycled paper.

 # Contents

Preface

Philosophers have long been interested in the subject of justice and questions of how to achieve a just society when differences exist between people. This anthology provides a way to think about the unique set of problems and challenges entwined in questions of justice and injustice in the United States in the 1990s. We think philosophy plays an important role in how we live and structure our society, and this anthology is meant to give both theoretical and practical guidance in responding to injustice in our society.

We begin each section with some basic questions of what would comprise a just society and then try to identify and analyze specific problems of injustice in our diverse society. We believe injustice is most often experienced in virtue of one's membership in a particular group, so we have identified those groups which face the most serious injustice: racial minorities, women, the poor, gays and lesbians, and persons with disabilities.

It is not enough to understand the theories about justice and injustice; readers must also see how they play out in actual experiences. We have focused on a few issues of paramount concern to our diverse society. As readers look at these issues, it is our hope that you will better understand the theories about justice and injustice and will be able to use what you learn to come to some conclusions about the issues.

Many people are left with feelings of despair and powerlessness when they recognize the pervasive character of injustice, but we believe there is real reason for optimism. There are strategies for social change that have been responsible for tremendous improvement, but these strategies must themselves survive philosophical and moral scrutiny. Hence, we end our anthology with a look at strategies for social transformation that seem realizable for the United States in the closing years of the twentieth century.

In putting this anthology together, we were guided by two aims: one was to give the reader an understanding of justice and injustice as well as an opportunity to see these concepts in action and a chance to reflect about how best to achieve a more just society. Our second aim was to allow members of the groups we have identified as suffering serious injustice to speak for themselves. When you begin to see injustice from the point of view of the people suffering from it, you may see the issues and responses from their point of view also.

There are disadvantages to this strategy. Readers may feel they are not getting enough "mainstream" views. This disadvantage is easy to address by reading and listening to those views; they will not be difficult to find, and instructors may well include such readings in their courses. The other disadvantage is that some readers will not be willing to hear so many points of view that they do not sympathize with or understand. All readers will find some of the views in this anthology new, thought-provoking, or even alarming, but we think that engaging these points of view is crucial to developing an understanding of the whole issue.

Philosophy has a mission that Socrates identified when he described himself as the gadfly of Athens: to hold up a mirror to society so that we can see ourselves in all our glory but with our warts and blemishes too. This is a constructive process, and without it we will never be able to engage in the kind of open and honest debate that we must have in order to transform our society into a more just one.

Acknowledgments

Many people have helped to bring this anthology to fruition. First, we thank the many contributors who allowed us to include their work. Our editor at Mayfield, Jim Bull, was a constant source of inspiration and constructive criticism. The book is better conceived, organized, and written because of his commitment to the project. We also thank Merlyn Holmes, production editor, and Linda Purrington, copyeditor, for their help during the production process. Mary Ann Shukait provided invaluable research. The following reviewers helped us fine tune the project: Ellen Fox, Illinois Institute of Technology; Karen Hanson, Indiana University; Jim Hill, Valdosta State University; Joan McGregor, Arizona State University; and Anita Silvers, San Francisco State University. Anu Arsalo worked tirelessly to unravel the permissions mysteries that came daily by fax and phone. Van Martin saw order in the earlier chaos and helped us to produce a book that was vibrant despite its leaner size. All the students in the Social Justice class at San Jose State University, who read many of the articles at earlier stages of the project, were of invaluable assistance. San Jose State provided both release time and funds for research and clerical assistance. We thank you all. Finally, we thank our families, whose encouragement and support made this project possible. Any omissions, confusions, or exaggerations are entirely our own.

PART 1

Social Justice

Any discussion of social justice must begin with an account of what would count as a just society. Philosophers have had a great deal to say about this, and hence it is impossible to include all their views in any anthology. This section reflects an understanding of what the central issues about justice are in a liberal democratic society such as that of the United States. The word "liberal" now has a set of connotations that make its use rather confusing. Many have come to understand a "liberal" as someone who would advocate a strong government presence in helping people to achieve a minimally decent life. In this section, we return to the more basic idea of what a liberal is, an idea that had its genesis in the work of such philosophers as Kant, Locke, and Mill. In this sense, a liberal is someone concerned with individual rights. Although liberals differ on what those rights are, how to rank them by priority, and how to adjudicate conflicts among them, it is generally agreed that liberty and equality have emerged as the most talked-about rights within this liberal tradition.

The first chapter in this section includes various discussions of what equality is, why it ought to be part of the just state, and ways in which people might meet this ideal. It also begins to address the tension between liberty rights and rights to equality. Libertarians, for example, argue that if we take liberty rights seriously, we would never interfere in social arrangements, no matter how unequal, that result from legitimate exercises of liberty rights. Others have argued that we must be concerned about equality in a just society and hence must find a way to balance liberty and equality. Bruce Ackerman provides an account of the liberal state that balances liberty and equality. He argues that both negative rights (rights understood as restrictions on the behavior of others) and positive rights (rights that imply duties to create more equal opportunities) ought to be part of the just liberal state.

Liberalism has usually accepted a distinction between the public and private arenas because of its concern to protect the individual exercise of choice. Susan Moller Okin notes that this distinction puts the family, which has been for many women the locus of their experience of injustice, outside the sphere of political debate. Her strategy is to show how liberalism can accommodate these concerns and place the family within the sphere of justice.

The liberal political tradition has been the subject of much debate, with Marxism providing both a powerful critique and an alternative vision of the just society. Rodney Peffer provides a Marxist account of justice, showing how it saves the most important moral value of liberalism (the importance of the individual) and responds to what he and other Marxists take to be its central failure (the inequality that liberalism often seems to justify). He gives a central role to equality, justifying state intervention to achieve a true equality of opportunity for all its citizens.

It is helpful to see how the often abstract ideas of philosophers handle real issues. Michael Katz gives us a powerful account of how our public school system fails to achieve the goal of equality, and he makes some suggestions about what it would mean to take equality seriously.

In the next chapter, we return to the notion of individual rights. Central to this notion is a picture of what an individual is and why people ought (or ought not) attribute rights to individuals. Alan White argues that moral rights belong to each of us in virtue of our status as persons. Elizabeth Wolgast worries that understanding all human interaction in terms of competing rights is confusing and often counterproductive. She offers examples where the appeal to rights is inappropriate. René Trujillo gives us a powerful example of how rights talk functions in a particular social context, showing how the concept of human rights motivated a change in the Spanish treatment of indigenous people during what is often referred to as the Age of Discovery.

The final concept discussed in this part of the book is autonomy. A strong sense of individuality is often described as a bedrock value in the United States, but people are not at all clear on what that concept involves. Does it refer to the strong, silent, self-sufficient (usually male) types who populate the big screen? Does it have its roots in a uniquely American experience? Rather than mine the cultural landscape for an understanding of this difficult concept, Chapter 2 offers Gerald Dworkin's careful description of what would be a philosophically defensible account of autonomy. Communitarian critics have noted the social problems caused by an excessive reliance on individuality, and Seyla Benhabib presents this line of thought. She defends a version of autonomy that centers it in the social organization within which people act.

Other concepts are also useful in discussions of social justice, and many of these concepts will be introduced in the other sections. After you have read the readings in this first part of the book you will have a foundation for thinking about social justice.

Justice and Equality

THE LIBERAL STATE

Bruce A. Ackerman

In this defense of the liberal state, Bruce Ackerman describes the central problem of civic society and offers four principles for its solution. The problem is that humans live under conditions of scarcity and typically resort to competition and the resulting inequality to respond to these conditions. The solution is to adopt four principles: rationality, consistency, neutrality, and undominated equality. (Source: Social Justice and the Liberal State *by Bruce Ackerman, pp. 3–30. Copyright © 1980 by Yale University Press. Reprinted by permission of Yale University Press.)*

1. The Struggle for Power

So long as we live, there can be no escape from the struggle for power. Each of us must control his body and the world around it. However modest these personal claims, they are forever at risk in a world of scarce resources. Someone, somewhere, will — if given the chance — take the food that sustains or the heart that beats within. Nor need such acts be attempted for frivolous reasons — perhaps my heart is the only thing that will save a great woman's life, my food sufficient to feed five starving men. No one can afford to remain passive while competitors stake their claims. Nothing will be left to reward such self-restraint. Only death can purchase immunity from hostile claims to the power I seek to exercise.

Not that all life is power lust. Social institutions may permit us to turn to better things — deterring the thief and killer while our attention is diverted. Even when our power is relatively secure, however, it is never beyond challenge in a world where total demand outstrips supply. And it is this challenge that concerns us here. Imagine someone stepping forward to claim control over resources you now take for granted. According to her, it is she, not you, who has the better right to claim them. Why, she insists on knowing, do you think otherwise? How can you justify the powers you have so comfortably exercised in the past?

A first response mixes annoyance with fear. Rather than justifying my claims to power, the urge is strong to suppress the questioner. There can be no question that her question is threatening: As soon as I begin to play the game of justification, I run the risk of defeat. I may not find it so easy to justify the powers I so thoughtlessly command. Perhaps the conversation will reveal that it is not she, but I, who is more properly called the thief in this affair. And if this is so, is it not better to suppress the conversation before it begins? This is no ordinary game; it may reveal that my deepest hopes for myself cannot be realized without denying the rights of others. If I succeed in suppressing the questioner, I may hope to live as if my power had never been challenged at all.

It is a tempting prospect which becomes more seductive as my effective power increases. Power corrupts: the more power I have, the more I can lose by
trying to answer the question of legitimacy; the more
power I have, the greater the chance that my effort at
suppression will succeed—at least for the time that
remains before I die. Yet this is not the path I mean to
follow; I hope to take the question of legitimacy seriously: What would our social world look like if no one
ever suppressed another's question of legitimacy,
where every questioner met with a conscientious attempt at an answer?

2. Culture and Right

And so we come to our first principle:

> *Rationality:* Whenever anybody questions the
> legitimacy of another's power, the power holder
> must respond not by suppressing the questioner
> but by giving a reason that explains why he is more
> entitled to the resource than the questioner is.

The first thing to notice about this formula is its generality. No form of power is immune from the question of legitimacy. By framing the Rationality requirement in this way, I hope to avoid the familiar
errors of partial critique: the blindness of the partisan
of laissez faire who fails to recognize that the private-
property owner must legitimate his power no less than
the government bureaucrat; the blindness of the communist who avoids this first mistake only to insulate
the power of Party leaders from the test of dialogue.

Nor are the institutions of property and government the only means by which some people get what
others want. Each person comes into the world with a
set of genetic abilities that helps determine his relative
power position; each is born into a particular system
of education, communication, and exchange that
gives some great advantages over others. Finally, there
is the tremendous fact of temporal priority: one generation can transform the cultural and material possibilities available to its successors—can deny them
life itself. None of these power structures can be accorded the immense privilege of invisibility; *each* person must be prepared[1] to answer the question of le-

gitimacy when *any* of his powers is challenged by *anyone* disadvantaged by their exercise.

This comprehensive insistence on dialogue forces
a break with one of the great myths of philosophy—
the idea of a "state of nature." While the myth takes
many forms, it always tells a story in which actors acquire "rights" that are prior to, and independent of,
their social interaction. How this trick takes place is a
matter of some dispute—some say by a silent act of
unchallenged appropriation, others merely stipulate
the "rights" their actors possess when they "first" encounter one another in a social situation. The important point, though, is the myth's assertion that people
have "rights" even before they confront the harsh fact
of the struggle for power.

In contrast, the Rationality principle supposes
that rights have a reality only *after* people confront the
fact of scarcity and begin to argue its normative implications. If you were completely confident that no
one would ever question your control over X, you
would never think of claiming a "right" over it; you'd
simply use it without a second thought. If you were
transported to an alien planet peopled by entities
whose symbolic code (if it existed) you could not
crack, there would be no point in claiming "rights" in
regulating your dealings with them. Instead, brute
force would remain the only option open.[2] Rights are
not the kinds of things that grow on trees—to be
plucked, when ripe, by an invisible hand. The only
context in which a claim of right has a point is one
where you anticipate the possibility of conversation
with some potential competitor. Not that this conversation always in fact arises—brute force also remains
a potent way of resolving disputes. Rights talk presupposes only the *conceptual* possibility of an alternative
way of regulating the struggle for power—one where
claims to scarce resources are established through a
patterned cultural activity in which the question of legitimacy is countered by an effort at justification.

Since the principle of Rationality conceives this
dialogue as the foundation of all claims of right, it requires a subtler, but no less decisive, break with a second familiar myth—the idea of "social contract."[3]
Although the parties to a social contract must speak
to one another while negotiating its terms, this conversation is understood in instrumental terms only. It

does not constitute the ground of the rights that emerge from the bargaining process but simply serves as a means to induce the parties to give their consent to the contract terms. Indeed, the most compelling versions of the contract myth try to cut through the chatter of precontractual negotiation by designing a bargaining situation in which no rational actor has any sensible choice but to sign on the dotted line. Protracted discussion about contract terms at the founding convention is often positively harmful—it can reveal strategic possibilities for bluffing and coalition formation that may make the terms of the contract indeterminate. And it is only each party's promise to abide by the contract that constitutes the basis of his social rights and duties—not the talk that precedes or follows the magic moment of promising.

In contrast, Rationality does not refer to some privileged moment of promising—existing apart from ordinary social life—as the foundation of everyday claims of right. It points instead to an ongoing social practice—the dialogue engendered by the question of legitimacy—as itself the constituting matrix for any particular claim of right. At a later point, I shall defend this view at greater length.[4] For now, though, it is enough to state the essence of my proposal: Rather than linking liberalism to ideas of natural right or imaginary contract, *we must learn to think of liberalism as a way of talking about power, a form of political culture.*

But there is another face to Rationality; one that deals with substance, not method. Consider, for example, the Nazi who answers the Jew's question of legitimacy by saying, "Jews are an intrinsically worthless people whose very existence is an insult to the morally superior races." While it is tempting to exclude such responses as ir-Rational under the first principle, I mean resolutely to resist. Rather than isolating the distinctive features of liberalism all by itself, Rationality simply points the would-be liberal in the general direction in which such a discovery is to be found: *If there is anything distinctive about liberalism, it must be in the kinds of reasons liberals rely on to legitimate their claims to scarce resources.* Nazis are not liberals because there is *something* about the reasons they give in support of their claims that is inconsistent with the organizing principles of liberal power talk. And what might that something be?

Before I try to answer this question, permit me a single preliminary move that is, substantively speaking, even emptier than the last. As a second principle in my model of legitimacy, I insist that like cases be treated alike.

> *Consistency.* The reason advanced by a power wielder on one occasion must not be inconsistent with the reasons he advances to justify his other claims to power.

Throughout the book, I shall remain content with an unanalyzed understanding of this second principle. The critical thing is that a power holder cannot justify his claim to X by saying, "Because Aryans are better than Jews" and then turn around and justify his claim to Y by announcing, "All men are created equal." Of course, Consistency simply requires the power wielder to resolve this tension in one way or another; it does not demand that he give up his Nazism. Thus, when standing alone, Consistency hardly has an obvious claim to its preeminence—a state that killed all Jews is more illegitimate than one that muddled its way to saving some. But Consistency does not stand alone. Its function is to safeguard the intelligibility of the dialogue demanded by Rationality. When a Jew is told that he is being killed because "Jews are intrinsically vicious beasts," he will be appalled by the answer he has received, *but he will find no difficulty understanding it.* This is true, however, only because the Jew decodes the utterance with the aid of the interpretive assumption that the Nazi would not knowingly contradict himself. If the Nazi's assertion were set against the background of an equally emphatic declaration that "Jews are as good as the rest of us," it would be wrenched into a context that puts its status as a reason into question. When a person is willing to assert R and $\overline{R}$ simultaneously, he has not given two reasons for his action. He has provided some noise that adds up to no argument at all.

3. Constrained Power Talk

The first two principles do one important thing—establish the centrality of reason giving to the concept of right. Whenever nothing intelligible can be said in justification of a power, its exercise is illegitimate. A sustained silence or a stream of self-contradictory noises are decisive signs that something very wrong is going on.

All this, it may be said, is very true but very weak stuff. Yet appearances are deceiving; with the addition of one final ingredient, we may brew a political solution with enormous resolving power. The missing idea is that particular kinds of conversation are often constrained by special rules restricting what may be appropriately said within them. We could hardly run our everyday lives if every utterance opened us up to an all-consuming conversation about everything under the sun. Even the most egregious boor recognizes that a conversation with the telephone operator is not a suitable vehicle for a blow-by-blow account of his life. It is this familiar sense of conversational constraint[5] that I mean to put to a new use. Just as there are constraints imposed in other conversations, I also want to constrain the dialogues in which people talk to one another about their claims to power. Not that I wish to constrain power talk by appealing to social etiquette. Notions of conventional propriety presuppose the legitimacy of the power structure, rather than vice versa. The question, instead, is whether fundamental philosophical arguments can be advanced to justify one or another constraint on power talk.

Suppose, for a moment, that the answer is Yes. Suppose that I can convince you that no argument of type Z should be permitted to count as a good argument in conversations about power. Given this achievement, it is easy to see how my first two principles can be transformed into a mighty philosophical engine. While it is a safe bet that *some* reason can be found to justify *any* power relationship, P_i, all bets are off once the propriety of a conversational constraint, Z, is conceded. For it might then turn out that the *only* reasons that can be advanced in support of P_i are among those eliminated by Z. Thus, once Z has done its work of exclusion, *all that may be left is silence.* And once a claimant to a scarce resource has been reduced to silence, Rationality requires him to recognize that his claim to power is illegitimate. In short, I propose to demonstrate the illegitimacy of a wide variety of power structures by reducing their proponents to silence. Call this way of delegitimating a power structure the method of *constrained silence.*

Now if this method can be deployed as a powerful engine of political appraisal, everything will depend on the choice of Z. To serve its purpose, Z must be designed with two ends in mind. First, the more reasons Z excludes, the more likely it is that at least some power structures will be unmasked as indefensible within the constraint it imposes. Ceteris paribus, the bigger the Z, the better. But this concern with quantity is worthless without an assessment of Z's quality. Thus, we will get nowhere with constraints of the form "*Only* reasons of Z type are good reasons in this conversation." For when the proponent of such a Z is asked to justify this constraint, he will be obliged to explain why Z is better than all competing substantive principles. Yet it is just this conversation which the constraint sought to avoid in the first place.

Things get more interesting if the constraint does not pretend to specify both necessary and sufficient conditions for a good reason but contents itself with stipulating only necessary conditions: "*No Z is a good reason*" rather than "*Only Z is a good reason.*" When framed in this way, a conversational constraint may seem plausible to many different people who bitterly disagree about lots of other things. For example, both communists and liberals may agree that Nazi arguments (defined in some clear way by Z) are bad reasons, though they reach this judgment by means of very different arguments — call them $\{c\}$ and $\{l\}$, respectively. Even more striking, the arguments contained in $\{c\}$ may be logically inconsistent with those contained in $\{l\}$. Nonetheless, *both groups will converge on Z by a process of argument that makes sense to them.*

Of course, the proposed "anti-Fascist" constraint is not, on its merits, a terribly incisive idea. Hitler may not have been smart enough to think of all the arguments for genocide. So if Z were carefully framed to exclude only the particular claims made by Hitler and his henchmen, our Z might not prevent someone from coming up with a new reason for genocide. If we are to hope for success from the method of constrained silence, we cannot frame our Z with a particular historical experience in mind but must proceed from more general philosophical considerations. Only in this way can we formulate a conversational constraint of such breadth that the proponents of particular power structures will find themselves speechless when called upon to defend their legitimacy.

But there are transparent dangers in broadening the constraints. The broader the Z, the harder it will be to frame a principle that will seem plausible to people with otherwise different views of the world. Nonetheless, the effort is not obviously hopeless; indeed, my object is to persuade you that the liberal tradition is best understood as precisely such an effort to define and justify broad constraints on power talk. Thus, I do not wish to claim any great novelty for the Z that will preoccupy us. To the contrary, constraints similar to mine can be found in any writer working within the historical liberal tradition.[6] The novelty is simply my claim that the notion of constrained conversation should serve as *the* organizing principle of liberal thought. When others have sought to give liberalism systematic form, they have turned to other ideas — most notably contract or utility — to serve as their organizing principle. In contrast, I hope to convince you that the idea of constrained conversation provides a far more satisfactory key to the liberal enterprise. And once the lock is turned, the liberal tradition will reveal unsuspected resources of methodological rigor and substantive depth.

4. Neutrality and Convergence

My particular Z taps the liberal's opposition to paternalism. The germ of the idea is that nobody has the right to vindicate political authority by asserting a privileged insight into the moral universe which is denied the rest of us. A power structure is illegitimate if it can be justified only through a conversation in which some person (or group) must assert that he is (or they are) the privileged moral authority:

Neutrality. No reason is a good reason if it requires the power holder to assert:

1. that his conception of the good is better than that asserted by any of his fellow citizens, *or*
2. that, regardless of his conception of the good, he is intrinsically superior to one or more of his fellow citizens.

I will defer important questions of interpretation to emphasize the main point — which is the way Neutrality promises to satisfy the two conditions we require for a potent Z. Since the breadth of the exclusion imposed by Neutrality is obvious, the critical question is whether the formulation suffers the defects of this virtue: Does its very breadth make it impossible to generate arguments that will justify its acceptance as a fundamental constraint on power talk?

Not at all. It is downright easy to think of several weighty arguments in support of Neutrality. The first is a skeptical argument: While everybody has an opinion about the good life, none can be known to be superior to any other. It follows that anyone who asserts that either he or his aims are intrinsically superior doesn't know what he's talking about. Yet this is precisely the move barred by Neutrality.

But there is no need to be a skeptic before you can reason your way to Neutrality. Even if you think you can *know* something about the good life, there are several good reasons for imposing liberal constraints on political conversation. Most obviously, you might think that you can only learn anything true about the good when you are free to experiment in life without some authoritative teacher intervening whenever he thinks you're going wrong. And if you think this, Neutrality seems made to order. But, once again, this view is only one of many that will provide a plausible path to Neutrality. Even if you don't think you need to experiment, you may adopt a conception of the good that gives a central place to autonomous deliberation and deny that it is possible to *force* a person to be good. On this view, the intrusion of non-Neutral argument into power talk will seem self-defeating at best — since it threatens to divert people from the true means of cultivating a truly good life. Assume, finally, that you think you know what the good life is and that it is of a kind that can be forced on others; then the only question is whether the right people will be doing the forcing. A single glance at the world suggests that this is no trivial problem. People adept in gaining power are hardly known for their depth of moral insight; the very effort to engross power corrupts — at least if your theory of the good embraces any number of familiar moral ideals.

Not that it is absolutely impossible to reason yourself to a rejection of Neutrality. Plato began systematic political philosophy with such a dream; medieval churchmen thought there were good reasons to confide ultimate secular authority to the pope. Only they recognized — as modern totalitarians do not — the depth of the reconceptualization required before a breach of Neutrality can be given a coherent justification. It is not enough to reject one or another of the basic arguments that lead to a reasoned commitment to Neutrality; one must reject *all* of them. And to do this does not require a superficial change of political opinions but a transformation of one's entire view of the world — both as to the nature of human values and the extent to which the powerful can be trusted to lead their brethren to the promised land.

In proposing Neutrality, then, I do not imagine I am defending an embattled citadel on the fringe of modern civilization. Instead, I am pointing to a place well within the cultural interior that can be reached by countless pathways of argument coming from very different directions. As time passes, some paths are abandoned while others are worn smooth; yet the exciting work on the frontier cannot blind us to the hold that the center has upon us.

5. Is Liberalism Consistent?

By the time we complete our journey, I will investigate the conceptual routes to Neutrality with greater care. Before we engage in extensive road repair, however, simple prudence requires us to attend to sober guides who warn us that all these highways lead nowhere. According to them,[7] liberalism is incapable of formulating a self-consistent response to the struggle for power. It is doomed instead to lurch from one self-contradiction to another in a vain effort to save the myth of Neutrality. Rather than making the same mistakes again, we must have the courage to discard the myth of Neutrality and search for a Something whose nature can only be glimpsed darkly through the gray mist that liberalism has bequeathed us. And though this Something is certainly elusive, yet surely it is better than the self-contradictory Nothing that liberalism provides. On then, into the darkness — for only there will we find our hidden Humanity.

Now I take this argument seriously. Yet, like all arguments, this one can be no better than its premises. The choice is between an obscure Something and a

self-contradictory Nothing only if it is conceded that liberalism is intellectually bankrupt, that it can propose no self-consistent way of resolving power conflict. And this is something that liberalism's critics are more apt to assert than prove. Not that I blame them: it is hard to prove a negative, and given their intimations of bankruptcy, they understandably prefer to spend their time on more constructive activities. For us, however, the case stands otherwise. There is a simple way to establish, once and for all, that the accusation of bankruptcy is wrong. And that is to provide a single example of a liberal theory equal to the conceptual task of providing a Neutral order to the struggle for power. In terms of our model of legitimacy, all we need propose is a single system for regulating power conflicts that can be justified by:

1. a self-consistent set of reasons (principles one and two) that

2. do *not* violate either branch of the Neutrality principle.

If there is even one such system of power relations, P_i, then the claim that liberalism is bankrupt is simply wrong. Of course, it may well turn out that any P_i that supports a thoroughgoing Neutral dialogue looks very different from the power structures within which we live our lives. But this means that liberalism, properly understood, requires a more sweeping critique of the existing power structure than is sometimes supposed. Rather than an empty bankrupt, liberalism emerges as a coherent set of ideals of enormous critical force.

Indeed, I may make an even stronger claim if the critics are only 99.99 percent right in their accusations of bankruptcy. Assume, for example, that a complete survey of the millions of possible reasons for claiming power reveals that *all but one* of them involved the claimant saying that he was intrinsically better than the next guy or that his ends in life were especially worthwhile. The discovery of such a unique reason, R, would have just the opposite consequences of bankruptcy. As we have seen, people may be persuaded by any number of very different reasons to embrace the ideal of Neutral discourse. Since R happens to be the *only* reason that passes the test of Neutral dialogue, anybody who has been convinced (for whatever reason) to accept my three principles of legitimacy has *no choice* but to accept R.[8] Thus, we may glimpse the old liberal dream of a philosopher's stone by which a commitment to a particular procedure of dispute resolution — here, the process of constrained conversation — can be transformed into a commitment to particular substantive outcomes.

Not that such a demonstration would induce instant conversion among those who would lead us to authoritarianism in the name of Humanity. Yet there would no longer be any hope of a cheap victory over some pitiful blob of self-contradiction. Instead, the partisans of authority will confront at least one well-specified power structure, P_i, that can be rationally defended within the conversational constraints imposed by liberal principles. Before they can reject P_i, they must proceed to do battle on far more difficult terrain — where success requires them to free themselves from the complex web of argument that binds them to Neutrality and Rationality.

But, alas, there is no a priori reason to think that things will work out so neatly. While the constraints imposed by Neutrality are broad, they may nonetheless permit more than one R to break the conversational barrier. Rather than pointing to a single kind of substantive discourse, liberalism would then be the name of a family of different substantive arguments that may lead to very different substantive conclusions concerning the right way to resolve one or another power conflict. Nonetheless, while the P_is may differ substantively, they all will share one family resemblance: all can be fathered by a rational conversation within Neutral constraints. Of course, the fact of common paternity will not then suffice to satisfy all the requirements of political evaluation. We would then be required to reach a new stage of liberal theory and articulate criteria for choosing the most promising child within the liberal family.

Before liberalisms can multiply, however, we must first establish that the ground yields any fruit whatever. Thus, most of this book will try to show how one particular R can be articulated in a way that is conceptually equal to the task of regulating all important forms of power struggle. While I do not claim that mine is the only R that will turn the trick, I can report that my own searches among the universe of possible reasons has not turned up a competitor. Unless somebody develops a formal proof of my R's uniqueness, however, the search for alternative liberal rationales must continue apace.

6. Liberalism and Equal Respect

Imagine that somebody finds that your claim to some resource interferes with his effort to pursue his good. Any resource will do — your questioner may challenge your right to use your body or some natural object or some cultural artefact or whatever. Anyway, he wants it and issues a conversational challenge:

Q: I want X.

A: So do I! And if I have my way, I'll use force to stop you from taking X.

Q: What gives you the right to do this? Do you think you're better than I am?

A: Not at all. But I think I'm just as good.

Q: And how is that a reason for your use of power?

A: Because you *already* have an X that's at least as good as mine is. If you take this X as well, you'd be better off than I am. And that's not right. Since I'm at least as good as you are, I should have power over an X that is at least as good as yours is.

Q: But haven't you just violated Neutrality?

A: Not at all. Neutrality forbids me from saying that I'm any better than you are; it doesn't prevent me from saying that I'm at least as good.

Q: But if I don't get this extra X, I won't achieve my ends in life.

A: That's not a good reason for your getting X, because the reason I'm claiming X is that I too want it to achieve my ends in life. And do you imagine that it is intrinsically more important for you to achieve your ends in life than it is for me?

Q: I can't say that within the constraints imposed by Neutrality.

A: So, then, what *can* you say in defense of your effort to get a better X than I have?

Q: And if I can't answer that?

A: Then you must recognize that I've given you a Neutral answer to your question of legitimacy, while you have backed up your power play with nothing that looks like a reason.

My purpose in producing this script must be kept clearly in mind. For the present, I do not care what you think of the *merits* of A's argument. Perhaps, upon finding out more facts about A, you will deny that he's as good as Q; perhaps, on thinking further, you will reject the idea that a person's assertion of *moral equality* implies a right to equality in *worldly possessions*. No such objection, however, defeats my purpose in presenting the script for your inspection. To pass the Neutrality test, I do not need to claim that A has presented a *convincing* argument for initial equality; instead, I need only establish that A has presented an *intelligible* argument on behalf of initial equality while keeping within Neutral ground rules. Even if you *disagree* with A when he says, "Since I'm at least as good as you are, I should have an X that is at least as good as yours is," there is something intelligible here with which to disagree. The only thing, then, that I want to say on behalf of my script is that *it can be said.*

And this, my reader, you already know to be true. For you've just read the dialogue and found no difficulty understanding it.

Yet this small concession is larger than it seems. It places the burden of articulation squarely upon those who seek an inegalitarian distribution of worldly advantage. While they may have all sorts of premonitions of superiority, they cannot engross a greater share of power within a liberal state unless they justify their claims in a way that passes the Neutrality constraint. And if they fail to articulate a Neutral justification, they can only succeed in the conversation over power by justifying a change in the conversational ground rules — explaining how they have reasoned their way free of all the arguments that lead to Neutrality. And if they fail in that, they will have no choice but to attack Rationality, joining with Nietzsche in celebrating the power of the powerful to transcend all talk of good and evil.

And if they do declare themselves supermen, they surely will understand me when I say that I'm willing to fight for my rival understanding of the world.

7. Finishing the Conversation

But I have gotten ahead of myself. There is lots of work to do before the stakes can get so high as this. To see why, consider two ways in which the first script is

incomplete. First, the dialogue does not end with an unconditional conversational victory by A, but simply establishes that Q cannot expect to win his claim so long as he remains silent. There is, however, no certainty that Q will remain silent. Instead, he can respond in one of two ways. On the one hand, he may reject A's claim that Q's X is at least as good as A's is. On the other hand, Q may accept A's characterization of their power relation and try to frame a Neutral reason why his X *ought* to be better than A's. If Q succeeds in either conversational move, the burden of conversational initiative will shift back to A — obliging him to explain, consistently with Neutrality, why he finds Q's reason unpersuasive; and so on, back and forth, until somebody fails to meet his conversational burden. It is only when this occurs that the silenced party's claim has been unmasked as illegitimate in a liberal state. To use a helpful legalism, our initial script merely describes a way that A might establish a prima facie case in support of the legitimacy of his power over X. A complete theory, however, must move beyond this first, prima facie stage of the conversation and describe the kinds of power structures that would be legitimated in a dialogue in which the parties are free to talk until they have nothing more to say.[9]

As this dialogue unfolds, I hope to show that it resolves a central ambivalence that has greatly weakened the liberal analysis of power. The ambiguity concerns the place of equality in a just society. On the one hand, certain forms of equal treatment — say, formal equality in the administration of justice — have been central to the liberal tradition. On the other hand, there has been a recurrent fear of a nightmare world where all human diversity has been destroyed in the name of an equality that levels everyone to the lowest common denominator. Haunted by these fears, liberals have too often accustomed themselves to an awkward position on the slippery slope, unable to explain what in principle distinguishes the equalities they cherish from those they detest. My thesis is that an extended conversation is precisely the therapy required to dispel this nightmare equality from our vision. While, as we have seen, Neutral dialogue begins with the affirmation of a right to equal shares, subsequent conversational moves will define a liberal conception of equality that is compatible with a social order rich in diversity of talents, personal ideals, and forms of community. The articulation of this distinctive conception of equality—I shall call it *undominated equality*—will be one of my major purposes.

To accomplish it, however, will require a remedy for a second kind of incompleteness in the initial script. Here the concern is not with the prima facie character of the text but with the dim background against which Q and A recite their lines. The stage directions simply describe two citizens struggling over some scarce resource, X, which both of them desire. But in the world as we know it, the struggle occurs over more concrete resources and takes many different forms: assailant versus victim; trespasser versus property owner; dissident versus bureaucrat; child versus parent; handicapped versus talented; and so forth. To understand the practical implications of liberal conversation, we must grasp the way it can discipline the concrete power struggle of our everyday lives.

In bringing the script down to earth, moreover, we must be careful about the way we fill in the dialogic background. While it is impossible to analyze every concrete institution that regulates the struggle for power, we must resist the temptation of a grossly simplified account. This is, perhaps, the most common mistake made by partisans of the liberal tradition. Time and again, these people speak as if the only significant power in society comes out of the smoking typewriter of a government bureaucrat. While they are tireless in their efforts to constrain this power by exacting standards of Neutrality, they often react with shocked surprise at the very idea of subjecting the powers of "private" citizens to an identical scrutiny. Yet, first of all, we live in a world in which the powers of government are routinely called upon to enforce (as well as define) all of these "private" entitlements. Without this reinforcement, there is no reason to think that those presently advantaged by the distribution of "private" rights would remain so. Second, even if something like the status quo could be maintained without a central government, Q could still ask A to justify his possession of "private" powers that Q also wants to exercise. And unless A can frame a Neutral answer, the three principles require him to recognize that his "private" power is illegitimate. Of course, in the absence of a central government, A might find it very easy to suppress Q and maintain control over "pri-

vate" powers he cannot justify. But this merely shows that a decentralized system of "private" power can be just as illegitimate as one in which a tyrannical central government holds sway. The task, then, is to deny *any* fundamental power structure the priceless advantage of invisibility—to define a world where *all* power is distributed so that each person might defend his share in a conversation that begins (but does not end) with the move: "because I'm at least as good as you are."

Notes

1. Is it enough to be *prepared* to answer the question of legitimacy? Must we drop everything and *actually engage* in a conversation *whenever* anybody challenges any of our claims to power? It would be silly to spend our entire lives in a discussion of the single question of legitimacy—at the expense of all talk and action on behalf of our personal ideals. Nonetheless, I cannot be permitted to evade questioning to such an extent that others are uncertain whether they have the power to call me to account at mutually convenient times and places. . . .

2. Of course, if the aliens were triumphant, you might try to warn earth that they did not recognize any "rights"—but that is plainly a derivative use of the term. . . .

3. While "state of nature" and "social contract" are commonly joined in familiar classics, it is not obvious that this is a necessary connection. Thus, Rawls tries to free contract from the fallacies of the state of nature, while Nozick returns the compliment by rescuing the state of nature from contract. Since I shall be rejecting both myths on their merits, I need not consider the extent to which, as a conceptual matter, they are indissolubly tied together. . . .

4. See Part Four of *Social Justice and the Liberal State.*

5. Elaborated illuminatingly by H. P. Grice, "Logic and Conversation," in Donald Davidson and Gilbert Harman, eds., *The Logic of Grammar* (Encino, Calif.: Dickinson, 1975), pp. 64–153.

6. Moreover, there are encouraging signs of a renewed appreciation of these constraints in recent liberal theorizing, see, e.g., Ronald Dworkin, "Liberalism" in Stuart Hampshire, ed., *Public and Private Morality* (Cambridge: Cambridge Univ. Press, 1978) pp. 113–43. No less encouraging is the emphasis upon conversational legitimation prevailing among the most creative workers in the Marxist tradition. See, e.g., Jurgen Habermas, *Legitimation Crisis* (Boston: Beacon Press, 1975).

7. See, e.g., Roberto Mangabeira Unger, *Knowledge and Politics* (New York, Free Press: 1976); Robert Paul Wolff,

In Defense of Anarchism (New York: Harper & Row, 1970).

8. The style of argument is similar to Kenneth Arrow's in his *Social Choice and Individual Values* (New Haven: Yale University Press, 2d ed., 1963). Like him, I propose to constrain collective choice by a set of principles each of which, taken individually, seems relatively uncontroversial. Given these constraints, I then inquire whether any principle for collective decision can be found that does not violate at least one of them. Unlike Arrow, however, I shall conclude that there is at least one *R* that does satisfy all constraints.

This conclusion, however, is not inconsistent with the famous negative result derived by Arrow's General Impossibility Theorem. Arrow works within the voluntarist tradition and is concerned with the problem of aggregating individual *preferences* into a consistent collective choice; I am working within the rationalist tradition and want to determine whether any of the *reasons* that can be given in defense of power survive plausible conversational constraints. If anything, Arrow's impossibility result can only invigorate inquiries of the kind attempted here. For if, as Arrow suggests, individual *preferences* cannot be aggregated in an uncontroversial way to legitimate social choice, it is even more important to isolate the kinds of *reasons* that may best legitimate the collective choices that must be made in the course of social life. . . .

9. An essay by H. L. A. Hart was important in suggesting to me the potential fruitfulness of this line of development. See his "The Ascription of Responsibility and Rights" in Anthony Flew, ed., *Logic and Language,* First Series (New York: Philosophical Library, 1951), pp. 145–66 in which the notion of a prima facie case is discussed in terms of "defeasible concepts." Unfortunately, Hart presented his analysis of defeasibility as part of a more ambitious — and much criticized — analysis of the nature of human action. See Peter Geach, "Ascriptivism," *Philosophical Review* 69(1960): 221; George Pitcher, "Hart on Action and Responsibility," ibid., p. 226. With characteristic thoughtfulness, Hart responded to these critics by abandoning his larger claims about human action. Nonetheless, even his critics recognize that Hart's point about defeasibility "seems to be true in one type of case, namely, that in which the action is bad and, in addition, is designated by a condemnatory verb" (p. 232). This is precisely the sort of case we are dealing with here. Q is condemning A's power play as illegitimate and A is trying to defend himself by asserting some reason in defense of his power.

For thoughtful efforts to save something of Hart's analysis, see Richard Epstein, "Pleadings and Presumptions," *University of Chicago Law Review* 40(1974): 556; Joel Feinberg *Doing and Deserving* (Princeton: Princeton Univ. Press, 1970), pp. 119–51.

THE FAMILY:
Beyond Justice?

Susan Moller Okin

Susan Moller Okin responds to two arguments about justice and the family. The first, recently articulated by Michael Sandel, is that the family is too elevated to need justice. The second, defended by Alan Bloom, is that the structure of the family is dictated by nature and hence justice is unnecessary. Okin argues that justice is a necessary virtue in real, nonidealized families. (Source: From Justice, Gender and the Family *by Susan Moller Okin. Copyright © 1989 by Basic Books, Inc. Reprinted by permission of Basic Books, a division of HarperCollins Publishers, Inc.)*

The substantial inequalities that continue to exist between the sexes in our society have serious effects on the lives of almost all women and an increasingly large number of children. Underlying all these inequalities is the unequal distribution of the unpaid labor of the family. Feminists who speak out against the traditional, gender-structured family are often unfairly attacked for being "anti-family." Some who have been so attacked have seemingly capitulated to these accusations and reverted to an unreflective defense of the family.[1] Others have responded more positively, stressing the ongoing need for feminists to "rethink the family"[2] and arguing that the family needs to be just. Moreover, these goals are necessary not only for the sake of women—though the injustice done to them is cause enough for challenging the gender-structured family—but for the sake of social justice as a whole.

In this chapter, I shall take up two different kinds of argument, both leading to the conclusion that to insist that families be internally just is misguided. These arguments have recently been made in widely read and much-praised books: Michael Sandel's *Liberalism and the Limits of Justice* and Allan Bloom's *The Closing of the American Mind*.[3] In the first type of argument, it is claimed that the family is "beyond" justice in the sense of being too elevated for it. In Sandel's view, the family is not characterized by the circumstances of justice, which operate only when interests differ and goods being distributed are scarce. An intimate group, held together by love and identity of interests, the family is characterized by nobler virtues. In the second type of argument, the family is held to be "beyond" justice in the sense that "nature" dictates its hierarchical structure. Bloom acknowledges frankly that the division of labor found within the gender-structured family is unjust, at least by prevailing standards of justice, but holds it to be both grounded in nature and necessary. A great deal of attention has been paid to Sandel's and Bloom's books; both are cherished by antiliberals. The former has flourished within academic circles and the latter, a popular best-seller, largely outside of them. However, it is testimony to the antifeminist climate of the 1980s that, with one notable exception, their claims about justice and the family have been virtually ignored.[4]

Justice and the Idealized Family

The notion that justice is not an appropriate virtue for families was most clearly expressed in the past by Rousseau and Hume. It is currently important because, as we have seen, it seems to be implicit, from their sheer disregard for family life and most aspects of gender, in the work of most contemporary theories of justice. It is rarely argued explicitly these days, but such a case is presented by Michael Sandel in his critique of John Rawls's liberal theory of justice, and I shall focus on this argument here. But first, let us take a brief look at the positions of Rousseau and Hume. On this, as on some other complex issues, Rousseau argues more than one side of the issue. Some of the time, he justifies his conclusion that the governance of the family, unlike that of political society, need not be accountable to its members or regulated by principles of justice by appealing to the notion that the family, unlike the wider society, is founded upon love. Thus unlike a government, he says, the father of a family, "in order to act right, . . . has only to consult his heart."5 Rousseau concludes that women can, without prejudice to their well-being, be both ruled within the family and denied the right to participate in the realm of politics, where their husbands will represent the interests of the family unit.

Hume argues similarly that the circumstances of family life are such that justice is not an appropriate standard to apply to them. He begins his discussion of justice by pointing out that in situations of "enlarged affections," in which every man "feels no more concern for his own interest than for that of his fellows," justice is useless, because unnecessary. He regards the family as one of the clearest instances of such enlarged affections, in which justice is inappropriate because "all distinction of property be, in a great measure, lost and confounded.... Between married persons, the cement of friendship is by the laws supposed so strong as to abolish all division of possessions; and has often, in reality, the force ascribed to it."6 The message is similar to Rousseau's: the affection and unity of interests that prevail within families make standards of justice irrelevant to them.

In his critique of Rawls, Sandel explicitly takes up and builds on Hume's vision of family life, in order to make the case that there are important social spheres in which justice is an inappropriate virtue. A central piece of his argument against Rawls, which he presents as a case against liberal accounts of justice in general, is based on a denial of Rawls's claim that justice is the primary moral virtue.7 This claim depends on the assumption that human society is characterized by certain "circumstances of justice." These include, first, the condition of moderate scarcity of resources, and second, the fact that, while persons have some similar or complementary needs and interests, they also have "different ends and purposes, and . . . make conflicting claims on the natural and social resources available."8 Does Rawls think the circumstances of justice apply *within* families? It seems — although he has not held consistently to this position — that he is one of the few theorists of justice who do. . . .

Sandel, however, argues that Rawls's claim for the primacy of justice is undermined by the existence of numerous social groupings in which the circumstances of justice do *not* predominate. Among such groupings, characterized by their "more or less clearly-defined common identities and shared pur-

poses," the family "may represent an extreme case."9 He argues that the existence of such associations refutes in two respects Rawls's claim that justice is the first or primary virtue of social institutions. First, he agrees with Hume that in such "intimate or solidaristic associations . . . the values and aims of the participants coincide closely enough that the circumstances of justice prevail to a relatively small degree." In "a more or less ideal family situation," spontaneous affection and generosity will prevail.10 Second, not only will justice not be the prevailing virtue in such associations, but if they were to begin to operate in accordance with principles of justice, an overall moral improvement would by no means necessarily result. Instead, the loss of certain "nobler virtues, and more favourable blessings" could mean that "in some cases, justice is not a virtue but a vice."11 Given such a possibility, the moral primacy of justice is demonstrated to be unfounded. Instead of being the primary virtue, as Rawls claims, in some situations justice is "a remedial virtue," called upon to repair fallen conditions.12

In both its eighteenth- and its twentieth-century manifestations, the argument that human associations exemplified by the family challenge the primacy of justice rests, in two respects, on faulty foundations. It misapprehends what is meant by the claim that justice is the first or primary virtue of social institutions; and it idealizes the family. When Rawls claims the primacy of justice, he does not mean that it is the highest or noblest of virtues. Rather, he means that it is the most fundamental or essential. This is implied by the simile he employs on the opening page of *A Theory of Justice:*

> Justice is the first virtue of social institutions, as truth is of systems of thought. A theory however elegant or economical must be rejected or revised if it is untrue; likewise laws and institutions no matter how efficient and well-arranged must be reformed or abolished if they are unjust.13

In the same way that theories can have qualities other than truth, some of which — brilliance or social utility, for example — might be more elevated than mere truth, so can social institutions have other moral qualities, some of which might be more elevated than mere justice. The point is that justice takes primacy because it is the most *essential*, not because it is the *highest,* of virtues. In fact, Rawls states explicitly his belief that there are moral principles and sentiments that are higher and nobler than justice. He refers to "supererogatory actions," such as "acts of benevolence and mercy, of heroism and self-sacrifice," as stemming from "higher-order moral sentiments that serve to bind a community of persons together."[14] He also indicates on several occasions that the members of families do commonly exhibit such higher moral virtues in relation to one another. But he considers that only saints and heroes, not ordinary persons, can *consistently* adhere to such standards of morality, which can require considerable sacrifice of self-interest, narrowly construed.[15] Furthermore, it is clear that, in Rawls's view, such moralities of supererogation, while they require *more* than the norms of right and justice, do not in any way contradict them. This is so both because their aims are continuous with these principles but extend beyond what they require and because such moralities need to rely upon the principles of justice when the claims of the goods they seek conflict.[16] Thus justice is first or primary among virtues in that such admittedly higher forms of morality depend upon it, both conceptually and in practice, in ways that it does not depend upon them.

When these points are taken into consideration, we can see that both the argument against the moral primacy of justice and that against justice as a central virtue for the family lose their force. The morality that often prevails in communities or associations that are governed in large part by affection, generosity, or other virtues morally superior to justice is a form of supererogation; individuals' narrowly construed interests give way to their concern for common ends or the ends of others they care about a great deal. Nevertheless, it is essential that such higher moral sentiments and actions, within the family as well as in society at large, be underwritten by a foundation of justice. Justice is needed as the primary, meaning most fundamental, moral virtue *even* in social groupings in which aims are largely common and affection frequently prevails.

We can learn more about why justice is a necessary virtue for families by examining the second flaw in Sandel's argument, which is that it relies upon an idealized, even mythical, account of the family. The picture drawn is, in fact, very close to Rawls's example of a circumstance in which he too agrees that justice is superfluous: "an association of saints agreeing on a common ideal."[17] But viewed realistically, human associations, including the family, do not operate so felicitously. And a theory of justice must concern itself not with abstractions or ideals of institutions but with their realities. If we were to concern ourselves only with ideals, we might well conclude that wider human societies, as well as families, could do without justice. The ideal society would presumably need no system of criminal justice or taxation, but that does not tell us much about what we need in the world we live in.

The vision of the family as an institution far above justice pays too little attention to what happens within such groupings when, as is surely common, they fail to meet this saintly ideal. Even a brief glance at the example that Hume regards as the paradigm setting for the exercise of moral virtues nobler than justice should serve to make us less than comfortable with his and Sandel's dismissal of the need for justice in such settings. The unity of the eighteenth-century family—enshrined in the ideology of the time and revived in the 1970s by family historians[18]—was based on the legal fiction of "coverture." The *reason* that, as Hume puts it, "the laws supposed . . . the cement of friendship [between married persons] so strong as to abolish all division of possessions," was that upon marrying, women became legal nonpersons. Contrary to what Hume's words suggest, the common law did not institute the shared or common ownership of the property of spouses. Rather, it automatically transferred all of a wife's personal property—as well as control over, and the income from, her real property—into the hands of her husband. As John Stuart Mill was later to put it: "the two are called 'one person in law,' for the purpose of inferring that whatever is hers is his, but the parallel inference is never drawn that whatever is his is hers."[19] Hume and others justified coverture by reference to the "enlarged affections" and unity of the family. This same idealized vision of the family as "the place of Peace; the shelter, not only from all injury, but from all terror, doubt, and division," as John Ruskin depicted it, was central to the arguments made by the opponents of married women's rights in the nineteenth century.[20] But *we* must realize that questions of distributive justice were not considered important in the context of this type of family because not only the wife's property but her body, her children, and her legal rights belonged to her husband. To revert in the late twentieth century to this account of family life in order to argue that the circumstances of justice are not so socially pervasive as liberals like Rawls think they are is not only grossly ahistorical. It does not allow for the fact that the account was a myth, and a far from harmless one. It served as the ideology that veiled the *in*justice called coverture.

What this example can teach us about justice and the family is that while it is quite possible for associations to appear to operate according to virtues nobler than justice, and thus to be morally preferable to those that are *just* just, we need to scrutinize them closely before we can conclude that this is really the case. In particular, we need to ask whether their members are entitled to their fair shares of whatever benefits and burdens are at issue when and insofar as the circumstances of justice arise — when interests or ends conflict and some resources are scarce (as tends to happen at least some of the time, except in communities of saints with common ends). Thus even if wives never had occasion to ask for their just share of the family property, due to the generosity and spontaneous affection of their husbands, we would be unable to assess the families in which they lived from a moral point of view unless we knew whether, if they did ask for it, they would be considered entitled to it. It is not difficult to imagine the kind of response that would have been received by most eighteenth-century wives if they had asked for their just shares of the family property! This should make us highly skeptical of reliance on the supposedly higher virtues embodied by such institutions.

. . . Sandel's argument against the primacy of justice also depends on a highly idealized view of the *contemporary* family. "Enlarged affections" are by no means the only feelings that occur, and are acted upon, in families. Since the 1970s, it has been "discovered" that a great deal of violence — much of it serious, some of it fatal — occurs within families. Our courts and police are increasingly preoccupied with family assault and with the sexual abuse of weaker

family members by more powerful ones. The family is also an important sphere of distribution. In the "more or less ideal family situation," Sandel says, the appeal to fairness is "preempted by a spirit of generosity in which I am rarely inclined to claim my fair share," and "the questions of what I get and what I am due do not loom large in the overall context of this way of life."[21] The implication seems to be that there are not likely to be *systematic* injustices. No account is taken of the fact that the socialization and role expectations of women mean that they are generally more inclined than men not to claim their fair share, and more inclined to order their priorities in accordance with the needs of their families. The supererogation that is expected in families often occurs at women's expense, as earlier ideologists of the family were well aware; Ruskin continues his vision by exhorting women to be "enduringly incorruptibly good; instinctively infallibly wise . . . , not for self-development but for self-renunciation."[22]

In fact, many social "goods," such as time for paid work or for leisure, physical security, and access to financial resources, typically are unevenly distributed within families. Though many may be "better than just," at least most of the time, contemporary gender-structured families are *not* just. But they *need* to be just. They cannot rely upon the spirit of generosity — though they can still aspire to it — because the life chances of millions of women and children are at stake. They need to be just, too, if they are to be the first schools of moral development, the places where we first learn to develop a sense of justice. And they need to be just if we are even to begin to approach the equality of opportunity that our country claims as one of its basic ideals.

It seems to be assumed by those who have held the position that I have been criticizing that justice somehow takes away from intimacy, harmony, and love. But why should we suppose that harmonious affection, indeed deep and long-lasting love, cannot coexist with ongoing standards of justice? Why should we be forced to choose and thereby to deprecate the basic and essential virtue, justice, by playing it off against what are claimed to be higher virtues? We are surely not faced with such a choice if, viewing human groupings like the family realistically, we insist that they be constructed upon a basis of justice. For this need not mean that we cannot also hope and expect more of them. We need to recognize that associations in which we *hope* that the best of human motivations and the noblest of virtues will prevail are, in fact, morally superior to those that are *just* just only if they are firmly built on a foundation of justice, however rarely it may be invoked. Since this is so, the existence of associations like families poses no problem for the moral primacy of justice. If they normally operate in accordance with spontaneous feelings of love and generosity, but provide justice to their members when, as circumstances of justice arise, it is needed, then they are just and better than just. But if they do not provide justice when their members have reason to ask it of them, then despite their generosity and affection, they are worse.

Thus, it is only when the family is idealized and sentimentalized that it can be perceived as an institution that undermines the primacy of justice. When we recognize, as we must, that however much the members of families care about one another and share common ends, they are still discrete persons with their own particular aims and hopes, which may sometimes conflict, we must see the family as an institution to which justice is a crucial virtue. When we recognize, as we surely must, that many of the resources that are enjoyed within the sphere of family life—leisure, nurturance, money, time, and attention, to mention only a few—are by no means always abundant, we see that justice has a highly significant role to play. When we realize that women, especially, are likely to change the whole course of their lives because of their family commitments, it becomes clear that we cannot regard families as analogous to other intimate relations like friendship, however strong the affective bonding of the latter may be. And now that it cannot be assumed, as it was earlier, that marriage is for life, we must take account of the fact that the decreasing permanence of families renders issues of justice within them more critical than ever. To substitute self-sacrifice and altruism for justice in the context of a unity that may dissolve before one's very eyes, without one's consent and to the great detriment of those one cares most about, would perhaps be better labeled lack of foresight than nobility.

The Unjust Family as Natural and Socially Necessary

While in Rousseau's *idealized* vision of family life, dependent, secluded, and subordinated wives could rely on their husbands' loving care and protection, he at times recognized the folly of trusting this account of family life. In his own fictional depictions, husbands and fathers fall far short of this ideal; they frequently neglect, abuse, and abandon those they are supposed to take care of.[23] Rousseau himself sent all his children off to foundling homes, against his wife's will. However, in spite of his own recognition of the fragility of the myth on which it was based, he could see no alternative to the dependent position of women that he regarded as imposed by nature. The "very law of nature," in Rousseau's view, leaving men uncertain of the paternity of the children they are expected to maintain, dictates that women are "at the mercy of men's judgments."[24] In Book 5 of *Emile*, having described in detail Sophie's careful preparation for a life of coquettish subordination to the multiple needs and whims of her husband, Rousseau frankly admits the injustice of it all:

> As she is made to obey a being who is so imperfect, often so full of vices, and always so full of defects as man, she ought to learn early to endure even injustice and to bear a husband's wrongs without complaining. It is not for his sake, it is for her own, that she ought to be gentle. The bitterness and the stubbornness of women never do anything but increase their ills and the bad behavior of their husbands.[25]

Thus, nature necessitates women's subjection to men, and the imperfections of men's nature necessitate the reinforcement of women's natural propensity for enduring injustice. The good of society and the continuation of the species make inevitable the rigid division of labor between the sexes and the subordination of women. Rather than delving further into Rousseau's reasons for believing this to be the case, let us now turn to the same argument as it appears in Allan Bloom's 1987 version. For two main reasons, it is important to pay attention to Bloom's variety of antifeminism: it is a strongly articulated, though somewhat extreme, version of notions that have considerable currency in powerful circles these days; and Bloom, because of his own political agenda, admits freely that the maintenance of sex roles in the family is inconsistent with liberal-democratic standards of justice.

The ostensible theme of Bloom's *The Closing of the American Mind* is that American liberal democracy is disintegrating because its universities are failing to educate the young elite. Without the education in rational thinking that can be provided only by serious study of the great books of Western philosophy and literature, young people are aimlessly wandering in the chaos of relativism—tolerance gone wild—that plagues our society. A major enemy, in Bloom's account of what has gone wrong since the early 1960s (when he thinks things were still basically on track), is feminism. For, while "nature should be the standard by which we judge our ... lives," feminism is "not founded on nature," defying as it does women's natural biological destiny.[26] Feminism is much to blame both for undermining the prestige of the great books and for hastening the decline of the already beleaguered family.

Bloom's arguments on both issues depend on completely unsubstantiated statements of alleged "fact." We are told, for example, that even in "relatively happy" homes, "the dreariness of the family's spiritual landscape passes belief," that "central to the feminist project is the suppression of modesty," that "there are two equal careers in almost every household composed of educated persons under thirty-five," and that, due to feminist activism, "offensive authors" are being expunged from college courses or included only to demonstrate the great books' distorting prejudices about women.[27] No evidence is cited for these or other such general allegations, which many of us who live in families, are active in the feminist movement, struggle to maintain our careers in the context of unequal family demands, or teach the great books known to be preposterous. The fact that Bloom's book, with its multiple inaccuracies and its disdain for evidence, topped the *New York Times'* nonfiction best-seller list throughout the summer of 1987 is, to my way of thinking, the clearest sign yet that there is indeed *something* wrong with American higher education.

At times, in Bloom's lament about the decline of the family, there appear hints of the idealized, better-than-just version of it. He writes of the family as "the intermediary ... that gave men and women unqualified concern for at least some others," thereby tempering individualism. But most of his argument runs counter to this notion. He assumes that men are by nature selfish creatures, who could not even be imagined as having "unqualified concern" for anyone but themselves. The problem, as Bloom sees it, is that "women are no longer willing to make unconditional and perpetual commitments on unequal terms." Arguing that feminism has eroded the family by its resistance to traditional sex roles, he says that it "ends, as do many modern movements that seek abstract justice, in forgetting nature and using force to refashion human beings to secure that justice."[28]*

Closely following Rousseau throughout his argument, he claims that if women refuse to be full-time mothers, men will refuse to be fathers at all, because they will no longer be gaining enough of what they expect from family life to have any commitment to it. Nature, according to Bloom, makes motherhood entirely different from fatherhood. Men have no natural desire or need for children. But women naturally want children, and therefore must take care of them. In order to get their children's fathers to support them while they do this, women must charm men into marriage (largely by withholding sex), and then must cater to their needs and take care of them. Recognizing the natural basis of their dependence, women should not develop careers, for this causes struggle and threatens family unity. They must accept the fact that "nothing can effectively make most men share equally the responsibilities of childbearing and childrearing." Bloom acknowledges that, by the egalitarian standards of modernity, this inequality of women is unjust.[29] But the writers of the great books all knew it to be natural and therefore necessary, which is why, by Bloom's own admission, they are all sexist. The only ones who do not *seem* to agree with Bloom about the proper role of women are either not great (Mill) or did not mean what they said (Plato).

---

*He does not explain how feminists have used force in pursuit of their aims. By chaining themselves to railings, or by learning self-defense, perhaps?

As Bloom says, feminist scholars during the last fifteen years or so have challenged many of the works that make up the tradition of what one has wittily called "malestream thought."[30] But the sexism of the great books has not been wantonly, angrily, and arbitrarily assaulted, as Bloom would like his readers to think. It has been carefully argued about. Feminists have brought the test of rational thought to what the great books have said about women and the family, and in many cases shown their assumptions to be unfounded and their arguments irrational. We have not, as Bloom alleges, gone on to conclude that these authors are worthless thinkers, to be relegated to the intellectual junkheap. We have, however, insisted that it would be wrong (not least because it is intellectually dishonest) to continue to teach their works as though they did not believe such things, or as though their statements about women were aberrations that can be conveniently forgotten because they have no effect on the "important" things the philosophers had to say. We have faced up to the challenge of learning what we can from great minds of the past and teaching it to our students, when most people in our society are no longer prepared to think about women in the ways they did.

What might happen if Bloom's complaint that feminism has undermined the teaching of the great books were transformed into policy? Would existing feminist criticisms, however rational, be banned? If so, would women (who would soon begin again to raise similar questions and to make similar objections) have to be forbidden from both teaching and studying in institutions of higher education? Who knows to what lengths we might have to go in order to protect the sexism of Aristotle, Rousseau, and Nietzsche from rational scrutiny. The world of Margaret Atwood's *The Handmaid's Tale,* in which women, as reproductive vessels, are no longer taught to read or write, might well be the logical conclusion of Bloom's train of thought.[31] From his point of view, there would appear to be nothing wrong with women's being uneducated, as long as they were dependent upon men and relatively powerless within the family, as he recommends.

Like many other antifeminists, Bloom relies heavily on "nature" and especially on reproductive biology to argue for the rationality and necessity of traditional sex roles. As we have seen, he uses the old trick of making child rearing by males look absurd by fusing it with male childbearing. He says that nature dictates, via female lactation, that women must stay home with children. Stooping to puerile humor, he remarks that paternity leave is "contrived and somewhat ridiculous," since the law cannot make male nipples give milk.[32] He does not seem to realize that the great majority of infants in the United States are at least partly bottle-fed, that nursing an infant is only a tiny part of raising a child, that flexibility of working and child-care conditions can allow wage-earning mothers both to breast-feed their infants and to share the care of them equally with fathers.

Bloom does not *want* to realize any of these things, of course. His fundamental case against feminist attempts to share more fairly the unpaid responsibilities of the family is that it undermines masculinity. "Here," he says, "is where the whole business turns nasty." (He means, of course, that the implications of feminism turn nasty; to my way of thinking it is his argument that gets rather nasty at this point.) He continues:

> The souls of men — their ambitious, warlike, protective, possessive character — must be dismantled in order to liberate women from their domination. Machismo — the polemical description of maleness or spiritedness, which was the central *natural* passion in men's souls in the psychology of the ancients, the passion of attachment and loyalty — was the villain, the source of the difference between the sexes. . . . With machismo discredited, the positive task is to make men caring, sensitive, even nurturing, to fit the restructured family. . . . And it is indeed possible to soften men. But to make them "care" is another thing, and the project must inevitably fail.[33]

The reason it must fail, he alleges, is that men cannot be forced to give up their natural selfishness, especially at a time when women are being more selfish. I need not go into just how wrong Bloom is about the ancients' view of male spiritedness; Martha Nussbaum has shown far better than I could how many of them, including those Bloom judges to be the best, believed that the needs of society required that such passions be modified.[34] But it is important to discuss his reliance upon what is natural.

"Nature," Bloom states, "should be the standard by which we judge our own lives and the lives of peoples. That is why philosophy . . . is the most important human science."[35] But what on earth, we must ask, is "nature"? And how is philosophy to help us discover it? It is unfortunate that Bloom is so contemptuous of Mill, who made arguments well worthy of his consideration about the political uses and abuses of *nature* and *the natural*.[36] One of the major sources of irrationality, Mill says, is that these words are sometimes used to mean the way things would be without human intervention and sometimes to mean the way things ought to be, as though the two are somehow synonymous. These words, Mill argues, have been used with such confusion and such proliferation of meanings that they have become "one of the most copious sources of false taste, false philosophy, false morality, and even bad law."[37] As we have seen, much of past and present feminism has dealt extensively with the subject of how "nature," and biological determinism in particular, has been used to oppress women.

Bloom, despite his reverence for philosophy, seems to feel no need to make arguments about what nature is or why it is good. He uses the words *nature* and *natural*—words crucial to his book's potential coherence, in a multitude of different ways, without ever defining them.* Unlike some scholars, such as Ruth Bleier and Anne Fausto-Sterling, who have given much thought to the matter,[38] he seems quite confident that he knows where the "natural" (which in this context seems to mean "biological") differences between the sexes begin and end. Yet he persists in the belief that child rearing as a whole is "naturally" women's responsibility. "Biology forces women to take maternity leaves," he pronounces. And he greets with sarcasm and deprecation women's claim that we

ourselves should have a major say in what constitutes "the feminine nature."[39]* Frequently falling into the fallacious way of thinking that Mill warns against, Bloom never confronts all the things that contemporary people, or even the Greeks, would have had to give up to return to nature, in the sense of letting biology take its course. He ridicules liberals whose concern for the natural environment leads them to protest the extinction of the snail darter, but who also defend the right to abortion. However, he has nothing to say about the fact that modern medicine and innumerable other life-preserving and life-enhancing aspects of modern life are manifest departures from the notion that biology is destiny. Most of the time, it is difficult to discern any consistent meaning in Bloom's references to "the natural," except that it is whatever preserves the dominance of the white male elite and enables its members, by philosophizing, to come to terms with their own mortality.

Ultimately, the only comprehensible way to read Bloom's book is the same way he wants us to read the *Republic*. According to Bloom, who ignores all reasoning to the contrary, Plato made the ridiculous proposal that the elite women should be treated equally with the men only in order to demonstrate the impossibility of his entire project. Bloom's own book about education purports, on one level at least, to be about the preservation of liberal democracy. But he is really, of course, a vehement defender of aristocracy. Among the reasons for his contempt for today's students is his (unfounded) belief that their instincts are wholly egalitarian: "Whenever they meet anyone," he alleges, "considerations of sex, color, religion, family, money, nationality, play no role in their reactions."[40] (Doubtless, both most of the students and the administrators of the colleges and universities now fraught with racist and sexist conflict might like to be reassured by Bloom's words, but the evidence before their eyes belies them.) His own belief in an aristocracy based on race, sex, and other natural indicators of "excellence" is evident over and over again in the

---

*One of the first uses in the book gives us an immediate clue to its author's misogyny: in the preface we learn that "nature, not the midwife" is the cause of the delivery of babies (p. 20). Where, we might ask, is the mother? One of the oddest uses comes on p. 105, where Bloom blames the sexual revolution and feminism for producing "an odd tension in which all the moral restraints governing nature disappeared, but so did nature." It is difficult to see why any tension should result from the lack of restraints on something that has disappeared.

---

*He says of the "recent feminist discussion" of the differences between men and women that "the feminine nature is a mystery to be worked out on its own, which can now be done because the male claim to it has been overcome."

book, such as when he remarks — seemingly with deliberate intent to insult — that the black students in the major universities "have, by and large, proved indigestible," or when he explains that white males still predominate in the natural sciences because it is only there that standards of excellence have not been eroded by affirmative action policies.[41]

As we should expect, *The Closing of the American Mind* can be read coherently only as a Straussian text, its superficial meaning veiling a deeper message.* It has obvious parallels in subject matter, and even in its ordering, with Plato's *Republic.* Here, as with Plato, the treatment of sexual relations and the family is of critical importance in unlocking the author's real meaning. Bloom does not take the risk, as he thinks Plato does, of "joking" about how women can be equal. Perhaps he fears that — as he thinks Plato was until the Straussian interpretation, and still is by most of us — he will be misread as meaning what he says. Instead, Bloom thinks he has shown that the equality of women would be impossible, ridiculous, unnatural, and socially devastating. By liberal democratic standards, then, a fundamental injustice must remain at the very foundation of the society. But this, more clearly than anything else, must show that all the other pretensions to human equality are equally doomed, the whole egalitarian enterprise of modernity misguided, and aristocracy vindicated.

For those of us who *are* still attached to democracy, to an egalitarian liberalism, and to feminism, Bloom's conclusions need hold no fearful portents. For the egalitarian family is not an absurd impossibility, but rather a necessary component of the society that we want to build. The things that make traditional families unjust are not matters of natural necessity, as reactionaries like Bloom would like to have

us believe. There is surely nothing in our natures that requires men not to be equal participants in the rearing of their children. Bloom says they won't do it because they are naturally selfish. Even if he were right, which I very strongly doubt, since when did we shape public policy around people's faults? Our laws do not allow kleptomaniacs to shoplift, or those with a predilection for rape to rape. Why, then, should we allow fathers who refuse to share in the care of their children to abdicate their responsibilities? Why should we allow the continuance of the peculiar contract that marriage has become, in which legal equality is assumed but actual inequality persists because women, whether or not they work for wages, are considerably hampered in developing skills or economic security, being caught up in doing the great bulk of the family's unpaid work? Why should we allow an injustice that is clearly harming large numbers of children, as well as women, to persist at the foundation of our political order?

Notes

1. See the account given in Judith Stacey, "Are Feminists Afraid to Leave Home? The Challenge of Conservative Pro-family Feminism," in *What Is Feminism? A Reexamination,* ed. Juliet Mitchell and Ann Oakley (New York: Pantheon, 1986).

2. See, for example, Barrie Thorne and Marilyn Yalom, eds., *Rethinking the Family: Some Feminist Questions* (New York: Longman, 1982), esp. Thorne's introductory "Overview."

3. Michael Sandel, *Liberalism and the Limits of Justice* (Cambridge: Cambridge University Press, 1982); Allan Bloom, *The Closing of the American Mind: How Higher Education Has Failed Democracy and Impoverished the Souls of Today's Students* (New York: Simon & Schuster, 1987).

4. The exception is Martha Nussbaum's brilliant review of Bloom, "Undemocratic Vistas," in the *New York Review of Books* 34, no. 17 (November 5, 1987).

5. *Discourse on Political Economy,* translated from Jean-Jacques Rousseau, *Oeuvres Complètes* (Paris: Pléiade, 1959–1969), vol. 3, pp. 241–42.

6. David Hume, *Enquiry Concerning the Principles of Morals,* ed. L. A. Selby-Bigge from the 1777 edition (Oxford: Oxford University Press, 1975), p. 185. See also *A Treatise of Human Nature,* ed. L. A. Selby-Bigge (Oxford: Oxford University Press, 1978), pp. 493–96.

---

*This method of political philosophizing originated with the work of Leo Strauss, who taught at the University of Chicago in the post–World War II years. The method depends heavily on the belief that all the great books of Western philosophy are written with two levels of meaning, one of which is easily accessible, the other — almost always containing a highly inegalitarian message — accessible only to the learned few, the "men of excellence." Not surprisingly, there are few female or black Straussians.

7. Sandel, *Limits of Justice,* pp. 30–35.

8. John Rawls, *A Theory of Justice* (Cambridge: Harvard University Press, 1971), p. 127.

9. Sandel, *Limits of Justice,* p. 31.

10. Ibid., pp. 30–31, 33.

11. Ibid., p. 34 (the first phrase is quoted from Hume, *A Treatise on Human Nature*).

12. Sandel, *Limits of Justice,* p. 31.

13. Rawls, *Theory,* p. 3.

14. Ibid., pp. 117, 192.

15. Ibid., pp. 129–30, 438–39.

16. Ibid., pp. 479, 191.

17. Ibid., p. 129.

18. Edward Shorter, *The Making of the Modern Family* (New York: Basic Books, 1975); Lawrence Stone, *The Family, Sex, and Marriage in England 1500–1800* (New York: Harper & Row, 1977); Randolph Trumbach, *The Rise of the Egalitarian Family* (New York: Academic Press, 1978).

19. *The Subjection of Women,* in *The Collected Works of John Stuart Mill,* ed. John M. Robson (Toronto: University of Toronto Press, 1984), p. 284.

20. John Ruskin, "Of Queen's Gardens," Lecture 2 of *Sesame and Lilies* (London: A. L. Burt, 1871), p. 85, quoted in Mary L. Shanley, "Marital Slavery and Friendship: John Stuart Mill's *The Subjection of Women,*" *Political Theory* 9, no. 2 (1981): 233. See also Shanley, *Feminism, Marriage and the Law in Victorian England 1850–1890* (Princeton: Princeton University Press, in press), esp. introduction and chap. 1.

21. Sandel, *Limits of Justice,* p. 33.

22. Ruskin, "Of Queen's Gardens," p. 86.

23. See Susan Moller Okin, *Women in Western Political Thought* (Princeton: Princeton University Press, 1979), chap. 8.

24. Rousseau, *Emile: or On Education,* trans. Allan Bloom (New York: Basic Books, 1979), p. 364. See also Okin, *Women in Western Political Thought,* esp. chaps. 6 and 7.

25. Rousseau, *Emile,* p. 370.

26. Bloom, *Closing,* pp. 38, 99–100.

27. Ibid., pp. 57, 101, 127, and 66 respectively.

28. Ibid., pp. 86, 115, 100.

29. Ibid., pp. 115, 128–31.

30. Mary O'Brien, *The Politics of Reproduction* (London: Routledge & Kegan Paul, 1981).

31. Margaret Atwood, *The Handmaid's Tale* (New York: Simon & Schuster, 1986).

32. Bloom, *Closing,* p. 131; see also p. 101.

33. Ibid., p. 129.

34. Nussbaum, "Undemocratic Vistas," pp. 23–24.

35. Bloom, *Closing,* p. 38.

36. John Stuart Mill, "Nature," from *Three Essays on Religion,* in *The Philosophy of John Stuart Mill,* ed. Marshall Cohen (New York: Random House, 1961), "The Subjection of Women," in *Collected Works of John Stuart Mill,* ed. J. M. Robson, vol. 21, (Toronto: University of Toronto Press, 1984), esp. pp. 269–70 and 276–82.

37. Mill, "Nature," p. 445; see also p. 487.

38. Ruth Bleier, *Science and Gender: A Critique of Biology and Its Theories on Women* (New York: Pergamon Press, 1984); Anne Fausto-Sterling, *Myths of Gender: Biological Theories About Women and Men* (New York: Basic Books, 1985).

39. Bloom, *Closing,* pp. 130, 105.

40. Ibid., p. 88.

41. Bloom, *Closing,* pp. 91, 351.

TOWARD AN ADEQUATE MARXIST
MORAL AND SOCIAL THEORY

R. G. Peffer

Rodney Peffer argues that government ought to guarantee rights to security and subsistence, equal basic liberty, equal opportunity, and equal participation. In addition, it should tolerate only those inequalities that would benefit the least advantaged, consistent with a just savings principle, and should not exceed levels that would jeopardize liberty or self-respect. (Source: From Marxism, Morality, and Social Justice *by R. G. Peffer. Copyright © 1990 by Princeton University Press. Reprinted by permission of Princeton University Press.)*

. . . [A]n adequate Marxist moral and social theory must have certain features. First, it must be based on a moral theory that is in wide reflective equilibrium with our considered moral judgments. Second, it must be informed by a correct set of empirical, social-scientific views. Third, it must account for the Marxist's basic normative political positions that (1) socialism is morally preferable to any form of capitalism (as well as to any other type of society possible under the historical conditions of moderate scarcity and moderate egoism), and (2) social and/or political revolution, if necessary (and sufficient) to effect the appropriate transformations, is *prima facie* morally justified.

. . .

On my reconstruction of this theory, Marx espouses the principle of *maximum equal freedom (both negative and positive)*, which, in turn, can be explicated as the following set of principles:

There is to be a maximum equal system of:

1. *negative freedom* (i.e., freedom from the undue interference of others), and
2. *positive freedom* (i.e., the opportunity to determine one's own life), including:
   a. the right to equal participation in social decision-making processes and
   b. the right of equal access to the means of self-realization, which entails:
      i. the right to an equal opportunity to attain social offices and positions, and
      ii. the right to an equal opportunity to acquire other social primary goods (income, wealth, leisure time, etc.).

Many of us, perhaps, will find that these principles come rather close to being in wide reflective equilibrium with our considered moral judgments. Thus it is arguable that they (or something very much like them) would be chosen by free and equal moral persons in the original position. But this theory (i.e., this set of moral principles concerning social arrangements), as it stands, is simply too general and vague to be considered an adequate moral theory as opposed to the bare outlines of one. Even if it is generally in accord with our considered moral judgments, it needs to be tightened up: the various terms ("interference," "access," "opportunity," etc.) need to be given more precise definitions; the notion of a "maximum equal system" needs to be clarified; decisions need to be made on what priority rules (if any) are to be established, etc.

. . .

I propose that the following principles — *listed in order of lexical priority* — make for an adequate, or at least more adequate, theory of social justice:

1. Everyone's security rights and subsistence rights shall be respected.
2. There is to be a maximum system of equal basic liberties, including freedom of speech and assembly; liberty of conscience and freedom of thought; freedom of the person along with the right to hold (personal) property; and freedom from arbitrary arrest and seizure as defined by the concept of the rule of law.
3. There is to be (a) a right to an equal opportunity to attain social positions and offices and (b) an equal right to participate in all social decision-making processes within institutions of which one is a part.

4. Social and economic inequalities are justified if, and only if, they benefit the least advantaged, consistent with the just savings principle, but *are not to exceed* levels that will seriously undermine equal worth of liberty or the good of self-respect.

. . .

Social Justice and Marxist Empirical Theory

It is obvious that the theory of social justice I am here putting forward is not a specifically Marxist moral theory. This should not be surprising. Not even Marx's implicit moral theory per se is a specifically Marxist theory. There is, in fact, no such thing as a specifically Marxist *moral theory.* There is, however, such a thing as a specifically Marxist *moral and social theory,* i.e., a theory which combines a moral theory with a set of empirical, social-scientific theses in order to judge alternative sets of social arrangements, programs, and policies. In fact, *any* moral and social theory that utilizes a recognizably Marxist set of empirical, social-scientific theses and supports a recognizably Marxist set of normative political positions qualifies as a *Marxist* moral and social theory.

Since there is no uniquely Marxist moral theory and no reason Marxists automatically ought to accept Marx's implicit moral theory as either definitive or correct, there will be as many different Marxist moral and social theories as there are moral theories that Marxists wish to combine with their empirical assumptions. Furthermore, there may be a considerable divergence among Marxists as to which empirical, social-scientific theses within the Marxist tradition are both relevant and true. But the real goal, of course, is not simply to develop a Marxist moral and social theory but to develop an *adequate* moral and social theory, i.e., one based on an adequate moral theory, on the one hand, and a true set of social-scientific theories, on the other. (Naturally, Marxists believe that the set of true social-scientific theories will be drawn largely from the Marxist tradition.)

If there is no set of Marxist empirical theses that meets these conditions, then, of course, the project of

developing an adequate Marxist moral and social theory is doomed. The truly monumental political questions of the day, it seems to me, turn on the truth or falsity of the Marxist's analysis of capitalism and the present world situation. If this analysis is essentially correct, then the Marxist's basic normative political positions will be justified; if it is essentially incorrect, then in all probability these normative political positions will not be justified. These positions . . . are that (1) socialism (i.e., democratic, self-managing socialism) is morally preferable to any feasible form of capitalism and to any other form of society possible in the present historical epoch (e.g., bureaucratic state-socialism), and (2) socialist revolution—if necessary and sufficient to effect the appropriate transformations—is *prima facie* morally justified. (Although there exist many kinds of capitalist society in terms of the type of government that prevails and there might be different types of state-socialist societies, at least in the sense that some of them will be more bureaucratic and/or repressive than others, I take these three forms of society—capitalism, state-socialism, and democratic, self-managing socialism—to be exhaustive of the *basic* types of society possible in this historical epoch.)

In what follows I shall first defend these normative political positions and then attempt to comment briefly on the empirical theses I have utilized in doing so. (That is, I shall delimit the minimal set of Marxist empirical assumptions of which I have previously spoken.) I shall not try to prove that these Marxist empirical theses are correct. Rather, I shall attempt to show which of them must be essentially correct in order for the Marxist's basic normative political positions to be justified. At this point I shall be painting a picture in fairly broad strokes: I shall not argue for the truth of the empirical theses put forward, nor shall I argue for the pedigree of the theses or the normative political positions I take them to support. Although it seems to me that they flow from the Classical Marxist tradition, I shall not argue the point here.[1]

Determining whether the first normative position is justified is simply a matter of determining whether democratic, self-managing socialism meets the four principles espoused by our theory of social justice better than any feasible form of capitalism or any form of state-socialism. One of the most important

Marxist empirical theses I will be utilizing is precisely that a democratic, self-managing socialist society is a real historical possibility. However, since many will deny this, another important question is whether capitalism is morally preferable to state-socialism if these are the only real choices open to us. A further complication is that our judgments may vary depending on whether we are speaking of an advanced, industrialized society or a developing society. Therefore, in reference to advanced, industrialized societies I shall consider (A) the choice between democratic, self-managing socialism and capitalism; (B) the choice between democratic, self-managing socialism and state-socialism; and (C) the choice between capitalism and state-socialism. With reference to the developing nations, I shall consider (D) the choice between revolutionary, post-capitalist societies (such as the People's Republic of China, Cuba, and — potentially — Nicaragua) and capitalism.

These issues cannot be intelligently decided, of course, unless we specify what sort of capitalist society we have in mind, as well as the severity of the violation of civil liberties and political rights in the state-socialist society we have in mind. Obviously, our choice will differ depending on whether we accept fascist Germany or contemporary Sweden as our model of capitalism, as well as on whether we accept Stalinist Russia of the 1930s or, say, contemporary Hungary as our model of state-socialism. In addition, these issues cannot be fully joined unless we bring both diachronic and international factors into consideration. Therefore, we shall have to consider variations of such societies along two parameters: (1) the tendencies of each of these types of society to change in certain ways over time, and (2) the relations of these types of societies to other societies that may exist (in particular, the developing societies of the Third World).

In attempting to come to terms with these issues within the framework of Classical Marxism, we will do well to keep in mind its claim that communism — or, for our purposes, democratic, self-managing socialism — can exist as a stable and continuing structure only on a worldwide scale, i.e., only in the absence of major capitalist powers that otherwise will attempt to undermine it economically and/or militarily. Thus the ultimate normative political position of Classical Marxism would seem to be that we are obligated to work toward the creation of a worldwide federation of democratic, self-managing socialist societies. After all, if democratic, self-managing socialism is to be preferred within an individual society then — barring any ill effects of their amalgamation — a worldwide system of such societies is to be preferred to any other historically possible world scenario. And far from having ill effects, Marxists maintain that a worldwide system of such societies will be the only insurance the world has against incessant war, international distributive injustices, the lack of cooperation in solving environmental and demographic problems, etc.

Democratic, Self-Managing Socialism vs. Capitalism

Given the theory of social justice advanced in the present chapter, it seems quite clear that a truly democratic, self-managing socialist society will be preferable to any historically possible form of capitalist society, even a capitalist society such as Sweden, which most of us, I think, will agree meets the principles of our theory of social justice as well or better than any capitalist society now extant and perhaps as well as any capitalist society can be expected to meet them. In brief, the reason a democratic, self-managing socialist society would be judged morally preferable is that while both sorts of society would meet the first two principles (the protection of basic rights to well-being and maximum equal liberty), a socialist society would quite probably better meet principles three and four. In reference to the third (equal opportunity) principle, though Swedish government-owned corporations like Volvo have introduced a certain amount of worker participation into the labor process, even these industries do not allow for genuine workers' democracy or, arguably, even as much of it as currently exists in many self-managed enterprises in Yugoslavia. Since a genuinely democratic, self-managing socialist society presumably will have a much greater degree of workers' self-management than present-day Yugoslavia, it would seem, based on this criterion, superior to Sweden or any "Swedenized" capitalist society.

As to the fourth principle, it must be kept in mind that while income differentials will exist in a socialist society, such a society—by hypothesis—will not be one in which systems of bureaucratic privilege exist. Since property is socially owned, neither will there exist the great differences in investment wealth (and income) that exist in capitalist societies. Although Sweden probably meets principle four as well or better than any other capitalist society, due to its extremely progressive taxation scheme and extensive welfare transfer programs, the investment wealth and, to a lesser extent, income are still severely skewed toward the Swedish capitalist class and, in particular, the famous "fifteen families."[2]

Since such a democratic, self-managing socialist society meets the first two principles as well as the best capitalist societies and meets the last two principles better, it must be judged morally superior. It does not, however, immediately follow that socialist revolution would be justified to transform a capitalist society like Sweden into a democratic, self-managing socialist society since, presumably, revolutions are justified only if the injustices of a society surpass certain limits (more on this presently). We should also keep in mind, of course, that the Swedish capitalist economy is part and parcel of the international capitalist economy and, as such, participates in the super-exploitation of the Third World.[3]

But even if a democratic, self-managing socialist society is morally preferable to any form of capitalism, the choice, many will maintain, is between such historically existing societies as the United States and the Soviet Union, and—it is argued—we must decide in favor of democratic capitalism over "totalitarian communism." The answer to this, it seems to me, if (1) this is not the choice facing us; (2) even if it were, the choice of a democratic capitalist society such as the U.S.A. would be incontrovertible *only* if we failed to take diachronic and international factors into consideration. (This issue is discussed later in this chapter.)

Democratic, Self-Managing Socialism vs. State-Socialism

Democratic, self-managing socialism is also quite obviously morally preferable to state-socialism. Even if they both were to meet the first principle concerning the protection of basic rights to well-being, a democratic, self-managing socialist society would almost

undoubtedly better meet principles two, three, and four. By definition, democratic, self-managing socialist societies protect civil liberties and instantiate not only political but also social and economic democracy; by definition, state-socialist societies do not. Thus the former will better meet principles two and three. Furthermore, while the former, by hypothesis, will *not* have a privileged bureaucracy, the latter—as a matter of both definition and empirical fact—do.[4] Thus democratic, self-managing socialism will probably better meet principle four as well.

The more interesting question concerns the view that the Classical Marxist tradition would (or should) take of presently existing post-capitalist societies. This is certainly one of the most controversial and divisive issues within the Marxist tradition as a whole. As pointed out previously, various Marxists describe these societies as communist (i.e., the higher stage of communism), as socialist (having reached the first stage of communism), as a bureaucratic-centralist, as state-capitalist, and as state-socialist. . . . [I]t is my contention that these societies should be described as *state-socialist*. Such societies are quite obviously not stateless, coercionless societies based on material superabundance. Therefore, they are not communist societies. Neither are they democratic enough to be classified as socialist societies (or, in Marx's words, as the first stage of communism). It would be inperspicuous to classify them as "state-capitalist" societies because they do not have classes of capitalists who can transfer investment wealth to their descendants, nor do such societies operate according to capitalist economic law of motion (i.e., according to the law of the maximization of exchange value). Finally, it would be misleading to classify them (along with fascist societies like Nazi Germany) as "bureaucratic-centralist" societies because this description ignores the fact that—unlike fascist societies—they have abolished capitalist production relations and successfully substituted the maximization of use value for the maximization of exchange value as the dominant economic law of motion.

More important than the label we attach to such societies are the normative political positions that seem to flow from the above descriptions. If the Marxist tradition is correct in its assertions that (1) capitalism is the chief cause of the world's social and economic problems and thus that capitalism must be eliminated on a worldwide scale in order to solve these problems and (2) the USSR and other so-called "communist countries" have eliminated capitalism, then whatever their drawbacks might be it would seem likely that a reversion to capitalism within such societies would be a major blow to the goal of developing a worldwide federation of democratic, self-managing socialist societies. Hence, it would seem that even though proponents of the tradition of Classical Marxism ought consistently to explain that state-socialist societies are not yet truly socialist and ought to call for implementation of democratic political, social, and economic institutions in such societies by evolutionary or, if necessary, revolutionary means, they ought also consistently to explain why such post-capitalist societies must be defended against the ideological, political, economic, and military attacks of the capitalist world. (Note that the revolutions in question would change the political and other decision-making superstructures rather than production relations—i.e., the economic substructure—and thus are classified by the Classical Marxist tradition as *political* rather than *social* revolutions.)[5]

In light of these considerations, it seems necessary to add two further positions to our list of the Classical Marxist's basic normative political positions, namely, that (3) *political* revolutions are justified in contemporary post-capitalist societies *if*, and only if, they are both necessary and sufficient to achieve genuinely democratic forms of socialism in those societies, and (4) contemporary post-capitalist societies—even though they, by no stretch of the imagination, meet the criteria of the Classical Marxists for being socialist societies in that they lack democratic institutions of workers' self-management—must be supported and defended in their struggles with capitalist and especially imperialist powers—except perhaps under extremely unusual circumstances.

State-Socialism vs. Capitalism

To decide between a capitalist and a state-socialist society we must specify what form of capitalism we have in mind as well as the degree of repression that exists in the state-socialist society. While this may seem to beg the question against state-socialist societies on the issue of the existence of repression, it is merely a definitional point: if a post-capitalist society is neither undemocratic nor repressive, then it is a genuinely socialist rather than a state-socialist society.

Since choosing between the worst-known form of capitalism (say, Nazi Germany of the 1930s and 1940s) and the worst form of state-socialism (say, Stalinist Russia of the late 1920s and the 1930s) is neither palatable nor enlightening, I shall for the present limit my discussion to presently existing forms of capitalism and state-socialism (both of which, I will assume, meet the first principle). It seems clear that *so long as this choice is made in isolation from diachronic and international factors,* a Swedenized form of advanced, industrialized capitalism is morally preferable to a state-socialist society because it better meets the second (maximum equal liberty) principle and at least the second part of the third principle, i.e., the part calling for political democracy. Similarly, in a decision between less egalitarian democratic capitalist societies (e.g., the contemporary U.S.A.) and state-socialist societies (e.g., the contemporary USSR), one would have to choose the former on precisely the same grounds—again, so long as the decision is made in isolation from diachronic and international considerations.

Attending to such diachronic and international considerations will quite probably not substantially weaken the case for preferring Sweden to state-socialist societies. Even though Swedish capital is, in part, international capital, Sweden has a relatively nonaggressive, egalitarian, and humanitarian foreign policy. However, attending to these factors will almost undoubtedly weaken the case for preferring such capitalist societies as the United States to state-socialist societies. Any such decision would also, of course, be contingent upon an analysis of the international and diachronic dimensions of contemporary state-socialist societies, in particular, their relations with other countries and their own potential for change toward a democratic form of socialism.

As to the first (diachronic) factor, it is an assumption of the Classical Marxist tradition that class struggle in capitalist societies is inevitable (or at least highly likely) and that capitalist societies such as the United States may well degenerate into dictatorial forms of government during the future course of this struggle. Although the claim that even hitherto stable capitalist democracies will quite possibly become authoritarian may at first seem outlandish, the historical evidence concerning the rise of fascism — as analyzed by Trotsky and others — points in another direction.[6]

In fact, the Marxist assessment of fascism as the ultimate defense of capitalism is an important empirical thesis in Marxism's defense of its normative political positions. Although this analysis is much disputed, it seems quite plausible that at least certain components of the capitalist class and the power elite that serves its interests will fight fervently for such a "solution" (i.e., a military dictatorship or fascist regime) if a revolutionary workers' movement actually begins to develop into a significant 'threat.' And Marxists — as opposed to some other sorts of socialists — are generally in agreement that not even the most prosperous and/or powerful capitalist society can keep the lid on the class struggle indefinitely. The logic of capitalism, so it is argued, will eventually lead to the capitalist class attempting to drive down the relative (and perhaps absolute) proportion of the surplus social product consumed by the working class and other subordinate classes, and this — conjoined with all of the other economic, social, and political crises of capitalism — will eventually lead to the radicalization of at least significant parts of these subordinate classes.

Furthermore, as pointed out in the previous discussion of the choice between democratic, self-managing socialism and state-socialism, another thesis of the Classical Marxist tradition is that there can be a democratic, self-managing form of socialism. A correlative thesis is that presently existing state-socialist societies — as well as presently existing capitalist societies — can by either evolutionary or revolutionary means be transformed into democratic, self-managing socialist societies. On this analysis, post-capitalist societies can, in the long run, also be expected to meet the second and third principles better than capitalist systems. Thus our theory of social justice will choose them as morally preferable. Ultimately, of course, the Marxist tradition demands that any real comparison be made on a world scale since it is assumed that capitalist and post-capitalist societies are incompatible and cannot indefinitely coexist. But if the above analysis is correct, the choice facing the

human species is *not* between bourgeois parliamentary democracy and "totalitarian communism," as many bourgeois polemicists and ideologues maintain, but — in the final analysis — between some form (perhaps, in time, an extremely democratic form) of socialism and some form (perhaps an extremely undemocratic or even a totalitarian form) of capitalism.

As to the second (international) parameter, it is an assumption not only of the Marxist tradition but of many non-Marxists as well that capitalism, in general, and such capitalist societies as the United States, in particular, are the major cause of the underdevelopment of the Third World and are thus responsible for the starvation, malnutrition, and abject poverty and misery of hundreds of millions of people.[7] Since the Marxist's view is that there is no chance of capitalism reforming itself to meet these problems, the conclusion is that the only way to solve the problems of the Third World is to transform both Third World societies and such advanced capitalist societies as the United States into socialist (or at least post-capitalist) societies. Therefore, post-capitalist societies are to be preferred to capitalist societies on a world scale because only the former will be able to ensure people's subsistence rights. This is assuming, of course, that there would be no comparable violations of security rights by such post-capitalist societies (due to mass torture, executions, slave-labor camps, etc.). Moreover, based on these assumptions even a worldwide state-socialist society may be morally preferable to a world that still contains major capitalist powers, since the principle providing for the protection of basic rights to well-being takes precedence over all other principles of social justice. (Fortunately, this is *not* the only alternative to capitalism if the Marxist tradition is correct.)

Opponents of Marxism often claim that post-capitalist societies — and especially a global post-capitalist society — will violate more basic rights to well-being than their capitalist counterparts due to torture, executions, and slave-labor camps. If this were true, then capitalism would be morally preferable to such post-capitalist societies. Abuses often cited are from 1930s Stalinist Russia: the massacre of millions of rich peasants and forced collectivization of the peasantry, the ruthless elimination of all political opposition both inside and outside the Communist

Party, the Gulag Archipelago, etc. Although it is beyond the purview of this work to attempt a systematic assessment of the development of the Soviet Union and other post-capitalist societies, some relatively plausible assertions made by non-Stalinist Marxists are: (1) such policies have no basis within the tradition of Classical Marxism, and it is of the utmost importance to distinguish Stalin and Stalinism from Marx and Marxism; [8] (2) the grain strike against the state, which led to Stalin's "liquidation" of the kulaks in the early 1930s, could in all probability have been avoided if the left opposition's program of gradual, voluntary collectivization and the prevention of the formation and solidification of a class of rich peasants had been accepted in the 1920s; (3) the abhorrent policies of the Soviet Union and other post-capitalist societies have largely resulted from the process of modernization and industrialization, which economically advanced capitalist societies had already undergone over a longer period of time, though not necessarily at less expense in terms of human misery;[9] (4) it was precisely the economic and political backwardness of the Soviet Union that resulted in its eventual degeneration into a totalitarian society; and (5) despite continued violation of civil rights and lack of democracy in the Soviet Union and other (now industrialized and modernized) post-capitalist societies, the past practices of mass executions, torture, and slave-labor camps have either been eliminated or severely curtailed.[10] Furthermore, it is arguable that capitalist rather than post-capitalist societies are today the worst violators of human rights.[11] Thus, rather than "communism" or Marxism being the primary cause of human-rights violations, as is often claimed, a strong case can be made for the view that today capitalism is the primary cause (more on this presently).

Although there is much talk of the "imperialism" of post-capitalist societies (as in "Soviet-socialist imperialism"), it is arguable that whatever state-socialist societies do to further their geopolitical interests, these interests are qualitatively different from those of capitalist societies. The geopolitical interests of capitalist powers like the United States (or, more precisely, the interests of the ruling classes and their allies within such societies) lie in maintaining what Noam Chomsky and others describe as a "favorable investment climate." This is because the laws of motion of capitalism demand an ever-expanding increase of capitalist investment and thus an ever-increasing penetration of the developing countries. Post-capitalist societies, however, are not subject to the same economic law of motion (namely, that of the maximization of exchange value or, more loosely, profit) and do not have the same economic interests or relations with developing countries. Although presently existing post-capitalist societies are interested in striking the best economic deals possible with such countries and often in supporting "friendly regimes," and — to a limited extent — supporting anti-capitalist movements around the world, they are not forced to maintain a favorable investment climate on an international scale. In short, unlike the imperialist capitalist powers, they are not compelled to undertake the role of maintaining a favorable economic status quo in every far-flung quarter of the world.

In addition, while we in the West (and especially in the United States) are told virtually every day of the "Soviet threat" and "international communist conspiracy," it is arguably the case that it is the United States that is committed to massive war expenditures and active military intervention around the world in order to protect "American interests" and "American security," i.e., to protect the right of the Western capitalist economy to have at its disposal favorable investment opportunities. It is also arguable that it is not the "international communist conspiracy" but the conditions of abject poverty and permanent misery engendered by capitalism in almost all (capitalist) developing countries that lead to the *indigenous* revolutionary movements. In short, it is arguably capitalism rather than "communism," and the United States rather than the USSR that is the main instigator of the arms race, the basic cause of revolutionary movements, and the primary aggressor in the world today.[12]

. . .

Revolution and Marxist Empirical Theory

Before setting out the minimal set of Marxist empirical theses upon which I believe an adequate Marxist moral and social theory should be based, I would like to make a few brief comments concerning the second basic normative political position I have attributed to Classical Marxism, namely, that socialist revolution — if necessary and sufficient to effect the appropriate transformations — is *prima facie* morally justified. . . .

[I]t seems to me that the justification of revolutions grows progressively weaker as we advance through our set of lexically ranked principles. I take it as fairly obvious that any system or government that by intentional action or negligence allows widespread violations of the first principle (which states that everyone's basic rights to well-being must be guaranteed) can legitimately be overthrown if there is a reasonable chance of replacing it with a system or government that will meet this principle. Similarly, I take it that systematic violations of the second (maximum equal liberty) principle give rise to a right to rebel unless they are justified by other extremely weighty moral considerations, e.g., meeting the first principle. And although justifications of revolution based on violations of the third and fourth principles are correspondingly weaker, if the violations of these principles were severe, unnecessary, and unending, then revolution might be justified (if it were both a necessary and sufficient condition to correct this situation).

· · ·

[O]bjections to the Marxist position in favor of socialist revolution in capitalist countries are sometimes based on misinterpretations of what Marxists are advocating. In this connection it is important to realize that for Marx and other Classical Marxists the means that advance socialist revolution are only those that advance the *mass* movement of the proletariat and its allies. (This is the empirical ground on which all Classical Marxists opposed terrorism as a means of social change.) The Classical Marxist view of revolution is one in which the majority of the population — or at least the majority of the working class and other oppressed segments of the population — is actively committed to radical social change and is forced into the use of violent means to protect themselves and their organizations (e.g., trade unions, workers' parties, and — in revolutionary situations — the popular organs of "dual power" that have begun to function as an alternate government) against the reactionary violence of the official police and military forces and/or fascist gangs or death squads. On this scenario the justification for workers' self-defense of their movements and organizations is essentially of the same sort as the justification that can be given for workers not allowing scabs to cross picket lines during a just labor strike.[13]

An adequate moral theory will certainly prohibit any violence not absolutely essential to a just struggle and may, besides, prohibit certain forms of violence (e.g., torture) under *any* circumstances. But the means proposed by the Classical Marxists — demonstrations, strikes, picket lines, the active and direct defense by workers and their allies of their organizations and movements, and (in extreme circumstances) rebellion and war — do not differ from the means most liberals (or most other people, for that matter) find permissible when essential for the successful prosecution of a just war or just struggle against oppression.[14] Although Marxists and non-Marxists may well disagree on the correct set of moral principles and/or the correct set of empirical theses involved in making such decisions, the point is that if a relatively egalitarian moral theory and a minimal set of Marxist empirical theses are essentially correct, then the Marxist position on socialist revolution is justified.

I wish now to discuss the minimal set of Marxist empirical theses I have utilized in justifying the Marxist's basic normative political positions. Previously I described three levels of Marx's empirical theories. In decreasing order of abstraction or generality they are: (1) historical materialism, (2) Marx's theory of classes and class conflict, and (3) Marx's more specific economic and sociological theories, including his analysis of the dysfunctions of capitalism and his projections concerning socialism. The theory of historical materialism seeks to account for epochal social transformations by relating the categories of forces of production, relations of production, and the political-legal-ideological superstructure by means of two laws (or statements of lawlike regularities). The "law" of *technological determinism* states that the forces of production in some sense determine the relations of production. The "law" of *economic determinism* states that the mode of production (i.e., the forces and relations of production taken together) in some sense determines the political-legal-ideological superstructure.

At the next level of abstraction comes Marx's theory of classes and class struggle. Some of the more important claims here are that (1) all societies having a significant surplus social product are divided into dominant and subordinate (or ruling and ruled) classes on the basis of how these classes of individuals are related to the means of production, (2) the economic interests of these classes are diametrically opposed to one another, and (3) the political-legal-ideological superstructures of such societies almost always support the interests of the dominant class. At the lowest level of abstraction we find the Marxist analysis of such dysfunctions of capitalism as depression, recession, inflation, imperialist wars, and (today) the problem of pollution and environmental destruction.

It is my contention that although historical materialism and Marx's theory of classes and class struggle (as applied to all surplus social product societies) can be given quite plausible interpretations, it is his theory of classes and class struggle *as specifically applied to capitalism,* together with the Marxist's analysis of the social and economic dysfunctions of capitalism and possibilities for post-capitalist societies, that composes the minimal set of Marxist empirical theses necessary to justify the Marxist's basic normative political positions. While the acceptance of the more abstract components of Marx's overall empirical theory may well give us more confidence in the lower-level claims, they are in principle dispensable for the justificatory purpose we have in mind.

Some writers hold that at least the "rational kernel" of historical materialism is relevant to or even necessary for the justification of these normative political positions since, the argument goes, this rational kernel is needed to show that socialism is possible.[15] But my answer to this is that (1) historical materialism does not show that socialism is possible (at least if we take "socialism" to mean democratic, self-managing socialism) and thus does not ensure that the Marxist's basic normative political positions are justified, and (2) since 1917 we haven't needed the theory of historical materialism to show us that at least some stable, ongoing form of post-capitalist society is possible. The point is that we may well have good reason to believe that post-capitalist societies in general and democratic, self-managing socialist societies in particular are historically possible, whether or not some

formulation of historical materialism (or of its rational kernel) is tenable.

Similarly, whether Marx's theory of classes and class struggle can be successfully applied to *all* specified societies seems irrelevant for our present justificatory purposes. I would venture the opinion that it may not even matter whether Marx's structural view or Max Weber's stratification view of classes (or some combination of the two) is ultimately correct so long as it is admitted that, on either account, it is reasonable to speak of dominant and subordinate classes and, in particular, of a ruling class. In fact, if Richard Miller's analysis is correct, asking whether there is a ruling class is not so much an abstract theoretical question as a practical and strategic political one. If we answer no, we seem to be implying that the less well-off segments of the population can pursue their interests and garner for themselves a fair share of the social wealth by legal and 'proper' means, while if we answer yes we seem to be implying the opposite view.[16]

Finally, this minimal set of theses will *not* include certain parts of Marx's less abstract economic and sociological theory either because they are demonstrably false or because, though plausible, they are irrelevant. The labor theory of value clearly falls into the first camp, while the thesis that there can be a completely classless and *stateless* society under modern conditions would seem to fall into the latter.

Under present historical circumstances this set of assumptions should, I think, include the following sociological and economic claims:

1. As a result of the logic of the maximization of exchange value, all capitalist societies — developed or developing, partially planned or completely unplanned — exhibit and will continue to exhibit certain economic and social problems (inflation, depression, recession, unemployment, poverty, failure to regulate environmental pollution sufficiently, etc.) that can be solved only by the institution of a planned (but not necessarily command) socialist economy.

2. Even the mixed, welfare-state capitalist societies of advanced, industrialized nations of the West exhibit severe social inequalities and — if sufficiently threatened by mass working-class movements for

social equality—will almost undoubtedly exhibit severe repression.

3. The world capitalist system causes in the Third World both extreme inequality and suffering, on the one hand, and (often) extremely repressive regimes, on the other.

4. So long as it is dominant or codominant on an international scale, the capitalist system will not allow the massive transfers of capital, technology, and knowledge necessary to solve the Third World's major social and economic problems.

5. Such conditions in the Third World make for perpetual social instability since those who are severely oppressed and/or deprived will organize and, if necessary, fight to better their condition or "the condition of their peoples."

6. The predictable response from the most powerful nations at the capitalist "center" (primarily the United States at this point in history and for the foreseeable future) is first to install and/or aid those Third World regimes or military cliques that can best suppress these mass movements for radical social change and, second, if that strategy fails, to intervene either directly with its own military forces or indrectly through proxy armies and "low-intensity warfare."

7. However else we may characterize contemporary post-capitalist societies, it seems clear that they are not the primary cause of the many indigenous revolutionary movements in the Third World and do not bear the primary responsibility for the nuclear arms race.

8. The bureaucracies of such post-capitalist societies genuinely want to reduce or eliminate arms expenditures in order to better satisfy the consumer appetites of their own populations.

9. Without the economic, diplomatic, and military pressure of the Western capitalist powers, such post-capitalist societies may well achieve significant democratization (by either evolutionary or revolutionary means).

10. Socialist transformations can occur in the advanced industrialized countries of the West, and

such transformations can lead to democratic forms of socialism; thus a worldwide federation of democratic, self-managing, socialist societies is a genuine historical possibility.

I am not saying that all of these claims are necessary for justifying the Marxist's basic normative political positions, although I would assert—barring extremely implausible counter-assumptions—that they are jointly sufficient. I put them forward as examples of the sorts of (seemingly plausible) claims that must be true in order for the Marxist's positions to be justified on any fairly egalitarian theory of social justice. If the vision of the present world social order expressed by this set of claims is not tenable, then, in all probability, neither are the Marxist's basic normative political positions.

As to the responsibilities of individuals, I here have very little to say. If both a relatively egalitarian theory of social justice (such as the one put forward here) and a minimal set of Marxist empirical assumptions are essentially correct, then our natural duty to support and promote just social institutions (on both a national and international level) would seem to require us to do our fair share in supporting and promoting various working-class and progressive causes within our own societies and, if possible, on an international scale. (Perhaps the most efficient way to support such causes on an international scale is to monitor and, if necessary, alter our own societies' foreign policy, investment and aid policies, etc.)

In any case, this would seem to include supporting the struggles of workers and labor unions, the struggles of poor people (and nations) for a just share of the world's wealth, the struggles of oppressed minorities, and the struggle for the liberation of women, as well as environmentalist movements, anti-nuclear and anti-interventionist movements, and organizations and movements committed to the protection of human rights. If Marxist political theory is correct, however, the most important sorts of movements and organizations we can (and should) support are *political parties* explicitly committed to eliminating capitalism and bringing into being a world federation of democratic, self-managing socialist societies.

The simple truth is that if a relatively egalitarian theory of social justice (and human rights) and the

Marxist's vision of contemporary social reality are essentially correct, then the only way we can respect other persons as free and equal moral beings—and, consequently, respect ourselves—is to do our fair share in supporting such movements, organizations, and struggles.

Notes

1. . . . I take the major figures of the Classical Marxist tradition to be Marx, Engels, Lenin, Luxemburg, Trotsky, and Gramsci. Contemporary Marxist political theorists whom I believe to be representative of the Classical Marxist tradition, and whom I believe would agree with much of what I say in the rest of this chapter, include Ernest Mandel, Ralph Miliband, Perry Anderson, Mihailo Marković, Svetozar Stojanović, and Roy Medvedev. (See references in the bibliography.) Although Alasdair MacIntyre probably never accepted enough of Marxist empirical theory to be classified as a Marxist, some of his early works are clearly sympathetic to the normative political positions of Classical Marxism. See *Marxism and Christianity,* and his essays on politics and political philosophy in part one of *Against the Self-Image of the Age.*

    I suspect that Noam Chomsky also would agree with most of the basic normative political positions for which I argue in this chapter, even though he is a self-proclaimed libertarian (i.e., left-wing) anarchist and, as such, is opposed in principle to certain Marxist claims having to do with the long-term legitimacy of a socialist state (since the state, for anarchists, is inherently evil) and the justifiability of a democratic-centralist—i.e., Marxist-Leninist—political party. (Anarchists are highly critical of *any* form of centralized power, even one that proclaims itself to be both democratic and temporary.) But see the references to Chomsky's works below, all of which provide unrelenting critiques of both contemporary capitalist and contemporary state-socialist societies.

2. For some relevant data and analyses concerning contemporary Sweden on this point, as well as the degree of social and economic democracy existing there, see the articles collected in *Limits of the Welfare State: Critical Views on Post-War Sweden* (J. A. Fry, ed.). According to the endnotes of Lennart Bernston's "Post-War Swedish Capitalism," in recent years, "The accumulation and concentration of wealth in the hands of Sweden's top fifteen families has continued and with government approval and support the number of annual mergers has increased. The position of finance capital in the Swedish economy has always been strong with the fifteen leading families clustered around three major banks [two of which have recently merged].

During recent years these financial institutions have extended their control over the most expansive sectors of industry both in monopoly and non-monopoly . . . controlled branches" (*Limits of the Welfare State,* p. 87).

    According to Stig Larsson and Kurt Sjöström in "The Welfare Myth in Class Society," "In general, no . . . income levelling [between social classes] has occurred in Sweden (with the exception of temporary phenomena). Even those who earlier tried to conceal class cleavages have been forced to concede their continued existence in spite of decades of social democratic rule . . . income levelling has stagnated during the post war period. The levelling effect of the taxation has been low—'approximately 90 per cent of inequality prior to tax remains after taxation'" (*Limits of the Welfare State,* p. 171). "Riches grow on one side and poverty spreads on the other. While the number of millionaires grows by a couple of hundred per year, the number of individuals who must seek social assistance . . . increases by about 50,000 annually. . . . 5 per cent of the population owns 50 per cent of the wealth . . . nearly one-half of the wage earners have an annual income of less than five thousands dollars (ibid., p. 172).

    The income and wealth differentials within a less egalitarian advanced capitalist society such as the United States are, of course, even more severe. See Ferdinand Lundberg, *America's Sixty Families,* Vanguard Press, 1937, and *The Rich and the Super-Rich: A Study in the Power of Money Today,* Lyle Stuart, 1968; and David Kotz, *Bank Control of Large Corporations in the United States,* University of California Press, Berkeley, 1978. Conversely, see Michael Harrington, *The Other America: Poverty in the United States,* Macmillan, N.Y., 1962, 1964, and *The New American Poverty,* Holt, Rinehart, and Winston, N.Y., 1984. The differentials in *power* resulting from the structures that create such wealth and income differentials are documented by William Domhoff in: *Who Rules America?* Prentice-Hall, Englewood Cliffs, N.J., 1967; *The Higher Circles: The Governing Class in America,* Random House, N.Y., 1970; *Fat Cats and Democrats: The Role of the Big Rich in the Party of the Common Man,* Prentice-Hall, Englewood Cliffs, N.J., 1972; *The Bohemian Grove and Other Retreats: A Study in Ruling Class Cohesiveness,* Harper & Row, N.Y., 1974; *Who Really Rules? New Haven and Community Power Reexamined,* Transaction Books, New Brunswick, N.J., 1978; *The Powers That Be: Process of Ruling Class Domination in America,* Random House, N.Y., 1979; *Who Rules America Now?: A View of the Eighties,* Prentice-Hall, Englewood Cliffs, N.J., 1983.

3. See the following articles in *Limits of the Welfare State* (J. A. Fry, ed.): Lennart Bernston, "Post-War Swedish Capitalism"; Karl Anders Larsson, "The

International Dependence of the Swedish Economy"; and Jan Annerstedt, "The Swedish Arms Industry and the Viggen Project."

4. For documentation of the rather extensive privileges of the political-military-managerial-technocratic bureaucracies of state-socialist societies, see Walter D. Connor, *Socialism Politics, and Equality: Hierarchy and Change in Eastern Europe and the USSR,* Columbia University Press, N.Y., 1979; Mervyn Matthews, *Privilege in the Soviet Union,* Allen & Unwin, London, 1978; Murray Yanowitch, *Social and Economic Inequality in the Soviet Union,* Myron Sharpe, N.Y., 1979; P. Wiles, *Distribution of Income: East and West,* North Holland Press, Amsterdam, 1974; Frank Parkin, *Class Inequality and Political Order: Social Stratification in Capitalist and Communist Societies,* Praeger, N.Y., 1971; and Victor Zaslavsky, "The Regime and the Working Class in the USSR," *Telos,* vol. 42 (1979–80), and "Socioeconomic Inequality and Changes in Soviet Ideology," *Theory and Society,* vol. 9, no. 2 (1980). Also, Trotsky's *The Revolution Betrayed* contains valuable information concerning the initial formation of a privileged bureaucracy in the Soviet Union.

Although this phenomenon is most well studied and well documented with respect to the Soviet Union and other Eastern European post-capitalist societies, it is clear that such privileged bureaucracies also exist (to one degree or another) in the People's Republic of China and other Third World post-capitalist societies. Cuba and Nicaragua, however, may be the least bureaucratized of all presently existing post-capitalist societies. One reason for this might be that they are among the most recently created post-capitalist societies. Perhaps an even more important reason, however, is that their anti-capitalist revolutions were not led by (already) Stalinized Communist Parties but by indigenous revolutionary socialist parties that either absorbed the smaller Communist Party after the revolution (as in the case of Castro's July 26th Movement in Cuba) or simply ignored it (as in the case of the Sandinista Party in Nicaragua). (These factors also may help account for the fact that both the leadership and the general population of these societies seem to exhibit the highest degree of revolutionary fervor to be found among presently existing post-capitalist societies. This, in turn, may account for the U.S. government's special antipathy toward them.)

Actually, since the process of socializing large-scale productive property has not to date been completed in Nicaragua, it is not quite accurate to classify it as a post-capitalist society. But it seems clear that barring the success of the U.S. policy of overthrowing the Sandinista government or completely bankrupting the Nicaraguan economy in order to ferment massive popular discontent and, thus, an internal revolt against the Sandinistas, Nicaragua eventually will complete the process of socialization of large-scale productive property and, thus, become a full-fledged post-capitalist society. (This does not mean that the Sandinista government will not let *some* productive enterprises remain in private hands or that they will not continue to rely on market mechanisms to some extent but . . . this would not necessarily count against classifying such a society as post-capitalist or even socialist.)

5. At the present time, as I am going over the copy edited version of this work, the student-led movement for greater freedom and democracy and less corruption on part of the privileged bureaucracy in China has just been brutally suppressed by the Chinese government. UPI has reported that the Red Cross in China estimated that 1400 people were killed and thousands wounded when the 27th Army cleared Tiananmen Square of demonstrators and retook Beijing, which had effectively been under the control of the students and the local population, who had surrounded and convinced numerous army units not to participate in the repression in the previous days. (Other estimates in the Western press range from 400 to 3,000 deaths.) Presently hundreds of students and workers who had supported them are being rounded up, imprisoned, beaten, forced to recant, and — in some cases — executed. There are reports that at least two generals and fifty officers from other army units that refused to participate in the bloody crackdown have also been executed.

Chinese government officials are now attempting to convince their own citizens (and anyone in the outside world willing to listen to them) that this mass movement on the part of students and workers was, in fact, a counterrevolutionary movement aimed at the overthrow of both the Communist Party and socialist property relations. The evidence, however, shows rather convincingly that this movement was not aimed at a social revolution to change property relations — i.e., at a reversion to capitalism — but, rather, at a political revolution to establish socialist democracy. (Actually, it is probably somewhat misleading to say that it was aimed at *any* sort of revolution, since the movement demanded only a dialogue with top government officials, publication of government leaders' assets and salaries, greater freedom of the press and other democratic rights, and price controls on consumer goods in the face of high inflation.) Assuming this analysis is basically correct, this is precisely the type of movement that Marxists and all those in favor of democratic socialism ought to advocate and support.

Not surprisingly, many capitalist politicians and ideologues in the West have hypocritically shed crocodile tears over Tiananmen Square while simultaneously supporting such brutally repressive, anti-democratic governments as those in Taiwan, South Korea, Chile, Guatemala, Honduras, and El Salvador. These figures, together with much of the bourgeois media in the West, have also trumpeted these events as signaling the "revolt against communism" and the "demise of socialism" rather than describing them as attempts to establish a more democratic and, therefore, more viable form of socialism. (That most of these individuals would not support pro-democracy movements in state-socialist societies if they really thought they would succeed can presumably be deduced from the fact that if such movements did succeed in transforming state-socialist societies into democratic, self-managing socialist societies, then these capitalist politicians and ideologues would lose their main argument for the superiority of capitalism — namely, that socialist property relations are incompatible with freedom and democracy — as well as their main rationale for savagely repressing anti-capitalist movements and/or installing pro-capitalist dictatorships around the world.) I would argue that while there is no evidence for the view that these events forebode a return to capitalism, they do seem to confirm the hypothesis that the entrenched bureaucracies in most state-socialist societies are not about to give up their privileges and their monopolies on political power without a serious struggle. (For an analysis of the political bureaucracy in China, see P'eng Shu-tse, *The Chinese Communist Party in Power,* Pathfinder Press, N.Y., 1980; Tom Kerry, *The Mao Myth and the Legacy of Stalinism in China,* Pathfinder Press, N.Y., 1977; and Leslie Evans, *China After Mao,* Pathfinder Press, N.Y., 1978. For a brief analysis of the recent events in China from the perspective of those Marxists in favor of democratic socialism, see Cliff DuRand, "Only through Socialism Can Full Democracy Be Realized: China's Socialists Have One Last Chance," *The Guardian* [N.Y.], June 21, 1989.)

6. See Trotsky's *The Struggle Against Fascism in Germany* and *The Spanish Revolution (1931–39)*; Daniel Guerin, *Fascism and Big Business,* Pathfinder Press, N.Y., 1973; Poulantzas, *Fascism and Dictatorship;* Rupert Palme Dutt, *Fascism and Social Revolution,* Proletarian Press, N.Y., 1936; Franz Neumann, *Behemoth: The Structure and Practice of National Socialism (1933–1944),* Harper & Row, N.Y., 1944; and David Schoenbaum, *Hitler's Social Revolution: Class and Status in Nazi Germany (1933–39),* W. W. Norton, N.Y., 1980.

7. For a defense of these claims, see Sweezy, *The Theory of Capitalist Development;* Baran, *The Political Economy of Growth;* Magdoff, *The Age of Imperialism;* Andre Gunder Frank, *Capitalism and Underdevelopment in Latin America,* Monthly Review Press, N.Y., 1967, and *Dependent Accumulation and Underdevelopment,* Monthly Review Press, N.Y., 1978; Immanuel Wallerstein, *The Capitalist World Economy: Essays,* Cambridge University Press, N.Y., 1979; Samir Amin, *Unequal Development: An Essay on the Social Formations of Peripheral Capitalism,* Monthly Review Press, N.Y., 1976, and *Imperialism and Unequal Development,* Monthly Review Press, N.Y., 1977; and Weisskopf, "Imperialism and the Economic Development of the Third World."

   See also Ronald H. Chilcote, *Theories of Development and Underdevelopment,* Westview Press, Boulder, Colo., 1984; Gabriel Kolko, *The Roots of American Foreign Policy,* Beacon Press, Boston, 1969; Robert Rhodes (ed.), *Imperialism and Underdevelopment,* Monthly Review Press, N.Y., 1970; Robert Owen and Bob Sutcliffe, *Studies in the Theory of Imperialism,* Longman, London, 1972; Michael Barratt-Brown, *The Economics of Imperialism,* Longman, London, 1973; Charles Wilber (ed.), *The Political Economy of Development and Underdevelopment,* Random House, N.Y., 1973; and Richard Barnet and Ronald Muller, *Global Reach: The Power of Multinational Corporation,* Simon & Schuster, N.Y., 1974.

   See also Michael Harrington, *The Vast Majority: A Journey to the World's Poor,* Simon & Schuster, N.Y., 1977; the Brandt Commission, *North-South: A Program for Survival,* MIT Press, Cambridge, Mass., 1980; Teresa Hayter, *The Creation of World Poverty: An Alternative View to the Brandt Report,* Pluto Press, London, 1981; and Castro, *The World Crisis.*

8. The claim that the violence against the Soviet population perpetrated by the Stalinist regime can be laid at the door of Marxist theory or values is debatable, to say the least. The Classical Marxists — including Lenin and Trotsky — never thought that the Soviet Union could, by itself, achieve a lasting democratic form of socialism but, rather, pinned their hopes on the spread of the socialist revolution to the industrialized West, especially to Germany. They neither thought necessary nor advocated the pernicious policies or methods here mentioned. Trotsky puts this in perspective when he writes: "Stalinism . . . [is] an immense bureaucratic reaction against the proletarian dictatorship in a backward and isolated country. The October Revolution abolished privileges, waged war against social inequality, replaced the bureaucracy with self-government of the toilers, abolished secret diplomacy, strove to render all social relationships completely transparent. Stalinism reestablished the most offensive forms of privileges, imbued inequality with a provocative character, strangled mass self-activity under police absolutism, transformed administration into a monopoly of the Kremlin oligarchy and regenerated the fetishism of power in forms that absolute monarchy dared not dream of.

". . . Stalinist frame-ups are not a fruit of Bolshevik 'amoralism'; no, like all important events in history, they are a product of the concrete social struggle, and the most perfidious and severest of all at that: the struggle of a new aristocracy against the masses that raised it to power.

"Verily boundless intellectual and moral obtuseness is required to identify the reactionary police morality of Stalinism with the revolutionary morality of the Bolsheviks" (*Their Morals and Ours*, p. 25).

On the phenomenon of Stalinism, see Trotsky, *The Revolution Betrayed;* R. Medvedev, *Let History Judge* and *On Stalin and Stalinism;* Ali (ed.), *The Stalinist Legacy;* and R. Tucker (ed.), *Stalinism.*

9. See Marx's description, in the first volume of *Capital,* of the plight of the emerging proletariat and dispossessed peasantry in England during and after the Industrial Revolution, or E. P. Thompson's account in *The Making of the English Working Class,* Vintage, N.Y., 1963, 1966.

10. See, however, Sidney Bloch and Peter Reddaway, *Psychiatric Terror,* Basic Books, N.Y., 1977; and Zhores Medvedev and Roy Medvedev, *Questions of Madness,* W. W. Norton, N.Y., 1979.

11. According to the American Friends Service Committee pamphlet, "Questions and Answers on the Soviet Threat and National Security" (Philadelphia, 1981): "The top ten recipients of US military and economic aid, according to Amnesty International, are also the world's top ten dictatorships or violators of human rights: South Korea, The Philippines, Indonesia, Thailand, Chile, Argentina, Uruguay, Haiti, Brazil, and formerly, Iran" (p. 16). (Needless to say, all of these countries are capitalist.)

12. In addition to the American Friends Service Committee pamphlet quoted above, see Robert Aldridge, *First Strike: The Pentagon's Strategy for Nuclear War,* South End Press, Boston, 1983, and *The Counterforce Syndrome: A Guide to U.S. Nuclear Weapons and Strategic Doctrine,* 2nd ed., Institute for Strategic Studies, Washington, D.C., 1979; Seymour Melmen, *Profits without Production,* Knopf, N.Y., 1983, and *The Permanent War Economy,* Touchstone, 1985; Daniel Ellsberg, "Call to Mutiny," *Protest and Survive* (E. P. Thompson and Dan Smith, eds.), Monthly Review Press, N.Y., 1981; Richard Barnet, *Roots of War: The Men and Institutions Behind U.S. Foreign Policy,* Penguin Books, N.Y., 1981; Noam Chomsky, *Towards a New Cold War: Essays on the Current Crisis and How We Got There,* Pantheon, N.Y., 1982; and Michael T. Klare and Peter Kornbluh (eds.), *Low Intensity Warfare: Counterinsurgency, Proinsurgency, and Antiterrorism in the Eighties,* Pantheon, N.Y., 1987. See also the following books by Michael T.

Klare: *War without End: American Planning for the Next Vietnams,* Knopf, N.Y., 1972; *Beyond the Vietnam Syndrome: U.S. Intervention in the 1980's,* Institute for Policy Studies, Washington, D.C., 1981; and *The American Arms Supermarket,* University of Texas Press, Austin, 1984.

For a Marxist defense of the view that the two superpowers are equally responsible for the arms race, however, see E. P. Thompson, "Notes on Exterminism, the Last Stage of Civilization," *New Left Review* 121 (May–June 1980); "Letter to America," *The Nation,* Jan. 24, 1981 (reprinted in *Protest and Survive*); *Exterminism and Cold War,* Schocken, N.Y., 1982; and *The Heavy Dancers,* Merlin Press, London, 1985. For a Marxist response to this position, see Roy Medvedev and Zhores Medvedev, "A Nuclear Samizdat on America's Arms Race," *The Nation,* Jan. 16, 1982.

13. See Trotsky, *Transitional Program for Socialist Revolution;* James P. Cannon, *Socialism on Trial,* Pathfinder Press, N.Y., 1970; Luxemburg, "The Mass Strike, the Political Party, and the Trade Unions"; and Gintis and Bowles, "Socialist Revolution in the United States: Goals and Means."

14. Although this form of reasoning is sometimes decried as crude consequentialism, it is not "consequentialist" in the strict philosophical sense of the term, since one can take human rights or principles of social justice as morally basic and make such judgments on the basis of minimizing the violation or maximizing the observance of such rights or principles. Such a mixed deontological view might be called a "teleology of rights."

For further philosophical discussions of these issues, from a leftist perspective, see Marcuse, "Ethics and Revolution"; Marković, "Violence and Human Self-Realization"; Petrović, "Socialism, Revolution and Violence"; Stojanović, "Revolutionary Teleology and Ethics"; Wolf, "On Violence"; Honderich, *Three Essays on Political Violence* and "Four Conclusions about Violence of the Left"; Harris, "The Marxist Conception of Violence"; and the following articles by Nielsen: "On the Choice Between Reform and Revolution," "On Justifying Revolution," "On the Ethics of Revolution," "On Justifying Violence," "Political Violence," "Capitalism, Socialism, and Justice," and "On Terrorism and Political Assassination."

15. See Levine, *Arguing for Socialism.* Although we disagree on this point, I find that we are in basic agreement on most others. The only other major disagreement I see us as having is that I believe a stronger case can be made for choosing socialism over capitalism. Levine argues that since only a weak case can be made for socialism at an abstract, theoretical level, and since these are not the sorts of beliefs in which we can have a great deal of confidence to begin with, it is best to

conceive of the choice situation as a Pascalian wager and thus choose the more attractive alternative, namely socialism. It seems to me that we can make a much stronger case for socialism once we descend from the abstract level on which we compare capitalism and socialism in terms of Pareto optimality, etc., and begin to compare them on their impact and potential future impact on the rights of people in developing nations, etc. In relation to this point, I do not understand how Levine can claim, in the last paragraph of his work, "Capitalism is not Hell on earth; and socialism, even in its most radically democratic forms, would not be Heaven" (p. 225). While I agree with the latter part of this statement, it seems to me that even cursory knowledge of capitalism's impact on people in the Third World falsifies the former part. Capitalism may not be hell on earth for everyone, but it *is* hell on earth for the hundreds of millions of persons who are unnecessarily starving to death or going hungry and who must watch their loved ones suffer and die in the same way.

16. See chapters 3 and 4 of Miller, *Analyzing Marx*. For other contemporary Marxist analyses of classes, see G. A. Cohen, *Karl Marx's Theory of History*, chapter 3; McMurtry, *The Structure of Marx's World-View*, chapter 3; Elster, *Making Sense of Marx*, chapter 6; Roemer, *A General Theory of Exploitation and Class*; Miliband, *Class Power and State Power* and "State Power and Class Interests"; Poulantzas, *Classes in Contemporary Capitalism* and *Political Power and Social Classes*; Laclau, "The Specificity of Political"; Therborn, *What Does the Ruling Class Do When It Rules?*; and the following works by Wright: *Class, Crisis and the State; Class Structure and Income; Classes;* and "Class Boundaries in Advanced Capitalist Societies."

EQUAL EDUCATIONAL OPPORTUNITY:
Reexamining a Liberal Ideal

Michael S. Katz

Michael Katz applies the concept of equality to primary and secondary public education. He argues that people do have a basic right to an education and this basic right is being systematically violated in this country. He ends by showing what kind of changes would be required if people took a right to an equal education seriously.

Equality of educational opportunity, however problematic the notion has been in the educational literature, can be intelligibly reconstructed and connected with a sensible conception of educating people for the twenty-first century. Moreover, it can be usefully connected to a commonsense notion of liberal social justice. Finally, a reformulated version of this principle can help us understand the tension underlying the gap between our faith in the possibilities of education and our growing skepticism about contemporary public schooling in America.

This essay addresses two central questions: How should we think about the concept of "equal educational opportunity," and how can this concept be usefully connected with a sensible version of social justice in society? The focus is primarily on the answer to the first question, but the final sections begin to touch on the second one.[1] The answers to these questions will take account of (1) a brief historical picture of the evolution of schooling, (2) some significant court cases dealing with schooling, and (3) some contemporary realities affecting education in America.

Equal Educational Opportunity: Two Historical Patterns

The promise of U.S. democracy is that each person will have sufficient freedom to pursue her own version of happiness and achieve her fair share of the commonly desired social goods (income, power, status, recognition) on the basis of merit, initiative, or talent. This is a promise of fair competition that deemphasizes the power of social circumstance, parental influence, or other accidents of birth. One of the most common metaphors for this promise of fair competition for an unequal distribution of social goods is that of a race, and schooling is the central vehicle or instrumentality through which fair competition in the social-economic marketplace can be achieved.[2]

Models of Equal Educational Opportunity: Some Relevant Contrasts

If we invoke the metaphor of a race to think about social opportunity, we can distinguish two ways in which fairness can be achieved within the race: (1) everyone can start the race at the same point, or (2) the competition can be regulated to favor those who have special needs or circumstances that might prevent them from competing on an equal footing with the rest. Following Ken Howe's taxonomy of distinctions, I shall call the first approach "the equal access" approach and the second approach the "compensatory" approach.[3]

The Substance of Educational Opportunities: Notions of Being Educated

If we were to translate the notion of "equal educational opportunity" into a predicate form and put it into a sentence, we might end up with something like "Person A and Person B have roughly the same opportunities to acquire an education." Another version of this notion might be "Group A and Group B have roughly the same opportunities to be educated." Before we can choose appropriate criteria for deciding when the notion of "roughly the same opportunities" makes sense, we must consider some competing notions of what it would mean to be educated. Do we have in mind here some elevated ideal of a liberally educated Renaissance person who possesses great breadth and depth of knowledge, sharply honed analytic reasoning capacities, a boundless curiosity for new information, and an abundance of experiential wisdom? Or will some more modest achievement be sufficient? Clearly "being educated" has both maximal and minimal forms, but it seems to me that the state's compelling interest in educating people, as Thomas Green has forcefully pointed out, are minimal rather than maximal, although its regulation of schooling may be more maximal than minimal.[4]

Even having said this, one must note that several competing notions of minimalist ideals can be found in the literature on education. One such view is Jefferson's notion — modified, revised or essentially endorsed by Howe, Strike, Guttman, and others — that one central aim of education be some form of political literacy or competence. As the plaintiffs unsuccessfully argued in *Rodriguez v. San Antonio School District* having the skills and understanding necessary to participate intelligently in the political process as a citizen seems to require educational opportunities. Intelligently exercising the First Amendment freedoms to vote, to assemble, and to develop and act on one's political convictions require some minimal set of understandings, reasoning skills, and political dispositions. Thus, the notion of "political literacy," which seems to capture the dispositional as well as the cognitive dimensions of this achievement, seems most appropriate. Nevertheless, it remains an open question exactly what this "political literacy" would look like, how we would recognize it or measure it, and what the necessary conditions for the provisions of opportunities to acquire it would consist of.[5]

A second modest but sensible aim in a minimal conception of being educated might be the development of a moral sensibility, a moral conscience, or a moral character. Despite disagreements over the substance of moral character or over the nature and source of moral judgments, one could argue, as recent Gallup

Polls on schooling in America suggest, that there may be a reasonable consensus on the development of moral virtues in young people, virtues that might include honesty, democracy, tolerance, responsibility, fairness, benevolence, and compassion.[6] Moreover, if we conceived of moral reasoning in either deontological or utilitarian terms, one could argue that teaching young people how to make rational moral judgments about right actions based on moral principles such as justice, the well-being of others, or respect for persons would be a legitimate aim of education. In any case, a crucial aim of education is to create moral persons. It lies at the heart of the educational enterprise. Recent feminists have provided critiques of traditional ethical theory and moral development and have suggested that a feminist moral sensibility is more attuned to nurturing and sustaining caring relationships with others than to matters of abstract moral reasoning. I use the word "sensibility" here deliberately to suggest that one's way of being-in-the-world clearly can reflect how one is related to significant others through care, concern, and compassion.[7]

A final aim of education is self-respect based on some meaningful level of self-knowledge. Self-respect, in contrast with self-esteem, depends on two dimensions that complement each other. One dimension is the cognitive and conative appreciation of oneself as having moral value as a person, as an end-in-oneself and not merely as a means or instrument to others' purposes. To have self-respect is to understand and act toward oneself as a person with basic rights, the right to dignity, the right not to be enslaved, exploited, degraded, or used. The other side of self-respect is more subjective; it is involved with aiming to live a certain kind of life, in accord with self-chosen values (both moral and nonmoral), in pursuit of certain goals. For Rawls the notion of self-respect is linked with self-esteem and the capacity to develop and act on one's life plan, but I am not convinced that one needs to have a full-blown life plan to have self-respect in the sense I am using it.[8]

Clearly, underlying all three of these aims — political literacy, a moral sensibility, and self-respect — is some capacity of critical thought and the disposition to be reasonable. Elsewhere I have called this "critical literacy," and like John Passmore, I think it is best thought of as a character trait rather than an isolated set of rational skills.[9] Clearly, my list of aims could be expanded or shortened. There is nothing magical about them, but they do call attention to the fact that "education" throughout most of its linguistic history was not a term synonymous with, or equivalent to, "schooling." The symbiotic, linguistic connection between education and schooling emerged only in the late nineteenth century as schools came to occupy more and more social space. By the twentieth century, the only kind of legitimated educational experiences were those certified by schooling diplomas or certificates. Thus, it is not uncommon for people to ask, "Where did you get your education?" or "How much are you spending on your children's education?" In such linguistic utterances, "education" has become synonymous with schooling.

That identification, however, has significant limitations. It assumes that all schooling experiences are, ipso facto, educational experiences, and that is clearly not so. It is not hard to imagine that much of what does, or might, occur in schools is fundamentally miseducative according to a variety of educational criteria, not simply mine. It also obscures what parents, informed laypersons, sociologists, and most teachers understand very, very well, namely, that families and communities, as well as religious institutions and the media (especially television), are exercising significant educative or miseducative influence on children's development. The quality of support that children receive from their family and community critically affects their educational growth and development.

Education as a Right and Moral Principle

Applying Joel Feinberg's scheme of rights, we may categorize "the right to education" (as he categorizes "the right to life" or "the right to liberty") as an ideal directive. Ideal directives, according to Feinberg, are endorsements of more or less vague ideals; they do not, by themselves, specify particular entitlements, that is, specific things one is allowed to do or have. Rather, they function as guiding principles deserving to be honored and commanding us to do our very best for the cause that is built into the expression.[10]

Since a significant degree of vagueness is associated with the principle of educating people toward political literacy, moral character, and self-respect, we can regard the right to education as a moral principle rather than as a specific moral rule.

In ordinary language, we often talk about principles and rules as if they were interchangeable notions. However, as Ronald Dworkin has pointed out, principles can usefully be distinguished from rules in several very subtle but important respects. A rule, according to Dworkin, sets out the conditions for its application in an all-or-nothing manner; that is, a rule either applies to a situation or it does not. Rules, therefore, can regulate specific conduct by permitting or prohibiting this conduct. In contrast, principles are more general; they do not regulate specific conduct, but they do have a dimension of weight that rules lack. In other words, if two principles, such as keeping your promises and being fair to others were in conflict, you would have to decide how much weight to attach to each principle in light of the circumstances. This is what Dworkin argues that judges do in "hard cases." They balance competing principles against each other in light of the specific facts at hand. Principles function as important considerations to take into account in arriving at a decision, but they do not, by themselves, prescribe the decision to be reached.[11]

My own view here of education as a rather vague right to be conceived of as a general principle does parallel Justice Marshall's dissenting opinion in *Rodriguez v. San Antonio School District*. In Marshall's dissenting view, to deny education that status of a constitutional right is to oversimplify and misrepresent its "fundamentality," for the Court had previously protected other fundamental interests that were not explicitly or implicitly spelled out in the Constitution, including the right to procreate and the right of access to criminal appellate processes. The fundamentality of education as an interest lies, according to Marshall, in the "nexus between specific constitutional guarantees and the nonconstitutional interests." If this nexus is a close one, the nonconstitutional interest — in this case, education — becomes fundamental. Marshall acknowledges that "this Court has never deemed the provision of free public education to be required by the Constitution." Nevertheless, his argument does underscore the fundamental interest citizens have in educational opportunities. According to Marshall, "the fundamental importance of education is amply indicated by the prior decisions of this Court, by the unique status accorded to public education in our society, and by the close relationship between education and some of our most basic constitutional values."[12]

Marshall's argument points to the flexibility to be gained in considering "the fundamental interest in education" not as a specific rulelike entitlement to some amount of schooling but as a guiding principle to be taken seriously into account. I do not think Marshall's dissent went far enough, and unfortunately his views do not constitute the law of the land. Education, in my view, however, remains a fundamental right intrinsically connected to the right to liberty in a democracy and the right to liberty remains a necessary condition of any just society. Since minority opinions are sometimes transmuted into majority views, it remains to be seen if education will emerge as a federal right. However, it seems clear from many state court decisions that education is a right of citizens within a state and this right has led several state supreme courts, even Texas's court, to deem inequitable financing schemes as unconstitutional.

Social Justice and Educational Opportunity

As Kenneth Strike has forcefully argued, social justice is a regulative ideal of a liberal society; it depends on the notion that everyone should earn her share of the social goods through merit or effort and not through inherited parental wealth or other social advantages passed on by the family. Liberal theory maintains the connection between fair competition and an unequal distribution of goods in the marketplace. Strike points to one central difficulty in reconciling traditional liberal notions of justice and the workings of educational opportunity. One difficulty is that some things that could be viewed as opportunities, such as receiving a university education, can also be viewed as rewards. Why is that a problem?

Strike suggests that such a dilemma of educational opportunities (such as acquiring a university education) overlapping with societal rewards seems to be rather intractable within liberal theory, for "it is the point of the schools to drive a wedge between reward and opportunity by making the conditions for acquiring marketable talent independent of wealth." However, such a view underestimates how strong the connection is between the parents' rewards and the child's opportunities. It is a connection so strong that it is not readily susceptible to social intervention, except the drastic kind of intervention into family life that liberals would not be likely to accept.[13]

Strike suspects that existing social science research indicating that schools, by themselves, cannot succeed in establishing equal opportunity, may not be foolproof. He thinks the verdict is not in on what future empirical approaches to educating students might yield. Such caution seems wise. However, recent social trends indicate that social inequalities between families and communities in U.S. society are widening rather than narrowing, and if the strong connection between familial and community support and educational achievement is validated by ongoing research, such a condition portends badly for increased equality of educational opportunity.

I shall now discuss just a few demographic particulars about family life in America; these "social realities" seem to suggest that contemporary families are able to be much less supportive of children than ever, and children born into black and Hispanic families are even more likely to face grim prospects. If this assertion is true, and it certainly seems plausible on its face, then increased social burdens will be placed on schools to compensate for these disadvantages. Reading the 1990 census, we find that poverty among families with children has increased from the mid-1960s with approximately 13.9 million children (22.9 percent of Americans under 18) living in "official poverty" (and it is estimated that official poverty statistics understate real poverty by 40 to 50 percent). Wallace Peterson, in a detailed economic analysis of the declining economic condition of the lower middle class since 1973, informs us that the incidence of poverty for black children living in poverty areas is much greater than that for white children—71.1 percent versus 12.3 percent. Overall poverty for black children was 46.7 percent and 38.2 percent for Hispanic children. Moreover, a University of Michigan study looking at family incomes over time indicates that the overwhelming majority of white children (73 percent) will escape poverty, but only a small minority of black children will (22 percent). Poverty in America remains very closely linked with race.

According to Peterson, increased numbers of working-class families, not officially listed as living in poverty, have experienced a decline in their living standards since the early 1970s, a slow but steady decline. This has placed increased stress on these families. Lillian Rubin in her compelling sociological analysis of 162 working-class families found that one out of five husbands or wives were now working split shifts just to meet the economic demands of family life.

Another very disturbing trend has been the dramatic increase in single-parent families, 90 percent of whom are headed by single mothers. In 1990, there were 13.5 million children living in families where the mother was the only parent. The number of children in single-parent families has risen from approximately 10 percent in 1970 to 25 percent in 1990. Among black people, 54.8 percent of children under age 18 lived in a single-parent family compared with 19.2 percent of white children. The increase in single mothers from 1980 to 1990 went from 5.8 million to 7.7 million—a 33 percent increase in only a decade. These single mothers were said to have a median income in 1990 of $9,353.

Still another trend is that growing poverty in financial resources seems to be accompanied by increasing poverty in the free time parents have for children. According to a report published in 1989 by the Family Research Council of Washington, D.C., the amount of time that parents spend with their children has dropped 40 percent during the last twenty-five years. In 1965, the average parent had roughly thirty contact hours with his or her children each week; by 1989, that figure had dropped to seventeen hours per week.[14]

One could extend this discussion with many more disturbing facts about the condition of families and youth in the United States; I present these particulars not as conclusive research findings but as prima facie evidence that many families are struggling to support their children adequately; and, many more are, in all likelihood, failing to support them in ways that will increase their educational opportunity.

If my prima facie conclusion about the increased difficulties that poor and working-class families are facing is true, what does this fact suggest for the challenge of reconciling educational policy and social reality? In my mind, it suggests that the relationship between social justice and equal educational opportunity must focus much more significantly on protecting and nurturing the well-being of families; it should also focus on creating supportive relationships between families and schooling. That we must provide more support for families without regulating them too seriously is one of the great policy challenges of the day, in my view.

James Coleman, the University of Chicago sociologist, whose 1966 study on equality of opportunity showed that the most powerful predictor of a student's ultimate nonschooling success was her socioeconomic class, recently concluded that another non-schooling variable was crucial to children's educational opportunities—the social capital of a supportive community. Coleman's own research indicates that the social capital in a community (which can include such things as making and enforcing rules that are similar from family to family, providing social support for their own and other children in times of distress, and even setting standards of dress and behavior) can offset to a significant extent the absence of parental support in a particular family.[15]

If we are to become clearer about the factors influencing equal educational opportunities and outcomes, we must continue to do research to determine more precisely what role families and communities play in influencing the educational outcomes of children. However we define the relationship between equal educational opportunities and equal educational outcomes—a topic I have not discussed here—it is clear that educational results are often the best indicators that opportunities have been exercised.[16]

Some Concluding Thoughts

Americans' faith in the possibilities of common, public schooling to solve our social problems and increase our socioeconomic opportunity is no longer unquestioned. There are no simple solutions to improving both the quality and the fairness with which we provide educational opportunities in a time of scarce public resources and growing public needs. Moreover, no philosophical account of social justice will determine, by itself, the hard judgments about how educational resources ought to be fairly distributed while creating minimally educated persons. No matter what we conclude as philosophers, some practical humility about changing the world of schooling is always called for, since schooling has acquired a life of its own quite independent of philosophers' conceptions of a good education and a good society.[17]

Nevertheless, adequate theoretical accounts of education can help us connect our ideals with the facts of everyday life. That is the best way for philosophical ideals and the principles that underlie them to function — to give us guidance in knowing what we should aim for and how we should take account of what we find. Ultimately, if we clarify how we want to live and what kind of social arrangements we wish to create, we will have guidance in pursuing our dreams. But we must not pursue them without a realistic sense of what is possible. In that regard, we must continue to reflect on our ideals. If Amy Guttman is correct, we may not have the luxury of devoting as many resources to education as is needed to maximize our children's life chances (what she calls the "maximization principle"). We may also not be able to raise the life chances of the least advantaged up to those of the most advantaged — her equalization principle — because "to equalize educational opportunity," the state would have to intrude so far into family life as to violate the important liberal ideal of family autonomy.[18] All that we may be able to do is to encourage the state to "take steps to avoid those inequalities that deprive children of educational attainment adequate to participation in the political processes."[19] This, I am sure, would not be an insignificant accomplishment, and although I have advocated a somewhat different minimalist conception of being educated than has Guttman, I think progress toward her social ideal would be welcome indeed, and not far from my own.

"Education," we must be reminded, primarily meant "proper child rearing" until the late nineteenth century when schools began to take up more and more social space. It also suggests the culture's effort to pass on its distinctive excellences to each new generation, so that a way of life could be both sustained and improved. If we remember these primary meanings of "education," we will not forget that education was, and always will be, a normative enterprise, informed by two complementary ideals — the ideal of a developed person living a meaningful life and the ideal of a good society. If Plato, Aristotle, and Dewey were correct, one ideal is not possible without the other.

Now, if I am correct, good societies need more than good schools and good persons; they also need good families and good communities for children. And, if my educational aims make sense, we must work to ensure that all children in the society achieve them, at least at a minimal level. Moreover, if education functions as a right in the sense I have argued, it provides us with an "ideal directive," pointing us in a certain direction; now it is up to us to head that way. We must do what is necessary as a society for schools, families, and communities to ensure that children achieve political literacy, moral character and self-respect. To aim for less is to aim too low.

Notes

I would like to thank my daughter Anessa Katz for assisting me in making this paper a more readable one. Her help was invaluable; she has made me proud to be involved in education as both a parent and a teacher.

1. For the richest and most sophisticated discussions of the relationship between social justice, educational policy, and equal educational opportunity, see Amy Guttman, *Democratic Education* (Princeton, NJ: Princeton University Press, 1984) and Kenneth A. Strike, *Educational Policy and the Just Society* (Chicago: University of Illinois Press. See also, Kenneth R. Howe, "In Defense of Outcomes-based Conceptions of Equal Opportunity," *Educational Theory* 39, no. 4 (fall 1989): 317–36; and Randall R. Curren, "Justice and the Threshold of Equality," *Philosophy of Education 1994,* ed. Michael S. Katz (Urbana: University of Illinois Press, 1994); and Kenneth R. Howe, "A Threshold of Inclusion, or a Threshold of Non-Exclusion?: A Response to Curren," *Philosophy of Education 1994,* ed. Michael S. Katz (Urbana: University of Illinois Press, 1994).

2. This is not to diminish the role of the parents or other social agencies, but to emphasize that the state,

in a liberal society, has chosen to exercise its primary locus of educational control over the school. It is not likely that the state would seek anything like the degree of regulation over families that it seeks over schools without seriously infringing on the autonomy of parents to bring up their children as they see fit. Guttman and Strike develop this point in much more detail.

3. See Kenneth R. Howe, "Equality of Educational Opportunity and the Criterion of Equal Educational Worth," *Studies in Philosophy and Education* 11, no. 4 (1993): 329–37. Howe's most provocative model is what he calls "Educational Opportunity of Equal Worth: The Participatory Interpretation." In this model, emphasis is placed on negotiating what the participants of education find.

4. Thomas F. Green, with the assistance of David L. Ericson and Robert H. Seidman, *Predicting the Behavior of the Educational System* (Syracuse, NY: Syracuse University Press, 1980), p. 24. See also Katz, "Critical Literacy."

5. All general educational aims function as principles that have a fundamental vagueness associated with them. This permits interesting disagreements about what the aims consist of and what policies or practices would best reflect them. People can agree or disagree about abstract principles, their concrete policy manifestations, and their implementation in practice, since there is no strictly logical move from principles to policies to practices.

6. See Stanley M. Elam, Lowell C. Rose, and Alec M. Gallup, "The 25th Annual Phi Delta Kappa Gallup Poll on the Public's Attitudes Towards the Public Schools," *Phi Delta Kappan* (October 1993), p. 145. Both in 1987 and in 1993, 69 percent of the public expressed their agreement with the proposition that people in their community could agree on a basic set of values to be taught in public schools. The individual values the public seems to agree should be taught are the following: honesty (97 percent), democracy (93 percent), acceptance of people of different races and ethnic backgrounds (93 percent), love of country (93 percent), caring for friends and family members (91 percent), the Golden Rule (90 percent), and acceptance of people with different religious beliefs (90 percent). To what degree public schools can inculcate moral values without intruding on an individual's freedom of conscience is an issue thoughtfully raised by Kenneth Strike; see Strike, *Educational Policy*, pp. 87–127.

7. For two important works in this tradition, see Nel Noddings, *Caring: A Feminine Approach to Ethics and Moral Education* (Berkeley: University of California Press, 1984), and Rita Manning, *Speaking from the Heart: A Feminist Perspective on Ethics* (Lanham, MD: Rowman and Littlefield, 1992). It should be noted that the concept of a "moral sensibility" is seldom used in this literature.

8. See Michael S. Katz, "Self-Respect Revisited," an unpublished paper delivered at the meeting of the California Association for Philosophers of Education, Cambridge, Massachusetts, May 3, 1991. See also David Sachs, "How to Distinguish Self-Respect from Self-Esteem," *Philosophy and Public Affairs* 10 (1981): 346–60, John Rawls, *A Theory of Justice* (Cambridge, MA: Harvard University Press, 1971), pp. 234, 440ff, 543–47, Thomas E. Hill, "Servility and Self-Respect," *Monist,* 57 (1973), Thomas Hill, "Self-Respect Reconsidered," in O. H. Green, ed., *Respect for Persons, Tulane Studies in Philosophy,* 31 (New Orleans: Tulane University, 1982): 129–37, Kenneth A. Strike, "Education, Justice, and Self-Respect: A School for Rodney Dangerfield," *Proceedings of the Philosophy of Education Society 1979,* ed. Jerrold R. Coombs (Normal, IL: Philosophy of Education Society), pp. 41–50.

9. See John Passmore, "On Teaching to Be Critical," in *The Concept of Education,* ed. R. S. Peters (London: Routledge & Kegan Paul, 1967), pp. 192–209.

10. Joel Feinberg, *Social Philosophy* (Englewood Cliffs, NJ: Prentice Hall, 1973). Much of this discussion was drawn from my earlier piece on "Critical Literacy," already cited.

11. Ronald Dworkin, "The Model of Rules," *University of Chicago Law Review* 35 (1967): 25–27. Dworkin's full-scale critique of legal positivism can be found in his *Taking Rights Seriously* (Cambridge, MA: Harvard University Press, 1978).

12. *Rodriguez v. San Antonio School District,* 411 US1 (1972), 111.

13. Strike, *Educational Policy and the Just Society,* p. 225. Neither Strike nor Guttman think the state can go very far in intervening in the affairs of the family.

14. These statistics and this analysis were gathered from various sources. For the sake of convenience I will simply list my sources together. Edward F. Zigler and Matia Finn Stevenson, *Children in a Changing World* (Belmont, CA: Wadsworth, 1993), pp. 480–84; Richard Louv, *Childhood's Future* (New York: Anchor, 1990), p. 15, Lillian B. Rubin, *Families on the Fault Line: America's Working Class Speaks About the Family, the Economy, Race, and Ethnicity* (New York: Harper Collins, 1994), "Single Mothers, Divorcees Show Sharp Rise in Poverty," *San Jose Mercury News,* February 18, 1994; Wallace C. Peterson, *Silent Depression: The Fate of the American Dream* (New York: Norton, 1994), pp. 129–70.

15. James S. Coleman, *Policy Perspectives: Parental Involvement in Education* (Washington, D.C.: Government Printing Office, 1991), pp. 7–11. See also James S. Coleman et al., *Report on Equality of Educational Opportunity* (Washington, D.C.: U.S. Government Printing Office, 1966).

16. To what degree "equal educational opportunity" should be thought of primarily in terms of "inputs" or "material conditions," or outcomes is a source of interesting controversy in the literature. See Kenneth Howe, "In Defense of Outcomes-Based Conceptions of Equal Educational Opportunity."

17. Guttman, pp. 127–71.

18. Ibid.

19. Guttman, p. 12.

Autonomy and Rights

WHOSE RIGHTS?

Alan R. White

Alan White explores the question of who has moral rights. He considers four answers to this question: those who have or take an interest, those who are beneficiaries of a duty, those who are treated rightly, and those who are persons. He argues that only the last criterion, personhood, is a condition for having rights. (Source: Reprinted from Rights *by Alan R. White. Copyright © 1984 by Alan R. White. Reprinted by permission of Oxford University Press.)*

Being Capable of Having a Right

Traditional discussions of rights have usually been confined to the rights of humans. The question whether anything other than a human being could sensibly be said to have a right, let alone whether it did or ought to have such, was rarely raised. Where the law wished to extend rights to other things, such as corporations, it did so by classifying them as 'legal persons'. Despite some remarks in the eighteenth century and a few books[1] in the nineteenth century on the rights of animals and, of course, a long legal tradition — enshrined in the doctrine of Deodand — of attributing blame and inflicting punishment on animals, railway engines, bricks, etc., which caused injuries to men, it is only recently, indeed, in the sixties and seventies of this century, that much attention has

seriously been given to the question whether rights can be possessed by what is not a human being. It is now debated, for example, not only whether generations of humans yet unborn, children, imbeciles, and the irremediably comatose can have rights, but also whether human foetuses and animals, plants, trees, material objects in nature, and even artistic creations in paint and sculpture can have them.

The question is usually approached by enquiring whether there are certain characteristics or a family of such characteristics which are either necessary or sufficient for the possible possession of a right. Are there certain kinds of subjects whose nature makes it logically impossible for them to have rights?

. . .

[I]t is difficult to see what conditions of substance could be suggested as either necessary or sufficient for the capacity to have rights at all which would not be one of those suggested for the capacity to have a right to a particular kind of thing. For instance, how could susceptibility to pain, the power of reason, or the capacity to take an interest in things, be either a necessary or a sufficient condition for something being capable of having rights without being necessary or sufficient for its being capable of having a right to a particular kind of thing, such as the right to be free from suffering, the right to exercise one's reasoning powers, or the right to what one was capable of having an interest in? Furthermore, any thesis that a particular characteristic is necessary or sufficient for the capacity to have a right to a particular kind of thing based on the coexistence of an instance of that characteristic and an instance of that right is disproved if other instances of the characteristic and of the right do not coexist.

. . .

Having an Interest

One of the commonest theses about the subjects of rights is that a necessary or sufficient condition for being capable of having a right is being capable of having, or actually having, an interest; a thesis which is also assumed in the traditional view, exemplified by Ihering and Bentham . . . that the actual possession of an interest is either a necessary or a sufficient condition of the actual possession of a right. This thesis is subscribed to both by some who assert and some who deny that, for example, animals or natural objects have rights, the former[2] arguing that because these are capable of having interests, they can have rights, and the latter[3] arguing that because they are incapable of having interests, they cannot have rights. Furthermore, the thesis can be taken in two ways because of an ambiguity, not always respected by holders of the thesis, in 'capable of having interests' between so and so's being of such a kind that something could be in its interest and so and so's being of such a kind that it could have (or even take) an interest in something.[4]

Clearly, something could be in the interests of so and so, although so and so could not have (or take) an interest in it or in anything. Thus, certain measures or changes could be in the interests of efficiency, peace, prosperity, the truth, or the economy, though none of these can have an interest in anything. It is even possibly arguable that something could be in the interests of an inanimate object, such as the land, one's car, or one's business, though these certainly cannot have (or take) an interest. The sorts of things in whose interests something could be are, it is plausible to say, very

various. On the other hand, whatever can have (or take) an interest in anything can have something in its interests. Furthermore, only the animate — and, perhaps, only the intelligent — can have (or take) an interest. Thus, a man or his dog can have (or take) an interest in certain food or in finding certain shelter; and such food or the discovery of such shelter can be in the interests of both. The class of what can have (or take) an interest is, therefore, much smaller than the class of what can have something in its interest.

However, neither the idea of something's being in so and so's interest nor the idea of so and so's having an interest in something will serve as a criterion for whether so and so is the kind of thing which can have a right.

First, neither being capable of having nor actually having something in its interests can be *sufficient* for something's being the kind of thing that can have a right, else many things, such as efficiency, peace, prosperity, the truth, the economy, and, perhaps, the land, one's car, and one's business, would be capable of having rights.[5] And no one would want to suggest that all these can have rights. Furthermore, there are many specific things which are capable of being or actually are in so and so's interest, as when it could be, or is, in my interest to be bigger than I am or to behave diplomatically, though I could not have a right to any of these. It is, therefore, a fallacy to argue, as is commonly done, that because a certain class of thing, whether animals, the environment, foetuses, generations yet to come, as well as babies, imbeciles, etc., is capable of having, or actually has, something in its interest, therefore it is capable of having a right.[6] On the other hand, though being capable of having, or actually having, something or other in its interest might conceivably be *necessary* for being the kind of thing that can have rights — a thesis for which, however, I know of no argument[7] — such a thesis would do very little to narrow the class of things which can have rights, since, as we have seen, what can have something in its interests is, arguably, very varied. Furthermore, it is not necessary that a particular item should be capable of being, or actually be, in so and so's interest for so and so to be capable of having a right to it. Even if it could not possibly be in my interests to criticize my betters, or could not even make sense to talk of its being in my interests to expect so and so, to feel disappointed or pleased at such and such, these are still things to which I could have a right.

Secondly, the capability of having (or taking) an interest in things equally fails to provide either a necessary or sufficient condition for the capability of having a right. It could not be a necessary condition if those who are incapable of having (or taking) an interest in anything at all are nevertheless capable of some rights, as when the dead have a right to a decent burial or my as yet unborn grandchildren to a share in my estate. And, of course, those who advocate the extension of rights to the inanimate, such as natural objects, or to the unintelligent, such as foetuses or even the comatose, could not accept it as a necessary condition. So and so's right to proper treatment or preservation is independent of its or his capability of having (or taking) an interest in this. More specifically, being capable of having, or actually having, an interest in a particular thing could not be a necessary condition of being capable of having a right to that. Individuals can be capable of having, and even have, rights to all sorts of things, such as higher education or a transferable vote, which for some reason, such as being children or unsophisticated adults, they are, at least at the time, incapable of having (or taking) an interest in. Even with those who are capable of having (or taking) an interest in a particular item, the possibility of their having a right to that is often quite unconnected with this capability, as when someone can have a right to what he has been promised.

Nor is being capable of having, or actually having, an interest a sufficient condition of being capable of having a right. There certainly is no such connection between particular interests and particular rights. One could be capable of having, or actually have, an interest in something, for example one's neighbour's progress, his actions or achievements, many of one's own conditions, such as one's age or size, and such things as the passing of the seasons or the rise and fall of empires, which it would make no sense to be capable of having a right to. Even when what one is capable of having, or actually has, an interest in is something one could have a right to, the former is not a sufficient condition for the latter, as where what one's actual or possible interest is in is, for example, one's actions or

one's achievements. Furthermore, if being capable of having, or actually having (or taking), an interest in a particular item is not sufficient for being capable of having a right to that or some related item, it is difficult to see how it could be sufficient for being the kind of a thing that can have rights, unless it is merely a criterion for some other quality, such as intelligence, which is itself posited as a sufficient condition for being capable of having rights.

It follows from all this that no valid argument can be given either for including or for excluding, for example, children, imbeciles, foetuses, animals, natural objects, unborn generations, as holders of rights on the ground that being capable of having a right ensures or necessitates being capable either of having something in one's interest or of being interested in something. Hence, the question whether animals, natural objects, etc., can or cannot have interests, either in the sense of something's being in their interest or in the sense of their being interested in something, is irrelevant to the question whether they can have rights and need not, therefore, be decided.[8]

Most of the multitude of other suggestions about the necessary or sufficient criteria for being the sort of thing which can have rights can with some plausibility be regarded as variations on either the broad idea of something's being in its interest or the narrow idea of its being interested in something.

Thus, to regard anything which is capable of having, or actually does have, a good, a benefit, an inherent value[9] or, as lawyers commonly suggest,[10] a need of protection, as being capable of having a right is similar to regarding anything whose interests can be affected as something which can have a right. And it is open to exactly the same objections, namely, that if it were a necessary criterion, it would exclude almost nothing as a possible holder of rights and, if it were sufficient, it would include many things to which no one would wish to attribute rights. In short, as a criterion for the possible possession of rights, each of these is, like the criterion of being in one's interests, too broad.

On the other hand, many criteria for the possible possession of rights consist in a narrowing, in different ways, of the suggestion that to be capable of having (or taking) an interest in something is a necessary or sufficient condition for a possible holder of a right. Such criteria range from the capability of being sentient[11] to the capability of suing in law,[12] through the capability of suffering,[13] of reasoning, of choosing,[14] of speaking a language, of making a claim, [15] of entering into a contract,[16] or of being morally conscious.[17] Many of these characteristics, such as the capability of making a contract or of suing in law, are clearly too restrictive to be necessary conditions of being the kind of thing that can have rights, though they might be necessary for the possible possession of some particular rights, such as the right to benefit from a contract or to bring an action. On the other hand, since most of these characteristics, such as the capability to sue in law, to enter into a contract, to make a claim, to speak a language, to choose, or to reason, are such that anything having any of them — and anything having any of them would seem to have most or all of them — is eligible for all, or almost all, of the attributes which, I shall later argue, logically pertain to the possessor of a right, then most of these characteristics are sufficient for being the kind of thing that can have rights, though not necessarily for being capable of having a particular right.

A variation on the first kind of 'interests criterion' which uses it to argue for the thesis that objects of art can and, indeed, do have rights, at least the right to protection from mistreatment, such as bad performance of music, trivialization of a painting, insensitive abridgement of a novel, while admitting that not all interests are sufficient for the actual or possible possession of rights, holds both that they are necessary and that certain kinds of interests are indeed sufficient.[18] But this variation is really only a version of the thesis that anything in regard to which one has an obligation has necessarily a right and, therefore, the capability of having a right, for the kind of interest which, this view holds, entails a right, is 'an obligation-generating interest.' A work of art's interest in not being mistreated is said to generate an obligation in us not to mistreat it and, hence, to give it a right not to be mistreated. To this the answer is twofold. First, the fact that something is in so and so's interest does not imply that there is any obligation to provide so and so with it. Many things may be in my interests, my country's interests, or my garden's interests, or in the inter-

ests of peace and prosperity, which I do not for one moment suppose anyone has an obligation to supply. Secondly, the assumption that what one has an obligation, or a duty, to do for so and so is something which so and so could have a right to, though commonly made,[19] is, as I shall now argue, mistaken.

Being Beneficiary of a Duty (or Obligation)

. . .

A duty (or obligation) in one subject does not imply the existence of another subject capable of having a right. First, one can have a duty (or obligation) to do something, for example to stand to attention or to be present at certain times and places, which does not imply the existence of any other subject. Secondly, one can have a duty (or obligation) which does imply the existence of another subject, but a subject which may be either one capable of having a right or one not so capable, as when one has a duty (or obligation) to punish an offender, to polish the silver, or to sweep the lawn. Where, as above, there is a duty (or obligation) *to do* something which is not a duty (or obligation) *to* anything, then clearly, even if there exists another subject, as there need not, or one capable of a right, as also there need not, this other's capability of having a right is not implied by the first's duty. Thirdly, one can have a duty (or obligation) *to something,* which is nevertheless not capable of having a right, as when one has a duty to one's country, one's conscience or one's art. Finally, even if that to which one's duty (or obligation) is owed is something which could have a right, its being capable of having a right does not follow from one's having a duty (or obligation) to it. A doctor's duty to his patient not to indulge her desire for drugs does not entail that she must be capable of having a right to such non-indulgence of her desires. Hence, if a duty (or obligation) in one subject does not necessarily imply even the possibility of a right in another either in regard to whom or even to whom the duty is owed, then whether we can have duties to animals, as Bentham and Mill insisted, or only to do something for animals, as Aquinas, Kant, Whewell, Ritchie, and Rickaby argued, it would not follow, as Feinberg[20] supposes, that they must be capable of having rights.

Equally, a duty (or obligation) in one subject is not implied by, and therefore not necessary to, the existence of another subject capable of having a right. For I may be capable of having, and even actually have, a right to treat people in certain ways, for example to teach, heal, protect, or punish them, without their having a duty (or obligation) to be treated or to allow themselves to be treated in these ways. No one has a duty (or obligation) corresponding to my right, much less to my capability of having a right, to assume, expect, hope for, or resent so and so. Scholars could have a right, and many in fact do have, to criticize Plato, though he could have no duty now to be, or to allow himself to be, criticized. I can have a right to look at my neighbour across our common fence without his having any duty to be looked at. *A fortiori,* one could have a right to treat animals and both natural and artistic objects in various ways even if they cannot have duties.

Being Treated Rightly

Finally, there is the common suggestion that if, and perhaps only if, so and so is something for which it is *right* for me to do such and such or for which I *ought* to do such and such, for example to provide it with this or protect it from that, then so and so is capable of having a right to that which it is right to do or which ought to be done. This suggestion is usually not distinguished from the more extreme suggestion that anything for which it is right to do such and such or for which such and such ought to be done has, *eo ipso,* actually a right to such and such, and vice versa. . . .

Among those who wish to extend the notion of a right beyond the rights of human beings, some shift quite unconsciously from the position that it is right for non-humans to be treated in certain ways to the position that such non-humans can be or are the possessors of rights,[21] while others explicitly, though without any careful argument, contend that the latter

position follows from the former.[22] Some, however, who sympathize with the desire to secure better treatment for non-humans recognize that it is sufficient to prove only that such treatment is something it is right to provide or which ought to be provided.[23] Others are eager to argue that non-humans can have rights because they think, possibly correctly in the current state of political thinking and the influence of the law, that to show that so and so has or could have a right to such and such is more persuasive in securing such and such treatment for it than to show merely that it is right for it to have it. Unfortunately, the fact that one conclusion has, in politics or the law, greater persuasive power than another does not show that it is correct or that it follows from that other. As a matter of fact, recent and current judicial treatment of children in English law still puts more emphasis on their welfare and interests than on their rights.[24] Moreover, it does not in general suggest that because they have interests they must have or be capable of having rights. Equally, the law, both English and American, has been reluctant to follow the advice of some jurisprudents, such as Stone and Tribe, that natural objects in the environment should be given, or be eligible for, a legal right against mistreatment.

The fact that it is right for so and so to have such and such cannot be either a necessary or a sufficient condition for so and so's being capable of having a right to such and such — much less for its actually having a right to it — for so and so could be something for which no question of a right can arise. Its being right for me to treat books, furniture, objections, exceptions, dangers, in such and such a way is not sufficient for any of these to be capable of having a right to be treated in that way. Some books which ought to be read may even deserve to be read, but are not, therefore, capable of a right to be read. Nor is it being right for me to treat a person in such and such a way necessary for him to be capable of having or even to have a right to such treatment. There are many things to which I have a right and more to which I could have a right, for example to assume this, to expect that, to punish one and reward another, which, for various reasons, it might not be right for me to do.

It is, therefore, conceptually important, however impolitic or bad strategy it may be, to keep quite distinct the question whether so and so could or does have a right to such and such and the question whether it would be or is right for it to have such and such. This is not, of course, to conclude wrongly, as some do, that there are no such things as (moral) rights or that the notion is superfluous.[25] The attribution of rights to various subjects also springs from a desire to protect their freedom. And it may be that just as some thinkers have confused rights with freedom or liberties, those who wish to extend rights to animals or nature do so because they seek to keep them free from suffering or the selfishness of humans. But to give something a protected freedom is not, as I shall argue later, necessarily to give it a right. We can keep animals free from suffering and fields free from spoliation without having to grant them rights or the capability of having rights.[26] The legal prohibition on the shooting of various sorts of birds and animals outside restricted seasons confers protection on their freedom, but does not give them a right or assume them to be capable of one.

Being a Person

Most discussions about the kinds of things which can possess rights centre on the kinds of capacities either necessary or sufficient for their possible possession, whether it be interests, rationality, sentience, the ability to claim, etc. Advocates of the various capabilities are usually torn between making them so strong, for example rationality or the ability to sue, that they exclude subjects to which they wish to allow rights, whether they be children, the feeble-minded, unborn generations, etc., and making them so weak that they include almost anything, whether they be inanimate objects, artefacts, abstract conceptions, etc.

I have tried to show that no criterion couched in terms of substantive characteristics is logically either sufficient or necessary in itself for the possible — or, indeed, the actual — possession of a right. What I would suggest is that such characteristics are at most a mark of a certain type of subject of which the question is whether that type of subject is logically capable of having a right. And the answer to that question depends on whether it is the sort of subject of which

it makes sense to use what may be called 'the full language of rights.'

A right is something which can be said to be exercised, earned, enjoyed, or given, which can be claimed,[27] demanded, asserted, insisted on, secured, waived, or surrendered; there can be a right to do so and so or have such and such done for one, to be in a certain state, to have a certain feeling or adopt a certain attitude. A right is related to and contrasted with a duty, an obligation, a privilege, a power, a liability. A possible possessor of a right is, therefore, whatever can properly be spoken of in such language; that is, whatever can intelligibly, whether truly or falsely, be said to exercise, earn, etc. a right, to have a right to such logically varied things, to have duties, privileges, etc. Furthermore, as I mentioned earlier, a necessary condition of something's being capable of having a right to V is that it should be something which logically can V.

In the full language of 'a right' only a *person* can logically have a right because only a person can be the subject of such predictions. Rights are not the sorts of things of which non-persons can be the subjects, however right it may be to treat them in certain ways. Nor does this, as some contend, exclude infants, children, the feeble-minded, the comatose, the dead, or generations yet unborn.[28] Any of these may be for various reasons empirically unable to fulfil the full role of a right-holder. But so long as they are persons — and it is significant that we think and speak of them as young, feeble-minded, incapacitated, dead, unborn *persons* — they are logically possible subjects of rights to whom the full language of rights can significantly, however falsely, be used. It is a misfortune, not a tautology, that these persons cannot exercise or enjoy, claim, or waive, their rights or do their duty or fulfil their obligations. The law has always linked together the notions of a person and of the bearer of rights, duties, privileges, powers, liberties, liabilities, immunities, etc., so that a change in application of one notion has accompanied a parallel change in application of the other.[29] Thus, at various times in the law, gods, idols, unborn and dead human beings, animals, inanimate things, corporations, and governments, have been treated as persons because they were conceived as possible subjects of such jural relations as rights, duties, etc. who can commit or be the victims of torts and crimes. In Roman law slaves were things, not persons, and, hence, had no rights. The attitudes of various legal systems to the possible rights of an unborn child depend on how far they are regarded as legal persons.[30]

What this legal practice brings out is the importance of using a set of concepts, for example rights, duties, privileges, obligations, etc. together and not isolating one of them, for example right, so that, as Wittgenstein might put it, the lone concept is only 'idling.' The concept of a right can, of course, be stretched — as when Trollope, for example talks of a house with certain grandiose features as having 'the right' to be called a castle — and debates about the rights of foetuses, animals, works of art, or of nature can become merely terminological. What is important is to ask what job, if any, is being done in such contexts by the notion of 'a right' as contrasted with that of 'right' when it is isolated from such normal companions as the notions of duty, obligation, power, etc.

Something capable only of sentience or of suffering would not necessarily be capable of exercising, owning, or enjoying a right, much less of claiming, asserting, insisting on, or fighting for its rights or of waiving or relinquishing them. Nor of having obligations, duties, privileges, etc. And though it would be capable of having something done for it or of being in a certain state, it would not necessarily be capable of performing tasks, assuming attitudes, or having emotions. Hence, its possible rights, if any, would be confined to the right to have something done for it, such as to be well treated or protected, or to be in a certain state, such as to be happy or free or to remain alive. Moreover, though sentience or capacity to suffer would be necessary for the possible possession of a right to anything relevant to these, such as a right to protection from suffering — because a right to V implies being logically able to V — they would not be sufficient. The fact that an animal can suffer from growing pains or a man suffer from doubt does not in itself prove that it or he is capable of a right to protection from these.

It is a misunderstanding to object to this distinction between the kinds of things which can have rights and those which cannot on the ground that it constitutes a sort of speciesism.[31] For it is not being argued that it is right to treat one species less considerately than another, but only that one species, that is,

a person, can sensibly be said to exercise or waive a right, be under an obligation, have a duty, etc., whereas another cannot, however unable particular members of the former species may be to do so.

Notes

1. Lawrence (1796–1798); Nicholson (1879); Salt (1892).
2. e.g. Nelson (1956); Feinberg (1974) and (1978); Godlevitch in Godlevitch and Harris (1973); Warren (1977).
3. e.g. McCloskey (1965).
4. Cp. White (1975), 118–20; Regan (1976); Frey (1980).
5. It might be objected that it cannot be inferred that because something is 'in the interests' of peace, prosperity, etc., therefore these 'have interests.' Quite so; but equally the fact that something can be in the interests of a foetus, an animal, a plant, or even a baby does not show that these have interests.
6. e.g. Nelson (1956); Feinberg (1974); Godlevitch (1973), 158; Warren (1977), 283–284. Regan (1976) interprets Feinberg as taking 'interests' in the psychological way, but in fact Feinberg seems unclear on the matter.
7. Narveson (1977), 175, says that interests are a necessary, but not a sufficient, condition for rights. Feinberg thinks they are both necessary and sufficient.
8. For opposing views on this latter question, contrast McCloskey and Frey with Nelson, Regan, and Godlevitch in the works cited above.
9. e.g. Regan (1979).
10. e.g. C. Morris (1964–5); Tribe (1974); Sagoff (1974); contrast Gray (1921). Salt and Nicholson also use the need of protection as a criterion for rights.
11. e.g. C. D. Stone (1974); Warren (1977); Linzey (1976), 26 ff.
12. e.g. C. D. Stone (1974).
13. e.g. Bentham, Nicholson, Regan, Singer, Warren, and Clark (1977).
14. e.g. Hart (1955).
15. e.g. Feinberg (1974).
16. e.g. Grice (1974). Cp. Hobbes, who on these grounds denied rights to children, though as regards animals he seems to have argued from their inability to understand the transfer of rights to their inability to make contracts, rather than vice versa; *Leviathan*, ch. 14.
17. e.g. Ross (1930); cp. Tooley (1972).
18. e.g. Tormey (1973); contrast Goldblatt (1976).
19. e.g. by Bradley (1876), ch. v; Nelson (1956); Ritchie (1894); Lowry (1975).
20. e.g. Feinberg (1978).

21. e.g. Schopenhauer; Singer (1976); Tooley (1972).

22. e.g. Salt (1892), following Herbert Spencer; Sprigge (1979); Warren (1977); Feinberg (1976), 196; Clark (1979), 180; Auxter (1979), 221 ff. Salt betrays his unease about this implication by frequently putting 'rights' in quotes.

23. e.g. Kant; Ritchie (1894); Hart (1955); Clark (1977); Frey (1980); Feinberg (1976); Hare (1975).

24. See the historical discussions in Freeman (1980); though contrast *M* v. *M* [1973] 2 All ER 81 at 85 where the court said that access was a 'right' of the child rather than of the parent.

25. e.g. Frey (1980), ch. I.

26. English law usually denies rights to animals, e.g. Kenny, *Criminal Law* (1958 edn.), 171–2. Feinberg's (1978) allegation that the Cruelty to Animals Act 1876, ss. 2 and 3, confers rights on animals is not borne out by the language of the Act. Tribe (1974), 1342, n. 27, quotes two rather old American cases— *State* v. *Karstandiek* 49 La. 1621, 22 So. 845 (1897) and *Stephens* v. *State* 65 Miss. 329, 3 So. 458 (1887) — which do allow animals rights on the grounds that it is wrong to be cruel to them.

27. The fact that a right can be claimed is no evidence for the mistaken thesis (e.g. Feinberg) that a right is a claim.

28. e.g. Lamont (1946), 83–5.

29. Cp. Pound (1959), IV. ch. 25 and references on p. 191, n. 1.

30. Cp. Lasok (1976); Louisell (1969); though Tooley (1972) goes too far in making 'is a person' and 'has a moral right to life' synonymous.

31. e.g. Singer (1976).

WRONG RIGHTS

Elizabeth H. Wolgast

Elizabeth Wolgast argues that rights talk assumes a model of independent, autonomous persons, but that this model does not accurately describe human society. When circumstances do not fit the model, such as in the case of sick people or children, she argues that rights talk is inappropriate. (Source: From Hypatia, *Winter 1987. Reprinted with permission of the author.)*

If the basic units of society are discrete and autonomous individuals, that fact must determine the way they should be treated. Thus it is a natural step from atomism to the concept of individual rights, rights that will attach to each individual regardless of his or her characteristics. As persons are independent, so their rights will be defined in a framework of independence. And as the indistinguishable atoms are equal, so their rights need to be equal. The concept of individual rights is a natural adjunct to atomism.

The language of rights is also a way of looking at wrongs, a conceptual grid, a schema. It both gives us a sense of *how* wrongs are wrong and points to the way to address them, that is, by establishing a right. Although it is a powerful and useful tool, still the schema of rights is sometimes unfit for the uses we make of it. It can bind us to a senseless stance, stereotype our reasoning, and lead to remedies that are grotesque. Our commitment to this language is deep, however; even in the face of bizarre consequences we hold it fast and view the consequent problems as demands for further rights. Thus our reasoning often goes on in an enclosed framework of rights, a framework from which counterexamples are excluded a priori. What does this commitment to rights mean to us, and how can it be sensibly limited?

I

Rights are often spoken of in the language of possessions. They are, Richard Wasserstrom writes, "distinctive moral 'commodities.'"[1] H. L. A. Hart spells out the metaphor: "Rights are typically conceived of as *possessed* or *owned by* or *belonging to* individuals, and these expressions reflect the conception of moral rules as not only prescribing conduct but as forming a kind of moral property of individuals to which they are as individuals entitled; only when rules are conceived in this way can we speak of *rights* and *wrongs* as well as right and wrong actions."[2] The idea of rights as moral property, as belonging to individuals the way property does, is an important aspect of the concept of rights. It focuses attention on the person to whom something is due, just as property law focuses attention on the possessor of property. The individual person with his needs and desires is the central motif.

This perspective is in contrast with one that focuses on the misdeeds of the offender, that condemns the misdeeds and castigates the doer. Instead of condemning, our perspective asserts something positive, namely, that a certain kind of thing—a *right*—exists. But what kind of thing is this, and how can we prove its existence? The answers given in response to this question are often vague, and they commonly lead to talk of "natural" rights as necessary features of human existence.[3] In the end we have something that sounds like a moral metaphysics. What is it that the possessor of a right holds? David Lyons explains:

> When *A* in particular, holds a certain right *against B, A* is a *claimant* against *B.* A "claimant" is one empowered to press or waive a claim against someone with a corresponding duty or obligation. He can, if he wishes, release the other from his obligation and cancel it, or he can insist upon its performance. . . . A claimant is thus one to whom the performance of a duty or obligation is *owed*— he is the one who holds the claim against the other and who is entitled to administer the claim as he chooses.[4]

Lyons describes an important feature of the language of rights: the power it puts in the hands of the owner to press his right against someone or some agency. Rights are there to be *claimed*—asserted, demanded, pressed—or, on the other hand, waived.[5] What the claimant is entitled to press for is no doubt a benefit;

rights are generally associated with benefits, if only the benefit of being able to do something one doesn't want to do. But a right can be distinguished from a benefit in that a beneficiary often need not do anything; the role can be described as passive, you might say, while a rightholder can choose to claim his right or not; his right enables him to act in a certain way or to decline to do so.

Thus a right puts its possessor in an assertive position in which he may claim something, and to claim something is to claim it against another. So a right to a free education may be claimed by any child *against* the state, the right to vote may be asserted by any citizen *against* anyone who would interfere, the right of habeas corpus may be demanded *against* the court by anyone charged with a crime, and so on. But these rights differ quite a bit from benefits, since a gift generally doesn't need to be claimed, and the giver doesn't owe it if it is.

II

Rights put the rightholder in the driver's seat; a rightholder may be seen as active while the recipient of a benefit is passive. Joel Feinberg captures the difference by comparing a world with rights to a world without them. He imagines "Nowheresville," a world without rights, and asks "what precisely [such] a world is missing . . . and why that absence is morally important." The crucial thing absent, he argues, is the activity of claiming: "Nowheresvillians, even when they are discriminated against invidiously, or left without the things they need, or otherwise badly treated, do not think to leap to their feet and make righteous demands against one another. . . . They do not have a notion of what is their due." Claiming depends on a prior right to claim, and although a right may be waived, rights' "characteristic use, and that for which they are distinctively well suited, is to be claimed, demanded, affirmed, insisted upon."[6]

Why do rights have such crucial moral importance? Feinberg answers that it is precisely the feature of claiming that "gives rights their special moral significance." It is "connected . . . with the customary rhetoric about what it is to be a human being. Having

rights enables us to 'stand up like men,' to look others in the eye, and to feel in some fundamental way the equal of anyone. To think of oneself as a holder of rights is not to be unduly but properly proud . . . and what is called 'human dignity' may simply be the recognizable capacity to assert claims." People need to think of themselves as equal to others and thus able to claim their rights against others: that is a large part of what it is to be in the fullest sense a person. Nothing is more appropriate to a person than the possession of individual rights, rights that by their nature are given equally to everyone. In Feinberg's view the claiming of these possessions has a moral value of its own: "the activity of claiming . . . as much as any other thing, makes for self-respect and respect for others [and] gives a sense to the notion of personal dignity."[7]

The language in which Feinberg praises rights is recognizably atomistic. He thinks of individuals as independent units whose self-respect is of prime important to them *as* separate entities. Further, their capacity to claim rights is an important part of their active pursuit of their own interests. In such ways the language of rights both confirms the main features of the atomistic model and relies on its implicit values.

My claim is that such a conception of individuals and their rights may not be an effective means of addressing some injustices.

III

Consider the issue of the maltreatment of patients by doctors and medical staff in hospitals. In a hospital a patient is entirely at the mercy of medical people, whose expertise and positions give them great power, and so they are vulnerable to abuses of that power. The patient who is weak and frightened is by definition dependent on the staff; and they, in virtue of their practical knowledge and ability, are in the position of his rescuers — can instruct him and help him to survive. Abuse of such power and authority is, in view of the patient's helplessness, a frightening possibility.

Michel Foucault argues that with the development of clinics and the opportunities they offer to study disease, a new doctor–patient relationship develops. In this impersonal, scientific context the doctor becomes an expert in diseases, and "if one wishes to know the illness from which he is suffering, one must abstract the individual, with his particular qualities."[8] The doctor must look through the patient at the disease.

On the one side of the patient is the family, whose "gentle, spontaneous care, expressive of love and a common desire for a cure, assists nature in its struggle against the illness"; on the other side is the hospital doctor, who "sees only distorted, altered diseases, a whole teratology of the pathological." The traditional family doctor, in contrast, cannot have the clinical detachment of the hospital doctor, but in his practice "must necessarily be respectful" of the patient.[9] Foucault's account provides a plausible explanation of how the problem of disrespectful treatment of patients in a modern hospital comes about; it is a natural, logical development. Inevitably, too, the search for knowledge and the holding of power go hand in hand, and as the doctor seeks knowledge of a scientific kind, his patient becomes increasingly an object under his control, and less and less someone to be dealt with in personal terms.

Here's the problem, then. The patient is weak, frightened, helpless, but needs to be treated in many ways as a normal person — needs to be respected, even in his wishes regarding treatment, and ultimately perhaps in his wish to die or to be sent home uncured. The issue may be addressed in various ways, but the most common way of dealing with it is to say that the patient has a *right* to respectful and considerate treatment, a right to have his wishes in regard to his treatment respected, a right to be informed about the character of his treatment, and so on. To force upon him decisions he might not accept if he weren't ill and dependent is then to subject him to a kind of domination. It is as if the patient could be mistreated *because he is ill,* and that thought recalls Samuel Butler's grotesque society Erewhon, where illness is a crime demanding punishment. There a judge trying a case of pulmonary congestion pronounces, "You may say that it is your misfortune to be criminal; I answer that it is your crime to be unfortunate."[10]

In the wake of protests over mistreatment of patients, the American Hospital Association instituted a code of patients' rights which has been widely adopted in this country. The first of these rights is the "the

right to considerate and respectful care," the fourth is the "right to refuse treatment to the extent permitted by law and to be informed of the medical consequences of his action," the eighth is the patient's "right to obtain information as to the existence of any professional relationships among individuals . . . who are treating him." Yet at the end we are told: "No catalog of rights can guarantee for the patient the kind of treatment he has a right to expect. . . . All [the hospital's various] activities must be conducted with an overriding concern for the patient, and above all, the recognition of his dignity as a human being."[11] Nonetheless, these rights are posted prominently in the hospital so that both patients and staff will be reminded of them as they go about their routines.

Now what can be wrong with this way of dealing with patient care? First, these rights, like the right not to be beaten by your spouse, call to mind the abuses they were designed to mitigate. They imply that hospital personnel are commonly guilty of unethical or insensitive conduct; otherwise there would be no need to protect patients against abuse. Second, the institution of rights focuses on a patient as complainant. As we have seen, the language of rights gives the rightholder a license to protest under certain circumstances; that is part of the language and the reason it's connected with self-respect. But as we have also remarked, the patient is not in a good position to exercise such rights. In his weakened condition, under medication, who is he to complain? Giving him rights puts him in the role of an assertive and able individual, but this role is inconsistent with being ill.

Someone who presses a claim and demands respect for his rights does so from the stance of a peer vis-à-vis the one complained against, as Feinberg says; but the doctor–patient relationship is not one of peers.[12] As one writer observes, "strong statements of patient rights imply a parity between physician and patient not usually possible in the situations under which . . . physician–patient relationships are developed." The patient needs the doctor; the doctor doesn't in the same way need him. Moreover, the patient "often enters into the arms of medicine as one might enter passionately into the arms of a lover — with great haste and need, but little forethought"; thus by definition a cool consideration of his situation is excluded."[13] Once recovered and out of the hospital, *then* the patient can exercise his rights — take the doctor and hospital administrator to court and sue for damages. But this remedy is no remedy at all. What a sick and dependent person needs is responsible treatment from others *while he is unable to press claims against anyone.*

How then ought the problem to be addressed? The moral difficulty comes to roost in the doctor–patient or staff–patient relationship: something isn't right there. As the Patient's Bill of Rights asserts, a doctor has to treat his patients with respect and concern, for that is his responsibility and part of his professional role. If he fails to do so, he is not a good doctor, no matter how knowledgeable he is. Then why is a set of rights given to the patient? It's the doctor who needs to be reminded of his charge, and that's where the focus ought to be, logically — on the doctor and his or her responsibility.

The doctor who sees the disease as the object of his interest, and sees the patient's idiosyncrasies as distractions from the pure case he wants to understand, is surely dehumanizing the patient. Foucault speaks of this outlook as a botanical view of medicine, for it is similar to the view found in botany, as well as in mechanics and physics.14 Moreover, if we regard medicine as a science, it is difficult to see why a doctor *should* take the patient seriously *as a person.* Such a view isn't *objective;* that isn't the way a physical scientist would view his subject. Humanity, sympathy, and sensitivity have no place in physical science. The problem of patient treatment, then, is connected with the way medicine is conceived, its claim to be a science, and its place in the community.

An obvious way to address the issue of disrespectful treatment of patients would be to approach the medical community with exactly this concern, a concern that pertains potentially to everyone. One can imagine penalties being imposed when an ethical code is violated. Medical practice might be monitored by people outside of the medical brotherhood. Various legal and institutional ways could be devised to deal with the problem; we don't need to decide here which ones would be the most practical.

There are barriers to this approach, however. In the atomistic model, connections of responsibility and dependency don't appear; there aren't any. In the same way that molecular theory cannot allow that some molecules take care of others or defer to them, independent autonomous beings cannot be connected. The language of rights reflects this atomistic fact, that relations of individuals to one another are relations between entities who are peers. And as we saw, these peer relations give rise to contracts in which both parties pursue their self-interests. Looking at the doctor–patient relation in this light, we see that there's no room for — no representation of — the doctor's *responsibility for the patient.* There is similarly no room in the model for anyone's responsibility for another; everyone is responsible for himself and that's all. Thus we are blocked from dealing with the problem in terms of the medical professional's responsibility for patients. Atomism prefers to give the patient rights.

But it doesn't make sense to do what we do in this case, to put the burden of straightening out the problem of medical negligence and disrespect on the shoulders of those already unable to handle the practical details of life — to say to such people, "Here are your rights; now you may press a claim against the doctor in whose care you placed yourself or waive your right, just as you please." The relationship between doctor and patient is appropriately one of trust, while this remedy implies the absence of trust.

It is no solution to assume that a patient has a healthy person to speak for him and press his rights. For even when such a person exists, the patient's dependency may still prevent his taking action against those who are supposed to care for him. When he is well (if he recovers), he and his representative can then bring suit against the doctor or whoever. But here again the right he possesses is a right appropriate to a well person, not a sick one. I conclude that the conception of patients' rights is irrational and impractical.

IV

Another area where rights are spoken of commonly but, as I will claim, inappropriately is the matter of children. The idea that children have a set of rights that their parents ought to respect is prompted by the prevalence of child neglect and child abuse, wrongs that undeniably exist. It's not in doubt that something needs to be done about such wrongs; wrongs are no less wrong when the perpetrators are the victim's own parents. Nonetheless, parents who abuse children present a difficult problem for the community.

The difficulty is with the strategy of putting rights in the hands of dependent children, rights they must exercise if they can against *those on whom they depend*. As with patients' rights, the model applied here is that of two equal and independent peers in a voluntary relationship—like that of parties to a contract. But that model doesn't fit this case. The child doesn't enter into its relationship with its parents voluntarily and isn't independent or a peer in relation to its parents. The main features of atomism are absent in this relationship.

Atomistic writers characteristically struggle with the place of children. Are they individuals with all the rights of individuals or not? Locke answers: "We are born free as we are born rational; not that we have actually the exercise of either: age, that brings one, brings with it the other too. And thus we see how *natural freedom* and *subjection to parents* may consist together."[15] Locke maintains both that children are free and rational and that they need their parents until they become rational. That is nothing less than a contradiction. Milton Friedman's answer is also problematic. He writes: "Freedom is a tenable objective only for responsible individuals. We do not believe in freedom for madmen or children. . . . We believe, and with good reason, that parents . . . can be relied on to protect them and to assure their development. . . . However we do not believe in the right of the parents to do whatever they will with their children. . . . Children are responsible individuals in embryo. They have ultimate rights of their own."[16] Both writers equivocate. They recognize that saying either that a child is independent or that it is altogether dependent is wrong. For the child its parents hold a unique position of intimacy and protection. The parent who abuses a child may also provide warmth and affection. The wrong, like the relationship, is complex.

The community's concern about the problem is commonly expressed by references to children's rights against their parents. But realistically, any pressing of such a claim against one's parents usually threatens the earliest and closest relationship a child has. The child is expected to court his or her own insecurity. The child's position, like the patient's, is dependent,

that of someone in need of the care and concern of another. But like the doctor–patient relationship, the parent–child relationship cannot be seen in our model. We protect children's interests by giving them rights, but in doing so blindly we ignore both the facts of human development and the various needs of children. Are children, who courts agree need protection, "dignified" by the possession of such rights or by the legal ability to claim them? They lack most ordinary rights because they are unready to use them, and generally are not good judges of the way they themselves should be treated. If there is an important right here, it should be the right to be given good parental care, but it is the parents that are responsible for providing such care. The alternative of giving children a right that they may claim is no substitute.

How should the wrongs of child abuse be addressed? As in the case of patients, we should speak to the wrong*doers* here; we need to restrain and admonish them, teach or punish them, remind them of the value and seriousness of parental roles, of the trust put in them by children on the one side and by society on the other. The matter at issue here is not only the place of the parent-culprit before the law but the place of the law in the parent–child relationship. The community has a profound interest here, not least because of its connection with the stature of its future citizens. Making the child and parent adversaries, encouraging the one to claim its rights against the other, is hardly a good way to pursue this interest.

Here, as in the medical case, we should be addressing the person in a *responsible* role and working with that relationship of responsibility, rather than dealing with the parties as independent peers. But the terms of atomism give us no purchase on this fundamental and complex relationship.

V

Another class of wrong rights affects women and the connections between them and their children. Consider the "equal rights" guaranteed to women who have committed substantial parts of their lives to raising a family and managing a home, and who then need work. The theory says that they have equal rights to a job, an equal opportunity in a free, competitive labor market. The image operating here is that of similar units—men and women of all ages—similarly situated, and in that case fair treatment would be identical treatment of them all. A woman is discriminated against and pays a penalty for her sex only if she is denied a job *when other factors are equal*. But if we suppose her situation to be as I have described it, then other factors are not equal. The model and its assumptions beg the essential question, namely, how she should be treated given that her situation is not like a man's. Affirmative action programs and a ban on "age discrimination" are stopgap efforts that inherently conflict with the model and bow in apology for the offense. They rest on the factors that distinguish people from one another, while in the model any distinctions of treatment are discriminatory and thus unfair.[17] Thus there is no theoretical solution to the problem. Measures that make reasonable moral sense are theoretically excluded.

Consider another issue, the debate over the constitutionality of mandated maternity leaves. The model requires this benefit to be couched in the language of equality; otherwise it appears as discriminatory against men. In order to avoid making a distinction between men and women, we assimilate maternity leaves to a disability or sickness leave, comparable to a leave one takes for the flu. When the benefit is thus clothed in sex-neutral terms, the question arises whether or not a right to maternity leave is an "equal right." The argument then turns on the importance of men's immunity to pregnancy. In such famous cases as *Miller-Wohl* and *California Federal Savings*,[18] the issue is exactly this: If a maternity leave is an equal right, it may be fair; otherwise it provides to women a benefit that is unavailable to men, and therefore it is unconstitutional under Title V of the Civil Rights Act. Thus the very document that was meant to ensure fairness in employment and education is used to frustrate a policy to accommodate the most fundamental process of human life, reproduction.

The reasoning that ensues from a concept of fairness defined as equality among autonomous agents is often strange. It is seriously asked, for instance, whether men have an equal maternity right because they could have such a leave *if they should become pregnant*. What a strange question—and how can a reasonable person answer? One legal writer discusses the Miller-Wohl case in these terms: "The equal treatment proponents . . . are thinking metaphysically. They approach the question [of the legality of maternity leave legislation] . . . by asking whether or not the statute conforms to a particular legal construct, i.e., the equal treatment principle. They focus the debate on legal theoretical levels, rather than starting with an analysis of the concrete material problems of women in the workforce."[19]

Realistically, maternity leaves are needed because childbirth is exhausting and because a newborn baby and its mother need care. In part it is the child's needs that dictate that its mother shouldn't work full time just after its birth. But if we introduce the mother–child complex into the argument, we lose the framework of individual rights. And how else can we deal with the issue?

If we consider the central position of a baby in birth, we may decide that the baby has the principal right. But the issue is obscure: first we need to know if the baby is an individual who can possess rights, and then we have the harder question of whether that individual can have a right to its mother's maternity leave. On the face of it, that notion makes no sense. A right, as we have seen, attaches directly to a person; one person can't have a right *for* another. Moreover, involving the child in the maternal right won't work because it isn't born during the last weeks of pregnancy, when, just because its birth is imminent, the mother needs extra rest and leave from work.

The language of individual rights makes this issue into a puzzle in which by ingenious distortion we force something into a form that's essentially alien to it. How many people are involved in childbirth and do they each have a right, or together have a joint right, to maternity leave? And how does this complex of mother-and-baby compare with the less complicated case of a man? If both sexes are equal, which sex sets the standard? And if we are talking of disabilities, what kind of "disability" is it that leads to the birth of a child and a subsequent commitment to its care? The model gives no answers. Common sense would say that pregnancy isn't an illness but a strenuous productive period culminating in new responsibilities for a creature whose existence is fragile and who requires care to survive. But the model can't admit this description. The dignity of a rightholder brings no dignity to the condition of pregnancy or the occasion of childbirth.

The argument that a right to a maternity leave is a special and unfair right of women unless it is extended and adapted to men is a consequence of individualism and the language of equal rights. In this case it puts men in the position of jealous siblings, watching for any sign of partiality shown to others. They are in the position of competing with pregnant women for favorable treatment, and in this stance they show a blind disregard for the realities of childbirth.

The debate about abortion also shows the inadequacies of a theory of rights in regard to reproduction. It is a subject of serious debate whether the fetus is an autonomous individual with equal rights. If so, then it has all the rights of any person and should be able to claim its rights against its mother-to-be. But how can we imagine such a thing?[20]

The fetus' need for its mother is more total and unqualified than that of an infant for its parents. But if a fetus isn't a person, what else can it be? Some people have proposed to deal with it as a kind of property, as belonging to the mother as part of her body. To be sure, we sometimes speak this way of a foot or a kidney, and even of self-respect and reputation. But a fetus *isn't* like a body part or reputation. It is a potential baby, which is to say a potential human being, and its birth is not like an amputation or organ removal but is the advent of a new member (albeit immature) into the community.

Either way of representing a fetus, as a person or as property, is fraught with difficulties. On the one hand we make too much of it, granting it rights that cannot apply to its case, and on the other we make too little of it, treating it as property whose owner can dispose of it any way she likes, for the point and virtue of ownership is one's right to do what one wants with one's property.

There are certainly two sides to the question of whether abortions should be restricted and what restrictions should be imposed; that's understandable. What is strange is the way we are forced to *present* the two sides, forced to caricature both the pregnant

woman and the fetus. We are forced to caricature them by our commitment to fit the issue into a grid that has room only for individuals who are autonomous, have property, and make contracts. But the reasoning is bizarre.

Imagine a Martian who has come to study us and make sense of our society. He hears arguments about whether the fetus is a person (in the full and legal sense) or a bit of property (in the tort-law sense). Wouldn't he consider us morally undeveloped or mentally handicapped? A human fetus is not like anything except another fetus, conceptually more like a rabbit fetus or a raccoon fetus or an elephant fetus than like a fully developed human. It is a stage in a process by which an infant comes into a community—a community of rabbits or raccoons or elephants or humans. Apart from this framework it's indefinable. It would be best to say, then, that a fetus is sui generis, its own kind of thing, and so irreducible to something else.

What is wrong with us, the Martian wonders, that we don't see this and persist in arguing about fetal personhood and fetal rights? But basically what is wrong here is the grid we press upon the facts of reproduction.

VI

One major problem with the model, as we have seen, is that it cannot show the variety of relationships in which people take responsibility and care for one another, some relationships of family, some of profession, some of simple concern. Its tendency to assimilate all relationships to that of independent, free, and self-interested persons also becomes a limitation in economic theory, as James Coleman observes. "Classical economic theory always assumes that the individual will act in his interest; but it never examines carefully the entity to which 'his' refers. Often, as when households are taken as the unit for income and consumption, it is implicitly assumed that 'the family' or 'the household' is this entity whose interest is being maximized. Yet this is without theoretical foundation, merely a convenient but slipshod device."[21] The "household" is a convenient device for preserving the outlines of atomism. But treating a family—which consists of more than one person — as a single individual "acting in its own interest" is at the same time at odds with the assumptions of atomism. The term *household* preserves the surface of atomism by making it a fictional person.

Rawls makes a similar adjustment, explaining that "the term 'person' is to be construed variously. . . . On some occasions it will mean human individuals, but in others it may refer to . . . business firms, churches, teams," and of course families. Each of these units is then regarded as a rational and self-interested entity.[22] How else can we conceive of families? As a voluntary association of autonomous persons? That notion doesn't square with the facts.

When autonomous persons enter into an agreement, each party agrees to make some concessions in return for advantages to himself: mutual self-interest is the explanatory factor in all bonds. Milton Friedman emphasizes its exclusive power: "If an exchange between two parties is voluntary, it will not take place unless both believe they will benefit from it." Thus it is that "economic order can emerge as the unintended consequence of the actions of many people, each seeking his own interest."[23]

Apply this picture to the sick person, who needs help, and to the doctor, who has what Friedman calls his "personal capacity" to sell. According to Friedman, the doctor's only motive in helping the patient is his own interest, although he concedes that this interest can be defined as more than "myopic selfishness." "It is whatever it is that interests the participants, whatever they value, whatever goals they pursue. The scientist . . . the missionary . . . the philanthropist . . . are all pursuing their interests, as they see them, as they judge them by their own values."[24] The doctor may or may not be acting selfishly; he may have a personal interest in the patient's health. There's no room for a distinction, in Friedman's theory, between the good doctor and the clever mercenary one. None has any *responsibility* to concern himself with anyone else's health.

Plato thought the distinction between good and bad doctors was clear enough. In the *Republic* he has Socrates ask Thrasymachus, "But tell me, your physician in the precise sense . . . is he a money-maker, an earner of fees, or a healer of the sick? And remember to speak of the physician who is really such." Later he asks:

"Then medicine . . . does not consider the advantage of medicine but of the body?" He concludes: "Can we deny, then . . . that neither does any physician in so far as he is a physician seek or enjoin the advantage of the physician but that of the patient? For we have agreed that the physician, 'precisely' speaking, is a ruler and governor of bodies and not a money-maker."[25]

Now if the doctor–patient relationship is a contract, and a sick person must approach a doctor who is motivated by his own gain, the contract is grossly unfair and susceptible to a multitude of exploitations, and therefore probably invalid. H. Tristram Engelhardt describes the initial approach like this: "The physician–patient relationship is likely to be assumed under circumstances that compromise the integrity of the patient. . . . At the very moments when much must be decided by the ill or dying person, he is often least able to decide with full competence. Disease not only places the patient at a general disadvantage . . . it also makes the patient dependent upon the physician."[26]

Here there is a relation governed by dependency, not autonomy, one in which most of the power and the clear options are on the side of the doctor. The patient is a poor example of the rational consumer. Given the doctor's motive and ability to get the best of him, it might be most rational in all self-interest for a patient not to approach him.

The best attitude of a sick person toward his doctor is trust, it is often remarked. The attitude intended is not trust that the doctor will fulfill a contract whose terms are unspecified, but trust in the doctor's concern. Without that sort of trust a doctor becomes a hired physiological consultant.

VII

A deeper question about the language of rights needs to be raised: Why, whenever we deal with a wrongful act or practice, do we feel impelled to refer to some right or other? Besides the influence of atomism, we think of a right as a justification for condemning something as wrong. Feinberg, for instance, says that claim rights are prior to and thus more basic than the duties with which they are correlated.[27] Thus they give a foundation for the demand that someone do or refrain from doing something and justify condemnation by showing the action as a violation of a (prior) right.

In practice the reasoning works like this. Burglary is wrong, everyone agrees; but what justifies us in calling it wrong? Some answer must exist, and one reasonable possibility is that it's wrong because a person has a right not to be burglarized, not to have his property invaded, abused, or stolen. Similarly we say that mugging is wrong, and then defend this judgment by arguing that it is wrong because a person has a right to walk down the street safely. Along these lines, murder is wrong because a person has a right to life; slander is wrong because a person has a right to be treated with respect; and so on. Rights proliferate as we seek justifications for every variety of things condemnable as wrong.

If justifications are needed, then the invocation of rights may make sense, but are such justifications necessary? Isn't murder simply wrong, wrong in itself? A common-sense answer might be yes—why should one need to justify such an obvious judgment? And if we reflect on the logical path that brought us here, we see that it is our conviction that we are justified in calling murder wrong that makes us sure that something must *justify* our judgment. We are of course justified; but does our justification imply that some separate justification lies behind it? What would happen if none did?

Murder's wrongness can be contrasted with the wrongness of something stipulated by a rule, such as moving a castle diagonally in chess. There a justification for the wrongness of the move clearly exists, that is, the rule that governs the way castles can move. And the wrongness of nonperformance of a contract has a justification, namely, that the contract specifies that one will do such-and-such. But in the case of some serious moral offenses it is less clear that analogous justifications exist. As Wittgenstein said of justifications of beliefs, "the chain of reasons has an end" and "at some point one has to pass from explanation to mere description."[28] Calling murder wrong is here like calling a certain color red, that is, what justifies us in using these terms is that the word means what it does. We are justified, but being justified is not the same as having a justification.

We have no particular reason to think that we need to invoke a right before we can call murder

wrong. The "right to life" is unnecessary, and by eschewing it we avoid the curious consequence that death, which negates life, is wrong. We also acquire an important general benefit. When we leave rights aside, our view of murder takes on a different appearance, just as the mistreatment of patients looks different when we stop focusing on patients' rights. Saying that Smith is wrong in murdering Jones because the murder violates Jones's right to life puts the focus on Jones and his rights, even makes it appear that there is something that Jones can do with this right after the fact, which is nonsense. What really concerns us in such a case is what Smith did; *his* action belongs in the center of our perspective, his culpability, not the violation of Jones's now-useless right. Seen this way, an emphasis on individual rights serves to obscure the focus of moral objection to killing rather than giving the objection a firm foundation.

Without doubt rights have an important place in our legal and political system and they often do give reasons for condemning actions that would be permissible without them. But since they are justifications in some instances—the right to vote, for example, justifies us in calling a poll tax wrong or unjust—we are led to think that they are always valuable, that without them our censure of wrongs is weakened and the substance of condemnation is in jeopardy. This conclusion is mistaken. Rights sometimes supply a justification, but sometimes they supply only the appearance or form of one. We should recognize that sometimes they are superfluous.

The corrective to the tendency to invoke rights as justifications is the realization that we know some things to be wrong more securely and fundamentally than we know what rights people have or ought to have. In discussing our demands for justifications for beliefs, Wittgenstein observed that "it is so difficult to find the *beginning*. Or, better: it is difficult to begin at the beginning. And not try to go further back."[29] We may distort our subject if we try always to find something deeper, look for another and another reason. There has to be an end to justifications, and with murder and lying and cheating we have hit bedrock.

This tendency to seek justifications has another, more unfortunate side. The notion that one really needs a justification for the wrongness of murder implies that one isn't sure that murder is wrong, and that its wrongness depends on the adequacy of some further proof. But in that case, one's moral judgment in regard to murder is uncertain, and if it is uncertain about murder, then a great deal of moral understanding is missing. In that event, it's unclear how the demand could be satisfied. Uncertainty about something so basic may put the questioner beyond the framework in which moral justifications are meaningfully asked for and given, and beyond that framework is a no-man's-land often identified with skepticism. The demand for justification thus threatens to weaken rather than support the structure of moral thinking. The move cannot do any good here.

I conclude that rights and their invocation are often important and valuable. The right to performance of contract and the right to vote and the right to assemble are all embodied in protective legislation and certainly justify court action against anyone who would prevent exercise of them. But three kinds of problems can arise when rights are invoked too freely. The first concerns their application to people who are not in a position to exercise them. There the invocation of a right is often a means of avoiding placing responsibility on someone in a position of strength and control. In such a case our moral focus is wrong. The second problem has to do with people in situations and connections that vitiate assumptions in other ways, as the situations of women and fetuses do. The third has to do with justifying the condemnation of offenses whose moral wrongness is perfectly clear and unequivocal. The invocation of a right does not automatically fortify a conviction but may echo a doubt, and in some.cases the doubt, once raised, cannot be put to rest, not by the invocation of a right or by any other means.[30]

Rights have their place, but their place is limited. They don't provide a moral panacea, a handy set of justifications to be called on when justification is desired. They need to be used with judgment and restraint, without a blanket commitment to the atomistic vision.

Notes

1. Richard Wasserstrom, "Rights, Human Rights, and Racial Discrimination," in *Rights,* ed. David Lyons (Belmont, Calif.: Wadsworth, 1979), p. 48.

2. H. L. A. Hart, "Are There Any Natural Rights?" in *Rights,* ed. Lyons, p. 19.

3. See Alasdair MacIntyre, *After Virtue* (Notre Dame: University of Notre Dame Press, 1981), pp. 68–70, for a good account of the relation between modern talk of rights and the ideas of the Enlightenment.

4. David Lyons, "Rights, Claimants, and Beneficiaries," in *Rights,* ed. Lyons, p. 60.

5. Joel Feinberg also emphasizes these options: if Nip has a claim against Tuck, he argues, then "Nip not only *has* a right, but he can choose whether or not to exercise it, whether to claim it, . . . even whether to release Tuck from his duty" ("The Nature and Value of Rights," in *Rights,* ed. Lyons, p. 85). For an interesting examination of the relation of rights and claims, see Alan White, "Rights and Claims," in *Law, Morality, and Rights,* ed. M. A. Stewart (Dordrecht: Reidel, 1983), pp. 139–60.

6. Feinberg, "Nature and Value of Rights," p. 84.

7. Ibid., pp. 87, 91.

8. Michel Foucault, *The Birth of the Clinic,* trans. A. M. Sheridan Smith (New York: Random House, 1975), p. 14.

9. Ibid., p. 17.

10. Samuel Butler, *Erewhon* (New York: Random House, 1927), p. 110.

11. American Hospital Association, "Statement on a Patient's Bill of Rights," *Hospitals* 4 (February 16, 1973). This statement, which was affirmed by the Board of Trustees of the Association on November 17, 1972, is reprinted in *Contemporary Issues in Bioethics,* ed. Tom L. Beauchamp and LeRoy Walters (Belmont, Calif.: Wadsworth, 1982). See also *Patient's Rights Handbook,* printed and distributed by the State of California under the administration of Governor Edmund Brown, Jr., which also assures a patient of "the right to decent living conditions and uncensored mail" (p. 13).

12. For a discussion of the relation of peers, see Elizabeth H. Wolgast, *Equality and the Rights of Woman* (Ithaca: Cornell University Press, 1980), chap. 3.

13. H. Tristram Engelhardt, "Rights and Responsibilities of Patients and Physicians," in *Contemporary Issues in Bioethics,* ed. Beauchamp and Walters, p. 136.

14. Foucault, *Birth of the Clinic,* p. 17.

15. John Locke, *Second Treatise on Civil Government,* in *Two Treatises on Government,* ed. Thomas I. Cook, (New York: Hafner, 1966), p. 150.

16. Milton Friedman, *Free to Choose* (New York: Harcourt Brace Jovanovich, 1979), pp. 32–33.

17. See Richard Wasserstrom, "Racism, Sexism, and Preferential Treatment: An Approach to the Topics," *UCLA Law Review,* July 1977, pp. 581–622, which argues for a model in which no sex differences are recognized, where both sexes are in detail treated alike. Wasserstrom's exercise shows how complex and deep the

theoretical problem is; if we are determined to deal with it in terms of equal rights, we have to reconstruct our society so that equal rights *will be fair*. For a discussion of Wasserstrom's argument, see my *Equality and the Rights of Women*, chap. 1; also see my "Is Reverse Discrimination Fair?" in *Law, Morality, and Rights*, ed. Stewart, pp. 295–314.

18. Miller-Wohl Co. v. Commissioner of Labor and Industry, State of Montana, 575 F. Supp. 1264 (D. Mont. 1981); California Federal Savings & Loan v. Guerra, 55 U.S. Law Week 4077 (1987).

19. Linda Krieger and Patricia Cooney, "The Miller-Wohl Controversy: Equal Treatment, Positive Action, and the Meaning of Women's Equality," *Golden Gate University Law Review* 13 (Summer 1983): 566. This article contains a good account of the theoretical problems presented by the maternity issue; however, the authors, like their opponents, couch the issue in terms of a *woman's* right, as if the problem involved no one else. For some suggestions about a different approach, see my *Equality and the Rights of Women*, chap. 4.

20. There is a wealth of literature debating the question whether a fetus is a person. Mary Anne Warren, "On the Moral and Legal Status of Abortion," in *Philosophy and Women*, ed. Sharon Bishop and Marjorie Weinzweig (Belmont, Calif.: Wadsworth, 1979), pp. 216–26, works out a defense of the proposition that the fetus, while potentially human, lacks some necessary features of a human being, and thus cannot be considered a peer of its potential parent.

21. James Coleman, *Papers on Non-Marketing Decision-Making*, quoted in Howard Margolis, *Selfishness, Altruism, and Rationality: A Theory of Social Choice* (Cambridge: Cambridge University Press, 1982), p. 1.

22. John Rawls, "Justice as Fairness," *Philosophical Review* 67 (April 1958): 166. One has to be careful here, as Rawls also thinks of the group interest as consolidating but not merging the interests of individuals. An excellent criticism of this aspect of Rawls's argument may be found in Michael Sandel, *Liberalism and the Limits of Justice* (Cambridge: Cambridge University Press, 1982), esp. chaps. 1 and 4.

23. Friedman, *Free to Choose*, pp. 13–14.

24. Ibid., p. 27. Rawls also supposes that the interests of a person are sometimes benevolent and social, but they needn't be, and the moral justification of state policies is neutral on the question of whether it is these interests or purely selfish ones that are represented.

25. Plato, *Republic*, trans. Paul Shorey, in *The Collected Dialogues of Plato*, ed. Edith Hamilton and Huntington Cairns (Princeton: Princeton University Press, 1961), V, 341c–342d.

26. Engelhardt, "Rights and Responsibilities of Patients and Physicians," p. 133.

27. Feinberg, "Nature and Value of Rights," p. 84. A. I. Melden also uses "rights" to mean moral rights, as ways to justify calling things morally wrong; see *Rights and Persons* (Berkeley: University of California Press, 1977), esp. chap. 4.

28. Ludwig Wittgenstein, *The Blue and Brown Books* (New York: Harper, 1958), p. 143, and *On Certainty*, ed. G. E. M. Anscombe and G. H. von Wright, trans. Denis Paul and Anscombe (New York: Harper & Row, 1969), 189.

29. Wittgenstein, *On Certainty*, 471.

30. For a parallel argument with regard to belief, see my *Paradoxes of Knowledge* (Ithaca: Cornell University Press, 1977), esp. chap. 4.

HUMAN RIGHTS IN THE "AGE OF DISCOVERY"

René Trujillo

René Trujillo describes the moral reflection that was occasioned by the Spanish conquest of indigenous peoples in the Western Hemisphere. The concept of human rights played a central role in this reflection and was a powerful foundation in the arguments for equitable treatment of indigenous peoples and their lands.

As we remember the "Age of Discovery" of the "New World" in terms of the brutality that attended it for the indigenous peoples of the Western Hemisphere, let us also remember what effect it had on conscientious European thinkers of the day. Let us learn not only from the mistakes of the conquest, but from the moral reflection that it occasioned.

In reply to the theology and philosophy of repression prevalent in his day, Francisco de Vitoria (1485–1546) proposed an alternative in his *Carta Constitucional de los Indios*. The major thesis of this work was expressed in three fundamental principles. First, the indigenous peoples had a fundamental right based on their humanity—that is, based on the fact that they were human beings—to be treated as free people. Second, they had a fundamental right to defend their own sovereignty. Third, and finally, they enjoyed the fundamental right of all peoples to work toward and to make peace and international solidarity. It was in light of these three beliefs that Vitoria both determined and evaluated the rights and concomitant obligations of the Spanish Crown to be in and remain in the "new" world. Ultimately, considering the transgressions suffered by the indigenous peoples, he concluded that Spain owed restitution to the natives.

The dispute that ensued between Juan Gines de Sepulveda (1490–1573), the official defender of the monarch, and Vitoria was based on the concept of the just war. They were concerned with the justifications for the actions of the Spanish Crown against the integrity of the societies of indigenous peoples with whom the Spanish conquerors had contact. More broadly, these two men were concerned with the concept of "justice" in general as it pertained to human rights and obligations.

The constitutional principles of Vitoria's alternative perspective can be understood on the basis of five points. In the first place, the Spaniards and indigenous peoples had to be understood as equal with regards to their humanity. This consideration spanned both actual and potential human characteristics. Second, any assertion of inhumanity in the indigenous peoples had to be understood as due to a lack of education and to their resultant barbaric customs. Some European thinkers of the day were enlightened enough to see that this same point might be leveled against the European communities within which they found themselves. Third, the indigenous peoples, in the same fashion as the Spanish, had property rights to their possessions and as such could not be dispossessed of them by virtue of any charge of lack of culture. This would follow for the same reasons as those which would serve to protect an uncultured individual in Spain. Fourth—and this might be very controversial today—the indigenous peoples might be entrusted to the tutelage of the Spaniards while still in an "underdeveloped state." This provision, of course, assumes that the aim of the tutelage would be the eventual autonomy of the indigenous peoples, and that the Spaniards had the requisite moral character and skill to undertake such a position. Finally, the consent of the indigenous peoples and their free choice were the ultimate grounds for any just Spanish intervention in the "new" world.

To better understand these assertions, and to see their relevance to us today, we must understand the motivation behind them. We might appropriately ask, What question do they answer? All demands placed on the indigenous peoples were justified in the minds of the Spanish based on their belief in the universal power of the Roman Catholic Church. Specifically, the appropriateness of their actions followed from the world authority of the pope, who, they thought, had sovereign power over all spiritual and temporal concerns. The papal "donation" of the Indies to the Catholic Kings (Fernando II el Catolico, king of Aragon and Castilla and Isabel I la Catolica, queen of Castilla) conferred the status of vassals (in a feudal sense) to the indigenous peoples, and established sovereignty for Spain over the "new" world. This condition of servitude was understood in Spain as "natural" and as having ample historical precedent. The latter belief was certainly clearly true; however, the issue of servitude, natural or otherwise, was to create a significant theological and moral crisis.

Along with their papal authority to govern came the mandate to evangelize the indigenous peoples, that is, to seek their free conversion to Christendom. It was understood as the duty of the indigenous peoples to accept evangelization — but what would this imply about the nature and humanity of these peoples? The Spanish monarchy wished to justify its wars against the indigenous peoples by establishing papal authority, Spanish sovereignty, and the right to evangelize. It wanted to be able to establish the submission, occupation, and enslavement of these peoples as the natural and inevitable consequence of the just war waged against indigenous rebellion and resistance. Much of this policy, however, rested on the notion that these indigenous individuals had some *duty* to comply. The resistance to these ideas, as evidenced in Vitoria's position, was based on a reevaluation of the necessary preconditions for moral duty. What sort of being has moral duties?

The resounding answer was "human beings." But human beings have not only moral duties and responsibilities, they have moral rights. They have human rights. Can one be held responsible for one's moral duties in the face of the systematic infringement of one's moral rights? Can one be morally disenfranchised within the community of moral beings, and still be expected to comply with moral law? These were some of the questions that motivated the opposition to come out against the policies and actions of the crown.

Today it is true, as it was five hundred years ago, that duty and obligation imply rights and benefits if they are to be considered just. To have the duties of a human being, one must be able to enjoy the rights that attend the human condition. If there are any moral duties to be defined within such a state, there must also be a sense of moral rights. The conclusion I draw from these observations is that morality requires humanity, and humanity depends on the recognition and observance of dignity. In the case of human beings, dignity is achieved not only through our duties and obligations to others, but also through the obligations and duties of others to ourselves. Human duties to ourselves or others only make sense in a reflective equilibrium that defines the rights that follow from these duties.

In today's communities there is an overabundance of duties talk in the face of a paucity of rights talk. When we do speak of rights, it is overwhelmingly in terms of personal rights and not the rights of others. We may in word understand that these rights depend on each other, but our deeds rarely conform to this understanding. If we are to secure the rights of any individuals whatsoever, we must secure the rights of all. If we are to establish the duties of any one person, we must confirm the basis for such a duty as rooted in the enjoyment of some right or privilege. Otherwise, we commit ourselves to the irrational: we ask of all disenfranchised human beings that they act systematically and freely against their own interests and that they trust in the beneficence of those who force them into such a dilemma.

Until we recognize that humanity manifests itself variously, we are in no position to judge either ourselves or others. Race, gender, class, and sexual orientation have historically been used as the basis for different duties and rights. These duties and rights have always been determined by the politically strong and the duties exacted with vengeance from the politically subordinate. We see continued evidence of this trend today. Take the recent Colorado state initiative to repeal all antigay discrimination protection legislation (as currently on the books in Boulder, Denver, and Aspen). How can we ask individuals to fully participate in a community where they are not deemed worthy of their full human rights with all the protection society is willing to offer others? The answer is, we cannot. To support the quality of our lives, each and every one of us must be committed to the quality of all lives. Otherwise, we will suffer the consequences.

THE NATURE OF AUTONOMY

Gerald Dworkin

Gerald Dworkin describes autonomy as a moral, political, and social ideal that limits the intrusions and interferences of other people in the lives of people who are themselves independent, self-determining, and worthy of respect. He also understands autonomy as a capacity to reflect on and change one's desires and by so doing give meaning to one's life. Given its central role in human life and social organization, the protection of autonomy is seen as a requirement of a just state.(Source: From The Theory and Practice of Autonomy *by Gerald Dworkin. Copyright © 1988 by Cambridge University Press. Reprinted with the permission of Cambridge University Press.)*

I

The concept of autonomy has assumed increasing importance in contemporary moral and political philosophy. Philosophers such as John Rawls, Thomas Scanlon, Robert P. Wolff, and Ronald Dworkin have employed the concept to define and illuminate issues such as the characterization of principles of justice, the limits of free speech, and the nature of the liberal state.

. . .

It is apparent that, although not used just as a synonym for qualities that are usually approved of, "autonomy" is used in an exceedingly broad fashion. It is used sometimes as an equivalent of liberty (positive or negative in Berlin's terminology), sometimes as equivalent to self-rule or sovereignty, sometimes as identical with freedom of the will. It is equated with dignity, integrity, individuality, independence, responsibility, and self-knowledge. It is identified with qualities of self-assertion, with critical reflection, with freedom from obligation, with absence of external causation, with knowledge of one's own interests. It is even equated by some economists with the impossibility of interpersonal comparisons. It is related to actions, to beliefs, to reasons for acting, to rules, to the will of other persons, to thoughts, and to principles. About the only features held constant from one author to another are that autonomy is a feature of persons and that it is a desirable quality to have.

It is very unlikely that there is a core meaning which underlies all these various uses of the term. Autonomy is a term of art and will not repay an Austinian investigation of its ordinary uses. It will be necessary to construct a concept given various theoretical purposes and some constraints from normal usage.

II

I shall begin by discussing the nature of autonomy. Given various problems that may be clarified or resolved with the aid of a concept of autonomy, how may we most usefully characterize the concept? I use the vague term "characterize" rather than "define" or "analyze" because I do not think it possible with any moderately complex philosophical concept to specify necessary and sufficient conditions without draining the concept of the very complexity that enables it to perform its theoretical role. Autonomy is a term of art introduced by a theorist in an attempt to make sense of a tangled net of intuitions, conceptual and empirical issues, and normative claims. What one needs, therefore, is a study of how the term is connected with other notions, what role it plays in justifying various normative claims, how the notion is supposed to ground ascriptions of value, and so on — in short, a theory.

. . .

Autonomy functions as a moral, political, and social ideal. In all three cases there is value attached to how things are viewed through the reasons, values, and desires of the individual and how those elements are shaped and formed.

As a political ideal, autonomy is used as a basis to argue against the design and functioning of political institutions that attempt to impose a set of ends, values, and attitudes upon the citizens of a society. This imposition might be based on a theological view, or secular visions of a good society, or on the importance of achieving excellence along some dimension of human achievement. In each case the argument favoring such imposition is made independently of the value of the institutions as viewed by each citizen. Those favoring autonomy urge that the process of justification of political institutions must be acceptable to each citizen, must appeal to considerations that are recognized to be valid by all the members of the society.

In particular, then, autonomy is used to oppose perfectionist or paternalistic views. It is also related to what Ronald Dworkin refers to as the notion of equal respect. A government is required to treat its citizens neutrally, in the sense that it cannot favor the interests of some over others. This idea is used by Dworkin to argue for the existence of various rights.

Conceptions of autonomy are also used, by Wolff and others, to argue for the illegitimacy of obedience to authority. The emphasis in this argument is on the individual making up his own mind about the merits of legal restrictions. This use of autonomy seems much closer in content to the ideal of moral autonomy. As a moral notion—shared by philosophers as divergent as Kant, Kierkegaard, Nietzsche, Royce, Hare, and Popper—the argument is about the necessity or desirability of individuals choosing or willing or accepting their own moral code. We are all responsible for developing and criticizing our moral principles, and individual conscience must take precedence over authority and tradition. I am not defending this line of reasoning, but it is certainly a body of thought which makes use of the notion of autonomy and has a corresponding set of problems connected with responsibility, integrity, and the will.[1] A theory of autonomy must throw some light on these problems, even if it does not accept (all of) the proposed solutions.

Finally, we have a set of issues concerning the ways in which the nonpolitical institutions of a society affect the values, attitudes, and beliefs of the members of the society. Our dispositions, attitudes, values, wants are affected by the economic institutions, by the mass media, by the force of public opinion, by social class, and so forth. To a large extent these institutions are not chosen by us; we simply find ourselves faced with them. From Humboldt, Mill, and DeTocqueville to Marcuse and Reismann, social theorists have worried about how individuals can develop their own conception of the good life in the face of such factors, and how we can distinguish between legitimate and illegitimate ways of influencing the minds of the members of society.

While Marxists have been most vocal in raising the issues of "false consciousness," and "true versus false needs," it is important to see that the question is one which a wide range of social theorists must address. For it is a reasonable feature of any good society that it is self-sustaining in the sense that people who grow up in such a society will acquire a respect for and commitment to the principles which justify and regulate its existence. It is very unlikely that the development of such dispositions is something over which individuals have much control or choice. Socialization into the norms and values of the society will have taken place at a very young age. It looks, then, as if we can only distinguish between institutions on the basis of what they convey, their content, and not on the basis that they influence people at a stage when they cannot be critical about such matters. It looks, therefore, as if autonomy in the acquisition of principles and values is impossible.

In all three areas—moral, political, social—we find that there is a notion of the self which is to be respected, left unmanipulated, and which is, in certain ways, independent and self-determining. But we also find certain tensions and paradoxes. If the notion of self-determination is given a very strong definition—the unchosen chooser, the uninfluenced influencer—then it seems as if autonomy is impossible. We know that all individuals have a history. They develop socially and psychologically in a given environment with a set of biological endowments. They mature slowly and are, therefore, heavily influenced by parents, peers, and culture. How, then, can we talk of self-determination?

Again, there seems to be a conflict between self-determination and notions of correctness and objectivity. If we are to make reasonable choices, then we must be governed by canons of reasoning, norms of conduct, standards of excellence that are not themselves the products of our choices. We have acquired them at least partly as the result of others' advice, example, teaching — or, perhaps, by some innate coding. In any case, we cannot have determined these for ourselves.[2]

Finally, there is a tension between autonomy as a purely formal notion (where what one decides for oneself can have any particular content), and autonomy as a substantive notion (where only certain decisions count as retaining autonomy whereas others count as forfeiting it). So the person who decides to do what his community, or guru, or comrades tells him to do cannot on the latter view count as autonomous. Autonomy then seems in conflict with emotional ties to others, with commitments to causes, with authority, tradition, expertise, leadership, and so forth.

What I shall try to do now is introduce a conception of autonomy . . . that is (1) relevant to the moral, political, and social issues mentioned above; (2) possible to achieve; and (3) able to avoid the difficulties and problems just enumerated.

III

The central idea that underlies the concept of autonomy is indicated by the etymology of the term: *autos* (self) and *nomos* (rule or law). The term was first applied to the Greek city state. A city had *autonomia* when its citizens made their own laws, as opposed to being under the control of some conquering power.

There is then a natural extension to persons as being autonomous when their decisions and actions are their own; when they are self-determining. The impetus for this extension occurs first when questions of following one's conscience are raised by religious thinkers. Aquinas, Luther, and Calvin placed great stress on the individual acting in accordance with reason as shaped and perceived by the person. This idea is then taken up by the Renaissance humanists. Pico della Mirandola expresses the idea clearly in his "Oration on the Dignity of Man." God says to Adam:

> We have given thee, Adam, no fixed seat, no form of thy very own, no gift peculiarly thine, that . . . thou mayest . . . possess as thine own the seat, the form, the gift which thou thyself shalt desire . . . thou wilt fix the limits of thy nature for thyself . . . thou . . . art the molder and the maker of thyself.[3]

The same concept is presented by Berlin under the heading of "positive liberty":

> I wish to be an instrument of my own, not other men's acts of will. I wish to be a subject, not an object . . . deciding, not being decided for, self-directed and not acted upon by external nature or by other men as if I were a thing, or an animal, or a slave incapable of playing a human role, that is, of conceiving goals and policies of my own and realizing them.[4]

But this abstract concept only can be understood as particular specifications are made of the notions of "self," "my own," "internal," and so forth. Is it the noumenal self of Kant, or the historical self of Marx? Which mode of determination (choice, decision, invention, consent) is singled out? At what level is autonomy centered — individual decision, rule, values, motivation? Is autonomy a global or a local concept? Is it predicated of relatively long stretches of an individual's life or relatively brief ones?

Let me begin by considering the relationship between the liberty or freedom of an individual and his autonomy. Are these two distinct notions? Are they linked, perhaps, in hierarchical fashion so that, say, interference with liberty is always interference with autonomy, but not vice-versa? Are they, perhaps, merely synonymous?

Suppose we think of liberty as being, roughly, the ability of a person to do what she wants, to have (significant) options that are not closed or made less eligible by the actions of other agents. Then the typical ways of interfering with the liberty of an agent (coercion and force) seem to also interfere with her autonomy (thought of, for the moment, as a power of self-determination). If we force a Jehovah's Witness to have a blood transfusion, this not only is a direct interference with his liberty, but also a violation of his ability to determine for himself what kinds of medical treatment are acceptable to him. Patient autonomy *is* the ability of patients to decide on courses of treatment, to choose particular physicians, and so forth.

But autonomy cannot be identical to liberty for, when we deceive a patient, we are also interfering with her autonomy. Deception is not a way of restricting liberty. The person who, to use Locke's example, is put into a cell and convinced that all the doors are locked (when, in fact, one is left unlocked) is free to leave the cell. But because he cannot — given his information — avail himself of this opportunity, his ability to do what he wishes is limited. Self-determination can be limited in other ways than by interferences with liberty.

Both coercion and deception infringe upon the voluntary character of the agent's actions. In both cases a person will feel used, will see herself as an instrument of another's will. Her actions, although in one sense hers because she did them, are in another sense attributable to another. It is because of this that such infringements may excuse or (partially) relieve a person of responsibility for what she has done. The normal links between action and character are broken when action is involuntary.

Why, then, should we not restrict our categories to those of freedom, ignorance, and voluntariness? Why do we need a separate notion of autonomy? One reason is because not every interference with the voluntary character of one's action interferes with a person's ability to choose his mode of life. If, as is natural, we focus only on cases where the person wishes to be free from interference, resents having his liberty interfered with, we miss an important dimension of a person's actions.

Consider the classic case of Odysseus. Not wanting to be lured onto the rocks by the sirens, he commands his men to tie him to the mast and refuse all later orders he will give to be set free. He wants to have his freedom limited so that he can survive. Although his behavior at the time he hears the sirens may not be voluntary — he struggles against his bonds and orders his men to free him — there is another dimension of his conduct that must be understood. He has a preference about his preferences, a desire not to have or to act upon various desires. He views the desire to move his ship closer to the sirens as something that is no part of him, but alien to him. In limiting his liberty, in accordance with his wishes, we promote, not hinder, his efforts to define the contours of his life.

To consider only the promotion or hindrance of first-order desires — which is what we focus upon in considering the voluntariness of action — is to ignore a crucial feature of persons, their ability to reflect upon and adopt attitudes toward their first-order desires, wishes, intentions.

It is characteristic of persons, and seems to be a distinctively human ability, that they are able to engage in this kind of activity. One may not just desire to smoke, but also desire that one not have that desire. I may not just be motivated by jealousy or anger, but may also desire that my motivations be different (or the same).

A person may identify with the influences that motivate him, assimilate them to himself, view himself as the kind of person who wishes to be moved in particular ways. Or, he may resent being motivated in certain ways, be alienated from those influences, prefer to be the kind of person who is motivated in different ways. In an earlier essay I suggested that it was a necessary condition for being autonomous that a person's second-order identifications be congruent with his first-order motivations.[5] This condition, which I called "authenticity," was to be necessary but not sufficient for being autonomous.

I now believe that this is mistaken. It is not the identification or lack of identification that is crucial to being autonomous, but the capacity to raise the question of whether I will identify with or reject the reasons for which I now act. There are a number of considerations that tell against my earlier view.

First, autonomy seems intuitively to be a global rather than local concept. It is a feature that evaluates a whole way of living one's life and can only be assessed over extended portions of a person's life, whereas identification is something that may be pinpointed over short periods of time. We can think of a person who today identifies with, say, his addiction, but tomorrow feels it as alien and who continues to shift back and forth at frequent intervals. Does he shift back and forth from autonomy to nonautonomy?

Second, identification does not seem to be what is put in question by obvious interferences with autonomy. The person who is kept ignorant or who is lobotomized or who is manipulated in various ways (all obvious interferences with autonomy) is not having his identifications interfered with, but rather his capacity or ability either to make or reject such identifications.

Third, there seems to be an implication of the position that is counterintuitive. Suppose that there is a conflict between one's second-order desires and one's first-order desires. Say one is envious but does not want to be an envious person. One way of becoming autonomous is by ceasing to be motivated by envy. But another way, on the view being considered here, is to change one's objections to envy, to change one's second-order preferences.

Now there may be certain limits on the ways this can be done that are spelled out in the other necessary condition which I elaborated: that of procedural independence. So, for example, it wouldn't do to have oneself hypnotized into identifying with one's envious motivations. But even if the procedures used were "legitimate," there seems to be something wrong with the idea that one becomes more autonomous by changing one's higher-order preferences.

Fourth, this view breaks the link between the idea of autonomy and the ability to make certain desires effective in our actions. On this view, the drug addict who desires to be motivated by his addiction, and yet who cannot change his behavior, is autonomous because his actions express his view of what influences he wants to be motivating him. This seems too passive a view. Autonomy should have some relationship to the ability of individuals, not only to scrutinize critically their first-order motivations but also to change them if they so desire. Obviously the requirement cannot be as strong as the notion that "at will" a person can change his first-order preferences. Indeed, there are certain sorts of inabilities of this nature that are perfectly compatible with autonomy. A person who cannot affect his desires to act justly or compassionately is not thought by that fact alone to be nonautonomous. Perhaps there is still the idea that if justice were not a virtue or that if, in a given case, hardness and not compassion were required, the agent could adjust his desires. Susan Wolf has suggested the requirement that a person "could have done otherwise if there had been good and sufficient reason."[6]

The idea of autonomy is not merely an evaluative or reflective notion, but includes as well some ability both to alter one's preferences and to make them effective in one's actions and, indeed, to make them effective because one has reflected upon them and adopted them as one's own.

It is important both to guard against certain intellectualist conceptions of autonomy as well as to be candid about the ways in which people may differ in their actual exercise of autonomy. The first error would be to suppose that my views imply that only certain types or classes of people can be autonomous. If we think of the process of reflection and identification as being a conscious, fully articulated, and explicit process, then it will appear that it is mainly professors of philosophy who exercise autonomy and that those who are less educated, or who are by nature or upbringing less reflective, are not, or not as fully, autonomous individuals. But a farmer living in an isolated rural community, with a minimal education, may without being aware of it be conducting his life in ways which indicate that he has shaped and molded his life according to reflective procedures. This will be shown not by what he says about his thoughts, but in what he tries to change in his life, what he criticizes about others, the satisfaction he manifests (or fails to) in his work, family, and community.

It may be true, however, that there is empirical and theoretical evidence that certain personality types, or certain social classes, or certain cultures are more (or less) likely to exercise their capacity to be autonomous. I do not suppose that the actual exercise of this capacity is less subject to empirical determination than, say, the virtue of courage. To the extent that this is borne out by the evidence, we must be on guard against the tendency to attribute greater value to characteristics which are more likely to be found in twentieth-century intellectuals than in other groups or cultures.

To return to our original question of the relation between autonomy and liberty, I would claim that the two are distinct notions, but related in both contingent and noncontingent ways. Normally persons wish to act freely. So, interfering with a person's liberty also interferes with the ways in which he wants to be motivated, the kind of person he wants to be, and hence with his autonomy. But a person who wishes to be restricted in various ways, whether by the discipline of the monastery, regimentation of the army, or even by coercion, is not, on that account alone, less autonomous. Further, I would argue that the condition of being a chooser (where one's choices are not defined by the threats of another) is not just contingently linked to being an autonomous person, but must be the standard case from which exceptions are seen as precisely that—exceptions. Liberty, power, control over important aspects of one's life are not the same as autonomy, but are necessary conditions for individuals to develop their own aims and interests and to make their values effective in the living of their lives.

Second-order reflection cannot be the whole story of autonomy. For those reflections, the choice of the kind of person one wants to become, may be influenced by other persons or circumstances in such a fashion that we do not view those evaluations as being the person's own. In "Autonomy and Behavior Control" I called this a failure of procedural independence.

Spelling out the conditions of procedural independence involves distinguishing those ways of influencing people's reflective and critical faculties which subvert them from those which promote and improve them. It involves distinguishing those influences such as hypnotic suggestion, manipulation, coercive persuasion, subliminal influence, and so forth, and doing so in a non ad hoc fashion. Philosophers interested in the relationships between education and indoctrination, advertising and consumer behavior, and behavior control have explored these matters in some detail, but with no finality.

Finally, I wish to consider two objections that can (and have) been raised to my views.[7] The first is an objection to introducing the level of second-order reflection at all. The second is why should we stop at the second level and is an infinite regress not threatened.

The first objection says that we can accomplish all we need to by confining our attention to people's first-order motivation. After all, on my own view of the significance of procedural independence, we have to find a way to make principled distinctions among different ways of influencing our critical reflections, so why not do this directly at the first level. We can distinguish coerced from free acts, manipulated from authentic desires, and so forth. My reply is that I think we fail to capture something important about human agents if we make our distinctions solely at the first level. We need to distinguish not only between the person who is coerced and the person who acts, say, to obtain pleasure, but also between two agents who are coerced. One resents being motivated in this fashion, would not choose to enter situations in which threats are present. The other welcomes being motivated in this fashion, chooses (even pays) to be threatened. A similar contrast holds between two patients, one of whom is deceived by his doctor against his will

and the other who has requested that his doctor lie to him if cancer is ever diagnosed. Our normative and conceptual theories would be deficient if the distinction between levels were not drawn.

The second objection is twofold. First, what is particularly significant about the second level? Might we not have preferences about our second-order preferences? Could I not regret the fact that I welcome the fact that I am not sufficiently generous in my actions? I accept this claim, at least in principle. As a theory about the presence or absence of certain psychological states empirical evidence is relevant. It appears that for some agents, and some motivations, there is higher-order reflection. If so, then autonomy will be thought of as the highest-order approval and integration. As a matter of contingent fact human beings either do not, or perhaps cannot, carry on such iteration at great length.

The second part of this objection concerns the acts of critical reflection themselves. Either these acts are themselves autonomous (in which case we have to go to a higher-order reflection to determine this, and since this process can be repeated an infinite regress threatens) or they are not autonomous, in which case why is a first-order motivation evaluated by a non-autonomous process *itself* autonomous. My response to this objection is that I am not trying to analyze the notion of autonomous *acts,* but of what it means to be an autonomous person, to have a certain capacity and exercise it. I do claim that the process of reflection ought to be subject to the requirements of procedural independence, but if a person's reflections have not been manipulated, coerced, and so forth and if the person does have the requisite identification then they are, on my view, autonomous. There is no conceptual necessity for raising the question of whether the values, preferences at the second order would themselves be valued or preferred at a higher level, although in particular cases the agent might engage in such higher-order reflection.

Putting the various pieces together, autonomy is conceived of as a second-order capacity of persons to reflect critically upon their first-order preferences, desires, wishes, and so forth and the capacity to accept or attempt to change these in light of higher-order preferences and values. By exercising such a capacity, persons define their nature, give meaning and coherence to their lives, and take responsibility for the kind of person they are.

Notes

1. See chaps. 3 and 4.

2. See chap. 4.

3. Quoted in P. O. Kristeller, "The Philosophy of Man in the Italian Renaissance," *Italica* 24 (1947), 100–1.

4. I. Berlin, *Four Essays on Liberty* (Oxford: Oxford University Press, 1969), 131.

5. G. Dworkin, "Autonomy and Behavior Control," *Hastings Center Report* (February 1976).

6. S. Wolf, "Asymmetric Freedom," *Journal of Philosophy* 77 (1980), 159.

7. I am indebted to an unpublished manuscript, "Autonomy and External Influence," of John Christman for his ideas on these points. For further discussion, see Irving Thalberg, "Hierarchical Analyses of Unfree Action," *Canadian Journal of Philosophy* 8 (June 1978) and Marilyn Friedman, "Autonomy and the Split-Level Self," *Southern Journal of Philosophy* 24 (1986, no. 1).

AUTONOMY, MODERNITY AND COMMUNITY
Communitarianism and Critical Social Theory in Dialogue

Seyla Benhabib

Seyla Benhabib defends Habermas's intersubjective notion of the self. On Habermas's and Benhabib's view, self identity is forged in a certain kind of activity with other humans. She argues that this view of the self does leave room for autonomy in the sense that people have the right to challenge traditions and social roles. The civic virtue for Benhabib is not conformity, but participation — having a say in the economic, political, and civic arrangements that define one's life. (Source: From Situating the Self *by Seyla Benhabib (1992), by permission of the publisher, Routledge, New York.)*

Political Theory and the Disenchantment with Modernity

. . .

In the evolving debate between liberalism, communitarians and post-modernist critics, where is contemporary critical social theory to be situated? The purpose of this chapter is to answer this question by bringing communitarianism and critical social theory and in particular the project of communicative ethics into dialogue.

Communitarianism and contemporary critical social theory share some fundamental epistemological principles and political views. The rejection of ahistorical and atomistic conceptions of self and society is common to both, as is the critique of the loss of public spiritedness and participatory politics in contemporary societies. While the critical theory of Jürgen Habermas, and more specifically his analysis of the contradictions of modern societies, can provide communitarianism with a more differentiated vision of the social problems of our societies, the communitarian insistence that contemporary moral and political theory enrich its understanding of the self and base its vision of justice upon a more vibrant view of political community offers a corrective to the excessive formalism of justice-centered and deontological theories.

As a political theory, "communitarianism" must primarily be identified *via negativa*, that is less in terms of the positive social and political philosophy it offers than in light of the powerful critique of liberalism it has developed. It is on account of their shared critique of liberalism that thinkers like Alasdair MacIntyre, Charles Taylor, Michael Walzer and Michael Sandel have been called communitarians.[1]

The communitarian critique of liberalism can be distinguished into an epistemological and a political component. The epistemological critique focuses on the incoherence of the Enlightenment project of justifying morality and of providing normative foundations for politics via the device of a voluntary contract between free and autonomous agents. The political critique of liberalism developed by communitarians is more varied. In the following I shall isolate two major issues of contention between communitarianism and critical social theory: (1) The critique of the "Unencumbered Self" and the Priority of the Right over the Good; (2) The Politics of Community and the Integrationist vs. Participatory Responses to Modernity.

The Critique of the "Unencumbered" Self and the Priority of the Right over the Good

The communitarians criticize the epistemic standpoint of the Enlightenment on the grounds that this standpoint and liberal political philosophies which proceed from it presuppose an incoherent and impoverished concept of the human self. In order to look at the world in the way suggested by those who believe in the Archimedean point of view, we must be certain kinds of people. But, argue communitarians, the kinds of people we are and the epistemic perspective required of us by Enlightenment liberalism are antithetical to each other. We can adopt "the view from nowhere" (Thomas Nagel) required of us by

75

Kantian liberalism, only if we can also conceive of ourselves as "unencumbered" selves. In his influential critique of John Rawls, Michael Sandel has sought to link this view of the unencumbered self to the commitment within liberal thought to the priority of the right over the good.

I shall not be concerned here to discuss in detail this criticism, or to evaluate the responses which have been formulated against Sandel in Rawls's defense.[2] What interests me is the following issue: despite the fact that Habermas also rejects the vision of the unencumbered self, he has not drawn some of the consequences which communitarians assume to follow from this rejection.[3] The intersubjective constitution of the self and the evolution of self-identity through the communicative interaction with others has been a key insight of Habermas's work since his early essay on "Labor and Interaction: Remarks on Hegel's *Jena Philosophy of Mind*."[4] Habermas often formulates this insight concerning the intersubjective constitution of self-identity in the language of George Herbert Mead. The "I" becomes an "I" only among a "we," in a community of speech and action. Individuation does not precede association; rather it is the kinds of associations which we inhabit that define the kinds of individuals we will become.[5]

. . .

In . . . moral justification as envisaged by communicative ethics, individuals do not have to view themselves as "unencumbered" selves. It is not necessary for them to define themselves independently either of the ends they cherish or of the constitutive attachments which make them what they are. In entering practical discourses individuals are not entering an "original position." They are not being asked to define themselves in ways which are radically counterfactual to their everyday identities. This model of moral argumentation does not predefine the set of issues which can be legitimately raised in the conversation and neither does it proceed from an unencumbered concept of the self. In communicative ethics, individuals do not stand behind any "veil of ignorance."

. . . [T]he very model of communicative ethics suggests that a procedural moral theory, which constrains what can be defined as the moral good in light of a conception of moral justification, need not sub-

scribe to an "unencumbered" concept of the self. In one crucial respect, communicative ethics endorses the modern understanding of the self and contends that moral autonomy means not only the right of the self to challenge religion, tradition and social dogma, but also the right of the self to distance itself from social roles and their content or to assume "reflexive role-distance." In their critique of the "unencumbered self," communitarians often fail to distinguish between the significance of constitutive communities for the formation of one's self-identity and a conventionalist or role-conformist attitude which would consist in an uncritical recognition of "my station and its duties" (F. H. Bradley). Communitarians often seem to conflate the philosophical thesis concerning the significance of constitutive communities for the formation of one's identity with a socially conventionalist and morally conformist attitude. The specifically *modern* achievement of being able to criticize, challenge and question the content of these constitutive identities and the "prima facie" duties and obligations they impose upon us should not be rejected.[6] Otherwise communitarians are hard put to distinguish their emphasis upon constitutive communities from an endorsement of social conformism, authoritarianism and, from the standpoint of women, of patriarchalism.[7] By contrast, communicative ethics develops a view of the person which makes this insight central and attributes to individuals the *ability* and the *willingness* to assume reflexive role-distance and the ability and the willingness to take the standpoint of others involved in a controversy into account and reason from their point of view. Naturally, these assumptions concerning the self are not "weak" and uncontroversial. They presuppose that individuals have the psychic-moral *Bildung* or formation which will make it motivationally plausible as well as rationally acceptable for them to adopt the reflexivity and universalism of communicative ethics.

As a procedural theory of moral argumentation, communicative ethics is based on certain *substantive* presuppositions. In my view this is unavoidable. All procedural theories must presuppose some substantive commitments. The issue is whether these substantive commitments are presented as theoretical certainties whose status cannot be further questioned, or whether we can conceive of ethical discourse in such a radically reflexive fashion that even the pre-suppositions of discourse can themselves be challenged, called into question and debated. . . . Since practical discourses do not theoretically predefine the domain of moral debate and since individuals do not have to abstract from their everyday attachments and beliefs when they begin argumentation, we cannot preclude that it will be not only matters of justice but those of the good life as well that will become thematized in practical discourses or that the presuppositions of discourse themselves will be challenged. A model of communicative ethics, which views moral theory as a theory of argumentation, need not restrict itself to the priority of justice. I see no reason as to why questions of the good life as well cannot become subject matters of practical discourses. Surely discourses will not yield conceptions of the good life equally acceptable to all, nor is it desirable that they do so. Yet, contrary to what Habermas at times suggests, our conceptions of the good life just like our conceptions of justice are matters about which inter-subjective debate and reflection is possible, even if consensus on these matters, let alone legislation, is not a goal. The line between matters of justice and those of the good life is not given by some moral dictionary, but evolves as a result of historical and cultural struggles. This is not to say that no such line needs to be drawn between matters of justice or those of the good life, between the public and the private spheres. . . . [I]t is not the moral classification of problems which will help in this task but the articulation of those normative principles and values which we would like to foster and cherish in a democratic polity.

In conclusion then I concur with critics of deontology like Williams, Taylor and Sandel that a strong deontological theory which views justice as the center of morality unnecessarily restricts the domain of moral theory, and distorts the nature of our moral experiences.[8] But a universalist and communicative model of ethics need not be so strongly construed. Such a theory can be understood as defending a "weak" deontology, according to which the argumentative establishment of norms is the central criterion of their validity. Such a theory can also allow moral debate about our conceptions of the good life, thus making them accessible to moral reflection and moral transformation. Of course, this is a far weaker result

than may be preferred by a strong teleologist but it remains for such a teleologist to show that under conditions of modernity one can indeed formulate and defend a univocal conception of the human good. So far Habermas is right: under conditions of modernity and subsequent to the differentiation of the value spheres of science, aesthetics, jurisprudence, religion and morals we can no longer formulate an overarching vision of the human good. Indeed, as Alasdair MacIntyre's definition of the good life, namely "the life spent in seeking the good life for man,"[9] very well reveals, as moderns we have to live with varieties of goodness. Whether the good life is to be fulfilled as an African famine relief fighter, a Warsaw ghetto resistant, a Mother Teresa or a Rosa Luxemburg, ethical theory cannot prejudge; at the most, modern moral theory provides us with some very general criteria by which to assess our intuitions about the basic validity of certain courses of action and the integrity of certain kinds of values. I regard neither the plurality and variety of goodnesses with which we have to live in a disenchanted universe nor the loss of certainty in moral theory to be a cause of distress. Under conditions of value differentiation, we have to conceive of the unity of reason not in the image of a homogeneous, transparent glass sphere into which we can fit all our cognitive and value commitments, but more as bits and pieces of dispersed crystals whose contours shine out from under the rubble.

The Politics of Community: The Integrationist Versus Participatory Responses to Modernity

The dispute over the concept of the self and deontology can be distinguished into a moral and a political aspect. In moral theory, deontology implies that conceptions of justice should precede those of the good life, both in the sense of limiting what can be legitimately defended as the good life and in the sense that conceptions of justice can be justified independently of *particular* conceptions of the good life. In the political realm, deontology means that the basic principles of a just order should be morally neutral, both in the sense of allowing many different conceptions of the good life to be freely pursued and cherished by citizens, and also in the sense that the basic liberties of citizens ought never to be curtailed for the sake of some specific conception of the social good or welfare. The arguments I have looked at so far concerned the moral claims for deontology only. Most communitarians reject deontology in the realm of moral theory, and argue that conceptions of justice necessarily imply certain conceptions of the good life. The political arguments for deontology usually weigh more heavily in the minds of liberal thinkers and it is around this issue that communitarian thinkers have been most severely criticized.

In their critique of Rawls, communitarians have neither focussed on the first principle of justice, namely the principle of the most extensive basic equal liberty,[10] nor have they questioned the ordering of the two principles of justice and the priority of liberty. It is partly this lack of explicitness on their part concerning the "priority of liberty" issue which has led their contemporary critics to assume that communitarians are advocates of small, homogeneous, undifferentiated social units, particularly prone to intolerance, exclusivism, and maybe even forms of racism, sexism and xenophobia.[11]

In his interesting analysis of these issues in *Patterns of Moral Complexity*, Charles Larmore maintains that communitarianism follows the tradition of "political romanticism" whose chief feature is the search for the reconciliation of personal and political ideals.[12] Defending a position which he names "modus vivendi" liberalism, Larmore writes:

> However, just this belongs at the core of the liberal tradition. Conceptions of what we should be as persons are an enduring object of dispute, toward which the political order should try to remain neutral. We do better to recognize that liberalism is not a philosophy of man, but a philosophy of politics. . . . This means that we must adopt a more positive attitude toward the liberal "separation of domains" than either political romantics or some liberals themselves have shown.[13]

I have doubts that one can defend liberalism without recourse to a "philosophy of man" or on the basis of what John Rawls has recently called "overlapping consensus" alone.[14] What interests me is Larmore's claim that the "reconciliation" of personal and political ideals

or of various social spheres is the mark of contemporary communitarianism as it has been the distinguishing characteristic of political romanticism since Herder and the conservative reaction to the French revolution. Communitarian political thought indeed contains two strains, a reconciliationist one or what I shall prefer to call an "integrationist strain" and a "participatory" one. It is the vacillation between these two strains that makes communitarian thought vulnerable to the charge of violating the priority of liberty.

According to the first conception, the problems of individualism, egotism, anomie and alienation in modern societies can only be solved by a recovery or a revitalization of some coherent value scheme. This coherent value scheme may be a religion, as Novalis and some German romantics had hoped for,[15] or it may be a "civic religion," the principles of which will inculcate citizen's virtue as Rousseau had dreamt of.[16] Then again one may view this value scheme as a "code of civility," which survives, on MacIntyre's view, in Orthodox Jewish, Greek and Irish communities,[17] or it may be a vision of friendship and solidarity which shapes moral character and lends it depth as Sandel evokes.[18] In each case, it is characteristic of the integrationist view that it emphasizes value revival, value reform, or value regeneration and neglects institutional solutions.

By contrast, the view that I shall name "participationist" sees the problems of modernity less in the loss of a sense of belonging, oneness and solidarity but more in the sense of a loss of *political agency and efficacy*. This loss of political agency is not a consequence of the separation of the personal from the political or of the differentiation of modern societies into the political, the economic, the civic and the familial-intimate realms. This loss may be a consequence of the contradiction between the various spheres which diminishes one's possibilities for agency in one sphere on the basis of one's position in another sphere (as for example when early bourgeois republics curtailed citizenship rights on the basis of income and occupation and denied wage-earners the vote). Or it may also result from the fact that membership in the various spheres becomes mutually exclusive because of the nature of the activities involved, while the mutual exclusivity of the spheres is reinforced by the system (take the duties of motherhood and the public aspirations of women in the economy, politics or science, and the fact that public funds are not used to support better, more readily available and more affordable forms of childcare).

The participationist view then does not see social differentiation as an aspect of modernity which needs to be overcome. Rather the participationist advocates the reduction of contradictions and irrationalities among the various spheres, and the encouragement of non-exclusive principles of membership among the spheres. Communitarian thinkers have not always been clear as to which perspective they want to emphasize in face of the problems of modern societies, and their liberal critics have been right to focus on this ambivalence.

Whether they focus upon the libertarianism of Nozick[19] or upon the welfare liberalism of Rawls, contemporary communitarians are concerned with the liberalism of the post World War II welfare state.[20] They focus upon a problem that is central to the welfare state as a political formation, namely the principles and criteria of distributive justice. Michael Walzer and Charles Taylor agree that there can be no single principle of distributive justice applicable to all social goods. As Walzer states: "different social goods ought to be distributed for different reasons, in accordance with different procedures, by different agents; and that all these differences derive from different understandings of the social goods themselves …."[21] Second, our societies operate on the basis of different and at times mutually exclusive principles of distribution, like need, membership, merit, contribution. "What all this means," writes Taylor, "is that we have to abandon the search for a single set of principles of distributive justice. On the contrary a modern society can be seen under different, mutually irreducible perspectives, and consequently can be judged by independent, mutually irreducible principles of distributive justice."[22] Third, the search for a single, overarching principle of distributive justice, applicable across spheres, appears plausible to contemporary liberals only because of the *philosophical framework* which they choose for stating the issue. Proceeding, in Taylor's words, from the perspective of the individual as bearer of rights, they claim to be able to frame the issue of distributive justice solely in terms of the conflicting rights claims of various individuals. Both

Taylor and Walzer agree that if the issue is framed in this fashion, then indeed such individuals would choose something like the Rawlsian difference principle.[23] Taylor rejects this framework on the grounds of his moral critique of deontology and argues that different principles of distributive justice are related to different conceptions of the good, and these in turn, are related to different understandings of the nature of our human associations.[24] Similarly, for Walzer the political community itself has to be adopted as the "appropriate setting for justice" and not some "original position,"[25] for the community itself is also a good, and perhaps the most important one, which gets distributed.

These criticisms of the search for a unified theory of distributive justice can also be stated in an "integrationist" or a "participatory" language. When Taylor and Walzer emphasize that the appropriate setting for justice is the political association itself, and that it is on the basis of shared understandings entertained by members of such a community that we have to proceed to think about justice, they follow the integrationist line. Modern societies are not communities integrated around a single conception of the human good or even a shared understanding of the value of belonging to community itself. Issues of distributive justice arise precisely because there is no such shared understanding among the members of the political community, but as Taylor and Walzer also acknowledge, such societies are marked by a "plurality" of visions of the good and of the good of association itself. If this is so, the search for a publicly acceptable scheme of just distribution is not as ill-guided as they would have us believe, for the question as to how one can distribute goods, services, income, etc., across primary groups which do not share the same moral conceptions is neither irrelevant nor foolhardy. In their epistemic critique of the perspective of the "right-bearing individual," Taylor and Walzer at times hypostatize what Taylor himself describes as the "philosophical framework" of community,[26] and treat this as if it were not only a methodological framework but also a living political reality.

Although Michael Walzer's aim in *Spheres of Justice* is to further an egalitarian, participatory conception of justice, the main task of which is to allow complex equality and to prevent the "illegitimate" domination of one set of goods by another (of public offices and votes by money, for example), in his continuous appeal to "shared understandings" of social goods Walzer also slides into the integrationist language. Since his aim is to proceed "immanently and phenomenologically,"[27] available and shared definitions and understandings of social meaning have to be his starting point. This beginning point, though, at times leads him to underestimate the degree to which what he is doing is not just a phenomenological re-description of what agents in our kinds of societies think about various goods; rather, Walzer is practicing a "normative hermeneutic," which is not very far removed from Rawlsian "reflective equilibrium" in its intentions. Proceeding from shared views and understandings of certain goods like citizenship or health-care, for example, Walzer is refining, systematizing, making coherent, criticizing and replacing by a "better" understanding the common views of these issues. *Spheres of Justice* abounds with such examples, but the most telling is Walzer's remarkable discussion of the issue of guest-workers in contemporary western societies. Walzer is not reluctant to go far beyond the prevailing political consensus on this issue both in Western Europe and in the United States to plead for the right to naturalization of such guest-workers, not just of the right to permanent residence but the right to citizenship. Walzer writes: "Democratic citizens, then, have a choice: if they want to bring in new workers, they must be prepared to enlarge their own member-ship; if they are unwilling to accept new members, they must find ways within the limits of the domestic labor market to get socially necessary work done."[28] Walzer does not contest the right of these communi-ties to make one or the other choice but he makes it very clear what he, as a political theorist, believes is right: "Political justice is a bar to permanent alien-age—either for particular individuals or for a class of changing individuals."[29] This last sentence in partic-ular is a good example of the "participatory" nature of Walzer's argument.

The distinction between these two modes of ap-proaching the problems of modernity and politics allows us to see more clearly the relation between Habermas's work and some contemporary communi-tarian projects. The defense of modernity in light of the principle of public participation has been an es-sential aspect of Habermas's work since his early essay on *The Structural Transformation of the Public Sphere.*[30] Reversing the pessimistic assessment of modernity as a "dialectic of Enlightenment," Habermas has empha-sized the extent to which modernity does not only sig-nify differentiation, individuation and bifurcation. The emergence of an autonomous public sphere of political reasoning and discussion is also central to the project of the moderns. The irrationalities of modern societies derive rather from several factors: first, access to the public sphere has always been limited by par-ticularistic considerations of class, race, gender and religion; second, increasingly not the consensual gen-eration of norms but money and power have become modes through which individuals define the social bond and distribute social goods. In Walzer's lan-guage, Habermas sees a trend in modern societies to-ward "simple equality" spurred on by the dominance of money and power as media of coordinating activ-ities. Third, as money and power become increasingly autonomous principles of social life, individuals lose a sense of agency and efficacy. They can neither see the nature of the social bond nor can they compre-hend its meaning. Political alienation, cynicism and anomie result. Fourth, the demands of increased role-distance and the continuing subjection of tradition to critique and revision in a disenchanted universe make it difficult for individuals to develop a coherent sense of self and community under conditions of moder-nity. These trends can only be counteracted by ex-panding individuals' cognitive participation in vari-ous branches of knowledge which today have become the monopoly of experts, and by increasing the possi-bilities for meaningful life-choices on the parts of in-dividuals. In other words, in each instance the solu-tion is to overcome the problems of modern societies by extending the principle of modernity, namely the unlimited and universally accessible participation of all in the consensual generation of the principles to govern public life.

Undoubtedly, Habermas has at times stated these insights in the language of traditional liberalism. Yet his participatory conception of public life and his in-sistence that only more democratization not less can solve the problems of modernity clearly transcend the traditional liberal preoccupation with negative and positive liberty in the direction of a participatorycommunalist critique of contemporary welfare-state societies. In his view then, the task of distributive justice would be to enhance the citizen's possibilities for the more effective exercise of political agency and control. In fact, it is because the emphasis is on participatory rather than distributive justice that "practical discourses" are so empty and yield no determinate solutions in Habermas's theory. Like Walzer, Habermas sees the attempt of the political theorist to provide citizens with a normative yardstick as a preemption of their right to democratic politics.[31]

If communitarian political theory is understood then as advocating a participationist rather than an integrationist restructuring of our political life, it cannot be subject to the charge of political romanticism, for participationism does not entail dedifferentiation, value homogeneity, or even value reeducation. Participationism is not an answer to the dilemmas of modern identity, estrangement, anomie and homelessness. For on the participationist model, the public sentiment which is encouraged is not reconciliation and harmony, but rather political agency and efficacy, namely the sense that we have a say in the economic, political and civic arrangements which define our lives together, and that what one does makes a difference. This can be achieved without value homogeneity among individuals. Of course, it is likely that a very atomized society will undermine one's options and motivation for political agency, while a vibrant, participatory life can become central to the formation and flourishing of one's self-identity. Equally, while the prevalence of certain kinds of public value systems will make the participationist option more or less likely, an increased sense of public-political agency and efficacy will contribute to the revitalization of certain kinds of values.

This emphasis on political participation and the widest-reaching democratization of decision-making processes in social life, is one that Jürgen Habermas's critical theory shares with the tradition usually referred to as that of "republican or civic virtue," and which extends from Aristotle to Machiavelli, to the Renaissance humanists, to Jefferson, Rousseau and Hannah Arendt. Clearly, this tradition has been a source of inspiration for contemporary communitarians as well. The crucial distinction between the participatory vision of contemporary critical theory and that of the tradition of

"civic virtue" is that thinkers of the latter tradition, more often than not, have formulated their views of participatory politics in express hostility toward the institutions of modern civil society, like the market. "Virtue" and "commerce" are thought to be antithetical principles. In Hannah Arendt's words, under conditions of modernity politics is reduced to administration. Participatory politics then is considered possible either for a land-based gentry of civic virtue or for the citizens of the Greek polis, but not for complex, modern societies with their highly differentiated spheres of the economy, the law, politics, civil and familial life.

We owe it to the work of Jürgen Habermas that it has enriched our understanding of the social and cultural possibilities of modernity in such a way that neither communities of virtue nor contracts of self-interest can be viewed as exhausting the modern project. His modernist and participatory vision distinguishes the politics of communicative ethics both from liberalism and from the republican tradition of "civic virtue."

Notes

This paper was originally delivered at the American Political Science Association convention in Chicago in 1987. It has appeared as my contribution to the Festschrift in honor of Jürgen Habermas's sixtieth birthday, published as *Cultural-Political Interventions in the Unfinished Project of Enlightenment,* ed. Axel Honneth, Thomas McCarthy, Claus Offe and Albrecht Wellmer (MIT Press, Cambridge, Mass., 1992). It has been revised for inclusion in this volume.

1. Of course, this approach should suggest neither that communitarianism is a school in the sense that one can speak of the Frankfurt School nor that there are no interesting and important differences among these thinkers. Since my goal is to establish *intraparadigmatic* dialogue, however, that is a dialogue across traditions, to some extent I shall have to minimize *interparadigmatic* differences.

   Although all the philosophical elements of the critique of liberalism defined as communitarian were contained already in Roberto M. Unger's *Knowledge and Politics* (Free Press, New York, 1975), pp. 29ff., Unger's position is more complicated insofar as his diagnosis of the condition of modern societies is centered less around the loss of community than around the paradoxes of the welfare state and the decline of the rule of law; cf. *Law in Modern Society* (Free Press, New York, 1976). In this respect Unger stands much closer to the tradition of critical social theory than do other communitarians, and his position would have required independent treatment.

Two recent essays by Charles Taylor and Michael Walzer, written in response to various liberal critics and reflecting upon their own positions "après la lutte" (so to speak), are highly significant for assessing the current state of the debate. See Charles Taylor, "Cross-Purposes: The Liberal–Communitarian Debate," in *Liberalism and the Moral Life* ed. Nancy L. Rosenblum (Harvard University Press, Cambridge, Mass., 1989), pp. 159–83; Michael Walzer, "The Communitarian Critique of Liberalism," *Political Theory,* 18.1 (Feb. 1990), pp. 6–23.

2. See Amy Gutmann, "Communitarian Critics of Liberalism," *Philosophy and Public Affairs,* 14.3 (Summer 1985), pp. 311ff.; Charles Larmore, *Patterns of Moral Complexity* (Cambridge University Press, New York, 1987); Will Kymlicka, *Liberalism, Community and Culture* (Oxford University Press, Oxford, 1989).

3. Will Kymlicka's clear and trenchant treatment of this issue in "Liberalism and Communitarianism," shows that communitarians themselves (Taylor, Sandel and MacIntyre in particular) are inconsistent in their positions, insofar as they also accept in some sense that "the *person* is prior to her ends" and not just "constituted" by her attachments. In *Philosophy and Public Affairs,* 18.2 (June 1988), pp. 181–204, here p. 192, emphasis in the text. Arguing for liberalism, Kymlicka emphasizes precisely those qualities of autonomous individuality which critical theory also valorizes: reflexivity vis à vis the setting of one's goals in life and the determination of one's interests; the ability to stand back and question those constitutive commitments into which we are born or into which sometimes we are "thrown," and I would add the ability to "act from principle." Both liberalism and critical theory are committed to a vision of the autonomous self. Disagreements emerge around another issue: inasmuch as philosophical liberals try to reformulate conceptions of the self without involving assumptions drawn from a comprehensive philosophical theory but in the light of articulating publicly shared conceptions of personality and agency, they weaken their own moral vision and are led into conceptual incoherence. The conceptual framework via which liberals state their views of the person follow a dualistic logic. On the one hand, there is the world of "causative" influences like language, culture and community which shape a person; these are so to speak the givens of phenomenal agency in this world. On the other hand, there are "the rational grounds" through which individuals assume an attitude of choice and reflection toward the given characteristics of their lives, bodies and communities—the position of noumenal agency. Kymlicka repeats this view in that he writes:

"In any event, this solution is in contrast with the liberal view, which desires a society that is transparently intelligible—where nothing works behind the back of its members—*Where all causes are turned into reasons*" (ibid. pp. 196–7, my emphasis). Hegelians would argue that this contrast between "causes" and "reasons" is spurious in understanding the reality of language, culture, society and institutions. As MacIntyre and Taylor have emphasized very well, in the explanation of human action, culture and societies the language of causality reduces the interpretive relation of the self to its world to the external relation of two bodies to each other. But human action can only be understood by understanding the language of reasons and the interpretive framework within which agents themselves view their world. Of course, a "causal" explanation going beyond mere hermeneutic interpretation is possible and even desirable. Such explanations in the social sciences must begin with an "already always interpreted reality." Critical social theorists, like the neo-Hegelians MacIntyre and Taylor, proceed from the primacy of the interpretive framework over the empiricist language of causes. Whereas for Kymlicka the view of a society that is "transparently intelligible" becomes a moral imperative, critical theorists along with Hegelians insist that the very contrast between "causes" and "reasons" needs to be reformulated in the light of the interpretive dimensions of human actions, institutions and culture. For an early statement, see Charles Taylor, "Interpretation and the Sciences of Man," *Review of Metaphysics,* 25 (1971), pp. 3–51; Alasdair MacIntyre, *Against the Self-Images of the Age* (University of Notre Dame Press, Notre Dame, 1978), chaps. 18–22 in particular; Jürgen Habermas, *On the Logic of the Social Sciences,* trans. Shierry Weber Nicholsen and Jerry A. Stalk (MIT Press, Cambridge, Mass., 1989); Richard J. Bernstein, *Restructuring Social and Political Theory* (University of Pennsylvania Press, Philadelphia, 1978).

4. In *Theory and Practice,* trans. John Viertel (Beacon, Boston, 1973), pp. 142–70.

5. J. Habermas, "Moral Development and Ego Identity," in *Communication and the Evolution of Society*, trans. and introd. Thomas McCarthy (Beacon, Boston, 1979), pp. 93ff.

6. Throughout history there have been exemplary moral individuals who in effect have become the moral heroes of our cultures and civilizations precisely because they could engage in such questioning and reflection: not only Socrates but Antigone as well, not only Buddha but Maimonides, not only the Stoics but the Prophet Amos have questioned the authority of conventional duties and obligations in their cultures and society. That they may have done so in the name of some other values which they held to be un-

questionable precisely because they were embedded in their cultural universe and carried its moral authority is not damaging to my argument. The "rationalization of value spheres" (Max Weber) under conditions of modernity means that increasingly all the "moral givens" of tradition are called into question but that furthermore, the attitude of moral rebellion and questioning which was once the privilege and virtue of heroes, prophets and moral sages now becomes "routinized" in everyday life, as modern societies define the duties and obligations which follow from social roles in increasingly abstract, formal and impersonal rules and norms. Simply put, as a co-worker in a modern company you stand today under no relationship of personal gratitude and obedience to your superiors beyond that which is dictated by the functional division of labor in that company. As social obligations become more abstract, they allow individuals greater latitude to fill in the "cracks" for themselves. That many female secretaries, for example, frequently make coffee for their usually male bosses, arrange golf appointments for them, or call up the cleaners is not part of the functional division of labor in the firm. One criticizes these patterns of interaction precisely because they continue paternalistic, patrimonial and premodern forms of dependence. This, of course, does not mean that the logic of gender differences and social roles would not assert itself in other ways in the modern workplace. Secretaries still continue to cook coffee, look pretty and presentable, and "mother" not only the boss but other co-workers as well. But a modern secretary who refuses to act in these ways and who questions what is expected of her is not being a moral sage or heroine, she is simply assuming one of the moral stances which life in the modern world allows her.

7. This point is cogently argued by Marilyn Friedman in "Feminism and Modern Friendship: Dislocating the Community," *Ethics,* 99.2 (Jan. 1989), pp. 275–90.

8. In his ethical theory, Habermas not only disregards self-regarding virtues, but restricts the sphere of justice to the public-institutional domain alone, thus disregarding *structures of informal justice* as they shape our everyday relations within the family and with friends. . . . one consequence of this bias in the theory is the exclusion of all *gender-related* issues from the domain of justice and their relegation to the private sphere. Cf. also Norma Haan, "An Interactional Morality of Everyday Life," in *Social Science as Moral Inquiry,* ed. N. Haan, R. Bellah, P. Rabinow and W. Sullivan (Columbia University Press, New York, 1983), pp. 218ff.

9. Alasdair MacIntyre, *After Virtue* (Notre Dame University Press, Notre Dame, Ind., 1981), p. 204.

10. See Rawls, *A Theory of Justice,* pp. 60ff.

11. See H. Hirsch, "The Threnody of Liberalism," in *Political Theory,* 14.3 (Aug. 1986), pp. 423–49; Iris Young, "The Ideal of Community and the Politics of Difference," in *Social Theory and Practice,* 12.1 (Spring 1986), pp. 2–25.

12. Charles Larmore, *Patterns of Moral Complexity* (Cambridge University Press, Cambridge, 1987), p. 119.

13. Ibid., p. 129.

14. John Rawls, "Justice as Fairness: Political, Not Metaphysical," *Philosophy and Public Affairs,* 14.3 (Summer 1985), pp. 223ff.

15. See Novalis, "Christendom or Europe," in *Hymns to the Night and Other Selected Writings,* trans. and introd. Charles E. Passage (Library of Liberal Arts, New York, 1960), pp. 45ff.

16. J. J. Rousseau, *Du Contrat Social,* first published 1762 (Garnier, Paris, 1962), pp. 327ff.

17. MacIntyre, *After Virtue,* pp. 234, 244–5.

18. Michael Sandel, "The Procedural Republic and the Unencumbered Self," *Political Theory,* 12.1 (1984), pp. 81ff.

19. Cf. Charles Taylor, "Legitimation Crisis?" and "The Nature and Scope of Distributive Justice," in *Philosophy and the Human Sciences,* pp. 248–318.

20. See Michael Walzer, *Spheres of Justice* (Basic Books, New York, 1983).

21. Ibid., p. 6.

22. Taylor, "The Nature and Scope of Distributive Justice," p. 312.

23. Walzer, *Spheres of Justice,* p. 79; Taylor, "The Nature and Scope of Distributive Justice," pp. 308ff.

24. Taylor, "The Nature and Scope of Distributive Justice," p. 291.

25. Walzer, *Spheres of Justice,* p. 29.

26. Taylor, "The Nature and Scope of Distributive Justice," pp. 297ff.

27. Walzer, *Spheres of Justice,* p. 26.

28. Ibid., p. 61.

29. Ibid.

30. An English translation of this work which was first published in 1962 is finally available, see J. Habermas, *The Structural Transformation of the Public Sphere,* trans. Thomas Burger (MIT Press, Cambridge, Mass., 1988).

31. See Michael Walzer, "Liberalism and the Art of Separation," *Political Theory* (Aug. 1984), pp. 315–30; J. Habermas, "Legitimation Problems in the Modern State," in *Communication and the Evolution of Society,* trans. T. McCarthy (Beacon, Boston, 1979), pp. 179ff.

PART 2

Social Injustice

The expression "That isn't fair" is used to refer to all sorts of morally objectionable behavior. The concept of justice, which is very close to fairness in everyday use, is usually restricted by philosophers to the economic, social, and political arenas—arenas where groups of people who are often strangers to each other interact. Although good arguments can be made that this is too restrictive, we have stayed fairly close to the standard use in picking out examples of injustice. The type of injustice discussed in this section is a persistent pattern of mistreatment based on one's group membership. For example, people experience racism on account of their perceived membership in a particular race. Obviously there are other forms of injustice than those treated in this section, such as ageism, but the illustrations chosen here—racism, sexism, classism, homophobia, and the exclusion of people with disabilities are perhaps the most pernicious forms of injustice in the contemporary United States.

This section begins with a discussion of racism, in part because the analysis of racism has been more fully developed than the analysis of some other forms of injustice. It is important to distinguish between two different kinds of racism. The first kind, which will be referred to as *individual racism,* is what comes to most people's minds when they think about racism. They imagine an individual who has negative beliefs and attitudes about someone of another race, on which the first person is often willing to act. Someone who taunts another with racial epithets is an example of this kind of racism. There are three features of this kind of racism: (1) beliefs that there are significant racial differences, and that one (or more) race is inferior to another; (2) negative attitudes ranging from discomfort to hatred about members of certain races; and (3) a willingness to act on the basis of these beliefs and attitudes. On this analysis, people can be a little bit racist or very racist, depending on their beliefs, attitudes, and actions. Jean Paul Sartre's essay is a detailed look at the phenomenology of individual racism.

But this is not the only kind of racism. Often people are puzzled when a charge of racism is made. They look into their own hearts, beliefs, and actions and do not see anything that looks like racism. Of course, we are all apt to deceive ourselves about some of our negative qualities, but it is possible that racism could exist even in the absence of individual racism, if institutions and traditional ways of doing things advantage members of certain races to the exclusion of others. This kind of racism is called *institutional racism*. Institutional racism involves three factors: (1) the mistreatment experienced by a group of people identified by race, (2) maintained by institutional arrangements through which (3) one group identified by race consistently gets a larger share of the economic, political, and social power. This kind of racism is often invisible to white people. An example of institutional racism is the different penalties for powdered cocaine versus crack cocaine. Powdered cocaine, which is the form of cocaine more often favored by white users, has significantly lower penalties in many jurisdictions than crack cocaine, which is more often favored by users of color. Here we see a social institution, the law, treating groups differently. One need not assume that this difference was *intended* to disadvantage users of color to describe this as an example of institutional racism.

Many people have argued that the only way we can get rid of racism is to get rid of the whole concept of race. This suggestion has something to recommend it. After all, it would be very difficult to discriminate on the basis of race if we stopped recognizing racial categories. There is another reason for abolishing the notion of race — it has no scientific basis. No set of biological or social characteristics distinguishes all members and *only* members of a particular race. Since race talk is unscientific and is the basis for racism, why not get rid of it? Well, it may turn out that a world without racial identifications is a better world than the one we live in, and then again it may not. Proponents of difference argue that the world would be a very boring and unstable place if we did not have differences and groups organized around their difference from other groups. Whether or not you agree about this, you must surely admit that we live in a world in which racism has a very solid foothold. In this world, it would be silly for members of oppressed races to pretend that no one else sees them as members of a race. Furthermore, racial groups might lose the solidarity that comes from recognizing their racial kin and their common oppression if they gave up the notion of race when it still has a social reality. These points are made by Tommy Lott in his essay. Naomi Zack takes a different tack on race, arguing that it is a concept that ought to be given up.

Sexism is similar in many ways to racism—women and girls are disadvantaged because of their group membership, in this case because they are female. It too has both an individual and an institutional form. The same features of individual and institutional racism exist for sexism as well. In the case of individual sexism, we see beliefs, attitudes, and actions. In the case of institutional sexism, mistreatment of females is maintained by institutional arrangements that result in males getting a bigger share of social benefits than females. The individual form is familiar to us as the "male chauvinist pig." This is a person who simply believes that women and girls are radically different from men and boys and inferior to males. Most individual sexists are willing to act on the basis of these beliefs. Indeed, just as in the case of racism, it is hard to imagine how someone could think that there are people who are different and inferior and yet never do or say anything that reflected this prejudice. There are characteristic beliefs that go along with sexism: that females are naturally different from males, that males deserve the attentions of females, that females have value only to the extent that they are valuable to males, that females are in some profound sense bodily creatures and that they are judged on their bodies. There is an institutional component of sexism as well. And again, as is the case of racism, it is possible to have institutional sexism even in the absence of individual sexism. The social expectation that women will be the primary caretakers of children might be cited as an example of an institutional arrangement that disadvantages women. Of course, if no one were an individual racist or sexist, the institutional versions would soon begin to be challenged and changed.

But there is another component to sexism that is present in racism as well—the effect on the psychology of the people in the disadvantaged group. This oppression is discussed in some detail by Marilyn Frye and Sandra Bartky. When we get to discussions of sexism, we note that racism and sexism can be experienced simultaneously. Ada Maria Isasi-Diaz describes how this double-pronged injustice affects Hispanas.

Classism can be analyzed in much the same way as racism and sexism. The individual version is exemplified by the snob, who thinks that persons of a "lower" social class are less worthy than those of a "higher" social class. Snobs are usually willing to act on the basis of their beliefs, jealously guarding their neighborhoods and country clubs against the incursions of the "lower" classes. But many would argue that individual classism, while still prevalent and hurtful, is less damaging than institutional classism. Some would argue that capitalism itself is a social, economic, and political arrangement that exploits the working class. The article by William Shaw presents this point of view. But even if you do not agree with this analysis, we can see many examples of institutional arrangements that give more benefits to the wealthy than to the poor. Thomas Geoghegan describes the National Labor Relations Act as one that makes it harder to organize workers in the United States than in any country outside the Third World. William Julius Wilson describes the patterns of industry location and urban organization that systematically disadvantage the inner-city poor.

The expression "homophobia" is not the best way to describe prejudice against gays, lesbians, and bisexuals, because it assumes that the cause of such prejudice is fear of homosexuality. This may be part of the story, but it is not the whole story. Some people have suggested "heterosexualism" instead. Since the term "homophobia" is the more common, it will be used in this text. The example of homophobia is again similar to racism, sexism, and classism. There is a clear individual version, illustrated in its worst form by gay bashers. These people believe that gays, lesbians, and bisexuals are fundamentally different from straight people and have a "lifestyle" that is inferior to that of heterosexuals. They are often willing to act out their beliefs and attitudes. The institutional arrangement is characterized by social institutions that make it harder for gays, lesbians, and bisexuals to share in social benefits than it is for heterosexuals. An example is the "Don't ask, don't tell" policy of the U.S. military, discussed here by René Trujillo. Richard Mohr and Morris Kaplan discuss additional institutional barriers. There is an additional component of homophobia that we did not see in racism, sexism, and classism. Heterosexuals have the benefit of sharing their personal lives and not having to hide their intimate sexual relationships, while gays, lesbians, and bisexuals are pressured to remain in the closet. In some ways then, homophobia is worse than racism, sexism, and classism because the social benefits denied to gays, lesbians, and bisexuals include the ability to freely and openly choose and enjoy one's most intimate relationships.

We can also think about discrimination against people who have disabilities on the same individual or institutional model. Many people do have negative beliefs and attitudes about people with disabilities. Indeed, not very long ago disabilities were seen as punishment for transgressions. Anita Silvers discusses the sense of the "normal" that underlies much thoughtless treatment of people with disabilities. Barbara Hillyer discusses ways in which these negative attitudes have counterparts in the negative attitudes toward women. But even if these negative beliefs and attitudes were disappearing, many institutional barriers still make it very hard for a person with a disability to share fully in social benefits. These barriers are often architectural—physical barriers. But there are other social barriers as well—such as mandatory forty-hour work weeks and equipment that cannot be used by people with particular disabilities. As Mary Johnson argues, in the wake of the Americans with Disabilities Act these institutional barriers will be increasingly challenged, but it will be a long time before they are all changed.

One might ask here which "ism" is the worst, or which is the most fundamental. Although this question is often raised and has been given various answers, it is not really the most helpful thing to ask. Asking it often causes splits between groups who have a lot in common and who could serve as very strong allies. In the section on social transformation, especially the discussions on separatism and coalitions politics, we will see how this can happen.

Racism

PORTRAIT OF AN ANTI-SEMITE

Jean-Paul Sartre

Jean-Paul Sartre paints a compelling portrait of the anti-Semite. He sees anti-Semitism as a freely chosen passion based on fear. This passion and fear makes the anti-Semite less than human. We can use Sartre's discussion to generalize about the psychology of all racists. (Source: From Anti-Semite and Jew *by Jean-Paul Sartre, translated by George Becker. Copyright © 1948 by Schocken Books Inc. Copyright renewed 1976 by Schocken Books Inc. Reprinted by permission of Schocken Books, published by Pantheon Books, a division of Random House, Inc.)*

If a man attributes all or part of his own misfortunes and those of his country to the presence of Jewish elements in the community, if he proposes to remedy this state of affairs by depriving the Jews of certain of their rights, by keeping them out of certain economic and social activities, by expelling them from the country, by exterminating all of them, we say that he has anti-Semitic *opinions.*

This word *opinion* makes us stop and think. It is the word a hostess uses to bring to an end a discussion that threatens to become acrimonious. It suggests that all points of view are equal; it reassures us, for it gives an inoffensive appearance to ideas by reducing them to the level of tastes. All tastes are natural; all opinions are permitted. Tastes, colors, and opinions are not open to discussion. . . . Anti-Semitism does not fall within the category of ideas protected by the right of free opinion.

Indeed, it is something quite other than an idea. It is first of all a *passion.* No doubt it can be set forth in the form of a theoretical proposition. The "moderate" anti-Semite is a courteous man who will tell you quietly: "Personally, I do not detest the Jews. I simply find it preferable, for various reasons, that they should play a lesser part in the activity of the nation." But a moment later, if you have gained his confidence, he will add with more abandon: "You see, there must be *something* about the Jews; they upset me physically."

This argument, which I have heard a hundred times, is worth examining. First of all, it derives from the logic of passion. For, really now, can we imagine anyone's saying seriously: "There must be something about tomatoes, for I have a horror of eating them"? . . .

I have questioned a hundred people on the reasons for their anti-Semitism. Most of them have confined themselves to enumerating the defects with which tradition has endowed the Jews. . . .

People speak to us also of "social facts," but if we look at this more closely we shall find the same vicious circle. There are too many Jewish lawyers, someone says. But is there any complaint that there are too many Norman lawyers? Even if all the Bretons were doctors would we say anything more than that "Brittany provides doctors for the whole of France"? Oh, someone will answer, it is not at all the same thing. No doubt, but that is precisely because we consider Normans as Normans and Jews as Jews. Thus wherever we turn it is the *idea of the Jew* which seems to be the essential thing.

It has become evident that no external factor can induce anti-Semitism in the anti-Semite. Anti-Semitism is a free and total choice of oneself, a comprehensive attitude that one adopts not only toward Jews but toward men in general, toward history and society; it is at one and the same time a passion and a conception of the world. No doubt in the case of a given anti-Semite certain characteristics will be more marked than in another. But they are always all present at the same time, and they influence each other. It is this syncretic totality which we must now attempt to describe.

I noted earlier that anti-Semitism is a passion. Everybody understands that emotions of hate or anger are involved. But ordinarily hate and anger have a *provocation:* I hate someone who has made me suffer, someone who contemns or insults me. We have just seen that anti-Semitic passion could not have such a character. It precedes the facts that are supposed to call it forth; it seeks them out to nourish itself upon them; it must even interpret them in a special way so that they may become truly offensive. Indeed, if you so much as mention a Jew to an anti-Semite, he will show all the signs of a lively irritation. If we recall that we must always *consent* to anger before it can manifest itself and that, as is indicated so accurately by the French idiom, we "put ourselves" into anger, we shall have to agree that the anti-Semite has *chosen* to live on the plane of passion. It is not unusual for people to elect to live a life of passion rather than one of reason. But ordinarily they love the *objects* of passion: women, glory, power, money. Since the anti-Semite has chosen hate, we are forced to conclude that it is the *state* of passion that he loves. Ordinarily this type of emotion is not very pleasant: a man who passionately desires a woman is impassioned because of the woman and in spite of his passion. We are wary of rea-

soning based on passion, seeking to support by all possible means opinions which love or jealousy or hate have dictated. We are wary of the aberrations of passion and of what is called monoideism. But that is just what the anti-Semite chooses right off.

How can one choose to reason falsely? It is because of a longing for impenetrability. The rational man groans as he gropes for the truth; he knows that his reasoning is no more than tentative, that other considerations may supervene to cast doubt on it. He never sees very clearly where he is going; he is "open"; he may even appear to be hesitant. But there are people who are attracted by the durability of a stone. They wish to be massive and impenetrable; they wish not to change. Where, indeed, would change take them? We have here a basic fear of oneself and of truth. What frightens them is not the content of truth, of which they have no conception, but the form itself of truth, that thing of indefinite approximation. It is as if their own existence were in continual suspension. But they wish to exist all at once and right away. They do not want any acquired opinions; they want them to be innate. Since they are afraid of reasoning, they wish to lead the kind of life wherein reasoning and research play only a subordinate role, wherein one seeks only what he has already found, wherein one becomes only what he already was. This is nothing but passion. Only a strong emotional bias can give a lightninglike certainty; it alone can hold reason in leash; it alone can remain impervious to experience and last for a whole lifetime.

The anti-Semite has chosen hate because hate is a faith; at the outset he has chosen to devaluate words and reasons. How entirely at ease he feels as a result. How futile and frivolous discussions about the rights of the Jew appear to him. He has placed himself on other ground from the beginning. If out of courtesy he consents for a moment to defend his point of view, he lends himself but does not give himself. He tries simply to project his intuitive certainty onto the plane of discourse. I mentioned awhile back some remarks by anti-Semites, all of them absurd: "I hate Jews because they make servants insubordinate, because a Jewish furrier robbed me, etc." Never believe that anti-Semites are completely unaware of the absurdity of their replies. They know that their remarks are frivolous, open to challenge. But they are amusing themselves, for it is their adversary who is obliged to use words responsibly, since he believes in words. The anti-Semites have the *right* to play. They even like to play with discourse for, by giving ridiculous reasons, they discredit the seriousness of their interlocutors. They delight in acting in bad faith, since they seek not to persuade by sound argument but to intimidate and disconcert. If you press them too closely, they will abruptly fall silent, loftily indicating by some phrase that the time for argument is past. It is not that they are afraid of being convinced. They fear only to appear ridiculous or to prejudice by their embarrassment their hope of winning over some third person to their side.

If then, as we have been able to observe, the anti-Semite is impervious to reason and to experience, it is not because his conviction is strong. Rather his conviction is strong because he has chosen first of all to be impervious.

He has chosen also to be terrifying. People are afraid of irritating him. No one knows to what lengths the aberrations of his passion will carry him — but he knows, for this passion is not provoked by something external. He has it well in hand; it is obedient to his will: now he lets go the reins and now he pulls back on them. He is not afraid of himself, but he sees in the eyes of others a disquieting image — his own — and he makes his words and gestures conform to it. Having this external model, he is under no necessity to look for his personality within himself. He has chosen to find his being entirely outside himself, never to look within, to be nothing save the fear he inspires in others. What he flees even more than Reason is his intimate awareness of himself. But someone will object: What if he is like that only with regard to Jews? What if he otherwise conducts himself with good sense? I reply that that is impossible. There is the case of a fishmonger who, in 1942, annoyed by the competition of two Jewish fishmongers who were concealing their race, one fine day took pen in hand and denounced them. I have been assured that this fishmonger was in other respects a mild and jovial man, the best of sons. But I don't believe it. A man who finds it entirely natural to denounce other men cannot have our conception of humanity; he does not see even those whom

he aids in the same light as we do. His generosity, his kindness are not like our kindness, our generosity. You cannot confine passion to one sphere.

. . . This man fears every kind of solitariness, that of the genius as much as that of the murderer; he is the man of the crowd. However small his stature, he takes every precaution to make it smaller, lest he stand out from the herd and find himself face to face with himself. He has made himself an anti-Semite because that is something one cannot be alone. The phrase, "I hate the Jews," is one that is uttered in chorus; in pronouncing it, one attaches himself to a tradition and to a community — the tradition and community of the mediocre.

We must remember that a man is not necessarily humble or even modest because he has consented to mediocrity. On the contrary, there is a passionate pride among the mediocre, and anti-Semitism is an attempt to give value to mediocrity as such, to create an elite of the ordinary. To the anti-Semite, intelligence is Jewish; he can thus disdain it in all tranquillity, like all the other virtues which the Jew possesses. They are so many ersatz attributes that the Jew cultivates in place of that balanced mediocrity which he will never have.

. . .

The anti-Semite is not too anxious to possess individual merit. Merit has to be sought, just like truth; it is discovered with difficulty; one must deserve it. Once acquired, it is perpetually in question: a false step, an error, and it flies away. Without respite, from the beginning of our lives to the end, we are responsible for what merit we enjoy. Now the anti-Semite flees responsibility as he flees his own consciousness, and choosing for his personality the permanence of rock, he chooses for his morality a scale of petrified values. Whatever he does, he knows that he will remain at the top of the ladder; whatever the Jew does, he will never get any higher than the first rung.

We begin to perceive the meaning of the anti-Semite's choice of himself. He chooses the irremediable out of fear of being free; he chooses mediocrity out of fear of being alone, and out of pride he makes of this irremediable mediocrity a rigid aristocracy. To this end he finds the existence of the Jew absolutely necessary. Otherwise to whom would he be superior? Indeed, it is vis-à-vis the Jew and the Jew alone that the anti-Semite realizes that he has rights. If by some miracle all the Jews were exterminated as he wishes, he would find himself nothing but a concierge or a shopkeeper in a strongly hierarchical society in which the quality of "true Frenchman" would be at a low valuation, because everyone would possess it. He would lose his sense of rights over the country because no one would any longer contest them, and that profound equality which brings him close to the nobleman and the man of wealth would disappear all of a sudden, for it is primarily negative. His frustrations, which he has attributed to the disloyal competition of the Jew, would have to be imputed to some other cause, lest he be forced to look within himself. He would run the risk of falling into bitterness, into a melancholy hatred of the privileged classes. Thus the anti-Semite is in the unhappy position of having a vital need for the very enemy he wishes to destroy.

. . .

The degree of integration of each anti-Semite with this society, as well as the degree of his equality, is fixed by what I shall call the temperature of the community. Proust has shown, for example, how anti-Semitism brought the duke closer to his coachman, how, thanks to their hatred of Dreyfus, bourgeois families forced the doors of the aristocracy. The equalitarian society that the anti-Semite believes in is like that of mobs or those instantaneous societies which come into being at a lynching or during a scandal. Equality in them is the product of the non-differentiation of functions. The social bond is anger; the collectivity has no other goal than to exercise over certain individuals a diffused repressive sanction. Collective impulsions and stereotypes are imposed on individuals all the more strongly because none of them is defended by any specialized function. Thus the person is drowned in the crowd, and the ways of thinking and reacting of the group are of a purely primitive type. Of course, such collectivities do not spring solely from anti-Semitism; an uprising, a crime, an injustice can cause them to break out suddenly. But those are ephemeral formations which soon vanish without leaving any trace.

. . .

We begin to understand that anti-Semitism is more than a mere "opinion" about the Jews and that it involves the entire personality of the anti-Semite. But we have not yet finished with him, for he does not confine himself to furnishing moral and political directives: he has a method of thought and a conception of the world all his own. In fact, we cannot state what he affirms without implicit reference to certain intellectual principles.

The Jew, he says, is completely bad, completely a Jew. His virtues, if he has any, turn to vices by reason of the fact that they are his; work coming from his hands necessarily bears his stigma. If he builds a bridge, that bridge, being Jewish, is bad from the first to the last span. The same action carried out by a Jew and by a Christian does not have the same meaning in the two cases, for the Jew contaminates all that he touches with an I-know-not-what execrable quality. The first thing the Germans did was to forbid Jews access to swimming pools; it seemed to them that if the body of an Israelite were to plunge into that confined body of water, the water would be completely befouled. Strictly speaking, the Jew contaminates even the air he breathes.

If we attempt to formulate in abstract terms the principle to which the anti-Semite appeals, it would come to this: A whole is more and other than the sum of its parts; a whole determines the meaning and underlying character of the parts that make it up. There is not *one* virtue of courage which enters indifferently into a Jewish character or a Christian character in the way that oxygen indifferently combines with nitrogen and argon to form air and with hydrogen to form water. Each person is an indivisible totality that has its own courage, its own generosity, its own way of thinking, laughing, drinking, and eating. What is there to say except that the anti-Semite has chosen to fall back on the spirit of synthesis in order to understand the world. It is the spirit of synthesis which permits him to conceive of himself as forming an indissoluble unity with all France. It is in the name of this spirit that he denounces the purely analytical and critical intelligence of the Jews.

. . .

Facile talkers speak of a Jewish will to dominate the world. Here again, if we did not have the key, the manifestations of this will would certainly be unintelligible to us. We are told in almost the same breath that behind the Jew lurks international capitalism and the imperialism of the trusts and the munitions makers, and that he is the front man for piratical Bolshevism with a knife between its teeth. There is no embarrassment or hesitation about imputing responsibility for communism to Jewish bankers, whom it would horrify, or responsibility for capitalist imperialism to the wretched Jews who crowd the rue des Rosiers. But everything is made clear if we renounce any expectation from the Jew of a course of conduct that is reasonable and in conformity with his interests, if, instead, we discern in him a metaphysical principle that drives him *to do evil* under all circumstances, even though he thereby destroy himself. This principle, one may suspect, is magical. On the one hand, it is an essence, a substantial form, and the Jew, whatever he does, cannot modify it, any more than fire can keep itself from burning. On the other hand, it is necessary in order to be able to hate the Jew — for one does not hate natural phenomena like earthquakes and plagues of locusts — that it also have the virtue of freedom. Only the freedom in question is carefully limited: The Jew is free *to do evil,* not good; he has only as much free will as is necessary for him to take full responsibility for the crimes of which he is the author; he does not have enough to be able to achieve a reformation. Strange liberty, which instead of preceding and constituting the essence, remains subordinate to it, is only an irrational quality of it, and yet remains liberty.

There is only one creature, to my knowledge, who is thus totally free and yet chained to evil; that is the Spirit of Evil himself, Satan. Thus the Jew is assimilable to the spirit of evil. His will, unlike the Kantian will, is one which wills itself purely, gratuitously, and universally to be evil. It is *the* will to evil. Through him Evil arrives on the earth. All that is bad in society (crises, wars, famines, upheavals, and revolts) is directly or indirectly imputable to him. The anti-Semite is afraid of discovering that the world is ill-contrived, for then it would be necessary for him to invent and modify, with the result that man would be found to be the master of his own destinies, burdened with an agonizing and infinite responsibility. Thus he localizes all the evil of the universe in the Jew. If nations war with each other, the conflict does not arise from the fact that the idea of nationality, in its present form, implies imperialism and the clash of interests. No, it is because the Jew is there, behind the governments, breathing discord. If there is a class struggle, it is not because the economic organization leaves something to be desired. It is because Jewish demagogues, hooknosed agitators, have seduced the workers.

Anti-Semitism is thus seen to be at bottom a form of Manichaeism. It explains the course of the world by the struggle of the principle of Good with the principle of Evil. Between these two principles no reconciliation is conceivable; one of them must triumph and the other be annihilated.

. . .

Manichaean anti-Semite puts his emphasis on destruction. What he sees is not a conflict of interests but the damage which an evil power causes society. Therefore Good consists above all in the destruction of Evil. Underneath the bitterness of the anti-Semite is concealed the optimistic belief that harmony will be re-established of itself, once Evil is eliminated. His task is therefore purely negative: there is no question of building a new society, but only of purifying the one which exists. In the attainment of this goal the cooperation of Jews of good will would be useless and even fatal, and anyhow no Jew could be a man of good will. Knight-errant of the Good, the anti-Semite is a holy man. The Jew also is holy in his manner — holy like the untouchables, like savages under the interdict of a taboo. Thus the conflict is raised to a religious plane, and the end of the combat can be nothing other than a holy destruction.

The advantages of this position are many. To begin with, it favors laziness of mind. We have seen that the anti-Semite understands nothing about modern society. He would be incapable of conceiving of a constructive plan; his action cannot reach the level of the methodical; it remains on the ground of passion. To a long-term enterprise he prefers an explosion of rage analogous to the running amuck of the Malays. His intellectual activity is confined to *interpretation;* he seeks in historical events the signs of the presence of an evil power. Out of this spring those childish and elaborate fabrications which give him his resemblance to the extreme paranoiacs. In addition, anti-Semitism channels revolutionary drives toward the destruction of certain men, not of institutions. An anti-Semitic mob will consider it has done enough when it has massacred some Jews and burned a few synagogues. It represents, therefore, a safety valve for the owning classes, who encourage it and thus substitute for a dangerous hate against their regime a beneficent hate against particular people. Above all this naive dualism is eminently reassuring to the anti-Semite himself. If all he has to do is to remove Evil, that means that the Good is already *given*. He has no need to seek it in anguish, to invent it, to scrutinize it patiently when he has found it, to prove it in action, to verify it by its consequences, or, finally, to shoulder the responsibilities of the moral choice he has made.

It is not by chance that the great outbursts of anti-Semitic rage conceal a basic optimism. The anti-Semite has cast his lot for Evil so as not to have to cast his lot for Good. The more one is absorbed in fighting Evil, the less one is tempted to place the Good in question. One does not need to talk about it, yet it is always understood in the discourse of the anti-Semite and it remains understood in his thought. When he has fulfilled his mission as holy destroyer, the Lost Paradise will reconstitute itself. For the moment so many tasks confront the anti-Semite that he does not have time to think about it. He is in the breach, fighting, and each of his outbursts of rage is a pretext to avoid the anguished search for the Good.

But that is not all, and now we touch on the domain of psychoanalysis. Manichaeism conceals a deep-seated attraction toward Evil. For the anti-Semite Evil is his lot, his Job's portion. Those who come after will concern themselves with the Good, if there is occasion. As for him, he is in the front rank of society, fighting with his back turned to the pure virtues that he defends. His business is with Evil; his duty is to unmask it, to denounce it, to measure its extent. That is why he is so obsessed with piling up anecdotes that reveal the lubricity of the Jew, his appetite for money, his ruses, and his treasons. . . .

What he contemplates without intermission, that for which he has an intuition and almost a taste, is Evil. He can thus glut himself to the point of obsession with the recital of obscene or criminal actions which excite and satisfy his perverse leanings; but since at the same time he attributes them to those infamous Jews on whom he heaps his scorn, he satisfies himself without being compromised. In Berlin I knew a Protestant in whom sexual desire took the form of indignation. The sight of women in bathing suits aroused him to fury; he willingly encouraged that fury and passed his time at swimming pools. The anti-Semite is like that, and one of the elements of his hatred is a profound sexual attraction toward Jews.

His behavior reflects a curiosity fascinated by Evil, but above all, I think, it represents a basic sadism. Anti-Semitism is incomprehensible unless one recalls that the Jew, object of so much execration, is perfectly innocent, I should even say inoffensive. Thus the anti-Semite takes pains to speak to us of secret Jewish organizations, of formidable and clandestine freemasonries. Yet if he meets a Jew face to face, it is as often as not a weak creature who is ill-prepared to cope with violence and cannot even defend himself. The anti-Semite is well aware of this individual weakness of the Jew, which hands him over to pogroms with feet and hands bound — indeed, he licks his chops over it in advance. Thus his hatred for the Jew cannot be compared to that which the Italians of 1830 felt toward the Austrians, or that which the French of 1942 felt toward the Germans. In these instances it was a case of oppressors, of hard, cruel, and strong men who had arms, money, and power and who could do more harm to the rebels than the latter could have dreamed of doing to them. In hatreds like these sadistic leanings have no place. But since Evil, to the anti-Semite, is incarnated in unarmed and harmless men, the latter never finds himself under the painful necessity of being heroic. It is *fun* to be an anti-Semite. One can beat and torture Jews without fear. At most they can appeal to the laws of the Republic, but those laws are not too rigorous.

The sadistic attraction that the anti-Semite feels toward the Jew is so strong that it is not unusual to see one of these sworn enemies of Israel surround himself with Jewish friends. To be sure, he says they are "exceptional Jews," insists that "these aren't like the rest." (In the studio of the painter whom I mentioned earlier, a man who in no way spoke out against the butchery at Lublin, there was in full view the portrait of a Jew who was dear to him and whom the Gestapo had shot.) Such protestations of friendship are not sincere, for anti-Semites do not envisage, even in their statements, sparing the "good Jews," and, while they recognize some virtues in those whom they know, they will not admit that their interlocutors may have been able to meet others equally virtuous. Actually they take pleasure in protecting these few persons through a sort of inversion of their sadism; they take pleasure in keeping under their eyes the living image of this people whom they execrate. Anti-Semitic women often have a mixture of sexual repulsion and attraction toward Jews. One woman I knew had intimate relations with a Polish Jew. She would often go to bed with him and allow him to caress her breasts and shoulders, but nothing more. She enjoyed feeling him respectful and submissive, divining his violently frustrated and humiliated desire. She afterward had normal sexual intercourse with other men.

There is in the words "a beautiful Jewess" a very special sexual signification, one quite different from that contained in the words "beautiful Rumanian," "beautiful Greek," or "beautiful American," for example. This phrase carries an aura of rape and massacre. The "beautiful Jewess" is she whom the Cossacks under the czars dragged by her hair through the streets of her burning village. And the special works which are given over to accounts of flagellation reserve a place of honor for the Jewess. But it is not necessary to look into esoteric literature. From the Rebecca of *Ivanhoe* up to the Jewess of "Gilles," not forgetting the works of Ponson du Terrail, the Jewess has a well-defined function in even the most serious novels. Frequently violated or beaten, she sometimes succeeds in escaping dishonor by means of death, but that is a form of justice; and those who keep their virtue are docile servants or humiliated women in love with indifferent Christians who marry Aryan women. I think nothing more is needed to indicate the place the Jewess holds as a sexual symbol in folklore.

A destroyer in function, a sadist with a pure heart, the anti-Semite is, in the very depths of his heart, a criminal. What he wishes, what he prepares, is the *death* of the Jew.

To be sure, not all the enemies of the Jew demand his death openly, but the measures they propose — all of which aim at his abasement, at his humiliation, at his banishment — are substitutes for that assassina-

tion which they meditate within themselves. They are symbolic murders. Only, the anti-Semite has his conscience on his side: he is a criminal in a good cause. It is not his fault, surely, if his mission is to extirpate Evil by doing Evil. The *real* France has delegated to him the powers of her High Court of Justice. No doubt he does not have occasion every day to make use of them, but we should not be misled on that account. These sudden fits of anger which seize him, these thundering diatribes which he hurls at the "Yids" are so many capital executions. The anti-Semite has chosen to be a criminal, and a criminal *pure of heart.* Here again he flees responsibilities. Though he censures his murderous instincts, he has found a means of sating them without admitting it to himself. He knows that he is wicked, but since he does Evil *for the sake of Good,* since a whole people waits for deliverance at his hands, he looks upon himself as a sanctified evildoer. By a sort of inversion of all values, of which we find examples in certain religions — for example, in India, where there exists a sacred prostitution — the anti-Semite accords esteem, respect, and enthusiasm to anger, hate, pillage, murder, to all the forms of violence. Drunk with evil, he feels in himself the lightness of heart and peace of mind which a good conscience and the satisfaction of a duty well done bring.

. . .

We are now in a position to understand the anti-Semite. He is a man who is afraid. Not of the Jews, to be sure, but of himself, of his own consciousness, of his liberty, of his instincts, of his responsibilities, of solitariness, of change, of society, and of the world — of everything except the Jews. He is a coward who does not want to admit his cowardice to himself; a murderer who represses and censures his tendency to murder without being able to hold it back, yet who dares to kill only in effigy or protected by the anonymity of the mob; a malcontent who dares not revolt from fear of the consequences of his rebellion. In espousing anti-Semitism, he does not simply adopt an opinion, he chooses himself as a person. He chooses the permanence and impenetrability of stone, the total irresponsibility of the warrior who obeys his leaders — and he has no leader. He chooses to acquire nothing, to deserve nothing; he assumes that everything is given him as his birthright — and he is not noble. He chooses finally a Good that is fixed once and for all, beyond question, out of reach; he dares not examine it for fear of being led to challenge it and having to seek it in another form. The Jew only serves him as a pretext; elsewhere his counterpart will make use of the Negro or the man of yellow skin. The existence of the Jew merely permits the anti-Semite to stifle his anxieties at their inception by persuading himself that his place in the world has been marked out in advance, that it awaits him, and that tradition gives him the right to occupy it. Anti-Semitism, in short, is fear of the human condition. The anti-Semite is a man who wishes to be pitiless stone, a furious torrent, a devastating thunderbolt — anything except a man.

DU BOIS ON THE INVENTION OF RACE

Tommy L. Lott

Tommy Lott explicates and critiques Du Bois's sociohistorical model of race and shows why competing models are deficient. Du Bois's notion was that race refers to a family of human beings that are generally of common blood and language, always of common history, and striving to accomplish shared goals. (Source: From The Philosophical Forum, *Vol. XXIV, No. 1–3, Fall–Spring 1992–93. Reprinted by permission.)*

In his well-known address to the newly founded American Negro Academy, W. E. B. Du Bois entertained the question of the fate and destiny of African-Americans as a group, asking somewhat rhetorically, "Does my black blood place upon me any more obligation to assert my nationality than German, or Irish or Italian blood would?"[1] His answer was that it is "the duty of the Americans of Negro descent, as a body, to maintain their race identity."[2] The argument he advanced to support this claim has sometimes been understood to suggest that African-Americans as a group are obligated to maintain and perpetuate their culture in order to retain their authenticity.[3] We should resist, however, becoming overly focused on this aspect of Du Bois's view, for it is fairly clear, on even the most cursory reading of his essay, that he was not particularly concerned with the African past as a standard for measuring the authenticity of African-American culture. Indeed, he proposed to resolve the dilemma of African-American double consciousness by appealing to a revisionist analysis of the concept of race that eschews a biological essentialist account of race identity.

. . .

Du Bois's argument for the claim that African-Americans are obligated to retain their race identity is connected with his early view of the role of culture in the African-American quest for social equality.[4] In particular, he maintained that the cultural integrity of African-Americans is crucial for their gaining acceptance as social equals. The view Du Bois stated in 1897 displays the late nineteenth-century historical context of African-American social thought; consequently, many features of the argument he presented can be found in the writings of his contemporaries. By contextualizing his argument I aim to show that he presented a notion of race that was in keeping with his own version of a race uplift theory of social change. According to my interpretation, his revisionist account represents a view of race identity that accorded with the prevailing African-American social philosophy at the turn of the century. I will begin with a brief discussion of his definition of race, followed by a sketch of some of the historical sources from which he may have drawn certain ideas to develop his argument for the duty of African-Americans to retain their race identity. I want to defend the plausibility of Du Bois's sociohistorical view of race identity against several, quite damaging, criticisms and thereby salvage the major thrust of his argument.

A Revisionist Concept of Race

With the aim of presenting an account tailored to fit his theory of social change, Du Bois proposed the following definition of race,

> It is a vast family of human beings, generally of common blood and language, always of common history, traditions and impulses, who are both voluntarily and involuntarily striving together for the accomplishment of certain more or less vividly conceived ideals of life.[5]

Unless we bear in mind why Du Bois was motivated to write about African-American identity, his definition of race will seem quite implausible, especially his stipulation that a racial group must *always* share a common history, traditions, and impulses, but need not always share a common blood or language. The reason Du Bois's proposal seems implausible is because he meant to implicitly contest the way the received view, which places a greater emphasis on common blood, has been socially constructed. Unfortunately, the insight that underlies his definition is diminished by the twofold nature of his account, an account which involves both a deconstruction of the received view as well as a reconstruction of his alternative conception.

Du Bois opened his essay with the statement that African-Americans are always interested in discussions regarding the origins and destinies of races because such discussions usually presuppose assumptions about the natural abilities, and the social and political status of African-Americans, assumptions that impede African-American social progress. He noted that the undesirable implications of some of these assumptions have fostered a tendency for African-Americans "to deprecate and minimize race distinctions."[6] He took himself to be giving voice to their aspiration for social equality by advancing a conception of African-Americans that would allow a discussion of racial distinctions while accommodating the tendency of African-Americans, under the dominating influence of racism, to want to minimize references to physical differences in such discussions.

Du Bois was interested in formulating non-biological criteria for a definition of race mainly because he wanted to provide a more adequate ground for the group identity he considered a crucial component in the African-American's social agenda. He made this clear when, with the reference to the idea of race in general, he spoke of "its efficiency as the vastest and most ingenious invention for human progress."[7] He suggested that, following the success model of other groups, African-Americans must *invent* a conception of themselves that will contribute to their social elevation as a group. His revisionist notion of race was therefore proposed at the outset as something African-Americans must self-consciously adopt for political purposes. We can notice that he did not fail to acknowledge the social construction of the concept of race when, in his citation of the eight distinct racial groups, he qualified his reference to them with the phrase "in the sense in which history tells us the word must be used."[8] What shows us that he aimed to deconstruct the received view, however, is the way he juxtaposed his sociohistorical concept of race with what he referred to as "the present division of races," viz., the scientific conception of the three main biological groups; for he goes on to point out that biology cannot provide the criteria for race identity because,

historically, there has been an "integration of physical differences."[9] This fact leads him to conclude that what really distinguishes groups of people into races are their "spiritual and mental differences."[10]

Some of Du Bois's readers have rejected his sociohistorical definition of race in favor of a definition based on physical differences.[11] What Du Bois's detractors tend to overlook, however, is the fact that his definition does not deny the obvious physical differences that constitute race, nor does his discussion of race display any special commitment to the sociohistorical view he sets forth. A close reading will reveal that he only meant to deny the *viability* of a strictly biological account of race, and, furthermore, to assert that an empirical study of history will show this to be the case. Based on his own survey of anthropological findings, he tells us that when different groups of people came together to form cities,

> The larger and broader differences of color, hair and physical proportions were not by any means ignored, but myriads of minor differences disappeared, and the sociological and historical races of men began to approximate the present division of races as indicated by physical researches.[12]

The aim of Du Bois's deconstruction of the concept of race was to create a means of employing the prevailing definition of race based on genetics, i.e., to allow him to continue speaking of "the black-blooded people of America," or the "people of Negro blood in the United States," while at the same time leaving room for him to question any undesirable implications of such definitions, i.e., to override definitions that imply that the physical differences which typically characterize the various races somehow justify social inequality.

The African-American Cultural Imperative

But what bearing does Du Bois's revised notion of race have on his argument for the claim that African-Americans have a duty to retain their race identity? As Boxill has noted, one important reason Du Bois cites to support this imperative is that African-Americans have a distinct cultural mission as a racial group.[13] On behalf of the Negro Academy, Du Bois asserted that, "We believe that the Negro people, as a race, have a contribution to make to civilization and humanity, which no other race can make."[14] But what exactly is this unique contribution? I am not sure whether Du Bois had an answer to this question. He weakly stated that African-Americans are "a nation stored with wonderful possibilities of culture," which suggests that they do not yet have any such cultural contribution to make. He then goes on to speak of "a stalwart originality which shall unswervingly follow Negro ideals."[15] And, although he makes passing references to "Pan-Negroism" and the "African fatherland," at no point does he advocate reclaiming any African cultural retentions.[16] Instead, he prefers to tell us that "it is our duty to conserve our physical powers, our intellectual endowments, our spiritual ideals."[17]

What then did Du Bois mean when he spoke of the duty of African-Americans to conserve their race identity in order to make a cultural contribution? His view of what constitutes African-American culture seems especially problematic when we consider some of his remarks regarding African-American identity. He states that,

> We are Americans, not only by birth and by citizenship, but by our political ideals, our language, our religion. Farther than that, our Americanism does not go. At that point, we are Negroes, members of a vast historic race that from the very dawn of creation has slept, but half awakening in the dark forests of its African fatherland.[18]

If African-Americans share the same language, religion, and political ideals with other Americans there does not seem to be much left for them to uniquely contribute to American culture.[19] Although, in some places, Du Bois spoke of the African-American's special mission in terms of a distinct cultural contribution he seems to have had more than simply culture in mind. I suspect that he really meant to speak of a *political* mission that culture in some way enables African-Americans to carry out. This is suggested, for instance, by his remarks regarding "that black to-morrow which is yet destined to soften the whiteness of the Teutonic to-day."[20] What Du Bois may have meant here is simply that, through the establishment of a culturally plu-

ralistic society, white cultures will no longer dominate. Instead, social equality will be fostered through a cultural exchange between the various races.

If we consider Du Bois's sociohistorical definition of race, along with his belief that African-Americans have a special mission, his rejection of biological essentialism and his failure to make use of the idea of African cultural retentions, begin to appear quite troublesome.[21] For, as Appiah has keenly observed, his stalk of Pan-Negroism requires that African-Americans and Africans share something in common other than oppression by whites.[22] This lacuna in Du Bois's argument can be explained to some extent by considering the *tentative* nature of the duty of African-Americans to conserve their race identity. According to Du Bois, this duty lasts only "until this mission of the Negro people is accomplished."[23] These remarks imply that the special mission of African-Americans has more to do with their struggle for social equality than with their making a cultural contribution; once social equality has been achieved, this duty no longer exists. We can see the explicitly *political* nature of this mission clearly expressed in the following remarks:

> (African-Americans) must be inspired with the Divine faith of our black mothers, that out of the blood and dust of battle will march a victorious host, a mighty nation, a peculiar people, to speak to the nations of earth a Divine truth that shall make them free.[24]

Although the imperative to make a cultural contribution has more to do with politics than with culture, there is nonetheless a link between them, for African-Americans must be inspired "out of the blood and dust of battle" to produce a unique culture that will contribute to world civilization. What makes African-American culture unique is its hybrid genesis within the context of racial oppression in America. The need for African cultural retentions is diminished given that the culture forged out of this experience will enable African-Americans to assume a role of political leadership among other black people. Du Bois's argument for the claim that African-Americans have a duty to conserve their race identity is backward-looking in the sense that it makes reference to the historical oppression of African-Americans, as a diaspora group, as a ground for this duty. His argument is forward-looking in the sense that it foresees an end to this oppression and, hence, an eventual release from the imperative.

. . .

Race, Ethnicity, and Biology

When Du Bois defines race in terms of sociohistorical, rather than biological, or physical, criteria he seems to have blurred an important distinction between race and ethnicity, where the former is understood to refer to biological characteristics and the latter refers chiefly to cultural characteristics.[25] Several commentators have taken him to task for lapsing into this confusion. Their criticisms, however, seem to presuppose that people can be divided into biologically distinct racial groups that develop in relative isolation. Du Bois's contention was that this ideal-type model of racial and ethnic groups lacks empirical validity, for sociohistorical factors have a greater significance for understanding the essentially *political* genesis, structure, and function of such groups.

Appiah, for instance, objects to Du Bois's sociohistorical definition on the ground that a group's history or culture *presupposes* a group identity and, therefore, cannot be a criterion of that group's identity.[26] He attempts to refurbish Du Bois's talk of a common history by adding a geographical criterion such that a group's history is to be understood as (in part) the history of people from the same place. This move, however, seems needless on two counts. First, Du Bois makes clear that an important part of the history of African-Americans is their African past, and since he had little concern with cultural retentions, his point was largely a matter of geography. Secondly, as a criterion of group identity, geography does not add much, given that there are racially and culturally diverse people in various locations.

A similar objection has been raised by Boxill who points out that it is simply false to maintain that every black American shares a common culture. Instead, Boxill offers a physical definition of race that is reflected in the way the racist classifies people into races, whether they share a common culture or not:

I propose that, insofar as black people are a race, they are people who either themselves look black — that is, have a certain kind of physical appearance — or are, at least in part, descended from such a group of people.[27]

Boxill, however, is a bit too hasty in his dismissal of the obvious fact that the American system of classification, constructed on the basis of a racist ideology, breaks down when people of mixed blood do not neatly fit into the prescribed racial categories. He makes reference to the notion of "passing" to show that, with regard to people of mixed blood, a physical definition of race still offers the best account. But he overlooks the fact that this notion is fairly limited to the United States and perhaps to similar societies with a majority white population.[28] Moreover, as I shall indicate shortly, many times the practice of racism, which informs Boxill's definition, seems to conveniently disregard the biological criteria he takes to be essential.

The best way to meet the objection that a definition of race based primarily on sociohistorical criteria confuses race with ethnicity is to accept it. In the United States the alleged confusion seems to have become a matter of institutionalized practice. College application forms, for instance, frequently display some such confusion when under the ethnic identity category they list *racial* designations such as "black" and "white" along with *ethnic* designations such as "Japanese" and "Hispanic." It becomes clear that such a system of racial and ethnic classification is constructed for political purposes when we take note of certain combined categories such as "Hispanic, not black."[29] As primarily a linguistic designation, the term "Hispanic" can apply to groups of people who consider themselves white, black, or mixed-blood. Why then is there a need for a special category which designates a racial distinction that only singles out black people?

The idea that various notions of race have been constructed by racists for political purposes was well recognized in nineteenth-century African-American social thought. In his 1854 essay, "The Claims of the Negro Ethnologically Considered," Douglass accused the slaveholders of seeking a justification in science for the oppression of slaves. He pointed out that by engaging arguments that amount to "scientific moonshine that would connect men with monkeys," they wanted "to separate the Negro race from every intelligent nation and tribe in Africa." Douglass surmised that "they aimed to construct a theory in support of a foregone conclusion."[30]

. . .

These nineteenth-century discussions of race indicate two of the most important factors underlying Du Bois's deconstruction of the biological concept of race, viz., racism and intermingling. Although the identity of every racial or ethnic group will involve both (a) physical or biological criteria and (b) cultural or sociohistorical criteria, whether, in any given society, (a) gains precedence over (b) seems to be a matter of politics, i.e., racism. But even in societies such as the United States where biological criteria have gained precedence, the fact of intermingling has rendered any attempt to establish rigid biological racial classifications problematic. When we consider groups such as Chicanos, Amerasians, or Cape Verdians it becomes clear that ethnic designations are needed to accommodate interminglings that have resulted in the creation of group identities that are based almost entirely on sociohistorical criteria.[31]

The Dilemma of Biological Essentialism

One major shortcoming of Du Bois's sociohistorical concept of race is that it fails to make clear how, in the face of racism, African-Americans are supposed to invent, or reconstruct, a concept of black identity that will contribute to the progress of the group. Racism is firmly grounded in scientific thinking regarding biologically determined racial types such that, for conceptual reasons, it seems undeniable that there are fundamentally yellow, black, and white people, despite any other ethnic, or cultural, designation that applies to them.[32] As Appiah has noted, Du Bois's proposal to replace the biological concept of race with a sociohistorical one "is simply to bury the biological conception below the surface, not to transcend it."[33] What is at issue, however, is whether the rigid dichotomy between race and ethnicity is tenable. Du Bois

introduced sociohistorical criteria as a way to give an account of African-American group identity without presupposing this dichotomy. His insight was to draw from the history of racial intermingling in the United States both an objection to the biological essentialism of scientific classifications, as well as a ground on which to reconstruct African-American group identity in a social context dominated by a racist ideology.

With regard to the political aspect of Du Bois's reconstructionist project there is a dilemma posed by the ideological competition between Pan-African nationalists and Pan-Indian nationalists, both of whom have made appeals for unity to the same mixed-blood populations.[34] Each nationalist group wants to lay claim to much of the same constituency as rightfully belonging to it, and each would justify this claim by reference to the relevant biological ancestry. Their respective injunctions regarding group loyalty make use of this essentialized conception of group membership for political purposes. In keeping with the biology inherent in their respective appeals for group loyalty, persons mixed with both African and Indian ancestry are asked to identify with the group that best represents their physical appearance.[35]

It is worth noting that the nationalist's motivation for establishing such rigid biological criteria for group membership is strictly political. Since black people and Indians are oppressed on the basis of race, rather than culture, the nationalists are rightfully inclined to seek to reconstruct the group identity of black people, or Indians, on strictly racial grounds. Du Bois, of course, recognized this and sought to achieve the same political ends as the nationalists, but without invoking the biological categories handed down from scientific racism. He wanted to accommodate the fact that intermingling had become an important feature of the history of African-Americans as a group. For Du Bois, then, group loyalty need not rely on a biological essentialism, given that most African-Americans are of mixed blood. As a criterion of group identity, he proposed to give culture a greater weight than physical characteristics.

The way biology is used to rationalize the American system of racial classification gives rise to an interesting puzzle regarding the dichotomy between race and ethnicity. Consider, for instance, the case in which two siblings are racially distinct, in some genetic sense, but have the same physical characteristics, as when a white male has offspring by both a black and a white female.[36] We can speak of the offspring as being racially distinct on wholly genetic grounds, given that one child has two white parents and the other is of mixed parentage. The fact that this particular genetic difference should matter with regard to racial classification suggests a reason for the belief that race and ethnicity are not interchangeable concepts, viz., only the offspring of two white parents can be considered white.[37]

This particular application of biological criteria becomes much more problematic, however, when the practice of tracing genetic background fails to neatly correlate with the practice of using physical characteristics as a basis for racial classification. We can see this problem by considering an example that involves a multiracial ethnic group that overlaps both black and white racial categories. Suppose that the female offspring of black/white mixed-blood parents has the same physical characteristics as the male offspring of non-black Hispanic parents, and further that they marry and have two children (a boy and a girl) who both, in turn, marry whites. Both are genetically black due to their mother's mixed blood, but since the girl no longer has a Spanish surname her children will be classified as white, while her brother's children will be classified as Hispanic. What this shows, I think, is not only that concepts of race and ethnicity are sometimes interchangeable, but also that, for sociological reasons, at some point genetics frequently drops out of consideration as a basis for racial classification.[38]

We might wonder whether the emphasis Du Bois placed on sociohistorical criteria avoids the nationalist dilemma that arises on the biological essentialist account. Suppose that there are two persons with the same racial and cultural profile, i.e., each is of mixed heritage (with one black parent), each has the physical characteristics of a white person, and each has been acculturated into a white community. What if one decides to adopt a black identity despite her white cultural background? Can her newly acquired consciousness allow her to transcend her cultural background? Given the American system of racial classification, based on genetics, she is entitled to claim a black identity, something which seems to be ruled out on strictly sociohistorical grounds.[39]

In many cases where members of multiracial ethnic groups seem to have pretty much adopted some version of Du Bois's sociohistorical criteria for their own group identity we can notice that the race–culture ambivalence engendered by the American system of racial classification is frequently resolved along cultural lines. For black Latinos, such as Puerto Ricans, Cubans, or Dominicans, language exerts an overriding influence on their group identity. Persons with black ancestry who have acculturated into these Latino groups would, in many instances, be more inclined to identify with people who share their cultural orientation than with people who share their physical characteristics, despite a great deal of pressure from the dominant society to abide by the prescribed racial classifications.[40]

Du Bois has been taken to task for giving insufficient attention to the cultural differences among different groups of black people in various parts of the world. Indeed, his sociohistorical notion seems to break down when applied to culturally distinct groups of black people. But if in many cases culture gains precedence over race as a basis for group identity, he must have thought that there is something universal, or essential, in the cultures of all the various black ethnic groups, viz., a common history of oppression. Appiah has objected to Du Bois's sociohistorical essentialism by pointing out that it fails to uniquely apply to black people, for African-Americans share a history of oppression with many groups other than Africans or diaspora black people. This objection must be questioned, for I do not think it does much damage to Du Bois's suggestion that a commonly shared history of oppression provides a basis for African-American identity and for Pan-African unity.

What Du Bois was after with his reconstructed notion of race is best exemplified by considering its application to Jews. Membership in this group is determined mainly, but not exclusively, by a blood relationship (i.e., matrilineal descent) with other members of the group.[41] Yet Jews are represented in all three of the biological races, most likely as a result of having intermingled.[42] Jewish identity does not seem to be strictly a matter of culture, i.e., religion, or language, for during the Inquisition many people who were Jewish "by birth" were forced to convert to Catholicism (hence the term "Jewish Catholic"), and, presently, there are many individuals who have chosen not to learn Hebrew, or to practice a religion, yet in both cases they would still be considered Jews, and by and large they would themselves accept this designation. What then is essential to having a Jewish identity?

One very important factor which plays a major role in the construction of Jewish identity is the history of oppression commonly shared by Jews of all races and cultures.[43] With regard to this oppression there is a sociohistorical continuity to the consciousness which unifies the group that is perpetuated by the persistence of antisemitism. Moreover, this consciousness seems to extend uniquely throughout the Jewish diaspora and, since the holocaust, has provided a rallying call for the maintenance of a homeland in Israel. What is important to notice in this regard is that contemporary Zionists in Israel have been accused of racism toward non-Jews, while anti-Semitism directed toward Jews seems to be virtually identical with other varieties of racism.[44] What this shows, I think, is that there seems to be some sense in which racist practices can be attributed to a multiracial ethnic group, and equally, a sense in which such groups can be considered the victims of racism.

In considering how Du Bois's reconstructed notion of race can be applied to multiracial ethnic groups we must not assume that this is always by virtue of intermingling in the sense of some form of racial amalgamation. In both the United States and in Latin American societies where so-called "miscegenation" has occurred, the mixed-blood populations are largely the result of involuntary sexual contact between white masters and their slaves.[45] In this historical context racism toward ex-slaves and their offspring has produced a value system such that "whitening" has become the racial ideal.[46] Although this is, understandably, a dominant tendency among oppressed Third World people generally, we must not allow the influence of racism to blind us to a quite different sense in which racial identities have been constructed.

Consider, for instance, the fact that British colonialists sometimes referred to the natives of India and Australia as "blacks" and "niggers." Pan-African nationalism may very well be viewed as a response to colonialism, but can it therefore be restricted to groups of people of black African origin? There seems to be a clear sense in which people who are not of black African descent share a common oppression with black Africans and diaspora black people. In Australia there has developed a black consciousness movement among the aboriginals, who have appropriated a black identity heavily influenced by the sixties Civil Rights struggle in the United States.[47] In England the term "black" is often used politically to include people of both West Indian and Asian descent. The reason for this development is that the Asian immigrant populations from Pakistan and India are politically aligned (in a way that is temporary and strained at times) with the West Indian immigrant population. The basis for the formation of this multiracial coalition under the rubric "black people" is the common history of oppression they share as ex-colonial immigrant settlers in Britain.[48] The extension of the racial term "black" to non-African people in Australia, as well as to Asians in contemporary Britain, provides some indication that there is a sense in which a racial concept can be reconstructed to extend to a multiracial group that has not intermingled in the sense of having mixed blood.

Du Bois's proposal regarding group identity requires an adjustment in the biological essentialist criteria to account for intermingling in the sense of racial amalgamation, but what about multiracial group coalitions? By shifting the emphasis to sociohistorical consciousness he wanted to modify the biological requirement (influenced by scientific racism) to specify only a vague blood tie. Given the fact of racial amalgamation in the United States, he rightly maintained that African-American identity can only reside in sociohistorical consciousness. It is far from clear that he would have embraced all that this implies, viz., that sociohistorical consciousness figures into the social formation of racial and ethnic groups on the model of multiracial group coalitions as well.

Racism and Color Stratification

What if a peculiar sort of cultural exchange were to suddenly occur such that the sociohistorical consciousness that once resided in the biological group now known as "black people" also begins to manifest itself in the biological group now known as "white people"? Suppose further that, at some time in the future, the former group is exterminated (by genocide) or disappears (through amalgamation), and that the latter group inherits this consciousness. To what extent do we continue to apply the term "black people"? It seems that on Du Bois's account some such transference of consciousness would be allowed as long as there is, perhaps, a blood tie (say, "traceable") and the inheritors have a sociohistorical connection with their ancestors. If we treat Du Bois's stipulation regarding common blood as inessential it seems that his sociohistorical criteria provide a sufficient ground on which to establish the black identity of this biological white group.[49]

While it may appear odd to speak of "white African-Americans," such an expression could conceivably be applied in some sense that parallels the present usage of the expression "black Anglo-Saxons," which does not seem odd.[50] In each instance the respective expression would be applied by virtue of a transference of consciousness from one biological group to another, even when there is no blood tie between them. The reason that the expression "white African-American" may seem odd is because in the United States the concept of race applies strictly to blacks and whites in the sense that "traceable ancestry" really means that to be white is to have *no* nonwhite ancestry and to be black is to have *any* black ancestry. With few exceptions we can safely assume that there will be only a one-way transference of consciousness, i.e., black people will acculturate into the dominant white mainstream.[51]

It would be a mistake, however, to rule out entirely the possibility of a group of white people appropriating something very much akin to the racial consciousness of African-Americans. In 1880 Gustave de Molinari documented his observation that the English press "allow no occasion to escape them of treating the Irish as an inferior race—a kind of white negroes."[52] What is most interesting about this instance of bigotry by one white ethnic group directed toward another is that it was justified by appealing to the same scientific racism used to justify the oppression of black people, i.e., the idea that the Irish were a lower species closer to the apes. Moreover, presently in Northern Ireland, Irish Catholics are sometimes referred to by Protestants as "white niggers"—and, in turn, have appropriated and politically valorized this appellation. The link between African-Americans

and, say, black South Africans is largely sociohistorical such that an important feature of African-American identity includes a commonly shared history of oppression, but only in this attenuated sense. Similarly, there is no reason to suppose that Irish Catholic identity could not conceivably include, as fellow colonial subjects, a commonly shared history of oppression, in this attenuated sense, with African-Americans and black South Africans.[53]

The oddness of the concept of "white Negroes" or "white African-Americans" is a result of a special norm that places black people into a rock bottom category to which others can be assimilated for political purposes.[54] The simianized portrayal of Irish Catholics figures into their oppression and degradation in a fashion similar to the function of such portrayals of African-Americans. What must be noted, however, is that black people are the paradigm for any such category.[55] This indicates that racism is an ideology regarding the superiority of white people and the inferiority of nonwhite people. Du Bois made reference to the fact that this color spectrum is defined mainly by the black and white extremes. Although certain white ethnic groups, such as the Irish and the Jews, have experienced their own peculiar brand of racial oppression by other whites, they are not above engaging in racial discrimination against blacks.

The most telling criticism of Du Bois's attempt to reconstruct an African-American identity in terms of culture, rather than biology or physical characteristics is the fact that so much racism is based on color discrimination.[56] Unlike most racial and ethnic groups, for black people physical characteristics are more fundamental than cultural characteristics with regard to racism. It is for this reason that black Jews experience discrimination by other Jews, or that there is a need to distinguish black Hispanics from all others.[57] Racism based on color indicates that black people occupy an especially abhorrent category such that even hybrid groups that include mulattoes discriminate against them.[58]

Although certain considerations regarding the intermingling of different racial and ethnic groups motivated Du Bois's revision of the notion of race his main concern was with the impact of racism on African-American group identity. He aimed to address the problem of color discrimination within the group by providing a concept of race that would bring

African-Americans of different colors together.[59] To the extent that color was an indication of class position among African-Americans he also dealt with the issue of group pride by rejecting the extremely divisive assimilationist racial ideal. He challenged the assimilationist doctrine of "whitening" by formulating the criteria of group identity in nonbiological terms, a strategy designed to include African-Americans on both ends of the color spectrum. Group elevation does not require amalgamation and self-obliteration. Instead, social progress for African-Americans requires a conservation of physical characteristics (already multiracial) in order to foster cultural development. The strength of a group lies in its cultural integrity, which has to be situated in a dynamic historical process, rather than in a biologically fixed category.

Notes

My research for this essay was partially supported by a Ford Postdoctoral Fellowship, 1989–90, and by a grant from Stanford University, 1991, hereby gratefully acknowledged.

1. W. E. B. Du Bois, "The Conservation of Races," in Howard Brotz (ed.), *Negro Social and Political Thought, 1850–1920* (New York: Basic Books, 1966), p. 491. All subsequent references to Du Bois will be to this work unless otherwise indicated.

2. Du Bois, p. 491.

3. Bernard R. Boxill, *Blacks and Social Justice* (Totowa, N.J.: Rowman & Allanheld, 1984), p. 180.

4. In this essay I do not take on the larger task of comparing Du Bois's claims in "The Conservation of Races" with modifications that appeared in his later writings. For useful analyses in this regard see the above cited works by DeMarco and Appiah.

5. Du Bois, p. 485.

6. Du Bois, p. 485.

7. Du Bois, p. 485.

8. Du Bois, p. 485.

9. Du Bois, pp. 486–87.

10. Du Bois, p. 486.

11. Boxill, *Blacks and Social Justice*, p. 178; Appiah, "The Uncompleted Argument," p. 28.

12. Du Bois, p. 487.

13. Boxill, *Blacks and Social Justice*, p. 183.

14. Du Bois, p. 491.

15. Du Bois, p. 488. Du Bois leaves open the question of whether Egyptian civilization was "Negro in its origin" and stresses that "the full, complete Negro message of the whole Negro race has not as yet been given to the world" (p. 487).

16. Du Bois, pp. 487 & 489.

17. Du Bois, p. 489.

18. Du Bois, p. 489. Du Bois's reference to Negroes in Africa as having "slept, but half awakening" reflects his lack of knowledge of African history at this early stage of his career. He later wrote the following about his reaction to Franz Boas's 1906 Atlanta University commencement address on the topic of black kingdoms south of the Sahara: "I was too astonished to speak. All of this I had never heard. . . ." *Black Folk: Then and Now* (New York: Henry Holt, 1939), p. vii.

19. Du Bois cites the fact that African Americans have given America "its only American music, its only American fairy tales, its only touch of pathos" (p. 489). Later Du Bois spoke of African-American music as "the greatest gift of the Negro people." *The Souls of Black Folk* (New York: Fawcett World Library, 1961), p. 181.

20. Du Bois, p. 489.

21. In a much later work Du Bois rejects what he calls "the physical bond" but goes on to assert that "the real essence of this kinship is its social heritage of slavery." *Dusk of Dawn: An Essay Toward an Autobiography of a Race Concept* (New York: Schocken, 1968), pp. 116–17, quoted in Appiah, "The Uncompleted Argument," p. 33.

22. Appiah, p. 32.

23. Du Bois, p. 491.

24. Du Bois, p. 489.

25. For a discussion of the rather tenuous racial basis for ethnicity see R. B. LePage and Andree Tabouret-Keller, *Acts of Identity: Creole-Based Approaches to Language and Ethnicity* (Cambridge: Cambridge University Press, 1985), pp. 207–49. Lucius Outlaw has argued a similar line regarding the social construction of race and ethnicity. See his "Toward a Critical Theory of 'Race'" in David L. Goldberg (ed.), *Anatomy of Racism* (Minneapolis: University of Minnesota Press, 1990), pp. 58–82.

26. Appiah, "The Uncompleted Argument," p. 27. In this regard Du Bois may have followed the view of Herder. According to Herder, "[Races] belong not, therefore, so properly to systematic natural history, as to the physico-geographical history of man." F. McEachran, *The Life and Philosophy of Johann Gottfried Herder* (Oxford: Clarendon Press, 1939), p. 298, cited in Cedric Dover, "The Racial Philosophy of Johann Herder," *British Journal of Sociology* Vol. 3, 1952, p. 125. See also Vernon J. Williams, Jr., *From A Caste to A Minority: Changing Attitudes of American Sociologists Toward*

Afro-Americans, 1896–1945 (New York: Greenwood Press, 1989), pp. 86–87.

27. Boxill, *Blacks and Social Justice,* p. 178.

28. For an historical account of racial classification see Michael Banton, "The Classification of Races in Europe and North America: 1700–1850," *International Social Science Journal* 111 (February 1987), pp. 45–60. According to Robert E. Park, "In South America and particularly in Brazil, where Negroes and mixed bloods constitute more than 60 per cent of the population, there is, strictly speaking, no color line . . . [although] the white man is invariably at the top, and the black man and the native Indian are at the bottom." *Race and Culture* (Glencoe, Ill.: Free Press, 1950), p. 381. Similarly, Julian Pitt-Rivers reports that "A man who would be considered Negro in the United States might, by traveling to Mexico, become *moreno* or *prieto,* then *canela* or *trigueno* in Panama, and end up in Barranquilla white." "Race, Color, and Class in Central America and the Andes" in John Hope Franklin (ed.), *Color and Race* (Boston: Houghton Mifflin Co., 1968), p. 270. With reference to black people of lighter skin Philip Mason tells us that "'The white man' in Jamaica sometimes means a well-to-do person who behaves as though he came from Europe and would often not be classed as 'white' in the United States." "The Revolt Against Western Values" in Franklin (ed.), *Color and Race,* p. 61.

29. See the California State University and University of Massachusetts Application Forms, 1991–92. For a discussion of the definitions of affirmative action categories see David H. Rosenbloom, "The Federal Affirmative Action Policy" in D. Nachimias (ed.), *The Practice of Policy Evaluation* (New York: Saint Martin's Press, 1980), pp. 169–86, cited in Dvora Yanow, "The Social Construction of Affirmative Action and Other Categories," a paper presented at the Fifth National Symposium on Public Administration Theory, Chicago, April 9–10, 1992. For a discussion of the political implications of treating the concepts of race and ethnicity as interchangeable see Michael Omi and Howard Winant, *Racial Formation in the United States: From the 1960s to the 1980s* (New York: Routledge & Kegan Paul, 1986), pp. 14–37.

30. Frederick Douglass, "The Claims of the Negro Ethnologically Considered" in Brotz, *Negro Social and Political Thought,* p. 250.

31. According to Margot Pepper, "Although *Chicano* has been misused to identify all Mexican Americans, it actually refers to a specific political and cultural attitude; it is not an ethnic category." "Resistance and Affirmation," *San Francisco Guardian* (June 26, 1991), p. 33. Velina Hasu Houston, president of the Amerasian League, informs us that "The term (*Amerasian*) referred to all multiracial Asians, whether their Ameri-

can half was Anglo, African American or Latino." "Broadening the Definition of Amerasians," *Los Angeles Times* (July 11, 1991), p. E5. Cape Verdians are a mixed Portuguese/African group who speak a creole language, but, in Massachusetts, are not classified as either black or Hispanic.

32. Cf. Ruth Benedict and Gene Weltfish, *The Races of Mankind,* Public Affairs Pamphlet No. 85 (September 1980), p. 8.

33. Appiah, "The Uncompleted Argument," p. 34. De-Marco suggests that Du Bois may have believed that the original world population was divided into the three different races, since he "characterized the growth of racial units as one which proceeds from physical heterogeneity to an increasing physical homogeneity." DeMarco, *Social Thought,* p. 41. Arnold Rampersad, however, has pointed out that by 1915 Du Bois shifted more toward a common ancestry view. *The Art and Imagination of W. E. B. Du Bois* (Cambridge, Mass.: Harvard University Press, 1976), pp. 230–31.

34. Cf. Robert A. Hill and Barbara Bair (eds.), *Marcus Garvey Life and Lessons* (Berkeley: University of California Press, 1987), p. 206, and V. R. H. de la Torre, "Indo-America" and "Thirty Years of Aprismo" in *The Ideologies of the Developing Nations* (New York: Simon & Schuster, 1972), pp. 790–800.

35. In 1885, Croatan Indians in Robeson County, North Carolina, sought to distinguish themselves from African-Americans, with whom they had mixed, by getting the legislature to pass laws that made them the final judges on questions of genealogy. They adopted the pragmatic definition, "an Indian is a person called an Indian by other Indians." Guy B. Johnson, "Personality in a White-Indian-Negro Community," in Alain Locke and Bernhard J. Stern (eds.), *When Peoples Meet* (New York: Progressive Education Association, 1942), p. 577.

36. See, for instance, Jean Fagan Yellin (ed.), Harriet Jacobs, *Incidents in the Life of a Slave Girl* (Cambridge, Mass.: Harvard University Press, 1987), p. 29.

37. In the mid-seventeenth century, Virginia enacted legislation that stipulated that children born of a black woman would inherit her status, even when the father was white. This measure allowed slaveholders to literally reproduce their own labor force. See Paula Giddings, *When and Where I Enter* (New York: Bantam, 1985), p. 37. Marvin Harris argues that the difference between the United States and Latin America in applying this rule of descent must be understood in terms of it being "materially advantageous to one set of planters, while it was the opposite to another." *Patterns of Race in the Americas* (New York: W. W. Norton, 1964), p. 81.

38. Indeed, in many cases where phenotypical characteristics are ambiguous with regard to an individual's genotype, self-identification (i.e., cultural criteria) becomes more of a possibility. C. Eric Lincoln informs us that "Reliable estimates on the basis of three hundred and fifty years of miscegenation and passing suggest that there are several million 'Caucasians' in this country who are part Negro insofar as they have Negro blood or Negro ancestry." "Color and Group Identity in the United States," in Franklin (ed.), *Color and Race*, p. 250. To see that the issue of genetic heritage is mostly a matter of politics we need only consider the fact that the Louisiana state legislature recently repealed a 1970 statute that established a mathematical formula to determine if a person was black. The "one thirty-second rule" was changed to "traceable amount." Frances Frank Marcus, "Louisiana Repeals Black Blood Law," *New York Times* (July 6, 1983), p. A10. For a detailed historical account of the politics surrounding the Louisiana law see Domínguez, Chapters 2 & 3. When Hawaii became a United States Territory in 1890 the "one thirty-second rule" was lobbied against by five large landholding companies. For economic reasons they favored the present law which requires 50% native blood to be eligible for a land grant. See Timothy Egan, "Aboriginal Authenticity to Be Decided in a Vote," *New York Times* (January 1, 1990), p. A12.

39. See the discussion of Hansen's Law by Werner Sollors in his *Beyond Ethnicity: Consent and Descent in American Culture* (New York: Oxford University Press, 1986), pp. 214–221. For a discussion of its application to Louisiana creoles see Domínguez, Chapter 7.

40. Boxill's definition of black people cannot accommodate such cases for he would insist on phenotype and descent as overriding factors such that black Latinos who operate with a primarily *cultural* identity must be viewed as in some sense "passing."

41. According to Israel's Law of Return anyone born to a Jewish mother who has not taken formal steps to adopt a different religion has the right to become a citizen of Israel.

42. Cf. Benedict and Weltfish, *The Races of Mankind*, p. 10; Abram Leon Sachar, *A History of the Jews* (New York: Alfred A. Knopf, 1979), p. 250.

43. According to Louis Wirth, "What has held the Jewish community together in spite of all disintegrating forces is . . . the fact that the Jewish community is treated as a community by the world at large." "Why the Jewish Community Survives" in Locke and Stern (eds.), *When Peoples Meet*, p. 493.

44. Cf. Peter Singer, "Is Racial Discrimination Arbitrary?," *Philosophia* 8, 2–3 (November 1978), p. 185. See also Edward W. Said, "Zionism from the Standpoint of Its Victims" in Goldberg *Anatomy of Racism*, pp. 210–46.

45. Webster's dictionary emphasizes the fact that this term applies primarily to marriage or interbreeding between whites and blacks.

46. See Thomas E. Skidmore, "Racial Ideas and Social Policy in Brazil, 1870–1940," in Richard Graham (ed.), *The Idea of Race in Latin America, 1870–1940* (Austin: University of Texas Press, 1990), pp. 7–36; and Parks, *Race and Culture*, p. 385.

47. For an account of the aboriginal struggle for social equality in Australia, see Roberta B. Sykes, *Black Majority* (Victoria, Australia: Hudson Publishing, 1989).

48. Consider, for instance, the following quote: "Now, a comment about the title of the book and why we have chosen the term 'black population.' What the immigrants from New Commonwealth and Pakistan (NCWP) and their children born have in common is the material consequences and, in very many cases, the direct experience of discrimination. Discrimination, as the studies, by Political and Economic Planning (PEP) have demonstrated, is based upon colour. Hence, the reference to Britain's black population. It can, of course, be argued that some immigrants and their children do not and would not want to be labelled as *black*. That is not denied, but the defence of this terminology in this context lies with the fact that, irrespective of their own particular beliefs, experiences and the wide range of cultural variations, racism and racial discrimination is a crucial determinant of their economic and social situation." The Runnymede Trust and The Radical Statistics Race Group, *Britain's Black Population* (London: Heinemann Educational Books, 1980), p. xii. See also Kobena Mercer, "'1968': Periodizing Postmodern Politics and Identity," in Lawrence Grossberg, Cary Nelson, Paula Treichler (eds.), *Cultural Studies* (New York: Routledge, 1992), pp. 424–38; Frank Reeves, *British Racial Discourse* (Cambridge: Cambridge University Press, 1983), p. 255; Lionel Morrison, *As They See It* (London: Community Relations Commission, 1976), pp. 35–49; Brian D. Jacobs, *Black Politics and Urban Crisis in Britain* (Cambridge: Cambridge University Press, 1986), pp. 41–62; Paul Gilroy, "*There Ain't No Black In The Union Jack*" (London: Hutchinson, 1987).

49. In *Worlds of Color*, written near his ninetieth birthday, Du Bois gave the following description of Jean Du Bignon: "a 'white Black Girl' from New Orleans; that is, a well educated young white woman who was classed as 'Colored' because she had a Negro great-grandfather." *Worlds of Color* (Millwood, N.Y.: Kraus-Thomson, 1976), p. 9. It should be noted here that

Du Bois seems to have inconsistently treated his own blood tie with his Dutch ancestors as inessential. Most likely this was due to his *cultural* identification with black people, as well as with his tacit commitment to the "census" definition of a black person—viz., that a black person is a person who "passes" for a black person in the community where he lives. See Parks, *Race and Culture*, p. 293.

50. In the nineteenth-century black Americans sometimes referred to themselves nonpejoratively as "Anglo-Africans." With a similar reference to a white cultural influence Nathan Hare's book, *The Black Anglo Saxons* (New York: Collier Books, 1965), was offered as a criticism of the assimilationist mentality of certain segments of the black middle class.

51. One notable exception is the white rap group, *Young Black Teenagers*, who explain their appropriation of this title (along with tunes such as "Proud to Be Black" and "Daddy Kalled Me Niga Cause I Likeded To Rhyme") as an expression of their having grown up in a predominantly black youth culture in New York City. See Joe Wood, "Cultural Consumption, From Elvis Presley to the Young Black Teenagers," *Village Voice Rock & Roll Quarterly*, pp. 10–11.

52. Quoted in L. Perry Curtis, Jr., *Apes and Angels: The Irishman in Victorian Caricature* (Washington, D.C.: Smithsonian Institution Press, 1971), p. 1.

53. In his very interesting documentary film, *The Black and the Green*, Saint Claire Bourne explores the theme of black consciousness in the Irish Catholics' struggle for social equality.

54. See Norman Mailer's "The White Negro" in his *Advertisements for Myself* (New York: Andre Deutsch, 1964).

55. Kobena Mercer cites a passage from Arthur Rimbaud's "A Season in Hell" (1873) in which the claim is made: "I am a beast, a Negro." Mercer, "'1968,'" p. 432.

56. With regard to his discussion of Du Bois's concept of race, Anthony Appiah was sharply criticized by Houston Baker for downplaying the role of color discrimination in everyday affairs. See his "Caliban's Triple Play" in Gates (ed.), *"Race," Writing, and Difference,* pp. 384–85, and Appiah's reply, "The Conservation of 'Race,'" *Black American Literature Forum*, Vol. 23, No. 1 (Spring 1989), pp. 37–60.

57. Cf. Morris Lounds, Jr., *Israel's Black Hebrews: Black Americans in Search of Identity* (Washington, D.C.: University Press of America, 1981), pp. 209–13.

58. Cf. Ozzie L. Edwards, "Skin Color as a Variable in Racial Attitudes of Black Urbanites," *Journal of Black Studies*, Vol. 3, No. 4 (June, 1972), pp. 473–83; Robert E. Washington, "Brown Racism and the Formation of a World System of Racial Stratification," *International Journal of Politics, Culture, and Society*, Vol. 4, No. 2, 1990; Lincoln, "Color and Group Identity," pp. 249–63.

59. With regard to the "self-questioning," "hesitation," "vacillation," and "contradiction" faced by mulattoes Du Bois remarked that "combined race action is stifled, race responsibility is shirked, race enterprises languish, and the best blood, the best talent, the best energy of the Negro people cannot be marshalled to do the bidding of the race" (p. 488).

THE ORDINARY CONCEPT OF RACE

Naomi Zack

Naomi Zack examines the concept of race during the colonial expansion into the Third World. She argues that there was not then, and is not now, any scientific way to support the concept of race. Instead, she locates this concept in its social context. Finally, she discusses the experience of people of "mixed" race, whose very existence challenges the concept of separate races. (Source: From Race and Mixed Race *by Naomi Zack. Copyright © 1993 by Temple University. Reprinted by permission of Temple University Press.)*

The History and Biology of the Concept of Race

Many historians trace references to racial differences back to antiquity. Less formally, some religious fundamentalists read racial differentiations in the biblical account of Noah's descendants.[1] However, there appears to be a contemporary consensus that the modern concept of race, which underlies the concept of race formed in the United States during the period of black slavery, has its roots in the European seventeenth-, eighteenth-, and nineteenth-century colonial expansions into what is now called the Third World.[2] The dominated and exploited non-European populations of this (present) Third World were conceptualized by Europeans as racial populations. It has been suggested that this racial conceptualization was developed by European invaders as a justification or rationalization of their domination of Third World peoples and of the subsequent European and American exploitation of the labor and natural resources of these peoples.[3] As the racial designations of the Third World populations were developed, these peoples were judged by Europeans to be less advanced culturally than Europeans. The allegedly less advanced non-European cultures were held to be inferior to European cultures — to the extent that Europeans acknowledged that Third World peoples even had cultures. In European thinking, this judged cultural inferiority of non-European peoples was linked to their non-white racial designations.[4]

It was generally believed during the colonial period that the racial designations of Third World peoples referred to biological characteristics, which were inherited within the races in question. The widespread model of racial inheritance was some kind of arithmetic mechanism which dictated the intergenerational transmission of racial characteristics through their division in the blood of offspring.[5] For example, in the United States, during the nineteenth century, it was believed that an individual with one black parent and one white parent was one-half white and one-half black. If that individual had a child with a white person, then the child would be one-quarter black. It was believed that a black individual was all black and that his or her descendants inherited their race in simple, divisible units, which, through the dilution of blood, became fractions of the resulting offspring. People whose blood had not thereby been mixed or diluted (before their birth) were racially pure. It is not difficult to see the relation between this theory of the dilution of the blood through racial mixing and the kinship schema of racial inheritance. It may be that as a model of racial designation, the kinship schema is the logical structure of practical applications of the blood theory.

By about 1900, biologists and anthropologists began to realize that there were serious empirical problems with both the fractional concept of racial inheritance and the idea of pure races. The problem with the fractional concept of racial inheritance is that the physical characteristics which can be used for racial designation are caused by genes that vary independently of one another during the process of human conception. In lay terms, these are the genetic facts that are now commonly accepted by scientists: Each individual receives a full complement of genes in two halves, one-half from each parent; each parent contributes one-half of his or her total of genetic material to the offspring. These genetic facts do not support the belief that there is, ever has been, or ever will be a pure race. All human beings are members of the same species, and all of the inheritable physical differences

110

among them are the result of their varied genetic makeup. It is not that racial characteristics are subject to dilution but that the genes that underlie racial characteristics are subject to dispersal into different combinations. Each gene responsible for a racial — or any other — characteristic retains its complete identity as long as it remains in the gene pool, i.e., as long as it is capable of being copied for combination with other genes at the time of conception. Even apart from this integrity of individual genes through inheritance, it does not make sense to think of 'old' or 'inherited' biological material persisting in descendants. Genes function by providing instructions for the development of new biological material — old biological material does not persist over generations in any form that can be diluted or mixed.

All human beings belong to the same species. All designated human races are capable of interbreeding. In scientific terms, a race is merely a self-contained breeding population that has a higher percentage of individuals with certain designated physical characteristics than some other population. *The scientific racial unit is the breeding population as a whole and not any individual within the population.* All individuals within a race do not have the same racial characteristics. The racial differences between any two individuals within a race may be greater than the racial differences (or physical differences designated as racial) between some individuals within that race and some individuals within another race. For example, there may be greater varieties in body structure among American blacks than between some blacks and some whites; some blacks have lighter skin than some whites; some whites have woolier hair than some blacks. Such variations in racial characteristics result from the fact that the genes which cause racial characteristics do not all get inherited together. Not all blacks have all of the genes that result in black racial designations. In logical, causal terms, there are no necessary, necessary and sufficient, or sufficient racial characteristics, or genes for such characteristics, which every member of a race has.[6]

As for the old idea of blood, there is nothing in the divisions of the major human blood groups which corresponds to the divisions of the major human racial groups. The four major human blood groups, which are identifiable in terms of their compatibility for transfusion purposes, are distributed somewhat geographically over the globe, but there is no connection between the racial characteristics of an individual's parents and that individual's blood group. Not only does blood not mix and not become diluted through interracial heredity but it is possible that close relatives of the same racial designation may have incompatible blood types for transfusion purposes.[7]

Ever since the 1920s, after Franz Boas corrected his earlier claims that cultural behavior was physically inheritable, social scientists have been careful to disassociate the behavioral or cultural characteristics of racially designated groups from the inheritance of physical racial characteristics. They have made this separation because there is no empirical evidence for such hereditary connections.[8] Many biologists and anthropologists are skeptical of the concept of race as a useful scientific tool because no racial population, past or present, has ever been completely isolated from other races in terms of breeding. Furthermore, there are too many variables in genetic combinations, including mutation, for individuals to breed 'true to type' over long periods of time. The scientific consensus that there are three main human racial groups is grudging, at best.[9]

Despite the scientific problems with biological concepts of race, social scientists have been reluctant to suggest that races do not exist in the sense in which the ordinary person believes that they exist. The reason for this reluctance seems to be not only that the ordinary belief in races is widespread but that this widespread belief is connected with strong feelings.[10] This reluctance should not be surprising, because while it may be part of the job of social scientists to analyze concepts which underlie human behavior, social scientists are not obligated to criticize such concepts. The criticism of a concept, such as the concept of physical race, is a task for philosophers (and perhaps other social critics).

The main philosophic criticism of the ordinary concept of physical race is this: There are no clear and uniform criteria by which the ordinary concept of race can be applied to every individual. And because racial designations have important consequences in the lives of individuals so designated, this lack of clarity and uniformity means that racial designations based on the ordinary concept of race are not fair.

It could be objected that there is nothing wrong with the ordinary concept of race, just as there is nothing wrong with the ordinary concepts of chair, cat, or tree. Many concepts are applied in varying ways based on different criteria of application, which may not even be predictable, independently of contexts, from application to application. This is not a problem with the concepts in question but merely a fact about the complexity of human meanings and cultural-linguistic behavior. Thus (the objection would continue) there are no necessary and sufficient conditions that all objects which can be counted as chairs must have. And there may be no *essences* possessed in common by all cats or all trees. Some individuals can be seen to be *paradigm* instances of racial whiteness and racial blackness, and their forebears had the same (respective) appearances as the observed individuals. Therefore the existence of a *slippery slope* in the form of individuals of mixed race does not mean that the primary concepts of pure race are illusory.

The answer to this objection needs to be as far-reaching as the objection itself, because the objection gestures toward the totality of those very habits of cultural life which the foregoing philosophical criticism of the ordinary concept of physical race attempts to challenge. First, it doesn't matter how concepts of things such as chairs are expanded and reinvented; but this expansion and reinvention are very important with concepts of people, which determine how those people will be treated. Second, concepts of cats and trees remain valid or appropriate without a cat or tree essence, because there are necessary and sufficient conditions that beings must fulfill in order to be counted as cats or trees. Lions, for example, are a natural kind that can be conceptualized without recourse to a lion essence, because they fulfill not only the necessary and sufficient conditions for membership in the group of cats but the necessary and sufficient conditions for membership in the subgroup of great cats and the sub-subgroup of lions. In contrast, those human groups that are designated as racial groups do not constitute a species or subgroup within the larger natural group of *Homo sapiens*. Races may be analogous to those subgroups known as 'breeds' among domestic animals. But while everyone acknowledges that collies and holsteins, for example, are the result of human control over animal reproduction, or human animal-breeding, it is less commonly acknowledged

that paradigm ideals of pure American blacks and pure American whites are the result of human control over human reproduction, i.e., the result of human–human breeding.

Thus there are no racial essences which give meaning to the concept of race, there are no necessary and sufficient conditions for racial membership, and races are not natural kinds. Finally, the existence of individuals who appear to be racially pure does not rescue the concept of race, because this concept requires that the majority of humans be and always have been racially pure. And racial purity is not a general truth about the human condition. Thus the slippery slope of mixed race is more than an unusual exception to a statistical norm or paradigm of racial purity. But even if instances of mixed race were statistical exceptions, these exceptions would be not a merely theoretical objection to concepts of racial purity but facts of human existence. Such facts of human existence, of the existence of human beings who belie commonsense racial concepts, ought to be an overriding axiological consideration. That is, if the existence of certain human beings causes problems for certain concepts or systems of categorization, then it is the concepts or systems of categorization and not the human existence which need to be criticized and changed.

The black emancipatory tradition in the United States has recognized the weakness of the concept of physical race for a long time, at least since W.E.B. Du Bois.[11] Du Bois was aware of the lack of an empirical foundation in nature for the concept of race. In the following literary exchange between himself as the narrator and a white man who would be considered a racist today, Du Bois suggests that the concept of the black race is the result of white injustice against blacks:

> "But what is this group; and how do you differentiate it; and how do you call it 'black' when you admit it is not black?"
>
> I recognize it quite easily and with full legal sanction; the black man is a person who must ride "Jim Crow" in Georgia.[12]

However, Du Bois and other important writers in the black emancipatory tradition resist racism on the basis of their own acceptance of the concept of race. This kind of resistance to the injustices that are perpetrated by whites against blacks obligates blacks to argue that their educational, moral, social, legal, and economic deficits in comparison to whites are not physically inherited or necessarily acquired.[13] But there is no sustained objection to ordinary racial designations within the tradition of black emancipation.

The ordinary concept of race in the United States has no scientific foundation. Yet rational people still retain this concept. The question is, why? What purpose does the ordinary concept of race serve? What prevents otherwise rational people from abandoning this concept as a means of designating individuals? To answer these questions, one must look at how racial designation determines ordinary identity in ordinary existence.

Notes

1. See, e.g., E. Ellis Cashmore and Barry Troyman, *Introduction to Race Relations* (London: Routledge & Kegan Paul, 1983), pp. 19–20.

2. See, e.g., Cashmore and Troyman, *Race Relations,* pp. 21–35; John Rex, *Race and Ethnicity* (Storey Stratford, England: Open University Press, 1986), pp. 1–37; Michael Leiris, "Race and Culture," in Leo Kuper, ed., *Race, Science and Society* (New York: Columbia University Press, 1965), pp. 135–72.

3. See, e.g., Max Gluckman, "New Dimensions of Change, Conflict and Settlement," in Kuper, ed., *Race, Science and Society,* pp. 320–39.

4. L. C. Dunn and Theodosius Dobzhansky, *Heredity, Race and Society* (New York: Mentor, 1960), pp. 114 and passim.

5. See, e.g., Dunn and Dobzhansky, *Heredity, Race and Society,* pp. 40–63; and L. C. Dunn, "Race and Biology," in Kuper, ed., *Race, Science and Society,* pp. 61–67.

6. For contemporary theories of blood groups and the genetics involved, see N. P. Dubinin, "Race and Contemporary Genetics," in Kuper, ed., *Race, Science and Society,* pp. 68–94.

7. See Otto Klineberg, "Race and Psychology," in Kuper, ed., *Race, Science and Society,* pp. 173–207.

8. See Dubinin, "Race and Contemporary Genetics," pp. 68–83, and idem, "Four Statements on the Race Question," originally published by UNESCO in 1950, 1951, 1964, 1967; reprint in Kuper, ed., *Race, Science and Society,* Appendix.

9. Ibid.

10. Ibid.

11. See W. E. B. Du Bois, "The Concept of Race" and "The White World," in idem, *The Dusk of Dawn: An Essay toward an Autobiography of a Race Concept,* reprinted in idem, *Du Bois Writings,* comp. Nathan Huggins, 1940; reprint (New York: Literary Classics of the U.S., 1986), pp. 549–651, 665–66.

12. Ibid., p. 666. It is interesting that it is Du Bois, not the white racist, who takes up the identification of an individual racially, based on how that individual is treated, as if to acknowledge that his definition of race is no more based on scientific facts than that of the racist but is taken up as a necessary reaction to what we would call "racism" today. Indeed, this was an insistent theme of Du Bois's throughout *Dusk of Dawn* and in his essays in *The Crisis* (1910–1934).

13. Leo Kuper, for example, in introducing his anthologized readings, which establish that cultural traits are not genetic, speaks of a "defense against racism" because "the arena of confrontation is essentially defined by racists" (*Race, Science and Society,* p. 14).

BLACK, WHITE, AND GRAY:
Words, Words, Words

I want to conclude . . . on an emancipatory but possibly conciliatory note that avoids hypocrisy. I do not wish to betray the alienation of persons of mixed race in the biracial American system. It is not that such persons have "difficulty" with their black identities but that they cannot conclusively choose any one racial identity.[1] The emancipation I aim for is that form of universalism that lies on the other side of diversity. I have to call it "liberalism." By 'liberalism' I mean a goal of the maximum amount of benevolence toward the maximum number of people, which is compatible with the maximum amount of respect for individual freedom. These maxima are matters of intuition: Benevolence is an intuitive good; freedom is a subjective necessity; subjective necessities override maximum social goods because individuals are the final sentient recipients of all goods.

Individual freedom cannot be defined absolutely for all time. It is a continual process of peeling away the onion of coercion, and what is seen to be coercive today would have been unthinkable as coercive yesterday. For example, before the 1920s white Anglo-Saxon Americans believed that Italian, Irish, and Polish immigrants were distinct races.[2] No one would suggest that now. The concept of black American race has no uniform factual or moral foundation, and when people are identified as racially black, they do not get the same treatment as people who are identified as racially white. So perhaps the time has come to reject the concept of a black American race, because that concept is coercive.

As a symbol of emancipatory liberalism, my mind dwells on a surprisingly obscure photograph. I came across the picture in a book about Pablo Picasso's life and work when I was taking a break. . . . An informally posed group of artists and writers stand in a semicircle and sit on the floor in Picasso's studio in March 1944. Picasso has read his play *Le Desire attrape par la queue.* Jean-Paul Sartre sits on the floor, his elbows resting on his knees and his ankles crossed; he is smoking a pipe and gazing owlishly off to his right. To Sartre's left, Albert Camus attends to a large standard poodle named "Kazbek," while Michael Leiris looks on. Picasso stands solidly behind Camus, his arms folded as he looks squarely at the camera. Between and behind Camus and Leiris stands Simone de Beauvoir. She is soberly dressed, with braids crowning her head, a book in her hands, and an old-fashioned reticule hanging from her arm. Others—Jacques Lacan, Cecile Eluard, Pierre Reverdy, Louise Leiris, Zanie Aubier, Jean Aubier, and Valentine Hugo—are also there.[3] But I was struck by the presence of Jean-Paul Sartre, Simone de Beauvoir, Michael Leiris, and Pablo Picasso in the same room toward the end of World War II. They were all strong liberals whose lives' works were based on themes of human freedom in ways that are meaningful to my own life and work.

. . . Simone de Beauvoir's *The Second Sex,* first published in 1949, was a fundamental component of the second wave of feminism in the twentieth century.[4] Michael Leiris was head of research at the Centre National de la Recherche Scientifique and a staff member of the Musée de l'Homme in Paris during the 1950s.[5] His work on race and culture was an important contribution to the international destruction of the paradigm that held that cultural traits were physically inheritable. The following passage by Leiris characteristically states this shift from genetics to history as an explanatory source of *difference:*

> In our own day, the task of the anthropologists is to study cultures diverging considerably from what with certain variants is the common culture of the Western nations. This must suggest the question whether there is a causal relationship between race and culture and whether each of the various ethnic groups has on balance a predisposition to develop certain cultural forms. However, such a notion cannot survive a scrutiny of the facts and it can be taken as established today that hereditary physical differences are negligible as causes of the differences in culture observable between the peoples. What should rather be taken into consideration is the history of those peoples.[6]

Although Picasso brought the horrors of the Spanish Civil War to mass cultural attention with his painting *Guernica,* art was probably more important to him than any political event or social situation.[7] Still, the lived autonomy of an artist always reinforces individual ideas about human freedom. Sartre, de Beauvoir, Leiris, and Picasso were all champions of human freedom—they were all liberals.

Richard Rorty says that a liberal is someone who will not accept cruelty: "I borrow my definition of 'liberal' from Judith Shklar, who says that liberals are the people who think that cruelty is the worst thing we do."[8] In this Shklar–Rorty sense, liberalism would be a species of utilitarianism, a public and political commitment to benevolence toward all. As Rorty is aware, a private sense of liberalism is also necessary for human freedom.[9] One should be as free from external restraints as possible in choosing who and what one is. A precise phenomenology of subjective freedom has yet to become a legitimate 'mainstream' philosophical subject. But I have been arguing throughout this work that in a context where a race is devalued, such as in the United States, racial designations are as racist, i.e., as cruel, as racist devaluations. Such racial designations limit individuals in their subjectivities, even when they take up the designations themselves, about themselves. The mythology about race which underlies racial devaluations and racial designations is evident in the language of race that is used in the United States. Everyone knows that racial epithets and slurs represent a breakdown of normal cooperative assumptions of communication—these derogatory *race-words* are insults and as such easily bridge gaps between words and action.[10] But people are less aware of the way in which seemingly neutral racial language is racist. Because the racism inherent in various concepts of race has already been discussed, it seems appropriate at this point to turn to the words themselves.

First, there is a general myopia about the black–white dichotomy. When Americans hear the word "race," they immediately assume it means "black" or "white." In many places, for long periods of time in American history, all people could be divided into black or white racial categories. This was before there were large numbers of Hispanic Americans, Asian Americans, and recognized Native Americans. It was before these other racial groups became large or strong enough to demand recognition or, as in the case of Native Americans, before they were permitted voices which could be heard by some of those in the society from which they had been alienated. The black–white racial dichotomy imposes a myopic linguistic convention, which holds that everyone belongs to a race but that there are only two races: Negro and Caucasian. Of course, even the most emphatic biracialists know that there are also Asians, but when the topic of race comes up they speak as if everyone were either black or white.

In Anglo-American cultural history, the words "black" and "white" are symbols with positive and negative moral connotations. Sin in the sense of sexual transgression, for example, is 'black,' and virginity and other traditional states of moral virtue are 'white.' Thus the black–white sin–virtue dichotomy was available historically as a justification for the exploitation of blacks by whites when Europeans first began to exploit Africa, the 'dark' continent.[11] (The moral-religious connotations of a black–white dichotomy are so exaggerated in American culture that it can be a locution of criticism, imputing ignorance, stupidity, and possibly insanity, to say that someone "sees" such and such "in black and white.")[12] In addition to this symbolism, there are other racist aspects of the American use of the black–white dichotomy of race.

There is no parity in the derivation of the words used for the two racial categories: Caucasian and Negro. The word "Caucasian" has a geographical reference to the Caucasus area and thereby derives from a proper name. The word "Negro" comes from the French or Spanish word *negro,* meaning the color black, which derives from the Latin word *niger,* having the same meaning.[13] Until the 1920s, American blacks were referred to as "negroes," with a small *n.* The insistence on the capital *N* was based on the demand for the acceptance of American blacks as a national group, like other national groups whose names were capitalized.[14] The insistence on the word "black" to refer to black Americans in the 1960s was, in this context, a change to an English translation of *negro.* When "black" is used to refer to black Americans as an ethnic group, it is capitalized. But when "black" is simply a racial designation in contrast to the racial designation "white," it is not capitalized. It is ironic that when American blacks insisted on racial respect, "Negro" became capitalized; and when Black Culture was revalued, "black" became the preferred racial designation. The word "white" as a racial designation is almost never capitalized these days, outside of white supremacist literature.

When American blacks are referred to as "African Americans," this appears to establish a parity of terminology with "Caucasian" because the word "African," like the word "Caucasian," is an adjective deriving from the proper name of a place. But people were first designated as Caucasian because of their resemblance to the physical appearance of people who inhabited the Caucasus geographical areas. By contrast, most American blacks are designated as African Americans on the basis of an assumption that they have forebears whose physical appearance resembled people who inhabit the geographical area of Africa. So again there is no parity.

The words "black" and "white" purport to categorize people racially on the basis of their skin color. There are some, but very few, Americans who have skin the actual colors of objects that are accurately described as having black and white surfaces. As colors, black and white are anomalous: In quasi-scientific language, black is the perceptual experience of the absence of all colors from the visible spectrum, and white is the perceptual experience of the presence of all colors from the visible spectrum.[15] (These optical facts make a joke out of the use of the sobriquet "of color" for all non-white people.) Still, it is possible to manufacture black and white pigments, and like all other colors that can be applied to the surfaces of objects, black and white can be mixed.

When the colors black and white are mixed, they produce various shades of gray. When people who are black and white "mix" genetically, it is commonly acknowledged that the skin colors of their offspring fall on a continuum of colors that are in the ranges of brown and tan. On one end of this continuum are those whose skin color would be called "white," in the absence of knowledge of their black forebears. On the other end of the continuum are those whose skin color would cause them to be racially designated black. Thus, as racial words, "black" and "white" purport to refer to skin color, but in fact they are only loosely related to the actual skin colors of human beings. In the case of individuals who are called "white" racially, the word "white" is not expected to refer either to their actual skin color or to the actual skin color of their ancestors. In the case of individuals who are called "black" racially, the word "black" may be believed to be a more accurate description of the skin color of their ancestors than of the individuals themselves.

By contrast, as Carl N. Degler describes the racial system in Brazil, there race is not determined by the race of a person's ancestors but by money. Thus a poor Brazilian mulatto is a Negro, whereas a rich Negro who is not visibly of mixed race is white. This has been called the "lightening" effect of money—and social class. American slave owners bred their slaves as a way of increasing their capital. This was less so in Brazil.[16] It may be that the strong hereditary aspect of American race derives from the strong property interest in the hereditary aspects of American slavery.[17] If this is so, it would suggest that Americans have stronger property traditions than Brazilians do. Even though Brazilians are now more "materialistic" about race, historically, Americans have been more materialistic about people, a form of materialism that lives on in all biracial American racial designations to this day. . . .

There is every reason to believe that Americans are just as sentient of colors as people who live in other countries. That is, only a small percentage of Americans are color blind, or perceive only black, white, and gray. So it is fairly clear that the racial words "black" and "white" are not the color words that they purport to be but labels that refer to nineteenth-century concepts of race, which associated nonphysical characteristics with racial designations.

The current scientific view of a race is that a race is a group of people who have more of some physical traits than do other groups of people. Skin color is not a particularly accurate standard for determining races, nor is skin color in combination with body types, facial features, hair textures, or any of the other physical characteristics associated with races. Henry Louis Gates, Jr., makes the point of how inadequate those physical criteria are that purport to be racial criteria, in a quote from a contemporary American work on "Left" political theory:

> The division of the human species into races is biologically—though not socially—arbitrary. We could differentiate humans along countless axes, such as height, weight and other physical features. It we assigned racial categories to groups of humans with different heights—for example, every foot of height from four feet up determines a new race—we would be more biologically precise than the usual racial designation by skin color. For no fixed biological boundary exists between Asian and Caucasian, black and Indian, whereas a fixed boundary does exist between those who are shorter than five feet and those who are between five and six feet.[18]

However, it is not racial-group membership that determines race in the United States but lines of descent—genealogy. As groups, races are not stable entities. In Melville J. Herskovits's often-quoted words, "Two human groups never meet but they mingle their blood." And of course, this has always been the case in the United States. But due to the alchemy of American racism, no new race ever results. Black and white do not make gray here, but black.

It is important to note that when the acknowledgment of a mixed-race individual does not go beyond a reference to the racial diversity of that individual's forebears, the individual is called "of mixed race." But if the individual is acknowledged to be a racial mixture *in himself,* then he would be called "mixed race," without the "of." The use of the word "of" in the designation "of mixed race" leaves open the question of what the mixed-race individual *is* racially, and this "of" is compatible with the American one-drop rule. But if "of" is left out and an individual is called simply "mixed race," it becomes more diffi-cult conceptually to designate that individual black (or white, for that matter).

It is interesting, however, that wherever there is some recognition that mixed-race people exist, as there was in the old lower South and as there still is in Brazil, the metaphors "black" and "white" are aban-doned in favor of color words which come closer to describing what it is that people see when they look at skin colors.[19] The skin colors of people of acknowl-edged mixed race are called words such as "coffee," "almond," "almond shell," "piney," "honey," "ivory," "mahogany," "tan," and so on.[20] It is almost as if, in the presence of those individuals who are perceived to be mixed black and white race, the reality of human perception reasserts itself, and an attempt is made to speak the truth about visual experience. As offensive as such mixed-race color words may be against the backdrop of a biracial system, they nevertheless have more human reality than those color words "black" and "white" (which most Americans could never ap-proximate in appearance without being badly burned or suffering massive blood loss).

However, once an American begins to formulate a theoretical entitlement to consideration as a mixed-race person, the word "gray" might look attractive as a racial name, for the sake of parity (even though it is now used to describe an appearance of illness in prac-tically everyone, without prejudice). Of course, it would be a more liberal society if all people could be described physically as other natural objects are de-scribed (without anachronistic metaphors that, if taken literally, refer to death and disease). It would be a far more liberal society if racial designations were *allowed* to go the inevitable way of all historically ves-tigial categories. And if there is an intention that this be so, in the interim between the world of today, when people are categorized like so many breeds of domes-tic animals, and tomorrow, when the dog show will be over, what should "black," "non-white," "gray," and perhaps "red" and "yellow" people be called? Call us what we are, plain and simple: "racially designated."

Notes

1. Contemporary Black Identity Theory holds that all designated black individuals experience predictable stages in developing black identities as part of their value-positive emancipation. See, e.g., William S. Hall, Roy Freedle, and William E. Cross, Jr., *Stages in the Development of a Black Identity* (Iowa City: Research and Development Division, American College Teach-ing Program, 1972). This theory omits the possibili-ties that individuals of mixed race may never acquire black identities and that it may not be necessary or even desirable for them to do so in order to achieve full, value-positive emancipation.

2. See R. Fred Wacker, *Ethnicity, Pluralism and Race* (Westport, Conn.: Greenwood, 1983), pp. 13–40.

3. William Rubin, ed., *Pablo Picasso* (New York: Museum of Modern Art, 1980), p. 353.

4. See, e.g., Martha Weinman Lear, "The Second Femi-nist Wave," in June Sochen, ed., *The New Feminism in Twentieth-Century America* (Lexington, Mass.: D. C. Heath, 1971), pp. 161–72.

5. See Michael Leiris, "Race and Culture," in Leo Kuper, ed., *Race, Science and Society* (New York: Columbia University Press, 1965), pp. 135–72.

6. Ibid., p. 159. See also the United Nations statements on the "Race Question" between 1950 and 1967, which restate Leiris's main theme that culture is not physically inherited, in Kuper, ed., *Race, Science and Society,* Appendix.

7. For example, the bull and several of the other figures in *Guernica* were developed in earlier paintings and drawings by Picasso. See Charles Harrison, "Picasso's Guernica," in *Images of The Spanish Civil War* (Wal-ton Hall, England: Open University Press, 1981), pp. 101–25.

8. Richard Rorty, *Contingency, Irony and Solidarity* (Cambridge: Cambridge University Press, 1988), p. xv.

9. Ibid., pp. 23–44, 77.

10. According to H. P. Grice, normal communication presupposes cooperation. On the assumption of co-operation, if certain obvious rules of discourse are broken, the listener has reason to infer a logical im-plication behind what the speaker has literally said. For example, if we are cooperating and I ask you how X's performance was last night and you tell me that X knew all her lines, I can infer, according to the Rule of Relevance, that X's performance was not very good, because you have flouted the Rule of Rele-vance. See H. P. Grice, "Logic and Conversation," in Donald Davidson and Gilbert Harman, eds., *The Logic of Grammar* (Encino, Calif.: Dickinson, 1975), pp. 64–153. Insults, especially racial insults and im-plied racial insults, do not merely flout the normal rules but signal that cooperation in communication is not present. This may be why insults lead so easily to acts of violence, i.e., they signal that verbal com-munication is no longer possible.

11. See John L. Hodge, "Equality: Beyond Dualism and Oppression," in David Theo Goldberg, ed., *Anatomy of Racism* (Minneapolis: University of Minnesota Press, 1990), pp. 89–108.

12. See Carl N. Degler, *Neither Black nor White* (Madison: University of Wisconsin Press, 1986), p. xviii.

13. See *Webster's New Collegiate Dictionary,* 2d ed. (1960), s.v. "Caucasian," "Negro."

14. See Degler, *Neither Black nor White,* p. 277.

15. William Cecil Dampier, *A History of Science* (Cambridge: Cambridge University Press, 1943), p. 176.

16. See Degler, *Neither Black nor White,* pp. 105–7.

17. Not only was there, in Brazil, a lack of interest in breeding slaves, as compared to the United States, but manumission was easier and more frequent in Brazil, especially in the case of slaves of mixed race. See ibid., pp. 19–20, 39–47, 61–67.

18. Henry Louis Gates, Jr., "Critical Remarks," in Goldberg, ed., *Anatomy of Racism,* p. 332.

19. Degler, *Neither Black nor White,* pp. 102–3; John C. Mencke, *Mulattoes and Race Mixture* (Ann Arbor: University of Michigan Institute of Research Press, 1979), pp. ix, 2–3; Joel Williamson, *New People* (New York: Free Press, 1980), pp. 23–24. It should be noted that the old racial words for mixed black and white race, e.g., "quadroon," "octaroon," etc., are no more naturalistically descriptive than the words for people who are racially pure.

20. The nineteenth-century fiction sympathetic to mulattoes was replete with such descriptions. Many writers claim that among contemporary American blacks, close attention is paid to gradations in skin color. See, e.g., Beth Day, *Sexual Life between Blacks and Whites* (New York: World, 1972), pp. 185–87. Also, there is a tradition in black letters of aesthetic racial pride, based on the variation in appearance among people who are designated as black in the United States. See. W. E. B. Du Bois, *The Dusk of Dawn,* in idem, *Du Bois Writings,* comp. Nathan Huggins (New York: Literary Classics of the U.S., 1986), pp. 657–58.

 Sexism

OPPRESSION

Marilyn Frye

Marilyn Frye spells out and defends a notion of oppression and shows that women are uniquely oppressed. Her analysis of the unique oppression of women points to the following factors: the restriction of the female body, the economic dependence of most women, the role of primary caretaker that largely falls to women, and violence against women. (Source: From The Politics of Reality: Essays in Feminist Theory. *Copyright © 1983 by Marilyn Frye. Published by The Crossing Press, Freedom, CA. Reprinted by permission.)*

It is a fundamental claim of feminism that women are oppressed. The word 'oppression' is a strong word. It repels and attracts. It is dangerous and dangerously fashionable and endangered. It is much misused, and sometimes not innocently.

The statement that women are oppressed is frequently met with the claim that men are oppressed too. We hear that oppressing is oppressive to those who oppress as well as to those they oppress. Some men cite as evidence of their oppression their much-advertised inability to cry. It is tough, we are told, to be masculine. When the stresses and frustrations of being a man are cited as evidence that oppressors are oppressed by their oppressing, the word 'oppression' is being stretched to meaninglessness; it is treated as though its scope includes any and all human experience of limitation or suffering, no matter the cause, degree or consequence. Once such usage has been put over on us, then if ever we deny that any person or group is oppressed, we seem to imply that we think they never suffer and have no feelings. We are accused of insensitivity; even of bigotry. For women, such accusation is particularly intimidating, since sensitivity is one of the few virtues that has been assigned to us. If we are found insensitive, we may fear we have no redeeming traits at all and perhaps are not real women. Thus are we silenced before we begin: the name of our situation drained of meaning and our guilt mechanisms tripped.

But this is nonsense. Human beings can be miserable without being oppressed, and it is perfectly consistent to deny that a person or group is oppressed without denying that they have feelings or that they suffer.

We need to think clearly about oppression, and there is much that mitigates against this. I do not want to undertake to prove that women are oppressed (or that men are not), but I want to make clear what is being said when we say it. We need this word, this concept, and we need it to be sharp and sure.

I

The root of the word 'oppression' is the element 'press.' *The press of the crowd; pressed into military service; to press a pair of pants; printing press; press the button.*

Presses are used to mold things or flatten them or reduce them in bulk, sometimes to reduce them by squeezing out the gasses or liquids in them. Something pressed is something caught between or among forces and barriers which are so related to each other that jointly they restrain, restrict or prevent the thing's motion or mobility. Mold. Immobilize. Reduce.

The mundane experience of the oppressed provides another clue. One of the most characteristic and ubiquitous features of the world as experienced by oppressed people is the double bind — situations in which options are reduced to a very few and all of them expose one to penalty, censure or deprivation. For example, it is often a requirement upon oppressed people that we smile and be cheerful. If we comply, we signal our docility and our acquiescence in our situation. We need not, then, be taken note of. We acquiesce in being made invisible, in our occupying no space. We participate in our own erasure. On the other hand, anything but the sunniest countenance exposes us to being perceived as mean, bitter, angry or dangerous. This means, at the least, that we may be found "difficult" or unpleasant to work with, which is enough to cost one one's livelihood; at worst, being seen as mean, bitter, angry or dangerous has been known to result in rape, arrest, beating and murder. One can only choose to risk one's preferred form and rate of annihilation.

Another example: It is common in the United States that women, especially younger women, are in a bind where neither sexual activity nor sexual inactivity is all right. If she is heterosexually active, a woman is open to censure and punishment for being loose, unprincipled or a whore. The "punishment" comes in the form of criticism, snide and embarrassing remarks, being treated as an easy lay by men, scorn from her more restrained female friends. She may have to lie and hide her behavior from her parents. She must juggle the risks of unwanted pregnancy and dangerous contraceptives. On the other hand, if she refrains from heterosexual activity, she is fairly constantly harassed by men who try to persuade her into it and pressure her to "relax" and "let her hair down"; she is threatened with labels like "frigid," "uptight," "manhater," "bitch" and "cocktease." The same parents who would be disapproving of her sexual activity may be worried by her inactivity because it suggests she is not or will not be popular, or is not sexually normal. She may be charged with lesbianism. If a woman is raped, then if she has been heterosexually active she is subject to the presumption that she liked it (since her activity is presumed to show that she likes sex), and if she has not been heterosexually active, she is subject to the presumption that she liked it (since she is supposedly "repressed and frustrated"). Both heterosexual activity and heterosexual nonactivity are likely to be taken as proof that you wanted to be raped, and hence, of course, weren't *really* raped at all. You can't win. You are caught in a bind, caught between systematically related pressures.

Women are caught like this, too, by networks of forces and barriers that expose one to penalty, loss or contempt whether one works outside the home or not, is on welfare or not, bears children or not, raises children or not, marries or not, stays married or not, is heterosexual, lesbian, both or neither. Economic necessity; confinement to racial and/or sexual job ghettos; sexual harassment; sex discrimination; pressures of competing expectations and judgments about *women, wives* and *mothers* (in the society at large, in racial and ethnic subcultures and in one's own mind); dependence (full or partial) on husbands, parents or the state; commitment to political ideas; loyalties to racial or ethnic or other "minority" groups; the demands of self-respect and responsibilities to others. Each of these factors exists in complex tension with every other, penalizing or prohibiting all of the apparently available options. And nipping at one's heels, always, is the endless pack of little things. If one dresses one way, one is subject to the assumption that one is advertising one's sexual availability; if one dresses another way, one appears to "not care about oneself" or to be "unfeminine." If one uses "strong language," one invites categorization as a whore or slut; if one does not, one invites categorization as a "lady" — one too delicately constituted to cope with robust speech or the realities to which it presumably refers.

The experience of oppressed people is that the living of one's life is confined and shaped by forces and barriers which are not accidental or occasional and hence avoidable, but are systematically related to each other in such a way as to catch one between and among them and restrict or penalize motion in any direction.

It is the experience of being caged in: all avenues, in every direction, are blocked or booby trapped.

Cages. Consider a birdcage. If you look very closely at just one wire in the cage, you cannot see the other wires. If your conception of what is before you is determined by this myopic focus, you could look at that one wire, up and down the length of it, and be unable to see why a bird would not just fly around the wire any time it wanted to go somewhere. Furthermore, even if, one day at a time, you myopically inspected each wire, you still could not see why a bird would have trouble going past the wires to get anywhere. There is no physical property of any one wire, *nothing* that the closest scrutiny could discover, that will reveal how a bird could be inhibited or harmed by it except in the most accidental way. It is only when you step back, stop looking at the wires one by one, microscopically, and take a macroscopic view of the whole cage, that you can see why the bird does not go anywhere; and then you will see it in a moment. It will require no great subtlety of mental powers. It is perfectly *obvious* that the bird is surrounded by a network of systematically related barriers, no one of which would be the least hindrance to its flight, but which, by their relations to each other, are as confining as the solid walls of a dungeon.

It is now possible to grasp one of the reasons why oppression can be hard to see and recognize: one can study the elements of an oppressive structure with great care and some good will without seeing the structure as a whole, and hence without seeing or being able to understand that one is looking at a cage and that there are people there who are caged, whose motion and mobility are restricted, whose lives are shaped and reduced.

The arresting of vision at a microscopic level yields such common confusion as that about the male door-opening ritual. This ritual, which is remarkably widespread across classes and races, puzzles many people, some of whom do and some of whom do not find it offensive. Look at the scene of the two people approaching a door. The male steps slightly ahead and opens the door. The male holds the door open while the female glides through. Then the male goes through. The door closes after them. "Now how," one innocently asks, "can those crazy womenslibbers say that is oppressive? The guy *removed* a barrier to the lady's smooth and unruffled progress." But each repetition of this ritual has a place in a pattern, in fact in several patterns. One has to shift the level of one's perception in order to see the whole picture.

The door-opening pretends to be a helpful service, but the helpfulness is false. This can be seen by noting that it will be done whether or not it makes any practical sense. Infirm men and men burdened with packages will open doors for able-bodied women who are free of physical burdens. Men will impose themselves awkwardly and jostle everyone in order to get to the door first. The act is not determined by convenience or grace. Furthermore, these very numerous acts of unneeded or even noisome "help" occur in counterpoint to a pattern of men not being helpful in many practical ways in which women might welcome help. What *women* experience is a world in which gallant princes charming commonly make a fuss about being helpful and providing small services when help and services are of little or no use, but in which there are rarely ingenious and adroit princes at hand when substantial assistance is really wanted either in mundane affairs or in situations of threat, assault or terror. There is no help with the (his) laundry; no help typing a report at 4:00 a.m.; no help in mediating disputes among relatives or children. There is nothing but advice that women should stay indoors after dark, be chaperoned by a man, or when it comes down to it, "lie back and enjoy it."

The gallant gestures have no practical meaning. Their meaning is symbolic. The door-opening and similar services provided are services which really are needed by people who are for one reason or another incapacitated—unwell, burdened with parcels, etc. So the message is that women are incapable. The detachment of the acts from the concrete realities of what women need and do not need is a vehicle for the message that women's actual needs and interests are unimportant or irrelevant. Finally, these gestures imitate the behavior of servants toward masters and thus mock women, who are in most respects the servants and caretakers of men. The message of the false helpfulness of male gallantry is female dependence, the invisibility or insignificance of women, and contempt for women.

One cannot see the meanings of these rituals if one's focus is riveted upon the individual event in all its particularity, including the particularity of the individual man's present conscious intentions and motives and the individual woman's conscious perception of the event in the moment. It seems sometimes that people take a deliberately myopic view and fill their eyes with things seen microscopically in order not to see macroscopically. At any rate, whether it is deliberate or not, people can and do fail to see the oppression of women because they fail to see macroscopically and hence fail to see the various elements of the situation as systematically related in larger schemes.

As the cageness of the birdcase is a macroscopic phenomenon, the oppressiveness of the situations in which women live our various and different lives is a macroscopic phenomenon. Neither can be *seen* from a microscopic perspective. But when you look macroscopically you can see it—a network of forces and barriers which are systematically related and which conspire to the immobilization, reduction and molding of women and the lives we live.

II

The image of the cage helps convey one aspect of the systematic nature of oppression. Another is the selection of occupants of the cages, and analysis of this aspect also helps account for the invisibility of the oppression of women.

It is as a woman (or as a Chicana/o or as a Black or Asian or lesbian) that one is entrapped.

"Why can't I go to the park; you let Jimmy go!"
"Because it's not safe for girls."

"I want to be a secretary, not a seamstress; I don't want to learn to make dresses."

"There's no work for negroes in that line; learn a skill where you can earn your living."[1]

When you question why you are being blocked, why this barrier is in your path, the answer has not to do with individual talent or merit, handicap or failure; it has to do with your membership in some category understood as a "natural" or "physical" category. The "inhabitant" of the "cage" is not an individual but a group, all those of a certain category. If an individual is oppressed, it is in virtue of being a member of a group or category of people that is systematically reduced, molded, immobilized. Thus, to recognize a person as oppressed, one has to see that individual *as* belonging to a group of a certain sort.

There are many things which can encourage or inhibit perception of someone's membership in the sort of group or category in question here. In particular, it seems reasonable to suppose that if one of the devices of restriction and definition of the group is that of physical confinement or segregation, the confinement and separation would encourage recognition of the group as a group. This in turn would encourage the macroscopic focus which enables one to recognize oppression and encourages the individuals' identification and solidarity with other individuals of the group or category. But physical confinement and segregation of the group as a group is not common to all oppressive structures, and when an oppressed group is geographically and demographically dispersed the perception of it as a group is inhibited. There may be little or nothing in the situations of the individuals encouraging the macroscopic focus which would reveal the unity of the structure bearing down on all members of that group.*

A great many people, female and male and of every race and class, simply do not believe that *woman* is a category of oppressed people, and I think that this is in part because they have been fooled by the dispersal and assimilation of women throughout and into the systems of class and race which organize men. Our simply being dispersed makes it difficult for women to have knowledge of each other and hence difficult to recognize the shape of our common cage. The dispersal and assimilation of women throughout economic classes and races also divides us against each other practically and economically and thus attaches *interest* to the inability to see: for some, jealousy of their benefits, and for some, resentment of the others' advantages.

---

*Coerced assimilation is in fact one of the policies available to an oppressing group in its effort to reduce and/or annihilate another group. This tactic is used by the U.S. government, for instance, on the American Indians.

To get past this, it helps to notice that in fact women of all races and classes *are* together in a ghetto of sorts. There is a women's place, a sector, which is inhabited by women of all classes and races, and it is not defined by geographical boundaries but by function. The function is the service of men and men's interests as men define them, which includes the bearing and rearing of children. The details of the service and the working conditions vary by race and class, for men of different races and classes have different interests, perceive their interests differently, and express their needs and demands in different rhetorics, dialects and languages. But there are also some constants.

Whether in lower, middle or upper-class home or work situations, women's service work always includes personal service (the work of maids, butlers, cooks, personal secretaries),* sexual service (including provision for his genital sexual needs and bearing his children, but also including "being nice," "being attractive for him," etc.), and ego service (encouragement, support, praise, attention). Women's service work also is characterized everywhere by the fatal combination of responsibility and powerlessness: we are held responsible and we hold ourselves responsible for good outcomes for men and children in almost every respect though we have in almost no case power adequate to that project. The details of the subjective experience of this servitude are local. They vary with economic class and race and ethnic tradition as well as the personalities of the men in question. So also are the details of the forces which coerce our tolerance of this servitude particular to the different situations in which different women live and work.

All this is not to say that women do not have, assert and manage sometimes to satisfy our own interests, nor to deny that in some cases and in some respects women's independent interests do overlap with men's. But at every race/class level and even across race/class lines men do not serve women as women serve men. "Women's sphere" may be understood as

_____

*At higher class levels women may not *do* all these kinds of work, but are generally still responsible for hiring and supervising those who do it. These services are still, in these cases, women's responsibility.

the "service sector," taking the latter expression much more widely and deeply than is usual in discussions of the economy.

III

It seems to be the human condition that in one degree or another we all suffer frustration and limitation, all encounter unwelcome barriers, and all are damaged and hurt in various ways. Since we are a social species, almost all of our behavior and activities are structured by more than individual inclination and the conditions of the planet and its atmosphere. No human is free of social structures, nor (perhaps) would happiness consist in such freedom. Structure consists of boundaries, limits and barriers; in a structured whole, some motions and changes are possible, and others are not. If one is looking for an excuse to dilute the word 'oppression,' one can use the fact of social structure as an excuse and say that everyone is oppressed. But if one would rather get clear about what oppression is and is not, one needs to sort out the sufferings, harms and limitations and figure out which are elements of oppression and which are not.

From what I have already said here, it is clear that if one wants to determine whether a particular suffering, harm or limitation is part of someone's being oppressed, one has to look at it *in context* in order to tell whether it is an element in an oppressive structure: one has to see if it is part of an enclosing structure of forces and barriers which tends to the immobilization and reduction of a group or category of people. One has to look at how the barrier or force fits with others and to whose benefit or detriment it works. As soon as one looks at examples, it becomes obvious that not everything which frustrates or limits a person is oppressive, and not every harm or damage is due to or contributes to oppression.

If a rich white playboy who lives off income from his investments in South African diamond mines should break a leg in a skiing accident at Aspen and wait in pain in a blizzard for hours before he is rescued, we may assume that in that period he suffers. But the suffering comes to an end; his leg is repaired by the best surgeon money can buy and he is soon recuperating in a lavish suite, sipping Chivas Regal. Nothing in this picture suggests a structure of barriers and forces. He is a member of several oppressor groups and does not suddenly become oppressed because he is injured and in pain. Even if the accident was caused by someone's malicious negligence, and hence someone can be blamed for it and morally faulted, that person still has not been an agent of oppression.

Consider also the restriction of having to drive one's vehicle on a certain side of the road. There is no doubt that this restriction is almost unbearably frustrating at times, when one's lane is not moving and the other lane is clear. There are surely times, even, when abiding by this regulation would have harmful consequences. But the restriction is obviously wholesome for most of us most of the time. The restraint is imposed for our benefit, and does benefit us; its operation tends to encourage our *continued* motion, not to immobilize us. The limits imposed by traffic regulations are limits most of us would cheerfully impose on ourselves given that we knew others would follow them too. They are part of a structure which shapes our behavior, not to our reduction and immobilization, but rather to the protection of our continued ability to move and act as we will.

Another example: The boundaries of a racial ghetto in an American city serve to some extent to keep white people from going in, as well as to keep ghetto dwellers from going out. A particular white citizen may be frustrated or feel deprived because s/he cannot stroll around there and enjoy the "exotic" aura of a "foreign" culture, or shop for bargains in the ghetto swap shops. In fact, the existence of the ghetto, of racial segregation, does deprive the white person of knowledge and harm her/his character by nurturing unwarranted feelings of superiority. But this does not make the white person in this situation a member of an oppressed race or a person oppressed because of her/his race. One must look at the barrier. It limits the activities and the access of those on both sides of it (though to different degrees). But it is a product of the intention, planning and action of whites for the benefit of whites, to secure and maintain privileges that are available to whites generally, as members of the dominant and privileged group. Though the existence

of the barrier has some bad consequences for whites, the barrier does not exist in systematic relationship with other barriers and forces forming a structure oppressive to whites; quite the contrary. It is part of a structure which oppresses the ghetto dwellers and thereby (and by white intention) protects and furthers white interests as dominant white culture understands them. This barrier is not oppressive to whites, even though it is a barrier to whites.

Barriers have different meanings to those on opposite sides of them, even though they are barriers to both. The physical walls of a prison no more dissolve to let an outsider in than to let an insider out, but for the insider they are confining and limiting while to the outsider they may mean protection from what s/he takes to be threats posed by insiders—freedom from harm or anxiety. A set of social and economic barriers and forces separating two groups may be felt, even painfully, by members of both groups and yet may mean confinement to one and liberty and enlargement of opportunity to the other.

The service sector of the wives/mommas/assistants/girls is almost exclusively a woman-only sector; its boundaries not only enclose women but to a very great extent keep men out. Some men sometimes encounter this barrier and experience it as a restriction on their movements, their activities, their control or their choices of "lifestyle." Thinking they might like the simple nurturant life (which they may imagine to be quite free of stress, alienation and hard work), and feeling deprived since it seems closed to them, they thereupon announce the discovery that they are oppressed, too, by "sex roles." But that barrier is erected and maintained by men, for the benefit of men. It consists of cultural and economic forces and pressures in a culture and economy controlled by men in which, at every economic level and in all racial and ethnic subcultures, economy, tradition—and even ideologies of liberation—work to keep at least local culture and economy in male control.*

---

*Of course this is complicated by race and class. Machismo and "Black manhood" politics seem to help keep Latin or Black men in control of more cash than Latin or Black women control; but these politics seem to me also to ultimately help keep the larger economy in *white* male control.

The boundary that sets apart women's sphere is maintained and promoted by men generally for the benefit of men generally, and men generally do benefit from its existence, even the man who bumps into it and complains of the inconvenience. That barrier is protecting his classification and status as a male, as superior, as having a right to sexual access to a female or females. It protects a kind of citizenship which is superior to that of females of his class and race, his access to a wider range of better paying and higher status work, and his right to prefer unemployment to the degradation of doing lower status or "women's" work.

If a person's life or activity is affected by some force or barrier that person encounters, one may not conclude that the person is oppressed simply because the person encounters that barrier or force; nor simply because the encounter is unpleasant, frustrating or painful to that person at that time; nor simply because the existence of the barrier or force, or the processes which maintain or apply it, serve to deprive that person of something of value. One must look at the barrier or force and answer certain questions about it. Who constructs and maintains it? Whose interests are served by its existence? Is it part of a structure which tends to confine, reduce and immobilize some group? Is the individual a member of the confined group? Various forces, barriers and limitations a person may encounter or live with may be part of an oppressive structure or not, and if they are, that person may be on either the oppressed or the oppressor side of it. One cannot tell which by how loudly or how little the person complains.

IV

Many of the restrictions and limitations we live with are more or less internalized and self-monitored, and are part of our adaptations to the requirements and expectations imposed by the needs and tastes and tyrannies of others. I have in mind such things as women's cramped postures and attenuated strides and men's restraint of emotional self-expression (except for anger). Who gets what out of the practice of those disciplines, and who imposes what penalties for improper relaxations of them? What are the rewards of this self-discipline?

Can men cry? Yes, in the company of women. If a man cannot cry, it is in the company of men that he cannot cry. It is men, not women, who require this restraint; and men not only require it, they reward it. The man who maintains a steely or tough or laid-back demeanor (all are forms which suggest invulnerability) marks himself as a member of the male community and is esteemed by other men. Consequently, the maintenance of that demeanor contributes to the man's self-esteem. It is felt as good, and he can feel good about himself. The way this restriction fits into the structures of men's lives is as one of the socially required behaviors which, if carried off, contribute to their acceptance and respect by significant others and to their own self-esteem. It is to their benefit to practice this discipline.

Consider, by comparison, the discipline of women's cramped physical postures and attenuated stride. This discipline can be relaxed in the company of women; it generally is at its most strenuous in the company of men.* Like men's emotional restraint, women's physical restraint is required by men. But unlike the case of men's emotional restraint, women's physical restraint is not rewarded. What do we get for it? Respect and esteem and acceptance? No. They mock us and parody our mincing steps. We look silly, incompetent, weak and generally contemptible. Our exercise of this discipline tends to low esteem and low self-esteem. It does not benefit us. It fits in a network of behaviors through which we constantly announce to others our membership in a lower caste and our unwillingness and/or inability to defend our bodily or moral integrity. It is degrading and part of a pattern of degradation.

Acceptable behavior for both groups, men and women, involves a required restraint that seems in itself

---

*Cf., *Let's Take Back Our Space: "Female" and "Male" Body Language as a Result of Patriarchal Structures,* by Marianne Wex (Frauenliteraturverlag Hermine Fees, West Germany, 1979), especially p. 173. This remarkable book presents literally thousands of candid photographs of women and men, in public, seated, standing and lying down. It vividly demonstrates the very systematic differences in women's and men's postures and gestures.

silly and perhaps damaging. But the social effect is drastically different. The woman's restraint is part of a structure oppressive to women; the man's restraint is part of a structure oppressive to women.

V

One is marked for application of oppressive pressures by one's membership in some group or category. Much of one's suffering and frustration befalls one partly or largely because one is a member of that category. In the case at hand, it is the category, *woman*. Being a woman is a major factor in my not having a better job than I do; being a woman selects me as a likely victim of sexual assault or harassment; it is my being a woman that reduces the power of my anger to a proof of my insanity. If a woman has little or no economic or political power, or achieves little of what she wants to achieve, a major causal factor in this is that she is a woman. For any woman of any race or economic class, being a woman is significantly attached to whatever disadvantages and deprivations she suffers, be they great or small.

None of this is the case with respect to a person's being a man. Simply being a man is not what stands between him and a better job; whatever assaults and harassments he is subject to, being male is not what selects him for victimization; being male is not a factor which would make his anger impotent — quite the opposite. If a man has little or no material or political power, or achieves little of what he wants to achieve, his being male is no part of the explanation. Being male is something he has going *for* him, even if race or class or age or disability is going against him.

Women are oppressed, *as women*. Members of certain racial and/or economic groups and classes, both the males and the females, are oppressed *as* members of those races and/or classes. But men are not oppressed *as men*.

> . . . and isn't it strange that any of us should have been confused and mystified about such a simple thing?

Note

1. This example is derived from *Daddy Was a Number Runner,* by Louise Meriwether (Prentice-Hall, Englewood Cliffs, New Jersey, 1970), p. 144.

ON PSYCHOLOGICAL OPPRESSION

Sandra Lee Bartky

Sandra Bartky argues that women are oppressed in much the same way as victims of racism and classism. She adopts Fanon's analysis of oppression — that it consists of stereotyping, cultural domination, and objectification — and applies it to women. (Source: Reprinted from Femininity and Domination: Studies in the Phenomenology of Oppression *(1990), by permission of the publisher, Routledge, New York.)*

In *Black Skin, White Masks,* Frantz Fanon offers an anguished and eloquent description of the psychological effects of colonialism on the colonized, a "clinical study" of what he calls the "psychic alienation of the black man." "Those who recognize themselves in it," he says, "will have made a step forward."[1] Fanon's black American readers saw at once that he had captured the corrosive effects not only of classic colonial oppression but of domestic racism too, and that his study fitted well the picture of black America as an internal colony. Without wanting in any way to diminish the oppressive and stifling realities of black experience that Fanon reveals, let me say that I, a white woman, recognize myself in this book too, not only in my "shameful livery of white incomprehension,"[2] but as myself the victim of a "psychic alienation" similar to the one Fanon has described. In this paper I shall try to explore that moment of recognition, to reveal the ways in which the psychological effects of sexist oppression resemble those of racism and colonialism.

To oppress, says Webster, is "to lie heavy on, to weigh down, to exercise harsh dominion over." When we describe a people as oppressed, what we have in mind most often is an oppression that is economic and political in character. But recent liberation movements, the black liberation movement and the women's movement in particular, have brought to light forms of oppression that are not immediately economic or political. It is possible to be oppressed in ways that need involve neither physical deprivation, legal inequality, nor economic exploitation;[3] one can be oppressed psychologically — the "psychic aliena-

tion" of which Fanon speaks. To be psychologically oppressed is to be weighed down in your mind; it is to have a harsh dominion exercised over your self-esteem. The psychologically oppressed become their own oppressors; they come to exercise harsh dominion over their own self-esteem. Differently put, psychological oppression can be regarded as the "internalization of intimations of inferiority."[4]

Like economic oppression, psychological oppression is institutionalized and systematic; it serves to make the work of domination easier by breaking the spirit of the dominated and by rendering them incapable of understanding the nature of those agencies responsible for their subjugation. This allows those who benefit from the established order of things to maintain their ascendancy with more appearance of legitimacy and with less recourse to overt acts of violence than they might otherwise require. Now, poverty and powerlessness can destroy a person's self-esteem, and the fact that one occupies an inferior position in society is all too often racked up to one's being an inferior sort of person. Clearly, then, economic and political oppression are themselves psychologically oppressive. But there are unique modes of psychological oppression that can be distinguished from the usual forms of economic and political domination. Fanon offers a series of what are essentially phenomenological descriptions of psychic alienation.[5] In spite of considerable overlapping, the experiences of oppression he describes fall into three categories: stereotyping, cultural domination, and sexual objectification. These, I shall contend, are some of the ways in which the terrible messages of inferiority can be delivered even to those who may enjoy certain material benefits; they are special modes of psychic alienation. In what follows, I shall examine some of the ways in which American women — white women and women of color — are stereotyped, culturally dominated, and sexually objectified. In the course of the discussion, I shall argue that our ordinary concept of oppression needs to be altered and expanded, for it is too restricted to encompass what an analysis of psychological oppression reveals about the nature of oppression in general. Finally, I shall be concerned throughout to show how both fragmentation and mystification are present in each mode of psychological oppression, although in varying degrees: fragmentation, the splitting of the whole person into parts of a person which, in stereotyping, may take the form of a war between a "true" and "false" self—or, in sexual objectification, the form of an often coerced and degrading identification of a person with her body; mystification, the systematic obscuring of both the reality and agencies of psychological oppression so that its intended effect, the depreciated self, is lived out as destiny, guilt, or neurosis.

=

The stereotypes that sustain sexism are similar in many ways to those that sustain racism. Like white women, black and brown persons of both sexes have been regarded as childlike, happiest when they are occupying their "place"; more intuitive than rational, more spontaneous than deliberate, closer to nature, and less capable of substantial cultural accomplishment. Black men and women of all races have been victims of sexual stereotyping: the black man and the black woman, like the "Latin spitfire," are lustful and hotblooded; they are thought to lack the capacities for instinctual control that distinguish people from animals. What is seen as an excess in persons of color appear as a deficiency in the white woman; comparatively frigid, she has been, nonetheless, defined by her sexuality as well, here her reproductive role or function. In regard to capability and competence, black women have, again, an excess of what in white women is a deficiency. White women have been seen as incapable and incompetent: no matter, for these are traits of the truly feminine woman. Black women, on the other hand, have been seen as overly capable, hence, as unfeminine bitches who threaten, through their very competence, to castrate their men.

Stereotyping is morally reprehensible as well as psychologically oppressive on two counts, at least. First, it can hardly be expected that those who hold a set of stereotyped beliefs about the sort of person I am will understand my needs or even respect my rights. Second, suppose that I, the object of some stereotype,

believe in it myself—for why should I not believe what everyone else believes? I may then find it difficult to achieve what existentialists call an authentic choice of self, or what some psychologists have regarded as a state of self-actualization. Moral philosophers have quite correctly placed a high value, sometimes the highest value, on the development of autonomy and moral agency. Clearly, the economic and political domination of women—our concrete powerlessness—is what threatens our autonomy most. But stereotyping, in its own way, threatens our self-determination too. Even when economic and political obstacles on the path to autonomy are removed, a depreciated alter ego still blocks the way. It is hard enough for me to determine what sort of person I am or ought to try to become without being shadowed by an alternate self, a truncated and inferior self that I have, in some sense, been doomed to be all the time. For many, the prefabricated self triumphs over a more authentic self which, with work and encouragement, might sometime have emerged. For the talented few, retreat into the *imago* is raised to the status of art or comedy. Muhammad Ali has made himself what he could scarcely escape being made into—a personification of Primitive Man; while Zsa Zsa Gabor is not so much a woman as the parody of a woman.

Female stereotypes threaten the autonomy of women not only by virtue of their existence but also by virtue of their content.[6] In the conventional portrait, women deny their femininity when they undertake action that is too self-regarding or independent. As we have seen, black women are condemned (often by black men) for supposedly having done this already; white women stand under an injunction not to follow their example. Many women in many places lacked (and many still lack) the elementary right to choose our own mates; but for some women even in our own society today, this is virtually the only major decision we are thought capable of making without putting our womanly nature in danger; what follows ever after is or ought to be a properly feminine submission to the decisions of men. We cannot be autonomous, as men are thought to be autonomous, without in some sense ceasing to be women. When one considers how interwoven are traditional female stereotypes with traditional female roles—and these, in turn, with the ways in which we are socialized—all this is seen in an even more sinister light: White women, at least, are psychologically conditioned not to pursue the kind of autonomous development that is held by the culture to be a constitutive feature of masculinity.

The truncated self I am to be is not something manufactured out there by an anonymous Other which I encounter only in the pages of *Playboy* or the *Ladies' Home Journal;* it is inside of me, a part of myself. I may become infatuated with my feminine persona and waste my powers in the more or less hopeless pursuit of a *Vogue* figure, the look of an *Essence* model, or a home that "expresses my personality." Or I may find the parts of myself fragmented and the fragments at war with one another. Women are only now learning to identify and struggle against the forces that have laid these psychic burdens upon us. More often than not, we live out this struggle, which is really a struggle against oppression, in a mystified way: What we are enduring we believe to be entirely intrapsychic in character, the result of immaturity, maladjustment, or even neurosis.

Tyler, the great classical anthropologist, defined culture as all the items in the general life of a people. To claim that women are victims of cultural domination is to claim that all the items in the general life of our people — our language, our institutions, our art and literature, our popular culture — are sexist; that all, to a greater or lesser degree, manifest male supremacy. There is some exaggeration in this claim, but not much. Unlike the black colonial whom Fanon describes with such pathos, women *qua* women are not now in possession of an alternate culture, a "native" culture which, even if regarded by everyone, including ourselves, as decidedly inferior to the dominant culture, we could at least recognize as our own. However degraded or distorted an image of ourselves we see reflected in the patriarchal culture, the culture of our men is still our culture. Certainly in some respects, the condition of women is like the condition of a colonized people. But we are not a colonized people; we have never been more than half a people.[7]

This lack of cultural autonomy has several important consequences for an understanding of the condition of women. A culture has a global character; hence, the limits of my culture are the limits of my world. The subordination of women, then, because it is so pervasive a feature of my culture, will (if uncontested) appear to be natural — and because it is natural, unalterable. Unlike a colonized people, women have no memory of a "time before": a time before the masters came, a time before we were subjugated and ruled. Further, since one function of cultural identity is to allow me to distinguish those who are like me from those who are not, I may feel more kinship with those who share my culture, even though they oppress me, than with the women of another culture, whose whole experience of life may well be closer to my own than to any man's.

Our true situation in regard to male supremacist culture is one of domination and exclusion. But this manifests itself in an extremely deceptive way; mystification once more holds sway. Our relative absence from the "higher" culture is taken as proof that we are unable to participate in it ("Why are there no great women artists?"). Theories of the female nature must then be brought forward to try to account for this.[8] The splitting or fragmenting of women's consciousness which takes place in the cultural sphere is also apparent. While remaining myself, I must at the same time transform myself into that abstract and "universal" subject for whom cultural artifacts are made and whose values and experience they express. This subject is not universal at all, however, but *male.* Thus, I must approve the taming of the shrew, laugh at the mother-in-law or the dumb blonde, and somehow identify with all those heroes of fiction from Faust to the personae of Norman Mailer and Henry Miller, whose *Bildungsgeschichten* involve the sexual exploitation of women. Women of color have, of course, a special problem: The dominant cultural subject is not only male, but *white,* so their cultural alienation is doubled; they are expected to assimilate cultural motifs that are not only masculinist but racist.[9]

Women of all races and ethnicities, like Fanon's "black man," are subject not only to stereotyping and cultural depreciation but to sexual objectification as well. Even though much has been written about sexual objectification in the literature of the women's movement, the notion itself is complex, obscure, and much in need of philosophical clarification. I offer the following preliminary characterization of sexual objectification: A person is sexually objectified when her sexual parts or sexual functions are separated out from the rest of her personality and reduced to the status of mere instruments or else regarded as if they were capable of representing her. On this definition, then, the prostitute would be a victim of sexual objectification, as would the *Playboy* bunny, the female breeder, and the bathing beauty.

To say that the sexual part of a person is regarded as if it could represent her is to imply that it cannot, that the part and the whole are incommensurable. But surely there are times, in the sexual embrace perhaps, when a woman might want to be regarded as nothing but a sexually intoxicating body and when attention paid to some other aspect of her person — say, to her mathematical ability — would be absurdly out of place. If sexual relations involve some sexual objectification, then it becomes necessary to distinguish situations in which sexual objectification is oppressive from the sorts of situations in which it is not.[10] The identification of a person with her sexuality becomes oppressive, one might venture, when such an identification becomes habitually extended into every area of her experience. To be routinely perceived by others in a sexual light on occasions when such a perception is inappropriate is to have one's very being subjected to that compulsive sexualization that has been the traditional lot of both white women and black men and women of color generally. "For the majority of white men," says Fanon, "the Negro is the incarnation of a genital potency beyond all moralities and prohibitions."[11] Later in *Black Skin, White Masks,* he writes that "the Negro is the genital."[12]

One way to be sexually objectified, then, is to be the object of a kind of perception, unwelcome and inappropriate, that takes the part for the whole. An example may make this clearer. A young woman was recently interviewed for a teaching job in philosophy by the academic chairman of a large department. During most of the interview, so she reported, the man stared fixedly at her breasts. In this situation, the woman is a bosom, not a job candidate. Was this department chairman guilty only of a confusion between business and pleasure? Scarcely. He stares at her breasts for his sake, not hers. Her wants and needs not only play no role in the encounter but, because of the direction of his attention, she is discomfited, feels humiliated, and performs badly. Not surprisingly, she fails to get the job. Much of the time, sexual objectification occurs

independently of what women want; it is something done to us against our will. It is clear from this example that the objectifying perception that splits a person into parts serves to elevate one interest above another. Now it stands revealed not only as a way of perceiving, but as a way of maintaining dominance as well. It is not clear to me that the sexual and nonsexual spheres of experience can or ought to be kept separate forever (Marcuse, for one, has envisioned the eroticization of all areas of human life); but as things stand now, sexualization is one way of fixing disadvantaged persons in their disadvantage, to their clear detriment and within a narrow and repressive eros.

Consider now a second example of the way in which that fragmenting perception, which is so large an ingredient in the sexual objectification of women, serves to maintain the dominance of men. It is a fine spring day, and with an utter lack of self-consciousness, I am bouncing down the street. Suddenly I hear men's voices. Catcalls and whistles fill the air. These noises are clearly sexual in intent and they are meant for me; they come from across the street. I freeze. As Sartre would say, I have been petrified by the gaze of the Other. My face flushes and my motions become stiff and self-conscious. The body which only a moment before I inhabited with such ease now floods my consciousness. I have been made into an object. While it is true that for these men I am nothing but, let us say, a "nice piece of ass," there is more involved in this encounter than their mere fragmented perception of me. They could, after all, have enjoyed me in silence. Blissfully unaware, breasts bouncing, eyes on the birds in the trees, I could have passed by without having been turned to stone. But I must be *made* to know that I am a "nice piece of ass": I must be made to see myself as they see me. There is an element of compulsion in this encounter, in this being-made-to-be-aware of one's own flesh; like being made to apologize, it is humiliating. It is unclear what role is played by sexual arousal or even sexual connoisseurship in encounters like these. What I describe seems less the spontaneous expression of a healthy eroticism than a ritual of subjugation.

Sexual objectification as I have characterized it involves two persons: the one who objectifies and the one who is objectified. But the observer and the one observed can be the same person. I can, of course, take pleasure in my own body as another might take pleasure in it and it would be naive not to notice that there are delights of a narcissistic kind that go along with the status "sex object." But the extent to which the identification of women with their bodies feeds an essentially infantile narcissism — an attitude of mind in keeping with our forced infantilization in other areas of life — is, at least for me, an open question. Subject to the evaluating eye of the male connoisseur, women learn to evaluate themselves first and best. Our identities can no more be kept separate from the appearance of our bodies than they can be kept separate from the shadow-selves of the female stereotype. "Much of a young woman's identity is already defined in her kind of attractiveness and in the selectivity of her search for the man (or men) by whom she wishes to be sought."[13] There is something obsessional in the preoccupation of many women with their bodies, although the magnitude of the obsession will vary somewhat with the presence or absence in a woman's life of other sources of self-esteem and with her capacity to gain a living independent of her looks. Surrounded on all sides by images of perfect female beauty — for, in modern advertising, the needs of capitalism and the traditional values of patriarchy are happily married — of course we fall short. The narcissism encouraged by our identification with the body is shattered by these images. Whose nose is not the wrong shape, whose hips are not too wide or too narrow? Anyone who believes that such concerns are too trivial to weigh very heavily with most women has failed to grasp the realities of the feminine condition.

The idea that women ought always to make themselves as pleasing to the eye as possible is very widespread indeed. It was dismaying to come across this passage in a paper written by an eminent Marxist humanist in defense of the contemporary women's movement:

> There is no reason why a woman's liberation activist should not try to look pretty and attractive. One of the universal human aspirations of all times was to raise reality to the level of art, to make the world more beautiful, to be more beautiful within given limits. Beauty is a value in itself; it will always be respected and will attract — to be sure various forms of beauty but not to the exclusion of physical beauty. A woman does not become a sex object in herself, or only because of her pretty appearance. She becomes a sexual object in relationship, when she allows a man to treat her in a certain depersonalizing, degrading way; and vice versa, a woman does not become a sexual subject by neglecting her appearance.[14]

It is not for the sake of mere men that we women — not just we women, but we women's liberation activists — ought to look "pretty and attractive," but for the sake of something much more exalted: for the sake of beauty. This preoccupation with the way we look and the fear that women might stop trying to make themselves pretty and attractive (so as to "raise reality to the level of art") would be a species of objectification anywhere; but it is absurdly out of place in a paper on women's emancipation. It is as if an essay on the black liberation movement were to end by admonishing blacks not to forget their natural rhythm, or as if Marx had warned the workers of the world not to neglect their appearance while throwing off their chains.

Markovic's concern with women's appearance merely reflects a larger cultural preoccupation. It is a fact that women in our society are regarded as having a virtual duty "to make the most of what we have." But the imperative not to neglect our appearance suggests that we can neglect it, that it is within our power to make ourselves look better — not just neater and cleaner, but prettier, and more attractive. What is presupposed by this is that we don't look good enough already, that attention to the ordinary standards of hygiene would be insufficient, that there is something wrong with us as we are. Here, the "intimations of inferiority" are clear: Not only must we continue to produce ourselves as beautiful bodies, but the bodies we have to work with are deficient to begin with. Even within an already inferiorized identity (i.e., the identity of one who is principally and most importantly a body), I turn out once more to be inferior, for the body I am to be, never sufficient unto itself, stands forever in need of plucking or painting, of slimming down or fattening up, of firming or flattening.

The foregoing examination of three modes of psychological oppression, so it appears, points up the need for an alteration in our ordinary concept of oppression. Oppression, I believe, is ordinarily conceived in too limited a fashion. This has placed undue restrictions both on our understanding of what oppression itself is and on the categories of persons we might want to classify as oppressed. Consider, for example, the following paradigmatic case of oppression:

> And the Egyptians made the children of Israel to serve with rigor; and they made their lives bitter with hard bondage, in mortar and in brick, and in all manner of service in the field; all their service wherein they made them serve, was with rigor.[15]

Here the Egyptians, one group of persons, exercise harsh dominion over the Israelites, another group of persons. It is not suggested that the Israelites, however great their sufferings, have lost their integrity and wholeness *qua* persons. But psychological oppression is dehumanizing and depersonalizing; it attacks the person in her personhood. I mean by this that the nature of psychological oppression is such that the oppressor and the oppressed alike come to doubt that the oppressed have the capacity to do the sorts of things that only persons can do, to be what persons, in the fullest sense of the term, can be. The possession of autonomy, for example, is widely thought to distinguish persons from nonpersons; but some female stereotypes, as we have seen, threaten the autonomy of women. Oppressed people might or might not be in a position to exercise their autonomy, but the psychologically oppressed may come to believe that they lack the capacity to be autonomous whatever their position.

Similarly, the creation of culture is a distinctly human function, perhaps the most human function. In its cultural life, a group is able to affirm its values and to grasp its identity in acts of self-reflection. Frequently, oppressed persons, cut off from the cultural apparatus, are denied the exercise of this function entirely. To the extent that we are able to catch sight of ourselves in the dominant culture at all, the images we see are distorted or demeaning. Finally, sexual objectification leads to the identification of those who undergo it with what is both human and not quite human—the body. Thus, psychological oppression is just what Fanon said it was—"psychic alienation"—the estrangement or separating of a person from some of the essential attributes of personhood.

Mystification surrounds these processes of human estrangement. The special modes of psychological oppression can be regarded as some of the many ways in which messages of inferiority are delivered to those who are to occupy an inferior position in society. But it is important to remember that messages of this sort are neither sent nor received in an unambiguous way. We are taught that white women and (among others) black men and women are deficient in those capacities that distinguish persons from nonpersons, but at the same time we are assured that we are persons after all. *Of course* women are persons; *of course* blacks are human beings. Who but the lunatic fringe would deny it? The Antillean Negro, Fanon is fond of repeating, is a *Frenchman.* The official ideology announces with conviction that "all men are created equal"; and in spite of the suspect way in which this otherwise noble assertion is phrased, we women learn that they mean to include us after all.

It is itself psychologically oppressive both to believe and at the same time not to believe that one is inferior—in other words, to believe a contradiction. Lacking an analysis of the larger system of social relations which produced it, one can only make sense of this contradiction in two ways. First, while accepting in some quite formal sense the proposition that "all men are created equal," I can believe, inconsistently, what my oppressors have always believed: that some types of persons are less equal than others. I may then live out my membership in my sex or race in *shame;* I am "only a woman" or "just a nigger." Or, somewhat more consistently, I may reject entirely the belief that my disadvantage is generic; but having still to account for it somehow, I may locate the cause squarely within myself, a bad destiny of an entirely private sort—a character flaw, an "inferiority complex," or a neurosis.

Many oppressed persons come to regard themselves as uniquely unable to satisfy normal criteria of psychological health or moral adequacy. To believe that my inferiority is a function of the kind of person I am may make me ashamed of being one of *this* kind. On the other hand, a lack I share with many others just because of an accident of birth would be unfortunate indeed, but at least I would not have to regard myself as having failed uniquely to measure up to standards that people like myself are expected to meet. It should be pointed out, however, that both of these "resolutions"—the ascription of one's inferiority to idiosyncratic or else to generic causes—produces a "poor self-image," a bloodless term of the behavioral sciences that refers to a very wide variety of possible ways to suffer.[16]

To take one's oppression to be an inherent flaw of birth, or of psychology, is to have what Marxists have characterized as "false consciousness." Systematically deceived as we are about the nature and origin of our unhappiness, our struggles are directed inward toward the self, or toward other similar selves in whom we may see our deficiencies mirrored, not outward upon those social forces responsible for our predicament. Like the psychologically disturbed, the psychologically oppressed often lack a viable identity. Frequently we are unable to make sense of our own impulses or feelings, not only because our drama of fragmentation gets played out on an inner psychic stage, but because we are forced to find our way about in a world which presents itself to us in a masked and deceptive fashion. Regarded as persons, yet depersonalized, we are treated by our society the way the parents of some schizophrenics are said by R. D. Laing to treat their children — professing love at the very moment they shrink from their children's touch.

In sum, then, to be psychologically oppressed is to be caught in the double bind of a society which both affirms my human status and at the same time bars me from the exercise of many of those typically human functions that bestow this status. To be denied an autonomous choice of self, forbidden cultural expression, and condemned to the immanence of mere bodily being is to be cut off from the sorts of activities that define what it is to be human. A person whose being has been subjected to these cleavages may be described as "alienated." Alienation in any form causes a rupture within the human person, an estrangement from self, a "splintering of human nature into a number of misbegotten parts."[17] Any adequate theory of the nature and varieties of human alienation, then, must encompass psychological oppression — or, to use Fanon's term once more, "psychic alienation."

Much has been written about alienation, but it is Marx's theory of alienation that speaks most compellingly to the concerns of feminist political theory. Alienation for Marx is primarily the alienation of labor. What distinguishes human beings from animals is "labor" — for Marx, the free, conscious, and creative transformation of nature in accordance with human needs. But under capitalism, workers are alienated in production, estranged from the products of their labor, from their own productive activity, and from their fellow workers.

Human productive activity, according to Marx, is "objectified" in its products. What this means is that we are able to grasp ourselves reflectively primarily in the things we have produced; human needs and powers become concrete "in their products as the amount and type of change which their exercise has brought about."[18] But in capitalist production, the capitalist has a right to appropriate what workers have produced. Thus, the product goes to augment capital, where it becomes part of an alien force exercising power over those who produced it. An "objectification" or extension of the worker's self, the product is split off from this self and turned against it. But workers are alienated not only from the products they produce but from their own laboring activity as well, for labor under capitalism is not, as labor should be, an occasion for human self-realization but mere drudgery which "mortifies the body and ruins the mind."[19] The worker's labor "is therefore not voluntary, but coerced; it is forced labor. It is therefore not the satisfaction of a need; it is merely a means to satisfy needs external to it."[20] When the free and creative productive activity that should define human functioning is reduced to a mere means to sustain life, to "forced labor," workers suffer fragmentation and loss of self. Since labor is the most characteristic human life activity, to be alienated from one's own labor is to be estranged from oneself.

In many ways, psychic alienation and the alienation of labor are profoundly alike. Both involve a splitting off of human functions from the human person, a forbidding of activities thought to be essential to a fully human existence. Both subject the individual to fragmentation and impoverishment. Alienation is not a condition into which someone might stumble by accident; it has come both to the victim of psychological oppression and to the alienated worker from without, as a usurpation by someone else of what is, by rights, *not his to usurp.*[21] Alienation occurs in each case when activities which not only belong to the domain of the self but define, in large measure, the proper functioning of this self, fall under the control of others. To be a victim of alienation is to have a part of one's being stolen by another. Both psychic alienation and the alienation of labor might be regarded as varieties of alienated productivity. From this perspective, cultural domination would be the estrangement or alienation of production in the cultural sphere; while the subjective effects of stereotyping as well as the self-objectification that regularly accompanies sexual objectification could be interpreted as an alienation in the production of one's own person.

All the modes of oppression—psychological, political, and economic—and the kinds of alienation they generate serve to maintain a vast system of privilege—privilege of race, of sex, and of class. Every mode of oppression within the system has its own part to play, but each serves to support and to maintain the others. Thus, for example, the assault on the self-esteem of white women and of black persons of both sexes prepares us for the historic role that a disproportionate number of us are destined to play within the process of production: that of a cheap or reserve labor supply. Class oppression, in turn, encourages those who are somewhat higher in the hierarchies of race or gender to cling to a false sense of superiority—a poor compensation indeed. Because of the interlocking character of the modes of oppression, I think it highly unlikely that any form of oppression will disappear entirely until the system of oppression as a whole is overthrown.

Notes

Several works that have appeared since the publication of this paper may interest the reader. Linda Tschirhart Sanford and Mary Ellen Donovan have written a lucid, detailed, and powerful account of the many sources of women's low self-esteem: *Women and Self-Esteem* (New York: Doubleday, 1984). Also recommended is Ann Wilson Schaef, *Women's Reality* (New York: Harper and Row, 1981). In *Common Differences: Conflicts in Black and White Feminist Perspectives* (New York: Anchor/Doubleday, 1981), Gloria Joseph and Jill Lewis examine differences, including psychological differences, between black and white women. Linda LeMoncheck has written an analytically acute monograph on the subject of sexual objectification, *Dehumanizing Women: Treating Persons as Sex Objects* (Totowa, N.J.: Rowman and Allanheld, 1985); she subjects my own view of sexual objectification to an extended discussion and critique. The exclusion of women in our society from cultural production, especially from art, literature, and music, has, of course, never been total. But since I wrote this paper, there

has been an enormous outpouring of work in these fields by creative women seeking very self-consciously to express a female and often a feminist perspective. Some of this work has reached a mass audience, for example, the art of Judy Chicago, the music of Holly Near and Tracey Chapman, and the novels of Toni Morrison, Marilyn French, Alice Walker, Marge Piercy, Erica Jong, and Gloria Naylor.

1. Frantz Fanon, *Black Skins, White Masks* (New York: Grove Press, 1967), p. 12.

2. Ibid.

3. For an excellent comparison of the concepts of exploitation and oppression, see Judith Farr Tormey, "Exploitation, Oppression and Self-Sacrifice," in *Women and Philosophy,* ed. Carol C. Gould and Marx W. Wartofsky (New York: G. P. Putnam's Sons, 1976), pp. 206–221.

4. Joyce Mitchell Cook, paper delivered at Philosophy and the Black Liberation Struggle Conference, University of Illinois, Chicago Circle, November 19–20, 1970.

5. Fanon's phenomenology of oppression, however, is almost entirely a phenomenology of the oppression of colonized *men.* He seems unaware of the ways in which the oppression of women by their men in the societies he examines is itself similar to the colonization of natives by Europeans. Sometimes, as in *A Dying Colonialism* (New York: Grove Press, 1968), he goes so far as to defend the clinging to oppressive practices, such as the sequestration of women in Moslem countries, as an authentic resistance by indigenous people to Western cultural intrusion. For a penetrating critique of Fanon's attitude toward women, see Barbara Burris, "Fourth World Manifesto," in *Radical Feminism,* ed. A. Koedt, E. Levine, and A. Rapone (New York: Quadrangle, 1973), pp. 322–357.

6. I have in mind Abraham Maslow's concept of autonomy, a notion which has the advantage of being neutral as regards the controversy between free will and determinism. For Maslow, the sources of behavior of autonomous or "psychologically free" individuals are more internal than reactive:

   Such people become far more self-sufficient and self-contained. The determinants which govern them are now primarily inner ones. . . . They are the laws of their own inner nature, their potentialities and capacities, their talents, their latent resources, their creative impulses, their needs to know themselves and to become more and more integrated and unified, more and more aware of what they really are, of what they really want, of what their call or vocation or fate is to be. *Toward a Psychology of Being,* 2d ed. [New York: D. Van Nostrand Co., 1968], p. 35).

   It would be absurd to suggest that most men are autonomous in this sense of the term. Nevertheless, insofar as there are individuals who resemble this portrait, I think it likelier that they will be men than women — at least white women. I think it likely that more white men than white women *believe* themselves to be autonomous; this belief, even if false, is widely held, and this in itself has implications that are important to consider. Whatever the facts may be in regard to men's lives, the point to remember is this: women have been thought to have neither the capacity nor the right to aspire to an ideal of autonomy, an ideal to which there accrues, whatever its relation to mental health, an enormous social prestige.

7. Many feminists would object vigorously to my claim that there has been no female culture (see, e.g., Burris, "Fourth World Manifesto"). I am not claiming that women have had no enclaves within the dominant culture, that we have never made valuable contributions to the larger culture, or even that we have never dominated any avenue of cultural expression — one would have to think only of the way in which women have dominated certain forms of folk art (e.g., quilting). What I am claiming is that none of this adds up to a "culture," in the sense in which we speak of Jewish culture, Arapesh culture, or Afro-American culture. Further, the fact that many women are today engaged in the self-conscious attempt to create a female culture testifies, I think, to the situation regarding culture being essentially as I describe it.

8. The best-known modern theory of this type is, of course, Freud's. He maintains that the relative absence of women from the higher culture is the consequence of a lesser ability to sublimate libidinal drives. See "Femininity" in *New Introductory Lectures in Psychoanalysis* (New York: W. W. Norton, 1933).

9. I take it that something like this forms the backdrop to the enjoyment of the average movie. It is daunting to consider the magnitude of the task of neutralization or transformation of hostile cultural messages that must fall constantly to the average female, nonwhite or even working class white male TV watcher or moviegoer. The pleasure we continue to take in cultural products that may disparage us remains, at least to me something of a mystery.

10. There might be some objection to regarding ordinary sexual relations as involving sexual objectification, since this use of the term seems not to jibe with its use in more ordinary contexts. For Hegel, Marx, and Sartre, "objectification" is an important moment in the dialectic of consciousness. My decision to treat ordinary sexual relations or even sexual desire alone as involving some objectification is based on a desire to remain within this tradition. Further, Sartre's phenomenology of sexual desire in *Being and Nothingness* (New York: Philosophical Library, 1966) draws heavily on a concept of objectification in an unusually com-

pelling description of the experienced character of that state:

> The caress by realizing the Other's incarnation reveals to me my own incarnation; that is, I make myself flesh in order to impel the Other to realize for-herself and for-me her own flesh, and my caresses cause my flesh to be born for me in so far as it is for the Other flesh causing her to be born as flesh. I make her enjoy my flesh through her flesh in order to compel her to feel herself flesh. And so possession truly appears as a double reciprocal incarnation. (p. 508)

What I call "objectification," Sartre here calls "incarnation," a refinement not necessary for my purposes. What he calls "sadism" is incarnation without reciprocity. Most of my examples of sexual objectification would fall into the latter category.

11. Fanon, *Black Skin, White Masks*, p. 177. Eldridge Cleaver sounds a similar theme in *Soul on Ice* (New York: Dell, 1968). The archetypal white man in American society, for Cleaver, is the "Omnipotent Administrator," the archetypal black man the "Super-Masculine Menial."

12. P. 180.

13. Erik Erikson, "Inner and Outer Space: Reflections on Womanhood," *Daedalus,* Vol. 93, 1961, pp. 582–606.

14. Mihailo Markovic, "Women's Liberation and Human Emancipation," in *Women and Philosophy,* pp. 165–166. In spite of this lapse and some questionable opinions concerning the nature of female sexuality, Markovic's paper is a most compelling defense of the claim that the emancipation of women cannot come about under capitalism.

15. Exod. 1:13–14.

16. The available clinical literature on the psychological effects of social inferiority supports this claim. See William H. Grier and Price M. Cobbs, *Black Rage* (New York: Grosset & Dunlap, 1969); Pauline Bart, "Depression in Middle-Aged Women," in *Women in Sexist Society,* ed. Vivian Gornick and Barbara Moran (New York: New American Library, 1971), pp. 163–186; also Phyllis Chesler, *Women and Madness* (New York: Doubleday, 1972).

17. Bertell Ollman, *Alienation: Marx's Conception of Man in Capitalist Society* (London and New York: Cambridge University Press, 1971), p. 135.

18. Ibid. p. 143.

19. Karl Marx, *The Economic and Philosophical Manuscripts of 1844,* ed. Dirk J. Struik (New York: International Publishers, 1964), p. 111.

20. Ibid.

21. The use of the masculine possessive pronoun is deliberate.

TOWARD AN UNDERSTANDING OF
FEMINISMO HISPANO IN THE U.S.A.

Ada Maria Isasi-Diaz

Ada Maria Isasi-Diaz describes the invisibility experienced by feminist Hispanas in the United States. She argues that overcoming this invisibility will require conscious effort by both feminist Hispanas and non-Hispana feminists. Here, the values of truth and empathy play a crucial role. (Source: Reprinted from Women's Consciousness, Women's Conscience, *ed. by Barbara Hilkert Andolsen, Christine E. Gudorf, and Mary D. Pellauer, 1985, Winston Press, Minneapolis.)*

How more invisible than invisible can you be? And yet there is a quality of invisible invisibility which many of us women, feminists, of other than the dominant culture have. A *Feminista Hispana* is at home nowhere. Invisible invisibility has to do with people not even knowing that they do not know you. As *Feministas Hispanas* we are so irrelevant that the mind constructs needed to think about us do not exist. Society at large thinks of us as Hispanics and the majority of Hispanics think of us as women. Only among our very few is our name understood: FEMINISTA HISPANA.

In the act of naming ourselves we are born. Our lives are a constant struggle to be called by name. We have not gone any further than that. We name ourselves because we are, but others cannot even imagine that we exist and, therefore, refuse to call us by name. For me this constitutes the highest form of oppression: others so define you that they refuse to recognize the way you define yourself. And, it is the task of all peoples of good will to recognize evil, fight against it, hope for good and work to bring it about. This is what makes us human for love cannot exist without justice and, in our world today, justice does not exist without people.

In this article I explore the four worlds in which the life of *Feministas Hispanas* unfolds. This will provide a framework to understand the invisible invisibility, the double burden of racial/ethnic diminishment and sexism that we endure, a burden which is often a triple one, for the feminization of poverty is a reality principally among racial/ethnic women.

However, before discussing these four worlds of the *Feminista Hispana*, I would like to propose that to understand what follows, the kind of understanding that leads to a conversion which precipitates action, there exist two prerequisites: commitment to truth and empathy.[1]

Commitment to Truth

In our world today there exists great awareness of justice and injustice. People are quick to claim their rights, to name their oppressors, to gather support and struggle for what is right. It is becoming increasingly hard to make someone understand that they are oppressors. It comes easy to claim we are oppressed, but we seldom bow our heads, accept the truth, and recognize our participation in oppressing others. We do not understand that being oppressed and being an oppressor are not mutually exclusive. Our commitment to justice makes it almost impossible for us to recognize our participation in systems that benefit us at the expense of someone else. Only our commitment to truth can help us to accept that the intricacies of our modern society often cause us to be oppressors while at the same time, without any doubt, being oppressed. Truth requires us to accept reality, while justice demands of us to struggle against oppression. One cannot exist without the other.

Empathy

Certain kinds of understanding require knowledge, intellectual comprehension, experiments, and even debates. The kind of understanding required for conversion necessitates more than anything else, empathy. Empathy is the ability of the heart to feel with the other person. It requires that we open ourselves not only at the intellectual level, but especially at the emotional level. To empathize is to risk, because it necessitates our being vulnerable.

Empathy does not ask that you feel the way I do, think the way I do, act the way I do. But empathy does demand that we listen with the heart. It is not only a matter of respecting what others say and do, who they are. Empathy asks that you seriously consider that what is true and good for others might well be true and good for you. That is the only way that new elements can enrich our society, our movement, for if not, those elements become mere appendages that can quietly and quickly be disposed of instead of becoming intrinsic parts of what is normative for all.

"You Came Here, You Learn Our Language"

He politely listened to me and then, embarrassed, while continuing to empty trash cans into the dumpster, he sheepishly answered me, "Ay don espik inglish." When I repeated my question in Spanish, his eyes lit up, and after telling me he had no idea where the address I was looking for was, he said to me, "*Ven aca, chica, tu eres cubana?*" When he realized I was a Cuban like him, you would have thought we were long-time friends! And we were. In Cuba we might have never thought that but in a foreign land, both of us being Cubans made us friends!

There is no need for me to delineate here the multifaceted oppression that Hispanics suffer in this country. Our lack of ability to speak the language makes education, the golden ladder in this society up to now, a very difficult road to travel. Many of us arrive here without a financial base. Starting over is an everyday affair. To attain positions of power, economic well-being, and prestige are almost impossibilities for us, simply because we do not belong to the dominant culture.

There is a much more subtle oppression, however, that few understand or talk about. That is the oppression we suffer when those values, traditions, and customs that are intrinsic to being Hispanic are not valued, are not remembered, are not celebrated. In our attempt to fit in this society, we are constantly asked to become assimilated, to become Americanized. Do

you know at what expense? To fit in this society means to accept the competitiveness intrinsic to this system which works directly against and to the detriment of our sense of community. To become Americanized means to adopt a "keeping up with the Joneses" mentality that requires a high degree of individualization. But we Hispanics value the person — the person, however, understood as a member of a family, of a community! To make it in this country we have to hide our emotions, and as we do, we die a thousand deaths. To be accepted as an American means having to give up our hyperbole and emotional binges, thus subscribing to an even flow of living which little by little kills our spirits.

We Hispanics feel oppressed in this society when we hear ourselves defined in negative terms: nondominant culture, minority, marginalized people. The oppression we suffer does not even have a name. We are included under the term racism, a word that only applies to us by extension: racism is oppression based on skin color and only lately has it come to mean also the systemic oppression of those belonging to a culture other than the dominant one. The oppression we Hispanics suffer has to do with struggling to explain what you mean only to realize that they will not understand because your patterns of conceptualization, your points of reference, your value system and loyalties are more foreign to them than the language your mother taught you — which they do not value enough to learn. "You came here, you learn our language," they say, so easily shrugging off the responsibility for the economic and political situations in our countries which obliged us to become refugees, for which they are at least partially responsible. And we then suffer the frustration not only of not being understood, but of not being able to influence actions.

Our oppression, our invisible invisibility as Hispanics is that sense you begin to have after you are here a short while that this society deals with you the way they do with a circus: they love our *mariachis, salsa, arroz con pollo, bacaladitos, margaritas* — we can really entertain them. With the oppressed of ancient times we say:

Beside the streams of Babylon
we sat and wept
at the memory of Zion,

leaving our harps
hanging on the poplars there.
For we had been asked
to sing to our captors,
to entertain those who had carried us off:
"Sing," they said
"Some hymns of Zion."

How could we sing
one of Yahweh's hymns
in a pagan country? . . .

— (Psalm 137)

The oppression and the invisible invisibility that are our lot as Hispanics in this country are the result of having the dominant culture's prejudices as the accepted and imposed societal norm.

For us *Feministas Hispanas,* to work against oppression is to work for liberation. We do not seek equal opportunities, we do not seek for success within the societal structures of this system. This system, and most probably the same can be said of the societal systems from which we come, functions in such a way that for us or for any group to be successful, other groups have to be oppressed. Because we believe that no one can be free until everyone is free, what we *Feministas Hispanas* seek is to participate in the community of struggle against all oppressive systems. This all-encompassing sense of liberation for which we struggle is a significant contribution that we *Feministas Hispanas* make to our own Hispanic people and to this society.

Horizontal Violence

The Anglo culture even sets up our bouts: we fight the blacks, we fight the indigenous people, we fight the Asians and Pacific people in America. Horizontal violence becomes intrinsic to survival and in the end, the winner is the loser; the only winner is the dominant culture which keeps us alive for its own benefit. If when you win you sense you have lost, then you know what invisible invisibility is all about.

Our black sisters and brothers have long struggled for justice for themselves. In the women's movement *Feministas Hispanas* often join hands with our black sisters in the struggle for inclusivity at all levels. But in the movement as well as in society at large, we are often pitted against each other. "Minority representation" often means either a black or a Hispanic. The term racism, as I already mentioned, further contributes to the invisibility of Hispanics. Limited funds for "participation of minorities" puts us in a position of vying against each other.

Compared to us Hispanics, and comparisons are always extremely limited and limiting, our black sisters are ahead of us in the struggle. Because they have been here longer than we have, consciousness of the oppression they suffer is more common in society than understanding what we Hispanics have to struggle against. Though indeed the advances made towards civil rights in this country are nothing to brag about, awareness of racism is at least a first step which has cost the black community long years of suffering, organizing, struggling, and dying.

Oppressed people need to know as much as possible about their oppressors in order to survive. Because the black women have been dealing with the dominant culture and race in this country longer than we have, they know their way around the streets of survival much better than we do. This is true not only in such areas as the welfare system of this country. Black women also have an understanding of how to deal with a racist mentality. For us Hispanic women, many of whom have come here and not been born here, many of whom have not experienced ethnic prejudice until the ages of eighteen, twenty-five, forty — whenever we moved here — to come to understand why we are being discriminated against takes a long time. To learn how to deal with it takes even longer.

Third, Hispanic women have the extra difficulty of not being fluent in the English language. Many of us who have studied and acquired a degree are still handicapped linguistically, especially when it comes to writing. Though most probably it is as difficult for black women to be published as it is for us Hispanic women, at least the black woman has a certain competency in writing English that we Hispanic women lack. And the same is true regarding our fluency in speaking English. Though the majority of us are bilingual, our fluency in both languages tends to be limited. In any meeting others will easily express themselves more precisely than we will and, therefore, will be more easily understood.

Finally, there are certain characteristics in our Hispanic culture that place us at a disadvantage in our dealings with black women as much as with Anglo women. To point out just two of them: in our culture, when attacked in public, we do not defend ourselves. Our concept of honor is a most important factor in our behavior. If you attack me, you have blemished my honor. My attitude will tend to be not to respond to you—whoever attacks me is not worthy of a response. Since duels are a thing of the past, my attitude will be to delete from my life anyone who has offended my honor by attacking me. Our silence is many times taken as timidity or maybe even acceptance. Our silence is instead our way of saying that, faithful to who we are, we do not believe it honorable to engage the person attacking us.

Another cultural trait which many times works against us is our indirect, circuitous way of dealing with people and problems. Two things are operative in this trait: first, by not dealing in such a direct way you allow the other person a way out. Though "saving face" is not as strong a cultural trait of Hispanics as it is of other cultures, it is more operative for us than it seems to be for both Anglos and blacks. Second, because emotions are such an important element of our understanding and behavior, we need more time to explain, to talk about things. We cannot go to the heart of the matter in one big jump, because the emotional element tends to make circumstances more complex, and therefore, I believe, more human.

Though undoubtedly Hispanics also have differences with other cultural/ethnic groups, up to now the majority of the so-called minority women that I have dealt with in the feminist movement have been black women. *Feministas Hispanas* have to understand what is at work in our dealings with our black sisters. Black women also have to realize and respect that we are different, that we wish our differences to be recognized and respected, and that we want to represent ourselves, to speak for ourselves and not to be included under the term racism as an afterthought, not to be referred to as women of color for many of us are white with a tinge of olive-brownness and a twist in our tongues that makes us Hispanic. Only

we, women who suffer the day-to-day oppression of racism, ethnic prejudice, classism, and sexism, can negate victory to the dominant culture by refusing to engage in a horizontal violence which makes losers of all of us.

Feministas Hispanas and White Feminists

You sit at a meeting with women friends, with feminists who are quick to call you sister, and you sense the tension mounting every time you mention Hispanics, or ask, "What about the Hispanics?" You go home with a sense that you are crazy: they invited you to be a Hispanic presence and voice at their meetings, yet any time you bring up and insist on the particularity and specificity of *Mujer Hispana,* tensions rise. Those of you who have been present at a meeting but not visible, you know what invisible invisibility is, what it feels like. And you cringe when, with a sincerity that could move mountains, they turn to you and say, "How can we integrate Hispanic women in the feminist movement?" How do you, one of you among many of them, tell them that that question is wrong, that it increases your invisibility? Will they ever understand that it is not a matter of baking a cake? *Feminismo Hispano* is not one more ingredient to add. *Feminismo Hispano* is to be there as a motivating force, at the level of conceptualization, understanding, definition, planning, or the feminist movement in the U.S.A. will continuously betray itself.

Of course white feminists know oppression and their sufferings often parallel those of *Feministas Hispanas.* We are not trying by any means to engage here in a dispute of which kind of oppression is more oppressive. That is exactly the mind-set that leads to horizontal violence. But without negating their oppression, white feminists have to seriously consider three facts: the possibility of their personal ethnic prejudices and racism; the definition of goals and strategies of the feminist movement, which in seeking for equality rather than for liberation, necessitates an oppressed group which will indeed be the ethnic/racial groups; finally, the lack of ability of the movement up to now to attract ethnic/racial groups is possibly due to the sense we have that white feminists want us to join their movement, instead of asking us to participate in redefining the movement so we could indeed call it ours.

Concretely, *Feministas Hispanas* ask of white feminists:[2]

—to assume responsibility for the systematic analysis of ethnic prejudice and racism, instead of depending on us to raise the issue and aggressively pursue it.

—out of a sense of justice and commitment to the process of liberation, white feminists should have a preferential option for us and all ethnic women and women of color. Such a preferential option has to be translated into concrete actions such as facilitating our attendance at meetings, providing translations when necessary, creating an environment in which the culture and personality of Hispanic women can be fully expressed and valued.

—we urge white feminists to seriously pursue a study of Hispanic culture so that our dealings with each one can be characterized by a sense of mutual empowerment and enabling which can only be born out of knowing each other, mutual acceptance, admiration, and respect.

—finally, we beg of white feminists to understand that the double and triple oppression we live under demands of us to participate equally in the struggle against ethnic/racial prejudice as in the struggle against sexism. Furthermore, we ask for their support and solidarity at the level of action in combating racial and ethnic prejudice.

Hispanic and Feminist: "Si Se Puede."

Invisible invisibility is what you feel when you sit among your own Hispanic people and, more and more, you feel like a stranger because they think of you as a threat. The male controlled and defined Hispanic movement in this country sees feminism and Hispanicness as mutually exclusive. Those of us *Feministas Hispanas* articulate enough to express our be-liefs, values, concerns, are called and seen as traitors because we refuse to participate in the struggle from any perspective other than one both feminist and Hispanic. Years back a black woman shared with us what she tells her black brothers: "I am not going to fight now against the whites for my rights as a black and then down the road have to fight against you for my rights as a woman. No way, I'm doing it both at the same time." That is the message of the *Feminista Hispana* to the Hispanic males in this country.

I believe that the fear and mistrust Hispanic males have of us are due to the following: first, they are threatened by a feminist stance just like any other male of any other culture or any other racial group is. Second, males of oppressed groups tend to vent the frustration they feel due to the prejudice they suffer at work and in society at large by treating those who historically have been "under" them the same way they are treated by those who have power over them. Finally, I do believe that the ideology of the Hispanic movement in the U.S.A. is one of equality instead of liberation. Therefore, Hispanic men do not want structural changes, but rather access to the structures of power from which they are barred at present. The sense of liberation of *Feministas Hispanas* which demands structural changes is, therefore, a threat to their understanding of what would be good for them. Of course, they "know" that what is good for them "has to be" good for all Hispanics.

Our challenge as *Feministas Hispanas* is to continue to find ways of living out our commitment to our people without having to betray our feminist understandings. Meanwhile, we challenge Hispanic men to understand that their unwillingness to see the interconnections between racist/ethnic prejudice, classism, and sexism makes us, *Feministas Hispanas,* women without a people. It is with deep regret and pain that we *Feministas Hispanas* at times have to admit that we are more sisters to feminists of other races and cultures than we are sisters to Hispanic men. The injustice that Hispanic men do to us by repeatedly demanding us to choose will continue to work against the liberation of all Hispanic people. Unless both Hispanic males and *Feministas Hispanas* engage in serious dialogue, history will judge us harshly for having been unable to join strengths to fight oppression.

Conclusion

The inability to stop or diminish the oppressive structures of society which make of our living a mere surviving, the bewilderment of being pitted against other oppressed sisters and brothers, the pain of being rejected by those you, *Feministas Hispanas,* have birthed, nurtured, cared for, the demand from the Anglo feminist that you participate, but, oh! participate the way they want, when they want — that is what invisible invisibility, oppression, is all about.

Our situation as *Feministas Hispanas* is not an enviable one, but for centuries oppressed people have managed to merely survive in the eyes of the oppressors, while living quite fully within their communities. Our most urgent need, therefore, is the creation of community among ourselves, *Feministas Hispanas.* We have to create our own space to be, our own support network, our own viable means of holding each other accountable. Neither the white feminists nor the Hispanic males are going to freely offer us the opportunity to do it. We must grasp the moment at hand and create as Hispanic women have done throughout history a sense of *familia* among ourselves. Justice to ourselves demands it; the memory of the oppression and struggle for liberation of Hispanic women down the ages makes it our duty. But above all, the cry that touches our hearts is the cry of our Hispanic people here in the U.S.A. To negate our feminism or our Hispanicness is to betray the trust that our people have always had in us. As *Feministas Hispanas* let us con-tinue to birth ourselves confident in the fullness of our womanhood and our deep-rootedness in our Hispanic culture and heritage.[3]

Notes

1. I would like to dedicate this article to so many people. Please know that if you are not mentioned by name it does not mean that it is not dedicated to you. First of all I wish to dedicate this to my mother, Nena. A woman of fierce spirit and unwavering determination, she taught me to demand much of myself and to struggle for what I believe. I also want to dedicate this to the four Hispanic women in the U.S.A. with whom I have shared in a significant way my struggle as *Feminista Hispana.* They are Yolanda Tarango, Margarita Castañada, Teresita Basso and Olga Villa-Parra. *Gracias, hermanas.* Thirdly, I want to remember five Anglo women who struggle unceasingly within the feminist movement against racism and with whom we can all count to have and exercise a preferential option for us Hispanic women: Mary Pellauer, Rosemary Radford Ruether, Rosalie Muschal-Reinhardt, Beverley Harrison and Marjorie Tuite. Finally I wish to acknowledge my debt of gratitude to two black feminists that have been true sisters to me and inspired me to better understand and to write about the struggle of the *Feminista Hispana:* Delores Williams and Katie Cannon. *VIVA LA HERMANDAD!*

2. Yolanda Tarango and I worked together at drafting some of the following recommendations to white feminists in the summer of 1982.

3. I realize that this article is incomplete without attempting to explain those dispositions and qualities of the *Feminista Hispana* which characterize her life and struggle. Such a study will be forthcoming.

Classism

THE NATURE OF CAPITALISM

William H. Shaw

William H. Shaw provides an analysis and brief historical overview of capitalism. He discusses several defenses of capitalism and then turns to moral objections to capitalism: that it leads to inequality, that it treats humans as mere economic creatures, that it breeds oligopolies, that it is not really competitive, and that it leads to the exploitation and alienation of workers. (Source: From Business Ethics *by William H. Shaw. Copyright © 1991 by Wadsworth Inc. Reprinted by permission.)*

The floor of the New York Stock Exchange, the heart of American capitalism, is a noisy and often chaotic place. Now, suddenly, it was becoming eerily quiet, as if someone had turned down the volume on a television set. The hustle and bustle of traders, brokers, and clerks scurrying across the massive floor practically ceased. All eyes were glued to the computer screens hanging above the floor's seventeen trading kiosks, some of which were suddenly and inexplicably going blank. It was Monday morning, October 19, 1987, and those on the stock market floor were witnessing the beginning of what was to be called the "panic of '87," the "market meltdown," or simply "black Monday."[1]

From 10:30 a.m. until 12:30 p.m., the Dow Jones industrial average fell as fast as anyone ever thought it could. Down 50 points in fifteen minutes. Down 100

in forty-five minutes. Down 167 in an hour. Down 200 in an hour and a half. A few traders left, unable to watch. "Holy sh—," someone said softly, "I just lost a million." "There was absolute terror," reported one broker, "things were collapsing all around you." Others simply described it as a "bloodbath." It was like "looking into the abyss," said Michael Starkman, a stockbroker for thirty years, as he recalled watching the plunging figures flicker across the Quotron machine in his Beverly Hills office.

By the end of the day stocks had lost almost a quarter of their value, twice as much as in the famous crash of October 1929, which had helped pave the way for the Great Depression. The loss of market value of U.S. securities was staggering. An incredible $500 billion blown in a single day. How did it happen? What did it mean? In the aftermath, experts debated the causes of the crash and its likely economic repercussions. Lots of opinions were aired, but nobody seemed to agree. One thing was clear, though. Wall Street's bust had quickly reverberated around the globe, with stocks tumbling in markets as far away as London, Tokyo, Australia, and Hong Kong.

That is not surprising. Capitalism is a worldwide system. Multinational firms operate without regard for traditional political boundaries, and the economies of capitalist nations are intricately interconnected. But what exactly is the nature of the economic system called capitalism? What is its underlying economic philosophy? What has it accomplished and what are its prospects for the future? This chapter examines these and related questions.

Looking back in history, one must definitely credit capitalism with helping to break the constraints of medieval feudalism, which had severely limited individual possibilities for improvement. In place of a stifling economic system, capitalism offered opportunities for those blessed with imagination, an ability to plan, and a willingness to work. In short, capitalism increased the possibilities for individualism and, many would argue, continues to do so.

Capitalism must also be credited with enhancing the numbers and diversity of goods beyond Adam Smith's wildest dreams. It has increased our ownership of material goods and our standard of living and has converted our cities from modest bazaars into treasure troves of dazzling merchandise.

In the light of such accomplishments and the acculturation process that tends to glorify them, it is possible to overlook capitalism's theoretical and operational problems, which have serious moral import. This chapter attempts to identify some of these problems and their moral implications. It provides some basic historical and conceptual categories for understanding the socioeconomic framework within which business transactions occur and moral issues arise. . . .

Capitalism

Capitalism can be defined ideally as an economic system in which the major portion of production and distribution is in private hands, operating under what is termed a profit or market system. The U.S. economy is the world's leading capitalistic economy. All manufacturing firms are privately owned, including those that produce military hardware for the government. The same applies to banks, insurance companies, and most transportation companies. All businesses— small, medium, and large—are also privately owned, as are power companies. With the exception of government expenditures for such things as health, education, welfare, highways, and military equipment,

no central governing body dictates to these private owners what or how much of anything will be produced. For example, officials at Ford, Chrysler, and General Motors set their own production goals according to anticipated consumer demand.

The private ownership and market aspects of capitalism contrast with its polar opposite, socialism. Ideally, *socialism* is an economic system characterized by public ownership of property and a planned economy. Under socialism a society's equipment is not owned by individuals (capitalists) but by public bodies. Socialism depends primarily on centralized planning rather than on the market system for both its overall allocation of resources and its distribution of income; crucial economic decisions are made not by individuals but by government. In the Soviet Union, for example, government agencies decide the number of automobiles—including models, styles, and colors— to be produced each year. Top levels of government formulate production and cost objectives, which are then converted to specific production quotas and budgets that individual plant managers must follow.

A hybrid economic system, advocated by some socialists and approximated by Yugoslavia, is *worker control socialism*.[2] Individual firms respond to a market in acquiring the necessary factors of production and in deciding what to produce. The work force of each enterprise controls the enterprise (although it may elect or hire managers to oversee day-to-day operations), and the profits accrue to the workers as a group to divide in whatever manner they agree upon. But although the workers manage their factories, the capital assets of each enterprise are owned by society as a whole and not by private individuals.

Historical Background of Capitalism

What we call capitalism did not fully emerge until the Renaissance, the rich outpouring of art, science, and philosophy in Europe during the fifteenth and sixteenth centuries. Prior to the Renaissance, business exchanges in medieval Europe were organized through guilds, which were associations of persons of the same trade, pursuit, or interests. People joined guilds for much the same reasons they have always joined clubs, groups, and organizations: for self-protection, mutual aid, maintenance of standards, furtherance of common goals.

Today if you want a pair of shoes, you head for a shoe store. There you find an array of shoes. If nothing strikes your fancy, you set out for another shop, and perhaps another, until at last you find what you want. Or still disappointed, you might tell the store clerk to order you a pair from "the manufacturer." You certainly wouldn't tell the clerk to have someone make you a pair of shoes.

Under the guild organization, shoemakers, who were also shoe sellers, made shoes only to fill orders. If they had no orders, they made no shoes. The shoemaker's sole economic function was to make shoes for people when they wanted them. His labor allowed him to maintain himself, not advance his station in life. When the shoemaker died, his business went with him — unless he had a son to inherit and carry on the enterprise. As for shoe quality and cost, the medieval shopper could generally count on getting a good pair of shoes at a fair price, since the shoemakers' guild strictly controlled quality and price.

Weaving was another big medieval trade. In fact, in the fourteenth century weaving was the leading industry in the German town of Augsburg. Little wonder, then, that an enterprising young man named Anton Fugger became a weaver when he settled there in 1380. But young Anton had ambitions that stretched far beyond the limits of the weaving trade and the handicraft guild system. And they were grandly realized, for within three short generations a family of simple weavers was transformed into a great German banking dynasty.[3]

Discontent with being a weaver, Anton Fugger began collecting and selling the products of other weavers. Soon he was employing lots of weavers, paying them for their labor, and selling their products as his own. His son, Jacob Fugger I, continued the business, which was expanded by Jacob Fugger II, the foremost capitalist of the Renaissance. Under his direction, the family's interests expanded into metals and textiles. Jacob Fugger II also lent large sums of money to the Hapsburg emperors to finance their wars, among other things. In return, he obtained monopoly rights on silver and copper ores, which he then traded. When Fugger bought the mines themselves, he had acquired all the props necessary to erect an extraordinary financial dynasty.

Like latter-day titans of American industry, Fugger employed thousands of workers and paid them wages, controlled all his products from raw material to market, set his own quality standards, and charged whatever the traffic would bear. In one brief century, what was once a handicraft inseparable from the craftsperson had become a company that existed outside any family members. What had once motivated Anton Fugger — maintenance of his station in life — had given way to gain for gain's sake, the so-called *profit motive*. Under Jacob Fugger II, the company amassed profits, a novel concept, that well exceeded the needs of the Fuggers. And the profits were measured not in goods or in land but in money.

Capitalism, like any other economic system, has undergone changes since then.[4] For example, the kind of capitalism that emerged in the Fuggers' time is often termed *mercantile capitalism*, which was based on mutual dependence between state and commercial interests. Implicit in mercantile capitalism are the beliefs that national good and merchant profit are complementary, that money is wealth, that political unification requires strong government, and that the role of government is to provide laws and economic policies designed to promote national supremacy.

In America in the period after the Civil War, *industrial capitalism* emerged, which is associated with the development of large-scale industry. The confluence of many post-war factors produced industrial expansion in America, including a sound financial base, the technology for mass production, expanding markets for cheaply manufactured goods, and a large and willing labor force. Exploiting these fortuitous conditions was a group of hard-driving, visionary entrepreneurs called robber barons by their critics and captains of industry by their supporters: Cornelius Vanderbilt, Cyrus McCormick, Andrew Carnegie, John D. Rockefeller, John Gates, and others.

As industrialization increased, so did the size and power of business. The private fortunes of a few individuals could no longer underwrite the accelerated growth of business activity. The large sums of capital necessary could be raised only through a corporate form of business, in which risk and potential profit were distributed among numerous investors.

As competition intensified, an industry's survival came to depend on its financial strength to reduce prices and either eliminate or absorb competition. To shore up their assets, industries engaged in *financial capitalism,* characterized by pools, trusts, holding companies, and an interpenetration of banking, insurance, and industrial interests. Hand in hand with this development, the trend continued toward larger and larger corporations, controlling more and more of the country's economic capacity.

The economic and political challenges of the Great Depression of the 1930s helped to usher in still another phase of capitalism, often called *state welfare capitalism,* in which government plays an active role in regulating economic activities in an effort to smooth out the boom-and-bust pattern of the business cycle. In addition, government programs like Social Security and unemployment insurance seek to enhance the welfare of the work force, and legislation legitimizes the existence of trade unions. Today state welfare capitalism prevails. Conservative politicians sometimes advocate less government control of business, but in reality the governments of all capitalist countries are deeply involved in the management of their economies.

While the study of capitalism's evolution is best left to economic historians, it is important to keep in mind capitalism's dynamic nature. There is nothing fixed and immutable about this or any other economic system; it is as susceptible to the social forces of change as any other institution. Nevertheless, the capitalism we know does have some prominent features that were evident in the earliest capitalistic businesses.

Key Features of Capitalism

Complete coverage of capitalism's features has filled many a book. Four features of particular significance here — the existence of companies, profit motive, competition, and private property — should be discussed briefly.

Companies

. . .

"It's not in the company's interests," "The company thinks that," "From the company's viewpoint," "As far as the company is concerned" — all of us have heard, perhaps even used, expressions that treat the business organization like a person or at least like a separate and distinct entity. Such personifications are not mere lapses into the figurative but bespeak a basic characteristic of capitalism: Capitalism permits the creation of companies or business organizations that exist separately from the people associated with them.

Today the big companies we're familiar with — Exxon, AT&T, Ford, IBM — are, in fact, incorporated businesses or corporations. The next chapter inspects the nature of the modern corporation, including its responsibilities and the positions of those who work inside it. Here it's enough to observe that, in the nineteenth century, Chief Justice John Marshall defined a *corporation* as "an artificial being, invisible, intangible, and existing only in the contemplation of law." Although a corporation is not something that can be seen or touched, it does have prescribed rights and legal obligations within the community. Like you or me, a corporation may enter into contracts and may sue or be sued in courts of law. It may even do things that the corporation's members disapprove of. The corporations that loom large on our economic landscape harken back to a feature of capitalism evident as early as the Fugger dynasty: the existence of the company.

Profit Motive

A second characteristic of capitalism lies in the motive of the company: to make profit. As dollar-directed and gain-motivated as our society is, most of us blithely assume that the human being is by nature an acquisitive creature who, left to his or her own devices, will pursue profit with all the instinctual vigor of a cat chasing a mouse. In fact, as economist Robert Heilbroner points out, the "profit motive, as we understand it, is a very recent phenomenon. It was foreign to the lower and middle classes of Egyptian, Greek, Roman, and medieval cultures, only scattered throughout the Renaissance times, and largely absent in most Eastern civilizations." The medieval Church taught that no Christian ought to be a merchant. "Even to our Pilgrim forefathers," Heilbroner writes, "the idea that gain ought to be a tolerable—even a useful—goal in life would have appeared as nothing short of a doctrine of the devil." Heilbroner concludes: "As a ubiquitous characteristic of society, the profit motive is as modern an invention as printing."[5]

Modern or not, *profit* in the form of money is the lifeblood of the capitalist system. Companies and capitalists alike are motivated by an insatiable appetite for more and more money profit. Indeed, the profit motive implies and reflects a critical assumption about human nature: that human beings are basically economic creatures, who recognize and are motivated by their own economic self-interests.

Competition

If self-interest and an appetite for money profit drive individuals and companies, then what stops them short of holding society up for exorbitant ransom? What stops capitalists from bleeding society dry?

Adam Smith provided an answer in his monumental treatise on commercial capitalism, *An Inquiry into the Nature and Causes of the Wealth of Nations* (1776). Free competition, said Smith, is the regulator that keeps a community activated only by self-interest from degenerating into a mob of ruthless profiteers. When traditional restraints are removed from the sale of goods and from wages, when all individuals have equal access to raw materials and markets (the doctrine of *laissez-faire,* from the French meaning "leave alone"), all of us are free to pursue our own interests. In pursuing our own interests, however, we come smack up against others similarly motivated. If any of us allows blind self-interest to dictate our actions—for example, by price gouging or employee exploitation—we will quickly find ourselves beaten out by a competitor who, let's say, charges less and pays a better wage. Competition thus regulates individual economic activity.

To sample the flavor of Smith's argument, imagine an acquisitive young woman who wants to pile up as much wealth as possible. She looks about her and sees that people need and want strong, twilled cotton trousers. So she takes her investment capital and sets up a jeans factory. She charges $45 for a pair and soon realizes handsome profits. The woman's success is not lost on other business minds, especially manufacturers of formal slacks and dresses, who observe a sharp decline in those markets. Wanting a piece of the jeans action, numerous enterprises start up jeans factories. Many of these start selling jeans for $40 a pair. No longer alone in the market, our hypothetical businesswoman must either check her appetite for profit by lowering her price or risk folding. As the number of jeans on the market increases, their supply eventually overtakes demand, and the price of jeans declines further and further. Inefficient manufacturers start dropping like flies. As the competition thins out, the demand for jeans slowly catches up with the supply, and the price regulates itself. Ultimately a balance is reached between supply and demand and the price of jeans is stabilized, yielding a normal profit to the efficient producer.

In much this way, Adam Smith tried to explain how economic competition steers individuals pursuing self-interest in a socially beneficial direction. By appealing to their self-interest, society can induce producers to provide it with what it wants—just as manufacturers of formal slacks and dresses were enticed into jeans production. But competition keeps prices for desired goods from escalating. High prices are self-correcting, because they call forth an increased supply.

Private Property

. . . "property" should not be identified only with physical objects like houses, cars, and video recorders. Nor should "ownership" be thought of as a simple relationship between the owner and the thing owned. First, one can have property rights over things that are not simple physical objects, as when one owns stock in a company. Second, property ownership involves a generally complex bundle of rights and rules governing how, under what circumstances, and in what ways both the "owner" and others can use, possess, dispose of, and have access to the thing in question.

Private property is central to capitalism. To put it another way, capitalism as a socioeconomic system is a specific form of private property. What matters for capitalism is not private property simply in the sense of personal possessions, because a socialist society can certainly permit people to own houses, television sets, and jogging shoes. Rather capitalism requires private ownership of the major means of production and distribution. The means of production and distribution include factories, warehouses, offices, machines, computer networks, trucking fleets, agricultural land, and whatever else makes up the economic resources of a nation. Under capitalism, private hands control these basic economic assets and productive resources. Thus the major economic decisions are made by individuals or groups acting on their own in pursuit of profit. These decisions are not directly coordinated with those of other producers, or are they the result of some overall plan. Any profits (or losses) that result from these decisions about production are those of the owners.

Capital, as an economic concept, is closely related to private property. Putting it simply, capital is money that is invested for the purpose of making more money. Individuals or corporations purchase various means of production or other related assets and use them to produce goods or provide services, which are then sold. They do this not for the purpose of being nice or of helping people out but rather in order to make money—more money, hopefully, than they spent to make the goods or provide the services in the first place. Using money to make money is at the heart of the definition of capitalism.

Moral Justifications of Capitalism

People tend to take for granted the desirability and moral legitimacy of the political and economic system within which they live. Americans are no exception. We are raised in a society that encourages individual competition, praises capitalism, promotes the acquisition of material goods, and worships economic wealth. Newspapers, television, records, movies, and other forms of popular culture celebrate these values, and rarely are we presented with fundamental criticisms of or possible alternatives to our socioeconomic order. Small wonder, then, that most of us blithely assume, without ever bothering to question, that our capitalist economic system is a morally justifiable one.

Yet as thinking people and moral agents, it is important that we reflect on the nature and justifiability of our social institutions. The proposition that capitalism is a morally acceptable system is very much open to debate. Whether or not we decide that capitalism is morally justified will depend, at least in part, on which general theory of justice turns out to be the soundest. . . .

The Natural Right to Property

As Americans, we live in a socioeconomic system that guarantees us certain property rights. Although we are no longer permitted to own other people, we are certainly free to own a variety of other things, from livestock to stock certificates, from our own homes to whole blocks of apartment buildings. A common defense of capitalism is the argument that people have a fundamental moral right to property and that our capitalist system is simply the outcome of this natural right.

. . . Locke attempted to base the right to property in human labor. When individuals mix their labor with the natural world, they are entitled to the results. And this idea seems plausible in many cases. For example, if Carl diligently harvests coconuts on the island he shares with Adam, while Adam himself idles away his days, then most of us would agree that Carl has an entitlement to those coconuts that Adam lacks. But property ownership as it actually exists in the real world today is a very complex, socially shaped phenomenon. This is especially true in the case of sophisticated forms of corporate and financial property—for example, bonds or stock options.

One could, of course, reject the whole idea of a natural right to property as a fiction, as, for example, utilitarians do. In their view, although various property systems exist, there is no natural right that things be owned privately, collectively, or in any particular way whatsoever. The moral task is to find that property system, that way of organizing production and distribution, with the greatest utility. Yet even if one believes that there is a natural right to property, at least under some circumstances, one need not believe that this right leads to capitalism or that it is a right to have a system of property rules and regulations just like the one we now have in the United States. That is, even if Carl has a natural right to his coconuts, there may still be moral limits on how many coconuts he can rightfully amass and what he can use them for. When he takes his coconuts to the coconut bank and receives further coconuts as interest, his newly acquired coconuts are not the result of any new labor on his part. When we look at capitalistic property — that is, at socioeconomic environments in which people profit from ownership alone — then we have left Locke's world far behind.

A defender of capitalism may reply, "Certainly, there's nothing unfair about Carl's accruing these extra coconuts through his investment; after all, he could have eaten his original coconuts instead." And, indeed, within our system this reasoning seems perfectly correct. It is the way things work in our society. But this fact doesn't prove that Carl has some natural right to use his coconuts to make more coconuts — that is, that it would be unfair or unjust to set up a different economic system (for example, one in which he had a right to consume his coconuts but no right to use them to earn more coconuts). The argument here is simply that the issue is not an all-or-nothing one. There may be certain fundamental moral rights to property, without those rights being unlimited and without them guaranteeing capitalism as we know it.

The Invisible Hand of Adam Smith

Relying on the idea of a natural right to property is not the only way and probably not the best way to defend capitalism. Another, very important argument defends capitalism in terms of the many economic benefits the system brings, claiming that a free and unrestrained market system, which exists under capitalism, is more efficient and more productive than any other possible system and is thus to be preferred on moral grounds. Essentially, this is a utilitarian argument, but one doesn't have to be a utilitarian to take it seriously. . . .

This section sketches Adam Smith's economic case for capitalism, as presented in *The Wealth of Nations*. Smith argues that when people are left to pursue their own interests, they will, without intending it, produce the greatest good for all. Each person's individual and private pursuit of wealth results — as if, in Smith's famous phrase, "an invisible hand" were at

work — in the most beneficial overall organization and distribution of economic resources. Although the academic study of economics has developed greatly since Smith's times, his classic arguments remain extraordinarily influential. Thus you should know what assumptions led Smith to his famous justification of capitalism.

The first of Smith's assumptions has already been mentioned: Human beings are acquisitive creatures. Self-interest and personal advantage, specifically in an economic sense, may not be all that motivate people, but they do seem to motivate most people much of the time. At any rate, they are powerful enough forces that any successful economic system must strive to harness them. We are, Smith thought, strongly inclined to act so as to acquire more and more wealth.

Second, humans have a natural propensity for trading. Unlike other species, we have an almost constant need for the assistance of others. Yet being creatures of self-interest, it is folly for us to expect others to act benevolently toward us. We can only secure what we need from others by offering something they need from us:

> Whoever offers to another a bargain of any kind, proposes to do this. Give me that which I want, and you shall have this which you want, is the meaning of every such offer; and it is in this manner that we obtain from one another the far greater part of those good offices which we stand in need of. It is not from the benevolence of the butcher, the brewer, or the baker that we expect our dinner, but from their regard to their own interest. We address ourselves, not to their humanity but to their self love, and never talk to them of our own necessities but of their advantages.[6]

This disposition to barter, said Smith, gives occasion to the division of labor — dividing the labor and production process into areas of specialization, which in theory increases capital and strengthens economic productivity.

Smith's third assumption is that individuals have natural endowments that should determine the kind of work they do. The disposition to trade will lead them to work that harmonizes with their talents. This collection of talents provides a common stock from which each of us can purchase whatever part of another's talent we need or desire.

The preceding assumptions led Smith to claim that the greatest utility will result from unfettered pursuit of self-interest. Individuals should be allowed unrestricted access to raw materials, markets, and labor. Government interference in private enterprise should be eliminated, free competition encouraged, and enlightened self-interest made the rule of the day. Because human beings are acquisitive creatures with natural talents, we will, if left free, engage in labor and exchange goods in a way that results in the greatest benefit to society. In our efforts to advance our own economic interests, we inevitably act so as to promote the economic well-being of society generally.

> Every individual is continually exerting himself to find the most advantageous employment for whatever capital he can command. It is his own advantage, indeed, and not that of the society, which he has in view. . . . [But] by directing that industry in such a manner as its produce may be of the greatest value, he [is] . . . led by an invisible hand to promote an end that was no part of his intention. . . . By pursuing his own interest he frequently promotes that of society more effectually than when he really intends to promote it.[7]

To explain why pursuit of self-interest necessarily leads to the greatest social benefit, Smith invoked the law of supply and demand, which was alluded to in discussing competition. The law of supply and demand tempers the pursuit of self-interest exactly as competition keeps the enterprising capitalist from becoming a ruthless profiteer. The law of supply and demand similarly solves the problems of adequate goods and fair prices.

The law of supply and demand even, some think, solves the problem of fair wages, for labor is another commodity up for sale like shoes or jeans. Just as the price of a new product at first is high, like the jeans in the hypothetical example, so too are the wages of labor in a new field. But as labor becomes more plentiful, wages decline. Eventually they fall to a point at which inefficient laborers are eliminated and forced to seek other work, just as the inefficient manufacturers of jeans were forced out of that business and into others. And like the price of jeans, the price of labor then stabilizes at a fair level. As for the inefficient laborers, they find work and a living wage elsewhere. In seeking new fields of labor, they help maximize the majority's opportunities to enjoy the necessities, conveniences, and trifles of human life.

Some modern capitalists still claim that capitalism operates as Smith envisioned and can be justified on the same utilitarian grounds. But others disagree.

Criticisms of Capitalism

The two major defenses of capitalism have not persuaded critics that it is a morally justifiable system. Their objections to capitalism generally fall into two categories, which are not mutually exclusive: theoretical and operational. Theoretical criticisms challenge capitalism's fundamental values, basic assumptions, or inherent economic tendencies. Operational criticisms focus more on capitalism's alleged deficiencies in actual practice (as opposed to theory) — in particular, on its failure to live up to its own economic ideals.

The following criticisms are a mix of both theoretical and operational concerns. They raise political, economic, and philosophical issues that cannot be fully assessed here; the debate over capitalism is a large and important one. The presentation that follows should be viewed as a stimulus to further discussion and not as the last word on the pros and cons of capitalism.

Inequality

. . . [P]rofound economic inequality exists in our capitalist society. The disparity in personal incomes is enormous; a minority of the population owns the vast majority of the country's productive assets; and in the last decade of the twentieth century, our society continues to be marred by poverty and homelessness. With divisions of social and economic class comes inequality of opportunity. A child born to a working-class family, let alone to an unwed teenager in an inner-city ghetto, has life prospects and possibilities that pale beside those of children born to wealthy, stock-owning parents. This reality challenges capitalism's claim of fairness, and the persistence of poverty and economic misfortune provides the basis for a utilitarian objection to it.

Few doubt that poverty and inequality are bad things, but defenders of capitalism make several responses to those who criticize it on these grounds:

1. A few extreme supporters of capitalism simply deny that it is responsible for poverty and inequality. Rather, they say, government interference with the market causes these problems. Left to itself, the market would eliminate unemployment and poverty, while ultimately lessening inequality. But neither theoretical economics nor the study of history supports this reply. Most economists and social theorists would agree that in this century activist government policies have done much, in all the Western capitalist countries, to reduce poverty and (to a lesser extent) inequality.

2. More moderate defenders of capitalism concede that, in its pure laissez-faire form, capitalism does nothing to prevent (and might even foster) inequality and poverty. But they argue that the system can be modified or its inherent tendencies corrected by political action, so that inequality and poverty are reduced or even eliminated. Critics of capitalism reply that the policies necessary to seriously reduce inequality and poverty are either impossible within a basically capitalist economic framework or unlikely to be carried out in any political system based on capitalism.

3. Finally, defenders of capitalism argue that the benefits of the system outweigh this weak point. Inequality is not so important if living standards are rising and even the poor have better lives than they did in previous times. This contention rests on an implicit comparison with what things would be like if society were organized differently and is, accordingly, hard to assess. Naturally, it seems more plausible to those who are relatively favored by, and content with, the present economic system than it does to those who are disadvantaged by it.

Some critics of capitalism go on to maintain that, aside from inequalities of income and ownership, the inequality inherent in the worker–capitalist relationship is itself morally undesirable. John Stuart Mill was one who found capitalism inferior in this respect to more cooperative and egalitarian economic arrangements. "To work at the bidding and for the profit of another," he wrote, "is not . . . a satisfactory state to human beings of educated intelligence, who have ceased to think themselves inferior to those whom they serve."[8] The ideal of escaping from a system of "superiors" and "subordinates" was well expressed by the great German playwright Bertolt Brecht when he wrote that "He wants no servants under him/And no boss over his head."[9]

Human Beings as Economic Creatures

The theory of capitalism rests on a view of human beings as rational economic creatures, individuals who recognize and are motivated largely by their own economic self-interests. Adam Smith's defense of capitalism, for instance, assumes that consumers have full knowledge of the diverse choices available to them in the marketplace. They are supposed to know the price structures of similar products, to be fully aware of product differences, and to be able to make the optimal choice regarding price and quality.

But the key choices facing today's consumers are rarely simple. From foods to drugs, automobiles to appliances, fertilizers to air conditioners, the modern marketplace is a cornucopia of products whose nature and nuances require a high level of consumer literacy. Even with government agencies and public interest groups to aid them, today's consumers are rarely an equal match for powerful industries that can influence prices and create and shape markets. The effectiveness of advertising, in particular, is hard to reconcile with the picture of consumers as the autonomous, rational, and perfectly informed economic maximizers that economics textbooks presuppose when they attempt to demonstrate the benefits of capitalism. Consumers frequently seem to be pawns of social and economic forces beyond their control.

According to some critics of capitalism, however, what is objectionable about capitalism's view of human beings as essentially economic creatures is not this gap between theory and reality but rather the fact that it presents little in the way of an ideal to which either individuals or societies may aspire. Not only does capitalism rest on the premise that people are basically acquisitive, individualistic, and materialistic; in practice, capitalism strongly reinforces those human tendencies. Capitalism, its critics charge, presents no higher sense of human mission or purpose, whereas other views of society and human nature do.

Christianity, for example, has long aspired to the ideal of a truly religious community united in *agape*, selfless love. And socialism, because it views human nature as malleable, hopes to see people transformed from the "competitive, acquisitive beings that they are (and that they are *encouraged* to be) under all property-dominated, market-oriented systems." In the more "benign environment of a propertyless, non-market social system," socialists believe that more cooperative and less selfish human beings will emerge.[10] Such positive ideals and aspirations are lacking in capitalism — or so its critics charge.

Capitalism Breeds Oligopolies

As early as the middle of the nineteenth century, the German philosopher and political economist Karl Marx (1818 – 1883) argued that capitalism leads to a concentration of property and thus a concentration of resources and power in relatively few hands. Exorbitant costs, complex machinery, increasing demand, and intense competition all work against the survival of small firms, said Marx. Many see proof of Marx's argument in today's economy.

The earlier economy of the Industrial Revolution was characterized by comparatively free and open competition, but today's is made up largely of a handful of enormous companies that can, to a distressing extent, conspire to fix prices, eliminate competition, and monopolize an industry. The food industry is a perfect example. According to Texas Commissioner of Agriculture Jim Hightower, the merger activity of giant firms has produced a series of shared monopolies in the food industry, with four or fewer firms controlling a majority of sales of a given product. Below are the levels of market control by just the top three brands in various categories.

Why is this kind of market control significant? When there is little competition, the "natural" regulator of prices is lost, and the consumer pays. "Once a

Share of Market Held by Top Three Brands

Product	Percentage of Market	Product	Percentage of Market
Table salt	91.7	Frostings	97.7
Flour	80.4	Spaghetti sauce	85.9
Catsup	86.1	Pickle relish	79.2
Mustard	76.2	Instant tea	86.0
Peanut butter	78.6	Frozen dinners	92.8
Salad and cooking oil	85.5	Corn and tortilla chips	86.7
Vinegar	84.1	Canned spaghetti and noodles	96.0
Gelatin desserts	98.4	Ready-to-serve dips	81.5
Whipped toppings	85.6	Nondairy cream substitutes	86.1
Canned evaporated milk	82.3	Pretzels	85.6
Marshmallows	98.2	Dry milk	80.1
Instant puddings	96.0	Add-meat dinner mixes	90.7
Shortenings	81.0	Canned stews	83.6
Jams and jellies	75.2	Instant potatoes	83.9
Nuts	80.7	Pizza mix	86.6
Honey	82.2	Instant breakfast products	90.8
Frozen potato products	82.2		

few firms gain a monopoly position in a product category," says Hightower, "the market for the category is considered to be 'mature,' . . . and the companies are able to 'harvest' it, meaning that they can push up prices. Taking one product at a time, such artificial inflation doesn't make a dramatic impression on shoppers—a few cents more on shortening, a little extra for the pizza mix. But when the whole market basket is pushed to the cash register, consumers have been nickle-and-dimed to death."11

It is true that antitrust actions have sometimes fostered competition and broken up monopolies, as in the cases of such corporate behemoths as Standard Oil and AT&T. But on the whole, such actions have proved largely ineffectual in halting the concentration of economic power in large, oligopolistic firms. In some cases, corporate giants have spawned even larger offspring, firms called multinationals that do business in several countries. And it is no secret that the cumulative power of business resulting from greater and greater profits has placed it in the position of a kind of industrial corporate state, an economic colossus that can negotiate independently with governments, solicit favorable franchises and tariffs, and influence self-serving legislation.

Robert Heilbroner suggests that the rise of such giant enterprises is changing the face of capitalism. Unable to function in the highly irrational system of ruthless competition, guided by some metaphysical "invisible hand," the big corporations attempt to alter the market setting through a system of public and private planning. The planning takes the form of efforts to create an atmosphere orderly and stable enough to allow the pursuit of profitable growth. Heilbroner says the planning assumes many guises, from union contracts that eliminate uncertainties in the labor market to sophisticated advertising calculated to create dependable product markets to cozy relationships with government in order to create programs that will ensure continuing high levels of demand. "At its worst," he writes, "we find it in the military-industrial complex—the very epitome of the new symbiotic business–government relations."12

True Competition Is Rare

As previously noted, free competition is theoretically the lifeblood of capitalism. Unfettered competition

supposedly serves the collective interest while offering the richest opportunities for the individual. And yet some of the same true believers who rabidly preach the doctrine of competition at home balk at applying it to international trade. There they want protection, not competition. Indeed, Robert Reich, for one, claims that America's basic industries lost the "habit of competing" over twenty years ago.13

Reich says that by the mid-1960s the industries forming the U.S. industrial base (for example, steel and auto) had become "stable oligopolies of three or four major firms, led by the largest and most entrenched." Woefully unprepared to compete in technology and price, American producers were quick to seek government protection from the influx of low-priced Japanese steel, autos, and televisions. The next twenty years witnessed a variety of protective measures. One of the most publicized were the restrictions that the United States forced Japan to impose on its auto exports. Among the lesser known, though not trivial, protections:

> Duties on $3.8 billion worth of imports from Southeast Asia and Latin America, which had the effect of protecting domestic manufacturers of car parts, electrical goods, fertilizers, and chemicals
>
> Special duties on 132 products, ranging from South Korean bicycles to Italian shoes, and including the lowly clothespin
>
> Special tax credits and tax depreciation allowances for specific industries threatened by foreign competition (total cost: $62.4 billion, or about 3 percent of the GNP)
>
> Federal loan guarantees for specific industries totaling $221.6 billion14

A Congressional Budget Office study estimated that business collects more than $60 billion annually through subsidy and credit programs.15 And at least one writer has contended that corporate America receives more in direct and indirect subsidies than it pays in taxes.16

Perhaps "free competition" is nice in theory but ultimately unworkable; government intervention is necessary to protect vital economic interests (as with protective tariffs). Or maybe latter-day capitalists have not kept the faith: They have abandoned or perverted the doctrine of free competition because it has become inconvenient or unprofitable to maintain it. Whatever the explanation, myriad indicators point to the fact that, insofar as competition is concerned, capitalism functions differently from how it was conceived to work. Business professor Robert B. Carson makes the point as follows:

> In surveying the American business system it is obvious that competition still exists; however, it is not a perfect competition. Often it is not price competition at all. With the possible exception of some farm markets where there are still large numbers of producers of similar and undifferentiated products (wheat, for instance), virtually every producer of goods and services has some control over price. The degree of control varies from industry to industry and between firms within an industry. Nevertheless, it does exist and it amounts to an important modification in our model of a free-enterprise economy.[17]

Exploitation and Alienation

Marx argued that, as the means of production become concentrated in the hands of the few, the balance of power between capitalists (bourgeoisie) and laborers (proletariat) tips further in favor of the bourgeoisie. Because workers have nothing to sell but their labor, said Marx, the bourgeoisie is able to exploit them by paying them less than the true value created by their labor. In fact, Marx thought, it is only through such an exploitative arrangement that capitalists make a profit and increase their capital. And the more capital they accumulate, the more they can exploit workers. Marx predicted that eventually workers would revolt. Unwilling to be exploited further, they would rise and overthrow their oppressors and set up an economic system that would truly benefit all.

The development of capitalist systems since Marx's time belies his forecast. Legal, political, and other institutions have tempered many of the greedy, exploitative dispositions of capitalism. The twentieth century has witnessed legislation curbing egregious worker abuse, guaranteeing a minimum wage, and ensuring a safer and more healthful work environment. The emergence of labor unions and their subsequent victories have significantly enlarged the worker's share of the economic pie. Indeed, many of the specific measures proposed by Marx and his collaborator Friedrich Engels in the *Communist Manifesto* (1848) have been implemented in capitalist countries: a program of graduated income tax, free education for all children

in public schools, investiture of significant economic control in the state, and so on.

Still, many would say that, although democratic institutions may have curbed some of the excesses of capitalism, they can do nothing to prevent the alienation of workers that results from having to do unfulfilling work. Again, because of the unequal positions of capitalist and worker, laborers must work for someone else — they must do work imposed on them as a means of satisfying the needs of others. As a result, they must eventually feel exploited and debased.

But what about workers who are paid handsomely for their efforts? They, too, said Marx, remain alienated, for as the fruits of their labor are enjoyed by someone else, their work ultimately proves meaningless to them. The following selection from Marx's "Economic and Philosophic Manuscripts" (1844) summarizes his notion of alienation as the separation of individuals from the objects they create, which in turn results in one's separation from other people, from oneself, and ultimately from one's human nature:

> The worker is related to the *product of his labor* as to an *alien* object. For it is clear on this presupposition that the more the worker expends himself in work the more powerful becomes the world of objects which he creates in face of himself, the poorer he becomes in his inner life, and the less he belongs to himself. . . . The worker puts his life into the object, and his life then belongs no longer to himself but to the object. The greater his activity, therefore, the less he possesses. What is embodied in the product of his labor is no longer his own. The greater this product is, therefore, the more he is diminished. The *alienation* of the worker in his product means not only that his labor becomes an object, assumes an *external* existence, but that it exists independently, *outside himself,* and alien to him, and that it stands opposed to him as an autonomous power. The life which he has given to the object sets itself against him as an alien and hostile force. . . .
>
> What constitutes the alienation of labor? First, that the work is *external* to the worker, that it is not part of his nature; and that, consequently, he does not fulfill himself in his work but denies himself, has a feeling of misery rather than well-being, does not develop freely his mental and physical energies but is physically exhausted and mentally debased. The worker, therefore, feels himself at home only during his leisure time,

whereas at work he feels homeless. His work is not voluntary but imposed, *forced labor*. It is not the satisfaction of a need, but only a *means* for satisfying other needs. Its alien character is clearly shown by the fact that as soon as there is no physical or other compulsion it is avoided like the plague. External labor, labor in which man alienates himself, is a labor of self-sacrifice, of mortification. Finally, the external character of work for the worker is shown by the fact that it is not his own work but work for someone else, that in work he does not belong to himself but to another person. . . .

We arrive at the result that man (the worker) feels himself to be freely active only in his animal functions — eating, drinking and procreating, or at most also in his dwelling and in personal adornment — while in his human functions he is reduced to an animal. The animal becomes human and the human becomes animal.

Eating, drinking and procreating are of course also genuine human functions. But abstractly considered, apart from the environment of human activities, and turned into final and sole ends, they are animal functions.

We have now considered the act of alienation of practical human activity, labor, from two aspects: (1) the relationship of the worker to the *product of labor* as an alien object which dominates him . . . [and] (2) the relationship of labor to the *act of production* within *labor*. This is the relationship of the worker to his own activity as something alien and not belonging to him. . . . This is *self-alienation* as against the above-mentioned alienation of the *thing*.[18]

In Marx's view, when workers are alienated they cannot be free. They may have the political and social freedoms of speech, religion, and governance. But even with these freedoms, individuals still are not fully free, because freedom from government interference and persecution does not necessarily guarantee freedom from economic exploitation. And it is for this kind of freedom, freedom from alienation, that Marx and Engels felt such passion.

Some would say that one need not wade through Marxist philosophy to get a feel for what he and others mean by worker alienation. Just talk to workers themselves, as writer Studs Terkel has done. In different ways the hundreds of workers from diverse occupations that Terkel has interviewed speak of the same thing: dehumanization.

Mike Fitzgerald . . . is a laborer in a steel mill. "I feel like the guys who built the pyramids. Somebody built 'em. Somebody built the Empire State Building, too. There's hard work behind it. I would like to see a building, say the Empire State, with a foot-wide strip from top to bottom and the name of every bricklayer on it, the name of every electrician. So when a guy walked by, he could take his son and say, 'See, that's me over there on the 45th floor. I put that steel beam in.' . . . Everybody should have something to point to."

Sharon Atkins is 24 years old. She's been to college and acidly observes, "The first myth that blew up in my face is that a college education will get you a worthwhile job." For the last two years she's been a receptionist at an advertising agency. "I didn't look at myself as 'just a dumb broad' at the front desk, who took phone calls and messages. I thought I was something else. The office taught me differently."

. . . Harry Stallings, 27, is a spot welder on the assembly line at an auto plant. "They'll give better care to that machine than they will to you. If it breaks down, there's somebody out there to fix it right away. If I break down, I'm just pushed over to the other side till another man takes my place. The only thing the company has in mind is to keep that machine running. A man would be more eager to do a better job if he were given proper respect and the time to do it."[19]

Today's Economic Challenges

Capitalism, as you have just seen, gives rise to a number of important critical questions, both theoretical and operational. These criticism are a powerful challenge to capitalism, especially in its pure laissez-faire form. But the capitalism that we know today is a long way from the laissez-faire model. Corporate behemoths able to control markets and sway governments have replaced the small-scale entrepreneurs and free-wheeling competition of an earlier day. And governments in all capitalist countries actively intervene in the economic realm; they endeavor to assist or modify Adam Smith's invisible hand; and over the years they have reformed or supplemented capitalism with programs intended to enhance the security of the work force and increase the welfare of their citizens.

This reality complicates the debate over capitalism. Its defenders may be advocating either the pure laissez-faire ideal or the modified state-welfare capitalism that we in fact have. Likewise, those who attack the laissez-faire ideal may do so on behalf of a modified, welfarist capitalism, or they may criticize both forms of capitalism and defend some kind of socialism, in which private property and the pursuit of profit are no longer governing economic principles. We thus have a three-way debate over the respective strengths and weaknesses of laissez-faire capitalism, state-welfare capitalism, and socialism.

. . .

Notes

1. See *Newsweek* (international edition), November 2, 1987, from which the details that follow are taken.

2. See David Schweickart, *Capitalism or Worker Control?* (New York: Praeger, 1980).

3. For a succinct treatment of the rise of the Fugger dynasty, see Ned M. Cross, Robert C. Lamm, and Rudy H. Turk, *The Search for Personal Freedom* (Dubuque, Iowa: Wm. C. Brown Company, 1972), 12.

4. Ibid., 13. See also Robert B. Carson, *Business Issues Today: Alternative Perspectives* (New York: St. Martin's Press, 1982), 3–30.

5. Robert Heilbroner, *The Worldly Philosophers*, 5th ed. (New York: Simon & Schuster, Touchstone edition, 1980), 22–23.

6. Adam Smith, *The Wealth of Nations* (New York: Modern Library, 1985), 16.

7. Ibid., 223-25.

8. As quoted by G. A. Cohen, *History, Labour, and Freedom* (Oxford: Oxford University Press, 1988), 273.

9. Ibid., 265.

10. Robert Heilbroner, *The Economic Problem* (Englewood Cliffs, N.J.: Prentice-Hall, 1972), 725.

11. Jim Hightower, "Food Monopoly: Who's Who in the Thanksgiving Business?" *Texas Observer,* November 17, 1978.

12. Heilbroner, *Worldly Philosophers,* 302.

13. Robert Reich, *The Next American Frontier* (New York: Penguin Books, 1983), 174.

14. Ibid., 178. See also Benjamin M. Friedman, *Day of Reckoning* (New York: Vintage Books, 1989), 57–58.

15. Doug Brandon, "Corporate America: Uncle Sam's Favorite Welfare Client," *Business and Society Review* 55 (Fall 1985): 48.

16. Martin Carnoy, *The State and Political Theory* (Princeton, N.J.: Princeton University Press, 1984), 246.

17. Carson, *Business Issues Today,* 29.

18. This entire extract is from *Karl Marx: Early Writings*, translated by T. B. Bottomore, 1963. Used with permission of McGraw-Hill Book Company.

19. Studs Terkel, "Here I Am a Worker," in Leonard Silk, ed., *Capitalism: The Moving Target* (New York: Quadrangle, 1974), 68–69. Copyright © 1974 by The New York Times Company. Reprinted by permission.

THE HIDDEN AGENDA

William Julius Wilson

William Julius Wilson argues that the severe disadvantages of African Americans are primarily the result of class discrimination—joblessness in the inner city—and not exclusively of race. He rejects the argument that inner-city poverty is caused by inner-city culture. Rather, he argues that culture emerges from one's specific circumstances and reflects one's class. He advocates nonracial solutions (full employment, balanced economic growth, and manpower training) in addition to traditional race-based solutions (affirmative action). (Source: From The Truly Disadvantaged *by William J. Wilson. Copyright © 1990 by University of Chicago Press. Reprinted by permission.)*

The Ghetto Underclass and Social Dislocations

. . .

Most unemployed blacks in the United States reside within the central cities. Their situation, already more difficult than that of any other major ethnic group in the country, continues to worsen. Not only are there more blacks without jobs every year; men, especially young males, are dropping out of the labor force in record proportions. Also, more and more black youth, including many who are no longer in school, are obtaining no job experience at all.

However, the growing problem of joblessness in the inner city exacerbates and is in turn partly created by the changing social composition of inner-city neighborhoods. These areas have undergone a profound social transformation in the last several years, as reflected not only in their increasing rates of social dislocation but also in the changing class structure of ghetto neighborhoods. In the 1940s, 1950s, and even the 1960s, lower-class, working-class, and middle-class black urban families all resided more or less in the same ghetto areas, albeit on different streets. Although black middle-class professionals today tend to be employed in mainstream occupations outside the black community and neither live nor frequently interact with ghetto residents, the black middle-class professionals of the 1940s and 1950s (doctors, lawyers, teachers, social workers, etc.) resided in the higher-income areas of the inner city and serviced the ghetto community. The exodus of black middle-class professionals from the inner city has been increasingly accompanied by a movement of stable working-class blacks to higher-income neighborhoods in other parts of the city and to the suburbs. Confined by restrictive covenants to communities also inhabited by the urban black lower classes, the black working and middle classes in earlier years provided stability to inner-city neighborhoods and perpetuated and reinforced societal norms and values. In short, their very presence enhanced the social organization of ghetto communities. If strong norms and sanctions against aberrant behavior, a sense of community, and positive neighborhood identification are the essential features of social organization in urban areas, inner-city neighborhoods today suffer from a severe lack of social organization.

Unlike in previous years, today's ghetto residents represent almost exclusively the most disadvantaged segments of the urban black community—including those families that have experienced long-term spells of poverty and/or welfare dependency, individuals who lack training and skills and have either experienced periods of persistent unemployment or have dropped out of the labor force altogether, and individuals who are frequently involved in street criminal activity. The term *ghetto underclass* refers to this heterogeneous group of families and individuals who inhabit the cores of the nation's central cities. The term suggests that a fundamental social transformation has taken place in ghetto neighborhoods, and the groups represented by this term are collectively different from and much more socially isolated than those that lived in these communities in earlier years.

The significance of changes embodied in the social transformation of the inner city is perhaps best captured by the concepts *concentration effects* and *social buffer*. The former refers to the constraints and opportunities associated with living in a neighborhood in which the population is overwhelmingly socially disadvantaged — constraints and opportunities that include the kinds of ecological niches that the residents of these communities occupy in terms of access to jobs, availability of marriageable partners, and exposure to conventional role models. The latter refers to the presence of a sufficient number of working- and middle-class professional families to absorb the shock or cushion the effect of uneven economic growth and periodic recessions on inner-city neighborhoods. The basic thesis is not that ghetto culture went unchecked following the removal of higher-income families in the inner city, but that the removal of these families made it more difficult to sustain the basic institutions in the inner city (including churches, stores, schools, recreational facilities, etc.) in the face of prolonged joblessness. And as the basic institutions declined, the social organization of inner-city neighborhoods (defined here to include a sense of community, positive neighborhood identification, and explicit norms and sanctions against aberrant behavior) likewise declined. Indeed, the social organization of any neighborhood depends in large measure on the viability of social institutions in that neighborhood. It is true that the presence of stable working- and middle-class families in the ghetto provides mainstream role models that reinforce mainstream values pertaining to employment, education, and family structure. But, in the final analysis, a far more important effect is the institutional stability that these families are able to provide in their neighborhoods because of their greater economic and educational resources, especially during periods of an economic downturn — periods in which joblessness in poor urban areas tends to substantially increase.

In underlining joblessness as an important aspect of inner-city social transformations, we are reminded that in the 1960s scholars readily attributed poor black family deterioration to problems of employment. Nonetheless, in the last several years, in the face of the overwhelming attention given to welfare as the major source of black family breakup, concerns about the importance of joblessness have diminished, despite the existence of evidence strongly suggesting the need for renewed scholarly and public policy attention to the relationship between the disintegration of poor black families and black male labor-market experiences.

Although changing social and cultural trends have often been said to explain some of the dynamic shifts in the structure of the family, they appear to have more relevance for changes in family structure among whites. And contrary to popular opinion, there is little evidence to support the argument that welfare is the primary cause of family out-of-wedlock births, breakups, and female-headed households. Welfare does seem to have a modest effect on separation and divorce, particularly for white women, but recent evidence indicates that its total effect on the proportion of all female householders is small.

By contrast, the evidence for the influence of joblessness on family structure is much more conclusive. Research has demonstrated, for example, a connection between an encouraging economic situation and the early marriage of young people. In this connection, black women are more likely to delay marriage and less likely to remarry. Although black and white teenagers expect to become parents at about the same ages, black teenagers expect to marry at later ages. The black delay in marriage and the lower rate of remarriage, each associated with high percentages of out-of-wedlock births and female-headed households, can be directly tied to the employment status of black males. Indeed, black women, especially young black women, are confronting a shrinking pool of "marriageable" (that is economically stable) men.

White women are not experiencing this problem. Our "male marriageable pool index" shows that the number of employed white men per one hundred white women in different age categories has either remained roughly the same or has only slightly increased in the last two decades. There is little reason, therefore, to assume a connection between the recent growth of female-headed white families and patterns of white male employment. That the pool of "marriageable" white men has not decreased over the years is perhaps reflected in the earlier age of first marriage and the higher rate of remarriage among white women. It is therefore reasonable to hypothesize that the rise in rates of separation and divorce among whites is due mainly to the increased economic independence of white women and related social and cultural factors embodied in the feminist movement.

The argument that the decline in the incidence of intact marriages among blacks is associated with the declining economic status of black men is further supported by an analysis of regional data on female headship and the "male marriageable pool." Whereas changes in the ratios of employed men to women among whites have been minimal for all regions of the country regardless of age from 1960 to 1980, the ratios among blacks have declined significantly in all regions except the West, with the greatest declines in the northeastern and north-central regions of the country. On the basis of these trends, it would be expected that the growth in numbers of black female-headed households would occur most rapidly in the northern regions, followed by the South and the West. Regional data on the "male marriageable pool index" support this conclusion, except for the larger-than-expected increase in black female-headed families in the West—a function of patterns of selective black migration to the West.

The sharp decline in the black "male marriageable pool" in the northeastern and north-central regions is related to recent changes in the basic economic organization in American society. In the two northern regions, the shift in economic activity from goods production to services has been associated with changes in the location of production, including an interregional movement of industry from the North to the South and West and, more important, a movement of certain industries out of the older central cities where blacks are concentrated. Moreover, the shrinkage of the male marriageable pool for ages sixteen to twenty-four in the South from 1960 to 1980 is related to the mechanization of agriculture, which lowered substantially the demand for low-skilled agricultural labor, especially during the 1960s. For all these reasons, it is often necessary to go beyond the specific issue of current racial discrimination to understand factors that contribute directly to poor black joblessness and indirectly to related social problems such as family instability in the inner city. But this point has not been readily grasped by policymakers and civil rights leaders.

The Limits of Race-Specific Public Policy

In the early 1960s there was no comprehensive civil rights bill and Jim Crow segregation was still widespread in parts of the nation, particularly in the Deep South. With the passage of the 1964 Civil Rights Bill there was considerable optimism that racial progress would ensue and that the principle of equality of individual rights (namely, that candidates for positions stratified in terms of prestige, power, or other social criteria ought to be judged solely on individual merit and therefore should not be discriminated against on the basis of racial origin) would be upheld.

Programs based solely on this principle are inadequate, however, to deal with the complex problems of race in America because they are not designed to address the substantive inequality that exists at the time discrimination is eliminated. In other words, long periods of racial oppression can result in a system of inequality that may persist for indefinite periods of time even after racial barriers are removed. This is because the most disadvantaged members of racial minority groups, who suffer the cumulative effects of both race and class subjugation (including those effects passed on from generation to generation), are disproportionately represented among the segment of the general population that has been denied the resources to compete effectively in a free and open market.

On the other hand, the competitive resources developed by the *advantaged minority members*—resources that flow directly from the family stability, schooling, income, and peer groups that their parents have been able to provide—result in their benefiting disproportionately from policies that promote the rights of minority individuals by removing artificial barriers to valued positions.

Nevertheless, since 1970, government policy has tended to focus on formal programs designed and created both to prevent discrimination and to ensure that minorities are sufficiently represented in certain positions. This has resulted in a shift from the simple formal investigation and adjudication of complaints of racial discrimination to government-mandated affirmative action programs to increase minority representation in public programs, employment, and education.

However, if minority members from the most advantaged families profit disproportionately from policies based on the principle of equality of individual opportunity, they also reap disproportionate benefits from policies of affirmative action based solely on their group membership. This is because advantaged minority members are likely to be disproportionately represented among those of their racial group most qualified for valued positions, such as college admissions, higher paying jobs, and promotions. Thus, if policies of preferential treatment for such positions are developed in terms of racial group membership rather than the real disadvantages suffered by individuals, then these policies will further improve the opportunities of the advantaged without necessarily addressing the problems of the truly disadvantaged such as the ghetto underclass.[1] The problems of the truly disadvantaged may require *nonracial* solutions such as full employment, balanced economic growth, and manpower training and education (tied to — not isolated from — these two economic conditions).

By 1980 this argument was not widely recognized or truly appreciated. Therefore, because the government not only adopted and implemented antibias legislation to promote minority individual rights, but also mandated and enforced affirmative action and related programs to enhance minority group rights, many thoughtful American citizens, including supporters of civil rights, were puzzled by recent social developments in black communities. Despite the passage of civil rights legislation and the creation of affirmative action programs, they sensed that conditions were deteriorating instead of improving for a significant segment of the black American population. This perception had emerged because of the continuous flow of pessimistic reports concerning the sharp rise in black joblessness, the precipitous drop in the black–white family income ratio, the steady increase in the percentage of blacks on the welfare rolls, and the extraordinary growth in the number of female-headed families. This perception was strengthened by the almost uniform cry among black leaders that not only had conditions worsened, but that white Americans had forsaken the cause of blacks as well.

Meanwhile, the liberal architects of the War on Poverty became puzzled when Great Society programs failed to reduce poverty in America and when they could find few satisfactory explanations for the sharp rise in inner-city social dislocations during the 1970s. However, just as advocates for minority rights have been slow to comprehend that many of the current problems of race, particularly those that plague the minority poor, derived from the broader processes of societal organization and therefore may have no direct or indirect connection with race, so too have the architects of the War on Poverty failed to emphasize the relationship between poverty and the broader processes of American economic organization. Accordingly, given the most comprehensive civil rights and antipoverty programs in America's history, the liberals of the civil rights movement and the Great Society became demoralized when inner-city poverty proved to be more intractable than they realized and when they could not satisfactorily explain such events as the unprecedented rise in inner-city joblessness and the remarkable growth in the number of female-headed households. This demoralization cleared the path for conservative analysts to fundamentally shift the focus away from changing the environments of the minority poor to changing their values and behavior.

However, and to repeat, many of the problems of the ghetto underclass are related to the broader problems of societal organization, including economic organization. For example, as pointed out earlier, regional differences in changes in the "male marriageable pool index" signify the importance of industrial shifts in the Northeast and Midwest. Related research clearly demonstrated the declining labor-market opportunities in the older central cities. Indeed, blacks tend to be concentrated in areas where the number and characteristics of jobs have been most significantly altered by shifts in the location of production activity and from manufacturing to services. Since an overwhelming majority of inner-city blacks lacks the qualifications for the high-skilled segment of the service sector such as information processing, finance, and real estate, they tend to be concentrated in the low-skilled segment, which features unstable employment, restricted opportunities, and low wages.

The Hidden Agenda:
From Group-Specific to
Universal Programs of Reform

. . .

The Great Society programs represented the country's most ambitious attempt to implement the principle of equality of life chances. However, the extent to which these programs helped the truly disadvantaged is difficult to assess when one considers the simultaneous impact of the economic downturn from 1968 to the early 1980s. Indeed, it has been argued that many people slipped into poverty because of the economic downturn and were lifted out by the broadening of welfare benefits. Moreover, the increase in unemployment that accompanied the economic downturn and the lack of growth of real wages in the 1970s, although they had risen steadily from 1950 to about 1970, have had a pronounced effect on low-income groups (especially black males).

The above analysis has certain distinct public policy implications for attacking the problems of inner-city joblessness and the related problems of poor female-headed families, welfare dependency, crime, and so forth. Comprehensive economic policies aimed at the general population but that would also enhance employment opportunities among the truly disadvantaged — both men and women — are needed. The research presented in this study suggests that improving the job prospects of men will strengthen low-income black families. Moreover, underclass absent fathers with more stable employment are in a better position to contribute financial support for their families. Furthermore, since the majority of female householders are in the labor force, improved job prospects would very likely draw in others.[2]

I have in mind the creation of a macroeconomic policy designed to promote both economic growth and a tight labor market.[3] The latter affects the supply-and-demand ratio and wages tend to rise. It would be necessary, however, to combine this policy with fiscal and monetary policies to stimulate noninflationary growth and thereby move away from the policy of controlling inflation by allowing unemployment to rise. Furthermore, it would be important to develop policy to increase the competitiveness of American goods on the international market by, among other things, reducing the budget deficit to adjust the value of the American dollar.

In addition, measures such as on-the-job training and apprenticeships to elevate the skill levels of the truly disadvantaged are needed. I will soon discuss in another context why such problems have to be part of a more universal package of reform. For now, let me simply say that improved manpower policies are needed in the short run to help lift the truly disadvantaged from the lowest rungs of the job market. In other words, it would be necessary to devise a national labor-market strategy to increase "the adaptability of the labor force to changing employment opportunities." In this connection, instead of focusing on remedial programs in the public sector for the poor and the unemployed, emphasis would be placed on relating these programs more closely to opportunities in the private sector to facilitate the movement of recipients (including relocation assistance) into more secure jobs. Of course there would be a need to create public transitional programs for those who have difficulty finding immediate employment in the private sector, but such programs would aim toward eventually getting individuals into the private sector economy. Although public employment programs continue to draw popular support, as Weir, Orloff, and Skocpol point out, "they must be designed and administered in close conjunction with a nationally oriented labor market strategy" to avoid both becoming "enmeshed in congressionally reinforced local political patronage" and being attacked as costly, inefficient, or "corrupt."[4]

Since national opinion polls consistently reveal strong public support for efforts to enhance work in America, political support for a program of economic reform (macroeconomic employment policies and labor-market strategies including training efforts) could be considerably stronger than many people presently assume.[5] However, in order to draw sustained public support for such a program, it is necessary that training or retraining, transitional employment benefits, and relocation assistance be available to all members of society who choose to use them, not just to poor minorities.

It would be ideal if problems of the ghetto underclass could be adequately addressed by the combination of macroeconomic policy, labor-market strategies, and manpower training programs. However, in the foreseeable future employment alone will not necessarily lift a family out of poverty.[6] Many families would still require income support and/or social services such as child care. A program of welfare reform is needed, therefore, to address the current problems of public assistance, including lack of provisions for poor two-parent families, inadequate levels of support, inequities between different states, and work disincentives. A national AFDC benefit standard adjusted yearly for inflation is the most minimal required change. We might also give serious consideration to programs such as the Child Support Assurance Program developed by Irwin Garfinkel and colleagues at the Institute for Research on Poverty at the University of Wisconsin, Madison.[7] This program, currently in operation as a demonstration project in the state of Wisconsin, provides a guaranteed minimum benefit per child to single-parent families regardless of the income of the custodial parent. The state collects from the absent parent through wage withholding a sum of money at a fixed rate and then makes regular payments to the custodial parent. If the absent parent is jobless or if his or her payment from withholdings is less than the minimum, the state makes up the difference. Since all absent parents regardless of income are required to participate in this program, it is far less stigmatizing than, say, public assistance. Moreover, preliminary evidence from Wisconsin suggests that this program carries little or no additional cost to the state.

Many western European countries have programs of family or child allowances to support families. These programs provide families with an annual benefit per child regardless of the family's income, and regardless of whether the parents are living together or whether either or both are employed. Unlike public assistance, therefore, a family allowance program carries no social stigma and has no built-in work disincentives. In this connection, Daniel Patrick Moynihan has recently observed that a form of family allowance is already available to American families with the standard deduction and the Earned Income Tax Credit, although the latter can only be obtained by low-income families. Even though both have been significantly eroded by inflation, they could represent the basis for a more comprehensive family allowance program that approximates the European model.

Neither the Child Support Assurance Program under demonstration in Wisconsin nor the European family allowances program is means tested; that is, they are not targeted at a particular income group and therefore do not suffer the degree of stigmatization that plagues public assistance programs such as AFDC. More important, such universal programs would tend to draw more political support from the general public because the programs would be available not only to the poor but to the working- and middle-class segments as well. And such programs would not be readily associated with specific minority groups. Nonetheless, truly disadvantaged groups would reap disproportionate benefits from such programs because of the groups' limited alternative economic resources. For example, low-income single mothers could combine work with adequate guaranteed child support and/or child allowance benefits and therefore escape poverty and avoid public assistance.

Finally, the question of child care has to be addressed in any program designed to improve the employment prospects of women and men. Because of the growing participation of women in the labor market, adequate child care has been a topic receiving increasing attention in public policy discussions. For the overwhelmingly female-headed ghetto underclass families, access to quality child care becomes a critical issue if steps are taken to move single mothers into education and training programs and/or full- or part-time employment. However, I am not recommending government-operated child care centers. Rather it would be better to avoid additional federal bureaucracy by seeking alternative and decentralized forms of child care such as expanding the child care tax credit, including three- and four-year-olds in preschool enrollment, and providing child care subsidies to the working-poor parents.

If the truly disadvantaged reaped disproportionate benefits from a child support enforcement program, child allowance program, and child care strategy, they would also benefit disproportionately from a program of balanced economic growth and tight-labor-market policies because of their greater vulnerability to swings in the business cycle and changes in economic organization, including the relocation of plants and the use of labor-saving technology. It would be shortsighted to conclude, therefore, that universal programs (i.e., programs not targeted at any particular group) are not designed to help address in a fundamental way some of the problems of the truly disadvantaged, such as the ghetto underclass.

By emphasizing universal programs as an effective way to address problems in the inner city created by historic racial subjugation, I am recommending a fundamental shift from the traditional race-specific approach of addressing such problems. It is true that problems of joblessness and related woes such as poverty, teenage pregnancies, out-of-wedlock births, female-headed families, and welfare dependency are, for reasons of historic racial oppression, disproportionately concentrated in the black community. And it is important to recognize the racial differences in rates of social dislocation so as not to obscure problems currently gripping the ghetto underclass. However, as discussed above, race-specific policies are often not designed to address fundamental problems of the truly disadvantaged. Moreover, as also discussed above, both race-specific and targeted programs based on the principle of equality of life chances (often identified with a minority constituency) have difficulty sustaining widespread public support.

Does this mean that targeted programs of any kind would necessarily be excluded from a package highlighting universal programs of reform? On the contrary, as long as a racial division of labor exists and racial minorities are disproportionately concentrated in low-paying positions, antidiscrimination and affirmative action programs will be needed even though they tend to benefit the more advantaged minority members. Moreover, as long as certain groups lack the training, skills, and education to compete effectively on the job market or move into newly created jobs, manpower training and education programs targeted at these groups will also be needed, even under a tight-labor-market situation. For example, a program of adult education and training may be necessary for some ghetto underclass males before they can either become oriented to or move into an expanded labor market. Finally, as long as some poor families are unable to work because of physical or other disabilities, public assistance would be needed even if the government adopted a program of welfare reform that included child support enforcement and family allowance provisions.

For all these reasons, a comprehensive program of economic and social reform (highlighting macroeconomic policies to promote balanced economic growth and create a tight-labor-market situation, a nationally oriented labor-market strategy, a child support assurance program, a child care strategy, and a family allowances program) would have to include targeted programs, both means tested and race-specific. However, the latter would be considered an offshoot of and indeed secondary to the universal programs. The important goal is to construct an economic-social reform program in such a way that the universal programs are seen as the dominant and most visible aspects by the general public. As the universal programs draw support from a wider population, the targeted programs included in the comprehensive reform package would be indirectly supported and protected. Accordingly, *the hidden agenda for liberal policymakers is to improve the life chances of truly disadvantaged groups such as the ghetto underclass by emphasizing programs to which the more advantaged groups of all races and class backgrounds can positively relate.*

I am reminded of Bayard Rustin's plea during the early 1960s that blacks ought to recognize the importance of fundamental economic reform (including a system of national economic planning along with new education, manpower, and public works programs to help reach full employment) and the need for a broad-based political coalition to achieve it. And since an effective coalition will in part depend upon how the issues are defined, it is imperative that the political message underline the need for economic and social reforms that benefit all groups in the United States, not just poor minorities. Politicians and civil rights organizations, as two important examples, ought to shift or expand their definition of America's racial problems and broaden the scope of suggested policy programs to address them. They should, of course, continue to fight for an end to racial discrimination. But they must also recognize that poor minorities are profoundly affected by problems in America that go beyond racial considerations. Furthermore, civil rights groups should also recognize that the problems of societal organization in America often create situations that enhance racial antagonisms between the different racial groups in central cities that are struggling to maintain their quality of life, and that these groups, although they appear to be fundamental adversaries, are potential allies in a reform coalition because of their problematic economic situations.

. . .

It is also important to recognize that just as we can learn from knowledge about the efficacy of alternative bargaining structures, we can also benefit from knowledge of alternative approaches to welfare and employment policies. Here we fortunately have the research of Alfred J. Kahn and Sheila Kamerman, which has convincingly demonstrated that countries that rely the least on public assistance, such as Sweden, West Germany, and France, provide alternative income transfers (family allowances, housing allowances, child support, unemployment assistance), stress the use of transfers to augment both earnings and transfer income, provide both child care services and day-care programs, and emphasize labor-market policies to enhance high employment. These countries, therefore, "provide incentives to work, supplement the use of social assistance generally because, even when used, it is increasingly only one component, at most, of a more elaborate benefit package." By contrast, the United States relies more heavily than all the other countries (Sweden, West Germany, France, Canada, Austria, the United Kingdom, and Israel) on public assistance to aid poorer families. "The result is that these families are much worse off than they are in any of the countries."[8]

In other words, problems such as poverty, joblessness, and long-term welfare dependency in the United States have not been addressed with the kinds of innovative approaches found in many western European democracies. "The European experience," argue Kamerman and Kahn, "suggests the need for a strategy that includes income transfers, child care services, and employment policies as central elements." The cornerstone of social policy in these countries is employment and labor-market policies. "Unless it is possible for adults to manage their work and family lives without undue strain on themselves and their children," argue Kamerman and Kahn, "society will suffer a significant loss in productivity, and an even more significant loss in the quantity and quality of future generations."[9]

The social policy that I have recommended above also would have employment and labor-market policies as its fundamental foundation. For in the final analysis neither family allowance and child support assurance programs, nor means-tested public assistance and manpower training and education programs can be sustained at adequate levels if the country is plagued with prolonged periods of economic stagnation and joblessness.

A Universal Reform Package and the Social Isolation of the Inner City

The program of economic and social reform outlined above will help address the problems of social dislocation plaguing the ghetto underclass. I make no claims that such programs will lead to a revitalization of neighborhoods in the inner city, reduce the social isolation, and thereby recapture the degree of social organization that characterized these neighborhoods in earlier years. However, in the long run these programs will lift the ghetto underclass from the throes of long-term poverty and welfare dependency and provide them with the economic and educational resources that would expand the limited choices they now have with respect to living arrangements. At the present time many residents of isolated inner-city neighborhoods have no other option but to remain in those neighborhoods. As their economic and educational resources improve they will very likely follow the path worn by many other former ghetto residents and move to safer or more desirable neighborhoods.

It seems to me that the most realistic approach to the problems of concentrated inner-city poverty is to provide ghetto underclass families and individuals with the resources that promote social mobility. Social mobility leads to geographic mobility. Geographic mobility would of course be enhanced if efforts to improve the economic and educational resources of inner-city residents were accompanied by legal steps to eliminate (1) the "practice at all levels of government" to "routinely locate housing for low-income people in the poorest neighborhoods of a community where their neighbors will be other low-income people usually of the same race"; and (2) the manipulation of zoning laws and discriminatory land use controls or site selection practices that either prevent the "construction of housing affordable to low-income families" or prevent low-income families "from securing residence in communities that provide the services they desire."[10]

This discussion raises a question about the ultimate effectiveness of the so-called self-help programs to revitalize the inner city, programs pushed by conservative and even some liberal black spokespersons.

In many inner-city neighborhoods, problems such as joblessness are so overwhelming and require such a massive effort to restabilize institutions and create a social and economic milieu necessary to sustain such institutions (e.g., the reintegration of the neighborhood with working- and middle-class blacks and black professionals) that it is surprising that advocates of black self-help have received so much serious attention from the media and policymakers.[11]

Of course some advocates of self-help subscribe to the thesis that problems in the inner city are ultimately the product of ghetto-specific culture and that it is the cultural values and norms in the inner city that must be addressed as part of a comprehensive self-help program.[12] However, cultural values emerge from specific circumstances and life chances and reflect an individual's position in the class structure. They therefore do not ultimately determine behavior. If ghetto underclass minorities have limited aspirations, a hedonistic orientation toward life, or lack of plans for the future, such outlooks ultimately are the result of restricted opportunities and feelings of resignation originating from bitter personal experiences and a bleak future. Thus the inner-city social dislocations emphasized in this study (joblessness, crime, teenage pregnancies, out-of-wedlock births, female-headed families, and welfare dependency) should be analyzed not as cultural aberrations but as symptoms of racial-class inequality.[13] It follows, therefore, that changes in the economic and social situations of the ghetto underclass will lead to changes in cultural norms and behavior patterns. The social policy program outlined above is based on this idea.

Before I take a final look, by way of summary and conclusion, at the important features of this program, I ought briefly to discuss an alternative public agenda that could, if not challenged, dominate the public policy discussion of underclass poverty in the next several years.

A Critical Look at an Alternative Agenda: New-Style Workfare

In a recent book on the social obligations of citizenship, Lawrence Mead contends that "the challenge to welfare statesmanship is not so much to change the extent of benefits as to couple them with serious work and other obligations that would encourage functioning and thus promote the integration of recipients." He argues that the programs of the Great Society failed to overcome poverty and, in effect, increased dependency because the "behavioral problems of the poor" were ignored. Welfare clients received new services and benefits but were not told "with any authority that they ought to behave differently." Mead attributes a good deal of the welfare dependency to a sociological logic ascribing the responsibilities for the difficulties experienced by the disadvantaged entirely to the social environment, a logic that still "blocks government from expecting or obligating the poor to behave differently than they do."[14]

Mead believes that there is a disinclination among the underclass to either accept or retain many available low-wage jobs. The problem of nonwhite unemployment, he contends, is not a lack of jobs, but a high turnover rate. Mead contends that because this kind of joblessness is not affected by changes in the overall economy, it would be difficult to blame the environment. While not dismissing the role discrimination may play in the low-wage sector, Mead argues that it is more likely that the poor are impatient with the working conditions and pay of menial jobs and repeatedly quit in hopes of finding better employment. At the present time, "for most jobseekers in most areas, jobs of at least a rudimentary kind are generally available." For Mead it is not that the poor do not want to work, but rather that they will work only under the condition that others remove the barriers that make the world of work difficult. "Since much of the burden consists precisely in acquiring skills, finding jobs, arranging child care, and so forth," states Mead, "the effect is to drain work obligation of much of its meaning."[15]

In sum, Mead believes that the programs of the Great Society have exacerbated the situation of the underclass by not obligating the recipients of social welfare programs to behave according to mainstream norms—completing school, working, obeying the law, and so forth. Since virtually nothing was demanded in return for benefits, the underclass remained socially isolated and could not be accepted as equals.

If any of the social policies recommended by conservative analysts are to become serious candidates for adoption as national public policy, they will more likely be based on the kind of argument advanced by Mead in favor of mandatory workfare. The laissez-faire social philosophy represented by Charles Murray is not only too extreme to be seriously considered by most policymakers, but the premise upon which it is based is vulnerable to the . . . criticism . . . that the greatest rise in black joblessness and female-headed families occurred during the very period (1972–80) when the real value of AFDC plus food stamps plummeted because states did not peg benefit levels to inflation.

Mead's arguments, on the other hand, are much more subtle. If his and similar arguments in support of mandatory workfare are not adopted wholesale as national policy, aspects of his theoretical rationale on the social obligations of citizenship could, as we shall see, help shape a policy agenda involving obligational state programs.

Nonetheless, whereas Mead speculates that jobs are generally available in most areas and therefore one must turn to behavioral explanations for the high jobless rate among the underclass, data . . . reveal (1) that substantial job losses have occurred in the very industries in which urban minorities are heavily concentrated and substantial employment gains have occurred in the higher-education-requisite industries that have relatively few minority workers; (2) that this mismatch is most severe in the Northeast and Midwest (regions that also have had the sharpest increases in black joblessness and female-headed families); and (3) that the current growth in entry-level jobs, particularly in the service establishments, is occurring almost exclusively outside the central cities where poor minorities are concentrated. It is obvious that these findings and the general observations about the adverse effects of the recent recessions on poor urban minorities . . . raise serious questions not only about Mead's assumptions regarding poor minorities, work experience, and jobs, but also about the appropriateness of his policy recommendations.

In raising questions about Mead's emphasis on social values as an explanation of poor minority joblessness, I am not suggesting that negative attitudes toward menial work should be totally dismissed as a contributing factor. The growing social isolation, and the concentration of poverty in the inner city, that have made ghetto communities increasingly vulner-

able to fluctuations in the economy, undoubtedly influence attitudes, values, and aspirations. The issue is whether attitudes toward menial employment account in large measure for the sharp rise in inner-city joblessness and related forms of social dislocation since the formation of the Great Society programs. Despite Mead's eloquent arguments the empirical support for his thesis is incredibly weak.[16] It is therefore difficult for me to embrace a theory that sidesteps the complex issues and consequences of changes in American economic organization with the argument that one can address the problems of the ghetto underclass by simply emphasizing the social obligation of citizenship. Nonetheless, there are clear signs that a number of policymakers are now moving in this direction, even liberal policymakers who, while considering the problems of poor minorities from the narrow visions of race relations and the War on Poverty . . . , have become disillusioned with Great Society–type programs. The emphasis is not necessarily on mandatory workfare, however. Rather the emphasis is on what Richard Nathan has called "new-style workfare," which represents a synthesis of liberal and conservative approaches to obligational state programs.[17] Let me briefly elaborate.

In the 1970s the term *workfare* was narrowly used to capture the idea that welfare recipients should be required to work, even to do make-work if necessary, in exchange for receiving benefits. This idea was generally rejected by liberals and those in the welfare establishment. And no workfare program, even Gov. Ronald Reagan's 1971 program, really got off the ground. However, by 1981 Pres. Ronald Reagan was able to get congressional approval to include a provision in the 1981 budget allowing states to experiment with new employment approaches to welfare reform. These approaches represent the "new-style workfare." More specifically, whereas workfare in the 1970s was narrowly construed as "working off" one's welfare grant, the new-style workfare "takes the form of obligational state programs that involve an array of employment and training services and activities — job search, job training, education programs, and also community work experience."[18]

According to Nathan, "we make our greatest progress on social reform in the United States when liberals and conservatives find common ground.

New-style workfare embodies both the caring commitment of liberals and the themes identified with conservative writers like Charles Murray, George Gilder, and Lawrence Mead." On the one hand, liberals can relate to new-style workfare because it creates short-term entry-level positions very similar to the "CETA public service jobs we thought we had abolished in 1981"; it provides a convenient "political rationale and support for increased funding for education and training programs"; and it targets these programs at the most disadvantaged, thereby correcting the problem of "creaming" that is associated with other employment and training programs. On the other hand, conservatives can relate to new-style workfare because "it involves a strong commitment to reducing welfare dependency on the premise that dependency is bad for people, that it undermines their motivation to self-support and isolates and stigmatizes welfare recipients in a way that over a long period feeds into and accentuates the underclass mind set and condition."[19]

The combining of liberal and conservative approaches does not, of course, change the fact that the new-style workfare programs hardly represent a fundamental shift from the traditional approaches to poverty in America. Once again the focus is exclusively on individual characteristics — whether they are construed in terms of lack of training, skills, or education, or whether they are seen in terms of lack of motivation or other subjective traits. And once again the consequences of certain economic arrangements on disadvantaged populations in the United States are not considered in the formulation and implementation of social policy. Although new-style workfare is better than having no strategy at all to enhance employment experiences, it should be emphasized that the effectiveness of such programs ultimately depends upon the availability of jobs in a given area. Perhaps Robert D. Reischauer put it best when he stated that: "As long as the unemployment rate remains high in many regions of the country, members of the underclass are going to have a very difficult time competing successfully for the jobs that are available. No amount of remedial education, training, wage subsidy, or other embellishment will make them more attractive to prospective employers than experienced unemployed workers."[20] As Reischauer also appropriately

emphasizes, with a weak economy "even if the workfare program seems to be placing its clients successfully, these participants may simply be taking jobs away from others who are nearly as disadvantaged. A game of musical underclass will ensue as one group is temporarily helped, while another is pushed down into the underclass."[21]

If new-style workfare will indeed represent a major policy thrust in the immediate future, I see little prospect for substantially alleviating inequality among poor minorities if such a workfare program is not part of a more comprehensive program of economic and social reform that recognizes the dynamic interplay between societal organization and the behavior and life chances of individuals and groups — a program, in other words, that is designed to both enhance human capital traits of poor minorities and open up the opportunity structure in the broader society and economy to facilitate social mobility. The combination of economic and social welfare policies discussed in the previous section represents, from my point of view, such a program.

Conclusion

. . . I have argued that the problems of the ghetto underclass can be most meaningfully addressed by a comprehensive program that combines employment policies with social welfare policies and that features universal as opposed to race- or group-specific strategies. On the one hand, this program highlights macroeconomic policy to generate a tight labor market and economic growth; fiscal and monetary policy not only to stimulate noninflationary growth, but also to increase the competitiveness of American goods on both the domestic and international markets; and a national labor-market strategy to make the labor force more adaptable to changing economic opportunities. On the other hand, this program highlights a child support assurance program, a family allowance program, and a child care strategy.

I emphasized that although this program also would include targeted strategies — both means tested and race-specific — they would be considered secondary to the universal program so that the latter are seen as the most visible and dominant aspects in the eyes of the general public. To the extent that the universal programs draw support from a wider population, the less visible targeted programs would be indirectly supported and protected. To repeat, the hidden agenda for liberal policymakers is to enhance the chances in life for the ghetto underclass by emphasizing programs to which the more advantaged groups of all class and racial backgrounds can positively relate.

Before such programs can be seriously considered, however, cost has to be addressed. The cost of programs to expand social and economic opportunity will be great, but it must be weighed against the economic and social costs of a do-nothing policy. As Levitan and Johnson have pointed out, "the most recent recession cost the nation an estimated $300 billion in lost income and production, and direct outlays for unemployment compensation totaled $30 billion in a single year. A policy that ignores the losses associated with slack labor markets and forced idleness inevitably will underinvest in the nation's labor force and future economic growth." Furthermore, the problem of annual budget deficits of around $200 billion dollars (driven mainly by the peacetime military buildup and the Reagan administration's tax cuts), and the need for restoring the federal tax base and adopting a more balanced set of budget priorities have to be tackled if we are to achieve significant progress on expanding opportunities.[22]

In the final analysis, the pursuit of economic and social reform ultimately involves the question of political strategy. As the history of social provision so clearly demonstrates, universalistic political alliances cemented by policies that provide benefits directly to wide segments of the population, are needed to work successfully for major reform.[23] The recognition among minority leaders and liberal policymakers of the need to expand the War on Poverty and race relations visions to confront the growing problems of inner-city social dislocations will provide, I believe, an important first step toward creating such an alliance.

Notes

1. James Fishkin covers much of this ground very convincingly. See his *Justice, Equal Opportunity and the Family* (New Haven, Conn.: Yale University Press, 1983).

2. Kathryn M. Neckerman, Robert Aponte, and William Julius Wilson, "Family Structure, Black Unemployment, and American Social Policy," in *The Politics of Social Policy in the United States,* ed. Margaret Weir, Ann Shola Orloff, and Theda Skocpol (Princeton, N.J.: Princeton University Press, forthcoming).

3. The essential features of such a policy are discussed in [William Wilson, *The Truly Disadvantaged,* University of Chicago Press, 1990] chap. 5, "The Case for a Universal Program."

4. Margaret Weir, Ann Shola Orloff, and Theda Skocpol, "The Future of Social Policy in the United States: Political Constraints and Possibilities," in Weir, Orloff, and Skocpol, *Politics of Social Policy in the United States.*

5. Theda Skocpol, "Brother Can You Spare a Job: Work and Welfare in the United States," paper presented at the Annual Meeting of the American Sociological Association, Washington, D.C., August 27, 1985.

6. Part of the discussion on welfare reform in the next several pages is based on Neckerman, Aponte, and Wilson, "Family Structure, Black Unemployment, and American Social Policy."

7. Irwin Garfinkel and Sara S. McLanahan, *Single Mothers and Their Children: A New American Dilemma* (Washington, D.C.: Urban Institute Press, 1986).

8. Sheila S. Kamerman and Alfred J. Kahn, "Income Transfers, Work and the Economic Well-being of Families with Children," *International Social Security Review* 3 (1982): 376.

9. Sheila S. Kamerman and Alfred Kahn, "Europe's Innovative Family Policies," *Transatlantic Perspectives,* March 1980, p. 12.

10. William L. Taylor, "*Brown,* Equal Protection, and the Isolation of the Poor," *Yale Law Journal* 95 (July 1986): 1729–30.

11. I have in mind the numerous editorials and op-ed columns on self-help in widely read newspapers such as the *Washington Post, New York Times, Wall Street Journal,* and *Chicago Tribune;* articles in national magazines such as *The New Republic* and *Atlantic Monthly;* and the testimony that self-help advocates, particularly black conservative supporters of self-help, have given before the U.S. Congress.

12. The most sophisticated and articulate black spokesperson of this thesis is Harvard University professor Glenn Loury. See, e.g., Glen Loury, "The Need for Moral Leadership in the Black Community," *New Perspectives* 16 (Summer 1984): 14–19.

13. Stephen Steinberg makes a compelling case for this argument in his stimulating book *The Ethnic Myth: Race, Ethnicity and Class in America* (New York: Atheneum, 1981).

14. Lawrence M. Mead, *Beyond Entitlement: The Social Obligations of Citizenship* (New York: Free Press, 1986), pp. 4, 61.

15. Ibid., pp. 73, 80.

16. See, for example, Michael Sosin's excellent review of *Beyond Entitlement* in *Social Service Review* 61 (March 1987): 156–59.

17. R. Nathan, "The Underclass—Will It Always Be with Us?" Paper presented at a symposium on the Underclass, New School for Social Research, New York, N.Y., November 14, 1986.

18. Ibid., p. 18.

19. Ibid., pp. 19-21. Although Lawrence Mead is highly critical of newstyle workfare (because it reinforces the sociological view of the disadvantaged by assuming that before the recipients can work, the program has to find the client a job, arrange for child care, solve the client's help problems, and so on), his elaborate theory of the social obligation of citizenship is being adopted by policymakers to buttress the more conservative side of the new workfare programs.

20. Robert D. Reischauer, "America's Underclass: Four Unanswered Questions," paper presented at The City Club, Portland, Oreg., January 30, 1986.

21. Robert D. Reischauer, "Policy Responses to the Underclass Problem," paper presented at a symposium at the New School for Social Research, November 14, 1986.

22. S. A. Levitan and C. M. Johnson, *Beyond the Safety Net: Reviving the Promising of Opportunity in America* (Cambridge, Mass.: Ballinger Publishing Co., 1984), pp. 169–70.

23. Skocpol, "Brother Can You Spare a Job?"

CITIZENS

Thomas Geoghegan

Thomas Geoghegan argues that in no country in the industrialized world is it tougher to organize a union than in the United States. He traces this problem to the anti-union provisions and probusiness enforcement of the National Labor Relations Act. (Source: From Which Side Are You On? by Thomas Geoghegan. Copyright © 1991 by Thomas Geoghegan. Reprinted by permission of Farrar, Straus & Giroux, Inc.)

A few years ago, Lane Kirkland, president of the AFL-CIO, a plodding, moderate man, called for the repeal of all the labor laws.

Blow them all up, repeal them all, he said, and just let labor and management go at it "*mano a mano.*"

Now, Kirkland is a man with about six pairs of galoshes. Those who saw the quote were shocked.

A friend of mine, a journalist, said, "He's bluffing, isn't he?"

"Maybe not," I said.

"Come on," my friend laughed. "Labor wouldn't survive five minutes without the labor laws."

He's right, I thought. We are bluffing.

"These laws protect your right to organize."

"But they don't," I said. "This is what Kirkland's trying to say."

I became excited. I said, "There is no right to organize. No Wagner Act. Nothing. It's gone. Over. No longer exists."

He looked at me and said, "I don't believe you."

I don't blame him. We used to impose sanctions on countries like Poland which didn't let their workers organize. We cheered on Lech Walesa. If labor is in decline, there must be another reason ("It's the culture, look at the Reagan vote," etc.). In high school, we all learned in American history that in the 1930s workers won the right to organize. It is burned into people's brains: "Workers have the right to organize."

On paper, the Wagner Act, passed in 1935, does grandly declare there is a right to join unions. But over the years, the right has become illusory. Against any normal employer opposition now, there's no practical way to enforce the right to organize. It is as unenforceable as a right set out in the Declaration of Independence.

I doubt today if any group of workers can form a union if their employer is truly determined to resist. The main reason is, employers can pick out and fire all the hard-core pro-union workers. They can do this flagrantly, almost admit they are doing it, yet can be assured they face no legal sanction for it, except maybe, *possibly,* having to cough up a tiny sliver of back pay, some $2,000 or $3,000 a body: and this is much later, three or four years from now, long after the drive is over and the union is in ashes.

Union busting now is almost a science. And the science is a pretty simple one: You go out and fire people. And keep firing until the organizing stops. Because at some point it always will. It is like sending people straight into a machine gun, and when the bodies pile up high enough, the drive is over and the employer has won.

"Come on," some will say, "that kind of thing went out years ago, didn't it?"

Actually, it did go out years ago. But then it came back.

When Congress in 1935 passed the National Labor Relations Act, popularly known as the Wagner Act, the new law did prohibit employers from firing workers for supporting a union. It created a new agency, the National Labor Relations Board (NLRB), to certify unions when a majority of the workers wanted them and then to require the employers to bargain with these unions "in good faith."

But the law was fatally weak from the start. The Board, for example, had no power to enforce its own orders. It had to petition for enforcement to the U.S. Court of Appeals, which could be a very time-consuming process. But for a while, this didn't matter, because employers seemed ready to obey the law.

Gradually, by the 1960s and 1970s, however, employers began to realize that the NLRB was weak. They could violate the Wagner Act, and nothing would happen. A whole profession of "labor consultants" had grown up, to tell them how to do it, to coach them in breaking the law. It was a sort of "cultural revolution," or mass civil disobedience, that began to occur, not among the workers, but among the employers, their bosses. It was like a civil rights movement in reverse.

In 1984, Professor Paul Weiler of Harvard Law School published a chilling study in the *Harvard Law Review*. He then estimated that about *one in twenty union supporters* would be fired in a typical organizing drive. He reached that number by taking for one year, 1980, the total number of cases in which the NLRB had made some award to a worker for an illegal firing in connection with an organizing drive. Then he divided that number (about 10,000) by the total number of pro-union votes cast in all elections that year (about 200,000). The number or ratio that came out, fifty years after the Wagner Act supposedly guaranteed the right to organize, was one in twenty.

Yet even this number, one in twenty, is probably an underestimate. First, Weiler was counting only the cases that end in final awards, and many workers, when fired, do not file charges, or they give up along the way. Second, his figures come from 1980, the last year of the Carter Board, which incidentally was not all that pro-union. They don't reflect PATCO, the Reagan era, or the "new permissiveness," when employers knew they could run wild and fire away, because the NLRB was full of "right-to-workers," right-to-lifers, and right-wing kooks. So the true ratio is not one in twenty: maybe it is one in fifteen, or even one in ten. It is really whatever ratio the employer wants.

In other words, if you put on a union button at work, in 1990, it can be shown to a reasonable certainty that you will be fired.

Weiler notes how illegal firings have increased over time. In 1939, for example, when the law was still new, the NLRB had to reinstate in that year 7,738 workers. But from 1939 to 1957, there is a downward trend, as employers came to accept the right of the workers to organize. In 1957, the NLRB reinstated only 922 workers. Then, from 1957 to 1980, as the labor consultants appear, there is a steady upward trend. By 1980, the year Weiler studied in detail, the number of reinstatements and other awards had risen *fifteen* times.

"But wait," some will say, "aren't the workers being reinstated?"

Yes, they can file charges. But the charges on average take over three years to resolve, more than a thousand days:

first, going through the General Counsel,

then to a full hearing before the Administrative Law Judge,

then an appeal to the whole Board,

then up to the U.S. Court of Appeals,

then maybe a remand back to the Board,

then back up to the Court of Appeals,

and then, at last, a final judgment enforcing the Board's order as modified.

Now the worker is reinstated. He has "won." But he has spent three or four years out in the darkness, gnashing his teeth. Also, when he comes back, the drive is over, and there is no union to protect him. Not only can he be fired again, but probably he will be fired again. Weiler found that 80 percent of those who win reinstatement are fired again within a year (oh, for something else, of course).

So if you put on a union button, it's not just that you'll be fired. You're fired and never coming back, ever: and if you try it, you'll be fired again within a year.

As a result, many workers don't file charges. Why bother? Perhaps if the worker could last it out, he could win some back pay, but it's usually peanuts. Under the Wagner Act, no matter how flagrant the violation, the employer can deduct from the back-pay award any other money the worker has earned. Unless the man was a total mope, he probably got another job, so the back pay won't be much, maybe a few thousand dollars. If he couldn't get another job, he probably settled the case a long time ago by agreeing to reinstatement without back pay, so he could cut the three-year wait and get back to work and feed his family.

Breaking the law, i.e., firing people, is absurdly cheap. Like jaywalking. The best deal in America, in cold business terms. There is a famous study, somewhere, that says a union on average will increase a company's wage bill by 20 percent. So let us say, at plant X there are 50 workers who make $25,000 a year. A union at this plant would cost an employer, then, about $250,000 *a year*. I don't even mention fringes, pensions, etc. And the penalty for violating the Wagner Act is . . . what, $3,000 a crack? Paid one time only, three or four years from now? An employer who didn't break the law would have to be what economists call an "irrational firm."

Actually, you don't have to break the law that much. My brother, who worked in personnel, saw a union try to organize his plant, which had about 40 or so workers. He said stopping the union was easy: "Our boss just picked out the two ringleaders and fired them."

That ended it. In any group of 40 people, he said, there are only one or two who make the drive happen. The heroes. So just fire them. This is what the consultants tell you. "Besides," my brother said, "one of these guys was a total jag-off," which is probably true, too.

Then he said to me, casually, "You know, I don't see how labor ever organizes a single plant."

By the way, my brother's employer was a good one. Even breaking the law, it was fairly humane. Most employers, to be on the safe side, would have fired a lot more workers.

Yes, the workers can be reinstated. But while their charges hang fire for three or four years, the company has made its point. And the point is not lost on the other workers, trembling, watching like the chorus. Most of us aren't heroes. We scare easy. And the workers today, the unorganized, who speak to us with their eyes, say, "We're sorry, we're not heroes, we don't want to be fired." They might be brave in a crowd, if they were 200,000 Czechs in Wenceslas Square, but nobody is that brave in a small shop, 40 or 50 workers, where most organizing occurs.

A few old union hands can't accept this. One I know will growl, "I've never believed the Board can win your strike." Then he will clench his fist and say, "The only thing the boss understands is . . ." Then he will take his right fist and pound it, *pow,* into his left palm. But the truth is, there are few union officials like him. The rest of us can dream of the 1930s, have a Yeats-like imagination of an insurrection, read the last stanzas of "Easter 1916," but we're going to wait for the Board to rule, even if it takes thirty years.

So do we really want to fight management *mano a mano?* No, we are bluffing. Yet I feel almost sorry for Lane Kirkland, with his secret, tormenting knowledge that there is no right to organize.

There's no other country (outside the Third World) where it's tougher legally to organize a union. It's getting even tougher than in South Korea.

Once, in the 1950s, before the mass firings began, American unions would win a stunning number of elections, even through the Board. I saw some of the statistics in Michael Goldfield's book *The Decline of Organized Labor in the United States.* In the 1950s, unions could count on organizing a new, additional *1 percent* of the work force annually. They often won over 80 percent of the Board elections. At the present time unions barely organize *0.3 percent* of the work force annually. They lose, many years, over 50 percent of the Board elections. Also, much of the 0.3 percent, the "new" organizing, comes in the public sector, where there are few illegal firings. There was little public-sector organizing in the 1950s, so the decline in private-sector organizing is worse than it seems. Organizing in the private sector has almost stopped.

As a result, the unionized share of our work force drops every year. The share is now 16 percent of the total work force and a bare 12 percent of the private sector work force (which excludes public employees). The new organizing cannot offset even the normal attrition or falloff in union membership, as older unionized companies go out of business or disappear. According to Goldfield, unions can still win a stunning number of elections even now, but only under one special set of circumstances: When the employer does not oppose or delay the election, or commit any legal violations, the unions currently win over *90 percent* of the time.

Otherwise, of course, we're screwed.

So far I have argued as if the Board were useless. Now, if the Board were only useless, that would not be so bad. But the Board is much worse that useless. The NLRB now seems to exist primarily to slow down the union, delay the election, ball things up, so the employer has even more time to fire people. In the extreme case, when the union threatens to win anyway, despite the firings, the Board will often step in and put everything on hold for eight years.

By the way, no country has anything like our NLRB, which can function like a bloodless, bureaucratic death squad. Look at Canada, for example. Oh, they have labor boards, etc. But when workers in Canada want to organize, they just sign cards saying, "I authorize the union to represent me." If 55 percent of the workers sign, there is a union, and the employer has to bargain. No hearings, no further elections, no years of litigation. Just the cards. Doesn't it sound simple, civilized, even fair?

Nothing like that happens here. Here we also collect "authorization" cards. But what is the last step in Canada is just a first, preliminary step here in a long, *Bleak House* type of legal proceeding that can go on, literally, for seven or eight years.

"O Canada," I whisper. Across that border is the free world. Now, I should say that in the U.S. a union needs only 30 percent of the cards to start the election process. But in practice, no sensible union would dare ask for an election without having 50 percent of the cards. So everything I now relate occurs only *after* a majority of the workers have come forth, by name, and said they want to join a union.

For ten years, I've represented the Illinois Nurses Association, or INA. This is a decent, honorable, and competent union, and in theory, the INA should be doing great, organizing like crazy. In the 1980s, everything seemed to fall into place. There was a nursing shortage, which made nurses hard to fire; but the same shortage also meant that nurses would work longer hours, in worse conditions. Nurses were mad, angry, and at the same time, they were feeling their oats. They were ready for a little labor unrest.

But organizing them is a nightmare. I know of Board cases pending for *seven* years. Think of it: Seven years ago, a union asked a group of nurses to sign cards, risk their jobs, and said at the time, perhaps, "Look, this'll go fast." Now, seven years later, the Board and the court are still trying to decide whether one little clutch of nurses should be in a union together — whether they are, in a legal sense, "an appropriate bargaining unit."

What, you say, is "an appropriate bargaining unit"? It means the unit or "election district" in which the group will vote whether to unionize. Should the unit be

1. registered nurses ("RNs") only;

2. RNs and licensed practical nurses (LPNs) only; or

3. RNs, LPNs, and maybe parking-lot attendants, electricians, and the grounds crew?

I list only three possibilities, but there are hundreds, maybe thousands, and a good management lawyer will raise each one. Not just raise it, but brief it, put on witnesses, ask for a ruling, and then do it all again for another permutation. And I, the Union lawyer, have to argue it, brief it, as if we are talking about something serious.

The hospital would like the Board to pick the silliest unit: let's say, RNs, LPNs, and parking-lot attendants. This, they tell the Board, is the only unit that makes sense. Then, if the Board says yes, the hospital will go to the parking-lot attendants and say, "Hey, do you guys want to be in a unit with *nurses?* Is that crazy or what?"

Meanwhile, the hospital is firing all the nurses it can.

And meanwhile, the Board is changing the rules for deciding what is "an appropriate bargaining unit." Since the cases drag on for years, the rules can change two or three times in the course of one case. A few years ago, the Board tried to codify the rules in a decision known as *St. Francis Hospital,* or *St. Francis I.* Then it came up with new rules in *St. Francis II.* Since a federal judge has just thrown out *St. Francis II,* we are now all waiting for *St. Francis III.* And after *St. Francis III,* there will be a puff of white smoke, and we will have *St. Francis IV,* and then one day, *St. Francis V,* in dynastic succession, like a long line of popes. One day, when I am old, and young lawyers are at my knee and asking me about *St. Francis XXIII,* maybe I will shock them by saying, "I remember *St. Francis I.*"

Meanwhile, the nurses wait and wait, their hair turns white. If a nurse is fired, I say to her, "You're going to file a charge, I hope."

"Where?" she says.

"The NLRB."

"THERE? *That* place?"

"Well, where did you think?"

"How long is this going to take?"

"Three years."

She looks at me as if I'm nuts. I don't even tell her the truth, which is that for three years she'll see her named dragged through the mud, with doctors, administrators, even parking-lot attendants coming in to say:

"She didn't change the patient's bedpan."

"I saw her yelling at a patient."

"I saw her flirting with a patient."

"I saw her having *sex* with a patient."

And finally: "She's on drugs."

And the hospital can swing away, since in a hearing it has absolute protection from libel.

Sure she should file a charge. Kafka would file a charge.

So I hate organizing. Oh sure, as a labor lawyer I go around telling unions, "Organize, organize," because we need the business, but I really feel like such a hypocrite. I would never be an organizer. In fact, I wonder if, ethically, we should even be asking people to organize. So I say, "Organize, organize," but thank God, it's not me doing it.

I bet somewhere right now union staffers are meeting and saying, "Yes, we've got to do more organizing." Then everyone looks around the room. O.K., who's going out there?

Organizers today are . . . well, they're professionals, naturally . . . Look, basically, they're outlaws. As a young lawyer at the UMW, I used to walk softly past our organizing department, like a child passing a haunted house. Sometimes I would look inside. Hellooo? Were they in there or out on the road? We, the staff, used to say, "Organize, organize," I think because we felt safer when they were out of the building. As bureaucrats, we felt guilty, too, because we depended on organizers for our little desk jobs. Because of them, we could live like quiet civil servants, drink at the Hay-Adams, and occasionally raise our eyes up to heaven and say, "Oh, where can we find good organizers?"

I would try the terrorist networks of Western Europe. That is what the Wagner Act has reduced us to.

I am being a romantic, though. I would like to think of an organizer as someone who can spend six weeks at a Holiday Inn in Kokomo, Indiana, reading novels like *The Day of the Jackal,* and then going out after dark to organize a ten-man machine shop; who sneaks around on private property; and who, after losing the election, can stub out his last cigarette, get in his car, and then, emotionless, drive down to Terre Haute, as if nothing happened.

But I know a few organizers, and none of them are like this. They aren't this romantic. I suppose to be a good organizer you can't have any imagination. Otherwise, going into a plant, you would feel like a virus or a bacillus, first infecting a lot of healthy workers and then getting them fired. After a while, I would go crazy. You have to recruit them. Get them to trust you. Be a father figure, mother figure, one-person support system. And then have to be perfectly neutral, when they are fired, as they turn on you, scream at you, shriek; and then you see how low and craven the human race can really be.

I could also never be an organizer, because I don't have the eye. I go to a meeting with an organizer, and two or three people are there, and I say, "Gee, this is pretty bad."

The organizer looks annoyed and says, "Actually, this is good."

So we go to the next meeting, and twenty people are there, and I say, "Gee, this is pretty good."

The organizer looks really annoyed and says, "Actually, this is bad."

Anyway, it is creepy to be there, knowing what I do about the Wagner Act, etc., and then to see workers come in, smiling, innocent, wearing union buttons. I think, "My God, take that *off* . . ." and I think of their families.

I look at the organizer, who shows no expression. When the employer wants to call a meeting, there is a full house. This is the so-called captive meeting. Everyone has to attend. The company president stands up, yells, rants, and, picking up a pay plan, says, "If you elect a union, I warn you, I'll be tearing this in two." Then he rips it up right in front of them. This is all within the law, of course.

Remember, this comes *after* a majority of workers have signed cards saying they want to be in a union. Foreigners, puzzled, will ask, "You mean, after the majority say they want to be in a union, the employer can still make these threats?"

"Yes," I say, "it's their First Amendment right."

"They don't have that right in my country."

"Well," I say, "you aren't a free country."

But we have rights, too. Under certain limited circumstances, which change year to year, we can wait outside in the parking lots and catch the workers as they come out. As people open their car doors, our organizer can say, "Psst . . . over here . . ."

＝

While I may worry whether, ethically, we should even try to organize, at least I am not a management lawyer. I wonder how some of them live with their consciences.

Once I dated a management lawyer. It was a blind date, and I didn't know she was a management lawyer. Besides, she turned out to be pretty, and she was even a Democrat. In fact, she was raising money for Dukakis at the time, more than I was doing.

"Well," I thought, "give her a chance."

We ordered drinks, and she talked about Dukakis. Then she talked about labor law. Since she spoke Spanish, she did a lot of work with Hispanics.

I said, "Do you work with a consultant?"

"Oh yes," she said. "His name is Jorge. He speaks Spanish, and he's very popular right now with the employers around town."

"Why?"

"Oh," she said, "you have to see him. He's tall and very charming. And when he goes out in the plant and talks to these Latino ladies . . . well, after that, they just can't vote *for* the union."

She laughed delicately. "They just can't vote against a man who's so handsome."

I could just see Jorge, tall and charming, out there on the shop floor, looking for people to fire.

I thought, "I'll finish this drink."

"Look," she said, "I'm not uncritical of my clients. Sometimes I tell them, 'Look, you brought this on yourself.' I have a client who uses illegal workers, and sometimes they have to change their names. If they do, he drops them to the bottom of the seniority list, even though he knows they are the same men. So a man can be working there ten or fifteen years, but have only one year of seniority."

I said, "Do you think that's right?"

"No," she said, "and I told him, my client, 'Look, you better clean up your act.'"

"Don't you think," I said, "maybe there should be a union here?"

She looked at me, and she was aghast. "*That's* no answer."

＝

I admit, once I saw a group of nurses organize at a private hospital in an NLRB election: so yes, even under the Wagner Act, it can be done. But let me explain why it was a freak occurrence.

The hospital was in Fairbury, Illinois, a small rural town not far from Peoria. I remember when I first saw the nurses. I came into Peoria on a tiny prop plane, where the stewardess gives you Beechnut chewing gum for the landing, and the nurses met me. Holding my suitcase, I felt with a slight thrill that at last I was an "organizer," the man from Big Labor, from shadowy big-city Chicago, and here I was, the man who would turn Fairbury upside down. I seemed pretty dangerous. I would organize these poor women.

It turns out, the nurses didn't want me to do that. They were already organized. They just needed a lawyer to sneak them around *St. Francis I,* or maybe by then, it was *II.* Anyway, I never even saw Fairbury but spent all my time in Peoria at the hearing. So the whole story collapses, and I wasn't a hero.

How these nurses had even gotten the idea of having a union, I am not too sure. It may have been the smallness of the town. The nurses of Fairbury knew each other socially. In fact, the "union" had started out as a club, like a social club or a book-reading club. Slowly, month by month, the club, the Fairbury Nurses Society, became a quasi-union. The hospital, horrified, called in a labor consultant. Then the nurses, horrified, called in the INA. This is how the battle of Fairbury, escalating week by week, came to be joined.

From the start, the nurses were "an appropriate bargaining unit," if not legally, then at least militarily. They had a sense of union like no other group of workers I ever knew. There were no class distinctions. One of the leaders, for example, was Bev, who was an LPN. Now, in Chicago, I cannot imagine an LPN ever being a leader or spokesperson for a group that included RNs within it. It is unthinkable. But here, in Fairbury, where everyone knew everyone, it was no big deal. Indeed, some of the younger RNs even seemed to look up to Bev, the LPN, and to take her as a model. This was good, because when two of the younger RNs were fired, this admiration would be tested.

We asked the Board to certify a unit of "all RNs, all LPNs, and all the lab workers." The hospital, of course, objected. The lawyer for the hospital was Mr. R., a tall, gangling man, who, unfortunately, like many downstate lawyers, had a Lincoln complex. He talked so slow, each word so slowly brought out, as if every word he said might show up one day in marble on the Lincoln Memorial. It was like hearing, over and over, on 16 rpm, the Second Inaugural Address. At first, Mr. Lincoln said our unit was too small. Then he said it was too big. In slow motion, he came up with every possible permutation (laundry workers, busboys, etc.).

The hearing dragged on and on. The hospital began firing nurses. The snow began to fall. I would sit in my room at night, at the Père Marquette Hotel, and think, "It's falling all over Illinois." What was I doing here? I had to call up a friend in New York and cancel a trip. "Why?" he asked. "I'm snowbound in Peoria," I said. I had a premonition that my body would be found frozen here, at the end of the hearings, after the last RN had been fired. It was insane, all this money being spent, all this time, just to decide if thirty women in a little Illinois town should be allowed just to have a *vote* whether to join a union. And here I was, all my dreams of being a great lawyer, Harvard Law School, etc., and all the time it was leading up to this, the 1980s, all these Reagan people in power, and Mr. Lincoln holding me captive down in Peoria, and reading at me over and over, for eternity, the Second Inaugural Address.

I worried about the firings. I thought the nurses would crack. I told them they shouldn't be discouraged, I wasn't.

"We're not," they said calmly.

One day, when we were crammed in a car together, about eight of us, Bev said to me, "We have a question."

I did not like the sound in her voice. I thought, "They're going to fold."

"Go ahead," I said, "ask it."

"It's not just my question," she said. "It's everyone's question."

"Go ahead, Bev, ask it."

"Well," she said, "why is it that a lawyer thirty-five years old still isn't married?"

Seven people in the car laughed.

Bev was such a sweet, grandmotherly lady. I used to wonder why they didn't fire her, because if they had, they might have stopped the drive. Either the hospital didn't know this or it simply wasn't ready to go all the way. I think that perhaps, sometimes, an employer tries to do the right thing, tries to start down the path of evil, but then, at the last minute, will stop, as if the president, Mr. A., whom the nurses mocked, didn't have the heart to fire any more.

After all, this was a small town, and a small hospital, with a community board. Everyone knew everyone. In the big city, nurses can be fired and just forgotten, dropped into Lake Michigan with weights tied to their feet. But in a small town like Fairbury, there is no place to dump the bodies. These are your neighbors, you keep running into them, at school, at church, even after they've been fired, like the undead, weightless, rising out of the lake and taking over the town. If you are Mr. A., then, and think of all this happening, maybe you get lost or confused and don't do what the consultants say.

Who knows? It could be the reason. I recall that once in Dixon, Illinois, another small town, the birthplace of Ronald Reagan, we represented fifteen nurses fired from a local hospital, and in the Dixon *Clarion* this story was front page for weeks. Six-column banner headlines, as if there had been an earthquake. Reporters would call us up. Our clients were celebrities. We all needed press agents. This may be the only way that any union, or any group of workers, can win these days, given the legal obstacles: to bring in the whole town, to gather people around and make them *look,* the way Jimmy Stewart or Gary Cooper could gather people around in a Frank Capra movie and make them bear witness, and make the big men like Mr. A. feel like little men and feel a sense of shame.

And here is the final reason we won at Fairbury:

The NLRB. The Board. The federal government. The Ronald Reagan people. In this one case, miraculously, they were on our side.

By dumb luck, our hearing officer turned out to be the head of the NLRB staff union in that region: that is, *he* knew what it was like.

I whispered to the nurses, "Thank God."

Over the weeks, I became certain he was on our side, from imperceptible glances, clicks in his voice, the tiniest rolling of his eyes when Mr. Lincoln droned on about the laundry workers. And Abe himself, I think, when the Board finally ruled in our favor, never knew what hit him, just like at Ford's Theater. When we won, I just whispered, like Booth . . . "Sic semper tyrannis."

No doubt by now the hearing officer has been fired by the NLRB, but he was there when we needed him, to get us past *St. Francis*.

I remember a story that a teacher of mine, Sam Beer, told me not long ago. When Sam was a young man, in the 1930s, he applied for a job at the NLRB, which was a brand-new federal agency. Sam asked the man who interviewed him, "Which side are we on?"

The man smiled. "We're neutral."

"Neutral?" Sam said. "*Neutral?* Neutral in the struggle between the bosses and the workers?"

"Yes," the man said, "but we're neutral on the side of the workers."

Well, that was back in the New Deal.

A few years ago, I read an article, "The Decline of Labor," by Seymour Martin Lipset, who wrote it for *The Wall Street Journal*. Professor Lipset is a neoconservative, and I don't much like his views, although I admire him in a way for even bothering to write about labor at all.

Professor Lipset tries to explain the sharp drop in union membership. He says that with Reagan, there has been a return to "individualism," a "resurgence of traditional values," a "new American patriotism," which has been fatal to organized labor. This is why today, no one wants to join.

And what about "Jorge," who's so handsome that all those Latino ladies simply can't vote for the union?

Now, Professor Lipset may be right. Maybe there is a "new American patriotism," etc., although labor's difficulties in organizing arose long before Reagan. But I take the Lipset thesis seriously, it may *be* the

"culture." I go to a shopping mall, or drive around a neighborhood, and people have TVs and VCRs, and no one seems to be starving, and I think, "Lipset is right, maybe these people don't want to be rank and file, and why don't I just leave them alone?" It is the land of Eisenhower, after all. But then on another day, same country, I can drive into a different neighborhood and think, "It's also the land of Jefferson, of Jackson, of the New Deal." So first, I don't know if it *is* the "culture," and second, I don't even know what the "culture" *is*.

In 1989, Nissan Motors, the Japanese automaker, beat back an organizing drive of the UAW at a new plant in Tennessee. On the TV that night, after the vote was announced, some of the Nissan workers stood before their Japanese bosses and sang the company song, "We're the Number One Team."

There may be a new "culture," but I'm not sure I'd call it the new American patriotism.

Anyway, Professor Lipset is a social scientist. Why not conduct a little experiment? Why not change the labor laws and let people decide, freely and without coercion, i.e., without being fired, whether they want to join a union? Then we don't have to argue, we can find out what people want to do. But I think conservatives, like Professor Lipset, don't want to conduct this little test.

We can talk "culture" until we all go mad. But isn't it possible that the law itself may help create the culture? The Jim Crow laws create one kind of culture, and the Civil Rights Act over time creates another. Likewise with the labor laws. If the laws are hostile to unionizing, and if the unions are weak and powerless as a result, then the laws are bound to influence the culture, i.e., the attitudes people hold about unions. In the 1980s, the boss looks strong, the unions look weak, and people identify with the boss and shrink from the union, without knowing why.

Actually, the 1980s should have been a boom time for union organizing. Real wages flat or falling, income gaps between rich and poor getting wider, the sense of class increasing. Yet it seems that the more the sense of class increases, the weaker labor becomes. There is more scabbing, more strikebreaking, fewer people voting to join. Also, the weaker labor becomes, the more (in the U.S. at least) it is resented. It holes up in a few bastions, shrinks into a smaller, privileged elite, where everyone makes $13.00 an hour, and everyone else is cut out. So labor, beaten to a pulp, helpless, in retreat on every front, appears more privileged, more remote, more irrelevant to the working majority. Yet this isn't labor's fault. Labor could not organize these people even if it wanted to. Labor, then, may look "arrogant," but this arrogance is thrust upon it. It does not want to be this weak, shrunken thing masquerading as a privileged elite.

But now I am sounding, like Professor Lipset, as if no one wants to join. The maddening thing is: we can't even organize the people who *want* to join.

Look, I am not naïve. I realize Americans are individualists. I know this is the culture of narcissism, and that community, solidarity, etc., are on the way out. But if the labor laws changed, if we had laws like France or Poland, I think Americans would join unions like crazy, simply out of self-interest, raw, Reaganite self-interest.

Let me give some examples:

1.   Baseball players. Look at the pros, the big stars. A bunch of young punk kids, multimillionaires, won't even sign autographs for free. The purest crystallizations we have of the Reagan culture.

But baseball players join unions like crazy. Why? Because they can get away with it, i.e., no one will fire them. And look at the salaries they get. *Unions raise your salary.* A lot.

If you can get away with it, it would be irrational not to join a union. Why would anyone, except Professor Lipset, think otherwise?

2.   Canadians. O.K., they're not Americans. But they have the same companies, like GM, the same TV shows. Technically, they're a foreign country, but it's like Minnesota being in NATO. Otherwise, they're just like us.

But Canadians join unions like crazy. Why? Because they can get away with it, i.e., no one will fire them. Canadian workers just sign cards, and bang, they're in a union. It goes so fast, there is no chance to fire them.

So in the last thirty years, while U.S. unions have dropped from 35 to 17 percent of the work force, Canadian unions have risen from 25 to 32 percent.

By the way, this fact casts doubt on the service-sector thesis, which says that unions will decline as the service sector grows. In Canada, this has not been true.

But then workers in Canada are like baseball players in the United States.

3.   Public employees. Also like baseball players, they're all in unions. Thank God, too. Without them, our share of the work force would be even below 16 percent.

Because federal labor law does not apply, the public sector is the only place where unions can organize without being maimed. It is like crossing into Canada. Here, in the public sector, the U.S. Constitution applies, so workers can't be fired simply for putting on a union button.

No wonder, then, that the Teamsters, the UAW, the Steelworkers, and AFSCME all fight to organize the same little clusters of public workers, battling like eagles over the same little nest of birds.

A Steelworkers officer I know is trying to organize the lawyers for the city of Chicago. I said, "What do you guys know about organizing lawyers?"

He growled at me. "Whose side are you on?"

4.   Blacks. No one doubts that blacks want to join unions like crazy. Every poll shows it. But blacks can't join unions, because they can't get away with it, i.e., someone *will* fire them.

Recently, the Supreme Court under Rehnquist has cut back, in some limited, technical ways, the protections afforded by the civil rights laws. I don't like these decisions either, but it mystifies me how liberals get worked up over fairly minor blips in the law and completely ignore the fact that, year after year, blacks are being denied a most basic civil right, the right to join a union without being fired.

If we only thought of the Wagner Act as a civil rights law, instead of a labor law, then maybe liberals would wake up and do something. Maybe one day I could walk around my city and not have the scary feeling that the whole south half of it is like Soweto.

=

There are two other groups to whom unions would have a natural appeal: Men and Women. I take them up in no particular order.

1.   Women. Even now, under the current laws, I keep waiting for women to rise up. What's holding them back? The "new American patriotism"? It seems to me they have to organize, in self-defense, to protect the strange double lives they lead as workers and mothers. Women are so vulnerable, so overextended, both on the job and off the job, that they have no choice.

Of course, I can walk into Barbara's Bookstore, and see fifty books by fifty women novelists, and not one word in any of them about unions.

If only we thought of the Wagner Act as a day-care law, instead of a labor law, then maybe liberals would wake up and do something.

As I write, a friend of mine, a feminist from England, tells me, "In England, there's some feeling that women don't join unions because the unions are sexist. Is that true in America?"

Maybe one day that'll be a reason . . . but we haven't reached that degree of sophistication yet.

2.   Men. You'd think they'd do it out of self-respect. What do these guys talk about when they're not in a union? When there is just "the Boss," and nothing but "the Boss"? I am thinking of Nissan Motors. Down at that plant in Tennessee, do they walk around thumping their chests, "Hey, we voted out the union"?

Of course, what do they talk about anywhere? Baseball. Football. I remember working in a non-union plant one summer in high school, and the only thing we could talk about, really, was baseball: that was about the limit of the right to speak, for the nonunion man . . . Baseball. We'd get dizzy talking about baseball, and at the end of the day, we'd clutch each other like exhausted dancers, still talking about baseball.

By the way, baseball players are not like this. Once, with some corporate lawyers, slobbering "sports," I went to a charity event, and we sat at a table with two major-league players. We peppered them with our questions, and the players would answer, polite but bored. Then one player asked me what kind of law I practiced.

"Labor law."

He seemed to wake up. "Union side?"

"Yes."

The two Sox looked at each other. "Do you know ERISA?"

"Sure."

For the next half hour, the two Sox, one of them a union rep, threw me one labor-law question after another. Most of them, I could field.

The corporate lawyers sat there, polite but bored.

———

. . . By the way, I can understand the Nissan workers, why they voted down the Union. Really, they're already in the UAW, and know it. So long as the UAW has organized 90 percent of the auto industry, Nissan has to match or even beat the UAW deal, and everyone knows it. The Nissan workers, then, can play both sides of the street, having the UAW bargaining for them, in effect, but not having to pay the dues.

Now, here is the new American individualism: getting a free ride, coasting on other people's solidarity. It is a rational enough thing to do. But to me, the Nissan workers should be buried in the bottom circle of hell.

The other day, coming back from O'Hare on the train, I was with an American Airlines employee. Computer reservations. Dallas, Texas. Garish red lipstick.

"I feel sorry for people in unions," she said. "We have such good management at American. We get the same benefits they do in the unions, and we don't have to pay any dues. I think the unions are just ripping people off."

I almost said, "It's not the unions ripping people off, lady. *You're* ripping people off. You . . . you take the union benefits and you don't pay your share of the dues."

I didn't put it quite that harshly, but I said something like it. Incredibly, the woman admitted it. She smirked. She was pleased with herself.

Dallas, Texas. What a jerk.

But I still don't quite understand the Nissan workers. Let's put aside higher wages, pension funds, health insurance, all of which the UAW brought about, because Nissan will match these things to keep the UAW out. Let's put aside work rules, too, and even seniority. I would just like to take up only the issue of job security, and ask this one question: Why would any adult, any sane or mature person, responsible to a family, ever choose voluntarily, rationally, to put himself in a position where he can be fired at any time, for any reason, on any whim?

O.K., I can understand why a twenty-four-year-old investment banker at Drexel Burnham might do it. But a forty-five-year-old autoworker? I don't get it.

I should explain here, for those who may not know, that every nonunion employee in the U.S. is an "employee at will." He can be fired for *any* reason, good or bad, for his tie, for the color of his eyes, or for no reason at all. It is amazing to me how many people, even bright, college-educated people, have no idea this is the case. They come to my office and say, "But I worked there for twelve years. How can they fire me?"

Some even believe that the civil rights laws of the 1960s apply to them, even though they are white males. They think these laws prohibit *all* discrimination, not just age, race, sex, but in the generic sense, unfairness of any kind.

When I try to explain the laws, they sit there in shock and say, "You mean it was just for *blacks?*"

I recently saw a man who was a dispatcher at a trucking company. He was a good employee for many years, and then one day he had a heart attack, and sometime later, "I got whacked, for no reason."

I felt sorry for him and wanted to help. I asked if there was anyone in the company, a fellow supervisor, for example, who could testify in his favor, say that he was a good employee.

No, he said, all his friends were in "management" (i.e., they were dispatchers or foremen), and they could be fired if they were to testify. He sat there, running through the names.

"No, I can't involve him.

"No, and not him either . . .

"Oh, there's T. He'd love to testify for me, but he'd get whacked, too, like me."

"Isn't there anyone?" I said.

He brightened. "Hey, why didn't I think of it? The guys in the *Union*. They can testify for me, and they can't get whacked."

The ones who drive the trucks. Because they were in a union, they couldn't be fired except for "just cause." They, unlike the supervisors, could stroll into court, testify, and just walk past the Boss and wave.

I thought, "Isn't that something? Maybe you're in a union, and maybe you're just a worker, and you should be ashamed. But at least you don't have to kiss anyone's ass, like this guy does. You can just go home at night and kiss your kids. And you know that, if you have to, you can walk into court, testify, and walk past the Boss and wave."

Tell me, Professor Lipset: Who is the real American?

Mostly because of the labor laws, the lack of a legal right to organize, I think we are at the end of the union era. What is to be done? Nothing, I suppose. All we need is a law, just a little law, like a civil rights law. But I know, in my heart of hearts, there will never be a law. We, in labor, sit there, riding low in the polls, and there will never be a law, because no one will ever lift a finger to help us.

Once, as a labor lawyer, I thought I should live in Chicago because it would be the last "union town" in America. But not even Chicago is safe anymore. The other day, I saw a priest, Father Egan, a man in his seventies, who has tried to help the unions for years, and he made this remark to me:

"I can walk down Michigan Avenue now, and see the Nikko Hotel, the Marriott Hotel, and they're all nonunion now, and I say to these union guys, 'How can you let that stand?' But I don't have to tell them. They know. They're scared.

"But what can they do? These hotels know, now, they don't have to let the unions in."

I don't have to walk down Michigan Avenue. I can go down my own street.

Not long ago, out of nowhere, a group of Korean ladies were out with picket signs, in my own neighborhood, just in front of my El stop. They came out of a small brown building, almost windowless, with just a tiny slit or two near the roof. The sign on the door said, "D & L Textiles." And I realized, for the first time, that I had been living next to a sweatshop, like a hundred other little windowless places all over the city, employing Latino, Filipino, and Korean ladies. We pass them all the time and don't even notice.

Sometimes a strike can make you look down a street and really see it for the first time.

All summer the women stood outside with their picket signs, which said, "AFL-CIO." Not even the name of a union. Just signs that said, "AFL-CIO." Meek and humble, like the women who held them.

All summer, I passed the women on the way to the El. All of us did, the lawyers, bankers, etc., on our way to the Loop. It was painful to see them every day. By now it was clear that the women had been fired, and after a while, it was annoying to have this painful thing go on, every single day, right in front of our condos. Even I, a labor lawyer, became annoyed, and I began to think, "What idiot had talked these women into going on strike?"

I knew, we all knew, up there on the El platform, that the women below us were doomed. From a distance, it must have been a tableau, the condo owners above, the women below, and we smiled down on them with compassion, but all of us felt helpless.

I think most of us up on the El were thinking, "The labor laws are supposed to work. Collective bargaining is supposed to work. If something is wrong, it can't be that serious."

No, there is just Big Business, Big Labor, and the Rest of Us. And the Rest of Us are like the Swiss, we are morally neutral, with our Swiss passports. A strike, even in our neighborhood, is none of our business.

These little strikes never make the news. But I can go into any law library, go way back in the stacks, to the old NLRB volumes, and read, in dry legal prose, one horror story after another. Thousands of pages, volumes and volumes, where some women try to pick up signs and then somebody drags them screaming away. I can sit there in the dark of the law library and read story after story.

I do not mean to sound so moral about this. If I were not a labor lawyer, I would be crossing picket lines, too, by now.

Anyway, one day, at the end of the summer, the little Korean ladies were no longer there, and I never saw them again. They probably have jobs now in other sweatshops, and they will never try this union stuff again. In Professor Lipset's phrase, they have returned to "traditional values."

I forgot about them until I was in New York a few months back. I was looking for what was then the fashionable new drink in the city, iced decaffeinated cappuccino. I was wandering around SoHo when a door swung open. For a split second, I could look inside, although it was dark, and I saw two or three women, possibly Korean, kneeling on the floor and sewing.

One of the women smiled at me shyly. I remember thinking, "It's filthy in there."

Then somebody slammed the door, and that was it.

I found the cappuccino, a few blocks away.

I think I would like to live in New York. And here is the part I dream about: Every morning I could go down in the subway and see the women reading Nabokov.

And I'd take my own copy of *Despair* and stand next to them and read.

But there'd be other women all around us.

The ones from Peoria. And still in Peoria.

Down in the darkness, without the right to vote.

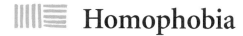 # Homophobia

INVISIBLE MINORITIES, CIVIC RIGHTS, DEMOCRACY:
Why Even Conservatives Should Support Gay Rights

Richard D. Mohr

Richard D. Mohr analyzes the concepts "civil rights" and "invisible minority." He applies these concepts to gays and lesbians and argues that if we take civil rights seriously, we are committed to making substantive changes in how we treat gays and lesbians. (Source: From Gays/Justice *by Richard D. Mohr. Copyright © 1988 by Columbia University Press. Reprinted with permission of the publisher.)*

This chapter advances three related arguments for the inclusion of sexual orientation in such legislation as the 1964 Civil Rights Act as a characteristic on the basis of which a person may not be discriminated against in employment, housing, and public services. For gay men and lesbians, such protections from discrimination are necessary enabling conditions for their having reasonably guaranteed access to an array of fundamental rights — both civic and political — which virtually everyone would agree are supposed to pertain equally to all persons. For gays, these rights are eclipsed, it is here argued, in consequence of the *indirect* results which widespread discrimination has when it affects individuals who are members of invisible minorities.

The arguments here are not, then, general arguments for civil rights legislation based on the *direct* or immediate deleterious effects which discrimination in employment, housing, and public services would have

on *any* person or even on society as a whole and which might on their own be sufficiently grave to justify a government ban on all but good faith discriminations in these areas — a ban which *per accidens* would catch gays within its broad protective reach. Such direct deleterious effects (as discussed in the prior chapter) include affronts to personal dignity, self-reliance, general prosperity, and individual flourishing.

Libertarians and other political minimalists tend to dismiss as irrelevant or inflated assessments of the nature and gravity of these possible direct effects and so have generally been unmoved by such arguments for civil rights legislation and its coercive intrusions into the private sector. But even if the direct effects of such discrimination were not as sufficient on their own as I think they are to warrant the state's deployment of its monopoly of preemptive coercive forces, still, if social realities are such that discrimination (actual or prospective) indirectly but determinately has the effect of denying access to certain universally recognized rights — the denial of which draws into doubt the very rule of law — then this effect does warrant state action on virtually any account of what constitutes legitimate state action.[1]

The arguments would apply equally well to other invisible minorities whose members are subject to widespread discrimination merely on the basis of their minority status rather than on the basis of their capacities, talents, or needs. By invisible minority I mean a minority whose members severally can be identified only through an act of will on someone's part rather than through the mere observation of the members' day-to-day actions in the public domain. Thus severely physically and mentally challenged people would rank along with racial classes, gender classes, and some ethnic and religious groups (like the Amish) as visible minorities, whereas diabetics, assimilated Jews, atheists, and released prisoners would rank along with gays as invisible minorities.

The arguments only presuppose the acceptability of a governmental system which is a constitutionally regulated representative democracy with a developed body of civic law. Such in broad outline is the government of the United States and its various states. The arguments, then, hold that gay civil rights are a necessary precondition for the proper functioning of this system. Specifically, they hold (1) that gay rights are necessary for gays having reasonably guaranteed access to judicial or civic rights, (2) that gay rights are necessary for gays having reasonably guaranteed access to the political rights of the sort found in the first amendment of the Constitution and (3) that gay rights are necessary if democracy is consistently and coherently to be given a preference-utilitarian rationale — that is, if democracy is at least in part justified as the form of government that tends to maximize goods and services in society by registering people's overall preferences.

Making Civic Rights Coherent

This section argues that civil rights legislation for gays is warranted as being a necessary precondition for gays having equitable access to civic rights. By civic rights I mean rights to the impartial administration of civil and criminal law in defense of property and person. In the absence of such rights there is no rule of law. An invisible minority historically subjected to widespread social discrimination has reasonably guaranteed access to these rights only when the minority is guaranteed nondiscrimination in employment, housing, and public services.

For an invisible minority, possessing civil rights has the same ethical justification as everyone's having the right when on criminal trial to have a lawyer at government expense. A lawyer through her special knowledge and skills provides her client with *access* to the substantive and procedural rights of the courts — rights to which a layman left to his own devices would not have reasonably guaranteed access. Without the guarantee of a lawyer, judicial rights are not equal rights but those of the well-to-do.[2]

All would agree that everyone ought to have judicial rights, and moreover — as in the case of having a lawyer at state expense — ought to have in that strong sense of rights by which an individual can make demand claims based on them. All individuals must be assured the right to demand from government access to judicial procedures. Judicial rights ought not to be debased to the level where government may simply be prevented from prohibiting judicial access, but need not guarantee it. This debasement would give judicial access the same status that abortion now has in the U.S.; it cannot be prohibited, but is not guaranteed for those who want or even (in most cases) need it. Civic rights ought not to be mere immunities and they ought not to be restricted only to certain classes.

Imagine the following scenario. Steve, who teaches math in a suburban high school and coaches the swim team, on a weekend night heads to the city to try his luck at Up and Coming, a popular gay cruise bar. There he meets Tom, a self-employed contractor, who in his former life sired two sons by a woman who now hates him, but who is ignorant of his new life. Tom and Steve decide to walk to Tom's nearby flat, which he rents from a bigot who bemoans the fact that the neighborhood is going gay and refuses to rent to people he supposes to be gay; Tom's weekend visitations from his sons are his cover.

Meanwhile, at a nearby Children's Aid Home for teenagers, the leader of the Anglo gang is taunting Tony, the leader of the Latino gang, by calling him a faggot. After much protestation to the contrary, Tony claims he will prove to the Anglos once and for all that he is not a faggot, and hits the streets with his gang members, who tote with them the blunt and not so blunt instruments of the queerbasher's trade. Like a hyena pack upon a wildebeest, they descend on Tom and Steve, downing their victims in a blizzard of strokes and blows. Local residents coming home from parties and others walking their dogs witness the whole event.

Imagine that two miracles occur. One, a squad car happens by, and two, the police actually do their job. Tony and another of the fleeing queerbashers are caught and arrested on the felony charges of aggravated assault and battery, and attempted murder. Other squad cars arrive and while witnesses' reports are gathered, Steve and Tom are taken to the nearest emergency room. Once Steve and Tom are in wards the police arrive to take statements of complaint from them, complaints which will engage the wheels of justice in what appears to be an open and shut case. But Steve knows the exposure of a trial will terminate his employment. And Tom knows the exposure of a trial would give his ex-wife the legal excuse she desires to deny his visitation rights and he knows he will eventually lose his apartment. So neither man can reasonably risk pressing charges. Tony is released, and within twelve hours of attempting murder, he returns to the Children's Aid Home hailed by all as a conquering hero. Gay rights are a necessary material condition for judicial access.

Any reader of gay urban tabloids, like Chicago's *Windy City Times,* San Francisco's *Bay Area Reporter,* Boston's *Gay Community News,* Toronto's *The Body Politic,* or *The Washington Blade,* knows that the events sketched here—miracles excepted—are typical. Every day gays are in effect blackmailed by our judicial system. Our judicial system's threat of exposure prevents gay access to judicial protections. The example given above of latter-day lynch law falls within the sphere of criminal justice. Even more obviously, the same judicial blackmail occurs in civil cases. Nor are the offending parties always outsiders to the group whose civic access is thus limited:

> Similarly, lesbians can be sexually harassed by other lesbians. Some lesbians may foist sexual attentions upon other lesbians who already have lovers, for example. To a large extent lesbians who are victims of nondiscriminatory [i.e., peer-on-peer] sexual harassment will be on their own. A lesbian will tend to reject any suggestion that she initiate a civil suit against her female harasser. Fearing that she will be laughed out of court, or doubting the wisdom of publicly proclaiming her sexual preference, the lesbian is apt to handle her problem in informal ways.[3]

These "informal ways," however, are bound to be unsatisfactory. For insofar as they try to circumvent the law and yet require for their warranted success the sort of justified coercion which is the exclusive preserve of the state's police powers, they will at a minimum result in violation of the law,[4] and more likely end in attempted usurpation of the law.[5]

It is unreasonable to expect anyone to give up that by which he lives, his employment, his shelter, his access to goods and services and loved ones in order for judicial procedures to be carried out equitably, in order to demand legal protections. Even if one were tempted to follow the libertarian and say that these are in fact reasonable expenses to pay for making the choice of living an open lifestyle, that a person always makes tradeoffs among his necessarily limited options, and that this condition does not warrant the state coercing *others* on his behalf—even if one believed all that, one would not, I think, go on and say that these costs are a reasonable price to pay to see one's assailants dealt justice or to enter a court of equity.

Now what is bitterly paradoxical about this blackmail by the judiciary is that it is a necessary concomitant of two major virtues of the fair administration of justice. The first is that trials are not star chamber affairs, but are open to scrutiny by public and press. The second is that defendants must be able to be confronted by the witnesses against them and have compulsory process for obtaining witnesses in their favor, while conversely prosecutors must have the tools with which to press cases on behalf of victims. In consequence, determinations of guilt and innocence must be based on a full examination of the facts. The result of these two virtues is that trials cast the private into the public realm.

The Supreme Court itself has recognized that public exposure of the private realm necessarily attends the workings of justice; thus wrote Chief Justice Burger for a unanimous Court in *United States v. Nixon:*

> [A]ll the values to which we accord deference for the privacy of all citizens . . . must yield . . . to our [nation's] commitment to the rule of law. This is nowhere more profoundly manifest than in our view that "the twofold aim [of criminal justice] is that guilt shall not escape or innocence suffer." We have elected to employ an adversary system of

criminal justice in which the parties contest all issues before a court of law. . . . The very integrity of the judicial system and public confidence in the system depend on full disclosure of all the facts.[6]

That trials cast the private into the public realm puts the lie to those condescending (would-be) liberals who claim that what gays do in private is no one else's business and should not be anyone else's business, so that on the one hand gays do not need rights, and on the other hand they do not deserve rights, lest they make themselves public. If the judiciary system is to be open and fair, it is necessary that gays be granted civil rights. Otherwise judicial access becomes a right only for the dominant culture.

In being *de facto* cast beyond the pale of civic procedures, gays, when faced with assaults on property and person, are left with only the equally unjust alternatives of the resignation of the impotent or the rage of man in a state of nature. Societies may remain orderly even when some of their members are denied civic procedures. Many tyrannies do. But such societies cannot be said to be civil societies which respect the rule of law.[7]

In October 1984, the governor of California signed a bill making actionable as civil suits assaults on gays which are motivated by an animus against gays.[8] In March of the same year, he had vetoed a civil rights bill which would have protected gays from private employment discrimination. Given the lived experience of gays, the former legislation will prove virtually pointless in the absence of the latter.

Making Political Rights Coherent

In the same 1938 case in which the Supreme Court programmatically withdrew its attention from the field of economic legislation, it set forth an agenda for itself in the area we now call civil liberties. The Court recognized *inter alia* that "legislation which restricts those political processes which can ordinarily be expected to bring about repeal of undesirable legislation" might need "to be subjected to more exacting judicial scrutiny under the general prohibitions of the Fourteenth Amendment than are most other types of legislation."[9] Even more perceptively the Court recognized that social, as opposed to legal, forces also might have the result for some groups of effectively excluding their participation in the political life of the nation: "Prejudice against discrete and insular minorities may be a special condition, which tends seriously to curtail the operation of those political processes ordinarily to be relied upon to protect minorities."[10]

Here it is argued that widespread *social* prejudice against gays has for them this very effect about which the Court, at the level of principle, so perceptively worried—the virtual eclipse of political rights. In the absence of gay civil rights legislation, gays are—over the range of issues which most centrally affect their minority status—effectively denied access to the political rights of the first amendment, that is, freedom of speech, freedom of press, freedom of assembly, and freedom to petition for the redress of grievances. Further, gays are especially denied the emergent constitutional right of association—the amalgam of the freedoms of speech and assembly—which establishes the right to join and be identified with other persons for common (political) goals.[11]

This eclipse of political access is most evident if we look at gays severally. Put concretely, does a gay person who has to laugh at and manufacture fag jokes in workplace elevators and around workplace coffee urns, in order to deflect suspicion from himself in an office which routinely fires gay employees, have freedom to express his views on gay issues? Is it likely that such a person could reasonably risk appearing in public at a gay rights rally? Would such a person be able to participate in a march celebrating the Stonewall Riots and the start of gay activism? Would such a person be able to sign, let alone circulate, a petition protesting the firing of a gay worker? Would such a person likely try to persuade workmates to vote for a gay-positive city-councilman? Would such a person sign a letter to the editor protesting abusive reportage of gay issues and events, or advocating the discussion of gay issues in high schools? The answer to all these questions is "obviously not!" Such a person is usually so transfixed by fear that it is highly unlikely that he or she could even be persuaded to write out a check to a gay rights organization.[12]

In the absence of 1964 Civil Rights Act protections, the vast majority of gays are effectively denied the ability to participate equally in first amendment rights, which are supposed to pertain equally to every citizen, and moreover pertain to every citizen *qua* individual. First amendment rights, like other such rights, apply directly to citizens or persons as individuals. They do not apply directly to groups and only derivatively to individuals. It will not do then to suggest that some, or even most, gays' inability to participate in politics is unproblematic on the alleged ground that other gays — those who *are* open about their minority status — may voice the interests of those who are not. This position simply confuses individual rights, like first amendment rights, with group "rights." The position further naïvely assumes that gays uniformly have the same interests and espouse the same views on any given gay issue, so that one simply needs to know one sociological fact — the percent of gays in the general population — to know the extent to which some publicly espoused gay interest is held.[13]

If further, for a moment, gays are viewed collectively as a potential political force, it should be clear that for a group that — fanciful contagion and recruitment theories of causation aside — is a permanent minority, it is hardly fair to be further encumbered by having the majority of its members absent through social coercion from the public workings of the political process.

If first amendment rights are not to be demoted to privileges to which only the dominant culture has access, then invisible minorities that are subject to widespread social discrimination will have to be guaranteed protection from those forces which maintain them in their position of invisibility. Civil rights protections are a very long step in that direction.

Now, it might be argued that first amendment rights are to be construed as mere immunities, that they merely prevent the government from interfering with certain types of actions, so that as long as the government and its agents do not, say, refuse parade permits to gays, smash up the gay press, deny the formation of gay student groups on state university campuses, and the like, then in fact gays do have first amendment rights just like everyone else.[14] In these circumstances, it would be reasonable to say that gays are *free from* active government interference in their political designs. Nevertheless, gays would still remain effectively denied the *freedom to act* politically.

Whatever else first amendment rights might be, they have as one of their chief rationales and purposes not merely *not making impossible* the procedures of democracy, but also actually promoting, enhancing, and making likely the proper working of democratic processes. To this end, then, first amendment rights need somehow to be construed not merely as immunities, as the mere absences of government interference, but as somewhat stronger rights. Indeed, they need to be realized as powers which place the government under a certain liability.

Democratic government should operate under the liability not only of removing its own possible interference with the dissemination of political views but also of removing those forces in society in general which block the *potentially effective* dissemination of political views.

At a minimum, potentially effective political activity requires that the political position espoused is widely and pointedly disseminated. Only with the widespread and lively dissemination of political ideas is it possible for a minority political position on social policy to have a chance of becoming the majority opinion and so of becoming government policy and law. If the majority of people never has the occasion to change its opinions to those of the minority, political rights would be otiose. It would seem incumbent upon government, then, to militate against those social conditions and mechanisms by which majority opinion perpetuates itself *simply by the elimination* of the hearing of alternative possible policies, or what is as good, *the reduction* of alternatives to the mere slogans of strawmen.

Now it is not a requirement for democratic process that minority opinions must at some point carry the day and become the majority opinion, as a sign that the system is working correctly. It is required only that minority opinions have their day in the court of the body politic, that majority opinion should not be allowed constantly to win out *by default*.

To this end, government must prohibit nongovernment agents from interfering with the political activities of individuals and groups. Thus, for instance, because we consider the freedom of assembly to be a power rather than merely an immunity, we not only insist that political rallies, say, should be immune from government interference but we also deem it a major obligation of government and its police actions to make actual as a power the rights of people to hold rallies by prohibiting goon squads and hecklers from disrupting political rallies. The goon performs an act considerably worse than simply assault when he strikes a speaker; the assassin worse than murder. A special need for police action against the goon and assassin arises over and above normal police activities of protecting civic rights.[15] Analogously, bigoted employers are the goon squads and hecklers that, when unrestrained by law, deny gays access to political rights. Civil rights legislation for gays should be considered an essential part of the police activities of the state.

Only when the government protects gays against discrimination in housing, employment, and public accommodation will gays have first amendment rights as powers. For all potentially effective political strategies involve *public* actions. More specifically, all the actions protected by the first amendment are public actions (speaking, publishing, petitioning, assembling, associating). Now, a person who is a member of an invisible minority and who must remain invisible, hidden, and secreted in respect to her minority status as a condition for maintaining a livelihood is not free to be public about her minority status or to incur suspicion by publicly associating with others who are open about their similar status. And so she is effectively denied all political power — except the right to vote. But voting aside, she will be denied the freedom to express her views in a public forum and to unite with or organize other like-minded individuals in an attempt to compete for votes which would elect persons who will support the policies advocated by her group. She is denied all effective use of legally available means of influencing public opinion before voting and all effective means of lobbying after elections are held.

Such denials to minorities of first amendment rights as powers differ in kind depending upon the minority affected, and remedies vary accordingly. Blacks, for instance, though constituting a visible minority, nevertheless, as the result of being in general poorer than whites, are effectively denied first amendment rights as powers, since blacks are, for financial reasons, effectively denied the political use of such expensive mass media tools as purchasing television time and newspaper space.[16]

For gays, it is not poverty *per se* which effectively denies them first amendment rights. Indeed gays are, as Kinsey showed, dispersed nearly homogeneously throughout all social and economic classes. Rather it is the recriminations that descend upon gays who are publicly gay that effectively deny them first amendment rights. Maybe such recriminations deny to them these rights even more effectively than poverty denies those rights to blacks, since the poor but visible at least have available to them such inexpensive but limited methods of public communications as sit-ins, marches, and demonstrations. Gays — as long as job discrimination is widespread — are effectively denied even these limited modes of public access.

On the one hand, the closeted condition of most gays has meant that nothing remotely approaching the widespread dissemination of views on gay issues necessary for any potentially effective political strategy has occurred in this country or any other. The condition has caused gay political organizations to be small, weak, inbred, ill-financed, impermanent, and subterranean. It greatly curtails any outreach to the nongay world, leaving such organizations largely "to preach to the converted." Membership tends to stand in inverse proportion to an organization's public profile; thus memberships in gay religious and other largely hermetic social organizations far outstrip those in gay political organizations.

In consequence, any widespread portrayal of gays and gay issues has been left entirely to the mercies of the mass media, which, however much they may preempt political discussion and activity, are no substitute for them. The general media have their own agenda, which includes politics largely to the extent that politics is entertaining. Regarding gays, the mass media have been able to see little beyond the titillation of fear and death. Such titillation after all is largely what keeps the mass media massive. It would be fanciful to say that hidden amongst the columns devoted to AIDS, Congressional scandals, and serial murderers is something like a robust national debate of gay issues. Little in this regard has changed in the last thirty years. Writing of the mainstream press during the period 1956–1960, historian John D'Emilio could summarize: "When articles did find their way into the press or periodicals, they tended to focus on scandal, tragedy, or stereotypical images of homosexual and lesbian life. Gay women and men rarely enjoyed the opportunity to express in print their own views about their lives."[17]

Can the liberal press serve as a proxy for gays in the discussion of gay issues? In December 1984, the Berkeley city council passed domestic partner legislation which gives gay couples the same city employment benefits as legally married couples. This was the first successful piece of domestic partner legislation in the country and so a major gay news story. Yet *The New York Times* thought this beacon worthy of but twenty-three words and failed even to mention that the law applied to and was designed for gays, choosing rather to focus its three-inch article on Eldridge Cleaver's presence at the council meeting.[18] Subsequently, Cleaver's presence was made a feature in *The Times'* Sunday "Ideas and Trends" column — where, however, no mention at all was made of the domestic partner legislation.[19]

It is ironic that the antigay polemics of the conservative press have done a better job of covering gay issues than the liberal press. The January 1985 issue of *Moral Majority Report* contains three articles on gay issues, the March issue four, covering AIDS, first amendment issues, privacy rights, CIA employment, gay parents, and domestic partner legislation. The cover of the February issue features a photograph of two gay men in affectionate embrace. In context, such reportage is but editorial fodder. Even so, to an extent, it inadvertently defeats itself in two ways. First, just the mention of gays begins to break down the taboo that has previously surrounded even the mention of homosexuality.[20] Second, what is intended to shock the reader and elicit an immediate sense of revulsion also, as a side-effect, informs and desensitizes the reader. He who sees men kissing in an image accompanying a conservative funding solicitation will be less surprised when he sees the original on the street. The more conservatives discuss gay issues, the less they can rely on automatic social responses which are fueled by fear of the unknown.[21] If a group's greatest political enemies are the best media aides it has available, the media can hardly be an adequate proxy for the wide dissemination of the group's views.

On the other hand, local dissemination of views is also impeded. Indeed, the closeted condition of gays blocks the most effective sort of political communication in which gays in particular might engage with others — personal conversation. Social reality is such that many people do not know or think they do not know any gay people firsthand. Such widespread ignorance is a breeding ground for vicious stereotypes. Problems compound when misunderstanding is added to ignorance. Many people *sort of* think they know that someone, say, a workmate is gay. But given the way the workmate acts, especially in avoiding certain topics, in being selectively "absent" from social intercourse or in confusingly broadcasting mixed messages, others think the gay person is embarrassed about his or her status and so do not initiate any discussion of it, and so further they are left with the impression that there is something wrong with gays because gays themselves seem to act as though there is. The nongay person oddly fails to realize that the gay person may have or — what comes to the same — may *suppose* he has solid prudential reasons for his skittish behavior.

When this widespread ignorance and misunderstanding combines with gut reactions to gays of fear and loathing or even just queasiness and discomfort, mere reportage (even accurate reportage) about gays or mere abstract discussion (even insightful discussion) of gay issues has little chance of success in changing the attitudes by which people conduct their lives. When people's attitudes are informed by deeply held emotional responses — ones perhaps central to their conceptions of themselves — reason's hope is slight. The most effective way of changing nongays' views about gays is for nongays to interact personally with some openly gay people.[22]

Such interaction is almost the only way to cut through stereotypes and fears, which when left unchecked tend mutually to aggravate each other into dangerous frenzy. At a minimum, personal contact generally reveals as sheer paranoia much of the fear some people have of gays. And yet such personal outreach of gays to the nongay person is not likely to occur, however willing the nongay person, as long as a gay person has to put her job and other major interests on the line to make the contact. It is after all at the job site and in certain public accommodations that people tend to have the sorts of contacts with others, initially strangers, which might lead to personal conversations. And yet it is exactly in these locations that a gay person is most likely to encounter discrimination if open about his status. And so the most effective avenue of communication for gays about the issues of importance to them as gays is effectively blocked in the absence of civil rights protections.

The California Supreme Court has taken cognizance of the adverse impact that employment discrimination has on political participation by gays. Prior to 1979, Pacific Telephone and Telegraph had an explicit company policy of firing gay employees. No systematic measures were taken by the company to find out who its gay employees were, but "manifest homosexuals," that is, gays who said they were gay or "made an issue of" being gay, were regularly fired. In a groundbreaking case, *Gay Law Students Assoc. v. PT&T Co.*,[23] the court ruled that such firings of 'manifest' gays violated the plaintiffs' political freedoms in violation of the sections of the California Labor Code which forbid employers from preventing employees from engaging or participating in politics.[24] The court recognized, for the first time in U.S. legal history, the special political plight of gays as an invisible minority. It acknowledged that if gays are to have political rights, they must be free to be open about who they are. After holding that the struggle for gay rights is political activity covered by the Code, the decision reads, in relevant part:

> A principal barrier to homosexual equality is the common feeling that homosexuality is an affliction which the homosexual worker must conceal from his employer and his fellow workers. Consequently, one important aspect of the struggle for equal rights is to induce homosexual individuals to "come out of the closet," acknowledge their sexual preferences and to associate with others in working for equal rights. In light of this factor in the movement for homosexual rights, the allegations of the plaintiffs' complaint assumes a special significance.[25]

Here the court recognizes that the ability to be openly gay is a necessary prerequisite for gays, *qua* gay, having any effective political rights. The California Labor Code, in its political dimension, stands to the first amendment as the 1871 Civil Rights Act, with its civil remedies for procedural abuses to equal protection, stands to the fourteenth amendment. These very general legislative acts turn the immunities of the amendments into effective powers.

Now, in the absence of such legislation the courts themselves should not take the step of construing constitutional guarantees as powers rather than as mere immunities,[26] by ruling, say, that first amendment rights entail rights to welfare and education as necessary enabling conditions for the equitable realization of first amendment rights. As long as the courts merely say in what ways the government *may not deploy* its monopoly of coercive forces against individuals and systematically avoid mandating (except as compensation for violations of constitutional immunities) that the government *must deploy* its monopoly on coercion in some way, then the courts, while retaining the legitimate capacity to construe constitutional rights broadly, avoid the conservative's common charge that in dilating constitutional guarantees, the courts mistakenly act like Platonic Guardians and usurp the proper power and function of legislatures.[27] But, the very last thing that Plato's Platonic Guardians do is to dispense to individuals immunities from state coercion. Their core activity, *like that of legislatures*, is essentially to deploy coercive force against individuals by either prohibiting or compelling acts in the private sector. If courts avoid coercing the private sector, they systematically avoid intruding into the essential activity of legislatures.

If, however, civil rights protections are to remain creatures of legislatures rather than the courts, the problem arises that the majority is left as the judge of its own fairness to minorities. Those most in need of such protections seem the least likely on their own to acquire them. Here the California case is instructive to political strategists. The labor code covers gays without explicitly mentioning them. Yet the omission is neither a rise nor an oversight. Rather, the labor code appeals to general principle and general social realities, and in doing so is broad enough in scope that many people will find it attractive legislation. For many can imagine themselves as potential beneficiaries of it. And so the likelihood of enacting such legislation is greatly enhanced.

That nonlegal social forces hinder robust political life to an even greater extent than does government coercion has been eloquently stated by John Stuart Mill:

> It is [social] stigma which is really effective [in stopping] the profession of opinions which are

under the ban of society. . . . In respect to all persons but those whose pecuniary circumstances make them independent of the good will of other people, opinion . . . is as efficacious as law; men might as well be imprisoned as excluded from the means of earning their bread. Our merely social intolerance roots out no opinions, but induces men to disguise them or to abstain from any active effort for their diffusion.[28]

Mill probably underestimated the effects of social intolerance in rooting out or even inverting opinions. He shows virtually no awareness of the possibility that members of a despised group may so thoroughly absorb the values of their culture regarding them that they become unwitting participants in their own oppression. Gays seem particularly prone to this mangling of their beliefs about themselves.[29] However, Mill is certainly correct in his general assessment of the effects of social ostracism and job discrimination in blocking the diffusion of unpopular beliefs and forcing their holders into lives of disguise. And though Mill never mentions homosexuals here or elsewhere in *On Liberty*, he could not have picked a clearer illustration for his general thesis.

Up to the AIDS crisis, the meager energies and monies of the gay rights movement had been directed almost exclusively at trying to get 1964 Civil Rights Act protections for gays.[30] Without these legislated rights, which would begin to bring gays into the procedures of democracy, gays have not even been able to begin thinking seriously about the substantial issues on which gays reasonably would want to exert influence in democratic policy making — issues, for instance, concerning sex and solicitation law, licensing, zoning, immigration policy, judicial and prison reform, military and police policy, tax law, educational, medical and aging policy, affirmative action, law governing living associations and the transfer of property, and 'family' law. By being effectively denied the public procedures of democracy, gays are incapable of defending their own interests on substantial issues of vital concern.

It is important to remember that the 1964 Civil Rights Act and similar legislation reasonably enough contain exemption provisions that allow for employment discrimination on the basis of an otherwise protected characteristic, *if* a business can show that the discrimination is reasonably necessary to the operation of the business — that is, that the discrimination is a discrimination in good faith. So, for example, it is reasonable for a bank to discriminate in its hiring practices against the invisible minority that consists of repeatedly convicted embezzlers, even though this minority may be organizing politically to try to reform embezzlement laws. However, given exemption provisions for discriminations based on *bona fide* occupational qualifications, ex-convicts, as an invisible minority subject to widespread discrimination, should be, as they are in a few jurisdictions, included within the reach of civil rights protections on the basis of the arguments advanced here. It is also important to note that the arguments for the inclusion of gays as an invisible minority within the reach of the 1964 Civil Rights Act hold good independently of whether gay sex acts are legal in any given jurisdiction.

Making Democracy Coherent

The previous section argued that the absence of civil rights protections for gays draws into doubt the fairness of current political *procedures* surrounding democratic voting. This section suggests that the same absence also draws into doubt the adequacy of certain *justifications* for democracy.

Perhaps the strongest argument for democracy is that democracy is justified on utilitarian grounds. Those who try to justify democracy as the institution which most directly gives expression to individual dignity simply overestimate the significance of political activity and voting in people's lives. The *consequences* of democratically enacted statute may be great for an individual, but for the vast majority of people, an individual's *contribution* to the democratic system — unless she is political by profession — is slight in her overall pattern of life. Campaigning and voting are sporadic activities. They are neither activities by which individuals sustain their day-to-day lives nor are they activities in which everyday activities culminate. At least one never nears anyone say "I work that I might vote" or "I live that I might vote." And so politics and voting are not integrative principles nor even integral parts of day-to-day life. They are not activities in terms of which any but a few do or should define their lives. The childless curmudgeon who religiously votes against school levies is no more dignified than the social worker who, caught up in a flurry of commitments, fails to vote. The resident alien is not deprived of essential human dignity by his inability to participate fully in the mechanisms of democracy.[31]

This is not to deny that many, even most, of the things that individuals do in their day-to-day lives do have political overtones. Since nearly all of everyday discourse is devoted to persuading people of this or that, or asserting to others the value of this or that, an individual's day-to-day activities will tend to shape other people's views in ways that may well register at the ballot box, but this registration is usually an entirely incidental and unconscious spinoff effect of day-to-day activities and not what motivates them or gives them importance in individuals' lives.

To make democratic politics the paradigmatically human activity is also to place it uncomfortably at odds with soundly held beliefs that voting should be restricted in what it may achieve. If one views voting as the paramount human value, and if voting is not to be made a merely formal activity, a hollow ritual, in virtue of having its effects voided, then one will be committed to a pure, direct democracy operating without substantive constitutional restraints and holding out the prospect that law can be the mere amassing of prejudice — a position virtually everyone would reject.[32]

Further, the right to vote ought not to be viewed even as a value on a moral par with other constitutional rights. The Court has persistently claimed for a century that voting if not *the* fundamental right is at least *a* "fundamental right" on the ground that voting is "preservative of all rights"[33] or, put somewhat more modestly, because voting is "preservative of other basic civil and political rights."[34] The Court, however, in these cases simply is conceptually confused. For democratic voting and its deployment of the state's coercive powers by majority rule are how fundamental constitutional rights, including "political" rights like speaking and assembling, are impinged and trampled. At best, the right to vote is how *legally* engendered rights, not constitutional rights, are preserved. That which is the vehicle for the destruction of rights cannot itself be viewed as on a par with them. Therefore, voting is a fundamental right not as other constitutional rights are fundamental, but in consequence of whatever role democracy properly plays in the constellation of just political institutions.[35]

In sum, democracy is a better registrar of desire than it is a vehicle of dignity. And as such, democracy is best justified in utilitarian terms.

It is reasonable to suppose that the policies that overall represent the wishes of the most people will be the policies which will most likely maximize utility. For given the complexity of *predicting* precise consequences of social policies for large and complex populations, relying on the *preferences* of the people in general rather than on the *predictions* of social engineers as likely indicators of future utility seems eminently reasonable.[36] It is precisely in the area of economics and areas which are productive of public goods — ones which each person wants but cannot get (or get efficiently) without the coercive coordinations of the state — that democracy is going to be the most accurate guide for social policy and least justifiably accused of irrationally burdening liberty.

However, if preferences pure and simple were the whole rationale involved in establishing social policy, social policies could be determined simply by direct democracy, as manifest in referenda and plebiscites.

For democracy coherently to have a preference-utilitarian justification, though, requires that a distinction be drawn between an individual's internal and external preferences. A person's internal preferences are her preferences for goods and services *for herself.* Her external preferences are preferences that she has for things *for persons other than herself.* To be *coherent* preference-justified democracy must discount and disregard a person's external preferences. For the person who has external preferences and who would have society act upon them is assuming for himself the role of social engineer — a role discredited by the very premises of the argument justifying democracy in terms of preferences.[37] Further, if democracy is to be an *accurate* gauge of likely utility maximization, it must for this reason also discount external preferences. For in general it is unlikely that anyone other than a person himself is going to know what is best for himself; hardly anyone will hold another's interest in the same regard that he holds his own.[38]

If, in consequence, external preferences are to be disregarded in the calculus of preferences, then direct democracy cannot be the instrument for this measurement. For referenda and plebiscites give equal weight to internal and external preferences; they give equal weight to the views of bigots and non-bigots. The remedy—where the distribution of powers rather than immunities is concerned—is a form of representative democracy in which it is hoped the elected official is rational enough and impartial enough to rise above popular prejudices and to take into account in her own voting only the internal preferences of her constituents. A legislator who discounts external preferences is not to suffer the accusation of moral elitism, for she is acting in accordance with sound democratic principles.[39]

Now, there are two sorts of external preferences which the rational legislator must discount. He must, on the one hand, discount the crass egoist's preferences for disutilities to be distributed to others and discount the possible attendant sadistic pleasures which the egoist might take in seeing other people's plans defeated.[40] On the other hand, the legislator must disregard the preferences of the altruist, who wishes to see the utilities of others promoted, and must discount the possible masochistic pleasures which the altruist might take in seeing the plans of others succeed.[41]

The rational legislator will sift through his mail, public debates, editorials, letter columns and all the other modes of public discussion of social policies and will winnow out external preferences. The legislator in this scheme is as justified in disregarding the altruistic opinions of the well-intended heterosexual (or would-be heterosexual) do-gooder who writes him supporting gay-positive legislation, as he is to disregard the opinion of the religious zealot who desires state persecution of gays.

If this system of justifications for democratic procedures is to work, it presupposes that people can present publicly their opinions on social policy as desires for things for themselves. They must be able to present themselves publicly as members of classes of which they in fact are members, so that they can promote legislation which benefits them as members of their classes.

For preference-utilitarianism to be a coherent rationale for democracy, everyone must be permitted to present himself in public debate as what he is. For preference democracy to be coherent, gays must be free to present themselves publicly as gays; and gays are effectively precluded this option, if the means by which they live can be removed from them at whim for being publicly gay. Civil rights protections for invisible minorities are a necessary prerequisite for coherent democratic processes.

Political Paradox and Political Decency

Current society puts gays in the queer position of not being able to fight for gay rights unless gays are already "out" and gays cannot be "out" unless gays already have gay rights. Paradoxically, gays cannot get gay rights, unless they already have them. This "particularly vicious circle" was noted over thirty years ago by an author himself closeted. Little has changed:

> On the one hand, . . . the social punishment of acknowledgment [of one's homosexuality is] so great that pretense is almost universal; on the other hand, only a leadership that would acknowledge [its homosexuality] would be able to break down the barriers . . . of discrimination. Until the world is able to accept us on an equal basis as human beings entitled to the full rights of life, we are unlikely to have any great numbers willing to become martyrs. . . . But until we are willing to speak out openly and frankly in defense of our activities and to identify ourselves with the millions pursuing these activities, we are unlikely to find the attitudes of the world undergoing any significant change.[42]

The author perhaps overestimates the potential effectiveness of martyrs;[43] but his main point is sound. As an invisible minority, gays cannot fight for the right to be open about being gay, unless gays are already open about it; and gays cannot reasonably be open about being gay, until gays have the right to be openly gay. One would hope that once society was made aware of this paradox, if society had any sense of decency and fair play, it would on its own move to establish civil rights for gays.

Notes

1. For libertarian argument against the 1964 Civil Rights Act generally, but for some government involvement in assuring access to courts and political processes, see for example Anne Wortham, "Individualism versus Racism" in Tibor R. Machan, ed., *The Libertarian Alternative,* pp. 403–7 (Chicago: Nelson-Hall, 1974).

2. See *Gideon v. Wainwright,* 372 U.S. 335 (1963) (held that the sixth amendment requires that states provide defendants in criminal trials with a lawyer).

3. Rosemarie Tong, "Lesbian Perspectives," in *Women, Sex, and the Law* (Totowa, N.J.: Rowman & Allanheld, 1984), p. 187.

4. Example: in December 1982, the only two women's bars in NYC—unwilling, not without reason, to rely on police protections—initiated a "women only" door policy to protect patrons from persistent harassment from nongay males. This action, of course, violated state liquor codes (among others) which bar gender discrimination. The result: both establishments lost their licenses and were closed by the state (Tong, *Women,* p. 186). I leave here as open questions whether such a door policy could be justified as a private sector affirmative action program or whether, given the historically central role of bars in the development and maintenance of lesbian and gay male culture and politics, the license revocations should be subject to successful challenge as violations of the constitutional right to (political) association. On this role, see John D'Emilio, *Sexual Politics, Sexual Communities: The Making of a Homosexual Minority in the United States, 1940–1970* (Chicago: University of Chicago Press, 1983), pp. 30–33, 49–51, and especially 97–99, 107, 186.

    Caveat emptor: usually, though not always, such Constitutional challenges to civil rights ordinances have worked against rather than in favor of gay male and lesbian interests, especially when religious rights have been invoked. See, for example, *Walker v. First Presbyterian Church,* 22 F E P Cases 762 (Cal. Super. Ct., 1980) (Free Exercise Clause voids application of municipal gay employment protections to gay church organist).

5. For a grisly example of such vigilantism—a case of revenge over an alleged violation of personal rights in which the avenger is in no position to seek recourse in the law—see Tong, *Women,* p. 189; for further examples and analysis, see "Lesbian Battering" *Gay Community News,* January 14, 1984, 11(25):13–17, and Kerry Lobel, ed., *Naming the Violence: Speaking Out About Lesbian Battering* (Seattle: The Seal Press, 1986).

6. 418 U.S. 683, 708, 713, 709 (1974).

7. I have not here intended to address a complementary problem of criminal justice for gays: whether, when gays stand accused of crime or pursue civil litigation, they get fair treatment from police, bench, and jury. For some eye-opening examples of patently prejudicial and abusive treatment of gays from the bench, see Rhonda R. Rivera's magisterial "Our Straight-Laced Judges: The Legal Position of Homosexual Persons in the U.S.," *Hastings Law Journal* (1979) 30:799–955 and for a history of police abuses of criminal procedures against gays, see D'Emilio, *Sexual Politics,* pp. 14–15, 30, 49–51, 70, 110–11, 120–21, 157, 182–84, 187–88, 193–94, 200–1, 202, 206–7.

    To the extent that civil rights legislation for a group tends to legitimate that group in the eyes of society as a whole, gay civil rights legislation would in fact increase the likelihood of gays getting fair trials. The issue is complex, but I doubt that this benefit outweighs the general inappropriateness of government throwing its weight behind one or another lifestyle or class. There is no guarantee that the government's symbolic actions are a ratchet that turns only in the direction of the good, so gays would do well to remember that what government may bless government may curse. I am inclined to agree with neoconservatives that gay civil rights legislation is not warranted *if* its main purpose and effect is simply a symbolic legitimizing of gays. See Jean Bethke Elshtain, "Homosexual Politics: The Paradox of Gay Liberation," *Salmagundi* (1982–1983) 58–59:255.

8. While I think that all assaults (or at least highly aggravated ones, as queerbashings almost always are) should *qua* assaults be actionable as civil suits, I do not think that they should be actionable (especially with punitive damages) *simply in virtue* of some political dimension of the assault, such that the only distinguishing feature between actionable and nonactionable assaults is simply the assailant's social or political beliefs and attitudes. Indeed, to the extent that a law draws a distinction based solely on the political dimension of some violent act, the law should be declared unconstitutional on first amendment grounds.

9. *United States v. Carolene Products Co.,* 304 U.S. 144, 152 n.4 (1938).

10. *Ibid.* In this circumstance, laws affecting discrete and insular minorities "may call for correspondingly more searching judicial inquiry." *Ibid.* To date, race, alienage and, to a lesser degree, gender and illegitimacy have in the Court's eyes marked out discrete and insular minorities warranting special judicial protections from the political process.

    If this section is correct, gays also ought to be considered a discrete and insular minority *on the very ground* that the Court gives in establishing the classification, namely, that prejudice tends to push the minority group out of the political process. See John Hart Ely, *Democracy and District* (Cambridge: Harvard University Press, 1980), pp. 162–64. See also Justice Brennan's dissent from denial of certiorari for *Rowland v. Mad River Local School District*, 470 U.S. 1009 (1985).

If given the status of a "suspect" class with attendant Constitutional protections under the fourteenth amendment, gays would be largely spared legislation that is targeted specifically against them. They would be guaranteed rights as *immunities* or certain negative freedoms, but this protection alone is nowhere near a sufficient guarantee of gay social justice. For as long as gays, even with immunity rights, still remain outside the political system, they will not be able to register their *interests,* however well protected their (immunity) *rights* may be. At a minimum, gays require for social justice that public policy take their interests into account.

11. See Lawrence Wilson and Raphael Shannon, "Homosexual Organizations and the Right of Association," *Hastings Law Journal* (1979) 30:1029–74 and Donald Solomon, "The Emergence of Associational Rights for Homosexual Persons," *Journal of Homosexuality* (1979–1980) 5(1–2):147–55.

12. Some organizations, like National Gay Rights Advocates, desperately aware of this last problem's magnitude, set up fund-raising account "fronts" with innocuous-sounding names, like "Legal Foundation for Personal Liberties," in an attempt to ease money, if not persons, out of the closet. Many organizations simply dissimulate, lying by omission or vagueness in assuming for themselves closeted names; thus the national gay political action committee baptizes itself "The Human Rights Campaign Fund."

13. The "Letters" columns of gay tabloids are regularly littered with frequently vituperative but always anonymous contributions of those who claim that open gays do not represent their interests, indeed positively destroy their interests. These authors though are in a nearly hopeless position politically; the column is their only outlet, an incredibly narrow one at that, and readers reasonably enough are going to doubt the convictions and the courage of conviction of those who resort to anonymity. Such doubt is the reason most mainstream tabloids decline publication of anonymously submitted letters.

More generally, as D'Emilio, writing of the years bridging 1980, claims: "the [gay] movement itself shows no unanimity as to the social rearrangements that equality would require," *Sexual Politics*, p. 247.

14. For the *status quaestionis* of gays and the first amendment, see José Gómez, "The Public Expression of

Lesbian/Gay Personhood as Protected Speech," *Journal of Law and Inequality* (1983) 1:121–53, and Paul Siegel, "Lesbian and Gay Rights as a Free Speech Issue: A Review of Relevant Caselaw," *Journal of Homosexuality,* (1988) vol. 15, in press. See also *National Gay Task Force v. Oklahoma City Board of Education*, 729 F.2d 1270 (10th Cir. 1984) (law permitting the dismissal of a teacher for advocating or encouraging homosexuality in a way that might come to be known at the teacher's school ruled unconstitutional on its face), aff'd mem. by an equally divided Court, 470 U.S. 903 (1985).

15. Meting out greater penalties to the goon or assassin than to a typical assailant or murderer does not punish the criminal simply on the basis of his political views, as it does in the case of the queerbasher (see note 8 above). Rather the criminal here is given a greater punishment because the result of his action is a greater offense — the disruption of legitimate government. It is true that but for his political views he probably would not have committed the greater offense, but that is irrelevant.

16. For a general defense of first amendment rights as powers and for an application of the view to blacks, see Alan Gewirth, *Human Rights* (Chicago: University of Chicago Press, 1982), pp. 310–28.

17. D'Emilio, *Sexual Politics,* p. 109.

18. "Berkeley Council Backs Friendship Benefits," *The New York Times*, December 7, 1984, p. Y12.

19. "The Trials of Cleaver," *The New York Times*, December 9, 1984, p. D7. See also note 43 below.

Paul Burstein summarizes the role of the mass media in the black civil rights movement thus:

> Media coverage had no independent effect on the outcome [of the civil rights movement]. That is not to say that the media were not important. It is very plausible, as so many have suggested, that media coverage of the activities of the civil rights movement was necessary if the movement was to succeed in getting the public concerned about the issue. But the media did not play an independent role. Coverage followed upon events; it did not, in the aggregate, precede them.

Paul Burstein, *Discrimination, Jobs, and Politics: The Struggle for Equal Employment Opportunity in the United States Since the New Deal* (Chicago: University of Chicago Press, 1985), p. 95.

20. On this important role of antigay polemics, see D'Emilio, *Sexual Politics,* p. 52.

21. Conservative attention to gay issues runs another risk as well. For many people the traditional taboo on even discussing gay issues may be one of the chief mechanisms by which homosexual desire is kept from

waxing into consciousness and act. See Michael Slote's "Inapplicable Concepts and Sexual Perversion" in *Philosophy and Sex,* Robert Baker and Frederick Elliston, eds., 1st ed., pp. 261–67 (Buffalo: Prometheus, 1975). See also Renaud Camus' forward to *Tricks: 25 Encounters* (New York: St. Martin's, 1981), p. xi: "Still other [homosexuals], and doubtless they are even today the majority, are unaware of such tastes because they live in such circumstances, in such circles, that their desires are not only for themselves inadmissible, but inconceivable, unspeakable. They possess no discourse of accommodation with which [they might] assume such desires and could change lives only by changing words."

22. The State of Oregon conducted a study of gay employment discrimination and found that positive attitudes toward gays in the workplace index closely to the degree of workers' firsthand acquaintance with gays. State of Oregon, Department of Human Resources, *Final Report of the Task Force on Sexual Preference* (Portland: State of Oregon, Department of Human Resources, 1978), pp. 73–87. For a review of the empirical literature on stereotyping of gays, see Alan Taylor, "Conceptions of Masculinity and Femininity as a Basis for Stereotypes of Male and Female Homosexuals," *Journal of Homosexuality* (1983) 9(1):37–53, especially 37–44.

23. *Gay Law Students Assn. v. Pacific Telephone and Telegraph Co.,* 24 Cal. 3d 458, 595 P.2d 592, 156 Cal. Rptr. 14 (1979).

24. Cal. Lab. Code, §§ 1101, 1102 (West 1971). These sections were passed in 1937.

25. *Gay Law Students Assoc. v. PT&T Co.,* 24 Cal. 3d at 488 (1979).

26. Exceptions are those few rights in the Constitution that explicitly are powers, namely, a defendant's right to compulsory process at criminal trials for producing witnesses on his behalf and thirteenth amendment rights against slavery and involuntary servitude.

27. See for example Chief Justice Burger's dissent in *Plyler v. Doe,* 457 U.S. 202, 242–43 (1982): "The Constitution does not constitute us as 'Platonic Guardians' nor does it vest in this Court the authority to strike down laws because they do not meet our standards of desirable social policy.... The Court employs, and in my opinion abuses, the Fourteenth Amendment in an effort to become an omnipotent and omniscient problem solver." This view simply confuses immunities and powers.

28. John Stuart Mill, *On Liberty,* Elizabeth Rapaport, ed., (Indianapolis: Hackett, 1978), pp. 30–31, cf. p. xv.

29. See Andrew Hodges and David Hutter, *With Downcast Gays: Aspects of Homosexual Self-Oppression,* 2d ed.

(1974; Toronto: Pink Triangle Press, 1979) and Barry Adam, *The Survival of Domination: Inferiorization and Everyday Life* (New York: Elsevier, 1978), especially chapter 4.

30. Successes have been few in number and their effects minimal. Municipal protections, in particular, tend to be limited in scope, have weak enforcement provisions, have frequently been voided by popular referendum, and have been successfully challenged as unconstitutional violations of state charter provisions which grant powers to cities.

31. For a critique of the view that politics represents the central medium for dignity and human value, see Gerald Doppelt, "Rawls' System of Justice: A Critique from the Left," *Nous* (1981) 15:259–307.

32. So correctly Ronald Dworkin arguing against John Hart Ely's *Democracy and Distrust* (note 10 above), which interprets constitutional rights essentially as only procedural rights. See Ronald Dworkin, *A Matter of Principle* (Cambridge: Harvard University Press, 1985), pp. 58–69.

33. *Yick Wo v. Hopkins,* 118 U.S. 356, 370 (1886).

34. *Reynolds v. Sims,* 377 U.S. 533, 562 (1964); cf. *Harper v. Virginia Board of Elections,* 383 U.S. 663, 667 (1966).

35. The Court is vaguely aware of this contingent status of what is fundamental about voting, even though the awareness stands at odds with the Court's "preservative of rights" analysis. Thus the Court correctly holds that "the right of suffrage is a fundamental matter *in a free and democratic society*" (*Reynolds v. Sims,* 377 U.S. at 561–62 [1964], emphasis added) and more fully, that "though not regarded strictly as a natural right, but as a privilege merely conceded by society according to its will, under certain conditions, nevertheless [voting] is regarded as a fundamental political right" (*Wick Yo v. Hopkins,* 118 U.S. at 370 [1886]).

The value of the role which democracy plays in any system of just institutions will more than sufficiently warrant bars to most democratically generated restrictions and regulations of the franchise — even if voting is not given the same rank of importance as those other constitutional rights which are implicit in the idea of ordered liberty. *Textually* the right to vote may be derived from the overall structure of the Constitution.... *Reynolds v. Sims* reaches the right result: infringements on the right to vote must pass the highest constitutional standards.

36. For a related argument to this end, see Ronald Dworkin, *Taking Rights Seriously* (Cambridge: Harvard University Press, 1977), p. 233.

37. This argument is similar to an argument that Dworkin makes only in passing to the effect that in many cases counting a person's external political preferences (say,

for some group not to get some scarce resource, when the person does not want or need the resource for himself) will simply be self-defeating from a utilitarian standpoint (*Taking*, p. 235 middle). I do not wish to commit my argument to Dworkin's assumptions that the right to treatment as an equal is the most fundamental of rights (*Taking*, p. 273) and that taking external preferences into account in social policy is wrong as violating that right (*Taking*, pp. 234–35, 275–76).

Even the necessary proviso in any utilitarian justification for democracy that each person's preferences are to count for one can be justified in purely utilitarian terms without appeals to general principles of equality. For, given the presumption that we are only considering conscious *homo sapiens* as voters and are not including in the franchise, say, comatose individuals or especially sensitive creatures from space, and given that people are more equal than unequal in their sensitivity and in the volume of their desires, then it seems likely that assigning one nonweighted vote to each will be a more accurate gauge in general of overall preference than if we try to establish some (unimaginable) mechanism to weight votes for small variations in either sensitivities or intensities of preferences.

38. See Mill, *On Liberty*, pp. 74–75.

39. So correctly Dworkin, *Taking*, p. 255, but contrast p. 276 bottom, where it is claimed that the mechanisms of democracy are incapable of winnowing internal and external preferences. In the latter passage, though, Dworkin simply runs together the mechanisms of direct democracy and representational democracy. The numerous cases in which city councils have passed gay civil rights legislation only to have it overturned by vast margins in referenda would suggest that legislators can on occasion rise above the prejudices of their constituents. The solution to the problem is not to abandon all hope that legislatures might effect a refined utilitarianism, opting instead for a democratic system awash in prejudices and checked only by constitutional immunities. The solution is for the Court to dust off the Guarantee Clause of the Constitution with its requirement that the federal government guarantee a *republican* form of government in the states (article IV, section 4), resurrect it from the deadletter

status to which it was assigned in the original reapportionment case, *Baker v. Carr*, 369 U.S. 186, 224 (1962), and with it void that decidedly nonrepublican mode of governance: the referendum. Cf. *Fortson v. Morris*, 385 U.S. 231, 249 (1966) (Fortas, J., dissenting).

40. I disagree with Dworkin that external preferences are no "less a source of pleasure when satisfied and displeasure when ignored, than purely personal preferences" (*Taking*, p. 276). The pleasure of external preferences satisfied is illusory in intensity. For such pleasures are parasitic upon a mere perceived *contrast* of one's situation to that of another—and are not consequences of anything one has done or experienced on one's own. Such pleasures have a similar status to mere absences or cessations of pains. One can discount such pleasures *even on a utilitarian account*. Again, one need not resort to a theory of rights to rid the utilitarian calculus of external preferences; see n. [37] above.

41. See Dworkin, *Taking*, pp. 235, 277 top. Whatever the moral worth of the altruist's acts and their masochistic pleasures, the intensity of the pleasures is again illusory based not upon anything that one's self has accomplished or experienced directly.

42. Donald Webster Cory [pseud.], *The Homosexual in America* (New York: Greenberg, 1951), p. 14. For the strange history of "Donald Webster Cory," subsequently the antigay polemicist Edward Sagarin, see D'Emilio, *Sexual Politics*, pp. 33, 57, 98, 139, 167–69.

43. Thus during the 1985 nationally televised Academy Awards, a seemingly ingenuous presenter could describe a documentary movie on the assassination of a gay activist elected official—*The Times of Harvey Milk*—merely as "a film about American values in conflict." *GayLife* [Chicago] March 28, 1985, 10(39), sect. X, p. 1. Had the film not won the "best documentary" award, no one in the audience of millions not already in the know would have learned that the film even had a gay content. As it was, the award recipients made mention only of their subject's pride, not his death, while those in the know were left with the suspicion that the Academy supposes that killing gays is an "American value."

AUTONOMY, EQUALITY, COMMUNITY:
The Question of Lesbian and Gay Rights[1]

Morris B. Kaplan

Morris B. Kaplan believes that liberty and privacy rights are not a sufficient grounding for gay and lesbian rights. He relies on case law and philosophical theories of justice to ground claims for fair treatment. He closes by discussing the potential for conflict among the diverse communities in our society. (Source: Reprinted with permission from Praxis International *11 (1991) 195–213.)*

In this paper I present an argument as to the principles at issue in the invocation of lesbian and gay rights. My immediate concern is to show the need for a more robust conception of lesbian and gay rights (and of human rights generally) than is implied in the analysis of such claims under the rubrics of liberty and of the right of privacy. Lesbian and gay rights will be analyzed in terms of three kinds of claims: for the decriminalization of private, consensual homosexual acts between adults; for protection against invidious discrimination; and for the recognition of the ethical and social status of lesbian and gay relationships and associations. By emphasizing the distinctive features of the third class of claims, I articulate a political-ethical framework in which conceptions of autonomy, equality, and community are mutually developed and examined.

I. What Are "Lesbian and Gay Rights"?[2]

Claims of lesbian and gay rights encompass a range of arguments regarding the right relationships between gay people and the state. As the movement for lesbian and gay rights has developed in the United States since the 1960's, these claims have come to include disparate demands on the political order, supported by diverse and potentially conflicting conceptions of the scope and limits of legitimate state action. This political situation has been exacerbated and made more urgent by the impact of the AIDS epidemic.

However, it remains important to identify and clarify the divergent strands of a movement for lesbian and gay rights. It may be useful to indicate three primary categories for such claims: (1) decriminalization of homosexual activities between consenting adults; (2) the prohibition of discrimination against lesbians and gays in employment, housing, and public accommodations; and (3) the legal and social recognition of the ethical status of lesbian and gay relationships and community institutions. Approximately one-half of the states continue to prohibit specified sexual activities (usually anal and oral intercourse) even when pursued in private between consenting adults; some jurisdictions proscribe such activities among "persons," others specifically target "persons of the same sex." Moral and political opposition to such criminalizing of intimate sexual behavior is generally articulated in terms derived from John Stuart Mill's classic essay *On Liberty*. Legal strategies seeking to invalidate such legislation as an unconstitutional infringement of individual "rights of privacy" culminated in the Supreme Court's 5–4 decision of *Bowers v. Hardwick*,[3] when the Court refused to overturn Georgia's laws banning consensual sodomy. Litigation in state courts premised on the provisions of state constitutions has met with some success.[4] What is important to note here is that the claim underlying demands for decriminalization is an individual right "to be let alone." At issue is the limitation of the state's authority to regulate individual behavior between consenting adults in which no one is harmed.

A somewhat different range of concerns informs opposition to invidious discrimination against lesbians and gays. Here the movement for lesbian and gay rights joins African-Americans, women, religious and ethnic minorities, and the handicapped in seeking the protections provided to some of these groups by the United States Congress in the Civil Rights Acts of 1964 and 1965 and by subsequent similar enactments by states and localities. When couched in constitutional terms, these claims invoke the "equal protection clause" of the 14th Amendment, whereas privacy claims depend on the "due process" clause. According to a recent survey in the *Harvard Law Review,* over 60 jurisdictions currently include sexual orientation among the categories protected against discrimination in their civil rights laws; however, this list includes only two states, Wisconsin and Massachusetts.[5] Of course, the federal civil rights laws do not include sexual orientation as a protected category. Civil rights legislation in general prohibits discrimination against specified groups in employment, housing, and public accommodations and provides a range of remedies from injunctive relief through compensation of damages to punitive damages. Claims by lesbians and gays for such protection envision a more positive role of the state in assuring lesbian and gay rights. Indeed, the demand of protection against discrimination asks the state to prohibit and regulate the conduct of private citizens to prevent them from exercising their prejudices against lesbians and gays in specified areas of commercial life. Richard Mohr has effectively marshalled the arguments favoring the inclusion of lesbians and gays in civil rights legislation, emphasized the importance of such legislation as a guarantor of fundamental rights, and indicated the need for transcending the terms of libertarian analysis.[6] Mohr articulated the role of the state in this context as that of a "civil shield."

A related but distinct class of claims emerge when we turn to the growing demand on states and the law for recognition of the status of lesbian and gay relationships, institutions and communal needs. Among the practical issues addressed here are: the right of lesbians and gays to marry or otherwise establish "domestic partnerships"; the entitlement of lesbian and gay partners to the benefits of health insurance, lease or rent stabilization privileges provided "spouses" or "family members," or the dignity of recognition within the institutions that provide for the sick and dying; the demands of lesbian and gay organizations for official status in public schools, universities, or professional associations; the status of lesbian and gay institutions in the politics and provision of health care during the AIDS crisis; the recognition of lesbian mothers and gay fathers as fit custodians of their own

children and of lesbians and gays generally as potential foster or adoptive parents.

At issue here is the demand for the recognition and respect of lesbian and gay relations and institutions within the broader legal, social, and ethical context. Let us note that: the state functions in these terms not only as a civil shield protecting lesbians and gays against invidious discrimination by private citizens, but also as a positive agency for actualizing the aspirations of lesbian and gay citizens. Moreover, the rights in question here are not simply those of individuals, but of couples, families, and voluntary associations. Ultimately what is at stake is the moral legitimacy and ethical validity of lesbian and gay ways of life. These claims may reveal the political and philosophical heart of the movement for lesbian and gay rights. Far from being "icing on the cake," such demands are the real "bread and butter" underlying more abstract and formal conceptualizations of lesbian and gay rights. These issues provide a focal point for comprehending the resistance to lesbian and gay rights as well as a perhaps surprising locus for potential reconciliation between lesbian and gay rights and traditionally formulated "family values" and community norms. Indeed, attention to the ethical and social status of lesbian/gay relations and institutions will permit us to probe and to clarify the problematic role of "community" in contemporary political thought and practice.

II. The Uses and Limits of Privacy

In this section I consider the development of a constitutional right of privacy as it bears on the question of lesbian and gay rights in particular. A fullblown conception of lesbian/gay rights requires that we go beyond the limitations of a right of privacy with its primarily negative connotation of a "right to be left alone." At best the right of privacy grounds arguments against the criminalization of private consensual homosexual acts between adults; it has little bearing on the regulation of discrimination or on the recognition of lesbian and gay relationships and institutions. Nevertheless, the recognition of a constitutional right of privacy with the implication of the equal enjoyment of such rights by all citizens is an important component of a fully articulated conception of lesbian and gay rights. Properly interpreted in the context of political theory and constitutional morality, the right of privacy encompasses basic principles concerning individual autonomy, limited government, political neutrality, and democratic pluralism. Unfortunately, although not decisive in philosophical terms, the constitutional right of privacy as articulated in *Griswold v. Connecticut* and subsequent cases has become problematic in relation to the jurisprudence and politics of the current Supreme Court. Nevertheless, an examination of the jurisprudence developed in the "right of privacy" cases will be of more than historical interest.

The great irony of the privacy jurisprudence is that it receives its most coherent and theoretically impressive formulation in Justice Blackmun's dissenting opinion in *Bowers v. Hardwick*.[8] In that case, the Court refused to invalidate Georgia's consensual sodomy laws as a violation of constitutionally-based privacy rights (at least insofar as the law applied to homosexuals). The concept of a constitutional right of privacy was first formulated in *Griswold v. Connecticut*,[9] in which the Court invalidated a state ban on the possession and use of contraceptive devices and substances. Although the result was supported by a majority of 7–2, the Justices offered quite diverse statements of the decision's rationale. As a result, the constitutional right of privacy has been the subject of a vigorous and heated academic and political debate, most recently and dramatically in the hearings on the nomination of Judge Robert Bork to the Supreme Court. Nonetheless, since 1965, the right of privacy has been applied to invalidate state laws aimed at regulating a variety of activities; the enjoyment of "obscene" materials in the home, in *Stanley v. Georgia*[10]; the availability of contraception to unmarried adults in *Eisenstadt v. Baird*,[11] and to minors; and, of course, the right of a woman to terminate her pregnancy by abortion in *Roe v. Wade*.[12]

The *Griswold* line of cases has been vehemently criticized as an instance of unprincipled judicial legislation with no support in the text or history of the Constitution. Full consideration of these arguments goes to the heart of contemporary constitutional theory and is beyond the scope of this paper. However, it is important to recognize this background in evaluating the Court's decision of *Bowers v. Hardwick*. Simply stated, to see the Court's retreat here as an instance of homophobia may be the optimistic view of the matter: one cannot rule out the possibility that the right of privacy as such no longer commands the support of a majority of Justices of the Supreme Court. If so, the implications extend quite beyond lesbian and gay rights; the Court's recent vacillations on a woman's right to abortion are further evidence in this regard. Political preferences aside, what is to be said on behalf of the constitutional right of privacy? What place does it play in a sound scheme of constitutional rights? What are its possibilities and limitations as a basis for lesbian and gay rights?

In his classic dissenting opinion in *Olmstead v. United States*,[13] Justice Brandeis identified the right of privacy as "the most comprehensive of rights and the right most valued by civilized men;" he defined it as "the right to be left alone." We must distinguish between privacy rights as defined by common law or by particular state or federal legislation and a right of privacy guaranteed by the United States Constitution. The latter, as formulated in *Griswold*, comes into play when a litigant seeks to have federal courts invalidate state legislation as an infringement of the due process clause of the 14th Amendment. It is noteworthy that in his opinion in *Griswold*, the great conservative jurist John Harlan found the issue relatively unproblematic: the Connecticut law was invalid because it constituted state interference in marital relations which have been insulated against government intervention by generations of history and tradition. Harlan found that the freedom of married couples to decide whether or not to have children was "implicit in the concept of ordered liberty," citing Justice Cardozo. The decision was not so easy to justify for Justice Douglas and his allies on the Court, who had expanded the reach of the due process clause by insisting that the 14th Amendment incorporated and applied to the states the specific provisions of the Bill of Rights. In part, this view was intended to protect individual rights at the same time that it limited the discretion of the Supreme Court by emphasizing that these rights were grounded in a literal reading of the text of the Constitution. This liberal literalism was developed as a corrective to the expansive and indeterminate reading of the 14th Amendment by which an earlier, conservative Court had employed doctrines of "substantive due process" to invalidate New Deal legislation. Justice Black, a leading proponent of the incorporationist view and a great defender of individual rights, actually dissented in *Griswold,* on the basis that he could find no textual basis for a constitutional right of privacy.

The political context of contemporary controversies over "strict construction" and "original intent" has served to obscure the fact that an earlier generation of constitutional fundamentalists like Black and Douglas urged a literal reading of the constitution to limit state action and expand the range of protected rights. Having rejected doctrines of "substantive due process" in favor of a thoroughgoing textualism, Justice Black was unable to find support for a constitutional right of privacy in the specific language of the Bill of Rights. For Douglas, who wrote the opinion of the court in *Griswold,* the task was to identify the general principles or values underlying the specific provisions of the Bill of Rights and to recognize their force as elements of due process of law. In his opinion, he found privacy to be a fundamental value underlying the First, Third, Fourth, Fifth, and Ninth Amendments. Justice Goldberg, in his concurring opinion, placed particular emphasis on the Ninth Amendment, which states that the enumeration of "certain rights" in the Constitution should not be construed as to "disparage other rights which are retained by the People." The language of the Ninth Amendment stands as a continuing rebuke to those who would limit constitutional rights to those enumerated literally in the other provisions of the Bill of Rights.

In retrospect, one may observe that Justice Douglas did not advance the cause of constitutional clarity by describing the source of the right of privacy as "penumbras and emanations" of the Bill of Rights. These are neither terms of art, nor especially artful terms. A generation of law professors has written its way to tenure by making fun of Douglas' rhetoric in *Griswold.* It is rather less easy to dismiss the analysis which identifies personal privacy as an underlying value protected by such specifics as the prohibition of unreasonable searches and seizures, the protection against compulsory self-incrimination, the guarantee of free exercise of religion, and the proscription of quartering soldiers in people's homes. What is at issue

in the right of privacy is the theory of limited government which informs the constitutional framework. For the framers, this theory was critically linked to the conception of natural rights, possessed by persons as such, independently of any positive legal or constitutional enactments. As Senator Joseph Biden insisted in his exchanges with Judge Bork at the confirmation hearings, rights are something one is born with; they are not given to us by the government. Although such theories have been out of fashion, especially among academics, for over a century, they played an important role in the philosophical defence of the American Revolution and were institutionalized in the Bills of Rights enacted as parts of the constitutions of the newly-independent states and eventually of the United States.[14] What attention to the Ninth Amendment emphasizes is that the enumeration of rights to be protected against infringement by the new governments was understood as a recognition and specification rather than a positive creation of individual rights. Thus the constitutional right of privacy appears as a belated formulation of a conception of the relation between individuals and their government which is central to the political philosophy of the Constitution. Indeed, the Federalists had initially opposed the adoption of an enumerated Bill of Rights as part of the Constitution on the grounds that it was unnecessary and potentially misleading. They feared that later generations might come to view such a list as exhaustive of constitutionally protected individual rights. Alexander Hamilton insisted that the Constitution created and defined the powers of a limited government whereas persons naturally possessed rights prior to the institution of government.[15] When the Bill of Rights was adopted in the first Congress, the Ninth Amendment was adopted as a prophylaxis against the "'strict construction" of personal rights.

In his dissent in *Bowers v. Hardwick,* Justice Blackmun summarizes the privacy jurisprudence in terms of the protection of zones of privacy which pertain to both the physical spaces persons occupy and the decisions they are entitled to make in the conduct of life. Privacy rights protect both places and personal choices from arbitrary interference by political authorities. The recognition of such zones of privacy does not constitute total insulation against all public regulation. Rather, the identification of fundamental rights of privacy requires that attempts by the government to intervene in private spaces and decisions be subject to critical scrutiny by courts enforcing constitutional standards. Such scrutiny seeks to strike a balance among individual rights and legitimate public objectives by considering the importance of the aim, the intrusiveness of the proposed means, and the possibility of less restrictive alternatives. The point here is that courts have developed over generations reasonable standards for striking the requisite balance once fundamental rights have been identified.

The issue in *Bowers v. Hardwick* was whether such a privacy right encompasses consensual homosexual acts between adults. The scope of privacy rights, like the reach of the due process clause generally, requires interpretive argument which identifies and analyzes competing private and public values in regard to the values, history, and political practice of the community. As Professor Cass Sunstein has recently stressed, adjudication under the due process clause tends to be conservative, looking to the history and traditions of the nation to identify cherished values and recognized constraints on government.[16] The difficulty always is to articulate persuasively the general principles which are embodied in such history and practice. The differences between Justice White, who wrote the opinion of the court, and Justice Blackmun, who dissented, may be seen in the very manner in which each formulates the right at issue in *Bowers v. Hardwick*. For White, Hardwick, who contested the constitutionality of the Georgia law, was seen as asserting a constitutional right of "homosexuals to engage in sodomy." One is hardly surprised at White's failure to find support in the Constitution for a right thus defined. For Blackmun, at issue is the right of individuals to pursue happiness through freely-chosen intimate associations with other persons.[17] For him, such a formulation states a moral and legal principle of constitutional magnitude, lying at the heart of the scheme of constitutional protections of individual rights. Further, he sees this principle as articulating the rationale which underlies the Court's previous privacy decisions. The recognition of a fundamental right of intimate association, which is infringed by the criminalization of consensual sexual conduct between adults, requires careful examination of the objectives of the state in enacting such a law. Blackmun concludes that the alleged public interest may not out-

weigh the personal rights at issue. His analysis of the state's interest in maintaining the community's professed standards of sexual morality leads beyond considerations of privacy as such into the broader issue of how the enforcement of public standards of morality is to be justified in a society committed to democracy and individual liberty. This question, critical for any theory of lesbian and gay rights, is the subject of the next section of this paper.

Let me summarize the discussion of the constitutional right of privacy so far. I am persuaded that the constitutional right of privacy enunciated in *Griswold* and its progeny has a legitimate and important place in constitutional adjudication. Consistent application of the relevant principles would have required the Supreme Court to invalidate Georgia's consensual sodomy law in *Bowers v. Hardwick*. At the very least, that decision is an unjustifiable retreat from the principles of the privacy cases. Such retreat may signal the willingness of a majority on the current Court to abandon the constitutional right of privacy altogether. However, it is not at all clear that a securely established constitutional right of privacy would be adequate to encompass the full range of lesbian and gay rights discussed in section I. In the remainder of this essay, I am concerned to explore more fully the range of ethical and political, as well as legal, principles at work in the movement for lesbian and gay rights. Further probing of the constitutional right of privacy will shed light on related aspects of our constitutional morality which may be less vulnerable than privacy rights to the vicissitudes of academic, political, and judicial fashion. In particular, I want to show how Justice Blackmun's analysis of the right of privacy may be developed in relation to an account of personal autonomy and public justification as concepts fundamental to our political culture.

III. The Individual Liberty/ Community Morality Debate[18]

Although lesbian and gay rights may not be adequately defined by opposition to the criminalization of homosexual acts between adults, the fact remains that the proscription of lesbian and gay sexuality is a central feature of the ethical and political situation.

What distinguishes lesbian and gay citizens from the members of other minority groups which have asserted their civil rights in recent decades is that lesbians and gays alone have been told that their freedom must be limited to accord with the moral standards of the community. Indeed, Justice White not only refused to recognize the rights asserted in *Bowers v. Hardwick,* but he characterized their assertion as "facetious." Here we confront a stumbling block to the movement for lesbian and gay rights which sometimes threatens to overwhelm all other issues. Lesbians and gays are seen as asserting individual liberties which conflict directly with the right of the community to use the criminal law to define standards of morality. In his dissent, Blackmun carefully examines and rejects the claim that Georgia may prohibit private consensual sodomy between adults as part of its effort to maintain "a decent society," that is, to enforce the alleged standards of community sexual morality as such. Here, the constitutional analysis intersects with the debate within academic philosophy and jurisprudence concerning "law, liberty, and morality." Indeed, Justice Blackmun cites Professor H. L. A. Hart of Oxford in support of his position.

Any contemporary discussion of lesbian and gay rights must include some mention of the Hart/Devlin controversy. The debate was occasioned by the recommendations of the Wolfenden Commission in Great Britain in 1957, which included the liberalization of laws governing prostitution and the decriminalization of private, consensual homosexual acts between adults. The Wolfenden Report specifically relied on J. S. Mill's formulation of the proper limits of the state's authority over the individual from *On Liberty.* Mill limited the jurisdiction of the state to the regulation of those actions which cause or threaten harm to specific interests of concrete individuals. He rejected the sovereignty of the state over individual or consensual activities where no one is hurt or threatened by harm, even where the community regards such activities as immoral. In a public lecture subsequently published as *The Enforcement of Morals,* the British jurist Lord Patrick Devlin challenged both the Commission's recommendations and its reliance on Mill's principle.

Devlin called into question Mill's distinction between self-regarding and other-regarding acts as well as his limitation of legitimate state concern to those other-regarding acts which cause or threaten to cause harm to distinct individuals. He urged that the state has a right, indeed a duty, to maintain the moral fabric of society through the use of criminal sanctions, even against private consensual conduct. He claimed that there was no more a right to commit private immorality than a right to commit private treason. Devlin argued that a society cannot survive without a shared morality and that the enforcement of moral standards through the criminal law is necessary social self-defense. Hence, Devlin proposed a defense of legal moralism in utilitarian rather than moral terms. In fact, the test which Devlin offered for identifying those moral principles which the state is justified in enforcing was the feelings of the ordinary citizen, "the man on the Clapham omnibus." Devlin proposed that the intensity of such feelings of "indignation, offense, and disgust" was a proper measure of their importance in maintaining the moral fabric of the community.

Devlin's argument evoked a considerable response, most notably from H. L. A. Hart in his article "Immorality and Treason," and subsequently in the lectures published as *Law, Liberty and Morality.* Hart rose to defend Mill's position, raising critical objections to Devlin in the process. This is not the place to rehearse the ensuing debate in detail. However, several comments are appropriate in this context. Hart insists that the moral status of criminal laws cannot be identified simply with the extent to which the conduct proscribed is felt by majoritarian sentiment to be immoral. Rather, he emphasizes the need to subject both the private behavior in question and its proscription to examination in terms of principles of critical morality. He insists that morality as a practice includes not only the evaluation of actions or courses of conduct, but also of the standards by which such particulars are to be judged. The specific instrument of critical morality he deploys is Mill's harm principle and the more general utilitarian ethic to which it is linked. He is particularly acute in calling attention to the suffering caused by the application of criminal penalties, not only to those actually punished, but to their families and friends as well as to the much larger population of those threatened with such punishment. Hart's analysis is invaluable in shifting the terms for an ethical evaluation of state regulation of individual sexuality. What is at issue in the criminalization of harmless consensual sexual activity between adults is not simply the striking of a balance between individual liberty and community morality. Rather, the question must be reformulated in terms of the morality of using the coercive apparatus of the state to enforce homogeneity of sexual conduct on those who neither cause nor threaten harm to others. The important philosophical question then comes to turn on the status of the harm principle itself and of the general standards of critical morality in terms of which the use of coercion to enforce conventional moral standards may be evaluated. These questions are the subject of Sections IV and V below.

The issues that emerge in the Hart/Devlin controversy may help to further focus this enquiry into the broader context of lesbian and gay rights. Although Devlin's account of morality seems to me fatally flawed (as Ronald Dworkin and others have argued in detail),[19] at a more general level he emphasizes a crucial point; the law exists as an expression and implementation of the moral standards of a community. Hart is correct in insisting on the need for critical moral standards which may be deployed in the moral and political evaluation of conventional social norms. However, such standards of critical morality must themselves be defined within the context of the moral practices of specific historical communities. What is required is a more complex model of social morality which includes both majoritarian beliefs and attitudes and practices of criticism and justification within the actual institutions and historical aspirations of a community. The public and institutional character of such practices is particularly evident when one considers the foundations and limits on the state's coercive regulation of individual conduct.[20] Devlin's argument combines an emotivism in ethics with a meta-ethical utilitarianism to justify the use of force to maintain the community's moral beliefs. Hart identifies the inadequacies of this view, but his own use of the harm principle is associated with a utilitarian ethic which does not comport easily with the rights-based framework of American liberal democracy. Within the context of American institutions, including a written constitution and a Supreme Court charged with its enforcement through judicial review, critical morality is itself often conceptualized in terms of constitutionalism. Actually, Americans are deeply ambivalent about the moral status of law, combining skepticism about government and its acts generally with something akin to reverence for the Constitution and the Supreme Court. This ambivalence is easily seen in popular attitudes toward lawyers. On the one hand, they are fast-talking shysters who make a living by putting one over on unsuspecting lay people. On the other, the most prestigious public office in the land turns out to be that of the Chief Justice of the Supreme Court, a lawyer. Alexis de Tocqueville quite early observed the central role of law and lawyers in the American democracy. Something more important is at stake here than a popular confusion between law and morality, which a healthy dose of positivism would remedy. Rather, the ethos of the American democracy, its politics, history and traditions, includes a "constitutional morality" which functions critically within our moral discourse as well as being institutionalized in the federal judiciary.[21] The specific tradition of the United States aspires to realize universal ideals of autonomy, equality, and community.

IV. Constitutional Morality

In this section, I return to Justice Blackmun's dissent in *Bowers v. Hardwick,* using his legal analysis to illuminate broader ethical and political principles implicated in the question of lesbian and gay rights. Blackmun's explication of privacy rights and rights of intimate association exhibits central features of a constitutional morality which encompasses and grounds the more narrow legal argument. The right of privacy gains plausibility as a constitutional principle because of its coherence with the theories of natural rights and limited government which inform the structure of the United States Constitution. In his dissent, Blackmun insisted that such principles invalidated Georgia's prohibition of consensual sodomy between adults. In Blackmun's rejection of the state's rationale for the necessity of such a law to maintain "a decent society," he deploys fundamental principles which explicate and clarify the reach of constitutional rights of privacy. Importantly, he invokes the authority of the First Amendment with its prohibition of the establishment of religion by the state and its guarantee of the free exercise of religion by the citizens. Although Georgia's sodomy statute was religiously "neutral," and Hardwick did not raise a conscientious defense of his sexual preferences, Blackmun used the principles underlying the First Amendment to reject the moral justification of the sodomy laws which played such a large part in the opinions of the majority. Blackmun does not reject the validity of a moral justification of the criminal law as such, but rather emphasizes the inadequacy of the conception of morality supporting the sodomy law. The moralistic defense fails for Blackmun because morality cannot be simply identified with the sentiments of a majority; neither the intensity nor the longevity of such sentiments immunize them from constitutional scrutiny. The derivation of such moral sentiments from a consensus within the Jewish and Christian traditions actually renders them suspect under that clause of the First Amendment which prohibits the establishment of religion. However, Blackmun is not simply applying a positive constitutional prohibition, but rather articulating and applying a critical principle of public morality in democratic society.

Like other specific provisions of the Bill of Rights, the First Amendment requires interpretation in historical and philosophical terms in order to yield moral and political principles. The establishment clause must be construed in terms of the sectarian controversies of the 17th and 18th centuries, as well as the oppression of dissenting minorities by the established churches and emergent states of Europe. Ironically, the identification of religious orthodoxy with established state power was reinforced in the 17th century as an "Erastian" solution to the problem of sectarian conflict and warfare. Peace would be ensured by empowering the sovereign political authority with the last word on potentially explosive differences of religious belief.[22] By the 18th century, liberal sentiment recognized the desirability of tolerance of diverse religious beliefs within the context of a securely established political order. This shift was made possible in part by the emergence of stable political structures and by a defusing of the politically subversive implications of sectarian difference. Thus, the rejection of an established religion by the Founding Fathers acknowledged the legitimacy of both an autonomous secular order of politics and a plurality of religious creeds and institutions. The free exercise clause underlines the conjunction of a secular politics

with religious pluralism. Critically, the plurality of religious institutions is to be guaranteed by protecting the authority of individual decision-making in this domain. However, the free exercise of religion is not simply an individual "right to be left alone." Religious practices require the existence of historical communities with their shared rituals and doctrines if religion is not to be reduced to a matter of mere private opinion. The point is that freedom in religious matters has to be with observance and activity in concert with like-minded others as well as with private belief.[23] The juxtaposition of religious freedom with the explicitly political rights protected in the First Amendment becomes more easily comprehensible when one notices the specifically public and associative dimensions of religious liberty.

By calling attention to the relevance of the First Amendment to the privacy issue, Blackmun develops both critical and positive aspects of constitutional morality. His analysis links up fundamental conceptions of political neutrality, moral community and individual autonomy within a constitutional framework. First, religious teaching alone cannot be used to legitimate state action: the moral principles underlying the criminal law require justification in secular terms acceptable to a community of diverse religious beliefs and varieties of unbelief as well. Secondly, a constitutional morality must recognize the centrality of individual autonomy in moral matters. Recognition of the right of individuals to determine freely their conduct is itself an element in the morality within which democratic politics is conducted. Restrictions on such individual autonomy cannot be justified in majoritarian terms, but rather in terms of the need to guarantee for all the right to make such choices. The secular framework within which competing moral claims and practices must be adjudicated is conjoined with a commitment to the equality of persons with regard to their rights. Thirdly, the rights to which each person is entitled under the dictates of constitutional morality will be expressed in their activities, often in association with other individuals. That is, constitutional rights are not simply individual but apply to concerted activities and to the institutions to which they give rise. Once again, Tocqueville early identified the centrality of voluntary associations in the ethos of American democracy. Justice Blackmun's analysis of the constitutional right of privacy shows the need for reaching beyond a "right to be alone" towards a recognition of the priority of the rights of association required by lesbian and gay citizens in creating and maintaining satisfying ways of life.

V. Autonomy, Pluralism, and Neutrality

Blackmun's dissent in *Bowers v. Hardwick* explicates the terms of a constitutional morality which informs legal reasoning and decision-making but which is also embodied in the "unwritten constitution" of moral discourse and political practice. In terms of lesbian and gay rights, Blackmun articulates a framework which may be applicable to lesbian and gay claims for state protection against discrimination and for the recognition by the state of lesbian and gay relationships and institutions as well as to decriminalization. In this section, I will briefly outline such an analysis in more general philosophical terms. The discovery of natural rights theories at the core of the privacy jurisprudence is not simply a matter of historical contingency. The principle which underlies the right of privacy is the affirmation of the centrality of uncoerced individual decision-making in important areas of human activity. In Kantian terms, morality requires recognition of the autonomy of the person. Such recognition implies the right to participate in the ethical life of a society in which each is free to join with others in creating the institutions necessary for pursuing a good life. The development of the political implications of moral autonomy was inherent in the social contract tradition which provides a relevant context for both Kantian ethics and the political practice of the American Founding Fathers.

The conceptual links between natural rights and social contract theories and Kantian moral philosophy have been most fully articulated in the work of John Rawls, especially *A Theory of Justice* and "Kantian Constructivism in Moral Theory."[24] Rawls has also explicated the egalitarianism required by such theories: autonomy is a characteristic of persons as such, and modern constitutional democracies are legitimated by the extent to which persons are recog-

nized as being equal in their rights. Finally, Rawls' theory emphasizes the centrality of moral pluralism among the circumstances of justice — of diverse conceptions of the good embodied in the practices of distinct associations within society, understood as a basic structure of fair cooperation. In his recent work[25] Rawls has emphasized the extent to which his theory of justice is an explication of the normative assumptions of the political culture of liberal democracy rather than a rational deduction of principles of justice *sub specie aeternitatis*. He has further emphasized the extent to which the conceptions of moral personality, the right, and the good, which are deployed within the theory, themselves function politically as conceptions appropriate to the public culture of constitutional democracy rather than as comprehensive philosophical doctrines. In the discussion which follows, I want to show how a Rawlsian analysis supplements and confirms the treatment of lesbian and gay rights developed thus far through a reading of Justice Blackmun's dissent in *Bowers v. Hardwick*.

Rawls does not explicitly address the issue of lesbian and gay rights, or of sexual freedom generally, except for some rather cryptic remarks in the course of an argument against perfectionism in *A Theory of Justice*. However, it is not difficult to construct a Rawlsian approach to the question. The central conception must be the priority of the right over the good. Rawls takes a plurality of conceptions of the good as one of the "circumstances of justice" in the modern world. The basic structure of society as a system of cooperation among free and equal persons cannot be grounded on a unitary or comprehensive conception of the good life. Rather, the theory of justice attempts to identify those principles by which rational agents may agree to be governed regardless of the conception of the good they may hold. The "original position" is the representational device by which Rawls attempts to delineate such principles. The conception of the person employed here is meant to embody the minimal requirements of moral personality; freedom, equality, and rationality. To make plausible the original position as a situation in which rational choice is possible. Rawls introduces the notion of primary social goods which function as a kind of all-purpose means such that they appear desirable across differing conceptions of a comprehensive good. In his later writings, Rawls appears to modify his interpretation of primary goods by developing the notion of an overlapping consensus by which a diversity of associations animated by distinct ways of life may nevertheless agree as to the desirability of some goods, such as income, food, medical care. These conceptions of Rawls are important and raise many technical problems. What is critical here is that Rawls insists on the necessity of establishing a basic structure of social cooperation that encompasses a plurality of conceptions of the good and consequent ways of life. The aspiration of a theory of justice is to articulate the general principles of right which are to govern the interactions of diverse moral communities within an encompassing social framework. The constraints which bind all the members of such a society of societies must be justified through an appeal which is neutral as to comprehensive conceptions of the good.

It is important to take seriously the extent to which Rawls' moral pluralism is more than simply a concession to the diversity and complexity of modern political communities. Rather, Rawls' analysis turns on the requirements of maintaining a basic structure of cooperation among free and equal moral personalities. The rights of citizenship implicated in a theory of justice are derived by unpacking the conception of moral personality. For Rawls, this conception consists in: 1) a capacity for developing, pursuing, and revising a conception of the good: and 2) a capacity for recognizing the constraints of justice which must be observed if we are to cooperate with others. The earlier and best known sections of *A Theory of Justice* are devoted to showing the adequacy of Rawls' two principles of justice as a description of the most general features of such a structure of cooperation among free and equal moral persons. Thus, the neutrality of principles of justice among differing conceptions of the good is a political requirement entailed by the conception of persons as autonomous individuals capable of forming, enacting, and revising their own conceptions of the good in a context of social cooperation.

Although the rational agents in Rawls' original position are ignorant of their moral and social particularities, including religious beliefs, gender, social class, sexual orientation, etc., they are endowed with some general, "non-controversial truths" concerning human nature and a "thin" conception of the good,

derived either from a theory of primary goods or from the political fact of overlapping consensus. Thus, although principles of justice cannot be tailored to a particular mode of sexual preference or personal morality, we know that persons will have some sexual desires and emotional needs for intimate association with others, however diverse the details might be. We know also that such desires and needs will play an important part in an individual's formulation and pursuit of a conception of the good life. The question for a theory of justice thus becomes whether any constraints on the fulfillment of personal sexual and associative desires would be accepted in advance by rational agents unaware of their particular psychosexual constitutions. In sexual matters as in most others, the function of the representational device of the original position is to emphasize the requirements of mutuality among free and equal persons with divergent conceptions of the good life. Regarding acceptable limitations on the freedom of individuals to pursue sexual satisfaction through relations with others, it appears likely that something very like Mill's harm principle would be chosen by rational agents in the original position. Respect for the autonomy of moral persons would seem to require permitting them to work out their sexual and emotional identities and needs in voluntary interaction with each other constrained only by the insistence on mutuality and the prohibition of harm. Public authority is justified only to protect persons against coercion and harm.[26]

Justice as fairness has fuller implications for lesbian and gay rights than the ratification of arguments for decriminalization. The central concern for the equal treatment of persons within a framework of justice also supports the prohibition of discrimination based on sexual orientation. Again, the device of the original position demonstrates the implications of reciprocity. Uncertain whether one is in fact destined to be a bigot or a victim of prejudice, rational agents with a concern to promote their own life prospects, whoever they turn out to be, would rule out the denial of primary goods to anyone based solely on the disapproval of others. In addition, Rawls' analysis of primary goods buttresses the emphasis here on the centrality of respect and recognition of the relationships and institutions through which lesbians and gays in fact pursue their life plans. For Rawls, a unifying theme, which links primary goods to each other in the rational life plan of a morally autonomous person, is the primary good of self-respect, or, as he sometimes clarifies, of the social bases of self-respect. The denial of legitimacy to an individual's affectional and sexual preferences would seem radically to undermine the self-respect of individuals so affected. Rawls is clear that in actual societies, as opposed to the original position, persons require associations with others in order to pursue the good, to formulate and fulfill a rational plan of life. Thus respect for the full autonomy of individual citizens entails the social recognition of the associations, intimate and otherwise, through which they express their moral personality. The neutrality of the state functions both to assure a political framework for the cooperation of disparate associates and to establish principles constraining all the citizens which may be justified from the perspective of each. Moral pluralism and political neutrality are required by respect for individual autonomy. The use of coercive political authority to enforce a particular morality on society at large violates individual autonomy and fundamental principles of justice.

V. The Ambiguities of Community

It is easy to see the question of lesbian and gay rights as reflecting the contemporary controversy between deontological liberals with their fundamental commitments to individual autonomy and human rights and the communitarian critics of liberalism with their stress on social contexts and moral/religious traditions.[27] However, the matter is not nearly so simple. Notice the multivalent sense of community at work in the analysis of lesbian and gay rights offered here. The simple dichotomy between individual liberty and community morality is inadequate to comprehend the complexity of ethical and social relations.[28] Even an exclusive focus on decriminalization requires explication of the conflicting community values at issue in the use of the coercive apparatus of the law to enforce majoritarian norms of sexual conduct on nonconforming adults. To seek state prohibition of discrimination against lesbians and gays is to appeal to professed community standards of fairness, some of

which are embodied in constitutional guarantees of fundamental rights. Ideals of respect for individual autonomy and insistence on the equal treatment of diverse groups are themselves incorporated in the moral discourse and social practice of liberal constitutional democracy. Moreover, these ideals are articulated as norms of human interaction. The communitarian component of the movement for lesbian and gay rights becomes more clearly visible in the demand for recognition of lesbian and gay intimate associations and ethical institutions.

The conception of "community" figures here in at least three distinct ways. First, and more familiarly, "community" is identified with the dominant moral attitudes and related beliefs of historical and contemporary majorities. This is the sense represented by Devlin's "man on the Clapham omnibus" whose gut reactions are to be taken as indicators of the shared values Devlin deems necessary to the survival of society as such. We may label this sense of community as "conventional." What defines it is the fact of agreement among a number of people. Defenders of conventional community emphasize the importance of traditions as providing individuals with values and beliefs which may orient and guide them in their activities and social relationships. These values and beliefs are transmitted by the institutions of socialization, such as childrearing, training, and education; they gain in force from the attachment of the members of the society to their fellows. The conventional communitarian is likely to emphasize the importance of feeling over intelligence, tradition over reason, the local over the universal, social solidarity over individual autonomy. From such a perspective, the fact that homosexual practices have been condemned by church, synagogue, state and public opinion over the centuries is entitled to great moral weight and may justify the use of criminal sanctions to enforce conformity. Other than Devlin, contemporary communitarians like Sandel and MacIntyre have not addressed questions of lesbian and gay rights. However, their treatment of community is consistent with the conventional sense developed here.

The inadequacy of conceptions of community as convention, especially for those sympathetic to community as a value and as a source of value, becomes clear as soon as one considers the fact of pluralism so central to modern politics. Quite simply, there are lesbian and gay communities as well as communities of fundamentalists, orthodox believers, and "moral majoritarians." Indeed, there are liberal communities bound together by a common commitment to respecting differences and encouraging diversity. One of the transformations in the movement for lesbian and gay rights in recent years, in part a response to the AIDS epidemic, has been the emergence of a sense of distinctive group identity, shared values, and cooperative effort. The fact of pluralism entails not only the possibility of conflicting collective norms of behaviour and ways of life, but also the need for developing a more complex model of individuality. One aspect of both communitarian and feminist critiques of liberal individualism focuses as much on its allegedly overindividualistic model of human nature as on any specific normative political doctrines. Both feminists and more conservative communitarians urge the need for conceiving of the individual as situated in concrete historical, social, and familial settings rather than as isolated and self-enclosed.[29] Such an understanding of human individuality underlies the insistence in this essay that the realization of equal rights requires the legal and social recognition of the associative and communal forms of lesbian and gay life. "Community" in this sense refers to the institutional dimension of human activity. Learning from Aristotle and Hegel, the proponents of institutional analysis emphasize the social contexts which condition and sustain individual and collective life. Clearly, the conception of community as institution overlaps and includes some components of community as convention. However, by focusing on the ways in which communities are realized in the development of concrete ways of life and modes of interaction, the emphasis on institutions escapes both the abstraction of talk about shared values and the atomism implicit in reducing community to matters of individual feeling or belief. A major defect of much communitarian analysis is its failure to recognize that in modern societies the individual is situated in a plurality of institutional settings. Thus, one may be a lesbian, a mother, a Jew, a daughter of working class parents, a university teacher, and a psychoanalyst. Such diversity of social roles may subject the individual to conflicting ethical demands which go to the very heart of her personal identity. The major point here is that recognition of the moral personality as socially situated in a plurality of communities leads back to acknowledgement of the centrality of individual choice in the shaping of a life.

The potential for conflict among a plurality of communities is heightened when one defines each community in terms of a distinct conventional system of moral, religious, and other beliefs. Understood rather as institutions through which groups may organize their specific ways of life, communities are more easily understood as interacting and overlapping. Here, liberal theory, especially as developed in Rawls' more recent work, emerges as something other than an individualist alternative to communitarianisms. Rather, the liberal articulation of fundamental individual rights and constraining principles of justice is an attempt to map the conditions of coexistence for disparate ethical and religious communities within the overarching unities of modern pluralistic states. Thus, Rawls in his account of the state as a "social union of social unions" (a community of communities?) is as much the liberal heir of the Federalists as of John Locke. It is in these terms that one may identify a distinctively political sense of community through which conflicting claims of distinct groups may be adjudicated and a basic structure of cooperation established and maintained. The arguments marshalled in support of a robust conception of lesbian and gay rights interpret modern constitutional democracy and the political morality which supports it as just such a framework, both constraining and supporting the efforts of diverse moral communities to maintain their own ways of life. Finally, the respect for human equality and moral autonomy which underlies claims of individual rights locates persons in diverse and interacting social contexts and insists on the primacy of mutual respect as the governing norm in an encompassing community of right.

Notes

1. Earlier versions of this essay were presented to the Society for Lesbian and Gay Philosophy at the meetings of the American Philosophical Association in New Orleans in April 1990; the Fourth Annual Conference on Lesbian and Gay Studies at Harvard in October 1990; the Society for Systematic Philosophy at the American Philosophical Association in Boston in December

1990; the Columbia University Seminar on Homosexualities in March 1991; as well as in lectures at Williams College and the Massachusetts Institute of Technology. I am grateful to all of those whose oral and written responses have helped me to clarify my arguments, including: Robert Anderson, Robert Berman, Ron Caldwell, Claudia Card, Wayne Dynes, Frank Farrell, Ellen Haring, Michael Koessel, Peter Lipton, Richard Mohr, Hart Murphy, Michael Sherman, Rosemarie Tong, Randolph Trumbach, Richard Winfield. Special thanks to Edward Stein, who first encouraged me to undertake this work and who has continued as a careful critic and generous friend.

2. The references to "lesbian and gay rights" throughout this paper are not intended to ellide historical differences in the treatment of the two nor to settle contested political issues by rhetorical fiat. However, as I hope the text will make clear, the range of issues defined by my second and third categories of claims apply in common to both gay men and lesbians. Exclusive attention to decriminalization sometimes serves to disguise the extent to which this is the case. I hope to address in a subsequent essay the more general question concerning the relationship between feminist theory and practice and movement for lesbian and gay rights.

3. 406 S. Ct 2841 (1986).

4. Cf., e.g., *People v. Onofre*, 51 N.Y. 2d476 (1981).

5. Developments in the law—sexual orientation and the law. *Harvard Law Review* 62 (January 1989) 617–36.

6. Richard Mohr, *Gays/Justice* (New York: Columbia University Press, 1990), especially chapters 5–7.

7. 381 U.S. 479 (1965).

8. See note 3 above.

9. See note 7 above.

10. 394 U.S. 557 (1969).

11. 405 U.S. 438 (1972).

12. 410 U.S. 113 (1973).

13. 277 U.S. 438 (1928).

14. The philosophical issues posed by natural rights theories will be considered more fully in Sections IV and V. . . .

15. See especially *The Federalist* No. 84.

16. C. R. Sunstein, "Sexual Orientation and the Constitution, a note on the relation between due process and equal protection," 55 *University of Chicago Law Review* (Fall 1988) 1161–79. Sunstein argues importantly that whereas the due process clause looks back upon the history and traditions of the nation the equal protection clause addresses its universalist aspirations.

17. See Karst, "The Freedom of Intimate Association," *Yale Law Journal* 89 (1980) 624.

18. The major contributions by the initial participants who have given their names to the controversy are: Patrick Devlin, *The Enforcement of Morals* (London: Oxford University Press, 1965) and H. L. A. Hart, *Law, Liberty and Morality* (Stanford, Cal.: Stanford University Press, 1963), and "Immorality and Treason," reprinted in R. Dworkin, *The Philosophy of Law* (London: Oxford University Press, 1977). This exchange has generated an extensive literature which will not be treated here.

19. See especially, Ronald Dworkin, *Taking Rights Seriously* (Cambridge, Mass.: Harvard University Press, 1977).

20. This analysis relies in part on the conception of "law as integrity" developed in Ronald Dworkin, *Law's Empire* (Cambridge, Mass.: Harvard University Press, 1986).

21. The concept of a "constitutional morality" has been developed in rich historical and legal detail in David A. J. Richards, *The Foundations of American Constitutionalism* (New York: Oxford University Press, 1990). My argument does not rely on the specifics of Richards' account. The general notion may be found at work in diverse forms in Dworkin's works cited above and in Alexander Bickel, *The Morality of Consent*.

22. On the general issue see David A. J. Richards, *Toleration and the Constitution* (New York: Oxford University Press, 1986). See also Kirstie McClure, "Difference, Diversity, and the Limits of Toleration." *Political Theory* 18 (August 1990) 361.

23. See, e.g., *Wisconsin v. Yoder* 406 U.S. 205 (1972), in which the Court upheld the right of the Amish community to raise their children in accordance with a religious way of life which conflicted with state laws on compulsory education. Of course, such rights are not unlimited and will be balanced against conflicting interests as in the cases of religious objections of the provision of necessary medical care to children.

24. John Rawls, *A Theory of Justice* (Cambridge, Mass.: Harvard University Press, 1971), "Kantian Constructivism in Moral Theory," *Journal of Philosophy* 77 (1980) 525.

25. See especially, John Rawls, "Justice as Fairness: Political Not Metaphysical," *Philosophy and Public Affairs* 14 (1985) 237. "The Idea of an Overlapping Consensus," *Oxford Journal of Legal Studies* 7 (1987) 4.

26. For a detailed argument analyzing the "due process" clause of the 14th Amendment in relation to the harm principle, see Richards, *op. cit.*, note 22 above.

27. See, e.g., A. MacIntyre, *After Virtue: A Study in Moral Theory* (London: Duckworth, 1981); C. Taylor, *Hegel and Modern Society* (Cambridge: Cambridge University Press, 1979); M. Sandel, *Liberalism and the Limits of Justice* (Cambridge: Cambridge University Press, 1982). This debate has generated a rich and interesting literature. For an assessment, see Amy Gutmann, "Communitarian Critics of Liberalism," *Philosophy and Public Affairs* 14 (1985) 319.

28. The centrality of these questions to contemporary work in political philosophy and social theory may be highlighted by noticing a convergence in the critique of liberalism by "conservative" and "left" communitarians and important strands in feminism and Marxism. A crucial text is Marx's essay "On the Jewish Question." In a separate essay, I hope to analyze the implications of Marx' analysis for lesbian and gay rights as well as consider contemporary radical critics of liberal, rights-based theories. The present essay is an effort to address a number of the substantive concerns for community within the context of liberal thought. Among the works contesting such a project, see Iris Marion Young, *Justice and the Politics of Difference* (Princeton, N.J.: Princeton University Press, 1990), and Nancy Fraser, "Rethinking the Public Sphere" in *Social Text* 8–9 (1990) 56.

29. See especially, S. Benhabib, "The Generalized and Concrete Other," in Benhabib and Cornell, *Feminism as Critique* (Minneapolis: University of Minnesota Press, 1987). See also, S. M. Okin, "Reason and Feeling in Thinking About Justice," *Ethics* 99 (January 1989) 229.

THE RIGHT TO FIGHT AND HOMOPHOBIC
EXCLUSION IN THE ROTC

René Trujillo

René Trujillo discusses two arguments for excluding gays, lesbians, and bisexuals from the U.S. military—that such people are vulnerable to blackmail and that their inclusion would undermine morale. He rejects both arguments and concludes that not only should the military drop the ban but that universities should ban ROTC until it does.

Whether anyone should orient his or her career goals around a life in the military is an open question I will not attempt to answer here. Yet I affirm the value of a civilian-trained officer corps, and argue that we must fight for free access to ROTC programs on university campuses.

Equal access to opportunities does not remedy the loss of personal rights associated with life in the military. However, it addresses the irrational and unethical discrimination currently defended by the U.S. Department of Defense (DOD) in its position on gay, lesbian, and bisexual exclusion from ROTC programs. No institutions affiliated with ROTC programs should aid and abet the DOD disenfranchisement of individuals expressing alternative sexual orientations. To do so would sanction the most destructive element of the political state—the power to silence dissent. It would affirm the right to perpetrate institutional violence against individuals for whose sake these same institutions were founded. We would thus dissolve the noblest aims of good government and commit ourselves to the most base aims.

The arguments the DOD most often uses to defend its discriminatory policy of exclusion are that homosexuals and bisexuals as a class are more vulnerable than heteros to blackmail, and that in the structure of military life they would make others so uncomfortable that their presence would compromise morale and the chain of command.

The first argument is easy to dismiss, since only the provincial, punitive, and irrational response the military has toward homosexuals and bisexuals makes for this vulnerability within its own ranks. Ending the need to lie about one's sexual orientation will rectify this vulnerability in military life. Also, the DOD must take responsibility for its role in perpetuating these irrational punitive responses.

The second argument is more interesting. It is undoubtedly true that many members of the military would be uncomfortable if gay, lesbian, and bisexual soldiers "came out." Indeed, it might very well adversely affect morale and threaten the chain of command in certain instances. However, none of this can be used as an argument for excluding homosexuals and bisexuals. It is rather an argument for providing therapeutic opportunities for the homophobic. This level of insecurity exposes a condition that makes them less equipped to deal with the demands of the progressive and tolerant world. The silver lining is that through their behavior these homophobic individuals are easy to diagnose, so therapy can begin right away.

The work of developing our society along democratic and socially progressive lines must be advanced at our colleges and universities. We in the academic community must stand up for the rights of all. The rights of any individual depend on the vigor with which we defend the rights of all individuals. Now more than ever we must renew our commitment to this task. Colleges and universities with ROTC programs must require the DOD to rescind its unethical and irrational exclusion policies. Absent such change we must sever our ties with such programs so that through our dissent we can bring the argument to a reasonable and equitable resolution.

▐▌▐▐▐▐ Disability and Equality

DISABLED AMERICANS PUSH FOR ACCESS

Mary Johnson

Mary Johnson discusses the Americans with Disabilities Act (ADA) in terms of both its promise and its vulnerabilities. She gives a wide range of examples where the ADA has been neutralized through local bargaining. Yet in the end, she is cautiously hopeful. (Source: Reprinted by permission from The Progressive, *August, 1991, 409 East Main Street, Madison, WI 53703.)*

Florida has a law requiring wheelchair access to big new hotels. But that didn't stop the architects of the Cocoa Beach Hilton from providing virtually none. And when local building officials refused to okay the blueprints, the Hilton chain simply got a waiver from the city attorney. Local disability-rights groups tried but failed to keep the hotel from opening in 1986, and now, five years and thousands of dollars in legal costs later, hotel and disability groups have settled out of court, with Hilton agreeing to only a few changes for access. Its claim: Since the hotel was already built, renovation for access would now be impractical.

Florida's law isn't just for hotels; it covers all new public buildings. Many states have had such disability protections on the books for years—with similar frustrations for those who would like to see them enforced. A year-old Federal law, the Americans with Disabilities Act (ADA), extends such protections—and others—nationwide, and the not-yet-final rules to implement the act are set to go into effect this summer. When rules on access to public accommodations were first proposed in February, Hilton told the press that the company had already begun to improve access at its hotels, and would "promptly move to be in accordance" with the final rules.

Activists in Florida and elsewhere are, to put it mildly, skeptical. Cheered last summer by passage of the law, they are now watching carefully to see that the rule-making process isn't used by big business to gut their hard-won victory.

Forty-three million Americans are said by the Census Bureau to have some sort of a physical or mental disability. In testimony before Congress leading to passage of the ADA, many of these individuals told of the lack of access and blatant discrimination they face in everyday life, from trying to find an apartment they can get into in a wheelchair to being refused a job because of a history of mental illness that makes potential employers nervous. Like racial and ethnic minorities, women, and gays, people with disabilities have been the target of systematic discrimination in this country ranging from exclusion due to lack of simple physical access to outright prejudice.

A growing disability-rights movement over the past fifteen years has reminded the public that this is the one minority to which we can all belong. Its activists have engaged in nonviolent direct action to secure a requirement that city buses have wheelchair lifts. They have fought legislative battles to change state building codes to require barrier-free access, and they have lobbied to be added to human-rights laws which prohibit discrimination against women and minorities. The movement has also had an effect on the news and entertainment industry in its efforts to see that people who have disabilities are portrayed without saccharine or tragic overtones.

The ADA of 1990 extends to the private sector protections first set out in 1973 in Title V of the Rehabilitation Act, which affected only companies with Federal contracts and groups receiving Federal funds. Besides requiring access and forbidding discrimination in such public accommodations as hotels, restaurants, shops, and service facilities — including state and local government — the ADA also prohibits discrimination against disabled people by employers of fifteen or more workers and requires employers to make "reasonable accommodation" to their disabilities. The law also requires access to transportation and telecommunications, including a national relay service for users of telecommunication devices for the deaf (TDDs). Title V was vague, but thanks to careful lobbying by disability-rights activists, the ADA is specific.

"The more prescriptive we could be in our statutory language, the less of a problem we'll have in court," says Patricia Wright, director of governmental affairs for the Disability Rights Education and Defense Fund. She should know, Title V was the focus of a Supreme Court ruling that went against disabled people; *Southeastern Community College v. Davis* exempted institutions from providing accommodation for disabled people if to do so caused an "undue" economic hardship.

Despite the disabled community's best efforts, that "undue-hardship" line wormed its way into the ADA, too. No other minority's rights are limited by such a legally explicit economic loophole. But, say lobbyists, the ADA would not have passed without it, so they compromised to have a law at all.

Knowing this to be its loophole, the business community tried this spring to get the Equal Employment Opportunity Commission, which is the rule-making authority for the ADA's employment protections, to allow even more leeway. The Equal Employment Advisory Council, a consortium of 225 of the nation's largest employers, wants the Commission to agree that if an employer "in good faith . . . concludes that a particular accommodation would be an 'undue hardship,'" the burden of proof shifts to the person with the disability — though normally it would be on the employer.

The business community also wants to fiddle with the formula for defining "undue hardship," since it didn't get everything it wanted when the legislation was before Congress. The formula — called "Factors to Be Considered" — is complicated, but specific. So business has come up with what's known as the "site-specific argument."

The Commission proposed rules, for example, that would allow franchises to get out of providing access no matter how big the parent firm is, if the unit — let's call it Hamburger Heaven — is locally owned and has limited finances and would thus face an "undue hardship." Never mind that the national Hamburger Heaven corporation licenses it to use its trademarks and menu, its architecture and color scheme, tells it how much special sauce to put on its burgers, how long to fry the fries, and at what temperature: The corporation need not take responsibility for telling its franchise-holders to accommodate disabled people.

The Council representing business also asked the Commission to agree that a business didn't have to fund its units' access "if that corporation puts a lot of autonomy in its individual units." The example it uses is a corporation owning a chain of convenience stores, each of which is an individual "cost center" on the corporate books and each of which may face its own "undue hardship" in providing access. This is the if-it's-bad-for-business-it-must-be-bad-for-disabled-people approach.

The Advisory Council warned the Commission that if the "broad degree of discretion" business needs in deciding what constitutes an "undue hardship" isn't in the final rules, a lawsuit will have to settle the matter. It wasn't exactly a veiled threat — but it didn't have to be. Business executives believe they can rely on the courts to shape this law to their liking — and they may be right. "The courts are not without bias in this situation," says Wright.

But nobody, in the fifteen-year history of the Rehabilitation Act's accommodation requirements, has ever gone bankrupt because of them, and that includes disability-rights groups all over the country which, as a matter of policy, hire disabled people and put people with severe disabilities in management jobs.

———

The conviction that access is too costly has prevailed in the building industry. Since 1988, amendments to the Fair Housing Act have required that new apartment units be "adaptable" to future disabled tenants. The National Association of Homebuilders has fought this requirement unrelentingly for the past three years.

Always vigilant of its members' freedom to continue to build inaccessible dwellings, the group has been especially worried this spring that the ADA may require that model homes be accessible. It insisted to the Architectural and Transportation Barriers Compliance Board, the agency that drafted the ADA's guidelines for access to places of public accommodation, that model homes should not have to be accessible. The houses, the Homebuilders acknowledge, are "temporarily used for sales purposes" and thus are "public accommodations." But, says Homebuilders President Mark Ellis Tipton, they are "ultimately sold as private residences. To require accessibility to these homes would change the essential character of the home." He also says, "It would be deceptive to the potential purchaser" to make a model home accessible, "since the actual home for sale would not incorporate accessibility functions."

The group has managed to forestall, almost entirely, access required under the 1988 legislation. Those who attended last January's Homebuilders convention got advice on how to circumvent the Fair Housing Act's access requirements, which were listed among "Barriers to Affordable Housing."

Eleanor Smith of Concrete Change, a direct-action housing-access group, derisively refers to the Association as the "National Association of Hypocritical Builders" because, she says, "they insist publicly that they want to help disabled people." She calls them the "chief enemy of the Fair Housing Act."

Does access cost too much? In the early 1980s, Ed Steinfeld, who teaches architecture at the State University of New York, Buffalo, and who has been involved in access issues for almost two decades, calculated costs for New York State when it implemented its access code in 1984. He came up with $440 as the extra cost of making a one-bedroom unit accessible. That cost hasn't risen much since.

Costs can still be as low as $500 per unit, admits Ray Kimsey of Niles Boulton Associates architectural firm, which developed cost estimates for the Homebuilders' group. However, the Association still puts out figures as high as $50,000 per unit. This can occur, says Kimsey, when much grading is required to make a hilly site flat for access. Access advocates say the group uses this "hilly-site" excuse to exempt units that could easily be built on flat parts of the site.

Complaints about cost are relative. Developers "will put in a hell of a lot of mirrors and Jacuzzis to sell the tiniest space," says Anne Emerman, head of New York Mayor David Dinkins's Office for People with Disabilities. "They don't seem to realize that the market out there might actually like to have the larger bathrooms and kitchens" adaptable housing would bring.

Terence Moakley, of the Eastern Paralyzed Veterans of America, says builders complain incessantly that they can't find kitchen cabinets that are easily modified to comply with access codes already in force in such places as New York City. His group located a cabinet-making firm that showed builders how to make the modification. It took about half an hour to do, Moakley says, and the builders complained they didn't have that kind of time to waste on the job.

"If building owners are required to spend a large portion of their remodeling budget to install accessibility features," Tipton warned the Compliance Board, "they may forgo renovation entirely." Better to have "gradual progress toward accessibility," he said, than "reduce the remodeling done."

———

Organized business and the housing industry weren't the only anti-access voices this spring. Places of public accommodation were angry at having to provide access — even the sort defined as "readily achievable."

Churches got themselves exempted from the law entirely. Then in the spring, churches represented by the Joint Baptist Committee and the National Association of Evangelicals complained that the public-accommodation rules required their soup kitchens, counseling centers, and day-care programs to be accessible.

The Children's Foundation was startled to discover day-care centers are defined in the law as public accommodations. The Foundation complained that to comply would be too burdensome.

Nursing homes insisted the law's guidelines for access are unfair. The seemingly modest proposal that 50 per cent of a nursing home's rooms be wheelchair-accessible was met with outrage: It was "overly restrictive" and "would add significant square footage and cost" to new nursing homes, according to the Alabama Nursing Home Association. Then, in a blatantly erroneous statement, Ann Mitchell of the Health Facilities Management Corporation insisted that "the handicapped population of long-term-care facilities is not greater than that of the general public, and thus only 5 per cent of the rooms need be accessible." And Gail Clarkson of MediLodge, in Romeo, Michigan, declared that nursing-home residents were content with their inaccessible rooms: "In my seventeen years in long-term care, I have never received a complaint regarding difficulty in this area."

The American Association of Homes for the Aging didn't see any sense in all nursing-home entrances being accessible, either.

But what the Taylor Living Center for Seniors in Taylor, Michigan, told rule-makers was perhaps the most direct. "We are not able to admit residents who have wheelchair needs," the Center wrote in a wonder of circular reasoning, "because our bathrooms were constructed for ambulatory seniors. Our building structure would be destroyed if the bathrooms would need to be expanded. It would be cost prohibitive and unnecessary." And Marla Turner, the Center's administrator, asked "that 'homes for the aged' be exempt" from having to comply with the access requirements of the ADA.

A member of the American Institute of Architects didn't see why "jury boxes, witness stands, and judges' benches" had to be accessible. "A wheelchair-bound person can either testify from his wheelchair or be assisted into the witness stand by attendants or bailiffs. Similarly, a judge or juror could be assisted. . . . To require lifts or ramps is impractical."

Hotel and motel owners were at pains to make sure they didn't have to make more than a small portion of their rooms accessible—no more than 1 per cent, insisted the Kansas City Motel and Hotel Association, which vowed that "no disabled person has ever been denied access to an accessible room in any hotel in Kansas City, ever."

The National Retail Federation was "particularly concerned" that only a few check-out aisles be required to be accessible. The American Banking Association didn't want bank-teller windows to be accessible: "Higher counters in banks are critical in order to protect employees and discourage robbery." In California, access laws have required such places as banks to provide access since the 1970s. But it took a disabled man's 1985 lawsuit against a bank for failing to provide access to the automatic teller machines, which the bank fought all the way to the California Supreme Court, to make the state's banks pay attention.

The American Bus Association, allowed decades of legal leeway in equipping coaches with lifts, complained this spring about a requirement to install a $100 TDD phone for deaf people in bus stations.

"In bus terminals having five or fewer public pay phones," the Association argued, "it is unlikely that use of the TDD device would be frequent enough to justify the cost." Using the same "we're-just-poor-folks" argument it used to avoid access, the Association insisted many small-town bus terminals are just mom-and-pop stores.

"The proprietors of these establishments sell bus tickets primarily as a community service. . . . If these small businesses were required to install a public pay phone equipped with a TDD, few if any would undertake to sell bus tickets," and "persons in small communities who rely on bus service would be seriously inconvenienced."

Never mind the disabled people with hearing losses who have never been able to call home from bus terminals in their lives. But such people, like those with other disabilities, have learned not to hold their breath when it comes to new laws. They have the same wait-and-see attitude about the ADA.

"I sincerely hope the ADA will be better implemented than the present requirement that all Federal agencies have TDDs," says Joan Cassidy of Sterling, Virginia. "Because if they have them, they don't use them."

NATURE AND TECHNOLOGY

Barbara Hillyer

Barbara Hillyer discusses the connection between feminism and disability. She discusses the concept of "body awareness" and shows its connection to both. Finally, she discusses the centrality of technology in meeting the needs of the disabled. (Source: From Feminism and Disability *by Barbara Hillyer. Copyright © 1993 by the University of Oklahoma Press. Reprinted by permission.)*

Since the mid-seventies, feminist theory has given increasing attention to women's problematic relationships with nature and with technology. Adrienne Rich's *Of Woman Born,* published in 1976, suggested that we separate ourselves from the patriarchal institution of motherhood by "thinking through our bodies," recognizing them as the "corporeal ground of intelligence."[1] By 1978, when Susan Griffin's *Woman and Nature* and Mary Daly's *Gyn/Ecology* were published, the ideas that men associate women with nature to the detriment of both and that women in fact have a closer relationship to nature which may save the world were widely accepted among feminists.

Women's supposed closeness to nature is both problematic and attractive to feminists as we struggle with biological, sociological, and ethical issues. Defined by our menstrual and childbearing capacities and excluded from male-defined "culture," we have cared for children and people with illnesses and claimed, renamed for ourselves, a positive relationship with cycles of growth and death.

Such closeness to nature may be seen as negative, as it excludes us from culture, power, and control, or positive, as it connects us with the environment and dissociates us from weaponry and chemical pollution. Thus we may be tempted to seek access to technological work on an "equal" basis with men or to withdraw romantically to the "natural" landscape to the considerable discomfort of our sisters who need respirators and ramps.

Women who live with disabilities have more reasons to understand the "corporeal ground of intelligence" than do the temporarily able-bodied and able-minded. They understand it in a way that illuminates women's relationships to nature and technology by providing or forcing a closer and more direct awareness of both.

Nature

The dualistic notion that nature is the opposite of culture and that it is the special province of women as culture is the province of men[2] has been discussed, disputed, and disclaimed by feminists — and sometimes embraced. Dualism itself is patriarchal or masculinist, yet our acculturation and the languages in which Westerners have learned to think have historically restricted our access to male-defined culture (and politics); at the same time, our work as mothers, midwives, and caregivers has made us aware of and responsive to the body and its rhythms, its needs.

The term "natural" is a cultural construction implying its opposite, the "social."[3] The idea that women's reproductive capacity and child-rearing activities make them "natural" has been used to confine women to the private, domestic sphere in contrast to men, whose ability to "reason" supposedly fits them for the political world.[4] Because the capacity to give birth is equated with a biological imperative to nurture children and others, political equality and work-force equity become by definition "unnatural." Thus women are required to participate in the patriarchal institution of motherhood, a profoundly social construction justified on the basis of our "natural" biological role in perpetuating the species.[5] White male fear of nature has repeatedly led our culture to identification of blacks and women with the body and with sexuality.[6] Physical disabilities are similar to racial and sex-role handicaps in this respect, as they evoke a similar fear of what is "natural";[7] they remind us that we are all, vulnerably, embodied.

The nature-culture dichotomy is by no means an outdated oversimplification now irrelevant to enlightened people. It has shaped not only our public policy, academic disciplines, and the organization of family life, but even—especially—our language. "These dichotomies are empirically false, but we cannot afford to dismiss them as irrelevant as long as they structure our lives and consciousnesses."[8] Even Jacques Lacan, whose theory some women consider a psychoanalytic model compatible with feminism, "puts the father on the side of culture and the mother on the side of nature" in his analysis of the Oedipal struggle, directly associating culture with language as an expression of social law.[9]

In light of this pervasive and discriminatory use of the nature–woman connection, it is not surprising that a significant amount of female energy has been used in demanding access to "culture" as defined by men and from which women have been excluded. It is equally predictable that women revaluing and renaming our own experience should take a romantic stance toward our identification with nature, especially in view of the negative, life-destroying aspects of male dominance over nature and the human interactivity of our caregiving, birthing, and child-rearing activities.

Ignoring the masculine Victorian concept of nature "red in tooth and claw," many feminists seem closer to the concept presented in "Tintern Abbey" of Wordsworth's sister as the emblem of the calm and peace that nature brings. Thus in Sally Gearhart's popular feminist science fiction, the characters live in a "sentimentalized nature, nature which is reliably benevolent and supportive as they themselves are benevolent and supportive."[10] Acknowledging that we do in fact bleed and die, the back-to-the-land feminist sees these facts as part of our affiliation with a benign natural world, whose cycles men seek to control in contrast to women's ability to cooperate with their flow. In contrast, Annette Kolodny's work on Americans' response to the frontier experience shows men as the ones who fantasized a harmony of man and nature based on the experience of the land as an embodiment of the female principle and women as the ones who literally cultivated the land, making gardens instead of embracing the wilderness.[11] While romantic William Wordsworth idealized his sister's peaceful relationship to nature, romantic Charlotte Brontë presented women characters who were not blessed by nature: Lucy Snowe and even Jane Eyre on the moors.

Autobiographical literature by women whose lives have been reshaped by someone else's disability or illness reflect an unromantic awareness of nature's arbitrariness. When Gerda Lerner was told by her husband's doctor that "nature respects the brain and is kind to it by numbing it first so one does not know," she responded, "But I'm watching it happen and writing it down. So nature is not kind to me."[12] And Suzanne Massie, whose son Bobby had hemophilia, appreciated the unsentimental attitude of fishermen to Bobby's disability: "They accepted Bobby's problem as another act of a capricious Nature—a nature they lived with and whose power they did not question. What had struck Bobby was the bolt of lightning that singles out one tree and not another, the wind that suddenly comes up from no one knows where, or the calamity when one fisherman and not another accidentally falls off his boat and sinks to the bottom like a stone."[13] The feminist retreat to a "natural" (nonurban) environment is fraught with more perils than insect bites and poison ivy for women with disabilities. I once participated in a feminist gathering where sleeping on the floor of a remodeled barn symbolized our lack of class distinctions—and created serious problems for those with even mild arthritis or back problems. After each Michigan Women's Music Festival, the letters column of *Off Our Backs* is full of letters about the problems that rural retreat causes women who use wheelchairs or respirators.

Recent feminist literature is full of warnings against romanticizing nature at the expense of political action. Janice Raymond, who herself has advocated an "ecofeminist" perspective, warns that "this emphasis should not be at the expense of avoiding the world of human affairs or of romanticizing the world of Nature, pitting the latter against the former or characterizing the world of public institutions and human artifacts as inherently patriarchal."[14] Rayna Rapp reminds us that nature is, after all, "a cultural product, continuously reinvented as part of the rhetorical strategies defining and defending slavery, empire, and technological triumphalism."[15] Mary Gordon, expressing her uneasiness about some feminists' argument that "surrogate" motherhood is "unnatural," warns that "simple-minded romance about the 'natural'" will prevent us from understanding, analyzing, and making laws in order to allow "certain groups like homosexuals and older couples to have children in ways that are satisfying to them."[16] And Bonnie Zimmerman, raising the question of whether lesbian separatism is "a white middle-class luxury," reminds us that "tempting as this dream of free lesbian tribes may be, we must consider that tribal cultures have fared poorly under the onslaught of advanced capitalism and imperialism."[17] In a similar political analysis, Charlotte Bunch asserts that we "must not romanticize pre-industrial cultures as the solution" because a viable plan for the future must be based on "what has been both useful and problematic in capitalist and socialist industrialization, as well as in agricultural societies." Bunch warns against such individual solutions as buying "health" foods or "going back to the land, where earth mothers again end up doing all the work from scratch."[18]

"Ecofeminism" is based on women's biological relationship to the natural world, a relationship women are thought to experience more directly than most men because most women menstruate and many of us raise children or care for people who are sick or have disabilities. Celebrants and mourners at the connection between birth and death, we see ourselves as participants in a natural rhythmic cycle. Yet our role in the celebration or the mourning, is human, is conscious. The mother giving birth may wish it were a vegetable process. Babies "should be picked up and held/root end up, soil spilling/from between their toes — /and how much easier it would be/later returning them to the earth."[19] The idea that birth and death are part of a natural process in which humans are participants but not in control may indeed come easier to women who give birth or attend it, especially since between birth and death caring directly for the body gives a sense of growth and change and of our intimate reliance on plants and other animals for our well-being. Such organic awareness nevertheless comes to us partly, perhaps entirely, through culture, as we know whatever it is we know about it through language and memory, which are culturally mediated. As Jane Caputi reminds us, "We have never fully known the organic or the natural, only the filmed version."[20] Similarly, a number of feminists have described the birth experience in Western industrial societies as less a bodily experience for the woman giving birth than an experience of her objectified

body *being seen* by the observing doctors, nurses, fetal monitors, and sometimes the child's father.[21] Female bodies, then, "are symbolic/material constructions, and reproduction is political."[22]

We may indeed be especially aware of the closeness of life and death to each other as we give birth or attend to the dying, but fixation on these two events as the "central defining moments" of life discounts the ongoing process of living itself, "the woman who is as she is."[23]

This is where the daily experience of body-aware authentic women who live close to the body's illness and its health, its disability and its individual ability, can clarify our sense of what being natural, in nature, means.

Body Awareness

If menstruation, childbirth, and caring for people with disabilities place women closer to the rhythms and processes of nature by promoting awareness of our own biology and showing us our relationship to other organic, living, dying, cyclic things, then disabilities that alter the body have the potential for increasing that connection as they increase body awareness. The problem with this theory is that it is by no means certain that women and people with disabilities (in mainstream Western culture at least) are in fact aware of what is really going on in their bodies. A substantial amount of literature, some of it feminist, has been published in the past few years about women's negative self-concept based on masculine objectification of the body, cultural standards of beauty, and various psychological or sociological pressures to change body shape. Eating disorders, inappropriate or harmful use of drugs, and denial of biological reality are common responses to these pressures. The closer the connection between self-image and body image in our culture, the greater the probability that the individual will define herself as worthless or worthwhile on that basis.[24] Unfortunately such congruence is rarely based on a genuine comfort in one's body, whatever its shape or size or abilities. Thus women's body awareness is likely to be acute but negative because societal or masculinist standards for beauty are so restrictive and beauty is the body characteristic most desired for women.[25] As Wendy Chapkis has observed, a white, Western, wealthy standard of beauty is increasingly being adopted throughout the world.[26]

Such body awareness is likely to focus on perceived defects in the body and not on a realistic assessment of its qualities. Many of our body processes are socially unmentionable or the subject of jokes; some are the source of shame. Most of our individual features are "wrong" by external cultural standards. Across American society both men and women feel "depersonalized," "which means that there is literally a sense of not being intimately unified with one's body—of regarding it with some detachment."[27] Indeed, women's objectification of their own bodies is sometimes so extreme that they undertake disfiguring surgery to change a body part. For example, 300,000 American women have had their breasts surgically enlarged, and 15–20,000 each year have their breasts reduced.[28] Stomach stapling, anorexia and bulimia, and chronic dieting are familiar symptoms of voluntary self-denial in North American society.[29] So is compulsive fitness training.[30] Self-denial is a psychologically accurate term. Linda Tschirhart Sanford and Mary Ellen Donovan found that most of the large number of women they interviewed had negative body images "because they saw themselves inaccurately" in terms of size, shape, or supposedly distorted body part.[31] This distorted perception of the woman's own body is grounded in gender duality.[32]

In light of the extreme negativity toward normal women's bodies, it is not surprising that women with disabilities react with even more negativity to their disabled bodies. Erik Erikson found that "in cases of morbid ego identity and in cripples, dreams occur where the dreamer tries to hide the painfully spotlighted body part, and others in which he accidentally loses it."[33] Like Erikson's "cripples," women who become ill see their bodies as the enemy and not as a partner with the mind in working toward health or toward management of the illness.[34]

"Patients," people whose illnesses or disabilities require medical care or other therapies, are usually objectified in the process to the extent that they perceive their bodies as literally belonging to someone else.[35] The experience reflects that of young children whose bodies, only recently separated from their mothers', are physically tended, moved, and interpreted by adults and told how they do and do not feel. Their bodies are often treated as psychological and physical possessions of their parents, just as the "patient's" body is treated as the possession of the doctor, physical therapist, or even an abstraction such as "the hospital."[36] As parents give childhood illnesses more attention, both negative and positive, than other behaviors,[37] adults with disabilities may relive both the guilt and the psychological boundary loss that go with the childhood experience.[38]

Nondisabled married women in body image therapy groups have described themselves as not owning their bodies, which they experienced "as utilitarian machines which gave birth to and nursed children and which sexually served their husbands," and then discounted "resentment at not owning their bodies as silly, trivial, or selfish."[39] To this culturally induced dissociation of the female self from her own body and her emotional reaction to its loss, the woman with disabilities adds pain, medical treatment (and sometimes medical abuse), surgeries, diagnostic procedures, and chronic unpredictability. She is likely to feel that her body has betrayed her and that it is an enemy very different from "self."

Physicians reinforce dissociation by ignoring information patients give about their own bodies, assuming that individuals know less about their own bodies than the "experts" do. Injuries and accidents to such physically fit people as dancers and athletes often result from training methods based on the concept of the body as adversary.[40] We are thus encouraged to ignore the body, to dissociate from it, even to abuse it; yet "highly generalized body awareness" such as that developed during severe childhood illnesses is strongly correlated with strong artistic, literary, and creative interests.[41] This fact provides a clue to the positive contribution that women with disabilities can make to feminist theory about our relationship through our bodies to nature.

Barbara MacDonald describes her changed relationship to her body as she recovered from a temporary disability: "Thus I healed myself and became whole again, connected to my aging body, wanting to live out my life in partnership with it, without feelings of humiliation because of its difference, and without the fear that I would so want to disclaim it that I would fail to protect it."[42] Partnership with her body prevents dissociation and enhances her sense of herself as a whole person whose aging, increasingly limited body is integral to her very positive self-concept. Feminist theory is full of discussions of the relationship between body and mind, especially in the contexts of sexuality and motherhood. Haunani-Kay Trask summarizes this literature as being about "the necessity for women and men to come to terms with the body's connection to the mind in the hopes of arriving at an intelligent, life-encouraging synthesis between mind and body, form and spirit."[43] What is different about MacDonald's statement is that it comes out of an experience of disability. The ideal of the physically fit, strong, active young feminist as the integrated physical-mental whole woman is transformed into a woman who is whole in her awareness of and acceptance of herself as someone whose fallible, human, aging body and mind are partners engaged in caring for her self. Positive body awareness thus comes not from striving for an ideal but from accepting the reality — that we age, change, become ill or disabled, and will die. MacDonald says, "I have this second chance to feel my body living out its own plan, to watch it daily change in the direction of its destiny."[44] Several of the contributors to *With the Power of Each Breath: A Disabled Women's Anthology* describe the profound acceptance of their bodies that has been part of their living with disabilities. An eloquent example is Stephanie Sugars's: "Watching how I live in the world in my body, I see how incredibly far I have come. I am coming to trust my body's integrity. . . . My body is such a sensitive indicator of my being. If I refuse to respond to my intuition, my body steps in with pain/discomfort/illness. I have a gate to my unconscious mind through my body."[45] So important is this kind of awareness that Stephanie and Carl Simonton have built a major cancer treatment strategy on training patients to respect and respond to "valuable feedback from their bodies."[46] Their patients' use of mental and spiritual strategies is firmly based on awareness of the body. Similarly, the Diabetes Self-Care Program, which has radically changed the treatment of that disease in the 1980s, is based on participants' learning through repeated blood tests to adjust their own insulin dosage based on awareness of their body's own characteristic reactions to changes in diet, exercise and stress.[47] And individuals with chronic pain are taught to know exactly the relationship between the pain and the environment, schedule, rest, food, clothing, "self-talk" — in short, to know how the body is related to all the other details of one's life.[48]

These holistic therapies are based on the concept of body awareness as awareness of *process,* a concept that is closely related to the idea that our female body processes are linked to the processes of growth and decay in "nature." Biofeedback for stress management does much more than teach us to continue to live in a harmful world. It helps us overcome cultural conditioning that "deprive[s] the self of the information it should have about its body — and mind — state."[49] With or without specific training, women with disabilities who stop fighting the body as an enemy or dissociating from it learn to access this information and use it. Fritz Perls believed that Gestalt therapy could give us such wisdom: "With full awareness you become aware of the organismic self-regulation, you can let the organism take over without interfering, without interrupting; we can rely on the wisdom of the organism."[50] What is missing from Perls's suggestions is the experience of people with illnesses or disabilities that require some medical or technological interference or interruption. Still, before such interventions can be integrated, acceptance of the biological self is essential.

Feminist celebration of the erotic and reproductive capacities of our bodies is a beginning. This "return to the body" sees the mother–daughter experience of infancy as "the time when love is learned through intimate care of the body."[51] By extension, intimate caring for another's body through nursing or attendance or caring for one's own body in daily living becomes part of our positive body awareness and of holistic female bonding, which includes physical and emotional ties. When such caring incorporates the use of prostheses, medication, or machines, there is potential for bridging the supposed gulf between nature and technology.

Technology

Even as disability requires body awareness and sensitivity to pace, rhythm, and process,[52] it requires reliance on technology as simple as typewriters and as sophisticated as dialysis machines. Specialized computers for people with hearing impairments, visual impairments, and cerebral palsy enhance communication and self-care. Braillers, tape recorders, hearing aids, special telephone equipment, motorized wheelchairs and carts, ramps, wheelchair lifts, adapted automobile controls, and many other devices are becoming ordinary parts of the lives of many people. Reproductive technology positively influences most American women's lives. Aerospace engineers work one on one with disabled people to devise new equipment to improve their daily lives.[53] Respirators and apnea monitors are readily used at home to save lives, and hospitals are full of life-saving and life-maintenance equipment.

The use of technology also has negative consequences. These range from neurological impairments that may be caused by mechanical ventilation of newborn children[54] to lung disease caused by exposure to asbestos or miscarriages caused by video display terminals. Electronic fetal monitoring sometimes causes fetal distress and frequently results in probably unnecessary caesarean sections.[55] Common industrial chemicals impair male fertility. Diethylstilbestrol (DES), formerly given to prevent miscarriages, causes reproductive abnormalities and cancer. The intrauterine device (IUD) greatly increases pelvic inflammatory disease.[56] And so on. Feminists have been among the most vocal in pointing out these problems. Science and technology are among the most conspicuous products of masculine values, so we are skeptical about their use and cautious about integrating them in our lives.

But women with disabilities and women who give care to people with disabilities rely heavily on technology to enhance and simplify daily life — and often just to survive. For these women, the issue is not whether to use technology but how best to integrate it with self-concept and with body awareness.

An interesting example is the experience of mothers of "thalidomide babies," who came into conflict with rehabilitation specialists about the use and interpretation of prostheses for the children's deformed or missing arms. The goal of the professionals was to integrate the prosthesis into the child's body image so that the child would feel that the device was part of the self. But the child's body image was already whole, so the prosthesis was experienced as a deformation. A more suitable goal would have been to see the prosthesis as a tool, useful only for specific purposes.[57] The psychological task the mothers were assigned was to convince the child that her or his body was not whole so that the technology would be seen as completing it. The mothers' response was to confuse themselves and the children and to frustrate the professionals by using the prostheses erratically and at random in terms of tasks to be performed.

In her research on people's responses to ambulatory devices, Caroline Kaufman's preliminary results found that individuals did not include the devices in their self-images, but maintained able-bodied images of themselves.[58] The prostheses are not, in fact, part of the body, however helpful they may be as tools. Similarly, a respirator is not part of the body, though it may breathe for the individual whose body will not survive without it. What we can learn from disability is how to incorporate the technology not into the body image but into its environment, so that it is experienced as "natural" in the same way that other aspects of the environment, positive and negative, are. When we remember that the mind is part of the body, is embodied (even as the body is part of nature), and is natural, it is not difficult to see how a respirator — the product of human intelligence — can be as integral to the breathing self as the allergen-laden south wind.

Susan Griffin suggests that one reason sexuality is so disturbing to people in our culture "is that in the sexual experience one is taken back to a profoundly physical state in which one can no longer deny that one is very deeply a part of nature and is therefore a dependent, mortal person."[59] I suggest that this is also what is disturbing about disabilities. What the disability tells the person whose relationship to it makes her fully, bodily aware is that she is a natural self, unseparated from the rest of nature. As Griffin says, "We breathe, we are born, we die, we eat, we get cold, we are part of the biosphere."[60] We also think and use tools, some of which enable some of us to be born, to eat, to breathe, to be our natural selves. When this is the case, and we can feel it in our bodies and implement the partnership with our minds, that sense of being inseparable from the rest of nature while highly individually aware of the embodied self is a spiritual experience that includes the technological support.

To use technology in such a framework is to re-shape the values by which it is made. We have been wisely suspicious of a technology made by men in opposition to nature, as we have been suspicious of other dichotomies. Technology that is used for control "first obscures the connective tissues that sustain us and then excises complex decisions from an ethical context."[61] We need not use technology merely because it exists,[62] nor must we use it to manipulate and control biological realities.[63] As the "thalidomide mothers" discovered, the value system that produces and interprets "correct" use of technology is not based on the wisdom of the body, but that does not mean that such values cannot or should not be developed.

In some American Indian and African cultures, health is harmony with nature, a balancing of physical, emotional, and spiritual factors. To live in harmony with nature is to accept it and to take from it only what is needed to live.[64] If technology were developed in or if its uses were determined by such a culture, presumably its use would be much more cooperative with nature than is the case in industrial societies such as ours. Sometimes a technological device may be what we take from nature because we need it in order to live. Women, dissociated as we have been from masculinist American-European culture, have been the carriers for that culture of physical and spiritual values. When we are body aware, as some disabilities enable us to be, we may be able to bridge the dichotomous gap between nature and technology.

Our experience not only with our female bodies but also with their illnesses and disabilities forces us to criticize the romantic view of nature (we need electricity at the music festivals and beds at the feminist retreat) and technological values (we need prostheses only as tools for our already complete bodies). We need to include technology and intellect in the politics of our cooperation with nature and the body. Our natural, living, breathing, dying, tool-using, whole selves are thus integrally a part of culture and nature.

Notes

1. Rich, *Of Woman Born*, 39.

2. Ortner, "Is Female to Male as Nature Is to Culture?" This is the germinal feminist essay on the subject.

3. Beverly Brown and Parveen Adams, "The Feminine Body and Feminine Politics," *m/f* (1979):51–58, cited in Swartz, "Is Thin a Feminist Issue?" 435.

4. DuBois et al., *Feminist Scholarship*. Chapter 3 provides a good summary of feminist literature responding to this tradition.

5. Rich, *Of Woman Born*. Bandarage, "Spirituality, Politics and Feminism Are One," 81. Allen, *Lesbian Philosophy*, 62–88.

6. Griffin, *Pornography and Silence*.

7. Chernin, *The Obsession*, 129–30.

8. Harding, "The Instability of the Analytical Categories," 662.

9. Brown, "Thinking About Food Prohibitions," 13.

10. Clausen, "Political Morality of Fiction," 19.

11. Kolodny, *The Lay of the Land; The Land Before Her*.

12. Lerner, *A Death of One's Own*, 188.

13. Massie and Massie, *Journey*, 111.

14. Raymond, *A Passion for Friends*, 230.

15. Rapp, "A Womb of One's Own," 10.

16. Gordon, "Baby M," 7.

17. Zimmerman, "The Politics of Transliteration," 674.

18. Bunch, "Food, Politics and Power," 93–94.

19. Linda Pasta, "Notes from a Delivery Room," quoted in Poston, "Childbirth in Literature," 30.

20. Caputi, "In Review: *Pure Lust: Elemental Feminist Philosophy*, by Mary Daly," 87–88.

21. Poston, "Childbirth in Literature," 20. Petchesky, "Fetal Images," 273, 277, 287.

22. Rapp, "A Womb of One's Own," 10.

23. Allen, *Lesbian Philosophy*, 72–73.

24. Squire, *The Slender Balance*, 101–102.

25. Wolf, *The Beauty Myth*. McBridge, "The Slender Imbalance," includes a good survey of the literature on women's negative body image.

26. Chapkis, *Beauty Secrets*. This was the most political of recent books on body image, before the publication of Wolf's *The Beauty Myth*.

27. Fisher, *Body-Consciousness*, 13–14. Fisher states that body depersonalization is more extreme for men, but his examples are drawn from the impact of fashion on women.

28. Chernin, *The Obsession*, 35.

29. This point is widely discussed in feminist literature. See, especially, Schoenfielder and Wieser, *Shadow on a Tightrope*.

30. Freedman, *Beauty Bound*, 45.

31. Sanford and Donovan, *Women and Self-Esteem*, 370.

32. Freedman, *Beauty Bound,* 18–19.

33. Erikson, *Identity, Youth and Crisis,* 60–61.

34. Sanford and Donovan, *Women and Self-Esteem,* 370–71.

35. Fisher, *Body-Consciousness,* 15–16, 83.

36. Ibid., 73–74. Fisher sees our reaction to this body anxiety of childhood as a direct cause of racism.

37. Ibid., 6–7. McCoy, *Coping with Teenage Depression,* 164.

38. Fisher, *Body-Consciousness,* 31.

39. Bergner, Remer, and Whetsell, "Transforming Women's Body Image," 34.

40. Browne, Connors, and Stern, *With the Power of Each Breath,* 246. Robbins, "Stroke," 18.

41. Fisher, *Body-Consciousness,* 137–38.

42. MacDonald, "Ageism in the Women's Movement," 35.

43. Trask, *Eros and Power,* 144.

44. MacDonald, "Ageism in the Women's Movement," 20.

45. Sugars, "Journal Piece," 266.

46. Simonton, Simonton, and Creighton, *Getting Well Again,* 196. Simonton, *The Healing Family,* 226.

47. Wallis, "Diabetes' New Gospel of Control," 75.

48. Whillans, "Adjusting to Chronic Pain," 52.

49. Brown, *Between Health and Illness,* 36–37, 59–60, 71–72.

50. Perls, *Gestalt Therapy Verbatim,* 17.

51. Trask, *Eros and Power,* 131.

52. Davis, "Time, Productivity and Disability." . . .

53. Broder, "'Space Program' to Benefit Disabled," 6.

54. Lyon, *Playing God in the Nursery,* 114.

55. McDonnell, *Not an Easy Choice,* 102.

56. Ibid., 110.

57. Roskies, *Abnormality and Normality,* 172–74. Just one of these mothers said that her child was so severely injured that "his prostheses are part of him; without prostheses he would not be a human being," 273–74.

58. Summary of work in progress by Caroline Kaufmann, "Disabled People and Enabling Technologies," 8–9.

59. Griffin, "Split Culture," 5.

60. Ibid., 4.

61. Diamond and Quinby. "American Feminism in the Age of the Body," 121.

62. Lyon, *Playing God in the Nursery,* 69.

63. Daniel Callahan quoted in McDonnell, *Not an Easy Choice,* 103.

64. Henderson and Bryan, *Psychosocial Aspects of Disability,* 101, 107.

References

Allen, Jeffner, ed. *Lesbian Philosophies and Cultures.* Albany: State University of New York Press, 1990.

Bergner, Mary, Pam Remer, and Charles Whetsell, "Transforming Women's Body Image: A Feminist Counseling Approach." *Women and Therapy* 4, no. 3 (Fall 1985): 25–38.

Broder, David S. "'Space Program' to Benefit Disabled." *Norman (Oklahoma) Transcript,* July 13, 1985, 6.

Browne, Susan, Debra Connors, and Nanci Stern, eds. *With the Power of Each Breath: A Disabled Women's Anthology.* San Francisco: Cleis, 1985.

Bunch, Charlotte. "Food, Politics and Power: A Feminist Perspective." *Heresies* 21 (1987): 92–94.

Chapkis, Wendy. *Beauty Secrets: Women and the Politics of Appearance.* Boston: South End Press, 1986.

Chernin, Kim. *The Obsession: Reflections on the Tyranny of Slimness.* New York: Harper & Row, 1981.

Clausen, Jan. "On the Political Morality of Fiction (Part One)." *Off Our Backs* 15, no. 6 (June 1985): 17–20.

Davis, Barbara Hillyer. "Time, Productivity and Disability." *Midwest Feminist Papers V.* Midwest Sociologists for Women in Society, 1985: 30–34.

Diamond, Irene, and Lee Quinby. "American Feminism in the Age of the Body." *Signs* 10, no. 1 (Autumn 1984): 119–25.

DuBois, Ellen Carol, Gail Paradise Kelly, Elizabeth Lapovsky Kennedy, Carolyn W. Korsmeyer, and Lillian S. Robinson. *Feminist Scholarship: Kindling in the Groves of Academe.* Urbana: University of Illinois Press, 1985.

Erikson, Erik H. *Identity, Youth and Crisis.* New York: Norton, 1968.

Fisher, Seymour. *Body-Consciousness: You Are What You Feel.* Englewood Cliffs, N.J.: Prentice-Hall, 1973.

Freedman, Rita. *Beauty Bound.* Lexington, Mass.: D. C. Heath, 1985.

Gordon, Mary. "Baby M: New Questions About Biology and Destiny." *Conscience* 8, no. 3 (May–June 1987): 7.

Griffin, Susan, *Pornography and Silence: Culture's Revenge Against Nature.* New York: Harper & Row, 1981.

———, "Split Culture." *Creative Woman* 8, no. 4 (Winter 1988): 4–7.

Harding, Sandra. "The Instability of the Analytic Categories of Feminist Theory." *Signs* 11, no. 4 (Summer 1986): 645–64.

Henderson, George, and Willie V. Bryan. *Psychosocial Aspects of Disability.* Springfield, Ill.: Charles C. Thomas, 1984.

Kolodny, Annette. *The Lay of the Land: Metaphor as Experience and History in American Life and Letters.* Chapel Hill: University of North Carolina Press, 1975.

Lerner, Gerda. *A Death of One's Own.* New York: Simon & Schuster, 1978.

Lyon, Jeff. *Playing God in the Nursery.* New York: Norton, 1985.

MacDonald, Barbara. "Ageism in the Women's Movement." *Broomstick* 8, no. 2 (March–April 1986): 6–9.

Massie, Robert, and Suzanne Massie. *Journey.* New York: Alfred A. Knopf, 1973.

McCoy, Kathleen. *Coping with Teenage Depression: A Parent's Guide.* New York: NAL Books, 1982.

McDonnell, Kathleen. *Not an Easy Choice: A Feminist Re-examines Abortion.* Boston: South End Press, 1984.

Ortner, Sherry. "Is Female to Male as Nature Is to Culture?" In *Women, Culture, and Society,* edited by Michelle Zimbalist Rosaldo and Louise Lamphere. Palo Alto, Calif.: Stanford University Press, 1974.

Poston, Carol. "Childbirth in Literature." *Feminist Studies* 4 no. 2 (June 1978): 18–31.

Rapp, Rayna. "A Womb of One's Own." *Women's Review of Books* 5, no. 7 (April 1988): 10.

Raymond, Janice G. *A Passion for Friends: Toward a Philosophy of Female Affection.* Boston: Beacon, 1986.

Rich, Adrienne. *Of Women Born: Motherhood as Experience and Institution.* New York: Norton, 1976.

Roskies, Ethel. *Abnormality and Normality: The Mothering of Thalidomide Children.* Ithaca: Cornell University Press, 1988.

Sanford, Linda Tschirhart, and Mary Ellen Donovan. *Women and Self-Esteem.* New York: Penguin, 1985.

Schoenfielder, Lisa, and Barb Wieser, eds. *Shadow on a Tightrope: Writings by Women on Fat Oppression.* Iowa City: Aunt Lute, 1983.

Squire, Susan. *The Slender Balance: Causes and Cures for Bulimia, Anorexia and the Weight-Loss/Weight-Gain Seesaw.* New York: G. P. Putnam's Sons, 1983.

Swartz, Leslie. "Is Thin a Feminist Issue?" *Women's Studies International Forum* no. 5 (1985): 429–37.

Trask, Huanani-Kay. *Eros and Power: The Promise of Feminist Theory.* Philadelphia: University of Pennsylvania Press, 1986.

Wolf, Naomi. *The Beauty Myth: How Images of Beauty Are Used Against Women.* New York: William Morrow, 1991.

Zimmerman, Bonnie. "The Politics of Transliteration: Lesbian Personal Narratives." *Signs* 9, no. 4 (Summer 1984): 663–82.

"DEFECTIVE" AGENTS:

Equality, Difference, and the Tyranny of the Normal

Anita Silvers

Anita Silvers examines the concept of "normality" and its relationship to disability. She offers a broad discussion of what it means to deserve rights and benefits. She closes by discussing the ADA and health care rationing. (Source: From Journal of Social Philosophy, *Volume XXV, 25th Anniversary Special Issue, 1994. Reprinted by permission.)*

(In)equality, (Ab)normality, and (Dis)ability

In a recent essay describing quality-of-life measures in health care and medical ethics, Dan Brock makes the following superficially sensible proposal about treating defective agents equitably:

> We also need to distinguish between the relative importance of a particular feature or condition, say as represented by a specific condition . . . in its contribution to a person having a good life, compared with what I shall call its broader moral importance. A simple example will suffice. One condition that may plausibly contribute to a person's quality of life or good life is his or her physical mobility. It may be possible to specify roughly a normal level of physical mobility for persons of a similar age at a particular historical stage and in a particular society, and then to specify roughly levels of mobility say 25 per cent below and 25 per cent above the norm, such that the effect on a person's quality of life in moving from 25 per cent below the norm up to the norm is quantitatively roughly the same as moving from the norm to 25 per cent above it. *While the degree of importance of the two changes in a person's quality of life or good life may be roughly the same, it can none the less be consistently held that these two comparable effects on the person's quality of life have different moral importance or priority. It might be held, for example, that on grounds of equality of opportunity bringing a person's mobility from 25 per cent below the norm has greater moral priority than increasing his mobility from the norm to 25 per cent above it.* [emphasis added][1]

At first glance, this approach to distributing scarce resources to individuals with disabilities appears most just to them, for surely it is more than fair to assign to defective agents more than equal call upon the resources which they require to normalize themselves. Nevertheless, a drawback does arise, for decreeing generous treatment of defective agents imparts to them the liability of their being perceived as burdensome in their consumption of resources. By setting a standard on which the equal treatment of individuals with disabilities authorizes what others perceive as overprivileging these persons, the conception of equality which informs Brock's discussion verges on being self-defeating.

I believe this dilemma to be common to distribution systems in which considerations of relative positionality construe equal treatment to require or permit differential allocation as a remedial or compensatory measure. Such systems expand the notion of *equal* treatment by reconceiving it to be, or to warrant, a program of *equalizing* treatment. The dilemma inherent in such an understanding of equality lies in its exposing those for whom fair treatment corresponds to preferential treatment to a backlash of resentment, as evidenced, for example, by the disdain visited upon women and minorities who are perceived, truly or falsely, to be favored by affirmative or preferential employment practices. In my experience, a similar but even more global disdain born from resentment against perceived privilege pervades the social interaction between normal and defective agents.

Here I propose to explore both the historical and the conceptual constructions which place disabled people in this predicament when they seek fair treatment which recognizes what they are. But because the problem of achieving accord between equality and difference seems to emerge wherever we pursue justice for previously marginalized kinds of persons, my study will go further. It will expose some equivocations and confusions which reach beyond the protracted social exclusion of individuals with disabilities to the fundamental framing of our egalitarian conceptualizations. It is the mechanism commonly brought into play to fabricate an agent-neutral point of view—regardless of whether agents differ so greatly as to defy reduction to each other, which will be at issue. To be equalized by being normalized is only to be neutralized, which proves to be no effective route to equality.

The Importance of Being Normal

Brock's remark about the moral importance of treating defective agents differentially recalls a similar discussion pursued in more detail by Amartya Sen.[2] Seeking a principle of equitable distribution of resources, Sen argues that unequal allocations are intuitively correct if they equalize individuals' capabilities for primary functionings. For instance, he finds nothing objectionable in allocating more resources to a needy cripple to buy a wheelchair than are given to needy able-bodied individuals who can attain that same degree of mobility with no extraordinary allocation of resources. Sen adds that this superior allocation of resources is required even if the impaired individual is so forbearing or selfless as to believe herself as well off as others—that is, as equal to them—regardless of her deficits. Of course, Brock takes the standard to be *normal* functioning, while Sen construes it as *basic* functioning, but the issue remains the same: individuals who fall below a specified level of functioning are fundamentally unequal—therefore, are inferior—and, consequently, egalitarianism demands allocating more than equal resources in order to elevate them to normal.

But there are more dimensions to the Brock–Sen illustration than are conspicuous. Despite what Brock suggests, the broadness of the moral import of the Brock–Sen illustration cannot lie in its exemplifying an intuitively obvious, morally inescapable, sweepingly broad principle of equitable allocation which secures more of certain resources for the disabled than for (some) other classes of agents. For it is not evident that of pairs of individuals, one defective and one normal, whose quality of life could be equally improved by the application of a scarce resource, that whoever would be made normal is more deserving of resources *per se* than whoever would be made superior.

In regard to equality of opportunity in a case like that which Brock cites, were the normally mobile person an otherwise disadvantaged individual whose only opportunity for achievement lies in superior athletic performance—while the defectively mobile person were a world-famous violinist whose impaired mobility does not equally threaten his opportunity for success—it is not implausible that the pair's opportunities are better equalized by elevating the former's mobility above normal than by normalizing the latter's. It is no more morally obvious that individuals with disabilities should be awarded priority in allocating *life-improving* resources (the distribution suggested by Brock's view) as that productive, law-abiding persons who happen to be disabled should defer to vicious but able-bodied criminals (so much the more dangerous because they are able-bodied) in the allocation of *life-saving* resources (an outcome implicitly or explicitly advanced, as we shall see, by some health care rationing plans). Further on, I will show what it is about the Brock–Sen approach to equality which leads them to think the proper resolution of the type of case they discuss is so obvious.

An instructive anomaly in some of these health care rationing discussions is the ease with which disabled individuals are offered greater than ordinary access to certain kinds of normalizing treatments, while simultaneously being denied mere equal access to life-saving treatments. Defective agents thus are represented as medically deserving only in regard to procedures which make them no longer themselves. What I have to say in this paper contributes, I hope, to understanding why we confront citizens with disabilities with such a conflicted sense of their personal value.

Nevertheless, Brock's illustration, and the considerations to which he chooses to appeal, do call into question a broader moral question. But this question is not, as he has it, whether we ought to furnish defective agents with equal opportunities. Rather, it is the more fundamental question of whether they have any claim at all on the opportunity to be treated equally. For it is usually supposed, at least within the framework of the ethics of justice, that equality is a relationship which holds between *normal* persons.

Looking within this framework, we can locate the source of the incentive which leads to Brock's assigning restorative treatment precedence over magnifying treatment. Increasing a defective individual's mobility to normal is thought to take moral priority over boosting a normal individual's mobility to superior just because it is believed that certain kinds of moral considerations — namely, those pertaining to equality — may not even be invoked unless those whose condition is being compared all fall within the parameters of normal functioning. This is because to act impartially — and therefore *prima facie* equitably — is to balance one's own standpoint, with its special interests and needs, by affording equal weight to what others want one to do from the viewpoint of their special interests and needs.

Of course, you can't really know what it is like to be me, so the moral exercise here is to abstract by imagining what other persons' ambitions in view of their interests and needs *normally* would be were they in my place or I in theirs. But performing major life functions such as moving one's body is so intimate an element of the fabric of our experience that one cannot accurately imagine how to live otherwise. Nor is the inability to envision what one's ambitions or desires would be in such an event merely a matter of the degree to which one's own experience of impairment fails to approximate that of a defective agent. For sometimes vast differences in functioning are occasioned by relatively small differences in impairment, while at other times relatively severe impairments are only minimally dysfunctional. There is no fixed proportional relation between the two.

Now, what we view as within our reach in the world around us — and thereby what we take as the objects of our ambition — is more directly a product of the scope of functioning than of the degree of impairment. This explains why disability is thought to narrow the scope of people's lives to such a degree that their abnormality or singularity marginalizes them morally. The moral status of individuals with disabilities is impaired because the stereotype of them defeats a condition imposed by most and perhaps all rational moral systems, namely, that reasons for action must not be opaque to normal adults. Individuals

perceived as irreparably impaired thus come to be seen as being beyond the scope of equality. Hence the compulsion to normalize them in order to satisfy a necessary condition for including them as subjects in conversations regarding the attainment of equality.

In respect to these conversations, we should note that modern moral thought has not construed disability as being like other particularities which differentiate moral agents one from another. Much more than in classical thought, in modern thought differences between persons are dismissed as contingent and external, and thus as accidental to a person's moral being; yet disability still is embraced as a morally essential attribute, one which assigns those who have it to the borderline of moral worth.

Since the prospect of being so impaired seems to paralyze the normalizing imagination, we cannot seem to operationalize impartial moral judgment when it comes to imagining ourselves in a disabled person's place. This consequence of the familiar persuasion that one's becoming disabled is unthinkable likely fosters Brock's sense of the pressing moral importance of repairing defective agents so as to return them to being normal and, consequently, potentially both equal and moral. Unhappily, as a reason for promoting reparative treatment, this devaluing perception ambiguates the position of individuals with disabilities — that is, those with irreparable deficits — in their moral relations with normal people.

The same malignant perception festers in public policy formation. The story of the State of Oregon's Health Plan illustrates the result of thrusting defective agents beyond equality. As originally proposed, the Oregon Health Plan made health care more or less deserved depending on whether a potential recipient was less or more damaged in an irremediable way. Being impaired in some way which defies medical restoration automatically reduced one's eligibility for various kinds of care because the system's conceptual framework assumed that to be disabled was without question to have an inferior life.

This ranking was arrived at by a telephone survey of able-bodied individuals who apparently surmised that they would rather be dead than confined to a wheelchair. Employed in the original version of the Oregon Health Plan as a factor in treatment rankings, this survey was used to impose somebody else's suicidal fantasies on disabled individuals, thereby diminishing their access to health care, and, as well, withholding from them recognition as equally important moral beings. Parenthetically, that the testimony compiled by the survey was distorted by myths about disability is evidenced by its lack of power to predict the actual behavior of persons with disabilities. The suicide rate among persons with disabilities would be much greater than it is if the survey had reported actual preferences instead of fearful fantasies.

Nevertheless, devaluing disabled individuals remained so pervasive a disposition among the Oregon policymakers that discriminatory provisions persisted throughout all revisions proposed by Oregon in its attempts to secure a federal waiver. Ultimately, the federal government was forced to set the condition that certain features of the plan be removed, as a March 20, 1983, *New York Times* story describes:

> In setting priorities for health care in its latest proposal, Oregon considered whether a particular treatment would remove all symptoms of injury or illness. The Federal Government objected to use of that feature and Oregon agreed to abandon it.[3]

Reconceptualizing Disability

The federal government's intervention in Oregon's health care policy was impelled by Public Law 101–336, the 1990 "Americans with Disabilities" Act (ADA), which extended the Constitution's Fourteenth Amendment to protect individuals whose physical or mental impairments substantially limit one or more major life activities, or who are perceived as having such impairment. Among the Congress's factual findings, reported in the Act itself, are the following:

> (2) historically, society has tended to isolate and segregate individuals with disabilities, and despite some improvements, such forms of discrimination against individuals with disabilities continue to be a serious and pervasive social problem.

> (7) individuals with disabilities are a discrete and insular minority who have been faced with restrictions and limitations, subjected to a history of purposeful unequal treatment, and relegated to a position of political powerlessness in our society based on characteristics that are beyond the control of such individuals and resulting from

stereotypic assumptions not truly indicative of the individual ability of such individuals to participate in, and contribute to society. [Congressional Findings which preface the 1990 "Americans with Disabilities" Act][4]

No explicit references to the delivery of health care occur in the language of this law. Initially, the ADA thus might seem at most tangential to health and medical policy. But this estimate is uninformed, as evidenced by the federal intervention in Oregon's decisions about the equitable allocation of health care. For the new law is especially far-reaching in that it reconceptualizes our understanding of "handicapping condition," transforming this notion from a state of a minority of people which naturally disadvantages them in society to a state of society which artificially disadvantages a minority of people.

The law thus transfigures individuals with disabilities from patients into persons, assigning them equal rights in public and proprietary transactions within, as well as beyond, the medical domain. As this paper progresses, we will begin to see the implications of this conceptual transformation. To understand why persons with disabilities require such legal safeguards against exclusionary practice, we need only notice the improbability of those same Oregon policymakers who espoused denial of health care based on disability, permitting themselves to be associated with any similar proposal for health care exclusions based on race or gender. This is because exclusion by explicit policy based on race or gender is now publicly inadmissible despite there being ample statistical evidence of the differential effectiveness of some medical procedures relative to race or gender. In contrast, the unabashed public proclamation of exclusionary practices based on disability abides in our society.

As the feminist historian Joan Scott puts it, "Equality, in the political theory of rights that lies behind the claims of excluded groups for justice, means the ignoring of differences between individuals . . . This presumes a social agreement to consider obviously different people as equivalent."[5] Regarding equality, the question is whether individuals with disabilities are so inescapably different as to unalterably defeat any agreement to be thought of as equivalent to persons not disabled. For if defective agents are impervious to such agreements to disregard their differences, they not only forfeit the protection of egalitarian concerns as these usually are understood but also constitute an insurmountable impediment to the social attainment of egalitarian ideals.

It is such a quandary which seems to prompt Charles Taylor to assign such individuals to the borders of equality, and thereby to equivocate as to whether or not they are irrevocably unequal. In his discussion of the foundation of the modern concept of equality in the essay "Multiculturalism and the Politics of Recognition," Taylor identifies "the basis for our intuitions of equal dignity" as "a universal human potential, a capacity that all humans share." But, he continues, "our sense of the importance of potentiality reaches so far that we extend this protection even to people who through some circumstance that has befallen them are incapable of realizing their potential in the *normal* way—handicapped people . . . for instance." (emphasis added)[6]

While it is no automatic error to qualify the scope of categorical claims to equality by stipulating that they are limited to "normal" people, care must be exercised to prevent any such qualification from being a merely arbitrary exclusion. For example, the characterization of women as being nothing more than defective males—and thereby inferior to men—is found in Aristotle, is disseminated in medieval thought and afterward, and emerges as a justification for treating women inequitably. Of course, today philosophers (almost) uniformly reject the belief that women are inferior by nature, and (almost) all public policymakers including those in Oregon would be reluctant to make such a belief an explicit consideration in the allocation of resources.

But this heretofore discredited way of thinking about individuals who deviate from the standard adult male resurfaces in Taylor's talk of "handicapped" people as being equal only by extension or derivation or fiction because they really don't possess the essentially humanizing capacity to fulfill their potential "normally." Yet a bit of reflection exposes the fallacy in purporting to delineate normal, or full, from abnormal, or restricted, realization of potential. For every human being, equally, has potentials that through circumstance remain unrealized, and whether these could have been fulfilled "in the normal way," and whether any loss accrues in not re-

alizing them, is merely speculative. We would not dream of declaring that an athletically gifted person who cannot realize his potential as a boxer only because he wants to play the violin is equal merely in some extended sense, so why place an artistically gifted person with a disability like the violinist Itzhak Perlman, who has not actualized his potential for boxing because he cannot walk normally, in this inferior category?

Naturalizing Inferiority

That a usually alert and thoughtful philosopher like Taylor reproduces stereotypic assumptions so unreflectively suggests how deeply these are embedded both in practice and in thought. Why so easily assent to portraying the lives of individuals with disabilities as so globally unfulfillable? To elucidate the dangers of such dismissive devaluation, consider a recently published view of this matter, which maintains that individuals with disabilities are essentially defective and consequently inferior. In a report on the ADA commissioned for the *Report from the Institute for Philosophy & Public Policy,* David Wasserman contends that nature has made persons with disabilities "less equal" than other Americans.

Because the report depicts individuals with disabilities as fundamentally impervious to social restructuring aimed at equalizing them, I propose to devote some care to examining its arguments. In particular, I will focus on the report's view that because the differentia of the class of persons the ADA protects is their impairments, this law cannot help but ultimately be self-defeating. That is, because the ADA definitively purports to safeguard persons who, according to the report, are disadvantaged due to a *natural* process, the report urges that no *civil* process suffices to grant them equality.

I do not know whether the report's author would care to be so blunt about the implications of his position.[7] But this is the unavoidable result of maintaining that there are natural or, as he calls them, "biological" differences which constitute the definitive characteristics of the class protected by the ADA. According to the report, these properties render the class's members irreparably inferior in respect to claims to fair or equitable treatment. The author's self-conviction is so compelling in this regard that we find him systematically misreporting the language of the law, as, for example, when he asserts:

> (the ADA) also recognizes *an objective category of biological impairment;* a person whose major life activities were limited *only* by other people's attitudes or practices would be "disabled" only in a derivative sense. (emphasis added)[8]

> The fact of *biological* impairment, recognized by the ADA in its definition of disability, makes the notion of "equal opportunity to benefit" problematic. This is a serious defect in a statute that treats the denial of such opportunity as a form of discrimination. (emphasis added)[9]

But the ADA *nowhere* mentions or otherwise recognizes "biological" impairment. While meticulously inclusive of both physical and mental impairment, the ADA does not legislate a biological explanation for all impairment. Nor are the impairments of members of the class it protects definitively or even preponderantly biological, in the way adherents of eugenics would have us believe. While some physical impairment originates genetically or chemically, much of it results instead from traumatic injury generally understood as a mechanical, not a biological, process.[10] Nor can the causes of all mental disabilities be inarguably reduced to biological terms, let alone legislated to be biological.

The line of argument promoted in this report is reminiscent of Aristotle's notorious attempts to establish that women and slaves are inferior by nature. The report applies views remarkably like Aristotle's to devalue disabled individuals. Worse, it presents these negative assessments as if they were definitively true or, at least, uncontentious. Moreover, the report abjures the Congressional Findings which trace the exclusion visited on disabled individuals to social causes, resting its case instead on the philosophically discredited ground that biological explanation is to be preferred because, according to the report, it is an "objective category."[11]

That is, the social exclusion visited on persons with disabilities is traced to a biological—that is, a nonsocial—source on the spurious ground that a social explanation of disabled persons' isolation cannot be as objective. Parenthetically, by suggesting that it is not objective to assign the repression of disabled individuals to social causes, this line of thought functions to absolve society from responsibility for remedying the adverse impact of socially sanctioned exclusionary practices. In rejecting the categorical obligation not to repress, or exclude, or discriminate against the disabled, this report proposes as a palliative that society agree to care for persons with disabilities, but only to the extent resources remain unstrained.

Social History and Disadvantage

Intent on making the ADA complicit in its own overthrow, the report charges, "The ADA itself recognizes that *the physical endowment* of people with disabilities *contributes to* their disadvantage" (emphasis added).[12] But the ADA *nowhere* cites a direct causal connection between physical state and disadvantage. On the contrary, the term "disadvantage" occurs in its text only in Finding 6, which assets that empirical research shows people with disabilities to "occupy an inferior status in our society, and (be) severely disadvantaged socially, vocationally, economically, and educationally." Thus, the language of the law explicitly conjoins the disadvantaged status of disabled persons not with inferior physical endowment but with the social status to which they are consigned.

Agreed that having a disability, or equally being believed to have one, is a *necessary* condition for triggering contemptuous interpersonal responses *to disability.* But this is nothing more than analytic. Only under certain social conditions does having a disability become a *sufficient* condition for being treated shoddily or victimized. The report's equivocation on the logical and empirical senses of "contributes to" in the citation above shifts the blame for being victimized to the victims and should remind us of how the myth of biological determinism has fueled eugenically sanctified liquidations of "defective" populations. In contrast, the ADA repudiates this sad history by banishing any legal presumption that "normal" and "disabled" are categories created by natural law.

So habitual are our feelings of superiority to individuals with disabilities that we may automatically acquiesce in the report's equating of disability with disadvantage. However, even though an impairment is no advantage, it does not follow that to be impaired or disabled is to be disadvantaged per se. For disadvantage is relative to both context and end. A specific impairment need have no natural or necessary deleterious impact on a life. Indeed, what counts as an impairment is itself relative to what is imagined to be normal, the last being, of course, a famously procrustean concept, as Brock rightly recognizes just prior to the passage with which I began when he observes that normal mobility is a standard relative to an individual's age, as well as to her social and historical environment.[13]

To illustrate, in an age of corrective lenses and supermarkets, your near-sightedness is not the disadvantage it would be for a Neanderthal hunter. Another illustration: deafness is not a natural disadvantage in interpersonal communication. Signing members of the deaf community communicate with one another as effectively as do hearing persons who speak to each other. That the majority of Americans know speech rather than sign may be thought of as simply another in a long list of practices imposed by the dominant group to suit its members while suppressing a minority whose practices are otherwise. Moreover, what counts as a "misfortune," another term imported by the report, is heavily dependent on taste and circumstance. While some may view it as a misfortune that I cannot ski, no one who does not ski and can't imagine choosing to spend time and money to get so cold pities me for this.

We should not protract the report's confusion of two very different questions: whether a departure from "normal" physical or mental states is remediable is a medical issue, but whether a deficit should be repaired, or adapted to, or exploited by society, is an open social and personal question which the report arbitrarily slams shut. The author is lured into doing this, I believe, by social arrangements which are centuries old.[14] By the 17th century, the virtue of according charitable benevolence to those in need clashed outright with the fear of creating a class of drones. Consequently, there emerged the concept of the "deserving" poor, those who would have worked but for their unfortunate impairments. To be a member of this class was to be distinguished from the undeserv-

ing, willfully malfunctioning poor, although careful attention to moral character was mandated to keep a disabled person from slipping over this social line.[15]

By definition, then, the deserving poor must be incompetent to be deserving. And their treatment, while technically benevolent, is designed to make their condition seem unattractive to those capable of work. In view of their definitively deficient state, the deserving poor are not conceivably capable themselves of the responsible use of whatever means charity bestows on them. So another social group emerged: caregivers, persons whose profession it became to channel charity by administering it to damaged individuals. Thus, as a social class, the disabled became required by definition to be nonproductive. They also became the means of production for members of another group, professional caretakers.

These conceptions, and the institutions they inform, forge conflicting imperatives. To demonstrate their commitment to contain the costs of benevolent practices, to discourage drones, and to prove their competent professionalism, caretakers need to alter some of their charges to the extent that they no longer require charity. But to mitigate the risk of rehabilitation's depleting the supply of those to be cared for, caretakers constantly are reassigning types of persons, who, they contend, have been assigned mistakenly to the class of undeserving poor, but who are in fact involuntarily rather than willfully flawed. Hence the drive to reconfigure substance abuse or violent behavior as medical rather than moral defects.[16]

Interjecting a Fishy Standard

Note that this model is unforgiving to those designated as abnormal, for it magnifies malfunctioning, expanding it beyond the involuntary inability to perform certain narrowly described physical or mental activities so as to imply an incapacity to shoulder social or moral responsibility, or to relate to others by acting equal to, rather than dependent on, them. Entrapped by this historical perspective, the report simply cannot comprehend that equal opportunity, not exceptional treatment, could be the objective of legislation protecting the disabled. The author seems convinced that a mandate for treating these individuals exceptionally benevolently must be the ultimate objective of the ADA, despite the explicit protestations found in the language of the law itself.

For instance, Congressional Finding 9, which prefaces the ADA, sets out for the nation the goal of remedying inequalities of opportunity which continue to handicap citizens with disabilities:

> (9) the continuing existence of unfair and unnecessary discrimination and prejudice denies people with disabilities the opportunity *to compete on an equal basis* and to pursue those opportunities for which our free society is justifiably famous, and costs the United States billions of dollars in unnecessary expenses resulting from dependency and nonproductivity. [emphasis added]

But by Wasserman's lights it is logically impossible for individuals with disabilities to compete on an equal basis, for he cannot discard the theory that it is their incompetence which defines the members of this class and which is the source of their need for social protection. Thus, counterfactually, he reports that the ADA relies on a stronger sense of "equal opportunity" than that central to earlier civil rights legislation.[17] (He defends this analysis on the ground that the ADA requires the removal of barriers created by covert or unintentionally prejudicial practices in addition to those arising from the intention to discriminate. To the contrary, it is nonsense to say that previous civil rights legislation has been directed only at explicitly intentional discriminatory practices, for we have had decades of judicial decisions mandating the elimination of *de facto* as well as *de jure* segregated systems and of practices which, regardless of being well or ill intentioned, have disparately adverse impact on protected classes.)

How can an individual with an impairment substantially limiting major life activities compete equally? The report's interpretation of the ADA's standard is that the law guarantees equal outcomes. In several places, the report declares that the law is flawed because such a warrant is absurd:

> More broadly, we cannot reasonably expect to raise all people with disabilities to a level of functioning where they can receive the same benefits from facilities and services as able-bodied people.[18] The fact of ... impairment ... makes the notion of "equal opportunity to benefit" problematic. ... However much they (the regulations) required, they would fall short of assuring equal mobility. The fact of ... impairment ... makes the notion of "equal opportunity to benefit" problematic. This is a serious defect in a statute that treats the denial of such opportunity as a form of discrimination.[19]

But the ADA does not demand that society render mobility-impaired individuals fully mobile and in so doing extricate them from the class the law protects. For instance, the law maintains that benefiting equally from public transportation means no more than being able to travel the same public routes with approximately the same expenditure of time and money as other individuals. The report's criticism that full implementation of the regulations on accessible transportation would still "leave most people with disabilities with a far greater burden of mobility than most able-bodied people" thus is worse than irrelevant.[20]

Does this criticism mean that the ADA is an ineffective law because it cannot make a cripple run, rather than wheel, a winning marathon? Not only is it demeaning to caricature disabled persons by imputing to them redemption fantasies which are someone else's obsession, but it is inconsistent to criticize the ADA on such a ground unless one also criticizes earlier civil rights legislation for failing to make black people white or to transform women into men. By importing a class structure which isolates a class of "deserving" dependents, confusing this with the class protected by the ADA, and then assuming that elevation from this class is the overriding desideratum, the report condemns the ADA by adopting the viewpoint of the social arrangements this law is designed to dislodge.

To argue as this report does is to interject a red herring, for neither the ADA, nor any disabled advocacy group I know of, proposes this kind of goal. Reforming disabled people to make them whole does not appear as a standard in the ADA. Nowhere does the ADA propose changing the members of the class it protects to make them more like other, more socially favored, people. To the contrary, the ADA proposes changing social practice to eliminate its favoring nondisabled persons.

Equality of Outcomes

What standard does the report erect in making its criticism of the ADA? Its charges seem to draw on the same equivocation between being normal and being equal embedded in the Sen–Brock illustration. But to take the metric engineered by this equivocation as a gauge of effective justice is odd because on it being just may require that resources be allocated to force individuals who do not wish to do so to function normally.

To offer one among many possible counterexamples which call into question the standard of equal functioning, there is a large group of hearing-impaired individuals who reject the surgical technology of cochlear implantation which could elevate their capability to hear. Indeed, persons of this persuasion would object to my describing the outcome of cochlear implantation as "elevating," for they contend that their lives would be in no degree wanting if only our social arrangements gave equal recognition to those who communicate nonaurally. And in this view they are protected by the ADA, for it was precisely in virtue of its imposing normal functioning as a standard which disabled citizens must submit to, that the treatment-ranking system of the Oregon Health Plan was judged to violate their civil rights. By declaring a class of individuals defined as defective to be equal, the ADA defies the equation of being normal with being equal, as well as the eugenic standard that an unimpaired or normal physical and mental state is a desideratum which should inform moral and social policy objectives.

As we have seen, to assume that physical or mental impairment, a contingent individual state, entails essential moral deficit—namely, the incapacity to be equal—neglects the extent to which the social arrangements to which we confine people insinuate into what we imagine those people to be, or not to be. Earlier, I observed that whether a deficit should be repaired is a personal and social question, not a medical one. How anyone answers it inevitably will be swayed by yet another consideration: Is inequality, cast as an unyielding aspect of a person's experience, definitive of individuals with disabilities, as the report seems to have, or is it merely the stubborn artifact of inequitable social arrangement?

In the everyday life of persons mobilizing in wheelchairs, their inequality—both as experienced by them and in the eyes of others—manifests itself not in the inability to walk but in exclusion from bathrooms, from theaters, from transportation, from places of work, and from life-saving medical treatment. In keeping with this reality, it is the strategy of the ADA to require that whoever operates a facility or program must accommodate individuals with disabilities unless doing so would constitute an undue hardship, as measured against the overall financial resources of the facility or program. (Operatively, other things being equal, the exemption places expenditure for access on a comparable—rather than on either a privileged or an inferior—basis with other expenditures on the facility or program.) What informs this mandate is recognition that accessibility would be a commonplace, not a novelty, were the majority, not the minority, of the population disabled.

Suppose that most persons used wheelchairs? Would we continue to build staircases rather than ramps? Suppose most were deaf? Closed-captioning would be open-captioning and would have been the standard for television manufacture long before July 1, 1993. By hypothesizing what society would do were persons with disabilities dominant rather than suppressed, it becomes evident that systematic exclusion of the disabled is a consequence not of their natural inferiority but of their minority social status. That is, they are inferior not because they are too defective, but rather because they are too few.

Moreover, by hypothesizing whether individuals with disabilities would be dysfunctional in an environment fashioned through social arrangements responsive to impairment, we are better positioned to separate natural or essential from artificially induced, socially contingent dysfunction. To understand why such counterfactual generalizations about public policy bear moral import, we may notice that they comply with the familiar rational procedure of universalizing, held by so many generations of philosophers to be the heart of moral thought. But rather than imagining how one personally would respond to joining the disabled minority through physical or mental affliction, here one simply considers what would be the rule in a kingdom in which one's unimpaired functioning had become so atypical as to be marginalized by social arrangements. This imaginative process reconfigures the operation of moral imagination so as to rely on social rather than psychological extrapolation.

My proposal thereby is responsive to the phenomenon, previously remarked on, that able-bodied persons do better at envisioning anyone but themselves as disabled. The proposal is also leveling in that it reduces the distance between those well-intentioned able-bodied individuals who are so well integrated socially and psychologically that they can internalize prevailing social norms, and those others, the marginalized disabled, whose vision is not so shielded from the perception of injustice.[21] Moreover, my proposal is not agent neutralizing in that it avoids liberal thought's habit of obscuring defective agents.

That is, liberalism typically treats discrepancies in knowledge, including knowledge of our own actual positions, as differences in advantage. Thus, liberalism idealizes the obscuring of differentiating relational characteristics by endorsing such homogenizing criteria as what people would choose if ignorant of their actual position. For example, in *Political Liberalism*, Rawls reintroduces the veil of ignorance as a device for preventing any party to a social compact from occupying an advantaged position from which to bargain.

But in positional bargaining, it is not what one knows about one's self, but what one knows about the other's interests and resources, which contributes to advantage. Indeed, accurate understanding of one's *own* interests is crucial to both positional and mutual interest bargaining. So to the extent veil-of-ignorance approaches restrict deliberation to idealized or normalized points of view, "defective" agents stand at an initial disadvantage, for there is no position within this system from which their interests are understood, and so in initial deliberations about justice they occupy no position at all.

Moreover, veil-of-ignorance arguments substitute a kind of generalized prudence for the motivating considerations which arise for each of us out of our personalized experiences of what we are and how we need to live. But, in abstraction, prudence rarely moves us to precautions against eventualities we find unthinkable. To illustrate, liberalism expects that, if I am ignorant of whether or not I am impaired, I will provide in the social arrangements I endorse for worst-case contingencies — for instance, for being seriously impaired. But demonstrably people's actual policies in this regard do not conform to what liberalism anticipates.

We can confirm this by noticing that, for almost every one of us, the onset of disability in one's self or one's intimates is unceasingly both possible and unpredictable. Yet, in actual social planning this possible future heretofore has almost always been repudiated, rather than provided for, as is evidenced by our systematic historical indifference to creating an environment suited to such eventualities. Egalitarian normalizing fails to provide for those whose future this may be by denying any standing to nontransparent viewpoints like those represented by individuals with disabilities. In contrast, counterfactually generalizing triumphs over this persistent diffidence because it concedes the opacity of disabled individuals' personal experience, while urging that exclusionary social conditions need not remain as they are.

Nor should the theoretical import of this last point be overlooked, for it elucidates why such veil-of-ignorance proposals as Ronald Dworkin's "prudent insurance" criterion for providing health care substitute what is normal for what is just.[22] Dworkin insists that any national coverage which taxes citizens for care that most would not individually choose to insure themselves for is unfair. For instance, because Dworkin imagines that most citizens, offered the choice between saving to pay for extraordinary measures taken to procure six extra months of life or expending the same amount to improve their lives while healthy, would choose the latter, he concludes that a public policy which extracts tax dollars to mandate the former at the expense of the latter is a "disservice to justice."[23] It is the public's sense of priorities which should guide decisions about what care is provided, Dworkin declares, praising Oregon's public polls and meetings as valuable sources of information while simultaneously acknowledging that very few of those whose care was being debated participated in the polls and meetings.[24]

The core conceptual mechanism of the "prudent insurance" criterion uses a process Dworkin describes as "speculating" about what, under fairer conditions than those which actually exist, would be prudent for most people, in order to guide us in selecting the health care that "justice demands everyone have now."25 He specifies these fairer conditions as (1) fair distribution of wealth and income, (2) all state-of-the-art knowledge about the costs and value and side effects of particular medical procedures is generally known by the public at large, and (3) no one has any information available about how likely any particular person is to acquire any specific medical condition. However, later in his discussion Dworkin slips from describing the criterion as what "we can speculate about what kind of medical care and insurance it would be prudent for most Americans to buy, for themselves" to a quite different criterion, namely "what most people would think prudent for themselves."26

This alteration marks an important difference, for what would be prudent for most people is far from what most people think is prudent as long as they are not now and do not know whether they will be impaired. Moreover, far from being democratic, this latter standard installs a tyranny of the normal. For by stipulating that fair judgment occurs when no one knows that she or he is impaired, Dworkin decrees that fair judgment is relative to unimpaired agents (that is, those unaware of being impaired) only.

The Illusion of Agent Neutrality

This is hardly an agent-neutral point of view. By authorizing the unimpaired as not just the majority but the sole viewpoint from which what is prudent may be discerned, Dworkin unfairly weights the speculative process he endorses against all those participants who under actual, as opposed to abstracted, conditions face a reasonable probability of becoming impaired. Yet it is precisely these individuals for whom the institution of a just health care system is most urgent. An agent-relative system of provisions surely is not just if the point of view which warrants it excludes all and only those who will need to use the system.

These observations suggest a more general point, which is that in the absence of a warranted exclusive perspective from which benefits can be assessed, sup-posedly agent-neutral relative benefit analyses cannot institute just distributions. As our consideration of the prudent insurance criterion indicated, we are hard put to identify a single point of view from which it is warranted to analyze benefits for even a single individual. Nor is it even clear that the perspective from which an individual sees himself as neediest is the most propitious one from which to judge what would best benefit him.

Do we owe it to a newly disabled person to accept his estimation of the incapacitating impact of his impairment and his assessment of what is owed him in regard or compensation of it? I do not think it can be so, for to assign precedence automatically to this point of view has a bizarre implication. A common experience in learning how to be disabled is to regret, when looking backward, one's initial debilitating panic and abdication. This process is recounted again and again in anecdotal and autobiographical material authored by persons with disabilities.

But if such a person's earlier verdict stands as authoritative, then as the result of their subsequently transformed points of view, persons reconciled to their disabilities seem vulnerable to the charge of being insensitive to, because dismissive of, their earlier despairing selves. But disabled persons no more owe it to their earlier selves to regard self-pity as credible than any disabled individual owes nondisabled persons acceptance of their verdict that the quality of his life is inferior. Nor do we owe either the despairing or the sanguine disabled person precedence regarding his own assessment of the quality of his life. Thus, no point of view is privileged here, not even that forbearing one to which, as mentioned earlier, Sen denies the standing to refuse to be the subject of compensatory allocations.

All of this suggests very strongly that cost–benefit approaches cannot offer just treatment to normal and defective agents alike. This is so regardless of whether the privileged point of view is the majority "normal" perspective or the rarer "impaired" perspective. That is, cost–benefit analyses must be inherently inequitable because they *necessarily privilege* one among several irreducible points of view.

In contrast, the ADA extends the constitutional guarantee of *equal* protection to defective agents. Nor is this measure satisfied by schemes which purport to compensate such persons for systematically inferior treatment by designating some limited respects in which to overprivilege them. Compensatory arrangements of this sort sometimes are offered by supporters of systems like the Oregon Health Plan as conciliations for compromised equal rights (but it would be incorrect to characterize the Brock–Sen compensatory proposal as conciliatory). But the posture adopted by the ADA rejects schemes like these as vestiges of the historically repressive practice of confining impaired individuals to roles reserved for the "deserving" poor.

Predictably, then, the rights established by the ADA cannot help but sanction claims against health care rationing systems that assess alternative outcomes by reference to such agent-relative benefits as the quality of one's well-being. Nor is there a conjecturally agent-neutral point of view from which just policy can be discerned. For far from being equalizing, idealized points of view appear infected by such contingencies of current social arrangement as what kind of person is, for the moment, most populous, most powerful, or most functional. To illustrate, we have seen that, far from being a benchmark of equality, the adoption of normality as a measure merely codifies the level of functioning of the most populous, and thereby the paramount, group.

Empirical Equality

Let us now reexamine the intuition which drives the Brock–Sen illustration in the light of our having disassociated being equal from being normal. No metamoral urgency can now be seen to attach to reparative procedures because all individuals, defective as well as superior, now are to be found together within equality's scope. Thus, equitable allocation schemes need not give moral priority to remedying people's impairments. But, of course, this does not preclude prioritizing such reparative treatment on economic grounds, for instance, that we cannot afford a social environment which induces nonproductivity in part of our population.

Because (dys)functioning associated with disability is in large part attributable to an environment artificially favoring those who are unimpaired, decisions regarding the extraordinary allocation of resources to defective individuals can be freed from the pressure to provide compensation only if allocation of resources to social ends sufficiently repairs the environment so as to secure conditions under which such persons' pursuit of opportunity becomes equitable. To the extent satisfaction of this standard remains incomplete, we will continue to be haunted by a compulsion to compensate defective agents for their dysfunction by allocating extraordinary resources for (some) reparative procedures. Simultaneously we will agonize over whether persons unsalvageable by means of such normalizing medical procedures have lives worth living or saving. It is my belief that, absent a society in which defective agents are sufficiently well integrated to have achieved equality of social treatment, we are in no fair position to ration any social cost by ranking the quality or value of "different" people's lives.

Finally, I want to comment on the propriety of my having seized on what are meant only as peripheral comments by Brock, Taylor, and Sen as a vehicle for my analysis of the prevailing conceptualization of disability. It is a fact that the vast bulk of philosophical writing on equality, difference, and related issues marginalizes individuals with disabilities to the extent that either they are the subject of scattered comments only, or they do not appear at all. Recently Ron Amundson, the late Gregory Kavka, and Susan Wendell all have remarked that contemporary philosophy alludes to disability almost solely in the context of discussions of killing and letting die.[27]

Thus, for individuals with disabilities, there has been little opportunity for reflective philosophical criticism to question either the practices or the concepts which devalue them. By asking how defective agents may be equal, and why they have not heretofore been comfortably acknowledged to be so, I hope in some part to remedy this neglect and, simultaneously, to illuminate why, in respect to these persons, some of our medical conceptualizations threaten to conflict so profoundly with the evolving social and legal understanding of them.

Notes

1. In *The Quality of Life,* pp. 99–100.

2. A. K. Sen, "Equality of What?" in S. McMurrin, ed., *Tanner Lectures on Human Values* (Cambridge, England: Cambridge University Press, 1980), p. 217.

3. *New York Times,* March 20, 1993, p. 8.

4. Section 2 of Public Law 101–336.

5. Joan W. Scott, "Deconstructing Equality-Versus-Difference," in *Conflicts in Feminism,* ed. Marianne Hirsch and Evelyn Fox Keller (New York: Routledge, 1990), p. 142.

6. Charles Taylor et al., *Multiculturalism and "The Politics of Recognition"* (Princeton, N.J.: Princeton University Press, 1992), pp. 41–42.

7. David Wasserman, "Disability, Discrimination, and Fairness," in *Report from the Institute for Philosophy & Public Policy* (College Park, Maryland) 13, no. 1/2 (Winter–Spring 1993): pp. 7–12.

8. Wasserman, p. 9.

9. Wasserman, p. 10.

10. Ron Amundson makes a similar point by carefully arguing the difference between disability and disease in "Disability, Handicap and the Environment," which Wasserman cites in his bibliography.

11. Wasserman, p. 9.

12. Wasserman, p. 8.

13. Brock, p. 99.

14. See my "Damaged Goods: Does Disability Disqualify People from Just Health Care?" *Mt. Sinai Journal of Medicine,* in press, for a more extensive review of the conceptual implications of the social history of disability.

15. For example, orthopedist R. C. Elmslie writes, "A failure in the moral training of a cripple means the evolution of an individual detestable in character, a menace and burden to the community." Quoted in H. Gallagher, *F.D.R.'s Splendid Deception* (New York: Dodd Mead, 1985), p. 30. R. C. Elmslie, *The Care of Invalid and Crippled Children in School* (1911). Elmslie's view of individuals with disabilities was progressive, for his argument was meant to gain entry to public education for crippled children.

16. On this subject, the work of Herbert Fingarette is illuminating and ahead of its time.

17. Wasserman, p. 9.

18. Ibid., p. 10.

19. Ibid., p. 10.

20. Ibid., p. 10. As a public policy analysis, Wasserman's argument functions to offer public officials an excuse for not enforcing regulations. In the case of the complaint filed on June 28, 1993, by the California Council of the Blind against the San Francisco Municipal Railroad System, Wasserman's position would excuse the MUNI's systematic, pervasive, and prolonged failure to comply with federal and state regulations requiring that stops be announced for visually impaired passengers. Note that enforcement of the regulation has no fiscal implications for MUNI, but being deposited at unfamiliar locations beyond their stops creates serious hazards for blind MUNI riders. Wasserman's position permits MUNI officials to excuse their practice of permitting drivers to ignore blind riders' requests to be notified aurally of their stop. It does so by reenforcing the drivers' attitude, once sanctified by exclusionary laws, that presence of people with disabilities in public is an imposition.

21. I have borrowed the idea that social marginalization is an enabling condition of the perception of injustice from Samuel Scheffler, *Human Morality* (Oxford, England: Oxford University Press, 1992), pp. 142–43.

22. Ronald Dworkin, "Is Clinton's Plan Fair?" in *The New York Review of Books* 66, nos. 1, 2, January 13, 1994, pp. 20–25.

23. Dworkin, p. 23.

24. Ibid., p. 24.

25. Ibid., p. 23.

26. Ibid.

27. This point has been commented on by Susan Wendell, "Toward a Feminist Theory of Disability," *Hypatia,* 4, no. 2 (Summer 1989); Gregory Kavka, *Social Philosophy & Policy* 9, no. 1 (1992); and Ron Amundson, "Disability, Handicap and the Environment," *Journal of Social Philosophy* 23, no. 1 (1992).

PART 3

Applications

Many issues provoke debate about social justice in a diverse society such as ours. In Part Three, we present issues that are particularly pressing in the 1990s: immigration, work and welfare, family and reproductive issues, and affirmative action.

Immigration has become one of the hottest political issues in this decade, but the discussion of immigration is too often filled with much heat and little light. Michael Walzer offers an account of the background moral issues in immigration debates, arguing that the possibility of belonging to a society is one of society's most important social goods.

Work and welfare are two issues that cannot be separated. It is not possible to survive in our society without either a job that pays a decent wage, or some sort of public assistance. And while some cry out for paring the welfare rolls, there has been little public debate about whether we have a moral obligation to offer jobs to all those who want them. Adina Schwartz argues that not only does everyone have the right to a job, but that we as a society have an obligation to see to it that everyone has the opportunity to be involved in work he or she sees as personally meaningful. Obviously, if Schwartz's recommendation were put into place, there would be no need for welfare for many people now on welfare (whether our society would continue to be an efficient player in the world economy is another question). But we do not live in a world where everyone who wants work can find it. Since this is so, many, including Carl Wellman, argue that we have a duty to provide welfare assistance to those who need it.

Discussions of welfare turn naturally to discussions of the family and reproductive issues. After all, if people were not having children, we would not need to discuss the need for aid to these children. Mary Gibson directly connects the issues of work and reproduction by showing how reproductive freedom has been abridged in the workplace. Angela Davis offers a penetrating historical analysis of the politics of reproduction from the African-American perspective, arguing that attempts to control both fertility and child rearing have often had hidden racist motivations. Jeffner Allen offers a quite different view on reproduction, viewing it as an important source of the oppression of women. The only solution, she argues, is for women to simply stop having children until their demands for full equality are met. Christine Pierce addresses another dimensions of the debate about family — gay and lesbian families. She argues that most arguments in favor of the family are equally supportive of gay and lesbian families.

Our final topic is affirmative action, a hotly debated strategy for social transformation. Affirmative action can be broadly defined as action taken to remedy and/or to prevent discrimination based on membership in certain disadvantaged groups, and/or to compensate people for past discrimination. People debate about many things when they debate about affirmative action. They disagree about whether discrimination has taken place and about what groups are the victims of discriminations. They disagree about what kind of strategies are permissible in cases of discrimination. They disagree about the consequences of various strategies. Many of these are empirical questions, such as whether groups are discriminated against, and can be settled by simply gathering the relevant information. Many other questions are value questions, which turn on notions of justice and equality. Discrimination is often understood as an unjust exclusion of a particular person or group of persons from some sphere of activity. Carol Locust expands this conception of discrimination. She argues that discrimination can be practiced against a whole group of persons and that it can involve the suppression of entire ways of life. When we see discrimination on this level, the focus of affirmative action on access to jobs and education for individuals begins to seem rather piecemeal and conservative. Alan Goldman turns to the more traditional understanding of affirmative action and focuses on one of its central issues — what it is to be qualified for a position. Richard Wasserstrom defends what he calls preferential treatment. Russell Abrams goes a bit further in his defense of affirmative action. Shelby Steele raises questions about the negative effects of affirmative action on those it is intended to help.

Immigration, Work, and Welfare

EL SONAVABITCHE

(for Aishe Berger)

Gloria Anzaldúa

(Source: From Borderlands/La Frontera: The New Mesitza. *Copyright © 1987 by Gloria Anzaldúa. Reprinted with permission from Aunt Lute Books (415) 826-1300.)*

Car flowing down a lava of highway
just happened to glance out the window
in time to see brown faces bent backs
like prehistoric boulders in a field
so common a sight no one
notices
blood rushes to my face
twelve years I'd sat on the memory
the anger scorching me
my throat so tight I can
barely get the words out.

I got to the farm
in time to hear the shots
ricochet off barn,
spit into the sand,
in time to see tall men in uniforms
thumping fists on doors
metallic voices yelling Halt!
their hawk eyes constantly shifting.

    When I hear the words, *"Corran muchachos"*
    I run back to the car, ducking,

see the glistening faces, arms outflung,
of the *mexicanos* running headlong
through the fields
kicking up clouds of dirt

see them reach the tree line
foliage opening, swishing closed behind them.
I hear the tussling of bodies, grunts, panting
squeak of leather squawk of walkie-talkies
sun reflecting off gunbarrels
    the world a blinding light
    a great buzzing in my ears
    my knees like aspens in the wind.
    I see that wide cavernous look of the hunted
    the look of hares
    thick limp blue-black hair
    The bare heads humbly bent
    of those who do not speak
    the ember in their eyes extinguished.

I lean on the shanty wall of that migrant camp
north of Muncie, Indiana.
Wets, a voice says.
I turn to see a Chicano pushing
the head of his *muchachita*
back into the *naguas* of the mother
a tin plate face down on the floor

tortillas scattered around them.
His other hand signals me over.
He too is from *el valle de Tejas*
I had been his kid's teacher.
I'd come to get the grower
to fill up the sewage ditch near the huts
saying it wouldn't do for the children
to play in it.

> Smoke from a cooking fire and
> shirtless *niños* gathered around us.

> *Mojados,* he says again,
> leaning on his chipped Chevy station wagon
> Been here two weeks
> about a dozen of them.
> The *sonavabitche* works them
> from sunup to dark — 15 hours sometimes.
> *Como mulas los trabaja*
> *no saben como hacer la perra.*
> Last Sunday they asked for a day off
> wanted to pray and rest,
> write letters to their *familias.*
> *¿Y sabes lo que hizo el sonavabitche?*
> He turns away and spits.
> Says he has to hold back half their wages
> that they'd eaten the other half:
> sack of beans, sack of rice, sack of flour.
> *Frijoleros sí lo son* but no way
> could they have eaten that many *frijoles.*
> I nod.

Como le dije, son doce — started out 13
five days packed in the back of a pickup
boarded up tight
fast cross-country run no stops
except to change drivers, to gas up
no food they pissed into their shoes —
those that had *guaraches*
slept slumped against each other
sabe Dios where they shit.
One smothered to death on the way here.

> Miss, you should've seen them when they
> stumbled out.
> First thing the *sonavabitche* did was clamp
> a handkerchief over his nose
> then ordered them stripped
> hosed them down himself
> in front of everybody.

> They hobbled about
> learning to walk all over again.
> *Flacos con caras de viejos*
> *aunque la mitá eran jóvenes.*

Como le estaba diciendo,
today was payday.
You saw them, *la migra* came busting in
waving their *pinche pistolas.*
Said someone made a call,
what you call it? Anonymous.
Guess who? That *sonavabitche,* who else?
Done this three times since we've been coming here
Sepa Dios how many times in between.

> Wets, free labor, *esclavos.*
> *Pobres jijos de la chingada.*
> This the last time we work for him
> no matter how *fregados* we are
> he said, shaking his head,
> spitting at the ground.
> *Vámonos, mujer, empaca el mugrero.*

> He hands me a cup of coffee,
> half of it sugar, half of it milk
> my throat so dry I even down the dregs.
> It has to be done.
> Steeling myself
> I take that walk to the big house.

Finally the big man lets me in.
How about a drink? I shake my head.
He looks me over, opens his eyes wide
and smiles, says how sorry he is immigration
is getting so tough
a poor Mexican can't make a living
and they sure do need the work.
My throat so thick the words stick.
He studies me, then says,
Well, what can I do you for?
I want two weeks wages
including two Saturdays and Sundays,
minimum wage, 15 hours a day.
I'm more startled than he.
Whoa there, sinorita,
wets work for whatever you give them
the season hasn't been good.
Besides most are halfway to Mexico by now.
Two weeks wages, I say,
the words swelling in my throat.

Miss uh what did you say your name was?
I fumble for my card.
You can't do this,
I haven't broken no law,
his lidded eyes darken, I step back.
I'm leaving in two minutes and I want cash
the whole amount right here in my purse
when I walk out.
No hoarseness, no trembling.
It startled both of us.

You want me telling every single one
of your neighbors what you've been doing
all these years? The mayor, too?
Maybe make a call to Washington?
Slitted eyes studied the card again.
They had no cards, no papers.
I'd seen it over and over.
Work them, then turn them in before paying them.

Well, now, he was saying,
I know we can work something out,
a sweet young thang like yourself.
Cash, I said. I didn't know anyone in D.C.
now I didn't have to.
You want to keep it for yourself?
That it? His eyes were pin pricks.
Sweat money, Mister, blood money,
not my sweat, but same blood.
Yeah, but who's to say you won't abscond
    with it?
If I ever hear that you got illegals on your land
even a single one, I'm going to come here
in broad daylight and have you
hung by your balls.
He walks slowly to his desk.
Knees shaking, I count every bill
taking my time.

Corran muchachos—Run boys.
muchachita—little girl
naguas—skirt
el valle de Tejas—Rio Grande Valley in Texas
mojados—wetbacks, undocumented workers, illegal immi-
    grants from Mexico and parts south
Como mulas los trabaja.—He works them like mules.
no saben como hacer la perra.—They don't know how to
    make the work easier for themselves.
¿Y sabes lo que hizo?—And you know what he did.
Frijoleros sí lo son.—Bean eaters they are.
Como le dije, son doce.—Like I told you, they're 12.
guarache—sandal
sabe Dios—God knows
Flacos con caras de viejos—skinny with old faces
aunque la mitá eran jóvenes—though half were youths
Como le estaba diciendo—as I was telling you
la migra—slang for immigration officials
pistolas—guns
esclavos—slaves
Pobres jijos de la Chingada—poor sons of the fucked one
fregados—poor, beaten, downtrodden, in need
Vámonos, mujer, empaca el mugrero.—Let's go, woman, pack
    our junk.

MEMBERSHIP

Michael Walzer

Michael Walzer argues that the most important good to be distributed is membership in the community. This has immediate consequences for immigration policy. Walzer argues that most rationales for excluding immigrants are flawed, though he recognizes the need to defend territory and way of life as legitimate, though defeasible, reasons to exclude immigrants.(Source: From Spheres of Justice: A Defense of Pluralism and Equality *by Michael Walzer. Copyright © 1983 by Basic Books, Inc. Reprinted by permission of Basic Books, a division of HarperCollins Publishers, Inc.)*

Members and Strangers

The idea of distributive justice presupposes a bounded world within which distributions takes place: a group of people committed to dividing, exchanging, and sharing social goods, first of all among themselves. That world, as I have already argued, is the political community, whose members distribute power to one another and avoid, if they possibly can, sharing it with anyone else. When we think about distributive justice, we think about independent cities or countries capable of arranging their own patterns of division and exchange, justly or unjustly. We assume an established group and a fixed population, and so we miss the first and most important distributive question: How is that group constituted?

I don't mean, How *was* it constituted? I am concerned here not with the historical origins of the different groups, but with the decisions they make in the present about their present and future populations. The primary good that we distribute to one another is membership in some human community. And what we do with regard to membership structures all our other distributive choices: it determines with whom we make those choices, from whom we require obedience and collect taxes, to whom we allocate goods and services.

Men and women without membership anywhere are stateless persons. That condition doesn't preclude every sort of distributive relation: markets, for example, are commonly open to all comers. But non-members are vulnerable and unprotected in the marketplace. Although they participate freely in the exchange of goods, they have no part in those goods that are shared. They are cut off from the communal provision of security and welfare. Even those aspects of security and welfare that are, like public health, collectively distributed are not guaranteed to non-members for they have no guaranteed place in the collectivity and are always liable to expulsion. Statelessness is a condition of infinite danger.

But membership and non-membership are not the only—or, for our purposes, the most important—set of possibilities. It is also possible to be a member of a poor or a rich country, to live in a densely crowded or a largely empty country, to be the subject of an authoritarian regime or the citizen of a democracy. Since human beings are highly mobile, large numbers of men and women regularly attempt to change their residence and their membership, moving from unfavored to favored environments. Affluent and free countries are, like élite universities, besieged by applicants. They have to decide on their own size and character. More precisely, as citizens of such a country, we have to decide: Whom should we admit? Ought we to have open admissions? Can we choose among applicants? What are the appropriate criteria for distributing membership?

The plural pronouns that I have used in asking these questions suggest the conventional answer to them: we who are already members do the choosing, in accordance with our own understanding of what membership means in our community and of what sort of a community we want to have. Membership as a social good is constituted by our understanding; its value is fixed by our work and conversation; and then we are in charge (who else could be in charge?) of its distribution. But we don't distribute it among ourselves; it is already ours. We give it out to strangers. Hence the choice is also governed by our relationships with strangers—not only by our understanding of those relationships but also by the actual contacts, connections, alliances we have established and the effects we have had beyond our borders. But I shall focus first on strangers in the literal sense, men and women whom we meet, so to speak, for the first time. We don't know who they are or what they think, yet we recognize them as men and women. Like us but not of us: when we decide on membership, we have to consider them as well as ourselves.

I won't try to recount here the history of Western ideas about strangers. In a number of ancient languages, Latin among them, strangers and enemies were named by a single word. We have come only slowly, through a long process of trial and error, to distinguish the two and to acknowledge that, in certain circumstances, strangers (but not enemies) might be entitled to our hospitality, assistance, and good will. This acknowledgment can be formalized as the principle of mutual aid, which suggests the duties that we owe, as John Rawls has written, "not only to definite individuals, say to those cooperating together in some social arrangement, but to persons generally."[1] Mutual aid extends across political (and also cultural, religious, and linguistic) frontiers. The philosophical grounds of the principle are hard to specify (its history provides its practical ground). I doubt that Rawls is right to argue that we can establish it simply by imagining "what a society would be like if this duty were rejected"[2] — for rejection is not an issue within any particular society; the issue arises only among people who don't share, or don't know themselves to share, a common life. People who do share a common life have much stronger duties.

It is the absence of any cooperative arrangements that sets the context for mutual aid: two strangers meet at sea or in the desert or, as in the Good Samaritan story, by the side of the road. What precisely they owe one another is by no means clear, but we commonly say of such cases that positive assistance is required if (1) it is needed or urgently needed by one of the parties; and (2) if the risks and costs of giving it are relatively low for the other party. Given these conditions, I ought to stop and help the injured stranger, wherever I meet him, whatever his membership or my own. This is our morality; conceivably his, too. It is, moreover, an obligation that can be read out in roughly the same form at the collective level. Groups

of people ought to help necessitous strangers whom they somehow discover in their midst or on their path. But the limit on risks and costs in these cases is sharply drawn. I need not take the injured stranger into my home, except briefly, and I certainly need not care for him or even associate with him for the rest of my life. My life cannot be shaped and determined by such chance encounters. Governor John Winthrop, arguing against free immigration to the new Puritan commonwealth of Massachusetts, insisted that this right of refusal applies also to collective mutual aid: "As for hospitality, that rule does not bind further than for some present occasion, not for continual residence."[3] Whether Winthrop's view can be defended is a question that I shall come to only gradually. Here I only want to point to mutual aid as a (possible) external principle for the distribution of membership, a principle that doesn't depend upon the prevailing view of membership within a particular society. The force of the principle is uncertain, in part because of its own vagueness, in part because it sometimes comes up against the internal force of social meanings. And these meanings can be specified, and are specified, through the decision-making processes of the political community.

We might opt for a world without particular meanings and without political communities: where no one was a member or where everyone "belonged" to a single global state. These are the two forms of simple equality with regard to membership. If all human beings were strangers to one another, if all our meetings were like meetings at sea or in the desert or by the side of the road, then there would be no membership to distribute. Admissions policy would never be an issue. Where and how we lived, and with whom we lived, would depend upon our individual desires and then upon our partnerships and affairs. Justice would be nothing more than non-coercion, good faith, and Good Samaritanism — a matter entirely of external principles. If, by contrast, all human beings were members of a global state, membership would already have been distributed, equally; and there would be nothing more to do. The first of these arrangements suggests a kind of global libertarianism; the second, a kind of global socialism. These are the two conditions under which the distribution of membership would never arise. Either there would be no such status to distribute, or it would simply come (to everyone) with birth. But neither of these arrangements is likely to be realized in the foreseeable future; and there are impressive arguments, which I will come to later, against both of them. In any case, so long as members and strangers are, as they are at present, two distinct groups, admissions decisions have to be made, men and women taken in or refused. Given the indeterminate requirements of mutual aid, these decisions are not constrained by any widely accepted standard. That's why the admissions policies of countries are rarely criticized, except in terms suggesting that the only relevant criteria are those of charity, not justice. It is certainly possible that a deeper criticism would lead one to deny the member/stranger distinction. But I shall try, nevertheless, to defend that distinction and then to describe the internal and the external principles that govern the distribution of membership.

The argument will require a careful review of both immigration and naturalization policy. But it is worth noting first, briefly, that there are certain similarities between strangers in political space (immigrants) and descendants in time (children). People enter a country by being both to parents already there as well as, and more often than, by crossing the frontier. Both these processes can be controlled. In the first case, however, unless we practice a selective infanticide, we will be dealing with unborn and hence unknown individuals. Subsidies for large families and programs of birth control determine only the size of the population, not the characteristics of its inhabitants. We might, of course, award the right to give birth differentially to different groups of parents, establishing ethnic quotas (like country-of-origin quotas in immigration policy) or class or intelligence quotas, or allowing right-to-give-birth certificates to be traded on the market. These are ways of regulating who has children and of shaping the character of the future population. They are, however, indirect and inefficient ways, even with regard to ethnicity, unless the state also regulates intermarriage and assimilation. Even well short of that, the policy would require very high, and surely unacceptable, levels of coercion: the dominance of political power over kinship and love. So the major public policy issue is the size of the population only — its growth, stability, or decline. To how many people do we distribute membership? The larger and philosophically more interesting questions — To what sorts of people?, and To what particular people? — are most clearly confronted when we turn to the problems involved in admitting or excluding strangers.

Analogies: Neighborhoods, Clubs, and Families

Admissions policies are shaped partly by arguments about economic and political conditions in the host country, partly by arguments about the character and "destiny" of the host country, and partly by arguments about the character of countries (political communities) in general. The last of these is the most important, in theory at least; for our understanding of countries in general will determine whether particular countries have the right they conventionally claim: to distribute membership for (their own) particular reasons. But few of us have any direct experience of what a country is or of what it means to be a number. We often have strong feelings about our country, but we have only dim perceptions of it. As a political community (rather than a place), it is, after all, invisible; we actually see only its symbols, offices, and representatives. I suspect that we understand it best when we compare it to other, smaller associations whose compass we can more easily grasp. For we are all members of formal and informal groups of many different sorts; we know their workings intimately. And all these groups have, and necessarily have, admissions policies. Even if we have never served as state officials, even if we have never emigrated from one country to another, we have all had the experience of accepting or rejecting strangers, and we have all had the experience of being accepted or rejected. I want to draw upon this experience. My argument will be worked through a series of rough comparisons, in the course of which the special meaning of political membership will, I think, become increasingly apparent.

Consider, then, three possible analogues for the political community: we can think of countries as neighborhoods, clubs, or families. The list is obviously not exhaustive, but it will serve to illuminate certain key features of admission and exclusion.

Schools, bureaucracies, and companies, though they have some of the characteristics of clubs, distribute social and economic status as well as membership; I will take them up separately. Many domestic associations are parasitic for their memberships, relying on the procedures of other associations: unions depend upon the hiring policies of companies; parent-teacher organizations depend upon the openness of neighborhoods or upon the selectiveness of private schools. Political parties are generally like clubs; religious congregations are often designed to resemble families. What should countries be like?

The neighborhood is an enormously complex human association, but we have a certain understanding of what it is like — an understanding at least partially reflected (though also increasingly challenged) in contemporary American law. It is an association without an organized or legally enforceable admissions policy. Strangers can be welcomed or not welcomed; they cannot be admitted or excluded. Of course, being welcomed or not welcomed is sometimes effectively the same thing as being admitted or excluded, but the distinction is theoretically important. In principle, individuals and families move into a neighborhood for reasons of their own; they choose but are not chosen. Or, rather, in the absence of legal controls, the market controls their movements. Whether they move is determined not only by their own choice but also by their ability to find a job and a place to live (or, in a society different from our own, to find a factory commune or a cooperative apartment house ready to take them in). Ideally, the market works independently of the existing composition of the neighborhood. The state upholds this independence by refusing to enforce restrictive covenants and by acting to prevent or minimize discrimination in employment. There are no institutional arrangements capable of maintaining "ethnic purity" — though zoning laws sometimes maintain class segregation.[4]* With reference to any formal criteria, the neighborhood is a random association, "not a selection, but rather a spec-

imen of life as a whole. . . . By the very indifference of space," as Bernard Bosanquet has written, "we are liable to the direct impact of all possible factors."[6]

It was a common argument in classical political economy that national territory should be as "indifferent" as local space. The same writers who defended free trade in the nineteenth century also defended unrestricted immigration. They argued for perfect freedom of contract, without any political restraint. International society, they thought, should take shape as a world of neighborhoods, with individuals moving freely about, seeking private advancement. In their view, as Henry Sidgwick reported it in the 1890s, the only business of state officials is "to maintain order over [a] particular territory . . . but not in any way to determine who is to inhabit this territory, or to restrict the enjoyment of its natural advantages to any particular portion of the human race."[7] Natural advantages (like markets) are open to all comers, within the limits of private property rights; and if they are used up or devalued by overcrowding, people presumably will move on, into the jurisdiction of new sets of officials.

Sidgwick thought that this is possibly the "ideal of the future," but he offered three arguments against a world of neighborhoods in the present. First of all, such a world would not allow for patriotic sentiment, and so the "casual aggregates" that would probably result from the free movement of individuals would "lack internal cohesion." Neighbors would be strangers to one another. Second, free movement might interfere with efforts "to raise the standard of living among the poorer classes" of a particular country, since such efforts could not be undertaken with equal energy and success everywhere in the world. And, third, the promotion of moral and intellectual culture and the efficient working of political institutions might be "defeated" by the continual creation of heterogeneous populations.[8] Sidgwick presented these three arguments as a series of utilitarian considerations that weigh against the benefits of labor mobility and contractual freedom. But they seem to me to have a rather different character. The last two arguments draw their force from the first, but only if the first is conceived in non-utilitarian terms. It is only if patriotic sentiment has some moral basis, only if communal cohesion makes for obligations and shared meanings, only if

---

*The use of zoning laws to bar from neighborhoods (boroughs, villages, towns) certain sorts of people — namely, those who don't live in conventional families — is a new feature of our political history, and I shall not try to comment on it here.[5]

there are members as well as strangers, that state officials would have any reason to worry especially about the welfare of their own people (and of *all* their own people) and the success of their own culture and politics. For it is at least dubious that the average standard of living of the poorer classes throughout the world would decline under conditions of perfect labor mobility. Nor is there firm evidence that culture cannot thrive in cosmopolitan environments, nor that it is impossible to govern casual aggregations of people. As for the last of these, political theorists long ago discovered that certain sorts of regimes — namely, authoritarian regimes — thrive in the absence of communal cohesion. That perfect mobility makes for authoritarianism might suggest a utilitarian argument against mobility; but such an argument would work only if individual men and women, free to come and go, expressed a desire for some other form of government. And that they might not do.

Perfect labor mobility, however, is probably a mirage, for it is almost certain to be resisted at the local level. Human beings, as I have said, move about a great deal, but not because they love to move. They are, most of them, inclined to stay where they are unless their life is very difficult there. They experience a tension between love of place and the discomforts of a particular place. While some of them leave their homes and become foreigners in new lands, others stay where they are and resent the foreigners in their own land. Hence, if states ever become large neighborhoods, it is likely that neighborhoods will become little states. Their members will organize to defend the local politics and culture against strangers. Historically, neighborhoods have turned into closed or parochial communities (leaving aside cases of legal coercion) whenever the state was open: in the cosmopolitan cities of multinational empires, for example, where state officials don't foster any particular identity but permit different groups to build their own institutional structures (as in ancient Alexandria), or in the receiving centers of mass immigration movements (early twentieth-century New York) where the country is an open but also an alien world — or, alternatively, a world full of aliens. The case is similar where the state doesn't exist at all or in areas where it doesn't function. Where welfare monies are raised and spent locally, for example, as in a seventeenth-century English parish, the local people will seek to exclude newcomers who are likely welfare recipients. It is only the nationalization of welfare (or the nationalization of culture and politics) that opens the neighborhood communities to whoever chooses to come in.

Neighborhoods can be open only if countries are at least potentially closed. Only if the state makes a selection among would-be members and guarantees the loyalty, security, and welfare of the individuals it selects, can local communities take shape as "indifferent" associations, determined solely by personal preference and market capacity. Since individual choice is most dependent upon local mobility, this would seem to be the preferred arrangement in a society like our own. The politics and the culture of a modern democracy probably require the kind of largeness, and also the kind of boundedness, that states provide. I don't mean to deny the value of sectional cultures and ethnic communities; I mean only to suggest the rigidities that would be forced upon both in the absence of inclusive and protective states. To tear down the walls of the state is not, as Sidgwick worriedly suggested, to create a world without walls, but rather to create a thousand petty fortresses.

The fortresses, too, could be torn down: all that is necessary is a global state sufficiently powerful to overwhelm the local communities. Then the result would be the world of the political economists, as Sidgwick described it — a world of radically deracinated men and women. Neighborhoods might maintain some cohesive culture for a generation or two on a voluntary basis, but people would move in, people would move out; soon the cohesion would be gone. The distinctiveness of cultures and groups depends upon closure and, without it, cannot be conceived as a stable feature of human life. If this distinctiveness is a value, as most people (though some of them are global pluralists, and others only local loyalists) seem to believe, then closure must be permitted somewhere. At some level of political organization, something like the sovereign state must take shape and claim the authority to make its own admissions policy, to control and sometimes restrain the flow of immigrants.

But this right to control immigration does not include or entail the right to control emigration. The political community can shape its own population in the one way, not in the other: this is a distinction that gets reiterated in different forms throughout the account of membership. The restraint of entry serves to defend the liberty and welfare, the politics and culture of a group of people committed to one another and to their common life. But the restraint of exit replaces commitment with coercion. So far as the coerced members are concerned, there is no longer a community worth defending. A state can, perhaps, banish individual citizens or expel aliens living within its borders (if there is some place ready to receive them). Except in times of national emergency, when everyone is bound to work for the survival of the community, states cannot prevent such people from getting up and leaving. The fact that individuals can rightly leave their own country, however, doesn't generate a right to enter another (any other). Immigration and emigration are morally asymmetrical.9 Here the appropriate analogy is with the club, for it is a feature of clubs in domestic society — as I have just suggested it is of states in international society — that they can regulate admissions but cannot bar withdrawals.

Like clubs, countries have admissions committees. In the United States, Congress functions as such a committee, though it rarely makes individual selections. Instead, it establishes general qualifications, categories for admission and exclusion, and numerical quotas (limits). Then admissible individuals are taken in, with varying degrees of administrative discretion, most on a first-come, first-served basis. This procedure seems eminently defensible, though that does not mean that any particular set of qualifications and categories ought to be defended. To say that states have a right to act in certain areas is not to say that anything they do in those areas is right. One can argue about particular admissions standards by appealing, for example, to the condition and character of the host country and to the shared understandings of those who are already members. Such arguments have to be judged morally and politically as well as factually. The claim of American advocates of restricted immigration (in 1920, say) that they were defending a homogeneous white and Protestant country, can plausibly be called unjust as well as inaccurate: as if non-white and non-Protestant citizens were invisible men and women, who didn't have to be counted in the national census!10 Earlier Americans, seeking the benefits of economic and geographic expansion, had created a pluralist society; and the moral realities of that society ought to have guided the legislators of the

1920s. If we follow the logic of the club analogy, however, we have to say that the earlier decision might have been different, and the United States might have taken shape as a homogeneous community, an Anglo-Saxon nation-state (assuming what happened in any case: the virtual extermination of the Indians who, understanding correctly the dangers of invasion, struggled as best they could to keep foreigners out of their native lands). Decisions of this sort are subject to constraint, but what the constraints are I am not yet ready to say. It is important first to insist that the distribution of membership in American society, and in any ongoing society, is a matter of political decision. The labor market may be given free rein, as it was for many decades in the United States, but that does not happen by an act of nature or of God; it depends upon choices that are ultimately political. What kind of community do the citizens want to create? With what other men and women do they want to share and exchange social goods?

These are exactly the questions that club members answer when they make membership decisions, though usually with reference to a less extensive community and to a more limited range of social goods. In clubs, only the founders choose themselves (or one another); all other members have been chosen by those who were members before them. Individuals may be able to give good reasons why they should be selected, but no one on the outside has a right to be inside. The members decide freely on their future associates, and the decisions they make are authoritative and final. Only when clubs split into factions and fight over property can the state intervene and make its own decision about who the members are. When states split, however, no legal appeal is possible; there is no superior body. Hence, we might imagine states as perfect clubs, with sovereign power over their own selection processes.*

But if this description is accurate in regard to the law, it is not an accurate account of the moral life of contemporary political communities. Clearly, citizens often believe themselves morally bound to open the

---

*Winthrop made the point clearly: "If we here be a corporation established by free consent, if the place of our habitation be our own, then no man hath right to come into us . . . without our consent."11 I will come back to the question of "place" later. . . .

doors of their country—not to anyone who wants to come in, perhaps, but to a particular group of outsiders, recognized as national or ethnic "relatives." In this sense, states are like families rather than clubs, for it is a feature of families that their members are morally connected to people they have not chosen, who live outside the household. In time of trouble, the household is also a refuge. Sometimes, under the auspices of the state, we take in fellow citizens to whom we are not related, as English country families took in London children during the blitz; but our more spontaneous beneficence is directed at our own kith and kin. The state recognizes what we can call the "kinship principle" when it gives priority in immigration to the relatives of citizens. That is current policy in the United States, and it seems especially appropriate in a political community largely formed by the admission of immigrants. It is a way of acknowledging that labor mobility has a social price: since laborers are men and women with families, one cannot admit them for the sake of their labor without accepting some commitment to their aged parents, say, or to their sickly brothers and sisters.

In communities differently formed, where the state represents a nation largely in place, another sort of commitment commonly develops, along lines determined by the principle of nationality. In time of trouble, the state is a refuge for members of the nation, whether or not they are residents and citizens. Perhaps the border of the political community was drawn years ago so as to leave their villages and towns on the wrong side; perhaps they are the children or grandchildren of emigrants. They have no legal membership rights, but if they are persecuted in the land where they live, they look to their homeland not only with hope but also with expectation. I am inclined to say that such expectations are legitimate. Greeks driven from Turkey, Turks from Greece, after the wars and revolutions of the early twentieth century, had to be taken in by the states that bore their collective names. What else are such states for? They don't only preside over a piece of territory and a random collection of inhabitants; they are also the political expression of a common life and (most often) of a national "family" that is never entirely enclosed within their legal boundaries. After the Second World War, millions of Germans, expelled by Poland and Czechoslovakia, were received and cared for by the two Germanies. Even if these states had been free of all responsibility in the expulsions, they would still have had a special obligation to the refugees. Most states recognize obligations of this sort in practice; some do so in law.

Territory

We might, then, think of countries as national clubs or families. But countries are also territorial states. Although clubs and families own property, they neither require nor (except in feudal systems) possess jurisdiction over territory. Leaving children aside, they do not control the physical location of their members. The state does control physical location— if only for the sake of clubs and families and the individual men and women who make them up; and with this control there come certain obligations. We can best examine these if we consider once again the asymmetry of immigration and emigration.

The nationality principle has one significant limit, commonly accepted in theory, if not always in practice. Though the recognition of national affinity is a reason for permitting immigration, nonrecognition is not a reason for expulsion. This is a major issue in the modern world, for many newly independent states find themselves in control of territory into which alien groups have been admitted under the auspices of the old imperial regime. Sometimes these people are forced to leave, the victims of a popular hostility that the new government cannot restrain. More often the government itself fosters such hostility, and takes positive action to drive out the "alien elements," invoking when it does so some version of the club or the family analogy. Here, however, neither analogy applies: for though no "alien" has a right to be a member of a club or a family, it is possible, I think, to describe a kind of territorial or locational right.

Hobbes made the argument in classical form when he listed those rights that are given up and those that are retained when the social contract is signed. The retained rights include self-defense and then "the use of fire, water, free air, *and place to live in,* and . . . all things necessary for life." (italics mine)[12] The right is not, indeed, to a particular place, but it is enforceable against the state, which exists to protect it; the state's claim to territorial jurisdiction derives ultimately from this individual right to place. Hence the right has a collective as well as an individual form, and these two can come into conflict. But it can't be said that the first always or necessarily supercedes the second, for the first came into existence for the sake of the second. The state owes something to its inhabitants simply, without reference to their collective or national identity. And the first place to which the inhabitants are entitled is surely the place where they and their families have lived and made a life. The attachments and expectations they have formed argue against a forced transfer to another country. If they can't have this particular piece of land (or house or apartment), then some other must be found for them within the same general "place." Initially, at least, the sphere of membership is given: the men and women who determine what membership means, and who shape the admissions policies of the political community, are simply the men and women who are already there. New states and governments must make their peace with the old inhabitants of the land they rule. And countries are likely to take shape as closed territories dominated, perhaps, by particular nations (clubs or families), but always including aliens of one sort or another—whose expulsion would be unjust.

This common arrangement raises one important possibility: that many of the inhabitants of a particular country won't be allowed full membership (citizenship) because of their nationality. I will consider that possibility, and argue for its rejection, when I turn to the specific problems of naturalization. But one might avoid such problems entirely, at least at the level of the state, by opting for a radically different arrangement. Consider once again the neighborhood analogy: perhaps we should deny to national states, as we deny to churches and political parties, the collective right of territorial jurisdiction. Perhaps we should insist upon open countries and permit closure only in non-territorial groups. Open neighborhoods together with closed clubs and families: that is the structure of domestic society. Why can't it, why shouldn't it be extended to the global society?

An extension of this sort was actually proposed by the Austrian socialist writer Otto Bauer, with reference to the old multinational empires of Central and Eastern Europe. Bauer would have organized nations into autonomous corporations permitted to tax their members for educational and cultural purposes, but denied any territorial dominion. Individuals would be free to move about in political space, within the empire, carrying their national memberships with them, much as individuals move about today in liberal and secular states, carrying their religious memberships and partisan affiliations. Like churches and parties, the corporations could admit or reject new members in accordance with whatever standards their old members thought appropriate.[13]

The major difficulty here is that all the national communities that Bauer wanted to preserve came into existence, and were sustained over the centuries, on the basis of geographical coexistence. It isn't any misunderstanding of their histories that leads nations newly freed from imperial rule to seek a firm territorial status. Nations look for countries because in some deep sense they already have countries: the link between people and land is a crucial feature of national identity. Their leaders understand, moreover, that because so many critical issues (including issues of distributive justice, such as welfare, education, and so on) can best be resolved within geographical units, the focus of political life can never be established elsewhere. "Autonomous" corporations will always be adjuncts, and probably parasitic adjuncts, of territorial states; and to give up the state is to give up any effective self-determination. That's why borders, and the movements of individuals and groups across borders, are bitterly disputed as soon as imperial rule recedes and nations begin the process of "liberation." And, once again, to reverse this process or to repress its effects would require massive coercion on a global scale. There is no easy way to avoid the country (and the proliferation of countries) as we currently know it. Hence the theory of justice must allow for the territorial state, specifying the rights of its inhabitants and recognizing the collective right of admission and refusal.

The argument cannot stop here, however, for the control of territory opens the state to the claim of necessity. Territory is a social good in a double sense. It is living space, earth and water, mineral resources and potential wealth, a resource for the destitute and the hungry. And it is protected living space, with borders and police, a resource for the persecuted and the stateless. These two resources are different, and we might conclude differently with regard to the kinds of claim that can be made on each. But the issue at stake should first be put in general terms. Can a political community exclude destitute and hungry, persecuted and stateless — in a word, necessitous — men and women simply because they are foreigners? Are citizens bound to take in strangers? Let us assume that the citizens have no formal obligations; they are bound by nothing more stringent than the principle of mutual aid. The principle must be applied, however, not to individuals directly but to the citizens as a group, for immigration is a matter of political decision. Individuals participate in the decision making, if the state is democratic; but they decide not for themselves but for the community generally. And this fact has moral implications. It replaces immediacy with distance and the personal expense of time and energy with impersonal bureaucratic costs. Despite John Winthrop's claim, mutual aid is more coercive for political communities than it is for individuals because a wide range of benevolent actions is open to the community which will only marginally affect its present members considered as a body or even, with possible exceptions, one by one or family by family or club by club. (But benevolence will, perhaps, affect the children or grandchildren or great-grandchildren of the present members — in ways not easy to measure or even to make out. I'm not sure to what extent considerations of this sort can be used to narrow the range of required actions.) These actions probably include the admission of strangers, for admission to a country does not entail the kinds of intimacy that could hardly be avoided in the case of clubs and families. Might not admission, then, be morally imperative, at least for *these* strangers, who have no other place to go?

Some such argument, turning mutual aid into a more stringent charge on communities than it can ever be on individuals, probably underlies the common claim that exclusion rights depend upon the territorial extent and the population density of particular countries. Thus, Sidgwick wrote that he "cannot concede to a state possessing large tracts of unoccupied land an absolute right of excluding alien elements."[14] Perhaps, in his view, the citizens can make some selection among necessitous strangers, but they

cannot refuse entirely to take strangers in so long as their state has (a great deal of) available space. A much stronger argument might be made from the other side, so to speak, if we consider the necessitous strangers not as objects of beneficent action but as desperate men and women, capable of acting on their own behalf. In *Leviathan*, Hobbes argued that such people, if they cannot earn a living in their own countries, have a right to move into "countries not sufficiently inhabited: where nevertheless they are not to exterminate those they find there, but constrain them to inhabit closer together and not range a great deal of ground to snatch what they find."[15] Here the "Samaritans" are not themselves active but acted upon and (as we shall see in a moment) charged only with nonresistance.

"White Australia" and the Claim of Necessity

The Hobbesian argument is clearly a defense of European colonization — and also of the subsequent "constraint" of native hunters and gatherers. But it has a wider application. Sidgwick, writing in 1891, probably had in mind the states the colonists had created: the United States, where agitation for the exclusion of immigrants had been at least a sporadic feature of political life all through the nineteenth century; and Australia, then just beginning the great debate over immigration that culminated in the "White Australia" policy. Years later, an Australian minister of immigration defended that policy in terms that should by now be familiar: "We seek to create a homogeneous nation. Can anyone reasonably object to that? Is not this the elementary right of every government, to decide the composition of the nation? It is just the same prerogative as the head of a family exercises as to who is to live in his own house."[16] But the Australian "family" held a vast territory of which it occupied (and I shall assume, without further factual reference, still occupies) only a small part. The right of white Australians to the great empty spaces of the subcontinent rested on nothing more than the claim they had staked, and enforced against the aboriginal population, before anyone else. That does not seem a right that one would readily defend in the face of necessitous men and women, clamoring for entry. If, driven by famine in the densely populated lands of Southeast Asia, thousands of people were to fight their way into an Australia otherwise closed to them, I doubt that we would want to charge the invaders with aggression. Hobbes's charge might make more sense: "Seeing every man, not only by Right, but also by necessity of Nature, is supposed to endeavor all he can, to obtain that which is necessary for his conservation; he that shall oppose himself against it, for things superfluous, is guilty of the war that thereupon is to follow."[17]

But Hobbes's conception of "things superfluous" is extraordinarily wide. He meant, superfluous to life itself, to the bare requirements of physical survival. The argument is more plausible, I think, if we adopt a more narrow conception, shaped to the needs of particular historical communities. We must consider "ways of life" just as, in the case of individuals, we must consider "life plans." Now let us suppose that the great majority of Australians could maintain their present way of life, subject only to marginal shifts, given a successful invasion of the sort I have imagined. Some individuals would be more drastically affected, for they have come to "need" hundreds or even thousands of empty miles for the life they have chosen. But such needs cannot be given moral priority over the claims of necessitous strangers. Space on that scale is a luxury, as time on that scale is a luxury in more conventional Good Samaritan arguments; and it is subject to a kind of moral encroachment. Assuming, then, that there actually is superfluous land, the claim of necessity would force a political community like that of White Australia to confront a radical choice. Its members could yield land for the sake of homogeneity, or they could give up homogeneity (agree to the creation of a multiracial society) for the sake of the land. And those would be their only choices. White Australia could survive only as Little Australia.

I have put the argument in these forceful terms in order to suggest that the collective version of mutual aid might require a limited and complex redistribution of membership and/or territory. Farther than this we cannot go. We cannot describe the littleness of Little Australia without attending to the concrete meaning of "things superfluous." To argue, for example, that living space should be distributed in equal amounts to every inhabitant of the globe would be to allow the individual version of the right to a place in the world to override the collective version. Indeed, it would deny that national clubs and families can ever acquire a firm title to a particular piece of territory. A high birthrate in a neighboring land would immediately annul the title and require territorial redistribution.

The same difficulty arises with regard to wealth and resources. These, too, can be superfluous, far beyond what the inhabitants of a particular state require for a decent life (even as they themselves define the meaning of a decent life). Are those inhabitants morally bound to admit immigrants from poorer countries for as long as superfluous resources exist? Or are they bound even longer than that, beyond the limits of mutual aid, until a policy of open admissions ceases to attract and benefit the poorest people in the world? Sidgwick seems to have opted for the first of these possibilities; he proposed a primitive and parochial version of Rawls's difference principle: immigration can be restricted as soon as failure to do so would "interfere materially . . . with the efforts of the government to maintain an adequately high standard of life among the members of the community generally — especially the poorer classes."[18] But the community might well decide to cut off immigration even before that, if it were willing to export (some of) its superfluous wealth. Its members would face a choice similar to that of the Australians: they could share their wealth with necessitous strangers outside their country or with necessitous strangers inside their country. But just how much of their wealth do they have to share? Once again, there must be some limit, short (and probably considerably short) of simple equality, else communal wealth would be subject to indefinite drainage. The very phrase "communal wealth" would lose its meaning if all resources and all products were globally common. Or, rather, there would be only one community, a world state, whose redistributive processes would tend over time to annul the historical particularity of the national clubs and families.

If we stop short of simple equality, there will continue to be many communities, with different histories, ways of life, climates, political structures, and economies. Some places in the world will still be more desirable than others, either to individual men and women with particular tastes and aspirations, or more generally. Some places will still be uncomfortable for at least some of their inhabitants. Hence immigration will remain an issue even after the claims of distributive justice have been met on a global scale—assuming, still, that global society is and ought to be pluralist in form and that the claims are fixed by some version of collective mutual aid. The different communities will still have to make admissions decisions and will still have a right to make them. If we cannot guarantee the full extent of the territorial or material base on which a group of people build a common life, we can still say that the common life, at least, is their own and that their comrades and associates are theirs to recognize or choose.

Refugees

There is, however, one group of needy outsiders whose claims cannot be met by yielding territory or exporting wealth; they can be met only by taking people in. This is the group of refugees whose need is for membership itself, a non-exportable good. The liberty that makes certain counties possible homes for men and women whose politics or religion isn't tolerated where they live is also non-exportable: at least we have found no way of exporting it. These goods can be shared only within the protected space of a particular state. At the same time, admitting refugees doesn't necessarily decrease the amount of liberty the members enjoy within that space. The victims of political or religious persecution, then, make the most forceful claim for admission. If you don't take me in, they say, I shall be killed, persecuted, brutally oppressed by the rulers of my own country. What can we reply?

Toward some refugees, we may well have obligations of the same sort that we have toward fellow nationals. This is obviously the case with regard to any group of people whom we have helped turn into refugees. The injury we have done them makes for an affinity between us: thus Vietnamese refugees had, in a moral sense, been effectively Americanized even before they arrived on these shores. But we can also be bound to help men and women persecuted or oppressed by someone else—if they are persecuted or oppressed because they are like us. Ideological as well as ethnic affinity can generate bonds across political lines, especially, for example, when we claim to embody certain principles in our communal life and encourage men and women elsewhere to defend those principles. In a liberal state, affinities of this latter sort

may be highly attenuated and still morally coercive. Nineteenth-century political refugees in England were generally not English liberals. They were heretics and oppositionists of all sorts, at war with the autocracies of Central and Eastern Europe. It was chiefly because of their enemies that the English recognized in them a kind of kin. Or, consider the thousands of men and women who fled Hungary after the failed revolution of 1956. It is hard to deny them a similar recognition, given the structure of the Cold War, the character of Western propaganda, the sympathy already expressed with East European "freedom fighters." These refugees probably had to be taken in by countries like Britain and the United States. The repression of political comrades, like the persecution of co-religionists, seems to generate an obligation to help, at least to provide a refuge for the most exposed and endangered people. Perhaps every victim of authoritarianism and bigotry is the moral comrade of a liberal citizen: that is an argument I would like to make. But that would press affinity too hard, and it is in any case unnecessary. So long as the number of victims is small, mutual aid will generate similar practical results; and when the number increases, and we are forced to choose among the victims, we will look, rightfully, for some more direct connection with our own way of life. If, on the other hand, there is no connection at all with particular victims, antipathy rather than affinity, there can't be a requirement to choose them over other people equally in need.* Britain and the United States could hardly have been required, for example, to offer refuge to Stalinists fleeing Hungary in 1956, had the revolution triumphed. Once again, communities must have boundaries; and however these are determined with regard to territory and resources, they depend with regard to population on a sense of relatedness and mutuality. Refugees must ap-

---

*Compare Bruce Ackerman's claim that "the *only* reason for restricting immigration is to protect the ongoing process of liberal conversation itself" (the italics are Ackerman's).[19] People publicly committed to the destruction of "liberal conversation" can rightfully be excluded—or perhaps Ackerman would say that they can be excluded only if their numbers or the strength of their commitment poses a real threat. In any case, the principle stated in this way applies only to liberal states. But surely other sorts of political communities also have a right to protect their members' shared sense of what they are about.

peal to that sense. One wishes them success; but in particular cases, with reference to a particular state, they may well have no right to be successful.

Since ideological (far more than ethnic) affinity is a matter of mutual recognition, there is a lot of room here for political choice—and thus, for exclusion as well as admission. Hence it might be said that my argument doesn't reach to the desperation of the refugee. Nor does it suggest any way of dealing with the vast numbers of refugees generated by twentieth-century politics. On the one hand, everyone must have a place to live, and a place where a reasonably secure life is possible. On the other hand, this is not a right that can be enforced against particular host states. (The right can't be enforced in practice until there is an international authority capable of enforcing it; and were there such an authority, it would certainly do better to intervene against the states whose brutal policies had driven their own citizens into exile, and so enable them all to go home.) The cruelty of this dilemma is mitigated to some degree by the principle of asylum. Any refugee who has actually made his escape, who is not seeking but has found at least a temporary refuge, can claim asylum—a right recognized today, for example, in British law; and then he cannot be deported so long as the only available country to which he might be sent "is one to which he is unwilling to go owing to well-founded fear of being persecuted for reasons of race, religion, nationality . . . or political opinion."[20] Though he is a stranger, and newly come, the rule against expulsion applies to him as if he had already made a life where he is: for there is no other place where he can make a life.

But this principle was designed for the sake of individuals, considered one by one, where their numbers are so small that they cannot have any significant impact upon the character of the political community. What happens when the numbers are not small? Consider the case of the millions of Russians captured or enslaved by the Nazis in the Second World War and overrun by Allied armies in the final offensives of the war. All these people were returned, many of them forcibly returned, to the Soviet Union, where they were immediately shot or sent on to die in labor camps.[21] Those of them who foresaw their fate pleaded for asylum in the West, but for expediential reasons (having to do with war and diplomacy, not with nationality and the problems of assimilation), asylum was denied

them. Surely, they should not have been forcibly returned—not once it was known that they would be murdered; and that means that the Western allies should have been ready to take them in, negotiating among themselves, I suppose, about appropriate numbers. There was no other choice: at the extreme, the claim of asylum is virtually undeniable. I assume that there are in fact limits on our collective liability, but I don't know how to specify them.

This last example suggests that the moral conduct of liberal and humane states can be determined by the immoral conduct of authoritarian and brutal states. But if that is true, why stop with asylum? Why be concerned only with men and women actually on our territory who ask to remain, and not with men and women oppressed in their own countries who ask to come in? Why mark off the lucky or the aggressive, who have somehow managed to make their way across our borders, from all the others? Once again, I don't have an adequate answer to these questions. We seem bound to grant asylum for two reasons: because its denial would require us to use force against helpless and desperate people, and because the numbers likely to be involved, except in unusual cases, are small and the people easily absorbed (so we would be using force for "things superfluous"). But if we offered a refuge to everyone in the world who could plausibly say that he needed it, we might be overwhelmed. The call "Give me . . . your huddled masses yearning to breathe free" is generous and noble; actually to take in large numbers of refugees is often morally necessary; but the right to restrain the flow remains a feature of communal self-determination. The principle of mutual aid can only modify and not transform admissions policies rooted in a particular community's understanding of itself.

Alienage and Naturalization

The members of a political community have a collective right to shape the resident population—a right subject always to the double control that I have described: the meaning of membership to the current members and the principle of mutual aid. Given these two, particular countries at particular times are likely to include among their residents men and women who are in different ways alien. These people may be members in their turn of minority or pariah groups, or they may be refugees or immigrants newly arrived. Let us assume that they are rightfully where they are. Can they claim citizenship and political rights within the community where they now live? Does citizenship go with residence? In fact, there is a second admissions process, called "naturalization," and the criteria appropriate to this second process must still be determined. I should stress that what is at stake here is citizenship and not (except in the legal sense of the term) nationality. The national club or family is a community different from the state, for reasons I have already sketched. Hence it is possible, say, for an Algerian immigrant to France to become a French citizen (a French "national") without becoming a Frenchman. But if he is not a Frenchman, but only a resident in France, has he any right to French citizenship?

One might insist, as I shall ultimately do, that the same standards apply to naturalization as to immigration, that every immigrant and every resident is a citizen, too — or, at least, a potential citizen. That is why territorial admission is so serious a matter. The members must be prepared to accept, as their own equals in a world of shared obligations, the men and women they admit; the immigrants must be prepared to share the obligations. But things can be differently arranged. Often the state controls naturalization strictly, immigration only loosely. Immigrants become resident aliens and, except by special dispensation, nothing more. Why are they admitted? To free the citizens from hard and unpleasant work. Then the state is like a family with live-in servants.

That is not an attractive image, for a family with live-in servants is — inevitably, I think — a little tyranny. The principles that rule in the household are those of kinship and love. They establish the underlying pattern of mutuality and obligation, of authority and obedience. The servants have no proper place in that pattern, but they have to be assimilated to it. Thus, in the pre-modern literature on family life, servants are commonly described as children of a special sort: children, because they are subject to command; of a special sort, because they are not allowed to grow up. Parental authority is asserted outside its sphere, over adult men and women who are not, and can never be, full members of the family. When this assertion is no longer possible, when servants come to be seen as

hired workers, the great household begins its slow decline. The pattern of living-in is gradually reversed; erstwhile servants seek households of their own.

The Athenian Metics

It is not possible to trace a similar history at the level of the political community. Live-in servants have not disappeared from the modern world. As "guest workers" they play an important role in its most advanced economies. But before considering the status of guest workers, I want to turn to an older example and consider the status of resident aliens (metics) in ancient Athens. The Athenian polis was almost literally a family with live-in servants. Citizenship was an inheritance passed on from parents to children (and only passed on if both parents were citizens: after 450 B.C., Athens lived by the law of double endogamy). Hence a great deal of the city's work was done by residents who could not hope to become citizens. Some of these people were slaves; but I shall not focus on them, since the injustice of slavery is not disputed these days, at least not openly. The case of the metics is harder and more interesting.

"We throw open our city to the world," said Pericles in his Funeral Oration, "and never exclude foreigners from any opportunity." So the metics came willingly to Athens, drawn by economic opportunity, perhaps also by the city's "air of freedom." Most of them never rose above the rank of laborer or "mechanic," but some prospered: in fourth-century Athens, metics were represented among the wealthiest merchants. Athenian freedom, however, they shared only in its negative forms. Though they were required to join in the defense of the city, they had no political rights at all; nor did their descendants. Nor did they share in the most basic of welfare rights: "Foreigners were excluded from the distribution of corn."[22] As usual, these exclusions both expressed and enforced the low standing of the metics in Athenian society. In the surviving literature, metics are commonly treated with contempt — though a few favorable references in the plays of Aristophanes suggest the existence of alternative views.[23]

Aristotle, though himself a metic, provides the classic defense of exclusion, apparently responding to critics who argued that co-residence and shared labor were a sufficient basis for political membership. "A citizen does not become such," he wrote, "merely by inhabiting a place." Labor, even necessary labor, is no better as a criterion: "you must not posit as citizens all those [human beings] without whom you could not have a city."[24] Citizenship required a certain "excellence" that was not available to everyone. I doubt that Aristotle really believed this excellence to be transmitted by birth. For him, the existence of members and non-members as hereditary castes was probably a matter of convenience. Someone had to do the hard work of the city, and it was best if the workers were clearly marked out and taught their place from birth. Labor itself, the everyday necessity of economic life, put the excellence of citizenship beyond their reach. Ideally, the band of citizens was an aristocracy of the leisured (in fact, it included "mechanics" just as the metics included men of leisure); and its members were aristocrats because they were leisured, not because of birth and blood or any inner gift. Politics took most of their time, though Aristotle would not have said that they ruled over slaves and aliens. Rather, they took turns ruling one another. The others were simply their passive subjects, the "material condition" of their excellence, with whom they had no political relations at all.

In Aristotle's view, slaves and aliens lived in the realm of necessity; their fate was determined by the conditions of economic life. Citizens, by contrast, lived in the realm of choice; their fate was determined in the political arena by their own collective decisions. But the distinction is a false one. In fact, citizens made all sorts of decisions that were authoritative for the slaves and aliens in their midst — decisions having to do with war, public expenditure, the improvement of trade, the distribution of corn, and so on. Economic conditions were subject to political control, though the extent of that control was always frighteningly limited. Hence slaves and aliens were indeed ruled; their lives were shaped politically as well as economically. They, too, stood within the arena, simply by virtue of being inhabitants of the protected space of the city-state; but they had no voice there. They could not hold public office or attend the assembly or serve on a jury; they had no officers or political organizations of their own and were never consulted about impending decisions. If we take them to be, despite Aristotle, men and women capable of rational deliberation, then we have to say that they were the subjects of a band of citizen-tyrants, governed without consent. Indeed, this seems to have been at least the implicit view of other Greek writers. Thus Isocrates's critique of oligarchy: when some citizens monopolize political power, they become "tyrants" and turn their fellows into "metics."[25] If that's true, then the actual metics must always have lived with tyranny.

But Isocrates would not have made that last point; nor do we have any record of metics who made it. Slavery was a much debated issue in ancient Athens, but "no vestige survives of any controversy over the *metoikia*."[26] Some of the sophists may have had their doubts, but the ideology that distinguished metics from citizens seems to have been widely accepted among metics and citizens alike. The dominance of birth and blood over political membership was part of the common understanding of the age. Athenian metics were themselves hereditary citizens of the cities from which they had come; and though this status offered them no practical protection, it helped, perhaps, to balance their low standing in the city where they lived and worked. They, too, if they were Greeks, were of citizen blood; and their relation with the Athenians could plausibly be described (as it was described by Lycias, another metic, and more ready than Aristotle to acknowledge his status) in contractual terms: good behavior in exchange for fair treatment.[27]

This view hardly applies, however, to the children of the first metic generation; no contractualist argument can justify the creation of a caste of resident aliens. The only justification of the *metoikia* lies in the conception of citizenship as something that the Athenians literally could not distribute given what they thought it was. All they could offer to aliens was fair treatment, and that was all the aliens could think to ask of them. There is considerable evidence for this view, but there is evidence against it, too. Individual metics were occasionally enfranchised, though perhaps corruptly. Metics played a part in the restoration of democracy in 403 B.C. after the government of the Thirty Tyrants; and they were eventually rewarded, despite strong opposition, with a grant of citizenship.[28] Aristotle made it an argument against large cities that "resident aliens readily assume a share in the exercise of political rights" — which suggests that there was no conceptual barrier to the extension of citizenship.[29] In any case, there is certainly no such barrier in contemporary democratic communities, and it is time now to consider our own metics. The question that apparently gave the Greeks no trouble is both practically and theoretically troubling today. Can states run their economies with live-in servants, guest workers, excluded from the company of citizens?

Guest Workers

I will not attempt a full description of the experience of contemporary guest workers. Laws and practices differ from one European country to another and are constantly changing; the situation is complex and unstable. All that is necessary here is a schematic sketch (based chiefly on the legal situation in the early 1970s) designed to highlight those features of the experience that are morally and politically controversial.[30]

Consider, then, a country like Switzerland or Sweden or West Germany, a capitalist democracy and welfare state, with strong trade unions and a fairly affluent population. The managers of the economy find it increasingly difficult to attract workers to a set of jobs that have come to be regarded as exhausting, dangerous, and degrading. But these jobs are also socially necessary; someone must be found to do them. Domestically, there are only two alternatives, neither of them palatable. The constraints imposed on the labor market by the unions and the welfare state might be broken, and then the most vulnerable segment of the local working class driven to accept jobs hitherto thought undesirable. But this would require a difficult and dangerous political campaign. Or, the wages and working conditions of the undesirable jobs might be dramatically improved so as to attract workers even within the constraints of the local market. But this would raise costs throughout the economy and, what is probably more important, challenge the existing social hierarchy. Rather than adopt either of these drastic measures, the economic managers, with the help of their government, shift the jobs from the domestic to the international labor market, making them available to workers in poorer countries who find them less undesirable. The government opens recruiting offices in a number of economically backward countries and draws up regulations to govern the admission of guest workers.

It is crucial that the workers who are admitted should be "guests," not immigrants seeking a new home and a new citizenship. For if the workers came as future citizens, they would join the domestic labor force, temporarily occupying its lower ranks, but benefiting from its unions and welfare programs and in time reproducing the original dilemma. Moreover, as they advanced, they would come into direct competition with local workers, some of whom they would outdo. Hence the regulations that govern their admission are designed to bar them from the protection of citizenship. They are brought in for a fixed time period, on contract to a particular employer; if they lose their jobs, they have to leave; they have to leave in any case when their visas expire. They are either prevented or discouraged from bringing dependents along with them, and they are housed in barracks, segregated by sex, on the outskirts of the cities where they work. Mostly they are young men or women in their twenties or thirties; finished with education, not yet infirm, they are a minor drain on local welfare services (unemployment insurance is not available to them since they are not permitted to be unemployed in the countries to which they have come). Neither citizens nor potential citizens, they have no political rights. The civil liberties of speech, assembly, association — otherwise strongly defended — are commonly denied to them, sometimes explicitly by state officials, sometimes implicitly by the threat of dismissal and deportation.

Gradually, as it becomes clear that foreign workers are a long-term requirement of the local economy, these conditions are somewhat mitigated. For certain jobs, workers are given longer visas, allowed to bring in their families, and admitted to many of the benefits of the welfare state. But their position remains precarious. Residence is tied to employment, and the authorities make it a rule that any guest worker who cannot support himself and his family without repeated recourse to state welfare programs, can be deported. In time of recession, many of the guests are forced to leave. In good times, however, the number who choose to come, and who find ways to remain, is high; soon some 10 percent to 15 percent of the industrial labor force is made up of foreigners. Frightened by this influx, various cities and towns establish residence quotas for guest workers (defending their neighborhoods against an open state). Bound to their jobs, the guests are in any case narrowly restricted in choosing a place to live.

Their existence is harsh and their wages low by European standards, less so by their own standards. What is most difficult is their homelessness: they work long and hard in a foreign country where they are not encouraged to settle down, where they are always strangers. For those workers who come alone, life in the great European cities is like a self-imposed prison term. They are deprived of normal social, sexual, and cultural activities (of political activity, too, if that is possible in their home country) for a fixed period of time. During that time, they live narrowly, saving money and sending it home. Money is the only return that the host countries make to their guests; and though much of it is exported rather than spent locally, the workers are still very cheaply had. The costs of raising and educating them where they work, and of paying them what the domestic labor market requires, would be much higher than the amounts remitted to their home countries. So the relation of guests and hosts seems to be a bargain all around: for the harshness of the working days and years is temporary, and the money sent home counts there in a way it could never count in a European city.

But what are we to make of the host country as a political community? Defenders of the guest-worker system claim that the country is now a neighborhood economically, but politically still a club or a family. As a place to live, it is open to anyone who can find work; as a forum or assembly, as a nation or a people, it is closed except to those who meet the requirements set by the present members. The system is a perfect synthesis of labor mobility and patriotic solidarity. But this account somehow misses what is actually going on. The state-as-neighborhood, an "indifferent" association governed only by the laws of the market, and the state-as-club-or-family, with authority relations and police, do not simply coexist, like two distinct moments in historical or abstract time. The market for guest workers, while free from the particular political constraints of the domestic labor market, is not free from all political constraints. State power plays a crucial role in its creation and then in the enforcement of its rules. Without the denial of political rights and civil liberties and the everpresent threat of deportation, the system would not work. Hence guest

workers can't be described merely in terms of their mobility, as men and women free to come and go. While they are guests, they are also subjects. They are ruled, like the Athenian metics, by a band of citizen-tyrants.

But don't they agree to be ruled? Isn't the contractualist argument effective here, with men and women who actually come in on contracts and stay only for so many months or years? Certainly they come knowing roughly what to expect, and they often come back knowing exactly what to expect. But this kind of consent, given at a single moment in time, while it is sufficient to legitimize market transactions, is not sufficient for democratic politics. Political power is precisely the ability to make decisions over periods of time, to change the rules, to cope with emergencies; it can't be exercised democratically without the ongoing consent of its subjects. And its subjects include every man and woman who lives within the territory over which those decisions are enforced. The whole point of calling guest workers "guests," however, is to suggest that they don't (really) live where they work. Though they are treated like indentured servants, they are not in fact indentured. They can quit their jobs, buy train or airline tickets, and go home; they are citizens elsewhere. If they come voluntarily, to work and not to settle, and if they can leave whenever they want, why should they be granted political rights while they stay? Ongoing consent, it might be argued, is required only from permanent residents. Aside from the explicit provisions of their contracts, guest workers have no more rights than tourists have.

In the usual sense of the word, however, guest workers are not "guests," and they certainly are not tourists. They are workers, above all; and they come (and generally stay for as long as they are allowed) because they need the work, not because they expect to enjoy the visit. They are not on vacation; they do not spend their days as they please. State officials are not polite and helpful, giving directions to the museums, enforcing the traffic and currency laws. These guests experience the state as a pervasive and frightening power that shapes their lives and regulates their every move — and never asks for their opinion. Departure is only a formal option; deportation, a continuous practical threat. As a group, they constitute a disenfranchised class. They are typically an exploited or oppressed class as well, and they are exploited or oppressed at least in part because they are disenfranchised, incapable of organizing effectively for self-defense. Their material condition is unlikely to be improved except by altering their political status. Indeed, the purpose of their status is to prevent them from improving their condition; for if they could do that, they would soon be like domestic workers, unwilling to take on hard and degrading work or accept low rates of pay.

And yet the company of citizens from which they are excluded is not an endogamous company. Compared with Athens, every European country is radically heterogeneous in character, and they all have naturalization procedures in place. Guest workers, then, are excluded from the company of men and women that includes other people exactly like themselves. They are locked into an inferior position that is also an anomalous position; they are outcasts in a society that has no caste norms, metics in a society where metics have no comprehensible, protected, and dignified place. That is why the government of guest worker looks very much like tyranny: it is the exercise of power outside its sphere, over men and women who resemble citizens in every respect that counts in the host country, but are nevertheless barred from citizenship.

The relevant principle here is not mutual aid but political justice. The guests don't need citizenship— at least not in the same sense in which they might be said to need their jobs. Nor are they injured, helpless, destitute; they are able-bodied and earning money. Nor are they standing, even figuratively, by the side of the road; they are living among the citizens. They do socially necessary work, and they are deeply enmeshed in the legal system of the country to which they have come. Participants in economy and law, they ought to be able to regard themselves as potential or future participants in politics as well. And they must be possessed of those basic civil liberties whose exercise is so much preparation for voting and office holding. They must be set on the road to citizenship. They may choose not to become citizens, to return home or stay on as resident aliens. Many—perhaps most—will choose to return because of their emotional ties to their national family and their native land. But unless they have that choice, their other

choices cannot be taken as so many signs of their acquiescence to the economy and law of the countries where they work. And if they do have that choice, the local economy and law are likely to look different: a firmer recognition of the guests' civil liberties and some enhancement of their opportunities for collective bargaining would be difficult to avoid once they were seen as potential citizens.

I should add that something of the same sort might be obtained in another way. The host countries might undertake to negotiate formal treaties with the home countries, setting out in authoritative form a list of "guest rights"—the same rights, roughly, that the workers might win for themselves as union members and political activists. The treaty could include a proviso stipulating its periodic renegotiation, so that the list of rights could be adapted to changing social and economic conditions. Then, even when they were not living at home, the original citizenship of the guests would work for them (as it never worked for the Athenian metics); and they would, in some sense, be represented in local decision making. In one way or another, they ought to be able to enjoy the protection of citizenship or potential citizenship.

Leaving aside such international arrangements, the principle of political justice is this: that the processes of self-determination through which a democratic state shapes its internal life, must be open, and equally open, to all those men and women who live within its territory, work in the local economy, and are subject to local law.* Hence, second admissions (naturalization) depend on first admissions (immigration) and are subject only to certain constraints of time and qualification, never to the ultimate constraint of closure. When second admissions are closed, the political community collapses into a world of members and strangers, with no political boundaries between the two, where the strangers are subjects of the

---

*It has been suggested to me that this argument doesn't plausibly apply to privileged guests: technical advisors, visiting professors, and so on. I concede the point, though I'm not sure just how to describe the category "guest workers" so as to exclude these others. But the others are not very important, and it is in the nature of their privileged positions that they are able to call upon the protection of their home states if they ever need it. They enjoy a kind of extra-territoriality.

members. Among themselves, perhaps, the members are equal; but it is not their equality but their tyranny that determines the character of the state. Political justice is a bar to permanent alienage — either for particular individuals or for a class of changing individuals. At least, this is true in a democracy. In an oligarchy, as Isocrates wrote, even the citizens are really resident aliens, and so the issue of political rights doesn't arise in the same way. But as soon as some residents are citizens in fact, all must be so. No democratic state can tolerate the establishment of a fixed status between citizen and foreigner (though there can be stages in the transition from one of these political identities to the other). Men and women are either subject to the state's authority, or they are not; and if they are subject, they must be given a say, and ultimately an equal say, in what that authority does. Democratic citizens, then, have a choice: if they want to bring in new workers, they must be prepared to enlarge their own membership; if they are unwilling to accept new members, they must find ways within the limits of the domestic labor market to get socially necessary work done. And those are their only choices. Their right to choose derives from the existence in this particular territory of a community of citizens; and it is not compatible with the destruction of the community or its transformation into yet another local tyranny.

Membership and Justice

The distribution of membership is not pervasively subject to the constraints of justice. Across a considerable range of the decisions that are made, states are simply free to take in strangers (or not) — much as they are free, leaving aside the claims of the needy, to share their wealth with foreign friends, to honor the achievements of foreign artists, scholars, and scientists, to choose their trading partners, and to enter into collective security arrangements with foreign states. But the right to choose an admissions policy is more basic than any of these, for it is not merely a matter of acting in the world, exercising sovereignty, and pursuing national interests. At stake here is the shape of the community that acts in the world, exercises sovereignty , and so on. Admission and exclusion are at the core of communal independence. They sug-

gest the deepest meaning of self-determination. Without them, there could not be *communities of character,* historically stable, ongoing associations of men and women with some special commitment to one another and some special sense of their common life.[31]

But self-determination in the sphere of membership is not absolute. It is a right exercised, most often, by national clubs or families, but it is held in principle by territorial states. Hence it is subject both to internal decisions by the members themselves (*all* the members, including those who hold membership simply by right of place) and to the external principle of mutual aid. Immigration, then, is both a matter of political choice and moral constraint. Naturalization, by contrast, is entirely constrained: every new immigrant, every refugee taken in, every resident and worker must be offered the opportunities of citizenship. If the community is so radically divided that a single citizenship is impossible, then its territory must be divided, too, before the rights of admission and exclusion can be exercised. For these rights are to be exercised only by the community as a whole (even if, in practice, some national majority dominates the decision making) and only with regard to foreigners, not by some members with regard to others. No community can be half-metic, half-citizen and claim that its admissions policies are acts of self-determination or that its politics is democratic.

The determination of aliens and guests by an exclusive band of citizens (or of slaves by masters, or women by men, or blacks by whites, or conquered peoples by their conquerors) is not communal freedom but oppression. The citizens are free, of course, to set up a club, make membership as exclusive as they like, write a constitution, and govern one another. But they can't claim territorial jurisdiction and rule over the people with whom they share the territory. To do this is to act outside their sphere, beyond their rights. It is a form of tyranny. Indeed, the rule of citizens over non-citizens, of members over strangers, is probably the most common form of tyranny in human history. I won't say much more than this about the special problems of non-citizens and strangers: henceforth, whether I am talking about the distribution of security and welfare or about hard work or power itself, I shall assume that all the eligible men and women hold a single political status. This assumption doesn't exclude other sorts of inequality further down the road, but it does exclude the piling up of inequalities that is characteristic of divided societies. The denial of membership is always the first of a long train of abuses. There is no way to break the train, so we must deny the rightfulness of the denial. The theory of distributive justice begins, then, with an account of membership rights. It must vindicate at one and the same time the (limited) right of closure, without which there could be no communities at all, and the political inclusiveness of the existing communities. For it is only as members somewhere that men and women can hope to share in all the other social goods—security, wealth, honor, office, and power—that communal life makes possible.

Notes

1. John Rawls, *A Theory of Justice* (Cambridge, Mass., 1971), p. 115. For a useful discussion of mutual aid as a possible right, see Theodore M. Benditt, *Rights* (Totowa, N.J., 1982), chap. 5.

2. Rawls, *Theory of Justice* [1], p. 339.

3. John Winthrop, in *Puritan Political Ideas: 1558–1794,* ed. Edmund S. Morgan (Indianapolis, 1965), p. 146.

4. On zoning, see Robert H. Nelson, *Zoning and Property Rights: An Analysis of the American System of Land Use Regulation* (Cambridge, Mass., 1977), pp. 120–21.

5. See the U.S. Supreme Court's decision in *Village of Belle Terre* v. *Boraas* (October term, 1973).

6. Bernard Bosanquet, *The Philosophical Theory of the State* (London, 1958), p. 286.

7. Henry Sidgwick, *Elements of Politics* (London, 1881), pp. 295–96.

8. Ibid., p. 296.

9. Cf. Maurice Cranston, on the common understanding of the right to move, in *What Are Human Rights?* (New York, 1973), p. 32.

10. See John Higham's account of these debates, *Strangers in the Land* (New York, 1968).

11. Winthrop, *Puritan Political Ideas* [3], p. 145.

12. Thomas Hobbes, *The Elements of Law,* ed. Ferdinand Tönnies (2nd ed., New York, 1969), p. 88, (part I, chap. 17, para. 2).

13. Bauer made his argument in *Die Nationalitätenfrage und die Sozialdemokratie* (1907); parts of it are ex-

cerpted in *Austro-Marxism,* ed. Tom Bottomore and Patrick Goode (Oxford, England, 1978), pp. 102–25.

14. Sidgwick, *Elements of Politics* [7], p. 295. Cf. John Stuart Mill's letter to Henry George on Chinese immigration to America, quoted in Alexander Saxton, *The Indispensable Enemy: Labor and the Anti-Chinese Movement in California* (Berkeley, 1971), p. 103.

15. Thomas Hobbes, *Leviathan,* part II, chap. 30.

16. Quoted in H. I. London, *Non-White Immigration and the "White Australia" Policy* (New York, 1970), p. 98.

17. Hobbes, *Leviathan,* part I, chap. 15.

18. Sidgwick, *Elements of Politics* [7], pp. 296–97.

19. Bruce Ackerman, *Social Justice in the Liberal State* (New Haven, 1980), p. 95.

20. E. C. S. Wade, and G. Godfrey Phillips, *Constitutional and Administrative Law,* 9th ed. revised by A. W. Bradley (London, 1977), p. 424.

21. For the whole ugly story, see Nikolai Tolstoy, *The Secret Betrayal: 1944–1947* (New York, 1977).

22. Victor Ehrenberg, *The People of Aristophanes* (New York, 1962), p. 153; I have drawn on the entire discussion of foreigners in fifth-century Athens, pp. 147–64.

23. David Whitehead, *The Ideology of the Athenian Metic,* Cambridge Philological Society supplementary volume no. 4 (1977), p. 41.

24. Aristotle, *The Politics* 1275a and 1278a; I have used the translation of Eric Havelock in *The Liberal Temper in Greek Politics* (New Haven, 1957), pp. 367–69.

25. Isocrates, quoted in Whitehead, *Athenian Metic* [23], pp. 51–52.

26. Whitehead, *Athenian Metic* [23], p. 174.

27. Ibid., pp. 57–58.

28. Ibid., pp. 154ff.

29. Aristotle, *The Politics* 1326b, trans. Ernest Barker (Oxford, 1948), p. 343.

30. In my account of guest workers, I rely chiefly on Stephen Castles and Godula Kosack, *Migrant Workers and Class Structure in Western Europe* (Oxford, England, 1973); and also on Cheryl Bernard, "Migrant Workers and European Democracy," *Political Science Quarterly* 92 (Summer 1979): 277–99, and John Berger, *A Seventh Man* (New York, 1975).

31. I have taken the term "communities of character" from Otto Bauer (see *Austro-Marxism* [13], p. 107).

MEANINGFUL WORK

Adina Schwartz

Adina Schwartz argues that everyone is entitled to be respected as an autonomous agent. Respecting people as autonomous requires that hierarchical division of labor be replaced by meaningful democratic divisions of labor. (Source: From Ethics 92 *by Adina Schwartz. Copyright © 1982 by University of Chicago Press. Reprinted by permission.)*

In the opening pages of *The Wealth of Nations,* Adam Smith describes how pins are made in a factory: "One man draws out the wire, another straights it, a third cuts it, a fourth points it,"[1] and so on to eighteen distinct operations. Some workers may perform two or three of these tasks; many repeatedly execute only one operation. In contemporary industrial societies, many people work at analogues of Smith's jobs: jobs in which persons are hired to perform series of set actions such as assembly line work, keypunching, or being a clerk on an automated checkout line.[2] These routine jobs provide people with almost no opportunities for formulating aims, for deciding on means for achieving their ends, or for adjusting their goals and methods in the light of experience. Smith's workers and their modern counterparts do not design the overall goals of the factories, offices, or service operations in which they are employed. More important, individual workers do not decide how to perform their particular jobs. Instead of being hired to achieve certain goals and left to select and pursue adequate means, workers are employed to perform precisely specified actions. Even the order in which they perform these operations, the pace at which they work, and the particular bodily movements they employ are largely determined by others' decisions. When the entire job consists of such mechanical activity, workers are in effect paid for blindly pursuing ends that others have chosen, by means that they judge adequate.

The existence of these jobs is of little concern to contemporary social and political philosophers.[3] This paper will argue, however, that this unconcerned stance is fundamentally at odds with the widely held view that a just society respects all its members as autonomous agents. If we care about the free development of all members of society, I will show, we must demand that no one be employed at the sorts of jobs that have just been described. We must also advocate a certain alternative to the current arrangement of industrial employment and must ask for government measures to effect this rearrangement.

I

My argument for these claims can best begin with a brief account of what I mean by 'autonomy.' I am concerned here with the central notion that is employed when philosophers argue that a society must grant extensive liberties in order to respect its members as autonomous agents. According to this conception, being autonomous is not simply a matter of having a capacity. Individuals are only free, or autonomous, persons to the extent that they rationally form and act on some overall conception of what they want in life. They also must adjust those conceptions to allow for changing circumstances and for faults in their original goals. This notion can be more sharply delineated by showing that it rules out certain claims about autonomous persons' behavior. An individual can decide on an overall system of aims without leading an autonomous life. Living autonomously means planning effectively to achieve one's aims instead of simply reacting to the circumstances that face one. Thus, autonomous agents take responsibility for decisions and rationally choose actions to suit their goals. For an autonomous agent, this activity is closely joined to the practice of revising goals and methods in the light of observations of the consequences of choices. These agents are also interested in learning of differences between their and others' decisions and in understanding how these differences result from various factual beliefs and normative commitments. Considering this, they attempt to decide rationally whether to revise or retain their beliefs, methods, and goals.

We can say, then, that people achieve autonomy to the extent that they lead lives of intelligence and initiative. It would be a mistake, however, to posit any straightforward correlation between how nearly autonomous people are and how many decisions they make. An autonomous agent makes certain *types* of decisions; rational choices informed by an awareness of alternatives. In addition, the actions of autonomous agents are not guided by series of unrelated choices, but by choices that are themselves guided by their overall conceptions of their purposes in life.

Proceeding from this brief account, we can show, I believe, that all who hold that a society should respect all its members as autonomous agents must be greatly concerned by the correlation that has so far obtained between industrialization and the existence of increasing numbers of the sorts of jobs described in the first paragraph of this article.[4] As we saw above, when persons are employed at these jobs, they are hired to pursue unquestioningly ends that others have chosen, by means that others judge adequate. The account of autonomy just given entitles us to claim that these jobs are degrading because persons cannot act as autonomous agents while performing them.

This claim might be met by the rejoinder, however, that an individual's work is not his or her whole life. We need not care, it might be argued, whether individuals have opportunities for framing, adjusting, and pursuing their own plans during their working hours or, indeed, at any particular time. What is important is that a society aid all its members to lead autonomous lives on the whole. There need be nothing wrong, then, with a social arrangement in which most adults devote large amounts of time to remunerative employment and in which some persons have jobs that consist mainly in the performance of machine-like tasks. This arrangement would be acceptable, according to this objection, so long as these persons were given opportunities in the rest of their lives for formulating goals and for rationally choosing means for effecting their ends.

Analogous arguments are not employed to justify restrictions on legal freedoms. No one claims that it is all right for persons to be legally prevented from framing and pursuing plans during considerable lengths of time so long as they are legally free to devote the rest of their lives to acting as autonomous individuals. It is widely held, instead, that if a society so restricts liberties, it degrades its members by preventing them from acting autonomously. It does not foster their autonomous development on the whole.

Granted that similar justifications are not advanced for curtailing legal freedoms, we do well to ask whether we can accept the above justification of the current arrangement of industrial employment if we respect all persons as autonomous beings. To answer this question, let us note that this justification stands or falls with the following premise; in general, when persons devote significant amounts of time to remunerative employment and when they are prevented from acting autonomously while performing their jobs, they are not caused to lead less autonomous lives on the whole. We can dismiss this premise on both empirical and conceptual grounds.

Taking the empirical grounds first, an opposing claim has been advanced both by contemporary psychologists and sociologists and by such noted social scientists as Adam Smith and Émile Durkheim. When persons work for considerable lengths of time at jobs that involve mainly mechanical activity, they tend to be made less capable of and less interested in rationally framing, pursing, and adjusting their own plans during the rest of their time. They are thereby caused to lead less autonomous lives on the whole. Durkheim's general enthusiasm for modern industrial developments did not prevent him from scoffing at the view that persons would not be made less autonomous by machine-like work if they were encouraged to devote other time to intellectual and cultural pursuits. "Who cannot see," he exclaimed, "that two such existences are too opposed to be reconciled and cannot be led by the same man!"[5] Similarly, although Smith praised the factory arrangements described in the first pages of *The Wealth of Nations,* he did not deny their dehumanizing effects. "The understandings of the greater part of men," he claimed, "are necessarily formed by their ordinary employments. The man whose whole life is spent in performing a few simple operations . . . has no occasion to exert his understanding, or to exercise his invention in finding out expedients for removing difficulties which never occur. He naturally loses, therefore, the habit of such exertion. . . . His dexterity at his own particular trade seems . . . to be acquired at the expense of his intellectual virtues."[6]

The empirical literature has thus consistently argued that persons are hindered from leading autonomous lives when their jobs provide them with almost no opportunities for rationally framing, adjusting, and pursuing their own plans. It seems to me, however, that there is an even more convincing a priori argument for that conclusion. Becoming autonomous is not a matter of coming to exercise intelligence and initiative in a number of separate areas of one's life. Rather, it is a process of integrating one's personality: of coming to see all one's pursuits as subject to one's activity of planning and to view all one's experiences as providing a basis for evaluating and adjusting one's beliefs, methods, and aims. This granted, concern for the autonomous development of all members of society commits us to objecting to institutional arrangements that prevent individuals from acting autonomously while at work, even if they encourage them to do so during their leisure time. Such arrangements foster schizophrenia. Given my analysis of autonomy, we must claim, instead, that a society must encourage all its members to pursue unified lives if it is to aid each one of them to achieve autonomy.

II

We can conclude, then, that persons' autonomous developments are stunted when their jobs severely restrict their opportunities for rationally framing, pursuing, and adjusting their own plans. If we care about the free development of all members of society, we thus are committed to considering how industrial employment could be restructured so that all persons' jobs allow them to act as autonomous individuals. To pursue this inquiry, we need to recognize that industrialization has been correlated with the rise of a distinctive type of division of labor. Once we see this, we can proceed to develop an account of how the current arrangement of industrial employment would need to be changed to allow all persons to act autonomously while at work. We can then show that these changes are both possible and desirable.

In all societies where there is production for exchange, there is a social division of labor. In other words, different productive specialties (e.g., hunting, fishing, being a medicine man or a physician) are pursued by various members of society, and the products produced by those specialities are exchanged in society at large. Only in industrial societies, however, has there also been a significant development of what Karl Marx called the detailed division of labor, a division that can also appropriately be termed the hierarchical division of labor.[7]

This detailed, or hierarchical, division obtains only when a productive specialty is divided into various tasks and when persons specialize in performing one, or at most a few, of those tasks. Under this division, a number of individuals cooperate to produce products that can be exchanged in society at large. This cooperation is essentially hierarchical. When specialists cooperate, under the detailed division of labor, to produce products that can be exchanged in society at large, some of these specialists are managers. These experts coordinate and schedule others' activities, deciding on what persons will do in their jobs and on the precise manner in which they will execute their tasks. The reverse side of this coin is that the detailed, or hierarchical, division of labor entails the existence of detail workers: persons whose jobs consist almost entirely in performing actions that others precisely specify and whose work thus prevents them from acting autonomously. . . .

It follows from this description that an alternative to the detailed, or hierarchical, division of labor is needed if industrial employment is to be meaningfully structured or, in other words, arranged to allow all persons to act as autonomous agents while performing their jobs. The reason for rejecting the detailed division of labor is not that it involves cooperation among specialists per se. Rather, that division of labor is objectionable because it is a cooperative arrangement in which some persons specialize in framing plans and in deciding how they are best pursued and others specialize in unquestioningly executing those decisions. Applying this criterion, we can now evaluate some contemporary proposals for the redesign of employment. Thereby, we can arrive at a relatively clear picture of what it would mean for industrial employment to be meaningfully structured.

Often, routine clerical or factory jobs are enlarged by a process of horizontal integration: instead of performing one mechanical task, a worker executes a number of routine operations. For example, assembly line workers may rotate jobs so that individuals can follow a product through all the stages in its production.[8] Or, bank tellers may sort returned checks when the loads at their counters are light.[9] Given our discussion, such horizontal restructurings clearly do not constitute a meaningful alternative to the current arrangement of employment. Although persons' tasks are made more various, their jobs consist, exactly as before, in performing actions that are precisely specified by others. Thereby, their work still prevents them from acting autonomously: from rationally framing, pursuing, and adjusting their own plans.

A similar criticism applies to proposals for employing some persons as detail workers and others as managerial experts but allowing all employees to participate in democratic decision making.[10] Even if all employees vote on administrators, mergers, hiring and financial policies, and so forth, the relations between managers and detail workers are still hierarchical. On the one hand, the managerial experts are employed to decide how to implement policies. On the other hand, the detail workers are hired to effect those decisions by repeatedly performing actions that those experts precisely specify. This daily distinction between those who decide and those who execute others' decisions seems to carry over to the roles that detail workers and managers assume when they both participate in democratic decision making. Under Yugoslav workers' self-management, at least, the managers' control of relevant information and their greater experience in making decisions appear to give them a powerful advantage in having their proposals accepted by others.[11]

If, then, industrial employment is to be restructured so that all persons can act autonomously while at work, detail workers cannot simply be assigned greater numbers of routine operations and formal democracy cannot simply be imposed on workplaces where the division of labor remains hierarchical. Rather, jobs must be democratically redesigned, tasks must be shared out in a way that abolishes the distinction between those who decide and those who execute others' decisions. A significant start in this direction was made in a dog-food plant opened by the General Foods Corporation in Topeka, Kansas, in 1971.[12] There, each worker was hired to be part of a small group of persons, each group was made responsible for intellectually demanding functions (e.g., maintaining and repairing machines, quality control operations), and all groups of workers shared in the routine work that was not eliminated by automation. Within each group, work was also democratically distributed. All workers were given opportunities to learn to perform all the tasks assigned to their group, no group member was mainly assigned to routine operations, and all the members of the group shared in supervising its operations, democratically deciding job assignments, pay raises, breaks, and so forth.

As a result of this sharing of supervisory functions and of routine and intellectually demanding production work, no person in this plant was employed mainly to perform actions that others precisely specified. Each person's job gave him or her significant opportunities for rationally framing, adjusting, and pursuing plans. Given, however, that the General Foods management unilaterally decided what should be produced, how fast it should be produced, how profits should be used, what hiring policies should be, and whether its democratic reforms should continue, the workers in this plant could only plan to implement policies that others set. If, then, industrial employment is to be meaningfully restructured to abolish the distinction between those who decide and those who execute others' decisions, labor must be still more democratically divided than it was by General Foods. In addition to functions being shared out so that no person is employed mainly at routine operations, there must be a sharing of information and provision of opportunities such that all persons can participate in shaping their enterprise's policies.

It seems to me that this discussion provides a general picture of what it would mean for industrial employment to be meaningfully structured, or, in other words, arranged so that all persons' jobs allow them to act as autonomous individuals and thus foster instead of stunt their autonomous development. Serious objections can be raised, however, as to the general practicability of such arrangements in a highly industrialized society, regardless of their desirability. These objections can be answered.

It might be argued, in the first place, that it would be impossible for an industrial society to institute a meaningful alternative to the detailed division of labor because the presence of that division is dictated by the presence of a machine technology. This claim is refuted by the facts. On the one hand, the factory arrangements of Adam Smith's time and current drives to routinize office employment show that a detailed division of labor may be imposed where there is little or no machinery.[13] On the other hand, automatic machine systems can be operated without a detailed division of labor. The machinery itself does not dictate that employees be divided into those who perform the routine tasks involved in assisting machine operations and those who decide how the machines are to be used.[14]

It might be objected, nonetheless, that my proposed alternative to the detailed division of labor should not be instituted because all moves away from this division would be inefficient. The current arrangement of employment in industrial societies is Pareto optimal: at lest some persons prefer that arrangement to any alternative. If, therefore, an industrial society were to seek to eliminate the detailed, or hierarchical, division of labor, it would pursue a Pareto-inefficient policy; one that violated some persons' preferences.

If we hold, however, that all members of society should be respected as autonomous individuals, our sole criterion for judging proposed reforms cannot be whether they would violate the preferences of some individuals. No one would seriously claim to care about all persons' autonomous development and yet argue that a dictatorship's restrictions on freedom of expression should be maintained because eliminating them would violate the rulers' preferences. All would agree that these preferences should not be respected because they are preferences for depriving others of liberties that they need for leading the rational, choosing lives of autonomous individuals. To generalize, respect for all persons' free development demands that we meet Paretian objections to proposed reforms by asking what preferences a given reform would satisfy or violate and whether, in doing so, it would foster the autonomous development of all members of society. Thus, in the case at hand, we need to consider why my proposed move away from the hierarchical division of labor might be expected to be Pareto inefficient. *Whose* preferences for *what* would this reform be

likely to violate? We can then show that our commitment to autonomy allows us to dismiss these individuals' objections.

It might be argued that owners would prefer that my alternative to the detailed division of labor not be instituted because instituting this reform would cause their profits to fall. If all workers are skilled, as they would be under this meaningful rearrangement of employment, none can be paid as low a wage as the detail worker whose entire job can be learned in a few weeks.[15] If all persons' jobs require significant training, as they would under my proposed alternative, owners will bear the cost of providing that training. These factual claims do not prove that my alternative to the detailed division of labor must decrease profits. Proving this, however, would not provide a reason for maintaining that hierarchical arrangement of employment. If we hold that social institutions should be arranged to respect all persons as autonomous, we cannot believe that individuals should be free to acquire wealth at the cost of others' development as free agents.

It might be urged, nonetheless, that industrial employment should not be meaningfully restructured because doing this would cause a society's level of production as a whole to fall. Many persons, whether workers or owners, would thereby suffer a decrease in wealth, presumably in violation of their preferences. We need to recognize, however, that the view that a society should foster all its members' autonomous development is incompatible with an unconditional commitment to economic growth. Certainly, it is desirable that a certain level of economic development be attained. How can persons be expected rationally to frame and evaluate beliefs, methods, and goals when they are starving or when poverty forces them to remain illiterate? Once a society attains a sufficient level of productivity, however, to provide all its members with the leisure time, educational opportunities, and level of health and material comfort that persons need for achieving autonomy, respect for autonomy does not demand further economic growth. To the contrary, increased productivity should not be pursued at the cost of depriving individuals of the liberties and working conditions that humans need for leading autonomous lives. This means, therefore, that the current arrangement of industrial employment could only justifiably be maintained if it were certain that my proposed alternative would so lower productivity that persons could not enjoy the material and educational prerequisites for achieving autonomy. The available evidence argues for the opposite conclusion. A special task force to the Secretary of Health, Education, and Welfare concluded in 1973 that American business enterprises could increase productivity by eliminating the detailed division of labor. "The redesign of work . . . *can* lower such business costs as absenteeism, tardiness, turnover, labor disputes, sabotage and poor quality. . . . The evidence suggests that meeting the higher needs of workers can, perhaps, increase productivity from 5% to 40%, the latter figure including the 'latent' productivity of workers that is currently untapped."[16] Such results have indeed been obtained by the General Foods Corporation plant described above. "Unit costs," *Business Week* reported in 1977, "are 5% less than under a traditional factory system. . . . This . . . should amount to a saving of $1 million a year."[17]

In sum, then, we cannot justify maintaining the detailed, or hierarchical, division of labor of claiming that it is the only technologically possible arrangement of industrial employment or the only one that is sufficiently profitable or productive. If we care about the free development of all members of society, we are therefore committed to demanding that this hierarchical division be replaced by a meaningful, or democratic, division of labor that will ensure that no one is employed mainly at routine operations, that all employees participate in shaping their enterprise's policies, and, consequently, that all persons' jobs allow them to act as autonomous individuals and thus foster instead of stunt their autonomous development.

Notes

Author's Note: Versions of this paper were read at a meeting of the New York Group of the Society of Philosophy and Public Affairs on February 14, 1978, to the philosophy department at Oberlin College on February 15, 1979, and at Douglass College of Rutgers University on February 6, 1979. I would like to thank those present for their comments. I would also like to thank Bruce A. Ackerman, Brian Barry, and Owen M. Fiss for helpful criticism and discussion.

1. Adam Smith, *An Inquiry into the Nature and Causes of the Wealth of Nations*, ed. Edwin Cannan, 2 vols. in 1 (Chicago: University of Chicago Press, Phoenix Books, 1976), 1:8.

2. Harry Braverman, *Labor and Monopoly Capital: The Degradation of Work in the Twentieth Century* (New York: Monthly Review Press, 1974), is the most detailed and illuminating account available of the routinization of work in contemporary industrial societies. Other useful empirical works include Elwood S. Buffa, *Modern Production Management: Managing the Operations Function*, 5th ed. (New York: John Wiley & Sons, 1977), pp. 207–36; Louis E. Davis and James C. Taylor, eds., *Designs of Jobs: Selected Readings* (Harmondsworth: Penguin Books, 1972); *Work in America: Report of a Special Task Force to the Secretary of Health, Education, and Welfare* (Cambridge, Mass.: MIT Press, 1973); and Studs Terkel, *Working* (New York: Avon Books, 1975).

3. Their existence is alluded to only in one vague paragraph of John Rawls, *A Theory of Justice* ([Cambridge, Mass.: Harvard University Press, 1971], p. 529). One of the main implications of the brief discussion in Robert Nozick, *Anarchy, State and Utopia* ([New York: Basic Books, 1974], pp. 246–50), is that political philosophers should not care about what persons do at work.

4. For a detailed argument showing that this correlation has obtained, see Braverman.

5. Émile Durkheim, *The Division of Labor in Society* (New York: Free Press, 1961), p. 372.

6. Smith, 2:302–3.

7. Karl Marx establishes and explores the concept of the detailed division of labor in vol. 1, pt. 4 of *Capital*, ed. Frederick Engels (New York: International Publishing Co., 1967), esp. chap. 14, sec. 4, pp. 350–59.

8. For this example and a general account of horizontal integration, see Buffa, p. 230.

9. For this example, see Braverman, p. 37.

10. There are more conservative and more radical versions of this reform. Democracy in the workplace may involve, as in West German codetermination, consulting selected workers about management's policies (see the article collectively written by the executive board of the West German Trade Union Federation [DGB]. "Co-Determination in the Federal Republic of Germany," in Hunnius, Garson, and Case, eds., pp. 191–210; and Helmut Schauer, "Critique of Co-Determination," in Hunnius, Garson, and Case, eds. pp. 210–24). Or, it may extend, as in Yugoslav workers' self-management, to allowing all employees to vote on policies (see Gerry Hunnius, "Workers' Self-Management in Yugoslavia," in Hun-

nius, Garson, and Case, eds., pp. 268–321). Likewise, workplace democracy may amount, as in many American experiments, only to allowing workers to decide relatively trivial matters such as the colors of their offices, the pace of the assembly lines on which they work, and so forth (see Buffa, pp. 232–33; Daniel Zwerdling, "Workplace Democracy: A Strategy for Survival," *Progressive* [August 1978], pp. 16–24, esp. pp. 18–19; and Richard Edwards, *Contested Terrain: The Transformation of the Workplace in the Twentieth Century* (New York: Basic Books, 1979), pp. 155–56). Or it may mean, as in the Yugoslav experience, that all major policy questions are decided by all employees (see Hunnius).

11. Hunnius, p. 297.

12. For descriptions of this plant, see *Work in America,* pp. 96–99; Zwerdling, pp. 17–18; and "Stonewalling Plant Democracy," *Business Week* (March 28, 1977), pp. 78–82.

13. For a description of the growing routinization or detailed division of office employment, see Braverman, chap. 15, pp. 293–358.

14. Ibid., chap. 9, esp. pp. 230–31. Also see Nehemiah Jordan, "Allocation of Functions between Man and Machines in Automated Systems," in Davis and Taylor, eds., pp. 91–99; and James G. Scoville, "A Theory of Jobs and Training," in Davis and Taylor, eds., pp. 225–44.

15. The nineteenth-century economist Charles Babbage "noted that: (1) wages paid were dictated by the most difficult or rarest skill required by the jobs; (2) the division of labor enabled skills to be made more homogeneous within jobs more easily; and (3) for each job, one could purchase exactly the amount of skill needed. The result would be a lower total labor cost" (Buffa, p. 208). Two of the most important developments contributing to the growth of the detailed division of labor, "scientific management under F. W. Taylor and motion study under Frank Gilbreth, about 1910, can be seen as an extension of the work of Babbage" (Davis and Taylor, eds., p. 16).

16. *Work in America,* p. 27.

17. "Stonewalling Plant Democracy," p. 78.

WELFARE RIGHTS

Carl Wellman

Carl Wellman argues that people have a right to welfare—to assistance provided to an individual because of his or her need. He begins with an analysis of what welfare rights are, and then goes on to argue that they are based on the civic right not to be unjustly impoverished. (Source: Reprinted by permission of the author.)

An essential preliminary to defining any right to welfare is some clear conception of what is, and what is not, included in welfare. Let us begin by reminding ourselves of the public welfare programs that constitute the paradigm instances of welfare in our society. These include Aid to Families with Dependent Children (AFDC), Supplemental Security Income (which replaced Old Age Assistance, Aid to the Blind, and Aid to the Permanently and Totally Disabled), Medicaid, Medicare, and unemployment insurance, all of which provide welfare benefits in the form of money. There are also other sorts of benefits. Public housing and Food Stamps, purchased by the recipient, constitute a form of benefit because they are subsidized by the government. Other benefits take the form of welfare services, such as legal services provided by the Office of Economic Opportunity, family services provided through the Aid to Families with Dependent Children, and vocational services provided by the Work Incentive Program. All are forms of assistance made available to individual recipients to provide an acceptable level of individual welfare or well-being. Accordingly, I propose to define a welfare benefit as some form of assistance provided to an individual in need. The word "welfare," in the special sense relevant to this book, is simply a collective name for any and all welfare benefits.

My proposed rough definition will serve to delimit for practical and even most theoretical purposes an identifiable and important area of individual, social, legal, and moral concern. Additional description might characterize the recipient of welfare benefits as financially needy, below the poverty level, one of the poor. In practice this is usually the case, but I do not wish to build this into my definition for two reasons.

First, some welfare benefits are actually provided for individuals who are in fact above the poverty level. For example, someone temporarily out of work is eligible to receive unemployment insurance without having exhausted his financial reserves, and the aged may be eligible for Medicare without being impoverished. Second, the concept of need is both somewhat elastic and partly independent of income. As a society becomes more affluent, its conception of what the individual needs in order to achieve an acceptable level of personal well-being changes. And I would not wish to rule out by definition the notion that a society might decide that middle-class individuals, clearly above the poverty level, need assistance of certain sorts, such as financial aid in financing higher education or in meeting certain categories of medical expenses, both of which are so expensive that they might disrupt individual and family life even for those who are not properly classified as poor. Therefore, I define welfare benefits in terms of an individual "in need" in the sense that the individual needs, or is judged to need, assistance in order to achieve an acceptable level of well-being. Thus, Peffer was on the right track when he introduced the notion of need into his definition of rights to well-being. But for our purposes, the relevant sense of need is not that of needing the good or service to satisfy a basic need, but that of being in need of assistance.

My definition of a welfare benefit as some form of assistance provided to an individual in need not only covers paradigm examples of welfare in the United States today; it also draws the line between what is and what is not welfare. For example, Medicaid payments are a form of welfare but payments on a Blue Cross or Blue Shield policy are not, because the former are assistance necessary to achieve an acceptable level of personal well-being, while the latter are payments rendered under the terms of a paid-up contract, independent of the need of the individual covered by the contract. Similarly, Old Age Assistance, or the newer Supplemental Security Income for the elderly, is a welfare benefit paid to the aged person, who is presumed to need assistance in maintaining an acceptable level of personal well-being; but the retirement benefits received by someone under an industry program or a company-subsidized retirement program are contractual rather than welfare benefits. Some of the social security benefits were, I think, originally intended to be similar contractual benefits under a public compulsory insurance system. If they were in fact nothing more than payments made in return for premiums paid, then their governmental source would not in and of itself convert them into welfare benefits in the relevant sense. But in point of fact, premiums paid into the social security insurance programs were supplemented out of the general treasury, and coverage was extended to persons who had paid few, if any, premiums into the insurance pool. Therefore, they have become a form of assistance to the needy rather than merely a public form of insurance.

Again, an AFDC payment is a form of assistance to an individual, usually a mother, who needs such assistance to maintain an acceptable level of personal welfare for herself and her dependent child or children; but an NSF or NEH grant or fellowship to support scientific research or humanistic scholarship is not welfare, because it is provided to assist in the pursuit of research. Finally, food stamps are, but postage stamps are not, welfare, even though both sorts of stamps are federally subsidized. Once more, this is because the former are, but the latter are not, a form of assistance to the individual in need.

Having established, or at least rendered plausible, my definition of a welfare benefit by showing that it fits clear cases, let us apply it to more controversial borderline cases. Is public education, especially on the elementary and secondary level, a form of public welfare? All residents of the United States are eligible for public education at the appropriate age and often in continuing education programs. Nevertheless, many families who elect to send their children could afford private education, so, public education in the United States today is not, strictly speaking, a form of public welfare. Yet one can imagine a society in which it would be: the affluent would be expected to pay for the education of their children, but education would be provided for those children whose families could not afford private education — either in free public schools, for which only the needy were eligible, or

through monetary grants to enable needy families to send their children to private schools.

Government programs relating to medical care take many forms, and it is not always clear which forms should be considered welfare programs. Medicaid is a paradigm case of public welfare, for only those judged to lack the financial resources to purchase private medical care are eligible for its benefits. Medicare is a less clear case, because retired persons or their spouses are eligible even when they could, if necessary, sell their homes or deplete their savings to obtain medical care. Still, it seems clear that the purpose of the legislation creating the Medicare program is to assist the elderly, who are generally presumed to have increasing needs for expensive medical care that they cannot provide for themselves on their limited fixed incomes, which become increasingly inadequate as inflation advances. Thus, even though Medicare is provided for all the elderly in our society, this is because the elderly are judged to be in need of such assistance.

Suppose medical payments were made available to all citizens of every age and financial situation by a universal, compulsory system of government medical insurance. Would this be a form of welfare? If the system were self-supporting through income derived from the payment of insurance premiums by the individuals covered by the system, and if the medical benefits were simply a return to which recipients were entitled on a contractual basis, it would not be public welfare any more than the Blue Cross and Blue Shield programs are a form of welfare. But if the income from premiums were supplemented by the general treasury and if individuals were eligible for medical benefits even though they had been unemployed or were unable to pay the usual premiums, then it would become a form of welfare. In its essential features it would be similar to other social security insurance programs that are a mixture between compulsory insurance schemes and outright welfare programs.

What would be the status of a universal national health service that would provide medical care for all citizens without cost or for a nominal charge? If the system were self-supporting and each eligible individual were required to pay his or her share of the total cost of the system, its governmental character would not be sufficient to make it into a welfare program; it would be comparable to a private group medical plan in which the recipients pay for all services rendered and in which eligibility is derived from payments made to the group medical care plan. But if the national medical service were made available to the citizens because they were incapable of providing adequate medical care for themselves in the private market, then it would become a form of assistance for those who need such assistance and would be a form of public welfare.

This suggests that the word "welfare" when it occurs in the expression "a welfare state" has a somewhat different meaning from the same word when it occurs in the expression "a welfare benefit" or "he is on welfare." I suppose any state that provides public programs of assistance to the needy could be considered a welfare state, but the ideal of the welfare state goes beyond this. The welfare state may well have a wide range of programs that contribute to the welfare of its citizens, perhaps national subsidies to the arts or support for higher education or nationalized transportation, that are not forms of governmental assistance to maintain personal well-being in those incapable of providing it for themselves. The welfare state may provide many services which its citizens could well provide for themselves but which, it is thought, could be better provided by the government for one reason or another.

. . .

Many more welfare benefits are provided by the family. There is an irony in the name of the best known public welfare program in the United States today, Aid to Families with Dependent Children. *All* families have dependent children, for every child is born completely dependent and remains so for years. Yet most families are ineligible for AFDC because they are not judged to be in need of public assistance. While most families can provide for the needs of their children without aid from the government, this should not blind us to the equally important fact that the children in even the most affluent families *do* need assistance. They obtain it, of course, from their parents or from other members of the family. The food, clothing, housing, and various forms of care from their families are welfare in the sense of assistance

provided to those who need it. Nor are these the only sorts of welfare benefits provided by the family. Usually the family, rather than Medicaid or Medicare, pays for a family member's needed medical care, feeds, clothes, and houses a high school graduate unable to find employment, and cares for the needs of the elderly, the blind, or the permanently and totally disabled. In short, every major public welfare program is a supplement to similar forms of welfare benefits normally provided by the family. I suggest that it would be entirely proper and quite illuminating to consider the assistance provided by the family to its needy members as welfare, for then we would recognize that the most important welfare institution in our society is the family.

We have finally arrived at an accurate definition of welfare, a collective noun used to refer to any and all forms of welfare benefits. A welfare benefit is any form of assistance—monetary payment, good, or service—provided to an individual because of his or her need. We can now define a primary welfare right as a right to some welfare benefit or benefits. Examples of welfare rights would be the legal right of a mother with one or more dependent children to AFDC payments, or the right of an elderly person entitled to social security payments to Medicare as well.

Such examples could be multiplied indefinitely, but even an extended list of primary welfare rights as we have defined them would not include most of the rights listed by the National Welfare Rights Organization in its "Bill of Welfare Rights." These include "the right to appeal a denial of aid and to be given a fair hearing" and "the right to be treated in a way which does not invade your privacy." The latter hardly seems a welfare right at all; as formulated, it is simply the right to privacy, a right that extends to many areas having nothing to do with any sort of welfare benefit. Still, one can understand its inclusion in a list of welfare rights. Welfare applicants' privacy is often violated when the welfare department investigates their personal affairs to determine their eligibility for aid, and the notorious midnight searches to find a man in the house have violated the right to privacy of many recipients of AFDC.

Again, the right to a fair hearing, although it is one aspect of the much more general right to due process, does have a meaning specific to our public welfare programs. It is defined especially in the *Code of Federal Regulations* section 205.10. Accordingly, I define a secondary welfare right as a right concerning, but not to, some welfare benefit. All of the rights listed in the NWRO "Bill of Welfare Rights" are either primary or secondary welfare rights, and I can think of no obvious examples of welfare rights that do not fall into one or the other category. I suggest, therefore, that we accept as our working definition of the concept of a welfare right a right to or concerning some welfare benefit or benefits.

Precisely what specific welfare rights exist is a matter to be determined only by detailed and prolonged investigation, but this conception of a welfare right allows for the possibility that a wide range of welfare rights exists. Surely there are many legal welfare rights, and there are probably a variety of ethical welfare rights as well. The human rights to social security and to an adequate standard of living are probably welfare rights — rights to assistance, in achieving these necessary conditions of an acceptable level of individual well-being. The child's moral right to special protection by its parents seems also to be a welfare right. Although one may wish to prevent the multiplication of welfare rights beyond necessity, one does not wish to rule any contender out of court arbitrarily and merely by definition. . . . A primary welfare right is a right to some welfare benefit — to some form of assistance provided to an individual in need. A secondary welfare right is a right concerning, but not to, some welfare benefit. . . .

The Right to Protection

The first example of an alleged ethical welfare right for which we need grounds is the human right to social security. At its core is an ethical claim of the individual human being against his or her society to be provided with a minimal livelihood in the event that he or she lacks the means of sustaining life because of circumstances beyond his or her control. The very name of this right suggests that the central function of any public system of social security is to protect the individual from some sort of insecurity. This in turn reminds us of the venerable tradition in political theory that holds that the central end of government is security and that the primary duty of any state is to protect its citizens, at least against the threat of foreign military attack and internal criminal activity. If the state really does owe protection to its citizens, then the individual citizens have a right to such protection. And if justice demands equal protection of the laws, this is because each citizen has a prior ethical claim to the protection of the state. Now if the individual does have an ethical right to protection by society and if the scope of this right reaches to protection from economic dangers, then the ground of the human right to social security might well be the more basic, or at least more traditional, human right to protection. Presumably, the core of any such right would consist of an ethical claim of the individual human being against the state to be protected to some specifiable degree against specific range of dangers. . . .

. . . The crux of the reasoning is the value and nature of the subject-sovereign relation. Primarily, this is a relation between the individual citizen and his or her state. Thus understood, the corresponding ethical right would seem to be a civic right, a right possessed by the individual *as a citizen.* But only a human right to protection, a right possessed by the individual *as a human being,* could ground a human right to social security. Does the right to protection extend beyond citizens to other human beings? In the broad sense in which I am using the term "citizen," resident aliens are citizens; they are members of the society. Illegal aliens and tourists, however, are not full members of the society. They are, however, subject to its laws. A visitor to a country becomes a temporary subject, for he or she is subject to its jurisdiction temporarily. Accordingly, for that period of living within the borders of the state, any human being stands in the relation of subject to sovereign and has the standing to claim protection from the state. The grounds are precisely the same as those of the ethical claim of the permanent and full citizen.

This does not imply, however, that the right to protection is a human right. Quite the contrary. A genuine human right is universal, but the right to protection holding against some state is possessed only by those human beings subject to jurisdiction. More fundamentally, the right to protection is not possessed by the individual as human, but as subject. What gives the individual standing to claim protection from a given state is standing at one end of the subject-sovereign relation. This implies that the right to protection is a civic right, an ethical right one possesses as a citizen. If this right extends beyond full citizens to illegal aliens and tourists, this is because they are temporary citizens. This has an important practical implication. While the alien or tourist remains within the jurisdiction of the state, the state has a duty to provide protection for the individual. But the state can extinguish this moral obligation, should it become onerous, by deporting the individual and thereby terminating his or her temporary and partial citizenship.

If my argument is accepted, it is not possible to ground any human right to social security in the human right to protection. At least, I have been unable to discover any grounds for any universal human right to state protection. At the same time, I have advanced what seem to me adequate grounds for an ethical claim of any individual subject to the jurisdiction of a given state against the state for protection from certain threats to life, limb, and property. This may well be the core of a civic right to protection, and upon this right one could ground a civic right to social security. . . .

Wrongful Harm

Having had something less than spectacular success in identifying adequate grounds for the alleged human right to social security, we may be well advised to turn to our other example of an ethical right to welfare, the alleged civic right to a fair share. As before, let us ignore its associated ethical elements and seek only a sufficient ground for its defining core, the ethical claim of the citizen who has been impoverished by the operations of the economic institutions that shape the distribution of goods and services in his or her society holding against the state to be provided with a fair share, that is with an amount of goods and services just sufficient to bring him or her up above the poverty line.

Proclamations of welfare rights are a modern phenomenon. Historically, the belief in the existence of ethical welfare rights has grown out of an increasing recognition of society's responsibility for the plight of the unemployed, the aged, children dependent upon impoverished families, and even the ill and the handicapped. More specifically, the underlying idea seems to be that society is morally responsible for providing social security because it is causally responsible for economic insecurity. Although the idea, or at least its widespread acceptance, is modern, the reality is ancient and universal. In every society, the income of the individual is determined by social institutions created or modified or regulated by state action. This suggests that ethical welfare rights might be grounded in the wrongful harm inflicted upon the individual by the state. To do so, one would need the ethical analogue of the central principle of tort law. An acceptable moral principle of remedy might be formulated as follows: a party wrongfully harmed by the action of a second party has an ethical claim-right holding against that second party to an appropriate remedy. This principle does not, of course, apply to natural harms, harms to the individual that do not result from human actions, for example the destruction of one's home by a tornado or a wound inflicted upon a camper by a wild animal. Nor does it confer any right to a remedy for harms arising from human actions that are not wrongful, such as just taxation that reduces one's wealth or the economic failure of an entrepreneur put out of business fairly by his or her competitors. Only wrongful harm serves to ground any ethical right to a remedy.

This moral principle of remedy is readily applicable to the case of an individual citizen impoverished by the operation of the social institutions that control the processes of economic distribution in his or her society. To be impoverished is certainly to be harmed, indeed harmed very seriously. Since the social institutions that control the distribution of goods and services in any society are formed and regulated by state action, to be impoverished in this way is to be impoverished by the state. And since every member of a society has a civic right not to be unjustly impoverished by the state, such state action, be it acts of commission or omission or both, is a wrongful violation of the ethical rights of the individual. In the last chapter, I have sketched, or at least hinted at, an argument to establish the existence of this civic right not to be unjustly impoverished. If this civic right is granted, and if one grants the moral principle of remedy, then the civic right to a fair share can be grounded readily in wrongful harm.

The reader wondering whether to accept the civic right not to be unjustly impoverished may be interested to note that its role in my ethical system is analogous to the role played by the Lockean Proviso in the moral philosophy of Robert Nozick, certainly no advocate of welfare rights. If Nozick recognizes the moral necessity to limit original acquisition of private property with the proviso that there is "enough and as good to spare," this is presumably because he recognizes that acquisition of private property can be just only so long as it does not arbitrarily exclude other individuals from similarly acquiring property of their own. Analogously, my civic right not to be unjustly impoverished is the recognition that society wrongs an individual if it arbitrarily excludes him or her from the processes of economic distribution by which individuals in the society acquire goods and services.

But let us suppose that some reader remains unconvinced by my argument for the existence of a civic right not to be unjustly impoverished. There is another way in which the civic right to a fair share can be grounded in wrongful harm. This right to a fair share can still be taken to be a remedial right demanding remedial action of the state regarding any citizen who has been impoverished by the arbitrary operations of the social institutions that determine the distribution of goods and services in that society. If the individual citizen has been reduced to poverty, then the citizen has surely been harmed. Moreover, if the citizen has been excluded from the processes of economic distribution arbitrarily, for no good reason such as his or her refusal to accept available employment, then the citizen has been *unnecessarily* harmed by the state. Sometimes the state harms the citizen

necessarily, under duress of compelling reasons. The state must tax away some of the citizen's wealth if it is to continue to function and perform its duties to the citizens. The state may have to conscript a citizen to defend itself and its very existence from military attack. But to inflict harm upon the citizen unnecessarily is wrongly to harm the citizen. Thus, arbitrary exclusion from the processes of economic distribution constitutes an action of inflicting unnecessary harm, and therefore wrongful harm, upon the individual member of society. Now a party wrongfully harmed by the action of a second party has an ethical claim-right holding against that second party to an appropriate remedy. The wrongful harm in this case is that of being impoverished by being excluded from the processes of economic distribution. Accordingly, the appropriate remedy would seem to be to be provided by the wrong-doer, the state, with the goods and services one would have received had one not been unjustly impoverished. This is precisely the content of the core ethical claim of the civic right to a fair share, for I have advocated an unjust impoverishment conception of the right to a fair share.

There are, then, two ways in which the civic right to a fair share can be grounded in wrongful harm. Both recognize that the state is responsible for the social institutions that control the distribution of goods and services in the society. Accordingly, if any citizen is left impoverished for no good reason by the processes of economic distribution, then the state has by its acts of commission or omission impoverished the citizen. Such impoverishment inflicts harm upon the citizen because it renders him or her incapable of meeting his or her basic needs. It is wrongful harm either because the individual citizen has an ethical right not to be unjustly impoverished or because the infliction of harm unnecessarily is morally wrong. Either way, wrongful harm serves as an adequate ground for the civic right to a fair share. . . .

Family and Reproductive Issues

RACISM, BIRTH CONTROL AND REPRODUCTIVE RIGHTS

Angela Davis

*Angela Davis argues for an expanded notion of a repro-
ductive right that would include the right not to be sterilized. This expanded notion is necessary to protect poor
women, in particular poor women of color, from being co-
ercively sterilized. (Source: From* Women, Race and Class
*by Angela Davis. Copyright © 1981 by Angela Davis. Re-
printed by permission of Random House, Inc.)*

When nineteenth-century feminists raised the
demand for "voluntary motherhood," the campaign for birth control was born. Its proponents were
called radicals and they were subjected to the same
mockery as had befallen the initial advocates of
woman suffrage. "Voluntary motherhood" was considered audacious, outrageous and outlandish by
those who insisted that wives had no right to refuse to
satisfy their husbands' sexual urges. Eventually, of
course, the right to birth control, like women's right to
vote, would be more or less taken for granted by U.S.
public opinion. Yet in 1970, a full century later, the call
for legal and easily accessible abortions was no less
controversial than the issue of "voluntary motherhood" which had originally launched the birth control movement in the United States.

Birth control — individual choice, safe contraceptive methods, as well as abortions when necessary —
is a fundamental prerequisite for the emancipation of
women. Since the right of birth control is obviously
advantageous to women of all classes and races, it
would appear that even vastly dissimilar women's
groups would have attempted to unite around this issue. In reality, however, the birth control movement
has seldom succeeded in uniting women of different
social backgrounds, and rarely have the movement's
leaders popularized the genuine concerns of working-
class women. Moreover, arguments advanced by birth
control advocates have sometimes been based on blatantly racist premises. The progressive potential of
birth control remains indisputable. But in actuality,
the historical record of this movement leaves much to
be desired in the realm of challenges to racism and
class exploitation.

The most important victory of the contemporary
birth control movement was won during the early
1970s when abortions were at last declared legal. Having emerged during the infancy of the new Women's
Liberation movement, the struggle to legalize abortions incorporated all the enthusiasm and the militancy of the young movement. By January, 1973, the
abortion rights campaign had reached a triumphant
culmination. In *Roe* v. *Wade* (410 U.S.) and *Doe* v.
Bolton (410 U.S.), the Supreme Court ruled that a
woman's right to personal privacy implied her right to
decide whether or not to have an abortion.

The ranks of the abortion rights campaign did not include substantial numbers of women of color. Given the racial composition of the larger Women's Liberation movement, this was not at all surprising. When questions were raised about the absence of racially oppressed women in both the larger movement and in the abortion rights campaign, two explanations were commonly proposed in the discussions and literature of the period: women of color were overburdened by their people's fight against racism; and/or they had not yet become conscious of the centrality of sexism. But the real meaning of the almost lily-white complexion of the abortion rights campaign was not to be found in an ostensibly myopic or underdeveloped consciousness among women of color. The truth lay buried in the ideological underpinnings of the birth control movement itself.

The failure of the abortion rights campaign to conduct a historical self-evaluation led to a dangerously superficial appraisal of Black people's suspicious attitudes toward birth control in general. Granted, when some Black people unhesitatingly equated birth control with genocide, it did appear to be an exaggerated — even paranoiac — reaction. Yet white abortion rights activists missed a profound message, for underlying these cries of genocide were important clues about the history of the birth control movement. This movement, for example, had been known to advocate involuntary sterilization — a racist form of mass "birth control." If ever women would enjoy the right to plan their pregnancies, legal and easily accessible birth control measures and abortions would have to be complemented by an end to sterilization abuse.

As for the abortion rights campaign itself, how could women of color fail to grasp its urgency? They were far more familiar than their white sisters with the murderously clumsy scalpels of inept abortionists seeking profit in illegality. In New York, for instance, during the several years preceding the decriminalization of abortions in that state, some 80 percent of the deaths caused by illegal abortions involved Black and Puerto Rican women.[1] Immediately afterward, women of color received close to half of all the legal abortions. If the abortion rights campaign of the early 1970s needed to be reminded that women of color wanted desperately to escape the back-room quack abortionists, they should have also realized that these same women were not about to express pro-abortion sentiments. They were in favor of *abortion rights,* which did not mean that they were proponents of abortion. When Black and Latina women resort to abortions in such large numbers, the stories they tell are not so much about their desire to be free of their pregnancy, but rather about the miserable social conditions which dissuade them from bringing new lives into the world.

Black women have been aborting themselves since the earliest days of slavery. Many slave women refused to bring children into a world of interminable forced labor, where chains and floggings and sexual abuse for women were the everyday conditions of life. A doctor practicing in Georgia around the middle of the last century noticed that abortions and miscarriages were far more common among his slave patients than among the white women he treated. According to the physician, either Black women worked too hard or

> . . . as the planters believe, the blacks are possessed of a secret by which they destroy the fetus at an early stage of gestation. . . . All country practitioners are aware of the frequent complaints of planters (about the) . . . unnatural tendency in the African female to destroy her offspring.[2]

Expressing shock that ". . . whole families of women fail to have any children,"[3] this doctor never considered how "unnatural" it was to raise children under the slave system. The previously mentioned episode of Margaret Garner, a fugitive slave who killed her own daughter and attempted suicide herself when she was captured by slavecatchers, is a case in point.

> She rejoiced that the girl was dead — "now she would never know what a woman suffers as a slave" — and pleaded to be tried for murder. "I will go singing to the gallows rather than be returned to slavery!"[4]

Why were self-imposed abortions and reluctant acts of infanticide such common occurrences during slavery? Not because Black women had discovered solutions to their predicament, but rather because they were desperate. Abortions and infanticides were acts of desperation, motivated not by the biological birth process but by the oppressive conditions of slavery. Most of these women, no doubt, would have expressed their deepest resentment had someone hailed their abortions as a stepping stone toward freedom.

During the early abortion rights campaign it was too frequently assumed that legal abortions provided a viable alternative to the myriad problems posed by poverty. As if having fewer children could create more jobs, higher wages, better schools, etc., etc. This assumption reflected the tendency to blur the distinction between *abortion rights* and the general advocacy of *abortions*. The campaign often failed to provide a voice for women who wanted the *right* to legal abortions while deploring the social conditions that prohibited them from bearing more children.

The renewed offensive against abortion rights that erupted during the latter half of the 1970s has made it absolutely necessary to focus more sharply on the needs of poor and racially oppressed women. By 1977 the passage of the Hyde Amendment in Congress had mandated the withdrawal of federal funding for abortions, causing many state legislatures to follow suit. Black, Puerto Rican, Chicana and Native American Indian women, together with their impoverished white sisters, were thus effectively divested of the right to legal abortions. Since surgical sterilizations, funded by the Department of Health, Education and Welfare, remained free on demand, more and more poor women have been forced to opt for permanent infertility. What is urgently required is a broad campaign to defend the reproductive rights of all women — and especially those women whose economic circumstances often compel them to relinquish the right to reproduction itself.

Women's desire to control their reproductive system is probably as old as human history itself. As early as 1844 the *United States Practical Receipt Book* contained, among its many recipes for food, household chemicals and medicines, "receipts" for "birth preventive lotions." To make "Hannay's Preventive Lotion," for example,

[t]ake pearlash, 1 part; water, 6 parts. Mix and filter. Keep it in closed bottles, and use it, with or without soap, immediately after connexion.[5]

For "Abernethy's Preventive Lotion,"

[t]ake bichloride of mercury, 25 parts; milk of almonds, 400 parts; alcohol, 100 parts; rosewater,

1000 parts. Immerse the glands in a little of the mixture. . . . Infallible, if used in proper time.[6]

While women have probably always dreamed of infallible methods of birth control, it was not until the issue of women's rights in general became the focus of an organized movement that reproductive rights could emerge as a legitimate demand. In an essay entitled "Marriage," written during the 1850s, Sarah Grimke argued for a ". . . right on the part of women to decide *when* she shall become a mother, how often and under what circumstances."[7] Alluding to one physician's humorous observation, Grimke agreed that if wives and husbands alternatively gave birth to their children, ". . . no family would ever have more than three, the husband bearing one and the wife two."[8] But, as she insists, ". . . the *right* to decide this matter has been almost wholly denied to women."[9]

Sarah Grimke advocated women's right to sexual abstinence. Around the same time the well-known "emancipated marriage" of Lucy Stone and Henry Blackwell took place. These abolitionists and women's rights activists were married in a ceremony that protested women's traditional relinquishment of their rights to their persons, names and property. In agreeing that as husband, he had no right to the "custody of the wife's person,"[10] Henry Blackwell promised that he would not attempt to impose the dictates of his sexual desires upon his wife.

The notion that women could refuse to submit to their husbands' sexual demands eventually became the central idea of the call for "voluntary motherhood." By the 1870s, when the woman suffrage movement had reached its peak, feminists were publicly advocating voluntary motherhood. In a speech delivered in 1873, Victoria Woodhull claimed that

(t)he wife who submits to sexual intercourse against her wishes or desires, virtually commits suicide; while the husband who compels it, commits murder, and ought just as much to be punished for it, as though he strangled her to death for refusing him.[11]

Woodhull, of course, was quite notorious as a proponent of "free love." Her defense of a woman's right to abstain from sexual intercourse within marriage as a means of controlling her pregnancies was associated with Woodhull's overall attack on the institution of marriage.

It was not a coincidence that women's consciousness of their reproductive rights was born within the organized movement for women's political equality. Indeed, if women remained forever burdened by incessant childbirths and frequent miscarriages, they would hardly be able to exercise the political rights they might win. Moreover, women's new dreams of pursuing careers and other paths of self-development outside marriage and motherhood could only be realized if they could limit and plan their pregnancies. In this sense, the slogan "voluntary motherhood" contained a new and genuinely progressive vision of womanhood. At the same time, however, this vision was rigidly bound to the lifestyle enjoyed by the middle classes and the bourgeoisie. The aspirations underlying the demand for "voluntary motherhood" did not reflect the conditions of working-class women, engaged as they were in a far more fundamental fight for economic survival. Since this first call for birth control was associated with goals which could only be achieved by women possessing material wealth, vast numbers of poor and working-class women would find it rather difficult to identify with the embryonic birth control movement.

Toward the end of the nineteenth century the white birth rate in the United States suffered a significant decline. Since no contraceptive innovations had been publicly introduced, the drop in the birth rate implied that women were substantially curtailing their sexual activity. By 1890 the typical native-born white woman was bearing no more than four children.[12] Since U.S. society was becoming increasingly urban, this new birth pattern should not have been a surprise. While farm life demanded large families, they became dysfunctional within the context of city life. Yet this phenomenon was publicly interpreted in a racist and anti-working-class fashion by the ideologues of rising monopoly capitalism. Since native-born white women were bearing fewer children, the specter of "race suicide" was raised in official circles.

In 1905 President Theodore Roosevelt concluded his Lincoln Day Dinner speech with the proclamation that "race purity must be maintained."[13] By 1906 he blatantly equated the falling birth rate among native-born whites with the impending threat of "race sui-

cide." In his State of the Union message that year Roosevelt admonished the well-born white women who engaged in "willful sterility — the one sin for which the penalty is national death, race suicide."[14] These comments were made during a period of accelerating racist ideology and of great waves of race riots and lynchings on the domestic scene. Moreover, President Roosevelt himself was attempting to muster support for the U.S. seizure of the Philippines, the country's most recent imperialist venture.

How did the birth control movement respond to Roosevelt's accusation that their cause was promoting race suicide? The President's propagandistic ploy was a failure, according to a leading historian of the birth control movement, for, ironically, it led to greater support for its advocates. Yet, as Linda Gordon maintains, this controversy ". . . also brought to the forefront those issues that most separated feminists from the working class and the poor."[15]

> This happened in two ways. First, the feminists were increasingly emphasizing birth control as a route to careers and higher education — goals out of reach of the poor with or without birth control. In the context of the whole feminist movement, the race-suicide episode was an additional factor identifying feminism almost exclusively with the aspirations of the more privileged women of the society. Second, the pro-birth control feminists began to popularize the idea that poor people had a moral obligation to restrict the size of their families, because large families create a drain on the taxes and charity expenditures of the wealthy and because poor children were less likely to be "superior."[16]

The acceptance of the race-suicide thesis, to a greater or lesser extent, by women such as Julia Ward Howe and Ida Husted Harper reflected the suffrage movement's capitulation to the racist posture of Southern women. If the suffragists acquiesced to arguments invoking the extension of the ballot to women as the saving grace of white supremacy, then birth control advocates either acquiesced to or supported the new arguments invoking birth control as a means of preventing the proliferation of the "lower classes" and as an antidote to race suicide. Race suicide could be prevented by the introduction of birth control among Black people, immigrants and the poor in general. In this way, the prosperous whites of solid Yankee stock could maintain their superior numbers within the population. Thus class-bias and racism crept into the birth control movement when it was still in its infancy. More and more, it was assumed within birth control circles that poor women, Black and immigrant alike, had a "moral obligation to restrict the size of their families."[17] What was demanded as a "right" for the privileged came to be interpreted as a "duty" for the poor.

When Margaret Sanger embarked upon her lifelong crusade for birth control—a term she coined and popularized—it appeared as though the racist and anti-working-class overtones of the previous period might possibly be overcome. For Margaret Higgins Sanger came from a working-class background herself and was well acquainted with the devastating pressures of poverty. When her mother died, at the age of forty-eight, she had borne no less than eleven children. Sanger's later memories of her own family's troubles would confirm her belief that working-class women had a special need for the right to plan and space their pregnancies autonomously. Her affiliation, as an adult, with the Socialist movement was a further cause for hope that the birth control campaign would move in a more progressive direction.

When Margaret Sanger joined the Socialist party in 1912, she assumed the responsibility of recruiting women from New York's working women's clubs into the party.[18] *The Call*—the party's paper—carried her articles on the women's page. She wrote a series entitled "What Every Mother Should Know," another called "What Every Girl Should Know," and she did on-the-spot coverage of strikes involving women. Sanger's familiarity with New York's working-class districts was a result of her numerous visits as a trained nurse to the poor sections of the city. During these visits, she points out in her autobiography, she met countless numbers of women who desperately desired knowledge about birth control.

According to Sanger's autobiographical reflections, one of the many visits she made as a nurse to New York's Lower East Side convinced her to undertake a personal crusade for birth control. Answering one of her routine calls, she discovered that twenty-eight-year-old Sadie Sachs had attempted to abort herself. Once the crisis had passed, the young woman asked the attending physician to give her advice on birth prevention. As Sanger relates the story, the doctor recommended that she ". . . tell (her husband) Jake to sleep on the roof."[19]

> I glanced quickly to Mrs. Sachs. Even through my sudden tears I could see stamped on her face an expression of absolute despair. We simply looked at each other, saying no word until the door had closed behind the doctor. Then she lifted her thin, blue-veined hands and clasped them beseechingly. "He can't understand. He's only a man. But you do, don't you? Please tell me the secret, and I'll never breathe it to a soul. Please!"[20]

Three months later Sadie Sachs died from another self-induced abortion. That night, Margaret Sanger says, she vowed to devote all her energy toward the acquisition and dissemination of contraceptive measures.

> I went to bed, knowing that no matter what it might cost, I was finished with palliatives and superficial cures; I resolved to seek out the root of evil, to do something to change the destiny of mothers whose miseries were as vast as the sky.[21]

During the first phase of Sanger's birth control crusade, she maintained her affiliation with the Socialist party—and the campaign itself was closely associated with the rising militancy of the working class. Her staunch supporters included Eugene Debs, Elizabeth Gurley Flynn and Emma Goldman, who respectively represented the Socialist party, the International Workers of the World and the anarchist movement. Margaret Sanger, in turn, expressed the anti-capitalist commitment of her own movement within the pages of its journal, *Woman Rebel,* which was "dedicated to the interests of working women."[22] Personally, she continued to march on picket lines with striking workers and publicly condemned the outrageous assaults on striking workers. In 1914, for example, when the National Guard massacred scores of Chicano miners in Ludlow, Colorado, Sanger joined the labor movement in exposing John D. Rockefeller's role in this attack.[23]

Unfortunately, the alliance between the birth control campaign and the radical labor movement did not enjoy a long life. While Socialists and other working-class activists continued to support the demand for birth control, it did not occupy a central place in their overall strategy. And Sanger herself began to underestimate the centrality of capitalist exploitation in her analysis of poverty, arguing that too many children caused workers to fall into their miserable predicament. Moreover, ". . . women are inadvertently perpetuating the exploitation of the working class," she believed, "by continually flooding the labor market with new workers."[24] Ironically, Sanger may have been encouraged to adopt this position by the neo-Malthusian ideas embraced in some socialist circles. Such outstanding figures of the European socialist movement as Anatole France and Rosa Luxemburg had proposed a "birth strike" to prevent the continued flow of labor into the capitalist market.[25]

When Margaret Sanger severed her ties with the Socialist party for the purpose of building an independent birth control campaign, she and her followers became more susceptible than ever before to the anti-Black and anti-immigrant propaganda of the times. Like their predecessors, who had been deceived by the "race suicide" propaganda, the advocates of birth control began to embrace the prevailing racist ideology. The fatal influence of the eugenics movement would soon destroy the progressive potential of the birth control campaign.

During the first decade of the twentieth century the rising popularity of the eugenics movement was hardly a fortuitous development. Eugenic ideas were perfectly suited to the ideological needs of the young monopoly capitalists. Imperialist incursions in Latin America and in the Pacific needed to be justified, as did the intensified exploitation of Black workers in the South and immigrant workers in the North and West. The pseudo-scientific racial theories associated with the eugenics campaign furnished dramatic apologies for the conduct of the young monopolies. As a result, this movement won the unhesitating support of such leading capitalists as the Carnegies, the Harrimans and the Kelloggs.[26]

By 1919 the eugenic influence on the birth control movement was unmistakably clear. In an article published by Margaret Sanger in the American Birth Control League's journal, she defined "the chief issue of birth control" as "more children from the fit, less from the unfit."[27] Around this time the ABCL heartily welcomed the author of *The Rising Tide of Color*

Against White World Supremacy into its inner sanctum.[28] Lothrop Stoddard, Harvard professor and theoretician of the eugenics movement, was offered a seat on the board of directors. In the pages of the ABCL's journal, articles by Guy Irving Birch, director of the American Eugenics Society, began to appear. Birch advocated birth control as a weapon to

> . . . prevent the American people from being replaced by alien or Negro stock, whether it be by immigration or by overly high birth rates among others in this country.[29]

By 1932 the Eugenics Society could boast that at least twenty-six states had passed compulsory sterilization laws and that thousands of "unfit" persons had already been surgically prevented from reproducing.[30] Margaret Sanger offered her public approval of this development. "Morons, mental defectives, epileptics, illiterates, paupers, unemployables, criminals, prostitutes and dope fiends" ought to be surgically sterilized, she argued in a radio talk.[31] She did not wish to be so intransigent as to leave them with no choice in the matter; if they wished, she said, they should be able to choose a lifelong segregated existence in labor camps.

Within the American Birth Control League, the call for birth control among Black people acquired the same racist edge as the call for compulsory sterilization. In 1939 its successor, the Birth Control Federation of America, planned a "Negro Project." In the Federation's words,

> (t)he mass of Negroes, particularly in the South, still breed carelessly and disastrously, with the result that the increase among Negroes, even more than among whites, is from that portion of the population least fit, and least able to rear children properly.[32]

Calling for the recruitment of Black ministers to lead local birth control committees, the Federation's proposal suggested that Black people should be rendered as vulnerable as possible to their birth control propaganda. "We do not want word to get out," wrote Margaret Sanger in a letter to a colleague,

> . . . that we want to exterminate the Negro population and the minister is the man who can straighten out that idea if it ever occurs to any of their more rebellious members.[33]

This episode in the birth control movement confirmed the ideological victory of the racism associated with eugenic ideas. It had been robbed of its progressive potential, advocating for people of color not the individual right to *birth control*, but rather the racist strategy of *population control*. The birth control campaign would be called upon to serve in an essential capacity in the execution of the U.S. government's imperialist and racist population policy.

The abortion rights activists of the early 1970s should have examined the history of their movement. Had they done so, they might have understood why so many of their Black sisters adopted a posture of suspicion toward their cause. They might have understood how important it was to undo the racist deeds of their predecessors, who had advocated birth control as well as compulsory sterilization as a means of eliminating the "unfit" sectors of the population. Consequently, the young white feminists might have been more receptive to the suggestion that their campaign for abortion rights include a vigorous condemnation of sterilization abuse, which had become more widespread than ever.

It was not until the media decided that the casual sterilization of two Black girls in Montgomery, Alabama, was a scandal worth reporting that the Pandora's box of sterilization abuse was finally flung open. But by the time the case of the Relf sisters broke, it was practically too late to influence the politics of the abortion rights movement. It was the summer of 1973 and the Supreme Court decision legalizing abortions had already been announced in January. Nevertheless, the urgent need for mass opposition to sterilization abuse became tragically clear. The facts surrounding the Relf sisters' story were horrifyingly simple. Minnie Lee, who was twelve years old, and Mary Alice, who was fourteen, had been unsuspectingly carted into an operating room, where surgeons irrevocably robbed them of their capacity to bear children.[34] The surgery had been ordered by the HEW-funded Montgomery Community Action Committee after it was discovered that Depo-Provera, a drug previously administered to the girls as a birth prevention measure, caused cancer in test animals.[35]

After the Southern Poverty Law Center filed suit on behalf of the Relf sisters, the girls' mother revealed that she had unknowingly "consented" to the operation, having been deceived by the social workers who handled her daughters' case. They had asked Mrs. Relf, who was unable to read, to put her "X" on a document, the contents of which were not described to her. She assumed, she said, that it authorized the continued Depo-Provera injections. As she subsequently learned, she had authorized the surgical sterilization of her daughters.[36]

In the aftermath of the publicity exposing the Relf sisters' case, similar episodes were brought to light. In Montgomery alone, eleven girls, also in their teens, had been similarly sterilized. HEW-funded birth control clinics in other states, as it turned out, had also subjected young girls to sterilization abuse. Moreover, individual women came forth with equally outrageous stories. Nial Ruth Cox, for example, filed suit against the state of North Carolina. At the age of eighteen — eight years before the suit — officials had threatened to discontinue her family's welfare payments if she refused to submit to surgical sterilization.[37] Before she assented to the operation, she was assured that her infertility would be temporary.[38]

Nial Ruth Cox's lawsuit was aimed at a state which had diligently practiced the theory of eugenics. Under the auspices of the Eugenics Commission of North Carolina, so it was learned, 7,686 sterilizations had been carried out since 1933. Although the operations were justified as measures to prevent the reproduction of "mentally deficient persons," about 5,000 of the sterilized persons had been Black.[39] According to Brenda Feigen Fasteau, the ACLU attorney representing Nial Ruth Cox, North Carolina's recent record was not much better.

> As far as I can determine, the statistics reveal that since 1964, approximately 65% of the women sterilized in North Carolina were Black and approximately 35% were white.[40]

As the flurry of publicity exposing sterilization abuse revealed, the neighboring state of South Carolina had been the site of further atrocities. Eighteen women from Aiken, South Carolina, charged that they had been sterilized by a Dr. Clovis Pierce during the early 1970s. The sole obstetrician in that small town, Pierce had consistently sterilized Medicaid recipients with two or more children. According to a nurse in his office, Dr. Pierce insisted that pregnant welfare women "will have to submit (sic!) to voluntary sterilization" if they wanted him to deliver their babies.[41] While he was ". . . tired of people running around and having babies and paying for them with my taxes,"[42] Dr. Pierce received some $60,000 in taxpayers' money for the sterilizations he performed. During his trial he was supported by the South Carolina Medical Association, whose members declared that doctors ". . . have a moral and legal right to insist on sterilization permission before accepting a patient, if it is done on the initial visit."[43]

Revelations of sterilization abuse during that time exposed the complicity of the federal government. At first the Department of Health, Education and Welfare claimed that approximately 16,000 women and 8,000 men had been sterilized in 1972 under the auspices of federal programs.[44] Later, however, these figures underwent a drastic revision. Carl Schultz, director of HEW's Population Affairs Office, estimated that between 100,000 and 200,000 sterilizations had actually been funded that year by the federal government.[45] During Hitler's Germany, incidentally, 250,000 sterilizations were carried out under the Nazis' Hereditary Health Law.[46] Is it possible that the record of the Nazis, throughout the years of their reign, may have been almost equaled by U.S. government-funded sterilizations in the space of a single year?

Given the historical genocide inflicted on the native population of the United States, one would assume that Native American Indians would be exempted from the government's sterilization campaign. But according to Dr. Connie Uri's testimony in a Senate committee hearing, by 1976 some 24 percent of all Indian women of childbearing age had been sterilized.[47] "Our blood lines are being stopped," the Choctaw physician told the Senate committee, "Our unborn will not be born . . . This is genocidal to our people."[48] According to Dr. Uri, the Indian Health Services Hospital in Claremore, Oklahoma, had been sterilizing one out of every four women giving birth in that federal facility.[49]

Native American Indians are special targets of government propaganda on sterilization. In one of the HEW pamphlets aimed at Indian people, there is a sketch of a family with *ten children* and *one horse*

and another sketch of a family with *one child* and *ten horses*. The drawings are supposed to imply that more children mean more poverty and fewer children mean wealth. As if the ten horses owned by the one-child family had been magically conjured up by birth control and sterilization surgery.

The domestic population policy of the U.S. government has an undeniably racist edge. Native American, Chicana, Puerto Rican and Black women continue to be sterilized in disproportionate numbers. According to a National Fertility Study conducted in 1970 by Princeton University's Office of Population Control, 20 percent of all married Black women have been permanently sterilized.[50] Approximately the same percentage of Chicana women had been rendered surgically infertile.[51] Moreover, 43 percent of the women sterilized through federally subsidized programs were Black.[52]

The astonishing number of Puerto Rican women who have been sterilized reflects a special government policy that can be traced back to 1939. In that year President Roosevelt's Interdepartmental Committee on Puerto Rico issued a statement attributing the island's economic problems to the phenomenon of overpopulation.[53] This committee proposed that efforts be undertaken to reduce the birth rate to no more than the level of the death rate.[54] Soon afterward an experimental sterilization campaign was undertaken in Puerto Rico. Although the Catholic Church initially opposed this experiment and forced the cessation of the program in 1946, it was converted during the early 1950s to the teachings and practice of population control.[55] In this period over 150 birth control clinics were opened, resulting in a 20 percent decline in population growth by the mid-1960s.[56] By the 1970s over 35 percent of all Puerto Rican women of childbearing age had been surgically sterilized.[57] According to Bonnie Mass, a serious critic of the U.S. government's population policy,

> . . . if purely mathematical projections are to be taken seriously, if the present rate of sterilization of 19,000 monthly were to continue, then the island's population of workers and peasants could be extinguished within the next 10 or 20 years . . . (establishing) for the first time in world history a systematic use of population control capable of eliminating an entire generation of people.[58]

During the 1970s the devastating implications of the Puerto Rican experiment began to emerge with unmistakable clarity. In Puerto Rico the presence of corporations in the highly automated metallurgical and pharmaceutical industries had exacerbated the problem of unemployment. The prospect of an ever-larger army of unemployed workers was one of the main incentives for the mass sterilization program. Inside the United States today, enormous numbers of people of color—and especially racially oppressed youth—have become part of a pool of permanently unemployed workers. It is hardly coincidental, considering the Puerto Rican example, that the increasing incidence of sterilization has kept pace with the high rates of unemployment. As growing numbers of white people suffer the brutal consequences of unemployment, they can also expect to become targets of the official sterilization propaganda.

The prevalence of sterilization abuse during the latter 1970s may be greater than ever before. Although the Department of Health, Education and Welfare issued guidelines in 1974, which were ostensibly designed to prevent involuntary sterilizations, the situation has nonetheless deteriorated. When the American Civil Liberties Union's Reproductive Freedom Project conducted a survey of teaching hospitals in 1975, they discovered that 40 percent of those institutions were not even aware of the regulations issued by HEW.[59] Only 30 percent of the hospitals examined by the ACLU were even attempting to comply with the guidelines.[60]

The 1977 Hyde Amendment has added yet another dimension to coercive sterilization practices. As a result of this law passed by Congress, federal funds for abortions were eliminated in all cases but those involving rape and the risk of death or severe illness. According to Sandra Salazar of the California Department of Public Health, the first victim of the Hyde Amendment was a twenty-seven-year-old Chicana woman from Texas. She died as a result of an illegal abortion in Mexico shortly after Texas discontinued government-funded abortions. There have been many more victims—women for whom sterilization has become the only alternative to the abortions, which are currently beyond their reach. Sterilizations continue to be federally funded and free, to poor women, on demand.

Over the last decade the struggle against sterilization abuse has been waged primarily by Puerto Rican, Black, Chicana and Native American women. Their cause has not yet been embraced by the women's movement as a whole. Within organizations representing the interests of middle-class white women, there has been a certain reluctance to support the demands of the campaign against sterilization abuse, for these women are often denied their individual rights to be sterilized when they desire to take this step. While women of color are urged, at every turn, to become permanently infertile, white women enjoying prosperous economic conditions are urged, by the same forces, to reproduce themselves. They therefore sometimes consider the "waiting period" and other details of the demand for "informed consent" to sterilization as further inconveniences for women like themselves. Yet whatever the inconveniences for white middle-class women, a fundamental reproductive right of racially oppressed and poor women is at stake. Sterilization abuse must be ended.

Notes

1. Edwin M. Gold *et al.,* "Therapeutic Abortions in New York City: A Twenty-Year Review" in *American Journal of Public Health,* Vol. LV (July, 1965), pp. 964–972. Quoted in Lucinda Cisla, "Unfinished Business: Birth Control and Women's Liberation," in Robin Morgan, editor, *Sisterhood Is Powerful: An Anthology of Writings From the Women's Liberation Movement* (New York: Vintage Books, 1970), p. 261. Also quoted in Robert Staples, *The Black Woman in America* (Chicago: Nelson Hall, 1974), p. 146.

2. Gutman, *op. cit.,* pp. 80–81 (note).

3. *Ibid.*

4. Aptheker, "The Negro Woman," p. 12.

5. Quoted in Baxandall *et al., op. cit.,* p. 17.

6. *Ibid.*

7. Lerner, *The Female Experience,* op. cit., p. 91.

8. *Ibid.*

9. *Ibid.*

10. "Marriage of Lucy Stone under Protest" appeared in *History of Woman Suffrage,* Vol. 1. Quoted in Schneir, *op. cit.,* p. 104.

11. Speech by Victoria Woodhull, "The Elixir of Life." Quoted in Schneir, *op. cit.,* p. 153.

12. Mary P. Ryan, *Womanhood in America from Colonial Times to the Present* (New York: Franklin Watts, Inc., 1975), p. 162.

13. Melvin Steinfeld, *Our Racist Presidents* (San Ramon, California: Consensus Publishers, 1972), p. 212.

14. Bonnie Mass, *Population Target: The Political Economy of Population Control in Latin America* (Toronto, Canada: Women's Educational Press, 1977), p. 20.

15. Linda Gordon, *Woman's Body, Woman's Right: Birth Control in America* (New York: Penguin Books, 1976), p. 157.

16. *Ibid.,* p. 158.

17. *Ibid.*

18. Margaret Sanger, *An Autobiography* (New York: Dover Press, 1971), p. 75.

19. *Ibid.,* p. 90.

20. *Ibid.,* p. 91.

21. *Ibid.,* p. 92.

22. *Ibid.,* p. 106.

23. Mass, *op. cit.,* p. 27.

24. Dancis, *op. cit.,* p. 96.

25. David M. Kennedy, *Birth Control in America: The Career of Margaret Sanger* (New Haven and London: Yale University Press, 1976), pp. 21–22.

26. Mass, *op. cit.,* p. 20.

27. Gordon, *op. cit.,* p. 281.

28. Mass, *op. cit.,* p. 20.

29. Gordon, *op. cit.,* p. 283.

30. Herbert Aptheker, "Sterilization, Experimentation and Imperialism," *Political Affairs,* Vol. LIII, No. 1 (January, 1974), p. 44.

31. Gena Corea, *The Hidden Malpractice* (New York: A Jove/HBJ Book, 1977), p. 149.

32. Gordon, *op. cit.,* p. 332.

33. *Ibid.,* pp. 332–333.

34. Aptheker, "Sterilization," p. 38. See also Anne Braden, "Forced Sterilization: Now Women Can Fight Back," *Southern Patriot,* September, 1973.

35. *Ibid.*

36. Jack Slater, "Sterilization, Newest Threat to the Poor," *Ebony,* Vol. XXVIII, No. 12 (October, 1973), p. 150.

37. Braden, *op. cit.*

38. Les Payne, "Forced Sterilization for the Poor?" *San Francisco Chronicle,* February 26, 1974.

39. Harold X., "Forced Sterilization Pervades South," *Muhammed Speaks,* October 10, 1975.

40. Slater, *op. cit.*

41. Payne, *op. cit.*

42. *Ibid.*

43. *Ibid.*

44. Aptheker, "Sterilization," p. 40.

45. Payne, *op. cit.*

46. Aptheker, "Sterilization," p. 48.

47. Arlene Eisen, "They're Trying to Take Our Future — Native American Women and Sterilization," *The Guardian,* March 23, 1972.

48. *Ibid.*

49. *Ibid.*

50. Quoted in a pamphlet issued by the Committee to End Sterilization Abuse, Box A244, Cooper Station, New York 10003.

51. *Ibid.*

52. *Ibid.*

53. Gordon, *op. cit.,* p. 338.

54. *Ibid.*

55. Mass, *op. cit.,* p. 92.

56. *Ibid.,* p. 91.

57. Gordon, *op. cit.,* p. 401. See also pamphlet issued by CESA.

58. Mass, *op. cit.,* p. 108.

59. Rahemah Aman, "Forced Sterilization," *Union Wage,* March 4, 1978.

60. *Ibid.*

MOTHERHOOD: THE ANNIHILATION OF WOMEN

Jeffner Allen

Jeffner Allen argues that motherhood is dangerous to women because it forces women to exist merely as wombs who produce for men. She argues instead for a radical separation from patriarchy, including the patriarchal institution of motherhood. (Source: From Lesbian Philosophy: Explorations, *Institute of Lesbian Studies, P.O. Box 25568, Chicago, IL 60625, 1986, pp. 61–88.)*

I would like to affirm the rejection of motherhood on the grounds that motherhood is dangerous to women. If woman, in patriarchy, is she who exists as the womb and wife of man, every woman is by definition a mother: she who produces for the sake of men. *A mother is she whose body is used as a resource to reproduce men and the world of men, understood as the biological children of patriarchy and as the ideas and material goods of patriarchal culture.* Motherhood is dangerous to women because it continues the structure within which females must be women and mothers and . . . because it denies to females the creation of a subjectivity and world that is open and free.

An active rejection of motherhood entails the development and enactment of a *philosophy of evacuation.*[1] Identification and analysis of the multiple aspects of motherhood not only show what is wrong with motherhood, but also point to a way out. A philosophy of evacuation proposes women's collective removal of ourselves from all forms of motherhood. Freedom is never achieved by the mere inversion of an oppressive construct, that is, by seeing motherhood in a "new" light. Freedom is achieved when an oppressive construct, motherhood, is vacated by its members and thereby rendered null and void.

A small and articulate group of radical feminist and radical lesbian authors agree that motherhood is oppressive to women. Simone de Beauvoir's position in *The Second Sex,* that woman's "misfortune is to have been biologically destined for the repetition of life,"[2] is reaffirmed in her recent interviews: "I think a woman must not fall into the trap of children and marriage. Even if a woman wants to have children, she must think very hard about the conditions in which she will have to bring them up, because childbearing, at the moment, is real slavery."[3] Shulamith Firestone, following de Beauvoir, finds that, "the heart of woman's oppression is her childbearing and childrearing roles."[4] That woman's "reproductive function . . . is the critical distinction upon which all inequities toward women are grounded" is also asserted by Ti-Grace Atkinson at the beginning of the second wave of the women's liberation movement.[5] Monique Wittig writes that a female becomes a woman and a mother when she is defined first of all, and above all else, in terms of "the capacity to give birth (biology)."[6]

The claim that a direct connection exists between woman's oppression and her role as breeder within patriarchy entails the recognition that men impose a type of sexuality on women through the institution of motherhood. De Beauvoir agrees that "frigidity seems . . . , in the present state of malaise created by the power relationship between men and women, a reaction at least more prudent and more reasonable [than woman being trapped in sexuality] because it reflects this malaise and makes women less dependent on men."[7] Atkinson answers affirmatively the more specific question, "Do you still feel that sexual instincts would disappear if 'sexual intercourse' no longer served the function of reproduction?"[8] Andrea Dworkin states, "There is a continuum of phallic control. In the male system, reproductive and nonreproductive sex are both phallic sex."[9] Wittig holds that, "Sexuality is for us [lesbians] an inevitable battleground insofar as we want to get outside of genitality and of the sexual economy imposed on us by the dominant heterosexuality."[10] I engage in a philosophy of evacuation as a radical lesbian who questions, analyzes, and describes how motherhood is dangerous to women.

Speaking of motherhood as the annihilation of women does not disclaim either women's past or present as mothers. Women as mothers make the best of motherhood. Women are mothers because within patriarchy women have no choice except motherhood. Without the institution of motherhood women could and would live otherwise. Just as no individual woman, or particular mother, is free in patriarchy, no token group of women, mothers in general, is free in patriarchy. Until patriarchy no longer exists, all females, as historical beings, must resist, rebel against, and avoid producing for the sake of men. Motherhood is not a matter of women's psychological or moral character. As an ideology by which men mark females as women, motherhood has nothing to do with a woman's selfishness or sacrifice, nurturance or nonviolence. Motherhood has everything to do with a history in which women remain powerless by reproducing the world of men and with a present in which women are expected to do the same. The central publication of the Soviet Women's Committee, for instance, writes, "Considering motherhood to be a woman's most important social function. . . ."[11]

I am endangered by motherhood. In evacuation from motherhood, I claim my life, body, world, as an end in itself.

Where Do Children Come From?

The question "Where do babies come from?" is frequently dismissed with a laugh, or cut short by recourse to scientific authority. In present-day discourse, both God's prescience and the stork are generally thought to be adequate responses. A satisfactory and "progressive" explanation is found in a scientific account of the union of egg and sperm. The appeal to science is misleading, however, for it ignores and conceals the social intercourse that first brings men and women together either directly, by means of physical copulation, or indirectly, through the use of medical technology.[12] The question "Where do babies come from?" might be approached more appropriately through the social and historical circumstances in which conception takes place: *Children come from patriarchal (male) sexuality's use of woman's body as a resource to reproduce men and the world of men.*

The scientific explanation of where children come from avoids placing conception within the continuum of social power relationships that constitute

motherhood and that often includes heterosexual intercourse, pregnancy, and childraising. Compulsion marks every aspect of the motherhood continuum: the mandatory heterosexuality imposed on women by men is thought "natural"; pregnancy is viewed as a biological "fact"; obligatory childraising by women is considered entirely "normal."[13]

Seduction and pregnancy, for instance, are remarkably similar: both eroticize women's subordination by acting out and deepening women's lack of power.[14]

> Male instinct can't help ITself; women need IT either because of their sexiness or their maternal instinct. IT, the penis, is big; IT, the child, is large. Woman's body is made for IT. Women's bodies have the right fit, or proportions. Women ask for IT, want IT. IT's a maturing experience in her becoming a woman. She takes IT. No real harm is done.

In seduction and pregnancy the power imbalance between men and women assumes the appearance of sexual difference, regardless of whether such activities are "affectionate" or "brutal."

> If women didn't want IT, IT wouldn't happen. Therefore, women must choose IT. Since many choose IT, IT must be part of their nature.[15]

I am defenseless within the motherhood continuum.

IT, "male instinct," passes through heterosexual intercourse to become the IT of motherhood. In motherhood, IT, male sexuality as a man-made social power construct, marks females with ITself. IT compels women to ITself: to male sexuality and its consequences, namely, birthing and raising men and the world of men. Children come from IT, from male-defined, male-dominated social intercourse. IT names ITself as "virility": belonging to, characteristic of a man; the power of procreation, especially for sexual intercourse; the masculine member, the generative organs; force, energy, drive considered typically masculine; to pursue, to hunt.[16] Virility comes from *vir,* which in Latin means "man." Women's "misfortune is to have been biologically destined for the repetition of life"[17] precisely because ITs power, force, energy, drive appropriates women's biological possibility in order to produce ITself. IT pursues ITs own continuation, silencing my questions: Is IT needed? Is IT desired? IT pursues ITs own evolution, constituting motherhood as a given, as compulsory for women, a danger to women.

———

One might object that children have not always come from patriarchal (male) sexuality's use of woman's body as a resource to reproduce men and the world of men. An appeal may even be made to a time in which motherhood is said to have had nothing to do with men's appropriation of women's bodies.

Çatal Hüyük, in particular, has been cited as "a very early urban culture which appears to have venerated women's activities, especially their procreative ones."[18] The Neolithic goddess at Çatal Hüyük who is claimed to clearly express "female experience and power" and the presence of "a positive female religious role" is described by Anne Barstow:

> Around 6200 B.C. the first goddess appears, in plaster outline on the wall, her legs spread wide, giving birth; below her, rows of plaster breasts, nipples painted red, are molded over animal skulls or jaws which protrude through the nipples. Already at her first appearance she is the deity of both life and death.[19]

Further examination of the context in which the Çatal Hüyük goddess appears shows, however, that care must be taken not to misconstrue the historical situation of women as mothers in early human culture. Females at Çatal Hüyük are represented exclusively in terms of maternal organs and attributes. Squatting in childbirth, usually with raised arms and legs, women are defined by their engagement in childbirth or, sometimes, pregnancy.[20] The female's head is less defined than the rest of her body, and often is not shown at all.[21] Synonymous with women's function as mother and maintainer of life at Çatal Hüyük is women's early death: "The average adult age [at Çatal Hüyük] was 34.3 years for men, 29.8 years for women."[22] The significantly shorter life-span of women at Çatal Hüyük demonstrates that although a culture may "venerate" women as mother, it may fail to empower individual women who spend much of their lives giving birth.

Examination of the context in which the Çatal Hüyük goddess appears makes evident, moreover, that the goddess was not alone. The goddess is regularly shown with the phallus: Neolithic figurines found as the cult inventory of shrines are "nearly always accompanied by an array of broken-off stalagmites or stalactites . . . many of the natural concretions suggest breasts or phalli."[23] Similar groupings of Neolithic female statuettes with amulets in the form of phalli are found in the Mesopotamian lowlands, at Chagar Bazar, and in Southern Iran, at Tepe Guran.[24] Even in the earlier Paleolithic period, the goddess is frequently accompanied by the phallus: "the clay models of a female bison [are] followed by a male placed against a projecting rock in a small chamber at the end of a long narrow passage in the Tuc d'Audoubert. . . . In a recess nearby were pieces of clay in the form of a phallus."[25]

Evidence concerning women as mothers at Çatal Hüyük does not support the claim that motherhood once existed outside patriarchy. The Çatal Hüyük goddess is usually surrounded by men more powerful than herself. She is often shown giving birth to a son, represented even in infancy as a bull, ram, or other horned animal.[26] The son's social status surpasses immediately that of the goddess, as is exemplified by the Çatal Hüyük leopard statue: "the goddesses stand behind the animals, whereas the boy god rides on it."[27] At Çatal Hüyük, as at many Paleolithic and Neolithic sites, the female power of life and death is consistently accompanied by the larger than life image of the male power of "wild life and death":

> As a symbol of male fertility an aurochs bull or a large ram was more impressive than man himself and the power of wild life and death was suitably symbolized in the leopard, the largest and fiercest wild animal in the region; in the destructive ferocity of the boar or in the impressive spectacle of flocks of Griffon vultures.[28]

Women's freedom is to be sought not by reclaiming the forms of motherhood that appear at Çatal Hüyük, but by engaging in an evacuation from motherhood in all its manifestations. That women at Çatal Hüyük were defined as mothers does not mean that such a definition was either natural or necessary. Indeed, without such an all-encompassing definition of woman's being, the goddess of Çatal Hüyük might have existed otherwise. *I separate from the deification and exploitation of women as womb and mother.*29

The Representation

The question remains: "Where do children come from?" If children are, and perhaps always have been, produced by IT, by male sexuality as a man-made social power construct: How does male sexuality appropriate women's biological possibility in order to reproduce ITself?

Motherhood is constituted by male sexuality's use of woman's body to represent ITself to ITself. As such, motherhood is a paradigmatic instance of men's creation of representational thinking and of men's appropriation of the "world" by means of representational thought.

Representational thinking does not mean the production of a picture, copy, or imitation *of* the world. Representational thinking means, rather, to conceive and grasp the world *as* picture.30 In representational thinking, man manipulates, pursues, and entraps the world in order to secure it as picture. Man brings into play his unlimited power for the calculating, planning, and molding of all things.31 By conceiving and grasping the world as picture, he gives the measure and draws up the guidelines for everything that is.32 He creates and determines what is real, and what is not. Not only is the man who has made the picture already in the picture, he is that which he pictures to himself. If man were to acknowledge himself as the picture, he would destroy himself as he who conceives and grasps the world as picture. Only by maintaining a privileged stand outside the picture can man claim to be the creator, and not the object, of the activity of representation. Withdrawn from representation as the represented, he enters into the picture as "the incalculable," "the gigantic."33

The object of representational thought is allowed to be only insofar as it can be overpowered — manipulated, pursued, entrapped — by representational thought. Once conceived and grasped as picture, the object is said to call forth, to provoke, the specific way

in which it is pictured and the activity of picturing as such.34 The object can, indeed, must repeat itself exactly as it has been thought. It must even claim to establish, maintain, and justify its objectification. Its sole "activity" is reproductive: the reiteration and reinforcement of itself as picture.

Reproductive thinking generates, unavoidably and of necessity, an ideology that is reproductive: motherhood. Athena is born from the head of Zeus alone; children are born from the head of man alone.35 Athena springs fully armed from the head of Zeus; a child springs from the head of its father, fully adorned with the markings of patriarchy. Zeus sees his world in his full-grown offspring; man pictures his world in his children who soon will be adults. Even if the child is female, man incorporates the female into his world as picture. The man with the child in his head, with the child as image in his head, represents himself to himself in the child he has made. In contrast, Athena's mother, Metis, cannot be manipulated, pursued, trapped. She cannot be bound, secured, by man's representational thought. Athena's mother, children's mothers, are not.

In representational thought, woman is made pregnable [from *prehendere*, Latin for "to take"], understood in its literal sense as vulnerable to capture, taken. She is compelled to have man's child, to reproduce throughout her world of experience men's thoughts, words, actions. She must reproduce the life of the species, that is, man and his immortality. Captured by representational thinking, woman can never be genuinely pregnant [*pre-gnas*, akin to *gignere*, to produce]: she cannot produce her own life and world. Woman as what-in-men's-eyes-she-seems-to-be36 is invisible, except insofar as her body is used by man to reproduce himself and his world. Motherhood passes through the mind of a man who does not see woman's body as her body. Throughout the motherhood continuum of heterosexual intercourse, pregnancy, and child raising, woman as what-I-am-in-my-own-eyes is not.

Key to the specific mode of representation that defines motherhood, including the articulation of woman's sexuality within the confines of motherhood, is male sexuality's setting of the bounds within which life and death are to be recognized. Man, the representer, assumes a greater-than-human power over life and death. Man, the representer, fixates on life and death as the central defining moments, or parts, of one's life. Man's representation of life and death reduces woman's body to a lifeless instrument, even when her body is a bearer of life and death. The manner in which man represents life and death precludes the experience of the continuity and discontinuity of an individual life, the strength and power of ongoing action in the world, the authentic subjectivity of the woman who is *as* she is.

While man is giving birth to himself, woman dies. *I, bound to the representation of woman as mother, leave that representation behind: evacuation to another way of thinking, to a productive empowering of the female who has been both woman and mother.*

The Mark

The question "Where do children come from?" may be answered in terms of that form of consciousness, the representation, and that form of existence, the mark, by which patriarchal (male) sexuality justifies the appropriation of women's bodies as a resource to reproduce men and the world of men.[37] Interpretation of the representation and the mark portray, when taken together, the social intercourse that is motherhood. A philosophy of evacuation proposes that from which women must collectively remove ourselves: patriarchal thinking, the representation, and patriarchal existence, the mark.

The mark imposed by patriarchy on the bodies of women compels women to exist as mothers. The mark of motherhood inscribes the domination of men into woman's body, making motherhood appear as a natural phenomenon. Yet, motherhood is not a natural phenomenon and mothers do not exist as a natural group. On the contrary, female biological possibilities are first "naturalized" by men as women's specific difference and then claimed as the reason for the existence of motherhood.[38] Through such "naturalization," the female's biological possibil-

ity to give birth is made to appear as the intrinsic cause of woman's place in motherhood and as the origin of woman's social, economic, and political place in the world. The female's biological capacity to bear a child becomes the defining characteristic of all women.

Marking focuses on isolated fragments of the female body.[39] Such fragments, vagina, breasts, etc., are marked with a significance that is presumed to be intrinsic, eternal, and to characterize the whole of the female body. Forms of activity and character traits termed "natural" to women are then deduced from the marking imposed on the body fragments.

The closer a mark is to the body, the more indelibly it is associated with the body and the more the individual as a whole is pursued, hunted, trapped.[40] In the case of woman, the mark has permanence, for woman's entire body, and the body of her world, is marked: MOTHER. The permanence of the mark is the sign of the permanence of the male domination that marks all women as mothers.

The object marked, woman as mother, experiences the mark as pain. The inscription of the mark of motherhood on women's bodies is never without pain — the pain of not "owning" our bodies, the pain of physical injury, the pain of being compelled to never produce a life or world of our own. Pain [from Greek *poinē*, punishment, penalty, payment] is the punishment, the penalty we must pay, for being marked by men as woman and mother. Pain has nothing to do with what we do, that is, our success or failure at being good, well-informed, or willing mothers. Pain is a sign that we, as women, are endangered by men who mark us. *If and when* the pain of the mark is not successfully "naturalized" by men, that is, is not or does not remain imprinted on females as belonging to our nature either physiologically or psychologically, we attempt to evade pain. Our pain breaks through the force of the mark. We do not endure the pain. We do not put up with the mark. We avoid, resist, the mark. We neither need nor desire the mark. We will get out of the mark. The immense amount of pain that marking entails is both an experience that accompanies the mark of motherhood and an experience that can lead to the end of the mark of motherhood.

Among those institutions created by marking, the institution of motherhood is unique: there is no other institution in which so many persons can be destroyed by the mark, and yet, a sufficient supply of persons to be marked remains. In all other forms of war, attrition eventually threatens the supply of persons who can be marked and thereby limits the activity of marking, at least for a time. The mark of motherhood is distinctive in that one of its by-products is the regeneration of more females to be marked as women and mothers.

Outside the social power relationship within which marking occurs, the mark does not exist.[41] Outside patriarchy, the mark of motherhood cannot even be imagined.

Women's daily life within patriarchy is shaped by the mark of motherhood. The genitalia and stomach are among the primary fragments of the female body which are so marked, as is woman's body as a whole.

Cut, carved, and literally burned into women's bodies are both the conditions under which our bodies will be open to the world, i.e., when, where, and to which individual men, and the world to which our bodies will be open, i.e., the world of men. From the mark of virginity to that of genital mutilation, our genitalia are marked: MOTHER.

In patriarchal society, the marking of women's genitalia is indelible, permanently closing us to alternative decisions within patriarchy, as well as to the decision to create other possible and non-patriarchal worlds. On 42nd Street in New York City, movies on excision are featured attractions.[42] Our genitalia are marked to give us "worth": the smaller the artificial passage made by genital mutilation, the greater our "value," the higher our brideprice. Without the operation we cannot get a husband. We are "worthless."[43] Our genitalia are marked to improve heterosexual intercourse: Dr. James Burt, a Dayton, Ohio, gynecologist, "reconstructs" women for "better" intercourse. For a fee of $1,500, he surgically tightens the vaginal opening of female patients to bring the vagina and the clitoris closer together.[44] To make us desire marriage our genitalia are marked: "Only when they [young girls] are ready to procreate is it [the clitoris] re-

moved — and once it is they feel deprived. Their desire then is concentrated in one place only and they promptly get married."[45] To regulate "madness" our genitalia are marked: "Circumcision, which . . . is confined to the clitoris, sets a barrier to the mad life of the girls," to the "lasciviousness" of eight-year-old females.[46] Marking is used as "social protection" against teenage heterosexual intercourse and pregnancy: "Why should not the United States and Europe be investigating the possibilities of hygienic experimentation with female circumcision as a social safeguard" from "teen sex" and "teen parenthood."[47] Marking as a "social safeguard" against rape: "infibulation is necessary to protect women from being raped."[48] Or, to "protect" the family.[49] One hundred percent of the female population of Somalia, Sudan, and Dijbouti,[50] sixty-five million women in those areas of Africa from which such estimates are available,[51] and increasing numbers of females in France, Norway, and Australia experience genital mutilation as the mark of motherhood.[52] Pain, illness, and death accompany the mark that initiates us into motherhood.[53]

The mark of motherhood imprints on us patriarchal (male) sexuality. It cuts, carves, and literally burns into our bodies men's "needs," men's "desires":

> A virgin body . . . what he alone is to take and to penetrate seems to be in truth created by man. And more, one of the ends sought by all desire is the using up of the desired object, which implies its destruction.[54]

From the idea of virginity to the act of genital mutilation, the mark of motherhood controls where we may walk in the world of men, and that we must walk only in the world of men.

Stamped, firmly imprinted on women's bodies, is the emblem that our bodies have been opened to the world of men: the shape of the pregnant woman's stomach. From conception to abortion, acts which are biologically different and yet symbolically the same, our stomachs are marked: MOTHER.

In present-day patriarchal society, the marking impressed on woman's stomach is man's proof of his virility, that he can reproduce himself. When the mark remains on women's stomachs from conception to the birth of an infant, male virility not only can, but does, reproduce itself. In contrast, when the mark remains imprinted on our stomachs from conception to the abortion of a fetus, male virility can, but does not — yet — reproduce itself. Either the time is judged as not right — yet, or the right time has passed by — already. When abortion is permitted in patriarchy, either officially or unofficially, there need not be an immediate and direct link between conception and the birth of an infant. There must, however, be an indirect link between male virility which can reproduce itself and male virility which does reproduce itself. The right time must eventually be found such that man both can and does reproduce himself, either by means of biological children or through the material goods and ideas of patriarchy. Indeed, within patriarchy the fact that abortion may sometimes be permitted does not make abortion a genuinely free choice, for women have no alternative but abortion if we are already impregnated and do not want to reproduce. Nor does the right to abortion make motherhood voluntary, for a woman in patriarchy cannot abort, or do away with, the mark of motherhood. The right to abortion in patriarchy cannot, in principle, recognize that women may choose abortion because we will not reproduce men and the world of men, because we will not be mothers.

The woman who does not remove the mark from her stomach, who does not have an abortion, may be killed: on the West Bank one such Arab woman a week is found "poisoned or burned to death and the murder is made to look accidental."[55] Women who survive an initial decision to not remove the mark from our stomachs, to not have an abortion, in defiance of the traditions of male virility, may be persecuted as nonvirgins and unmarried mothers.[56] Yet, the women who do remove the mark from our stomachs, who abort, may also die. Five thousand women a year are estimated to die in Spain and Portugal alone as a result of complications arising from illegal abortions.[57] In Latin America, abortion causes twenty percent to fifty percent of all maternal deaths.[58] . . . A woman undergoing a properly performed abortion has six times less risk of death from complications than a woman having a child.[59] In childbirth our bodies as a whole are stamped with the mark of pain, terror, and possible death.

To speak of birth without violence is to ignore the violence of childbirth.[60] The most frequent cause of death of women is childbirth.[61]

. . .

Already, as female children, women as a whole are marked — "undesirable." College students in the United States, for instance, favor what amounts to a decrease in female births, with the overall ratio of girls to boys desired designated at 100:116.[62] In addition, "from sixty-six to ninety-two percent of men have been found to want an only child to be a boy . . . , and from sixty-two to eighty percent prefer a first child to be a boy," a chilling thought as the United States, like Western Europe, moves toward zero growth.

As female fetuses, women as a whole are stamped "to be aborted." A recent Chinese report, for example, shows that when sex determination tests were performed on one hundred fetuses for the sole purpose of determining the fetuses' gender, twenty-nine of the forty-six female fetuses, but only one of the fifty-three male fetuses, were aborted.[63]

As female infants, women as a whole are marked "dead." Men, rather than regulate men and men's use of women, claim that because there is not enough food, resources, etc., "female fertility" must be controlled by the elimination of women.[64] From antiquity to the present, infanticide has been, largely and for the most part, femicide.[65]

Women as mothers are marked: dead. Man the marker continues with himself, his sons, his mark.

The Society of Mothers

Man remains with his representation and his mark. Women need not remain. The representation and the mark, and not existing females, are integral to motherhood. If and when the representation and the mark of motherhood can be affixed to something other than the female body, women may not exist at all.

The society of mothers, comprised of all women within motherhood, is dangerous to all its members.[66] The society of mothers continues, by definition, the ideology and institution of motherhood as oppressive to women. The motherhood lived out by the society of mothers is the annihilation of women.

The forms of annihilation by which the society of mothers is endangered are multiple. Whenever motherhood involves men's representation and marking of females, motherhood entails the death of a world in which women are free, and motherhood may entail the physical death and non-existence of women as mothers and as female infants. In the contemporary ideology and institution of motherhood, women's annihilation may also be brought about when men represent and mark objects from the domain of the sciences and technology of reproduction to reproduce men and the world of men, such that the class, women as mothers, has no further use function, and thus, need no longer exist. The specifically contemporary manifestation of motherhood, however, shows clearly that women are not necessary to motherhood. Patriarchal men must represent and mark something as MOTHER, but that which is so designated need not be women.

In a patriarchal context, even the production of females by parthenogenesis need not alter the social and historical circumstances of the society of mothers into which such females would be born.[67] Men may or may not continue to impose patriarchal (male) sexuality on women. Regardless of whether men relate to women in explicitly sexual modes, women may still be kept in a service function as the society of mothers.

Members of the society of mothers who reproduce the material goods and ideas of patriarchal culture may manifest the ideology and institution of motherhood in differing ways. Despite such differences, the women remain mothers. The limitation of the society of mothers to those who reproduce only the biological children of men is to ignore that men use women's bodies in a multitude of ways to reproduce patriarchal life. Women who do not give birth to biological children are still involved in the "regeneration" of men, in virtue of our work, unpaid and paid, to continue the products, both ideal and material of motherhood.

The representation and mark of motherhood claim not just the surface, but the whole of women,

such that the society of mothers not only reproduces, but often defends, the patriarchal world of men: "Confined to their cities the mothers were no longer separate, free, complete individuals and they fused into an anonymous collective consciousness."[68] So strong is the force of the representation and mark that the society of mothers often maintains its own repetition.

In the production of the son for the father, in the production of goods for the father, for the benefit of the son, we are not our bodies, we are not ourselves. A means to men's ends, never an end in ourselves, we are selfless, worldless, annihilated. *The experience of our servitude takes seriously our danger and holds, firmly and strongly, to the conviction that we must get out of motherhood.*

Priorities and Alternatives

To show how motherhood, in its many forms, is dangerous to women is also to suggest how women may get out of motherhood. *Central to a philosophy of evacuation from motherhood is the primacy of women's daily lives and the power of our possible, and sometimes actual, collective actions.* In breaking free from motherhood, I no longer focus on birth and death as the two most important moments of my life. I give priority to my life and my world. I — my activities, body, sexuality — am articulated by my actions and choices which, apart from patriarchy, may be made in the openness of freedom. New modes of thinking and existing emerge. I, as an individual female, and we, as the community of all females, lay claim to our freely chosen subjectivities, to the priorities and alternatives we create as our own.

The evacuation from motherhood does not simply seek to alter motherhood as it exists currently. Its focus is not specifically the development of alternative means of intercourse, pregnancy, or child care.[69] Women who use artificial insemination and whose children have no known father and women who live as lesbian mothers clearly challenge, but need not break with, the ideology and institution of motherhood. Each of these alternatives is significant for women's survival within patriarchy, but none is sufficient for women's effective survival, that is, for the creation of the self-chosen, non-patriarchal, existence of all women.

A precondition for women's effective survival may be established, instead, by a female's power to not have children. A decision not to have children may be made, not because a female's biological capacity causes the ideology of motherhood, but because:

> To not have children opens a time-space for the priority of claiming my life and world as my own and for the creative development of radically new alternatives.

> The biology from which a child is born does not determine or control the course of that child's life. Females and males, younger and older, create the shapes of our lives through our actions.

> Women who wish to be with younger females or males can do so collectively, with others of similar interests, or individually.

At present, and for several thousands of years past, women have conceived, borne, and raised multitudes of children without any change in the conditions of our lives as women. In the case that all females were to decide not to have children for the next twenty years, the possibilities for developing new modes of thought and existence would be almost unimaginable.

The necessary condition for women's evacuation from motherhood is the claiming of our bodies as a source. Our bodies are not resources to be used by men to reproduce men and the world of men while, at the same time, giving death to ourselves. If necessary, women must bear arms, but not children, to protect our bodies from invasion by men. For our effective survival, women's repetitive reproduction of patriarchy must be replaced by the creative production of ourselves. In particular, the areas of food, literacy, and energy sources and supplies for women must be examined as crucial to claiming our bodies as a source.

Women's hunger is one of the specific conditions affecting the possibility for men's continuing success in representing and marking women as mothers. In the current patriarchal economy, women are the majority of the world's farmers, but women, on a global basis, do not have access to sufficient food to feed ourselves.[70] In many areas where malnutrition is prevalent, up to half the cultivated acreage is growing crops for export to those who can afford them, rather than food stuffs for those who need them. Nor do women have access to the money necessary to purchase food: women living in poverty constitute twelve percent of the total, world-wide, female population and seventy-five percent of all people living in poverty.[71]

Women's literacy is the second specific condition that enhances the possibility for men's continuing success in maintaining the ideology and institution of women as mothers. Women have insufficient access to the basics of literacy, that is, reading, writing, and simple arithmetic. Women are two-thirds of the illiterate people of the world.[72] In almost all countries, "girls already begin school in fewer numbers than boys; on the average, the difference even at the start of school is ten to twenty percent. By the time higher education is reached, the ratio between boys and girls is at least two to one, but in many cases more."[73] The education gap between men and women is growing throughout the developing world.[74] Even in industrialized societies, women have almost no access to determining which areas of research are the most urgent, or what constitutes an education.

Energy sources and supplies for women are a third area that undermines women's endeavors to break free of motherhood. In many villages in Africa and Asia, women work about three hours per day more than men because women are expected to gather the food, water, and fuel necessary for survival. Technological information on alternative means of energy is usually not made available to these women, any more than it is to most women in industrialized countries. In all societies, women's non-control of energy sources and supplies necessary to our survival keeps us in subordination to men.

Female-defined access to food, education, and energy forms a necessary condition for women's collective evacuation from motherhood in that such access claims as a source the whole of our bodies and world. To get out of the reproduction of motherhood, females of all ages must work together to establish alternatives that express and fulfill our current needs and desires. As females who engage in evacuation from motherhood, we shape the whole of ourselves and our world in the present of our own lifetimes.

Notes

1. I would like to thank Julie Murphy for suggesting the phrase, "a philosophy of evacuation."
2. Simone de Beauvoir, *The Second Sex,* trans. H. M. Parshley (New York: Vintage, 1974), p. 72.
3. de Beauvoir, "Talking to de Beauvoir," *Spare Rib* (March, 1977), p. 2.
4. Shulamith Firestone, *The Dialectic of Sex* (New York: Bantam, 1971), p. 72.
5. Ti-Grace Atkinson, *Amazon Odyssey* (New York: Links Books, 1974), p. 1.
6. Monique Wittig and Sande Zeig, *Brouillon pour un dictionnaire des amantes* (Paris: Grasset, 1976), p. 94; Wittig, "One is not born a Woman," *Feminist Issues,* vol. 1, no. 2 (Winter, 1981), p. 1.
7. de Beauvoir, "Talking to de Beauvoir," p. 2.
8. Atkinson, "Interview with Ti-Grace Atkinson," *Off Our Backs,* vol. 9, no. 11 (December, 1973), p. 3.
9. Andrea Dworkin, *Pornography: Men Possessing Women* (New York: Perigree, 1981), p. 222.
10. Wittig, "Paradigm," *Homosexualities and French Literature,* eds. George Stambolian and Elaine Marks (Ithaca: Cornell University Press, 1979), pp. 118, 119.
11. *WIN News,* vol. 7, no. 4 (1981), p. 68. Citation from the Soviet Women's Committee, "Soviet Women's Committee" booklet.
12. A more "sophisticated" appeal to science is misleading for similar reasons. Feminist biologists are currently questioning accounts of egg and sperm production, for instance, in an attempt to dislodge sexist assumptions with respect to their production and union.
13. *WIN News,* vol. 6, no. 2 (1980), p. 76. U.S. Department of Labor, "Facts About Women Heads of Households and Heads of Families."
14. Catherine MacKinnon, *Sexual Harassment of Working Women* (New Haven: Yale University Press, 1979), p. 221.
15. Iion Wieder, "Accouche!" *questions féministes* no. 5 (February, 1979), pp. 53–72.
16. *The Oxford English Dictionary* (Oxford: Clarendon Press, 1933), p. 236.
17. de Beauvoir, *The Second Sex,* p. 72.
18. Ranya Rapp, "Women, Religion and Archaic Civilizations: An Introduction" *Feminist Studies,* vol. 4, no. 3 (October, 1978), p. 1.

19. Anne Barstow, "The Neolithic Goddess at Çatal Hüyük," *Feminist Studies,* vol. 4, no. 3 (October, 1978), p. 12.
20. James Mellart, *The Archaeology of Ancient Turkey* (London: Bodley Head, 1978), p. 20; E. O. James, *The Cult of the Mother Goddess* (London: Thames & Hudson, 1958), pp. 22.
21. James, *The Cult of the Mother Goddess,* p. 23.
22. Mellart, *The Neolithic Near East* (London: Thames & Hudson, 1975), p. 99.
23. Ibid., p. 107.
24. Ibid., p. 167.
25. James, *op. cit.,* pp. 17, 18.
26. Mellart, *Çatal Hüyük* (New York: McGraw-Hill, 1967), p. 183; Mellart, *The Archaeology of Ancient Turkey,* p. 20.
27. Ibid., p. 142.
28. Mellart, *Çatal Hüyük,* p. 181.
29. Catherine Deudon, "Le Colonialism hétéro," *Actuel,* no. 38 (1974), p. 15.
30. Martin Heidegger, "The Age of the World Picture," *The Question of Technology,* trans. William Lovitt (New York: Harper & Row, 1977), pp. 129–130.
31. Ibid., p. 135.
32. Ibid., p. 134.
33. Ibid., p. 135.
34. Dworkin, *Pornography,* pp. 108, 109.
35. Jane Harrison, *Prolegomena to the Study of Greek Religion,* 3rd ed. (Cambridge: Cambridge University Press, 1922), pp. 302, 303.
36. de Beauvoir, *The Second Sex,* p. 155.
37. Colette Guillaumin, "Race et Nature: Système des marques. Idée de groupe naturel et rapports sociaux," *Pluriel,* no. 11 (1977), pp. 39–55. Guillaumin develops the concept of the mark to analyze racial oppression.
38. Ibid., pp. 48, 54, 55.
39. Ibid., p. 49.
40. Ibid., p. 45.
41. Ibid., p. 55.
42. Fran Hosken, "The Case Histories: The Western World," *The Hosken Report,* 2d rev. ed. (Lexington, Massachusetts, 1979), p. 11.
43. Ibid., "Medical Facts and Summary," p. 2.
44. Ibid., "Case Histories," p. 9.
45. Ibid., "The Reasons Given," p. 5.
46. Ibid., p. 6.
47. *WIN News,* vol. 7, no. 2 (1981), p. 39. Citation from *The New National Black Monitor,* (October, 1980).

48. Hosken, "Forward," *The Hosken Report,* p. 3.

49. Ibid.

50. *WIN News,* vol. 6, no. 2 (1980), p. 30. From Edna Adan Ismail, *Genital Operations: Their Physical and Mental Effects and Complications.*

51. Hosken, "Medical Facts and Summary," *The Hosken Report,* p. 6.

52. *WIN News,* vol. 6, no. 4 (1980), p. 45. From the New South Wales Humanist Society, "Report on Genital Mutilation from Australia."

53. Hosken, "The Reasons Given," *The Hosken Report,* p. 4.

54. *WIN News,* vol. 7, no. 4 (1981), p. 34. Report by Dr. Abu Hassan Abu in "Workshop on Eradicating Female Circumcision in the Sudan."

55. *WIN News,* vol. 7, no. 2 (1981). From *Journal-American* (January 3, 1981).

56. *International Tribunal on Crimes Against Women,* eds. Diana Russell and Nicole Van de Ven (California: Les Femmes, 1976), pp. 31–33.

57. *WIN News,* vol. 7, no. 3 (1981), p. 22. From AGENOR, "Abortion: The Facts/European Survey."

58. *WIN News,* vol. 7, no. 4 (1981), p. 17. From World Health Organization, "Towards a Better Future: Maternal and Child Health."

59. *WIN News,* vol. 7, no. 3 (1981), p. 22. From AGENOR, "Abortion: The Facts/European Survey."

60. Wieder, *op. cit.,* p. 69.

61. *WIN News,* vol. 7, no. 4 (1981), p. 24; vol. 7, no. 3 (1981), p. 16. From The Population Institute, *International Dateline.*

62. Jalna Hammer, "Sex Predetermination, Artificial Insemination and the Maintenance of Male-Dominated Culture," *Women, Health, and Reproduction,* ed. Helen Roberts (London: Routledge & Kegan Paul, 1981), pp. 167, 168.

63. Ibid., p. 176.

64. Jalna Hammer and Pat Allen, "La Science de la reproduction — solution finale?" *questions féministes,* vol. 5 (February, 1979), p. 39.

65. Elizabeth Fisher, *Woman's Creation* (New York: Doubleday, 1980), p. 335.

66. Hammar and Allen, *op. cit.,* p. 39.

67. Wittig and Zeig, *Lesbian Peoples: Material for a Dictionary* (New York: Doubleday, 1980), p. 76.

68. Julie Murphy, personal communication, December, 1981.

69. *WIN News,* vol. 7, no. 4 (1981), pp. 23, 24. From The Population Institute, *International Dateline.* See Jeffner Allen, "Women and Food: Feeding Ourselves," *The Journal of Social Philosophy,* 1984, pp. 34–41.

70. *WIN News,* vol. 7, no. 4 (1981), p. 73. From the National Commission on Working Mothers, "Women at Work: News about the 80%."

71. Hosken, "Editorial," *WIN News,* vol. 7, no. 2 (1981), p. 1.

72. *WIN News,* vol. 7, no. 1 (1981), p. 21. From World Bank Headquarters, Education: A World Bank Sector Policy Paper.

73. Hosken, "Editorial," *WIN News,* vol. 6, no. 3 (1980), p. 1.

74. *WIN News,* vol. 7, no. 4 (1981), p. 6. From U.N. Conference on New and Renewable Sources of Energy, "Conference Report."

THE CASE OF AMERICAN CYANAMID

Mary Gibson

Mary Gibson argues that all people have a reproductive right—the right to make one's own decisions about whether and when to have children and to carry out these decisions. This has implications for the workplace: women should not be discriminated against merely because they are of child-bearing age. (Source: From Worker's Rights *by Mary Gibson. Copyright © 1983 by Mary Gibson. Reprinted by permission of Rowman & Littlefield.)*

Workers' rights must be examined in terms of the concrete realities of the everyday lives of real human beings. The following newspaper article describes the choice that was thrust upon women workers in West Virginia: to be sterilized or to lose their jobs. This story raises compelling issues concerning the rights of workers: the right of workers to a safe and healthful workplace, reproductive rights, privacy, paternalism, protective policies, discrimination. These are the issues that will be explored in this chapter.

> WILLOW ISLAND, W. Va. — The giant American Cyanamid Corp. has what could be described only as a corporate public relations nightmare on its hands here.
>
> What began a year ago as a drive, according to the chemical conglomerate's spokesmen, to shift its female employees out of positions at the company's plant here where exposure to lead could harm their unborn children has backfired into charges by five of the women that they had to get themselves surgically sterilized to hang onto their jobs.
>
> The women, who range in age from 26 to 43, said in interviews that they reluctantly allowed themselves to be sterilized at a local hospital only after they were pressured to get the operations by American Cyanamid officials at the company's Ohio River chemical complex.
>
> Two other women who did not have operations were transferred out of the plant's pigment division into lesser-paying janitor's jobs in October.
>
> The entire 17-women component of the company's production force here has sought advice on what to do next from a local lawyer and their union, the Oil, Chemical and Atomic Workers, has vowed to make their case a national issue.
>
> "These women were forced to make a Draconian choice that nobody should have to make," said Anthony Mazzocchi, the union's vice president. "It's an outrageous situation and American Cyanamid is not the only company that is trying to force women out of the workplace rather than clean it up," said Mazzocchi. "Women who have been able to enter these jobs as a result of their own struggle are now being confronted with the dismal choice of relinquishing their right to have children or their jobs."
>
> Spokesmen for the chemical company emphatically denied that American Cyanamid was responsible for the sterilization of the women. They said the policy was aimed solely at protecting unborn children.
>
> "Our doctor met with all of the women in September when our policy was announced," said a spokesman here. "At that time we said that we discourage sterilization and that if it was done we did not sanction it."
>
> A spokesman at the firm's corporate headquarters in Wayne, N.J., said, "from a moral point of view the company feels it is on the side of the angels in this thing." . . .
>
> Other firms, such as General Motors, reportedly have refused to assign women to jobs with lead exposure and the policy has drawn fire from women's groups. The Equal Employment Opportunity Commission has also indicated that such blanket exclusionary policies could violate federal civil rights laws. In 1977, American Cyanamid tried to bar women from jobs with harmful chemicals at its Linden, N.J., plant but the company dropped its policy after opposition from the United Steelworkers.
>
> In the American Cyanamid situation here, however, the company's spokesmen claim the case against lead is so well documented that they decided to restrict all women workers under 50 with childbearing capacity to two sections of the plant where no lead is used.

. . . Women in the plant said they were told by company officials at the time that the policy eventually would be expanded to cover all but the two non-lead departments "within a few months."

Last January, the women were told during two meetings with plant officials in Willow Island that some of the chemicals at the plant and lead were potentially dangerous to pregnant women and that their jobs would be shifted.

"They told us we could go to the janitorial department but that if there weren't enough jobs there some of us might have to leave," said Betty Moler, one of the women who was sterilized. Janitorial department workers make less money and have less chance for overtime, she said.

Moler and the other women interviewed said the two departments left open to the women for transfer out of the janitorial department were both staffed with men with seniority over them and with no openings. All the women said that company officials pressured them directly or indirectly to accept sterilization.

In an interview at her home in Belmont near here Moler, who is 27 and has one son, said she told company officials her husband already had had a vasectomy. She was told, she said, that did not matter.

Another of the women, Lola Rymer, 43, said they offered to sign papers so the company would not be held liable for any lead exposure problems. That was also rejected, she said.

The women all said they went ahead with the operations because of pressure from company officials and because they stood to lose several thousand dollars in overtime pay if they shifted jobs.

The company's lead policy apparently contradicts federal regulations on the metal which were issued in October by the Occupational Safety and Health Administration.

The new regulations cut the allowable level of airborne lead in the workplace to 50 micrograms per cubic meter of air from the former 200 microgram level. In addition, the regulations set a 30 microgram "action level" at which a company must initiate special monitoring. The regulations warn of possible neurological damage to a fetus at lead levels above 30 micrograms and to all adults at over a 50 microgram reading.

The new regulations were strongly opposed by the lead industry, including American Cyanamid.

Supposedly, if the regulations are followed there should be no harm to a fetus. "Given the data in this record," the regulations state, "OSHA believes there is no basis whatsoever for the claim that women of childbearing age should be excluded from the workplace in order to protect the fetus."

American Cyanamid declined requests from The Washington Post to be allowed to see the company's measurements of lead dust in the air of the pigment section, where paint is mixed. The company also refused to allow photographs of the area. [Washington Post–L.A. Times News Service, printed in Home News, New Brunswick, N.J. January 3, 1979.]

Lead poisoning was first recognized as an occupational disease when lead miners suffered from it in ancient times (Stellman, 1977, 178). There are two kinds of lead, inorganic and organic (or tetraethyl) lead. Both are highly toxic, though their effects are somewhat different.

Inorganic lead is typically found in pigments and in grinding operations. It enters the body mainly through inhalation, and is stored in the bones, where it affects the blood-forming tissue in the bone marrow. Chronic exposure results in insomnia, fatigue, constipation, anemia, colic, neuritis, tremors, headache, loss of appetite, weakness, double vision, brain damage (sometimes severe enough to cause permanent retardation in children), high blood pressure and kidney failure.

Organic lead is found mainly in leaded gasoline. It is readily absorbed through the skin; its other main route of entry is inhalation. It is stored in the brain, resulting in mental disturbance, insomnia, anxiety, and (from acute exposure) delirium and death.

. . .

Reproductive effects of lead exposure include high rates of miscarriage and stillbirth (both for women directly exposed and for wives of exposed men), reducing male libido and fertility (prolonged exposure can result in atrophy of testes), and sperm abnormalities. Lead is known to be capable of crossing the placental barrier and entering fetal blood and tissue, and animal tests suggest that it is teratogenic (capable of causing birth defects as a result of such fetal exposure). There is also evidence of genetic damage, making it a suspected mutagen. Mutagens, of course, can act through both males and females.

. . .

Moreover, even if one wanted to include consideration of these costs, among the most important of them are noneconomic ones (pain, suffering, loss of life, bereavement), and there is no appropriate way of comparing them with the financial costs of cleaning up the workplace. Controversy over the role of economic feasibility or cost-benefit studies is one of many ongoing battles in the efforts of the Occupational Safety and Health Administration (OSHA) to carry out the mandate of the OSH Act.[1]

While the legal right to a safe and healthful workplace may be subject to various interpretations and rulings based on technicalities, loopholes, enforcement difficulties, claims of ruinous effects on industry, etc., the right that the law seems clearly intended to recognize and protect is the right not to be exposed to unnecessary risks to life, safety or health for the sake of greater convenience or profit for the employer—and not to be forced to choose between accepting the risks and forfeiting the job.

In view of the harmful effects of lead on exposed adults (diminished health, in the language of the OSH Act) and of its known and suspected reproductive effects on both men and women (functional capacity), it seems clear that the exclusion of fertile women from high lead exposure jobs involves, in one way or another, violation of the rights of all of the workers involved. Workers remaining on the job face health and reproductive risks that violate their rights under the OSH Act; the women who are sterilized to keep their jobs are forced to accept diminished functional capacity as a condition of employment, while the health risks to themselves remain substantially as before. And the women excluded from the jobs have their rights against sex discrimination, as provided by Title VII of the Civil Rights Act and Executive Order No. 11246, violated. (Title VII of the Civil Rights Act of 1964, as amended by the Equal Employment Opportunity Act of 1972, provides that no one shall be discriminated against on the basis of sex, race, color, or national origin in the area of employment. Executive Order No. 11246 forbids discrimination in employment by the federal government and by federal government contractors.)

Let us look briefly now at the reproductive and privacy rights involved in this case. Reproductive rights are not yet generally spelled out in law in the United States. The legal status of abortion has been treated as a matter of the right of privacy, specifically in the relation between a woman and her physician. More generally one would expect reproductive rights and privacy rights to overlap extensively, especially in a society where reproductive decisions and activities are considered among the most personal and private aspects of life, and are thought to be at the core of what is called the private sphere. It seems to me unlikely that reproductive rights can be entirely reduced to or subsumed under privacy rights. Still, persons who may be skeptical about reproductive rights could object to the Cyanamid policy on privacy grounds. The Department of Health, Education and Welfare (now the Department of Health and Human Services) has, as of March 8, 1979, regulations governing federal financial participation in sterilization programs which establish certain rights and protections against involuntary sterilization in federally funded programs. The application of these regulations is, of course, limited, but they may be seen as expressing recognition of certain reproductive rights. Thus, while the existence of reproductive rights seems to be fairly widely acknowledged today, there is no official or widely recognized statement, definition or interpretation of those rights. For present purposes, let me suggest that reproductive rights involve, among other things, the right to make one's own decisions about whether and when to have children and at what risk (there are always some risks), and about how best to carry out those decisions—whether by use of contraceptives and if so by which method, or by sterilization and if so of which partner and by which method, whether to abort an unplanned pregnancy or one involving special risks to mother or child, etc. If this is even approximately correct, it seems clear that American Cyanamid's policy violated the reproductive rights of the sterilized women, and I suggest it did so in an area where reproductive and privacy rights overlap, thus violating their rights to privacy as well.

Two objections are likely to arise. First, it may be objected that the company was only doing the responsible thing—that it would be irresponsible to allow the women to continue working at those jobs when they might become pregnant (recall the company spokesman's statement that, "from a moral point of view the company feels it is on the side of the angels in this thing"). Second, it may be objected that the women were not deprived of the right to make their own decisions: they could have chosen to give up their jobs.

Let us consider the first objection. Employers offer the following arguments for the claim that exclusion of fertile women from certain jobs is justified: a woman may become pregnant even if she doesn't intend to; pregnancy is often not discovered for several weeks and the early weeks of pregnancy are the period of greatest fetal susceptibility to teratogens; exposure levels safe for adults may still be dangerous to fetuses; thus the morally responsible policy is to protect the potential offspring. This is best achieved by the exclusion of fertile women because reduction of exposure levels sufficient to ensure safety of the fetus is often economically or technologically unfeasible; and finally, exclusion affects negligible numbers of women, since few are employed in the industries in question. (*Women's Occupational Health Resource Center News*, 1979; Lehmann, undated, 4–5)

This objection does not deny that the policy restricts reproductive freedom, rather it claims that under the circumstances such restriction is justified.

In response to this claim, it is worth noting that our society generally leaves to the individual parents decisions about risks to potential children. As Joan Bertin of the American Civil Liberties Union notes:

> Women workers are being required to make this agonizing decision even where the "risk" associated with their employment is wholly speculative or less, for example, than that posed by drinking coffee or alcoholic beverages or smoking cigarettes. The risk they face is surely less than that faced daily by couples with known genetic or other characteristics which increase the chance that their children may be born with Down's Syndrome, hemophilia, Tay-Sachs disease, sickle cell disease, Huntington's Chorea, or similar condition. Yet in all these situations, it is the right of the parents to choose. Why should it be different for women workers? [Bertin, 1982, 216]

Consistency seems to require that the right to make one's own reproductive choices be treated the same in the workplace as it is elsewhere in our society—or that a justification be given for differential treatment.

In any event, whether or not our first objector claims that the sterilization-or-exclusion policy constitutes (1) a (justified) violation, or (2) no violation of reproductive rights will depend on whether he or she holds (1) that rights that are overridden are (justifiably) violated, or (2) that to say that an act or policy violates a right carries with it the claim that the act or policy is unjustified, as well as on (3) whether she or he holds that there are reproductive rights of the sort proposed above. These are not questions we need to—or can—settle here.

The justifiability of the sterilization-or-exclusion policy, then, may depend, entirely or to some degree, on whether or not the relevant reproductive rights exist and on their relative weight vis-a-vis the considerations raised in favor of the policy. In this case, the objector cannot show conclusively that the policy is justified without settling these difficult and controversial matters. We might, however, be able to decide, on other grounds, that the policy is unjustified or that its justification is at best doubtful. In assessing whether the policy ought to be adopted, all things considered, the possibility that it would violate reproductive rights could, then, count as an additional consideration against it.

Let us turn now to the second objection—that the women were not deprived of the right to make their own decisions because they could have chosen to give up their jobs rather than be sterilized. This objection raises important and difficult questions about the relative freedom or coerciveness of various choices and choice situations. Some of these questions arise in relation to choices concerning terms and conditions of employment in general, and thus connect directly with the question of whether the employment contract is ever the result of a voluntary agreement between equal parties in a free and open market.... In relation to the particular case at hand, it might be argued, in support of the claim that the women's reproductive rights were violated, that there is a fairly strong similarity between this case and cases where women are told they must "consent" to be sterilized or lose their eligibility for welfare and/or medicaid benefits. This practice is now widely condemned as sterilization abuse and a clear violation of reproductive rights. It is expressly prohibited in the recently adopted Health and Human Services (H & HS) regulations for federally funded sterilization programs mentioned above. In such cases, this argument goes, consent is not genuine, even though the person has chosen between two (unattractive) alternatives.

But, our objector may respond, a person can be forced to choose among unattractive alternatives by circumstances that are beyond anyone's control, and it does not seem correct to say that consent is always lacking in such cases. For example, following an accident, if a person forced to choose between having a leg amputated and almost certain death decides on the amputation, it is appropriate to say he or she was forced to choose amputation, or even that he or she had no choice. But this surely does not imply that she or he did not genuinely consent to the operation.

The point is well taken. This suggests that we must distinguish between being *forced* and being *coerced.* The genuineness of consent is undermined by coercion but not (at least not always) by force-of-circumstances. The kinds of sterilization abuse prohibited by H & HS are objectionable because they are coercive. Was the Cyanamid policy coercive?

Several different accounts of coercion have been offered by philosophers over the past dozen or so years, so the answer to this question is likely to be controversial.[2] It does seem clear, however, that coerciveness is often a matter of degree. To the degree, then, that the company coerced the women by requiring them to choose between their jobs and their fertility, to that degree their reproductive rights were violated. To that degree the women who were sterilized were sterilized without their genuine consent. And to that degree the policy may be seen as sterilization abuse.

That degree seems to me to be substantial, especially in view of the alternative that could have been made available to them and was not: that the dangers

be fully and accurately presented to them, steps be taken to minimize exposure of all workers as far as possible, remaining exposure levels be carefully monitored and the workers informed of them, and then the women decide for themselves whether to remain in the division, and if so, whether to have themselves sterilized.

In addition, to the extent that coercion involves *preventing* someone from having a preferred alternative, it seems worth noting that the distinction between *preventing* someone's having such an alternative and *not helping* someone to have it is not always clear.[3] Where this is the case, the distinction between being coerced and being forced by circumstances will also be blurred. This is so especially where patterns of action and inaction of many persons acting more or less independently result in the unavailability of the preferred alternative. To a large extent these patterns are themselves the results, not necessarily intended, of other human decisions and actions which create and maintain the framework of social institutions, expectations, and attitudes within which the previously mentioned actions and inactions occur. Whether or not we decide to say that situations in which persons are forced to choose among alternatives restricted by such patterns of action and inaction are coercive, let us say that a person in such a situation is at least less free than she or he might be. And where human action could alter the patterns and/or frameworks so that the preferred alternative(s) could be made available, such a person is unnecessarily unfree. Clearly both of these — freedom or lack of it and necessity or lack of it — will be matters of degree.[4] Nevertheless, where the degrees are high enough, we may want to say that persons ought not to be unnecessarily unfree in certain ways. And, since freedom is a good, this would be a reason for acting to provide the preferred alternative even independently of whether not providing it violated rights.

Let us turn now to discussion of the interrelated issues of protective policies, paternalism and discrimination.

To bring out some of the ways in which these issues are, or may be related, we can set forth the following general questions, which it will be useful to keep in mind during the course of the discussion, though it is doubtful that any of them will be conclusively answered.

1. When, if ever, are protective policies paternalistic?

2. When, if ever, are protective policies discriminatory?

3. When, if ever, are protective policies protective?

4. How are the answers to 1–3 related to each other?

The history of protectionism, that is of special labor laws or policies applying only to women, purportedly to protect them from certain job hazards, is complex and paradoxical. Male workers sometimes supported "protective" policies in order to prevent women from entering certain occupations, competing for "men's" jobs, and depressing wages. That the restricted kinds of jobs available to women forced them to accept lower wages, and that men often did not recruit or even admit women into their unions so that they could command higher wages, made this a vicious cycle. Thus, some women opposed all protective policies as mere rationalizations for discrimination. Yet conditions were so bad that some women accepted the restrictions, welcoming whatever relief they could get. And protective legislation, defended on sexist and discriminatory grounds, has in several instances paved the way for significant improvements in conditions for all workers. One example is the ten-hour day.[5]

In general, in response to question 2 above, it seems to me that protective policies are discriminatory and unjustifiable. If job conditions are such that women should be protected from them, then men should be protected as well. Whether there are any exceptions to this general rule is a more difficult question, one to which we shall return specifically in connection with exclusionary policies.

Let us turn now to paternalism. For purposes of this discussion, we shall adopt what has come to be the standard philosophical conception of paternalism, i.e., what John Stuart Mill argues against in *On Liberty* and Gerald Dworkin discusses in his essay, "Paternalism." Later on we shall explore a somewhat different way of thinking about paternalism, but for now let us proceed on the basis of Dworkin's characterization: "By paternalism I shall understand roughly the interference with a person's liberty of action justified by reasons referring exclusively to the welfare, good, happiness, needs, interests or values of the person being coerced" (G. Dworkin, 1971, 108).

A note of clarification: The word "justify" may be used in two different ways. On one usage, to say that an act or policy is justified by certain reasons is to say that an act or policy is, in fact, justified. On another usage, to say that an act or policy is justified (by an agent) by reference to certain reasons does not imply that those reasons actually suffice to justify the act or policy in question. The reasons are offered as justification, but the attempted justification may or may not succeed. It seems that we must understand Dworkin, in the passage just quoted, to be using the term in the latter way. For if it is taken in the former way, there could be no such thing as *un*justified paternalism, and this clearly is not his intention.

Without pausing to discuss the many substantive difficulties involved, let me suggest for now that paternalism, in Dworkin's sense, may be (actually) justified in some cases where it is necessary to preserve or expand the freedom or autonomy of the individual in question. Dworkin makes a similar suggestion and proposes some guidelines intended to place the burden of proof on those who would impose paternalistic measures (G. Dworkin, 1971, 118–26). His proposal seems likely to permit a far wider range of paternalism than I think justifiable, but the basic approach seems correct. What is striking, though, when one looks at actual cases where the issue of paternalism arises, is how very rare genuine instances of paternalism, as characterized in the preceding paragraph, seem to be.[6] Thus, to the question whether or not the apparent paternalism in a particular case is justified, there is the prior question of whether it is indeed an instance of paternalism in the relevant sense.

Let us consider, then, whether our example counts as a case involving paternalism at all. Assuming the conception of paternalism characterized above, there are at least two reasons why it might be said not to. First, it might be said that the policy is not paternalistic because it is aimed, not at the good of the women employees, but at the prevention of harm to their potential offspring. Second, it might be claimed that the policy is not paternalistic because, despite initial appearances, it is not motivated solely (if at all) by consideration of the good of the potential mothers *or* children, but by the company's concern to protect itself against potential lawsuits by or on behalf of damaged offspring.

. . .

Why, it may be asked, am I so skeptical about the company's motives? Granted that self interest may have had a role in their decision, might not genuine concern over potential harm to the unborn have been involved too? Of course, as we noted above, it is often difficult or impossible to tell in practice what really motivates an agent. But there are, it seems to me, fairly strong reasons for skepticism in this case.

Excessive lead exposure is known to be extremely harmful to adult men and women, and to their already existing children. Moreover, lead is known to affect the male as well as the female reproductive system. Why, then, Cyanamid's single-minded effort to exclude fertile women from lead exposure areas while willfully exposing other workers to excessive levels . . . ? As Jeanne Stellman notes in her excellent book, *Women's Work, Women's Health,* "There seems to be an aura of sanctity about a fertilized egg, a sort of fetus fetish, that apparently disappears when a child is born or matures into a working person" (Stellman, 1977, 179–80). Why so much concern about the unborn and so little about the living?

The most plausible explanation has two related parts: (1) potential costs of law suits to the company, and (2) stereotyped and discriminatory attitudes toward women and reproduction.

Under present state workers' compensation laws there are fixed, and usually very low, maximum limits on the rates to be paid for any occupationally caused injury or disease. They do not permit employees covered by workers' compensation to sue their employers in cases of occupationally related illness or injury. In cases of disease, such as those associated with lead poisoning (in contrast to clear-cut injuries, such as having one's hand mangled in a machine) they generally place the burden of proof on the worker to establish that the condition was caused by his or her job, and not by personal habits or lifestyle (e.g., smoking), general environmental exposure to toxins, or the "normal aging process." Thus the potential cost to the company resulting from lead poisoning of the workers themselves is predictable and fairly small. The poten-

tial children of workers, however, are not barred from suing, and workers cannot, even if they want to, waive their potential children's right to sue. Clearly, then, the company wants to protect itself against suits by future children with birth defects attributable to genetic or fetal damage for which the company may be found responsible.

But why do they restrict their concern to birth defects transmitted through the mother? There is in our society at the present time, a deeply ingrained identification of women with reproduction. Thus we tend to think of reproductive hazards only in terms of women — and of women's occupational health problems only in terms of reproduction. (The first major scientific conference on the occupational health of women workers was almost entirely taken up with such topics as the risks of toxic substances on future generations, birth defects, miscarriages, reproductive dangers, and pregnancy (Stellman, 1977, 81).) This identification gives rise to the "myth of perpetual pregnancy" (Stellman, 1977, 179) according to which any fertile woman is presumed pregnant until proven otherwise. Thus women are not thought of as able to choose whether or not to become pregnant or to continue an unplanned pregnancy. And this makes it seem reasonable and right that they not be permitted to choose whether or not to continue working at a job involving reproductive risks. This attitude helps to explain why the company's policy seems to acknowledge the possible teratogenic (fetal damage) but not mutagenic (genetic damage) effects of lead, since teratogens act only through the female. This emphasis is most convenient for the company, too, since acknowledging mutagenic risks would not allow the appearance that the problem could be dealt with simply by excluding certain people rather than cleaning up the entire operation. Finally, at least one source suggests that a birth defect resulting from maternal exposure would be easier to establish in court than one resulting from paternal exposure.[7] It is not clear to me why this should be the case (unless it is because the attitudes we have been discussing would also influence judges and juries), but the company may, rightly or wrongly, believe it to be. Hence, Cyanamid's policy seems to me to be the result of a desire to protect itself from expensive law suits combined with a stereotypic, discriminatory attitude toward women, rather than from any genuine concern over the welfare of the women or their potential children.

. . .

Let us now consider whether a policy of excluding fertile women from jobs involving exposure to reproductive hazards could be a justifiable way of preventing birth defects. Would it, for example, be justifiable for OSHA to promulgate such a policy? Note that, although the Cyanamid case stands out due to the explicit nature of the choice presented — your fertility or your job — any policy specifically excluding fertile women implicitly presents that same choice.

The facts of this particular case are such that the policy cannot be justified regardless of who is responsible for it. It does not eliminate the danger of birth defects, and it allows remaining workers to continue working in an environment that is dangerous to their own health. A more effective and nondiscriminatory approach is available: make the job safe for all workers by reducing the exposure levels. But what if the facts were different, as they may turn out to be in some other cases, and what about women who actually are pregnant, since fetuses may in fact be more vulnerable than adults to toxic substances, especially in the early weeks?

On the more general question first, if dangers really were only to and/or through women, would it be justifiable to bar them from certain workplaces? In general, I claim it would not be justifiable to bar women from workplaces in such cases. To do so would be to accept, or require, blatant discrimination against women. Employers should be required to make workplaces safe for both men and women. This is so for a combination of reasons.

First, there is the matter of the violation of reproductive and privacy rights discussed above. These considerations would apply regardless of what person or agency instituted the policy. Thus, even if they are not decisive, they must be placed in the balance.

Second, women constitute slightly more than half the population of the United States. To treat what is a threat to a substantial portion of the population (it need not be a majority, or even near one) as a special vulnerability, a misfortune and inconvenience for the individuals but not the responsibility or concern of society as a whole, much less of private corporations,

is more and more coming to be viewed as unacceptable and unjust.

It might be objected that by barring women, society and/or the corporations would be showing their concern and exercising their responsibility. But the point is that excluding them places the entire burden — cost, inconvenience, possible stigma, etc. — upon those in the threatened group, without even any choice about how that burden shall be borne. Thus it is becoming accepted that public facilities and jobs must be made accessible to those confined to wheelchairs, the blind, etc. This way of thinking is reflected, for example, in the Rehabilitation Act of 1973 and Department of Labor regulations which require that federal contractors and subcontractors take affirmative action, including individualized accommodation if necessary to employ and advance qualified handicapped individuals. Insofar as possible, public facilities, workplaces, and social institutions in general should be made flexible enough to adapt to the diversity within the population, rather than requiring individuals to adapt or be excluded. This seems to me correct as a general rule, and its application to the situations under consideration is clear.

It should be mentioned that this rule is by no means universally accepted.[8] Employers in private industry especially tend to push hard in the other direction. If a certain proportion of workers exposed to a substance get rashes, or asthma, or cancer, or byssinosis (brown lung disease of cotton workers), or berylliosis (beryllium disease), the response of the employers — almost universally as far as I have seen — is to claim that certain individuals are "allergic" or "sensitive" to the substance in question, which is otherwise quite safe. The employee may quit, seek a transfer, or go on suffering continued exposure and deteriorating health. It is her or his problem. Opponents argue that, not only is this approach unfair to those directly affected, but their response to the substances in question should be taken as an indication that the substances are probably harmful to humans generally at the exposure levels involved. Individual sensitivity and reaction to harmful substances naturally vary, and the harmful effects of some substances appear only after some time (e.g., ten to forty years for some carcinogens). Hence, the fact that some workers do not suffer acute symptoms is no indication that they are not being harmed.

. . .

Finally, in addition to the general objections against exclusionary policies, the history and continued practice of discrimination against women makes barring them even more objectionable than it might otherwise be. A point which was passed over earlier is relevant here. The employers' argument . . . ends with the point that the number of women affected by exclusionary policies is negligible, since few women are employed in the industries in question. Since this fact is the result of past discrimination, it should count against, not for, additional discriminatory measures. Moreover, general acceptance of the practice of excluding fertile women from jobs involving reproductive hazards could shut them out of some 20 million or more jobs.[9] These factors render highly suspect even temporary acceptance of exclusionary practices while industry finds ways to make the workplace safe for everyone.

On the relation between protective policies and discrimination, it is interesting to note that, while exclusionary policies have been adopted in many of the higher paying, traditionally male jobs, no such policies are applied in the traditional women's jobs where known reproductive hazards abound: operating room personnel (anesthetic gases); x-ray technicians and flight attendants (radiation); beauticians (propellants — now being phased out for environmental reasons, mutagenic and carcinogenic hair dyes); drycleaning (tetrachlorethylene, a mutagen); meatwrapping (polyvinylchloride); and so on (Wright, 1979, 304–5; *WOHRC News*, 1979). Moreover, historically, protective legislation has not applied to women in low-paid women's jobs. Regulations restricting night work and heavy lifting, for example, were not extended to female hospital workers, who continued to work nights and to lift patients and heavy equipment, or to waitresses who also worked nights and lifted heavy trays (Stellman, 1977, 176–77).

For all these reasons, exclusionary policies ought generally to be avoided even where a hazard is known to work only on or through members of one sex. And we ought to be extremely suspicious of claims that it is not technologically possible or economically feasible to make the workplace safe for all. Still, we must recognize that there may be rare cases in which such a claim is true.

For those few instances where the requirement that the workplace be made safe for all workers may be genuinely unworkable, the recently formed Coalition for the Reproductive Rights of Workers (CRROW) has proposed the following guidelines. An exclusionary policy can be justified only if the employer can prove that (1) it has cleaned up the workplace in compliance with OSHA regulations; (2) substantial scientific evidence exists on the effects of the substance in question on both sexes; (3) this evidence shows that the risk is to only one sex or group; (4) no alternative means exist for reducing or eliminating the risk; (5) the company's policy is to displace as few workers as possible, and these workers are assured of the same pay rate and seniority after transfer (*WOHRC News*, 1979, 6). This seems a reasonable approach, keeping the responsibility upon the company and at the same time recognizing that there may be exceptional cases where exclusion is justified.

Some may argue that no exclusion can be justified — that in the above kind of case, what the company should be required to do is to make the job as safe as possible, fully inform members of the group at risk what the dangers are, and let the individuals make the final decision on whether or not to accept the risks. Not allowing the individual to make that choice seems paternalistic.

In light of our earlier discussion, some may wish at this point to distinguish cases where the danger is exclusively or primarily to the worker from cases where actual fetuses and/or potential offspring are threatened. The charge of unjustified paternalism could then be directed quite forcefully against the former sort of case, the argument being that where only their own lives or health are at risk, once they are fully informed of the nature and extent of the risk, surely only they have the right to decide. (Responses pointing to the burden on society should the individual become disabled would presumably be persuasive only to someone willing to forego freedom of choice in many areas where we normally expect it.) The latter cases would be more complex and controversial, but no doubt some would still maintain that only the individual worker should have the final choice.

I have a great deal of sympathy for this position. I am hesitant to endorse it, however, because I fear that such an approach would tend to shift the total burden of responsibility onto the individual worker. That is, (1) companies would maintain that if, after being fully informed of the risks, a worker chose to stay on, then the company should be absolved of all future liability. (2) Companies would tend to use this "voluntary" approach rather than clean up the workplace, whereas, in order to institute an exclusionary policy they would have to show that they already had cleaned up, at least enough to meet OSHA's standards. While I am not optimistic about enforcement in either case, it seems likely that there would be better and stricter enforcement in the latter one. (3) Companies would be less likely to provide genuinely acceptable alternatives to workers already employed in a risk area. Workers transferred out of a risk area under an exclusionary policy would have to be provided alternative employment at no loss in pay or seniority, according to the CRROW proposal outlined earlier. Would a similar requirement be applicable and enforceable for individual workers who "chose" to leave a risk area?

The words "voluntary" and "chose" appear in scare quotes. This is because whether or not a decision is a voluntary choice depends at least sometimes on what the available alternatives are. And I fear that where matters are left up to individual arrangements between employer and employee, the alternatives will be to choose to stay on and continue to be exposed — at your own risk — or quit.

So I am inclined to think that a very strictly enforced set of restrictions and requirements on exclusionary policies might be preferable to the individual choice approach. Insofar as this is needed — not to protect the workers from themselves, but to prevent the kind of slippage in the burden of responsibility described above — it would not be paternalistic. Still, there is a serious question whether the requirement that all possible alternatives such as additional clean-up beyond OSHA standards, changing production processes, and substitution of less hazardous substances be preferred to exclusion would be genuinely enforceable. Thus, it might be best in the end to bar both the individual choice approach and the exclusionary one and simply require that employers find ways to make workplaces safe.

In cases where a woman is actually pregnant and there is reason to believe that the fetus is at risk, similar considerations apply. Certainly, she should be guaranteed the opportunity for a temporary transfer or leave if no safe work is available out of the area of exposure, with no loss in pay or seniority and the right to return to her original job after the danger is past. Ideally, perhaps, she should be free, given these conditions, to make whatever individual arrangements are, in her judgment, best suited to her particular situation. Here again, though, I would be hesitant to leave these arrangements to be worked out on a "voluntary" individual basis between employer and employee. This is not because the employee might not make the rational or the right decision, but because she might be placed at an extreme disadvantage.

To sum up, then, exclusionary policies are generally unjustifiable at least under existing social conditions. They *may* be justifiable in extremely rare cases, but only if properly restricted. If, in those rare cases, the policies serve to prevent employers from abusing workers' individual vulnerability, they would not be paternalistic. But primary emphasis should be placed on making workplaces safe for everyone, and if even restricted exclusionary policies would undermine this goal, then they are not justifiable at all. Temporary transfers or leaves with pay-rate and seniority retention should, of course, be made available to pregnant women in all jobs where the fetus might be endangered.

Notes

1. Since this [essay] was written, this controversy has been at least partially resolved by the Supreme Court in the Cotton Dust case (*American Textile Manufacturer's Institute* v. *Donovan* 452 U.S. [1981]). In 1981, the Court found that, in the OSH Act, "Congress itself defined the basic relationships between costs and benefits, by placing the 'benefit' of worker health above all other considerations save those making attainment of this benefit unachievable." Thus, cost–benefit studies were deemed inappropriate for the setting of OSHA standards, and "feasibility" was interpreted broadly as consistency with the continued viability of the industry as a whole.

2. See, for example, Nozick, 1969; Pennock and Chapman, 1972; Frankfurt, 1973; Lyons, 1975; Cohen, 1979; Zimmerman, 1981; Fowler, 1982; and Cohen, 1983.

3. See Zimmerman, 1981.

4. Obviously, we have to do here with what might be called "natural necessity," not logical necessity.

5. For other examples, details and discussion, see Stellman, 1977, 35–39 and 178–200; and Milkman, 1980, entire.

6. Reflection upon this fact is what led me to the somewhat different way of thinking about paternalism . . . discussed in Chapter Two [of the book from which this reading is excerpted].

7. Women's Occupational Health Resources Center *News,* Nov./Dec. 1979, 6.

8. The reasoning in two Supreme Court decisions upholding the constitutionality of restrictions on the funding of abortions for poor women (*Maher* v. *Roe,* 1977, and *Harris* v. *McRae,* 1980) is a potentially devastating rejection of this way of thinking. The Court held that although government may not place obstacles in the way of a person's exercise of a constitutionally protected right, it need not remove obstacles not of its own creation.

9. Keeping in mind that reproductive hazards can affect men as well as women, note that widespread acceptance of the practice of employing only infertile workers in these jobs would lead to the creation of a subclass of "drones" in our society. A person who genuinely chooses to have him- or herself sterilized because having children does not fit into his or her life-plan is not at issue; a class of workers required to be sterilized in order to get and hold their jobs is.

References

Dworkin, G. 1971. "Paternalism." In Richard A. Wasserstrom, ed., *Mortality and the Law.* Belmont, CA: Wadsworth Publishing Co.

Cohen, G. 1979. "Capitalism, Freedom and the Proletariat." In Alan Ryan, ed., *The Idea of Freedom: Essays in Honor of Isaiah Berlin.* Oxford: Oxford University Press.

———. 1983. "The Structure of Proletarian Unfreedom." *Philosophy & Public Affairs,* 12, no. 1: 3–33.

Fowler, M. 1982. "Coercion and Practical Reason." *Social Theory and Practice* 8, no. 83: 329–55.

Frankfurt, H. 1973. "Coercion and Moral Responsibility." In T. Honderich, *Social Ends and Political Means.* London: Routledge and Kegan Paul. 1976.

Lehmann, P. (n.d.) "Protecting Women Out of Their Jobs." Somerville, MA: New England Free Press. (pamphlet)

Lyons, D. 1975. "Welcome Threats and Coercive Offers." *Philosophy* 50: 425–36.

Milkman, R. 1980. "Organizing the Sexual Division of Labor: Historical Perspectives on 'Women's Work' and the American Labor Movement." *Socialist Review* 49: 95–150.

Nozick, R. 1969. "Coercion." In *Philosophy, Science and Method,* S. Morgenbesser et al., eds. New York: St. Martin's Press.

Pennock, J. R., and J. W. Chapman, eds. 1972. *Coercion.* Vol. 14 of the NOMOS series. Chicago/New York: Aldine-Atherton.

Stellman, J. M. 1977. *Women's Work, Women's Health.* New York: Pantheon Books.

WOHRC NEWS. 1979. Vol. 1, No. 3. New York: Columbia University, Women's Occupational Health Resource Center (WOHRC).

Wright, M. J. 1979. "Reproductive Hazards and 'Protective' Discrimination." *Feminist Studies* 5, No. 2: 302–9.

Update

In March 1991, the Supreme Court ruled, in the case of *Automobile Workers* v. *Johnson Controls,* that the fetal protection policy at Johnson Controls violated the Civil Rights Act of 1964, which prohibits sexual discrimination in the workplace. This ruling put an end to practices like the ones described at American Cyanamid.

GAY MARRIAGE

Christine Pierce

Christine Pierce argues that lesbians and gay men should be allowed to enter into legal marriages. In making this case, she cites the same values that are appealed to in defense of opposite-sex marriage: equality, privacy, justice, liberation, and dignity. (Source: From Journal of Social Philosophy, *Volume XXVI, No. 2, Fall 1995. Reprinted by permission.)*

"The effort to legalize gay marriage will almost certainly emerge as a major issue in the next decade"[1] says law professor Nan D. Hunter in the October 1991 *Nation*. Why is this so? In part, what drives this issue is the practice of most U.S. employers and many institutions (such as the IRS) to give *significant* benefits including health, life, disability and dental insurance, tax relief, bereavement and dependent care leave, tuition, use of recreational facilities, and purchase discounts on everything from memberships at the local Y to airline tickets only to those in conventional heterosexual families. Although employee benefits are sometimes referred to as "fringe" benefits, they, in fact, make up a hefty portion of compensation. As such, married people are paid more than their nonmarried counterparts. Whether or not favoring the institution of marriage is justified, there remains the problems that those in heterosexual relationships at least have the option (indeed, the right) to marry, whereas lesbians and gay men in relationships do not (at least in the United States).[2]

Although I find monetary and benefit arguments convincing, what follows is a discussion of other types of considerations — legal, historical, ethical and psychological — that are relevant to the issue of gay marriage. Of these, I find the so-called psychological ones most persuasive. Moreover, since some benefits can be gained by domestic partnership plans, the question of the comparative merits of marriage and domestic partnership needs to be addressed.

Legal Arguments

Although I will not dwell on the subject of law, a May 1993 Hawaii Supreme Court decision described by the Lambda Legal Defense and Education Fund as "astonishing" and possibly opening the door to gay marriage is worthy of mention. In *Baehr v. Lewin*, the first same-sex marriage case to reach a State Supreme Court in twenty years, the Hawaii Supreme Court held that "denying marriage licenses to same-sex couples appears to violate the State constitutional guarantee of equal protection on the basis of sex."[3] Overturning a lower court decision, the Hawaii Supreme Court sent the issue back for a trial at which the State must show compelling reasons for its discriminatory policy. According to Lambda, the Hawaii court refused to be satisfied with the "tortured and conclusory sophistry" of past court hearings on gay marriage and rejected the "tautological and circular nature" of the state's argument that same-sex couples cannot marry because marriage is inherently for opposite-sex couples.[4] Indeed, the argument from definition cited so recently in the Hawaii case, has been around for a long time. In 1971, the Minnesota Supreme Court defined marriage as "a union of man and woman"[5] and in 1974, two men were denied a marriage license "because of the nature of marriage itself."[6] As Richard Mohr puts it so nicely, "the courts [have held] that gay access to marriage must be a form of grand theft."[7] The charge, says Mohr, is "theft of essence."[8] ". . . [S]traights wouldn't really be married," he says, "if gays were . . . the meaning of marriage would be revised beyond recognition if gays could marry."[9] Similar claims about the concept of "family" are commonplace in right-wing rhetoric today; it is said that so-called true families will be undermined if the concept of family is extended to include lesbian and gay couples.

Other possibilities for legal argument include privacy rights[10] and Kenneth Karst's interesting suggestion that the Constitutional freedom of intimate association "extends to homosexual associations."[11] These ideas I simply mention concluding my remarks on legal reasoning by noting the importance of a 1967 Supreme Court case, *Loving* v. *Virginia*,[12] which established the right to marry as a fundamental legal right. *Loving* overturned laws against interracial marriage in the United States. Presumably one can make an equal protection argument to the effect that even as the government cannot restrict choice of a marital partner by insisting on a particular race, so the government cannot restrict such a choice on the basis of sex. Of course, such an argument would only work in a state like Hawaii, where the category of sex is constitutionally protected from discrimination. In sum, what is new on the legal scene is that gay advocates of gay marriage are making serious arguments that are at long last being taken seriously.

Queer Versus Straight: Historical Arguments

As the title of a recent article conveys, however, "Some Gays Aren't Wedded to the Idea of Same-Sex Marriage."[13] Journalist Anna Quindlen expands on this issue when she says, "Gay marriage is a radical notion for straight people and a conservative notion for gay ones. After years of being sledgehammered by society, some gay men and [lesbians] are deeply suspicious of participating in an institution that seems to have 'straight world' written all over it."[14] Queer things — queer theory, Queer Nation, the protest chant, "We're here, we're queer, we're fabulous, get used to us" — assume that respect for distinctiveness, an opportunity to pursue a life that is "not straight" is what is wanted.[15] Although some traditionalists have called same-sex marriage a slap in the face of tradition and some queer theorists have repudiated the institution of marriage as not queer, both may have reason to pause. If Yale historian John Boswell is right, Christian marriage rites between same-sex partners date back to the fourth century, earlier than the widespread performance of heterosexual ceremonies in the eleventh century.[16] Boswell claims to have found gay marriage rites in liturgical manuals and early legal documents that constitute clear evidence that "gay unions were comparable to heterosexual marriages."[17] "Both men and women were married using these rites, though evidence for lesbian unions is not as geographically widespread nor as ancient," Boswell says.[18] He theorizes that "gay marriage rites . . . appear to have started as a religious ceremony and were based principally on love, . . . includ[ing] an erotic dimension."[19] He contrasts this history with heterosexual marriage, which he says started as a civil ceremony concerned with property exchange and later, when appropriated by the church, emphasized progeny and worldly success.[20] So, it appears that queer theorists could claim or reclaim an institution that is part of their history. Indeed, the good history — the part about love and eroticism — is queer.

Equality, Justice, Liberation

Whether being able to marry is a desirable political goal is a question pretty much outside of law and history. At the least, it is a question that requires ethical analysis of matters such as equality, justice, oppression, and dignity. Attorney Paula Ettelbrick,[21] who doubts that marriage is the path to liberation for anyone, argues against lesbian and gay marriages on the grounds that they will not alter the elitist character of marriage, that they will at best "minimally transform" the oppressive character of marriage by "diluting its patriarchal dynamic" and that they will not transform society or bring about a just world.

On the subject of a just world, Ettelbrick says,

Gay marriages will not help us address the systematic abuses inherent in a society that does not provide decent health care to all of its citizens . . . nor will it address the pain of the unmarried lesbian who . . . is prohibited from entering the intensive care unit . . . solely because she is not a spouse or family member. Likewise, marriage will not help the gay victim of domestic violence who, because he chose not to marry, finds no protection under the law to keep his violent lover away.[22]

Of course, allowing lesbians and gay men to marry will not address the issue of decent health care. Why, one might (indeed, should) ask, must one be employed by a company or an institution of a certain size or be married to someone who is in order to get health insurance? Presumably, in a just world, folks could get health care because they are valuable. Ettelbrick is absolutely correct in her view about the notions of "equality" or "rights" or "equal rights" when she says, "A pure 'rights' analysis often fails to incorporate a broader understanding of the underlying inequities that operate to deny justice to a fuller range of people and groups."[23] Despite her claim that rights and justice should be combined, she goes on to argue that gay marriage will gain rights for a few, will make some lesbians and gays "insiders," but will not correct the imbalance of power between the married and the nonmarried. Thus, "justice would not be gained."[24]

One answer to Ettelbrick is that she herself has put her finger on the way equality arguments usually work. They work on a limited scale. They do not do big jobs such as bring about a just society. As Mary Midgley puts it so clearly,

> [E]quality . . . is a rather abstract ideal. . . . Who is to be made equal to whom, and in what respect? Historically the answers given have mostly concerned rather narrow groups. . . . The formula needed is something like "let those who are already equal in respect x be, as is fitting, equal also in respect y." . . . Outsiders . . . who are currently not equal in respect x, cannot benefit from this kind of argument. . . . The notion of equality is a tool for rectifying injustices within a given group, not for widening that group or deciding how it ought to treat those outside it.[25]

Ettelbrick least understands the limited and painfully slow way that equality arguments normally work when she suggests that "more marginal members of the lesbian and gay community (women, people of color, working class and poor) are less likely [than those who are more acceptable to the mainstream] to see marriage as having relevance to our struggles for survival."[26] The fact that achieving the right to marry will not benefit everyone or everyone equally or solve all the world's problems is not an argument against it. What good, asks Ettelbrick, "is the

affirmation of our relationships (that is, marital relationships) if we are rejected as women, blacks, or working class?"[27] The answer to the question "What good is a job in philosophy if I am discredited as a woman?" is "A lot." Moreover, the exclusion of lesbian relationships from legal recognition directly affects survival issues that cut across class and race. As Attorney Ruthann Robson notes, "a member of a lesbian couple who becomes incapacitated can be controlled by a person determined in accordance with relationships recognized under the rule of law, such as the father who does not believe she is a lesbian, the brother who abused her, or the husband she has not seen for twenty years but never divorced."[28]

Ettelbrick dismisses the importance of equality not only because it is of more use to those "closer to the norm or to power"[29] but also because "the concept of equality . . . only supports sameness."[30] She continues, "The moment we argue . . . that we should be treated as equals because we are really just like married couples and hold the same values to be true, we . . . begin the dangerous process of silencing our different voices."[31] I have argued elsewhere against the assumption that equality is similarity. In brief, whether or not differences are relevant depends on what kind of equality one is talking about. If one is talking about equal opportunity, differences should be ignored; however, if one is talking about equal representation, differences are important.[32] Even if equality did entail similarity, sameness is not always bad. Of course, sometimes sameness is bad and that is part of Ettelbrick's worry. She says lesbians and gay men "end up mimicking all that is bad about the institution of marriage in our effort to appear to be the same as straight couples."[33]

Others who disagree with Ettelbrick think that the participation of lesbians and gay men in the institution of marriage will alter the institution for the better. For example, Thomas Stoddard says, "marriage may be unattractive and even oppressive as it is currently structured and practiced, but enlarging [it] to embrace same-sex couples would necessarily transform it into something new."[34] Susan Moller Okin in her recent book, *Justice, Gender and the Family,*[35] certainly makes a strong case against what she calls *gender-structured* marriage, thereby tempting others to suggest that an alternative, especially an alternative that is not gender structured, has got to be better. Marriage and the family as currently practiced in our society, Okin says, "constitute the pivot of a . . . system of gender that renders women vulnerable to dependency, exploitation, and abuse."[36] The conventional family, she says, "is the linchpin of gender"[37] and gendered relationships, private and public, are thoroughly unjust. Martha Nussbaum in her review of Okin's book says, "[Okin] plainly has a strong preference for the nuclear family in something like its modern Western form. . . . But she never tells us what benefits she believes the modern Western family provides, or why, in view of the many alternatives that have been conceived, she still prefers the pattern that has proven, as she herself demonstrates, so resistant to reform in the name of justice."[38]

If same-sex couples could marry, says Nan Hunter,

> . . . the profoundly gendered structure at the heart of marriage would be radically disrupted. Who *would* be the "husband" in a marriage of two men, or the "wife" in a marriage of two women? And either way—if there can be no such thing as a female husband or a male wife, as the right-wing argues with contempt; or indeed in some sense there *can* be, as lesbian and gay couples reconfigure these roles on their own terms—the absolute conflation of gender with role is shattered. What would be the impact on heterosexual marriage?[39]

Unfortunately, Hunter does not answer this question. As we have seen, Thomas Stoddard is hopeful, Paula Ettelbrick is doubtful and Martha Nussbaum wants to try something new because heterosexual marriage and the nuclear family are unjust institutions. I would not rest a case for the legalization of lesbian and gay marriage on the possibility that lesbians and gay men might improve the institution of marriage, for transformative values may not come about. Nonetheless, I am with Nussbaum here. We ought to pull the pin and see what happens. However, at the least, arguments against lesbian and gay marriages based on the oppressive character of marriage should be rejected if the oppressive character referred to is due to the currently accepted gender requirements of marriage. This type of argument, exemplified in the

following remarks by Ruthann Robson and S. E. Valentine, is widespread in lesbian writings: "Underlying the lesbian critique of marriage is the gendered perspective on marriage developed by feminists. . . . Marriage has remained interwoven with both the development and the perpetuation of patriarchy and women's status within patriarchy."[40] Even if the oppressive nature of marriage historically did count as a reason for devaluing marriage per se, and therefore gay marriage, it still could be argued that lesbians and gay men should have the right to marry.[41] It is perfectly coherent to assert that lesbians and gay men should have the option to marry without claiming the value of marriage even as one can coherently claim that lesbians and gay men should have the option to serve in the military while not valuing the military.[42]

Paula Ettelbrick has one last formulation of her anti-equality argument. She says the idea of marriage is inconsistent with the goal of gay liberation, which is to recognize the legitimacy of many different kinds of relationships.[43] Interestingly, she favors domestic partnership plans, which, she argues, better accomplish this goal. Such plans—on the part of municipalities and employers—almost universally define domestic partners to include lesbian and gay couples as well as unmarried heterosexual partners and extend to them some of the rights accorded to married couples. The qualifications for benefits approximate the qualifications for marriage although in many instances they are more stringent. For example, domestic partnership requires couples to give evidence of commitment, whereas marriage does not.[44] On Ettelbrick's view, marriage is a "two-tier system of the 'haves' and the 'have-nots'"[45] and same-sex marriage simply perpetuates "the elevation of married relationships and of 'couples' in general, . . . further eclipsing other relationships of choice."[46] Domestic partnership plans, on the other hand, "validate non-marital relationships"[47] thereby contributing to the goal mentioned above of recognizing many different kinds of relationships. It does seem that the idea of domestic partnership is more inclusive of diverse relationships than is marriage although domestic partnership does not abolish the privileging of some relationships. Sisters who are really sisters and not closeted lesbians posing as sisters could get minimal benefits if they set up a household and are financially interdependent.

Kinship Arguments

Despite the attractive potential of registered partnerships, I think a separate and compelling argument can be made for lesbian and gay marriages. Although lesbians and gay men have made some progress in the area of individual rights in the United States, until very recently, there has been an almost total nonrecognition of gay families. A chapter title of a recent book illustrates the exile of gays from kinship: "Is Straight to Gay as Family Is to No Family?"[48] Again Justice White, speaking for the Supreme Court majority's view that homosexual sex between consenting adults in their own bedroom is not protected by the right to privacy, said, in *Bowers v. Hardwick* in 1986, "No connection between family, marriage, or procreation on the one hand and homosexual activity on the other has been demonstrated."[49] The right to privacy in *Bowers* protects only marital privacy. Gay people were not seen by Justice White as being in relationships. Lesbians and gay men were not visible to him as couples, partners, families, kin. Had the Court interpreted the right to privacy as a right to sexual autonomy, gay people might have been seen, for all the Court had to be able to see was individuals who desired autonomy and who had some kind of a sexual life. But when the Court said the right to privacy is the right to marital privacy, then they saw no connection between marriage and gay people. A legal system or an ethical system based on principle will not be of any use to lesbians and gay men if they are not seen as the sorts of folks to whom these principles can apply.

Worse yet, think about an ethic based on sentiment. Take, for example, Mary Midgley's view: those nearest to us have special claims — claims that diminish in proportion to distance, either physical or social. Fortunately, Midgley says that those most distant need not always come at the end of the queue. Unfortunately, priority rankings among various kinds of claims are determined by the cultural maps worked out by individual societies, and nearness and kinship are real and important factors in our psychological makeup. The psychology presented here seems right

to me. I care more about Morgan, my Maine Coon cat, than I do about the kid I don't know who lives six blocks down the street. These feelings I have really matter however much those folks who believe in universalizing ethical principles say that physical and social distance should not matter. However, appealing to sentiment as a way of justifying behavior as *ethical* can be as dangerous as it is comforting. It is, of course, comforting to hear that those folks one already cares about are just the ones one ought to care about (or ought to care most about). Such a psychology explains, at least in part, why ethical views based on sentiment have not been applied to lesbians and gay men, who are perceived as strangers and not as kin in our society.

One would expect lesbians and gay men to get a better deal from ethics based on principle, but arguments based on principle often do not work for gay people, as evidenced by the 1986 *Bowers* case. A more recent example is the debate over Colorado Amendment 2, which illustrates how all civil rights of lesbians and gay men can be jeopardized because lesbians and gay men are not perceived as kin or as having important relationships. In July 1993, the state Supreme Court ruled that the voter initiative to outlaw gay rights laws must prove a compelling state interest in order to meet constitutional standards. The state's attorney general said, "the State's desire to promote 'family values' provide[s] such a compelling interest."[50] Amendment 2 was declared unconstitutional by a district court judge on December 13, 1993 on grounds that it violated equal protection by usurping "the fundamental right of an identifiable group to participate in the political process,"[51] and it may be that the Colorado Supreme Court and the United States Supreme Court will continue in this lead. Nevertheless, the fact that anyone would offer "family values" as a good reason for the denial of equal rights is a measure of just how far lesbians and gay men are from being viewed as kin in our society. As one California court put it, in rejecting a similar initiative in Riverside, California, "All that is lacking is a sack of stones for throwing."[52]

In short, moral arguments based on existing sentiment will not work for gay people; arguments based on principle should work, but often do not in part because sentiment plays a role in even principled ethics and law. Until current sentiments in our society are changed, lesbians and gay men will not be able to expect that ethical (and legal) principles will be applied fairly to them. Thus, it is important for the sake of creating new sentiments to press for gay marriage so that lesbians and gay men can become visible as couples, partners, families, and kin. Pressing for registered partnerships — or what some have called gay near-marriage — may not do the job. Those folks who in 1986 could not even imagine lesbians and gay men in relationship need to know that many lesbians and gay men — to quote the Supreme Court — view their relationships as "noble" and "intimate to the degree of being sacred."[53]

Conclusion

In sum, I have raised the following issues: Married people are paid more than their nonmarried counterparts while the possibility of choice regarding whether or not to marry has not been extended to lesbians and gay men. Marriage has been rejected as an undesirable political goal on the ground that it is not queer, presumably meaning to a degree that marriage is not part of lesbian and gay history. But John Boswell's new discoveries of historical evidence indicate that marriage is in a very important sense queer. I have argued that the pursuit of equality should not be abandoned simply because it is often compatible with injustice. Nor should equality be discarded because it supposedly means "sameness" and sameness is bad. I have suggested that our assessment of the comparative merits of marriage and domestic partnership is to some extent a reflection of the respective values we place on equality and diversity. Although I have expressed my doubts about the transformative power of same-sex marriage, it seems to me that objections to gay marriage based on the gender structure of heterosexual marriage are misplaced. Lastly, I have argued that Americans have been allowed for too long to view lesbians and gay men only as individuals (that is, not in relationship) and as strangers (that is, not as kin). I think that gay marriage needs to be on the political agenda for the sake of gaining a certain level of social awareness and acceptance of serious lesbian and gay relationships. I do not worry, as do some

queer theorists, that pursuing a goal such as marriage will result in assimilation into invisibility or, as Ettelbrick puts it, "[let us] fade into the woodwork."[54] I think it is a far greater worry that the current invisibility as family is threatening to destroy any kind of a decent life at all for lesbians and gay men in the United States.

Notes

Author's Note: My thanks to the CHASS (College of Humanities and Social Sciences) Research Fund and Humanities Foundation Travel Grants at North Carolina State University for funds to travel to the Kinsey Institute; the Kinsey Institute for Research in Sex, Gender, and Reproduction, Bloomington, Indiana, for their staff time and bibliographical assistance; and the audience of the Midwest Society for Women in Philosophy, University of Cincinnati, October 2, 1993, for their comments.

1. Nan D. Hunter, "Sexual Dissent and the Family," *The Nation,* October 1991, p. 441. Nan Hunter was formerly an attorney with the American Civil Liberties Union. The ACLU has endorsed lesbian and gay marriage since 1986.

2. Gay civil marriage is legal in Denmark.

3. Docket Update, *Baehr v. Lewin, The Lambda Update: The Newsletter of Lambda Legal Defense and Education Fund* 10, no. 2 (summer 1993): 14.

4. Evan Wolfson, "Hawaii Supreme Court Paves Way for Same-Sex Marriage," *The Lambda Update: The Newsletter of Lambda Legal Defense and Education Fund* 10, no. 2 (summer 1993): 23.

5. *Baker v. Nelson,* 291 Minn. 310 (1971) *appeal dismissed,* 409 U.S. 810 (1972).

6. *Singer v. Hara,* 11 Wash. App. 247 (1974).

7. Richard D. Mohr, *Gay Ideas: Outing and Other Controversies* (Boston: Beacon Press, 1992), p. 90.

8. Ibid.

9. Ibid. Not everyone thinks gay marriage is a threat to straight marriage. Andrew Sullivan, for example, argues that "[g]ay marriage . . . [u]nlike domestic partnership . . . merely asks that gays be allowed to join in. . . . Gay marriage could only delegitimize straight marriage if it were a real alternative to it." In other words, gay marriage does not challenge the value of "a deeper and harder-to-extract-yourself-from commitment to another human being [which] would foster social cohesion, emotional security, . . . economic prudence" and a nurturing environment for children. Andrew Sullivan, "The Case for Gay Marriage," *The New Republic,* August 28, 1989, p. 22.

10. See, for example, Hannah Swarzschild, "Same-Sex Marriage and Constitutional Privacy: Moral Threat and Legal Anomaly," *Berkeley Woman's Law Journal* 4, no. 94 (1988).

11. Kenneth L. Karst, "Freedom of Intimate Association," 89 *Yale Law Journal* 624 (1980): 682.

12. *Loving v. Virginia,* 388 U.S. 1 (1967).

13. Peter Freiberg, "Some Gays Aren't Wedded to the Idea of Same-Sex Marriage," *The Advocate,* 530, no. 16 (1989).

14. Anna Quindlen, "Evan's Two Moms," *The New York Times,* February 5, 1992, p. A15.

15. One variant of this protest chant does not seek social acceptance of even things queer: "We're here, we're queer, we're fabulous, don't fuck with us."

16. Steve Bryant and Demian, "The Ancient History of Same-Sex Marriage," in *An Indispensable Guide for Gay and Lesbian Couples: What Every Same-Sex Couple Should Know* (Seattle: Sweet Corn Productions, 1993), p. 43. This article consists of notes on a public lecture given by John Boswell. Boswell's book on the history of same-sex marriages is forthcoming.

17. Ibid.

18. Ibid.

19. Ibid.

20. Ibid.

21. Paula Ettelbrick is public policy director of the National Center for Lesbian Rights, New York City office.

22. Paula Ettelbrick, "Since When Is Marriage a Path to Liberation?" *Outlook* 6, no. 8 (1990): 17.

23. Ibid., p. 14.

24. Ibid.

25. Mary Midgley, *Animals and Why They Matter* (London: Penguin Books, 1983), p. 67.

26. Ettelbrick, p. 16.

27. Ibid.

28. Despite her recognition that these practical difficulties arise from the fact that lesbian partners are legal strangers, Robson opposes both gay marriage and domestic partnership arguing instead that marriage should be abolished. Attorney Thomas Stoddard welcomes abolishing marriage for all couples as an alternative to extending the right to marry to lesbians and gay men, but finds the replacement of marriage by a new legal entity unlikely. Ruthann Robson, *Lesbian (Out)Law: Survival Under the Rule of Law* (Ithaca, NY: Firebrand Books, 1992), pp. 117, 126–27; Thomas Stoddard, "Why Gay People Should Seek the Right to Marry," *Outlook* 6, no. 8 (1990): 13.

29. Ettelbrick, p. 16.

30. Ibid., p. 15.

31. Ibid., p. 14.

32. Christine Pierce, "Postmodernism and Other Skepticisms," *Feminist Ethics,* ed. Claudia Card (Lawrence: University Press of Kansas, 1991), p. 66.

33. Ettelbrick, p. 15.

34. Stoddard, p. 13.

35. Susan Moller Okin, *Justice, Gender, and the Family* (New York: Basic Books, 1989).

36. Ibid., pp. 135–36.

37. Ibid., p. 170.

38. Martha Nussbaum, "Justice for Women!" *The New York Review of Books* 39, no. 16 (October 8, 1992): 46.

39. Hunter, p. 411.

40. Ruthann Robson and S. E. Valentine, "Lov(h)ers: Lesbians as Intimate Partners and Lesbian Legal Theory," 63 *Temple Law Review* 511 (1990): 536. For further examples of arguments to the effect that gay marriage should be rejected because marriage is "het" or "patriarchal" or oppressive to women, see Frieberg, p. 18; Catherine Saalfield, "Lesbian Marriage . . . [K]not!" in *Sisters, Sexperts, Queers: Beyond the Lesbian Nation,* ed. Arlene Stein (New York: Penguin Books, 1993), p. 191; Suzanne Sherman, ed., *Lesbian and Gay Marriage: Private Commitments, Public Ceremonies* (Philadelphia: Temple University Press, 1992), pp. 113, 217.

41. Thomas Stoddard takes this position.

42. See Claudia Card, *Lesbian Choices and Values,* chap. 10, New York: Columbia University Press, in press.

43. Ettelbrick, p. 16.

44. Marrying for the sake of a green card is an exception here.

45. Ettelbrick, p. 17.

46. Ibid., p. 16.

47. Ibid., p. 17.

48. See Kath Weston, *Families We Choose: Lesbians, Gays, Kinship* (New York: Columbia University Press), 1991.

49. *Bowers v. Hardwick,* 106 S. Ct. 2841, 2844 (1986).

50. Dirk Johnson, "Colorado Ban on Gay Rights Laws Is Ruled Unconstitutional," *The New York Times,* December 14, 1993, p. A11.

51. "Colorado Gay Rights Ban Ruled Unconstitutional," *The Washington Post,* December 15, 1993, p. A24.

52. Tamar Lewin, "Colorado Ban on Gay Rights Laws Is Ruled Unconstitutional," *The New York Times,* December 14, 1993, p. A11.

53. Stoddard, p. 12.

54. Freiberg, p. 18.

▥ Affirmative Action

WOUNDING THE SPIRIT:
Discrimination and Traditional
American Indian Belief Systems

Carol Locust

Carol Locust discusses the various ways in which Native Americans are discriminated against in the area of spiritual belief or cultural teachings. She implicates the dominant culture's educational system as perpetuating the crime against belief and spirit. In making this case, she gives a powerful example of how discrimination must be understood as broader than discrimination against particular individuals. (Source: From U.S. Race Relations in the 1980s and 1990s: Challenges and Alternatives, *ed. Gail E. Thomas. Copyright © 1990 Hemisphere Publishing Corporation. Reprinted by permission.)*

Discrimination against one's beliefs is the most insidious kind of injustice. Ridicule of one's spiritual beliefs or cultural teachings wounds the spirit, leaving anger and hurt that is usually masked by a proud silence. For American Indians[1] this discrimination exists in the extreme against their traditional beliefs, especially when such beliefs conflict with those of the dominant culture's educational systems.

When Europeans first came to North America their hearts were hungry for one thing—freedom from being discriminated against because of their belief systems. The United States of America was founded on the principle of religious freedom, yet the indigenous peoples whose land was used to establish this country were denied this freedom. Incredibly, American Indians were not granted religious freedom until 1978, when Congress passed the American Indian Religious Freedom Act (Public Law 95-341). The passage of a law, however, cannot bring change quickly after decades of discrimination; racist attitudes toward traditional Indian religions still exist even today.

These attitudes manifest themselves in the U.S. educational system, which was not designed to honor diverse racial and cultural groups. In earlier years Indian children did not have easy access to public schools so they were placed in a military-like educational system of boarding schools established by the Bureau of Indian Affairs in 1819 (Roessel, 1963). Neither the public schools nor the military system was designed to accommodate tribal religions, ceremonies, cultural differences, or language differences. Change is very slow in coming to educational systems in the United States; very few public or Bureau schools respect Indian traditions and beliefs.

To change this situation in the schools, teachers and administrators must begin to understand that belief systems among Indian people are sacred and holy; moreover, Indians do not separate the sacred from the secular aspects of life. For example, when a medicine person works with an individual to bring about healing of an illness, it is not just an act of obtaining medical help such as going to see a physician for a cold remedy. Healing and worship cannot be separated, as there is little difference between religious and traditional healing practices of American Indians (Aberle, 1966). Jerrold Levy (1963) has described the social behavior of the Indian as inseparable from the culture, sacred narratives, and religion. Clyde Kluckhohn and Dorothy Leighton (1962) noted that there is no distinct term in the Navajo language for "religion" in the Western sense. While doing a study of Tohono O'odham ceremonies, Marvin Kahn et al. (1975) observed that no distinction was made between healing and worship. Carol Locust (1985) stated that there is little or no difference between religion and medicine, between a church and a hospital in the Indian belief system. Carl Hammerschlag (1985), a friend to Indian people and a former psychiatrist at the Phoenix Indian Medical Center, points out that for Indian people the concept of health is not just a physical state, but a spiritual one as well (p. 2). As these studies show, American Indian beliefs about health may be identified as the core beliefs of the cultures themselves. Educators need to learn more about these concepts since they are fundamental to both the traditional ways of Indian life and to the health and spirituality of tribal members. Without this understanding, there can only be discrimination—discrimination that wounds the spirit of Indian people.

There is a long history of misunderstanding of Indian beliefs on the part of the dominant culture. Early, widely referenced scholars (e.g., Morgan, 1892; Reagan, 1930) seem to have assumed that American Indians were pagans (had no religion) or that they worshiped idols, animals, or devils. Such misunderstandings may have occurred because these scholars did not know the language or the customs of the people, and therefore interpreted Indian ceremonies from the perspectives of their own religious backgrounds. For example, eyewitness accounts of Apache culture and religion written by Thomas Morgan (1892) and Albert Reagan (1930) have serious flaws. Thomas Mails (1974) documented his misgivings about the account of the Apaches written by Reagan: Reagan's

comments are based on what he saw in only nine months on the western Apache reservations. He was a captain in the Third Cavalry who was among the Apaches from July 1901 until May of 1902. His interpretations of the real meanings and purposes of some acts he saw performed by the medicine men and the Ghan (Mountain spirit) dancers should not be taken as gospel. More probably, excepting those instances where acts were explained to him, he was not informed or sympathetic enough to make a reliable and profound statement. The fact is that tribal belief systems contain highly structured theological organization, protocol, and ritual, just as other religions do around the world. In most Indian traditions every element of existence and every second of time is perceived as being holy, thereby implying that worship is a constant daily function. The fact that there were no familiar religious objects (no alters, crosses, books) for early observers to see contributed to their conclusion that Indians were "pagan."

One of the reasons non-Indian people do not understand much about Indian beliefs is that they vary from tribe to tribe and from clan to clan. For example, Apaches believe that supernatural spirits seek out an individual to become a medicine person. The Tohono O'odham, on the other hand, believe that one must be born into a lineage of medicine people or must be a twin in order to become a medicine person. Yet in spite of these differences, most systems are built on a common set of beliefs. In a previous work I have identified ten common beliefs that are basic to most Indian tribes in the United States (Locust, 1985). These beliefs are presented here as general statements and should be taken as indicators or guides for further study, not as universals or absolute truths for any one Indian tribal belief system. An understanding of each will help non-Indians begin to comprehend how educational systems suppress and discriminate against the belief systems of Indians.

Several factors may influence the beliefs of an American Indian: subtribe or clan affiliation, tribal sodality (society) membership, formal education, influence of an outside religion, marriage, and length of time and/or experience off the reservation. A tribal member may or may not know many traditional beliefs, and may or may not identify with those that are known. However, the following statements are applicable to the majority of tribal members:

1. American Indians believe in a Supreme Creator. In this belief system there are lesser beings also.

2. Humans are threefold beings made up of a spirit, mind, and body.

3. Plants and animals, like humans, are part of the spirit world. The spirit world exists side by side with and intermingles with physical world.

4. The spirit existed before it came into a physical body and will exist after the body dies.

5. Illness affects the mind and spirit as well as the body.

6. Wellness is harmony in spirit, mind, and body.

7. Unwellness is disharmony in spirit, mind, and body.

8. Natural unwellness is caused by the violation of a sacred or tribal taboo.

9. Unnatural unwellness is caused by witchcraft.

10. Each of us is responsible for his or her own wellness.

Educators need to understand the meaning of these beliefs because Indian sociocultural behaviors rooted in these traditional beliefs strongly affect their formal educational experiences. But an understanding of Indian beliefs is not enough for educators; they must also be able to identify how such beliefs manifest themselves in Indian attitudes and behaviors toward formal educational systems. Below I discuss each of these ten common beliefs and outline ways in which U.S. educational practices come in conflict with these beliefs.

1.   *American Indians believe in a Supreme Creator. In this belief system there are lesser beings also.* Most tribes identify a Supreme Creator by a name and a personage and usually identify a place of residence for that entity. Although often identified as male, the Supreme Creator is considered both male and female. The name of the Supreme Creator is seldom spoken, for it is sacred. Prayer is usually addressed to the Supreme Creator by a term of reverence and en-

dearment, such as "Grandfather." The Creator is usually perceived as omnipotent, in command of all the elements of existence, and as being anthropomorphic but spiritual rather than physical (Lukert, 1977).

Many tribal groups believe in other spirit beings that are associated with the Supreme Creator, such as a partner, co-creator, mate, or offspring. These lesser beings may or may not be impersonated in ceremony. More frequently they are considered exemplary models after which humans are to pattern their own lives. Most Indian tribes also recognize an assemblage of spirit helpers that assist humans. These beings are not gods, nor do they belong to the hierarchy of sacredness; therefore they are not worshipped or prayed to, but they command respect and thanks as angels and saints do in Western religious traditions. These beneficent spirit helpers may be identified (Locust, 1985) as Kachinas (Hopi), Ghan (Apache), or Yei (Navajo).

2.   *Humans are threefold beings made up of a spirit, mind, and body.* "Come into this house that has been prepared for you" is a phrase from a Hopi song welcoming an infant into the world. The "house" is the physical body the parents have prepared for the spirit to inhabit. The "I AM" of each person is the spirit that dwells within the physical body. Of the three elements — spirit, mind, and body — the spirit is the most important, for it is the essence of the being. The instrument by which the spirit may express itself is the body. It can learn spiritual lessons and may progress toward the ultimate goal of being united with the Supreme Creator. The mind is the link between the spirit and body and functions as an interpreter between the two. For example, a person hears a truth by means of the ears of the physical body, and recognizes the truth on a spiritual level. The mind, being aware of the disparity between human desires and spiritual truths, then makes adjustments in the thinking and response systems in the consciousness to incorporate this new truth.

The element of existence that gives vitality to all creation is often called "energy" or "power." The Supreme Creator is all powerful; all things he has created have power. This power (energy) is spiritual, so someone referred to as a "powerful" medicine person is identified as a person who has extremely strong personal energy. A stone (such as a crystal) or a plant (tobacco) may be powerful as well. Eagles have very powerful energy, for they fly closest to the sky, the abode of the Supreme Creator. Animals are sensitive to human energy; they can sense if someone is friendly or not. Humans can sense energies also, but most people are not aware of it. For example, a person may meet a stranger that he or she likes immediately and another person that he or she dislikes immediately. Personal energy is spiritual, and if the personal energy of a newborn infant is extremely strong, medicine people will know that the baby is a medicine person. It is difficult to deceive people who can "see," because energies betray what an individual really is.

Unlike Indian medicine, Western medicine does not incorporate the concept of spiritual illness, which can create problems for Indian children in non-Indian schools. For example, suppose an Indian child is absent from school because of a spiritual sickness. What happens if the school requires a doctor's note to the effect that he or she was seen by a physician, and no note is forthcoming? Non-Indian doctors cannot treat illnesses they do not recognize and were not trained to treat. A spiritual unwellness is frequently more devastating than a physical illness, yet this phenomenon is not recognized by many school nurses. Moreover, the concept of spiritual illness means that an individual's illness can affect the group (family and friends) and that group efforts are required to return all members of the group to wellness. As a result, students who are not ill may be absent from school in order to assist a sick relative in returning to wellness. Although this group effort is of vital importance to tribal, clan, and family members, it becomes a point of antagonism between group membership requirements and school rules, resulting in discriminating actions by school authorities.

Furthermore, many tribal customs revolves around the belief that the body and spirit need not be in the same place at all times. What non-Indians may perceive as inattention, "spacing out," or perhaps a petit mal seizure may be a matter of "spirit traveling" for the Indians. The term "spacing out"

implies the act of thinking or seeing things in one's mind, either in recall or in imagination, but confined to creation within the mind. "Spirit traveling" refers to the spirit's traveling to another location, assessing the activities and/or situation there (such as in reconnoitering during warfare), and being able to give an account of the information gathered during the travel. The ability to project the consciousness from the body appears to be common among tribal members, as many people have spoken about it to this researcher. However, it can create conflict in the classroom for students who have not yet learned adequate control of it.

Some tribal groups seem to possess the unique ability to "travel in their spirit bodies," or to manifest themselves in bodily form in another location, as part of the projected consciousness. This ability of bilocation may create frustration for teachers, whose Indian students may leave the physical body sitting at a desk in the classroom while their consciousness and spirit bodies go elsewhere (Locust, 1987).

3. *Plants and animals, like humans, are part of the spirit world. The spirit world exists side by side with and intermingles with the physical world.* Most American Indians believe that all creation has a spiritual component because all things were made by the Supreme Creator. The earth is our mother, the sky our father, and the animals our brothers and sisters. Water is our friend, and every living thing is a relative. Traditionally, thanks and a small gift were given to any animal or plant from which life was taken. No life was taken for sport or fun; hunting, fishing, and harvesting were done to obtain food. Most Indian tribes consider the mutilation of a body to be a direct violation of a brother or sister and believe that what is done to others will be done to them in return. This traditional belief comes in conflict with the practice in high school biology classes of requiring students to dissect animals. When faced with the choice of failing the class or bringing terrible consequences into their own lives or the lives of family members by mutilating an animal's body, most Indian students will fail the class (Locust, 1986a).

The idea that spirit forms inhabit the same living space as humans is not uncommon among Indian people. "My [deceased] father came to see me today" is a common statement, although each tribe may attach a different set of meanings to the visitation. Animals, birds, and fish may also manifest themselves in spirit form without a physical body. When an Indian seeks the meaning of his or her life (this is often called a vision quest), an animal from the spirit world may make itself visible to him or her, thus becoming the symbol for his or her life. Traditionally, American Indian people have been visionaries and have had the ability to see into the spirit world. Tribal members with an extraordinary ability in this area become medicine people.

Indian students are frequently reluctant to express their views about spirit beings because they fear ridicule. Non-Indians tend to think of spirit beings as terrifying specters, or else they scoff at anything that smacks of the supernatural. Indian people who acknowledge the spirit world as a normal part of existence have difficulty with both of these non-Indian views; further, they may refuse to debate the issue because of traditional respect for spirit beings.

4. *The spirit existed before it came into a physical body and will exist after the body dies.* The Indian belief in the immortality of the spirit parallels the non-Indian belief in everlasting life. However, unlike some organized religions that define immortality as beginning with birth and moving forward in a continuum of time, American Indians conceive of immortality as circular in nature, having no beginning and no end. In the Indian belief system, when one physical body is worn out, it is shed like an old garment and the spirit is free to inhabit another body. When that one is worn out, the cycle is repeated until the spirit reaches perfection and returns to the Supreme Creator. This "returning" is basic to the beliefs of most tribes, and although it is also a central concept for many cultures throughout the world, it is frequently a point of ridicule for those whose beliefs differ.

Traditional Indian belief systems do not incorporate an ultimate place of punishment for individuals who have transgressed in this life. Hell as a place of fire is not part of traditional Indian religion, although a state of torment is identified for departed spirits who have transgressed and who need chastisement to remind them not to repeat the same errors when they return in another body. Conversely, a peaceful land of rest and plenty occupies a place in Indian religion, but as a place where existence is carried on rather than a place of eternal sleep, as in Christian religions. This belief affects burial practices: Indian people provide their deceased with the necessities of life in the next world.

5. *Illness affects the mind and spirit as well as the body.* The concept of spirit, body, and mind interacting in humans is basic to most Indian beliefs and traditional healing methods. When Indians become ill, they often ask themselves why they are ill, since the cause of a sickness is as important as the illness itself. If the spiritual energy around a person is strong, he or she will not become ill, and negative things cannot happen to him or her. If an Indian does become ill or experiences difficulties (family problems, for example), he or she must find out why his or her personal energy is low and take steps to correct the situation; otherwise he or she will continue to have problems. And if the source of a student's spiritual weakness is the school, that student may not attend classes until his or her spiritual energy is strong again.

Modern medicine tends to treat the body for illness without treating the spirit. In the Western approach, bodies are cut open, repaired, put back together, cleaned, medicated, and bandaged; but most Western doctors give no thought to the spirit. If the situation indicates emotional or mental problems, the doctor may refer the patient to another doctor who specializes in such illnesses. The physical — and perhaps mental — side of an illness may be taken care of; the spirit, however, is not treated by Western medicine. For this reason many Indians prefer to see a medicine person at the same time that they are being treated by a physician. For example, an Indian may go to the Indian Health Center to have a broken leg cared for. The physician takes care of the physical injury, but to the Indian the spirit must also be cared for properly. Treating the spirit is the process of finding out why the broken leg occurred, understanding the events in a spiritual rather than a physical sense, and then beginning the process of changing whatever it was in the body, mind, or spirit that was out of harmony enough to warrant a broken leg.

In the schools, misunderstandings frequently arise because of the difference between the school systems' definition of "sickness" and the Indian concept of unwellness. Schools may have a list of physical symptoms for which students are automatically sent home: for instance, fever, upset stomach, headache, vomiting, and other obvious symptoms of distress. These physical symptoms are not cause for alarm, however, in most Indian families, whose members have learned to live with minor discomforts and realize that such suffering is usually transient. As a result, Indian parents may be labeled by the school authorities as uncaring, irresponsible, ignorant, or lazy when they send their children to school with a runny nose or a cough, when in fact those symptoms are so common in their culture that they are not considered evidence of illness. In contrast, a child may be kept home several days for traditional treatments for "ghost sickness," a malady of lethargy, apathy, and general nonspecific unwellness caused by the spirits of dead relatives calling for the child to join them. The child may face punishment for his or her absence upon returning to school, since the school's list of excusable illnesses may not include "ghost sickness," and a note from a traditional medicine person — if it could be obtained — may not be considered adequate. Furthermore, a healing ceremony may call for burning powerful, often pungent herbs and enveloping the ill person in the smoke. This treatment usually includes an admonition not to bathe the afflicted person for several days, a practice that precludes the student's returning to school.

6. *Wellness is harmony in spirit, mind, and body.* Harmony is the peaceful, tranquil state of knowing all is well with one's spirit, mind, and body. To be in harmony is to be at "oneness" with life, eternity, the Supreme Creator, and oneself. Many Indians who are visionaries describe the energy (aura) around an individual who has harmony as a light or radiance of being, to which all life forms react with joy. But harmony is not found within the environment, nor does it come from others; it comes from within and from the Supreme Creator. It is toward this harmony that American Indians strive, despite the poverty and deprivation in their lives and discrimination against them for their belief in harmony itself.

Harmony is wellness, but it is not utopia, as an older Cherokee man explained. When asked about harmony, an elderly Hopi responded that each person has his proper set of relationships for being in harmony and that no two people are alike. John Coulehan (1980) found a similar perspective among the Navajo. A person can be in harmony, Indians believe, despite the condition of the body, the mind, or the environment. One person's harmony may include compensating for failing vision. It is not the events that happen to a person, but his or her responses to those events that create harmony. Every human chooses his responses, and thus chooses harmony or disharmony.

7. *Unwellness is disharmony in spirit, mind, and body.* In contrast to wellness or harmony, unwellness is characterized by disharmony. One cannot be in a state of disharmony that is caused by suppressed anger, frustration, heartache, or fear without sooner or later developing unwellness in the physical body from that disharmony. Disharmony may be a vague feeling of things "not being right" in one's life, and a time of meditation may be needed in which to discover what is not right. One can be affected by terminal cancer, but if the spirit, mind, and body are in harmony the cancer becomes part of the harmony and the person is at peace.

Indian tribes tend to allow each person his or her harmony without forcing absolute conformity to all cultural standards. This custom allows the individuals who are less capable mentally to find a meaningful place in their society in simple physical tasks, such as wood gathering. A beautiful Hopi man once wept when he recounted the story of his friend "Bear," a big, loving, mentally retarded boy who was the village water carrier. The Bureau of Indian Affairs social worker insisted that Bear go to a school in the city. Bear went, but he was terribly homesick and became violent. He spent the next twenty years in the state hospital for the criminally insane and then returned to his village to die. What a tragic waste of human life! Bear was in harmony in his village carrying water. His retardation was part of his harmony; the state hospital was not.

Avoiding disharmony is desirable in Indian cultures; disharmony is negative and pervasive and destroys an individual's harmony. For instance, Indian parents frequently refuse to go to the school when called because they have learned that being called means their child is in trouble. The negative situation that is certain to develop among school officials, the child, and the parents brings disharmony for all concerned and can result in illness if spiritual energy becomes low. Therefore the parents may choose not to be involved with the disharmony at the school and instead to counsel the child at home in a positive manner. Non-Indians, whose culture dictates swift and painful punishment for students who transgress school rules, may view the Indian response as too lenient or as pampering the child, and may become angry because Indian parents do not respond in the manner they think appropriate. The disparity between the cultural expectations of parental responsibilities and control of children may create dissension and hostility between school officials and tribal members.

Students who are faced with a disharmonic situation at school may choose to remove themselves from it in an effort to avoid the possibility of disharmony in their own lives. Physically removing themselves — through leaving school or hiding — is the first defense against disharmony. However, if a student is called before a school official and forced to listen to a tirade full of loud, angry reprimands and accusations, and is therefore endangered by being in close proximity to such negativity, the student may choose to protect his or her spirit by removing it through spirit travel if he or she cannot escape physically. At the first available opportunity, the student may also choose to take the physical body along on the spirit travel and leave an empty chair and a furious school official behind. But to Indians, escaping disharmony does not mean escaping the consequences of an action. Indian children are taught early in life that every thought and every ac-

tion creates a ripple in their being and that the consequences of those actions are inescapable.

8.   *Natural unwellness is caused by the violation of a sacred or tribal taboo.* Most American Indians' tribal beliefs include a distinction between those illnesses that are the result of natural causes and those that result from unnatural causes. Natural unwellness is a consequence of violating a taboo, whether it was done intentionally or unintentionally, and can affect the offender or his or her family. Although the word *taboo* is not a perfect translation of the concept, it is closer than any other word in English to the meaning of the concept. However, taboo, in the Indian sense, carries cultural and religious implications, and to violate a taboo brings spiritual as well as physical consequences.

Each tribe has its own taboos, with specific consequences. In some tribes there is a definite relationship between breaking a certain taboo and experiencing identical consequences. Mutilating an animal's paw or leg, for example, always results in injury to the mutilator's foot or leg. In other tribes, a particular reptile may be seen as a carrier of negative energy, and getting near the reptile may cause a variety of illnesses secondary to "reptile illness."

Most tribes recognize cultural and moral taboos that relate to personal conduct, such as never laughing at a disabled person or at an animal (Gifford, 1940). Religious taboos may concern proper observance of rituals. Some of the prevalent tribal taboos concern death, incest, the female menstrual cycle, witchcraft, certain animals, some types of phenomena such as lightning or an eclipse, particular foods, dead bodies, marrying into one's own clan, and strict observance of religious and ceremonial protocol.

One particular taboo, based on the belief that bodies are sacred to their owners, often creates conflict in schools. For Indians, exposing one's bodily sacredness to the indiscriminate view of others violates the holiness of the being. Thus, violation of the sacredness of the body occurs when students are required to change clothes or shower as part of their physical education classes, since many of the schools do not provide private showers or changing rooms. Rather than commit this sacrilegious act of exposing their bodies, many Indian students fail physical education, because changing clothes and showering are required to pass the course. Non-Indian educational systems have been extremely slow to respond to the Indians' need for privacy in regard to this issue.

9. *Unnatural unwellness is caused by witchcraft.* For almost all tribes, evil is a real and powerful adversary, and one must continually be on guard against it. Evil is seen as a power, and it is also identified as an entity, either human or animal. As part of an attempt to develop a clear definition of evil in Indian belief systems, this writer asked several Indians to explain how they perceived evil. The terms they most often used to identify evil were *bad power, bad energy, negative energy, negative power,* or *dark side.* While non-Indians often personify evil as a red being with horns, a tail, and a pitchfork, some tribes see the bear as a personification of evil, and others see evil as being an owl or a reptile. Most tribes identify a legendary cultural figure associated with evil, but unlike the Christian concept of Satan as an entity that creates evil, traditional cultural figures usually only represent it. Evil may manifest itself in a multitude of shapes and forms, and it can be manipulated by witchcraft.

According to some Indian belief systems, an individual may choose not to walk in the spirit of harmony, and instead choose to walk in the power of malevolent spirits and to do harm to other humans. Indians refer to these individuals as *witches* and to their activities as *witchcraft.* Hopi Indians refer to these individuals as *buaka.* In the Yaqui language it is *yesisivome.* These terms are not synonymous with Western concepts of witches and witchcraft — actually there are no English terms for the Indian concept. The Hopi word *buaka* might be translated as "those who go around at night" or "those from the dark side," as compared with non-witches, who are "beings of light." The Yaqui word *yesisivome* means "one who is on the bad side" of using supernatural power. The Indian term for witch refers to both males and females. Tribal groups differ on what the terms *witches* and *witchcraft* mean in their language, but most Indian people understand the use of negative energy against one another. But

one need not be a witch to cast a spell or to "witch" another person, for most Indians know how to manipulate energy (power), especially mental energy. In intense, destructive cases of witchcraft, however, the witch involved makes skillful, professional use of negative power.

Witching usually follows one of two patterns: It may affect the environment around the victim, which in turn affects the person; or it may affect the person directly. If the intended victim's personal power is so strong that the witchcraft cannot affect him or her, a member of the family who is weak will fall victim. Incidences of witchcraft related by Indian people of various tribes indicate that sudden physical illness, sharp pains, accidents, depression, irrational thinking, and unusual behavior are often suspected as having been caused by witchcraft. Protective objects, such as medicine bags, certain stones, bits of organic material, and symbolic items of a religious or spiritual nature, are frequently worn on the body; their removal (which is often required by school officials) can often create a dangerous vulnerability for the individual.

Keeping one's personal energy strong is the best defense against negative energy. Parents are responsible for the personal protection of their children and of any older, weak family members in their household. When the house is filled with love, caring, and kindness, evil cannot find a weakness by which to enter. If it does enter, therefore, one knows that there is a weakness somewhere and that it must be corrected before more harm is done. Staying away from situations that cause an Indian's personal energy to become weak is a survival behavior that may be frustrating to non-Indians. First, such behavior is not part of their culture, and second, the identification of a harmful situation is culturally determined and frequently causes conflict in school settings and, consequently, discrimination.

Medicine people are on the "good side" of the use of energy and are frequently prevailed upon to counteract the negative energy of witchcraft. If the spell is not strong, the victim, with the help of his or her family, may be able to dissolve it. If the negative energy is strong, however, or if the individual does not know where his or her weakness lies, a medicine person may assist the victim in these areas. (Medicine people never claim to "heal" anyone or to "take off" a spell; properly speaking, they assist other people in healing themselves or in dissolving the negative energy around them.) Medicine people are also healers of the physical body; one may specialize in bones and another in childbirth. The visionaries also work with positive energy to counteract negativity, for they have the ability to perceive spiritual matters. In some tribes, healers dedicate themselves to "light" and therefore can never intentionally harm anyone; in others a medicine person may heal someone today and harm someone else tomorrow, depending on the situation. Traditionally, however, medicine people are warriors for "light," and witches are perpetrators of "darkness."

10. *Each of us is responsible for our own wellness.* Many American Indians believe they are responsible for their own wellness. They can make themselves well and they can make themselves unwell. If an individual allows himself or herself to become upset by something, he or she has allowed disharmony to enter his or her life. This disharmony may create physical symptoms such as a headache or indigestion. Thus, that individual has caused the headache or indigestion by allowing himself or herself to become upset. If an individual's spiritual energy is so low that he or she can be affected by witchcraft, then the individual has allowed the witchcraft to affect him or her. Therefore, keeping one's energy strong and keeping oneself in harmony preclude unwellness.

When an Indian is in harmony, his or her spirit, mind, and body are so attuned to the self, the environment, and the universe that transgressions against moral, religious, or cultural taboos do not occur; further, negative energy from witchcraft cannot find a weakness by which to affect him or her. The idea of this powerful protective shield of harmony is articulated in song by the Navajo: "Beauty is above me, beauty is before me, beauty is all around me."

Most tribes believe that a spirit chooses the body it will inhabit. In the case of a handicapped body, the spirit chooses that body knowing its limitations but choosing to use it for some purpose determined by that spirit and the Supreme Creator. Further-

more, tribal members envision the spirit inside a handicapped body as being whole and perfect and capable of understanding everything that goes on in the environment, even when it appears that the physical body cannot comprehend anything. One might express sympathy for the physical conditions of the body in which a spirit chose to express itself, to learn lessons, and to teach lessons. One might express respect and honor for the spirit that is strong and wise enough to inhabit such a body, and assist it in accomplishing whatever it came to the earth to accomplish. Indians distinguish between a spirit in a handicapped body and the body itself: The causes of a body's being handicapped may lie with the parents (as in the case of fetal alcohol syndrome), and consequently the blame for (prenatal) mutilation of a body falls on the parents; the choice of being in the body, however, remains with the spirit in the body, not the parents.

Consider, though, that the concept of handicaps is culturally determined; what may be a handicap to a non-Indian may not be considered a handicap to an Indian. Many Navajo, for instance, are born with a congenital hip deformity, but the condition does not disable them and therefore they are not handicapped. When surgery is performed, however, they become unable to sit on a horse comfortably and therefore become disabled, for riding is still an important mode of transportation in many areas (Rabin, Barnett, Arnold, Freiberger & Brooks, 1967).

In school systems, children may be considered mentally retarded while within their own community they are not retarded but function as contributing members of their society (consider the case of Bear described earlier). Most traditional Indian languages do not have words for retarded, disabled, or handicapped. Dee Brown's (1970) book *Bury My Heart at Wounded Knee* contains many names of individuals that are descriptive of disabilities — No-Eyes, Big-Head, One-Who-Walks-With-a-Limp, Hump, One-Arm — but categories such as "cripples" do not appear in the literature. The Hopi people identify some individuals with the white or snow kachina (albinos), and legends tell them that one deity who was incarnated as a human, the kachina Kokopeli, was humpbacked; neither of these two conditions constitutes a handicap to the Hopi people (Locust, 1986b). A beautiful term for describing a disabled person comes from the Yaquis: *not completed yet* (Locust, 1987).

Obtaining an education has been a necessity for all Indian children. Traditionally, children who learned at a slower pace than others were as normal as children who learned faster than others. Little differences existed in the way they were treated. Only when formal education came to the Indian Nations were labels applied to the differences between children. Public Law 94-142, the Education for All Handicapped Children Act (1975), was a two-edged sword for Indian people. On the one hand, it provided educational opportunities for severely disabled children who were once institutionalized off the reservation by the Bureau of Indian Affairs, but on the other hand, it caused multitudes of children to be labeled mentally retarded or learning disabled who up until that time were not considered handicapped in their cultures (Joe & Miller, 1987). This is because American Indian cultures reinforce non-verbal communication and alternative avenues of communication, including visual/spatial memory, visual/motor skills, and sequential visual memory, but not verbal skills. Psychological evaluations include verbal skills as a large portion of the tests Indian children are given. Tests are conducted in English, a second language to many Indian children. Small wonder, then, that non-Indian tests identify disproportionate numbers of Indian children who score very low in verbal skills.

The formal education process, including standardized achievement and intelligence tests, is designed to assist and measure mental functions desirable in the dominant culture. It is a fact that use of such tests for other cultures is discriminatory; nevertheless, little change has occurred to adjust either the educational or the testing process to accommodate the language or cognition styles of other cultures.

Discussion

Belief systems are integrated into the total being of the American Indian, and discrimination against these beliefs occurs in ways that non-Indians do not easily understand. Indians view immortality and existence as circular rather than linear and appear to learn best when information is presented to them in a circular manner (Emerson, 1987). Traditional ceremonies are based on the concept of circular completion, just as the spirit continues on the medicine wheel until it reaches completion. Formal education, in contrast, is composed of linear lessons, each of which occupies a linear spot on the year's time chart. Completion is from the top to the bottom of the chart, year after year, until the final year has been reached. Traditional education of Indian youth is not linear and frequently not verbal. Indian children learn by watching elders, by having the grandparents identify for them the whole of the task, the complete circle, the perfection of completion.

One of the most blatant issues of discrimination against American Indian belief systems involves traditional ceremonial times. School calendars include holidays based on Christian tradition and on national historical events. Children from other religious backgrounds — those who are Jewish, for instance — typically enjoy the freedom to participate in religious activities without penalty for absences from their classes. In most school systems American Indian children do not enjoy this religious freedom and are penalized for being absent from classes while participating in traditional tribal ceremonies. Consider the case of the Pascua Yaqui Indians near Tucson, Arizona, who attend classes in the Tucson Unified School District. Hundreds of years ago, traditional Yaqui religion was combined with Catholicism, producing a unique belief system with strict religious procedures, ceremonies, and observances in the weeks before the Running of the Gloria (corresponding with Easter Sunday). Each year scores of Yaqui children were absent from school twice a week for several weeks preceding the Lenten season in the spring, and each year the children suffered the humiliation of having to justify their absences. Each year it was the same; excusable absences did not include participation in traditional tribal functions. However, in 1986 the culturally sensitive school board amended its attendance policy so that the observance of traditional Indian ceremonies and feast days became excusable absences. Unfortunately, this bold step toward religious equality in the educational system is an exception, not the norm, for school boards.

The dominant culture's lack of understanding of the tribal concept that the unity of a group is binding also leads to discrimination against Indian people. In years past, it was the unity of the tribe, clan, or even family that enabled its members to survive. This survival instinct is still present in Indian communities, and it dictates behaviors that are frequently misunderstood by non-Indians. For example, the group's survival depends on everyone working together and sharing. All members work together and contribute to the group, supporting each other in times of stress, for they know that they will find the same network of support for themselves should they require it. Children are expected to contribute to their group as soon as they are mature enough, and thus a 4-year-old may have the responsibility of looking after a toddler, and a 6-year-old Navajo may act as a shepherd. With this kind of early responsibility comes an early breaking of the maternal bond; children as young as 9 and 10 "break the apron strings" and are respected as adults since they participate as adults in the group effort. Responsibility, loyalty, and proper codes of behavior are taught to the children by grandparents, who are the traditional teachers in Indian communities. The U.S. educational system has dealt a severe blow to this group bonding behavior by separating children from the home to send them to school, thus removing from the grandparents the opportunity to teach them properly. Frequently, children are still accorded respect as adults at an early age, but too often they have not had the advantage of traditional teachings. This creates freedom without knowledge of how to accept responsibility, and consequently Indian children are called "delinquent," "wild," and "uncontrolled" by a social system that created this situation for them.

Another aspect of the group membership concept often conflicts with educational systems: that of justifying membership in the group through one's contribution and loyalty. Junior high school girls stay home to babysit younger siblings while their parents work, enabling the family to have two incomes without the cost of child care. Young boys, pressed to go to work to help buy food and unable to find employment because of their age, may turn to stealing in order to contribute to the group. So strong is the membership bonding that students go hungry rather than ask their parents for lunch money, for in asking they would be putting their needs in front of the group's needs. For the same reason, Indian students may not participate in group sports that require uniforms or equipment that they must purchase, for money spent on those things means that someone else must go without. In an era when unemployment among American Indians is 62% on and near reservations (Bureau of Indian Affairs, 1987), and the average annual income of all Indian families in the United States consistently runs $6,000 to $7,000 below that of the general population, money is a great concern (Northern Arizona University and the University of Arizona, 1987, p. 6).

Belief systems are the framework upon which cultures and societies function. The belief system is the bond that holds civilizations together, and it is the small voice inside each of us that urges us to be true to what we have been taught. As Native people, we cannot separate our spiritual teachings from our learning, nor can we separate our beliefs about who and what we are from our values and our behaviors. As Indian people, we ask that educational systems recognize our right to religious freedom and our right, as Sovereign Nations, to live in harmony as we were taught. However, non-Indians must be educated about the traditional beliefs that Indian people may have before they can understand what changes may be needed.

Tribal beliefs vary, and the extend to which a tribe embraces its traditional cultural beliefs varies. Each tribal group has distinct and unique beliefs that are basic to that tribe's culture. Most tribes cling to the Old Teachings because they know that, once gone, it means the death of their culture. Educational systems could make it easier to maintain endangered cultures by abandoning the idea that all non-WASPS (White Anglo-Saxon Protestants) wish to become WASP-like and vanish into the melting pot of America. The majority of American Indians wish to maintain their identity as Sovereign Nations under the Constitution of the United States, and they wish to maintain their tribal and cultural belief systems and life-styles. We remain positive that, once understanding has been established between tribal cultures and established educational systems, discrimination will cease.

Note

1. As defined in Public Law 93-638, the Indian Self-Determination and Education Assistance Act (1975), an Indian means "a person who is a member of an Indian tribe. An Indian tribe means any Indian tribe, band, nation, or other organized group or community, including any Alaska Native village, regional, or village corporation as defined or established pursuant to the Alaska Native Claims Settlement Act (1971) which is recognized as eligible for the special programs and services provided by the United States to Indians because of their status as Indians. Tribal organization means the recognized governing body of any Indian tribe; any legally established organization of Indians which is controlled, sanctioned, or chartered by such governing body or which is democratically elected by the adult members of the Indian community to be served by such organization and which includes the maximum participation of Indians in all phases of its activities."

References

Aberle, D. (1966). *The peyote religion among the Navajo.* Chicago: University of Chicago Press.

Alaska Native Claims Settlement Act, 85 Stat. 688 (1971).

American Indian Religious Freedom Act (Public Law 95-341), 42 U.S.C. 1966 (1978).

Brown, D. (1970). *Bury my heart at Wounded Knee.* New York: Holt, Rinehart & Winston.

Bureau of Indian Affairs, Department of the Interior. (1987). *Indian service population and labor estimates.* Washington, DC: Author.

Coulehan, J. (1980). Navajo Indian medicine: Implications for healing. *Journal of Family Practice, 10,* 55–61.

Education For All Handicapped Children Act (Public Law 94-142), 20 U.S.C. 1400–1485 (1975).

Emerson, L. (1987). *Self-determination through culture and thought processes.* Paper presented at the Indigenous People's World Conference, University of British Columbia, Vancouver, British Columbia, Canada.

Gifford, E. W. (1940). Cultural elements distributions: XII, Apache-Pueblo. *Anthropological Records, 4*(1).

Hammerschlag, C. (1985, April). *The spirit of healing in groups.* Monograph from a modified text of the Presidential address delivered to the Arizona Group Psychotherapy Society, Phoenix Indian Medical Center, Oracle, AZ.

Joe, J., & Miller, D. (1987). *American Indian cultural perspectives on disability* (Monograph). Tucson: Native American Research and Training Center, College of Medicine, University of Arizona.

Kahn, M., Williams, C., Calvez, E., Lujero, L., Conrad, R., & Goldstein, G. (1975). The Papago psychological service: A community mental health program on an American Indian reservation. *American Journal of Community Psychology, 3,* 81–96.

Kluckhohn, C., & Leighton, D. (1962). *The Navajo* (rev. ed.). New York: Anchor Books.

Levy, J. (1963). *Navajo health concepts and behaviors: The role of the Anglo medical man in the Navajo healing process.* (Report to the U.S. Public Health Service, Indian Health Systems). Bethesda, MD: U.S. Public Health Service.

Locust, C. (1985). *American Indian beliefs concerning health and unwellness* (Monograph). Tucson: Native American Research and Training Center, College of Medicine, University of Arizona.

Locust, C. (1986a). *Apache beliefs about unwellness and handicaps* (Monograph). Tucson: Native American Research and Training Center, College of Medicine, University of Arizona.

Locust, C. (1986b). *Hopi Indian beliefs about unwellness and handicaps* (Monograph). Tucson: Native American Research and Training Center, College of Medicine, University of Arizona.

Locust, C. (1987). *Yaqui Indian beliefs about unwellness and handicaps* (Monograph). Tucson: Native American Research and Training Center, College of Medicine, University of Arizona.

Lukert, K. (1977). *Navajo mountain and rainbow bridge religion* (Museum of Northern Arizona series on American Tribal Religions). Flagstaff: Museum of Northern Arizona.

Mails, T. E. (1974). *The people called Apache.* Englewood Cliffs, NJ: Prentice-Hall.

Morgan, T. J. (1892). *Report of Indian commissioners.* Washington, DC: National Archives.

Northern Arizona University and University of Arizona. (1987). *A study of the special problems and needs of American Indians with handicaps both on and off the reservation, Volume II* (Report prepared for the U.S. Department of Education, Office of Special Education and Rehabilitative Services, Rehabilitation Services Administration). Washington, DC: U.S. Department of Education.

Rabin, D. L., Barnett, C. R., Arnold, W. E., Freiberger, R. H., & Brooks, G. (1967). Untreated hip disease. *American Public Health Association Supplement Edition, 55*(2), 1–44.

Reagan, A. (1930). *Notes on the Indians of the Fort Apache region* (Anthropological Publications No. 31). New York: American Museum of Natural History.

Roessel, R. A., Jr. (1963). *San Carlos Apache Indian education* (Monograph). Tempe: Indian Education Center, Arizona State University.

AWARDING POSITIONS BY COMPETENCE

Alan H. Goldman

Alan H. Goldman examines the awarding of positions by competence and the issue of past discrimination. He offers a social contract argument and discusses both libertarian and egalitarian alternatives. (Source: From Justice and Reverse Discrimination *by Alan H. Goldman. Copyright © 1979 by Princeton University Press. Reprinted by permission of Princeton University Press.)*

... In recent political debates on the subject of reverse discrimination or preferential hiring the principle of hiring by competence has seemed to remain sacrosanct, at least if one is to judge from the lip service paid to it by all sides of the discussion. Proponents of affirmative action at the level of hiring in universities go to great lengths to distinguish minority "goals" from quotas. While strict quotas for raising percentages of blacks and women employed by a fixed date, which would result in strong reverse discrimination, are acknowledged to be incompatible with the maintenance of strict competence standards, percentage goals for minorities are held to encourage minority hiring while maintaining existing standards. Some affirmative action supporters also argue that because minority-group members have suffered discrimination in the past, their real competence cannot be judged in terms of their "paper credentials," that some women and blacks who appear to have lower qualifications on paper (in terms of degrees, experience, etc.) may actually raise the general level of competence if hired and given the chance formerly denied them to develop and use their talents. Opponents of the policy, on the other hand, seem to feel that affirmative action programs in universities can be shown to be unjust by demonstrating that academic standards of excellence suffer and that the most qualified individuals fail to receive positions through pressure for reverse discrimination. They seem to believe the argument won if they can only show that affirmative action in practice violates the rule of hiring by competence.

Despite the apparent unanimity regarding hiring by competence in the context of this public debate, the principle has recently come under attack in more sophisticated philosophical circles from both the right and left. Libertarians argue or imply that corporations or organizations with positions to fill can give them to whomever they choose, that society has no right to interfere in this free process. Corporations, like individuals, have the right to control their legitimately acquired assets and to disburse them to whomever they choose; the right to hire freely is part of this more general right. Egalitarians, on the other hand, hold the principle of hiring by competence to be unjust because it rewards initial social positions and purely native talents that individuals do not deserve and for which they can claim no responsibility. I shall argue here that these attacks are misguided....[1] I hold that hiring the most competent probably meets the stringent criterion of justice by being in the interests of all in society in the long run (as opposed to alternative rules), and is hence capable of being willed as a distributive principle by all contractors regardless of social position.

Philosophical clarification regarding the issue of preferential hiring for minorities demands prior consideration of the justification of hiring by competence for two reasons. First, reverse discrimination, or first-order discrimination for that matter, can only be precisely defined relative to some rule for hiring that is held to be just. Discrimination, as the concept is used in this context, involves treating relevantly similar persons differently or relevantly different people the same. Any award of scarce goods or positions requires some differentiation among those individuals considered; such differentiation amounts to unjust discrimination only when the characteristics on the basis of which it is made are irrelevant to the rewards from a moral point of view. But to know whether discrimination is occurring in practice, we must first know what constitutes relevant distinctions in the area under consideration.[2] In our context this means knowing what rule should govern the award of positions. Second, unless some just distributive rule is violated by the practice of reverse discrimination, and unless certain people acquire at least prima facie *rights* to positions by satisfying the criteria stipulated in this rule, reverse discrimination will never be seriously unjust. The question of its morality would then be decided on utilitarian grounds, which I hold to be largely irrelevant.

Thus I shall be concerned . . . with two central questions: (1) Does society have the right to impose and enforce any rule of hiring against corporations with positions to fill? (2) If the answer to (1) is affirmative, which principle for awarding positions ought to be adopted from the point of view of justice? I shall argue that society does have this right, both to protect its own welfare as a consumer of goods and services and to protect equal opportunity for its members. The principle of awarding positions by competence will be seen to satisfy our strong criterion in all probability, and certainly to satisfy the liberal criterion. Enforcement of this principle, it will be argued, overrides rights of corporations to control their assets by hiring whomever they please and is more just than seemingly egalitarian alternatives. Once the awarding of positions on the basis of competence is accepted as a just initial rule, the question . . . becomes that of deciding when principles of compensation require departures from the distributive rule. But the general rule must be established against possible alternatives before that question becomes relevant.

The Rule for Awarding Desirable Positions

The first question to be faced here is why one system of hiring or awarding positions can be judged more just than another. . . . To say that principles of hiring are a matter of distributive social *justice* is to imply that certain individuals acquire distributive *rights* to certain positions and that to refuse them these positions is to refuse to grant them what is legitimately due them. Part of the reason that we do in fact recognize such rights is that one's career or social position affects the quality of one's life as much as any other single factor. Having attained a particular position

through effort or work is for many a crucial ingredient in a sense of self-accomplishment, satisfaction, or self-respect, as it is a central element in the respect that one enjoys from the community. . . .

It might be objected that those in our society who begin with social advantages for attaining desirable positions will not be concerned with such equality or fairness; in fact, they may well be concerned to prevent it. But certainly hypothetical contractors unaware of their initial social positions will be anxious to ensure their ability to work for desirable positions and to prevent the denial of these positions on capricious or arbitrary grounds. Barring individuals from achieving goals for which they have productively worked is to deprive them of an important source of satisfaction, a source that is somewhat independent of the other benefits attached to the desirable positions. Positions assigned in a totally capricious or arbitrary way could not rationally serve as sources of self-respect. It is the achievement of a goal for which one has worked that serves as this source. Therefore, if the attainment of self-respect and a sense of accomplishment is an important good; if the achievement of a position for which one has worked is a part of this good; if all contractors would wish to preserve the opportunity to pursue this good; and if the liberal contractual model provides a test of moral rules; then we have moral reason for creating some general rule for awarding desirable positions fairly. The rule would have to be such as to prevent the denial of opportunity to pursue and achieve these positions through effort and work. Acceptance of the rule would in turn create prima facie rights to positions for individuals who satisfy the criteria stipulated by it. At this point we can say that individuals would acquire rights not to be excluded on grounds other than those deemed acceptable as criteria by the rule. These rights would become ingredients in a general right to fair or equal opportunity.

Clearly, if any right to equal opportunity is to be recognized, we cannot allow jobs and positions in professional schools to be awarded capriciously, especially given the deep-seated prejudices known to exist in our society. An opportunity to compete with others and to be judged on the basis of one's performance, rather than on the basis of native factors alone, is a necessary condition for an equal opportunity to acquire all other goods. Since one's ability to acquire other social goods is a function mainly of one's job, equal opportunity for social goods does not exist without equal opportunity for decent jobs. While redistributive taxation, open housing, and integrated schools are advocated in the name of this right, they amount to little when jobs can be denied to those who have managed to acquire superior qualifications after escaping other forms of social deprivation. Thus the enforcement of some rule for hiring that is not based purely upon inborn or initial chance factors is the first prerequisite for equality of opportunity. Contractors ignorant of race, sex, and social position would want to ensure that effort and accomplishment play major roles in satisfying criteria for positions, not only because they will want to preserve the attainment of positions as a source of pride and self-respect, but also because they will recognize that it is worse to be prevented from attempting to achieve that for which one is willing to work than it is to lack that which one might not want to make efforts to acquire.[3] Moreover, the frustration of not being allowed to compete is greater than that of ultimately losing in competition. From the point of view of their own self-interest, then, and to prevent frustration, the contractors would want some rule stipulating initial rights to positions on the basis of criteria that give priority to effort, work, and achievement.

A critic might recognize that once we build the artificial constraints of equality into our contractual position via a Rawls-type "veil of ignorance," egalitarian rights like that to equal opportunity must emerge from it. But he might question once more our reason for building in these constraints. Here we are taken back to fundamental intuitions regarding the nature of morality itself. Part of the justification of the liberal moral framework is that recognition of moral equality among agents is central to a moral point of view. Placing the interests of all on the same level entails accepting only social rules that could be freely accepted by rational contractors defined as equal in certain respects. Although this framework creates a presumption of equality in distributions from which departures need to be justified, it is clear that such contractors would permit certain departures from

strict equality. They would do so first in order to create incentives for individuals to develop their capacities and competencies, so as to be able to contribute more to the total pool of goods and services and to benefit all by so doing.[4] For these incentives to succeed, those who develop competence must be rewarded by being given those positions for which they are most competent.

Thus we have another reason why the rule of awarding positions to those most competent is just as an initial distributive rule, and why rights are created in relation to it. Inequalities are permissible in the first place partly to encourage individuals to be maximally productive. When individuals are encouraged in this way to direct their efforts toward maximal social productivity, differentials achieved in productivity or potential productivity cannot then be justly ignored. It would be possible to encourage productivity on the job by differential reward without initially assigning positions according to reasonable estimates of potential productivity. But this inconsistency would violate this purpose of differential rewards. Many positions require prior training, and we want people to train for positions in advance for the same reasons that we want them to perform competently in those positions. Contractors adopting rules by which to shape society would want to encourage efforts in early years toward attaining skills required for various positions, and the obvious inducement is the ultimate reward of the positions with their different pay scales. Once a rule for rewarding competence is adopted, it would be unjust not to reward those who satisfy its criteria. The rights that they acquire to positions for which they are most competent can then be seen as rights to have society fulfill its contractual obligations. The adoption of the rule results in contractual relations with those who work to satisfy its criteria: these individuals acquire the rights that their legitimate expectations to the positions be fulfilled.

To the fundamental presumption of equality, then, we must add limits to degrees of justified inequalities and means to ensure equal opportunity to attain the better shares of justified inequalities. The right to equal opportunity itself follows from the fundamental right to have one's interests counted on the same scale with those of others, since one's interests are not counted equally unless one is given an equal chance to satisfy those interests. According to the line of reasoning pursued here, this right is to be interpreted not as a right to equal or random chances to attain the better shares of justified inequalities, but as an equal chance to achieve those shares through work.

Thus, in addition to their desire to preserve their chances to succeed through effort, contractors would wish to adopt a rule giving initial rights to positions to those who best qualify in order to create a maximum pool of quality goods and services. This second reason relates not to those who will come to occupy the positions in question but to the public, to whom those in socially important positions are responsible for providing needed goods and services. Desirable positions, to which respect and high monetary reward attach, are generally positions of social responsibility, whose occupants have significant effects upon the satisfaction of social needs and demands. To have such positions of responsibility filled capriciously or arbitrarily results in sharply diminished utility to the public. This consideration motivates adoption of a rule for assigning positions by competence or potential competence. In fact, if we compare this general rule with any other fully general rule as a basis for assigning positions, it seems likely that its adoption would result not only in utility maximization across society, but also in a strong Pareto improvement, that is, in gains to all members of society in overall goods and services. Of course, some who might occupy desirable positions under some other rule will not do so under the rule that rewards competence or potential competence. But it seems probable that losses to these individuals will be more than offset — even for them — by gains in other goods and services derived from having individuals of maximum competence occupying those positions. It therefore seems likely that the rule for hiring the competent meets our strongest criterion for acceptability: it could be rationally willed by all actual members of society. Even if this weighing of goods is inaccurate, and even if some actual individuals would be willing to sacrifice quality and quantity of other goods and services in order to occupy desirable positions that they could not occupy according to criteria of competence, our weaker criterion is nevertheless satisfied by the adoption of this initial general rule as opposed to alternatives. Contractors ignorant of the positions they might come to occupy under different possible rules would certainly want to adopt the rule that maximizes the provision of quality goods and services to the community as a whole.

It is true that we have not barred knowledge of natural abilities from our hypothetical contractors. Those who know that they lack talents and are below average in mental abilities might therefore prefer rules that place less emphasis upon qualifications, the acquisition of which is greatly aided by talent or intelligence. But if we disallow advantages for acquiring qualifications deriving from initial social positions (as our contractors would), then those within a normal range of intelligence will recognize that attainment of qualifications for most positions will vary largely with the degree of effort made to acquire them. Given that a wide range of positions might be available as goals for individuals with normal capacities, given that all will suffer when unqualified persons occupy many positions, and given that special forms of compensation can be established for individuals with subnormal capacities, it is plausible that our contractors would all agree upon a rule with competence criteria. Few would prefer that positions requiring superior intelligence or talent for adequate performance be filled by individuals who lack those characteristics. Positions exist to satisfy social needs and demands. Even those individuals who lack the requisite potentials to attain such positions will recognize that there is little point to making one who could not defend clients a lawyer, or one who could not diagnose disease a doctor, or one who could not instruct a professor, or one who could not play an instrument well a musician, etc. They would recognize the rationality of a rule requiring qualifications, even if they felt that they might fare better under some alternative. Of course, only some positions require relative excellence. The rule for hiring unskilled labor might reasonably differ from the rule for awarding positions that call for special skills. The former might require hiring on a first-come or other random basis. But of primary interest here is a rule for awarding positions that offer above-average reward or respect.

A final consideration regarding award of these positions is that a person could derive only limited satisfaction from occupying a position in which he could not perform well. Increased monetary benefits to unqualified individuals who might gain positions under other rules would need to be weighed not only against decreased goods and services in general, but also against frustrations from trying to do jobs they could not really do.

Combining these two motivations behind the adoption of a rule for awarding desirable positions — the first of which calls for rewarding effort, or at least for permitting attainment of positions through effort and achievement, and the second of which calls for rewarding social productivity or potential productivity — we derive a rule for rewarding socially productive effort. Socially productive effort amounts to competent performance on a job or the attainment of qualifications for performing a job before one applies for it. There may be some question, however, as to the ease with which these two motivations can be combined. Even when we correct for advantages derived from initial social positions (which contractors ignorant of social position would want to do), productivity and achievement are not perfect measures of effort. Where these two criteria might conflict, I believe that the contractual model implies that productivity itself should normally serve as the basis for differential rewards, while estimates of potential productivity would become the criterion for award of positions. The contractors' motivation for rewarding effort appealed to effort as a measure of desire and to the fact that a lack of opportunity to acquire goods through effort frustrates desire more than does a lack of willingness to make efforts to acquire those goods. Given roughly equal natural abilities and correction for socially relative differences, however, productivity itself is some measure of effort and desire. While certainly not exact, it is questionable whether more exact measures could be institutionalized into social rules for differential rewards that could be applied fairly, consistently, and without excessive costs. Second, from the contractors' point of view, the prospect of unrewarded effort, representing frustrated desires for goods, would be more than offset by the prospect of increased goods and services made available by having maximally competent persons occupying various positions and being rewarded for producing at full capacity. Since awarding positions by competence rather than on some other basis entails increased goods and services for all society, it is difficult to see how contractors unaware of their initial or ultimate positions and interested in maximizing their prospective goods could choose any other principle.

. . .

In concluding this section, we may use another approach to support inductively the adoption of a rule for awarding positions generally by competence, an approach that is closer to the issue at hand. This is our conviction that first-order discrimination against minority-group members and women is not only wrong but seriously unjust, that is, in violation of their rights. Certainly our distributive principles ought to explain this conviction. Those who defend reverse discrimination by arguing that no one has prima facie rights to positions and that such rights therefore cannot be violated by the practice must be careful not to defend first-order discrimination on this ground as well. It certainly seems that if white males can never have distributive rights to positions, minority-group members can never have these rights either, and that if they can never have right to positions, we cannot treat them unjustly in hiring practices. One possible way around this point is to counterargue that the rights violated by first-order discrimination are rights to equal consideration rather than to positions, or rights not to be invidiously insulted. Regarding the former suggestion, equal consideration amounts to nothing if there is no rule stipulating criteria for appointment or if one can be dismissed despite satisfying these criteria. Regarding the latter suggestion, I would imagine that most blacks care less about the opinions that whites may have of them than about getting decent jobs. Exclusion from positions is felt to be the most serious injustice, not the insults associated with exclusion, although the latter may add to the overall injustice of first-order discrimination.

The most plausible reason why first-order discriminatory practices are unjust is that they exclude individuals from social benefits or opportunities for benefits on grounds of unalterable characteristics unrelated to performance. Such practices would not be seriously unjust unless there were a rule that created rights to positions violated by the practices. But if such rights exist for minority-group members, then according to our reversal test, they must also exist for white males who satisfy the criteria stipulated by the rule. Of course, a rule that creates rights to positions would not necessarily require that competence be rewarded. For all that our argument has established so far, the rule might rather call for some fair random process for awarding positions. But the depth of our reaction to first-order discrimination indicates that this practice is unjust, not merely in relation to some abstractly possible rule, according to which *all* current hiring would be unjust, but rather in relation to a rule widely accepted and applied often to nonminority candidates for positions. This would be the rule for awarding positions according to competence or potential competence, which stipulates that it is most unjust when a woman or minority-group member is rejected at the level of hiring when most qualified, and that it is also unjust when individuals are denied the chance given others to attain qualifications. But this rule also demands that the most qualified white males as well must acquire initial or prima facie distributive rights to positions.

Thus both the contractual framework and inductive arguments by analogy from other cases imply that the most competent individuals have prima facie rights to positions. It is in the context of such rights that the debate over reverse discrimination takes form. Before deciding which other rights conflict with these in the present context, and which ought to override others, I want to consider in somewhat more detail the motivations for denying the existence of these prima facie rights and the question of how we decide who is most competent for various positions.

Rejection of Alternative Rules

The Libertarian Position

The libertarian denies that applicants for positions in private corporations could have rights to those positions. Such rights would conflict with the rights of the corporations to control their own assets or property and with the rights of their members to associate with whom they please. A corporation may be said to have a property right in the positions it chooses to fill by virtue of having legitimately acquired the assets with which to fund the positions. The freedom to control

its own assets is empty unless it is free to disburse them as or to whom it chooses. Since present members of the corporation must associate with new appointees, the freedom to associate with whom one pleases may also be cited in support of the libertarian position here. A mandatory rule for hiring may force present members to work closely with others against their will, making their work unpleasant for them. And the friction created by this forced close association may be detrimental to the continued smooth operation of the company or organization. The corporation's property rights to control the disbursement of its assets and the right of free association of its members can then be held to imply a specific right of the corporation to hire whom it pleases without interference from society. The only rule that a libertarian would accept in this area would be one permitting private corporations to hire whomever they choose.

I argued in the previous section that rights to positions are recognized as part of a more general demand for equal opportunity, and as part of society's interest in generating a maximal pool of quality goods and services. Regarding the latter, the libertarian will ask how a social interest in more material goods and services can override recognized rights of individuals or private corporations within the society, such as the rights of property and free association. (Remember that the libertarian does not demand rational self-interest in contracts made or rules accepted. He accepts only actual contracts among actual individuals, not hypothetical contracts establishing rules among hypothetically rational or equal agents. Real individuals must be left free to make their own contracts and exchanges.) To determine a social interest is not necessarily to demonstrate the right of society or the state to further that interest, especially when individual or private corporation rights are apparently ignored in the process. For one principal purpose of recognizing individual rights within a system of social justice is to protect individuals from losses whenever utilitarian calculations run against them in particular cases.

Recognition of the right to property, for example, means that a person will not be dispossessed whenever another is in greater need, although such forced transfer would raise total or average utility in particular cases. The recognition of a right in relation to a certain interest determines in advance that the person whose right is at stake will take precedence over others with different and conflicting interests, even if the latter should seem greater in a given situation. Considerations of utilitarian balancing and maximization are not allowed to determine the relative priority of these interests. The rights to property and free association, it could therefore be argued, should not be overridden here by the social interest in maximizing goods and services. A private corporation with assets to disburse for jobs should be free to hire whomever it pleases, even when this results in lower efficiency in its production of goods and services. Efficiency cannot be permitted to override recognized rights, or our rights and freedoms would be fragile indeed. Thus while it may be in the interest of all, even of those in power in corporations, to have the most competent hired, the rights of free choice allow corporations to ignore this maximization of interest satisfaction.

As a counterargument, we might first state that, while utilities are not permitted to override rights once these are recognized, we do not recognize a prospective right when the consequences of accepting it are worse than the consequences of not recognizing it. Since the consequences of recognizing a right of corporations to hire whom they please are detrimental to the interests of individuals, we ought not to recognize this right.[6] But the libertarian might point here to other cases in which we recognize rights even when not doing so might maximize utility for all. For example, even if there were some proven scientific method of matching spouses that increased their chances for happiness, we would undoubtedly continue to recognize the right of individuals to choose their own spouses.[7] Hence we cannot argue simply that when acceptance of a right lowers prospective welfare we ought not to recognize it. For the libertarian, freedom of choice normally takes precedence over welfare considerations. Since we do recognize a right to property and the freedom to control and disburse legitimately acquired assets, and since this seems to entail a freedom to hire by choice, consistency appears to require that we refuse to recognize rights of applicants to positions.

I would argue nevertheless that the libertarian misrepresents here the way that rights are ordered, and that the analogy with choosing spouses is misleading. Regarding the latter, aside from the difference in the interest that the public takes in who occupies positions of responsibility as opposed to who marries whom, there is a difference in the rights at stake. In the case of one's right to choose a spouse, what is at stake is the right over one's own person and body — perhaps the most fundamental of all rights. But in the case of hiring, what is at stake is only a portion of corporations' right to control the disbursement of their assets. And we already recognize many exceptive clauses in rights to property, clauses that express the priority of competing interests. My right to dispose of my property as I please does not include a right to dispose of my knife in an enemy's chest; my right to use my property according to my own wishes does not include a right to play my stereo near my neighbor at deafening volumes; and my right to spend my assets as I like does not allow me to buy nerve gas, even if I keep it sealed in my basement vault. Which exceptive clauses are applied in the recognition of a particular right depends upon the ranking of the particular values to be embodied in the system. If there is to be any system of rights, however, there must be an ordering of each in relation to the others, and this means that there must be exceptive clauses expressing these precedence relations. I can dispose of my knife as I please, except in an adversary's chest, because the rights to life and not to be assaulted take precedence over rights to disposition of personal property, which therefore include this exceptive clause. Much political debate — and indeed, much of the debate over reverse discrimination as a social policy — concerns the recognition of new exceptive clauses in previously recognized rights when these appear to conflict. Since we recognize various exceptive clauses in property rights, and since a restriction on hiring practices removes only a small part of the right of corporations to control their assets, it seems reasonable to accept this exceptive clause in the name of equal opportunity and public welfare. The same can be said of a restriction of rights to free association. We already recognize restrictions in public contexts in which access to important benefits is at stake — for example, access of minority-group members to privately owned restaurants, etc.

The libertarian will reply that freedoms, including those of disbursing property and associating with those of one's choice, may be limited only to prevent wrongful harm. A defender of this position undoubtedly would want to press the distinction between the interests of individuals in maximizing available goods and services, and any potential harm to them from the exercise of these freedoms on the part of corporations in hiring. He would grant that we cannot use our property in ways that directly harm other people, but he would allow total freedom short of this, including the freedom to ignore rational self-interest (to allow some to impose their conception of rational self-interest on others leads to repressive regimes, in his view). Nor will he recognize any such right as that to equal opportunity. He would hold that people have a right to what they have legitimately acquired and that no general right like that of equal opportunity should be recognized because it would involve violations of individuals' rights to their legitimately acquired property in excess of those permissible under the harm principle.

Let us, however, first consider the distinction in this context between preventing harm and maximizing welfare. I am not certain that this distinction can be maintained in relation to many positions of responsibility in society, such as those of pilots, doctors, lawyers, police, and even automobile, home, or toy manufacturers. Having relative incompetents in these positions entails not only losses in efficiency but also serious potential harm. Thus the harm principle itself, if it allows prevention of unnecessary risk or potential harm — which it must to be at all plausible — may require enforcement of a rule for hiring the most competent in many positions. With respect to a right to equal opportunity, which would include prima facie rights to positions as one facet, we argued in the previous section that this follows from the fundamental moral demand to accept the moral equality of others. In accepting the outcome of all "free" exchanges, even though these often result from the desperation of those who initially occupy lower positions, the libertarian fails to guarantee just distributive results. Rules or conditions that can be recognized only as the outcome of grudging transactions between haves and have-nots cannot be accepted as moral on that basis alone, since the haves may have inherited their advantages without deserving them and the have-nots may have begun where they are through no fault of their own. That some condition or distribution has

been arrived at through transactions entered into "freely" by have-nots does not afford the same guarantee of its morality or fairness as when a distribution has been arrived at through the operation of a set of rules freely and rationally willed by those in the lower positions. Justice and morality demand placing the interests of all agents on the same scale, thereby limiting inequalities among them and granting them equal opportunity to satisfy those interests.

But we are not simply placing welfare considerations over freedoms, an ordering rejected by the libertarian? Have we arrived at a dead end in moral argument? This apparent impasse occurs because we have argued so far as though freedom is to be balanced against equality and welfare. But we can point out also that absolute liberty with respect to property and association may not result in the overall maximization of freedom that is apparently desired by the libertarian. For poverty and the lack of satisfaction of basic needs that poverty entails constitutes an impediment to freedom as well, that is, to the basic freedom to formulate and pursue a meaningful life plan and to control one's life as one desires. This is perhaps the most essential liberty of all; if it is denied through the operation of a social system that totally frustrates some so that others may totally control their property, we can view this as an unwarranted conventional constraint upon liberty (property is only protected and indeed created in the first place by the social system). It follows that a rule of hiring that results in more goods and services for all, and especially for those whose freedom is compromised by want, can be adopted not only in the name of welfare or utility but also to increase freedom. This does not mean that every increase in welfare is to be counted as an increase in freedom, or that despotic states with higher GNP's are to be preferred, but only that no social system that abandons those at the bottom to an enforced circle of dire poverty can be justified in the name of freedom. A free market society with severe racial biases and no rule for hiring results in that situation. Thus we again arrive at the conclusion that society has the right to impose a rule for hiring against private corporations, justified this time in the name of freedom. Restrictions upon the freedom of corporations to choose capriciously or invidiously in hiring are necessary to protect or create more basic freedoms. Equality of opportunity is itself a necessary condition for these most important and fundamental freedoms.

That there must be an enforceable rule governing appointments to positions does not mean that the rule must be enforced in all situations — for example, in the cases of an individual's hiring someone for temporary help or a businessman's giving a job to his son. The first distinction between the case of a small business or individual and the large corporation is the interest of the public in their products and services. If a small business is the only source of a vital service or product in a given area, it may be reasonable to demand competents in positions of responsibility. Otherwise, it may be unreasonable to demand that the proprietor take the time and bear the cost of advertising the positions, etc. This is especially clear in such cases as my hiring someone for the afternoon to unload my rented truck. The right of free association is also more central in the case of a small business, and this may have been part of the reasoning of Congress in applying nondiscriminatory regulations only to businesses with more than twenty-five employees. Since these differences are real, and since equality of opportunity and social welfare do not require that literally every position in society be open to all, but only a certain proportion of them, we may in applying these rationales establish a rule for hiring only for corporations over a certain size, recognizing that a precise demarcation will be somewhat arbitrary.

Thus the rights of individuals to equal opportunity and of the public to be spared potential harm justify enforcement of a rule that restricts the rights of larger corporations to control their assets by hiring or admitting whomever they choose. But is equal opportunity truly compatible with awarding positions by competence? We turn next to the objections of the egalitarian.

The Egalitarian Position

The egalitarian attempts to refute the above justification by arguing that those abilities relevant to awarding jobs on the basis of efficiency, that is, competence qualifications, are irrelevant from the point of view of justice. Because it rewards native talent and intelligence, the practice of awarding positions by competence is arbitrary from a moral point of view. Individuals deserve only those benefits they have earned. They have not earned their native advantages and so do not deserve those benefits, including good jobs, that flow from such advantages throughout their lives. A child born intelligent stands a far better chance than do other children of acquiring competence qualifications for desirable positions later in life; yet he cannot be said to deserve the better chance from the point of view of justice, nor therefore the job he eventually gets. Thus increments to social welfare from hiring by competence are a matter of social utility from which questions of justice must be separated. The egalitarian appears to have uncovered a conflict between the two criteria for a just rule for hiring that were advanced in the first section of this chapter. Maximization of utility through hiring by competence seems inconsistent with equality of opportunity in the deepest sense, and the egalitarian claims that considerations of equality take precedence over those of social utility.

In reply, I do not think that any such radical separation of analyses of justice and efficiency could accord with our intuitions regarding the former, as these are aroused by specific examples. Although we may not all be utilitarians, it seems we must grant that welfare does count at least as a positive consideration, and certainly at the extreme involved in this issue. I would argue, for example, that a practice or rule that generates a sum total of fifteen units of goods to be distributed in a hypothetical society of four individuals in shares of 4, 4, 4, and 3 is preferable from the point of view of justice to one that generates eight units to be distributed in shares of 2, 2, 2, and 2, despite the greater inequality of the former distribution. In other words, those who could have received four units under the first plan could legitimately claim injustice at having their shares reduced to equal the lowest share under the second (given no differences in desert among the individuals in the first and second situations).[8] If a claim of injustice or unfairness at having one's reward so reduced is justified, then aggregate utility in itself must be a consideration of distributive justice. Plans or rules that result in larger aggregates must be prima facie preferable. To deny this is perhaps to grant too large a moral force to the feelings of envy and pride. For even the person with the lowest share in our hypothetical case is better off under the first plan than under the second, except that others around him have more.

There may appear to be a complication here in that those with less relative (though more absolute) income may be in a worse position to bid for scarce goods. But the alternatives in relation to choices between hiring by competence and other rules may be taken to refer to goods available and not simply to income. The argument is that more goods will be available to all if competents occupy productive positions; this is what the egalitarian wrongly claims to be irrelevant to the choice of a just rule for hiring. Furthermore, the rule for awarding positions is itself independent of the degree of inequality of wealth and income throughout society. It is not as if the adoption of this rule increases inequalities between rich and poor. It affects not the relative positions themselves, but only who will occupy them. The egalitarian can press for equalization of pay scales and redistribution of wealth without altering the rule that determines who gets the better shares of justified inequalities. Unlike abandoning the practice of hiring by competence, the readjustment contemplated toward equalization of pay scales would perhaps not result in great losses of efficiency, but it would take massive coercion or drastic changes toward more social or altruistic attitudes on the part of businessmen and professionals.

Given that this demand for equalization is independent of the rule for awarding positions, a rule that creates a larger share of goods without affecting degrees of inequality certainly seems preferable to alternatives. But there remains the charge of injustice relating to reward of native talents. Since inequalities do exist in our society beyond those that might be justified as incentives or on grounds of differential productivity, it can be argued that it is crucial that the better shares not be assigned on morally arbitrary bases or on the basis of unearned native characteristics. An egalitarian could argue that although moving away from awarding positions by competence would not in itself result in a more equal distribution of goods, a more random process would at least equalize the chances of all individuals for acquiring the benefits of an unequal distribution. The point can be pressed that equal chances to unequal shares are fairer than unequal chances to unequal shares. The real question is whether the fact that native intelligence has some effect on the ability to acquire competence qualifications for many positions nullifies competence as a just basis for assigning positions.

To answer this challenge to our rule, we may question first whether the nullification of the effects of intelligence would itself be just, and second, whether there are alternative rules that do not also nullify factors that we consider to be intuitively plausible bases for differential rewards. Regarding the first counterquestion, the rights of individuals over their own bodies seem to indicate rights to what they can produce through the exercise and development of their capacities. The intuitions that one has this right to keep what one makes or contributes to a joint venture, and that the less intelligent have no initial right to the item or efforts of those more intelligent, in themselves appear to offset the claim that we should nullify all effects of differences in intelligence in granting rewards. That an individual does not deserve something, or that he can claim no responsibility for it, does not imply that he is not entitled to it or to what he can obtain by using it, especially if the advantage in question is an inherent feature of the individual. Furthermore, as we argued above, the justification of inequalities as incentives to encourage maximal productivity also justifies the reward of competence independently of its causal source.

Thus, even if society were able to nullify differential effects of differences in intelligence without affecting other relevant variables, it might not have the right to do so. The antecedent of the previous sentence is also false. The failure of the egalitarian argument becomes more clear if we seriously consider its alternative to hiring by competence as a general distributive principle. Presumably, the egalitarian would advocate greater randomization in the process of sorting people for positions, in order to equalize the chances of all. The central question is whether a more random process would indeed be more fair. The egalitarian's central complaint against hiring by competence is that it tends to reward initial differences for which individuals can claim no responsibility. To be blessed with native intelligence is a matter of good fortune or chance. And the rewarding of chance factors for which the agent can claim no responsibility is morally arbitrary, whether the reward is jobs or other benefits. But certainly a process of random selection in the job market, aside from losses in efficiency, comes out worse on this score. It was admitted that differences in competence for various positions constitute only imperfect barometers of prior efforts to acquire competence. But the acquisition of qualifications for positions still represents the expenditure of some effort in a socially desirable way; and the question is whether it is more just to ignore socially productive effort altogether and make all reward a matter of pure chance, which seems implausible or inconsistent if the only complaint against hiring by competence is that it rewards chance factors to some degree. The effect of randomization at any level is to negate differences in previous efforts. If the cost of negating differences in native factors is to render all effort and productivity negligible as measures of desert as well, it hardly seems worthwhile from the point of view of distributive justice. Even if the efforts of some are undeservedly doomed to failure, it still seems preferable to reward those who have made efforts and succeeded than to ignore effort entirely. If the complaint against the reward of native factors is that they are undeserved, then some other factors must be presupposed as entering into desert. Presumably, these will not consist in being lucky in some random selection, but rather in some such factor as socially productive effort. The question then becomes how to measure this in a social rule — and we are back to the argument that actual attainment of competence seems as fair a measure as can be fairly applied, if we correct for initial social differences.

In rewarding the attainment of competence we are *not* rewarding a native characteristic, although native characteristics enter as causal factors. Since the latter is the source of the egalitarian's complaint against our rule, his complaint can be seen to rest upon a false principle. This principle states that all causal antecedents of features that enter into criteria for desert must themselves be deserved. That it is false can be made clear by the example of a character like Soapy in the O'Henry story "The Cop and the Anthem." After an inspirational moment in church, Soapy vows to reform his ways and work hard from that moment on. If our character escapes Soapy's fate

and fulfills his vow, we cannot say that he does not deserve the fruits of his labor simply because he did not deserve the inspirational moment that motivated it. By tracing back far enough we can always find causes for actions that create deserts that are themselves not deserved.

The real contrast, then, reduces to that between rewarding chance versus rewarding effort and social contribution; and it still seems that randomization in the award of positions, while it equalizes chances, is the worst possible choice by these criteria. Where there is no ulterior social purpose in the reward of some benefit than the distribution of some windfall good, and where no previous actions of the individuals in question can be seen to create differential rights or deserts to the goods, then a random process of distribution is fairest. This follows from the presumption of equality of persons in a moral point of view. But when positions are assigned for socially productive purposes, and when individuals are therefore encouraged to direct their efforts toward fulfilling these purposes, past and potential productivity achieved through these efforts cannot be justly ignored. To avoid this unfair waste, positions might be assigned by some random process earlier in life. But the only relevant difference between this determination and the operation of original chance differences against which the egalitarian complains is that this assignment of positions would be more rigid and would involve losses in social utility as compared with more open competition for productive positions. Furthermore, randomization restricts the important liberty to pursue the career of one's choice. It might be assumed that randomization would increase this liberty for many, since it would allow all who wish to pursue a given position to do so merely by applying. But, as argued before, the meaningful pursuit of what one considers valuable and worth achieving involves effort and even struggle, and part of the enjoyment of reward is the feeling of success as a consequence of effort. Such real pursuit is rendered meaningless when positions are awarded by chance. Dignity or a sense of personal worth beyond the mere dignity of being human — often mentioned in egalitarian arguments — derives from a sense of having accomplished, not from winning by chance. An equal right to positions at all levels is bought at the expense of an equal chance to meaningful achievement through effort. Alternatives like randomization or assignment of positions proportionately to members of various groups in the population block this freedom to achieve.

Of course, in reality the egalitarian advocates randomization in the award of positions at higher levels only for those who can demonstrate a certain minimal level of competence. For him this represents a concession to efficiency rather than a consideration of justice, which is distinct. Thus arguments against this and other alternatives that purport to equalize chances for positions are well founded when they criticize such alternatives for nullifying variables that are indeed relevant to just distributions and for restricting individuals' freedom to pursue personal achievement. The egalitarian might reply, however, that a sense of dignity or achievement can be developed through performing well on a job rather than in the process of acquiring it, and that his system equalizes chances for the former type of achievement. But aside from the fact that this downgrades accomplishments culminating the first twenty-five years or so of a person's life, the sense of dignity or achievement of those who acquire positions through a random process most likely would not be appreciably enhanced. Could they be expected to perform well, having never found the need to do so earlier and possibly not having the capacity to do so? The prestige of the positions themselves and the self-respect that goes with them would soon diminish with the knowledge that they were attained by chance. Since prestige and self-respect are themselves sources of inequality, the egalitarian might welcome this change. But since not everyone seeks satisfaction through trying to attain a particular position, why deny this source to those who do? If all had equal chances to all positions, then none could pursue positions or feel any satisfaction at having achieved them. Furthermore, if competence were later demanded on the job, a series of firings and hirings would take place until competent people filled the positions, resulting in resentment among those who proved to be incompetent. If only those who achieved a certain level of competence through effort could apply for positions, moreover, why ignore all achievements beyond that level? (If several applicants are at or predicted to be at the same level of competence, then a random process of choosing does become prima facie proper.)

We do not want to reward purely native characteristics — to do so is generally unfair — but it is an empirical fact that there are few desirable positions in which successful performance demands only native talents. But despite all this argument, we may continue to be bothered by the inability of some people to acquire maximal qualifications for some positions no matter how hard they try. Some people simply do not have the native intelligence or talent, and any system of distributing positions in which efficiency is an important consideration will bar these individuals from certain desirable positions. If this seems sad or unfair, it is nevertheless a fact of life that cannot be justifiably improved by alternative rules of hiring. The point was made above that no matter how narrowly we construe the concept of justice and just reward, no one would seriously advocate randomization to fill the many positions crucial to social welfare and safety, which demand maximum competence. In general, those positions that stress or require excellence or intelligence are the ones that we would least want to open to a random process. Moreover, individuals have the best chance for satisfaction in positions that challenge without exceeding their capacities. This requires that applicants not be placed in positions for which they are not competent and, just as important, that applicants not be placed in positions for which they are overqualified and in which they are hence likely to become bored. From the viewpoints of both the public and the applicants, then, the egalitarian must appear like the skeptic regarding knowledge of the external world in the philosophy classroom when he attacks hiring by competence as an initial general rule, as someone not to be taken seriously in practice.

To say this is not to defend the present system of hiring in our society, for we have hired the most competent only within a very restricted initial class. Nor is it to defend the grossly unequal schedule of rewards that attaches to different positions. But if we lean toward egalitarianism, the only intelligent program is to press for compensatory programs where these are owed, for the creation of equal opportunity as far as possible, and for readjustment of pay scales, no matter how difficult to accomplish. The achievement of these reforms may well take priority over the further application of the rule to award all positions by competence. But if we are to have an initial distributive rule for awarding positions, a rule that creates prima facie rights to positions and prevents the denial of equal opportunity through invidious or capricious awards, it seems that it must be the rule of competence. There simply are no reasonable, practical alternatives.

Qualifications

No discussion of hiring by competence in the context of the debate on reverse discrimination would be complete without some clarification of the nature of competence qualifications and credentials for various positions. I said in my initial argument that a social rule for hiring could be justified in terms of universal increases in utility, and that hiring the most competent entails more goods and services for all. This must now be qualified, for the entailment holds only when competence is defined in terms of actual performance on the job. The problem of course is that in an actual hiring situation, future performance must be predicted on the basis of past achievements that are sometimes indirectly related to tasks required on the job. The question regarding the kinds of achievements or characteristics of applicants that should be made the basis of such predictions constitutes an independent issue in this context.

This complication does not affect my previous arguments or justification of hiring the competent, since the conclusion is still that we want to *aim* at universal increases in utility by having a rule calling upon us to hire the most competent, given the limits upon our ability to predict competence. Such practical limitations do not affect the adoption of ideal distributive rules of the level of specificity of the rule for hiring, just as at the most general level we are always called upon to do what is right, even though it may be difficult in complex situations to figure out what specific action is right. If we could never predict competence at all, then our distributive rules would be different, just as if we could never figure out what is

right, we might have no morality at all. Happily, neither antecedent holds. The problem of qualifications in the context of reverse discrimination is that disagreements over which characteristics should be used to predict future competence can generate arguments over when discrimination and reverse discrimination occur in practice. It is therefore necessary to achieve some clarification regarding the nature of competence qualifications before we can know when arguments regarding the justice or injustice of reverse discrimination are to be applied. Without some settlement of this still preliminary issue, opponents of my later general position could always circumvent the arguments by claiming that what appears to be reverse discrimination according to a certain set of narrowly construed competence criteria actually satisfies the rule for hiring the competent according to a broader and more reasonable set of qualification criteria. We want some guidelines for deciding how far to accept such claims.

The necessary distinctions can be drawn more clearly in relation to a comparison between qualifying for a job and qualifying to win a prize in some athletic or scholarly contest.[9] In the latter case there is a threefold distinction to be drawn among: (1) credentials, in terms of which the outcome could be predicted in advance (in the case of a race, previous running times; in the case of an essay competition, previous writing samples); (2) qualifications or abilities (physical condition or aptitude; composition skills); and (3) actual performance or qualification for the prize as stipulated in the rules of the contest (crossing the finish line first; writing the best essay or one judged best). The person with the best credentials may not be the one currently in the best physical condition or with the most aptitude, since the other contestants may have had bad luck in the past or have improved greatly since their last contest. Similarly, the person with the best actual physical or mental qualifications may not win the race or the essay competition, again owing to factors that we attribute to luck or chance. In the former case he might trip or develop a cramp despite his condition; in the latter he might happen to write one bad essay or one that does not appeal to the judges. These possibilities necessitate the distinctions. If the chance factors did not exist, and if there were not a regularity to human (and animal) performance nevertheless, enabling us to predict with some reliability (2) from (1) and (3) from (2), there would be neither horse racing nor reasonable social rules for hiring, since similar distinctions can be drawn in the case of predicting job performance.

In the area of hiring, we can again distinguish among: credentials—for example, previous test scores, academic records, or evaluations of performance on prior jobs; qualifications, that is, abilities or knowledge or skills needed on the job; and actual performance on the job. (One apparent difference between the cases is that good or best performance on the job will not be mechanically determinable by the application of a fixed set of rules. But this is not always the case with contests either—for example, essay competitions.) While qualifications constitute the actual capacity to do well on the job, credentials are past achievements presented as evidence of this capacity, which is not testable until the future. It is important to note that when certain types of credentials do not prove predictive of real qualifications or performance, they are downgraded and other, more reliable ones are substituted (assuming that the motive is to satisfy the rules or make a true prediction). In the case of athletic contests and their prizes, the credentials to be used are obvious, that is, previous records from similar contests. When these prove unreliable in the case of a given individual or team, we simply lament their inconsistency and hold our bets, since there will generally be no more reliable barometers available. But in the case of hiring, applicants' credentials will usually reflect achievements different in kind from those required on the jobs in question; therefore more conscious efforts must be made to tailor credentials according to their predictive capacities regarding performance on particular jobs. And there's the rub.

Many who wish to have more women and minority-group members hired argue that credentials previously and still used for various categories of jobs are not "objective," that is, not predictive of real differentials in job performance, and that what appears to be reverse discrimination in favor of such individuals may actually satisfy the rule for hiring competents to a greater degree than do past and current practices. Again, this argument attempts to cut the ground from under the compensatory issues that we

shall discuss later; for while we might show that real reverse discrimination has only limited justifiability, our arguments will be inapplicable if what seems to be preferential treatment really amounts only to the implementation of more objective or predictive systems of credentials.

Before assessing the validity of the various forms of this argument, we must examine a number of preliminary points. First, disputes over credentials are sometimes confounded with disputes over actual tasks to be performed on the job itself or over what abilities are required for performance on the job. For example, is scholarship or publication a legitimate part of the duties of a university teacher, and if so, how is it to be weighted against actual teaching ability? Is public relations part of the job of a policeman, or should courage, fairness, and physical ability constitute the only qualifications? These questions regarding relevant performance or qualifications for various jobs relate only indirectly, however, to the issue of reverse discrimination (it might be claimed or shown, for example, that women, although not as physically adept as males, tend to be better at police–community relations, or that statistically, women teachers happen to excel at teaching, although they are not as successful at publishing). In light of more urgent features of the line of argument under consideration, they need not occupy us further. It would be impossible for us in any case to discuss the nature of every relevant job.

Second, there is an important distinction to be made between acceptance of criteria or credentials that are fair or predictive in themselves but that historically have not been applied impartially or fairly, and acceptance of credentials or tests that are themselves unpredictive or unfair and discriminatory. Much discrimination has been caused by hiring officers who misapply or simply ignore criteria that are accepted as theoretically fair. While the application of merit criteria has perhaps been fairer historically in academia than elsewhere, that is, one's social class, accent, and ethnic or national origin has not mattered much (which partially explains the overrepresentation of Jews, who were long barred from other fields), this point must ring hollow to women or blacks, who have often been passed over because wrongly or biasedly assessed, or even when recognized as most competent. (The "old buddy" system of hiring among chairmen of academic departments has been unfair to many others as well.) Although violations in other sectors have been far more glaring, this is only to admit that discrimination has occurred and that fair rules have been ignored; it is not to say that we cannot easily detect such unfair practice in various areas, and reverse discrimination as well, by considering the rule and its current specification of relevant credentials. The argument under consideration here holds not only that the criteria or credentials currently accepted have not been applied fairly, but also that they are inherently discriminatory, that even when applied fairly or impartially they do not indicate future performance or allow us to identify real preferential treatment.

The more obvious forms of this argument make such claims as that tests for school admissions or jobs are totally irrelevant to future tasks, that they are intentionally biased against certain groups or individuals, or that they are ultimately shaped by the preconceptions of those in power in order to measure qualities considered important by them. An initial point to be made here is that in a truly competitive situation market pressures will militate against the use of irrelevant criteria or credentials. In a situation in which a corporation or institution survives only by satisfying social demands — for example, where many universities and colleges now compete for scarce funds, students, and recognition through the achievements of their faculty members — there will not be much room for intentional manipulation or rigging of credentials criteria; nor can they be as arbitrary as some have claimed. We have nevertheless seen that a partial market economy does not guarantee that the most competent are always hired even within the limits of predictability, that biases can alter motivations and color perceptions. Until recently, when the qualifications of certain individuals could simply be ignored, more subtle efforts to rig credentials criteria were unnecessary for the purposes of the racist or sexist. After the federal government and the courts began to be sensitive to such gross violations of law, there were undoubtedly attempts by unscrupulous hiring officers in some fields to overstress certain, mostly irrelevant deficiencies associated with minority-group members or women (such as physical strength for police) in order to continue to exclude them from em-

ployment. Not that such activities are being detected and monitored in those areas, it is probably easier once again to ignore fair criteria when discrimination can be gotten away with than to manipulate consideration of credentials.

Thus it still seems a good rule of thumb to apply the reversal test . . . to detect either first-order or reverse discrimination. In a case of possible first-order discrimination, we can ask: If the candidate in question were white and male (if the person turned down is black or female), would he have gotten the job? If we want to detect reverse discrimination, we can ask the same question when the person hired is black or female. (Other variations are possible as well.) More subtle attacks on currently used credentials debate the applicability of this simple test. It may be argued first that in the current context being a minority-group member or woman should itself be considered a qualification for many positions, although it is not according to standard criteria. Or it may be claimed that members of such groups cannot be accurately judged according to standard credentials, since they have been denied the opportunity to acquire such credentials at lower levels in the educational system. Here it is claimed that present credentials will not measure the true potential of such individuals, who may prove more competent than rivals when hired through apparently preferential policies.

Let us consider first when sex or race should become a qualification. This may appear obviously true in a smaller number of cases, such as singing or acting roles or rest-room attendants (although in Europe attendants of the opposite sex fail to cause bladder problems). In such cases sex or race is generally conceded to be relevant. Attempts to press this line more broadly include such claims as that women or blacks teach some college courses more understandingly (for example, female psychology or black history); that female or minority-group students are more receptive to or more communicative with teachers of their own race or sex (in their roles as advisors as well as teachers); that persons living in ghetto communities feel more at ease with police of their own race; that minority-group members need lawyers of their own race or ethnic or national background, who know the community and can communicate better with clients and potential witnesses; that white students gain from having to learn in a mixed classroom because students of different races and backgrounds bring different viewpoints and accustom the whites to a mixed environment; and that women or minority-group members in positions of responsibility provide role models for students, and that this is required to create motivation, which is an essential ingredient of equal opportunity.

. . . Here I shall offer some guidelines and some reasons why, in attempting to identify and justify preferential treatment, these arguments should for the most part be construed as narrowly as possible. There are two necessary and distinct considerations to be applied to claims such as these: first, are they factually accurate (on the basis of what empirical evidence are they advanced); and second, if they are empirically true, should they be morally accepted as creating qualification rights to jobs in accord with the rule for hiring the most competent. It is not at all clear, for example, that women students learn better from women teachers or men from men, nor that heterogeneous classrooms are more conducive to learning, although there may be other reasons for demanding them, at least at lower levels (in Sweden students of homogeneous backgrounds seem to learn no less than here). Nor must we suppose that women are better teachers of female psychology or blacks of black history (not only Europeans can teach Western history or Romance languages, few adolescent psychology courses could be taught by teen-agers, and not many toddlers could improve upon Piaget's theories, whatever we think of his experimental methods).

But more important than these empirical questions is whether race or sex should be given any moral weight for determining rights to various jobs. That they should be given little if any seems clear from another application of our reversal test, the exercise that calls upon us to switch the roles in the context in question. Suppose it were found that male students learn better from men or that white students learn better in all-white classrooms? Do we want to cater to such racist or sexist attitudes, and why on the part of women and blacks and not males and whites (unless we think it fair to let minorities exercise their baser attitudes for a while; but that does not constitute an acceptance of the argument under consideration)? It seems morally and pragmatically preferable from the point of view of women and minority-group members as well, since they may want to teach a variety of courses or work for Wall Street rather than ghetto law firms, to disallow such objectionable utility benefits from entering into consideration of qualifications. The rule for hiring the competent was justified in the first place partially in terms of the increases in social utility that would flow from it as opposed to alternatives. But these are universal increases that can be built into the formulation of the rules and the rights it determines; other, temporary increases for certain groups are prohibited by other rights that protect individuals.

Furthermore, according to our original argument justifying the social rule for hiring the most competent, an individual acquires a right to a position by satisfying the rule *through his own effort*. Insofar as we want to make competence some barometer of previous effort (and rewarding effort rather than chance was part of our justification for the rule as well), we shall not want to base competence qualifications on native characteristics. Considerations of universal utility may leave us unable or unwilling to rule out native intelligence, because it is difficult to separate its effects from those of effort and because ruling it out, even if possible, would almost destroy the idea of competence as the basis of hiring. But the same considerations do not apply to race or sex as qualifications for given positions, since they produce only limited and temporary utility. We want criteria that serve the public interest and toward which an individual can aim his efforts; and these must be applied consistently and with an attempt to guarantee equality of opportunity, so as to give maximum weight to choice and effort. Out of moral considerations then, and pragmatic ones regarding women and minority-group members as well, we should not consider race or sex as direct qualifications for positions.

For the same reason, and for reasons of clarity as well, it is better not to think of the policy of reverse discrimination, where justified, as creating new qualifications for jobs in terms of its justifications. We sometimes tend to think of qualifications for other types of benefits simply in terms of the overall purposes or justifications of the policies according to which the benefits are distributed. For example, wealth disqualifies one from a scholarship, and so having an income under a certain level can be considered one qualification for this benefit designed to remove economic handicaps. (There is a distinction here that I have not stressed between qualifying for entering a competition and qualifying to win it, but that is irrelevant in the case of jobs.) Although I have claimed that qualifications for jobs are to be recognized in relation to a general distributive rule for hiring the competent, this is not to say that this rule and the prima facie rights it creates (or rights subject to a limited number of exceptive clauses) cannot be overridden by considerations relating to other just rules, such as compensation for past harm or creation of greater equality of opportunity than empirically exists now. (If these rules were not also relevant to particular hiring decisions, the issue would be far simpler. . . .) Numerous utilitarian justifications, such as increased social harmony, have been put forth to justify preferential policies for minorities, and they are at least intelligible and in need of evaluation. But if we think of race or sex (or poverty or past harm) as qualifications created through accepted justifications for preferential treatment, we might complete this circle of reasoning by arriving at the conclusion that what appears to be preferential is really not: reverse discrimination is really hiring the most qualified in terms of a comprehensive and just hiring policy. This reasoning obscures the identification of reverse discrimination and, perhaps more importantly, of first-order discrimination as well, and it disguises the nature of the justification for the former.

Therefore, rather than making race a qualification in order to atone for past discrimination, we should consider reverse discrimination as a way of honoring the right to compensation. And rather than making sex a qualification in order to help to restore women's self-respect, we might consider preferential hiring as a means to honor the right to self-respect and to help to make up for past affronts to that right. The latter language has the virtue of clarifying the special compensatory nature of the proposed policy and its relation to earlier violations of the general distributive rule, rather than obscuring the existence of preferential practices. While qualifications are defined relative to the distributive purposes of awarding jobs, I repeat that these must be general distributive goals and not shifting, special purposes; thus initial rights of individuals to jobs are conceived in terms of qualifications that all individuals can aim at acquiring, and discrimination of *both* types is to be defined and identified in terms of those rights.

Let us turn to the second form of the argument under consideration, namely, the claim that the true potential of women and minority-group members cannot be accurately assessed in terms of standard or "paper" credentials, since these will mask previous discriminatory practices that prevented the accumulation of impressive résumés. This version too seems inconsistent, especially if combined with a plea on behalf of the same individuals for compensation for past injury from discrimination. It seems that if past discrimination has been harmful, the handicaps will be real and not merely apparent, as reflected in misleading credentials. The opportunities denied will most likely be opportunities denied not only for acquiring credentials but also for acquiring real qualifications. That members of certain groups score lower on certain tests because of inferior prior education does not in itself prove the tests to be discriminatory; the question in this context is always whether the tests are predictive of future performance. Where lower scores are the result of poor education, the fault lies not in the present tests but in the past injustices. If the acquisition of necessary skills has been prevented or denied at lower levels, as reflected in the only tests available or suggested (if the plea is not for specifically different and more predictive tests but only for handicapping the scores of minority-group members or women on the same criteria), it is unlikely that such skills could suddenly appear without remedial help at the graduate level or on the job. At the higher levels it is hard to believe that educational deprivation, where it has occurred, has not resulted in a lack of requisite skills but only in the lack of ability to demonstrate them on tests, or that such abilities, which took years for those who had the opportunities to develop them, can be immediately acquired by others without special help. This of course is not to say that past denial of opportunity is not grounds for present compensatory measures, such as remedial programs, for those individuals injured through such unjust denial. Such apparently just measures, and the variations of them that are currently possible and available, will be evaluated in the next chapter. The point here is that the claim that credentials assessment is in itself biased or unpredictive in light of earlier discrimination is likely to be false, and again it overshadows the type of policy that ought to be advocated in light of such past injustice. It also obscures the nature of the possible justifications for remedial policies.

Sometimes the claim is made that tests or credentials criteria are racially or culturally biased even apart from discrimination or denial of opportunity at a lower level in the educational system. Reliance on such culture-bound tests is said to have the effect of excluding blacks or Spanish-speaking Americans from the higher professions, just as more overt or less subtle discrimination did in the past. But if the earlier injustices are claimed to be causally unrelated to the inability to compete on tests or to the acquisition of credentials now, this begins to sound racist; if not, then the arguments of the last paragraph apply. The causes of poor test performance will be hard to separate in practice, as the only relevant sample is the group of minority-group members who have had full educational opportunities. In the case of blacks, for example, this sample may be relatively small. In the absence of suggestions for more objective tests applied to all, tests more predictive of job performance, the claim that tests are culturally biased is indistinguishable in terms of its predictive consequences from the recognition that individuals in certain groups tend to be less qualified for certain positions on average than others. These same individuals seem to have a higher drop-out rate when accepted to graduate programs, despite test scores, confirming the predictive value of the tests.[10] (Nor, for example, should the fact that small differentials in medical school admissions tests fail to accurately predict relative success of doctors twenty years later cause us to dismiss the tests, given the extremely good credentials of all persons previously admitted to medical schools.) In light of past large-scale injustice in the educational system toward these individuals, and the unsupported racist implications of attributing the differences to other causes, blame should be placed upon the former and compensatory considerations applied.

If tests are culture-bound, graduate school and professional tasks may be as well, which is only to say that we live in a cultural setting in which certain types of conceptual skills are valued and required in certain professions. While culture-bound tests may not measure native intelligence, they may be the only reasonable barometers of qualifications for culture-bound tasks. But to suggest that individuals from certain racial or ethnic groups are incapable of acquiring these skills is a far more implausible claim, one rightly condemned as an expression of the essence of racism and as an excuse for empirically unfounded bias and injustice. In the unlikely event that this claim proved true on the average, justice might require vast changes in our entire social structure and hierarchy of jobs (in light of a deeper conflict between utility and equal opportunity than acknowledged in the last section); yet the claim that credentials are misleading would again be a far too weak and misleading way of expressing the problem. But in the present context the belief that prior massive injustice in the educational system (as well as extreme differences in economic levels) is at fault for present differences in credentials *and* qualifications should guide our search for a just policy.

Finally, the claim is sometimes made that differences in the credentials of women result not always from denial of educational opportunity or inherently unfair tests, but simply from unfair grading of women by male teachers. While this may occur occasionally—rare individual teachers may allow any irrational bias or neurotic dislike to influence their grading—it is equally plausible that some male teachers grade some of their female students less harshly than average. One implication of this version of the argument regarding evaluation of credentials should be that women previously hired in competitive situations, when their credentials were superior, should do better on the average than their male colleagues in professional life. If lower credentials mark equal qualifications, then equal credentials should indicate superior qualifications and predict superior performance. Here the empirical evidence is more relevant than a priori conjecture. While sufficient to dispel the myth that women tend to work less steadily in positions than do men, the available studies do not indicate relative overachievement either. One study of woman doctorates in America, for example, shows that in terms of scholarly achievement (as measured by books and articles), women do not compare favorably on the average.[11] This can be discounted by other variables, that is, the fact that relatively fewer women teach at large universities that have ample research facilities, possibly because of discrimination in hiring. Discrimination against women by journal editors and publishers might also be claimed, although there is no independent evidence for this conjecture. The essential point here is that when claims with empirical predictive consequences are made in this area, they should be held to exact evaluation of the evidence. Much prior discrimination was based upon absurd factual assumptions—for example, that blacks are lazy, or that women are unpredictable and unreliable. We must be careful not to base reverse discrimination upon opposite stereotypes of these same individuals as overly hardworking and overly qualified but held down at every step by unfair tests and biased grades.

Thus none of the above claims goes far toward justifying race or sex as a qualification for jobs or toward discounting credentials of minority-group members as inherently misleading indicators of qualifications. Certainly, problems arise from the conceptual gap between credentials and qualifications and between qualifications and performance. Presently accepted credentials that prove irrelevant or unpredictive should be changed or redesigned, not handicapped in favor of minority-group members. Nor need we place exclusive reliance upon "mechanical tests." It may be, for example, that given widespread past patterns of discrimination and economic deprivation, certain individuals who make it through college thereby demonstrate a higher motivational level than others; this can certainly be taken into account in predicting future performance. But it is important to note that this is a factor that can be applied to anyone from an economically deprived background; it is not equivalent to considering race or sex a qualification, or to judging the credentials of all women or minority-group members more leniently in assessing real qualifications.

While such nonmechanical criteria can be applied legitimately, it is in the interest of all candidates for positions generally that credentials considered be limited, standard, and publicized. For example, the personality of a prospective teacher might be taken into account in the extreme case that it might substantially affect his or her teaching ability, but in general, personality factors, as they relate to compatibility with colleagues, should be discounted in order to prevent both discrimination and unwarranted reverse discrimination. Standard criteria, such as degrees, publications, student ratings, etc., should be emphasized to ensure fair application of the rule for hiring. The same points apply to positions for which only a fixed level of competence rather than open-ended degrees of excellence are possible. The rule for hiring the competent must still be interpreted narrowly and applied impartially, the only difference being that more applicants will have equal qualifications according to this criterion and that positions will therefore be awarded more frequently on utilitarian grounds or by a random process.

Even if, contrary to all the above considerations, the criteria of credentials for some fields were found to be inherently discriminatory, this would only constitute a reason for finding more predictive or objective criteria and for compensating victims of past application of the unfair set, not for regarding race and sex as qualifications for hiring in the future. This can be made clearer in comparison with a hypothetical case. Suppose that at a school where women account for 50 percent of the enrollment only 10 percent of the persons on the dean's list are women, and from this it is concluded that discrimination in grading or test designing has occurred. Surely we would not attempt to remedy this situation by insisting that being female is henceforth to be a qualification for the dean's list or that credentials of female students be more leniently evaluated on the same scale, since such moves would tend to destroy the notion of a dean's list as an indication of merit or achievement. Rather, we would insist that tests and other grading criteria be more fairly designed and applied and take steps to ensure this. Similarly, the idea of using race and sex as general qualifications for positions or of judging the credentials of individuals from certain groups more leniently than those of others in an attempt to apply the rule for hiring the most competent is self-defeating. If certain tests have on the average proved unpredictive of future performance by individuals in certain groups, there is no guarantee that keeping the same tests but grading them easier for all individuals of those groups will result in generally more competent people being chosen. Rather, more objective tests should be designed and applied to all. The feeling that at present the same tests cannot be applied fairly to all is a result of the past discrimination and economic deprivation that have handicapped some. But as argued above, the fact of discrimination and deprivation shows that compensatory programs are in order, not that the tests or credentials used are in themselves discriminatory or unpredictive of qualifications. Again, we should advocate reverse discrimination where justified and recognize the costs, not disguise them with misleading talk of native qualifications.

A significant part of the liberal trend in Western nations in the last two centuries has been the gradual elimination of native differences like race or sex as determinants of social roles and benefits. (That intelligence cannot be justly eliminated, however, shows the danger of oversimplification.) We have come to see common humanity as a sufficient reason to demand the satisfaction of basic human needs and, above that level, to distribute benefits more according to individual contributions and potential contributions to the public good. Progress has been slow and impatience warranted in the face of continuing injustice. But the current calls for reversing this trend are perhaps the most disturbing aspect of the debate over reverse discrimination, especially when the policies can be straightforwardly advocated for those individuals who deserve them for compensatory or equalizing reasons. The charge that certain credentials are unpredictive of true qualifications and performance on the job warrants attention and attempts to alter criteria of appointment so as to make them more predictive. This is especially important when present criteria, in addition to being unpredictive, tend to operate against members of groups that have suffered from overt forms of discrimination. But there remains a difference between criteria that individuals can attempt to satisfy through their own efforts, whether predictive or not, and those that count purely native characteristics as credentials in themselves. The latter, where avoidable, are not only inefficient but also unjust in denying equal opportunity.

The point of this section has been that the arguments to follow in favor of the policy of reverse discrimination should not be confused with appeals to abandon impersonal merit criteria regarding credentials and qualifications under the distributive rule for awarding positions. It is important here to separate distributive from compensatory considerations, although, as we shall see, the latter follow from the former.

Notes

1. For libertarian arguments, see Nozick, *Anarchy, State, and Utopia*, chaps. 7, 8; also Judith Thomson, "Preferential Hiring," *Philosophy & Public Affairs*, 2 (1973), 364–84. For the egalitarian position, see Thomas Nagel, "Equal Treatment and Compensatory Discrimination," *Philosophy & Public Affairs*, 2, (1973), 348–63; also Rawls, *Theory of Justice*, pp. 75–90.

2. Compare Louis Katzner, "Is the Favoring of Women and Blacks in Employment and Educational Opportunities Justified?" in Joel Feinberg and Hyman Gross, eds., *Philosophy of Law* (Encino, Calif.: Dickenson, 1975), p. 291.

3. Compare J. Sterba, "Justice as Desert," *Social Theory & Practice*, 3 (1974), 101–16.

4. For the justification of inequalities as incentives, see Rawls, *Theory of Justice*, pp. 305–6, 311.

5. Need is of course another criterion of distribution and a basic source of claims to social goods. But I ignore it here as irrelevant to the award of positions, since persons do not have special needs to occupy specific positions.

6. This argument is found in Gertrude Ezorsky, "It's Mine," *Philosophy & Public Affairs*, 3 (1974), 321–30.

7. The analogy is from Thomson, "Preferential Hiring."

8. Compare Nicholas Rescher, *Distributive Justice* (Indianapolis: Bobbs-Merrill, 1966), pp. 90–93.

9. Joel Feinberg makes this comparison in "Justice and Personal Desert," in his *Doing and Deserving* (Princeton: Princeton University Press, 1970). Much of the following discussion draws from his illuminating chapter.

10. See, for example, the testimony of Millard Ruud in the *DeFunis* case as to the success of CLEO program graduates in law schools. This is reproduced in Ann F. Ginger, ed., *DeFunis versus Odegaard and The University of Washington*, 3 vols. (New York: Oceana, 1974), 1, 68.

11. Helen S. Astin, *The Woman Doctorate in America* (New York: Russell Sage Foundation, 1969), p. 85.

IS PREFERENTIAL HIRING FAIR?

Russell Abrams

Russell Abrams examines whether it is ever fair to hire someone according to criteria other than ability to do the job. He argues that when we consider what qualifications usually depend on, we will agree that it is sometimes fair.

Is the practice of preferential hiring ever fair? By preferential hiring, I mean hiring based on factors that go beyond a candidate's ability to do the job, that is, his or her qualifications. All hiring, of course, must take qualifications into account. Hiring is *preferential* when additional factors are also considered. The question I want to investigate here is, Under what conditions, if any, is a systematic practice of preferential hiring morally justified? I would like you to think of this discussion as applying primarily to hiring in the public sector; however, the ensuing arguments should also be applicable to hiring practice in private industry.

The foregoing definition of preferential hiring — hiring based on factors in addition to qualifications — is intended to be free of all positive or negative value judgments. This is important, because the everyday terminology in this area is so value-laden that we often find it difficult to carry on an objective discussion. People unfortunately tend to conclude without argument that preferential hiring is unfair simply because a negative value judgment is already built into the term. The definition I am proposing, by contrast, should allow us to distinguish freely between fair and unfair instances of preferential hiring.

My concern here is not with questions of efficiency but with those of fairness. Notice that in our society the assignment of a job accomplishes two things. First, it determines a person's role in the society's means of production, for jobs are mechanisms by which society integrates the individual into the society's productive machinery. Second, the assignment of a job determines, to a great extent, the size of the jobholder's share of social goods. For most people their job is the main determinant of their wealth and prestige, and the various social goods that wealth and prestige make possible. So in assigning jobs we are really deciding who is to get the greater and who the lesser share of the available social goods. Efficiency is primarily relevant to the first function of job assignment — integrating the individual into the society's productive machinery. Fairness is primarily relevant to this second function of job assignment — determining of one's share of social goods.

Since I am concerned here with fairness, my focus will be on this second function of job assignment. To sidestep the need to worry about the other aspect of job assignment, efficiency, I am going to assume — in the examples put forward — that all the competing candidates are highly qualified for the jobs in question. Some will be better qualified than others but all will be highly qualified. This means that decisions in these cases concerning who gets the job will not have a material impact on efficiency, productivity, or overall welfare. Who should get the job in these cases will be primarily an issue of fairness? (By the way, sometimes instead of saying that it is *fair* that a certain candidate get a particular job, I will say that the candidate *deserves* to get the job, or that this is *morally appropriate* or *justified*. I mean the same thing by all four expressions.)

It is commonplace to extol the moral virtues of hiring someone because he or she is the best person for the job. We say, "May the best person win" in a way that suggests that something morally important turns on it. Or we often hear pronounced with pride, "I chose her because she was the best person for the job." Even President Bush, in nominating Clarence Thomas to the Supreme Court, justified his choice by claiming that Thomas was the most highly qualified candidate available. But such talk by itself doesn't settle the question of whether the most highly qualified candidate really does deserve the job.

Let's begin to address this question by analyzing the factors that affect a person's qualifications. Roughly speaking, people qualifications depend on three independent factors: their efforts, their aptitudes and talents, and their external circumstances. We can call these for short *effort, talent,* and *circumstance*. Of these three, the only one that is even arguably under the individual's control is effort. Some claim, for instance, that no matter what one's circumstances one is always free to fully exert oneself or not. Many would disagree with this claim, but let us accept it for the sake of argument. By contrast, a person's aptitudes — innate intelligence and raw talents — are clearly not under his or her control. Finally, external circumstances, by which I mean circumstances forced on us from the outside, are by definition beyond an individual's personal control. The circumstances I have in mind here would include early family environment, early education, deeply entrenched social structures, acts of nature, and so forth. In summary, much if not most of what determines an individual's qualifications are not things that the individual is responsible for. Therefore, it may be argued, it is not fair to distribute jobs, the chief determinant of one's social goods, solely on the basis of qualifications.

Consider, for example, two brothers, Dunster and Brad, brought up in the same household and provided with the same educational opportunities, which they have pursued with equal diligence. They are now applying for the same job, as an attorney, for which they are both highly qualified. However, Brad is slightly better qualified than Dunster, for one reason — Brad is smarter than Dunster. Now, the basic question is "Is it fair that Brad be awarded the job, and the share of social goods that go along with it, based on his better qualifications?" Certainly Brad is not morally responsible for his being more qualified than Dunster. He didn't work any harder. His better qualifications are due purely to his luck in being born with more intelligence. And luck, it would seem, should not be the basis for distributing such an important gateway commodity as a job.

The argument we are considering is really quite simple: Since one's qualifications are determined by a number of factors beyond one's control, it is not fair to award jobs and their attendant benefits solely on the basis of those qualifications. Let me pause here and consider a couple of opposing arguments. The first, which I will call the *opportunity argument,* goes as follows: Although people's skills differ, each deserves an equal opportunity to exercise those skills to the fullest extent possible. This equality of opportunity will most likely be realized if jobs are given to the most qualified candidate. For only in this way is the person with mathematical talent likely to get the job in mathematics, and the person with musical talent the job in music, and so forth.

In order to see through this argument, we need to distinguish carefully between innate talents and acquired skills. If the opportunity argument has any validity at all, it seems to support an equal opportunity to exercise innate talents, not acquired skills. But rewarding qualifications is basically equivalent to rewarding acquired skills. Why shouldn't acquired skills always be rewarded? Because acquired skills depend on previous opportunities, and these opportunities may not have been made equally available to everyone. The rewarding of acquired skills may not be fair if the opportunity to acquire those skills was not fairly distributed among the population.

Consider, for example, two piano players equal in innate musical talent and equally hardworking. The first, as a child, was given a superior musical education; the second, an average one. The first developed somewhat greater skill at her instrument. The two are not applying for the same job — for which they are both highly qualified — as a dance studio piano player. Now if qualifications are used as the sole criterion, then the job will automatically go to the better piano player. And this *will* result in the player with the greater skill getting the opportunity to use this skill. But it is not at all intuitively clear that the player with the greater skill really deserves the job. The reason, of course, is that the first player has the greater skill only because of an educational opportunity she had but the other didn't. Thus, it can be argued, she doesn't deserve to be better or to receive a reward based on her being better. We are assuming here, of course, that both candidates would do a fine job in the position.

A second attempt at providing a moral justification for distributing jobs on the basis of qualifications alone might be called the *expectation argument.* The initial premise of the argument is that people in our society have been led to expect that jobs will be awarded strictly on the basis of qualifications. Society has made a kind of implicit promise to its members that this will be so. Based on this assurance people have made vast commitments of time, energy, and resources. Therefore, so the argument concludes, it is unfair to change the rules of the game midstream and award jobs on some other basis.

The expectation argument is not convincing because (1) the initial premise is probably false, and even if it weren't, (2) the argument as a whole can be counterbalanced by other considerations. As for the first, I don't see that anyone really has received assurances that qualifications will be the sole determining factor in hiring. Certainly qualifications have not in the past *been* the sole determining factor: Consider, for example, past racial and gender discriminations, veterans preferences, and seniority preferences. Nor is it clear that anyone or any institution in the position of doing so has guaranteed us that qualifications will be the sole hiring basis. As for the second, even if people had been led to expect that hiring would be based solely on qualifications, this still doesn't mean that such expectations should never be disrupted. Notice that the expectation argument could be used to justify any social practice, no matter how evil, as long as it has existed for a significant period of time. For example, slaveowners could use it to justify the continuance of slavery, arguing that they had arranged their lives and businesses based on the expectation that slavery would continue.

In any case, even if the opportunity and expectation arguments carry some slight weight in the direction of relying solely on qualifications, they still must operate in an environment in which jobs and major social benefits are closely linked. So these arguments cannot by themselves establish the fairness of awarding jobs on the basis of qualifications alone.

I now want to look at a third argument for basing hiring solely on qualifications, at least insofar as these are the result of effort and talent. This argument addresses head on the linkage between jobs and social benefits. Proposed by the Harvard philosopher John Rawls, it attempts to establish the moral acceptability of hiring based on qualifications, even though (1) qualifications depend on innate talent, and (2) jobs requiring better qualifications are in our society more highly paid. The basic principle behind Rawls's argument is that it is OK to give special rewards to talent-based qualifications, if those with the least amount of talent are made better off in the

process. This may sound paradoxical, but it isn't really. If talent-based qualifications are highly rewarded, so the argument goes, then the people with the talent will be more motivated to develop and use it. The result will be a more productive society with a higher standard of living for everyone, including the least talented. In such a situation the least talented—though likely to be rewarded less handsomely than the more talented—will still be better off than if talent were not rewarded differentially at all. Many believe that the economies of eastern Europe and the former Soviet Union, for example, are in such sad shape because they failed to reward talent.

This is an interesting theoretical argument as far as it goes. What it leaves open is *how much* we should reward talent: that is, what is a fair difference between the pay scale of the most talented and the least talented? The theory is clear enough—keep enlarging the difference until further enlargement no longer benefits the least talented. But, as you might imagine, it is very difficult in practice to locate this stopping point. I will not go into this issue now, and I will leave it to you to think about.

In any case, even if—based on this argument—we favor the direct rewarding of qualifications insofar as they depend just on effort and talent, we are still left with the third factor affecting qualifications, namely circumstances. Even Rawls's argument cannot be used to justify hiring solely by qualifications once we take into account this third factor.

The term *circumstance,* you will recall, was intended to cover all those external conditions over which we have no control, conditions that are thrust on us from the outside. These include such things as acts of nature; early childhood upbringing and education; socially imposed systems of punishment, opportunity, and reward; and so forth. Because circumstance includes factors that are man-made, either individually or societally, many of them may be appropriately classified as either just or unjust. Thus, circumstance may have direct bearing on questions of justice and fairness in the realm of hiring. In fact, I believe that the basic principle connecting circumstance with fairness in hiring is the following: If, in the pursuit of qualifications, I am helped—or my competitors hindered—by unfair actions of men or unjust social institutions, then this casts into doubt my deserving a job based on my superior qualifications.

Let's start with an example involving an unfair act of an individual. Suppose Charlie Cheater and Andy Honest are just out of law school and are applying for the same job as a tax attorney. Let's assume that they are equally talented and hardworking. They are both highly qualified for the job. Charlie, however, is slightly better qualified because he went to Harvard Law School, while Andy went to Golden Gate. Charlie Cheater managed to squeak into the last slot in Harvard Law's first-year class by cheating on his LSAT exam. He cheated by copying some of his answers — in areas where he knew he was weak — from Andy's exam. As a result he just managed to bump Andy out of the Harvard slot that Andy would have gotten if Charlie hadn't cheated.

Now the question is "Does Charlie deserve the job over Andy based on his superior qualifications?" Clearly not. True, he has superior qualifications, but he does not deserve to have them and therefore he does not deserve to be rewarded for them. It seems appropriate here — given that both are highly qualified — that the job go to Andy. In fact, giving the job to Andy would balance accounts in two ways: it would compensate Andy for the loss he suffered at the hands of Charlie and it would punish Charlie for his evil deed. It seems clear, then, that under the described circumstances the fair thing to do is to award the job to the person who does not have the best qualifications, that is, to practice preferential hiring. The main point I am trying to make here is that if the circumstances surrounding the pursuit of qualifications unfairly favors or disfavors one of the participants, then it is not fair to base the awarding of the job solely on those qualifications.

Of course, the circumstances relevant to the kind of preferential hiring we are most concerned with here are not those created by a single aberrant individual. Rather, they are those connected with the injustice of a whole social system. I mean, of course, institutional or systematic racism, sexism, and prejudice. For 300 of the 330 years of U.S. history, great segments of our society were deprived *by law* of their human rights. These classes of people were systematically denied the opportunity to obtain the qualifications that would allow them to compete fairly for our society's gateway commodity — a good job. Our founding fathers were slaveowners, woman suffrage was not won until the early part of this century, and the last of our racist statutes were not expunged from the lawbooks until the 1960's. Those who claim that in the last 30 years we, as a society, have completely reversed the course of 300 years of history are, in my opinion, either naive or disingenuous. We have, of course, made a great deal of progress, but that is not the issue. The issue is whether there are still large numbers of people who are applying for jobs today who have been deprived by our social system of a fair opportunity to obtain qualifications. I think that an excellent case can be made for the claim that there are, though I will not argue this here. I will simply assume that this is the case.

Consider, now, a job competition between Bill and Whitney, two equally talented and equally hardworking people. Bill is black and was born and raised in a poor black ghetto. Whitney is white and was raised in a white, upper middle class community. Bill is highly qualified for the job in question. Whitney is even better qualified. Finally, let us assume that the reason that Bill is less qualified than Whitney is that Bill has had to pursue his qualifications in the face of racial prejudice. Question: Is it fair to award Whitney the job based on her better qualifications? I think the answer again has to be "no" with the reasoning similar to that used before. Whitney's superior qualifications are, by hypothesis, due to the fact that Bill has been treated unfairly. Thus Whitney doesn't deserve to have superior qualifications or be rewarded for them. In short, this is a situation in which it is fair to look beyond superior qualification, that is, to practice preferential hiring.

Someone might object to the foregoing argument by pointing out that there is a significant disanalogy between the case of cheating and the case of an unjust social system. In the cheating case Charlie himself performed an evil deed and thus, perhaps, deserved to be punished by the loss of the job. But in the case of Bill and Whitney, it is quite possible that Whitney did nothing evil. She may have simply been an innocent participant who happened to benefit from an unjust social system. She may have had no role in either setting up the social system or perpetuating it. Is it fair under these conditions that she be punished? I think the answer has to be no. It is not fair that she be punished, for the simple reason she did nothing evil. This doesn't mean, however, that it is unfair for her not to get the job.

Consider, by analogy, a race between two horses in which the horse with the slower time has been drugged with a sedative. The horse with the faster time will not be declared the winner and the owner of that horse will not collect the prize money, even if the owner had nothing to do with the drugging. Notice that the owner of the horse with the faster time is not being punished. He is merely being denied what was never fairly his in the first place. The point is that he cannot be allowed to profit from circumstances that gave him an unfair advantage over his competitors, even though he played no role in bringing those circumstances about. Similarly, Whitney should not be allowed to benefit from circumstances that gave her an unfair advantage in the job competition, even though she played no role in bringing those circumstances about. In neither case is someone being unfairly deprived of something that was hers. Each is merely not being given something that she did not deserve.

Let us consider the possible sources of Whitney's unfair advantage over Bill and see if these might affect the issue of fairness here. By hypothesis, at least part of Whitney's advantage is due to Bill's having been unfairly held back by racial prejudice. Has Whitney, in addition, gained something positive that she doesn't deserve, or even something positive at Bill's expense? Has her education, for example, been better than it would have been because of resources unfairly taken from Bill? If Bill and Whitney were real people in our society, I think that the answer might well be yes. Prejudice is not completely blind. Behind it is often insight into the personal benefits of prejudice, the benefits of appropriating resources for oneself and justifying it in sexist or racial terms. But the important point here is that for the purposes of justifying preferential hiring, it doesn't matter. All that is necessary is that the inequality or differences in qualifications between Bill and Whitney be undeserved. This may be the result solely of Bill's being unfairly held back in his pursuit of qualifications without any undeserved benefits to Whitney. Or it may have been the result of Bill's being unfairly held back *plus* Whitney's unfairly receiving extra benefits (perhaps not at Bill's expense). Or it may have been the result of resources unfairly taken from Bill and given directly or indirectly to Whitney. Any of these scenarios would justify preferential hiring, that is, taking into account considerations other than qualifications.

The foregoing line of reasoning answers a common objection to preferential hiring, one that turns on the idea that preferential hiring is unfair to white or male candidates. Opponents of preferential hiring sometimes concede that a minority candidate may well deserve special consideration. But they quickly add that if this special consideration entails unfair treatment of white or male candidates, then this special consideration must be foregone. The idea is that though perhaps Bill has been unfairly held back, Whitney may have received no special advantages. And if this is true, then it is unfair to deprive Whitney of the job for which she is better qualified. But what I am arguing here is that the fact that minority competitors have been unfairly held back in the pursuit of their qualifications *already* makes the inequality undeserved, and therefore makes hiring based on that inequality unfair. There is no need to make any additional assumptions about white candidates having received extra support they didn't deserve or extra support taken directly or indirectly from the minority candidate.

I want now to look at one final argument against preferential hiring. This is the argument that the law should be blind to gender, color, race, ethnicity, and religious preference. Why should one's gender or skin color, it is often asked, affect whether one gets a particular job? The answer is that these characteristics should not, per se, make any difference. One color or gender does not intrinsically deserve any more consideration than another. What should make a difference is whether or not one has been unfairly held back by the society in the pursuit of one's qualifications. And it may be that the most practical method—or even the only practical method—of picking out those that have been unfairly held back is to use some extraneous property like skin color or gender. It's not *because* of one's skin color that one deserves a special advantage; it's because one's skin color—in this particular time and place—happens to be a reasonably reliable indicator of whether or not one has been unfairly treated.

Of course, such indicators can never be 100% accurate, so they are bound to "pass" some individuals who have *not* been unfairly disadvantaged. Is this drawback significant enough to justify dropping the use of such indicators? The answer must come, I think, from weighing the net benefits of using such indicators against the alternative. The alternative is to require individuals to prove, on a case-by-case basis, that they have been unfairly disadvantaged in the pursuit of qualifications. In principle there seems to be nothing wrong with this. In practice, however, it has spelled the virtual end of preferential hiring.

There are at least two reasons for this. The first is the great difficulty in proving in an individual case that one has been disadvantaged by prejudice. Because of the subtlety of prejudicial discrimination, much of the supporting data involves statistical and attitudinal evidence derived from large populations. This type of evidence can establish that it is highly likely that a member of a certain ethnic or gender group has, over a certain period, experienced prejudicial discrimination. But it cannot establish certainty in individual cases. Second, when it is required that prejudicial discrimination be proved on a case-by-case basis, the burden of proof is placed on those very individuals who — if their cases are just — are least able to successfully press their case. These are, of course, the economically disadvantaged and the poorly educated. And these individuals will be required to press their cases against the most powerful elements in the society, namely, those who control access to jobs. For these two reasons, the requirement that prejudicial discrimination be proved on a case-by-case basis is virtually tantamount to abandoning the vast majority of those who deserve relief. If this complete abandonment of justice is the alternative to using a simple ethnic or racial indicator for purposes of preferential hiring, then it seems clear that the disadvantages of using such indicators are vastly outweighed by their advantages. I might add that, in my opinion, those who ultimately do not want to see any relief given in any of these cases, no matter how justified, often hide behind the principle that prejudicial discrimination must be proved on a case-by-case basis. They understand very well that in practice this means nothing will be changed.

Let me quickly review and sum up what I have covered so far. I began by defining preferential hiring. I then drew a distinction between two functions of job assignment — integrating the individual into the society's productive machinery and determining the jobholder's share of social goods. I pointed out that fairness in job assignment is relevant primarily to this second function. I then proceeded to analyze three independent factors that affect a person's job qualifications — effort, talent, and circumstance. I noted that of these, three factors are not within an individual's control and suggested that this makes the distribution of important social goods on the basis of qualifications alone unlikely to be fair. I then considered and, I believe, refuted two arguments in favor of using qualifications alone — the opportunity argument and the expectation argument. I then considered a third argument, Rawls's argument, for rewarding qualifications, at least insofar as these are attributable to effort and talent. But I noted that even this argument is powerless in the face of the contribution of unfair or unjust circumstances to the development of qualifications. I then noted how the existence of an unjust system — which unfairly prevents certain members of society from developing qualifications nullifies any presumption that morality demands that jobs be awarded solely on the basis of such qualifications. This is true, I argued, even if nonminorities themselves receive no special advantages. All that is necessary is that a minority or gender class be unfairly deprived of opportunities to develop qualifications. Finally, I explained why using color, gender, or other indicators to demarcate populations deserving preferential hiring is (1) consistent with our beliefs that the law should be color and gender blind, and (2) justifiable even though such indicators are not perfectly accurate indicators of past injustice for all members of these classes.

AFFIRMATIVE ACTION:
The Price of Preference

Shelby Steele

Shelby Steele discusses what he sees as the remarkable escalation of affirmative action. According to Steele, affirmative action programs are pernicious because they encourage African Americans to exploit the past. (Source: From The Content of Our Character *by Shelby Steele. Copyright © 1990 by Shelby Steele. Reprinted by permission of St. Martin's Press, Inc., New York, NY.)*

In a few short years, when my two children will be applying to college, the affirmative action policies by which most universities offer black students some form of preferential treatment will present me with a dilemma. I am a middle-class black, a college professor, far from wealthy, but also well removed from the kind of deprivation that would qualify my children for the label "disadvantaged." Both of them have endured racial insensitivity from whites. They have been called names, have suffered slights, and have experienced firsthand the peculiar malevolence that racism brings out in people. Yet, they have never experienced racial discrimination, have never been stopped by their race on any path they have chosen to follow. Still, their society now tells them that if they will only designate themselves as black on their college applications, they will likely do better in the college lottery than if they conceal this fact. I think there is something of a Faustian bargain in this.

Of course, many blacks and a considerable number of whites would say that I was sanctimoniously making affirmative action into a test of character. They would say that this small preference is the meagerest recompense for centuries of unrelieved oppression. And to these arguments other very obvious facts must be added. In America, many marginally competent or flatly incompetent whites are hired everyday — some because their white skin suits the conscious or unconscious racial preference of their employer. The white children of alumni are often grandfathered into elite universities in what can only be seen as a residual benefit of historic white privilege. Worse, white incompetence is always an individ-

ual matter, while for blacks it is often confirmation of ugly stereotypes. The Peter Principle was not conceived with only blacks in mind. Given that unfairness cuts both ways, doesn't it only balance the scales of history that my children now receive a slight preference over whites? Doesn't this repay, in a small way, the systematic denial under which their grandfather lived out his days?

So, in theory, affirmative action certainly has all the moral symmetry that fairness requires — the injustice of historical and even contemporary white advantage is offset with black advantage; preference replaces prejudice, inclusion answers exclusion. It is reformist and corrective, even repentant and redemptive. And I would never sneer at these good intentions. Born in the late forties in Chicago, I started my education (charitable term in this case) in a segregated school and suffered all the indignities that come to blacks in a segregated society. My father, born in the South, only made it to the third grade before the white man's fields took permanent priority over his formal education. And though he educated himself into an advanced reader with an almost professorial authority, he could only drive a truck for a living and never earned more than ninety dollars a week in his entire life. So, yes, it is crucial to my sense of citizenship, to my ability to identify with the spirit and the interests of America, to know that this country, however imperfectly, recognizes its past sins and wishes to correct them.

Yet good intentions, because of the opportunity for innocence they offer us, are very seductive and can blind us to the effects they generate when implemented. In our society, affirmative action is, among other things, a testament to white goodwill and to black power, and in the midst of these heavy investments, its effects can be hard to see. But after twenty years of implementation, I think affirmative action has shown itself to be more bad than good and that blacks — whom I will focus on in this essay — now stand to lose more from it than they gain.

In talking with affirmative action administrators and with blacks and whites in general, it is clear that supporters of affirmative action focus on its good intentions while detractors emphasize its negative effects. Proponents talk about "diversity" and "pluralism"; opponents speak of "reverse discrimination," the unfairness of quotas and set-asides. It was virtually impossible to find people outside either camp. The closest I came was a white male manager at a large computer company who said, "I think it amounts to reverse discrimination, but I'll put up with a little of that for a little more diversity." I'll live with a little of the effect to gain a little of the intention, he seemed to be saying. But this only makes him a halfhearted supporter of affirmative action. I think many people who don't really like affirmative action support it to one degree or another anyway.

I believe they do this because of what happened to white and black Americans in the crucible of the sixties when whites were confronted with their racial guilt and blacks tasted their first real power. In this stormy time white absolution and black power coalesced into virtual mandates for society. Affirmative action became a meeting ground for these mandates in the law, and in the late sixties and early seventies it underwent a remarkable escalation of its mission from simple anti-discrimination enforcement to social engineering by means of quotas, goals, timetables, set-asides, and other forms of preferential treatment.

Legally, this was achieved through a series of executive orders and EEOC guidelines that allowed racial imbalances in the workplace to stand as proof of racial discrimination. Once it could be assumed that discrimination explained racial imbalances, it became easy to justify group remedies to presumed discrimination, rather than the normal case-by-case redress for proven discrimination. Preferential treatment through quotas, goals, and so on is designed to correct imbalances based on the assumption that they always indicate discrimination. This expansion of what constitutes discrimination allowed affirmative action to escalate into the business of social engineering in the name of anti-discrimination, to push society toward statistically proportionate racial representation, without any obligation of proving actual discrimination.

What accounted for this shift, I believe, was the white mandate to achieve a new racial innocence and the black mandate to gain power. Even though blacks had made great advances during the sixties without quotas, these mandates, which came to a head in the very late sixties, could no longer be satisfied by anything less than racial preferences. I don't think these mandates in themselves were wrong, since whites clearly needed to do better by blacks and blacks needed more real power in society. But, as they came together in affirmative action, their effect was to distort our understanding of racial discrimination in a way that allowed us to offer the remediation of preference on the basis of mere color rather than actual injury. By making black the color of preference, these mandates have reburdened society with the very marriage of color and preference (in reverse) that we set out to eradicate. The old sin is reaffirmed in a new guise.

But the essential problem with this form of affirmative action is the way it leaps over the hard business of developing a formerly oppressed people to the point where they can achieve proportionate representation on their own (given equal opportunity) and goes straight for the proportionate representation. This may satisfy some whites of their innocence and some blacks of their power, but it does very little to truly uplift blacks.

A white female affirmative action officer at an Ivy League university told me what many supporters of affirmative action now say: "We're after diversity. We ideally want a student body where racial and ethnic groups are represented according to their proportion in society." When affirmative action escalated into social engineering, diversity became a golden word. It grants whites an egalitarian fairness (innocence) and blacks an entitlement to proportionate representation (power). *Diversity* is a term that applies democratic principles to races and cultures rather than to citizens, despite the fact that there is nothing to indicate that real diversity is the same thing as proportionate representation. Too often the result of this on campuses (for example) has been a democracy of colors rather than of people, an artificial diversity that gives the appearance of an educational parity between black and white students that has not yet been achieved in reality. Here again, racial preferences allow society to leapfrog over the difficult problem of developing blacks to parity with whites and into a cosmetic diversity that covers the blemish of disparity—a full six years after admission, only about 26 percent of black students graduate from college.

Racial representation is not the same thing as racial development, yet affirmative action fosters a confusion of these very different needs. Representation can be manufactured; development is always hard-earned. However, it is the music of innocence and power that we hear in affirmative action that causes us to cling to it and to its distracting emphasis on representation. The fact is that after twenty years of racial preferences, the gap between white and black median income is greater than it was in the seventies. None of this is to say that blacks don't need policies that ensure our right to equal opportunity, but what we need more is the development that will let us take advantage of society's efforts to include us.

I think that one of the most troubling effects of racial preferences for blacks is a kind of demoralization, or put another way, an enlargement of self-doubt. Under affirmative action the quality that earns us preferential treatment is an implied inferiority. However, this inferiority is explained—and it is easily enough explained by the myriad deprivations that grew out of our oppression—it is still inferiority. There are explanations, and then there is the fact. And the fact must be borne by the individual as a condition apart from the explanation, apart even from the fact that others like himself also bear this condition. In integrated situations where blacks must compete with whites who may be better prepared, these explanations may quickly wear thin and expose the individual to racial as well as personal self-doubt.

All of this is compounded by the cultural myth of black inferiority that blacks have always lived with. What this means in practical terms is that when blacks deliver themselves into integrated situations, they encounter a nasty little reflex in whites, a mindless, atavistic reflex that responds to the color black with alarm. Attributions may follow this alarm if the white cares to indulge them, and if they do, they will most likely be negative—one such attribution is intellectual ineptness. I think this reflex and the attributions that may follow it embarrass most whites today; therefore, it is usually quickly repressed. Nevertheless,

on an equally atavistic level, the black will be aware of the reflex his color triggers and will feel a stab of horror at seeing himself reflected in this way. He, too, will do a quick repression, but a lifetime of such stabbings is what constitutes his inner realm of racial doubt.

The effects of this may be a subject for another essay. The point here is that the implication of inferiority that racial preferences engender in both the white and black mind expands rather than contracts this doubt. Even when the black sees no implication of inferiority in racial preferences, he knows that whites do, so that—consciously or unconsciously—the result is virtually the same. The effect of preferential treatment—the lowering of normal standards to increase black representation—puts blacks at war with an expanded realm of debilitating doubt, so that the doubt itself becomes an unrecognized preoccupation that undermines their ability to perform, especially in integrated situations. On largely white campuses, blacks are five times more likely to drop out than whites. Preferential treatment, no matter how it is justified in the light of day, subjects blacks to a midnight of self-doubt, and so often transforms their advantage into a revolving door.

Another liability of affirmative action comes from the fact that it indirectly encourages blacks to exploit their own past victimization as a source of power and privilege. Victimization, like implied inferiority, is what justifies preference, so that to receive the benefits of preferential treatment one must, to some extent, become invested in the view of one's self as a victim. In this way, affirmative action nurtures a victim-focused identity in blacks. The obvious irony here is that we become inadvertently invested in the very condition we are trying to overcome. Racial preferences send us the message that there is more power in our past suffering than our present achievements—none of which could bring us a *preference* over others.

When power itself grows out of suffering, then blacks are encouraged to expand the boundaries of what qualifies as racial oppression, a situation that can lead us to paint our victimization in vivid colors, even as we receive the benefits of preference. The same corporations and institutions that give us preference are also seen as our oppressors. At Stanford University minority students—some of whom enjoy as much as $15,000 a year in financial aid—recently took over the president's office demanding, among other things, more financial aid. The power to be found in victimization, like any power, is intoxicating and can lend itself to the creation of a new class of super-victims who can feel the pea of victimization under twenty mattresses. Preferential treatment rewards us for being underdogs rather than for moving beyond that status—a misplacement of incentives that, along with its deepening of our doubt, is more a yoke than a spur.

But, I think, one of the worst prices that blacks pay for preference has to do with an illusion. I saw this illusion at work recently in the mother of a middle-class black student who was going off to his first semester of college. "They owe us this, so don't think for a minute that you don't belong there." This is the logic by which many blacks, and some whites, justify affirmative action—it is something "owed," a form of reparation. But this logic overlooks a much harder and less digestible reality, that it is impossible to repay blacks living today for the historic suffering of the race. If all blacks were given a million dollars tomorrow morning it would not amount to a dime on the dollar of three centuries of oppression, nor would it obviate the residues of that oppression that we still carry today. The concept of historic reparation grows out of a man's need to impose a degree of justice on the world that simply does not exist. Suffering can be endured and overcome, it cannot be repaid. Blacks cannot be repaid for the injustice done to the race, but we can be corrupted by society's guilty gestures of repayment.

Affirmative action is such a gesture. It tells us that racial preferences can do for us what we cannot do for ourselves. The corruption here is in the hidden incentive *not* to do what we believe preferences will do. This is an incentive to be reliant on others just as we are struggling for self-reliance. And it keeps alive the illusion that we can find some deliverance in repayment. The hardest thing for any sufferer to accept is that his suffering excuses him from very little and never has enough currency to restore him. To think otherwise is to prolong the suffering.

Several blacks I spoke with said they were still in favor of affirmative action because of the "subtle" discrimination blacks were subject to once on the job. One photojournalist said, "They have ways of ignor-

ing you." A black female television producer said, "You can't file a lawsuit when your boss doesn't invite you to the insider meetings without ruining your career. So we still need affirmative action." Others mentioned the infamous "glass ceiling" through which blacks can see the top positions of authority but never reach them. But I don't think racial preferences are a protection against this subtle discrimination; I think they contribute to it.

In any workplace, racial preferences will always create two-tiered populations composed of preferred and unpreferreds. This division makes automatic a perception of enhanced competence for the unpreferreds and of questionable competence for the preferreds—the former earned his way, even though others were given preference, while the latter made it by color as much as by competence. Racial preferences implicitly mark whites with an exaggerated superiority just as they mark blacks with an exaggerated inferiority. They not only reinforce America's oldest racial myth but, for blacks, they have the effect of stigmatizing the already stigmatized.

I think that much of the "subtle" discrimination that blacks talk about is often (not always) discrimination against the stigma of questionable competence that affirmative action delivers to blacks. In this sense, preferences scapegoat the very people they seek to help. And it may be that at a certain level employers impose a glass ceiling, but this may not be against the race so much as against the race's reputation for having advanced by color as much as by competence. Affirmative action makes a glass ceiling virtually necessary as a protection against the corruptions of preferential treatment. This ceiling is the point at which corporations shift the emphasis from color to competency and stop playing the affirmative action game. Here preference backfires for blacks and becomes a taint that holds them back. Of course, one could argue that this taint, which is, after all, in the minds of whites, becomes nothing more than an excuse to discriminate against blacks. And certainly the result is the same in either case—blacks don't get past the glass ceiling. But this argument does not get around the fact that racial preferences now taint this color with a new theme of suspicion that makes it even more vulnerable to the impulse in others to discriminate. In this crucial yet gray area of perceived competence, preferences make whites look better than they are and blacks worse, while doing nothing whatever to stop the very real discrimination that blacks may encounter. I don't wish to justify the glass ceiling here, but only to suggest the very subtle ways that affirmative action revives rather than extinguishes the old rationalizations for racial discrimination.

In education, a revolving door; in employment, a glass ceiling.

I believe affirmative action is problematic in our society because it tries to function like a social program. Rather than ask it to ensure equal opportunity we have demanded that it create parity between the races. But preferential treatment does not teach skills, or educate, or instill motivation. It only passes out entitlement by color, a situation that in my profession has created an unrealistically high demand for black professors. The social engineer's assumption is that this high demand will inspire more blacks to earn Ph.D.'s and join the profession. In fact, the number of blacks earning Ph.D.'s has declined in recent years. A Ph.D. must be developed from preschool on. He requires family and community support. He must acquire an entire system of values that enables him to work hard while delaying gratification. There are social programs, I believe, that can (and should) help blacks *develop* in all these areas, but entitlement by color is not a social program; it is a dubious reward for being black. . . .

I would also like to see affirmative action go back to its original purpose of enforcing equal opportunity — a purpose that in itself disallows racial preferences. We cannot be sure that the discriminatory impulse in America has yet been shamed into extinction, and I believe affirmative action can make its greatest contribution by providing a rigorous vigilance in this area. It can guard constitutional rather than racial rights, and help institutions evolve standards of merit and selection that are appropriate to the institution's needs yet as free of racial bias as possible (again, with the understanding that racial imbalances are not always an indication of racial bias). One of the most important things affirmative action can do is to define exactly what racial discrimination is and how it might manifest itself within a specific institution. The impulse to discriminate *is* subtle and cannot be ferreted out unless its many guises are made clear to people. Along with this there should be monitoring of institutions and heavy sanctions brought to bear when actual discrimination is found. This is the sort of affirmative action that America owes to blacks and to itself. It goes after the evil of discrimination itself, while preferences only sidestep the evil and grant entitlement to its *presumed* victims.

But if not preferences, then what? I think we need social policies that are committed to two goals: the educational and economic development of disadvantaged people, regardless of race, and the eradication from our society — through close monitoring and severe sanctions — of racial, ethnic, or gender discrimination. Preferences will not deliver us to either of these goals, since they tend to benefit those who are not disadvantaged — middle-class white women and middle-class blacks — and attack one form of discrimination with another. Preferences are inexpensive and carry the glamour of good intentions — change the numbers and the good deed is done. To be against them is to be unkind. But I think the unkindest cut is to bestow on children like my own an undeserved advantage while neglecting the development of those disadvantaged children on the East Side of my city who will likely never be in a position to benefit from a preference. Give my children fairness; give disadvantaged children a better shot at development — better elementary and secondary schools, job training, safer neighborhoods, better financial assistance for college, and so on. Fewer blacks go to college today than ten years ago; more black males of college age are in prison or under the control of the criminal justice system than in college. This despite racial preferences.

The mandates of black power and white absolution out of which preferences emerged were not wrong in themselves. What was wrong was that both races focused more on the goals of these mandates than on the means to the goals. Blacks can have no real power without taking responsibility for their own educational and economic development. Whites can have no racial innocence without earning it by eradicating discrimination and helping the disadvantaged to develop. Because we ignored the means, the goals have not been reached, and the real work remains to be done.

PART 4

Social Transformation

Not every one will agree about the correct account of social injustice, but even if we all shared the same sense of what is unjust about our society, we would still have much disagreement about what to do about it. This section deals with five common strategies to transform our society into a more just one: education, violence or nonviolence, assimilation, separatism, and coalition politics. We need not limit ourselves to accepting only one of these strategies; some of them could be easily combined with some others, but some of them are clearly incompatible.

Many people have a great deal of faith in education. They argue that if we could change the children then we could have a new generation that would not have the prejudices of its elders. If we could raise such a generation, then its members would be willing to make the institutional changes that would be necessary to make our society truly just. The chapter on education offers some suggestions for ways to change our educational system to make for a more just society. Nel Noddings describes changes that in her view ought to be made in elementary and high school education. Lawrence Blum and Tessie Liu describe how higher education must change in our increasingly diverse society.

But education alone may turn out to be insufficient. There are tremendous temptations for a person who comes from a privileged group to keep social arrangements that benefit him or her, even when they have been educated to see the injustice of such arrangements. And there is another problem with education as well: how do you change the educational system in order to get rid of social injustice when many of the people who benefit from this injustice do not want it to change? And even if we could assume that everyone was altruistic and willing to sacrifice unjust benefits, not everyone would agree about how we ought to change, and hence how education ought to change.

Civil disobedience has been a favored strategy for social change in the United States since the Boston Tea Party. Many philosophers, from Plato to Rawls, have debated the morality of civil disobedience. But even where civil obedience might seem justified, the question of whether violent disobedience is justified is deeply controversial. Some pacifists argue that violence is never justified, no matter how intolerable the situation. They base this position on the sanctity of life. This position is illustrated by Mohandas Gandhi's essay. Victoria Davion wonders whether violence is compatible with another ethical ideal — an ethic of care. Just-war theorists say that violence is justified when the injustice is serious enough, when all nonviolent remedies have failed, when the violence will likely end the injustice, and when the plan for violence avoids, insofar as it can, harm to civilians. Other theorists and activists say that we should resist injustice in whatever way we can. Some argue that violence dehumanizes us; some, such as Franz Fanon, say it is the only way to regain the humanity lost through oppression.

Another strategy that has many adherents is assimilation. Some defenders of assimilation argue that we should respond to injustice based on group membership by becoming as similar to the dominant group as we can. But there is a more sophisticated account and defense of assimilation. This version, defended by Richard Wasserstrom, says that we should be able to maintain our private differences while we shape our public selves in terms of norms that are acceptable to all. Communitarians, such as Iris Marion Young, argue that even this version of assimilation gives up too much. They want to acknowledge the profound influence and value of group difference. But assimilation should not be a one-way street, as it all too often is. Paula Gunn Allen points out the profound influence of Native American traditions on U.S. culture and institutions. And even if assimilation were a morally defensible and effective strategy for social transformation, it would still have its personal costs. In her essay, Trinh Minh-ha poignantly describes some of these costs. She also raises the question of whether it is ever really possible for someone to totally assimilate.

The defenders of group difference often argue for separatism and identity politics. Larry Kramer points out the tremendous costs borne by two highly assimilated groups: Jews during the Holocaust and gays during what he calls the AIDS holocaust. He sees their assimilation as a source of their respective tragedies. Separatists come in different varieties, but most argue that members of certain disadvantaged groups are better off separating, insofar as they can, from the dominant society and banding together. Political issues should be negotiated by cohesive groups, where members of groups share an identity, usually based on a common heritage as well as a history of oppression. Sarah Hoaglund gives an argument for separating from heterosexualism. Maria Lugones and Elizabeth Spelman describe the need for a separate feminist space as well as the attitudes that are needed to make this space respectful and friendly.

Others have pointed out the practical, personal, and moral shortcomings of separatism. The practical problem is that the separated group may be unable to exercise as much power as it needs to in order to combat oppression. The personal problems are faced by people within the group. Suppose you are an African-American, female, lesbian musician, with two children. What group are you a member of? What personal costs will you have to pay to limit your interaction with other groups? Cornel West describes some of these problems as they arose in the Clarence Thomas hearings. The moral objection turns on the perceived motivation for separating. Separatism is often viewed as motivated by a distaste for those outside one's group, which is incompatible with respect and concern for all persons. Some people are no doubt motivated by distaste and even hatred of those who are members of other groups, but a separatist need not be motivated by a lack of respect and concern for people outside one's group. A separatist may simply see separatism as a temporary strategy to end injustice — a way to build up the group cohesion, economic power, and self-esteem that the group needs to resist.

Coalition politics is a way of preserving much of what is valuable about separatism while responding to the practical, personal, and moral objections. Coalitions can be built between cohesive groups. Such coalitions may be temporary and shallow and based on a short-term shared goal, or they may be long term and deep, and based on shared values and commitments. In any case, coalitions will be more powerful than individual groups. They will also give people with a multiplicity of identities a way to interact with others who share their interests. In this final chapter, Ann Ferguson and Nellie Wong describe and defend socialist coalitions. Coalitions based on mutual respect and friendship are an exemplar of respect and concern for persons, but in practice coalitions often fail to live up to these standards. Haunani-Kay Trask sounds a cautionary note in her essay on coalitions between native Hawaiians and nonnatives.

Education and the Transformation of Consciousness

EDUCATING FOR A MORALITY OF EVIL

Nel Noddings

Nel Noddings describes evil as a real presence and related to states of consciousness. She contrasts these states with salutary states of consciousness, like caring. Finally, she discusses the way in which education can encourage positive states of consciousness. (Source: From Women and Evil, *by Nel Noddings, pages 229–245. Copyright © 1989 The Regents of the University of California. Reprinted by permission.)*

The purpose of this last chapter is to bring together the recommendations of the preceding chapters and to direct them toward education. The main task of the book has been to examine evil from women's perspective. To do so it has been necessary to analyze traditional views of evil, to consider our culture's expectations for women and for men, and to explore what we might call the logic of women's experience. What have we learned in our long history as the second sex? What positions are logically compatible with the view from our experiential standpoint?

Early on I rejected the notion held long ago by Socrates and recently by Hannah Arendt that evil is simply the absence of knowledge or good.[1] Evil is a real presence, and moral evil is often the result of trying to do something either genuinely thought to be good or rationalized layer on layer in gross bad faith.

Evil is thus intimately bound up in disputes over good. Nor do I believe that evil is necessarily ugly or that people cannot think on that which is ugly. De Sade showed us vividly how untrue these notions are. Although Sartre was technically right when he said that we cannot sustain a choice to do evil for its own sake (we do evil mainly in opposition to some perceived evil and therefore choose something we rationalize as right or good), this only points up the power of mystification and repression. We cannot think for long on our own evil motives, so we think about obedience, the knowledge to be gained, the cause to be won, and the safety of our lives, and we evaluate all these as good. But this slippery bit of thinking comes into question when we regard evil as relational and positively real. When we acknowledge that pain, separation, and helplessness are the basic states of consciousness associated with evil and that moral evil consists in inducing, sustaining, or failing to relieve these conditions, we can no longer ignore that we *do* think on and intend evil when we perform such acts. Just as disease is real and not just an illusion or absence of health, evil is real, and to control it we need to understand it and accept that the tendency toward it dwells in all of us.

If we believe this, a primary purpose of education should be to reduce pain, separation, and helplessness by encouraging people to explore the nature of evil and commit themselves to continue the search for understanding. Further, faced with the temptation or apparent need to do something evil, appropriately educated people should ask themselves: Is there a different way to accomplish my goal? Is the goal *itself* evil or tainted with evil? What good am I trying to achieve? Thinking this way should govern our political and social relations as well as our personal lives. Because such thinking requires analytical skill, all students need practice in considering their lives philosophically. And because we should not reduce such consideration to a purely contemplative state divorced from action, philosophy *becomes* largely as John Dewey advised—philosophy of education, that is, philosophy of life. An important purpose of education should be to combat mystification. This chapter explores topics of special importance to educators: curriculum and instruction, relational virtues, and the possibility of spirituality.

Curriculum and Instruction

Literacy on evil comes to mind as a reasonable aim to guide the selection and presentation of content. A few days ago in a graduate class on curriculum theory a student drew our attention to the current campus debate on courses in Western culture. His theme was the "bleaching of history," and he circulated several beautifully illustrated books that pictured the great figures of Greek and biblical history as Nordic types. Although he was a humanities major, this young man had come to believe that Western culture has so demeaned people of color and women that we should abandon it as an educational requirement. A substantial number of people have already pressed for curricular changes that would introduce courses in non-Western cultures and include female writers and writers of color. Many—but by no means all of us—agree that this is a move in the right direction.

The arguments that have led to change have largely followed the liberal tradition. They argue from conceptions of equality. When we examine the situation from the perspective adopted throughout this book, another sort of argument begins to develop, and a different solution emerges. It takes account of—even though it ultimately rejects—the rationale many scholars offer to retain required courses in Western culture. Even though this culture and the works chosen to represent it are filled with arrogance, cruelty, gross injustice, and distorted arguments for Western male dominance, this *is* our heritage. This is the thinking that has controlled our troubled rise to high culture and technology. We teach it, they argue, not only to admire its intellectual grandeur but to critique it, to understand and grow beyond it.

This strikes me as a powerful argument if it is honest. But people who make it—if they have learned the lessons supposedly taught by their beloved material—should know that the very requirement of this material honors it. It is not enough for the enlightened professor, usually white and male, to hold forth on the errors and injustices revealed in the works we study with such reverence. At the least the critical perspectives of those injured should be included and attended to with material written and spoken in their own voices. If we require students to read Aristotle, Augustine, and Aquinas, then we should require them as well to read Mary Daly, James Baldwin, Susan Moller Okin, and other critics where their works are directly relevant. We would not dream of requiring our students to read old works of science riddled with errors. In the rare cases when we do so because of some allegedly great literary value, we make sure that other material in the curriculum corrects the errors. In the case of the great works in humanities, it is not simply a matter of error; it is a matter of *evil* enshrined in a culture that does not really want to forsake it.

In earlier sections I referred to the glories and horrors of *The Iliad* and *The Odyssey*. Should all students read these books? I think the books should be available—present in the curriculum—for those who are led to or choose to study them, but students should study them with attention to details that traditional instruction has regularly overlooked. Penelope is often used as a model of the faithful and passive wife (totally unproductive—weaving and tearing out, weaving and tearing out, day after day), and Telemachus is interpreted developmentally. Many interpretations portray Telemachus as a compassionate figure who begs his father to spare Medon and Phemiosa, but part of his growing up involves his ability to assert total control over the women in his household, including his mother, who is lost in admiration for his newly acquired manliness. In contrast to the mercy he encourages for Medon and Phemiosa, his treatment of the slave women — whose only apparent crime was succumbing to the romantic overtures of the wooers — exceeds in cruelty the demands of his father. Odysseus had ordered him to have the twelve unfaithful women clean up the great hall that was littered with the bodies and blood of the slain wooers. After their cleaning, he wanted the women taken outside and slain with swords. But Telemachus in the full fire of manhood says, "God forbid that I should take these women's lives by a clean death, these that have poured dishonor on my head and on my mother, and have lain with the wooers." (I should note that these same women may have "lain with" Odysseus in the past, given that such use of women was common among Homeric princes.) Homer proceeds to describe Telemachus's action in graphic terms:

> With that word he tied the cable of a dark-prowed ship to a great pillar and flung it round the vaulted room, and fastened it aloft, that none might touch the ground with her feet. And even as when thrushes, long of wing, or doves fall into a net that is set in a thicket, as they seek to their roosting-place, and a loathly bed harbors them, even so the women held their heads all in a row, and about all their necks nooses were cast, that they might die by the most pitiful death. And they writhed with their feet for a small space, but for no long while.2

What we should impress on students is not only the cruelty of Telemachus — in the next passage he and his fellows cut off the nostrils, hands, feet, and ears of Melanthius and throw his "vitals" to the dogs — but the pattern of his development. He grows in direct opposition to all that is feminine and exhibits a large part of his manhood in his control of women. The women he murders are not even named, and they behave passively — like caught thrushes or doves — even in the face of death.

When we treat material of this sort in the classroom, we should address the great themes of torture, cruelty, and misogyny in some depth. Students should not leave with the idea that people no longer do such dreadful things to one another. The results of Hiroshima, for example, were a sanitized form of torture. No one played bold Telemachus stringing up meek women or tearing the guts out of a shamed enemy. But people were nevertheless gutted and burned and strangled, and many suffered for years, not simply "for no long while." Nor did misogyny end with Telemachus and his hero father. Curriculum makers should begin to assemble appropriate materials for following up on *these* themes and not just on the traditional themes of the warrior's courage, the wife's faithfulness, the son's obedience and "growth," the hero's triumph, and the alleged victory of good over evil. (The dreadful scenes just described include many references to vengeful acts as righteous, as defeats of evil.) If we are concerned, as we continually say we are, with the development of our children, then we must carefully consider the development of Telemachus and ask whether that is the pattern we wish to perpetuate. We may answer that we should indeed admire and encourage *part* of the pattern. In trying to redress an imbalance and reject obvious tendencies to evil, I do not mean to throw out everything associated with a model that contains both admirable and despicable qualities.

. . . Education requires changes not only within the subjects now taught but also in the constellation of topics now addressed as "subjects." Jane Roland Martin cautions that we should "not delude ourselves that education can be created anew."3 She is thoroughly familiar with the discouraging literature on schooling and change. In our theoretical work, however, we *should* create education anew. We can then use the vision we create to guide the actual changes we find feasible. Without such a vision we have no way to order our priorities or to seize opportunities when they present themselves. Similarly, I have argued throughout this book that without a morality of evil we lack the questions needed to prevent us from continuing to ratify evil.

Martin, who also wants the school curriculum to include the activities and interests of women, argues for a dramatic change in subjects and also for changes in the ways we teach traditional subjects. She recommends that "caring, concern, and connection" be made goals of education:

I do not mean by this that we should fill up school time with courses in the 3 Cs of caring, concern, and connection. In an education that gives Sophie, Sarah, and the reproductive processes of society their due, Compassion 101a need no more be listed in a school's offering than Objectivity 101a is now. Just as the general curricular goals of rationality and individual autonomy derive from the productive processes of society, so too the reproductive processes yield general goals.[4]

The difficulty here is even greater than Martin admits. The notion of objectivity is peculiarly compatible with courses, teacher dominance, grading, and hierarchical structures of school organization. That is why Objectivity 101a is not needed. Even if schools added courses in caring, concern, and connection to the curriculum (and we can imagine at least one such course being added as a sop to feminist academics), this move would not accomplish our purpose. Indeed, it might vitiate the sort of program I envision. Converting a way of being in the world to a set of courses is more likely to destroy the way of being than to transform the curriculum, which by its structure belongs to the world of male dominance. Objectivity 101a would remain in the implicit curriculum.

With this realization we face a hard point that Catherine MacKinnon makes repeatedly: sex and gender are not mere differences; gender is a hierarchy marked by male dominance.[5] The structures of this dominance pervade our entire society, and they do not depend on the active malevolence of individual men. On the contrary, individual men of goodwill are as much caught in their tentacles as are women. In such a society—one in which the separation and helplessness of women has defined the ego strength and identity of men—it will not be easy to make changes that signify an upward evaluation of women's ways and experience. Madeleine Grumet vividly describes the ways in which the school curriculum is a masculine project. In the early years of schooling, for example, children learn in semiformal ways reminiscent of the mother's way; they learn to live together in play, song, dance, art, and story. But from third or fourth grade on, the curriculum becomes discrete—separated into well-defined subjects—and the children learn "to master the language, the rules, the games and the names of the father."[6]

Schooling has not remained recalcitrant because of a lack of critics. Critics have always been plentiful. Most of them want only to strengthen the existing structures. Some want to reform schools along Marxist or neo-Marxist lines.[7] Some want to deschool and, as we saw, even believe that schools will collapse under the weight of their own corruption.[8] A few see the need for teacher–student relations to become more genuinely collaborative and for teaching to become an act of empowerment. Maxine Greene, for example, concludes a call for critical pedagogy by saying, "In 'the shadow of silent majorities,' then, as teachers learning along with those we try to provoke to learn, we may be able to inspire hitherto unheard voices. We may be able to empower people to rediscover their own memories and articulate them in the presence of others, whose space they can share. Such a project demands the capacity to unveil and disclose."[9]

"To unveil and disclose" is the first essential task, and the second is to subvert the structures of dominance by challenging standard grading practices, administrative hierarchies, and whatever practices clearly support relations of dominance/submission. Some things we can do. We can change the content of standard subjects (such as the themes in literature), augment the subjects themselves, and guide our modes of instruction by our desire to educate people who will commit evil infrequently and with great regret. I have already described the influence of competitive processes in our schools as largely pernicious—as ways of creating rivals and making enemies. Cooperative processes can certainly be substituted for at least some competitive ones. We can also replace some authoritarian practices with more genuinely participatory ones.

But I must emphasize again that we cannot fully describe education in terms of subjects and instruction. Something else, a fuller experience, is essential. Marxist thinkers like Antonio Gramsci recommend, for example, that education dedicate itself to producing working-class intellectuals.[10] How can this project succeed? Surely not by turning working-class children into nonlaboring intellectuals who will then speak in abstractions about the dignity of labor! It can succeed only by incorporating into education itself real work—both physical and intellectual—that will be at least partly planned, executed, evaluated, and revised by students and teachers working together. A working-class intellectual is one, or ought to be one, who works and thinks and theorizes. The long-range goal would be to have a society of worker-thinkers and no classes. Similarly, if we want people to internalize the logic of feminine experience with respect to good and evil, we have to provide children with opportunities to engage in the activities that have induced this logic in women. It is not simply a matter of talking about tasks, but of doing them. It is a way of living and relating.

Now, of course, the full power of an entrenched patriarchy is likely to descend on us. How can schools accomplish all this, some will ask, when they cannot accomplish the tasks now assigned to them? I cannot answer that question satisfactorily here, but the first part of the answer has to be simply that the schools are now largely engaged in irrelevant tasks that are meaningless to many students. The schools are not providing education for fully human *being*. Rather, they are trying desperately to perform tasks necessary to sustain the pain of separation and helplessness. Students could learn everything worthwhile that the schools now teach more easily and rapidly in a situation that also provides opportunities to work and to live together.

In this short section on curriculum and instruction I have suggested four sorts of changes to consider: changes within the subjects of the standard curriculum (such as themes in literature and history), the augmentation of the standard curriculum with new subjects that attend to the traditional concerns of women, changes in instructional patterns, and a total reorganization of the patterns of schooling. Realistically the first and third are to some degree feasible and desirable. The second might be distorted and used to maintain the subordination of women. The last is next to impossible, and yet it must be our goal.

Relational Virtues

. . .

An ethic of caring is based on a relational ontology; that is, it takes as a basic assumption that all human beings—not just women—are defined in relation. It is not just that I as a preformed continuous individ-

ual enter *into* relations; rather, the *I* of which we speak so easily is itself a relational entity. *I* really am defined by the set of relations into which my physical self has been thrown. This is not to adopt a total determinism, because *relation* involves affective response in each of the emerging entities, and this response is at least partly under the control of the present occupants of the relation. We cannot escape our relational condition, but we can reflect on it, evaluate it, move it in a direction we find good. We are neither totally free and separate in our affective and volitional lives, as many existentialists would have us believe, nor totally determined by the physical conditions of our past.

Caring is not an individual virtue, although certain virtues may help sustain it. Rather, caring is a relational state or quality, and it requires distinctive contributions from carer and cared for. A relation may deteriorate either because no one takes *care*—that is, attends to the messages and needs of the other—or because there is no response from the cared for. When either party rivets attention on himself or herself, for example, as the self-sacrificial and virtuous carer, a pathological condition arises. A child may be smothered, for example, by a woman who "lives" for her children; such a woman sees only her contribution to the relation. In general, pathologies of caring, whether public or private, manifest themselves in actual helplessness or feelings of helplessness in those "cared for."

Relational virtues are two kinds: virtues that belong to the relation itself and individual virtues that enhance relations. Caring, friendship, companionship, and empathy are of the first kind, although they are not discrete. The task of philosophers with respect to this class of relational virtues is to describe the contributions of each member of the relation, the conditions under which the relation develops positively or negatively, and the place of such virtues with respect to individual virtues and vices. The task of educators is to encourage the actual growth of relational virtues, to explore relational themes in literature and history, and to establish learning conditions that permit people to contribute to their own relational growth.

Closely related to relational virtues are relational tasks. Teaching, parenting, advising, mediating, and helping are all relational tasks. Their success depends not only on the goodwill, sensitivity, and skills of the more powerful member of the relation, but also on the goodwill, skills, and responsiveness of the less powerful member. It is ridiculous to study any of these relational tasks by focusing only on the teacher, parent, adviser, mediator, or helper. Research that radically separates teacher and student into treatments and outcomes inadvertently ratifies the evils of separation and helplessness. It supposes that something the teacher-as-treatment does causes a particular effect in a class of students. Even in studies that acknowledge an interaction between what the teacher does and what particular students are capable of doing, we find the same defect. There is no way to account for the obvious fact that teaching–learning is relational, not just interactive. A student may do better, achieve more, out of love for his or her teacher (or out of hate), out of rivalry with another student (or as a result of helping another student), or out of understanding a concept (or catching on to the awful truth that understanding is irrelevant). Clearly, achieving a slightly higher grade on some test may be something to rejoice over, something to deplore, or something to safely ignore. It tells us nothing about the student's likely contribution to good or evil in the world.

The second class of relational virtues is the set of individual virtues that contributes to the quality of relations. Schools have always attended to the so-called virtues of character. Early in this century the Character Development League published *Character Lessons in American Biography,* a guide to character education for use in "public schools and home instruction." It extolled, grade by grade, the traits of obedience, honesty, truthfulness, unselfishness, sympathy, consecration to duty, usefulness, industry, perseverance, patience, self-respect, purity, self-control, fortitude, courage, heroism, contentment, ambition, temperance, courtesy, comradeship, amiability, kindness to animals, justice, habits, fidelity, determination, imagination, hopefulness, patriotism, and character—the last established by the practice of the preceding "principles of morality."[11] I have taken the trouble to reproduce the entire list because it illustrates vividly the task we need to undertake. Almost every trait on the list needs analysis from the relational perspective. *Character Lessons* introduces fidelity, for example, as "an essential in crystallizing habits"—as a virtue students should cultivate in connection to principles, not

in connection to persons and relations. These meanings are not, of course, entirely separate. One may cultivate a habit faithfully out of genuine concern for others, but the focus of such fidelity is still oneself and one's status with respect to a principle. The point is that almost every virtue has a dark side that we must examine in the context of relation.

Not only should schools teach the relational nature of virtue thematically and directly, but they should also approach conflicts and disputes relationally. In studying past and present conflicts, such as those between the Israelis and the Palestinians, the Sandinistas and the contras, and Iran and Iraq, a relational perspective should be enlightening. Students need not take sides or decide who is right. Their task should be to study the problem with questions of reconciliation as a guide. How can these people come together to live in peace? Students are not, of course, in a position to effect the policies they might create in response to such a question, but both their present learning and their future attitudes may be deeply affected as a result.

Some may object that a study plan of this sort induces a lack of commitment. After all, is not one side usually more right than the other? Should we not commit ourselves to standing by those nations and groups that share our principles? The answer to this objection is to stop thinking in terms of a zero-sum game, in terms of either/or. We should stand by both parties. We should stand sympathetically between the apparently evil and the apparently good and work toward reconciliation. The naive temptation, as we have seen, is to attribute good qualities to our allies and monstrous ones to our opponents. We see this inclination regularly even at the highest levels of government. But an opposite danger also arises. During the Vietnam War many intellectuals rejected the naive temptation. They saw clearly that the United States was supporting a repressive regime and that their own government was committing shameful deeds. This realization led some to suppose that the other side must be right. (Someone must be right, and if our side is wrong, then . . .)

Thinking in oppositional terms supports partisanship and reduces the likelihood of reconciliation. Further, it makes the development of beneficent patriotism very difficult. Intelligent students are often disillusioned and make the mistake noted above, namely, that their own government is totally wrong. Those exposed to little inquiry and critical thinking embrace a simplistic version of chauvinistic patriotism. Careful study from a relational perspective should reveal both strengths and weaknesses in the nation's past activities and present policies. There are things of which American citizens can be proud. That more people want to enter the United States than to leave it is something to be proud of. We can be proud also of our unfortified borders. The economic hegemony that reduces the need for border fortification should be a matter of far less pride. The point is that identifying and analyzing faults in ourselves or in our friends should not lead to abandonment and betrayal but to a deeper appreciation of how hard it is to avoid evil and a greater sense of affiliation with those we might otherwise label enemies.

In the relational study of conflict the parties should be allowed as nearly as possible to speak in their own voices. Textbooks generally reduce the discussion of conflict to an abstract recital of "facts." Sometimes they attempt to present a balanced picture, but the passion of genuine conflict dissolves in the bland language of an impartial recorder. The relational perspective demands restoration of the aggrieved voices. We should hear the hate, fear, terror, cruelty, and all the excesses that accompany conflict in their most eloquent expressions. When we *live* with warring parties, we often find it hard to take sides. What we want to do is to stop the suffering, to explain each side to the other, to mediate. For women "to mediate" does not mean to decide who is right and what the loser should pay to the winner; it means to bring together, to reconcile. We do not expect all the good deeds to be on one side and all the monstrous ones on the other.

Adopting a relational approach is in itself a form of deep commitment. It signifies that we care enough about each other to learn more about human relations. Clearly it will also identify new models of relations and individual behavior for special attention and emulation. Moderation in the pursuit of wealth would, for example, become an admirable trait. Some time ago the nightly news reported a survey of the "heroes" teachers selected to present to their students. Several teachers selected Lee Iacocca. Why? Because,

they said, his success proves that a person can make it in this country by striving. A far better model from the relational perspective would be Atticus Finch, the small-town lawyer and wonderful father in *To Kill a Mockingbird*.[12] In Atticus (so addressed even by his children) we find a model of steady integrity, of fidelity to persons—both to his children and to the innocent black man he was assigned to defend—of reasonable contentment with ordinary life and its achievable dignity. Atticus did not admire great wealth. Great personal wealth can no longer be a criterion of health and success; pursuing it must be seen as a sign of sickness in the individual and in the society that encourages such pursuit.

Educational efforts to encourage moderation are essential. States can redistribute wealth by force and adopt ideologies to justify the redistribution. But unless people understand and admire moderation as a relational virtue, their longing to contend, surpass, and prove themselves superior to others will result in behavior very like the pursuit of wealth. Power or fame may substitute for wealth. Before people can safely emerge from oppression they must have models of moderation, and so the education of such models must be part of the pedagogy of both oppressors and oppressed.

Moderation as I have described it does not entail mediocrity. Just as Finny in *A Separate Peace* found joy in surpassing his own previous performances, so most of us can strive for higher levels of performance in many things we do so long as the effort does not destroy others or lead to a debilitating neglect of relation. We must understand and choose moderation. We might then experience a tremendous sense of freedom, well-being, and renewed interest in the wonders of everyday life.

A relational approach suggests the careful study of relational virtues—both those that belong to relations and those individual virtues that contribute to positive relations. It also suggests the meticulous analysis of virtues, traits, and ways of life such as *striving*. We should pick apart each item of the long list in *Character Lessons* to locate the evil that so often accompanies individual virtue. Educators should commit themselves to this analysis and to the study of themes and counterthemes that arise as a result. Instructional arrangements should reflect this commitment by establishing conditions in which positive relations may flourish.

The Possibility of Spirituality

I have taken a critical attitude toward traditional religion throughout this book. This attitude does not mean that I believe — with Freud — that people must be liberated from religion. Rather, I believe that the subject needs demystification. As we have seen, some theologians and philosophers of religion have worked and are working on projects that might remove much nonsense at the level of theoretical doctrine. But unless they work on the education of ordinary people and the doctrine preached from ordinary pulpits, mystification will remain. We must discuss religion critically, much as we discuss "problems of American democracy." Although schools do not often perform at the critical level we would like . . . at least the topics are present in the curriculum. Religion, in contrast, is usually entirely absent from public school offerings.

Some people want prayer and Bible reading in the schools without critical discussion. Such activities are clearly out of the question if our goal is demystification. Many others oppose any form of religious discussion in schools out of an avowed fear of indoctrination. I suspect a deeper fear lurks behind the one spoken. There is an understandable fear that religion will look foolish unclothed by critical eyes. So it might. Critical thought should challenge many, many practices and beliefs scattered throughout the major religions. Should not students be aware of and reflect critically on magic rituals that change wine into blood, prayers that thank God for making the one praying a man and not a woman, rules that condemn unrepentant women to hell for having abortions, practices that exclude persons of certain classes or gender from some rituals, elaborate hierarchies of divine and semi-divine persons, doctrines that establish an elite, a chosen, or an elect, and the pervasive notion that God is male? We talk about a liberal education — one that frees its participants — but we avoid discussing the topics that might actually free us. If helplessness is evil, then mystification is a great moral evil and the failure to reduce it is also a moral evil.

To avoid indoctrination the major religions should be presented in the words of their own spokespersons, in words appropriate to the level of instruction. The idea is to share beliefs and practices respectfully, to question, to wonder. Children so challenged should go home with lots of questions, and parents in turn may have questions for their religious leaders. They may even begin to wonder why priests and ministers *preach* instead of teaching in the open, critical way they admire in real teachers. It will not do to say that such discussion destroys the traditional respect we have had for free religious determination. There is nothing respectful about a conspiracy of silence. To the contrary, honest and interested questions are a genuine mark of respect, and any religious position that rejects dialogue deserves to look foolish.

It follows that free critical discussion should be the approach to creationism. Why go on fussing over whether secular humanism is a religion? Let the voices speak, and let it be clear who is speaking and with what social backing. It is true that students may become bewildered. They may come to a point where they say, "I don't know what to think anymore." That is the time when real study makes sense, when the spirit hungers for knowledge. The teacher's job, then, is not to give an answer but to direct the inquiry in a defensible fashion.

This discussion brings us back to the earlier material on curriculum. When we consider those things that matter most deeply to human beings — the meaning of life, the possibility of gods, birth and parenting, sexuality, death, good and evil, love, happiness — we may well wonder how the standard set of subjects became our curriculum. The usual answer is that people can study all these important matters at home and in religious institutions and that schools are specially organized to teach those subjects that cannot easily be taught in other settings. But one wonders whether the real reason might not be different. Perhaps the great topics of life are not used to organize the curriculum because it is not in the interests of those in power to encourage free critical inquiry on such important questions. In rebuttal we could argue that the curriculum was once so organized (roughly) and that religious indoctrination was the result. This historical warning is no reason to reject reform, but it is an important reminder that no plan designed to seek something better — to reduce evil — is entirely free of the potential for evil.

God is a psychic reality, Jung said, and in this assessment he seems closer to the truth than was Freud. Human beings long for God "as the hart panteth after the water brook." The quest is neither juvenile nor primitive. There is, after all, the fact of the universe, the fact of our existence, the fact, as Unamuno pointed out, of our longing after life, and life, and more life. But it should be clear that we cannot really know the form or nature of God any more than we can answer the questions: What came before time? What was there before something?

It is just whimsy or personal longing to consider God male or female. Scott Peck (and many men) feel God as male. To me, when that longing for holy communication arises, God is clearly female. As I hold a new infant, or dive through a marvelous ocean wave, or spot one of my grown children at the airport, or feel the warmth of the sun on my back as I garden, or listen to a gentle snore from my sleeping husband, I speak thanks to someone like Ceres — a deity who loved her child as I would like to be loved. It is, as I said, a bit of whimsy at one level and at another an expression of wonder and longing.

It is also a mode of learning, for Ceres was not perfect. Was she right or wrong to let the earth go to ruin over her personal grief? From the perspective of women's experience this is not the question to ask. Surely her reaction was problematic. What can I learn from it? So far as She is *my* god, then She contains my aspirations and my faults as well. I, like Her, may love my own children too fiercely and so may neglect others who need my care. When I see this, however, I also see that the many others who have been created in Her image (or who have shared in creating Her) have the same aspirations and faults. They too love their children fiercely. This realization induces prudence. To preserve the lives of my own children I must maintain positive relations with others who have the same project.

As I leave the mystical mode, I can drop the name Ceres and the capital letters on *she* and *her* and *god*. What a wrenching loss it is to do so! But after all I do not want to spend my intellectual and spiritual life describing Ceres, justifying her in the face of evil's real-

ity, or trying to convert others to her worship. I do not want to build a relation with her that can be used to dominate others. Instead, I may use this spiritual longing to connect myself to real human beings in whom spirit is manifest and to learn more about good and evil in myself and in them.

Education has — at least in modern times — been guided by optimism and notions of progress (notions that are, I think, peculiarly masculine). Perhaps we should now consider an education guided by a tragic sense of life, a view that cannot claim to overcome evil (any more than we can overcome dust) but claims only to live sensitively with as little of it as possible. Even as I write this, I realize that the expression "tragic sense of life" will not quite work. It has been used to describe experience that is essentially male, and it points to the male hero who strives courageously with or against a deity — a god good or evil but often aloof or absent. The sense of sadness is right, but the response is wrong. It includes the notion Ricoeur endorsed: "Man enters into the ethical world through fear and not through love."[13] We cannot deny that fear inspires some ethical thinking, but so does love. The desire to be like a loving parent is a powerful impetus toward ethical life, and so is the desire to remain in loving relation. A woman's view has to find new language or at least to modify language as it seeks expression. It should not be articulated as mere opposition, but rather as a positive program for human living. From this perspective, in agreement with those who adopt a tragic sense of life, life is at bottom sad. All the more reason for us to give and take what joy we can from each other.

Notes

1. Hannah Arendt takes this position both in *Eichmann in Jerusalem* (New York: Penguin Books, 1965) and in *The Life of the Mind: Thinking* (New York: Harcourt Brace Jovanovich, 1977).

2. Homer, *The Odyssey of Homer,* trans. S. H. Butcher and A. Lang (New York: Modern Library, n.d.), 22:352.

3. Jane Roland Martin, *Reclaiming a Conversation* (New Haven: Yale University Press, 1985), p. 198.

4. Ibid., p. 197.

5. Catherine A. MacKinnon, *Feminism Unmodified* (Cambridge, Mass.: Harvard University Press, 1987).

6. Madeleine R. Grumet, "Conception, Contradiction and Curriculum," *Journal of Curriculum Theorizing* 3, no. 1 (1981): 287–298, 293; see also Grumet, *Bitter Milk* (Amherst: University of Massachusetts Press, 1988).

7. Among many examples, see Samuel Bowles and Herbert Gintis, *Schooling in Capitalist America* (London: Routledge & Kegan Paul, 1977); Michael W. Apple, *Ideology and Curriculum* (Boston: Routledge & Kegan Paul, 1979); Apple, *Education and Power* (Boston: Routledge & Kegan Paul, 1982); Daniel Liston, "Faith and Evidence: Examining Marxist Explanations of Schools," *American Journal of Education* 96, no. 3 (1988): 323–350.

8. See Ivan Illich, *Deschooling Society* (New York: Harper & Row, 1971).

9. Maxine Greene, "In Search of a Critical Pedagogy," in *Teachers, Teaching, and Teacher Education,* ed. Margo Okazawa-Rey, James Anderson, and Rob Traver (Cambridge, Mass.: Harvard Educational Review, 1987), p. 248.

10. See Antonio Gramsci, *Selections from the Prison Notebooks,* ed. and trans. Quinton Hoare and Geoffrey Newell Smith (New York: International Press, 1978).

11. James Terry White, *Character Lessons in American Biography* (New York: Character Development League, 1909), table of contents.

12. Harper Lee, *To Kill a Mockingbird* (Philadelphia: J. B. Lippincott, 1960).

13. Paul Ricoeur, *The Symbolism of Evil,* trans. Emerson Buchanan (Boston: Beacon Press, 1969), p. 30.

ANTIRACISM, MULTICULTURALISM, AND INTERRACIAL COMMUNITY:

Three Educational Values for a Multicultural Society

Lawrence Blum

Lawrence Blum discusses values in educational curricula and concludes that there is a plurality of values that need to be taught. Antiracism is one such value and it, like other values, ought to be offered to all students as part of a multicultural education. (Source: Reprinted with permission from "Antiracism, Multiculturalism, and Interracial Community: Three Educational Values for a Multicultural Society," Distinguished Lecture Series, 1991–92, November 1991, Office of Graduate Studies and Research, University of Massachusetts at Boston. Copyright (© 1992 by Lawrence A. Blum.)

In the past year and a half or so multicultural education has garnered an extraordinary amount of media attention, most of it negative. My own involvement in this area predates the recent hoopla and has its source in my own children's working their way through the public schools of Cambridge, Massachusetts. I have been struck by how extraordinarily different their educational and social experience has been, and will continue to be, than was my own, attending almost all-white schools in the 1950s. Charges of so-called political correctness cannot mask the extraordinary demographic and social changes our society is undergoing that ground the need for a philosophy of education suited to an increasingly multiracial, multicultural society.

I approach that task from my own background in moral philosophy and the philosophy of value. I want to ask what values I would want my own and other children to be taught in schools, as well as in their families, to prepare them for life in the multicultural United States. I assume here that moral and value education must be a part of precollege education, and in doing so I ally myself with educators across a wide political spectrum.

My work in this area does not by and large focus on education at the college level, though I assume that *some* of what I have to say will have implications for colleges and their curricula. I also think it instructive for adults concerned with our current and future state of racial and ethnic relations to focus on younger children, where we sometimes get a glimpse of possibilities otherwise difficult to envision.

I want to argue that there are a *plurality* of values that one would want taught in schools and families. None of these can be reduced to the others, nor can any take the place of the others. Without claiming comprehensiveness for my list I want to suggest that there are at least four values, or families of values, essential to a program of value education for a multiracial society. I will describe all four values briefly and will then talk about each in more detail. (I recognize that the labels on these are somewhat arbitrary.)

I realize that multicultural education has its critics and detractors. I will not attempt today to defend or justify the four values but only to articulate them, so that it will be clearer what it is that needs defense and justification.

The first value is *antiracism* or *opposition to racism*:

Racism is the denial of the fundamental moral equality of all human beings. It involves the expression of attitudes of superior worth or merit justifying or underpinning the domination or unjust advantage of some groups over others. Antiracism as a value involves striving to be without racist attitudes oneself as well as being prepared to work against both racist attitudes in others and racial injustice in society more generally.

The second value is *multiculturalism*:

Multiculturalism involves an understanding, appreciation and valuing of one's own culture, and an informed respect and curiosity about the ethnic culture of others. It involves a valuing of other cultures, not in the sense of approving of all aspects of those cultures, but of attempting to see how a given culture can express value to its own members.

The third value is a sense of *community,* and in particular an *interracial community:*

> This involves a sense, not necessarily explicit or articulated, that one possesses human bonds with persons of other races and ethnicities. The bonds may, and ideally should, be so broad as to encompass all of humanity; but they may also be limited to the bonds formed in friendships, schools, workplaces, and the like.

The fourth value is *treating persons as individuals:*

> This involves recognizing the individuality of each person — specifically, that while an individual person is a member of an ethnic or racial group, and while that aspect may be an important part of who she is, she is more than that ethnic or racial identity. It is the lived appreciation of this individuality, not simply paying lip service to it, that constitutes the value I will call treating persons as individuals. (I will not have the opportunity to discuss this value further on this occasion.)

Again, I claim that these four are distinct though related values, and that all of them are essential to multicultural value education. Failure to appreciate their distinctness poses the danger that one of them will be neglected in a value education program. At the same time there are natural convergences and complementarities among the four values taken in any combination; there are ways of teaching each value that support the promotion of each one of the other values. On the other hand, I will claim, there can also be tensions, both practical and theoretical, between various of the values; that is, some ways of teaching one of the values may work against the conveying of one of the others. Since the values can be either convergent or in tension, it will be crucial to search for ways of teaching them that minimize the tension and support the convergences.

I have designated *antiracism* as the first value for this value education. In contrast to the three others, this one is stated negatively — in opposition to something rather than as a positive goal to be striven for. Why do I not refer to this value positively as "racial equality" or "racial justice"? One reason is that the oppositional definition brings out that a central aspect of the value of antiracism involves countering an evil and not just promoting a good. An important com-

ponent of what children need to be taught is how to notice, to confront, to oppose, and to work toward the elimination of manifestations of racism. Particular moral abilities and traits of character, involving certain forms of empowerment, are required for activities of *opposition* that are not required merely for the promotion of a good goal. Of course, antiracism does presuppose the positive value of racial justice; hence, the positive element is implicitly contained in the value of antiracism.

To understand the value of antiracism we must first understand *racism.* The term racism, while a highly charged and condemnatory one, has no generally agreed upon meaning. On the other hand all can agree that using a racial slur, telling a Chicano student that one does not like Chicanos and wishes they were not in one's school, or carving "KKK" on the door of the African-American student's door, are racist acts. At the same time the conservative writer Dinesh D'Souza has given voice to a suspicion, shared I am sure by others, that the term "racism" is in danger of losing its meaning and moral force through a too broad usage.

I agree that there has sometimes been a tendency to inflate the meaning of the word racism so it becomes virtually a catchall term for any behavior concerning race or race relations that its user strongly condemns. This development ill serves those like myself who wish racism to be taken more seriously than it presently is. Like the boy who cried "wolf," the inflation of the concept of racism to encompass phenomena with questionable connection to its core meaning desensitizes people to the danger, horror, and wrongfulness of true racism.

Here is my definition of racism, which I present without further defense: Racism refers both to an institutional or social structure of racial domination or injustice — as when we speak of a racist institution — and also to individual actions, beliefs, and attitudes, whether consciously held or not, which express, support or justify the superiority of one racial group to another. Thus, on both the individual levels, racism involves denying or violating the equal dignity and worth of all human beings independent of race; and, on both levels, racism is bound up with dominance and hierarchy.

Note that on my definition several practices or attitudes sometimes thought of as automatically racist are not (necessarily) racist, though they may involve racism in particular instances. One is *racial ignorance* or *insensitivity,* an example being a black high school student, who had what he thought were good white friends; but when Martin Luther King's birthday came around the white students did not understand why the black student cared about the celebration of King's birthday. This seems to be an example of racial ignorance or insensitivity, but not of racism. A second is *making racial distinctions.* We are all familiar with the view that merely to make a distinction between people on the basis of race is itself racist. A related example is when simply mentioning or noticing someone's race is seen as racist. A false model of nonracism as "color blindness" leads us to confuse making racial distinctions with racism itself. But unless making the racial distinction is grounded in an attribution of inferiority or lesser worth to one of the groups involved, racism (on my definition) is not present.

A third example is *racial exclusiveness* on the part of people of color, as when African-American or Hispanic students sit together in the school cafeteria. This too is not normally a racist practice, for it is not normally premised on an attitude of superiority toward nonblacks (or non-Hispanics), but may be simply a sense of comfort with those like oneself. A final example is *racial discomfort,* that is, a discomfort with people of other races; this too is not necessarily racist, though, of course, it can be.

Some of these practices or attitudes may be objectionable or regrettable without being racist. After all, ignorance and insensitivity are bad things. And racial exclusiveness can be detrimental to a sense of interracial community. But conflating them with racism makes it difficult to deal *either* with racism or with whatever *other* disvalue these practices may involve.

The point I am making here—and one I mean to emphasize in my work on multiculturalism—is that there are a *plurality* of values needed in a multicultural society, and, conversely, a plurality of things that can go wrong in multicultural and multiracial interaction.

There are three components of (the value of) *antiracism* as I see it.

One is the belief in the equal worth of all persons regardless of race, not just as an intellectual matter,

but rooted more deeply in one's attitudes and emotions; this is to have what one might call a *nonracist* moral consciousness. But it is not enough to learn to be nonracist as an individual; students must also be taught to *understand* the particularity of racism as a psychological and historical phenomenon. This is partly because one aspect of antiracism is learning to perceive racism and to recognize when it is occurring. Just being nonracist cannot guarantee this. For one may sincerely subscribe to the right principles of racial justice and yet not see particular instances of racism right under one's nose, in either institutional or individual forms; for example, not recognizing unintended patterns of exclusion of people of color, or not recognizing a racial stereotype.

There are three components to this second feature of antiracism (understanding racism). The first is the *psychological* dynamic of racism, such as scapegoating and stereotyping, rigidity and fear of difference, rationalization of privilege and power, projecting of unwanted wishes onto others, and other psychological processes contributing to racist attitudes. The second is the *historical* dynamic of racism in its particular forms: slavery, colonialism, segregation, Nazism, the mistreatment of native Americans, and the like. Involved also must be learning about movements *against* racism, such as abolitionism, civil rights movements, and the black power movement; and learning about institutional racism as well. The third component is the role of *individuals* in sustaining or resisting racist institutions, patterns, and systems—how individuals can change racist structures; how they may contribute to or help to perpetuate racist patterns even if they themselves are not actually racist.

Studying the historical dynamics of racism necessarily involves teaching the victimization of some groups by others. While some conservative critics of multicultural education ridicule and derogate focusing on a group's history as victims of racism, it would nevertheless be intellectually irresponsible not to do so. One can hardly understand the historical experience of African-Americans without slavery, of Jews without the Holocaust, of Asian-Americans without the historic barriers to citizenship and to family life and without the World-War-II internment camps.

Nevertheless, from the point of view of historical accuracy as well as that of value education, it is vital not to *confine* the presentation of a group to its status as victim. One needs to see subordinate groups as agents in their own history — not just as suffering victimization but as responding to it, sometimes by active resistance both cultural and political, sometimes by passive resistance, sometimes by accommodation. The study of social history is invaluable here in providing the framework for seeing that victims made their own history in the face of their victimization, and for giving concrete embodiment to the philosophical truth that human beings retain the capacity for agency even when oppressed and dominated by others.

The third component of antiracist education (in addition to nonracism and understanding racism) is *opposition to racism;* for nonracism implies only that one does all one can to avoid racism in *one's own* actions and attitudes. This is insufficient, for students need also to develop a sense of responsibility concerning manifestations of racism in other persons and in the society more generally. For example, since students will almost inevitably witness racist acts, to confine their own responsibility simply to ensuring that they individually do not participate in such actions themselves is to give students a mixed message about how seriously they are being asked to take racism.

A teacher in my children's school elicited from her class occasions on which they had witnessed racist remarks. Two examples were of store clerks, one of whom said, "You Puerto Ricans are always stealing things; get out of my store," and the other, "Don't be a dirty Jew — give him the money." As this teacher did, truly antiracist education should help pupils think through what they themselves might do in such situations, how to assess the gains and risks of various courses of action. Discussions of this sort might help secure two goals. The first is that by encouraging students to bring up incidents of racism and by discussing them seriously, the teacher conveys to the class that racism is serious business, and is everyone's responsibility. The second is that such conversations help to develop students' own skills, abilities, and sense of competence in the complex tasks of active engagement with a society and world far from embodying ideals of racial justice.

Let me now examine antiracist education in the context of "citizenship" education, currently being touted across a broad political spectrum as an important component of secondary school education. A very useful text here is the *California History/Social Science Framework,* officially adopted by the state of California as a guideline for the writing and the adoption of textbooks for secondary schools.[1] (Some textbooks have now been adopted that conform to this framework.) This is an intellectually and pedagogically impressive document, written by a variety of educators and scholars, including Diane Ravitch, an influential educational historian and theorist, and currently an Assistant U.S. Education Secretary.

The *History/Social Science Framework* sees the development of the commitments and skills of active citizenship — a citizenship whose purpose is to sustain and protect democratic institutions — as a central task of secondary school education. The *Framework* also takes up racial issues much more fully than, say, the education that I received in the 1950s. Yet there is very little recognition in the *Framework* that the responsibilities of citizenship in a democratic society should include antiracist commitments. To give just one illustration, the *Framework* speaks of learning to respect the rights of the minority, even a minority of one. But how about learning when to *be* such a minority of one, oneself? When should one be the person to speak out, to call attention to an injustice that others prefer not to think about?

James Baldwin in his book *The Fire Next Time* powerfully describes an incident from the early sixties in his own life that exemplifies such a failure of citizenship in the area of race.[2]

> A civilization is not destroyed by wicked people; it is not necessary that people be wicked but only that they be spineless. I and two Negro acquaintances, all of us well past thirty, and looking it, were in the bar in Chicago's O'Hare airport several months ago, and the bartender refused to serve us, because, he said, we looked too young. It took a vast amount of patience not to strangle him and great insistence and some luck to get the manager, who defended the bartender, on the ground that he was "new" and had not yet, presumably, learned how to distinguish a Negro "boy" of twenty and a Negro "boy" of thirty-seven. Well, we were served, finally, of course, but by this time no amount of Scotch would have helped us. The bar was very crowded and our altercation had been very noisy,

yet not one customer in the bar had done anything to help us. (77 f.)

One goal of citizenship education should surely be for people to come to believe that they ought to intervene in some way in such situations, and to come away from their education with some guidelines about how to do so. On this, antiracist, feature of citizen education the *California History/Social Science Framework* is almost entirely silent.

The *Framework's* failure here has two interconnected aspects. First, its conception of the forms of activity appropriate to a citizenry committed to upholding justice (as a feature of a democratic society) is too limited. It largely omits citizens' responsibility to *counter injustices* in their society. The second failure is the inadequate attention to racism as a *primary instance* of the sort of injustice that a future democratic citizenry needs to be educated to understand and to counteract.

The second educational value, *multiculturalism,* encompasses the following three subvalues: (1) affirming one's own cultural identity; learning about and valuing one's own cultural heritage; (2) respecting and desiring to understand and learn about (and from) cultures other than one's own; (3) valuing and taking delight in cultural diversity itself; that is, regarding the existence of distinct cultural groups within one's own society as a positive good to be treasured and nurtured. The kind of respect involved in the second condition (respecting others) is meant to be an informed (and not uncritical) respect grounded in an understanding of another culture. It involves an attempt to see the culture from the point of view of its members and in particular to see how members of that culture value the expression of their own culture. It involves an active interest in and ability in some way to enter into and to enjoy the cultural expressions of other groups.

Such an understanding of another culture in no way requires an affirmation of every feature of that culture as positively good, as some critics of multiculturalism fear (or at least charge). It does not preclude criticism, on the basis either of norms of that culture itself which particular practices in that culture might violate, or of standards external to that culture. Of course when it is legitimate to use a standard external to a culture (e.g. a particular standard of equality between men and women drawn from the Western liberal tradition) is a complex issue. And multiculturalism always warns both against using a legitimate criticism of some feature of a culture as moral leverage to condemn the culture as a whole — declaring it not worthy of serious curricular attention, or disqualifying it as a source of moral insight to those outside that culture, for example — as well as alerting us to the difficult-to-avoid failure to scrutinize the basis of that criticism for its own cultural bias. Nevertheless, multiculturalism need not and should not identify itself with the view that members of one culture never have the moral standing to make an informed criticism of the practices of another culture.

The outward directedness of the second feature of multiculturalism (respecting other cultures) is an important complement to the inward focus of the first feature (learning about and valuing one's own culture). This dual orientation meets the criticism sometimes made of multiculturalism that it creates divisions between students. For the second feature prescribes a reaching out beyond one's own group and thus explicitly counters the balkanizing effect of the first dimension of multiculturalism alone. Nevertheless, that first feature — learning about and valuing one's own culture — is an integral part of multiculturalism, not merely something to be tolerated, treated as a response to political pressure, or justified simply on the grounds of boosting self-esteem. An individual's cultural identity is a deeply significant element of herself, and understanding of her own culture should be a vital part of the task of education. An understanding of one's own culture as contributing to the society of which one is a part is a significant part of that first element of multiculturalism.

The third component of multiculturalism is the valuing of diversity itself. Not only do we want our young people to respect specific other cultures but also to value a school, a city, a society in which diverse cultural groups exist. While this diversity may certainly present problems for young people, one wants them to see the diversity primarily as something to value, prefer, and cherish.

Three dimensions of culture seem to be deserving of curricular and other forms of educational attention in schools. The first is the *ancestor culture* of the ethnic group, nation, or civilization of origin. For Chinese-Americans this would involve understanding Chinese culture, including ancient Chinese cultures, philosophies, religions, and the like. For Irish-Americans it would be Irish history and culture. For Mexican-Americans it would include attention to some of the diverse cultures of Mexico—the Aztec, the Mayan, as well as the Spanish, and then the hybrid Spanish/indigenous culture which forms modern Mexican culture.

While all ethnic cultures have an ancestor culture, not all current groups bear the same relationship to that ancestor culture. For example, African-Americans' connection to their ancestor culture is importantly different from that of immigrant groups like Italians, Eastern European Jews, and Irish. Although scholars disagree about the actual extent of influence of various African cultures on current African-American cultural forms, it was a general feature of American slavery systematically to attempt to deprive African slaves of their African culture. By contrast voluntary immigrant groups brought with them an intact culture, which they renegotiated in the new conditions of the United States. In fact the label "African-American" can be seen as an attempt to forge a stronger analogy between the experience of black Americans and that of other immigrant groups than do other expressions, such as "black" or even "Afro-American." The former conceptualization emphasizes that American blacks are not simply a product of America but do indeed possess an ancestor culture, no matter how brutally that culture was attacked. Note, however, that there is an important difference between this use of "African-American" and that applied, for example, to second-generation Ethiopian-Americans. The latter is a truer parallel to white ethnic "hyphenate Americans."

Other differences among groups, such as the current ethnic group's distance in time from its original emigration, variations and pressures to assimilate once in the United States, and the effects of racism affect the significance of the ancestor culture for a current ethnic group. Nevertheless ancestor culture plays some role for every group.

A second dimension of culture to be encompassed by multicultural education is the *historical experience* of the ethnic group within the United States. Generally it will attend to the historical experiences, ways of life, triumphs and setbacks, art and literature, contributions and achievements, of ethnic groups in the United States. The latter point is uncontroversial; all proponents of multicultural education agree in the need to correct the omission in traditional curricula and text books of many ethnic groups' experiences and contributions to our national life. But distinguishing this dimension from the ancestor culture and giving attention to both of them is crucial. For the culture of the Chinese-American is *not* the same as the culture of traditional or modern China; it is a culture with its own integrity: neither the purer form of ancestor culture nor that of middle-America. It can be called "intercultural," influenced by more than one culture (as indeed the ancestor culture itself may have been), yet forming a culture in its own right.

A third dimension of culture is the *current ethnic culture* of the group in question. This is the dimension most directly embodied in the student member of that culture. This current ethnic culture—family ethnic rituals, foods, customs regarding family roles and interactions, values, musical and other cultural preferences, philosophies of life, and the like—bears complex relationships to the ancestor culture as well as to the group's historical ethnic experience in the United States. It changes over time and is affected in myriad ways by the outer society. As with ancestor culture and historical ethnic experience, the student's current ethnic culture must be given respect. What such respect consists in is a complex matter, as the following examples indicate.

In one case respect can involve allowing Arab girls to wear traditional headgear in school if they so desire. In another it can mean seeing a child's remark in class as containing an insight stemming from her cultural perspective that might otherwise be missed or seem off the mark. Another form of respect for culture involves, for example, recognizing that a Vietnamese child's failure to look a teacher in the eye is not a sign of evasiveness or lack of interest but a way of expressing a deference to teachers and authority, culturally regarded as appropriate. Thus, respect for ethnic cultures sometimes involves a direct valorizing of a part of that culture; at other times neither valorizing nor disvaluing, but allowing for its expression because it is important to the student. In another context, it can involve reshaping one's own sense of what is educationally essential, to take into account another culture's difference. Finally, it can sometimes involve seeing a cultural manifestation as a genuine obstacle to learning but respecting the cultural setting in which it is embedded and the student's own attachment to that cultural feature, and finding ways to work with or around that obstacle to accomplish an educational goal.

In summary, ancestor culture, ethnic historical experience in the United States, and current ethnic culture are three dimensions of ethnic culture requiring attention in a multicultural education. They are all dimensions that children need to be taught and taught to respect — both in their own and other's cultures.

The context of multicultural education presupposes a larger society consisting of various cultures. Thus, teaching an attitude of appreciation toward a particular one of these cultures in the three dimensions just mentioned will have both a particular and a general aspect. We will want students to appreciate cultures in their own right, but also in their relationship to the larger society. This simple point can help us to avoid two familiar, and contrasting, pitfalls of multicultural education, that can be illustrated with the example of Martin Luther King, Jr.

One pitfall would be exemplified by a teacher who portrayed King as an important leader of the black community, but who failed to emphasize that he should be seen as a great *American* leader more generally — as a true hero for all Americans, indeed, for all humanity, and not *only* for or of African-Americans. The teacher fails to show the non-African-American students that they too have a connection with King simply as Americans.

Yet an exactly opposite pitfall is to teach appreciation of the contribution of members of particular cultures *only* insofar as those contributions can be seen in universal terms or in terms of benefiting the entire society. This pitfall would be exemplified by seeing Dr. King only in terms of his contribution to humanity or to American society more generally, but *not* acknowledging him as a product and leader specifically of the African-American community. Multicultural education needs to enable non-African-

American students (whether white or not) to be able to appreciate a leader of the African-American community in that role itself, and not *only* by showing that the leader in question made a contribution to everyone in the society. Thus, multicultural education needs to emphasize both the general or full society dimension of each culture's contributions and heroes and also the particular or culture-specific dimension.

Many people associate multiculturalism with the idea of moral *relativism* or cultural relativism and specifically with the view that because no one from one culture is in a position to judge another culture, no one is in a position to say which culture should be given priority in the allocation of respect, curricular inclusion, and the like. Therefore, according to this way of thinking, every culture has a claim to equal inclusion and respect, because no one is in a position to say which ones are *more* worthy of respect. While the philosophic relativism on which this version of multiculturalism rests needs to be taken seriously — it has a long and distinguished philosophic history — there is an alternative, quite different and nonrelativistic, philosophic foundation for multiculturalism as well. This view — which might be called *pluralistic* — agrees that cultures manifest different values but affirms that the values of a given culture can be, or can come to be, appreciated (as well as assessed) by someone from a different culture. Thus, while cultures are different, they are at least partly accessible to one another.

According to this pluralist, nonrelativist line of thought, multicultural education should involve exposing students to, and helping them to appreciate the range of, values embodied in different cultures. Both whites and Cambodian immigrant students can come to appreciate Toni Morrison's novels of black life in America. African-American students can come to understand and appreciate Confucian philosophy. This pluralist view should not minimize the work often necessary to see beyond the parochial assumptions and perspectives of one's own culture in order to appreciate the values of another culture. Indeed, one of the undoubted contributions of the multicultural movement has been to reveal those obstacles as well as the dominant culture's resistance to acknowledging them. Nevertheless, the fact that such an effort can be even partially successful provides a goal of multicultural education that is barely conceivable within the pure relativist position.

I want now to explore the complex relationship between the two values that I have discussed so far — antiracism and multiculturalism. First, to establish the differences: Both multiculturalism and antiracism are concerned with groups and group identities; but the groups are constituted differently from an antiracist than from a multicultural standpoint. From an antiracist standpoint a group is constituted by its place in the hierarchy of racial dominance (roughly, by whether it is a dominant group or a subordinate group). Thus, in the United States whites, as a racial group, are dominant, while African-Americans, Native-Americans, and Latinos or Hispanics are subordinate. But from a multicultural perspective African-Americans, Latinos, and Native-Americans are not single cultural groups. Mexicans are culturally very different from Puerto Ricans though both are Latino. Black Americans whose roots in this country go back to slavery are culturally distinct from much more recent immigrants, for example, from Haiti, whose native language is Haitian Creole, as well as from English-speaking blacks from other Caribbean countries. Haitians have a heritage as citizens of the first black republic in the New World and the only one set up as a result of a successful slave revolt. This gives Haitians a very different sense of the significance of their race and racial history than that of United States slave descendants. Elaine Pinderhughes, an African-American professor of social work and the author of *Understanding Race, Ethnicity, and Power,* quotes a Haitian-American whose racial and ethnic identity illustrates this: "As a child I never understood why my father insisted on identifying himself as Haitian whenever the issue of race came up. Later I understood that he wanted us to dissociate ourselves from black Americans."[3]

In fact, it is partly because racist attitudes are generally *not* sensitive to these cultural and ethnic distinctions that an antiracist perspective divides groups up in a somewhat different way from a multicultural perspective. This point is made powerfully and tragically by the case of a Chinese-American, Vincent Chin, who was killed by a white autoworker resentful towards the Japanese because competition from the Japanese auto industry contributed to unemployment of American auto workers. The point suggested by a documentary film concerning this incident (*The Killing of Vincent Chin*) is not so much that the white killer mistook a Chinese-American for a Japanese-American, as that he had no clear sense that there was a difference between these two Asian-American groups. So racism's existence gives subordinate groups that are culturally distinct, common cause to identify and unite on a common racial basis in opposition to, for example, anti-Asian racism.

This difference between the antiracist and the multicultural perspectives applies to the categorization of dominant groups as well as to that of subordinate or vulnerable ones, in that the antiracist perspective ignores cultural differences within the dominant groups. Jewish-, Polish-, and Irish-Americans exemplify this. Irish-Americans, once viciously discriminated against by Anglo-Protestants in this country and viewed in derogatory terms similar to African-Americans, are no longer a victimized group; rather, Irish-Americans are now part of, are seen by non-white minorities as part of, and generally see themselves as part of the majority white group — a group which in fact perpetuates disadvantage and injustice to nonwhite groups.

Yet, despite the common racial designation as "white," Irish-Americans are a culturally distinct group from Jewish-Americans and Polish-Americans; they have a distinct ancestor culture and historic ethnic experience, distinctive music, rituals, language, backgrounds, foods and the like. These deserve to be valued and appreciated by members of other ethnic groups, including nonwhite ethnic groups, as part of a multicultural program. Yet from a purely antiracist perspective Irish-Americans have no distinct group identity; they are just "whites." White students often object to being lumped together, as discussions of racism may do. The multicultural perspective is meant to speak to one legitimate source of this discomfort or protest. (Another is socioeconomic class, a large factor in this context, but unfortunately one beyond my scope here.) Whites aren't *just* whites; they too have ethnicities that are important sources of identity and that differentiate them from other whites. Nevertheless, the classification yielded by the lens of race — of Irish-Americans or Polish-Americans as "white" is not a *false* one; it is simply *partial*. Antiracism and multiculturalism constitute two distinct and complementary lenses, yielding different categorizations of a common social reality. Both lenses highlight a truth about that reality. *Antiracism:* the truth that groups are arranged in a hierarchy of dominance and subordination, security and vulnerability, advantage and disadvantage; *multiculturalism:* the truth that groups have distinct cultures.

The metaphor of antiracism and multiculturalism as complementary lenses on a complex reality should not mislead us as to the reality of race and ethnicity. The identities of both racial and ethnic cultural groups are not simply givens but are historical and social constructs. What people at a given time think of as distinct racial or ethnic groups is a product of social categorization both situationally determined and subject to change. Thus, southern and eastern European immigrant groups in this country in the early part of the twentieth century are now regarded unequivocally as white, but at that time were often seen as distinct races; they were thought by many to have racially based psychological characteristics, such as industry, irresponsibility, intelligence, and the like. To the extent that the notions of "white" and "black" were used, members of these immigrant groups did not always think of themselves as either one. Another example: in England the term "black" is currently used to refer to east Asians as well as to Afro-Caribbeans; in the United States only the latter are regarded as "black."

A third difference is that multiculturalism and antiracism involve distinct approaches to the study of a particular cultural group that has been a target of racism. While antiracism highlights victimization and resistance, multiculturalism highlights cultural life, cultural expression, achievements, and the like.

In particular the two perspectives yield distinct (though complementary) approaches to the study of the *contributions* of different groups. Multiculturalism's thrust is to highlight (especially hitherto neglected or undervalued) contributions. Yet merely highlighting contributions of different cultural groups does not, by itself, address the deficiencies in traditional education that the multicultural education movement (broadly construed) hopes to address. For one effect of racism has been to prevent subordinate groups from fully developing their capacities for such accomplishments and contributions. Indeed, what it means for a society to be characterized by systemic and institutional racism is precisely for it to place obstacles, on the basis of race, in the way of equal opportunity to develop precisely those capacities that allow a cultural group to make contributions both to their own people and to the wider society. Hence, the multicultural perspective is needed to highlight (often neglected or underappreciated) contributions of a group, while the antiracist perspective focuses on the racist obstacles in the path of that group's development toward (among other things) making such contributions.

A fourth difference between the antiracist and the multicultural perspectives lies in the basic values in which each is grounded and which guide the forms of education under each rubric. Antiracism is grounded in the idea of the equal dignity of all persons and of the consequent wrongness of any group dominating or suppressing any other. Equal dignity is a value rooted in a *sameness* among persons; a humanity *shared* by all persons. By contrast, multiculturalism is a value rooted in *differences* among persons; multiculturalism calls for a respect for cultures, not in spite of their differences from oneself, but precisely *for* those differences. Both of these values — of shared humanity, and of cultural difference — are essential; neither one encompasses the other. The strength of antiracism — in its grounding in individual dignity and shared humanity — is also the source of its limitation. While antiracism says that it is wrong for one group to dominate or persecute another because of race, it does not by itself involve a positive appreciation of ethnic groups as embodying distinct *cultures* which deserve to be valued. Common dignity can be affirmed without a positive valuing of the individual's culture in its concrete particularity. Multiculturalism involves the converse value limitation, for, while highlighting respect and appreciation for cultural difference, it does *not* focus on our common humanity or shared dignity. These two values are not inconsistent with one another; children can and need to learn both what they share with others as well as an appreciation of their differences.

A striking example of the difference between multiculturalism and antiracism regarding this valuational foundation can be found in a comprehensive study of non-Jewish rescuers of Jews during the Holocaust, a book called *The Altruistic Personality,* by Samuel and Pearl Oliner.[4]

Most of the rescuers of Jews studied by the Oliners — people of various nationalities and occupations — expressed in some way an appreciation of the equal dignity of all persons and the irrelevance of race, nationality, and religion to that dignity. It was this acute appreciation of dignity, this strong antiracist consciousness, that provided an important part of their willingness to put themselves at great personal risk to rescue Jews during the Nazi occupation. However, only rarely did any rescuers show an appreciation of Jewishness as a cultural form having value in its own right. The rescuees were seen as having dignity *independent of,* and even *despite* their Jewishness. The Jewishness was not seen as a source of value, a value that was at risk in Hitler's attempt to exterminate Jewishness as well as Jews. The rescuers either lacked a general sense of multicultural value or failed to appreciate that value in the case of Jews. Similar points can be made about Turkish rescuers of Armenians during the Armenian genocide of 1915–16, according to research by Richard Hovanissian.

A final significant difference between the antiracist and the multicultural perspectives is that while antiracism directly challenges racial domination and racial injustice, multiculturalism, by contrast, poses no strong or pointed challenge to inequalities of power and opportunity between groups. Multiculturalism tends to promote the attitude of respect for other cultures, primarily within the existing structure and inequality between groups. While some multicultural education theorists, such as Christine Sleeter and Carl Grant, have argued that a fully realized program of multicultural education does challenge inequalities of power,[5] I think this point is better put by saying that a multicultural program needs to have a strong and central antiracist component, as well as a multicultural one in the sense I have outlined here.

I hope I have succeeded in showing both that antiracism and multiculturalism provide distinct perspectives and guiding values; that these perspectives are complementary; and that both are essential to a value education for a multiracial, multiethnic society.

The third value for an educational program that I want to discuss is the *sense of community* — specifically a sense of community that embraces racial and cultural differences. While the idea of a multiracial integrated community has historically been linked with the struggle against racism, I think there is reason for focusing on it as a value distinct from antiracism. The sense of community that I mean involves a sense of bond with other persons, a sense of shared identification with the community in question (be it a class, a school or workplace), a sense of loyalty to and involvement with this community. I will make the further assumption that the experience of interracial community in such institutions is an important contributor to being able fully to experience members of other races and cultures as fellow citizens and fellow human beings throughout one's life.

It is true that the achievement of or the experience of interracial community is likely to contribute to a firm commitment to nonracist and antiracist values. Nevertheless, there is an important difference between the two families of values. A sense of community is defeated not only by racist attitudes, in which members of one group feel themselves superior to members of another group, but simply by experiencing members of other races and cultural groups as *other,* as distant from oneself, as people with whom one does not feel comfortable, and has little in common. As I suggested earlier, racial discomfort, racial sensitivity, and racial ignorance should be distinguished from racism itself; yet all of the former run contrary to a sense of interracial community. What defeats a sense of community is to see members of a group primarily as a *they,* as a kind of undifferentiated group counterposed to a *we,* defined by the group one identifies with oneself. One becomes blind to the individuality of members of the *they* group. One experiences this group as deeply different from oneself, even if one cannot always account for or explain that sense of difference. This anticommunal consciousness can exist in the absence of actual racist attitudes toward the other group, although the former is a natural stepping stone toward the latter. I think many students in schools, of all races and cultures, never do achieve the experience of interracial community, never learn to feel comfortable with members of other racial and ethnic groups, even though these students do not really have racist attitudes in the strict sense. Rather, the sense of group difference simply overwhelms any experiencing of commonality and sharing that is necessary for developing a sense of community.

Moreover, and unfortunately, despite the ways that antiracism and interracial community can be mutually supportive, there can also be tensions between certain aspects of antiracist education and the achievement of interracial community. On the most general level, antiracist education puts racial identity in the forefront of concern; one talks about groups — whites, blacks, Hispanics, etc. Yet, an overfocus on racial identity can give children a message that the most important thing about persons is their racial identity, and that people who differ from oneself racially necessarily differ in all kinds of other fundamental ways. It is perhaps ironic that an antiracist perspective that affirms the shared humanity and equal dignity of all persons independent of race can sometimes contribute to this *we/they* consciousness. Nevertheless, this "racialization" of consciousness, to use Michael Omi and Howard Winant's term,[6] can contribute to a sense of distance and estrangement, or at least to a lack of comfort with members of other races. It can thereby harm the achievement of interracial community. This is not of course an argument against antiracist education, for, even if the two values were irrevocably in tension — and I will argue that they aren't — it might be interracial community that should be sacrificed to the more urgent task of antiracist education.

This tension presents a situation in which the tasks of value education might appear different to members of subordinate groups than of dominant groups, especially to parents in those different groups. African-American and other parents of color face the difficult task of teaching their children to be wary of and prepared for the racism that they will probably experience at some point, while yet not becoming so paranoid as to lump all whites together and to be entirely distrustful of them. I bring this point up partly because I think many white people fail to recognize, or don't take seriously enough, the pervasive and often subtle racism experienced by people of color, and incorrectly regard this self-protective attitude on their part as hypersensitivity. Because of their greater stake in countering racism, the ideal of interracial community might seem like a luxury to a subordinate group parent; nevertheless, I think it is a value that needs to have some place in their children's education as well.

Fortunately, we need not choose between the values of interracial community and antiracism; rather, we should search for ways of teaching antiracist values that minimize the potential for harming or preventing interracial community. I will briefly mention two general guidelines in this regard. One is constantly to emphasize the internal variety within a group being studied; not to say "whites" and "blacks" all the time as if these were monolithic groups. For example, in discussing slavery, make clear that not all blacks were slaves during the period of slavery, that there were many free blacks. Similarly, most whites did *not* own slaves, and a few whites even actively aligned themselves with the cause of abolition, aiding free blacks who organized the underground railroads and the like. Exhibiting such internal variety within "white," "black," and other groups helps to prevent the formation of rigid or undifferentiated images of racial groups that lend themselves readily to a *we/they* consciousness that undermines community.

A second guideline is to try to give students the experience (in imagination at least) of being both discriminated against, excluded, or demeaned, and also being the discriminator, the excluder, the advantaged one. One first grade teacher I know discusses discrimination and racism by asking all the children in her class if they feel that they have been discriminated against in any way. Children feel discriminated against, excluded, or vulnerable to exclusion for all sorts of reasons — because they are short, or because they once didn't have a certain toy that other children had, or didn't know the characters of some television program being discussed. In one discussion in this teacher's class, a heavyish boy said that other kids made fun of him because of his size. In discussing this all the children were helped to see and to be sensitized in a personal, meaningful way to the damage done by all sorts of discrimination; and this is a lesson that this teacher extended to other forms of discrimination as well, including more socially significant ones, such as racism and sexism.

Encouraging students to attempt as much as possible to experience the vantage points of advantaged and disadvantaged, included and excluded, and the like, provides an important buffer to a "we/they" consciousness in the racial domain. This buffering is accomplished not so much by encouraging, as the first guideline does, the appreciation of internal diversity in a given group, as by bridging the gulf between the experience of the dominant and that of the subordinate. This is achieved by showing children that there is at least *some* dimension of life on which they occupy the dominant, and on others the subordinate, position (even if these dimensions are not of equal significance).

There is a similar process of potential convergence as well as potential tension between *community* and *multiculturalism.* These are distinct values. The positive bond and sense of connection involved in interracial community is not guaranteed by multiculturalism, which emphasizes *respect, interest,* and *understanding;* while such attitudes may help to inform and enrich a sense of community, they are quite compatible with its absence, and with a sense of distance from those of the respected, interesting "other culture." Some forms of multicultural education can even further divide students from one another while teaching respect, by *overemphasizing* cultural differences and mutual inaccessibility of different cultures to one another. Analogously to antiracism, this kind of faulty teaching of multiculturalism can lead to a similarly rigidified *we/they* consciousness.

The converse is true as well. Interracial community can not provide all the values involved in multiculturalism. For, while interracial community does encompass people who are culturally, racially, different from one another, it does not by itself promote a definite, positive appreciation of cultural differences and of distinct cultural values. And a single-minded attempt to foster interracial community can lead easily to an avoidance of fully acknowledging these racial/cultural differences, for fear that such acknowl-

edgment will foster a we/they attitude inimical to community.

Thus, interracial community and multiculturalism are distinct values that are both essential to a value education program, but that can be in tension with one another. Nevertheless, there are ways of teaching multiculturalism that minimize these tensions. Some broad guidelines are the following: (1) Invite children's participation in cultures studied, so as to make "other" cultures as accessible as possible to nonmembers. For example, have children in the class interview one another, posing questions about each others' cultures that the questioners feel will help them to comprehend the culture in question. Establish an "intercultural dialogue" among students. This approach will use a recognition of genuine cultural differences to bring children together rather than keep them apart. (2) Recognize cultures' internal variety (even contradictory strands within a given culture), their change over time, and (where appropriate) their interaction with other cultures — rather than presenting cultures as frozen in time, monolithic, and totally self-contained. (3) Recognize cultural universals and commonalities. It is not contrary to the spirit of multiculturalism — to the acknowledgment of authentic cultural differences — to see that distinct cultures may share certain broad features. For example, every culture responds to certain universal features of human life, such as birth, death, the rearing of children, a search for meaning in life. Both (2) and (3) prevent an inaccurate and community-impairing "theyness" in the presentation of other cultures.

Finally, our conception of interracial community must itself allow for the recognition of difference. A powerful, but misleading, tradition in our thinking about community is that people only feel a sense of community when they think of themselves as "the same" as the other members of the community. On this view, recognition of difference is threatening to community. But, as Robert Bellah and his colleagues argue in *Habits of the Heart,* the kind of community needed in the United States is *pluralistic* community, one which involves a sense of bond and connection stemming from shared activity, condition, task, location, and the like — and grounded ultimately in an experience of shared humanity — yet recognizing and valuing cultural differences (and other kinds of differences as well).[7]

I have discussed three crucial educational values for a multiracial, multicultural society: opposition to racism, multiculturalism, and interracial community. I have argued that these are distinct values, and that all three are essential to a responsible program of value education in a multicultural society. I have argued also that there can be tensions between different values. But the values can also be mutually supportive, and I have suggested some guidelines for maximizing the support and minimizing the tensions.

Notes

1. *History-Social Science Framework for California Public Schools, Kindergarten Through Grade Twelve* (Sacramento: California State Department of Education, 1988).

2. James Baldwin, *The Fire Next Time* (New York: Dell, 1962).

3. Elaine Pinderhughes, *Understanding Race, Ethnicity, and Power: The Key to Efficacy in Clinical Practice* (New York: Free Press, 1989).

4. Samuel and Pearl Oliner, *The Altruistic Personality: Rescuers of Jews in Nazi Europe* (New York: Free Press, 1988).

5. See among other writings, Carl Grant and Christine Sleeter, "An Analysis of Multicultural Education in the United States," *Harvard Educational Review* (Nov. 1987).

6. Michael Omi and Howard Winant, *Racial Formation in the United States: From the 1960's to the 1980's* (New York: Routledge, 1986).

7. Robert Bellah et al., *Habits of the Heart: Individualism and Commitment in American Life* (Berkeley: University of California Press, 1985).

TEACHING THE DIFFERENCES AMONG WOMEN
FROM A HISTORICAL PERSPECTIVE
Rethinking Race and Gender as Social Categories

Tessie Liu

Tessie Liu stresses the connection between racism and sexism and describes the changes that must be made in higher education to address both problems. She discusses several strategies that she thinks inadequate and then defends her own alternative. (Source: Reprinted with permission from Women's Studies International Forum, Vol. 14, No. 4, 1991, Elsevier Science Ltd., Pergamon Imprint, Oxford, England.)

During the week-long SIROW institute in 1989 on teaching Women's Studies from an international perspective, I experienced several epiphanal moments when a number of my research and teaching preoccupations melded and came into sharper focus. What follows is a progress report on my ruminations on this subject in the year since the institute. In particular, I would like to share the conceptual inversions and reexamination of received categories through which this problem has led me.

What has emerged from this journey is a clearer vision that feminist scholars must not only talk about diversity, but also must better understand how the differences among women are constituted historically in identifiable social processes. In this paper, I explore the importance of race as an analytical tool for investigating and understanding the differences among women. To do so, we must recognize that race is a *gendered* social category. By exploring the connections between race oppression and sex oppression, specifically how the former is predicated on the latter, we will also gain new insights into the relationship between gender and class.

Epiphanal moments, in many ways, occur only when one is primed for them. The lectures and workshops in the week-long seminar addressed questions with which I had been grappling throughout the academic year. My first set of concerns came out of a graduate course in comparative women's history that

I taught at the University of Arizona with a colleague who specializes in Latin American history and women's history. Through the semester, students and instructors asked one another what we were trying to achieve by looking at women's experiences comparatively. Beyond our confidence that appreciating diversity would enrich us personally, as well as stimulate in us new questions to pose to our own areas of specialization, we raised many more questions than we found definitive answers. One set of questions, in particular, troubled me. Throughout the semester, I wondered about the relationship between the kinds of comparisons in which we were engaged and feminist theory more generally. Were we looking for some kind of underlying sameness behind all the variations in women's experiences? Was our ultimate goal to build a unified theory of gender that would explain all the differences among women? Much later, I realized that my questions centered on the status of diversity in feminist theory and politics. Especially troubling to me was the lack of discussion on such questions as these: How do feminists explain the differences among women? Are there contradictions between the focus on differences and the claim to a universal sisterhood among women? How can these tensions be resolved?

The second set of concerns that I brought to this week-long workshop came out of ongoing discussions with my colleagues in the History Department over how to restructure and teach Western Civilization if we were to live up to our mandate to incorporate race, class, and gender.[1] Both sets of concerns address the problems of teaching cultural diversity. In this paper, I point out that the intellectual issues raised by adopting a more cross-cultural or international perspective in Women's Studies parallel the emotional and conceptual hurdles that my colleagues and I encountered in our attempts to integrate race, class, and gender into courses in western civilization. Further, I suggest that the rethinking required to restructure such courses can be instructive to feminist scholars in offering an opportunity to reassess our own understanding of the relationships among race, class, and gender in feminist analysis.

The mandate to incorporate race, gender, and class into the western-civilization curriculum originated as a political move. But even those of us who pushed for this integration did not have a clear idea of the fundamental intellectual changes entailed. We were initially motivated by the wish to establish diversity. This task is most easily accomplished thematically: that is, every so often, we add a lecture on women, on African Americans, on Native Americans, and so on, aiming for a multicultural representation. Although it marked a good-faith beginning, this approach is particularly problematic in the context of courses like Western Civilization. This attempt to introduce diversity merely sprinkles color on a white background, as Abena Busia commented in her lecture to the summer institute. One unintended but very serious effect of merely adding women, other cultures, or even discussions of class conflict and colonialism without challenging the basic structure of the idea of western civilization is that non-Europeans, all women, the poor, and all intersecting subsets of these identities appear in the story only as victims and losers.

One problem I had not anticipated was the capacity of my students, who are primarily white and middle class, for sympathy and yet distance. To put this more starkly: to many students, they themselves embody the universal norm. In their heart of hearts, they believe that *white* establishes not merely skin color, but the norm from which blacks, browns, yellows, and reds deviate. They condemn racism, which they believe is a problem out there between racists and the people they attack. Analogously, many male students accept the reality of sexism, feel bad about it for women, but think that they are not touched by it. Even though they sympathize, for these students poverty, racism, and even sexism are still other people's problems. Teaching them, I learned an important lesson about the politics of inclusion. For those who have been left out of the story of western civilization, it is perfectly possible to be integrated and still remain marginal.

Teaching students to appreciate cultural differences with the aim of promoting tolerance may not be a bad goal in itself, but the mode of discourse surrounding tolerance does not challenge the basically Eurocentric world view enshrined in western-civilization courses. At best, tolerance teaches us to accept differences; at worst, it teaches the necessity of accepting what we fear or dislike. In fact, it often encourages an ethnocentric understanding of differences because this form of comparison does not break down the divisions between *us* and *them*, between *self/subject* and *other*. Most of all, it does encourage us to realize that we are implicated in these differences — that our own identities are constituted relationally within them.

Maintaining the divide between *us* and *them*, I suspect, is one way of distancing the uncomfortable reality of unequal power relations, which come to the fore once we include those previously excluded. Classically, western-civilization courses eschew such discussions of power. The purpose of such courses, structured by very Hegelian notions of the march of progress, is to present world history as the inevitable ascent of Europeans. The noted Islamicist Marshall Hodgson (1963) aptly described this as the "torch theory of civilization": the torch was first lit in Mesopotamia, passed on to Greece and then to Rome, and carried to northern Europe; ultimately, it came to rest on the North American continent during and after the Second World War. In this story, Europeans and their descendants bear the torch. The privileged subject is white and male, usually a member of the ruling elite, and the multiple social relationships that sustain his privilege are rarely, if ever, examined.

In light of these complexities, the basic problem in reforming western-civilization courses changed. Our new problem was how to de-center the privileged white male (and sometimes female) subject — the *I* — in the story of western civilization, which, not coincidentally, corresponds closely to the subjectivity students have been socialized to develop in relation to the world. We could not possibly modify or reform this strong underlying message with a sprinkle of diversity. The Euro(andro-)centric viewpoint is embedded in categories of analysis, in notions of historical significance, in beliefs about who the important actors are, and in the causal logic of the story. We cannot integrate race, class, and gender without completely restructuring a course: critiquing foundations, developing new categories, telling a new story. The critical part of the decentering, however, is the painful process of self-examination. Needless to say, the intellectual and emotional hurdles of such a project must not be underestimated. We are teaching against the grain.

African-American feminists in the United States have long argued that the historically privileged white male is paralleled in American feminist discourse by the white female subject. The problem is perhaps most explicitly and succinctly articulated in the title *All the Women Are White, All the Men Are Black, But Some of Us Are Brave: Black Women's Studies* (Hull et al., 1982). Introducing and more fully representing women in all their diversity, although a good-faith beginning, is not sufficient in itself to correct the problems. The problem for black women, as just one example, lies not just in their initial invisibility, but also in the manner in which they enter the mainstream. The real possibility of black (and other nonwhite) women being brought in as second-class citizens forces us to consider how we as feminists account for and explain the differences among women. What is the status of these differences in feminist theory and politics, especially with respect to the claims of universal sisterhood?

To illustrate the depth of these unresolved problems, let me refer to our discussions on sameness and difference throughout the week-long institute. My personal history is relevant in explaining my reactions. I am an immigrant born on Taiwan to parents who were political refugees from China; my education, however, is completely western. My feminist consciousness was formed in the context of elite educational institutions, and my specialization is European history. Not surprisingly, I have lived with the contradictions of being simultaneously an insider and an outsider all of my life. The task of explaining why I do not fit anyone's categories is a burden I had long ago accepted. All the same, the week's discussions on sameness and difference stirred within me the undercurrents of unresolved issues and brought into clearer focus how much this problem pervades feminist politics.

The first note of disquiet came in the first day when someone in my discussion group used the term *women of color.* A Palestinian woman, two Chicanas, and I looked at each other and winked knowingly. All of a sudden we were *others,* strangers to each other but placed in the same group. We were all at this conference as feminist scholars, as insiders to the movement, yet suddenly we became outsiders because we had this special affiliation. This concept of diversity (however well meant) begs the question: where is the feminist standpoint in theorizing about the differences among women? Who is the feminist self and, to borrow from Aihwa Ong (1988), "who is the feminist other?" In the previous paragraph, I deliberately used *difference* in the singular rather than *differences* in the plural because I believe that there is an important distinction. *Difference* has become a crucial concept in feminist theory, yet in this context, we are tempted to ask, "different from what or whom?" As *women of color,* we were classed together, in spite of our obvious diversity, simply because we are not white. However well-intentioned such acts of inclusion are, they raise the question: who is doing the comparing? Unless there is an Archimedean point outside of social ties from which one could neutrally compare, as feminist scholars we must recognize that all discussions of differences and sameness are themselves inseparable from the power relations in which we live (see Jehlen, 1982; Mohanty, 1984). In this sense, I maintain, there is no true international or cross-cultural perspective. We can view the world only from where we stand.

Failure to recognize this fundamental limitation leads to the kind of ethnocentrism hidden in works like Robin Morgan's anthology *Sisterhood Is Global* (1984). Without doubt, Morgan's anthology is an impressive achievement. Covering 70 countries, it provides a wealth of information on women's lives and their legal, economic, and political status. As reviewers Hackstaff and Pierce (1985) point out, however, the implicit argument that women everywhere are fundamentally and similarly oppressed is extremely problematic. In *Sisterhood Is Global,* differences are treated as local variations on a universal theme. As a result, *why* women's experiences differ so radically is never seriously examined. Moreover, the reviewers point out a Western bias implicit in the uncritical and unselfconscious use of crucial terms like *feminism, individual rights,* and *choice,* which retain definitions developed by Western feminists from industrialized countries, however inappropriate such working definitions may be in other cultural and social contexts. The problem is not only that women in other cultures define *feminism* or *self* in distinct ways that Morgan should have acknowledged. More fundamentally, an unproblematic assumption of common sisterhood overlooks the social reality within which texts like *Sisterhood Is Global* are created. Morgan's vision of global feminism does not question the relative power and advantages from which feminists in North America and Western Europe claim the authority to speak in the name of others on the oppression of all women (see Mohanty, 1984; Ong, 1988).

This curious result—a catalog of difference in which the relations among those who are different play no role—is symptomatic of a more general problem with what might be called a *cross-cultural perspective*. The classic anthropological use of *culture* understands the values, beliefs, and politics of various groups and societies as concrete realizations within the compass of human possibility. In an intellectual move with obvious benefits for liberal politics, difference is made a raw fact, irreducible to any hierarchical orderings of evolution or mental progress. A cross-cultural perspective rests on the notion of a transcendental or universal humanness, an essential similarity that makes it possible to understand the beliefs and behavior of others, however strange (Clifford, 1985).

This is a political vision with clear and obvious benefits. In the hands of members of a society that enjoys advantages of wealth and power over those with different cultures, however, it conceals more than it reveals. By not focusing on the unequal distribution of power which permeates relations between groups, the liberal humanist discourse elides the necessary discussion of power. To assert that the differences among women conceal an essential sisterhood is not enough: this quick achievement of solidarity comes at the expense of a real examination of the nature of the connections that actually do exist, by virtue of the fact that we occupy different positions in a world inadequately described as a congeries of reified, discrete *cultures*.[2] Instead, we must understand difference in social structural terms, in terms of interests, of privileges, and of deprivation. Only then can we see the work required to make *sisterhood* more than a rhetorical assertion of common substance. The crucial alternative analytical framework, I argue, entails exploring how diverse women's experiences are constituted reciprocally within relations of power.

On these highly charged issues within feminist politics, Charlotte Bunch (1987), our first speaker in the institute, brought an important perspective on thinking about the differences among women, arguing that we must take differences as the starting point, as the feminist standpoint. In the process of exploring diversity, Bunch assured the audience, the similarities in women's experiences will emerge. For Bunch, however, *difference* is not opposed to *sameness*. Rather, recognizing the differences among women should lead us to ask how our different lives and experiences are connected. In contrast to Morgan, Bunch argues that sisterhood is not a natural category, stemming from an organic community. Rather, an international (or cross-cultural or cross-class) sisterhood is constructed out of common political strategies. In this sense, the possibility of sisterhood begins with the recognition that, despite the vast differences which could divide us, our fates are linked and that very connectedness necessitates common action and common solutions. The fact of difference, however, means that a common cause needs to be constructed; it cannot simply be asserted.

Bunch's perspective is wholly consistent with the general goal of understanding differences across cultures. Yet I think that she asks us to investigate and appreciate diversity not just for its own sake, but also for its strategic importance to feminist politics. The goal of studying women's conditions across regions and cultures is not to demonstrate the sameness of women's oppression, but to understand the connections among the different ways in which women are oppressed (and, perhaps, to understand the connection between some women's privileges and others' deprivations). Because the *connectedness* of experience allows us to formulate strategies for common action, our study of differences must focus on how differences are constituted relationally. As a historian, I interpret these remarks through the possible contributions of my discipline. Methodologically, social history has much to add to the goal of understanding differences relationally. By situating experience as part of specific social processes, social history understands experience as the result of particular actions and actors, actions that establish connections among people and among groups.

In terms of understanding connections, the lessons I have drawn from revising the curriculum for Western Civilization are particularly instructive. Moreover, once we change the content of the course from the story of European ascendency to a critical history of European dominance, the global scale and time frame of the modern half of the course (post-1500) offer a framework for thinking through and empirically studying how the differences among women were relationally constituted.[3] This framework is important, I believe, because differences in the world that we have inherited are not neutral facts. The diversity of lived experiences that we encounter today within a single society and among societies around the globe cannot be abstracted from the legacy of colonialization, forced contact, expropriation, and continuing inequalities. Of course, the cultures of subjugated peoples cannot be reduced to the fact of their domination alone, any more than the culture of colonizers can be reduced to conquest. Yet no analysis of cultural diversity can be complete without study of the forces that have so fundamentally shaped experience.

In the remainder of this paper, I offer the broad outlines of a conceptual inversion entailed in remaking courses in western civilization to serve our goal of understanding the differences among women. At present, although within Women's Studies we speak often of race, class, and gender as aspects of experience, we continue to organize our courses around gender as the important analytical category. This focus is both understandable and logical because, after all, our subject is women. Yet I would like to suggest the usefulness of organizing courses around the concept of race. By understanding how race is a *gendered* social category, we can more systematically address the structural underpinnings of the questions why women's experiences differ so radically and how these differences are relationally constituted.

In order to place race at the center of feminist inquiry, we need first to rethink how we conceptualize race as an analytical category. We tend to think that race is a relevant social category only when we encounter racism as a social phenomenon, in the form

of bigotry, for example. Scholars have tried to understand racial hatred by analyzing characteristics like skin color, skull size, and intelligence, which racist ideology deems important, and much of this scholarship has consisted of testing and refuting racial categories. As a result, scholars have let the ideologies of racism set the agenda for discussions of racism within the academy. Although this work is important, I think the scope is too narrow. I would like to suggest that it is fruitful to inquire into the social metaphors that allow racial thinking, that is, the kind of logic or type of reasoning about human relationships that allows racists to believe in the reality of their categories. In other words, we need to move beyond the belief that racial thinking is purely an outgrowth of (irrational) prejudices, because such a belief in fact exoticizes racism, in the sense that it makes racism incomprehensible to those who do not share the hatred. Rather, as I will specify below, the more radical position holds that race is a widespread principle of social organization.

Once we ask what kind of reasoning about the nature of human relationships allows racists to believe in the reality of their categories, we find racial metaphors in benign situations as well as under conditions of discrimination, overt hatred, and even genocide. In other words, even those of us who do not hate on the basis of skin color must realize that racial thinking is disturbingly close to many of the acceptable ways that we conceptualize social relationships. In this sense, placing race at the intellectual center of courses like Western Civilization is de-centering, for it attempts to break established habits of categorizing in terms of *self* and *others*. My ideas on this subject, I should add, are still in the formative stages. I have sketched with broad strokes very complex and nuanced social situations in the hope of capturing simple patterns that have been overlooked. In making bold and overly schematic generalizations, I also hope to provoke opposition and controversy as one way to assess the usefulness of these ideas for further inquiry.

Let me begin with several dictionary definitions of race that I found quite surprising and illuminating. Under the first definition in the *Oxford English Dictionary,* we find *race* as "a group of persons, animals, or plants connected by common descent or origin." As illustrations, the dictionary lists "the offspring or posterity of *a* person; a set of children or descendants; breeding, the production of offspring; (rarely): a generation." In a second set of usages, the *OED* defines *race* as "a limited group descended from a common ancestor; a house, family, kindred." We find as examples "a tribe, nation, or people, regarded as common stock; a group of several tribes or peoples regarded as forming a distinct ethnic stock; one of the great divisions of mankind, having certain peculiarities in common." The last is qualified by this comment: "this term is often used imprecisely; even among anthropologists there is no generally accepted classification or terminology." These definitions are then followed by explanations of the meaning of *race* when applied to animals, plants, and so forth.

It is clear from the first two sets of usage that ideas about descent, blood ties, or common substance are basic to the notion of *race*. What struck me, in particular, was the second set of synonyms for *race:* house, family, kindred. Louis Flandrin (1979) made the reverse discovery when he looked up *family* in a French dictionary, *Petit Robert. Family* refers to "the entirety of persons mutually connected by marriage or filiation" or "the succession of individuals who descend from one another," that is to say, "a line," "a race," "a dynasty." Only secondarily does *Petit Robert* define family in the way we usually mean, as "related persons living under one roof," "more specifically, the father, the mother, the children." These dictionary definitions, taken all together, suggest that race as a social category is intimately linked to one of the basic ways in which human beings have organized society, that is, by kinship. As Flandrin points out, etymologically, at least in England and France, *race* as a kinship term, usually to denote the *patronymic* or *family name*—called literally, the name of the race or *le nom de race*—predated our current usage of the term, which denotes distinct large populations.

Although the specific referent in notions of race is kinship, in order to understand the significance of racial thinking, we need to move beyond these neutral dictionary distinctions. When kinship becomes the key element in a stratified social order, as in dynastic politics or caste systems, the concept of race becomes important. Thus, European society, before actual contact with peoples of different skin tones and different cultures and customs, was organized by racial princi-

ples. The operating definition of race was based not on external physical characteristics but on blood ties—or, more precisely, some common substance passed on by fathers. In early modern Europe, when patriarchal rule and patrilineal descent predominated, political power, social station, and economic entitlements were closely bound to blood ties and lineage. Thus, race also encapsulated the notion of class. But class in this society was an accident of birth: either according to birth order (determining which rights and privileges the child inherited) or, more generally, according to the family into which one was born (noble or common, propertied or not). The privileges or stigmas of birth, in this system, were as indelible and as discriminatory as any racial system based on skin color or some other trait. The notion of legitimate and illegitimate birth indicates that blood ties did not extend to all who shared genetic materials, but only those with a culturally defined "common substance" passed on by fathers.

Understanding race as an element of social organization directs our attention to forms of stratification. The centrality of reproduction, especially in the transmission of common substance through heterosexual relations and ultimately through birth as the differentiating mark of social entitlements, for example, allows us to see the gendered dimensions of the concept of race. For societies organized by racial principles, reproductive politics are closely linked to establishing the boundaries of lineages. In a male-dominated system, regulating social relationships through racial metaphors necessitates control over women. The reproduction of the system entails not only regulating the sexuality of women in one's own group, but also differentiating between women according to legitimate access and prohibition. Considered in these terms, race as a social category functions through controlling sexuality and sexual behavior.

To borrow from Benedict Anderson's (1983) insights about the nature of nationalism, racial thinking, as a principle of social organization, is a way to imagine communities. Basic to the notion of race is that an indelible common substance unites the people who possess it in a special community. Importantly, the community described with racial metaphors is always limited; the intent is to exclude in the process of including. Metaphors of common substance simultaneously articulate the quality of relationship among the members of a group and specify who belongs and who does not, asserting a natural, organic solidarity among people whose relations are described as indelible and nonvoluntary. Thus, it is not accidental that racial thinking borrows its language from biology, particularly from a systemic vision of the natural world wherein hierarchies, differences, and even struggles are described as functional to the survival and health of the whole.

These core concepts in racial thinking are powerful and flexible. Racial metaphors are rife in other forms of community-building. By analogy, kinship terms — *family, brotherhood, sisterhood,* each with its own specific meanings — are often invoked to create a sense of group affiliation: they can be applied to small communities mobilized for political action or to an entire society, in the sense of the body politic. Most notably, such metaphors are central to nationalist movements and nation-building, wherein common language and culture are often linked to blood and soil. The invocation of common substance and frequent use of kinship terms to describe the relationships among members of the political community emphasize the indelible and nonvoluntary quality of the ties and de-emphasize conflict and opposing interests. The familiarity of racial metaphors, however, should not lead us to over-generalize the phenomenon. Racial metaphors are used to build particular kinds of communities, with a special brand of internal politics on which I will later elaborate, but we must remember that forms of community-building exist which do not draw on racial metaphors. For example, there are communities, even families, conceived as voluntary associations built on common values and commitment to common goals, not on indelible ties.

The power and flexibility of racial metaphors lie, I think, in the malleability of notions of common substance. In the colonial societies that Europeans and their descendants created around the world, the older notion of race articulating a lineage-based system of entitlements and privileges was expanded and became the organizing concept through which Europeans attempted to rule subjugated populations. Only in this context of colonization did skin color become the mark of common substance and the differentiat-

ing feature between colonizers and the colonized, and, in many cases, between freedom and enslavement. Of course, the qualities designated as superior had power only because of the military force and other forms of coercion which reinforced the political and social privileges accompanying them.

Although colonial societies in the Americas, Africa, and Asia differed greatly in the taxonomy of racial categories and in the degree to which they tolerated sexual unions between colonizers and colonized and thus had different miscegenation laws and roles from *mestizos,* the underlying problem of creating a hierarchal system of differentiation was similar. As Ann Stoler notes,

> Colonial authority was constructed on two powerful, but false premises. The first was the notion that Europeans in the colonies made up an easily identifiable and discrete biological and social entity; a "natural" community of class interests, racial attributes, political and social affinities and superior culture. The second was the related notion that the boundaries separating colonizer from colonized were thus self-evident and easily drawn. (1989, p. 635).

As scholars of colonial societies are quick to point out, neither premise reflected colonial realities. The rulers, divided by conflicting economic and political goals, differed even on which methods would best safeguard European (or white) rule. Yet colonial rule itself was contingent on the colonists' ability to construct and enforce legal and social classifications for who was *white* and who was *native,* who counted as *European* and by what degree, which progeny were legitimate and which were not.

Because racial distinctions claim that common substance is biologically transmitted, race as a social reality focuses particular attention on all women as reproducers of human life (as well as the social life of the group) and at the same time necessarily separates them into distinct groups with special but different burdens. To the degree that colonial authority was based on racial distinctions, then, one could argue that colonial authority itself was fundamentally structured in gendered terms. Although in reality there may have been many types of prohibited unions and contested relationships, "ultimately," as Stoler points out, "inclusion or exclusion required regulating the sexual, conjugal and domestic life of both Europeans in the colonies and their colonized subjects" (1989, p. 635), especially in a racially based slaveholding society like the American South, where the children of a slave woman were slaves and the children of a free woman were free. Under this juridical system, regulating who had sexual access to which group of women involved economic decisions as well.

In colonial societies as different as Dutch Indonesia (Taylor, 1983), British Nigeria (Callaway, 1987), and the American plantation South (Fox-Genovese, 1988), we find bifurcated visions of womanhood. Women of European descent became the guardians of civilization. Thus, the Victorian cult of domesticity in the colonial world must be seen in the context of demarcations between groups. Because the structure of colonial race privileges focused particularly on limiting access to Europeans status, the elevation of white women as civilization's guardians also confined them within narrow spheres. As the reproducers of the ruling elite, they established through their daily actions the boundaries of their group identity; hence their behavior came under group scrutiny.

By contrast, the images and treatment of colonized women resulted from more complex projections. On the other hand, colonized women were not viewed as women at all in the European sense; they were spared neither harsh labor nor harsh punishment. On the other hand, as the reproducers of the labor force, colonized women were valued as one might value a prize broodmare. Equally, men of European descent eroticized colonized women as exotic, socially prohibited, but available and subjugated sexual objects. In this case, prohibition and availability are intimately connected to desire. Because such unions were socially invisible, the progeny from the union could be denied. Sex, under these conditions, became a personal rather than a community or racial matter. In other words, in sexual unions with women from a socially prohibited category, men could step outside the normal restrictions and obligations imposed on sexual activity by shirking responsibility for their progeny.[4]

The same bifurcated images of women appear in European societies as the result of similar processes of creating hierarchy and class distinctions. Students of European history are not used to thinking about race as a relevant category for societies on European soil; these historians, including historians of women, much more readily accept class as the fundamental divide. Yet, despite the presence of more democratically oriented notions of meritocracy in industrial society and the dissemination of Enlightenment notions of contractual polity, we should not underestimate the degree to which older (lineage-based) racial thinking rooted in kinship and family alliances remained basic to the accumulation and concentration of capital in propertied families. Racial metaphors (concerns over purity of stock and preservation of social boundaries) pervaded the rationale behind marriage alliances and inheritance. The European upper classes literally thought of themselves as a *race* apart from the common rabble. Belief in the reality of these social distinctions constructed around biological metaphors pervaded bourgeois imagination and social fears. Respectability centered on domestic virtues defended by the upper-class woman, the angel of the hearth. Just as the bourgeoisie championed its own vision of domestic order as a model for civic order, they feared the disorder and contagion of the working class.

This fear is evident in perceptions of 19th-century elite social reformers, particularly on such seemingly neutral subjects as social hygiene. In their studies of English and French attempts to control venereal diseases, historians Judy Walkowitz (1980) and Jill Harsin (1985) have shown that regulation focused particularly on policing female prostitutes and not their male clients. As Walkowitz has demonstrated for the port cities of England, forcing working-class women who occasionally stepped out with sailors to register on police blotters as prostitutes created a distinct outcast group, in a sense professionalizing these women while at the same time isolating them from their working-class neighbors. The ideological assumptions behind such police actions were more explicitly articulated in the French case. As Harsin shows, police regulations explicitly considered street prostitutes, called *les filles publiques* or public women, the source of contagion. Although ostensibly the problem concerned public health and the spread of venereal disease, the solutions reveal that elite social reformers like Parent du Chatelet saw poor working-class women not only as the source of disease, but as infectants of civic order, as sources of social disorder.[5]

The improbability that impoverished street prostitutes could threaten civic order demonstrates the power of the biological metaphors that linked questions of physical health metaphorically to the health of the society (of the body politic). The perception of danger bespeaks how the French upper-class imagination represented working-class women. As the dialectical opposite of the pure and chaste bourgeois angel of the hearth, poor women of the streets symbolized dirt and sexual animality. Whether these perceptions accurately reflected real circumstances is immaterial. It is more important for us to see that elite reformers and the police acted as if their perceptions were true, putting into practice elaborate controls that had material effects on the lives of working class women and, indirectly, of upper-class women as well. The perception of danger and disorder rests on that prior social reasoning which I have identified as racial metaphors.

The previous analysis of the relationship between prostitution and public health demonstrates both the malleability and the power of racial thinking to structure the terms of political debates and actions. In recent European history, we can find many other examples where racial metaphors provide the basic vocabulary for political discourse. In the latter half of the 19th century, the imperatives of competition for empire in a world already carved up by Europeans filtered back into European domestic politics in the form of anxiety over population decline and public health. In the eyes of the state, responsibility for the fitness of the nation rested on woman's reproductive capacity, their place in the economy, and their role as mothers in protecting the welfare of children (the future soldiers for the empire) (Davin, 1978). Debates over the Woman Question, in the form of feminist demands for greater equality within marriage and for political, economic, and reproductive rights, were debated in the context of colonial politics and concerns over the vitality of the master European races. Competition among European nations for colonial empire and their anxieties about themselves as colonizers set the terms for curtailing women's demands for greater freedom of action and autonomy. Anti-

feminist projects such as economically restrictive protective legislation, bans on birth control, and pronatalist policies went hand in hand with the campaign against women's suffrage.

In the 20th century, within the European heartland, German National Socialists took these shared assumptions about the relation between national fitness and women's activities to their terrifying extreme. As Gisela Bock's study of women's reproductive rights in Nazi Germany indicates, obsession with race purity and population strength led to a policy of compulsory motherhood with the criminalization of abortion for Aryan women of the superior race and forced sterilization for the inferior races as part of their ultimate extermination (Bock, 1984). This study of the differential effects of racial policy on women's reproductive rights shocks us into recognizing that the division of women into breeders and nonbreeders is wholly consistent with the logic of racial thinking, whether we encounter such divisions in European dynastic politics or as part of the effort to establish boundaries between colonizers and the colonized. The most disturbing aspect of racial thinking is that it is *not* limited to the terrifying circumstances of genocide for some and compulsory motherhood for others. It is, in many respects, its very banality which should trouble us.

This brief survey of the common use and implications of what I have called racial metaphors in colonial contexts as well as in the home countries of colonizers, while hardly satisfactory in terms of detail, has at minimum I hope, suggested an interesting point of departure for rethinking the connections among gender, race, and class. As Bock's study shows us, racism and sexism are not just analogous forms of oppression; institutionalized racism is a form of sexism. One form of oppression is predicated on the other. Racism is a kind of sexism which does not treat all women as the same, but drives wedges between us on the basis of our daily experiences, our assigned functions within the social order, and our perceived interests and mobilization. Although women everywhere have struggled against prescriptive images and have fought for greater autonomy and control, it should not be surprising that, given their different positions within the system and the vastly different material conditions of their lives, women have fashioned different notions of self, have had different grievances against their circumstances, and have often developed different strategies.

Thinking about differences in the ways that I have suggested in this paper requires overcoming very strong emotional and intellectual barriers. We are all products of societies that have taught us to hate others or, worse, to be indifferent to their suffering and blind to our own privileges and to those who labor to provide them. The historical legacy of these differences makes common bonds difficult to conceive. That which divides us may also connect us, but will not easily unite us. Still, if sisterhood beyond the boundaries of class, race, ethnicity, and nation is a meaningful goal, we must try to develop common strategies for change. As a first step, we can become aware that some of the most fundamental differences arise from our distinct locations within a social system that underprivileges all women, but in different ways. To bridge these differences, we must, as Peggy Pascoe has urged, take a candid look at the shameful side,[6] recognizing that we cannot bury the past or wipe the slate completely clean. We can only strive for empathy and mutual understanding. Some of us face the painful process of re-examining our definitions of *self* and *other* and of challenging the categories of analysis and conceptions of historical development which support our intimate vision of ourselves in the world. Others face the equally painful task of letting go of anger, not enough to forget it entirely, but enough to admit the possibility of common futures and joint strategies for transformation.

We cannot fully capture and understand the kinds of differences between women based on race and class by such phrases as *diversity of experiences*. By focusing on race as an analytical category in accounting for the differences among women, we are in fact studying race as a principle of social organization and racial metaphors as part of the process of defining hierarchies and constituting boundaries of privilege. The core notion of common substance transmitted through heterosexual intercourse and birth underscores the gendered nature of the concept of race. In a male-dominated society, this concept focuses particular attention on women's activities, on reproductive politics, and more generally, on control over sexuality and sexual behavior. Understanding this process allows us to see how much the identities of different groups of women in the same society are implicated in one another. Although their experiences of oppression differ dramatically, these differences are nonetheless relationally constituted in identifiable social processes.

Notes

Author's Note: This paper has benefitted enormously from Ken Dauber's intellectual support and careful readings. I would also like to thank Karen Anderson, Jan Monk, Amy Newhall, and Pat Seavey for their insights and editorial suggestions.

1. Since 1987, all students earning the Bachelor of Arts and Sciences at the U of A have been required to take one course, selected from a designated list, which focuses on gender, class, race, or ethnicity.

2. For a critique of this view of *culture,* see Worsley (1981) and Clifford (1988).

3. Although I am vulnerable, in this move, to the charge that even in the posture of critique, I still privilege a Western perspective, I do so as a politically conscious first step. With regard to my earlier concerns with some of the problems of cross-cultural comparison, a focus on colonialism forces us to keep in the center of our vision the relationship between differences and power.

4. I am indebted to Ken Dauber for this insight. For European parallels in relationships between upper-class men and working-class women, see Davidoff (1983).

5. For interesting parallels see White (1983, 1986) and Guy (1988).

6. Pascoe's talk at Western History Conference in Santa Fe, New Mexico, 1989. See also Pascoe (1990).

References

Anderson, Benedict. (1983). *Imagined communities: reflections on the origins and spread of nationalism.* London: Verso.

Bock, Gisela. (1984). Racism and sexism in Nazi Germany: motherhood, compulsory sterilization, and the state. In Renate Bridenthal, Atina Grossman, & Marion Kaplan (Eds.), *When biology became destiny: women in Weimar and Nazi Germany* (pp. 271–296). New York: Monthly Review Press.

Bunch, Charlotte. (1987). Bringing the global home. In Charlotte Bunch (Ed.), *Passionate politics* (pp. 328–345). New York: St. Martin's Press.

Callaway, Helen. (1987). *Gender, culture and empire: European women in colonial Nigeria.* London: Macmillan.

Clifford, James. (1986). On ethnographic allegory. In James Clifford & George Marcus (Eds.), *Writing culture: the poetics and politics of ethnography* (pp. 98–121). Berkeley: University of California Press.

Clifford, James. (1988). *The predicaments of culture: twentieth century ethnograpy, literature, and art.* Cambridge, MA: Harvard University Press.

Davin, Anna. (1978). Imperialism and motherhood. *History Workshop, 5,* 9–56.

Davidoff, Lenore. (1983). Class and gender in Victorian England. In Judith L. Newton, Mary P. Ryan, & Judith R. Walkowitz (Eds.), *Sex and class in women's history* (pp. 16–71). London: Routledge & Kegan Paul.

Flandrin, Jean-Louis. (1979). *Families in former times: kinship, household, and sexuality in early modern France,* Richard Southern (Trans.). Cambridge: Cambridge University Press.

Fox-Genovese, Elizabeth. (1988). *Within the plantation household: the black and white women of the Old South.* Chapel Hill: University of North Carolina Press.

Guy, Donna J. (1988). White slavery, public health and the socialist position on legalized prostitution in Argentina 1913–1936. *Latin American Research Review, 23*(3), pp. 60–80.

Hackstaff, Karla, & Pierce, Jennifer. (1985). Is sisterhood global? *Berkeley Journal of Sociology, 30,* 189–204.

Harsin, Jill. (1985). *Policing prostitution in nineteenth century Paris.* Princeton: Princeton University Press.

Hodgson, Marshall. (1963). The interrelations of societies in history. *Comparative Studies in Society and History, 5,* 227–250.

Hull, Gloria T., Scott, Patricia Bell, & Smith, Barbara. (1982). *All the women are white, all the men are black, but some of us are brave: black women's studies.* Westbury, NY: Feminist Press.

Jehlen, Myra. (1982). Archimedes and the paradox of feminist criticism. In Nannerl Keohane, Michelle

Rosaldo, & Barbara Gelpi (Eds.), *Feminist theory: a critique of ideology* (pp. 189–215). Chicago: University of Chicago Press.

Mohanty, Chandra Talpade. (1984). Under western eyes: feminist scholarship and colonial discourses. *Boundaries, 2*(12/13), 333–358.

Morgan, Robin. (1984). *Sisterhood is global.* New York: Anchor Press/Doubleday.

Ong, Aihwa. (1988). Colonialism and modernity: feminist re-presentations of women in non-western societies. *Inscriptions (Journal of the Group for the Study of Discourse in Colonialism), 3/4,* 79–93.

Pascoe, Peggy. (1990). At the crossroads of culture. *Women's Review of Books, 7*(5), 22–23.

Stoler, Ann L. (1989). Making empire respectable: the politics of race and sexual morality in twentieth century colonial cultures. *American Ethnologist, 16,* 634–660.

Taylor, Jean. (1983). *The world of Batavia.* Madison: University of Wisconsin Press.

Walkowitz, Judith. (1980). *Prostitution and Victorian society: women, class, and the state.* Cambridge: Cambridge University Press.

White, Luise. (1986). Prostitution, identity and class consciousness in Nairobi during World War II. *Signs, 11,* 255–273.

White, Luise. (1983). A colonial state and an African petty bourgeoisie: prostitution, property and class struggle in Nairobi, 1936–1940. In Frederick Cooper (Ed.), *Struggle for the city: migrant labor, capital, and the state in urban Africa* (pp. 167–193). Beverly Hills, CA: Sage.

Worsley, Peter. (1981). Marxism and culture: the missing concept. *Dialectical Anthropology, 6,* 103–123.

 Violent and Nonviolent Action

NON-VIOLENT RESISTANCE

M. K. Gandhi

Mohandas Gandhi argues against violence and in favor of noncooperation as a strategy for social transformation. His argument against violence is that it leaves the door at the moral level of his or her enemies, and it violates a basic principle of ahisma — *sacredness of life. He defends noncooperation, which is not merely passive acceptance of the status quo, as both effective and morally desirable. (Source: Excerpts from* Non-Violent Resistance *by M. K. Gandhi. Copyright © 1951 by Schocken Books, Inc. Reprinted by permission of the Navajivan Trust, India.)*

Neither a Saint Nor a Politician

A kind friend has sent me the following cutting from the April number of the *East and West:*

"Mr. Gandhi has the reputation of a saint but it seems that the politician in him often dominates his decisions. He has been making great use of *hartals* [direct actions] and there can be no gainsaying that under his direction *hartal* is becoming a powerful political weapon for uniting the educated and the uneducated on a single question of the day. The *hartal* is not without its disadvantages. It is teaching direct action, and direct action however potent does not work for unity. Is Mr. Gandhi quite sure that he is serving the highest behests of *ahimsa*, harmlessness? His proposal to commemorate the shooting at Jalianwala Bagh is

not likely to promote concord. It is a tragic incident into which our Government was betrayed, but is the memory of its bitterness worth retaining? Can we not commemorate the event by raising a temple of peace, to help the widows and orphans, to bless the souls of those who died without knowing why? The world is full of politicians and petti-foggers who, in the name of patriotism, poison the inner sweetness of man and, as a result, we have wars and feuds and such shameless slaughter as turned Jalianwala Bagh into a shambles. Shall we not now try for a larger symbiosis such as Buddha and Christ preached, and bring the world to breathe and prosper together? Mr. Gandhi seemed destined to be the apostle of such a movement, but circumstances are forcing him to seek the way of raising resistances and group unities. He may yet take up the larger mission of uniting the world."

I have given the whole of the quotation. As a rule I do not notice criticism of me or my methods except when thereby I acknowledge a mistake or enforce still further the principles criticized. I have a double reason for noticing the extract. For, not only do I hope further to elucidate the principles I hold dear, but I want to show my regard for the author of the criticism whom I know and whom I have admired for many years for the singular beauty of his character. The critic regrets to see in me a politician whereas he expected

394

me to be a saint. Now I think that the word *saint* should be ruled out of present life. It is too sacred a word to be lightly applied to anybody, much less to one like myself who claims only to be a humble searcher after truth, knows his limitations, makes mistakes, never hesitates to admit them when he makes them, and frankly confesses that he, like a scientist, is making experiments about some 'of the eternal verities' of life, but cannot even claim to be a scientist because he can show no tangible proof of scientific accuracy in his methods or such tangible results of his experiments as modern science demands. But though by disclaiming sainthood I disappoint the critic's expectations, I would have him to give up his regrets by answering him that the politician in me has never dominated a single decision of mine, and if I seem to take part in politics, it is only because politics encircle us today like the coil of a snake from which one cannot get out, no matter how much one tries. I wish therefore to wrestle with the snake, as I have been doing with more or less success consciously since 1894, unconsciously, as I have now discovered, ever since reaching years of discretion. Quite selfishly, as I wish to live in peace in the midst of a bellowing storm howling round me, I have been experimenting with myself and my friends by introducing religion into politics. Let me explain what I mean by religion. It is not the Hindu religion, which I certainly prize above all other religions, but the religion which transcends Hinduism, which changes one's very nature, which binds one indissolubly to the truth within and which ever purifies. It is the permanent element in human nature which counts no cost too great in order to find full expression and which leaves the soul utterly restless until it has found itself, known its Maker and appreciated the true correspondence between the Maker and itself.

It was in that religious spirit that I came upon *hartal*. I wanted to show that it is not a knowledge of letters that would give India consciousness of herself, or that would bind the educated together. The *hartal* illuminated the whole of India as if by magic on the 6th of April, 1919. And had it not been for the interruption of the 10th of April, brought about by Satan whispering fear into the ears of a Government conscious of its own wrong and inciting to anger a people that were prepared for it by utter distrust of the Government, India would have risen to an unimaginable height.

The *hartal* had not only been taken up by the great masses of people in a truly religious spirit but it was intended to be a prelude to a series of direct actions.

But my critic deplores direct action. For, he says, "it does not work for unity." I join issue with him. Never has anything been done on this earth without direct action. I rejected the word *passive resistance* because of its insufficiency and its being interpreted as a weapon of the weak. It was direct action in South Africa which told and told so effectively that it converted General Smuts to sanity. He was in 1906 the most relentless opponent of Indian aspirations. In 1914, he took pride in doing tardy justice by removing from the Statute Book of the Union a disgraceful measure which, in 1909 he had told Lord Morley, would be never removed, for he then said South Africa would never tolerate repeal of a measure which was twice passed by the Transvaal Legislature. But what is more, direct action sustained for eight years left behind it not only no bitterness but the very Indians who put up such a stubborn fight against General Smuts ranged themselves round his banner in 1915 and fought under him in East Africa. It was direct action in Champaran which removed an agelong grievance. A meek submission when one is chafing under a disability or a grievance which one would gladly see removed, not only does not make for unity, but makes the weak party acid, angry and prepares him for an opportunity to explode. By allying myself with the weak party, by teaching him direct, firm, but harmless action, I make him feel strong and capable of defying the physical might. He feels braced for the struggle, regains confidence in himself and knowing that the remedy lies with himself, ceases to harbour the spirit of revenge and learns to be satisfied with a redress of the wrong he is seeking to remedy.

It is working along the same line that I have ventured to suggest a memorial about Jalianwala Bagh. The writer in *East and West* has ascribed to me a proposal which has never once crossed my mind. He thinks that I want "to commemorate the shooting at Jalianwala Bagh." Nothing can be further from my thought than to perpetuate the memory of a black deed. I dare say that before we have come to our own we shall have a repetition of the tragedy and I will prepare the nation for it by treasuring the memory of the innocent dead. The widows and the orphans have been and are being helped, but we cannot "bless the souls of those who died without knowing why," if we will not acquire the ground which has been hallowed by innocent blood and there erect a suitable memorial for them. It is not to serve, if I can help it, as a reminder of a foul deed, but it shall serve as an encouragement to the nation that it is better to die helpless and unarmed and as victims rather than as tyrants. I would have the future generations remember that we who witnessed the innocent dying did not ungratefully refuse to cherish their memory. As Mrs. Jinnah truly remarked when she gave her mite to the fund, the memorial would at least give us an excuse for living. After all it will be the spirit in which the memorial is erected that will decide its character.

What was the larger 'symbiosis' that Buddha and Christ preached? Buddha fearlessly carried the war into the enemy's camp and brought down on its knees an arrogant priesthood. Christ drove out the money-changers from the temple of Jerusalem and drew down curses from Heaven upon the hypocrites and the pharisees. Both were for intensely direct action. But even as Buddha and Christ chastized they showed unmistakable gentleness and love behind every act of theirs. They would not raise a finger against their enemies, but would gladly surrender themselves rather than the truth for which they lived. Buddha would have died resisting the priesthood, if the majesty of his love had not proved to be equal to the task of bending the priesthood. Christ died on the cross with a crown of thorns on his head defying the might of a whole empire. And if I raise resistances of a non-violent character I simply and humbly follow in the footsteps of the great teachers named by my critic.

Lastly, the writer of the paragraph quarrels with my 'grouping unities' and would have me to take up 'the larger mission of uniting the world.' I once told him under a common roof that I was probably more cosmopolitan than he. I abide by that expression. Unless I group unities I shall never be able to unite the whole world. Tolstoy once said that if we would but get off the backs of our neighbours the world would be quite all right without any further help from us. And if we can only serve our immediate neighbours by ceasing to prey upon them, the circle of unities thus grouped in the right fashion will ever grow in circumference till at last it is conterminous with that of the whole world. More than that it is not given to any man to try or achieve. **यथा पिंडे तथा ब्रह्मांडे*** is as true today as ages ago when it was first uttered by an unknown *rishi*.[1]

The Law of Suffering

No country has ever risen without being purified through the fire of suffering. Mother suffers so that her child may live. The condition of wheat growing is that the seed grain should perish. Life comes out of Death. Will India rise out of her slavery without fulfilling this eternal law of purification through suffering?

If my advisers are right, evidently India will realize her destiny without travail. For their chief concern is that the events of April, 1919, should not be repeated. They fear non-co-operation because it would involve the sufferings of many. If Hampdon had argued thus he would not have withheld payment of ship-money, nor would Wat Tyler have raised the standard of revolt. English and French histories are replete with instances of men continuing their pursuit of the right irrespective of the amount of suffering involved. The actors did not stop to think whether ignorant people would not have involuntarily to suffer. Why should we expect to write our history differently? It is possible for us, if we would, to learn from the mistakes of our predecessors to do better, but it is impossible to do away with the law of suffering which is the one indispensable condition of our being. The way to do better is to avoid, if we can, violence from our side and thus quicken the rate of progress and to introduce greater purity in the methods of suffering. We can, if we will, refrain, in our impatience, from bending the wrong-doer to our will by physical force as Sinn Feiners are doing today, or from coercing our neighbours to follow our methods as was done last year by some of us in bringing about *hartal*. Progress is to be measured by the amount of suffering undergone by the sufferer. The purer the suffering, the greater is the progress. Hence did the sacrifice of Jesus suffice to free a sorrowing world. In his onward march he did not count the cost of suffering entailed upon his neighbours whether it was undergone by them voluntarily or otherwise. Thus did the sufferings of a Harishchandra

---

*As the atom, so the universe.

suffice to re-establish the kingdom of truth. He must have known that his subjects would suffer involuntarily by his abdication. He did not mind because he could not do otherwise than follow truth.

I have already stated that I do not deplore the massacre of Jalianwala Bagh so much as I deplore the murders of Englishmen and destruction of property by ourselves. The frightfulness at Amritsar drew away public attention from the greater though slower frightfulness at Lahore where attempt was made to emasculate the inhabitants by slow processes. But before we rise higher we shall have to undergo such processes many more times till they teach us to take up suffering voluntarily and to find joy in it. I am convinced that the Lahorians never deserved the cruel insults that they were subjected to; they never hurt a single Englishman; they never destroyed any property. But a willful ruler was determined to crush the spirit of a people just trying to throw off his chafing yoke. And if I am told that all this was due to my preaching Satyagraha, my answer is that I would preach Satyagraha all the more forcibly for that so long as I have breath left in me, and tell the people that next time they would answer O'Dwyer's insolence not by opening shops by reason of threats of forcible sales but by allowing the tyrant to do his worst and let him sell their all but their unconquerable souls. Sages of old mortified the flesh so that the spirit within might be set free, so that their trained bodies might be proof against any injury that might be inflicted on them by tyrants seeking to impose their will on them. And if India wishes to revive her ancient wisdom and to avoid the errors of Europe, if India wishes to see the Kingdom of God established on earth instead of that of Satan which has enveloped Europe, then I would urge her sons and daughters not to be deceived by fine phrases, the terrible subtleties that hedge us in, the fears of suffering that India may have to undergo, but to see what is happening today in Europe and from it understand that we must go through suffering even as Europe has gone through, but not the process of making others suffer. Germany wanted to dominate Europe and the Allies wanted to do likewise by crushing Germany. Europe is no better for Germany's fall. The Allies have proved themselves to be just as deceitful, cruel, greedy and selfish as Germany was or would have been. Germany would have avoided the sanctimonious humbug that one sees associated with the many dealings of the Allies.

The miscalculation that I deplored last year was not in connection with the sufferings imposed upon the people, but about the mistakes made by them and violence done by them owing to their not having sufficiently understood the message of Satyagraha. What then is the meaning of non-co-operation in terms of the law of suffering? We must voluntarily put up with the losses and inconveniences that arise from having to withdraw our support from a Government that is ruling against our will. Possession of power and riches is a crime under an unjust Government, poverty in that case is a virtue, says Thoreau. It may be that in the transition state we may make mistakes; there may be avoidable suffering. These things are preferable to national emasculation.

We must refuse to wait for the wrong to be righted till the wrong-doer has been roused to a sense of his iniquity. We must not, for fear of ourselves or others having to suffer, remain participators in it. But we must combat the wrong by ceasing to assist the wrong-doer directly or indirectly.

If a father does an injustice it is the duty of his children to leave the parental roof. If the headmaster of a school conducts his institution on an immoral basis, the pupils must leave the school. If the chairman of a corporation is corrupt the members thereof must wash their hands clean of his corruption by withdrawing from it; even so if a Government does a grave injustice the subjects must withdraw co-operation wholly or partially, sufficiently to wean the ruler from his wickedness. In each case conceived by me there is an element of suffering whether mental or physical. Without such suffering it is not possible to attain freedom.[2]

How to Work Non-Co-Operation

Perhaps the best way of answering the fears and criticism as to non-co-operation is to elaborate more fully the scheme of non-co-operation. The critics seem to imagine that the organizers propose to give effect to the whole scheme at once. The fact however is that the organizers have fixed definite, progressive four stages. The first is the giving up of titles and resignation of honorary posts. If there is no response or if the response received is not effective, recourse will be had to the second stage. The second stage involves much previous arrangement. Certainly not a single servant will be called out unless he is either capable of supporting himself and his dependents or the Khilafat Committee is able to bear the burden. All the classes of servants will not be called out at once and never will any pressure be put upon a single servant to withdraw himself from Government service. Nor will a single private employee be touched, for the simple reason that the movement is not anti-English. It is not even anti-Government. Co-operation is to be withdrawn because the people must not be party to a wrong—a broken pledge—a violation of deep religious sentiment. Naturally, the movement will receive a check, if there is any undue influence brought to bear upon any Government servant, or if any violence is used or countenanced by any member of the Khilafat Committee. The second stage must be entirely successful, if the response is at all on an adequate scale. For no Government—much less the Indian Government—can subsist if the people cease to serve it. The withdrawal therefore of the police and the military—the third stage—is a distant goal. The organizers however wanted to be fair, open and above suspicion. They did not want to keep back from Government or the public a single step they had in contemplation even as a remote contingency. The fourth, i.e. suspension of taxes, is still more remote. The organizers recognize that suspension of general taxation is fraught with the greatest danger. It is likely to bring a sensitive class in conflict with the police. They are therefore not likely to embark upon it, unless they can do so with the assurance that there will be no violence offered by the people.

I admit, as I have already done, that non-co-operation is not unattended with risk, but the risk of supineness in the face of a grave issue is infinitely greater than the danger of violence ensuing from organizing non-co-operation. To do nothing is to invite violence for a certainty.

It is easy enough to pass resolutions or write articles condemning non-co-operation. But it is no easy task to restrain the fury of a people incensed by a deep sense of wrong. I urge those who talk or work against non-co-operation to descend from their chairs and go down to the people, learn their feelings and write, if they have the heart, against non-co-operation. They will find, as I have found, that the only way to avoid violence is to enable them to give such expression to their feelings as to compel redress. I have found nothing save non-co-operation. It is logical and harmless. It is the inherent right of a subject to refuse to assist a government that will not listen to him.

Non-co-operation as a voluntary movement can only succeed, if the feeling is genuine and strong enough to make people suffer to the utmost. If the religious sentiment of the Mohammedans is deeply hurt and if the Hindus entertain neighbourly regard towards their Muslim brethren, they both will count no cost too great for achieving the end. Non-co-operation will not only be an effective remedy but will also be an effective test of the sincerity of the Muslim claim and the Hindu profession of friendship.[3]

How and When to Act

The following is a statement issued by the Non-co-operation Committee for public information and guidance:

Many questions have been asked of the Non-co-operation Committee as to its expectation and the methods to be adopted for beginning non-co-operation.

The Committee wish it to be understood that whilst they expect every one to respond to their recommendation to the full, they are desirous of carrying the weakest members also with them. The Committee want to enlist the passive sympathy, if not the active co-operation, of the whole of the country in the method of non-co-operation.

Those, therefore, who cannot undergo physical sacrifice will help by contributing funds or labour to the movement.

Should non-co-operation become necessary, the Committee has decided upon the following as part of the first stage:

1. Surrender of all titles of honour and honorary offices.

2. Non-participation in Government loans.

3. Suspension by lawyers of practice and settlement of civil disputes by private arbitration.

4. Boycott of Government schools by parents.

5. Boycott of the Reformed Councils.

6. Non-participation in Government parties, and such other functions.

7. Refusal to accept any civil or military post, in Mesopotamia, or to offer as Units for the army especially for service in the Turkish territories now being administered in violation of pledges.

8. Vigorous prosecution of Swadeshi, inducing the people, at the time of this national and religious awakening, to appreciate their primary duty to their country by being satisfied with its own productions and manufactures.

Swadeshi must be pushed forward without waiting for the 1st of August, for it is an eternal rule of conduct not to be interrupted even when the settlement arrives.

In order not to commit themselves, people will refrain now from taking service either civil or military. They will also suspend taking Government loans, new or old.

For the rest, it should be remembered that non-co-operation does not commence before 1st August next.

Every effort is being, and will still be, made to avoid resort to such a serious breach with the Government by urging His Majesty's Ministers to secure the revision of a Treaty which has been so universally condemned.

Those who realize their responsibility and gravity of the cause will not act independently, but in concert with the Committee. Success depends entirely upon disciplined and concerted non-co-operation and the later is dependent upon strict obedience to instructions, calmness and absolute freedom from violence.[4]

. . .

Non-Violence and Swadeshi

Before a crowded meeting of Mussalmans in the Muzaffarabad at Bombay held on the 29th July, speaking on the impending non-co-operation which commenced on the 1st of August, Mr. Gandhi said the time for speeches on non-co-operation was past and the time for practice had arrived. But two things were needful for complete success: an environment free from any violence on the part of the people and a spirit of self-sacrifice. Non-co-operation, as the speaker had conceived it, was an impossibility in an atmosphere surcharged with the spirit of violence. Violence was an exhibition of anger and any such exhibition was dissipation of valuable energy. Subduing of one's anger was a storing up of national energy, which, when set free in an ordered manner, would produce astounding results. His conception of non-co-operation did not involve rapine, plunder, incendiarism and all the concomitants of mass madness. His scheme presupposed ability on their part to control all the forces of evil. If, therefore, any disorderliness was found on the part of the people which they could not control, he for one would certainly help the Government to control them. In the presence of disorder it would be for him a choice of evil, and evil though he considered the present Government to be, he would not hesitate for the time being to help the Government to control disorder. But he had faith in the people. He believed that they knew that the cause could only be won by non-violent methods. To put it at the lowest, the people had not the power, even if they had the will, to resist with brute strength the unjust Governments of Europe who had, in the intoxication of their success, disregarding every canon of justice, dealt so cruelly by the only Islamic Power in Europe.

Matchless Weapon

In non-co-operation they had a matchless and powerful weapon. It was a sign of religious atrophy to sustain an unjust Government that supported an injustice by resorting to untruth and camouflage. So long therefore as the Government did not purge itself of the canker of injustice and untruth, it was their duty to withdraw all help from it, consistently with their ability to preserve order in the social structure. The first stage of non-co-operation was, therefore, so arranged as to involve minimum of danger to public peace and minimum of sacrifice on the part of those who participated in the movement. And if they might not help an evil Government nor receive any favours from it, it followed that they must give up all titles of honour which were no longer a proud possession. Lawyers, who were in reality honorary officers of the Court, should cease to support Courts that upheld the prestige of an unjust Government and the people must be able to settle their disputes and quarrels by private arbitration. Similarly, parents should withdraw their children from the public schools and they must evolve a system of national education or private education totally independent of the Government. An insolent Government, conscious of its brute strength, might laugh at such withdrawals by the people especially as the Law Courts and schools were supposed to help the people, but he had not a shadow of doubt that the moral effect of such a step could not possibly be lost even upon a Government whose conscience had become stifled by the intoxication of power.

Swadeshi

He had hesitation in accepting Swadeshi as a plank in non-co-operation. To him Swadeshi was as dear as life itself. But he had no desire to smuggle in Swadeshi through the Khilafat movement, if it could not legitimately help that movement. But conceived as non-co-operation was in a spirit of self-sacrifice, Swadeshi had a legitimate place in the movement. Pure Swadeshi meant sacrifice of their liking for fineries. He asked the nation to sacrifice its liking for the fineries of Europe and Japan and be satisfied with the coarse but beautiful fabrics woven on their handlooms out of yarns spun by millions of their sisters. If the nation had become really awakened to a sense of the danger to its religions and its self-respect, it could not but perceive the absolute and immediate necessity of the adoption of Swadeshi in its intense form, and if the people of India adopted Swadeshi with religious zeal he begged to assure them that its adoption would arm them with a new power and would produce an unmistakable impression throughout the whole world. He, therefore, expected the Mussalmans to give the lead by giving up all the fineries they were so fond of and adopt the simple cloth that could be produced by the manual labour of their sisters and brethren in their own cottages. And he hoped that the Hindus would follow suit. It was a sacrifice in which the whole nation, every man, woman and child, could take part.[5]

Programme for Satyagraha

[From a letter written by Gandhiji to Hakim Ajmal Khan from Sabarmatl Jail, dated 12th March, 1922.]

A staunch Mussalman, you have shown in your own life what Hindu–Muslim unity means.

We all now realize, as we have never before realized, that without that unity we cannot attain our freedom, and I make bold to say that without that unity the Mussalmans of India cannot render the Khilafat all the aid they wish. Divided, we must ever remain slaves. This unity, therefore, cannot be a mere policy to be discarded when it does not suit us. We can discard it only when we are tired of Swaraj. Hindu–Muslim unity must be our creed to last for all time and under all circumstances.

Nor must that unity be a menace to the minorities — the Parsees, the Christians, the Jews or the powerful Sikhs. If we seek to crush any of them, we shall some day want to fight each other.

I have been drawn so close to you chiefly because I know that you believe in Hindu–Muslim unity in the full sense of the term.

This unity, in my opinion, is unattainable without our adopting non-violence as a firm policy. I call it a policy because it is limited to the preservation of that unity. But it follows that thirty crores of Hindus and Mussalmans, united not for a time but for all time, can defy all the powers of the world and should consider it a cowardly act to resort to violence in their dealings with the English administrators. We have hitherto feared them and their guns in our simplicity. The moment we realize our combined strength, we shall consider it unmanly to fear them and, therefore, ever to think of striking them. Hence am I anxious and impatient to persuade my countrymen to feel non-violent, not out of our weakness but out of our strength. But you and I know that we have not yet evolved the non-violence of the strong. And we have not done so, because the Hindu–Muslim union has not gone much beyond the stage of policy. There is still too much mutual distrust and consequent fear. I am not disappointed. The progress we have made in that direction is indeed phenomenal. We seem to have covered in eighteen months' time the work of a generation. But infinitely more is necessary. Neither the classes nor the masses feel instinctively that our union is necessary as the breath of our nostrils.

For this consummation we must, it seems to me, rely more upon quality than quantity. Given a sufficient number of Hindus and Mussalmans with almost a fanatical faith in everlasting friendship between the Hindus and the Mussalmans of India, we shall not be long before the unity permeates the masses. A few of us must first clearly understand that we can make no headway without accepting non-violence in thought, word and deed for the full realization of our political ambition. I would, therefore, beseech you and the members of the Working Committee and the All-India Congress Committee to see that our ranks contain no workers who do not fully realize the essential truth I have endeavoured to place before you. A living faith cannot be manufactured by the rule of majority.

To me the visible symbol of all-India unity and, therefore, of the acceptance of non-violence as an indispensable means for the realization of our political ambition is undoubtedly the *charkha,* i.e. khaddar. Only those who believe in *cultivating* a non-violent spirit and eternal friendship between Hindus and Mussalmans will daily and religiously spin. Universal hand-spinning and the universal manufacture and use of hand-spun and hand-woven khaddar will be a substantial, if not absolute, proof of real unity and non-violence. And it will be a recognition of a living kinship with the dumb masses. Nothing can possibly unify and revivify India as the acceptance by all India of the spinning wheel as a daily sacrament and khaddar wear as a privilege and a duty.

Whilst, therefore, I am anxious that more title-holders should give up their titles, lawyers law-courts, scholars Government schools or college, Councillors the Councils, and the soldiers and the civilians their posts, I would urge the nation to restrict its activity in this direction only to the consolidation of the results already achieved and to trust its strength to command further abstentions from association with a system we are seeking to mend or end.

Moreover, the workers are too few. I would not waste a single worker today on destructive work when we have such an enormous amount of constructive work. But perhaps the most conclusive argument against devoting further time to destructive propaganda is the fact that the spirit of intolerance which is a form of violence has never been so rampant as now. Co-operators are estranged from us; they fear us. They say that we are establishing a worse bureaucracy than the existing one. We must remove every cause for such anxiety. We must go out of our way to win them to our side. We must make Englishmen safe from all harm from our side. I should not have to labour the point, if it was clear to every one as it is to you and to me that our pledge of non-violence implies utter humility and goodwill even towards our bitterest opponent. This necessary spirit will be automatically realized, if only India will devote her sole attention to the work of construction suggested by me.

I flatter myself with the belief that my imprisonment is quite enough for a long time to come. I believe in all humility that I have no ill-will against any one. Some of my friends would not have to be as non-violent as I am. But we contemplated the imprisonment of the most innocent. If I may be allowed that claim, it is clear that I should not be followed to prison by anybody at all. We do want to paralyze the Government considered as a system — not, however, by intimidation, but by the irresistible pressure of our innocence. In my opinion it would be intimidation to fill the jails anyhow. And why should more innocent men seek imprisonment till one considered to be the most innocent has been found inadequate for the purpose.

My caution against further courting of imprisonment does not mean that we are now to shirk imprisonment. If the Government will take away every *non-violent* non-co-operator, I should welcome it. Only it should not be because of our civil disobedience, defensive or aggressive. Nor, I hope, will the country fret over those who are in jail. It will do them and the country good to serve the full term of their imprisonment. They can be fitly discharged before their time only by an act of the Swaraj Parliament. And I entertain an absolute conviction that universal adoption of khaddar is Swaraj.

I have refrained from mentioning untouchability. I am sure every good Hindu believes that it has got to go. Its removal is as necessary as the realization of Hindu–Muslim unity.

I have placed before you a programme which is in my opinion the quickest and the best. No impatient Khilafatist can devise a better. May God give you health and wisdom to guide the country to her destined goal.[6]

. . .

More Objections Answered

I do not know from where the information has been derived that I have given up the last two stages of non-co-operation. What I have said is that they are a distant goal. I abide by it. I admit that all the stages are fraught with some danger but the last two are fraught with the greatest — the last most of all. The stages have been fixed with a view to running the least possible risk. The last two stages will not be taken up unless the Committee has attained sufficient control over the people to warrant the belief that the laying down of arms or suspension of taxes will, humanly speaking be free from an outbreak of violence on the part of the people. I do entertain the belief that it is possible for the people to attain the discipline necessary for taking the two steps. When once they realize that violence is totally unnecessary to bend an unwilling Government to their will and that the result can be obtained with certainty by dignified non-co-operation, they will cease to think of violence even by way of retaliation. The fact is that hitherto we have not attempted to take concerted and disciplined action from the masses. Some day, if we are to become truly a self-governing nation, that has to be made. The present, in my opinion, is a propitious movement. Every Indian feels the insult to the Punjab as a personal wrong, every Mussalman resents the wrong done to the Khilafat. There is, therefore, a favourable atmosphere for expecting cohesive and restrained movement on the part of the masses.

So far as response is concerned, I agree with the Editor that the quickest and the largest response is to be expected in the matter of suspension of payment of taxes, but as I have said, so long as the masses are not educated to appreciate the value of non-violence even whilst their holdings are being sold, so long must it be difficult to take up the last stage into any appreciable extent.

I agree too that a sudden withdrawal of the military and the police will be a disaster if we have not acquired the ability to protect ourselves against robbers and thieves. But I suggest that when we are ready to call out the military and the police on an extensive scale, we would find ourselves in a position to defend ourselves. If the police and the military resign from patriotic motives, I would certainly expect them to perform the same duty as national volunteers, not as hirelings but as willing protectors of the life and liberty of their countrymen. The movement of non-co-operation is one of automatic adjustment. If the Government schools are emptied, I would certainly expect national schools to come into being. If the lawyers as a whole suspended practice, they would devise arbitration courts and the nation will have expeditious and cheaper method of settling private disputes and awarding punishment to the wrong-doer. I may add that the Khilafat Committee is fully alive to the difficulty of the task and is taking all the necessary steps to meet the contingencies as they arise.

Regarding the leaving of civil employment, no danger is feared, because no one will leave his employment, unless he is in a position to find support for himself and family either through friends or otherwise.

Disapproval of the proposed withdrawal of students betrays, in my humble opinion, lack of appreciation of the true nature of non-co-operation. It is true enough that we pay the money wherewith our children are educated. But when the agency imparting the education has become corrupt, we may not employ it without partaking of the agent's corruption. When students leave schools or colleges I hardly imagine that the teachers will fail to perceive the advisability of themselves resigning. But even if they do not, money can hardly be allowed to count where honour or religion are the stake.

As to the boycott of the councils, it is not the entry of the Moderates or any other persons that matters so much as the entry of those who believe in non-co-operation. You may not co-operate at the top and non-co-operate at the bottom. A councillor cannot remain in the council and ask the *gumasta* who cleans the council table to resign.[7]

Answers to Questions

My experience of last year shows me that in spite of aberrations in some parts of India, the country was entirely under control, that the influence of Satyagraha was profoundly for its good and that where violence did break out, there were local causes that directly contributed to it. At the same time I admit that even the violence that did take place on the part of the people and the spirit of lawlessness that was undoubtedly shown in some parts should have remained under check. I have made ample acknowledgment of the miscalculation I then made. But all the painful experience that I then gained did not in any way shake my belief in Satyagraha or in the possibility of that matchless force being utilized in India. Ample provision is being made this time to avoid the mistakes of the past. But I must refuse to be deterred from a clear course because it may be attended by violence totally unintended and in spite of extraordinary efforts that are being made to prevent it. At the same time I must make my position clear. Nothing can possibly prevent a Satyagrahi from doing his duty because of the frown of the authorities. I would risk, if necessary, a million lives so long as they are voluntary sufferers and are innocent, spotless victims. It is the mistakes of the people that matter in a Satyagraha campaign. Mistakes, even insanity must be expected from the strong and the powerful, and the moment of victory has come when there is no resort to the mad fury of the powerful but a voluntary, dignified and quiet submission, but not submission to the will of the authority that has put itself in the wrong. The secret of success lies, therefore, in holding every English life and the life of every officer serving the Government as sacred as those of our own dear ones. All the wonderful experience I have gained now during nearly 40 years of conscious existence, has convinced me that there is no gift so precious as that of life. I make bold to say that the moment Englishmen feel that although they are in India in a hopeless minority, their lives are protected against harm not because of the matchless weapons of destruction which are at their disposal, but because Indians refuse to take the lives even of those whom they may consider to be utterly in the wrong, that moment will see a transformation in the English nature in its relation to India, and that moment will also be the moment when all the destructive cutlery that is to be had in India will begin to rust. I know that this is a far-off vision. That cannot matter to me. It is enough for me to see the light and to act up to it, and it is more than enough when I gain companions in the onward march. I have claimed in private conversations with English friends that it is because of my incessant preaching of the gospel of non-violence and my having successfully demonstrated its practical utility that so far the forces of violence, which are undoubtedly in existence in connection with the Khilafat movement, have remained under complete control.

I consider non-co-operation to be such a powerful and pure instrument, that if it is enforced in an earnest spirit, it will be like seeking first the Kingdom of God and everything else following as a matter of course. People will have then realized their true power. They would have learnt the value of discipline, self-control, joint action, non-violence, organization and everything else that goes to make a nation great and good, and not merely great.

I do not know that I have a right to arrogate greater purity for myself than for our Mussalman brethren. But I do admit that they do not believe in my doctrine of non-violence to the full extent. For them it is a weapon of the weak, an expedient. They consider non-co-operation without violence to be the only thing open to them in the way of direct action. I know that if some of them could offer successful violence, they would today. But they are convinced that humanly speaking it is an impossibility. For them, therefore, non-co-operation is a matter not merely of duty but also of revenge. Whereas I take up non-co-operation against the Government as I have actually taken it up in practice against members of my own family. I entertain very high regard for the British Constitution. I have not only no enmity against Englishmen but I regard much in English character as worthy of my emulation. I count many as my friends. It is against my religion to regard any one as an enemy. I entertain similar sentiments with respect to Mohammedans. I find their cause to be just and pure. Although therefore their view-point is different from mine I do not hesitate to associate with them and invite them to give my method a trial, for, I believe that the use of a pure weapon even from a mistaken motive does not fail to produce some good, even as the telling of truth, if only because for the time being it is the best policy, is at least so much to the good.[8]

Non-Co-Operation Explained

A representative of this journal[9] called on Mr. M. K. Gandhi yesterday at his temporary residence in the Pursewalkum High Road for an interview on the subject of non-co-operation. Mr. Gandhi, who has come to Madras on a tour to some of the principal Muslim centres in Southern India, was busy with a number of workers discussing his programme; but he expressed his readiness to answer questions on the chief topic which is agitating Muslims and Hindus.

"After your experience of the Satyagraha agitation last year, Mr. Gandhi, are you still hopeful and convinced of the wisdom of advising non-co-operation?"

"Certainly."

"How do you consider conditions have altered since the Satyagraha movement of last year?"

"I consider that people are better disciplined now than they were before. In this I include even the masses whom I have had opportunities of seeing in large numbers in various parts of the country."

"And you are satisfied that the masses understand the spirit of Satyagraha?"

"Yes."

"And that is why you are pressing on with the programme of non-co-operation?"

"Yes. Moreover, the danger that attended the civil-disobedience part of Satyagraha does not apply to non-co-operation, because in non-co-operation we are not taking up civil disobedience of laws as a mass movement. The result hitherto has been most encouraging. For instance, people in Sindh and Delhi, in spite of the irritating restrictions upon their liberty by the authorities, have carried out the Committee's instructions in regard to the Seditious Meetings Proclamation and to the prohibition of posting placards on the walls which we hold to be inoffensive but which the authorities consider to be offensive."

"What is the pressure which you expect to bring to bear on the authorities if co-operation is withdrawn?"

"I believe, and everybody must grant, that no Government can exist for a single moment without the co-operation of the people, willing or forced, and if people suddenly withdraw their co-operation in every detail, the Government will come to a stand-still."

"But is there not a big 'If' in it?"

"Certainly, there is."

"And how do you propose to succeed against the big 'If'?"

"In my plan of campaign expediency has no room. If the Khilafat movement has really permeated the masses and the classes, there must be adequate response from the people."

"But are you not begging the question?"

"I am not begging the question, because so far as the data before me go, I believe that the Muslims keenly feel the Khilafat grievance. It remains to be seen whether their feeling is intense enough to evoke in them the measure of sacrifice adequate for successful non-co-operation."

"That is, your survey of the conditions, you think, justifies your advising non-co-operation in the full conviction that you have behind you the support of the vast masses of the Mussalman population?"

"Yes."

"This non-co-operation, you are satisfied, will extend to complete severance of co-operation with the Government?"

"No; nor is it at the present moment my desire that it should. I am simply practising non-co-operation to the extent that is necessary to make the Government realize the depth of popular feeling in the matter and the dissatisfaction with the Government that all that could be done has not been done either by the Government of India or by the Imperial Government, whether on the Khilafat question or on the Punjab question."

"Do you, Mr. Gandhi, realize that even amongst Mohammedans there are sections of people who are not enthusiastic over non-co-operation however much they may feel the wrong that has been done to their community?"

"Yes, but their number is smaller than those who are prepared to adopt non-co-operation."

"And yet does not the fact that there has not been an adequate response to your appeal for resignation of titles and offices and for boycott of elections of the Councils indicate that you may be placing more faith in their strength of conviction than is warranted?"

"I think not; for the reason that the stage has only just come into operation and our people are always most cautious and slow to move. Moreover, the first stage largely affects the uppermost strata of society, who represent a microscopic minority though they are undoubtedly an influential body of people."

"This upper class, you think, has sufficiently responded to your appeal?"

"I am unable to say either one way or the other at present. I shall be able to give a definite answer at the end of this month."

"Do you think that without one's loyalty to the King and the Royal Family being questioned, one can advocate non-co-operation in connection with the Royal visit?"

"Most decidedly; for the simple reason that if there is any disloyalty about the proposed boycott of the Prince's visit, it is disloyalty to the Government of the day and not to the person of His Royal Highness."

"What do you think is to be gained by promoting this boycott in connection with the Royal visit?"

"I want to show that the people of India are not in sympathy with the Government of the day and that they strongly disapprove of the policy of the Government in regard to the Punjab and Khilafat, and even in respect of other important administrative measures. I consider that the visit of the Prince of Wales is a singularly good opportunity to the people to show their disapproval of the present Government. After all, the visit is calculated to have tremendous political results. It is not to be a non-political event, and seeing that the Government of India and the Imperial Government want to make the visit a political event of first-class importance, namely, for the purpose of strengthening their hold upon India, I for one consider that it is the bounden duty of the people to boycott the visit which is being engineered by the two Governments in their own interest which at the present moment is totally antagonistic to the people."

"Do you mean that you want this boycott promoted because you feel that the strengthening of the

hold upon India is not desirable in the best interests of the country?"

"Yes. The strengthening of the hold of a Government so wicked as the present one is not desirable for the best interests of the people. Not that I want the bond between England and India to become loosened for the sake of loosening it, but I want that bond to become strengthened only in so far as it adds to the welfare of India."

"Do you think that non-co-operation and the non-boycott of the Legislative Councils are consistent?"

"No; because a person who takes up the programme of non-co-operation cannot consistently stand for Councils."

"Is non-co-operation, in your opinion, an end in itself or a means to an end, and if so, what is the end?"

"It is a means to an end, the end being to make the present Government just, whereas it has become mostly unjust. Co-operation with a just Government is a duty; non-co-operation with an unjust Government is equally a duty."

"Will you look with favour upon the proposal to enter the Councils and to carry on either obstructive tactics or to decline to take the oath of allegiance as consistent with your non-co-operation?"

"No; as an accurate student of non-co-operation, I consider that such a proposal is inconsistent with the true spirit of non-co-operation. I have often said that a Government really thrives on obstruction, and so far as the proposal not to take the oath of allegiance is concerned, I can really see no meaning in it; it amounts to a useless waste of valuable time and money."

"In other words, obstruction is no stage in non-co-operation?"

"No."

"Are you satisfied that all efforts at constitutional agitation have been exhausted and that, non-co-operation is the only course left us?"

"I do not consider non-co-operation to be unconstitutional, but I do believe that of all the constitutional remedies now left open to us, non-co-operation is the only one left for us."

"Do you consider it constitutional to adopt it with a view merely to paralyze Government?"

"Certainly, it is not unconstitutional, but a prudent man will not take all the steps that are constitutional if they are otherwise undesirable, nor do I advise that course. I am resorting to non-co-operation in progressive stages because I want to evolve true order out of untrue order. I am not going to take a single step in non-co-operation unless I am satisfied that the country is ready for that step, namely, non-co-operation will not be followed by anarchy or disorder."

"How will you satisfy yourself that anarchy will not follow?"

"For instance, if I advise the police to lay down their arms, I shall have satisfied myself that we are able by voluntary assistance to protect ourselves against thieves and robbers. That was precisely what was done in Lahore and Amritsar last year by the citizens by means of volunteers when the military and the police had withdrawn. Even where Government had not taken such measures in a place, for want of adequate force, I know people have successfully protected themselves."

"You have advised lawyers to non-co-operate by suspending their practice. What is your experience? Has the lawyers' response to your appeal encouraged you to hope that you will be able to carry through all stages of non-co-operation with the help of such people?"

"I cannot say that a large number has yet responded to my appeal. It is too early to say how many will respond. But I may say that I do not rely merely upon the lawyer class or highly educated men to enable the Committee to carry out all the stages of non-co-operation. My hope lies more with the masses so far as the later stages of non-co-operation are concerned."

Love

I accept the interpretation of *ahimsa*, namely, that it is not merely a negative state of harmlessness but it is a positive state of love, of doing good even to the evil-doer. But it does not mean helping the evil-doer to continue the wrong or tolerating it by passive acquiescence. On the contrary, love, the active state of *ahimsa*, requires you to resist the wrong-doer by dissociating yourself from him even though it may offend him or injure him physically. Thus if my son lives

a life of shame, I may not help him to do so by continuing to support him; on the contrary, my love for him requires me to withdraw all support from him although it may mean even his death. And the same love imposes on me the obligation of welcoming him to my bosom when he repents. But I may not by physical force compel my son to become good. That in my opinion is the moral of the story of the Prodigal Son.

Non-co-operation is not a passive state, it is an intensely active state — more active than physical resistance or violence. Passive resistance is a misnomer. Non-co-operation in the sense used by me must be non-violent and, therefore, neither punitive nor vindictive nor based on malice, ill-will or hatred. It follows therefore that it would be sin for me to serve General Dyer and co-operate with him to shoot innocent men. But it will be an exercise of forgiveness or love for me to nurse him back to life, if he was suffering from a physical malady. I would co-operate a thousand times with this Government to wean it from its career of crime, but I will not for a single moment co-operate with it to continue that career. And I would be guilty of wrong-doing if I retained a title from it or "a service under it or supported its Law Courts or schools." Better for me a beggar's bowl than the richest possession from hands stained with the blood of the innocents of Jalianwala. Better by far a warrant of imprisonment than honeyed words from those who have wantonly wounded the religious sentiment of my seventy million brothers.[10]

. . .

The Non-Co-Operation of a Satyagrahi

Q: It has been suggested in Bombay that you went to the Governor uninvited, in fact you forced yourself upon his attention. If so, was it not co-operation even without response? What could you have to do with the Governor, I wonder?

A: My answer is that I am quite capable even of forcing myself upon the attention of my opponent when I have strength. I did so in South Africa. I sought interviews after interviews with General Smuts when I knew that I was ready for battle. I pleaded with him to avoid the untold hardships that the Indian settlers must suffer, if the great historic march had to be undertaken. It is true that he in his haughtiness turned a deaf ear; but I lost nothing. I gained added strength by my humility. So would I do in India when we are strong enough to put a real fight for freedom. Remember that ours is a non-violent struggle. It pre-supposes humility. It is a truthful struggle and consciousness of truth should give us firmness. We are not out to destroy men. We own no enemy. We have no ill-will against a single soul on earth. We mean to convert by our suffering. I do not despair of converting the hardest-hearted or the most selfish Englishman. Every opportunity of meeting him is, therefore, welcome to me.

Let me distinguish. Non-violent non-co-operation means renunciation of the benefits of a system with which we non-co-operate. We, therefore, renounce the benefits of schools, courts, titles, legislatures and offices set up under the system. The most extensive and permanent part of our non-co-operation consists in the renunciation of foreign cloth which is the foundation for the vicious system that is crushing us to dust. It is possible to think of other items of non-co-operation. But owing to our weakness or want of ability, we have restricted ourselves to these items only. If then I go to any official for the purpose of seeking the benefits above-named, I co-operate. Whereas if I go to the meanest official for the purpose of converting him, say to khaddar, or weaning him from his service or persuading him to withdraw his children from Government schools, I fulfil my duty as a non-co-operator. I should fail, if I did not go to him with that definite and direct purpose.[11]

Civil Disobedience

Civil disobedience was on the lips of every one of the members of the All India Congress Committee. Not having really ever tried it, every one appeared to be enamoured of it from a mistaken belief in it as a sovereign remedy for our present-day ills. I feel sure that it can be made such if we can produce the necessary atmosphere for it. For individuals there always is that atmosphere except when their civil disobedience is certain to lead to bloodshed. I discovered this exception during the Satyagraha days. But even so a call may come which one dare not neglect, cost it what it may. I can clearly see the time coming to me when

I *must* refuse obedience to every single State-made law, even though there may be a certainty of bloodshed. When neglect of the call means a denial of God, civil disobedience becomes a peremptory duty.

Mass civil disobedience stands on a different footing. It can only be tried in a calm atmosphere. It must be the calmness of strength not weakness, of knowledge not ignorance. Individual civil disobedience may be and often is vicarious. Mass civil disobedience may be and often is selfish in the sense that individuals expect personal gain from their disobedience. Thus in South Africa, Kallenbach and Polak offered vicarious civil disobedience. They had nothing to gain. Thousands offered it because they expected personal gain also in the shape, say, of the removal of the annual poll-tax levied upon ex-indentured men and their wives and grown-up children. It is sufficient in mass civil disobedience if the resisters understand the working of the doctrine.

It was in a practically uninhabited tract of country that I was arrested in South Africa when I was marching into prohibited area with over two to three thousand men and some women. The company included several Pathans and others who were able-bodied men. It was the greatest testimony of merit the Government of South Africa gave to the movement. They knew that we were as harmless as we were determined. It was easy enough for that body of men to cut to pieces those who arrested me. It would have not only been a most cowardly thing to do, but it would have been a treacherous breach of their own pledge, and it would have meant ruin to the struggle for freedom and the forcible deportation of every Indian from South Africa. But the men were no rabble. They were disciplined soldiers and all the better for being unarmed. Though I was torn from them, they did not disperse, nor did they turn back. They marched on to their destination till they were, every one of them, arrested and imprisoned. So far as I am aware, this was an instance of discipline and non-violence for which there is no parallel in history. Without such restraint I see no hope of successful mass civil disobedience here.

We must dismiss the idea of overawing the Government by huge demonstrations every time some one is arrested. On the contrary, we must treat arrest as the normal condition of the life of a non-co-operator. For we must seek arrest and imprisonment, as a soldier who goes to battle seeks death. We expect to bear down the opposition of the Government by courting and not by avoiding imprisonment, even though it be by showing our supposed readiness to be arrested and imprisoned *en masse*. Civil disobedience then emphatically means our desire to surrender to a single unarmed policeman. Our triumph consists in thousands being led to the prisons like lambs to the slaughter house. If the lambs of the world had been willingly led, they would have long ago saved themselves from the butcher's knife. Our triumph consists again in being imprisoned for no wrong whatsoever. The greater our innocence, the greater our strength and the swifter our victory.

As it is, this Government is cowardly, we are afraid of imprisonment. The Government takes advantage of our fear of gaols. If only our men and women welcome gaols as health-resorts, we will cease to worry about the dear ones put in gaols which our countrymen in South Africa used to nickname His Majesty's Hotels.

We have too long been mentally disobedient to the laws of the State and have too often surreptitiously evaded them, to be fit all of a sudden for civil disobedience. Disobedience to be civil has to be open and non-violent.

Complete civil disobedience is a state of peaceful rebellion—a refusal to obey every single State-made law. It is certainly more dangerous than an armed rebellion. For it can never be put down if the civil resisters are prepared to face extreme hardships. It is based upon an implicit belief in the absolute efficiency of innocent suffering. By noiselessly going to prison a civil resister ensures a calm atmosphere. The wrong-doer wearies of wrong-doing in the absence of resistance. All pleasure is lost when the victim betrays no resistance. A full grasp of the conditions of successful civil resistance is necessary at least on the part of the representatives of the people before we can launch out on an enterprise of such magnitude. The quickest remedies are always fraught with the greatest danger and require the utmost skill in handling them. It is my firm conviction that if we bring about a successful boycott of foreign cloth, we shall have produced an atmosphere that would enable us to in-

augurate civil disobedience on a scale that no Government can resist. I would, therefore, urge patience and determined concentration on Swadeshi upon those who are impatient to embark on mass civil disobedience.[12]

Civil Disobedience

We dare not pin our faith solely on civil disobedience. It is like the use of a knife to be used most sparingly if at all. A man who cuts away without ceasing cuts at the very root, and finds himself without the substance he was trying to reach by cutting off the superficial hard crust. The use of civil disobedience will be healthy, necessary, and effective only if we otherwise conform to the laws of all growth. We must therefore give its full and therefore greater value to the adjective 'civil' than to 'disobedience.' Disobedience without civility, discipline, discrimination, non-violence is certain destruction. Disobedience combined with love is the living water of life. Civil disobedience is a beautiful variant to signify growth, it is not discordance which spells death.[13]

The Right of Civil Disobedience

I wish I could persuade everybody that civil disobedience is the inherent right of a citizen. He dare not give it up without ceasing to be a man. Civil disobedience is never followed by anarchy. Criminal disobedience can lead to it. Every State puts down criminal disobedience by force. It perishes, if it does not. But to put down civil disobedience is to attempt to imprison conscience. Civil disobedience can only lead to strength and purity. A civil resister never uses arms and hence he is harmless to a State that is at all willing to listen to the voice of public opinion. He is dangerous for an autocratic State, for he brings about its fall by engaging public opinion upon the matter for which he resists the State. Civil disobedience therefore becomes a sacred duty when the State has become lawless, or which is the same thing, corrupt. And a citizen that barters with such a State shares its corruption or lawlessness.

It is therefore possible to question the wisdom of applying civil disobedience in respect of a particular act or law; it is possible to advise delay and caution. But the right itself cannot be allowed to be questioned. It is a birthright that cannot be surrendered without surrender of one's self-respect.

At the same time that the right of civil disobedience is insisted upon, its use must be guarded by all conceivable restrictions. Every possible provision should be made against an outbreak of violence or general lawlessness. Its area as well as its scope should also be limited to the barest necessity of the case.[14]

Aggressive *v.* Defensive

It is now necessary to understand the exact distinction between aggressive civil disobedience and defensive. Aggressive, assertive or offensive civil disobedience is non-violent, wilful disobedience of laws of the State whose breach does not involve moral turpitude and which is undertaken as a symbol of revolt against the State. Thus disregard of laws relating to revenue or regulation of personal conduct for the convenience of the State, although such laws in themselves inflict no hardship and do not require to be altered, would be assertive, aggressive or offensive civil disobedience.

Defensive civil disobedience, on the other hand, is involuntary or reluctant non-violent disobedience of such laws as are in themselves bad and obedience to which would be inconsistent with one's self-respect or human dignity. Thus formation of volunteer corps for peaceful purposes, holding of public meetings for like purposes, publication of articles not contemplating or inciting to violence in spite of prohibitory orders, is defensive civil disobedience. And so is conducting of peaceful picketing undertaken with a view to wean people from things or institutions picketed in spite of orders to the contrary. The fulfilment of the conditions mentioned above is as necessary for defensive civil disobedience as for offensive civil disobedience.[15]

Notes

1. *Young India,* 12–5–'20.
2. *Young India,* 16–6–'20.
3. *Young India,* 5–5–'20.
4. *Young India,* 7–7–'20.
5. *Young India,* 4–8–'20.
6. *Young India,* 16–3–'22.
7. *Young India,* 18–8–'20.
8. *Young India,* 2–6–'20.
9. The present article is the report of a talk the representative of *The Madras Mail* had with Gandhiji. It was reproduced in the *Young India* from that paper. *Young India,* 18–8–'20.
10. *Young India,* 25–8–'20.
11. *Young India,* 27–5–'26.
12. *Young India,* 4–8–'21.
13. *Young India,* 5–1–'22.
14. *Young India,* 5–1–'22.
15. *Young India,* 9–2–'22.

PACIFISM AND CARE

Victoria Davion

In this article, Victoria Davion argues there is no pacifist commitment implied by the practice of mothering, contrary to what Ruddick suggests. Using violence in certain situations is consistent with the goals of this practice. Furthermore, she uses Ruddick's valuable analysis of the care for particular individuals involved in this practice to show why pacifism may be incompatible with caring passionately for individuals. If giving up passionate attachments to individuals is necessary for pacifist commitment, as Gandhi claims, then the price is too high. (Source: From Hypatia, *5 (1990). Reprinted with permission of the author.)*

This paper questions the relationship between the practice of mothering and care. In recent feminist literature the assumption is widespread that an ethic of care somehow implies a pacifist commitment.[1] Although this connection is usually assumed rather than argued for, Sara Ruddick argues in favor of it in "Preservative Love and Military Destruction: Some Reflections on Motherhood and Peace" (1984b). I shall examine her arguments in this paper and argue that the practice does not imply a pacifist commitment at all. Thus, because the practice of mothering exemplifies an ethic of care, I shall argue that an ethic of care need not imply a pacifist commitment at all.

In an earlier work, "Maternal Thinking," Ruddick analyzes what she calls the practice of mothering as a discipline having as its goal the production of a healthy adult (1984a). She maintains that it is possible to identify interests that seem to govern maternal practice throughout the species, which she believes are part of the discipline she calls maternal practice. In "Preservative Love and Military Destruction," Ruddick claims that the practice of mothering involves in its very nature a pacifist commitment on behalf of mothers. It involves this commitment because of the goal of producing a healthy adult. Ruddick calls the activity that mothers engage in when they attempt to fulfill this basic goal "preservative love," which is the activity of keeping a child alive and healthy in an indifferent or hostile world (1984b, 240). Because this activity involves preventing damage to the child, Ruddick argues

that it is fundamentally opposed to destruction and therefore to war. Because mothers wish to prevent damage to their children, Ruddick argues, non-violent conflict resolution is fundamental to the practice of mothering. Ruddick does not claim that all mothers are actually non-violent in practice, something which is obviously false. Rather, she claims that non-violence is a conceptual good or an ideal which is fundamental to the goals of mothering. She therefore speaks of the "pacifist commitment" which she says is part of maternal thinking.

Ruddick contrasts this so-called "pacifist commitment" with pacifism as articulated by Gandhi. She maintains that the pacifist commitment in maternal practice is based on "concrete thinking." This style of thinking involves paying attention to particular concrete situations, particular individuals and their particular needs. In contrast, Gandhian pacifism is based on abstract principles. Ruddick claims that abstraction is dangerous and can lead to war because it doesn't focus on particular individuals as individuals. It thus fails to encourage empathy. Hence, she argues that pacifists of the Gandhian variety have something to learn from the pacifist commitment in maternal thinking.

I will argue that there are really two pacifist commitments discussed in Ruddick's analysis, and that neither of them is implied by her analysis of mothering. While I find her analysis of the practice of mothering to be extremely useful and accurate, I do not think that it implies any pacifist commitment whatsoever. Rather, Ruddick's analysis can be used to show that any true pacifist commitment would be unreasonable for mothers to make, and also point to why such a commitment may be unreasonable for anyone else to make either. Thus, I think Ruddick's analysis shows something very important, but it is not what Ruddick thinks it shows. One can use Ruddick's analysis to show that the goal of protecting and preserving the life of a child can involve the use of violence, and that violence may be a reasonable choice in certain situations. I do not agree, therefore, with Ruddick's position that pacifists can become better pacifists by learning from maternal thinkers. I conclude that pacifists can learn to abandon pacifism altogether as a doctrine. Finally I will argue that although Ruddick has found a problem with pacifism, the problem is not a matter of abstraction versus concreteness. It concerns the particular abstract principle involved in pacifism. I will begin with a discussion of the two senses of pacifist commitment I find in Ruddick's work.

Ruddick offers a very clear definition of what she calls the pacifist commitment:

> . . . commitment to avoid battle whenever possible, to fight necessary battles non-violently, and to take, as aim of every battle, reconciliation between opponents and restoration of connection and community. (1984b, 239)

This type of commitment is one that is normally associated with pacifism. It involves the renunciation of physical violence as a method of doing battle. While non-violent resistance is permitted, even encouraged, physically damaging the opponent is not considered an option.

There is, however, another kind of pacifist commitment discussed by Ruddick, although she does not call it by that name. In her discussion of the pacifist commitment mentioned above, Ruddick recognizes that mothers might have a tendency to be violent toward people harming their children. She talks about a legitimate interest that mothers have in the particular well-being of their own children. However, Ruddick states that mothers can come to see that the good of their children is entwined with the good of all children, because no child can grow up to be healthy in a world threatened by violence. Hence, Ruddick argues that mothers are in a good place to see the necessity of creating a world without violence. The commitment to helping create a world without violence is a second kind of pacifist commitment. One might argue that while Ruddick's analysis of mothering doesn't imply a pacifist commitment in the first sense, it does imply a pacifist commitment in the second sense. And the second sense allows for the possibility of using violence as a way of creating a world where violence doesn't exist.

I will argue that neither commitment is implied by Ruddick's analysis, and thus that neither is im-

plied by the practice of mothering as she presents it. I shall also argue that this is a good thing. I shall begin with a discussion of the first type of pacifist commitment, the commitment not to engage in violence.

Ruddick states that central to the practice of mothering is the goal of producing a healthy being. This involves nurturing that being. To nurture a being is to help it grow. At a minimum, this will involve providing conditions in which it can survive. Once this is accomplished, the nurturer can strive not only to provide such conditions, but also to improve upon them in an attempt to provide an environment in which the being cannot only survive but be healthy and thrive. Providing and maintaining such conditions can be extremely difficult in a world which is often indifferent or hostile. The commitment to nurture one particular being can often involve the necessity of destroying something else. Here the image of a mother defending her child against an attacker comes to mind. The mother's goal is the preservation of the life of her particular child. Accomplishing this may involve the use of violence against the attacker. This is a case in which the use of violence would certainly be consistent with the goal of preserving the child's life.

Another way that nurturing a child can involve the use of violence is less direct. Rather than using violence herself the mother may decide to instruct her child in the use of violent techniques as a means of self-defense. The job of nurturing not only involves caring in terms of providing necessary conditions for the growth and health of a child, but also involves teaching the child how to maintain such conditions for herself. This includes teaching the child certain necessary skills such as cooking. In a world in which there already exists violence, and in which there is a probability that one's child may be attacked, it may be necessary to teach the child to employ violence. It is understandable that a mother should wish to do this as a way of protecting her child. Here again there is nothing about teaching and condoning the use of violence which is in any way in contradiction with the goals of preserving the life of a child.

One might object that the goal of mothering involves not only keeping a child alive but also producing a healthy adult, and that teaching a child to use violence, even in dangerous situations, will itself damage the child. It may be true that it would be healthiest for a child not to be exposed to any kind of violence. But health admits of degrees. There will always be factors beyond a mother's control which can damage both the physical and mental health of her child. These include disease, injuries not caused by violence, disappointment and fear. The goal of a mother is more realistically described as that of raising the healthiest child possible given certain conditions. While raising a perfectly healthy child (whatever that means) may be an ideal, the raising of even a fairly healthy child can be regarded as a success.

Because the environment will always challenge mothers, they must settle for the best alternative available. In many cases, people find themselves in violent situations which they have not created. Thus, being the target of someone else's violent behavior is in many cases a risk foisted upon one just like the risks of catching certain diseases. A mother cannot control the environment to the point where she can prevent the possibility that her child may be attacked. Thus, she must make a choice about how to handle this reality. A pacifist might argue that in teaching a child to use violence one creates a moral monster, thus ruining the health of the child. However, another attitude might be that it is healthy to be willing to fight for oneself, and that the attitude that oneself is worth fighting for is healthy. Of course it would be best if children never even had to think about how to respond to violence. However, in the real world violence is out there. I think that one can argue that given this reality raising a healthy child can include teaching it to fight back using violence in certain situations. In fact, in at least some situations, showing a willingness to use violence can actually prevent an attack. Many women report that standing in a fighting stance and yelling "no" intimidates rapists.

Whether a mother will choose to teach her child to fight back will depend upon what she thinks about the relationship between a willingness to use violence and health. Some will choose pacifism and others will not. However, I do not think that a pacifist commitment, where this means teaching children to be pacifists, necessarily follows from the goals of raising a healthy child at all. Hence, I do not believe that a pacifist commitment of this sort necessarily follows from the goals central to the practice of mothering as Ruddick describes them.

One final way that mothering can involve condoning the use of violence and even war is as follows: If conditions are so terrible that a child cannot be expected to survive for any length of time within them, a mother may encourage others to fight in order to bring change for her child. Hence, a mother may support a war-effort while her child is young in the hope that the fighting will eventually bring better conditions for her child. Here again there doesn't seem to be anything present in the goals of maternal thinking that makes this self-defeating.

In each of the examples discussed above, the use of violence seems perfectly compatible with the goal of mothering as Ruddick defines it, namely the preservation and protection of the child. Because of this, it seems odd that Ruddick should say that there is any kind of pacifist commitment present in maternal thinking.

One might object that the examples I have chosen are examples involving violence towards others and not by a mother towards her own children. Perhaps the latter is the pacifist commitment Ruddick has in mind, namely the commitment not to use violence against one's own children. Ruddick claims that the pacifist commitment is fundamental to maternal thinking because it defeats the goal of preserving a healthy child and producing a healthy adult to use violence against that child. In other words, it is somehow self-defeating to damage the very thing one wishes to protect. So it is self-contradictory to act violently towards one's own children. I am not in favor of violence towards children. Yet I am not entirely sure that the problem is best described as in contradiction with a mother's goals. A mother may use violence as a means of disciplining a child so that it does not injure itself. While this may not be the wisest solution, I see no contradiction in the mother's reasoning. There would be a contradiction if she did nothing to try to prevent the child from injuring itself and yet actually cared about the child's safety. Using corporal punishment, I would argue, is not a wise solution to the problem, but I am not sure it exemplifies a contradiction. Even in the seemingly most obvious case, it isn't clear that there is anything that a commitment not to use violence towards one's children is implied by the practice of mothering. However, even if one grants that there is some contradiction in a mother's using violence against her own children, I cannot see this as a basis for attributing a pacifist commitment. This becomes obvious when one looks at what Ruddick says about how mothers can be expected to act towards their enemies.

Ruddick is willing to grant that mothers are not reliably non-violent towards those perceived as enemies. She states:

> Toward one group of combatants however, a mother is not reliably non-violent, namely the families and children of her own enemies class. . . . Political or religious allegiance, misguided desire for purity, and order, the sheer lust to see one's own children privileged, all may fuel a violence otherwise too crude to tolerate. The repulsive, contorted faces of white mothers shouting at Black children seeking to enter school rooms may haunt most women. But they are the faces of maternal practice and represent a temptation to which mothers are liable. (1984b, 244)

Ruddick realizes that a mother may be particularly prone to violence in situations in which she believes that the welfare of her own children is at stake. Yet all of the examples Ruddick presents deal with situations in which a more enlightened mother would see that violence is uncalled for. When as a result of her own prejudice or narrow mindedness, a mother perceives great danger to her children, this is certainly a shame. Because of bias, she misperceives a situation as dangerous. The examples presented above are definitely of this sort. However, by using only these kinds of examples, Ruddick makes it appear that violence is usually uncalled for. This may be true, but it does not show that there are no situations which, owing to real and imminent danger, call for a violent response in order to protect a particular child. The point is that although there may be situations in which it is wrong for a mother to employ violence, it doesn't follow that there aren't any situations in which violence is appropriate. Ruddick's examples do not show a problem with ever using violence, but rather a problem of when it is appropriate. Hence Ruddick does not show that violence is always contrary to a mother's aims, nor that a mother never should use violence.

Ruddick states that the pacifist commitment in the practice of mothering is similar to the pacifism in Gandhi's *Satyagraha*. A comparison of these two, however, reveals some important differences which cannot be ignored. According to Gandhi:

> Not to hurt any living thing is no doubt a part of ahimsa (non-violence). But it is its least expression. The principle of ahimsa is hurt by every evil thought, by undue haste, by lying, by hatred, by wishing ill to anybody.
>
> Ahimsa really means that you may not offend anybody, you may not harbor an uncharitable thought even in connection with one who may consider himself to be your enemy. (1961, 43)

Gandhi's pacifist commitment is a commitment in the first sense of pacifist commitment discussed in the introduction, namely the commitment of an agent not to employ violence herself. Certainly Gandhi would favor a world in which nobody uses violence. However he is unwilling to consider the possibility that violence could be used in the creation of such a world, and if this was necessary he would forfeit its creation.

As I have argued above, Ruddick's analysis of mothering doesn't seem to imply this kind of pacifist commitment. Mothers are likely to use violence in order to protect their children. I argue that in many situations this may be appropriate, and this is one of the reasons I cannot consider myself a pacifist in the first sense. What is more interesting is that Gandhi, realizing that close affiliations may ruin a person's ability to stick to this type of a pacifist commitment, warns against forming families at all. He states:

> The man who is wedded to Truth and worships Truth alone, proves unfaithful to her, if he applies his talents to anything else. How then can he minister to the senses? A man, whose activities are wholly consecrated to the realization of Truth, which requires utter selflessness, can have no time for the selfish purpose of begetting children and running a household. (1961, 43)

Gandhi realizes that interest in a special group of people is dangerous to the cause of pacifism. This is also evident in what he says about marriage:

> Ahimsa means universal love. If a man gives his love to one woman, or a woman to one man, what is there left for all the world besides? It simply means, "we two first, and the devil take all the rest of them." (1961, 43)

Pacifism relies upon a person's ability not to be self interested, or interested in some special other, so that one can be willing to give up one's life, or the life of the special other, in order to avoid using violence. Gandhian pacifism involves not only not using violence when attacked, but being willing to go out and make oneself a possible target for attack by protesting against social wrongs. One must be willing to stand up to those prepared to use violence and perhaps allow those people to kill one if it comes down to that. Because mothers can be expected to take a certain special interest in their own children, and because violence towards their children's enemies is consistent with this special interest, it cannot be said that they have a "pacifist commitment." Rather, what they have is the kind of interest in some special group of others which is exactly what Gandhian pacifism attempts to discourage. The implication here is that in order to be successful pacifists in the Gandhian sense, we need to learn to care about other people as individuals less rather than more. Even if this could bring about a world with less violence in it, I doubt that it would be worth the sacrifice. After all, it is caring passionately about others that often makes life worth living in the first place. I shall return to this point later.

Ruddick is certainly not insensitive to the fact that mothers are not reliably pacifists in their settlement of conflicts with those who are perceived as a threat to their children. And she realizes that perhaps the pacifist commitment as articulated by Gandhi demands way too much. She thus argues that pacifists have something to learn from mothers. She characterizes the problem in terms of what she calls abstract versus concrete thinking. "Abstraction refers to a cluster of interrelated dispositions to simplify, dissociate, generalize and sharply define." She opposes this style of thinking to concreteness which "respects complexity, connection, particularity, and ambiguity" (1984b, 249). She argues that the style she calls abstraction is more pronounced in men and is most likely to lead to war. "Willing warriors are loyal to abstract causes and abstract states. They are encouraged to develop an abstract hatred for the enemy that will allow them to kill" (1984b, 250). Those who think concretely, on the other hand, "are more likely to consider their opponents, to understand the pain their coercion causes, and of course the suffering which they choose to

bear" (1984b, 251). Ruddick believes that the pacifist commitment in maternal thinking is based on concreteness rather than abstraction and is, therefore, more conducive to peace.

There seems to be an obvious problem in Ruddick's discussion. It is that Gandhian pacifism, which is certainly based on abstract principles about the use of violence, is a peaceful rather than a warlike doctrine. This seems to contradict Ruddick's claim that abstract thinking is warlike. One of the greatest pacifists of our time based his doctrine on exactly the kind of thinking Ruddick believes is dangerous. Ruddick acknowledges this:

> If pacifists require (as our draft boards demand) that a person abjure from violence in every place, at every time, or that s/he take as opponents those who choose differently, then pacifism, too, is asking for abstract commitment. This may show that abstraction has its place in peace as in war; I myself think it shows that pacifists should learn from maternal practice to attend to the battle at hand. . . . Many people refuse to rule out in advance the violence that might be necessary to protect one's loved ones from immediate danger. (1984b, 252)

Why should pacifists give up this advance commitment? The giving up of such a commitment amounts to the rejection of pacifism altogether and would cause former pacifists to hold beliefs about the use of violence which are similar to many non-pacifists, such as violence is a very terrible thing and shouldn't be resorted to unless there is no alternative. The belief just described may be reasonable, but it is the opposite of pacifism. For even if it is granted that there could theoretically be just one situation in which violence is called for, the new belief is in logical opposition to the old. Hence, if I am right about this, Ruddick is actually saying that pacifists should learn from maternal thinkers that pacifism is somehow unreasonable. I tend to agree with Ruddick about this point, yet I do not see the problem as one of abstract thinking versus concrete thinking. I shall now explain why not.

It is certainly true that viewing one's enemies abstractly can allow one to treat them in ways that viewing them as full human beings would not. The propaganda that accompanies wars testifies to this; as such, propaganda encourages people to see the enemy as evil, somehow less than human. I, therefore, agree that viewing people only in the abstract can be dangerous. I agree that often soldiers in a war fight for abstract causes against abstract enemies, and that this allows them to kill or destroy with a certain amount of ease. Yet it must be remembered that there is a flip side of the coin. Often what motivates a soldier to enter battle is love for particular human beings. Soldiers are often told that they owe it to their families and loved ones to go fight, and it is this love which propels them onto the battlefield. Thinking concretely about one's family can often lead one to think abstractly about other people, as each human being can only pay very close attention to a limited number of situations. Also, if one does believe in a pacifism based on what Ruddick would call abstraction, it is thinking concretely about one's loved ones which may cause one to be violent rather than peaceful, for this can cause one to fight anyone who attacks them.

I do not believe that thinking abstractly is necessarily more likely to lead to warlike behavior than thinking concretely. It depends upon what principles one is using. For, if the principle that one is holding is pacifist in the Gandhian sense, thinking concretely about one's loved ones may, in fact, cause one to violate the principle and become violent. Also it should be noticed that Ruddick's entire analysis of mothering is itself quite abstract. She discusses the goals of a practice in an abstract way and argues that a principle of non-violence is implied by them. It cannot be that all abstract thinking is dangerous. In addition, much of the time it is impossible to view one's enemies in a war as anything but abstractions. Even if one learns facts about them, one is not going to really get to know them. If we need to honestly be able to think concretely about people we do not know in order to establish a more peaceful world, I fear we are all in trouble.

Because the practice of mothering doesn't seem to imply a pacifist commitment of the Gandhian sort, one might think that it is a pacifist commitment in the second sense that Ruddick has in mind. Perhaps the practice of mothering involves a commitment to seek a world without violence altogether. In speaking of the fact that mothers have a special interest in their own children, Ruddick argues that mothers can learn that the health and well-being of their particular children is connected with the health and well-being of other children. She says:

> Mothers can, I believe, come to realize that the good of all children, that in a world divided between exploiter and exploited no children can be good and strong, that in a world at war all children are endangered. (1984b, 239)

Ruddick here implies that mothers should be in favor of a peaceful world rather than a world at war.

I agree with this in the abstract. However, this does not mean that mothers can be expected to refrain from violence. If obtaining a peaceful world involves the sacrifice of lives, it will be understandable, given the goals of maternal thinking, for mothers whose children are at least relatively well-off not to encourage their children to enter into the struggle. Entering involves a gamble that one will lose what one has, understandably a gamble a mother would not wish to take. While it is true that a world without violence may be an ideal, it may be contrary to the goals of many mothers to sacrifice their children to the struggle of acquiring such a world. This is because the goal of each mother, as Ruddick defines it, is the preservation of the particular lives of her own children, rather than the goal of making life better for children in general. And if her children are doing at least relatively well, it would contradict a mother's goals to desire her children to sacrifice themselves for others. Thus, although I can see that mothers may wish for a peaceful world, I do not see the practice of mothering, which is concerned with the preservation and health of each mother's own individual child, as implying a readiness to make very great sacrifices to create a world without violence. In fact, children often have to argue a great deal with their mothers about decisions to risk themselves for any cause.

Finally, it is interesting to note that the commitment to a world without violence is itself quite abstract, probably the product of abstract rather than concrete thinking. Even the term violence is an abstraction. Thus, in order to sacrifice children who are doing even moderately well for the sake of producing a world without violence seems to be contrary to, rather than in accordance with, the goals of mothering. Here it is helpful to remember Ruddick's criticism of the abstract nature of Gandhian pacifism. She argues that it requires one to put aside the battles at hand for the sake of abstract goals and principles. It would seem that for many mothers whose children are doing fairly well even though they live in a world containing some violence, a willingness to sacrifice their children in an attempt to create a violence-free world would be to sacrifice them to an abstract cause, something which Ruddick says is a mistake, and not the product of the kind of thinking she believes is part of the practice of mothering.

In conclusion, I have argued that there is no pacifist commitment implied by the practice of mothering. This is because mothers think concretely rather than abstractly. In addition, I think we can learn why pacifism may be unreasonable as well as unattractive by examining the passionate feelings mothers have towards their own children. As Gandhi realized, being a pacifist (I think in either of the two senses discussed) means being willing to sacrifice individuals for the sake of abstract principles or abstract goals. Caring a great deal about certain individuals is likely to get in the way of one's being able to do this. Hence, Gandhi warns against it. I argue that if being a pacifist means having to renounce passionate feelings towards specific individuals, the price is too high. Without these passionate attachments life might not even be worth living for many of us. If having some violence in the world is the cost of loving passionately, I believe it may be worth it. I hope that I have used Ruddick's intelligent and sensitive account of what is beautiful in the practice of mothering, namely the ability to really care about others, to show why.

Notes

Special thanks to Claudia Card and Elaine Marks for their help with earlier drafts.

1. Carol Gilligan (1982) speaks of an ethic of care where relationships are viewed as primary. She contrasts this with an ethic of rights which values individuals as autonomous right holders. The primary concern in an ethic of care is the continuation of the relationship, while in an ethic of rights the primary concern is the balancing of claims between individuals. Ruddick refers to Gilligan in the articles discussed in this paper, and it is clear that she views "maternal practice" as an example of an ethic of care.

References

Gandhi, M. K. 1961. *Non-violent resistance.* New York: Shocken Books.

Gilligan, Carol. 1982. *In a different voice.* Cambridge, MA: Harvard University Press.

Ruddick, Sarah. 1984a. Maternal thinking. In *Mothering.* Joyce Trebilcot, ed. Totowa, NJ: Rowman and Allenheld.

Ruddick, Sara. 1984b. Preservative love and military destruction: Some reflections on mothering and peace. In *Mothering.* Joyce Trebilcot, ed. Totowa, NJ: Rowman and Allenheld.

CONCERNING VIOLENCE

Frantz Fanon

Frantz Fanon argues that only violence will lead to social transformation. His reasons are two: first, the oppressor rules by force and will not give up without a fight. Second, only through violent struggle do the oppressed regain their sense of themselves as full human beings. (Source: From The Wretched of the Earth *by Frantz Fanon, translated by Constance Farrington. Copyright © 1963 by Presence Africaine. Used by permission of Grove/Atlantic, Inc.)*

National liberation, national renaissance, the restoration of nationhood to the people, commonwealth: whatever may be the headings used or the new formulas introduced, decolonization is always a violent phenomenon. At whatever level we study it — relationships between individuals, new names for sports clubs, the human admixture at cocktail parties, in the police, on the directing boards of national or private banks — decolonization is quite simply the replacing of a certain "species" of men by another "species" of men. Without any period of transition, there is a total, complete, and absolute substitution. It is true that we could equally well stress the rise of a new nation, the setting up of a new state, its diplomatic relations, and its economic and political trends. But we have precisely chosen to speak of that kind of *tabula rasa* which characterizes at the outset all decolonization. Its unusual importance is that it constitutes, from the very first day, the minimum demands of the colonized. To tell the truth, the proof of success lies in a whole social structure being changed from the bottom up. The extraordinary importance of this change is that it is willed, called for, demanded. The need for this change exists in its crude state, impetuous and compelling, in the consciousness and in the lives of the men and women who are colonized. But the possibility of this change is equally experienced in the form of a terrifying future in the consciousness of another "species" of men and women: the colonizers.

Decolonization, which sets out to change the order of the world, is, obviously, a program of complete disorder. But it cannot come as a result of magical practices, nor of a natural shock, nor of a friendly understanding. Decolonization, as we know, is a historical process: that is to say that it cannot be understood, it cannot become intelligible nor clear to itself except in the exact measure that we can discern the movements which give it historical form and content. Decolonization is the meeting of two forces, opposed to each other by their very nature, which in fact owe their originality to that sort of substantification which results from and is nourished by the situation in the colonies. Their first encounter was marked by violence and their existence together — that is to say the exploitation of the native by the settler — was carried on by dint of a great array of bayonets and cannons. The settler and the native are old acquaintances. In fact, the settler is right when he speaks of knowing "them" well. For it is the settler who has brought the native into existence and who perpetuates his existence. The settler owes the fact of his very existence, that is to say, his property, to the colonial system.

Decolonization never takes place unnoticed, for it influences individuals and modifies them fundamentally. It transforms spectators crushed with their inessentiality into privileged actors, with the grandiose glare of history's floodlights upon them. It brings a natural rhythm into existence, introduced by new men, and with it a new language and a new humanity. Decolonization is the veritable creation of new men. But this creation owes nothing of its legitimacy to any supernatural power; the "thing" which has been colonized becomes man during the same process by which it frees itself.

In decolonization, there is therefore the need of a complete calling in question of the colonial situation. If we wish to describe it precisely, we might find it in the well-known words: "The last shall be first and the first last." Decolonization is the putting into practice of this sentence. That is why, if we try to describe it, all decolonization is successful.

The naked truth of decolonization evokes for us the searing bullets and bloodstained knives which emanate from it. For if the last shall be first, this will only come to pass after a murderous and decisive struggle between the two protagonists. That affirmed intention to place the last at the head of things, and to make them climb at a pace (too quickly, some say) the well-known steps which characterize an organized society, can only triumph if we use all means to turn the scale, including, of course, that of violence.

You do not turn any society, however primitive it may be, upside down with such a program if you have not decided from the very beginning, that is to say from the actual formulation of that program, to overcome all the obstacles that you will come across in so doing. The native who decides to put the program into practice, and to become its moving force, is ready for violence at all times. From birth it is clear to him that this narrow world, strewn with prohibitions, can only be called in question by absolute violence.

The colonial world is a world divided into compartments. It is probably unnecessary to recall the existence of native quarters and European quarters, of schools for natives and schools for Europeans; in the same way we need not recall apartheid in South Africa. Yet, if we examine closely this system of compartments, we will at least be able to reveal the lines of force it implies. This approach to the colonial world, its ordering and its geographical layout will allow us to mark out the lines on which a decolonized society will be reorganized.

The colonial world is a world cut in two. The dividing line, the frontiers are shown by barracks and police stations. In the colonies it is the policeman and the soldier who are the official, instituted go-betweens, the spokesmen of the settler and his rule of oppression. In capitalist societies the educational system, whether lay or clerical, the structure of moral reflexes handed down from father to son, the exemplary honesty of workers who are given a medal after fifty years of good and loyal service, and the affection which springs from harmonious relations and good behavior — all these aesthetic expressions of respect for the established order serve to create around the exploited person an atmosphere of submission and of inhibition which lightens the task of policing considerably. In the capitalist countries a multitude of moral teachers, counselors and "bewilderers" separate the exploited from those in power. In the colonial countries, on the contrary, the policeman and the soldier, by their im-

mediate presence and their frequent and direct action maintain contact with the native and advise him by means of rifle butts and napalm not to budge. It is obvious here that the agents of government speak the language of pure force. The intermediary does not lighten the oppression, nor seek to hide the domination; he shows them up and puts them into practice with the clear conscience of an upholder of the peace; yet he is the bringer of violence into the home and into the mind of the native.

The zone where the natives live is not complementary to the zone inhabited by the settlers. The two zones are opposed, but not in the service of a higher unity. Obedient to the rules of pure Aristotelian logic, they both follow the principle of reciprocal exclusivity. No conciliation is possible, for of the two terms, one is superfluous. The settlers' town is a strongly built town, all made of stone and steel. It is a brightly lit town; the streets are covered with asphalt, and the garbage cans swallow all the leavings, unseen, unknown and hardly thought about. The settler's feet are never visible, except perhaps in the sea; but there you're never close enough to see them. His feet are protected by strong shoes although the streets of his town are clean and even, with no holes or stones. The settler's town is a well-fed town, an easygoing town; its belly is always full of good things. The settlers' town is a town of white people, of foreigners.

The town belonging to the colonized people, or at least the native town, the Negro village, the medina, the reservation, is a place of ill fame, peopled by men of evil repute. They are born there, it matters little where or how; they die there, it matters not where, nor how. It is a world without spaciousness; men live there on top of each other, and their huts are built one on top of the other. The native town is a hungry town, starved of bread, of meat, of shoes, of coal, of light. The native town is a crouching village, a town on its knees, a town wallowing in the mire. It is a town of niggers and dirty Arabs. The look that the native turns on the settler's town is a look of lust, a look of envy; it expresses his dreams of possession — all manner of possession: to sit at the settler's table, to sleep in the settler's bed, with his wife if possible. The colonized man is an envious man. And this the settler knows very well; when their glances meet he ascertains bitterly, always on the defensive, "They want to take our place." It is true, for there is no native who does not dream at least once a day of setting himself up in the settler's place.

This world divided into compartments, this world cut in two is inhabited by two different species. The originality of the colonial context is that economic reality, inequality, and the immense difference of ways of life never come to mask the human realities. When you examine at close quarters the colonial context, it is evident that what parcels out the world is to begin with the fact of belonging to or not belonging to a given race, a given species. In the colonies the economic substructure is also a superstructure. The cause is the consequence; you are rich because you are white, you are white because you are rich. This is why Marxist analysis should always be slightly stretched every time we have to do with the colonial problem.

Everything up to and including the very nature of precapitalist society, so well explained by Marx, must here be thought out again. The serf is in essence different from the knight, but a reference to divine right is necessary to legitimize this statutory difference. In the colonies, the foreigner coming from another country imposed his rule by means of guns and machines. In defiance of his successful transplantation, in spite of his appropriation, the settler still remains a foreigner. It is neither the act of owning factories, nor estates, nor a bank balance which distinguishes the governing classes. The governing race is first and foremost those who come from elsewhere, those who are unlike the original inhabitants, "the others."

The violence which has ruled over the ordering of the colonial world, which has ceaselessly drummed the rhythm for the destruction of native social forms and broken up without reserve the systems of reference of the economy, the customs of dress and external life, that same violence will be claimed and taken over by the native at the moment when, deciding to embody history in his own person, he surges into the forbidden quarters. To wreck the colonial world is henceforward a mental picture of action which is very clear, very easy to understand and which may be assumed by each one of the individuals which constitute the colonized people. To break up the colonial world does not mean that after the frontiers have been abolished

lines of communication will be set up between the two zones. The destruction of the colonial world is no more and no less that the abolition of one zone, its burial in the depths of the earth or its expulsion from the country.

. . .

As soon as the native begins to pull on his moorings, and to cause anxiety to the settler, he is handed over to well-meaning souls who in cultural congresses point out to him the specificity and wealth of Western values. But every time Western values are mentioned they produce in the native a sort of stiffening or muscular lockjaw. During the period of decolonization, the native's reason is appealed to. He is offered definite values, he is told frequently that decolonization need not mean regression, and that he must put his trust in the qualities which are well-tried, solid, and highly esteemed. But it so happens that when the native hears a speech about Western culture he pulls out his knife — or at least he makes sure it is within reach. The violence with which the supremacy of white values is affirmed and the aggressiveness which has permeated the victory of these values over the ways of life and of thought of the native mean that, in revenge, the native laughs in mockery when Western values are mentioned in front of him. In the colonial context the settler only ends his work of breaking in the native when the latter admits loudly and intelligibly the supremacy of the white man's values. In the period of decolonization, the colonized masses mock at these very values, insult them, and vomit them up.

This phenomenon is ordinarily masked because, during the period of decolonization, certain colonized intellectuals have begun a dialogue with the bourgeoisie of the colonialist country. During this phase, the indigenous population is discerned only as an indistinct mass. The few native personalities whom the colonialist bourgeois have come to know here and there have not sufficient influence on that immediate discernment to give rise to nuances. On the other hand, during the period of liberation, the colonialist bourgeoisie looks feverishly for contacts with the elite and it is with these elite that the familiar dialogue concerning values is carried on. The colonialist bourgeoisie, when it realizes that it is impossible for it to maintain its domination over the colonial countries, decides to carry out a rearguard action with regard to culture, values, techniques, and so on. Now what we must never forget is that the immense majority of colonized peoples is oblivious to these problems. For a colonized people the most essential value, because the most concrete, is first and foremost the land: the land which will bring them bread and, above all, dignity. But this dignity has nothing to do with the dignity of the human individual: for that human individual has never heard tell of it. All that the native has seen in his country is that they can freely arrest him, beat him, starve him: and no professor of ethics, no priest has ever come to be beaten in his place, nor to share their bread with him. As far as the native is concerned, morality is very concrete; it is to silence the settler's defiance, to break his flaunting violence — in a word, to put him out of the picture. The well-known principle that all men are equal will be illustrated in the colonies from the moment that the native claims that he is the equal of the settler. One step more, and he is ready to fight to be more than the settler. In fact, he has already decided to eject him and to take his place; as we see it, it is a whole material and moral universe which is breaking up. The intellectual who for his part has followed the colonialist with regard to the universal abstract will fight in order that the settler and the native may live together in peace in a new world. But the thing he does not see, precisely because he is permeated by colonialism and all its ways of thinking, is that the settler, from the moment that the colonial context disappears, has no longer any interest in remaining or in co-existing. It is not by chance that, even before any negotiation* between the Algerian and French governments has taken place, the European minority which calls itself "liberal" has already made its position clear: it demands nothing more nor less than twofold citizenship. By setting themselves apart in an abstract manner, the liberals try to force the settler into taking a very concrete jump into the unknown. Let us admit it, the settler knows perfectly well that no phraseology can be a substitute for reality.

---

*Fanon is writing in 1961.—Trans.

Thus the native discovers that his life, his breath, his beating heart are the same as those of the settler. He finds out that the settler's skin is not of any more value than a native's skin; and it must be said that this discovery shakes the world in a very necessary manner. All the new, revolutionary assurance of the native stems from it. For if, in fact, my life is worth as much as the settler's, his glance no longer shrivels me up nor freezes me, and his voice no longer turns me into stone. I am no longer on tenterhooks in his presence; in fact, I don't give a damn for him. Not only does his presence no longer trouble me, but I am already preparing such efficient ambushes for him that soon there will be no way out but that of flight.

We have said that the colonial context is characterized by the dichotomy which it imposes upon the whole people. Decolonization unifies that people by the radical decision to remove from it its heterogeneity, and by unifying it on a national, sometimes a racial, basis. We know the fierce words of the Senegalese patriots, referring to the maneuvers of their president, Senghor: "We have demanded that the higher posts should be given to Africans; and now Senghor is Africanizing the Europeans." That is to say that the native can see clearly and immediately if decolonization has come to pass or not, for his minimum demands are simply that the last shall be first.

But the native intellectual brings variants to this petition, and, in fact, he seems to have good reasons: higher civil servants, technicians, specialists—all seem to be needed. Now, the ordinary native interprets these unfair promotions as so many acts of sabotage, and he is often heard to declare: "It wasn't worth while, then, our becoming independent . . ."

. . .

A world divided into compartments, a motionless, Manicheistic world, a world of statues: the statue of the general who carried out the conquest, the statue of the engineer who built the bridge; a world which is sure of itself, which crushes with its stones the backs flayed by whips: this is the colonial world. The native is a being hemmed in; apartheid is simply one form of the division into compartments of the colonial world. The first thing which the native learns is to stay in his place, and not to go beyond certain limits. This is why the dreams of the native are always of muscular prowess;

his dreams are of action and of aggression. I dream I am jumping, swimming, running, climbing; I dream that I burst out laughing, that I span a river in one stride, or that I am followed by a flood of motorcars which never catch up with me. During the period of colonization, the native never stops achieving his freedom from nine in the evening until six in the morning.

The colonized man will first manifest this aggressiveness which has been deposited in his bones against his own people. This is the period when the niggers beat each other up, and the police and magistrates do not know which way to turn when faced with the astonishing waves of crime in North Africa. We shall see later how this phenomenon should be judged. When the native is confronted with the colonial order of things, he finds he is in a state of permanent tension. The settler's world is a hostile world, which spurns the native, but at the same time it is a world of which he is envious. We have seen that the native never ceases to dream of putting himself in the place of the settler — not of becoming the settler but of substituting himself for the settler. This hostile world, ponderous and aggressive because it fends off the colonized masses with all the harshness it is capable of, represents not merely a hell from which the swiftest flight possible is desirable, but also a paradise close at hand which is guarded by terrible watchdogs.

The native is always on the alert, for since he can only make out with difficulty the many symbols of the colonial world, he is never sure whether or not he has crossed the frontier. Confronted with a world ruled by the settler, the native is always presumed guilty. But the native's guilt is never a guilt which he accepts; it is rather a kind of curse, a sort of sword of Damocles, for, in his innermost spirit, the native admits no accusation. He is overpowered but not tamed; he is treated as an inferior but he is not convinced of his inferiority. He is patiently waiting until the settler is off his guard to fly at him. The native's muscles are always tensed. You can't say that he is terrorized, or even apprehensive. He is in fact ready at a moment's notice to exchange the role of the quarry for that of the hunter. The native is an oppressed person whose permanent dream is to become the persecutor. The symbols of social order — the police, the bugle calls in the barracks, military parades and the waving flags — are at one and the same time inhibitory and stimulating: for

they do not convey the message "Don't dare to budge"; rather, they cry out "Get ready to attack." And, in fact, if the native has any tendency to fall asleep and to forget, the settler's hauteur and the settler's anxiety to test the strength of the colonial system would remind him at every turn that the great showdown cannot be put off indefinitely. That impulse to take the settler's place implies a tonicity of muscles the whole time; and in fact we know that in certain emotional conditions the presence of an obstacle accentuates the tendency toward motion.

The settler–native relationship is a mass relationship. The settler pits brute force against the weight of numbers. He is an exhibitionist. His preoccupation with security makes him remind the native out loud that there he alone is master. The settler keeps alive in the native an anger which he deprives of outlet; the native is trapped in the tight links of the chains of colonialism. But we have seen that inwardly the settler can only achieve a pseudo petrification. The native's muscular tension finds outlet regularly in bloodthirsty explosions — in tribal warfare, in feuds between septs, and in quarrels between individuals.

. . .

At the decisive moment, the colonialist bourgeoisie, which up till then has remained inactive, comes into the field. It introduces that new idea which is in proper parlance a creation of the colonial situation: non-violence. In its simplest form this non-violence signifies to the intellectual and economic elite of the colonized country that the bourgeoisie has the same interests as they and that it is therefore urgent and indispensable to come to terms for the public good. Non-violence is an attempt to settle the colonial problem around a green baize table, before any regrettable act has been performed or irreparable gesture made, before any blood has been shed. But if the masses, without waiting for the chairs to be arranged around the baize table, listen to their own voice and begin committing outrages and setting fire to buildings, the elite and the nationalist bourgeois parties will be seen rushing to the colonialists to exclaim, "This is very serious! We do not know how it will end; we must find a solution — some sort of compromise."

This idea of compromise is very important in the phenomenon of decolonization, for it is very far from being a simple one. Compromise involves the colonial system and the young nationalist bourgeoisie at one and the same time. The partisans of the colonial system discover that the masses may destroy everything. Blown-up bridges, ravaged farms, repressions, and fighting harshly disrupt the economy. Compromise is equally attractive to the nationalist bourgeoisie, who since they are not clearly aware of the possible consequences of the rising storm, are genuinely afraid of being swept away by this huge hurricane and never stop saying to the settlers: "We are still capable of stopping the slaughter; the masses still have confidence in us; act quickly if you do not want to put everything in jeopardy." One step more, and the leader of the nationalist party keeps his distance with regard to that violence. He loudly proclaims that he has nothing to do with these Mau-Mau, these terrorists, these throat-slitters. At best, he shuts himself off in a no man's land between the terrorists and the settlers and willingly offers his services as go-between; that is to say, that as the settlers cannot discuss terms with these Mau-Mau, he himself will be quite willing to begin negotiations. Thus it is that the rear guard of the national struggle, that very party of people who have never ceased to be on the other side in the fight, find themselves somersaulted into the van of negotiations and compromise — precisely because that party has taken very good care never to break contact with colonialism.

Before negotiations have been set afoot, the majority of nationalist parties confine themselves for the most part to explaining and excusing this "savagery." They do not assert that the people have to use physical force, and it sometimes even happens that they go so far as to condemn, in private, the spectacular deeds which are declared to be hateful by the press and public opinion in the mother country. The legitimate excuse for this ultra-conservative policy is the desire to see things in an objective light; but this traditional attitude of the native intellectual and of the leaders of the nationalist parties is not, in reality, in the least objective. For in fact they are not at all convinced that this impatient violence of the masses is the most efficient means of defending their own interests. Moreover, there are some individuals who are convinced of the ineffectiveness of violent methods; for them, there is no doubt about it, every attempt to break colonial

oppression by force is a hopeless effort, an attempt at suicide, because in the innermost recesses of their brains the settler's tanks and airplanes occupy a huge place. When they are told "Action must be taken," they see bombs raining down on them, armored cars coming at them on every path, machine-gunning and police action . . . and they sit quiet. They are beaten from the start. There is no need to demonstrate their incapacity to triumph by violent methods; they take it for granted in their everyday life and in their political maneuvers. They have remained in the same childish position as Engels took up in his famous polemic with that monument of puerility, Monsieur Dühring:

> In the same way that Robinson [Crusoe] was able to obtain a sword, we can just as well suppose that [Man] Friday might appear one fine morning with a loaded revolver in his hand, and from then on the whole relationship of violence is reversed: Man Friday gives the orders and Crusoe is obliged to work. . . . Thus, the revolver triumphs over the sword, and even the most childish believer in axioms will doubtless form the conclusion that violence is not a simple act of will, but needs for its realization certain very concrete preliminary conditions, and in particular the implements of violence; and the more highly developed of these implements will carry the day against primitive ones. Moreover, the very fact of the ability to produce such weapons signifies that the producer of highly developed weapons, in everyday speech the arms manufacturer, triumphs over the producer of primitive weapons. To put it briefly, the triumph of violence depends upon the production of armaments, and this in its turn depends on production in general, and thus . . .on economic strength, on the economy of the State, and in the last resort on the material means which that violence commands.[1]

In fact, the leaders of reform have nothing else to say than: "With what are you going to fight the settlers? With your knives? Your shotguns?"

It is true that weapons are important when violence comes into play, since all finally depends on the distribution of these implements. But it so happens that the liberation of colonial countries throws new light on the subject. For example, we have seen that during the Spanish campaign, which was a very genuine colonial war, Napoleon, in spite of an army which reached in the offensives of the spring of 1810 the huge figure of 400,000 men, was forced to retreat. Yet the French army made the whole of Europe tremble by its weapons of war, by the bravery of its soldiers, and by the military genius of its leaders. Face to face with the enormous potentials of the Napoleonic troops, the Spaniards, inspired by an unshakeable national ardor, rediscovered the famous methods of guerrilla warfare which, twenty-five years before, the American militia had tried out on the English forces. But the native's guerrilla warfare would be of no value as opposed to other means of violence if it did not form a new element in the worldwide process of competition between trusts and monopolies.

. . .

Thus there exists a sort of detached complicity between capitalism and the violent forces which blaze up in colonial territory. What is more, the native is not along against the oppressor, for indeed there is also the political and diplomatic support of progressive countries and peoples. But above all there is competition, that pitiless war which financial groups wage upon each other. A Berlin Conference was able to tear Africa into shreds and divide her up between three or four imperial flags. At the moment, the important thing is not whether such-and-such a region in Africa is under French or Belgian sovereignty, but rather that the economic zones are respected. Today, wars of repression are no longer waged against rebel sultans; everything is more elegant, less bloodthirsty; the liquidation of the Castro regime will be quite peaceful. They do all they can to strangle Guinea and they eliminate Mossadegh. Thus the nationalist leader who is frightened of violence is wrong if he imagines that colonialism is going to "massacre all of us." The military will of course go on playing with tin soldiers which date from the time of the conquest, but higher finance will soon bring the truth home to them.

This is why reasonable nationalist political parties are asked to set out their claims as clearly as possible, and to seek with their colonialist opposite numbers, calmly and without passion, for a solution which will take the interests of both parties into consideration. We see that if this nationalist reformist tendency which often takes the form of a kind of caricature of trade unionism decides to take action, it will only do so in a highly peaceful fashion, through stoppages of work in the few industries which have been set up in the towns, mass demonstrations to cheer the leaders, and the boycotting of buses or of imported commodities. All these forms of action serve at one and the same time to bring pressure to bear on the forces of colonialism, and to allow the people to work off their energy. This practice of therapy by hibernation, this sleep-cure used on the people, may sometimes be successful; thus out of the conference around the green baize table comes the political selectiveness which enables Monsieur M'ba, the president of the Republic of Gabon, to state in all seriousness on his arrival in Paris for an official visit: "Gabon is independent, but between Gabon and France nothing has changed; everything goes on as before." In fact, the only change is that Monsieur M'ba is president of the Gabonese Republic and that he is received by the president of the French Republic.

The colonialist bourgeoisie is helped in its work of calming down the natives by the inevitable religion. All those saints who have turned the other cheek, who have forgiven trespasses against them, and who have been spat on and insulted without shrinking are studied and held up as examples. On the other hand, the elite of the colonial countries, those slaves set free, when at the head of the movement inevitably end up by producing an ersatz conflict. They use their brothers' slavery to shame the slavedrivers or to provide an ideological policy of quaint humanitarianism for their oppressors' financial competitors. The truth is that they never make any real appeal to the aforesaid slaves; they never mobilize them in concrete terms. On the contrary, at the decisive moment (that is to say, from their point of view the moment of indecision) they brandish the danger of a "mass mobilization" as the crucial weapon which would bring about as if by magic the "end of the colonial regime." Obviously there are to be found at the core of the political parties and among their leaders certain revolutionaries who deliberately turn their backs upon the farce of national independence. But very quickly their questionings, their energy, and their anger obstruct the party machine; and these elements are gradually isolated, and then quite simply brushed aside. At this moment, as if there existed a dialectic concomitance, the colonialist police will fall upon them. With no security in the towns, avoided by the militants of their former party and rejected by its leaders, these undesirable firebrands will be stranded in county districts. Then it is that they will realize bewilderedly that the peasant masses catch on to what they have to say immediately, and without delay ask them the question to which they have not yet prepared the answer: "When do we start?"

. . .

There is however no definite subject matter and no political or social program. There is a vague outline or skeleton, which is nevertheless national in form, what we describe as "minimum requirements." The politicians who make speeches and who write in the nationalist newspapers make the people dream dreams. They avoid the actual overthrowing of the state, but in fact they introduce into their readers' or hearers' consciousness the terrible ferment of subversion. The national or tribal language is often used. Here, once again, dreams are encouraged, and the imagination is let loose outside the bounds of the colonial order; and sometimes these politicians speak of "We Negroes, we Arabs," and these terms which are so profoundly ambivalent take on during the colonial epoch a sacramental signification. The nationalist politicians are playing with fire: for, as an African leader recently warned a group of young intellectuals, "Think well before you speak to the masses, for they flare up quickly." This is one of the terrible tricks that destiny plays in the colonies.

When a political leader calls a mass meeting, we may say that there is blood in the air. Yet the same leader very often is above all anxious to "make a show" of force, so that in fact he need not use it. But the agitation which ensues, the coming and going, the listening to speeches, seeing the people assembled in one place, with the police all around, the military demonstrations, arrests, and the deportation of the leaders—all this hubbub makes the people think that the moment has come for them to take action. In these times of instability the political parties multiply their appeals to the left for calm, while on their right they scan the horizon, trying to make out the liberal intentions of colonialism.

In the same way the people make use of certain episodes in the life of the community in order to hold themselves ready and to keep alive their revolutionary zeal. For example, the gangster who holds up the police set on to track him down for days on end, or who dies in single combat after having killed four or five policemen, or who commits suicide in order not to give away his accomplices—these types light the way for the people, form the blueprints for action and become heroes. Obviously, it's a waste of breath to say that such-and-such a hero is a thief, a scoundrel, or a reprobate. If the act for which he is prosecuted by the colonial authorities is an act exclusively directed against a colonialist person or colonialist property, the demarcation line is definite and manifest. The process of identification is automatic.

We must also notice in this ripening process the role played by the history of the resistance at the time of the conquest. The great figures of the colonized people are always those who led the national resistance to invasion. Behanzin, Soundiata, Samory, Abdel Kader—all spring again to life with peculiar intensity in the period which comes directly before action. This is the proof that the people are getting ready to begin to go forward again, to put an end to the static period begun by colonization, and to make history.

The uprising of the new nation and the breaking down of colonial structures are the result of one of two causes: either of a violent struggle of the people in their own right, or of action on the part of surrounding colonized peoples which acts as a brake on the colonial regime in question.

A colonized people is not alone. In spite of all that colonialism can do, its frontiers remain open to new ideas and echoes from the world outside. It discovers that violence is in the atmosphere, that it here and there bursts out, and here and there sweeps away the colonial regime—that same violence which fulfills for the native a role that is not simply informatory, but also operative. The great victory of the Vietnamese people at Dien Bien Phu is no longer, strictly speaking, a Vietnamese victory. Since July, 1954, the question which the colonized peoples have asked themselves has been, "What must be done to bring about another Dien Bien Phu? How can we manage it? Not a single colonized individual could ever again doubt the possibility of a Dien Bien Phu; the only problem was how best to use the forces at their disposal, how to organize them, and when to bring them into action. This encompassing violence does not work upon the colonized people only; it modifies the attitude of the colonialists who become aware of manifold Dien Bien Phus. This is why a veritable panic takes hold of the colonialist governments in turn. Their purpose is to capture the vanguard, to turn the movement of liberation toward the right, and to disarm the people: quick, quick, let's decolonize. Decolonize the Congo before it turns into another Algeria. Vote the constitutional framework for all Africa, create the French *Communauté*, renovate that same *Communauté*, but for God's sake let's decolonize quick. . . . And they decolonize at such a rate that they impose independence on Houphouët-Boigny. To the strategy of Dien Bien Phu, defined by the colonized peoples, the colonialist replies by the strategy of encirclement — based on the respect of the sovereignty of states.

But let us return to that atmosphere of violence, that violence which is just under the skin. We have seen that in its process toward maturity many leads are attached to it, to control it and show it the way out. Yet in spite of the metamorphoses which the colonial regime imposes upon it in the way of tribal or regional quarrels, that violence makes its way forward, and the native identifies his enemy and recognizes all his misfortunes, throwing all the exacerbated might of his hate and anger into this new channel. But how do we pass from the atmosphere of violence to violence in action? What makes the lid blow off? There is first of all the fact that this development does not leave the settler's blissful existence intact. The settler who "understands" the natives is made aware by several straws in the wind showing that something is afoot. "Good" natives become scarce; silence falls when the oppressor approaches; sometimes looks are black, and attitudes and remarks openly aggressive. The nationalist parties are astir, they hold a great many meetings, the police are increased and reinforcements of soldiers are brought in. The settlers, above all the farmers isolated on their land, are the first to become alarmed. They call for energetic measures.

The authorities do in fact take some spectacular measures. They arrest one or two leaders, they organize military parades and maneuvers, and air force displays. But the demonstrations and warlike exercises, the smell of gunpowder which now fills the atmosphere, these things do not make the people draw back. Those bayonets and cannonades only serve to reinforce their aggressiveness. The atmosphere becomes dramatic, and everyone wishes to show that he is ready for anything. And it is in these circumstances that the guns go off by themselves, for nerves are jangled, fear reigns and everyone is trigger-happy. A single commonplace incident is enough to start the machine-gunning: Sétif in Algeria, the Central Quarries in Morocco, Moramanga in Madagascar.

The repressions, far from calling a halt to the forward rush of national consciousness, urge it on. Mass slaughter in the colonies at a certain stage of the embryonic development of consciousness increases that consciousness, for the hecatombs are an indication that between oppressors and oppressed everything can be solved by force. It must be remarked here that the political parties have not called for armed insurrection, and have made no preparations for such an insurrection. All these repressive measures, all those actions which are a result of fear are not within the leaders' intentions: they are overtaken by events. At this moment, then, colonialism may decide to arrest the nationalist leaders. But today the governments of colonized countries know very well that it is extremely dangerous to deprive the masses of their leaders; for then the people, unbridled, fling themselves into *jacqueries*, mutinies, and "brutish murders." The masses give free rein to their "bloodthirsty instincts" and force colonialism to free their leaders, to whom falls the difficult task of bringing them back to order. The colonized people, who have spontaneously brought their violence to the colossal task of destroying the colonial system, will very soon find themselves with the barren, inert slogan "Release X or Y."* Then colonialism will release these men, and hold discussions with them. The time for dancing in the streets has come.

---

*It may happen that the arrested leader is in fact the authentic mouthpiece of the colonized masses. In this case colonialism will make use of his period of detention to try to launch new leaders.

In certain circumstances, the party political machine may remain intact. But as a result of the colonialist repression and of the spontaneous reaction of the people the parties find themselves out-distanced by their militants. The violence of the masses is vigorously pitted against the military forces of the occupying power, and the situation deteriorates and comes to a head. Those leaders who are free remain, therefore, on the touchline. They have suddenly become useless, with their bureaucracy and their reasonable demands; yet we see them, far removed from events, attempting the crowning imposture — that of "speaking in the name of the silenced nation." As a general rule, colonialism welcomes this godsend with open arms, transforms these "blind mouths" into spokesmen, and in two minutes endows them with independence, on condition that they restore order.

So we see that all parties are aware of the power of such violence and that the question is not always to reply to it by a greater violence, but rather to see how to relax the tension.

What is the real nature of this violence? We have seen that it is the intuition of the colonized masses that their liberation must, and can only, be achieved by force. By what spiritual aberration do these men, without technique, starving and enfeebled, confronted with the military and economic might of the occupation, come to believe that violence alone will free them? How can they hope to triumph?

It is because violence (and this is the disgraceful thing) may constitute, in so far as it forms part of its system, the slogan of a political party. The leaders may call on the people to enter upon an armed struggle. This problematical question has to be thought over. When militarist Germany decides to settle its frontier disputes by force, we are not in the least surprised; but when the people of Angola, for example, decide to take up arms, when the Algerian people reject all means which are not violent, these are proofs that something has happened or is happening at this very moment. The colonized races, those slaves of modern times, are impatient. They know that this apparent folly alone can put them out of reach of colonial oppression. A new type of relations is established in the world. The underdeveloped peoples try to break their chains, and the extraordinary thing is that they succeed. It could be argued that in these days of sputniks it is ridiculous to die of hunger; but for the colonized masses the argument is more down-to-earth. The truth is that there is no colonial power today which is capable of adopting the only form of contest which has a chance of succeeding, namely, the prolonged establishment of large forces of occupation.

As far as their internal situation is concerned, the colonialist countries find themselves faced with contradictions in the form of working-class demands which necessitate the use of their police forces. As well, in the present international situation, these countries need their troops to protect their regimes. Finally there is the well-known myth of liberating movements directed from Moscow. In the regime's panic-stricken reasoning, this signifies "If that goes on, there is a risk that the communists will turn the troubles to account and infiltrate into these parts."

In the native's eagerness, the fact that he openly brandishes the threat of violence proves that he is conscious of the unusual character of the contemporary situation and that he means to profit by it. But, still on the level of immediate experience, the native, who has seen the modern world penetrate into the furthermost corners of the bush, is most acutely aware of all the things he does not possess. The masses by a sort of (if we may say so) childlike process of reasoning convince themselves that they have been robbed of all these things. That is why in certain underdeveloped countries the masses forge ahead very quickly, and realize two or three years after independence that they have been frustrated, that "it wasn't worth while" fighting, and that nothing could really change. In 1789, after the bourgeois revolution, the smallest French peasants benefited substantially from the upheaval. But it is a commonplace to observe and to say that in the majority of cases, for 95 per cent of the population of underdeveloped countries, independence brings no immediate change. The enlightened observer takes note of the existence of a kind of masked discontent, like the smoking ashes of a burnt-down house after the fire has been put out, which still threaten to burst into flames again.

So they say that the natives want to go too quickly. Now, let us never forget that only a very short time ago they complained of their slowness, their laziness, and their fatalism. Already we see that violence used in specific ways at the moment of the struggle for freedom does not magically disappear after the ceremony of trooping the national colors. It has all the less reason for disappearing since the reconstruction of the nation continues within the framework of cutthroat competition between capitalism and socialism.

This competition gives an almost universal dimension to even the most localized demands. Every meeting held, every act of repression committed, reverberates in the international arena. The murders of Sharpeville shook public opinion for months. In the newspapers, over the wavelengths, and in private conversations Sharpeville has become a symbol. It was through Sharpeville that men and women first became acquainted with the problem of apartheid in South Africa. Moreover, we cannot believe that demagogy alone is the explanation for the sudden interest the big powers show in the petty affairs of underdeveloped regions. Each *jacquerie*, each act of sedition in the Third World makes up part of a picture framed by the Cold War. Two men are beaten up in Salisbury, and at once the whole of a bloc goes into action, talks about those two men, and uses the beating-up incident to bring up the particular problem of Rhodesia, linking it, moreover, with the whole African question and with the whole question of colonized people. The other bloc however is equally concerned in measuring by the magnitude of the campaign the local weaknesses of its system. Thus the colonized peoples realize that neither clan remains outside local incidents. They no longer limit themselves to regional horizons, for they have caught on to the fact that they live in an atmosphere of international stress.

· · ·

Let us return to considering the single combat between native and settler. We have seen that it takes the form of an armed and open struggle. There is no lack of historical examples: Indo-China, Indonesia, and of course North Africa. But what we must not lose sight of is that this struggle could have broken out anywhere, in Guinea as well as Somaliland, and moreover today it could break out in every place where colonialism means to stay on, in Angola, for example. The existence of an armed struggle shows that the people are decided to trust to violent methods only. He of whom *they* have never stopped saying that the only language he understands is that of force, decides to give utterance by force. In fact, as always, the settler has shown him the way he should take if he is to become free. The argument the native chooses has been furnished by the settler, and by an ironic turning of the tables it is the native who now affirms that the colonialist understands nothing but force. The colonial regime owes its legitimacy to force and at no time tries to hide this aspect of things. Every statue, whether of Faidherbe or of Lyautey, of Bugeaud or of Sergeant Blandan — all these conquistadors perched on colonial soil do not cease from proclaiming one and the same thing: "We are here by the force of bayonets. . . ."* The sentence is easily completed. During the phase of insurrection, each settler reasons on a basis of simple arithmetic. This logic does not surprise the other settlers, but it is important to point out that it does not surprise the natives either. To begin with, the affirmation of the principle "It's them or us" does not constitute a paradox, since colonialism, as we have seen, is in fact the organization of a Manichean world, a world divided up into compartments. And when in laying down precise methods the settler asks each member of the oppressing minority to shoot down 30 or 100 or 200 natives, he sees that nobody shows any indignation and that the whole problem is to decide whether it can be done all at once or by stages.†

This chain of reasoning which presumes very arithmetically the disappearance of the colonized people does not leave the native overcome with moral indignation. He has always known that his duel with the settler would take place in the arena. The native loses no time in lamentations, and he hardly ever seeks for justice in the colonial framework. The fact is that if the settler's logic leaves the native unshaken, it

---

*This refers to Mirabeau's famous saying: "I am here by the will of the People; I shall leave only by the force of bayonets." — *Trans.*

†It is evident that this vacuum cleaning destroys the very thing that they want to preserve. Sartre points this out when he says: "In short by the very fact of repeating them [concerning racist ideas] it is revealed that the simultaneous union of all against the natives is unrealizable. Such union only recurs from time to time and more over it can only come into being as an active groupment in order to massacre the natives — an absurd though perpetual temptation to the settlers, which even if it was feasible would only succeed in abolishing colonization at one blow." (*Critique de la Raison Dialectique*, p. 346.)

is because the latter has practically stated the problem of his liberation in identical terms: "We must form ourselves into groups of two hundred or five hundred, and each group must deal with a settler." It is in this manner of thinking that each of the protagonists begins the struggle.

For the native, this violence represents the absolute line of action. The militant is also a man who works. The questions that the organization asks the militant bear the mark of this way of looking at things: "Where have you worked? With whom? What have you accomplished?" The group requires that each individual perform an irrevocable action. In Algeria, for example, where almost all the men who called on the people to join in the national struggle were condemned to death or searched for by the French police, confidence was proportional to the hopelessness of each case. You could be sure of a new recruit when he could no longer go back into the colonial system. This mechanism, it seems, had existed in Kenya among the Mau-Mau, who required that each member of the group should strike a blow at the victim. Each one was thus personally responsible for the death of that victim. To work means to work for the death of the settler. This assumed responsibility for violence allows both strayed and outlawed members of the group to come back again and to find their place once more, to become integrated. Violence is thus seen as comparable to a royal pardon. The colonized man finds his freedom in and through violence. This rule of conduct enlightens the agent because it indicates to him the means and the end.

· · ·

It is understandable that in this atmosphere, daily life becomes quite simply impossible. You can no longer be a fellah, a pimp, or an alcoholic as before. The violence of the colonial regime and the counter-violence of the native balance each other and respond to each other in an extraordinary reciprocal homogeneity. This reign of violence will be the more terrible in proportion to the size of the implantation from the mother country. The development of violence among the colonized people will be proportionate to the violence exercised by the threatened colonial regime. In the first phase of this insurrectional period,

the home governments are the slaves of the settlers, and these settlers seek to intimidate the natives and their home governments at one and the same time. They use the same methods against both of them. The assassination of the Mayor of Evian, in its method and motivation, is identifiable with the assassination of Ali Boumendjel. For the settlers, the alternative is not between *Algérie algérienne* and *Algérie française* but between an independent Algeria and a colonial Algeria, and anything else is mere talk or attempts at treason. The settler's logic is implacable and one is only staggered by the counter-logic visible in the behavior of the native insofar as one has not clearly understood beforehand the mechanisms of the settler's ideas. From the moment that the native has chosen the methods of counter-violence, police reprisals automatically call forth reprisals on the side of the nationalists. However, the results are not equivalent, for machine-gunning from airplanes and bombardments from the fleet go far beyond in horror and magnitude any answer the natives can make. This recurring terror de-mystifies once and for all the most estranged members of the colonized race. They find out on the spot that all the piles of speeches on the equality of human beings do not hide the commonplace fact that the seven Frenchmen killed or wounded at the Col de Sakamody kindles the indignation of all civilized consciences, whereas the sack of the douars* of Guergour and of the dechras of Djerah and the massacre of whole populations—which had merely called forth the Sakamody ambush as a reprisal—all this is of not the slightest importance. Terror, counter-terror, violence, counter-violence: that is what observers bitterly record when they describe the circle of hate, which is so tenacious and so evident in Algeria.

In all armed struggles, there exists what we might call the point of no return. Almost always it is marked off by a huge and all-inclusive repression which engulfs all sectors of the colonized people.

· · ·

But it so happens that for the colonized people this violence, because it constitutes their only work,

---

*Temporary village for the use of shepherds. — *Trans.*

invests their characters with positive and creative qualities. The practice of violence binds them together as a whole, since each individual forms a violent link in the great chain, a part of the great organism of violence which has surged upward in reaction to the settler's violence in the beginning. The groups recognize each other and the future nation is already indivisible. The armed struggle mobilizes the people; that is to say, it throws them in one way and in one direction.

The mobilization of the masses, when it arises out of the war of liberation, introduces into each man's consciousness the ideas of a common cause, of a national destiny, and of a collective history. In the same way the second phase, that of the building-up of the nation, is helped on by the existence of this cement which has been mixed with blood and anger. Thus we come to a fuller appreciation of the originality of the words used in these underdeveloped countries. During the colonial period the people are called upon to fight against oppression; after national liberation, they are called upon to fight against poverty, illiteracy, and underdevelopment. The struggle, they say, goes on. The people realize that life is an unending contest.

We have said that the native's violence unifies the people. By its very structure, colonialism is separatist and regionalist. Colonialism does not simply state the existence of tribes; it also reinforces it and separates them. The colonial system encourages chieftaincies and keeps alive the old Marabout confraternities. Violence is in action all-inclusive and national. It follows that it is closely involved in the liquidation of regionalism and of tribalism. Thus the national parties show no pity at all toward the caids and the customary chiefs. Their destruction is the preliminary to the unification of the people.

At the level of individuals, violence is a cleansing force. It frees the native from his inferiority complex and from his despair and inaction; it makes him fearless and restores his self-respect. Even if the armed struggle has been symbolic and the nation is demobilized through a rapid movement of decolonization, the people have the time to see that the liberation has been the business of each and all and that the leader has no special merit. From thence comes that type of aggressive reticence with regard to the machinery of protocol which young governments quickly show. When the people have taken violent part in the national liberation they will allow no one to set themselves up as "liberators." They show themselves to be jealous of the results of their action and take good care not to place their future, their destiny, or the fate of their country in the hands of a living god. Yesterday they were completely irresponsible; today they mean to understand everything and make all decisions. Illuminated by violence the consciousness of the people rebels against any pacification. From now on the demagogues, the opportunists and the magicians have a difficult task. The action which has thrown them into a hand-to-hand struggle confers upon the masses a voracious taste for the concrete. The attempt at mystification becomes, in the long run, practically impossible.

Note

1. Friedrich Engels: *Anti-Dühring*, Part II, Chapter III, "Theory of Violence," p. 199.

Assimilation and Cultural Pluralism

RACISM AND SEXISM

Richard A. Wasserstrom

Richard A. Wasserstrom argues in favor of the ideal of assimilation. His argument is that group difference is neither natural nor necessary but arbitrary and that we can develop and defend standards of equality and justice that are unambiguous and that apply without discrimination to members of all groups and that maximize the individual choice of all. (Source: From Philosophy and Social Issues *by Richard A. Wasserstrom. Copyright © 1980 by University of Notre Dame Press. Used by permission of the publisher.)*

Racism and sexism are two central issues that engage the attention of many persons living within the United States today. But while there is relatively little disagreement about their importance as topics, there is substantial, vehement, and apparently intractable disagreement about what individuals, practices, ideas, and institutions are either racist or sexist — and for what reason. In dispute are a number of related questions concerning how individuals and institutions ought to regard and respond to matters relating to race or sex.

. . .

There are four questions, or domains of inquiry, that I think it essential to distinguish and keep separate. The first is what I call the question of the social realities. Within this domain, one is concerned with asking what is the correct, complete description of the existing social arrangements in respect to either the characteristic of race or sex. Under the category of social arrangements I mean to include such things as the existing institutional structures, laws, practices, places in society, attitudes, and ideologies — and within the idea of an ideology I include both beliefs about the facts and beliefs about the appropriateness of the existing set of arrangements.

The second question is devoted to the task of explanation. Given a description of what the social reality at any given time and place is, one can certainly ask how things got that way and by what mechanisms they tend to be perpetuated or changed. There can be, and typically is, an array of competing explanatory theories concerning the causes of the social reality and the determinants of social change and stability. For example, much of the literature about the social relations between men and women is focused upon this question of explanation. Complex and sophisticated theories utilizing the ideas of Freud, Levi-Strauss, and Marx have been developed to explain the past and present oppression of women.[1] Alternative theories, drawing upon such things as the behavior of animals, the nature of early human societies, and the psychological and physiological differences between men and women, have also been offered to explain the dominance of males.[2]

The third question is what I call the question of ideals. Within this domain one is concerned with asking the question of how things ought be arranged: if we had the good or the just society in respect to race or sex, if the social reality were changed so that it in fact conformed to our vision of what the social arrangements ought to be as to these characteristics, what would that society's institutions, practices, and ideology be in respect to matters of racial and sexual differentiation? In other words, what, if anything, would be the social significance of race or sex in a society which got things right as to these two characteristics; when, if at all, would either individuals or institutions ever care about and make social decisions concerning the race or sex of the individuals in that society?

The fourth and final question is that of instrumentalities. Once one has developed the correct account of the social realities, and the most defensible conception of the nature of the good society, and the most adequate theory of how the social realities came about and are maintained, then the remaining question is the broadly instrumental one of the appropriate vehicle of social change. How, given all of this, might a society most effectively and fairly move from the existing state of affairs to a closer approximation of the ideal?

It is a central part of my thesis that many of the debates over matters pertaining to race or sex are less illuminating than they otherwise would be because they neglect to take into account these four different domains, each of which is important and deserving of separate consideration, and to identify clearly which of these four questions is in fact being addressed. . . . When the issues are properly disentangled, one thing that is possible is that what might be an impermissible way to take race or sex into account in the ideal society, may nonetheless be a desirable and appropriate way to take race or sex into account, given the social realities.

. . .

Just as we can and must ask what is involved in our or any other culture in being of one race or one sex rather than the other, and how individuals are in

fact viewed and treated, we can also ask a different question, namely, what would the good or just society make of an individual's race or sex, and to what degree, if at all, would racial and sexual distinctions ever properly be taken into account there? Indeed, it could plausibly be argued that we could not have a wholly adequate idea of whether a society was racist or sexist unless we had some conception of what a thoroughly nonracist or nonsexist society would look like. This question is an extremely instructive as well as an often neglected one. Comparatively little theoretical literature that deals with either racism or sexism has concerned itself in a systematic way with this issue, but as will be seen it is in some respects both a more important and a more complicated one where sex is concerned than where race is involved.[3] Moreover, as I shall argue, many discussions of sexual differences which touch upon this question do so inappropriately by concentrating upon the relatively irrelevant question of whether the differences between males and females are biological rather than social in origin.

The inquiry that follows addresses and seeks to answer two major questions. First, what are the major, plausible conceptions of what the good society would look like in respect to the race and sex of individuals, and how are these conceptions to be correctly characterized and described? And second, given a delineation of the alternatives, what is to be said in favor or against one or another of them? Here, the focus is upon two more specific issues. One concerns the relevance and force of the various arguments founded upon nature and the occurrence of natural differences for the preservation of sex roles and sexual or racial differences in the good society. The other concerns some of the central moral arguments for the elimination of sex roles and the diminution, if not elimination, of the importance of distinctions connected with one's sex or race.

In order to ask more precisely what some of the possible ideals are of desirable racial or sexual differentiation, it is necessary to ask: Differentiation in respect to what? And one way to do this is to distinguish in a crude way among three levels or areas of social and political arrangements and activities. First, there is the area of basic political rights and obligations, including such things as the rights to vote and to travel, and the obligation to pay taxes. Second, there is the area of important, but perhaps less primary institutional benefits and burdens of both governmental and nongovernmental types. Examples are access to and employment in the significant economic markets, the opportunity to acquire and enjoy housing in the setting of one's choice, the right of persons who want to marry each other to do so, and the duties (nonlegal as well as legal) that persons acquire in getting married. And third, there is the area of individual, social interaction, including such matters as whom one will marry, have as friends, and, perhaps, what aesthetic preferences one will cultivate and enjoy.

As to each of these three areas we can ask, for example, whether in a nonracist or a nonsexist society it would be thought appropriate ever to take the race or sex of an individual into account. It is, for instance, a widely held, but by no means unanimously accepted, view that we would have the good society in respect to race if race were to be a wholly unimportant characteristic of individuals—if, that is, race were to function in the lives of individuals in the way in which eye color now does.

Thus, one conception of a nonracist society is that which is captured by what I shall call the assimilationist ideal: a nonracist society would be one in which the race of an individual would be the functional equivalent of the eye color of individuals in our society today.[4] In our society no basic political rights and obligations are determined on the basis of eye color. No important institutional benefits and burdens are connected with eye color. Indeed, except for the mildest sort of aesthetic preferences, a person would be thought odd who even made private, social decisions by taking eye color into account. It would, of course, be unintelligible, and not just odd, were a person to say today that while he or she looked blue-eyed, he or she regarded himself or herself as really a brown-eyed person. Because eye color functions differently in our culture than does race, there is no analogue to passing for eye color. Were the assimilationist ideal to become a reality, the same would be true of one's race. In short, according to the assimilationist idea, a nonracist society would be one in which an individual's race was of no more significance in any of these three areas than is eye color today.

What is a good deal less familiar is an analogous conception of the good society in respect to sexual differentiation—one in which an individual's sex were to become a comparably unimportant characteristic. An assimilationist society in respect to sex would be one in which an individual's sex was of no more significance in any of the three areas than is eye color today. There would be no analogue to transsexuality, and, while physiological or anatomical sex differences would remain, they would possess only the kind and degree of significance that today attaches to the physiologically distinct eye colors persons possess.

It is apparent that the assimilationist ideal in respect to sex does not seem to be as readily plausible and obviously attractive here as it is in the case of race. In fact, many persons invoke the possible realization of the assimilationist ideal as a reason for rejecting the Equal Rights Amendment and indeed the idea of women's liberation itself. The assimilationist ideal may be just as good and just as important an ideal in respect to sex as it is in respect to race, but it is important to realize at the outset that this appears to be a more far-reaching proposal when applied to sex rather than race and that many more persons think there are good reasons why an assimilationist society in respect to sex would not be desirable than is true for the comparable racial ideal. Before such a conception is assessed, however, it will be useful to provide a somewhat fuller characterization of its features.

To begin with, it must be acknowledged that to make the assimilationist ideal a reality in respect to sex would involve more profound and fundamental revisions of our institutions and our attitudes than would be the case in respect to race. On the institutional level we would, for instance, have to alter significantly our practices concerning marriage. If a nonsexist society is a society in which one's sex is no more significant than eye color in our society today, then laws which require the persons who are getting married to be of different sexes would clearly be sexist laws.

More importantly, given the significance of role differentiation and ideas about the psychological differences in temperament that are tied to sexual identity, the assimilationist ideal would be incompatible with all psychological and sex-role differentiation. That is to say, in such a society the ideology of the society would contain no proposition asserting the inevitable or essential attributes of masculinity or femininity; it would never encourage or discourage the ideas of sisterhood or brotherhood; and it would be unintelligible to talk about the virtues or the disabilities of being a woman or a man. In addition, such a society would not have any norms concerning the appropriateness of different social behavior depending upon whether one were male or female. There would be no conception of the existence of a set of social tasks that were more appropriately undertaken or performed by males or by females. And there would be no expectation that the family was composed of one adult male and one adult female, rather than, say, just two adults—if two adults seemed the appropriate number. To put it simply, in the assimilationist society in respect to sex, persons would not be socialized so as to see or understand themselves or others as essentially or significantly who they were or what their lives would be like because they were either male or female. And no political rights or social institutions, practices, and norms would mark the physiological differences between males and females as important.[5]

Were sex like eye color, these kinds of distinctions would make no sense. Just as the normal, typical adult is virtually oblivious to the eye color of other persons for all significant interpersonal relationships, so, too, the normal, typical adult in this kind of nonsexist society would be equally as indifferent to the sexual, physiological differences of other persons for all significant interpersonal relationships. Bisexuality, not heterosexuality or homosexuality, would be the typical intimate, sexual relationship in the ideal society that was assimilationist in respect to sex.[6]

To acknowledge that things would be very different is, of course, hardly to concede that they would thereby be undesirable—or desirable for that matter. But still, the problem is, perhaps, with the assimilationist ideal. And the assimilationist ideal is certainly not the only possible, plausible ideal.

There is, for instance, another one that is closely related to, but distinguishable from that of the assimilationist ideal. It can be understood by considering how religion rather than eye color tends to be thought about in our culture today and incorporated within social life today. If the good society were to match the present state of affairs in respect to one's religious identity, rather than the present state of affairs in respect to one's eye color, the two societies would be different, but not very greatly so. In neither would we find that the allocation of basic political rights and duties ever took an individual's religion into account. And there would be a comparable indifference to religion even in respect to most important institutional benefits and burdens—for example, access to employment in the desirable vocations, the opportunity to live where one wished to live, and the like. Nonetheless, in the good society in which religious differences were to some degree socially relevant, it would be deemed appropriate to have some institutions (typically those which are connected in an intimate way with these religions) which did in a variety of ways properly take the religion of members of the society into account. For example, it would be thought both permissible and appropriate for members of a religious group to join together in collective associations which have religious, educational, and social dimensions, and when it came to the employment of persons who were to be centrally engaged in the operation of those religious institutions (priests, rabbis and ministers, for example), it would be unobjectionable and appropriate explicitly to take the religion of job applicants into account. On the individual, interpersonal level, it might also be thought natural and possibly even admirable, were persons to some significant degree to select their associates, friends, and mates on the basis of their religious orientation. So there is another possible and plausible ideal of what the good society would look like in respect to a particular characteristic in which differences based upon the characteristic would be to some degree maintained in some aspects of institutional and interpersonal life. The diversity of the religious beliefs of individuals would be reflected in the society's institutional and ideological fabric in a way in which the diversity of eye color would not be in the assimilationist society. The picture is a more complex, somewhat less easily describable one than that of the assimilationist ideal.

There could be at least two somewhat different reasons why persons might think it preferable to have some ideal different from that of the assimilationist one in respect to religion. They might, for instance, think that heterodoxy in respect to religious belief and practice was a positive good. On this view they would see it as a loss—they would think it a worse society—

were everyone to be a member of the same religion. Or they might, instead, view heterodoxy in respect to religious belief and practice more as a necessary, lesser evil. On this view they would see nothing intrinsically better about diversity rather than uniformity in respect to religion, but they might also think that the evils of achieving anything like homogeneity far outweighed the possible benefits. That is to say, persons holding this position might believe, for instance, that there was one correct religion and that it would be good were everyone to accept and be a member of that religion, but they might also believe that it would be undesirable and wrong to try to structure the social and political institutions, or the socialization of persons in the society, in such a way that social benefits and burdens were distributed in accordance with one's religion or that significantly different norms of social behavior ought to be connected with being of one religion or the other. Because persons favoring religious diversity for either reason would desire and expect different religions to exist in the good society, and because religions themselves are composed of and require certain institutional structures of varying degrees of formality and complexity, the good society modeled upon this ideal would necessarily contain some acceptable social and interpersonal differentiation based upon the religious identity of the individuals in the society. As such, the rendering of the precise description of the right degree of differentiation based upon religion would be a more complex and more difficult undertaking than is true for the assimilationist ideal.

Nonetheless, it may be that in respect to sex, and conceivably, in respect to race, too, something more like this ideal of diversity in respect to religion is the right one. But one problem then — and it is a more substantial one than is sometimes realized — is to specify with a good deal of precision and care what that ideal really comes to in the matter of sexual or racial identity and degree of acceptable sexual or racial differentiation. Which institutional and personal differentiations would properly be permissible and which would not be? Which attitudes, beliefs, and role expectations concerning the meaning and significance of being male or female would be properly introduced and maintained in the good society and which would not be? Which attitudes, beliefs, and practices

would continue in the good society to constitute the meaning of ethnicity as a racial concept and which would have to be purged? Part, but by no means all, of the attractiveness of the assimilationist ideal is its clarity and simplicity. In the good society of the assimilationist sort we would be able to tell easily and unequivocally whether any law, practice, attitude, or form of socialization was in any respect either racist or sexist. Part, but by no means all, of the unattractiveness of any more pluralistic ideal concerning sex or race is that it makes the question of what is racist or sexist a much more difficult and complicated one to answer. But although simplicity and lack of ambiguity may be virtues, they are not the only virtues to be taken into account in deciding among competing ideals. We quite appropriately take other considerations to be relevant to an assessment of the value and worth of alternative, possible conceptions of nonracist and nonsexist societies. What has been said so far by no means settles the question.

Nor do I even mean to suggest that all persons who reject the assimilationist ideal in respect to sex would necessarily embrace something like the kind of pluralistic ideal I have described as matching something like our present arrangements and ideas concerning the relevance of religious identity — although these do seem to exhaust the plausible ideals in respect to race. Some persons might think the right ideal was one in which substantially greater sexual differentiation and sex-role identification were retained than would be the case within a good society of that general type. Thus, someone might believe, for instance, that the good society was, perhaps, essentially like the one they think we now have in respect to sex: equality of basic political rights, such as the right to vote, but all of the sexual differentiation in both legal and nonlegal, formal and informal institutions, all of the sex-role socialization and all of the differences in matters of temperament that are characteristic of the way in which our society has been and still is ordered. And someone might also believe that the prevailing ideological concomitants of these arrangements are the correct and appropriate ones to perpetuate.[7]

This could, of course, be regarded as a version of the pluralistic ideal described above, with the emphasis upon the extensive character of the institutional, normative, and personal differences connected with sexual identity. Whether it is a form of this plu-ralistic ideal or a different ideal altogether turns, I think, upon two things: first, how pervasive the sexual differentiation is in terms of the number, impor-tance, and systemic interconnectedness of the institu-tions and role expectations connected with being of one sex or the other, and, second, whether the ideal contains within it a conception of the appropriate-ness of significant institutional and interpersonal in-equality, e.g., that the woman's job is in large measure to serve and be dominated by the male. The more ei-ther or both of these features is present, the clearer is the case for regarding this as an ideal, distinctively dif-ferent from either of the other two described so far. I shall indicate later why I think these two features make such a difference.

But the next question is that of how a choice is rationally to be made among these different, possible ideals. One general set of issues concerns the empiri-cal sphere, because the question of whether some-thing is a plausible and attractive ideal does turn in part on the nature of the empirical world. If it is true, for example, that any particular characteristic, such as an individual's race or sex, is not only a socially sig-nificant category in our culture but that it is largely a socially created one as well, then for many people a number of objections to the assimilationist ideal ap-pear immediately to disappear. The other general set of issues concerns the relevant normative considera-tions. Here the key questions concern the principles and considerations by which to assess and evaluate different conceptions of how persons ought to be able to live and how their social institutions ought to be constructed and arranged. I begin with the empirical considerations and constraints, although one heuris-tic disadvantage in doing so is that this decision may appear to give them greater weight than, as I shall ar-gue, they in fact deserve.

What opponents of assimilationism and propo-nents of schemes of strong sexual differentiation seize upon is that sexual difference appears to be a naturally occurring category of obvious and inevitable rele-vance for the construction of any plausible concep-tion of the nature of the good society.[8] The problems with this way of thinking are twofold. To begin with, a careful and thorough analysis of the social realities would reveal, I believe, that it is the socially created

sexual differences which constitute most of our con-ception of sex differences and which tend in fact to matter the most in the way we live our lives as persons of one sex or the other. For, it is, I think, sex-role dif-ferentiation and socialization, not the physiological and related biological differences — if there are any — that make men and women as different as they are from each other, and it is these same sex-role-created differences which are invoked to justify the necessity or the desirability of most sexual differentiation pro-posed to be maintained at any of the levels of social arrangements and practices described earlier.[9]

It is important, however, not to attach any greater weight than is absolutely necessary to the truth or fal-sity of this causal claim about the source of the degree of sexual distinctions that exist in our or other cul-tures. For what is significant, although seldom recog-nized, is the fact that the answer to that question al-most never goes very far in settling the question of what the good society should look like in respect to any particular characteristic of individuals. And the answer certainly does not go as far as many persons appear to believe it does to settle that question of the nature of the good society.

Let us suppose that there are what can be called "naturally occurring" sexual differences and even that they are of such a nature that they are in some sense of direct prima facie social relevance. It is essential to see that this would by no means settle the question of whether in the good society sex should or should not be as minimally significant as eye color. Even if there are major or substantial biological differences be-tween men and women that are in this sense "natural" rather than socially created, this does not determine the question of what the good society can and should make of these differences — without, that is, begging the question by including within the meaning of "ma-jor" or "substantial" or "natural" the idea that these are things that ought to be retained, emphasized, or oth-erwise normatively taken into account. It is not easy to see why, without begging the question, it should be thought that this fact, if it is a fact, settles the question adversely to anything like the assimilationist ideal. Persons might think that truths of this sort about na-ture or biology do affect, if not settle, the question of what the good society should look like for at least two different reasons.

In the first place, they might think the differences are of such a character that they substantially affect what would be *possible* within a good society of human persons. Just as the fact that humans are mortal necessarily limits the features of any possible good society, so, they might argue, the fact that males and females are physiologically or biologically different limits in the same way the features of any possible good society.10

In the second place, they might think the differences are of such a character that they are relevant to the question of what would be *desirable* in the good society. That is to say, they might not think that the differences determine or affect to a substantial degree what is possible, but only that the differences are appropriately taken into account in any rational construction of an ideal social existence.

The second reason seems to be a good deal more plausible than the first. For there appear to be very few, if any, respects in which the ineradicable, naturally occurring differences between males and females *must* be taken into account. The industrial revolution has certainly made any of the general differences in strength between the sexes capable of being ignored by the good society for virtually all significant human activities.11 And even if it were true that women are naturally better suited than men to care for and nurture children, it is also surely the case that men can be taught to care for and nurture children well.12 Indeed, the one natural or biological fact that seems *required* to be taken into account is the fact that reproduction of the human species requires that the fetus develop *in utero* for a period of months. Sexual intercourse is not necessary, for artificial insemination is available. Neither marriage nor the nuclear family is necessary either for conception or child rearing. Given the present state of medical knowledge and what might be termed the natural realities of female pregnancy, it is difficult to see why any important institutional or interpersonal arrangements are constrained to take the existing biological differences as to the phenomenon of *in utero* pregnancy into account.

But to say all this is still to leave it a wholly open question to what degree the good society *ought* to build upon any ineradicable biological differences, or to create ones in order to construct institutions and sex roles which would thereby maintain a substantial degree of sexual differentiation. The way to answer that question is to consider and assess the arguments for and against doing so. What is significant is the fact that many of the arguments for doing so are less persuasive than they appear to be upon the initial statement of this possibility.

It might be argued, for instance, that the fact of menstruation could be used as a premise upon which to base the case for importantly different social roles for females than for males. But this could only plausibly be proposed if two things were true: first, that menstruation would be debilitating to women and hence relevant to social role even in a culture which did not teach women to view menstruation as a sign of uncleanliness or as a curse;13 and, second, that the way in which menstruation necessarily affected some or all women was in fact necessarily related in an important way to the role in question. But even if both of these were true, it would still be an open question whether any sexual differentiation ought to be built upon these facts. The society could still elect to develop institutions that would nullify the effect of these natural differences and it would still be an open question whether it ought to do so. Suppose, for example, what seems implausible — that some or all women will not be able to perform a particular task while menstruating, e.g., guard the border of a country. It would be possible, even easy, if the society wanted to, to arrange for substitute guards for the women who were incapacitated. We know that persons are not good guards when they are sleepy, and we make arrangements so that persons alternate guard duty to avoid fatigue. The same could be done for menstruating women, even given the implausibly strong assumptions about menstruation.

The point that is involved here is a very general one that has application in contexts having nothing to do with the desirability or undesirability of maintaining substantial sexual differentiation. It has to do with the fact that humans possess the ability to alter their natural and social environment in distinctive, dramatic, and unique ways. An example from the nonsexual area can help bring out this too seldom recognized central feature. It is a fact that some persons born in human society are born with congenital features such that they cannot walk or walk well on their legs. They are born naturally crippled or lame.

However, humans in our society certainly possess the capability to devise and construct mechanical devices and institutional arrangements which render this natural fact about some persons relatively unimportant in respect to the way they and others will live together. We can bring it about, and in fact are in the process of bringing it about, that persons who are confined to wheelchairs can move down sidewalks and across streets because the curb stones at corners of intersections have been shaped so as to accommodate the passage of wheelchairs. And we can construct and arrange buildings and events so that persons in wheelchairs can ride elevators, park cars, and be seated at movies, lectures, meetings, and the like. Much of the environment in which humans live is the result of their intentional choices and actions concerning what that environment shall be like. They can elect to construct an environment in which the natural incapacity of some persons to walk or walk well is a major difference or a difference that will be effectively nullified vis-à-vis the lives that they, too, will live.

Nonhuman animals cannot do this in anything like the way humans can. A fox or an ape born lame is stuck with the fact of lameness and the degree to which that will affect the life it will lead. The other foxes or apes cannot change things. This capacity of humans to act intentionally and thereby continuously create and construct the world in which they and others will live is at the heart of what makes studies of nonhuman behavior essentially irrelevant to and for most if not all of the normative questions of social, political, and moral theory. Humans can become aware of the nature of their natural and social environment and then act intentionally to alter the environment so as to change its impact upon or consequences for the individuals living within it. Nonhuman animals cannot do so. This difference is, therefore, one of fundamental theoretical importance. At the risk of belaboring the obvious, what it is important to see is that the case against any picture of the good society of an assimilationist sort — if it is to be a defensible critique — ought to rest on arguments concerned to show why some other ideal would be preferable; it cannot plausibly rest in any significant respect upon the claim that the sorts of biological differences typically alluded to in contexts

such as these require that the society not be assimilationist in character.

There are, though, several other arguments based upon nature, or the idea of the "natural" that also must be considered and assessed. First, it might be argued that if a way of doing something is natural, then it ought to be done that way. Here, what may be meant by "natural" is that this way of doing the thing is the way it would be done if culture did not direct or teach us to do it differently. It is not clear, however, that this sense of "natural" is wholly intelligible; it supposes that we can meaningfully talk about how humans would behave in the absence of culture. And few if any humans have ever lived in such a state. Moreover, even if this is an intelligible notion, the proposal that the natural way to behave is somehow the appropriate or desirable way to behave is strikingly implausible. It is, for example, almost surely natural, in this sense of "natural," that humans would eat their food with their hands, except for the fact that they are, almost always, socialized to eat food differently. Yet, the fact that humans would naturally eat this way, does not seem in any respect to be a reason for believing that that is thereby the desirable or appropriate way to eat food. And the same is equally true of any number of other distinctively human ways of behaving.

Second, someone might argue that substantial sexual differentiation is natural not in the sense that it is biologically determined not in the sense that it would occur but for the effects of culture, but rather in the sense that substantial sexual differentiation is a virtually universal phenomenon in human culture. By itself, this claim of virtual universality, even if accurate, does not directly establish anything about the desirability or undesirability of any particular ideal. But it can be made into an argument by the addition of the proposition that where there is a widespread, virtually universal social practice or institution, there is probably some good or important purpose served by the practice or institution. Hence, given the fact of substantial sex-role differentiation in all, or almost all, cultures, there is on this view some reason to think that substantial sex-role differentiation serves some important purpose for and in human society.

This is an argument, but it is hard to see what is attractive about it. The premise which turns the fact of sex-role differentiation into any kind of a strong reason for sex-role differentiation is the premise of conservatism. And it is no more or less convincing here than elsewhere. There are any number of practices or institutions that are typical and yet upon reflection seem without significant social purpose. Slavery was once such an institution; war perhaps still is.

More to the point, perhaps, the concept of "purpose" is ambiguous. It can mean in a descriptive sense "plays some role" or "is causally relevant." Or, it can mean in a prescriptive sense "does something desirable" or "has some useful function." If "purpose" is used descriptively in the conservative premise, then the argument says nothing about the continued desirability of sex-role differentiation or the assimilationist ideal. If "purpose" is used prescriptively in the conservative premise, then there is no reason to think that premise is true.[14]

To put it another way, the question that seems fundamentally to be at issue is whether it is desirable to have a society in which sex-role differences are to be retained in the way and to the degree they are today — or even at all. The straightforward way to think about the question is to ask what would be good and what would be bad about a society in which sex functioned like eye color does in our society; or alternatively, what would be good and what would be bad about a society in which sex functioned in the way in which religious identity does today; or alternatively, what would be good and what would be bad about a society in which sex functioned in the way in which it does today. We can imagine what such societies would look like and how they might work. It is hard to see how thinking about answers to this question is substantially advanced by reference to what has typically or always been the case. If it is true, for instance, that the sex-role-differentiated societies that have existed have tended to concentrate power and authority in the hands of males, have developed institutions and ideologies that have perpetuated that concentration, and have restricted and prevented women from living the kinds of lives that persons ought to be able to live for themselves, then this, it seems to me, says far more about what may be wrong with any strongly nonassimilationist ideal than does the conservative premise say what may be right about any strongly nonassimilationist ideal.

This does not, however, exhaust the reasons why persons might think that the question of whether sex differences are naturally occurring differences is an important or relevant one. There are at least two others. First, if the differences are natural, rather than socially created, it might be thought that there is less of an obligation to correct or alter the impact or effect that those differences will play in the lives people will be able to live in the society. That is to say, if it is nature, or biology, that accounts for the differences that result, then the society is not causally responsible and for that reason is not to blame for or accountable for those differences. The cause is not society, but nature. If society were the cause, and if the differences produced arrangements that seemed unequal or unfair, then the fault would be society's and its obligation to remedy the situation would be clearer, more direct, and more stringent. But since it is not, the causal chain is different and society is, for this reason, off the hook of accountability. An argument such as this one is seldom made explicit, but it underlies, I suspect, much of the motivation for the belief in the relevance of the search for natural as opposed to social causation.

The difficulty here is that only if the question is cast in terms of a certain very particular conception of compensatory justice does the causal issue assume genuine relevance or importance. What remains unexplained is why that perspective should be seen to be the obviously correct or appropriate one from which to look at matters. For if the question were to be cast, instead, in terms of a conception of distributive justice — one that was, say, founded upon the importance of a *resulting* equality of distributional treatment — then the cause of the initial differences or inequalities becomes a substantially less significant issue. And, if the focus were to be on the more general question of what kind of society it would be desirable to have, then the correct causal explanation would be still less important. Consider again the fact that some persons are born lame while others are not. Even though social institutions did not cause the lameness at all, it is difficult to understand how that is at all decisive to the question of what the good society would do in the way of seeking to nullify the natural consequences of lameness through having certain institutions and arrangements rather than others. If the cause of undesirable existing inequalities or differences is socially created, then there is an additional argument of a compensatory sort for requiring that the society make the alterations necessary to change the operative social mechanisms. But the absence of such an argument in no way implies that things may therefore be appropriately or justly left the way nature has produced them.

The other argument is that if the differences are natural, then there are considerations of efficiency that come into play. If some persons are naturally less equipped or suited to do some things, then it will be less efficient than would otherwise be the case to bring it about that they will end up being able to do those things—either because they will not be able to do them as well as others, or because it will be most costly to bring it about that they will be able to do them as well as others who are differently endowed can do them. Here, too, there is, I think, something to the argument, but not as much as is typically supposed. If it is possible to arrange things so that the natural differences can be nullified, and if there are reasons of justice (or reasons of morality) for doing so, then it is as hard here, as elsewhere, to see why considerations of efficiency should necessarily be thought overriding.

There are, in fact, several different issues and arguments that may be involved here, and it is worthwhile trying to disentangle them. One issue is whether what underlies this line of thought is the view that all persons ought to be *required* to do whatever it is they are naturally endowed to do, and that, therefore, the social institutions should be designed so as to bring that state of affairs into being. On this view, if a person were naturally endowed to be a brain surgeon, or a garbage collector, the social institutions ought to at least direct if not require the person to end up in that role or place—irrespective of the person's desires and irrespective of the kind and quality of life allotted to the persons with differing natural endowments. A society organized in this fashion would, doubtless, be highly efficient in terms of the correspondence between natural endowments and places in society and the degree to which each person was living the life he or she was "naturally" suited for, but I do not see how one could easily argue that such a "naturally" ordered society would be either just or morally desirable. Apart from everything else, if one wanted a nice

philosophical example of a case of viewing persons wholly as a means—a case of using persons as objects—a society organized and justified along these lines would seem to be an obvious candidate.

But the argument about nature and efficiency may not be this sweeping. Perhaps instead the claim is only that in the good society at least those persons who are especially able or competent ought to be permitted to do what they are naturally able or competent to do. This is a substantially weaker thesis, and I shall assume for purposes of argument that it is defensible. This thesis is not, however, fundamentally at issue. The primary question is whether the society ought to be organized so that the less well endowed will be able to do things, live their lives, in a way that is more fully adequate and satisfactory. If some are naturally able to do certain things well, while others are less able naturally to do them, one complaint the better endowed could have about attempts to increase the abilities and opportunities of the less well endowed is that based upon the overall social cost involved in doing so. But the better endowed do not have a claim that, just because they happen to be better endowed by nature, they *alone* should have the opportunity to participate in institutions that depend upon or require certain abilities, talents, dispositions, and the like. They can claim that different social structures may be less efficient in terms of overall cost of having those social structures than ones in which they alone participate. But if there are considerations of justice or morality that favor these alternative "more expensive" arrangements, it seems plausible that considerations of efficiency should at least to some degree give way.

Perhaps, though, they have one other argument, namely, that if alternative social arrangements are to be preferred, then the society will be one in which the institutions do not permit them to utilize their natural talents to the fullest extent. This may be just a restatement of the argument from efficiency, or it may be an argument that the better endowed deserve to be able always to utilize their natural talents to the fullest.[15]

I do not think they can claim to deserve to be able always to utilize their natural talents to the fullest. They cannot claim this because, *ex hypothesi* since these are natural talents or capabilities, they manifestly did nothing to deserve these natural attributes. And while it may be good to permit them to utilize their talents—in terms of the happiness of those who are naturally better endowed—there is no reason to give their claims any greater weight than the claims of others on the ground that their talents or characteristics are naturally rather than socially produced. And it even seems plausible, for reasons analogous to those offered by Rawls for the difference principle, that if there are sacrifices of any sort to be made, it is fairer that they be made or borne by the naturally better rather than naturally worse off.

So, even supposing that there is a clear sense of natural endowments or capabilities based on sexual physiology, and even supposing that the natural differences between males and females were as strongly present "in nature" as the preceding arguments require, the conclusions to be drawn vis-à-vis the character of the good society would be appreciably weaker and more indeterminate than is typically supposed by those who focus upon the possible existence of biological differences between the sexes. The primary point that emerges is that the question of whether there are natural differences (in any of the above senses) between males and females (or even persons of different races) tends to get disputed on the wrong grounds. The debate tends to focus upon whether biology or society is the cause of the differences. The debate ought to attend instead to the question of why it matters. The debaters ought to address first the unasked question of within what theoretical inquiry the issue is even relevant. When the question is one of ideals, of what the good society would make of sexual or racial characteristics, the issue of natural as opposed to social causation is a strikingly irrelevant one. There do not, therefore, appear to be any very powerful, let alone conclusive, arguments against something like the assimilationist society that can be based on any of the different, possible appeals to nature and the natural.

If the chief thing to be said in favor of something like the assimilationist society in respect to sex is that some arguments against it are not very relevant, that does not by itself make a very convincing case. Such is not, however, the way in which matters need to be left. There is an affirmative case of sorts for something like the assimilationist society.

One strong, affirmative moral argument on behalf of the assimilationist ideal is that it does provide for a kind of individual autonomy that a substantially nonassimilationist society cannot provide. The reason is because any substantially nonassimilationist society will have sex roles, and sex roles interfere in basic ways with autonomy. The argument for these two propositions proceeds as follows.

Any nonassimilationist society must have some institutions and some ideology that distinguishes between individuals in virtue of their sexual physiology, and any such society will necessarily be committed to teaching the desirability of doing so. That is what is implied by saying it is nonassimilationist rather than assimilationist. And any substantially nonassimilationist society will make one's sexual identity an important characteristic so that there will be substantial psychological, role, and status differences between persons who are male and those who are female. That is what is implied by saying that it is substantially nonassimilationist. Any such society will necessarily have sex roles, a conception of the places, characteristics, behaviors, etc., that are appropriate to one sex or the other but not both. That is what makes it a *sex* role.

Now, sex roles are, I think, morally objectionable on two or three quite distinct grounds. One such ground is absolutely generic and applies to all sex roles. The other grounds are less generic and apply only to the kinds of sex roles with which we are familiar and which are a feature of patriarchal societies, such as our own. I begin with the more contingent, less generic objections.

We can certainly imagine, if we are not already familiar with, societies in which the sex roles will be such that the general place of women in that society can be described as that of the servers of men. In such a society individuals will be socialized in such a way that women will learn how properly to minister to the needs, desires, and interests of men; women and men will both be taught that it is right and proper that the concerns and affairs of men are more important than and take precedence over those of women; and the norms and supporting set of beliefs and attitudes will be such that this role will be deemed the basic and appropriate role for women to play and men to expect. Here, I submit, what is objectionable about the connected set of institutions, practices, and ideology— the structure of the prevailing sex role—is the role itself. It is analogous to a kind of human slavery. The fundamental moral defect — just as is the case with slavery — is not that women are being arbitrarily or capriciously assigned to the social role of server, but that such a role itself has no legitimate place in the decent or just society. As a result, just as is the case with slavery, the assignment on *any* basis of individuals to such a role is morally objectionable. A society arranged so that such a role is a prominent part of the structure of the social institutions can be properly characterized as an *oppressive* one. It consigns some individuals to lives which have no place in the good society, which restrict unduly the opportunities of these individuals, and which do so in order improperly to enhance the lives and opportunities of others.

But it may be thought possible to have sex roles and all that goes with them without having persons of either sex placed within a position of general, systemic dominance or subordination. Here, it would be claimed, the society would not be an oppressive one in this sense. Consider, for example, the kinds of sex roles with which we are familiar and which assign to women the primary responsibilities for child rearing and household maintenance. It might be argued first that the roles of child rearer and household maintainer are not in themselves roles that could readily or satisfactorily be eliminated from human society without the society itself being deficient in serious, unacceptable ways. It might be asserted, that is, that these are roles or tasks that simply must be filled if children are to be raised in a satisfactory way. Suppose this is correct, suppose it is granted that society would necessarily have it that these tasks would have to be done. Still, if it is also correct that, relatively speaking, these are unsatisfying and unfulfilling ways for humans to concentrate the bulk of their energies and talents, then, to the degree to which this is so, what is morally objectionable is that if this is to be a *sex* role, then women are unduly and unfairly allocated a disproportionate share of what is unpleasant, unsatisfying, unrewarding work. Here the objection is the degree to which the burden women are required to assume is excessive and unjustified vis-à-vis the rest of society, i.e., the men. Unsatisfactory roles and tasks, when they are substantial and pervasive, should surely be allocated and filled in the good society in a way which seeks to distribute the burdens involved in a roughly equal fashion.

Suppose, though, that even this feature were eliminated from sex roles, so that, for instance, men and women shared more equally in the dreary, unrewarding aspects of housework and child care, and that a society which maintained sex roles did not in any way have as a feature of that society the systemic dominance or superiority of one sex over the other, there would still be a generic moral defect that would remain. The defect would be that any set of sex roles would necessarily impair and retard an individual's ability to develop his or her own characteristics, talents, capacities, and potential life-plans to the extent to which he or she might desire and from which he or she might derive genuine satisfaction. Sex roles, by definition, constitute empirical and normative limits of varying degrees of strength — restrictions on what it is that one can expect to do, be, or become. As such, they are, I think, at least prima facie objectionable.

To some degree, all role-differentiated living is restrictive in this sense. Perhaps, therefore, all role differentiation in society is to some degree troublesome, and perhaps all strongly role-differentiated societies are objectionable. But the case against sex roles and the concomitant sexual differentiation they create and require need not rest upon this more controversial point. For one thing that distinguishes sex roles from many other roles is that they are wholly involuntarily assumed. One has no choice about whether one shall be born a male or female. And if it is a consequence of one's being born a male or a female that one's subsequent emotional, intellectual, and material development will be substantially controlled by this fact, then it is necessarily the case that substantial, permanent, and involuntarily assumed restraints have been imposed on some of the most central factors concerning the way one will shape and live one's life. The point to be emphasized is that this would necessarily be the case, even in the unlikely event that substantial sexual differentiation could be maintained without one sex or the other becoming dominant and developing oppressive institutions and an ideology to support that dominance and oppression. Absent some far stronger showing than seems either reasonable or possible that potential talents, abilities, interests, and the like are inevitably and irretrievably distributed between the sexes in such a way that the sex roles of the society are genuinely congruent with and facilitative of the development of those talents, abilities, interests, and the like that individuals can and do possess, sex roles are to this degree incompatible with the kind of respect which the good or the just society would accord to each of the individual persons living within it. It seems to me, therefore, that there are persuasive reasons to believe that no society which maintained what I have been describing as *substantial* sexual differentiation could plausibly be viewed as a good or just society.

What remains more of an open question is whether a society in which sex functioned in the way in which eye color does (a strictly assimilationist society in respect to sex) would be better or worse than one in which sex functioned in the way in which religious identity does in our society (a nonoppressive, more diversified or pluralistic one). For it might be argued that especially in the case of sex and even in the case of race much would be gained and nothing would be lost if the ideal society in respect to these characteristics succeeded in preserving in a nonoppressive fashion the attractive differences between males and females and the comparably attractive differences among ethnic groups. Such a society, it might be claimed, would be less bland, less homogeneous and richer in virtue of its variety.

I do not think there is any easy way to settle this question, but I do think the attractiveness of the appeal to diversity, when sex or race are concerned, is less alluring than is often supposed. The difficulty is in part one of specifying what will be preserved and what will not, and in part one of preventing the reappearance of the type of systemic dominance and subservience that produces the injustice of oppression. Suppose, for example, that it were suggested that there are aspects of being male and aspects of being female that are equally attractive and hence desirable to maintain and perpetuate: the kind of empathy that is associated with women and the kind of self-control associated with men. It does not matter what the characteristic is, the problem is one of seeing why the characteristic should be tied by the social institutions to the sex of the individuals of the society. If the characteristics are genuinely ones that all individuals ought to be encouraged to display in the appropriate circumstances, then the social institutions and ideology ought to endeavor to foster them in all individuals. If it is good for everyone to be somewhat empathetic all of the time or especially empathetic in some circumstances, or good for everyone to have a certain a degree of self-control all of the time or a great deal in some circumstances, then there is no reason to preserve institutions which distribute these psychological attributes along sexual lines. And the same is true for many, if not all, vocations, activities, and ways of living. If some, but not all persons would find a life devoted to child rearing genuinely satisfying, it is good, surely, that that option be open to them. Once again, though, it is difficult to see the argument for implicitly or explicitly encouraging, teaching, or assigning to women, as opposed to men, that life simply in virtue of their sex. Thus, while substantial diversity in individual characteristics, attitudes, and ways of life is no doubt an admirable, even important feature of the good society, what remains uncertain is the necessity or the desirability of continuing to link attributes or behaviors such as these to the race or sex of individuals. And for the reasons I have tried to articulate there are significant moral arguments against any conception of the good society in which such connections are pursued and nourished in the systemic fashion required by the existence and maintenance of *sex* roles.

Notes

1. For an example of this kind of theory see Rubin, "The Traffic in Women" in Reiter (ed.), *Toward an Anthropology of Women* (New York: Monthly Review Press, 1975), pp. 157–210.

2. For an example of this kind of theory see Tiger, *Men in Groups* (New York: Random House, 1969).

3. One of the few thorough and valuable explorations of this question as it relates to sexual difference is Jaggar's "On Sexual Equality," 84 *Ethics* 275 (1974). The article also contains a very useful analysis of the views of other feminist writers who have dealt with this topic.

4. There is a danger in calling this ideal the "assimilationist" ideal. That term often suggests the idea of incorporating oneself, one's values, and the like into the dominant group and its practices and values. No part of that idea is meant to be captured by my use of the term. Mine is a stipulative definition.

5. Jaggar describes something fairly close to the assimilationist view in this way:

   "The traditional feminist answer to this question [of what the features of a non-sexist society would be] has been that a sexually egalitarian society is one in which virtually no public recognition is given to the fact that there is a physiological sex difference between persons. This is not to say that the different reproductive function of each sex should be unacknowledged in such a society nor that there should be no physicians specializing in female and male complaints, etc. But it is to say that, except in this sort of context, the question whether someone is female or male should have no significance. . . .

". . . In the mainstream tradition, the nonsexist society is one which is totally integrated sexually, one in which sexual differences have ceased to be a matter of public concern." Jaggar, *supra* note 3, at 276–77.

6. In describing the assimilationist society in this fashion, I do not mean thereby to be addressing the question of how government and laws would regulate all of these matters, or even whether they would. I am describing what laws, practices, attitudes, conventions, ideology, behavior, and the like one would expect to find. These might be reasons, for example, why it would be undesirable to have laws that regulated interpersonal relationships and personal preferences. We have no such laws concerning eye color and interpersonal relationships and yet it is generally irrelevant in this area. If the entire cultural apparatus were different from what it now is in respect to race or sex, we can imagine that race and sex would lose their significance in the analogous ways, even in the absence of laws which regulated all dimensions of social life.

7. Thus, for example, a column appeared a few years ago in the *Washington Star* concerning the decision of the Cosmos Club to continue to refuse to permit women to be members. The author of the column (and a member of the club) defended the decision on the ground that women appropriately had a different status in the society. Their true distinction was to be achieved by being faithful spouses and devoted mothers. The column closed with this paragraph:

"In these days of broken homes, derision of marriage, reluctance to bear children, contempt for the institution of family — a phase in our national life when it seems more honorable to be a police-woman, or a model, or an accountant than to be a wife or mother — there is a need to reassert a traditional scale of values in which the vocation of homemaker is as honorable and distinguished as any in political or professional life. Such women, as wives and widows of members, now enjoy in the club the privileges of their status, which includes [*sic*] their own drawing rooms, and it is of interest that they have been among the most outspoken opponents of the proposed changes in

club structure." Groseclose, "Now — Shall We Join the Ladies?" *Washington Star,* Mar. 13, 1975.

8. This is not to deny that certain people believe that race is linked with characteristics that prima facie are relevant. Such beliefs persist. They are, however, unjustified by the evidence. *See, e.g.,* Block & Dworkin, "IQ, Heritability and Inequality," 3 *Phil & Pub. Aff.* 331 (1974); 4 *id.* 40 (1974). More to the point, even if it were true that such a linkage existed, none of the characteristics suggested would require that political or social institutions, or interpersonal relationships, would have to be structured in a certain way.

9. *See, e.g.,* authorities cited in note 15, *supra*; Mead, *Sex and Temperament in Three Primitive Societies* (New York: Morrow, 1935).

"These three situations [the cultures of the Anapesh, the Mundugumor, and the Tchambuli] suggest, then, a very definite conclusion. If those temperamental attitudes which we have traditionally regarded as feminine — such as passivity, responsiveness, and a willingness to cherish children — can so easily be set up as the masculine pattern in one tribe, and in another to be outlawed for the majority of women as well as for the majority of men, we no longer have any basis for regarding such aspects of behaviour as sex-linked. . . .

". . . We are forced to conclude that human nature is almost unbelievably maleable, responding accurately and contrastingly to contrasting cultural conditions. . . . Standardized personality differences between the sexes are of this order, cultural creations to which each generation, male and female is trained to conform." *Id.,* at 190–91.

A somewhat different view is expressed in Sherman, *On the Psychology of Women* (Springfield, Ill.: C. C. Thomas, 1975). There the author suggests that there are "natural" differences of a psychological sort between men and women, the chief ones being aggressiveness and strength of sex drive. *See id.* at 238. However, even if she is correct as to these biologically based differences, this does little to establish what the good society should look like. *See* pp. 30–38 *infra.*

Almost certainly the most complete discussion of this topic is Maccoby & Jacklin, *The Psychology of Sex Differences* (Stanford, Cal.: Stanford U. Press, 1974). The authors conclude that the sex differences which are, in their words, "fairly well established," are: (1) that girls have greater verbal ability than boys; (2) that boys excel in visual-spatial ability; (3) that boys excel in mathematical ability; and (4) that males are aggressive. *Id.* at 351–52. They conclude, in respect to the etiology of these psychological sex differences, that there appears to be a biological component to the greater visual-spatial ability of males and to their greater aggressiveness. *Id.* at 360.

10. As H. L. A. Hart has observed in a different context, if humans had a different physical structure such that they were virtually invulnerable to physical attack or assault by other humans, this would alter radically the character or role of substantial segments of the criminal and civil law. Hart, *The Concept of Law* (Oxford: At the Clarendon Press, 1961), p. 190. But humans are, of course, not like this at all. The fact that humans are vulnerable to injury by others is a natural fact that affects the features of any meaningful conception of the good society.

11. As Sherman observes, "Each sex has its own special physical assets and liabilities. The principal female liability of less muscular strength is not ordinarily a handicap in a civilized, mechanized, society. . . . There is nothing in the biological evidence to prevent women from taking a role of equality in a civilized society." Sherman, *supra* note 9, at 11.

    There are, of course, some activities that would be sexually differentiated in the assimilationist society, namely, those that were specifically directed toward, say, measuring unaided physical strength. Thus, I think it likely that even in this ideal society, weight-lifting contests and boxing matches would in fact be dominated, perhaps exclusively so, by men. But it is hard to find any significant activities or institutions that are analogous. And it is not clear that such insignificant activities would be thought worth continuing, especially since sports function in existing patriarchal societies to help maintain the dominance of males . . .

    It is possible that there are some nontrivial activities or occupations that depend sufficiently directly upon unaided physical strength that most if not all women would be excluded. Perhaps being a lifeguard at the ocean is an example. Even here, though, it would be important to see whether the way lifeguarding had traditionally been done could be changed to render such physical strength unimportant. If it could be changed, then the question would simply be one of whether the increased cost (or loss of efficiency) was worth the gain in terms of equality and the avoidance of sex-role differentiation. In a nonpatriarchal society very different from ours, where sex was not a dominant social category, the argument from efficiency might well prevail. What is important, once again, is to see how infrequent and peripheral such occupational cases are.

12. Once again, though, I believe there is substantial evidence that to sex-role socialization and not to biology is far more plausibly attributed the dominant causal role in the relative child-rearing capacities and dispositions of men and women in our and other societies.

13. *See, e.g.,* Paige, "Women Learn to Sing the Menstrual Blues," in C. Tavis (ed.), *The Female Experience* (Del Mar, Cal.: CRM, Inc., 1973), p. 17.

    "I have come to believe that the 'raging hormones' theory of menstrual distress simply isn't adequate. All women have the raging hormones, but not all women have menstrual symptoms, nor do they have the same symptoms for the same reasons. Nor do I agree with the 'raging neurosis' theory, which argues that women who have menstrual symptoms are merely whining neurotics, who need only a kind pat on the head to cure their problems.

    "We must instead consider the problems from the perspective of women's subordinate social position, and of the cultural ideology that so narrowly defines the behaviors and emotions that are appropriately 'feminine.' Women have perfectly good reasons to react emotionally to reproductive events. Menstruation, pregnancy and childbirth—so sacred, yet so unclean—are the woman's primary avenues of achievement and self-expression. Her reproductive abilities define her femininity; other routes to success are only second-best in this society. . . .

    ". . . My current research on a sample of 114 societies around the world indicates that ritual observances and taboos about menstruation are a method of controlling women and their fertility. Men apparently use such rituals, along with those surrounding pregnancy and childbirth, to assert their claims to women and their children.

    ". . . The hormone theory isn't giving us much mileage, and it's time to turn it in for a better model, one that looks to our beliefs about menstruation and women. It is no mere coincidence that women get the blue meanies along with an event they consider embarrassing, unclean—and a curse." *Id.* at 21.

14. *See also,* Joyce Trebilcot, "Sex Roles: The Argument from Nature," 85 *Ethics* 249 (1975).

15. Thomas Nagel suggests that the educationally most talented deserve, as a matter of "educational justice," the opportunity to develop their talents to the fullest. Thomas Nagel, "Equal Treatment and Compensatory Discrimination," 2 *Phil. & Pub. Aff.* 348, 356 (1973).

    I do not find the concept of educational justice a clear or even wholly intelligible one. Nor, I think, has Nagel adequately explained why this is a matter of desert at all.

SOCIAL MOVEMENTS AND THE POLITICS OF DIFFERENCE

Iris Marion Young

The idea that I think we need today in order to make decisions in political matters cannot be the idea of a totality, or of the unity, of a body. It can only be the idea of a multiplicity or a diversity. . . . To state that one must draw a critique of political judgment means today to do a politics of opinions that at the same time is a politics of Ideas . . . in which justice is not placed under a rule of convergence but rather a rule of divergence. I believe that this is the theme that one finds constantly in present day writing under the name "minority."

— Jean-François Lyotard

Iris Young argues against assimilation and in favor of what she calls the politics of difference. Her arguments against assimilation are that it denies the reality and desirability of social groups, fails to recognize that privilege and discrimination are on the basis of group membership, and that ignoring group differences has negative consequences. Her positive argument for the politics of difference are that it is liberatory and recognizes the reality and value of group difference. (Source: From Justice and the Politics of Difference. *Copyright © 1990 by Princeton University Press. Reprinted by permission of Princeton University Press.)*

There was once a time of caste and class, when tradition decreed that each group had its place, and that some are born to rule and others to serve. In this time of darkness, law and social norms defined rights, privileges, and obligations differently for different groups, distinguished by characteristics of sex, race, religion, class, or occupation. Social inequality was justified by church and state on the grounds that people have different natures, and some natures are better than others.

Then one day Enlightenment dawned, heralding a revolutionary conception of humanity and society. All people are equal, the revolutionaries declared, inasmuch as all have a capacity for reason and moral sense. Law and politics should therefore grant to everyone equal political and civil rights. With these bold ideas the battle lines of modern political struggle were drawn.

For over two hundred years since those voices of Reason first rang out, the forces of light have struggled for liberty and political equality against the dark forces of irrational prejudice, arbitrary metaphysics, and the crumbling towers of patriarchal church, state, and family. In the New World we had a head start in this fight, since the American War of Independence was fought on these Enlightenment principles, and our Constitution stood for liberty and equality. So we did not have to throw off the yokes of class and religious privilege, as did our Old World comrades. Yet the United States had its own oligarchic horrors in the form of slavery and the exclusion of women from public life. In protracted and bitter struggles these bastions of privilege based on group difference began to give way, finally to topple in the 1960s.

Today in our society a few vestiges of prejudice and discrimination remain, but we are working on them, and have nearly realized the dream those Enlightenment fathers dared to propound. The state and law should express rights only in universal terms applied equally to all, and differences among persons and groups should be a purely accidental and private matter. We seek a society in which differences of race, sex, religion, and ethnicity no longer make a difference to people's rights and opportunities. People should be treated as individuals, not as members of groups; their life options and rewards should be based solely on their individual achievement. All persons should have the liberty to be and do anything they want, to choose their own lives and not be hampered by traditional expectations and stereotypes.

We tell each other this story and make our children perform it for our sacred holidays—Thanksgiving Day, the Fourth of July, Memorial Day, Lincoln's Birthday. We have constructed Martin Luther King Day to fit the narrative so well that we have already forgotten that it took a fight to get it included in the canon year. There is much truth to this story. Enlightenment ideals of liberty and political equality did and do inspire movements against oppression and

445

domination, whose success has created social values and institutions we would not want to lose. A people could do worse than tell this story after big meals and occasionally call upon one another to live up to it.

The very worthiness of the narrative, however, and the achievement of political equality that it recounts, now inspires new heretics. In recent years the ideal of liberation as the elimination of group difference has been challenged by movements of the oppressed. The very success of political movements against differential privilege and for political equality has generated movements of group specificity and cultural pride.

In this chapter I criticize an ideal of justice that defines liberation as the transcendence of group difference, which I refer to as an ideal of assimilation. This ideal usually promotes equal treatment as a primary principle of justice. Recent social movements of oppressed groups challenge this ideal. Many in these movements argue that a positive self-definition of group difference is in fact more liberatory.

I endorse this politics of difference, and argue that at stake is the meaning of social difference itself. Traditional politics that excludes or devalues some persons on account of their group attributes assumes an essentialist meaning of difference; it defines groups as having different natures. An egalitarian politics of difference, on the other hand, defines difference more fluidly and relationally as the product of social processes.

An emancipatory politics that affirms group difference involves a reconception of the meaning of equality. The assimilationist ideal assumes that equal social status for all persons requires treating everyone according to the same principles, rules, and standards. A politics of difference argues, on the other hand, that equality as the participation and inclusion of all groups sometimes requires different treatment for oppressed or disadvantaged groups. To promote social justice, I argue, social policy should sometimes accord special treatment to groups. I explore pregnancy and birthing rights for workers, bilingual-bicultural rights, and American Indian rights as three cases of such special treatment. Finally, I expand the idea of a heterogeneous public here by arguing for a principle of representation for oppressed groups in democratic decisionmaking bodies.

Competing Paradigms of Liberation

In "On Racism and Sexism," Richard Wasserstrom (1980a) develops a classic statement of the ideal of liberation from group-based oppression as involving the elimination of group-based difference itself. A truly nonracist, nonsexist society, he suggests, would be one in which the race or sex of an individual would be the functional equivalent of eye color in our society today. While physiological differences in skin color or genitals would remain, they would have no significance for a person's sense of identity or how others regard him or her. No political rights or obligations would be connected to race or sex, and no important institutional benefits would be associated with either. People would see no reason to consider race or gender in policy or everyday interactions. In such a society, social group differences would have ceased to exist.

Wasserstrom contrasts this ideal of assimilation with an ideal of diversity much like the one I will argue for, which he agrees is compelling. He offers three primary reasons, however, for choosing the assimilationist ideal of liberation over the ideal of diversity. First, the assimilationist ideal exposes the arbitrariness of group-based social distinctions which are thought natural and necessary. By imagining a society in which race and sex have no social significance, one sees more clearly how pervasively these group categories unnecessarily limit possibilities for some in existing society. Second, the assimilationist ideal presents a clear and unambiguous standard of equality and justice. According to such a standard, any group-related differentiation or discrimination is suspect. Whenever laws or rules, the division of labor, or other social practices allocate benefits differently according to group membership, this is a sign of injustice. The principle of justice is simple: treat everyone according to the same principles, rules, and standards. Third, the assimilationist ideal maximizes choice. In a society where differences make no social difference people can develop themselves as individuals, unconstrained by group norms and expectations.

There is no question that the ideal of liberation as the elimination of group difference has been enormously important in the history of emancipatory politics. The ideal of universal humanity that denies natural differences has been a crucial historical development in the struggle against exclusion and status differentiation. It has made possible the assertion of the equal moral worth of all persons, and thus the right of all to participate and be included in all institutions and positions of power and privilege. The assimilationist ideal retains significant rhetorical power in the face of continued beliefs in the essentially different and inferior natures of women, Blacks, and other groups.

The power of this assimilationist ideal has inspired the struggle of oppressed groups and the supporters against the exclusion and denigration of these groups, and continues to inspire many. Periodically in American history, however, movements of the oppressed have questioned and rejected this "path to belonging" (Karst, 1986). Instead they have seen self-organization and the assertion of a positive group cultural identity as a better strategy for achieving power and participation in dominant institutions. Recent decades have witnessed a resurgence of this "politics of difference" not only among racial and ethnic groups, but also among women, gay men and lesbians, old people, and the disabled.

Not long after the passage of the Civil Rights Act and the Voting Rights Act, many white and Black supporters of the Black civil rights movement were surprised, confused, and angered by the emergence of the Black Power movement. Black Power advocates criticized the integrationist goal and reliance on the support of white liberals that characterized the civil rights movement. They encouraged Blacks to break their alliance with whites and assert the specificity of their own culture, political organization, and goals. Instead of integration, they encouraged Blacks to seek economic and political empowerment in their separate neighborhoods (Carmichael and Hamilton, 1967; Bayes, 1982, chap. 3; Lader, 1979, chap. 5; Omi and Winant, 1986, chap. 6). Since the late 1960s many Blacks have claimed that the integration successes of the civil rights movement have had the effect of dismantling the bases of Black-organized social and economic institutions at least as much as they have lessened Black-white animosity and opened doors of opportunity (Cruse, 1987). While some individual Blacks may be better off than they would have been if

these changes had not occurred, as a group, Blacks are no better off and may be worse off, because the Blacks who have succeeded in assimilating into the American middle class no longer associate as closely with lower-class Blacks (cf. Wilson, 1978).

While much Black politics has questioned the ideal of assimilation in economic and political terms, the past twenty years have also seen the assertion and celebration by Blacks of a distinct Afro-American culture, both as a recovery and revaluation of an Afro-American history and in the creation of new cultural forms. The slogan "Black is beautiful" pierced American consciousness, deeply unsettling the received body aesthetic which . . . continues to be a powerful reproducer of racism. Afro-American hairstyles pronounced themselves differently stylish, not less stylish. Linguistic theorists asserted that Black English is English differently constructed, not bad English, and Black poets and novelists exploited and explored its particular nuances.

In the late 1960s Red Power came fast on the heels of Black Power. The American Indian Movement and other radical organizations of American Indians rejected perhaps even more vehemently than Blacks the goal of assimilation which has dominated white–Indian relations for most of the twentieth century. They asserted a right to self-government on Indian lands and fought to gain and maintain a dominant Indian voice in the Bureau of Indian Affairs. American Indians have sought to recover and preserve their language, rituals, and crafts, and this renewal of pride in traditional culture has also fostered a separatist political movement. The desire to pursue land rights claims and to fight for control over resources on reservations arises from what has become a fierce commitment to tribal self-determination, the desire to develop and maintain Indian political and economic bases in but not of white society (Deloria and Lytle, 1983; Ortiz, 1984, pt. 3; Cornell, 1988, pt. 2).

These are but two examples of a widespread tendency in the politics of the 1970s and 1980s for oppressed, disadvantaged, or specially marked groups to organize autonomously and assert a positive sense of their cultural and experiential specificity. Many Spanish-speaking Americans have rejected the traditional assumption that full participation in American society requires linguistic and cultural assimilation.

In the last twenty years many have developed a renewed interest and pride in their Puerto Rican, Chicano, Mexican, or other Latin American heritage. They have asserted the right to maintain their specific culture and speak their language and still receive the benefits of citizenship, such as voting rights, decent education, and job opportunities. Many Jewish Americans have similarly rejected the ideal of assimilation, instead asserting the specificity and positive meaning of Jewish identity, often insisting publicly that Christian culture cease to be taken as the norm.

Since the late 1960s the blossoming of gay cultural expression, gay organization, and the public presence of gays in marches and other forums have radically altered the environment in which young people come to sexual identity, and changed many people's perceptions of homosexuality. Early gay rights advocacy had a distinctly assimilationist and universalist orientation. The goal was to remove the stigma of being homosexual, to prevent institutional discrimination, and to achieve societal recognition that gay people are "no different" from anyone else. The very process of political organization against discrimination and police harassment and for the achievement of civil rights, however, fostered the development of gay and lesbian communities and cultural expression, which by the mid 1970s flowered in meeting places, organizations, literature, music, and massive street celebrations (Altman, 1982; D'Emilio, 1983; Epstein, 1987).

Today most gay and lesbian liberation advocates seek not merely civil rights, but the affirmation of gay men and lesbians as social groups with specific experiences and perspectives. Refusing to accept the dominant culture's definition of healthy sexuality and respectable family life and social practices, gay and lesbian liberation movements have proudly created and displayed a distinctive self-definition and culture. For gay men and lesbians the analogue to racial integration is the typical liberal approach to sexuality, which tolerates any behavior as long as it is kept private. Gay pride asserts that sexual identity is a matter of culture and politics, and not merely "behavior" to be tolerated or forbidden.

The women's movement has also generated its own versions of a politics of difference. Humanist feminism, which predominated in the nineteenth century and in the contemporary women's movement

until the late 1970s, finds in any assertion of difference between women and men only a legacy of female oppression and an ideology to legitimate continued exclusion of women from socially valued human activity. Humanist feminism is thus analogous to an ideal of assimilation in identifying sexual equality with gender blindness, with measuring women and men according to the same standards and treating them in the same way. Indeed, for many feminists, androgyny names the ideal of sexual liberation—a society in which gender difference itself would be eliminated. Given the strength and plausibility of this vision of sexual equality, it was confusing when feminists too began taking the turn to difference, asserting the positivity and specificity of female experience and values (see Young, 1985; Miles, 1985).

Feminist separatism was the earliest expression of such gynocentric feminism. Feminist separatism rejected wholly or partly the goal of entering the male-dominated world, because it requires playing according to rules that men have made and that have been used against women, and because trying to measure up to male-defined standards inevitably involves accommodating or pleasing the men who continue to dominate socially valued institutions and activities. Separatism promoted the empowerment of women through self-organization, the creation of separate and safe spaces where women could share and analyze their experiences, voice their anger, play with and create bonds with one another, and develop new and better institutions and practices.

Most elements of the contemporary women's movement have been separatist to some degree. Separatists seeking to live as much of their lives as possible in women-only institutions were largely responsible for the creation of the women's culture that burst forth all over the United States by the mid 1970s, and continues to claim the loyalty of millions of women—in the form of music, poetry, spirituality, literature, celebrations, festivals, and dances (see Jaggar, 1983, pp. 275–86). Whether drawing on images of Amazonian grandeur, recovering and revaluing traditional women's arts, like quilting and weaving, or inventing new rituals based on medieval witchcraft, the development of such expressions of women's culture gave many feminists images of a female-centered beauty and strength entirely outside capitalist patriarchal definitions of feminine pulchritude. The separatist impulse also fostered the development of the many autonomous women's institutions and services that have concretely improved the lives of many women, whether feminists or not—such as health clinics, battered women's shelters, rape crisis centers, and women's coffeehouses and bookstores.

Beginning in the late 1970s much feminist theory and political analysis also took a turn away from humanist feminism, to question the assumption that traditional female activity expresses primarily the victimization of women and the distortion of their human potential and that the goal of women's liberation is the participation of women as equals in public institutions now dominated by men. Instead of understanding the activities and values associated with traditional femininity as largely distortions and inhibitions of women's truly human potentialities, this gynocentric analysis sought to revalue the caring, nurturing, and cooperative approach to social relations they found associated with feminine socialization, and sought in women's specific experiences the bases for an attitude toward the body and nature healthier than that predominant in male-dominated Western capitalist culture.

None of the social movements asserting positive group specificity is in fact a unity. All have group differences within them. The Black movement, for example, includes middle-class Blacks and working-class Blacks, gays and straight people, men and women, and so it is with any other group. The implications of group differences within a social group have been most systematically discussed in the women's movement. Feminist conferences and publications have generated particularly fruitful, though often emotionally wrenching, discussions of the oppression of racial and ethnic blindness and the importance of attending to group difference among women (Bulkin, Pratt, and Smith, 1984). From such discussions emerged principled efforts to provide autonomously organized forums for Black women, Latinas, Jewish women, lesbians, differently abled women, old women, and any other women who see reason for claiming that they have as a group a distinctive voice that might be silenced in a general feminist discourse. Those discussions, along with the practices feminists instituted to structure discussion and interaction among differ-

ently identifying groups of women, offer some beginning models for the development of a heterogeneous public. Each of the other social movements has also generated discussion of group differences that cut across their identities, leading to other possibilities of coalition and alliance.

Emancipation Through the Politics of Difference

Implicit in emancipatory movements asserting a positive sense of group difference is a different ideal of liberation, which might be called democratic cultural pluralism (cf. Laclau and Mouffe, 1985, pp. 166–71; Cunningham, 1987, pp. 186–99; Nickel, 1987). In this vision the good society does not eliminate or transcend group difference. Rather, there is equality among socially and culturally differentiated groups, who mutually respect one another and affirm one another in their differences. What are the reasons for rejecting the assimilationist ideal and promoting a politics of difference?

As I [have] discussed . . . some deny the reality of social groups. For them, group difference is an invidious fiction produced and perpetuated in order to preserve the privilege of the few. Others, such as Wasserstrom, may agree that social groups do now exist and have real social consequences for the way people identify themselves and one another, but assert that such social group differences are undesirable. The assimilationist ideal involves denying either the reality or the desirability of social groups.

Those promoting a politics of difference doubt that a society without group differences is either possible or desirable. Contrary to the assumption of modernization theory, increased urbanization and the extension of equal formal rights to all groups has not led to a decline in particularist affiliations. If anything, the urban concentration and interactions among groups that modernizing social processes introduce tend to reinforce group solidarity and differentiation (Rothschild, 1981; Ross, 1980; Fischer, 1982). Attachment to specific traditions, practices, language, and other culturally specific forms is a crucial aspect of social existence. People do not usually give up their social group identifications, even when they are oppressed.

Whether eliminating social group difference is possible or desirable in the long run, however, is an academic issue. Today and for the foreseeable future societies are certainly structured by groups, and some are privileged while others are oppressed. New social movements of group specificity do not deny the official story's claim that the ideal of liberation as eliminating difference and treating everyone the same has brought significant improvement in the status of excluded groups. Its main quarrel is with the story's conclusion, namely, that since we have achieved formal equality, only vestiges and holdovers of differential privilege remain, which will die out with the continued persistent assertion of an ideal of social relations that make differences irrelevant to a person's life prospects. The achievement of formal equality does not eliminate social differences, and rhetorical commitment to the sameness of persons makes it impossible even to name how those differences presently structure privilege and oppression.

Though in many respects the law is now blind to group differences, some groups continue to be marked as deviant, as the Other. In everyday interactions, images, and decisions, assumptions about women, Blacks, Hispanics, gay men and lesbians, old people, and other marked groups continue to justify exclusion, avoidance, paternalism, and authoritarian treatment. Continued racist, sexist, homophobic, ageist, and ableist institutions and behavior create particular circumstances for these groups, usually disadvantaging them in their opportunity to develop their capacities. Finally, in part because they have been segregated from one another, and in part because they have particular histories and traditions, there are cultural differences among social groups — differences in language, style of living, body comportment and gestures, values, and perspectives on society.

Today in American society, as in many other societies, there is widespread agreement that no person should be excluded from political and economic activities because of ascribed characteristics. Group differences nevertheless continue to exist, and certain groups continue to be privileged. Under these circumstances, insisting that equality and liberation entail ignoring difference has oppressive consequences in three respects.

First, blindness to difference disadvantages groups whose experience, culture, and socialized capacities differ from those of privileged groups. The strategy of assimilation aims to bring formerly excluded groups into the mainstream. So assimilation always implies coming into the game after it is already begun, after the rules and standards have already been set, and having to prove oneself according to those rules and standards. In the assimilationist strategy, the privileged groups implicitly define the standards according to which all will be measured. Because their privilege involves not recognizing these standards as culturally and experientially specific, the ideal of a common humanity in which all can participate without regard to race, gender, religion, or sexuality poses as neutral and universal. The real differences between oppressed groups and the dominant norm, however, tend to put them at a disadvantage in measuring up to these standards, and for that reason assimilationist policies perpetuate their disadvantage. [There are] . . . examples of facially neutral standards that operate to disadvantage or exclude those already disadvantaged.

Second, the ideal of a universal humanity without social group differences allows privileged groups to ignore their own group specificity. Blindness to difference perpetuates cultural imperialism by allowing norms expressing the point of view and experience of privileged groups to appear neutral and universal. The assimilationist ideal presumes that there is a humanity in general, an unsituated group-neutral human capacity for self-making that left to itself would make individuality flower, thus guaranteeing that each individual will be different . . . [b]ecause there is no such unsituated group-neutral point of view, the situation and experience of dominant groups tend to define the norms of such a humanity in general. Against such a supposedly neutral humanist ideal, only the oppressed groups come to be marked with particularity; they, and not the privileged groups, are marked, objectified as the Others.

Thus, third, this denigration of groups that deviate from an allegedly neutral standard often produces an internalized devaluation by members of those groups themselves. When there is an ideal of general human standards according to which everyone should be evaluated equally, then Puerto Ricans or Chinese Americans are ashamed of their accents or their parents, Black children despise the female-dominated kith and kin networks of their neighborhoods, and feminists seek to root out their tendency to cry, or to feel compassion for a frustrated stranger. The aspiration to assimilate helps produce the self-loathing and double consciousness characteristic of oppression. The goal of assimilation holds up to people a demand that they "fit," be like the mainstream, in behavior, values, and goals. At the same time, as long as group differences exist, group members will be marked as different—as Black, Jewish, gay—and thus as unable simply to fit. When participation is taken to imply assimilation the oppressed person is caught in an irresolvable dilemma: to participate means to accept and adopt an identity one is not, and to try to participate means to be reminded by oneself and others of the identity one is.

A more subtle analysis of the assimilationist ideal might distinguish between a conformist and a transformational ideal of assimilation. In the conformist ideal, status quo institutions and norms are assumed as given, and disadvantaged groups who differ from those norms are expected to conform to them. A transformational ideal of assimilation, on the other hand, recognizes that institutions as given express the interests and perspective of the dominant groups. Achieving assimilation therefore requires altering many institutions and practices in accordance with neutral rules that truly do not disadvantage or stigmatize any person, so that group membership really is irrelevant to how persons are treated. Wasserstrom's ideal fits a transformational assimilation, as does the group-neutral ideal advocated by some feminists (Taub and Williams, 1987). Unlike the conformist assimilationist, the transformational assimilationist may allow that group-specific policies, such as affirmative action, are necessary and appropriate means for transforming institutions to fit the assimilationist ideal. Whether conformist or transformational, however, the assimilationist ideal still denies that group difference can be positive and desirable; thus any form of the ideal of assimilation constructs group difference as a liability or disadvantage.

Under these circumstances, a politics that asserts the positivity of group difference is liberating and empowering. In the act of reclaiming the identity the dominant culture has taught them to despise (Cliff, 1980), and affirming it as an identity to celebrate, the oppressed remove double consciousness. I am just what they say I am—a Jewboy, a colored girl, a fag, a dyke, or a hag—and proud of it. No longer does one have the impossible project of trying to become something one is not under circumstances where the very trying reminds one of who one is. This politics asserts that oppressed groups have distinct cultures, experiences, and perspectives on social life with humanly positive meaning, some of which may even be superior to the culture and perspectives of mainstream society. The rejection and devaluation of one's culture and perspective should not be a condition of full participation in social life.

Asserting the value and specificity of the culture and attributes of oppressed groups, moreover, results in a relativizing of the dominant culture. When feminists assert the validity of feminine sensitivity and the positive value of nurturing behavior, when gays describe the prejudice of heterosexuals as homophobic and their own sexuality as positive and self-developing, when Blacks affirm a distinct Afro-American tradition, then the dominant culture is forced to discover itself for the first time as specific: as Anglo, European, Christian, masculine, straight. In a political struggle where oppressed groups insist on the positive value of their specific culture and experience, it becomes increasingly difficult for dominant groups to parade their norms as neutral and universal, and to construct the values and behavior of the oppressed as deviant, perverted, or inferior. By puncturing the universalist claim to unity that expels some groups and turns them into the Other, the assertion of positive group specificity introduces the possibility of understanding the relation between groups as merely difference, instead of exclusion, opposition, or dominance.

The politics of difference also promotes a notion of group solidarity against the individualism of liberal humanism. Liberal humanism treats each person as an individual, ignoring differences of race, sex, religion, and ethnicity. Each person should be evaluated only according to her or his individual efforts and achievements. With the institutionalization of formal equality some members of formerly excluded groups have indeed succeeded, by mainstream standards. Structural patterns of group privilege and oppression nevertheless remain. When political leaders of oppressed groups reject assimilation they are often affirming group solidarity. Where the dominant culture refuses to see anything but the achievement of autonomous individuals, the oppressed assert that we shall not separate from the people with whom we identify in order to "make it" in a white Anglo male world. The politics of difference insists on liberation of the whole group of Blacks, women, American Indians, and that this can be accomplished only through basic institutional changes. These changes must include group representation in policymaking and an elimination of the hierarchy of rewards that forces everyone to compete for scarce positions at the top.

Thus the assertion of a positive sense of group difference provides a standpoint from which to criticize prevailing institutions and norms. Black Americans find in their traditional communities, which refer to their members as "brother" and "sister," a sense of solidarity absent from the calculating individualism of white professional capitalist society. Feminists find in the traditional female values of nurturing a challenge to a militarist world-view, and lesbians find in their relationships a confrontation with the assumption of complementary gender roles in sexual relationships. From their experience of a culture tied to the land American Indians formulate a critique of the instrumental rationality of European culture that results in pollution and ecological destruction. Having revealed the specificity of the dominant norms which claim universality and neutrality, social movements of the oppressed are in a position to inquire how the dominant institutions must be changed so that they will no longer reproduce the patterns of privilege and oppression.

From the assertion of positive difference the self-organization of oppressed groups follows. Both liberal humanist and leftist political organizations and movements have found it difficult to accept this principle of group autonomy. In a humanist emancipatory politics, if a group is subject to injustice, then all those interested in a just society should unite to combat the powers that perpetuate that injustice. If many groups are subject to injustice, moreover, then they should unite to work for a just society. The politics of difference is certainly not against coalition, nor does it hold that, for example, whites should not work against racial injustice or men against sexist injustice. This politics of group assertion, however, takes as a basic principle that members of oppressed groups need separate organizations that exclude others, especially those from more privileged groups. Separate organization is probably necessary in order for these groups to discover and reinforce the positivity of their specific experience, to collapse and eliminate double consciousness. In discussions within autonomous organizations, group members can determine their specific needs and interests. Separation and self-organization risk creating pressures toward homogenization of the groups themselves, creating new privileges and exclusions. . . . But contemporary emancipatory social movements have found group autonomy an important vehicle for empowerment and the development of a group-specific voice and perspective.

Integration into the full life of the society should not have to imply assimilation to dominant norms and abandonment of group affiliation and culture (Edley, 1986; cf. McGary, 1983). If the only alternative to the oppressive exclusion of some groups defined as Other by dominant ideologies is the assertion that they are the same as everybody else, then they will continue to be excluded because they are not the same.

Some might object to the way I have drawn the distinction between an assimilationist ideal of liberation and a radical democratic pluralism. They might claim that I have not painted the ideal of a society that transcends group differences fairly, representing it as homogeneous and conformist. The free society envisaged by liberalism, they might say, is certainly pluralistic. In it persons can affiliate with whomever they choose; liberty encourages a proliferation of life styles, activities, and associations. While I have no quarrel with social diversity in this sense, this vision of liberal pluralism does not touch on the primary issues that give rise to the politics of difference. The vision of liberation as the transcendence of group difference seeks to abolish the public and political significance of group difference, while retaining and promoting both individual and group diversity in private, or nonpolitical, social contexts. . . . [T]his way of distinguishing public and private spheres, where the public represents universal citizenship and the private individual differences, tends to result in group exclusion from the public. Radical democratic pluralism acknowledges and affirms the public and political significance of social group differences as a means of ensuring the participation and inclusion of everyone in social and political institutions.

Reclaiming the Meaning of Difference

Many people inside and outside the movements I have discussed find the rejection of the liberal humanist ideal and the assertion of a positive sense of group difference both confusing and controversial. They fear that any admission by oppressed groups that they are different from the dominant groups risks justifying anew the subordination, special marking, and exclusion of those groups. Since calls for a return of women to the kitchen, Blacks to servant roles and separate schools, and disabled people to nursing homes are not absent from contemporary politics, the danger is real. It may be true that the assimilationist ideal that treats everyone the same and applies the same standards to all perpetuates disadvantage because real group differences remain that make it unfair to compare the unequals. But this is far preferable to a reestablishment of separate and unequal spheres for different groups justified on the basis of group difference.

Since those asserting group specificity certainly wish to affirm the liberal humanist principle that all persons are of equal moral worth, they appear to be faced with a dilemma. Analyzing W. E .B. Du Bois's arguments for cultural pluralism, Bernard Boxill poses the dilemma this way: "On the one hand, we must overcome segregation because it denies the idea of human brotherhood; on the other hand, to overcome segregation we must self-segregate and therefore also deny the idea of human brotherhood" (Boxill, 1984, p. 174). Martha Minow finds a dilemma of difference facing any who seek to promote justice for currently oppressed or disadvantaged groups. Formally neutral rules and policies that ignore group differences often perpetuate the disadvantage of those whose difference is defined as deviant; but focusing on difference risks recreating the stigma that difference has carried in the past (Minow, 1987, pp. 12–13; cf. Minow, 1985; 1990).

These dilemmas are genuine, and exhibit the risks of collective life, where the consequences of one's claims, actions, and policies may not turn out as one intended because others have understood them differently or turned them to different ends. Since ignoring group differences in public policy does not mean that people ignore them in everyday life and interaction, however, oppression continues even when law and policy declare that all are equal. Thus I think for many groups and in many circumstances it is more empowering to affirm and acknowledge in political life the group differences that already exist in social life. One is more likely to avoid the dilemma of difference in doing this if the meaning of difference itself becomes a terrain of political struggle. Social movements asserting the positivity of group difference have established this terrain, offering an emancipatory meaning of difference to replace the old exclusionary meaning.

The oppressive meaning of group difference defines it as absolute otherness, mutual exclusion, categorical opposition. This essentialist meaning of difference submits to the logic of identity. One group occupies the position of a norm, against which all others are measured. The attempt to reduce all persons to the unity of a common measure constructs as deviant those whose attributes differ from the group-specific attributes implicitly presumed in the norm. The drive to unify the particularity and multiplicity of practices, cultural symbols, and ways of relating in clear and distinct categories turns difference into exclusion.

Thus I explored in the previous two chapters how the appropriation of a universal subject position by socially privileged groups forces those they define as different outside the definition of full humanity and citizenship. The attempt to measure all against some universal standard generates a logic of difference as hierarchical dichotomy — masculine/feminine, civilized/savage, and so on. The second term is defined negatively as a lack of the truly human qualities; at the same time it is defined as the complement to the valued term, the object correlating with its subject, that which brings it to completion, wholeness, and identity. By loving and affirming him, a woman serves as a mirror to a man, holding up his virtues for him to see (Irigaray, 1985). By carrying the white man's burden to tame and educate the savage peoples, the civilized will realize universal humanity. The exotic orientals are there to know and master, to be the completion of reason's progress in history, which seeks the unity of the world (Said, 1978). In every case the valued term achieves its value by its determinately negative relation to the Other.

In the objectifying ideologies of racism, sexism, anti-Semitism, and homophobia, only the oppressed and excluded groups are defined as different. Whereas the privileged groups are neutral and exhibit free and malleable subjectivity, the excluded groups are marked with an essence, imprisoned in a given set of possibilities. By virtue of the characteristics the group is alleged to have by nature, the ideologies allege that group members have specific dispositions that suit them for some activities and not others. Difference in these ideologies always means exclusionary opposition to a norm. There are rational men, and then there are women; there are civilized men, and then there are wild and savage peoples. The marking of difference always implies a good/bad opposition; it is always a devaluation, the naming of an inferiority in relation to a superior standard of humanity.

Difference here always means absolute otherness; the group marked as different has no common nature with the normal or neutral ones. The categorical opposition of groups essentializes them, repressing the differences within groups. In this way the definition of difference as exclusion and opposition actually denies difference. This essentializing categorization also denies difference in that its universalizing norms preclude recognizing and affirming a group's specificity in its own terms.

Essentializing difference expresses a fear of specificity, and a fear of making permeable the categorical border between oneself and the others. This fear . . . is not merely intellectual, and does not derive only from the instrumental desire to defend privilege, though that may be a large element. It wells from the depths of the Western subject's sense of identity, especially, but not only, in the subjectivity of privileged groups. The fear may increase, moreover, as a clear essentialism of difference wanes, as belief in a specifically female, Black, or homosexual nature becomes less tenable.

The politics of difference confronts this fear, and aims for an understanding of group difference as indeed ambiguous, relational, shifting, without clear borders that keep people straight — as entailing neither amorphous unity nor pure individuality. By asserting a positive meaning for their own identity, oppressed groups seek to seize the power of naming difference itself, and explode the implicit definition of

difference as deviance in relation to a norm, which freezes some groups into a self-enclosed nature. Difference now comes to mean not otherness, exclusive opposition, but specificity, variation, heterogeneity. Difference names relations of similarity and dissimilarity that can be reduced to neither coextensive identity nor nonoverlapping otherness.

The alternative to an essentializing, stigmatizing meaning of difference as opposition is an understanding of difference as specificity, variation. In this logic, as Martha Minow (1985; 1987; 1990) suggests, group differences should be conceived as relational rather than defined by substantive categories and attributes. A relational understanding of difference relativizes the previously universal position of privileged groups, which allows only the oppressed to be marked as different. When group difference appears as a function of comparison between groups, whites are just as specific as Blacks or Latinos, men just as specific as women, able-bodied people just as specific as disabled people. Difference thus emerges not as a description of the attributes of a group, but as a function of the relations between groups and the interaction of groups with institutions (cf. Littleton, 1987).

In this relational understanding, the meaning of difference also becomes contextualized (cf. Scott, 1988). Group differences will be more or less salient depending on the groups compared, the purposes of the comparison, and the point of view of the comparers. Such contextualized understandings of difference undermine essentialist assumptions. For example, in the context of athletics, health care, social service support, and so on, wheelchair-bound people are different from others, but they are not different in many other respects. Traditional treatment of the disabled entailed exclusion and segregation because the differences between the disabled and the able-bodied were conceptualized as extending to all or most capacities.

In general, then, a relational understanding of group difference rejects exclusion. Difference no longer implies that groups lie outside one another. To say that there are differences among groups does not imply that there are not overlapping experiences, or that two groups have nothing in common. The assumption that real differences in affinity, culture, or privilege imply oppositional categorization must be challenged. Different groups are always similar in some respects, and always potentially share some attributes, experiences, and goals.

Such a relational understanding of difference entails revising the meaning of group identity as well. In asserting the positive difference of their experience, culture, and social perspective, social movements of groups that have experienced cultural imperialism deny that they have a common identity, a set of fixed attributes that clearly mark who belongs and who doesn't. Rather, what makes a group a group is a social process of interaction and differentiation in which some people come to have a particular *affinity* (Haraway, 1985) for others. My "affinity group" in a given social situation comprises those people with whom I feel the most comfortable, who are more familiar. Affinity names the manner of sharing assumptions, affective bonding, and networking that recognizably differentiates groups from one another, but not according to some common nature. The salience of a particular person's group affinities may shift according to the social situation or according to changes in her or his life. Membership in a social group is a function not of satisfying some objective criteria, but of a subjective affirmation of affinity with that group, the affirmation of that affinity by other members of the group, and the attribution of membership in that group by persons identifying with other groups. Group identity is constructed from a flowing process in which individuals identify themselves and others in terms of groups, and thus group identity itself flows and shifts with changes in social process.

Groups experiencing cultural imperialism have found themselves objectified and marked with a devalued essence from the outside, by a dominant culture they are excluded from making. The assertion of a positive sense of group difference by these groups is emancipatory because it reclaims the definition of the group by the group, as a creation and construction, rather than a given essence. To be sure, it is difficult to articulate positive elements of group affinity without essentializing them, and these movements do not always succeed in doing so (cf. Sartre, 1948, p. 85; Epstein, 1987). But they are developing a language to describe their similar social situation and relations to one another, and their similar perceptions and perspectives on social life. These movements engage in the project of cultural revolution . . . , insofar

as they take culture as in part a matter of collective choice. While their ideas of women's culture, Afro-American culture, and American Indian culture rely on past cultural expressions, to a significant degree these movements have self-consciously constructed the culture that they claim defines the distinctiveness of their groups.

Contextualizing both the meaning of difference and identity thus allows the acknowledgment of difference within affinity groups. In our complex, plural society, every social group has group differences cutting across it, which are potential sources of wisdom, excitement, conflict, and oppression. Gay men, for example, may be Black, rich, homeless, or old, and these differences produce different identifications and potential conflicts among gay men, as well as affinities with some straight men.

Respecting Difference in Policy

A goal of social justice, I will assume, is social equality. Equality refers not primarily to the distribution of social goods, though distributions are certainly entailed by social equality. It refers primarily to the full participation and inclusion of everyone in a society's major institutions, and the socially supported substantive opportunity for all to develop and exercise their capacities and realize their choices. American society has enacted formal legal equality for members of all groups, with the important and shameful exception of gay men and lesbians. But for many groups social equality is barely on the horizon. Those seeking social equality disagree about whether group-neutral or group-conscious policies best suit that goal, and their disagreement often turns on whether they hold an assimilationist or culturally pluralist ideal. In this section I argue for the justice of group-conscious social policies, and discuss three contexts in which such policies are at issue in the United States today: women's equality in the workplace, language rights of non-English speakers, and American Indian rights. . . .

The issue of formally equal versus group-conscious policies arises primarily in the context of workplace relations and access to political power. I have already discussed one of the primary reasons for preferring group-conscious to neutral policies: policies that are universally formulated and thus blind to differences of race, culture, gender, age, or disability often perpetuate rather than undermine oppression. Universally formulated standards or norms, for example, according to which all competitors for social positions are evaluated, often presume as the norm capacities, values, and cognitive and behavioral styles typical of dominant groups, thus disadvantaging others. Racist, sexist, homophobic, ageist, and ableist aversions and stereotypes, moreover, continue to devalue or render invisible some people, often disadvantaging them in economic and political interactions. Policies that take notice of the specific situation of oppressed groups can offset these disadvantages.

It might be objected that when facially neutral standards or policies disadvantage a group, the standards or policies should simply be restructured so as to be genuinely neutral, rather than replaced by group-conscious policies. For some situations this may be appropriate, but in many the group-related differences allow no neutral formulation. Language policy might be cited as paradigmatic here, but as I will discuss shortly, some gender issues may be as well.

More important, however, some of the disadvantages that oppressed groups suffer can be remedied in policy only by an affirmative acknowledgment of the group's specificity. The oppressions of cultural imperialism that stereotype a group and simultaneously render its own experience invisible can be remedied only by explicit attention to and expression of the group's specificity. For example, removing oppressive stereotypes of Blacks, Latinos, Indians, Arabs, and Asians and portraying them in the same roles as whites will not eliminate racism from television programming. Positive and interesting portrayals of people of color in situations and ways of life that derive from their own self-perceptions are also necessary, as well as a great deal more positive presence of all these groups than currently exists.

These considerations produce a second reason for the justice of group-conscious policies, in addition to their function in counteracting oppression and disadvantage. Group-conscious policies are sometimes necessary in order to affirm the solidarity of groups, to allow them to affirm their group affinities without suffering disadvantage in the wider society.

Some group-conscious policies are consistent with an assimilationist ideal in which group difference has no social significance, as long as such policies are understood as means to that end, and thus as temporary divergences from group-neutral norms. Many people look upon affirmative action policies in this way, and as I shall discuss shortly, people typically understand bilingual education in this way. A culturally pluralist democratic ideal, however, supports group-conscious policies not only as means to the end of equality, but also as intrinsic to the ideal of social equality itself. Groups cannot be socially equal unless their specific experience, culture, and social contributions are publicly affirmed and recognized.

The dilemma of difference exposes the risks involved both in attending to and in ignoring differences. The danger in affirming difference is that the implementation of group-conscious policies will reinstate stigma and exclusion. In the past, group-conscious policies were used to separate those defined as different and exclude them from access to the rights and privileges enjoyed by dominant groups. A crucial principle of democratic cultural pluralism, then, is that group-specific rights and policies should stand together with general civil and political rights of participation and inclusion. Group-conscious policies cannot be used to justify exclusion of or discrimination against members of a group in the exercise of general political and civil rights. A democratic cultural pluralism thus requires a dual system of rights: a general system of rights which are the same for all, and a more specific system of group-conscious policies and rights (cf. Wolgast, 1980, chap. 2). In the words of Kenneth Karst:

> When the promise of equal citizenship is fulfilled, the paths to belonging are opened in two directions for members of cultural minorities. As full members of the larger society, they have the option to participate to whatever degree they choose. They also may look inward, seeking solidarity within their cultural group, without being penalized for that choice. (Karst, 1986, p. 337)

If "cultural minority" is interpreted to mean any group subject to cultural imperialism, then this statement applies to women, old people, disabled people, gay men and lesbians, and working-class people as much as it applies to ethnic or national groups. I will now briefly consider three cases in which group-specific policies are necessary to support social equality: women, Latinos, and American Indians.

1.   Are women's interests best promoted through gender-neutral or group-conscious rules and policies? This question has been fiercely debated by feminists in recent years. The resulting literature raises crucial questions about dominant models of law and policy that take equality to mean sameness, and offers some subtle analyses of the meaning of equality that do not assume identity (see Vogel, 1990). Most of this discussion has focused on the question of pregnancy and childbirth rights in the workplace.

   Advocates of an equal treatment approach to pregnancy argue that women's interests are best served by vigorously pressing for the inclusion of pregnancy leaves and benefits within gender-neutral leave and benefit policies relevant to any physical condition that renders men or women unable to work. The history of protective legislation shows that women cannot trust employers and courts not to use special classification as an excuse for excluding and disadvantaging women, and we are best protected from such exclusion by neutral policies (Williams, 1983). Even such proponents of equal treatment, however, agree that gender-neutral policies that take male lives as the norm will disadvantage women. The answer, according to Nadine Taub and Wendy Williams, is a model of equality in the workplace that recognizes and accommodates the specific needs of all workers; such a model requires significant restructuring of most workplace policy (Taub and Williams, 1986).

   In my view an equal treatment approach to pregnancy and childbirth is inadequate because it either implies that women do not have any right to leave and job security when having babies, or assimilates such guarantees under the supposedly gender-neutral category of "disability." Such assimilation is unacceptable because pregnancy and childbirth are usually normal conditions of normal women, because pregnancy and childbirth themselves count as socially necessary work, and because they have unique and variable characteristics and needs (Scales, 1981; Littleton, 1987). Assimilating pregnancy and childbirth to disability tends to stigmatize these processes as

"unhealthy." It suggests, moreover, that the primary or only reason that a woman has a right to leave and job security is that she is physically unable to work at her job, or that doing so would be more difficult than when she is not pregnant and recovering from childbirth. While these are important considerations, another reason is that she ought to have the time to establish breast-feeding and develop a relationship and routine with her child, if she chooses. At issue is more than eliminating the disadvantage women suffer because of male models of uninterrupted work. It is also a question of establishing and confirming positive public recognition of the social contribution of childbearing. Such recognition can and should be given without either reducing women to childbearers or suggesting that all women ought to bear children and are lacking if they do not.

   Feminists who depart from a gender-neutral model of women's rights generally restrict this departure to the biological situation of childbirth. Most demand that parental leave from a job, for example, should be gender-neutral, in order not to perpetuate the connection of women with the care of children, and order not to penalize those men who choose more than average childrearing responsibilities. I myself agree with gender-neutral policy on this issue.

   Restricting the issue of group-conscious policies for women to childbirth, however, avoids some of the hardest questions involved in promoting women's equality in the workplace. Women suffer workplace disadvantage not only or even primarily because of their birthing capacity, but because their gender socialization and identity orients the desires, temperaments, and capacities of many women toward certain activities and away from others, because many men regard women in inappropriately sexual terms, and because women's clothes, comportment, voices, and so on sometimes disrupt the disembodied ideal of masculinist bureaucracy. Differences between women and men are not only biological, but also socially gendered. Such gender differences are multiple, variable, and do not reduce men and women to segregating essences. Perhaps such differences should not exist, but without doubt they do now. Ignoring these differences sometimes disadvantages women in public settings where masculine norms and styles predominate.

In a model she calls "equality as acceptance," Christine Littleton argues for a gender-conscious approach to policy directed at rendering femininely gendered cultural attributes costless for women. This model begins with the assumption of structured social gender differences—for example, gender-dominated occupational categories, woman-dominated childrearing and other family member caretaking, and gender differences in the sports people wish to pursue. None of these are essences; it is not as though all men or all women follow the gendered patterns, but the patterns are identifiable and apply broadly to many people's lives. Littleton's model of equality as acceptance supports policies which not only will not disadvantage women who engage in traditionally feminine activity or behavior, but which value the feminine as much as the masculine:

> The focus of equality as acceptance, therefore, is not on the question of whether *women* are different, but rather on the question of how the social fact of gender asymmetry can be dealt with so as to create some symmetry in the lived-out experience of all members of the community. I do not think it matters so much whether differences are "natural" or not; they are built into our structures and selves in either event. As social facts, differences are created by the interaction of person with person or person with institution; they inhere in the relationship, not in the person. On this view, the function of equality is to make gender differences, perceived or actual, costless relative to each other, so that anyone may follow a male, female, or androgynous lifestyle according to their natural inclination or choice without being punished for following a female lifestyle or rewarded for following a male one. (Littleton, 1987, p. 1297)

The acceptance model of equality, then, publicly acknowledges culturally based gender differences, and takes steps to ensure that these differences do not disadvantage. Though Littleton does not emphasize it, this model implies, first, that gender differences must not be used implicitly or explicitly as a basis for excluding persons from institutions, positions, or opportunities. That is, general rights to equal opportunity, as well as other civil and political rights, must obtain. Over and above this, equality as acceptance explicitly revalues femininely coded activity and behavior as the equal of masculine-coded activity.

Comparable worth policies are a widely discussed strategy for revaluing the culturally feminine. Schemes of equal pay for work of comparable worth require that predominantly male and predominantly female jobs have similar wage structures if they involve similar degrees of skill, difficulty, stress, and so on. The problem in implementing these policies, of course, lies in designing methods of comparing different jobs. Most schemes of comparison still choose to minimize sex differences by using supposedly gender-neutral criteria, such as educational attainment, speed of work, whether the work involves manipulation of symbols, pleasantness of work conditions, decisionmaking ability, and so on. Some writers have suggested, however, that standard classifications of job traits may be systematically biased to keep specific kinds of tasks involved in many female-dominated occupations hidden (Beatty and Beatty, 1981; Treiman and Hartman, 1981, p. 81). Many female-dominated occupations involve gender-specific kinds of labor—such as nurturing, smoothing over social relations, or the exhibition of sexuality—which most task observation ignores (Alexander, 1987). A fair assessment of the skills and complexity of many female-dominated jobs may therefore involve paying explicit attention to gender differences rather than applying gender-blind categories of comparison (cf. Littleton, 1987, p. 1312).

Littleton offers sports as another area of revaluation. An "equality as acceptance" approach, she suggests, would support an equal division of resources between male and female programs rather than divide up the available sports budget per capita (Littleton, 1987, p. 1313). If the disparities in numbers of people involved were too great, I do not think this proposal would be fair, but I agree with the general principle Littleton is aiming at. Women who wish to participate in athletic activities should not be disadvantaged because there are not more women who currently wish to; they should have as many well-paid coaches, for example, as do men, their locker room facilities should be as good, and they should have access to all the equipment they need to excel. More importantly, femininely stereotyped sports, such as synchronized swimming or field hockey, should receive a level of support comparable to more masculine sports like football or baseball.

2.   In November 1986 the majority of voters in California supported a referendum declaring English the official language of that state. The ramifications of this policy are not clear, but it means at least that state institutions have no obligation to print ballots and other government literature or provide services in any language other than English. The California success has spurred a national movement to declare English the official language of the United States, as well as many additional local movements, especially in regions with fast-growing populations of people whose first language is not English. In winter 1989, for example, an English-only proposal went before the legislature of Suffolk County, Long Island, that even some English-first advocates thought was too strong. Not only would it have made English the official language of Suffolk County, but it would have forbidden public service providers from speaking to clients in any language other than English (Schmitt, 1989).

Many English-only advocates justify their position as another of many measures that should be taken to cut the costs of government. But the movement's primary appeal is to a normative ideal of the unity of the polity. As a nation, the United States was founded by English speakers; non-English speakers are not "real" Americans, no matter how many generations they can trace on American soil. A polity cannot sustain itself without significant commonality and mutual identification among its citizens, this argument goes, and a common language is one of the most important of such unifying forces. Linguistic and cultural pluralism leads to conflict, divisiveness, factionalism, and ultimately disintegration. Giving public preference to English supports this unity and encourages non-English speakers to assimilate more quickly.

There are at least three arguments against this appeal to the unity of a single harmonious polity. First, it is simply unrealistic. From its beginnings the United States has always harbored sizable linguistic and cultural minorities. Its history of imperialism

and annexation and its immigration policy have resulted in more. In the past twenty-five years U.S. military and foreign policy has led to a huge influx of Latin Americans and Asians. Some estimate, moreover, that by the year 2000 Hispanic and Asian populations in the United States will have increased by 84 and 103 percent respectively (Sears and Huddy, 1987). Many individuals belonging to cultural minorities choose to assimilate, as do some whole groups. But many do not. Even without official support for their doing so and with considerable pressures against it, many groups have retained distinct linguistic and cultural identities, even some whose members have lived in the United States for several generations. Spanish speakers may be the most salient here because their relative numbers are large, and because their connections with Puerto Rico, Mexico, or other parts of Latin America remain strong. Given the determination of many linguistic and cultural minorities to maintain a specific identity even as they claim rights to the full benefits of American citizenship, a determination which seems to be increasing, the desire of the English-only movement to create unity through enforced language policy is simply silly.

Second, as I have already argued at several points, this norm of the homogeneous public is oppressive. Not only does it put unassimilated persons and groups at a severe disadvantage in the competition for scarce positions and resources, but it requires that persons transform their sense of identity in order to assimilate. Self-annihilation is an unreasonable and unjust requirement of citizenship. The fiction, poetry, and songs of American cultural minorities brim over with the pain and loss such demands inflict, documenting how thoroughly assimilationist values violate basic respect for persons.

Thus, third, the normative ideal of the homogeneous public does not succeed in its stated aim of creating a harmonious nation. In group-differentiated societies conflict, factionalism, divisiveness, civil warfare, do often occur between groups. The primary cause of such conflict, however, is not group difference per se, but rather the relations of domination and oppression between groups that produce resentment, hostility, and resistance among the oppressed. Placing a normative value on homogeneity only exacerbates division and conflict, because it gives members of the dominant groups reason to adopt a stance of self-righteous intractability.

I [have] argued . . . that a just polity must embrace the ideal of a heterogeneous public. Group differences of gender, age, and sexuality should not be ignored, but publicly acknowledged and accepted. Even more so should group differences of nation or ethnicity be accepted. In the twentieth century the ideal state is composed of a plurality of nations or cultural groups, with a degree of self-determination and autonomy compatible with federated equal rights and obligations of citizenship. Many states of the world embrace this ideal, though they often realize it only very imperfectly (see Ortiz, 1984, pt. 2). English-only advocates often look with fear at the large and rapidly growing cultural minorities in the United States, especially the Spanish-speaking minority, and argue that only enforcing the primacy of English can prevent us from becoming a culturally plural society like Canada. Such arguments stubbornly refuse to see that we already are.

The difference between an assimilationist and a culturally pluralist ideal becomes particularly salient in educational policy. Bilingual education is highly controversial in the United States today, partly because of the different cultural meanings given to it. In 1974 the Supreme Court ruled that the state has an obligation to remedy the English-language deficiency of its students so they will have equal opportunity to learn all subjects; but the Court did not specify how this should be done. The Bilingual Education Act, passed in 1978 and amended several times, sets aside federal funds for use by school systems to develop bilingual education programs (see Minow, 1985; Kleven, 1989). Even so, in 1980, 77 percent of Hispanic children in the United States received no form of special programming corresponding to their linguistic needs (Bastian, 1986, p. 46). In 1986 in Texas, 80 percent of school districts were found out of compliance with a state-mandated bilingual education program (Canter, 1987).

There are several different models of language support programs. Some, like English as a Second Language, provide no instruction in the student's native language, and are often not taught by persons who can speak the student's language. Others, called immersion programs, involve English-language instruction primarily, but are taught by bilingual instructors whom the student can question in his or her native language. Transitional bilingual education programs involve genuinely bilingual instruction, with the proportions of English and native language changing as the student progresses. Transitional programs instruct students in such subjects as math, science and history in their native language at the same time that they develop English-language skills; they aim to increase the amount of time of instruction in English.

All these programs are assimilationist in intent. They seek to increase English proficiency to the point where native-language instruction is unnecessary; none has the goal of maintaining and developing proficiency in the native language. The vast majority of programs for students with limited English proficiency in the United States take one of these forms. The use of transitional bilingual programs instead of ESL or immersion programs is hotly debated. The majority of Americans support special language programs for students with limited English, in order to help them learn English; but the more programs instruct in a native language, especially when they instruct in subjects like math or science, the more they are considered by English speakers to be unfair coddling and a waste of taxpayer dollars (Sears and Huddy, 1987). Transitional bilingual educational programs, on the other hand, are usually preferred by linguistic minorities.

Another model of bilingual education is rarely practiced in the United States, and is hardly on the public agenda: bilingual–bicultural maintenance programs. These aim to reinforce knowledge of the students' native language and culture, at the same time that they train them to be proficient in the dominant language, English. Few advocates of cultural pluralism and group autonomy in the United States would deny that proficiency in English is a necessary condition for full participation in American society. The issue is only whether linguistic minorities are recognized as full participants in their specificity, with social support for the maintenance of their language and culture. Only bilingual–bicultural maintenance programs can both ensure the possibility of the full inclusion and participation of members of linguistic minorities in all society's institutions and at the same time preserve and affirm their group-specific identity (cf. Nickel, 1987, p. 119).

3.   American Indians are the most invisible oppressed group in the United States. Numbering just over one million, they are too small a proportion of most regional populations to organize influential pressure groups or threaten major disruptions of the lives of white society. Federal and state policy often can safely ignore Indian interests and desires. Many Indians live on reservations, where non-Indians have little contact with them. Even in cities Indians often form their own support systems and networks, mingling little with non-Indians (Cornell, 1988, pp. 132–37). Whether on or off the reservation, Indians suffer the most serious marginalization and deprivation of any social group; by every measure — income, unemployment rates, infant mortality, and so on — Indians are the poorest Americans.

At the same time, Indians are the most legally differentiated people in the United States, the only group granted formally special status and rights by the federal government. Indians represent the *arche*-difference that from the beginning subverts the claim to origin, to a New World, that founds the myth of America as the home of English-speaking farmers, traders, and inventors. Agents of the U.S. government have poisoned, burned, looted, tricked, relocated, and confined Indians many times over, in persistently genocidal policies, attempting to purge this difference within. Legal history and the string of federal treaties, however, also testify to a begrudging acknowledgment of the Indian peoples as independent political entities with which the government must negotiate. Until the twentieth century the special legal status of Indians was conceptualized almost entirely as a relation of wardship and dependence between an inferior savage people and a superior civilized sovereign, and the shadow of this conceptualization darkens even recent legal decisions (Williams, 1987). As with women, Blacks, and the feebleminded, Indian difference was codified in nor-

malizing law as an inferior infantile nature that justified less than full citizenship.

At the turn of the century policymakers assumed that an end to this position of tutelage and wardship implied assimilation to the dominant culture. Thus the land reallocation policies of the late 1800s were intended to encourage Indians to value private property and the virtues of yeoman husbandry. In the 1920s, when Congress voted to grant Indians full U.S. citizenship, federal policy forced assimilation by forbidding Indian children to speak their native language in the boarding schools to which they were transported, sometimes thousands of miles from home. During the same period Indians were prohibited from practicing many of their traditional religious rites.

In the 1930s the Indian Reorganization Act eliminated and reversed many of these policies, creating the contemporary system of federally recognized tribal governments. But in the 1950s the pendulum swung back with the effort by Congress to terminate the federal relationship with tribes, withdrawing all recognition of Indians as distinct peoples, and once again attempting to force Indians to assimilate into white society. This brutal seesaw history of U.S.–Indian relations caused Indians to change and adapt their values, practices, and institutions and even their identities. Many distinct Indian identities have disappeared, as Indian groups merged or reorganized their relations with one another under the oppression of white policies. Throughout this history, however, assimilation was not a live option for the Indians. While many individuals may have left their groups and successfully integrated into the dominant white culture, Indians as groups persistently preserved their differences from white society against the fiercest opposition. Many Indians today find much fault with the present organization of the tribes, the definition of their role, and their legal relationship with the U.S. government, but few would propose the elimination of the tribal system that formally recognizes specific independently defined Indian groups and guarantees them specific rights in defining and running tribal affairs.

The case of American Indians especially exemplifies the arguments of this chapter because it is

perhaps clearest here that justice toward groups requires special rights, and that an assimilationist ideal
amounts to genocide. Such special rights, however,
should not justify exclusion from full participation
in the American dream of liberty, equal opportunity, and the like. The justice of recognizing both
specific needs of a group and rights of full participation and inclusion in the polity has clear precedence
in U.S.–Indian law. Indians are the only group to
have what almost amounts to a dual citizenship: as
members of a tribe they have specific political, legal,
and collective rights, and as U.S. citizens they have
all the civil and political rights of other citizens
(Deloria and Lytle, 1984, pp. 3–4). Recognized
Indian tribes have specific rights to jurisdictional
and territorial sovereignty, and many specific religious, cultural, and gaming rights (see Pevar, 1983).

Many Indians believe this system of particular
rights remains too much at the discretion of the federal government, and some have taken their claims
for greater self-determination to international judicial bodies (Ortiz, 1984, pp. 32–46). Justice in the
form of unambiguous recognition of American Indian groups as full and equal members of American
society requires, in my view, that the U.S. government relinquish the absolute power to alter or eliminate Indian rights.

Even in the absence of full justice the case of
Indians provides an important example of the combination of general rights and particular rights
which, I have argued, is necessary for the equality
of many oppressed or disadvantaged groups. The
system of tribal rights, and their relation to general
rights, is certainly complex, and there is often disagreement about the meaning and implications of
these rights. Many Indians believe, moreover, that
their rights, especially territorial rights to make decisions about land, water, and resources, are not sufficiently recognized and enforced because economic
interests profit from ignoring them. I do not wish
to argue that this system of particular rights, or the
bureaucratic form it takes, should extend to other
oppressed or disadvantaged social groups. The specificity of each group requires a specific set of rights
for each, and for some a more comprehensive system than for others. The case of American Indians,
however, illustrates the fact that there is a precedent for a system of particular rights that a group
wants for reasons of justice, namely, because they
enforce the group's autonomy and protect its interests as an oppressed minority.

The Heterogeneous Public and Group Representation

I have argued that participatory democracy is an element and condition of social justice. Contemporary
participatory democratic theory, however, inherits
from republicanism a commitment to a unified public that in practice tends to exclude or silence some
groups. Where some groups are materially privileged
and exercise cultural imperialism, formally democratic processes often elevate the particular experiences and perspectives of the privileged groups, silencing or denigrating those of oppressed groups.

In her study of the functioning of a New England
town meeting government, for example, Jane Mansbridge demonstrates that women, Blacks, working-
class people, and poor people tend to participate less
and have their interests represented less than whites,
middle-class professionals, and men. White middle-
class men assume authority more than others, and
they are more practiced at speaking persuasively;
mothers and old people find it more difficult than
others to get to meetings (Mansbridge, 1980, chap. 9).
. . . Amy Gutmann [gives an] example of how increasing democracy in some school systems led to increased segregation because the more numerous, materially privileged, and articulate whites were able to
promote their perceived interests against Blacks' just
demand for equal treatment in an integrated system
(Gutmann, 1980, pp. 191–202).

In these and similar cases, the group differences of
privilege and oppression that exist in society have an
effect on the public, even though the public claims to
be blind to difference. Traditionally political theory
and practice have responded to evidence of such bias
by attempting yet once again to institute a genuinely
universal public. Such a pure perspective that transcends the particularity of social position and consequent partial vision . . . is impossible. If the unified
public does not transcend group differences and often

allows the perspective and interests of privileged groups to dominate, then a democratic public can counteract this bias only by acknowledging and giving voice to the group differences within it.

I assert, then, the following principle: a democratic public should provide mechanisms for the effective recognition and representation of the distinct voices and perspectives of those of its constituent groups that are oppressed or disadvantaged. Such group representation implies institutional mechanisms and public resources supporting (1) self-organization of group members so that they achieve collective empowerment and a reflective understanding of their collective experience and interests in the context of the society; (2) group analysis and group generation of policy proposals in institutionalized contexts where decisionmakers are obliged to show that their deliberations have taken group perspectives into consideration; and (3) group veto power regarding specific policies that affect a group directly, such as reproductive rights policy for women, or land use policy for Indian reservations.

Specific representation for oppressed groups in the decisionmaking procedures of a democratic public promotes justice better than a homogeneous public in several ways, both procedural and substantial (cf. Beitz, 1988, pp. 168–69). First, it better assures procedural fairness in setting the public agenda and hearing opinions about its items. Social and economic privilege means, among other things, that the groups which have it behave as though they have a right to speak and be heard, that others treat them as though they have that right, and that they have the material, personal, and organizational resources that enable them to speak and be heard. As a result, policy issues are often defined by the assumptions and priorities of the privileged. Specific representation for oppressed groups interrupts this process, because it gives voice to the assumptions and priorities of other groups.

Second, because it assures a voice for the oppressed as well as the privileged, group representation better assures that all needs and interests in the public will be recognized in democratic deliberations. The privileged usually are not inclined to protect or advance the interests of the oppressed, partly because their social position prevents them from understanding those interests, and partly because to some degree their privilege depends on the continued oppression of others. While different groups may share many needs, moreover, their difference usually entails some special needs which the individual groups themselves can best express. If we consider just democratic decisionmaking as a politics of need interpretation, as I have already suggested, then democratic institutions should facilitate the public expression of the needs of those who tend to be socially marginalized or silenced by cultural imperialism. Group representation in the public facilitates such expression.

In the previous section I argued for the assertion of a positive sense of difference by oppressed groups, and for a principle of special rights for those groups. I discussed there the legitimate fears of many in emancipatory social movements that abandoning group-blind policies and adopting group-specific ones will restigmatize the groups and justify new exclusions. Group representation can help protect against such a consequence. If oppressed and disadvantaged groups can self-organize in the public and have a specific voice to present their interpretation of the meaning of and reasons for group-differentiated policies, then such policies are more likely to work for than against them.

Group representation, third, encourages the expression of individual and group needs and interests in terms that appeal to justice, that transform an "I want" into an "I am entitled to," in Hannah Pitkin's words. . . . I [have] argued that publicity itself encourages this transformation because a condition of the public is that people call one another to account. Group representation adds to such accountability because it serves as an antidote to self-deceiving self-interest masked as an impartial or general interest. Unless confronted with different perspectives on social relations and events, different values and language, most people tend to assert their perspective as universal. When social privilege allows some group perspectives to dominate a public while others are silent, such universalizing of the particular will be reaffirmed by many others. Thus the test of whether a claim upon the public is just or merely an expression of self-interest is best made when those making it must confront the opinion of others who have explicitly different, though not necessarily conflicting, experiences, priorities, and needs (cf. Sunstein, 1988,

p. 1588). As a person of social privilege, I am more likely to go outside myself and have regard for social justice when I must listen to the voice of those my privilege otherwise tends to silence.

Finally, group representation promotes just outcomes because it maximizes the social knowledge expressed in discussion, and thus furthers practical wisdom. Group differences are manifest not only in different needs, interests, and goals, but also in different social locations and experiences. People in different groups often know about somewhat different institutions, events, practices, and social relations, and often have different perceptions of the same institutions, relations, or events. For this reason members of some groups are sometimes in a better position than members of others to understand and anticipate the probable consequences of implementing particular social policies. A public that makes use of all such social knowledge in its differentiated plurality is most likely to make just and wise decisions.

I should allay several possible misunderstandings of what this principle of group representation means and implies. First, the principle calls for specific representation of social groups, not interest groups or ideological groups. By an interest group I mean any aggregate or association of persons who seek a particular goal, or desire the same policy, or are similarly situated with respect to some social effect—for example, they are all recipients of acid rain caused by Ohio smokestacks. Social groups usually share some interests, but shared interests are not sufficient to constitute a social group. A social group is a collective of people who have affinity with one another because of a set of practices or way of life; they differentiate themselves from or are differentiated by at least one other group according to these cultural forms.

By an ideological group I mean a collective of persons with shared political beliefs. Nazis, socialists, feminists, Christian Democrats, and anti-abortionists are ideological groups. The situation of social groups may foster the formation of ideological groups, and under some circumstances an ideological group may become a social group. Shared political or moral beliefs, even when they are deeply and passionately held, however, do not themselves constitute a social group.

A democratic polity should permit the expression of all interests and opinions, but this does not imply specific representation for any of them. A democratic public may wish to provide representation for certain kinds of interests or political orientations; most parliamentary systems, for example, give proportional representation to political parties according to the number of votes they poll. The principle of group representation that I am arguing for here, however, refers only to social groups.

Second, it is important to remember that the principle calls for specific representation only of oppressed or disadvantaged groups. Privileged groups are already represented, in the sense that their voice, experience, values, and priorities are already heard and acted upon. The faces of oppression . . . provide at least beginning criteria for determining whether a group is oppressed and therefore deserves representation. Once we are clear that the principle of group representation refers only to oppressed social groups, then the fear of an unworkable proliferation of group representation should dissipate.

Third, while I certainly intend this principle to apply to representative bodies in government institutions, its application is by no means restricted to that sphere. . . . I have argued that social justice requires a far wider institutionalization of democracy than currently obtains in American society. Persons should have the right to participate in making the rules and policies of any institution with authority over their actions. The principle of group representation applies to all such democratized publics. It should apply, for example, to decisionmaking bodies formed by oppressed groups that aim to develop policy proposals for a heterogeneous public. Oppressed groups within these groups should have specific representation in such autonomous forums. The Black caucus should give specific representation to women, for example, and the women's caucus to Blacks.

This principle of group representation, finally, does not necessarily imply proportional representation, in the manner of some recent discussions of group representation (see Bell, 1987, chap. 3; Beitz, 1988, p. 163). Insofar as it relies on the principle of "one person one vote," proportional representation retains the assumption that it is primarily individuals who must be represented in decisionmaking bodies. Certainly they must, and various forms of proportional representation, including proportional representation of groups or parties, may sometimes be an important vehicle for representing individuals equally. With the principle I argue for here, however, I am concerned with the representation of group experience, perspectives, and interests. Proportional representation of group members may sometimes be too little or too much to accomplish that aim. A system of proportional group representation in state and federal government in the United States might result in no seats for American Indians, for example. Given the specific circumstances and deep oppression of Indians as a group, however, the principle would certainly require that they have a specific voice. Allocating strictly half of all places to women, on the other hand, might be more than is necessary to give women's perspectives an empowered voice, and might make it more difficult for other groups to be represented.

A principle of group representation has been implicitly and sometimes explicitly asserted in several contemporary social movements struggling against oppression and domination. In response to the anger and criticism that women, Blacks, gays and lesbians, American Indians, and others have leveled against traditionally unitary radical groups and labor unions, many of them have implemented some form of group representation in their decisionmaking bodies. Some political organizations, unions, and feminist groups have formal caucuses for Blacks, Latinos, women, gay men and lesbians, disabled people, and old people, whose perspectives might be silenced without explicit representation. Frequently these organizations have procedures for giving the caucuses a voice in organization-wide discussion and caucus representation in decisionmaking. Some organizations also require representation of members of disadvantaged groups in leadership bodies.

At the height of efforts to occupy nuclear power construction sites, for example, many anti-nuclear power actions and organizations responded to criticisms by feminists or people of color that the movement was dominated by straight white men. Social group affinity groups formed and were generally encouraged, providing solidarity and representation to formerly invisible groups. The National Women's Studies Association, to take another example, has a complex and effective system of representation for group caucuses in its decisionmaking bodies.

The idea of a Rainbow Coalition expressed a heterogeneous public with forms of group representation. The traditional coalition corresponded to the idea of a unified public that transcends particular differences of experience and concerns. In traditional coalitions diverse groups work together for specific ends which they agree interest or affect them all in a similar way, and they generally agree that the differences of perspective, interests, or opinion among them will not surface in the public statements and actions of the coalition. This form ideally suits welfare state interest-group politics. In a Rainbow Coalition, by contrast, each of the constituent groups affirms the presence of the others as well as the specificity of their experience and perspective on social issues (Collins, 1986). In the Rainbow public Blacks do not simply tolerate the participation of gays, labor activists do not grudgingly work alongside peace movement veterans, and none of these paternalistically concede to feminist participation. Ideally, a Rainbow Coalition affirms the presence and supports the claims of each of the oppressed groups or political movements constituting it, and arrives at a political program not by voicing some "principles of unity" that hide difference, but rather by allowing each constituency to analyze economic and social issues from the perspective of its experience. This implies that each group maintains significant autonomy, and requires provision for group representation. Unfortunately, the promise of the Jesse Jackson campaign to launch a viable grassroots organization expressing these Rainbow Coalition ideas has not been fulfilled.

A principle of representation for oppressed or disadvantaged groups has been implemented most frequently in organizations and movements that challenge politics as usual in welfare capitalist society. Some more mainstream organizations, however, also have implemented this principle in some form. The National Democratic Party has had rules requiring representation of women and people of color as delegates, and many state Democratic parties have had similar rules. Many nonprofit agencies call for representation of specific groups, such as women, Blacks, Latinos, and disabled people, on their boards of directors. In a program that some of them call "valuing difference," some corporations have instituted limited representation of oppressed social groups in corporate discussions. One can imagine such a principle of group representation extended to other political contexts. Social justice would be enhanced in many American cities, for example, if a citywide school committee formally and explicitly represented Blacks, Hispanics, women, gay men and lesbians, poor and working-class people, disabled people, and students.

Some might object that implementing a principle of group representation in governing bodies would exacerbate conflict and divisiveness in public life, rendering decisions even more difficult to reach. Especially if groups have veto power over policies that fundamentally and uniquely affect members of their group, it seems likely, it might be claimed, that decisionmaking would be stalled. This objection presupposes that group differences imply essential conflicts of interest. But this is not so; groups may have differing perspectives on issues, but these are often compatible and enrich everyone's understanding when they are expressed. To the extent that group differences produce or reflect conflict, moreover, group representation would not necessarily increase such conflict and might decrease it. If their differences bring groups into conflict, a just society should bring such differences into the open for discussion. Insofar as structured relations of privilege and oppression are the source of the conflict, moreover, group representation can change those relations by equalizing the ability of groups to speak and be heard. Thus group representation should mitigate, though not eliminate, certain kinds of conflict. If, finally, the alternative to stalled decisionmaking is a unified public that makes decisions ostensibly embodying the general interest which systematically ignore, suppress, or conflict with the interests of particular groups, then stalled decisionmaking may sometimes be just.

A second objection might be that the implementation of this principle can never get started. For to implement it a public must be constituted to decide which groups, if any, deserve specific representation in decisionmaking procedures. What principles will guide the composition of such a "constitutional convention"? Who shall decide what groups should receive representation, and by what procedures shall this decision be made? If oppressed groups are not represented at this founding convention, then how will their representation be ensured at all? And if they are represented, then why is implementation of the principle necessary?

These questions pose a paradox of political origins which is not specific to this proposal, and which no philosophical argument can resolve. No program or set of principles can found a politics, because politics does not have a beginning, an original position. It is always a process in which we are already engaged. Normative principles such as those I have proposed in this chapter can serve as proposals in this ongoing political discussion, and means of envisioning alternative institutional forms, but they cannot found a polity. In actual political situations application of any normative principle will be rough and ready, and always subject to challenge and revision. If democratic publics in American society accept this principle of group representation, as I have suggested a few have, they also are likely to name candidates for groups within them that deserve specific representation. Such an opening might sensitize the public to the need for other groups to be represented. But if it does not, these groups will have to petition with arguments that may or may not be persuasive. I see no practical way out of this problem of origin, but that does not stand as a reason to reject this or any other normative principle.

One might ask how the idea of a heterogeneous public which encourages self-organization of groups and group representation in decisionmaking differs from the interest-group pluralism I [have] criticized. . . . Interest-group pluralism, I suggest, operates precisely to forestall the emergence of public discussion and decisionmaking. Each interest group promotes its own specific interest as thoroughly and forcefully as it can, and need not consider the other interests competing in the political marketplace except strategically, as potential allies or adversaries in its own pursuit. The rules of interest-group pluralism do not require justifying one's interest as right, or compatible with social justice. A heterogeneous public, however, is a *public*, where participants discuss together the issues before them and come to a decision according to principles of justice. Group representation, I have argued, nurtures such publicity by calling for claimants to justify their demands before others who explicitly stand in different social locations.

Implementing principles of group representation in national and local politics in the United States, or in restructured democratic publics within particular institutions such as factories, offices, universities, churches, and social service agencies, would obviously require creative thinking and flexibility. There are no models to follow. European models of consociational democratic institutions, for example, cannot be removed from the contexts in which they have evolved, and even within them it is not clear that they constitute models of participatory democracy. Reports of experiments with institutionalized self-organization among women, indigenous peoples, workers, peasants, and students in contemporary Nicaragua offer an example closer to the conception I am advocating (Ruchwarger, 1987).

Social justice entails democracy. Persons should be involved in collective discussion and decisionmaking in all the settings that depend on their commitment, action, and obedience to rules — workplaces, schools, neighborhoods, and so on. When such institutions privilege some groups over others, actual democracy requires group representation for the disadvantaged. Not only do just procedures require group representation in order to ensure that oppressed disadvantaged groups have a voice, but such representation is also the best means to promote just outcomes of the deliberative process.

I have argued that the ideal of the just society as eliminating group differences is both unrealistic and undesirable. Instead justice in a group-differentiated society demands social equality of groups, and mutual recognition and affirmation of group differences. Attending to group-specific needs and providing for group representation both promotes that social equality and provides the recognition that undermines cultural imperialism.

References

Alexander, David. 1987. "Gendered Job Traits and Women's Occupations." Ph.D. dissertation, Economics, University of Massachusetts.

Altman, Dennis, 1982. *The Homosexualization of American Society.* Boston: Beacon.

Bayes, Jane H. 1982. *Minority Politics and Ideologies in the United States.* Novato, Calif.: Chandler and Sharp.

Beatty, Richard W. and James R. Beatty. 1981. "Some Problems with Contemporary Job Evaluation Systems." In Helen Remick, ed., *Comparable Worth and Wage Discrimination: Technical Possibilities and Political Realities.* Philadelphia: Temple University Press.

Beitz, Charles. 1979. *Political Theory and International Relations.* Princeton: Princeton University Press.

———. 1988. "Equal Opportunity in Political Representation." In Norman Bowie, ed., *Equal Opportunity.* Boulder: Westview.

Boxill, Bernard. 1984. *Blacks and Social Justice.* Totowa, N.J.: Rowman and Allanheld.

Canter, Norma V. 1987. "Testimony from Mexican American Legal Defense and Education Fund." *Congressional Digest* (March).

Carmichael, Stokeley and Charles Hamilton. 1967. *Black Power.* New York: Random House.

Collins, Sheila. 1986. *The Rainbow Challenge: The Jackson Campaign and the Future of U.S. Politics.* New York: Monthly Review Press.

Cornell, Stephen. 1988. *The Return of the Native: American Indian Political Resurgence.* New York: Oxford University Press.

Cruse, Harold. 1987. *Plural but Equal: Blacks and Minorities and America's Plural Society.* New York: Morrow.

Cunningham, Frank. 1987. *Democratic Theory and Socialism.* Cambridge: Cambridge University Press.

Deloria, Vine and Clifford Lytle. 1984. *The Nations Within.* New York: Pantheon.

D'Emilio, Joseph. 1983. *Sexual Politics, Sexual Communities.* Chicago: University of Chicago Press.

Epstein, Steven. 1987. "Gay Politics, Ethnic Identity: The Limits of Social Constructionism." *Socialist Review* 17 (May/August): 9–54.

Fischer, Claude. 1982. *To Dwell among Friends: Personal Networks in Town and City.* Chicago: University of Chicago Press.

Gutmann, Amy. 1980. *Liberal Equality.* Cambridge: Cambridge University Press.

Haraway, Donna. 1985. "Manifesto for Cyborgs." *Socialist Review* 80 (March/April): 65–107.

Irigaray, Luce. 1985. *Speculum of the Other Woman.* Ithaca: Cornell University Press.

Jaggar, Alison. 1983. *Feminist Politics and Human Nature.* Totowa, N.J.: Rowman and Allanheld.

Karst, Kenneth. 1986. "Paths to Belonging: The Constitution and Cultural Identity." *North Carolina Law Review* 64 (January): 303–77.

Kleven, Thomas. 1988. "Cultural Bias and the Issue of Bilingual Education." *Social Policy* 19 (Summer): 9–12.

Laclau, Ernesto and Chantal Mouffe. 1985. *Hegemony and Socialist Strategy.* London: Verso.

Lader, Laurence. 1979. *Power on the Left.* New York: Norton.

Littleton, Christine. 1987. "Reconstructing Sexual Equality." California Law Review 75 (July): 1279–1337.

Mansbridge, Jane. 1980. *Beyond Adversarial Democracy.* New York: Basic.

Miles, Angela. 1985. "Feminist Radicalism in the 1980's." *Canadian Journal of Political and Social Theory* 9:16–39.

Minow, Martha. 1985. "Learning to Live with the Dilemma of Difference: Bilingual and Special Education." *Law and Contemporary Problems* 48 (Spring): 157–211.

Nickel, James. 1988. "Equal Opportunity in a Pluralistic Society." In Ellen Frankel Paul, Fred D. Miller, Jeffrey Paul, and John Ahrens, eds., *Equal Opportunity.* Oxford: Blackwell.

Omi, Michael and Howard Winant. 1983. "By the Rivers of Babylon: Race in the United States, Part I and II." *Socialist Review* 71 (September/October): 31–66; 72 (November/December): 35–70.

Ortiz, Roxanne Dunbar. 1984. *Indians of the Americas.* New York: Praeger.

Ross, Jeffrey. 1980. Introduction to Jeffrey Ross and Ann Baker Cottrell, eds., *The Mobilization of Collective Identity.* Lanham, Md.: University Press of America.

Rothschild, Joseph. 1981. *Ethnopolitics.* New York: Columbia University Press.

Said, Edward. 1978. *Orientalism.* New York: Pantheon.

Scales, Ann. 1981. "Towards a Feminist Jurisprudence." *Indiana Law Journal* 56 (Spring): 375–444.

Schmitt, Eric. 1989. "As the Suburbs Speak More Spanish, English Becomes a Cause." *New York Times,* 26 February.

Scott, Joan. 1988. "Deconstructing Equality-versus-Difference: Or the Uses of Post-Structuralist Theory for Feminism." *Feminist Studies* 14 (Spring): 33–50.

Sears, David O. and Leonie Huddy. 1987. "Bilingual Education: Symbolic Meaning and Support among Non-Hispanics." Paper presented at the annual meeting of the American Political Science Association, Chicago, September.

Sunstein, Cass R. 1988. "Beyond the Republican Revival." *Yale Law Journal* 97 (July): 1539–90.

Taub, Nadine and Wendy Williams. 1985. "Will Equality Require More than Assimilation, Accommodation or Separation from the Existing Social Structure?" *Rutgers Law Review* 37 (Summer): 825–44.

Treiman, Donald J. and Heidi I. Hartman. 1981. *Women, Work and Wages.* Washington, D.C.: National Academy Press.

Wasserstrom, Richard. 1980a. "On Racism and Sexism." In *Philosophy and Social Issues.* Notre Dame: Notre Dame University Press.

Williams, Wendy. 1983. "Equality's Riddle: Pregnancy and the Equal Treatment/Special Treatment Debate." *New York University Review of Law and Social Change* 13: 325–80.

WHO IS YOUR MOTHER?
Red Roots of White Feminism

Paula Gunn Allen

Paula Gunn Allen argues that the rejection of tradition is a major feature of life in the United States, but that tradition gives people a sense of identity and lessens conflict. The tradition she urges us to recapture is the Native American tradition, which, she goes on to show, profoundly influenced life in the United States. (Source: From The Sacred Hoop *by Paula Gunn Allen. Copyright © 1986, 1992 by Paula Gunn Allen. Reprinted by permission of Beacon Press.)*

At Laguna Pueblo in New Mexico, "Who is your mother?" is an important question. At Laguna, one of several of the ancient Keres gynocratic societies of the region, your mother's identity is the key to your own identity. Among the Keres, every individual has a place within the universe — human and nonhuman — and that place is defined by clan membership. In turn, clan membership is dependent on matrilineal descent. Of course, your mother is not only that woman whose womb formed and released you — the term refers in every individual case to an entire generation of women whose psychic, and consequently physical, "shape" made the psychic existence of the following generation possible. But naming your own mother (or her equivalent) enables people to place you precisely within the universal web of your life, in each of its dimensions: cultural, spiritual, personal, and historical.

Among the Keres, "context" and "matrix" are equivalent terms, and both refer to approximately the same thing as knowing your derivation and place. Failure to know your mother, that is, your position and its attendant traditions, history, and place in the scheme of things, is failure to remember your significance, your reality, your right relationship to earth and society. It is the same as being lost — isolated, abandoned, self-estranged, and alienated from your own life. This importance of tradition in the life of every member of the community is not confined to Keres Indians; all American Indian Nations place great value on traditionalism.

The Native American sense of the importance of continuity with one's cultural origins runs counter to contemporary American ideas: in many instances, the immigrants to America have been eager to cast off cultural ties, often seeing their antecedents as backward, restrictive, even shameful. Rejection of tradition constitutes one of the major features of American life, an attitude that reaches far back into American colonial history and that now is validated by virtually every cultural institution in the country. Feminist practice, at least in the cultural artifacts the community values most, follows this cultural trend as well.

The American idea that the best and the brightest should willingly reject and repudiate their origins leads to an allied idea — that history, like everything in the past, is of little value and should be forgotten as quickly as possible. This all too often causes us to reinvent the wheel continually. We find ourselves discovering our collective pasts over and over, having to retake ground already covered by women in the preceding decades and centuries. The Native American view, which highly values maintenance of traditional customs, values, and perspectives, might result in slower societal change and in quite a bit less social upheaval, but it has the advantage of providing a solid sense of identity and lowered levels of psychological and interpersonal conflict.

Contemporary Indian communities value individual members who are deeply connected to the traditional ways of their people, even after centuries of concerted and brutal effort on the part of the American government, the churches, and the corporate system to break the connections between individuals and their tribal world. In fact, in the view of the traditionals, rejection of one's culture — one's traditions, language, people — is the result of colonial oppression and is hardly to be applauded. They believe that the roots of oppression are to be found in the loss of tradition and memory because that loss is always accompanied by a loss of a positive sense of self. In short, Indians think it is important to remember, while Americans believe it is important to forget.

The traditional Indians' view can have a significant impact if it is expanded to mean that the sources of social, political, and philosophical thought in the Americas not only should be recognized and honored by Native Americans but should be embraced by American society. If American society judiciously modeled the traditions of the various Native Nations, the place of women in society would become central, the distribution of goods and power would be egalitarian, the elderly would be respected, honored, and protected as a primary social and cultural resource, the ideals of physical beauty would be considerably enlarged (to include "fat," strong-featured women, gray-haired, and wrinkled individuals, and others who in contemporary American culture are viewed as "ugly"). Additionally, the destruction of the biota, the life sphere, and the natural resources of the planet would be curtailed, and the spiritual nature of human and nonhuman life would become a primary organizing principle of human society. And if the traditional tribal systems that are emulated included pacifist ones, war would cease to be a major method of human problem solving.

Re-membering Connections and Histories

The belief that rejection of tradition and of history is a useful response to life is reflected in America's amazing loss of memory concerning its origins in the matrix and context of Native America. America does not seem to remember that it derived its wealth, its values, its food, much of its medicine, and a large part of its "dream" from Native America. It is ignorant of the genesis of its culture in this Native American land, and that ignorance helps to perpetuate the longstanding European and Middle Eastern monotheistic, hierarchical, patriarchal cultures' oppression of women, gays, and lesbians, people of color, working class, unemployed people, and the elderly. Hardly anyone in America speculates that the constitutional system of government might be as much a product of American

Indian ideas and practices as of colonial American and Anglo-European revolutionary fervor.

Even though Indians are officially and informally ignored as intellectual movers and shapers in the United States, Britain, and Europe, they are peoples with ancient tenure on this soil. During the ages when tribal societies existed in the Americas largely untouched by patriarchal oppression, they developed elaborate systems of thought that included science, philosophy, and government based on a belief in the central importance of female energies, autonomy of individuals, cooperation, human dignity, human freedom, and egalitarian distribution of status, goods, and services. Respect for others, reverence for life, and, as a by-product, pacifism as a way of life; importance of kinship ties in the customary ordering of social interaction; a sense of the sacredness and mystery of existence; balance and harmony in relationships both sacred and secular were all features of life among the tribal confederacies and nations. And in those that lived by the largest number of these principles, gynarchy was the norm rather than the exception. Those systems are as yet unmatched in any contemporary industrial, agrarian, or postindustrial society on earth.

As we have seen in previous essays, there are many female gods recognized and honored by the tribes and Nations. Femaleness was highly valued, both respected and feared, and all social institutions reflected this attitude. Even modern sayings, such as the Cheyenne statement that a people is not conquered until the hearts of the women are on the ground, express the Indians' understanding that without the power of woman the people will not live, but with it, they will endure and prosper.

Indians did not confine this belief in the central importance of female energy to matters of worship. Among many of the tribes (perhaps as many as 70 percent of them in North America alone), this belief was reflected in all of their social institutions. The Iroquois Constitution or White Roots of Peace, also called the Great Law of the Iroquois, codified the Matrons' decision-making and economic power:

> The lineal descent of the people of the Five Fires [the Iroquois Nations] shall run in the female line. Women shall be considered the progenitors of the Nation. They shall own the land and the soil.

Men and women shall follow the status of their mothers. (Article 44)

The women heirs of the chieftainship titles of the League shall be called Oiner or Otinner [Noble] for all time to come. (Article 45)

If a disobedient chief persists in his disobedience after three warnings [by his female relatives, by his male relatives, and by one of his fellow council members, in the order], the matter shall go to the council of War Chiefs. The Chiefs shall then take away the title of the erring chief *by order of the women in whom the title is vested.* When the chief is deposed, the women shall notify the chiefs of the League . . . and the chiefs of the League shall sanction the act. The women will then select another of their sons as a candidate and the chiefs shall elect him. (Article 19) (Emphasis mine)[1]

The Matrons held so much policy-making power traditionally that once, when their position was threatened they demanded its return and consequently the power of women was fundamental in shaping the Iroquois Confederation sometime in the sixteenth or early seventeenth century. It was women

> who fought what may have been the first successful feminist rebellion in the New World. The year was 1600, or thereabouts, when these tribal feminists decided that they had had enough of unregulated warfare by their men. Lysistratas among the Indian women proclaimed a boycott on lovemaking and childbearing. Until the men conceded to them the power to decide upon war and peace, there would be no more warriors. Since the men believed that the women alone knew the secret of childbirth, the rebellion was instantly successful.

> In the Constitution of Deganawidah the founder of the Iroquois Confederation of Nations had said: "He caused the body of our mother, the woman, to be of great worth and honor. He purposed that she shall be endowed and entrusted with the birth and upbringing of men, and that she shall have the care of all that is planted by which life is sustained and supported and the power to breathe is fortified: *and moreover that the warriors shall be her assistants.*"

The footnote of history was curiously supplied when Susan B. Anthony began her "Votes for Women" movement two and a half centuries later. Unknowingly the feminists chose to hold their founding convention of latter-day suffragettes in the town of Seneca [Falls], New York. The site was just a stone's throw from the old council house where the Iroquois women had plotted their feminist rebellion. (Emphasis mine)[2]

Beliefs, attitudes, and laws such as these became part of the vision of American feminists and of other human liberation movements around the world. Yet feminists too often believe that no one has ever experienced the kind of society that empowered women and made that empowerment the basis of its rules of civilization. The price the feminist community must pay because it is not aware of the recent presence of gynarchical societies on this continent is unnecessary confusion, division, and much lost time.

The Root of Oppression Is Loss of Memory

An odd thing occurs in the minds of Americans when Indian civilization is mentioned: little or nothing. As I write this, I am aware of how far removed my version of the roots of American feminism must seem to those steeped in either mainstream or radical versions of feminism's history. I am keenly aware of the lack of image Americans have about our continent's recent past. I am intensely conscious of popular notions of Indian women as beasts of burden, squaws, traitors, or, at best, vanished denizens of a long-lost wilderness. How odd, then, must my contention seem that the gynocratic tribes of the American continent provided the basis for all the dreams of liberation that characterize the modern world.

We as feminists must be aware of our history on this continent. We need to recognize that the same forces that devastated the gynarchies of Britain and the Continent also devastated the ancient African civilizations, and we must know that those same materialistic, antispiritual forces are presently engaged in wiping out the same gynarchical values, along with the peoples who adhere to them, in Latin America. I am convinced that those wars were and continue to be about the imposition of patriarchal civilization over the holistic, pacifist, and spirit-based gynarchies they supplant. To that end the wars of imperial conquest have not been solely or even mostly waged over the land and its resources, but they have been fought within the bodies, minds, and hearts of the people of the earth for dominion over them. I think this is the reason traditionals say we must remember our origins, our cultures, our histories, our mothers and grandmothers, for without that memory, which implies continuance rather than nostalgia, we are doomed to engulfment by a paradigm that is fundamentally inimical to the vitality, autonomy, and self-empowerment essential for satisfying, high-quality life.

The vision that impels feminists to action was the vision of the Grandmothers' society, the society that was captured in the words of the sixteenth-century explorer Peter Martyr nearly five hundred years ago. It is the same vision repeated over and over by radical thinkers of Europe and America, from François Villon to John Locke, from William Shakespeare to Thomas Jefferson, from Karl Marx to Friedrich Engels, from Benito Juarez to Martin Luther King, from Elizabeth Cady Stanton to Judy Grahn, from Harriet Tubman to Audre Lorde, from Emma Goldman to Bella Abzug, from Malinalli to Cherrie Moraga, and from Iyatiku to me. That vision as Martyr told it is of a country where there are "no soldiers, no gendarmes or police, no nobles, kings, regents, prefects, or judges, no prisons, no lawsuits. . . . All are equal and free," er so Friedrich Engels recounts Martyr's words.[3]

Columbus wrote:

> Nor have I been able to learn whether they [the inhabitants of the islands he visited on his first journey to the New World] held personal property, for it seemed to me that whatever one had, they all took shares of. . . . They are so ingenuous and free with all they have, that no one would believe it who has not seen it; of anything that they possess, if it be asked of them, they never say no; on the contrary, they invite you to share it and show as much love as if their hearts went with it.[4]

At least that's how the Native Caribbean people acted when the whites first came among them; American Indians are the despair of social workers, bosses, and missionaries even now because of their deeply ingrained tendency to spend all they have, mostly on others. In any case, as the historian William Brandon notes,

the Indian *seemed* free, to European eyes, gloriously free, to the European soul shaped by centuries of toil and tyranny, and this impression operated profoundly on the process of history and the development of America. Something in the peculiar character of the Indian world gave an impression of classlessness, of propertylessness, and that in turn led to an impression, as H. H. Bancroft put it, of "humanity unrestrained . . . in the exercise of liberty absolute."[5]

A Feminist Heroine

Early in the women's suffrage movement, Eva Emery Dye, an Oregon suffragette, went looking for a heroine to embody her vision of feminism. She wanted a historical figure whose life would symbolize the strengthened power of women. She found Sacagawea (or Sacajawea) buried in the journals of Lewis and Clark. The Shoshoni teenager had traveled with the Lewis and Clark expedition, carrying her infant son, and on a small number of occasions acted as translator.[6]

Dye declared that Sacagawea, whose name is thought to mean Bird Woman, had been the guide to the historic expedition, and through Dye's work Sacagawea became enshrined in American memory as a moving force and friend of the whites, leading them in the settlement of western North America.[7]

But Native American roots of white feminism reach back beyond Sacagawea. The earliest white women on this continent were well acquainted with tribal women. They were neighbors to a number of tribes and often shared food, information, child care, and health care. Of course little is made of these encounters in official histories of colonial America, the period from the Revolution to the Civil War, or on the ever-moving frontier. Nor, to my knowledge, has either the significance or incidence of intermarriage between Indian and white or between Indian and Black been explored. By and large, the study of Indian-white relations has been focused on government and treaty relations, warfare, missionization, and education. It has been almost entirely documented in terms of formal white Christian patriarchal impacts and assaults on Native Americans, though they are not often characterized as assaults but as "civilizing the savages." Particularly in organs of popular culture and miseducation, the focus has been on what whites imagine to be degradation of Indian women ("squaws"), their equally imagined love of white government and white conquest ("princesses"), and the horrifying misleading, fanciful tales of "bloodthirsty, backward primitives" assaulting white Christian settlers who were looking for life, liberty, and happiness in their chosen land.

But, regardless of official versions of relations between Indians and whites or other segments of the American population, the fact remains that great numbers of apparently "white" or "Black" Americans carry notable degrees of Indian blood. With that blood has come the culture of the Indian, informing the lifestyles, attitudes, and values of their descendants. Somewhere along the line—and often quite recently—an Indian woman was giving birth to and raising the children of a family both officially and informally designated as white or Black—not Indian. In view of this, it should be evident that one of the major enterprises of Indian women in America has been the transfer of Indian values and culture to as large and influential a segment of American immigrant populations as possible. Their success in this endeavor is amply demonstrated in the Indian values and social styles that increasingly characterize American life. Among these must be included "permissive" childrearing practices, for . . . imprisoning, torturing, caning, strapping, starving, or verbally abusing children was considered outrageous behavior. Native Americans did not believe that physical or psychological abuse of children would result in their edification. They did not believe that children are born in sin, are congenitally predisposed to evil, or that a good parent who wishes the child to gain salvation, achieve success, or earn the respect of her or his fellows can be helped to those ends by physical or emotional torture.

The early Americans saw the strongly protective attitude of the Indian people as a mark of their "savagery"—as they saw the Indian's habit of bathing frequently, their sexual openness, their liking for scant clothing, their raucous laughter at most things, their suspicion and derision of authoritarian structures, their quick pride, their genuine courtesy, their willingness to share what they had with others less fortu-

nate than they, their egalitarianism, their ability to act as if various lifestyles were a normal part of living, and their granting that women were of equal or, in individual cases, of greater value than men.

Yet the very qualities that marked Indian life in the sixteenth century have, over the centuries since contact between the two worlds occurred, come to mark much of contemporary American life. And those qualities, which I believe have passed into white culture from Indian culture, are the very ones that fundamentalists, immigrants from Europe, the Middle East, and Asia often find the most reprehensible. Third- and fourth-generation Americans indulge in growing nudity, informality in social relations, egalitarianism, and the rearing of women who value autonomy, strength, freedom, and personal dignity—and who are often derided by European, Asian, and Middle Eastern men for those qualities. Contemporary Americans value leisure almost as much as tribal people do. They find themselves increasingly unable to accept child abuse as a reasonable way to nurture. They bathe more than any other industrial people on earth—much to the scorn of their white cousins across the Atlantic, and they sometimes enjoy a good laugh even at their own expense (though they still have a less developed sense of the ridiculous than one might wish).

Contemporary Americans find themselves more and more likely to adopt a "live and let live" attitude in matters of personal sexual and social styles. Two-thirds of their diet and a large share of their medications and medical treatments mirror or are directly derived from Native American sources. Indianization is not a simple concept, to be sure, and it is one that Americans often find themselves resisting; but it is a process that has taken place, regardless of American resistance to recognizing the source of many if not most of American's vaunted freedoms in our personal, family, social, and political arenas.

This is not to say that Americans have become Indian in every attitude, value, or social institution. Unfortunately, Americans have a way to go in learning how to live in the world in ways that improve the quality of life for each individual while doing minimal damage to the biota, but they have adapted certain basic qualities of perception and certain attitudes that are moving them in that direction.

An Indian-Focused Version of American History

American colonial ideas of self-government came as much from the colonists' observations of tribal governments as from their Protestant or Greco-Roman heritage. Neither Greece nor Rome had the kind of pluralistic democracy as that concept has been understood in the United States since Andrew Jackson, but the tribes, particularly the gynarchical tribal confederacies, did. It is true that the *oligarchic* form of government that colonial Americans established was originally based on Greco-Roman systems in a number of important ways, such as its restriction of citizenship to propertied white males over twenty-one years of age, but it was never a form that Americans as a whole have been entirely comfortable with. Politics and government in the United States during the Federalist period also reflected the English common law system as it had evolved under patriarchal feudalism and monarchy—hence the United States' retention of slavery and restriction of citizenship to propertied white males.

The Federalists did make one notable change in the feudal system from which their political system derived on its Anglo side. They rejected blooded aristocracy and monarchy. This idea came from the Protestant Revolt to be sure, but it was at least reinforced by colonial America's proximity to American Indian nonfeudal confederacies and their concourse with those confederacies over the two hundred years of the colonial era. It was this proximity and concourse that enabled the revolutionary theorists to "dream up" a system in which all local polities would contribute to and be protected by a central governing body responsible for implementing policies that bore on the common interest of all. It should also be noted that the Reformation followed Columbus's contact with the Americas and that his and Martyr's reports concerning Native Americans' free and easy egalitarianism were in circulation by the time the Reformation took hold.

The Iroquois federal system, like that of several in the vicinity of the American colonies, is remarkably similar to the organization of the federal system of the United States. It was made up of local, "state," and federal bodies composed of executive, legislative, and judicial branches. The Council of Matrons was the executive: it instituted and determined general policy. The village, tribal (several villages), and Confederate councils determined and implemented policies when they did not conflict with the broader Council's decisions or with theological precepts that ultimately determined policy at all levels. The judicial was composed of the men's councils and the Matron's council, who sat together to make decisions. Because the matrons were the ceremonial center of the system, they were also the prime policymakers.

Obviously, there are major differences between the structure of the contemporary American government and that of the Iroquois. Two of those differences were and are crucial to the process of just government. The Iroquois system is spirit-based, while that of the United States is secular, and the Iroquois Clan Matrons formed the executive. The female executive function was directly tied to the ritual nature of the Iroquois politic, for the executive was lodged in the hands of the Matrons of particular clans across village, tribe, and national lines. The executive office was hereditary, and only sons of eligible clans could serve, at the behest of the Matrons of their clans, on the councils at the three levels. Certain daughters inherited the office of Clan Matron through their clan affiliations. No one could impeach or disempower a Matron, though her violation of certain laws could result in her ineligibility for the Matron's council. For example, a woman who married *and took her husband's name* could not hold the title Matron.

American ideas of social justice came into sharp focus through the commentaries of Iroquois observers who traveled in France in the colonial period. These observers expressed horror at the great gap between the lifestyles of the wealthy and the poor, remarking to the French philosopher Montaigne, who would heavily influence the radical communities of Europe, England, and America, that "they had noticed that in Europe there seemed to be two moities, consisting of the rich 'full gorged' with wealth, and the poor, starving 'and bare with need and povertie.' The Indian tourists not only marveled at the division, but marveled that the poor endured 'such an injustice, and that they took not the others by the throte, or set fire on their house.' "[8] It must be noted that the urban poor eventually did just that in the French Revolution. The writings of Montaigne and of those he influenced provided the theoretical framework and the vision that propelled the struggle for liberty, justice, and equality on the Continent and later throughout the British empire.

The feminist idea of power as it ideally accrues to women stems from tribal sources. The central importance of the clan Matrons in the formulation and determination of domestic and foreign policy as well as in their primary role in the ritual and ceremonial life of their respective Nations was the single most important attribute of the Iroquois, as of the Cherokee and Muskogee, who traditionally inhabited the southern Atlantic region. The latter peoples were removed to what is now Oklahoma during the Jackson administration, but prior to the American Revolution they had regular and frequent communication with and impact on both the British colonizers and later the American people, including the African peoples brought here as slaves.

Ethnographer Lewis Henry Morgan wrote an account of Iroquoian matriarchal culture, published in 1877,[9] that heavily influenced Marx and the development of communism, particularly lending it the idea of the liberation of women from patriarchal dominance. The early socialists in Europe, especially in Russia, saw women's liberation as a central aspect of the socialist revolution. Indeed, the basic ideas of socialism, the egalitarian distribution of goods and power, the peaceful ordering of society, and the right of every member of society to participate in the work and benefits of that society, are ideas that pervade American Indian political thought and action. And it is through various channels — the informal but deeply effective Indianization of Europeans, and christianizing Africans, the social and political theory of the confederacies feuding and then intertwining with European dreams of liberty and justice, and, more recently, the work of Morgan and the writings of Marx and Engels — that the age-old gynarchical systems of egalitarian government found their way into contemporary feminist theory.

When Eva Emery Dye discovered Sacagawea and honored her as the guiding spirit of American womanhood, she may have been wrong in bare historical fact, but she was quite accurate in terms of deeper truth. The statues that have been erected depicting Sacagawea as a Matron in her prime signify an understanding in the American mind, however unconscious, that the source of just government, of right ordering of social relationships, the dream of "liberty and justice for all" can be gained only by following the Indian Matrons' guidance. For, as Dr. Anna Howard Shaw said of Sacagawea at the National American Woman's Suffrage Association in 1905:

> Forerunner of civilization, great leader of men, patient and motherly woman, we bow our hearts to do you honor! . . . May we the daughters of an alien race . . . learn the lessons of calm endurance, of patient persistence and unfaltering courage exemplified in your life, in our efforts to lead men through the Pass of justice, which goes over the mountains of prejudice and conservatism to the broad land of the perfect freedom of a true republic; one in which men and women together shall in perfect equality solve the problems of a nation that knows no caste, no race, no sex in opportunity, in responsibility or in justice! May 'the eternal womanly' ever lead us on![10]

Notes

1. The White Roots of Peace, cited in *The Third Woman: Minority Women Writers of the United States,* ed. Dexter Fisher (Boston: Houghton Mifflin, 1980), p. 577. Cf. Thomas Sanders and William Peek, eds., *Literature of the American Indian* (New York: Glencoe Press, 1973), pp. 208–239. Sanders and Peek refer to the document as "The Law of the Great Peace."

2. Stan Steiner, *The New Indians* (New York: Dell, 1968), pp. 219–220.

3. William Brandon, *The Last Americans: The Indian in American Culture* (New York: McGraw-Hill, 1974), p. 294.

4. Brandon, *Last Americans,* p. 6.

5. Brandon, *Last Americans,* pp. 7–8. The entire chapter "American Indians and American History" (pp. 1–23) is pertinent to the discussion.

6. Ella E. Clark and Margot Evans, *Sacagawea of the Lewis and Clark Expedition* (Berkeley: University of California Press, 1979), pp. 93–98. Clark details the fascinating, infuriating, and very funny scholarly escapade of how our suffragette foremothers created a feminist hero from the scant references to the teenage Shoshoni wife of the expedition's official translator, Pierre Charbonneau.

7. The implications of this maneuver did not go unnoticed by either whites or Indians, for the statues of the idealized Shoshoni woman, the Native American matron Sacagawea, suggest that American tenure on American land, indeed, the right to be on this land, is given to whites by her. While that implication is not overt, it certainly is suggested in the image of her that the sculptor chose: a tall, heavy woman, standing erect, nobly pointing the way westward with upraised hand. The impression is furthered by the habit of media and scholar of referring to her as "the guide." Largely because of the popularization of the circumstances of Sacagawea's participation in the famed Lewis and Clark expedition, Indian people have viewed her as a traitor to her people, likening her to Malinalli (La Malinche, who acted as interpreter for Cortés and bore him a son) and Pocahontas, that unhappy girl who married John Rolfe (not John Smith) and died in England after bearing him a son. Actually none of these women engaged in traitorous behavior. Sacagawea led a long life, was called Porivo (Chief Woman) by the Comanches, among whom she lived for more than twenty years, and in her old age engaged her considerable skill at speaking and manipulating white bureaucracy to help in assuring her Shoshoni people decent reservation holdings.

   A full discussion is impossible here but an examination of American child-rearing practices, societal attitudes toward women and exhibited by women (when compared to the same in Old World cultures) as well as the foodstuffs, medicinal materials, countercultural and alternative cultural systems, and the deeply Indian values these reflect should demonstrate the truth about informal acculturation and cross-cultural connections in the Americas.

8. Brandon, *Last Americans*, p. 6.

9. Lewis Henry Morgan, *Ancient Society or Researches in the Lines of Human Progress from Savagery Through Barbarism to Civilization* (New York, 1877).

10. Clark and Evans, *Sacagawea*, p. 96.

COMMITMENT FROM THE MIRROR-WRITING BOX

Trinh T. Minh-ha

Trinh-Minh-ha describes her triple bind: being a woman of color, a writer, and a writer of color. We can put this article in the context of assimilation and separatism by seeing her experience as typical of "hyphenated Americans." Assimilation is never really possible, and separatism can call for tremendous personal sacrifices. (Source: From Women, Native, Other *by Trinh Minh-ha. Reprinted by permission of Indiana University Press.)*

The Triple Bind

Neither black/red/yellow nor woman but poet or writer. For many of us, the question of priorities remains a crucial issue. Being merely "a writer" without doubt ensures one a status of far greater weight than being "a woman of color who writes" ever does. Imputing race or sex to the creative act has long been a means by which the literary establishment cheapens and discredits the achievements of non-mainstream women writers. She who "happens to be" a (non-white) Third World member, a woman, and a writer is bound to go through the ordeal of exposing her work to the abuse of praises and criticisms that either ignore, dispense with, or overemphasize her racial and sexual attributes. Yet the time has passed when she can confidently identify herself with a profession or artistic vocation without questioning and relating it to her color-woman condition. Today, the growing ethnic-feminist consciousness has made it increasingly difficult for her to turn a blind eye not only to the specification of the writer as historical subject (who writes? and in what context?), but also to writing itself as a practice located at the intersection of subject and history — a literary practice that involves the possible knowledge (linguistical and ideological) of itself as such. On the one hand, no matter what position she decides to take, she will sooner or later find herself driven into situations where she is made to feel she must choose from among three conflicting identities. Writer of color? Woman writer? Or woman of color? Which comes first? Where does she place her loyalties? On the other hand, she often finds herself at odds with language, which partakes in the white-male-is-norm ideology and is used predominantly as a vehicle to circulate established power relations. This is further intensified by her finding herself also at odds with her relation to writing, which when carried out uncritically often proves to be one of domination: as holder of speech, she usually writes from a position of power, creating as an "author," situating herself *above* her work and existing *before* it, rarely simultaneously *with* it. Thus, it has become almost impossible for her to take up her pen without at the same time questioning her relation to the material that defines her and her creative work. As focal point of cultural consciousness and social change, writing weaves into language the complex relations of a subject caught between the problems of race and gender and the practice of literature as the very place where social alienation is thwarted differently according to each specific context.

Silence in Time

Writing, reading, thinking, imagining, speculating. These are luxury activities, so I am reminded, permitted to a privileged few, whose idle hours of the day can be viewed otherwise than as a bowl of rice or a loaf of bread less to share with the family. "If we wish to increase the supply of rare and remarkable women like the Brontës," wrote our reputed foresister Virginia Woolf, "we should give the Joneses and the Smiths rooms of their own and five hundred [pounds] a year. One cannot grow fine flowers in a thin soil."[1] Substantial creative achievement demands not necessarily genius, but acumen, bent, persistence, time. And time, in the framework of industrial development, means a wage that admits of leisure and living conditions that do not require that writing be incessantly interrupted, deferred, denied, at any rate subordinated to family responsibilities. "When the claims of creation cannot be primary," Tillie Olsen observes, "the results are atrophy; unfinished work; minor effort and accomplishment; silences." The message Olsen conveys in *Silences* leaves no doubt as to the circumstances under which most women writers function. It is a constant reminder of those who never come to writing: "the invisible, the as-innately-capable: the born to the wrong circumstances — diminished, excluded, foundered."[2] To say this, however, is not to say that writing should be held in veneration in all milieus or that every woman who fails to write is a disabled being. (What Denise Paulme learned in this regard during her first period of fieldwork in Africa is revealing. Comparing her life one day with those of the women in an area of the French Sudan, she was congratulating herself on not having to do a chore like theirs — pounding millet for the meals day in and day out — when she overheard herself commented upon by one of the women nearby: "That girl makes me tired with her everlasting paper and pencil: what sort of a life is that?" The lesson, Paulme concluded, "was a salutary one, and I have never forgotten it.")[3] To point out that, in general, the situation of women does not favor literary productivity is to imply that it is almost impossible for them (and especially for those bound up with the Third World) to engage in writing as an occupation without their letting themselves be consumed by a deep and pervasive sense of guilt. Guilt over the selfishness implied in such activity, over themselves as housewives and "women," over their families, their friends and all other "less fortunate" women. The circle in which they turn proves to be vicious, and writing in such a context is always practiced at the cost of other women's labor. Doubts, lack of confidence, frustrations, despair: these are sentiments born with the habits of distraction, distortion, discontinuity and silence. After having toiled for a number of years on her book, hattie gossett exclaims to herself:

> Who do you think you are [to be writing a book]? and who cares what you think about anything enough to pay money for it . . . a major portion of your audience not only cant read but seems to think readin is a waste of time? plus books like this arent sold in the ghetto bookshops or even in airports?[4]

The same doubt is to be heard through Gloria Anzaldúa's voice:

> Who gave us permission to perform the act of writing? Why does writing seem so unnatural for me? . . . The voice recurs in me: *Who am I, a poor Chicanita from the sticks, to think I could write?* How dared I even consider becoming a writer as I stooped over the tomato fields bending, bending under the hot sun. . . .

> How hard it is for us to *think* we can choose to become writers, much less *feel* and *believe* that we can.[5]

Rites of Passage

S/he who writes, writes. In uncertainty, in necessity. And does not ask whether s/he is given the permission to do so or not. Yet, in the context of today's market-dependent societies, "to be a writer" can no longer mean purely to perform the act of writing. For a laywo/man to enter the priesthood — the sacred world of writers — s/he must fulfill a number of unwritten conditions. S/he must undergo a series of rituals, be baptized and ordained. S/he must *submit* her writings to the law laid down by the corporation of literary/literacy victims and be prepared to *accept* their verdict. Every woman who writes and wishes to become established as a writer has known the taste of *rejection*. Sylvia Plath's experience is often cited. Her years of darkness, despair and disillusion, her agony of slow rebirth, her moments of fearsome excitement at the start of the writing of *The Bell Jar*, her unsuccessful attempts at re-submitting her first book of poems under ever-changing titles and the distress with which she upbraided herself are parts of the realities that affect many women writers:

> Nothing stinks like a pile of unpublished writing, which remark I guess shows I still don't have a pure motive (O it's-such-fun-I-just-can't-stop-who-cares-if-it's-published-or-read) about writing . . . I still want to see it finally ritualized in print.[6]

Accumulated unpublished writings do stink. They heap up before your eyes like despicable confessions that no one cares to hear; they sap your self-confidence by incessantly reminding you of your failure to incorporate. For publication means the breaking of a first seal, the end of a "no-admitted" status, the end of a soliloquy confined to the private sphere and the start of a possible sharing with the unknown other—the reader, whose collaboration with the writer alone allows the work to come into full being. Without such a rite of passage, the woman-writer-to-be/woman-to-be-writer is condemned to wander about, begging for permission to join in and be a member. If it is difficult for any woman to find acceptance for her writing, it is all the more so for those who do not match the stereotype of the "real woman"—the colored, the minority, the physically or mentally handicapped. Emma Santos, who spent her days running to and fro between two worlds—that of hospitals and that of the "normal" system—equally rejected by Psychiatry and by Literature, is another writer whose first book has been repeatedly dismissed (by twenty-two publishing houses). Driven to obsession by a well-known publisher who promised to send her an agreement but never did, she followed him, spied on him, called him twenty times a day on the phone, and ended up feeling like "a pile of shit making after great men of letters." Writing, she remarks, is "a shameful, venereal disease," and Literature, nothing more than "a long beseeching." Having no acquaintance, no friend to introduce her when she sought admission for her work among the publishers, she describes her experience as follows:

> I receive encouraging letters but I am goitrous. Publishers, summons, these are worse than psychiatrists, interrogatories. The publishers perceive a sick and oblivious girl. They would have liked the text, the same one, without changing a single word, had it been presented by a young man from the [Ecole] Normale Superieure, *agrégé* of philosophy, worthy of the Goncourt prize.[7]

The Guilt

To capture a publisher's attention, to convince, to negotiate: these constitute one step forward into the world of writers, one distress, one guilt. One guilt among the many yet to come, all of which bide their time to loom up out of their hiding places, for the path is long and there is an ambush at every turn. Writing: not letting it merely haunt you and die over and over again in you until you no longer know how to speak. Getting published: not loathing yourself, not burning it, not giving up. Now I (the all-knowing subject) feel almost secure with such definite "not-to-do's." Yet, I/i (the plural, non-unitary subject) cannot set my mind at rest with them without at the same time recognizing their precariousness. i (the personal race- and gender-specific subject) have, in fact turned a deaf ear to a number of primary questions: Why write? For whom? What necessity? What writing? What impels you and me and hattie gossett to continue to write when we know for a fact that our books are not going to be "sold in the ghetto bookshops or even in airports?" And why do we care for their destinations at all? "A writer," proclaims Toni Cade Bambara, "like any other cultural worker, like any other member of the community, ought to try to put her/his skills in the service of the community." It is apparently on account of such a conviction that Bambara "began a career as the neighborhood scribe," helping people write letters to faraway relatives as well as letters of complaint, petitions, contracts and the like.[8] For those of us who call ourselves "writers" in the context of a community whose major portion "not only cant read but seems to think readin is a waste of time" (gossett), being "the neighborhood scribe" is no doubt one of the most gratifying and unpretentious ways of dedicating oneself to one's people. Writing as a social function—as differentiated from the ideal of art for art's sake—is the aim that Third World writers, in defining their roles, highly esteem and claim. *Literacy* and *literature* intertwine so tightly, indeed, that the latter has never ceased to imply both the ability to read and the condition of being well read—and thereby to convey the sense of *polite learning* through the arts of *grammar* and *rhetoric*. The illiterate, the ignorant versus the wo/man of "letters" (of wide reading), the highly educated. With such discrimination and opposition, it is hardly surprising that the writer should be viewed as a social parasite. Whether s/he makes common cause with the upper classes or chooses to disengage her/himself by adopting the myth of the bohemian artist, the writer is a kept wo/man who for her/his living largely relies on the generosity of that portion of society called the literate. A room of one's own and a pension of five hundred pounds per year solely for making ink marks on paper: this, symbolically speaking, is what many people refer to when they say the writer's activity is "gratuitous" and "useless." No matter how devoted to the vocation s/he may be, the writer cannot subsist on words and mere fresh air, nor can s/he really "live by the pen," since her/his work — arbitrarily estimated as it is — has no definite market value. Reading in this context may actually prove to be "a waste of time," and writing, as Woolf puts it, "a reputable and harmless occupation." Reflecting on her profession as a writer (in a 1979 interview), Toni Cade Bambara noted that she probably did not begin "getting really serious about writing until maybe five years ago. Prior to that, in spite of all good sense, I always thought writing was rather frivolous, that it was something you did because you didn't feel like doing any work." The concept of "writing" here seems to be incompatible with the concept of "work." As the years went by and Toni Cade Bambara got more involved in writing, however, she changed her attitude and has "come to appreciate that it is a perfectly legitimate way to participate in struggle."9

Commitment as an ideal is particularly dear to Third World writers. It helps to alleviate the Guilt: that of being privileged (Inequality), of "going over the hill" to join the clan of literates (Assimilation), and of indulging in a "useless" activity while most community members "stoop over the tomato fields, bending under the hot sun" (a perpetuation of the same privilege). In a sense, committed writers are the ones who write both to awaken to the consciousness of their guilt and to give their readers a guilty conscience. Bound to one another by an awareness of their guilt, writer and reader may thus assess their positions, engaging themselves wholly in their situations and carrying their weight into the weight of their communities, the weight of the world. Such a definition naturally places the committed writers on the side of Power. For every discourse that breeds fault and guilt is a discourse of authority and arrogance. To say this, however, is not to say that all power discourses produce equal oppression or that those established are necessary. Discussing

African literature and the various degrees of propaganda prompted by commitment, Ezekiel Mphahlele observes that although "propaganda is always going to be with us" — for "there will always be the passionate outcry against injustice, war, fascism, poverty" — the manner in which a writer protests reflects to a large extent her/his regard for the reader and "decides the literary worth of a work." "Commitment," Mphahlele adds, "need not give rise to propaganda: the writer can make [her/]his stand known without advocating it . . . in two-dimensional terms, i.e., in terms of one response to one stimulus."10 Thus, in the whirlwind of prescriptive general formulas such as: Black art must "respond *positively* to the reality of revolution" or Black art must "expose the enemy, *praise* the people, and *support* the revolution" (Ron Karenga, my italics), one also hears distinct, unyielding voices whose autonomy asserts itself as follows:

> Black pride need not blind us to our own weaknesses: in fact it should help us to perceive our weaknesses. . . .
>
> I do not care for black pride that drugs us into a condition of stupor and inertia. I do not care for it if leaders use it to dupe the masses.11

> To us, the man who adores the Negro is as sick as the man who abominates him.12

Freedom and the Masses

The notion of *art engagé* as defined by Jean-Paul Sartre, an influential apologist for socially effective literature, continues to grow and to circulate among contemporary engaged writers. It is easy to find parallels (and it is often directly quoted) in Third World literary discourses. "A free man addressing free men," the Sartrian writer "has only one subject — freedom." He writes to "appeal to the reader's freedom to collaborate in the production of his work" and paints the world "only so that free men may feel their freedom as they face it."13 The function of literary art, in other words, must be to remind us of that freedom and to defend it. Made to serve a political purpose, literature thus places itself within the context of the proletarian fight, while the writer frees himself from his dependence on elites — or in a wider sense, from any privilege — and creates, so to speak, an art for an unrestricted public known as "art for the masses." From the chain of notions dear to Sartre — choice, responsibility, contingency, situation, motive, reason, being, doing, having — two notions are set forth here as being most relevant to Third World engaged literary theories: freedom and the masses. What is freedom in writing? And what can writing-for-the-masses be? Reflecting on being a writer, "female, black, and free," Margaret Walker, for example, defines freedom as "a philosophical state of mind and existence." She proudly affirms:

> My entire career in writing . . . is determined by these immutable facts of my human condition. . .
>
> Writing is my life, but it is an avocation nobody can buy. In this respect I believe I am a free agent, stupid perhaps, but *me* and still free. . . .
>
> The writer is still in the avant-garde for Truth and Justice, for Freedom, Peace, and Human Dignity. . . . Her place, let us be reminded, is anywhere she chooses to be, doing what she has to do, creating, healing, and always being herself.[14]

These lines agree perfectly with Sartre's ideal of liberty. They may be said to echo his concepts of choice and responsibility — according to which each person, being an absolute choice of self, an absolute emergence at an absolute date, must assume her/his situation with the proud consciousness of being the author of it. (For one is nothing but this "being-in-situation" that is the total contingency of the world, of one's birth, past and environment, and of the fact of one's fellow wo/man.) By its own rationale, such a sense of responsibility (attributed to the lucid, conscientious, successful man of action) renders the relationship between freedom and commitment particularly problematic. Is it not, indeed, always in the name of freedom that My freedom hastens to stamp out those of others? Is it not also in the name of the masses that My personality bestirs itself to impersonalize those of my fellow wo/men? Do the masses become masses by themselves? Or are they the result of a theoretical and practical operation of "massification"? From where onward can one say of a "free" work of art that it is written for the infinite numbers which constitute the masses and not merely for a definite public stratum of society?

For the People, by the People and from the People

Like all stereotypical notions, the notion of the masses has both an upgrading connotation and a degrading one. One often speaks of the masses as one speaks of the people, magnifying thereby their number, their strength, their mission. One invokes them and pretends to write on their behalf when one wishes to give weight to one's undertaking or to justify it. The Guilt mentioned earlier is always lurking below the surface. Yet to oppose the masses to the elite is already to imply that those forming the masses are regarded as an aggregate of average persons condemned by their lack of personality or by their dim individualities to stay with the herd, to be docile and anonymous. Thus the notion of "art *for* the masses" supposes not only a split between the artist and her/his audience — the spectator-consumer — but also a passivity on the part of the latter. For art here is not attributed to the masses; it is ascribed to the active few, whose role is precisely to produce *for* the great numbers. This means that despite the shift of emphasis the elite-versus-masses opposition remains intact. In fact it must remain so, basically unchallenged, if it is to serve a conservative political and ideological purpose — in other words, if (what is defined as) "art" is to exist at all. One of the functions of this "art for the masses" is, naturally, to contrast with the other, higher "art for the elite," and thereby to enforce its elitist values. The wider the distance between the two, the firmer the stand of conservative art. One can no longer let oneself be deceived by concepts that oppose the artist or the intellectual to the masses and deal with them as with two incompatible entities. Criticisms arising from or dwelling on such a *myth* are, indeed, quite commonly leveled against innovators and more often used as tools of intimidation than as reminders of social interdependency. It is perhaps with this perspective in mind that one may better understand the variants of Third World literary discourse, which claims not exactly an "art for the masses," but an "art for the people, by the people and from the people." In an article on *"Le poète noir et son peuple"* (The Black Poet and His People), for example,

Jacques Rabemananjara virulently criticized Occidental poets for spending their existence indulging in aesthetic refinements and subtleties that bear no relation to their peoples' concerns and aspirations, that are merely sterile intellectual delights. The sense of dignity, Rabemananjara said, forbids black Orpheus to go in for the cult of art for art's sake. Inspirer inspired by his people, the poet has to play the difficult role of being simultaneously the torch lighting the way for his fellowmen and their loyal interpreter. "He is more than their spokesman: he is their voice." His noble mission entitles him to be "not only the messenger, but the very message of his people."[15] The concept of a popular and functional art is here poised against that of an intellectual and aesthetic one. A justified regression? A shift of emphasis again? Or an attempt at fusion of the self and the other, of art, ideology and life? Let us listen to other, perhaps less didactic voices; that of Aimé Césaire in *Return to My Native Land:*

> I should come back to this land of mine and say to it: "Embrace me without fear. . . . If all I can do is speak, at least I shall speak for you."
>
> And I should say further: "My tongue shall serve those miseries which have no tongue, my voice the liberty of those who founder in the dungeons of despair."
>
> And I should say to myself: "And most of all beware, even in thought, of assuming the sterile attitude of the spectator, for life is not a spectacle, a sea of griefs is not a proscenium, a man who wails is not a dancing bear."[16]

that of Nikki Giovanni in *Gemini:*

> Poetry is the culture of a people. We are poets even when we don't write poems. . . . We are all preachers because we are One. . . . I don't think we younger poets are doing anything significantly different from what we as a people have always done. The new Black poetry is in fact just a manifestation of our collective historical needs.[17]

and that of Alice Walker in an essay on the importance of models in the artist's life:

> It is, in the end, the saving of lives that we writers are about. . . . We do it because we care. . . . We care because we know this: *The life we save is our own.*[18]

One may say of art for art's sake in general that it is itself a reaction against the bourgeois "functional" attitude of mind which sees in the acquisition of art the highest, purest form of consumption. By making explicit the gratuitousness of their works, artists show contempt for their wealthy customers, whose purchasing power allows them to subvert art in its subversiveness, reducing it to a mere commodity or a service. As a reaction, however, art for art's sake is bound to be "two-dimensional" — "one response to one stimulus" (Mphahlele) — and, therefore, to meet with no success among writers of the Third World. "I cannot imagine," says Wole Soyinka, "that our 'authentic black innocent' would ever have permitted himself to be manipulated into the false position of countering one pernicious Manicheism with another."[19] An art that claims to be at the same time sender and bearer of a message, to serve the people and "to come off the street" (Cade Bambara), should then be altogether "functional, collective, and committing or committed" (Karenga). The reasoning circle closes on the notion of commitment, which again emerges, fraught with questions.

Notes

1. Virginia Woolf, *Women and Writing* (New York: Harcourt Brace Jovanovich, 1979), 54.

2. Tillie Olsen, *Silences* (1978, rpt. New York: Delta/Seymour Lawrence Ed., 1980), 13, 39.

3. Denise Paulme, ed., *Women of Tropical Africa,* tr. H. M. Wright (1963, rpt. Berkeley: University of California Press, 1974), 2.

4. hattie gossett, "Who Told You Anybody Wants to Hear from You? You Ain't Nothing But a Black Woman!" *This Bridge Called My Back: Writings by Radical Women of Color,* ed. Cherrie Moraga & Gloria Anzaldúa (Watertown, MA: Persephone Press, 1981), 175.

5. Gloria Anzaldúa, "Speaking in Tongues: A Letter to 3rd World Women Writers," *This Bridge Called My Back,* 166.

6. Sylvia Plath, *The Bell Jar* (1971, rpt. New York: Bantam Books, 1981), 211. See Biographical Note by Lois Ames.

7. Emma Santos, *L'Itinéraire psychiatrique* (Paris: Des Femmes, 1977), 46–47. For previous quotes see pp. 47, 50, 125 (my translations).

8. Toni Cade Bambara, "What It Is I Think I'm Doing Anyhow," *The Writer on Her Work,* ed. J. Sternburg (New York: W. W. Norton, 1980), 167.

9. "Commitment: Toni Cade Bambara Speaks," interview with Beverly Guy-Sheftall in *Sturdy Black Bridges: Visions of Black Women in Literature,* ed. R. P. Bell, B. J. Parker, & B. Guy-Sheftall (New York: Anchor/ Doubleday, 1979), 232.

10. Ezekiel Mphahlele, *Voices in the Whirlwind* (New York: Hill & Wang, 1972), 186–87.

11. Ibid., 196.

12. Franz Fanon, *Black Skin, White Masks,* tr. Charles Lam Markmann (New York: Grove Press, 1967), 8.

13. Jean-Paul Sartre, *Situations, II Qu'est-ce que la littérature?* (Paris: Gallimard, 1948), 97, 112.

14. Margaret Walker, "On Being Female, Black, and Free," *The Writer on Her Work,* 95, 102, 106.

15. Jacques Rabemananjara. "Le Poète noir et son peuple," *Présence Africaine* 16 (Oct.–Nov. 1957), 10–13.

16. Aimé Césaire, *Return to My Native Land* (Paris; Présence Africaine, 1971), 60–62.

17. Nikki Giovanni, *Gemini: An Extended Autobiographical Statement on My First Twenty-Five Years of Being a Black Poet* (New York: Viking Press, 1971), 95–96.

18. Alice Walker, "Saving The Life That Is Your Own: The Importance of Models in the Artist's Life," *The Third Woman: Minority Women Writers of the United States,* ed. D. Fisher (Boston: Houghton Mifflin, 1980), 158.

19. Wole Soyinka, *Myth, Literature, and the African World* (New York: Cambridge University Press, 1976), 138.

Identity Politics and Separatism

I CAN'T BELIEVE YOU WANT TO DIE*

Larry Kramer

Larry Kramer argues that assimilation requires gays and lesbians to live their lives in the closet. But pretending that we are all the same will not protect those who are oppressed. He cites two powerful examples: the Holocaust and the AIDS epidemic. Both Jews in pre-War Germany and gays in the pre-AIDS United States were well assimilated. But this assimilation undermined group solidarity and group institutions that might have protected them from these two holocausts. (Source: From Reports from the Holocaust: The Making of an AIDS Activist *by Larry Kramer. Copyright © 1981, 1982, 1983, 1984, 1985, 1987, 1988, 1989, by Larry Kramer. Reprinted by permission of the author.)*

We have little to be proud of this Gay Pride Week. One by one, we are being picked off by the enemy. They are killing us.

I don't think you are going to like what I am going to say. It is the last time I am going to say it. I'm making a farewell appearance. I am not overly tired. I am certainly not suffering from burnout. I have a lot of piss and vinegar left in me—too much, in fact. No. I'm not tired.

Not physically tired, at any rate. I am, of course, as are you, very tired of many things. I am tired of what *they* are doing to us. I am tired of what *they* aren't doing for us. I am tired of seeing so many of my friends die—I'm exceptionally tired of that, as I know you are too.

I'm also tired of people coming up to me on the street and saying, "Thank you for what you're doing and saying." They mean it as a compliment, I know. But now I scream back, "Why aren't you doing it and saying it, too?" Why are there so few people out there screaming and yelling? You're dying too!

I'm telling you they are killing us! We are being picked off one by one, and half the men reading this could be dead in five years, and you are all still sitting on your asses like weaklings, and therefore we, the gay community, are not strong enough and our organizations are not strong enough and we are going to die for it!

I have come to the terrible realization that I believe this gay community of ours has a death wish and that we are going to die because we refuse to take responsibility for our own lives.

Yes, most of all, I'm tired of you. I'm tired of the death wish of the gay community. I'm tired of our colluding in our own genocide. I'm tired of you, by your own passivity, actively participating in your own genocide.

*Speech delivered on June 9, 1987, to the Boston Lesbian and Gay Town Meeting, held in Faneuil Hall, to kick off their Gay Pride Weekend. It was reprinted in many of the major gay newspapers across the country.

How many of you have given a thousand dollars or more at any one time to any gay organization or gay charity? Ten thousand? (For the rich readers: one hundred thousand dollars? A million?)

How many of you have left anything in your wills to anything gay?

How many of you have spent at least one hour a week volunteering for a gay organization? Ten hours?

And if you don't like any of the gay organizations, how many of you have spent how much time to make any of them better? Instead of just bitching them into further weakness? Or helped them raise money to make themselves better?

How many of you have bothered to consider that by helping to raise $80,000 a year, you could fund a lobbyist in Washington to fight for us all year long—to join with a network of other gay lobbyists, paid for by groups in other cities, so that we could have as many lobbyists as General Motors or the National Rifle Association or the National Council of Churches or the American Medical Association, all of whom get what *they* want?

Is it such a big deal to get a group together to raise $80,000 to save your lives? (Did anyone notice that when Paul Popham died, he asked that contributions be made to AIDS Action Council, a lobbying group, and not Gay Men's Health Crisis, which he cofounded, and in whose ability to do anything but look after funerals he had lost confidence and faith?)

How many of you have written consistently or even irregularly to an elected official or testified at an official hearing on the subject of AIDS, or regarding treatment, or official lethargy in this city and state and country?

How many of you really trust the NIH to be capable of coordinating research around a crisis of this scope?

How many of you even know what the NIH is, or how important it is in your life? And that your very own life is in its hands? You didn't know that, did you? That your very own life is in the hands of an agency you don't know anything about.

How many of you believe there is sufficient education to contain what is happening?

How many of you have children? How many of you have spoken to a school board about sex education?

How many of you have had sex with more than one person in the last ten years?

How many of you have protested actively against mandatory testing?

How many of you are willing to face up to the fact that the FDA is fucked up, the NIH is fucked up, the CDC is *very* fucked up—and that, entering the seventh year of what is now a pandemic, the boys and girls running the show at these organizations have been unable to make whatever system they're operating work?

How long are you prepared to wait for these systems to work?

How long are you prepared to wait before our own AIDS organizations provide us with adequate information on available treatments?

How many hours and days are you prepared to spend on the phone attempting, in vain, to find out what is going on where and how it's doing and why your dying friends can't get it immediately?

How many of you believe you have no responsibility to take action on any of these matters?

How many of you need to die or become infected before you feel you can take action on why every single branch of government in charge of AIDS, both local and federal, is dragging its ass?

What's the number of dead friends at which you can decide to stop just sitting quietly like the good little boys and girls we were all brought up to be—and start taking rude, noisy, offensive political action? One? Ten? *One hundred?*

It always amazes me when I tell people they have power, and they answer me, "Power? Me? What power?" How can you be so conservative, dumb, blind? You know what is going on better than anybody, and yet you are silent, you constantly, consistently, and continuously sit on your collective asses and refuse to use your power.

Your voice is your power! Your collective voices! Your group power! Your political power! Your names all strung together on one long list is your power. Your bank accounts are your power, if you weren't all so devastatingly stingy when it comes to funding anything gayer than a Halloween costume. Your bodies are your power, your *living* bodies all strung together in one long line that reaches across this country and could reach to the moon if we only let it.

You know that this country is not responding on a national political level or a local political level, and yet you sit by along with everyone else and watch our men being picked off one by one by one by one by one.

No one is in charge of this pandemic, either in this city or this state or this country! It is as simple as that. And certainly no one who is compassionate and understanding and knowledgeable and efficient is even anywhere near the top of those who are in charge. Almost every person connected with running the AIDS show everywhere is second-rate. I have never come across a bigger assortment of the second-rate in my life. And you have silently and trustingly put your lives in their hands. You—who are first-rate—are silent. And we are going to *die* for that silence.

You know, it's not even a question of government funding anymore. For six long years we fought so hard to get the money. Finally Congress has appropriated masses of money. *Can you believe me when I tell you that it is not being spent?* Two years ago, nineteen official AIDS treatment centers, called ATEUs (AIDS Treatment Evaluation Units), were set up by the NIH—and they still aren't being utilized beyond a fraction of their humane possibilities and intentions. One year ago the NIH was given $47 million just for testing new AIDS drugs—*and they aren't spending it!* Why didn't we know that? Where have we been for these long two years? Why didn't we know that this precious, precious time—during which how many dear friends of ours died—was being thrown out in the garbage because we didn't get on the phone and inquire politely: "Please, sirs, can you tell me what you're doing with all that nice money Congress gave you last May?" How could we have been so lazy and irresponsible—and *trusting?* We, of all people in this world, should know better, and know how not to trust. Where were our gay leaders? Where were all our AIDS organizations? Where were our people in Washington? Where was I? For I blame myself more than I blame anyone else. God fucking damn it, I trusted too!

When I found out about three months ago that $47 million was actually lying around not being used when I knew personally that at least a dozen drugs and treatments just as promising as AZT and in many cases much less toxic were not being tested and were not legally available to us, I got in my car and drove down to Washington. I wanted to find out what was going on. Like most people, I have no notion of how

the system works down there, who reports to whom, which agency is supposed to do what. What I found out sent me into as profound a depression as I have been in since this epidemic started.

My first meeting was at the White House, with the President's Domestic Policy Adviser, Gary Bauer, who advises Ronald Reagan on AIDS. I asked him if ignoring AIDS was intentional. He answered me that he had not seen enough evidence that the Black Plague was going on yet. He was particularly interested to hear from me that the current evidence indicates that the gay male population of the major cities is on its way to becoming totally exposed to the virus. He asked me if I thought female-to-male transmission was as potent as male-to-male. I said the statistics were about the same. He said his advisers told him otherwise. I asked him if gay people who were AIDS experts could be on the President's Commission, and he told me No. I asked him why the President had refused to put anyone in charge—to appoint an AIDS czar? He told me the President *was* the AIDS czar. I asked him why the President had not only not read Surgeon General Koop's AIDS report, or the National Academy of Sciences AIDS report—both of which were then over six months old and both of which beg for immediate, all-out action—but he hadn't even met with Koop personally, his own Surgeon General, and he answered me that the chain of command dictates that, in matters of health, the President talks only to his Secretary of Health and Human Services, Dr. Otis R. Bowen. It turns out that Dr. Koop has absolutely no power; his position is simply that of figurehead. They do not like what he is saying, and I think that if you listen to what he is beginning to say now, you will see that Dr. Koop is being pulled back into line.

Dr. Otis R. Bowen would not see me. He is Reagan's *third* Secretary of Health and Human Services, and he is supposed to be in charge of AIDS. Until he appeared as the closing speaker at the Third International AIDS Conference, where I am happy to say he was roundly booed—were any of *you* there to boo him?—he had not been heard to say anything substantial at all about AIDS. The Secretary of the main department of your government in charge of AIDS—the one single man who can report to the President on the state of this nation's health—had yet to be heard saying anything about AIDS, at the beginning of the seventh year of this pandemic.

I discovered that Dr. Bowen had passed the AIDS buck over to his Assistant Secretary of Health and Human Services, Dr. Robert Windom. Dr. Windom has been in his job all of one year. He's never worked in government before. He was a private physician in Sarasota, Florida, and I figure he got his wonderful opportunity to work so close to his idol, Ronald Reagan, by contributing $55,000 to Republican candidates between 1979 and 1984. He is exceptionally ill-informed about AIDS. On a recent NBC Radio coast-to-coast call-in show, he answered two of his questions incorrectly. My favorite description of Dr. Windom comes from a top legislative congressional aide: "If his IQ were any lower, you'd have to water him."

You laugh — and Dr. Windom is in charge of your life! An uncaring, dumb stooge who knows next to nothing about any of the drugs or treatments or research is in charge of your life, and you are laughing! Over half the men here could be dead in less than five years, and you are laughing at this crack about Dr. Windom!

Dr. Windom reports to Dr. Bowen who reports to the President.

Dr. Windom has passed the AIDS buck to his assistant, Dr. Lowell Harmison. Dr. Harmison is sort of the power behind the power behind the throne. Dr. Harmison does not like gays. Dr. Harmison has been described to me by several congressional contacts as "evil." "You cannot say enough bad things about Lowell Harmison," I was told by more than one. He is so frightened of gay people that he was terrified we would intentionally give blood in order to pollute the nation's blood supply — *on purpose.*

Dr. Harmison reports to Dr. Windom who reports to Dr. Bowen who reports to the President.

Bauer, Bowen, Windom, Harmison. These are the four top men in charge of AIDS in the United States government, the government of all the American people. Your government. God (if there is one) help us — because these four idiots won't.

I am here to tell you that I know more about AIDS than any of these four inhumane men, and that any one of you here who has AIDS or who tends to someone with AIDS, or who reads all the newspapers and watches TV, knows more about AIDS than any of

these four monsters. And they are the four fuckers who are in charge of AIDS for your government — the bureaucrats who have the ultimate control over your life.

Next I went to the National Institutes of Health. The National Institutes of Health receives $6.2 billion *each and every year* to look after the health of the American people. "To improve the health of the American people" is how the U.S. Government Manual describes the NIH's mission. How many of you can tell me the name of the head of NIH?

You don't know the name of the man who is given $6.2 billion each and every year to help make you better if you have AIDS? You should be ashamed of yourselves.

His name is Dr. James Wyngaarden, and he has never been heard to speak out publicly about AIDS either. He is given $6.2 *billion* every year, and not only doesn't he speak out *about* AIDS, but you don't even know his name!

Dr. Wyngaarden reports to Dr. Windom who reports to Dr. Bowen who reports to the President.

The NIH is like a college campus. It looks like Amherst, or like something from an old MGM musical. It's really made up of twelve institutes, which are sort of like dorms, or fraternities, all part of the whole. The grounds are manicured and you can't see any shit on the ground.

Seven years ago, when AIDS was first noticed, and you would have thought NIH would jump on it fast, this is what happened. You would have thought that because there was a cancer involved, called Kaposi's sarcoma, it should have gone to the institute in charge of cancer, the National Cancer Institute of the National Institutes of Health. The National Cancer Institute is the richest fraternity at NIH. In 1981, when AIDS first showed up and should have gone into this rich fraternity, the head of this fraternity didn't want it. So he blackballed it. He had $1 billion of research money "to improve the health of the American people," and the head of NCI didn't want it. Now, how many of you can tell me the name of the head of NCI, then and now?

The man who is in charge of the most important cancer research institute in the entire world — and you don't know his name? You should be ashamed of yourselves.

His name is Dr. Vincent T. Devita. In 1981 he didn't want AIDS, he didn't like the smell of it, and he didn't want to spend any of his institute's $1 billion a year on it, so he too passed the buck.

Dr. Devita reports to Dr. Wyngaarden who reports to Dr. Windom who reports to Dr. Bowen who reports to the President.

Dr. Devita passed the buck to a poor relation, a much smaller institute named the National Institute for Allergy and Infectious Diseases of the National Institutes of Health, which had a budget one-fourth of his and which was not nearly so popular a fraternity to rush and was then run by a man named Dr. Richard Krause, who didn't want AIDS either. He must have smelled the shit about to hit the fan because he quickly resigned as head of NIAID, and he was replaced by — now I am sure you can tell me the name of the man who is now the director of NIAID, the man who reports to Dr. Wyngaarden who reports to Dr. Windom who reports to Dr. Bowen who reports to the President — the single most important name in AIDS today, the name of the man who has probably more effect on your future than anybody else in the world.

How many of you know this man's name?

His name is Dr. Anthony Fauci. He's real cute. He's an Italian from Brooklyn, short, slim, compact; he wears aviator glasses and is a natty dresser, a very energetic and dynamic man. After a recent meeting a bunch of us from New York had with him, during which absolutely nothing was accomplished, he asked me what we thought of the meeting. I told him: "Everyone thought you were real cute." And he blushed to his roots.

You are smiling, and this is the man who has more effect on your future than anyone else, and he is not spending that $47 million — *which was given to him specifically to test AIDS drugs* — and you are smiling!

Everybody likes Dr. Fauci and everybody thinks Dr. Fauci is real cute and every scientific person I spoke to whispers off to the side, "Yes, he's real cute, but he's in way over his head."

Dr. Fauci is an ambitious bureaucrat who is the recipient of all the buck-passing and dumping-on from all of the above. He staggers, without complaint, under his heavy load. No loud-mouth Dr. Koop he.

Dr. Fauci, with his devoted staff of several dozen — that's right, folks, no more than a couple dozen doctors and scientists are fighting against AIDS at NIAID; I guess $47 million doesn't buy what it used to — is chief administrator of the nineteen AIDS-designated treatment units around the country, called ATEUs, and of all AIDS research and testing for the entire country, and no major decision can be made without him. He works eighteen-hour days, his wife is an AIDS nurse in his hospital, he must summon committees, preside over meetings, supervise the selection of drugs to test, monitor their results, deal with pharmaceutical companies, keep up on all the latest information, attend conferences all over the world, and put up with complaints from absolutely everyone.

Dr. Fauci, of all the names in this article, is certainly not the enemy. Because he is not, and because I think he does care, I am even more angry at him for what he is not doing — no matter what his excuses, and he has many.

Instead of screaming and yelling for help as loudly as he can, he tries to make do, to make nice, to negotiate quietly, to assuage. An ambitious bureaucrat doesn't make waves. Yes, Dr. Fauci reports to Dr. Wyngaarden who reports to Dr. Windom who reports to Dr. Bowen who reports to the President.

Dr. Fauci has had this $47 million for a year, and worse — the beds in his AIDS wards are empty! A whole floor in America's state-of-the-art hospital, $47 million given him to test new treatments, and his beds are empty, just as the majority of places on the treatment protocols at those nineteen ATEUs around the country are empty.

What the fuck is going on here? Are they actually afraid they might learn something that might save us?

Research at NIH? I have not space to go into the gory details. Let me just say that the research rivalries in and among *all* the institutes at NIH could make a TV series to rival "Dynasty" and "Falcon Crest" in competitiveness, hostility, selfishness, and greed. (Why doesn't the press write about these scandals as they do about all others? Why doesn't the press ever investigate NIH? Is it so holy — like the Vatican?)

Now you know why NIH stands for Not Interested in Homosexuals.

What the fuck is going on here, and what the fuck are you doing about it?

If I use gross language — go ahead, be offended — I don't know how else to reach you, how to reach everybody. I tried starting an organization: I co-founded GMHC, which becomes more timid as it becomes richer day by day. I tried writing a play. I tried writing endless articles in the *Native* and *The New York Times* and *Newsday* and screaming on "Donahue" and at every TV camera put in front of me. I helped start ACT UP, a small bunch of too few very courageous people willing to make rude noises. I don't know what else to do to wake you up!

I will tell you something else to try to wake you up: If AIDS does not spread out widely into the white, non-drug-using, heterosexual population, as it may or may not do, then the white, non-drug-using population is going to hate us even more — for scaring them, for costing them a fucking fortune, for our "lifestyle," which they will say caused this. AIDS will stay a disease of blacks and Hispanics and gays, and it will continue to be ignored, it will be ignored even more.

The straight world is scared now because they're worried it's going to happen to them. What if it doesn't? Think about that for a while. If all this lethargy is going on now, think what will happen then — just as you are coming down with it and facing death.

Who is fighting back in any and all of this? Twenty-four million gay men and lesbians in this country, and who is fighting back? We have a demonstration at the White House and we have three hundred people and we think we're lucky! We get our pictures in all the magazines and newspapers for one or two days and we feel real proud. Sixty thousand Catholics march in Albany. Two hundred fifty thousand Jews march in New York against the treatment of Soviet Jews. One million people march for nuclear disarmament.

What does it take to get you off your fucking asses?

"You want to die, Felix? Die!" That's a line from *The Normal Heart*. In his immense frustration, Ned Weeks yells it at his dying lover. That's how I feel about all of you.

What does it take to make people hate? I hate Ed Koch because he is the one person in this entire world who could have done something in the beginning and didn't and it took us almost two years even to get a meeting with him (we must always remember that, as Dr. Mathilde Krim tells us, "this is an epedimic that could have been contained"), and he has put yet an-

other powerless wimp in place as his Commissioner of Health, and gay men and women in New York still kiss Koch's ass, as gay men and women still think Ronald Reagan is peachy wonderful, and gay people in Massachusetts think that Ted Kennedy is wonderful, and he is in charge of health issues in the Senate and he has been silent and cowardly about AIDS for six long years, and how many dead brothers have to be piled up in a heap in front of your faces before you learn to fight back and scream and yell and demand and take some responsibility for your own lives?

I am telling you they are killing us and we are letting them!

Yes, I am screaming like an hysteric. I know that. I look and sound like an asshole. I told you this was going to be my last tirade and I am going to go out screaming so fucking rudely that you will hear this coarse, crude voice of mine in your nightmares. You are going to die and you are going to die very, very soon unless you get up off your fucking tushies and fight back!

Unless you do — you will forgive me — you deserve to die.

I never thought I would come to say anything like that. Nobody *deserves* to die.

I recently spoke at a *Village Voice* AIDS Forum in New York on a panel with Dr. Ron Grossman, who has one of the largest gay practices in New York. "Larry," he said to me, "our most outrageous early pronouncements are short of the mark. And so have been our efforts. We are so *behind*."

AIDS is our holocaust. Tens of thousands of our precious men are dying. Soon it will be hundreds of thousands. AIDS is our holocaust and Reagan is our Hitler. New York City is our Auschwitz.

"Holocaust" is another word for "genocide."

"Genocide" is a word I hear myself and others using more and more frequently. You don't hear it as much as you hear words like "mandatory testing" or "no sex education in the schools" or "no condom ads on TV."

Why doesn't everybody realize that all the screaming and yelling going on about "education" and "mandatory testing" is one whale of a red herring?

Why doesn't everyone realize that while all the hatred and fury from the right wing, from the fundamentalists, Mormons, Southern Baptists, born-agains,

Charismatics, Orthodox Jews, Hasidic Jews, Phyllis Schlafly, Paul Cameron, Governor Deukmejian, Representative Dannemeyer, Jesse Helms, Jerry Falwell — and all their equally as vocal supporters — goes on, that while they are screaming and yelling about the naughtiness of condoms and sex education and homosexuality, the killing culprit virus continues to spread and spread and spread and kill and kill and kill. While Rome burns, the Falwells fiddle, fanning their fundamentalists into fury against the faggots — and the junkies and the niggers and the spics and the whores and . . .

And they *know* it!

It is perfectly clear to me — no matter what Ronald Reagan and his henchmen say — that no substantial battle for a cure will be mounted while he is in office and that we must endure, at the least, another eighteen months of untended, *intended* death.

Very consciously they *know* that the more noise they can make, the more stalling tactics they can put into action, with the aid of their President, who supports them, and with the aid of his staff and his Cabinet and his Vice-President and his Attorney General and his Justice Department and his Supreme Court and his Secretary of Education and his various Secretaries and Assistant Secretaries of Health and Human Services and his director of the National Institutes of Health and his Centers for Disease Control — the more gays and blacks and Hispanics will die.

They *know* this! I believe it is a conscious act.

And we are allowing it!

We have fallen into their trap!

Our leaders — such as they are — their energies are consumed fighting these battles against mandatory testing and for better education — and no one is fighting the NIH for drugs and increased protocol testing and faster research. I am telling you that there are drugs and treatments out there that can prolong the quality of our lives and you are not getting them and no one is fighting for them and these drugs and treatments are caught up in so much red tape that they are strangled in the pipeline and the Reagan administration knows this, knows all this, and does nothing about untangling the red tape and half the gay men here can die because of it.

Yes, by our own passivity we are actively colluding with, and participating in, our own genocide.

We are allowing ourselves to be knocked off one by one. Half the gay men here could be dead in five years.

Our gay organizations are weak and *still* don't work with each other and our AIDS organizations have *all* been co-opted by the very systems they were formed to make accountable and you all sit by and allow it to happen when it's your lives that are going down the tubes.

Politicians understand only one thing: PRESSURE. You don't apply it — you don't get anything. Simple as that.

And it must be applied day by week by month by year. You simply can't let up for one single second. Or you don't get anything. Which is what is happening to us.

For six years I have been trying to get the gay world angry enough to exert this pressure. I have failed and I am ashamed of my failure. I blame myself — somehow I wasn't convincing enough or clever enough or cute enough to break through your denial or self-pity or death wish or self-destruction or whatever the fuck is going on. I'm very tired of trying to make you hear me.

I'm shutting up and going away. The vast majority of the gay world will not listen to what is so simple and plain. That there are so few voices as strident as mine around this country is our tragedy. That there is not one single gay leader who has any national recognition like Gloria Steinem or Cardinal O'Connor or Jerry Falwell or Jesse Jackson is also our tragedy. Why is that? Why does every gay spokesperson finally just collapse under the apathy of trying to make you listen — and failing, failing utterly.

Don't you ask yourselves quite often the Big Question: Why am I still alive? Untouched? At some point I did something the others did. How have I escaped?

Don't you think that obligates you to repay God or fate or whomever or whatever, if only your conscience, for this miraculous fact: I am still alive. I must put back something into this world for my own life, which is worth a tremendous amount. By not putting back, you are saying that your lives are worth shit, and that we deserve to die, and that the deaths of all our friends and lovers have amounted to nothing.

I can't believe that in your heart of hearts you feel this way. I can't believe you want to die.

Do you?

I guess this is the angriest speech I have ever delivered. I was pretty fed up and tired. Boston was an unlikely city to deliver it—they're a quiet, polite bunch up there, and the local gay papers had never been very kind to me. But this group kept calling me up, offering me a thousand bucks (I'd never been paid to speak before), and I decided I was going to diva-out and make my farewell appearance. And what better place than historic Faneuil Hall?

And for a while, I really meant it. Even though, much to my surprise, because as I'd harangued them they'd sat there stone-faced, I received a standing ovation; even though, much to my surprise, I got letters from as far away as France and places like Utah and Nevada, from strangers begging me not to quit. I'd had it.

I don't know why I can't confess to burnout when it happens to me, but I can't. I told everyone that I was quitting activism. I'd devote my energy to writing my plays and trying to get them on and writing another novel and trying again to get *The Normal Heart* made into a movie. You'll see, you'll see, I said. Larry's never going to make another speech again.

None of my friends believed me.

WHOSE CONSTITUTION IS IT, ANYWAY?

. . .

"It is no mere accident," Arendt wrote in "The Moral of History," "that the catastrophic defeats of the peoples of Europe began with the catastrophe of the Jewish people, a people in whose destiny all others thought they could remain uninterested."

It's not too early to see AIDS as the homosexuals' holocaust. I have come reluctantly to believe that genocide is occurring: that we are witnessing—or *not* witnessing—the systematic, planned annihilation of some by others with the avowed purpose of eradicating an undesirable portion of the population.

I know that straight Jews, and other heterosexuals, find this comparison of holocausts repugnant.

I certainly don't know what it was like to witness six million die. When I say that I have lost some five hundred acquaintances and friends over the past seven years, I have been told point-blank by straight Jewish people that "their" extermination is the only "holy" one; ours, by contrast, is piddling. Evidently I must not get so upset, because my deaths are less than their deaths.

Does it appear that I am intentionally trying to escalate our horror to that of the Supreme Horror? I am not unfamiliar with charges of hysteria and hyperbole. To read Primo Levi is to know that our suffering, as of this moment, is still small in comparison. But Primo Levi also writes, "A certain dose of rhetoric is perhaps indispensable for memory to persist."

One inadvertent fallout from *the* Holocaust is the growing inability to view any other similar tragedies as awful. Jews themselves are partly responsible for this: memory must in no way be tampered with. But, important as this memory is, the insistence on its primogeniture frustrates efforts to arouse equal public concern when the newest children on the block arrive, demanding immediate succor.

What Hannah Arendt was trying to tell the Jews was that, whether they knew it or not, they have been able to survive thus far because, like it or not, they constituted a political community, and if they wanted to survive they had to break, as Ron H. Feldman puts it in his introduction to *The Jew as Pariah,* "with the past in which accident reigned supreme and take conscious control of their destiny."

The years Arendt writes about were ones in which "being a Jew does not give any legal status in the world." It is hard for young Jews to remember this time, and it is hard for gays to believe Jews were once as unrecognized as gays are now. Gays remain pretty unconvinced when told that it took World War II to organize the Jewish population finally and effectively—those of them who were left.

(Because I am also Jewish, and find so many similarities in the historic plights of both Jews and gays, I find it painful that my religion is, in most instances, so unkind, uncharitable, and in some instances—that of the Orthodox and Hasidim—downright murderous.

People, if they learn lessons at all, learn them, it would appear, only for themselves, and then only if they are lucky. The benefits are evidently neither transferable generally or assignable specifically.)

"The realization that millions of Jews had gone to their deaths without resistance resulted in a change in Jewish consciousness," Feldman writes, then quoting Arendt: "Gone, probably forever, is that chief concern of the Jewish people for centuries: survival at any price. Instead, we find something essentially new among Jews, the desire for dignity at any price."

This longing for dignity at any price has overtaken the gay population in the largest cities. Our holocaust has done that for us. We have learned, if not how to fight, or become "political," how to grieve magnificently. We have established organizations, many of them now huge and rich, to cater to the dying. It is almost as if, rather than bother anyone with our problems, certainly rather than fight to correct what caused them, we shall clutch them possessively to our bosoms and suffer as nobly as we can. It is indeed heroic to witness the amazing devotion that so many, gay and straight, lavish on their dying friends. I do not mean to diminish these sad rituals, though indeed I personally find them slightly ghoulish.

Of course I want to be attended to by those I love when my time comes. I am just slightly stunned when I witness so many electing to give such large amounts of energy, devotion, and caring to those morbid activities, rather than attempting to right the wrongs in a system that's made these activities necessary in the first place. I look at faces at countless memorial services and cannot comprehend why the connection isn't made between these deaths and going out to fight so that more of these deaths, including possibly one's own, can be staved off. Huge numbers regularly show up in cities for Candlelight Marches, all duly recorded for the television cameras. Where are these same numbers when it comes to joining political organizations, with either their dollars or their skills, or plugging in to the incipient civil disobedience movement represented in ACT UP?

I find in these actions a defeatism that is depressingly negative: Gays are hated, these actions seem to say, and there's nothing to be done about it, gays will always be hated, so let's accept this as we bury our dead.

That an increasingly large number of these saints — and I do think there's also a margin of saintliness inherent here, as well as a yearning for such saintliness — are straight women I find both disturbing and gratifying. But it's as if, not only do we tell ourselves that fighting for our lives is a useless occupation, but now we are joined by heterosexual representatives telling us the same thing and helping us to nail our coffins.

I submit that there are different kinds of holocausts. After all, the word is defined, in my *American Heritage Dictionary,* as "any widespread destruction." Hitler gave it new and grotesque meaning, but despite the Jewish insistence that the word is not totally attached to their own destruction, it is perversely inhuman to deny its attachment to other conflagrations. At this moment in history, it is perhaps thought that such a holocaust as Hitler perpetrated can never happen again, and Jews fight mightily to keep this notion alive, even though there certainly have been mighty holocausts since: Stalin's and Ethiopia's, as well as incomprehensible slaughters in Biafra, Cambodia, and Lebanon, are only the few that come immediately to mind. The Jewish outrage that automatically erupts whenever another endangered minority, under threat of destruction, claims that a holocaust is occurring is selfishly counterproductive to confronting yet another example of man's seemingly innate inhumanity to man.

Certainly, a holocaust does not require a Hitler to be effective. Certainly, a holocaust does not require *deliberate* intentionality on the part of one or several or many or a bureaucracy to be effective. Holocausts can occur, and probably most often do occur, because of *inaction.* This inaction can be unintentional or deliberate. How one defines the line, or level, of intentionality or unintentionality is often a difficult question. How does one accuse a bureaucrat of looking the other way, or of paying no attention, or of paying less attention than he should, when he can counter — as Adolf Eichmann did — with the defense, "I was only doing my job as best I could"?

In all my investigations over these past years into why AIDS has not been attended to with the dispatch it warrants, I have been told at almost every juncture that "all is being done that can be done." Indeed, I'm often accused of being "ungrateful" for this "activity," and that more has been learned about this condition in a shorter time than in any other health emergency. To this hyperbole, I usually add my own: If AIDS were happening to Jews, or to American Legionnaires, or to white tennis players at country clubs, we would be much farther along the road to treatment and cure than we are, which, despite all protestations to the contrary, is not very far at all.

The one facet of the AIDS epidemic that I think almost everyone prefers to overlook is this: *Something infectious is going around.* Whatever the cause (and, as I have said, and it bears repeating, like almost everything connected with this epidemic, I tend to view any statement of definite fact with doubt, so many have been contradicted, contravened, or proved downright wrong since these statements of "fact" started appearing in 1981), it is apparently being transmitted infectiously, and it is not stopping. Nothing has changed since the onset about the most important prediction: There may never be a cure. As Dr. Linda Laubenstein, a hematologist at New York University Medical Center and one of the first doctors to note AIDS in patients and to this day one of the leading doctors treating it, says, "We don't have a very good record of dealing with viruses. There isn't a virus yet that's been cured or eliminated. The best we can hope for, and this is a long way from ever happening, is that there will be some kind of treatment that will be suppressive without being too toxic to use over a lifetime — the way diabetics take insulin."

Opponents of increased AIDS funding use, as one of their excuses, the high fatalities from other horrors, such as lung cancer, various lymphomas, heart disease, even auto accidents. These, they say, are just as much in need of attention. "But they're not infectious," is Dr. Laubenstein's curt response to this kind of thinking.

If I harp on my holocaust comparisons, it is because it is my firm belief that we are in but the early stages of destruction by AIDS of huge swaths of the world's population. And the hideously alarming World Health Organization figures don't seem to do the trick of convincing any powers-that-be. There have been, over these past three years, four damning reports prepared for President Reagan or at his behest: two by the National Academy of Sciences, one by his Surgeon General, Dr. C. Everett Koop, and one, most recently, by his own Presidential Commission

on the Human Immunodeficiency Virus Epidemic. Each has said more or less the same thing. The leading editorial in the Sunday *New York Times* of June 5th, 1988, congratulating the commission for its "findings," noted (in words that could as justifiably be applied to the *Times* itself): "The Administration's response to AIDS has from the start been torpid, fitful, fragmented and riven with prejudice against those infected with the virus." The Commission's Report itself says that government leadership "has been inconsistent and not properly coordinated"; the federal response has been "slow, halting, and uneven"; the Food and Drug Administration and the National Institutes of Health were particularly criticized for going *very* slowly indeed.

Amazingly enough, it is no longer even a question of money. Over very long years, Congress has gradually increased its appropriations, so that now there appears to be enough to go around. What Congress is not finding is that this money isn't being spent, or is being spent unwisely, and that no one is in charge of supervising its proper allocation. To cite just one heinous example of malfeasance, Dr. Anthony Fauci, the director of the National Institute for Allergy and Infectious Diseases — that branch of the NIH under which most AIDS treatment research falls — was recently raked over the coals, first at hearings conducted by Representative Ted Weiss and his House Subcommittee on Human Resources, and subsequently by Senator Edward Kennedy, at Senate hearings conducted by his Committee on Labor and Human Resources, who accuse Fauci of "doubletalk." Dr. Fauci has had at his disposal some $374 million. He has been unable to set up a network of hospital treatment centers around the country to test, quickly, promising new drugs (calculated, as I mentioned, to be some two hundred by medical reporter Susan Spencer on "CBS Evening News," and most of them unavailable legally in this country until they *are* tested by the NIH and approved by the FDA). After two years, not only is this system not functioning in any coherent way, but 80 percent of the studies Dr. Fauci and one of his many, many committees, and subcommittees, have approved are still only with AZT, a problematic drug that, in any case, has *already* been approved by the FDA. Because of the snail-like pace of Dr. Fauci's work, and because of the equal lethargy of response from the FDA, which must license any treatment that is approved (and certainly because of the lack of effective pressure from gays or AIDS organizations like GMHC), most of these two hundred untested drugs must be obtained by sufferers as best they can. Hence these treatments are unavailable to any but the rich or the most persistently cagy. Dr. Fauci has been described as "a bumbler" by one of the members of the President's AIDS Commission. I myself have called him, in print, an incompetent idiot.

It is not possible to condemn the stupidities of the NIH without adding those of the FDA. They are a dog-and-pony show. The system is such that you can't have one without the other. A drug tested at the NIH must still be approved by the FDA. Dr. Fauci's culpabilities are equal in size to those of Dr. Frank Young, the FDA's director. Despite repeated promises, despite pressure from congressional subcommittees, presidential reports, and even from Vice-President Bush himself, Dr. Young has done nothing to lessen the eight to nine years' time required for a drug to wend its way leisurely through the FDA approval process. (The average length of time AIDS patients have to live is five years.) Dr. Young loudly trumpeted some new regulations about a year ago—ones that would allow drugs that showed promising efficacy to be available to American patients; but in practice he and his staff have demanded *proof* of this efficacy, not just promise of it, and the time required for that proof to be proved to the FDA is eight to nine years.

A particularly inhumane example of what *is* going on scientifically involves an NIH-sponsored study to test the effectiveness of intravenous immune globulin (an existing pharmaceutical product that anyone can get) on four hundred babies with AIDS or ARC. These babies have an average age of eighteen months to two years. Almost all of them are black or Hispanic. It takes four to eight hours for each intravenous infusion. An infusion is administered once every twenty-eight days, for a period of two years. Previous research has revealed that a higher number of the babies have to be *physically restrained* during the infusion. Half of the babies will receive a useless placebo. Even those babies receiving placebos must be hooked up to an IV and restrained; because it is assumed that many of the babies will pick up typical hospital infections, the NIH wants to make sure these infections are equally

distributed among those receiving both placebo and the actual drug. As if this type of enforced experimentalization was not cruel enough, and as if making half the babies receive a placebo under the same circumstances was not cruel enough, it turns out that it was not necessary to use placebos at all. There already are in existence earlier results to utilize for statistical comparisons. When these earlier studies were presented to the NIH, studies that would save two hundred babies from a needless and painful ordeal, the NIH elected to proceed with the study nevertheless.

The Presidential Commission Report, its strong condemnations and recommendations—they are all words gay men have longed to hear. But, as I said, we've heard them all before, in those three earlier reports, which produced as little result as, in our despondency, we expect this new report to duplicate. There is no gay man who believes that anything helpful will actually be accomplished while President Reagan is in office. (Or if George Bush is elected.) His Commission's Report is seen as window dressing, perfectly timed so that he doesn't have to do anything, for he'll be out of office shortly after its receipt. Again, with the exception of Jesse Jackson, not one of the many candidates who recently competed for their party's nomination mentioned AIDS, dealt with AIDS, addressed any AIDS issues, or presented a plan for the future—a future that, without any doubt, is going to burden any administration with mountainous problems far surpassing any of the ones these candidates *are* willing to discuss. They know that AIDS is not a topic the electorate wishes to hear about. And no one ever seems to ask, nor does any of these four reports address the questions: Just why is it so many people take drugs? Just why is it so many gay men were promiscuous? Just why is it so many people are homeless?

If it is not possible to locate one Hitler responsible for allowing this AIDS destruction to multiply so, it is possible to locate a number of junior candidates. "We don't have one Hitler," a friend of mine said; "we have many Mengeles."

Ronald Reagan, Dr. Bowen, Dr. Wyngaarden, doctors at the NIH and FDA, are equal to Hitler and his Nazi doctors performing their murderous experiments in the camps—not because of similar intentions, but because of similar results.

"You either wait while six million die, which is complicity, or you do something about it. It is just as sinful to let people die as to gas them." This was said by my best friend, Rodger McFarlane, who then went on to recite to me sentences from Christian theology — about sins of commission and omission — from a religion he no longer believes in.

With all due respect, it doesn't appear piddling to me to place my five hundred dead friends on the altar of history, and to posit the possibility that, at the rate we are going, we are now in a situation historically equivalent to, say, the German Jews circa 1938–1940, when the looming danger was, for the most part, also pooh-poohed. And that there will be millions of gay men dead before our holocaust is over. How can everyone avoid seeing this? How can straight and gay people continue to deny the viciousness of the AIDS epidemic? Why do gay men need to be *convinced* that we are being murdered?

Reluctantly, though for some time I denied this, and fought against it, for I know it is hugely counterproductive, I have found myself coming to hate heterosexuals. All heterosexuals. The ones, naturally, who sit by and ignore or simply observe what is happening to us. The ones who offer me condolences for all the awful things happening to us now, as they would in passing along kind words for a sick friend or relief from a cold that won't go away. The ones who invite me for Thanksgiving and Christmas and offer up prayers to God for a surcease to "Larry's friends who are suffering so much" before commencing to consume the turkey. The ones who help us bury so many dead and do not recognize that such deaths need not continue to occur. I hate them for not doing what I am unable to do — change all this. The same reason they hate me.

The greatest criminal of the century was, to Arendt, the "jobholder and the good family man" who did everything out of "kind concern and earnest concentration on the welfare of his family." "In contrast to the earlier units of the SS men and the Gestapo, Himmler's overall organization relied not on fanatics, nor on congenital murderers, nor on sadists; it relied entirely upon the normality of jobholders and family men."

The family. The family. How these words are repeated and repeated in America — from campaign rhetoric to television commercials. This is a country that prides itself on proclaiming family values, as if there were no others, as if every family was homespun and united and loving, as if it is necessary to produce a child — like a product — to justify or countenance a sexual act. AIDS goes against *all* family values: It is perceived as happening mostly to gay men; it is spread sexually (as if heterosexuals did not have sex); it is an embarrassment. Well, I am a member of a family, too. Or I once thought so. Every gay man has two parents, and other relatives, too. How convenient for them all to have disposed of us so expeditiously, just when we need them most. But the ranks are closed, something is happening to gay men, and we are suddenly no longer affiliated with *the* family. Where do they think we came from? The cabbage patch?

Most gay people see little to admire or to emulate in heterosexual life. It seems filled with hypocrisies we have worked hard to avoid. We see few happy straight marriages and many dishonest ones — husbands and wives cheating on each other, children taking more drugs than we ever took, and people ignoring values that we have made important in our lives: taste, style, education, directness, honesty, energy, friendships. We feel particularly blessed by so many and such strong friendships. We have turned to our friends to take the place of families. "Your friends are your family" is something often heard in conversations of gay people gathered together. We look at Ronald and Nancy Reagan, and the books their own children have written about them, and we watch our President and his wife talk constantly about "family values in America," and we laugh. At least our promiscuity was *honest.*

I spoke earlier about Luke, the appealing man who offered me love. After five dates, I decided not to see him anymore. I offer here a reasonable facsimile of the thoughts that crisscrossed my consciousness while he held me in his arms:

I don't want to die, this is killing me, my need to love can't be worth this — he is so nice, I want him so, he is so gentle and he makes me feel good — he takes me for what I am, and he is kind to me, and he is all the things I have always longed for in a relationship, but my work, my work must come first, I have too much yet to say, I cannot abandon my work, and yet

why might it not work out?, why might we not be carriers?, why not take the chance?: But the chance is
Russian roulette and the risks are too great, the odds
are too much against us, and, too, I might kill him, I
might be the carrier, and his life is precious, his youth,
he has so much he wants to give to the world. . . .

What it amounts to is that I cannot stand the torture that each coupling brings to our lovemaking, and
the nightmares that come into my dreams, and the
walking dialogue that plagues me every time I think
of it. It constantly jams itself into my thoughts: You
must be crazy, you must be out of your mind, you are
gambling with your life. Suddenly it doesn't seem to
be worth it. When he leaves me, I promise myself I
won't see him again. I cannot wait for him to leave. He
keeps kissing me goodbye, tenderly, as he goes off to
take the GMHC volunteer training—he wants to become a Crisis Counselor, like his sister-in-law, helping
to tend the dying. But when he is gone, I miss him already, and I wonder if somehow we can't work it out.
No. I must hold firm to my decision. But I miss him.
Why didn't I ask him to come back tonight? He has no
place to stay before returning to the training tomorrow, without going home to his parents in New Jersey.
"Check in," I said, noncommittally, when he left. Will
he? When? What will I say then? Do a Nancy Reagan
and "Just say no"?

Hours later I am still trying not to think of him.
But it's there inside me, my desire for him, my sweet
memories, the ingestion of him, symbolic, but perhaps, accidentally, actual. I try to deny these feelings
and get to work. Work! I must work. Another hour
later, I vomit.

I find I've made this note in my diary after he left,
after our fifth night together: When we hold each
other, there are three people in bed and one of them
is Death. I confide in no one, not even Rodger, who
was my former lover and with whom I share everything. In one of our many daily phone conversations,
he volunteers, "I think Jesus would have to carry me
in his arms to Paris for me to put out."

I am going to say a few words about "gay promiscuity," and let it go. Promiscuity is a loaded word and
a controversial subject, and what exactly constitutes
promiscuity—how many more than one encounter
with how many more than one person?—seems to

differ depending on whom you ask. In any event, as
Professor Boswell of Yale writes: "There does not seem
to be any evidence that gay people are more or less
sexual than others." Dr. Richard Isay, a practicing psychoanalyst and Clinical Associate Professor of Psychiatry at Cornell Medical College, writes in his forthcoming book, *Being Homosexual:* "Human males in
general are more interested in variations of sexual
partners than females." To which Dr. Kinsey's words
can be added: "This is the history of his anthropoid
ancestors, and this is the history of unrestrained males
everywhere." Promiscuity is liberating for some people while for others it's dehumanizing, and thus it's
hard to come down on one side or the other without
taking into account who's being promiscuous. But the
gay community, both before and after the arrival of
AIDS, has taken a bad rap for it. The entire heterosexual world, it sometimes seems to me, perceives the
entire homosexual world as busily involved in doing
nothing but performing endless acts of sexual intercourse. Some of us did and most of didn't (and now
pretty much all of us don't). But it's an issue that must
be addressed because if AIDS is transmitted sexually
in any way, then there's no question that the promiscuity of some gay men was unwittingly responsible
for AIDS killing so many of us. And it's this, of course,
that we are being blamed for (particularly by religious
groups)—spreading AIDS.

The concept of making a virtue out of sexual freedom, i.e., promiscuity, came about because gay men
had nothing else to call their own *but* their sexuality.
The heterosexual majority has for centuries denied us
every possible right of human dignity (which the doctrines of all religions and most "free" countries, as well
our own Constitution, are meant to guarantee for all).
The right to marry. The right to tax advantages and
employee benefits that married couples enjoy. The
right to own property jointly without fear that the law
will disinherit the surviving partner. The right to hold
a job as an openly gay person. The right to have children. The right not to be discriminated against in just
about every area. Indeed—the right to walk down
the street holding hands, as heterosexual people can
do freely when they are in love. The right to love. We
are denied the right to love. Can any heterosexual
imagine being denied the right to love? I ask you to try

to imagine how you might feel if you had to hide from the whole world the fact that you loved your wife or husband.

So, rightly or wrongly—wrongly, as it turned out—many gay men decided to make a virtue of the only thing the straight world didn't have control of: our sexuality. Had we possessed these rights denied us, had we been allowed to live respectably in a community of equals, I think a good case could be made that there would never have been an AIDS epidemic such as we are seeing. Had we been allowed to marry, many of us would not have felt the obligation to be promiscuous. (While we may not see much to emulate in heterosexual marriages, this does not preclude our desire to try it ourselves. It wouldn't be the first time we've demonstrated to the straight world that we can do something better.) Thus I think a good case also can be made that the AIDS pandemic is the fault of the heterosexual white majority.

"Our society does not now want gay men to be in stable, responsible, mutually gratifying relationships," Dr. Isay writes. "The visibility of such couples is too shattering to the sense of masculinity of men in most segments of our culture." Until this change comes—a change that will benefit both gay men and society alike—the destruction of American homosexuals by the heterosexual majority will continue. It is unrealis-tic to think that, even with AIDS, an entire population will be able to stop having sex. The irony, of course, is that being promiscuous is a characteristic that straight men congratulate each other on achieving, at the same time they condemn us for the same acts.

The leveling of this blame for the AIDS epidemic is perhaps better understood if an extension of this argument is presented: that the poor, black, and Hispanic have also been forced into AIDS by oppression. The awfulness of their destitution and deprivation, the absolutely zero chance so many of them face in bettering their lot in this world, forces them to seek peaceful respite and brief relief in the only oblivion available to them—the never-never land of drugs. And these drugs, for all the Just Say No mentality of an imbecilic First Lady, this society makes remarkably available through inept law enforcement and just plain looking the other way. It's almost as if a conscious decision had been made somewhere in government to let all these people drug themselves to death.

AIDS having thus been caused to seed and sprout, it was *allowed* to grow and fester and increase a millionfold by the inaction of our government. As I noted earlier, everyone is more interested in *managing* this epidemic than in stopping it, than in taking any time to search for and begin to solve the root causes of what is going on.

SEPARATING FROM HETEROSEXUALISM

Sarah Lucia Hoagland

Sarah Lucia Hoagland provides an argument for separating from heterosexualism, which she describes as a political institution that ensures a male right of physical, economic, and emotional access to women. She argues that separatism is a central option, both as a political strategy and a personal one. (Source: From Lesbian Ethics: Toward New Value *by Sarah Lucia Hoagland. Reprinted by permission of Institute of Lesbian Studies, P.O. Box 25568, Chicago, IL 60625.)*

In writing a book on Lesbian Ethics, I am concerned with moral change. And given that lesbians are oppressed within the existing social framework, I am concerned with questioning the values of such a framework as well as with considering different values around which we can weave a new framework. In other words, I am interested in moral revolution. Significantly, however, within traditional ethics the only type of moral change we tend to acknowledge is moral reform. Thus in this chapter I want to explore the existing social framework and raise the issue of separating from it.

Moral reform is the attempt to bring human action into greater conformity with existing ethical principles and thereby alleviate any injustice which results from the breach of those principles. In addressing the question of moral change, Kathryn Pyne Addelson argues:

> The main body of tradition in ethics has occupied itself with the notions of obligation, moral principle, justification of acts under principle, justification of principle by argument. When moral change was considered at all, it was seen as change to bring our activities into conformity with our principles, as change to dispel injustice, as change to alleviate suffering.[1]

She goes on to suggest:

> But moral reform is not the only type of moral change. There is also moral revolution. Moral

revolution has not to do with making our principles consistent, not to do with greater application of what we *now* conceive as justice. That is the task of moral reform, because its aim is the preservation of values. But the aim of moral revolution is the creation of values.[2]

In recognizing only moral reform, traditional ethics discourages us from radically examining the values around which existing principles revolve, or the context in which we are to act on those principles (such as oppression), or the structure which gives life to just those values. Traditional ethics concerns itself almost exclusively with questions of obligation, justification, and principle, and does not leave room for us to examine underlying value or create new value. As a result, Kathryn Pyne Addelson argues, "the narrow focus of traditional ethics makes it impossible to account for the behavior of the moral revolutionary *as* moral behavior."[3]

For example, someone engaged in moral reform might question the use of the concept of 'evil': she might question the concept of 'woman' as evil (the myth of eve) or the concept of 'jew' as evil (the jewish blood libel*), or she might question the concepts of 'black' and 'darkness' as sinister and evil, suggesting that these are all inappropriate applications of 'evil'. Nevertheless, she would not question the concept of 'evil' itself; her concern would be with its application.

On the other hand, someone engaged in moral revolution might question the concept of 'evil,' arguing that 'evil' is a necessary foil for 'good' — that there must be something designated as evil to function as a scapegoat for the shortcomings or failures of that

---

*This is the myth that jews slaughter christian children on easter and use their blood during passover, for example, in baking matzoh. It is the myth which justified the christian slaughter of jews during easter which dates back to the middle ages. Similar muslim persecutions of jews date back to the fifteenth century, and there are references to use of the libel by muslims as late as the nineteenth century.[4]

which is designated as good. She might point out that 'good' requires 'evil' and therefore that evil can never be eradicated if good is to prevail. She might suggest that we could create a moral value in which we had no need of the concepts of 'good' or 'evil.'

I want a moral revolution. I don't want greater or better conformity to existing values. I want change in value. Our attempts to reform existing institutions merely result in reinforcing the existing social order.

For example, a woman may elect to teach a women's studies course using writings on women's rights. She may present classic arguments in favor of women's rights: exposing the contradiction of denying women's rights while affirming democratic ideals, or exposing the hypocrisy in recruiting women during times of need and yet espousing an ideology which negates women's competence. And she could include absurd anti-feminist documents, such as material by a woman doctor denying that women should be professional, or a piece which argues that a woman should stand by her man — no matter what — for the "good" of "society." To give the illusion of objectivity, she might even invite speakers to present arguments against equal rights for women, thereby airing "both sides" of the issue.

However, in addressing and defending women's rights, she is implicitly acknowledging that women's rights are debatable. She is, by that very act, affirming that there is a legitimate question concerning women's rights, even if she is quite clear about the answer she espouses. And she is agreeing that society has a "right" to determine women's place.

Significantly, however, she cannot broach or even formulate a question about men's rights or men's competence without appearing radical beyond reason. That is, men's rights are not debatable. Thus, in agreeing to defend women's rights, she is solidifying status quo values which make women's but not men's rights debatable in a democracy.

A feminist challenging sexist values by defending women's rights is actually coerced into agreeing with the sexist structure of society at a more basic level. And insofar as her challenge appeals to ethical questions of justice, it is subject to consideration of whether such rights are consistent with the existing social order.

I want a moral revolution.

. . .

Understanding heterosexism, as well as homophobia,* involves analyzing, not just women's victimization, but also how women are defined in terms of men or not at all, how lesbians and gay men are treated — indeed scapegoated — as deviants, how choices of intimate partners for both women and men are restricted or denied through taboos to maintain a certain social order. (For example, if sexual relations between men were openly allowed, then men could do to men what men do to women[6] and, further, (some) men could become what women are. This is verboten. In addition, if love between women were openly explored, women might simply walk away from men, becoming 'not-women'. This, too, is verboten.) Focusing on heterosexism challenges heterosexuality as an institution, but it can also lead lesbians to regard as a political goal our acceptance, even assimilation, into heterosexual society: we try to assure heterosexuals we are normal people (that is, just like them), that they are being unjust in stigmatizing us, that ours is a mere sexual preference.

In her ground-breaking work on compulsory heterosexuality, Adrienne Rich challenges us to address heterosexuality as a political institution which ensures male right of physical, economical, and emotional access to women.[7] Jan Raymond develops a theory of hetero-reality and argues: "While I agree that we are living in a heterosexist society, I think the wider problem is that we live in a hetero-relational society where most of women's personal, social, political, professional, and economic relations are defined by the ideology that woman is for man."[8] I go a bit further.

Understanding heterosexualism involves analyzing the relationship between men and women in which

---

*Celia Kitzinger suggests we stop using 'homophobia' altogether. She argues that the term did not emerge from within the women's liberation movement but rather from the academic discipline of psychology. She questions characterizing heteropatriarchal fear of lesbians as irrational, she challenges the psychological (rather than political) orientation of 'phobia,' and she notes that within psychology, the only alternative to 'homophobia' is liberal humanism.[5]

both men and women have a part. Heterosexualism is men dominating and de-skilling women in any of a number of forms, from outright attack to paternalistic care, and women devaluing (of necessity) female bonding as well as finding inherent conflicts between commitment and autonomy and consequently valuing an ethics of dependence. Heterosexualism is a way of living (which actual practitioners exhibit to a greater or lesser degree) that normalizes the dominance of one person in a relationship and the subordination of another. As a result, it undermines female agency.

What I am calling 'heterosexualism' is not simply a matter of males having procreative sex with females.[9] It is an entire way of living which involves a delicate, though at times indelicate, balance between masculine predation upon and masculine protection of a feminine object of masculine attention.* Heterosexualism is a particular economic, political, and emotional relationship between men and women: men must dominate and women must subordinate themselves to men in any of a number of ways.[†] As a result, men presume access to women while women remain riveted on men and are unable to sustain a community of women.

In the u.s., women cannot appear publicly without some men advancing on them, presuming access to them. In fact, many women will think something is wrong if this doesn't happen. A woman simply is someone toward whom such behavior is appropriate. When a woman is accompanied by a man, however, she is usually no longer considered fair game. As a result, men close to individual women — fathers, boyfriends, husbands, brothers, escorts, colleagues —

become protectors (theoretically), staving off advances from other men.

The value of special protection for women is prevalent in this society. Protectors interact with women in ways that promote the image of women as helpless: men open doors, pull out chairs, expect women to dress in ways that interfere with their own self-protection.[12] And women accept this as attentive, complimentary behavior and perceive themselves as persons who need special attention and protection.*

What a woman faces in a man is either a protector or a predator, and men gain identity through one or another of these roles.[13] This has at least five consequences. First, there can be no protectors unless there is a danger. A man cannot identify himself in the role of protector unless there is something which needs protection. So it is in the interest of protectors that there be predators. Secondly, to be protected, women must be in danger. In portraying women as helpless and defenseless, men portray women as victims . . . and therefore as targets.

Thirdly, a woman (or girl) is viewed as the object of male passion and thereby its cause. This is most obvious in the case of rape: she must have done something to tempt him — helpless hormonal bundle that he is. Thus if women are beings who by nature are endangered, then, obviously, they are thereby beings who by nature are seductive — they actively attract predators. Fourthly, to be protected, women must agree to act as men say women should: to appear feminine, prove they are not threatening, stay at home, remain only with the protector, devalue their connections with other women, and so on.

---

*I think the main model for personal interaction for women and lesbians has been heterosexual. However, for men in the anglo-european tradition there has also been a model of male homosexual interaction — a form of male bonding, even though sex between men has come to be persecuted. And while it is not my intention here to analyze the model, I will suggest that it revolves around an axis of dominance and submission, and that heterosexualism is basically a refined male homosexual model.[10]

[†]Julien S. Murphy writes: "Heterosexuality is better termed hetero-economics, for it pertains to the language of barter, exchange, bargain, auction, buy and sell. . . . Heterosexuality is the economics of exchange in which a gender-based power structure continually reinstates itself through the appropriation of the devalued party in a duo-gendered system. Such reinstatement happens through each instance of 'striking a deal' in the market of sex."[11]

---

*In questioning the value of special protection for women, I am not saying that women should never ask for help. That's just foolish. I am talking about the ideal of women as needing sheltering. The concept of children needing special protection is prevalent and I challenge that concept when it is used to abrogate their integrity "for their own good." But at least protection for children theoretically involves ensuring that (male) children can grow up and learn to take care of themselves. That is, (male) children are protected until they have grown and developed skills and abilities they need to get on in this world. No such expectation is included in the ideal of special protection for women: the ideal of special protection of women does not include the expectation that women will ever be in a position to take care of themselves (grow up).

Finally, when women step out of the feminine role, thereby becoming active and "guilty,"* it is a mere matter of logic that men will depict women as evil and step up overt physical violence against them in order to reaffirm women's victim status. For example, as the demand for women's rights in the u.s. became publicly perceptible, the depiction of lone women as "sluts" inviting attack also became prevalent. A lone female hitchhiker was perceived, not as someone to protect, but as someone who had given up her right to protection and thus as someone who was a target for attack. The rampant increase in pornography—entertainment by and for men about women—is men's general response to the u.s. women's liberation movement's demand of integrity, autonomy, and dignity for women.

What radical feminists have exposed through all the work on incest (daughter rape) and wife-beating is that protectors are also predators. Of course, not all men are wife- or girlfriend-beaters, but over half who live with women are. And a significant number of u.s. family homes shelter an "incestuous" male.[15]

Although men may exhibit concern over womanabuse, they have a different relationship to it than women; their concerns are not women's concerns. For example, very often men become irate at the fact that a woman has been raped or beaten by another man. But this is either a man warming to his role of protector—it rarely, if ever, occurs to him to teach her self-defense—or a man deeply affected by damage done to his "property" by another man. And while some men feel contempt for men who batter or rape, Marilyn Frye suggests it is quite possible their contempt arises, not from the fact that womanabuse is happening, but from the fact that the batterer or rapist must accomplish by force what they themselves can accomplish more subtly by arrogance.[16]

The current willingness of men in power to pass laws restricting pornography is a matter of men trying to reestablish the asexual, virginal image of (some) women whom they can then protect in their homes. And they are using as their excuse right-wing women as well as feminists who appear to be asking for protection, like proper women, rather than demanding liberation. Men use violence when women don't pay attention to them. Then, when women ask for protection, men can find meaning by turning on the predators—particularly ones of a different race or class.

In other words, the logic of protection is essentially the same as the logic of predation. Through predation, men do things to women and against women all of which violate women and undermine women's integrity. Yet protection objectifies just as much as predation. To protect women, men do things to women and against women; acting "for a woman's own good," they violate her integrity and undermine her agency.

Protection and predation emerge from the same ideology of male dominance, and it is a matter of indifference to the successful maintenance of male domination which of the two conditions women accept. Thus Sonia Johnson writes:

> Our conviction that if we stop studying and monitoring men and their latest craziness, that if we abandon our terrified clawing and kicking interspersed with sniveling and clutching—our whole sick sadomasochistic relationship with the masters—they will go berserk and kill us, is the purest superstition. With our eyes fully upon them they kill us daily; with our eyes riveted upon them they have gone berserk.[17]

. . .

Complementing the protector/predator function of men is the concept of 'woman,' particularly as it functions in mainstream u.s. society. Consider what the concept lacks. It lacks (1) a sense of female power, (2) any hint that women as a group have been the targets of male violence, (3) any hint either of collective or individual female resistance to male domination and control, and (4) any sense of lesbian connection.

The concept of 'woman' includes no real sense of female power. Certainly, it includes no sense of woman as conquering and dominating forces. More significantly, it includes no sense of strength and competence. I am not denying that there are many strong women. And where women encourage each other in

---

*In her analysis of fairy tales, Andrea Dworkin points out that an active woman is portrayed as evil (the stepmother) and a good woman is generally asleep or dead (snow white, sleeping beauty).[14]

defiance of the dominant valuation, significant images appear. But over time, under heterosexualism, these images tend to be modified by appeals to femininity or are used against women. Without sufficient deference to men, women will find 'castrating bitch' or 'dyke' or comparable concepts used to keep them in line.

Men of a given group will partially modify 'femininity' in order to emphasize female competence and skill when they absolutely need extra help: during wars—Rosie the riveter, for example—or on small nebraska farms or in revolutionary movements or in kibbutzim when the state is unstable or in a community deeply split under oppression. But once their domain is more firmly established, men drag up the feminine stereotype (while nevertheless expecting women to do most of the work with none of the benefits).

In her essay for black women in the cities, Pat Robinson connects the loss of a people's self-awareness and power with the loss of their deities. She states, "When a group must be controlled, you always take away from them their gods, their very reflections of themselves and their inner being."[18] Where we find reference to goddesses of any culture in dominant anglo-european scholarship, they are being kidnapped or raped, and/or they are mothers. Significantly, the one female figure present in anglo-european thought is the virgin Mary, remnant of an ancient goddess transformed into a model rape victim, reputed to have said to a god, "Do unto me as thou willest."

Pat Robinson goes on to note that to control a people, while one must take from them their very reflections of themselves, one must first use force.[19] (This, of course, is the initial process of colonization.) A second notable lack in the concept of 'woman' is a sense that force is ever used against women as a group. Feminist literature has appeared about the massacre of european witches. But the vast majority of u.s. women today remain unaware of the witch burnings. One might wonder how mass destruction could be eradicated from consciousness. Perhaps it was simply suppressed. But when a social order requires the extermination of a particular group and that extermination virtually succeeds, subsequent memory of the process can be eradicated by renaming. The massacre of witches in europe over a three-hundred-fifty-year

period has endured just such a renaming. The caricature of witches assaults us annually in the form of a u.s. mass-media event: halloween.

The use of force or violence against women as a group has not been limited to europe. Mary Daly among others has attempted to bring into u.s. feminist consciousness the fact that such force has been and continues to be used against women in every part of the world.[20] And while the practice of indian dowry murders has been acknowledged as a problem, it is only because men in power have recently named it a problem. Further, while in china the fathers deemed footbinding uneconomical and therefore immoral, our memory and awareness of what led to it and why it was perpetuated for so long is fading. And female infanticide has taken its place as an expression of misogyny.

Because there is no sense that violence has ever been directed at women as a group, it is difficult to gain a perspective on the magnitude of the force used against women now. While u.s. women may be horrified at the specter of african genital mutilation and indian dowry deaths, african (particularly nigerian) and indian students in my classes are no less horrified at the incidence of rape and the amount of pornography which form a daily part of u.s. women's lives. Except for radical feminists, no one in the united states perceives the phenomenal rate of incest (daughter rape), wife beating, rape, forced prostitution, and the ideology of pornography—depicted not only in men's magazines but on television, billboards, in grocery stores, in schools, and in general in every public and private sector a woman goes—as any kind of concerted assault on women. There is no general sense that, as Sonia Johnson points out, men have declared war on women;[21] rather this assault—because men are paying attention to women—is called "attraction," even "admiration."

Thirdly, the concept of 'woman' includes no sense of female resistance—either collective or individual—to male domination. While there is evidence that amazons once lived in north africa, in china, in anatolia (turkey), and between the black and the caspian seas, amazons are repeatedly treated as a joke or buried. Yet as Helen Diner writes:

At the celebrations in honor of the dead, Demosthenes, Lysias, Himerios, Isocartes, and Aristeides praise the victory over the Amazons as more important than that over the Persians or any other deed in history. . . . The wars between the Greeks and Persians were wars between two male-dominated societies. In the Amazon war, the issue was which of the two forms of life was to shape European civilization in its image.[22]

Significantly, even feminists and lesbian-feminists shun amazons, apparently for fear of appearing out of touch with reality (with the consensus). With a few notable exceptions, we are not responding to Maxine Feldman's call, "Amazon women rise."[23] There is little celebration of amazons (even though we are beginning to hear again of goddesses and witches). We do not acknowledge the amazons even as symbolic defenders of womanhood—and this at a time when male violence against women is blatant. Instead, even radical feminists push for greater police and state protection. The amazons—as well as female warriors such as those of the dahomey or the nootka societies—simply do not fit within the concept of 'woman' of mainstream u.s. society.[24]

Because there is no mythological, much less historical, memory of female resistance to male domination, isolated and individual acts of female resistance are also rendered imperceptible as resistance, particularly, as I argue below, through the concept of 'femininity.' A 'woman' is one whose identity comes through her alliance with a man to such an extent that any woman who resists male violence, male advances, and male access is not a real woman.

The value of 'woman,' thus, excludes a sense of female presence, skill, and power, an awareness that violence has been and is perpetrated against women as a group, and a sense of female resistance to male domination. It also excludes a sense of lesbian connection. Adrienne Rich took on the task of addressing (1) the bias "through which lesbian experience is perceived on a scale ranging from deviant to abhorrent, or simply rendered invisible;" (2) "how and why women's choice of women as passionate comrades, life partners, co-workers, lovers, tribe, has been crushed, invalidated, forced into hiding and disguise;" and (3) "the virtual or total neglect of lesbian existence in a wide range of writings, including feminist scholarship."[25] As Harriet Ellenberger writes:

A central taboo in patriarchy is the taboo against women consorting with women—and yet that tabooed consorting, allying, connecting has gone on and goes on in front of their noses, and men and most women don't think it's real.[26]

What the concept of 'woman' includes is equally significant. Given the masculinist naming of women, a 'woman' is (1) male-identified, someone whose identity emerges through her relationship to a man, (2) someone who makes herself attractive to men, (3) an object to be conquered by men, and (4) a breeder (of boys).

A woman's identity is incorporated in her relationship with a man: she is first and foremost some man's but not some woman's mother, wife, mistress, or daughter. As the radicalesbians argued in 1970:

We are authentic, legitimate, real to the extent that we are the property of some man whose name we bear. To be a woman who belongs to no man is to be invisible, pathetic, inauthentic, unreal.[27]

A woman belonging to no man either doesn't exist or is trying to be a man. Further, a 'woman' is responsible for the sexual servicing of men.[28] Her goodness or badness, her ethical status, is based on her sexual availability, cost, and fidelity to men.[29] Ultimately, a 'woman' is a virgin or a whore—that is, related through sex to a man.

Secondly, a 'woman' is someone who is attractive to men. If she does not try to make herself attractive to men, she is considered to have a serious problem. In mainstream u.s. society, attractiveness means she is white anglo, upper middle class, virtually anorexic (that is, unhealthy), and young enough to have no character lines on her face, though occasionally she may be dark and "exotic." Those women who fall outside these categories, while not entirely discounted as women, are nevertheless made to feel poor substitutes for a woman.* Further, a 'woman' is one who must be protected from what is evil (that is, dark) unless she is dark (that is, evil) herself—in which case, other women must be protected from her. The whiter she is,

---

*In other areas of the world different standards apply. In some places being catholic is essential to womanhood, or being fat or being dark, not pale. The model of 'woman' in terms of physical manifestation tends to adhere to the values of the men in power in a given location.

the purer she is. The darker she is, the more dangerously sexual she is. Again, she is a virgin or a whore — that is, white or black.

Thirdly, a 'woman' is someone who must be conquered by a man. The ideology of pornography, from soft porn to snuff, portrays a woman as an object (someone to be acted upon — in this case, attacked and overcome), someone who exists to be dominated. She is characterized by her sexual desire, and she is to be dominated through violation — which violation she will ultimately crave. The ideology of romanticism (popularly portrayed in the harlequin romances) is the same: A woman is an object (someone to be acted upon — in this case, protected and seduced), someone who exists to be conquered. She is characterized by her lack of sexual desire — she is to reject (male) sexual advances in order to display her modesty; and hence men know that when she says "no," she really means "yes." Thus she, too, is to be dominated through violation — violation of her integrity — which violation she suddenly starts to crave. Both pornography and romanticism tell us that a woman is to be conquered and dominated by the force of masculine will.

Finally, a 'woman' is a breeder. A woman is fulfilled through breeding, her basic ethical possibility is selfless giving and nurturing, and anything which interferes with this process is suspect. Further, whenever a people are in jeopardy because men play war, men stress breeding to the exclusion of all else, and carefully supervise it. In anglo-european, eurasian, and all mainstream american societies (central, south, and north), this function cannot be entrusted to her. Her body is not hers to determine. For example, the issue of abortion, as it is being played out in the u.s., is not a woman's issue. For the question concerns, simply, which men will control women's abortions — the state or individual men.[30] And doctors exercising their paternalistic concern for social order sterilize women they deem inappropriate mothers, such as poor black and poor puerto rican women.[31] A 'woman' is a breeder, and breeders need caretakers who make breeding decisions, including genetic reconstruction. Further, of course, when a woman breeds successfully, what she breeds is male — that is, someone who carries on her husband's line.

A 'woman,' thus, is a sex object essentially submissive to and dependent on men, one whose function is to perpetuate the race (while protectors and predators engage in their project of destroying it). No, one is not born a woman.

I want a moral revolution.

. . .

'Femininity' is a concept which goes a long way in the social construction of heterosexual reality. A movement of women could withdraw from that framework and begin to revalue that reality and women's choices within it. A movement of women can challenge the feminine stereotype, discover women's resistance, and provide a base for more effective resistance. A movement of women can challenge the consensus that made the individual act of sabotage plausible.

Yet if that movement does not challenge the concept of 'femininity,' ultimately it will not challenge the consensus, it will not challenge the dominance and subordination of heterosexualism. For example, radical feminists and revolutionary feminists in england criticize the women's work at greenham common for appealing too much to traditional feminine stereotypes, including woman as nurturer and peacemaker as well as sacrificer for her children. As a result, they argue, the peace movement coopts feminism.[32]

Further, feminism itself is in danger of perpetuating the value of 'femininity' in interpreting and evaluating individual women's choices. Feminists continue to note how women are victims of institutional and ordinary behavior, but many have ceased to challenge the concept of 'woman' and the role of men and male institutions play as "protectors" of women. And feminism is susceptible to what Kathleen Barry calls 'victimism', which in effect portrays women as helpless and in need of protection.[33]

So much of our moral and political judgment involves either blaming the victim[34] or victimism. Victimism is the perception of victims of acknowledged social injustice, not as real persons making choices, but instead as passive objects of injustice. Kathleen Barry explains that in order to call attention to male violence and to prove that women are harmed by rape, feminists have portrayed women who have been raped by men as victims pure and simple—an understandable development. The problem is that

> the status of "victim" creates a mind set eliciting pity and sorrow. Victimism denies the woman the integrity of her humanity through the whole experience, and it creates a framework for others to know her not as a person but as a victim, someone to whom violence was done. . . . Victimism is an objectification which establishes new standards for defining experience; those standards dismiss any question of will, and deny that the woman even while enduring sexual violence is a living, changing, growing, interactive person.[35]

For my purposes, blaming the victim involves holding a person accountable not only for her choice in a situation but for the situation itself, as if she agreed to it. Thus in masculinist thought, a woman will be judged responsible for her own rape. Victimism, on the other hand, completely ignores a woman's choices. In other words, victimism denies a woman's moral agency. Under victimism, women are still passive, helpless, and in need of special protection—still feminine.

A movement which challenges the dominant valuation of women will focus on women as agents in a relationship rather than as a type. A woman is not a passive being to whom things unfortunately or intentionally happen. She is a breathing, judging being, acting in coerced and oppressive circumstances. Her judgments and choices may be ineffective on any given occasion, or wrong, but they are decisions nevertheless. She is an agent and she is making choices. More than a victim, Kathleen Barry suggests, a woman caught in female sexual slavery is a survivor, making crucial decisions about what to do in order to survive. She is a moral agent who makes judgments within a context of oppression in consideration of her own needs and abilities.

By perceiving women's behavior, not through the value of 'femininity,' but rather as actions of moral agents making judgments about their own needs and abilities in coerced and oppressive circumstances, we can begin to conceive of ourselves and each other as agents of our actions (though not creators of the circumstances we face under oppression). And this is a

step toward realizing an ethical existence under oppression, one not caught up with the values of dominance and subordination.

Further, we can also begin to understand women's choices which actually embrace the feminine stereotype. Some women embrace 'femininity' outright, man-made though it is, or embrace particular aspects of it which involve some form of ritual or actual subordination to men, in the pursuit of what these women judge to be their own best interests. Some women embrace 'femininity' in a desperate attempt to find safety and to give some meaning to their existence.

In the first chapter of *Right-Wing Women*, Andrea Dworkin analyzes the choices of some white christian women, arguing that "from father's house to husband's house to a grave that still might not be her own, a woman acquiesces to male authority in order to gain some protection from male violence."[36] She argues that such acquiescence results from the treatment girls and women receive as part of their socialization:

> Rebellion can rarely survive the aversion therapy that passes for being brought up female. Male violence acts directly on the girl through her father or brother or uncle or any number of male professionals or strangers, as it did and does on her mother, and she too is forced to learn to conform in order to survive. A girl may, as she enters adulthood, repudiate the particular set of males with whom her mother is allied, run with a different pack as it were, but she will replicate her mother's patterns in acquiescing to male authority within her own chosen set. Using both force and threat, men in all camps demand that women accept abuse in silence and shame, tie themselves to hearth and home with rope made of self-blame, unspoken rage, grief, and resentment.[37]

Andrea Dworkin also argues that some women continue to submit to male authority because they finally believe it is the only way they can make sense of and give meaning to their otherwise apparently meaningless existence as women.[38] They find meaning through being bound to their protectors and having a common enemy. Their anger is thus given form and a safety valve, and is thereby deflected from its logical target. They become antisemites, queer-haters, and racists, and so create purpose in their existence.

Andrea Dworkin's analysis highlights two points of interest here. First, these women have the same information that radical feminists have (they know what men do), yet they are making different choices. Secondly, their choices stem from judgments they make about their own best interests. That is, they are choosing what they consider their best option from among those available. These are survival choices made in circumstances with restricted options.

Another group of women embrace 'femininity' from a different direction. In discussing why more black women are not involved in activist women's groups, instead considering themselves "Black first, female second" and embracing a version of the feminine ideal, Brunetta R. Wolfman presents a number of factors. She points to the traditionally greater independence black women enjoy from black men in the united states, since the legal end of slavery, than white women have enjoyed from white men. And she points to the commitment of women to the black church, in terms of time and loyalty, whereby a "scrub woman or maid could aspire to be the head of the usher board and a valuable, respected member of the congregation."39

However, she notes that the pattern in the black church here as well as in civil rights groups such as the n.a.a.c.p. or the urban league, has been one of women assuming secondary roles in deference to male leadership. She also points to the romantic sense of nobility, purity, and race pride personified in the stereotype of 'the black woman' and promulgated by nationalistic ideologies such as that of Marcus Garvey or the black muslims:

> The Muslims have taken the idealized Euro-American image of the middle-class wife and mother and made it the norm for the sect so that the women members must reject the traditional independence of black women, adopting another style in the name of a separatist religious ideology. In return, Muslim men must respect and protect their women, a necessary complement to demands placed on females.40

This point is reiterated by Jacquelyn Grant as she argues:

> It is often said that women are the "backbone" of the church. . . . It has become apparent to me that most of the ministers who use this term are referring to location rather than function. What they really mean is that women are in the background and should be kept there: they are merely support workers.41

Brunetta R. Wolfman goes on to discuss demands placed on black women by the black community as well as community expectation of a subordinate position for women. For example, she points out that women in the movement '60s were expected to keep black men from involving themselves with white women. She argues that this "duty is in keeping with a traditional feminine role, that of modifying or being responsible for the behavior of the group in general and the males in particular.42 Further, she points out how feminist values such as control of one's own body were undermined as black (and white) men told black women there was no choice but to bear children in order to counterattack the white racist plan of black genocide being carried out through birth control programs.

While noting that the women's liberation movement included many demands that would help the social and economic position of black women, Brunetta R. Wolfman suggests that (many) black women have not responded to it, instead becoming a conservative force in the black community, partly because they have a strong sense of self as contributor to the survival of the black community and partly because they have been identified by american society as the polar opposite of the feminine ideal.43 That is, since they have been excluded from the feminine ideal, they now embrace it.

The jeopardy of racial genocide stemming from an external enemy and used to justify the ideology of male domination is real for u.s. black and other women of color in a way that it is not for u.s. right-wing christian white women. Nevertheless, the choice of embracing 'femininity' and male authority is similar in both cases, as is the threat members of each group face from men.

Further, such choices are not qualitatively different from choices made by feminists to defer to men and men's agendas and to soothe male egos in the pursuit of women's rights. (And such choices do not preclude acts of sabotage of the sort I've discussed when male domination encroaches too far upon a woman's sense of self.) They are survival choices. And what we can consider from outside the feminine valuation is whether such choices in the long run are self-enhancing or self-defeating.

The answers are varied and complex. But insofar as they lean toward the idea that embracing 'femininity' is not self-defeating, they also perpetuate what it means to be a 'woman': to be a 'woman' is to be subject to male domination and hence to be someone who enacts her agency through manipulation — exercising (some modicum of) control from a position of subordination. Should she act in any other way, she is, under heterosexualism, not only unnatural but also unethical.

Thus, while promoting an ethic for females, heterosexualism is a set of values which undermines female agency outside the master/slave values. Women hang on to those values out of fear, out of a choice to focus on men while taking women for granted, and out of a lack of perception of any other choices. As a result, although many women individually have resisted male domination — in particular, men's attempts to make women mere extensions of men's will — it is less clear that (with a few notable exceptions), as Simone de Beauvoir suggested, women as a group dispute male sovereignty. However, in claiming this, I am not suggesting that disputing male sovereignty means attempting to oppose men as men have opposed women. Rather, I am suggesting that it seems, for the most part, that women, whether as saboteurs or acceptors of male domination, have not disputed the entire dominance/subordination game of heterosexualism.

I want a moral revolution.

Separation

Significantly, just as traditional ethics does not recognize moral revolution, so it does not acknowledge separation as an option for moral agents. Withdrawal or separation is not perceived as an option when the game played appears to be the only game in town and so is taken for reality. In a sense the game is reality, but its continued existence is not a matter of fact so much as a matter of agreement. The game is an agreement in value which players breathe life into.

And this suggests that participation in the system at some level — support, reform, rebellion — must be an unquestioned norm and hence not itself perceived as a choice.

Consider, again, that shelters for women who have been beaten by their husbands lose funding if shelter workers are suspected of encouraging those seeking refuge to withdraw or separate from the particular batterer or from marriage or from heterosexuality in general. Ethical considerations forced on most women whom men beat involve how to maintain the family unit, how to work with their husband's problems, how to restore his "dignity," how to help the children adjust — in short, how to go on as a (heterosexual) woman. Such judgments hold in place the feminine, in this case feminine virtue, and the function of such judgments is not to encourage the integrity of the individual in her choices. It is rather to maintain the social order and specific relationships and avenues of hierarchy within it.

I want to suggest that it is crucial to acknowledge withdrawal, separatism, as an option if we are to engage in moral revolution. Separation is a central option both as a political strategy and as a consideration in individual relationships. We may withdraw from a particular situation when it threatens to dissolve into a relationship of dominance and subordination. And we may withdraw from a system of dominance and subordination in order to engage in moral revolution.

To withdraw from a system, a conceptual framework, or a particular situation is to refuse to act according to its rules. A system can only function if there are participants. A king can direct his domain only if most everyone else acknowledges him as king, if the couriers carry his messages.[43] If the messengers dump their messages and go on to something else, not only is the king's communication interrupted, so is his status, for the couriers are no longer focused on him and are therefore declaring themselves no longer couriers. If enough couriers lay down their messages, the king will not be able to amass sufficient power to force those messengers to again focus on him.

When we separate, when we withdraw from someone's game plan, the game becomes meaningless, at least to some extent, ceasing to exist for lack of acknowledgment. Of course if a tree falls in the forest, there are sound waves, whether or not there are human or other animals ears, or whether there are any other sorts of mechanisms in addition to the king's own ears to detect them. But if the listeners, the messengers, have withdrawn, then the sound waves can't be translated or even acknowledged. Thus the messages of the king in a certain respect make no sense, and in a certain respect have ceased to exist. So has the king . . . as a king.

Separation is a legitimate moral and political choice. (I mean by saying it is legitimate that it has a political and moral function.) That is, to engage in a situation or a system in order to try to change it is one choice. To withdraw from it, particularly in order to render it meaningless, is another choice. Within a given situation or at a given moment there are often good reasons for either choice. Further, both choices involve considerable risk; neither one comes with guarantees: while directly challenging something can validate it, withdrawing may allow it to continue essentially unhampered.

What is significant to me is that the choice to separate is not *acknowledged* as a legitimate ethical choice. There are considerable prohibitions in all quarters against withdrawal. Depending on various factors, including the location within the power hierarchy of the perceiver, the choice to withdraw is judged to be (1) functionally equivalent to collaborating with the enemy, (2) cowardly hiding from the situation and foolishly hoping it will go away, (3) an indication of dull-wittedness or an admission of defeat, (4) a refusal to be politically responsible, or (5) a denial of reality, indicating insanity.

For example, during a war—that is, a struggle over who will dominate—those in power regard draft dodgers and even conscientious objectors not as moral challengers but as immoral quitters, not significantly different from those who collaborate with the enemy. In time of war this moral equation is drawn because, to be successful, those who wage war must have grand-scale cooperation in order to defeat the enemy. And when social organization must be very tight, those who dissent and withdraw are perceived as no different from those who attack. (To some degree, this is an accurate perception.)

Those who withdraw may be perceived by their peers as cowardly hiding from the situation and hoping it will go away or as foolishly ignoring reality. For example, one who withdraws from a fight will often be considered a coward. Such labeling, of course, is an attempt to coerce participation. Alternatively, some who have opposed united states draft dodgers and conscientious objectors charge them with failing to recognize that if the enemy won, they would no longer have the right to dissent. And because of our (at least partial) withdrawal from the institution of heterosexuality, lesbians are accused of foolishly ignoring half the human race and hence of denying reality.

Certainly, there are those who believe problems will just go away. But I am concerned with the choice to withdraw as a political strategy. For example, the danes refused to cooperate with the nazi policy of identifying jews. This was a refusal to participate in the debate over who should be saved, and as a result it rendered the nazi effort at "purification" meaningless. Pacifism, too, is a withdrawal. And during world ii, pacifists were perceived as cowards. In fact, the label 'passive resistance,' itself a contradiction of terms, is an attempt to discredit the actions of those who refuse to play the games of dominance and subordination—Gandhi's strategy was hardly passive.

Political activists will often perceive withdrawing or separating as simply being politically irresponsible. For example, many will show overt hostility toward those who refuse to participate in the u.s. election process, even though they themselves are horrified by what passes for candidates, campaigning, and voting in this country. Those who refuse to vote, on the other hand, refuse to participate in the illusion. As one female nonvoter stated, "Oh, I never vote, it encourages them so."[43]

Lesbian separatists, too, are perceived as not caring about or wanting to end injustice. Separatists are often judged by liberals, socialists, and coalitionists as almost more morally reprehensible than those who control the system. As a result, lesbian separatists are scapegoated.

In certain respects, to engage, to participate, in a situation or in a system is to affirm its central values. This is true whether we actively uphold the system, attempt to change it through designated avenues of reform, or rebel against it through designated avenues of rebellion (act in ways named evil or bad within the system). For in acting in any of these capacities, we are operating within the system's parameters and are thus giving the system meaning by helping to hold its axis (what goes unquestioned) in place.

While a great deal is accomplished through reform, the change that occurs must fit within the (usually unacknowledged) parameters of the system. Thus "votes for women" was achieved only when women's suffrage was generally perceived as not altering the structure and value of patriarchal, heterosexual society. As Kate Millett points out in *Sexual Politics,* the first wave of the feminist movement failed to challenge the institution of the family, thereby ending in reform rather than revolution. She argues that without radical change in value, that which reformers found most offensive — "the economic disabilities of women, the double standard, prostitution, venereal disease, coercive marital unions and involuntary parenthood" — could not be eradicated.46 Reform perpetuates existing value.

In the first place, feminist reform forces women to focus on men and address men's conceptions of women rather than creating and developing women's values about themselves. It forces women to focus on men's reactions and mass media stereotypes of women; it forces women to respond by means of apology to masculinist depictions of witches, manhaters, lesbians, and amazons. It forces women to prove that men's fears are unfounded — to prove that women, or "real" women, are not lesbians or manhaters. It forces women to appear feminine and prove they are not threatening. Feminist reform forces women to attend male fantasies and validate masculinist value. As a result men are invited to act out and are given even greater license to project their insecurities on women, while women must soothe and tend male egos. In other words, reform keeps women focused on finding ways of seducing men. I want a moral revolution.

Secondly, feminist reform makes the actual success of women's efforts depend on the intelligence, willingness, and benevolence of the men they're seeking to convince to enact reform. Efforts in this regard may at times gain relief for women, relief which is badly needed even if selective. But it is a relief of symptoms, not a removal of causes.47 In this respect reform forces the reformer to restrict her imagination and efforts to the limits of those she's trying to convince. A feminist striving for change by working for reform within the dominant/subordinate framework

is like a starving person seeking nourishment in junk food.

Finally, feminist reform sets up women to value change in men more highly than change in women. It makes any failure a failure of effort on women's part, not a refusal on men's part. And it sets up women to fear risking any small gain they might have gotten. As a result, to avoid offending men, they promote lesbian erasure, thereby reinforcing heterosexualism. This is one of the reasons some french-speaking radical lesbians insist that feminism is the last stronghold of patriarchy.48

Aside from reform, there are also serious problems with rebellion, particularly when that rebellion fits the parameters of what counts as rebellion from the dominant perspective. For example, a young woman might rebel against her family by getting pregnant, or a high school student might rebel by becoming addicted to heroin. These actions, while not in conformity with what is called good in society, nevertheless support and uphold it; though they are designated as evil within the system, they are not real threats to it. Further, as I have suggested above, there are serious dangers involved in sabotage when a movement is afoot, when a group is interacting in ways which begin to challenge the consensus which made the individual act of sabotage plausible for the saboteurs.

Another form of rebellion — the male pornographic rebellion against the establishment — has been challenged by Mary Daly, Susan Griffin, Catharine A. MacKinnon, and Andrea Dworkin, each in her own way. For while pornographic sons rebel against church fathers, they nevertheless operate out of the same conceptual framework — a framework which gives rise to necrophilic hatred of the body.49 Far from undermining the system, they infuse it with meaning. And when things get too far out of hand, protectors can target pornographers, launching a crusade to clean up our minds, all the while polluting our minds with church imagery which gives rise to pornography.

Significantly, the so-called sexual "revolution" is hardly a revolution of values but simply a reversal of certain polarities within the same value system. Thus, rather than being a "proper lady," a woman is now a "hot mama." Either way her sexual subordination to men remains unchallenged. The "sexual revolution" has displaced the women's movement in the media.

Advocates of sadomasochism also claim to be rebelling against the system, yet they are neither resisting it nor striving for change. In emulating nazi/jew or master/slave scenes, for example, sadomasochists contribute to the context which allows such institutions to flourish, thereby validating them. And rather than shock us into political awareness, as can a parody, such practices lull us into acceptance and resignation.[50]

In general, the system of the fathers designates as evil what it can tolerate and uses it as a safety valve. When things threaten to get out of hand, those in power can then scapegoat that which they designate as evil to explain why that which they designate as good — marriage, business, education, religion, medicine, for example — isn't working. And this suggests that withdrawal from and change in central values, rather than evil, are the real threats to the traditional framework of ethics and politics.

Upon examining the system, we may find we actually agree with the underlying value and structure. Alternatively, we may find we disagree significantly with it but judge that it is the best structure around or that the existing structure is better than no structure or better than the risk involved in creating a new one. We might even feel that a new structure would be preferable but that the current situation is a crisis which needs immediate relief, even though this results in incomplete solution and co-optation. After all, working to create a new value system hardly solves an immediate problem of starvation.

But what is missing from the focus of traditional ethics as well as from lesbian community ethics is acknowledgment that these choices involve agreement with the system in certain key ways, acknowledgment that such agreement is a choice, and acknowledgment that there is another choice. What is missing from traditional ethics is acknowledgment that there are ethical choices at this level, that participation is one of those choices, and that separation — at the very least from the belief system — is another.

Now beyond noting that withdrawal or separation is a crucial moral option, I want to suggest that such a choice is central to lesbian moral agency. What I am calling separation or withdrawal is not a set of rules we live up to, particularly in an attempt to be

purists. It is rather a general approach to the world which involves various choices in various circumstances, choices which depend on various factors but which are choices from a lesbian center.

In her history and analysis of *Lavender Woman*, a chicago lesbian newspaper published between 1971 and 1976, Michal Brody offers a basic definition of separatism which, while apparently clear-cut, invited "universes of interpretation":

> The fundamental core of separation was separation of women from men. This was desirable for two basic reasons: 1) there was too much frustration and aggravation involved in trying to work or deal with men. Sexism, once perceived, became intolerable, and 2) it became urgent to understand the meaning and essence of womanhood as only we could define it for ourselves.[51]

I named myself separatist in 1976 in lincoln, nebraska, a little over a year after I came out and while teaching at the university of nebraska, as the result of a very simple statement from Julia Penelope [Stanley]. I had just returned from the second national women's music festival, where I observed Meg Christian and Holly Near defend women-only concerts and Holly Near participate in a group discussion on the issue. I was confused. They were all talking about separating from men, yet all they seemed to talk about was men. I, too, knew about men, but I didn't comprehend what the big issue was. Standing at her kitchen sink peeling potatoes, Julia said, quite simply, "Power." This made sense to me. Since that time, how and why I conceive and enact separatism has developed. What follows are those aspects of separatism I consider central to the continuing creation of lesbian community and meaning.

Separatism is, first, a way of pulling back from the existing conceptual framework, noting its patterns, and understanding their function regardless of the mythology espoused within the framework. For example, within the framework it is said that women don't resist male domination. However, by stepping out of the framework, we can detect quite another story. Separatism is a matter of deconstructing and revaluing existing perceptions and judgments.

In this way, withdrawing or separating is not the opposite of participating; rather, it is a form of engagement. While it is important for survival to stay in touch with what is going on, by becoming detached from belief in heterosexual values, we can move through the system in very different ways, noting very different things.[52]

Secondly, separatism is a way of undermining heterosexual patterns. As Marilyn Frye argues, feminist separation is

> separation of various sorts or modes from men and from institutions, roles and activities which are male-defined, male-dominated and operating for the benefit of males and the maintenance of male privilege — this separation being initiated or maintained, at will, *by women.*

The point of this is to undermine male parasitism:

> that it is, generally speaking, the strength, energy, inspiration and nurturance of women that keeps men going, and not the strength, aggression, spirituality and hunting of men that keeps women going.[53]

Marilyn Frye goes on to argue that male parasitism means males must have access to females, that total power is unconditional access, that the first act of challenging this must be denying access in order to create a power shift, and that such a denial of access is also to claim the power of naming for oneself: "The slave who excludes the master from her hut thereby declares herself *not a slave.*"[54]

Thirdly, separatism is "paring away the layers of false selves from the Self," as Mary Daly suggests.[55] What draws us to each other, I believe, is a sense of female agency, a sense of inner strength. Separatism allows us to expand our imaginations and hence our risks beyond the boundaries of heterosexuality. It allows us an ethical option to the de-moralization that results when we resign ourselves to the categories of the fathers and lose each other.[56] Thus, it allows us the possibility of developing female agency outside the master/slave virtues of heterosexuality.

Consequently, fourthly, lesbian separatism is a withdrawal from heterosexualism. Following Simone de Beauvoir's perception that we are not born women, Monique Wittig announces that lesbians are not women.[57] She argues:

> The refusal to become (or to remain) heterosexual always meant to refuse to become a man or a women, consciously or not. For a lesbian this goes

further than the refusal of the *role* "woman." It is the refusal of the economic, ideological, and political power of a man.[58]

Withdrawal or separatism is a refusal to participate in the heterosexual social construction of reality; to practice separatism is to deconstruct the dominant/subordinate relationship of men and women.

Monique Wittig goes on to argue that our task is to define oppression in materialist terms:

> to make it evident that women are a class, which is to say that the category "woman" as well as the category "man" are political and economic categories not eternal ones.[59]

She suggests that our strategy must be to

> suppress men as a class, not through a genocidal, but a political struggle. Once the class "men" disappears, "women" as a class will disappear as well, for there are no slaves without masters.[60]

Thus she does not advocate resisting male domination by trying to oppose men as men have opposed women, as Simone de Beauvoir seems to imply women must do if women are to resist male sovereignty. However, neither is her strategy a separatist one. She anticipates a struggle between men and women similar to a class struggle, a struggle in which gender categories will finally disappear, thereby ending the economic, political, and ideological order which perpetuates the dominance and subordination of heterosexuality:

> The class struggle is precisely that which resolves the contradictions between two opposed classes by abolishing them at the same time it constitutes them as classes. The class struggle between women and men, which should be undertaken by all women, is that which resolves the contradictions between the sexes, abolishing them at the same time as it makes them understood.[61]

Once this struggle breaks out, the violence of the categories (dominant/suppressed, male/female) becomes apparent, and what was considered natural differences now can be understood as material opposition.

While I agree that heterosexualism is a violent opposition between men and women, my focus is different. I agree with the goal of deconstructing heterosexualism and the categories 'man' and 'woman.' But in my opinion there can be slaves without masters, there can be women without men. Thus, even though 'lesbian' is a concept beyond the categories of sex, nevertheless we tend to embrace the existing categories both in assimilation and in resistance. More often than not, we embrace the values of dominance and subordination.

We tend to seek meaning by subordinating ourselves to a higher order or system because we seek the semblance of security in something constructed outside of us in which we can participate. Heterosexualism is such a system. In another context Marilyn Frye writes of the "mortal dread of being outside the field of vision of the arrogant eye":

> We fear that if we are not in that web of meaning there will be no meaning: our work will be meaningless, our lives of no value, our accomplishments empty, our identities illusory.[62]

My concern is involved with the sense in which it is true that there are no 'masters' without 'slaves,' for in that same sense there are no 'men' without 'women.' A king cannot be king without his messengers attending him. And patriarchy cannot persist without female complicity, regardless of how that complicity is commandeered, complicity that persists as women and lesbians back away from our power to invent.[63] My concern in pursuing withdrawal or separation, both ethically and politically, involves pursuing lesbian agency outside the dominant/subordinate values of heterosexualism. To separate, withdraw, refocus, is to cease attending to the existing system. As Alice Molloy wrote:

> return no thing to evil, that is the basis of separatism. give it no energy, no time, no attention. no nourishment.[64]

The no-saying and the struggle are essential, but so is the ability to withdraw from the existing ground of meaning. If we remain riveted on their categories, we will not succeed in creating new ones.

Thus, separatism is, most importantly, a refocusing, a focusing on lesbians and a lesbian conceptual framework. Through our focus, our attention, we determine what is significant and what is not. Attending is active and creative. And by focusing on ourselves and each other as lesbians in all our diversity, we determine, not that we exist in relation to a dominant

other, but rather that we can create new value, lesbian meaning. By focusing on ourselves and each other, we make lesbianism possible. In calling for withdrawal from the existing heterosexual value system, I am calling for a moral revolution.

Now, beginning with the first aspect of separatism, by withdrawing or separating from the conceptual framework of heterosexualism we can understand a number of things central to lesbian moral agency and the creation of new value. We can realize male domination persists through both predation and protection. We can realize that what it means to be a woman is a creation of the patriarchy, and that 'femininity' makes male domination appear natural. We can realize that what men call 'difference' is actually 'opposition,' and that women have resisted male domination, though not necessarily by challenging heterosexualism. We can perceive women as moral agents, making choices as best they can within the framework of heterosexualism. And we can also understand that lesbians have made other choices, choices not among the designated options.

* . . .

The need to control and be controlled in relationships is central to the dominant/subordinate values of heterosexualism, and, . . . it is central to the values of the anglo-european tradition of ethics.

Through all of this, I am not trying to argue that heterosexualism is the "cause" of oppression. I do mean to suggest, however, that any revolution which does not challenge it will be incomplete and will eventually revert to the values of oppression. Heterosexualism is the form of social organization through which other forms of oppression, at times more vicious forms, become credible, palatable, even desirable. Heterosexualism — that is, the balance between masculine predation upon and masculine protection of a feminine object of masculine attention — de-skills a woman, makes her emotionally, socially, and economically dependent, and allows another to dominate her "for her own good" all in the name of "love." In no other situation are people expected to love, identify with, and become other to those who dominate them to the extent that women are supposed to love, identify with, and become other to men.[65]

It is heterosexualism which makes us feel that it is possible to dominate another for her own good, that one who resists such domination is abnormal or doesn't understand what is good for her, and that one who refuses to participate in dominant/subordinate relationships doesn't exist. And once we accept all this, imperialism, colonialism, and ethnocentrism, for example, while existing all along, become more socially tolerable in liberal thought. They become less a matter of exercising overt force and more a matter of the natural function of (a) social order.

Heterosexualism is a conceptual framework within which the concept of 'moral agency' independent of the master/slave virtues cannot find fertile ground. And it combines with ethical judgments to create a value whose primary function is not the moral development of individuals but rather the preservation of a patriarchal social control. Thus I want to challenge our acceptance and use of that ethics. . . .

In discussing what I call Lesbian Ethics, I do not claim that lesbians haven't made many of the choices (heterosexual) women have made or that lesbians haven't participated in the consensus of straight thinking or that lesbians have withdrawn from the value of dominance and subordination and the security of established meaning we can find therein. I am not claiming that lesbians have lived under different conceptual or material conditions. I am claiming, however, that lesbian choice holds certain possibilities. It is a matter of further choice whether we go on to develop these possibilities or whether instead we try to fit into the existing heterosexual framework in any one of a number of ways.

Thus I am claiming that the conceptual category 'lesbian' — unlike the category 'woman' — is not irretrievably tied up with dominance and subordination as norms of behavior. And I am claiming that by attending each other, we may find the possibility of ethical values appropriate to lesbian existence, values we can choose as moral agents to give meaning to our lives as lesbians. In calling for withdrawal from the existing heterosexual value system, I am calling for a moral revolution, a revolution of lesbianism.

Notes

1. Kathryn Pyne Parsons [Addelson], "Nietzsche and Moral Change," in *Woman in Western Thought*, ed. Martha Lee Osborne (New York: Random House, 1979), p. 235.

2. Ibid.

3. Ibid.

4. Note David K. Shipler, *Arab and Jew: Wounded Spirits in a Promised Land* (New York: Random House/Times Books, 1986). Bette S. Tallen brought this to my attention.

5. Celia Kitzinger, "Heteropatriarchal Language: the Case Against 'Homophobia'," *Gossip* 5, pp. 15–20.

6. Conversation, Marilyn Frye. Note Andrea Dworkin, *Pornography: Men Possessing Women* (New York: G. P. Putnam's Sons, 1979), p. 61.

7. Adrienne Rich, "Compulsory Heterosexuality and Lesbian Existence," *Signs* 5, no. 4 (Summer 1980): 647; reprinted in *Women-Identified-Women*, ed. Trudy Darty and Sandee Potter (Palo Alto, Calif.: Mayfield Publishing Co., 1984), p. 133.

8. Janice G. Raymond, *A Passion for Friends*, p. 11.

9. Conversation, Ariane Brunet.

10. Note, e. g., Andrea Dworkin, *Pornography*, pp. 61–2.

11. Julien S. Murphy, "Silence and Speech in Lesbian Space," paper presented at Mountain Moving Coffeehouse, Chicago, Ill., 1984.

12. For further development of this point, note Marilyn Frye, "Oppression," in *The Politics of Reality: Essays in Feminist Theory* (Trumansburg, N.Y.: The Crossing Press, 1983, now in Freedom, Calif.), pp. 5–6.

13. Note Susan Griffin, "Rape: The All-American Crime," in *Feminism and Philosophy*, ed. Mary Vetterling-Braggin, Frederick A. Elliston, & Jane English (Totowa, N.J.: Littlefield, Adams & Co., 1977), especially p. 320.

14. Andrea Dworkin, *Woman Hating* (New York: E. P. Dutton & Co., 1974), pp. 29–49.

15. Sonia Johnson, presidential campaign speech, Chicago, Ill., 1984; conversation, Pauline Bart.

16. Marilyn Frye, "In and Out of Harm's Way: Arrogance and Love," *Politics of Reality*, p. 72.

17. Sonia Johnson, "Excerpts from the last chapter of *Going Out of Our Minds and Other Revolutionary Acts of the Spirit*," *Mama Bears News & Notes* 3, no. 2 (April/May 1986): 15; also in *Going Out of Our Minds: The Metaphysics of Liberation* (Freedom, Calif.: The Crossing Press, 1987), p. 336.

18. Pat Robinson and Group, "A Historical and Critical Essay for Black Woman in the Cities," in *The Black Woman*, ed. Toni Cade [Bambara] (New York: New American Library, 1970), p. 202.

19. Pat Robinson et al., "Essay for Black Women in the Cities," p. 202.

20. Mary Daly, "The Second Passage," in *Gyn/Ecology: The Metaethics of Radical Feminism* (Boston: Beacon Press, 1978).

21. Sonia Johnson, presidential campaign speech, Chicago, Ill., 1984; also *Going Out of Our Minds*, p. 244.

22. Helen Diner, *Mother and Amazons* (New York: Doubleday, 1973), pp. 95–105.

23. Maxine Feldman, "Amazon," recorded on the album *Closet Sale* (Galaxia, P. O. Box 212, Woburn, MA 01801). Some exceptions include Susan Cavin, *Lesbian Origins* (San Francisco: Jism Press, 1985); Mary Daly, *Gyn/Ecology*; Audre Lorde, *The Black Unicorn* (New York: W. W. Norton & Co., 1978); Merlin Stone, *When God Was a Woman* (New York: Harcourt, Brace, Jovanovich/Harvest, 1976); Monique Wittig, *Les Guérillères* (New York: Avon, 1969), and Monique Wittig and Sande Zeig, *Lesbian Peoples: Material for a Dictionary* (New York: Avon, 1979); Carol Moorefield and Kathleen Valentine, "Matriarchy: A Guide to the Future?," in *For Lesbians Only: A Separatist Anthology*, ed. Sarah Lucia Hoagland and Julia Penelope, forthcoming, Onlywomen Press, London; "Amazons," in *The Woman's Encyclopedia of Myths and Secrets*, Barbara G. Walker (New York: Harper & Row, 1983), pp. 24–7; Judy Grahn, *Another Mother Tongue: Gay Words, Gay Worlds* (Boston: Beacon Press, 1984); Anne Cameron, *Daughters of Copper Woman* (Vancouver, B.C.: Press Gang Publishers, 1981); Micheline Grimard-Leduc, "The Mind-Drifting Islands," *Trivia* 8 (Winter 1986): 28–36, published in *l'île des amantes: essai/poèmes*, Micheline Grimard-Leduc, C.P. 461, Station N, Montréal, Québec, H2X 3N3, Canada, 1982; and Jeffner Allen, *Lesbian Philosophy: Explorations* (Palo Alto, Calif.: Institute of Lesbian Studies, 1986).

24. For reference to the Dahomey, note Audre Lorde, *The Black Unicorn*, p. 119; also Carol Moorefield and Kathleen Valentine, "Matriarchy: A Guide to the Future?" for reference to the Nootka, note Anne Cameron, *Daughters of Copper Woman*.

25. Adrienne Rich, "Compulsory Heterosexuality and Lesbian Existence," p. 632 or pp. 119–20.

26. Harriet Desmoines [Ellenberger] "There Goes the Revolution . . . ," *Sinister Wisdom* 9 (Spring 1979): 22.

27. Radicalesbians, "The Woman Identified Woman," in *Notes from the Third Year*, 1971, reprinted in *Radical Feminism*, p. 244. Note also Anita Cornwell, "Some Notes on the Black Lesbian and the Womin-Identified Womin Concept," in *Black Lesbian in America* (Tallahassee, Fla.: The Naiad Press, 1983), pp. 26–30.

28. Kathleen Barry, *Female Sexual Slavery*.

29. Julia P. Stanley [Julia Penelope] "Paradigmatic Woman: The Prostitute," in *Papers in Language Variation*, ed. David L. Shores and Carole P. Hines (Birmingham: University of Alabama Press, 1977), pp. 303–21.

30. This point was made in a talk by Marilyn Frye.

31. Claudia Dreifus, "Sterilizing the Poor," in *Seizing Our Bodies: The Politics of Women's Health*, ed. Claudia Dreifus (New York: Vintage Books/Random House, 1978), pp. 105–20.

32. Note, for example, *Breaching the Peace: A Collection of Radical Feminist Papers* (London: Onlywomen Press, 1983).

33. Kathleen Barry, *Female Sexual Slavery*, pp. 43–6.

34. William Ryan, *Blaming the Victim* (New York: Vintage Books, 1976).

35. Kathleen Barry, *Female Sexual Slavery*, p. 45.

36. Andrea Dworkin, *Right-Wing Women* (New York: G. P. Putnam's Sons/Perigee, 1983), p. 14.

37. Ibid., p. 15.

38. Ibid., pp. 17, 21.

39. Brunetta R. Wolfman, "Black First, Female Second," in *Black Separation and Social Reality: Rhetoric and Reason*, ed. Raymond L. Hall (New York: Pergamon Press, 1977), p. 228.

40. Ibid., p. 229.

41. Jacquelyn Grant, "Black Women and the Black Church," in *But Some of Us Are Brave*, p. 141.

42. Brunetta R. Wolfman, "Black First, Female Second," p. 230.

43. Ibid., p. 231.

44. I've adapted this from Franz Kafka, "Couriers," in *Parables*, trans. Willa and Edwin Muir (New York: Schocken Books, 1946), pp. 268–78; however, Kafka's point is not about change and his parable contains no king to begin with.

45. Reported to me by Juana María Paz and Bette S. Tallen.

46. Kate Millett, *Sexual Politics*, p. 157.

47. Communication, Marilyn Frye.

48. Conversation, Ariane Brunet.

49. Susan Griffin, "Sacred Images," in *Pornography and Silence* (New York: Harper & Row, 1981), pp. 8–81; Mary Daly, *Gyn/Ecology*; Catharine A. MacKinnon, *Feminism Unmodified: Discourse on Life and Law* (Cambridge, Mass.: Harvard University Press, 1987); Andrea Dworkin, *Pornography*.

50. For an earlier development of this argument note Sara Lucia Hoagland, "Sadism, Masochism, and Lesbian-Feminism," in *Against Sadomasochism: A Radical Feminist Analysis*, ed. Robin Ruth Linden, Darlene R. Pagano, Diana E. H. Russell, and Susan Leigh Star (East Palo Alto, Calif.: Frog in the Well, 1982), pp. 153–63.

51. Michal Brody, *Are We There Yet? A Continuing History of 'Lavender Woman': A Chicago Lesbian Newspaper,*

1971–1976 (Iowa City: Aunt Lute Book Co., 1985, now Spinsters/Aunt Lute, San Francisco), p. 184.

52. Communication, Claudia Card.

53. Marilyn Frye, "Some Reflections on Separatism and Power," in *Politics of Reality,* pp. 96, 98–9.

54. Ibid, pp. 103–5.

55. Mary Daly, *Gyn/Ecology,* p. 381.

56. Resignation is one of the plastic passions Mary Daly names in *Pure Lust,* pp. 200–26.

57. Monique Wittig, "The Straight Mind," *Feminist Issues* 1, no. 1 (Summer 1980): 110.

58. Monique Wittig, "One Is Not Born a Woman," *Feminist Issues* 1, no. 2 (Winter 1981): 49.

59. Ibid., p. 50.

60. Ibid.; note also Monique Wittig, "The Category of Sex," *Feminist Issues* 2, no. 2 (Fall 1982): 64.

61. Monique Wittig, "Category of Sex," p. 64.

62. Marilyn Frye, "In and Out of Harm's Way," p. 80.

63. Conversation, Harriet Ellenberger.

64. Alice Molloy, *In Other Words,* p. 39.

65. This point has been made many times before; for example note Shulamith Firestone, *The Dialectic of Sex: The Case For Feminist Revolution* (New York: Bantam/William Morrow & Co., 1972), chapter 6; Ti-Grace Atkinson, *Amazon Odyssey* (New York: Links Books, 1974), p. 43; and more recently, noting the reverse — namely, that in "no other form of slavery are those in power called upon to love those whom they have found to be inferior and despicable" — Kathleen Barry, *Female Sexual Slavery,* p. 136.

HAVE WE GOT A THEORY FOR YOU!

Feminist Theory, Cultural Imperialism and the Demand for "The Woman's Voice"

Maria C. Lugones and Elizabeth V. Spelman

Maria Lugones and Elizabeth Spelman show how feminist theorizing needs to change in order to take the interests and experience of all women into account. But this can also be read as a primer on building coalitions. They show that even within groups (for example, feminists) coalitions must be built between members who recognize and respect each other, and more importantly, come together in friendship. (Source: From Women's Studies International Forum, *Vol. 6, No. 6 (1983). Reprinted by permission of the authors.)*

Prologue

(In an Hispana voice) A veces quisiera mezclar en una vos el sonido canyenge, tristón y urbano del porteñismo que llevo adentro con la cadencia apacible, serrana y llena de corage de la hispana nuevo mejicana. Contrastar y unir

> el piolín y la cuerda
> el traé y el pepéname
> el camión y la troca
> la lluvia y el llanto

Pero este querer se me va cuando veo que he confundido la solidaridad con la falta de diferencia. La solidaridad requiere el reconocer, comprender, respetar y amar lo que nos lleva a llorar en distintas cadencias. El imperialismo cultural desea lo contrario, por eso necesitamos muchas voces. Porque una sola voz nos mata a las dos.

No quiero hablar por ti sino contigo. Pero si no aprendo tus modos y tu los mios la conversación es sólo aparente. Y la apariencia se levanta como una barrera sin sentido entre las dos. Sin sentido y sin sentimiento. Por eso no me debes dejar que te dicte tu ser y no me dictes el mio. Porque entonces ya no dialogamos. El diálogo entre nosotras requiere dos voces y no una.

Tal vez un diá jugaremos juntas y nos hablaremos no en una lengua universal sino que vos me hablarás mi voz y yo la tuya.

Preface

This paper is the result of our dialogue, of our thinking together about differences among women and how these differences are silenced. (Think, for example, of all the silences there are connected with the fact that this paper is in English — for that is a borrowed tongue for one of us.) In the process of our talking and writing together, we saw that the differences between us did not permit our speaking in one voice. For example, when we agreed we expressed the thought differently; there were some things that both of us thought were true but could not express as true of each of us; sometimes we could not say "we"; and sometimes one of us could not express the thought in the first person singular, and to express it in the third person would be to present an outsider's and not an insider's perspective. Thus the use of two voices is central both to the process of constructing this paper and to the substance of it. We are both the authors of this paper and not just sections of it but we write together without presupposing unity of expression or of experience. So when we speak in unison it means just that — there are two voices and not just one.

Introduction

(In the voice of a white/Anglo woman who has been teaching and writing about feminist theory) Feminism is, among other things, a response to the fact that women either have been left out of, or included in demeaning and disfiguring ways in what has been an al-

most exclusively male account of the world. And so while part of what feminists want and demand for women is the right to move and to act in accordance with our own wills and not against them, another part is the desire and insistence that we give our *own* accounts of these movements and actions. For it matters to us what is said about us, who says it, and to whom it is said: having the opportunity to talk about one's life, to give an account of it, to interpret it, is integral to leading that life rather than being led through it; hence our distrust of the male monopoly over accounts of women's lives. To put the same point slightly differently, part of human life, human living, is talking about it, and we can be sure that being silenced in one's own account of one's life is a kind of amputation that signals oppression. Another reason for not divorcing life from the telling of it or talking about it is that as humans our experiences are deeply influenced by what is said about them, by ourselves or powerful (as opposed to significant) others. Indeed, the phenomenon of internalized oppression is only possible because this is so: one experiences her life in terms of the impoverished and degrading concepts others have found it convenient to use to describe her. We can't separate lives from the accounts given of them; the articulation of our experience is part of our experience.

Sometimes feminists have made even stronger claims about the importance of speaking about our own lives and the destructiveness of others presuming to speak about us or for us. First of all, the claim has been made that on the whole men's accounts of women's lives have been at best false, a function of ignorance; and at worst malicious lies, a function of a knowledgeable desire to exploit and oppress. Since it matters to us that falsehood and lies not be told about us, we demand, of those who have been responsible for those falsehoods and lies, or those who continue to transmit them, not just that we speak but that they learn to be able to hear us. It has also been claimed that talking about one's life, telling one's story, in the company of those doing the same (as in consciousness-raising sessions), is constitutive of feminist method.[1]

And so the demand that the woman's voice be heard and attended to has been made for a variety of reasons: not just so as to greatly increase the chances that true accounts of women's lives will be given, but also because the articulation of experience (in myriad ways) is among the hallmarks of a self-determining individual or community. There are not just epistemological, but moral and political reasons for demanding that the woman's voice be heard, after centuries of androcentric din.

But what more exactly is the feminist demand that the woman's voice be heard? There are several crucial notes to make about it. First of all, the demand grows out of a complaint, and in order to understand the scope and focus of the demand we have to look at the scope and focus of the complaint. The complaint does not specify *which* women have been silenced, and in one way this is appropriate to the conditions it is a complaint about: virtually no women have had a voice, whatever their race, class, ethnicity, religion, sexual alliance, whatever place and period in history they lived. And if it is as women that women have been silenced, then of course the demand must be that women as women have a voice. But in another way the complaint is very misleading, insofar as it suggests that it is women as women who have been silenced, and that whether a woman is rich or poor, Black, brown or white, etc., is irrelevant to what it means for her to be a woman. For the demand thus simply made ignores at least two related points: (1) it is only possible for a woman who does not feel highly vulnerable with respect to other parts of her identity, e.g., race, class, ethnicity, religion, sexual alliance, etc., to conceive of her voice simply or essentially as a "woman's voice"; (2) just because not all women are equally vulnerable with respect to race, class, etc., some women's voices are more likely to be heard than others by those who have heretofore been giving—or silencing—the accounts of women's lives. For all these reasons, the women's voices most likely to come forth and the women's voices most likely to be heard are, in the United States anyway, those of white, middle-class, heterosexual Christian (or anyway not self-identified non-Christian) women. Indeed, many Hispanas, Black women, Jewish women—to name a few groups—have felt it an invitation to silence rather than speech to be requested—if they are requested at all—to speak about being "women" (with the plain wrapper—as if there were one) in distinction from speaking about being Hispana, Black, Jewish, working-class, etc., women.

The demand that the "woman's voice" be heard, and the search for the "woman's voice" as central to feminist methodology, reflects nascent feminist theory. It reflects nascent empirical theory insofar as it presupposes that the silencing of women is systematic, shows up in regular, patterned ways, and that there are discoverable causes of this widespread observable phenomenon; the demand reflects nascent political theory insofar as it presupposes that the silencing of women reveals a systematic pattern of power and authority; and it reflects nascent moral theory insofar as it presupposes that the silencing is unjust and that there are particular ways of remedying this injustice. Indeed, whatever else we know feminism to include — e.g., concrete direct political action — theorizing is integral to it: theories about the nature of oppression, the causes of it, the relation of the oppression of women to other forms of oppression. And certainly the concept of the woman's voice is itself a theoretical concept, in the sense that it presupposes a theory according to which our identities as human beings are actually compound identities, a kind of fusion or confusion or our otherwise separate identities as women or men, as Black or brown or white, etc. That is no less a theoretical stance than Plato's division of the person into soul and body or Aristotle's parcelling of the soul into various functions.

The demand that the "woman's voice" be heard also invites some further directions in the exploration of women's lives and discourages or excludes others. For reasons mentioned above, systematic, sustained reflection on being a woman — the kind of contemplation that "doing theory" requires — is most likely to be done by women who vis-à-vis other women enjoy a certain amount of political, social and economic privilege because of their skin color, class membership, ethnic identity. There is a relationship between the content of our contemplation and the fact that we have the time to engage in it at some length — otherwise we shall have to say that it is a mere accident of history that white middle-class women in the United States have in the main developed "feminist theory" (as opposed to "Black feminist theory," "Chicana feminist theory," etc.) and that so much of the theory has failed to be relevant to the lives of women who are not white or middle class. Feminist theory — of all kinds — is to be based on, or anyway touch base with, the variety of real life stories women provide about themselves. But in fact, because, among other things, of the structural political and social and economic inequalities among women, the tail has been wagging the dog: feminist theory has not for the most part arisen out of a medley of women's voices; instead, the theory has arisen out of the voices, the experiences, of a fairly small handful of women, and if other women's voices do not sing in harmony with the theory, they aren't counted as women's voices — rather, they are the voices of the woman as Hispana, Black, Jew, etc. There is another sense in which the tail is wagging the dog, too: it is presumed to be the case that those who do the theory know more about those who are theorized than vice versa; hence it ought to be the case that if it is white/Anglo women who write for and about all other women, the white/Anglo women must know more about all other women that other women know about them. But in fact just in order to survive, brown and Black women have to know a lot more about white/Anglo women — not through the sustained contemplation theory requires, but through the sharp observation stark exigency demands.

(*In an Hispana voice*) I think it necessary to explain why in so many cases when women of color appear in front of white/Anglo women to talk about feminism and women of color, we mainly raise a complaint: the complaint of exclusion, of silencing, of being included in a universe we have not chosen. We usually raise the complaint with a certain amount of disguised or undisguised anger. I can only attempt to explain this phenomenon from a Hispanic viewpoint and a fairly narrow one at that: the viewpoint of an Argentinian woman who has lived in the US for 16 years, who has attempted to come to terms with the devaluation of things Hispanic and Hispanic people in "America" and who is most familiar with Hispano life in the Southwest of the US. I am quite unfamiliar with daily Hispano life in the urban centers, though not with some of the themes and some of the salient experiences of urban Hispano life.

When I say "we,"[2] I am referring to Hispanas. I am accustomed to use the "we" in this way. I am also pained by the tenuousness of this "we" given that I am not a native of the United States. Through the years I have come to be recognized and I have come to recognize myself more and more firmly as part of this "we." I also have a profound yearning for this firmness since I am a displaced person and I am conscious of not being of and I am unwilling to make myself of—even if this were possible—the white/Anglo community.

When I say "you" I mean not the non-Hispanic but the white/Anglo woman that I address. "We" and "you" do not capture my relation to other non-white women. The complexity of the relation is not addressed here, but it is vivid to me as I write down my thoughts on the subject at hand.

I see two related reasons for our complaint-full discourse with white/Anglo women. Both of these reasons plague our world, they contaminate it through and through. It takes some hardening of oneself, some self-acceptance of our own anger to face them, for to face them is to decide that maybe we can change our situation in self-constructive ways and we know fully well that the possibilities are minimal. We know that we cannot rest from facing these reasons, that the tenderness towards others in us undermines our possibilities, that we have to fight our own niceness because it clouds our minds and hearts. Yet we know that a thoroughgoing hardening would dehumanize us. So, we have to walk through our days in a peculiarly fragile psychic state, one that we have to struggle to maintain, one that we do not often succeed in maintaining.

We and you do not talk the same language. When we talk to you we use your language: the language of your experience and of your theories. We try to use it to communicate our world of experience. But since your language and your theories are inadequate in expressing our experiences, we only succeed in communicating our experience of exclusion. We cannot talk to you in our language because you do not understand it. So the brute facts that we understand your language and that the place where most theorizing about women is taking place is your place, both combine to require that we either use your language and distort our experience not just in the speaking about it, but in the living of it, or that we remain silent. Complaining about exclusion is a way of remaining silent.

You are ill at ease in our world. You are ill at ease in our world in a very different way than we are ill at ease in yours. You are not of our world and again, you are not of our world in a very different way than

we are not of yours. In the intimacy of a personal relationship we appear to you many times to be wholly there, to have broken through or to have dissipated the barriers that separate us because you are Anglo and we are raza. When we let go of the psychic state that I referred to above in the direction of sympathy, we appear to ourselves equally whole in your presence but our intimacy is thoroughly incomplete. When we are in your world many times you remake us in your own image, although sometimes you clearly and explicitly acknowledge that we are not wholly there in our being with you. When we are in your world we ourselves feel the discomfort of having our own being Hispanas disfigured or not understood. And yet, we have had to be in your world and learn its ways. We have to participate in it, make a living in it, live in it, be mistreated in it, be ignored in it, and rarely, be appreciated in it. In learning to do these things or in learning to suffer them or in learning to enjoy what is to be enjoyed or in learning to understand your conception of us, we have had to learn your culture and thus your language and self-conceptions. But there is nothing that necessitates that you understand our world: understand, that is, not as an observer understands things, but as a participant, as someone who has a stake in them understands them. So your being ill at ease in our world lacks the features of our being ill at ease in yours precisely because you can leave and you can always tell yourselves that you will be soon out of there and because the wholeness of your selves is never touched by us, we have no tendency to remake you in our image.

But you theorize about women and we are women, so you understand yourselves to be theorizing about us, and we understand you to be theorizing about us. Yet none of the feminist theories developed so far seems to me to help Hispanas in the articulation of our experience. We have a sense that in using them we are distorting our experiences. Most Hispanas cannot even understand the language used in these theories—and only in some cases the reason is that the Hispana cannot understand English. We do not recognize ourselves in these theories. They create in us a schizophrenic split between our concern for ourselves as women and ourselves as Hispanas, one that we do not feel otherwise. Thus they seem to us to force us to assimilate to some version of Anglo culture, however revised that version may be. They seem to ask that we leave our communities or that we become alienated so completely in them that we feel hollow. When we see that you feel alienated in your own communities, this confuses us because we think that maybe every feminist has to suffer this alienation. But we see that recognition of your alienation leads many of you to be empowered into the remaking of your culture, while we are paralyzed into a state of displacement with no place to go.

So I think that we need to think carefully about the relation between the articulation of our own experience, the interpretation of our own experience, and theory making by us and other non-Hispanic women about themselves and other "women."

The only motive that makes sense to me for your joining us in this investigation is the motive of friendship, out of friendship. A non-imperialist feminism requires that you make a real space for our articulating, interpreting, theorizing and reflecting about the connections among them—a real space must be a non-coerced space—and/or that you follow us into our world out of friendship. I see the "out of friendship" as the only sensical motivation for this following because the task at hand for you is one of extraordinary difficulty. It requires that you be willing to devote a great part of your life to it and that you be willing to suffer alienation and self-disruption. Self-interest has been proposed as a possible motive for entering this task. But self-interest does not seem to me to be a realistic motive, since whatever the benefits you may accrue from such a journey, they cannot be concrete enough for you at this time and they may not be worth your while. I do not think that you have any obligation to understand us. You do have an obligation to abandon your imperialism, your universal claims, your reduction of us to your selves simply because they seriously harm us.

I think that the fact that we are so ill at ease with your theorizing in the ways indicated above does indicate that there is something wrong with these theories. But what is it that is wrong? Is it simply that the theories are flawed if meant to be universal but accurate so long as they are confined to your particular group(s)? Is it that the theories are not really flawed but need to be translated? Can they be translated? Is

it something about the process of theorizing that is flawed? How do the two reasons for our complaint-full discourse affect the validity of your theories? Where do *we* begin? To what extent are our experience and its articulation affected by our being a colonized people, and thus by your culture, theories and conceptions? Should we theorize in community and thus as part of community life and outside the academy and other intellectual circles? What is the point of making theory? Is theory making a good thing for us to do at this time? When are we making theory and when are we just articulating and/or interpreting our experiences?

Some Questionable Assumptions About Feminist Theorizing

(*Unproblematically in Vicky's and Maria's voice*) Feminist theories aren't just about what happens to the female population in any given society or across all societies; they are about the meaning of those experiences in the lives of women. They are about beings who give their own accounts of what is happening to them or of what they are doing, who have culturally constructed ways of reflecting on their lives. But how can the theorizer get at the meaning of those experiences? What should the relation be between a woman's own account of her experiences and the theorizer's account of it?

Let us describe two different ways of arriving at an account of another woman's experience. It is one thing for both me and you to observe you and come up with our different accounts of what you are doing; it is quite another for me to observe myself and others much like me culturally and in other ways and to develop an account of myself and then use that account to give an account of you. In the first case you are the "insider" and I am the "outsider." When the outsider makes clear that she is an outsider and that this is an outsider's account of your behavior, there is a touch of honesty about what she is doing. Most of the time the "interpretation by an outsider" is left understood and most of the time the distance of outsidedness is understood to mark objectivity in the interpretation. But why is the outsider as an outsider interpreting your behavior? Is she doing it so that you can understand how she sees you? Is she doing it so that other outsiders will understand how you *are*? Is she doing it so that *you* will understand how you are? It would seem that if the outsider wants you to understand how she sees you and you have given your account of how you see yourself to her, there is a possibility of genuine dialogue between the two. It also seems that the lack of reciprocity could bar genuine dialogue. For why should you engage in such a one-sided dialogue? As soon as we ask this question, a host of other conditions for the possibility of a genuine dialogue between us arise: conditions having to do with your position relative to me in the various social, political and economic structures in which we might come across each other or in which you may run face to face with my account of you and my use of your account of yourself. Is this kind of dialogue necessary for me to get at the meaning of your experiences? That is, is this kind of dialogue necessary for feminist theorizing that is not seriously flawed?

Obviously the most dangerous of the understanding of what I—an outsider—am doing in giving an account of your experience is the one that describes what I'm doing as giving an account of who and how you are whether it be given to you or to other outsiders. Why should you or anyone else believe me; that is, why should you or anyone else believe that you are as I say you are? Could I be right? What conditions would have to obtain for my being right? That many women are put in the position of not knowing whether or not to believe outsiders' accounts of their experiences is clear. The pressures to believe these accounts are enormous even when the woman in question does not see herself in the account. She is thus led to doubt her own judgment and to doubt all interpretation of her experience. This leads her to experience her life differently. Since the consequences of outsiders' accounts can be so significant, it is crucial that we reflect on whether or not this type of account can ever be right and if so, under what conditions.

The last point leads us to the second way of arriving at an account of another woman's experience, viz., the case in which I observe myself and others like me culturally and in other ways and use that account to give an account of you. In doing this, I remake you in my own image. Feminist theorizing approaches this remaking insofar as it depends on the concept of women as women. For it has not arrived at this concept as a consequence of dialogue with many women who are culturally different, or by any other kind of investigation of cultural differences which may include different conceptions of what it is to be a woman; it has simply presupposed this concept.

Our suggestion in this paper, and at this time it is no more than a suggestion, is that only when genuine and reciprocal dialogue takes place between "outsiders" and "insiders" can we trust the outsider's account. At first sight it may appear that the insider/outsider distinction disappears in the dialogue, but it is important to notice that all that happens is that we are now both outsider and insider with respect to each other. The dialogue puts us both in position to give a better account of each other's and our own experience. Here we should again note that white/Anglo women are much less prepared for this dialogue with women of color than women of color are for dialogue with them in that women of color have had to learn white/Anglo ways, self-conceptions, and conceptions of them.

But both the possibility and the desirability of this dialogue are very much in question. We need to think about the possible motivations for engaging in this dialogue, whether doing theory jointly would be a good thing, in what ways and for whom, and whether doing theory is in itself a good thing at this time for women of color or white/Anglo women. In motivating the last question let us remember the hierarchical distinctions between theorizers and those theorized about and between theorizers and doers. These distinctions are endorsed by the same views and institutions which endorse and support hierarchical distinctions between men/women, master race/inferior race, intellectuals/manual workers. Of what use is the activity of theorizing to those of us who are women of color engaged day in and day out in the task of empowering women and men of color face to face with them? Should we be articulating and interpreting their experience for them with the aid of theories? Whose theories?

Ways of Talking or Being Talked About That Are Helpful, Illuminating, Empowering, Respectful

(*Unproblematically in Maria's and Vicky's voice*) Feminists have been quite diligent about pointing out ways in which empirical, philosophical and moral theories have been androcentric. They have thought it crucial to ask, with respect to such theories: who makes them? for whom do they make them? about what or whom are the theories? why? how are theories tested? what are the criteria for such tests and where did the criteria come from? Without posing such questions and trying to answer them, we'd never have been able to begin to mount evidence for our claims that particular theories are androcentric, sexist, biased, paternalistic, etc. Certain philosophers have become fond of—indeed, have made their careers on—pointing out that characterizing a statement as true or false is only one of many ways possible of characterizing it; it might also be, oh, rude, funny, disarming, etc.; it may be intended to soothe or to hurt; or it may have the effect, intended or not, of soothing or hurting. Similarly, theories appear to be the kinds of things that are true or false; but they also are the kinds of things that can be, e.g., useless, arrogant, disrespectful, ignorant, ethnocentric, imperialistic. The immediate point is that feminist theory is no less immune to such characterizations than, say, Plato's political theory, or Freud's theory of female psychosexual development. Of course this is not to say that if feminist theory manages to be respectful or helpful it will follow that it must be true. But if, say, an empirical theory is purported to be about "women" and in fact is only about certain women, it is certainly false, probably ethnocentric, and of dubious usefulness except to those whose position in the world it strengthens (and theories, as we know, don't have to be true in order to be used to strengthen people's positions in the world).

Many reasons can be and have been given for the production of accounts of people's lives that plainly have nothing to do with illuminating those lives for the benefit of those living them. It is likely that both the method of investigation and the content of many accounts would be different if illuminating the lives of the people the accounts are about were the aim of the studies. Though we cannot say ahead of time how feminist theory making would be different if all (or many more) of those people it is meant to be about were more intimately part of the theory-making process, we do suggest some specific ways being talked about can be helpful:

1. The theory or account can be helpful if it enables one to see how parts of one's life fit together, for example, to see connections among parts of one's life one hasn't seen before. No account can do this if it doesn't get the parts right to begin with, and this cannot happen if the concepts used to describe a life are utterly foreign.

2. A useful theory will help one locate oneself concretely in the world, rather than add to the mystification of the world and one's location in it. New concepts may be of significance here, but they will not be useful if there is no way they can be translated into already existing concepts. Suppose a theory locates you in the home, because you are a woman, but you know full well that is not where you spend most of your time? Or suppose you can't locate yourself easily in any particular class as defined by some version of Marxist theory?

3. A theory or account not only ought to accurately locate one in the world but also enable one to think about the extent to which one is responsible or not for being in that location. Otherwise, for those whose location is as oppressed peoples, it usually occurs that the oppressed have no way to see themselves as in any way self-determining, as having any sense of being worthwhile or having grounds for pride, and paradoxically at the same time feeling at fault for the position they are in. A useful theory will help people work out just what is and is not due to themselves and their own activities as opposed to those who have power over them.

It may seem odd to make these criteria of a useful theory, if the usefulness is not to be at odds with the issue of the truth of the theory; for the focus on feeling worthwhile or having pride seems to rule out the possibility that the truth might just be that such-and-such a group of people has been under the control of others for centuries and that the only explanation of that is that they are worthless and weak people, and will never be able to change that. Feminist theorizing seems implicitly if not explicitly committed to the moral view that women *are* worthwhile beings, and the metaphysical theory that we are beings capable of bringing about a change in our situations. Does this mean feminist theory is "biased"? Not any more than any other theory, e.g., psychoanalytic theory. What is odd here is not the feminist presupposition that women are worthwhile but rather that feminist theory (and other theory) often has the effect of empowering one group and demoralizing another.

Aspects of feminist theory are as unabashedly value-laden as other political and moral theories. It is not just an examination of women's positions, for it includes, indeed begins with, moral and political judgments about the injustice (or, where relevant, justice) of them. This means that there are implicit or explicit judgments also about what kind of changes constitute a better or worse situation for women.

4.   In this connection a theory that is useful will provide criteria for change and make suggestions for modes of resistance that don't merely reflect the situation and values of the theorizer. A theory that is respectful of those about whom it is a theory will not assume that changes that are perceived as making life better for some women are changes that will make, and will be perceived as making, life better for other women. This is *not* to say that if some women do not find a situation oppressive, other women ought never to suggest to the contrary that there might be very good reasons to think that the situation nevertheless *is* oppressive. But it is to say that, e.g., the prescription that life for women will be better when we're in the workforce rather than at home, when we are completely free of religious beliefs with patriarchal origins, when we live in complete separation from men, etc., are seen as slaps in the face to women whose life would be better if they could spend more time at home, whose identity is inseparable from their religious beliefs and cultural practices (which is not to say those beliefs and prac-

tices are to remain completely uncriticized and unchanged), who have ties to men — whether erotic or not — such that to have them severed in the name of some vision of what is "better" is, at that time and for those women, absurd. Our visions of what is better are always informed by our perception of what is bad about our present situation. Surely we've learned enough from the history of clumsy missionaries, and the white suffragists of the 19th century (who couldn't imagine why Black women "couldn't see" how crucial getting the vote for "women" was) to know that we can clobber people to destruction with our visions, our versions, of what is better. *But:* this does not mean women are not to offer supportive and tentative criticism of one another. But there is a very important difference between (a) developing ideas together, in a "pre-theoretical" stage, engaged as equals in joint enquiry, and (b) one group developing, on the basis of their own experience, a set of criteria for good change for women — and then reluctantly making revisions in the criteria at the insistence of women to whom such criteria seem ethnocentric and arrogant. The deck is stacked when one group takes it upon itself to develop the theory and then have others criticize it. Categories are quick to congeal, and the experiences of women whose lives do not fit the categories will appear as anomalous when in fact the theory should have grown out of them as much as others from the beginning. This, of course, is why any organization or conference having to do with "women" — with no qualification — that seriously does not want to be "solipsistic" will from the beginning be multi-cultural or state the appropriate qualifications. How we think and what we think about does depend in large part on who is there — not to mention who is expected or encouraged to speak. (Recall the boys in the *Symposium* sending the flute girls out.) Conversations and criticism take place in particular circumstances. Turf matters. So does the fact of who if anyone already has set up the terms of the conversations.

5.   Theory cannot be useful to anyone interested in resistance and change unless there is reason to believe that knowing what a theory means and believing it to be true have some connection to resistance and change. As we make theory and offer it

up to others, what do we assume is the connection between theory and consciousness? Do we expect others to read theory, understand it, believe it, and have their consciousness and lives thereby transformed? If we really want theory to make a difference to people's lives, how ought we to present it? Do we think people come to consciousness by reading? only by reading? Speaking to people through theory (orally or in writing) is a *very* specific context-dependent activity. That is, theory makers and their methods and concepts constitute a community of people and of shared meanings. Their language can be just as opaque and foreign to those not in the community as a foreign tongue or dialect.[3] Why do we engage in *this* activity and what effect do we think it ought to have? As Helen Longino has asked: "Is 'doing theory' just a bonding ritual for academic or educationally privileged feminist women?" Again, whom does our theory making serve?

Some Suggestions About How to Do Theory That Is Not Imperialistic, Ethnocentric, Disrespectful

(*Problematically in the voice of a woman of color*) What are the things we need to know about others, and about ourselves, in order to speak intelligently, intelligibly, sensitively, and helpfully about their lives? We can show respect, or lack of it, in writing theoretically about others no less than in talking directly with them. This is not to say that here we have a well-worked out concept of respect, but only to suggest that together all of us consider what it would mean to theorize in a respectful way.

When we speak, write, and publish our theories, to whom do we think we are accountable? Are the concerns we have in being accountable to "the profession" at odds with the concerns we have in being accountable to those about whom we theorize? Do commitments to "the profession," method, getting something published, getting tenure, lead us to talk and act in ways at odds with what we ourselves (let alone others) would regard as ordinary, decent behavior? To what extent do we presuppose that really understanding another person or culture requires our

behaving in ways that are disrespectful, even violent? That is, to what extent do we presuppose that getting and/or publishing the requisite information requires or may require disregarding the wishes of others, lying to them, wresting information from them against their wills? Why and how do we think theorizing about others provides *understanding* of them? Is there any sense in which theorizing about others is a short-cut to understanding them?

Finally, if we think doing theory is an important activity, and we think that some conditions lead to better theorizing than others, what are we going to do about creating those conditions? If we think it not just desirable but necessary for women of different racial and ethnic identities to create feminist theory jointly, how shall that be arranged for? It may be the case that at this particular point we ought not even try to do that — that feminist theory by and for Hispanas needs to be done separately from feminist theory by and for Black women, white women, etc. But it must be recognized that white/Anglo women have more power and privilege than Hispanas, Black women, etc., and at the very least they can use such advantage to provide space and time for other women to speak (with the above caveats about implicit restrictions on what counts as "the women's voice"). And once again it is important to remember that the power of white/Anglo women vis-a-vis Hispanas and Black women is in inverse proportion to their working knowledge of each other.

This asymmetry is a crucial fact about the background of possible relationships between white women and women of color, whether as political co-workers, professional colleagues, or friends.

If white/Anglo women and women of color are to do theory jointly, in helpful, respectful, illuminating and empowering ways, the task ahead of white/Anglo women because of this asymmetry, is a very hard task. The task is a very complex one. In part, to make an analogy, the task can be compared to learning a text without the aid of teachers. We all know the lack of contact felt when we want to discuss a particular issue that requires knowledge of a text with someone who does not know the text at all. Or the discomfort and impatience that arise in us when we are discussing an issue that presupposes a text and someone walks into the conversation who does not know the text. That person is either left out or will impose herself on us and either try to engage in the discussion or try to change the subject. Women of color are put in these situations by white/Anglo women and men constantly. Now imagine yourself simply left out but wanting to do theory with us. The first thing to recognize and accept is that you disturb our own dialogues by putting yourself in the left-out position and not leaving us in some meaningful sense to ourselves.

You must also recognize and accept that you must learn the text. But the text is an extraordinarily complex one: vis., our many different cultures. You are asking us to make ourselves more vulnerable to you than we already are before we have any reason to trust that you will not take advantage of this vulnerability. So you need to learn to become unintrusive, unimportant, patient to the point of tears, while at the same time open to learning any possible lessons. You will also have to come to terms with the sense of alienation, of not belonging, of having your world thoroughly disrupted, having it criticized and scrutinized from the point of view of those who have been harmed by it, having important concepts central to it dismissed, being viewed with mistrust, being seen as of no consequence except as an object of mistrust.

Why would any white/Anglo woman engage in this task? Out of self-interest? What in engaging in this task would be, not just in her interest, but perceived as such by her before the task is completed or well underway? Why should we want you to come into our world out of self-interest? Two points need to be made here. The task as described could be entered into with the intention of finding out as much as possible about us so as to better dominate us. The person engaged in this task would act as a spy. The motivation is not unfamiliar to us. We have heard it said that now that Third World countries are more powerful as a bloc, westerners need to learn more about them, that it is in their self-interest to do so. Obviously there is no reason why people of color should welcome white/Anglo women into their world for the carrying out of this intention. It is also obvious that white/Anglo feminists should not engage in this task under this description since the task under this description would not lead to joint theorizing of the desired sort: respectful, illuminating, helpful and empowering. It would be helpful and empowering only in a one-sided way.

Self-interest is also mentioned as a possible motive in another way. White/Anglo women sometimes say that the task of understanding women of color would entail self-growth or self-expansion. If the task is conceived as described here, then one should doubt that growth or expansion will be the result. The severe self-disruption that the task entails should place a doubt in anyone who takes the task seriously about her possibilities of coming out of the task whole, with a self that is not as fragile as the selves of those who have been the victims of racism. But also, why should women of color embrace white/Anglo women's self-betterment without reciprocity? At this time women of color cannot afford this generous affirmation of white/Anglo women.

Another possible motive for engaging in this task is the motive of duty, "out of obligation," because white/Anglos have done people of color wrong. Here again two considerations: coming into Hispano, Black, Native American worlds out of obligation puts white/Anglos in a morally self-righteous position that is inappropriate. You are active, we are passive. We become the vehicles of your own redemption. Secondly, we couldn't want you to come into our worlds "out of obligation." That is like wanting someone to make love to you out of obligation. So, whether or not you have an obligation to do this (and we would deny that you do), or whether this task could even be done out of obligation, this is an inappropriate motive.

Out of obligation you should stay out of our way, respect us and our distance, and forego the use of whatever power you have over us — for example, the power to use your language in our meetings, the power to overwhelm us with your education, the power to intrude in our communities in order to research us and to record the supposed dying of our cultures, the power to engrain in us a sense that we are members of dying cultures and are doomed to assimilate, the power to keep us in a defensive posture with respect to our own cultures.

So the motive of friendship remains as both the only appropriate and understandable motive for white/Anglo feminists engaging in the task as described above. If you enter the task out of friendship with us, then you will be moved to attain the appropriate reciprocity of care for your and our well-being as whole beings, you will have a stake in us and in our world, you will be moved to satisfy the need for reciprocity of understanding that will enable you to follow us in our experiences as we are able to follow you in yours.

We are not suggesting that if the learning of the text is to be done out of friendship, you must enter into a friendship with a whole community and for the purpose of making theory. In order to understand what it is that we are suggesting, it is important to remember that during the description of her experience of exclusion, the Hispana voice said that Hispanas experience the intimacy of friendship with white/Anglo women friends as thoroughly incomplete. It is not until this fact is acknowledged by our white/Anglo women friends and felt as a profound lack in our experience of each other that white/Anglo women can begin to see us. Seeing us in our communities will make clear and concrete to you how incomplete we really are in our relationships with you. It is this beginning that forms the proper background for the yearning to understand the text of our cultures that can lead to joint theory making.

Thus, the suggestion made here is that if white/Anglo women are to understand our voices, they must understand our communities and us in them. Again, this is not to suggest that you set out to make friends with our communities, though you may become friends with some of the members, nor is it to suggest that you should try to befriend us for the purpose of making theory with us. The latter would be a perversion of friendship. Rather, from within friendship you may be moved by friendship to undergo the very difficult task of understanding the text of our cultures by understanding our lives in our communities. This learning calls for circumspection, for questioning of yourselves and your roles in your own culture. It necessitates a striving to understand while in the com-

fortable position of not having an official calling card (as "scientific" observers of our communities have); it demands recognition that you do not have the authority of knowledge; it requires coming to the task without ready-made theories to frame our lives. This learning is then extremely hard because it requires openness (including openness to serve criticism of the white/Anglo world), sensitivity, concentration, self-questioning, circumspection. It should be clear that it does not consist in a passive immersion in our cultures, but in a striving to understand what it is that our voices are saying. Only then can we engage in a mutual dialogue that does not reduce each one of us to instances of the abstraction called "woman."

Notes

1. For a recent example, see MacKinnon, Catharine. 1982. Feminism, Marxism, method and the state: An agenda for theory. *Signs* 7 (3): 515–544.

2. I must note that when I think this "we," I think it in Spanish—and in Spanish this "we" is gendered, "nosotras." I also use "nosotros" lovingly and with ease and in it I include all members of "La raza cosmica" (Spanish-speaking people of the Americas, la gente de colores: people of many colors). In the US, I use "we" contextually with varying degrees of discomfort: "we" in the house, "we" in the department, "we" in the classroom, "we" in the meeting. The discomfort springs from the sense of community in the "we" and the varying degrees of lack of community in the context in which the "we" is used.

3. See Bernstein, Basil. 1972. Social class, language, and socialization. In Giglioli, Pier Paolo, ed., *Language and Social Context,* pp. 157–178. Penguin, Harmondsworth, Middlesex. Bernstein would probably, and we think wrongly, insist that theoretical terms and statements have meanings *not* "tied to a local relationship and to a local social structure," unlike the vocabulary of, e.g., working-class children.

BLACK LEADERSHIP AND THE
PITFALLS OF RACIAL REASONING

Cornel West

Cornel West describes the "racial reasoning" that went on during the Clarence Thomas hearings. He argues that racial reasoning should be given up in favor of moral reasoning with an emphasis on a mature black identity, coalitionist strategy, and cultural democracy. (Source: From Race-ing Justice, En-gendering Power *by Toni Morrison, editor. Copyright © 1992 by Cornel West. Compilation copyright © 1992 by Toni Morrison. Reprinted by permission of Pantheon Books, a division of Random House, Inc.)*

The most depressing feature of the Clarence Thomas/ Anita Hill hearings was neither the mean-spirited attacks of the Republicans nor the spineless silences of the Democrats — both reveal the predictable inability of most white politicians to talk candidly about race and gender. Rather, what most disturbed me was the low level of political discussion in black America about these hearings — a crude discourse about race and gender that bespeaks a failure of nerve of black leadership.

This failure of nerve was already manifest in the selection and confirmation process of Clarence Thomas. Bush's choice of Thomas caught most black leaders off guard. Few had the courage to say publicly that this was an act of cynical tokenism concealed by outright lies about Thomas being the most qualified candidate regardless of race. The fact that Thomas was simply unqualified for the Court — a claim warranted by his undistinguished record as a student (mere graduation from Yale Law School does not qualify one of the Supreme Court!); his turbulent eight years at the EEOC, where he left thirteen thousand age-discrimination cases dying on the vine for lack of investigation; and his mediocre performance during a short fifteen months as an appellate court judge — was not even mentioned. The very fact that no black leader could utter publicly that a black appointee for the Supreme Court was *unqualified* shows how captive they are to white-racist stereotypes about black intellectual talent. The point here is not simply that if Thomas were white they would have no trouble uttering this fact from the rooftops, but also that their silence reveals that they may entertain the possibility that the racist stereotype is true. Hence their attempt to cover Thomas's mediocrity with silence. Of course, some privately admit his mediocrity then point out the mediocrity of Judge Souter and other Court judges — as if white mediocrity is a justification for black mediocrity. No double standards here, this argument goes, if a black man is unqualified, one can defend and excuse him by appealing to other unqualified white judges. This chimes well with a cynical tokenism of the lowest common demoninator — with little concern about shattering the racist stereotype or furthering the public interest in the nation. It also renders invisible highly qualified black judges who deserve serious consideration for selection to the Court.

How did much of black leadership get in this bind? Why did so many of them capitulate to Bush's cynical strategy? Three reasons loom large. First, Thomas's claim to racial authenticity — his birth in Jim Crow Georgia, his childhood spent as the grandson of a black sharecropper, his undeniably black phenotype degraded by racist ideals of beauty, and his gallant black struggle for achievement in racist America. Second, the complex relation of this claim to racial authenticity to the increasing closing-ranks mentality in black America. Escalating black-nationalist sentiments — the notion that America's will to racial justice is weak and therefore black people must close ranks for survival in a hostile country — rests principally upon claims to racial authenticity. Third, the way in which black-nationalist sentiments promote and encourage black cultural conservatism, especially black patriarchal (and homophobic) power. The idea of black people closing ranks against hostile white Americans reinforces black male power exercised over black women (e.g., to protect, regulate, subordinate, and hence usually, though not always, use and abuse women) in order to preserve black social order under circumstances of white-literal attack and symbolic assault.

Most black leaders got lost in their thicket of reasoning and thus got caught in a vulgar form of racial reasoning: *black authenticity — black closing-ranks mentality — black male subordination of black women in the interests of the black community in a hostile white-racist country.* This line of racial reasoning leads to such questions as "Is Thomas really black?"; "Is he black enough to be defended?"; "Is he just black on the outside?" et al. In fact, these kind of questions were asked, debated, and answered throughout black America in barber shops, beauty salons, living rooms, churches, mosques, and schoolrooms.

Unfortunately, the very framework of this line of racial reasoning was not called into question. Yet as long as racial reasoning regulates black thought and action, Clarence Thomases will continue to haunt black America — as Bush and his ilk sit back, watch, and prosper. How does one undermine the framework of racial reasoning? By dismantling each pillar slowly and systematically. The fundamental aim of this undermining and dismantling is to replace racial reasoning with moral reasoning, to understand the black-freedom struggle not as an affair of skin pigmentation and racial phenotype but rather as a matter of ethical principles and wise politics, and to combat black-nationalist views of subordinating the issues and interests of black women by linking mature black self-love and self-respect to egalitarian relations within and outside black communities. The failure of nerve of black leadership is to refuse to undermine and dismantle the framework of racial reasoning.

Let us begin with the claim to racial authenticity — a claim Bush made about Thomas, Thomas made about himself in the hearings, and black nationalists make about themselves. What is black authenticity? Who is really black? First, blackness has no meaning outside of a system of race-conscious people and practices. After centuries of racist degradation, exploitation, and oppression in America, blackness means being minimally subject to white supremacist abuse and being part of a rich culture and community that has struggled against such abuse. All people with black skin and African phenotype are subject to potential white-supremacist abuse. Hence, all black Americans have some interest in resisting racism — even if their interest is confined solely to themselves as individuals rather than to larger black communities. Yet how this "interest" is defined and how individuals and communities are understood vary. So any claim to black authenticity — beyond being the potential object of racist abuse and heir to a grand tradition of black struggle — is contingent on one's political definition of black interest and one's ethical understanding of how this interest relates to individuals and communities in and outside black America. In short, blackness is a political and ethical construct. Appeals to black authenticity ignore this fact; such appeals hide and conceal the political and ethical dimension of blackness. This is why claims to racial authenticity trump political and ethical argument — and why racial reasoning discourages moral reasoning. Every claim to racial authenticity presupposes elaborate conceptions of political and ethical relations of interests, individuals, and communities. Racial reasoning conceals these presuppositions behind a deceptive cloak of racial consensus — yet racial reasoning is seductive because it invokes an undeniable history of racial abuse and racial struggle. This is why Bush's claims to Thomas's black authenticity, Thomas's claims about his own black authenticity, and black-nationalist claims about black authenticity all highlight histories of black abuse and black struggle.

But if claims to black authenticity are political and ethical conceptions of the relation of black interests, individuals, and communities, then any attempt to confine black authenticity to black-nationalist politics or black male interests warrants suspicion. For example, black leaders failed to highlight the problematic claims Clarence Thomas made about his sister, Emma Mae, regarding her experience with the welfare system. In front of a conservative audience in San Francisco, Thomas made her out to be a welfare scrounger dependent on state support. Yet, like most black women in American history, Emma Mae is a hardworking person, sensitive enough to take care of her sick aunt, and she was unable to work for a short period of time. After she got off welfare, she worked two jobs — until three in the morning! This episode reveals not only a lack of integrity and character on Thomas's part; failure to highlight it by black leaders discloses a conception of black authenticity confined to black male interests, individuals, and communities. In short, the refusal to give weight to the interests of black women by most black leaders was already apparent before Anita Hill appeared on the scene.

The claims to black authenticity that feed on the closing-ranks mentality of black people are dangerous precisely because this closing of ranks is usually done at the expense of black women. It also tends to ignore the divisions of class and sexual orientation in black America—divisions that require attention if *all* black interests, individuals, and communities are to be taken into consideration. Thomas's conservative Republican politics does not promote a closing-ranks mentality; instead, his claim to black authenticity is for the purpose of self-promotion, to gain power and prestige. All his professional life he has championed individual achievement and race-free standards. Yet when he saw his ship sinking, he played the racial card of black victimization and black solidarity at the expense of Anita Hill. Like his sister Emma Mae, Anita Hill could be used and abused for his own self-interested conception of black authenticity and racial solidarity.

Thomas played this racial card with success—first with appeals to his victimization in Jim Crow Georgia and later to his victimization by a "high-tech lynching"—primarily because of the deep cultural conservatism in white and black America. In white America this cultural conservatism takes the form of a chronic racism, sexism, and homophobia. Hence, only certain kinds of black people deserve high positions, that is, those who accept the rules of the game played by white America. In black America, this cultural conservatism takes the form of an inchoate xenophobia (e.g., against whites, Jews, and Asian Americans), systemic sexism, and homophobia. Like all conservatisms rooted in a quest for order, the pervasive disorder in white and, especially, black America fans and fuels the channeling of rage toward the most vulnerable and degraded members of the community. For white America this means primarily scapegoating black people, women, gays, and lesbians. For black America the targets are principally black women and black gays and lesbians. In this way black-nationalist and black-male-centered claims to black authenticity reinforce black cultural conservatism. The support of Louis Farrakhan's Nation of Islam for Clarence Thomas—despite Faraakhan's critique of Republican Party racist and conservative policies—highlights this fact. It also shows how racial reasoning leads disparate viewpoints in black America to the same dead end—with substantive ethical principles and savvy, wise politics left out.

The undermining and dismantling of the framework of racial reasoning—especially the basic notions of black authenticity, the closing-ranks mentality, and black cultural conservatism—leads toward a new framework for black thought and method. This new framework should be a *prophetic* one of moral reasoning, with its fundamental ideas of a mature black identity, coalition strategy, and black cultural democracy. Instead of cathartic appeals to black authenticity, a prophetic viewpoint bases mature black self-love and self-respect on the moral quality of black responses to undeniable racist degradation in the American past and present. These responses assume neither a black essence that all black people share nor one black perspective to which all black people should adhere. Rather, a prophetic framework encourages *moral* assessment of the variety of perspectives held by black people and selects those views based on black dignity and decency that eschew putting any group of people or culture on a pedestal or in the gutter. Instead, blackness is understood to be either the perennial possibility of white-supremacist abuse or the distinct styles and dominant modes of expression found in black cultures and communities. These styles and modes are diverse—yet they do stand apart from those of other groups (even as they are shaped by and shape those of other groups). And all such styles and modes stand in need of ethical evaluation. Mature black identity results from an acknowledgment of the specific black responses to white-supremacist abuses and a moral assessment of these responses such that the humanity of black people does not rest on deifying or demonizing others.

Instead of a closing-ranks mentality, a prophetic framework encourages a coalition strategy that solicits genuine solidarity with those deeply committed to antiracist struggle. This strategy is neither naive nor opportunistic; black suspicion of whites, Latinos, Jews, and Asian Americans runs deep for historical reasons. Yet there are slight though significant antiracist traditions among whites, Asian Americans, and especially Latinos, Jews, and indigenous people that must not be cast aside. Such coalitions are important precisely because they not only enhance the plight of black people but also because they enrich the quality of life in the country.

Lastly, a prophetic framework replaces black cultural conservatism with black cultural democracy. Instead of authoritarian sensibilities that subordinate women or degrade gays and lesbians, black cultural democracy promotes the equality of black women and men and the humanity of black gays and lesbians. In short, black cultural democracy rejects the pervasive patriarchy and homophobia in black American life.

If most black leaders had adopted a prophetic framework of moral reasoning rather than a narrow framework of racial reasoning, the debate over the Thomas–Hill hearings would have proceeded in a quite different manner in black America. For example, both Thomas and Hill would be viewed as two black conservative supporters of some of the most vicious policies to beseige black working and poor communities since Jim and Jane Crow segregation. Both Thomas and Hill supported an unprecedented redistribution of wealth from working people to well-to-do people in the form of regressive taxation, deregulation policies, cutbacks and slowdowns in public service programs, takebacks at the negotiation table between workers and management, and military build-ups at the Pentagon. Both Thomas and Hill supported the unleashing of unbridled capitalist market forces on a level never witnessed before in this country that have devastated black working and poor communities. These market forces took the form principally of unregulated corporative and financial expansion and intense entrepreneurial activity. This tremendous ferment in big and small businesses — including enormous bonanzas in speculation, leveraged buy-outs and mergers, as well as high levels of corruption and graft — contributed to a new kind of culture of consumption in white and black America. Never before has the seductive market way of life held such sway in nearly every sphere of American life. This market way of life promotes addictions to stimulation and obsessions with comfort and convenience. These addictions and obsessions — centered primarily around bodily pleasures and status rankings — constitute market moralities of various sorts. The common denominator is a rugged and ragged individualism and rapacious hedonism in quest of a perennial "high" in body and mind.

In the hearings Clarence Thomas emerged as the exemplary hedonist, addicted to pornography and captive to a stereotypical self-image of the powerful black man who revels in sexual prowess in a racist society. Anita Hill appears as the exemplary careerist addicted to job promotion and captive to the stereotypical self-image of the sacrificial black woman who suffers silently and alone. There should be little doubt that Thomas's claims are suspect — those about his sister, his eighteen-year silence about *Roe* v. *Wade*, his intentions in the Heritage Foundation speech praising the antiabortion essay by Lewis Lehrman, and the contours of his conservative political philosophy. Furthermore, his obdurate stonewalling in regard to his private life was symptomatic of all addicts — passionate denial and irrational cover-up. There also should be little doubt that Anita Hill's truth-telling was a break from her careerist ambitions. On the one hand, she strikes me as a person of integrity and honesty. On the other hand, she indeed put a premium on job advancement — even at painful personal cost. Yet her speaking out disrupted this pattern of behavior and she found herself supported only by people who opposed the very conservative policies she otherwise championed, namely, progressive feminists, liberals, and some black folk. How strange she must feel being a hero to her former foes. One wonders whether Judge Bork supported her as fervently as she did him a few years ago.

A prophetic framework of moral reasoning would have liberated black leaders from the racial guilt of opposing a black man for the highest court in the land and feeling as if one had to choose between a black woman and a black man. Like the Congressional Black Caucus (minus one?), black people could simply oppose Thomas based on qualifications and principle. And one could choose between two black conservatives based on their sworn testimonies in light of the patterns of their behavior in the recent past. Similarly, black leaders could avoid being duped by Thomas's desperate and vulgar appeals to racial victimization by a white male Senate committee who handled him gently (no questions about his private life, no queries about his problematic claims). Like

Senator Hollings, who knows racial intimidation when he sees it (given his past experiences with it), black leaders could see through this rhetorical charade and call a moral spade a moral spade.

Unfortunately, most of black leadership remained caught in a framework of racial reasoning — even when they opposed Thomas and/or supported Hill. Rarely did we have a black leader highlight the moral content of a mature black identity, accent the crucial role of coalition strategy in the struggle for justice, or promote the ideal of black cultural democracy. Instead, the debate evolved around glib formulations of a black "role model" based on mere pigmentation, an atavistic defense of blackness that mirrors the increasing xenophobia in American life and a silence about the ugly authoritarian practices in black America that range from sexual harassment to indescribable violence against women. Hence, a grand opportunity for substantive discussion and struggle over race and gender was missed in black America and the larger society. And black leadership must share some of the blame. As long as black leaders remain caught in a framework of racial reasoning, they will not rise above the manipulative language of Bush and Thomas — just as the state of siege (the death, disease, and destruction) raging in much of black America creates more wastelands and combat zones. Where there is no vision, the people perish; where there is no framework of moral reasoning, the people close ranks in a war of all against all. The growing gangsterization of America results in part from a market-driven racial reasoning prevalent from the White House to the projects. In this sense, George Bush, David Duke, and gangster rap artists speak the same language from different social locations — only racial reasoning can save us. Yet I hear a cloud of witnesses from afar — Sojourner Truth, Wendell Phillips, Emma Goldman, A. Philip Randolph, Ella Baker, Fannie Lou Hamer, Michael Harrington, Abraham Joshua Heschel, Tom Hayden, Harvey Milk, Robert Moses, Barbara Ehrenreich, Martin Luther King, Jr., and many anonymous others — who championed the struggle for freedom and justice in a prophetic framework of moral reasoning. They understood that the pitfalls of racial reasoning are too costly in mind, body, and soul — especially for a downtrodden and despised people like black Americans. The best of our leadership have recognized this valuable truth — and more must do so in the future if America is to survive with any moral sense.

SOCIALIST-FEMINIST AND ANTIRACIST POLITICS:
Toward Sexual Democracy

Ann Ferguson

Ann Ferguson suggests that both assimilationism and separatism have proven to be ineffective strategies for countering injustice. She argues for a third option: group autonomy and solidarity and coalitions between groups with some shared goals. She describes the goals that she thinks ought to be shared in the coalitions. (Source: From Sexual Democracy: Women, Oppression, and Revolution *by Ann Ferguson. Copyright © 1991 by Westview Press, Inc. Reprinted by permission of Westview Press, Boulder, Colorado.)*

Strategies for a Better Progressive Coalition Politics in the United States

Since the New Deal of the 1930s, there had not really been an effective coalition politics in the United States that has managed to challenge simultaneously our three primary systems of social domination: racism, sexism, and capitalism. From the popular-front anti-Nazi politics of the 1930s and 1940s to the civil rights, Black Power, student, and anti-Vietnam New Left politics of the 1960s and the women's and gay liberation movements of the 1970s and 1980s, there have been two conflicting tendencies in popular social movements: cultural separatism and van-

guardism on the one hand and coalitionist assimilationism on the other. Cultural separatism, whether it be the hippie, Black Power, student "free university," or lesbian separatist movements, involves rejecting the hegemony of the dominant culture by creating a culture of resistance that defines its values, visions, and priorities independently of the dominant culture. Usually those involved in such cultural movements have also developed a sense of themselves as a vanguard of change for those fellow victims of oppression still locked in the false consciousness of the dominant culture. Marxist sectarian socialist parties have also been vanguardist, though their concern has been less with building an oppositional culture than with party formation.

The other pole of popular social movements, assimilationism, attempts to find a niche for oppressed groups by extending to them the values and opportunities open to dominants in the status quo. This has often involved a coalitionist and integrationist strategy. For example, while black nationalism tried to set up Black Power community schools outside of the public school system to reinforce the idea that "black is beautiful," liberal antiracists like the Southern Christian Leadership Conference, the National Urban League, and the National Association for the Advancement of Colored People (NAACP) worked to integrate the public schools. Similarly, while radical feminists set up autonomous women's community schools that would empower women to challenge male domination, liberal feminists' organizations like the National Organization of Women and the National Women's Political Caucus (NWPC) supported abortion rights, the Equal Rights Amendment, and affirmative action initiatives to guarantee women equal access to higher education and jobs.

Although separatist and assimilationist tendencies are both necessary tools to organize certain popular sectors, neither alone can prove an effective avenue for radical social change of the sort needed to eliminate racism, sexism, and economic class inequalities in this country. Separatist politics tends to focus on building a counterculture of pride and resistance. But such countercultures, though necessary, are not sufficient for change: They can be repressed by the coercive state apparatus, as were the Black Panthers, or co-opted by consumerist capitalism, as have some women's businesses. Or else they are rendered ineffective by the structural forces of the dominant system, for example, black unemployment, inferior schools in the ghettos, and the sexual division of wage labor in which women's work is paid less than men's. Because the majority of people tend to be influenced more by status quo economic, political, and social structures than by countercultures, there is also the danger that the separatists lose contact with the "troops" they are trying to empower and become static, self-enclosed subcultures that persuade only a small minority to join them.

Mainstream liberal labor unions, black organizations, and women's groups, though they, too, are necessary institutions, cannot by themselves lead to real change because of their tendency to become co-opted. The legalization of collective bargaining in the Wagner Act has meant that national trade union leaderships end up enforcing the agreements made with management over more radical local unions and caucuses. Manning Marable (1985) documents how President Lyndon Johnson's Great Society reforms have benefited only a small segment of blacks, those in the professional and business class, while a huge underclass of people of color has developed (cf. Wilson, 1987). NOW and NWPC have spent much en-

ergy pushing for the passage of the Equal Rights Amendment, which, even if it were enacted, would not guarantee equal work for women: Only comparable worth legislation that guarantees that work of comparable skill in different job categories will be paid equally would be likely to do this. Furthermore, liberal feminist pro-choice groups like the National Abortion Rights Action League (NARAL) have defined the fight for reproductive rights too narrowly to deal with issues of forced sterilization, medicaid payments for abortion, available and affordable quality childcare, or even gay and lesbian rights—all issues that have greater impact on working-class and poor people of color than on middle- and upper-class white feminists.

In the 1970s the socialist-feminist women's unions attempted to deal with the dilemma of separatism versus assimilationism by distinguishing a third option: autonomy. The idea is that there is a dual need, both for a separate political space for members of an oppressed group (for example, women) to work out their strategy and for coalitions and alliances with allies of the dominant group (for example, men) in order to challenge the multifaceted nature of social domination in our society. We used to joke that autonomy meant that you had to go to twice as many meetings—for example, women's caucus or group meetings as well as mixed male and female leftist organization meetings. Another 1970s group, the Black Liberation Army, left its membership open to whites but explicitly involved anticapitalist and black nationalist politics. Autonomy, in other words, could be the mean between the two extremes of separatism and assimilationism, but only if social conditions provide enough ferment to allow for a principled coalition-building between groups also involved in organizing multilayered movements of resistance.

Unfortunately, the New Left social movements that socialist-feminists relied on to make plausible the autonomy option have dissipated in most areas of the country, leaving only pockets of activism, usually around solidarity with Central American anti-imperialist struggles, some progressive union struggles, and some local community-building projects of peoples of color. What remains is the initially hopeful but now mainstreamed presidential electoral campaign efforts of Jesse Jackson and the Rainbow

Coalition, some student activism around divestiture of stocks in apartheid South Africa, and small socialist and feminist organizations and projects like the secretaries' organization (Nine to Five), the Democratic Socialists of America, Solidarity, and the Reproductive Rights National Network. There are also radical gay and lesbian groups and networks (for example, the AIDS Coalition to Unleash Power, or ACT-UP), which because of their work in the AIDS issue have come to target the connections among capitalism, antiracism, and homophobia for the failure of the U.S. medical research and health care systems to deal adequately with the problem.

Though the situation for the Left in general, and for socialist-feminism and antiracist activists in particular, looks grim today, I think we should take heart from the recent radical upheavals in the state socialist societies of Eastern Europe, the Soviet Union, and China. After all, only a few years ago right-wing ideologues like Jeane Kirkpatrick were arguing that such totalitarian countries could never change from within, suggesting no hope for a democratization of those countries. If those countries can transform so radically and unexpectedly, what does this suggest about the possibility for radical change in this country? Though the Jackson coalition has lost its early promise because of its co-optive turn toward a centralized, hierarchical decisionmaking structure with the single goal of getting Jackson elected president, the Rainbow Coalition's initial success in connecting local activists around issues of gender, race, class, and heterosexist domination does show that such a populist movement is possible in this country and is just waiting to be organized.

Principled coalitions between dominants and subordinates are only plausible in historical periods of crisis when the systems of social domination in place in a social formation (in our case, capitalist, patriarchal welfare state racism) are increasingly unable to meet the material and social expectations the dominant ideology promises, even for those in prominent positions. Luckily for advocates of radical social change, the United States today is in such a crisis. Though whites' material and status interests have been constructed in opposition to those of people of color, and men's material and sex/affective interests have been pitted against women's, the contradictory values and realities of our society today, together with its growing economic crisis, set the stage for a massive historical redefinition and reconstruction of both our values and understanding of our material interests. We need to organize around a vision . . . which would resolve the current racial, class, and sex/affective contradictions of our society and begin to cure our class, racial, and sexual alienation.

We need a new coalitionist strategy that can develop a radical politics of the majority that nonetheless supports a radical pluralism. That is, we must understand the need for separatist cultures of empowerment for oppressed people as well as the need for a counterhegemonic culture with a general world view of a social alternative with which to replace the dominant order. We must develop a radical vision of an alternative United States that takes into account the demands of all oppressed groups and minorities and yet has a viable analysis of how such demands can simultaneously be realized. In my opinion the only feasible approach to this, given our historical values and present resources, is some form of decentralized democratic socialist society.

A progressive coalition should have as its basic operating procedure a commitment to participatory democracy. It would encourage an anarcho-socialist-feminist process in which self-defining caucuses of those with particular interests would separate from the whole to develop their demands and ideas, yet come back together in a coalition group or network. The coalition would have a common platform or set of demands developed out of the special interest groups.

Unlike the classical Marxist-Leninist strategy of vanguard party-building, our strategy of participatory democracy in leftist coalitions should not deny autonomous subgroups within such coalitions. It would differ from a liberal pluralist strategy both in its understanding that simple reforms to the existing state structure are not sufficient and in its inclusive rather than competitive process of defining the common interest of the coalition — not by the least common denominator but by the most common divisions! Less paradoxically, we can say that such coalitions would be looking to add rather than subtract differences from the group's agenda. For example, such coalitions should support the right to a gay or lesbian life-style even though only 10 percent of the coalition is lesbian and gay, and the right of single mothers to adequate child support payments even though single mothers are a minority of the coalition. The coalition should be proud of its diversity — in fact should think of itself as representing the majority of people by protecting a number of special interest groups (workers, lesbians and gays, women, racial minorities, single mothers, the homeless, the poor) that together make up a majority of the population of the United States.

Is it plausible to maintain that men and women, on the one hand, and blacks and whites, on the other, can work together politically to challenge sexism, racism, and capitalism? After all, the theory of racial genders . . . implies that these overlapping social domination systems give rise to differences rather than similarities in personal identities. Marxism, liberal pluralism, and separatist identity politics, such as radical feminism and black nationalism, tend to assume unified theories of self, thus supposing that interest groups that are in conflict with one another cannot be involved in coalition politics. The feminist aspect theory of self that I maintain, however, holds that there is no unified theory of self. This connects to the view that there is no unified gender, racial, or class identity that automatically cuts across lines of the other two categories. Rather, whether one sees oneself as unified or divided by gender, race, or class differences is relative to particular social practices.

Thus, even though men are opposed to women, blacks and other racial minorities are opposed to whites, gays to straights, and different economic classes are opposed in some key social practices in the state, family, economy, and community, in other practices we may be allied. That is, our interests may be adversarial in some ways and blend in others. The structure of left-wing organizations and coalitions must acknowledge the need to struggle about the oppositional aspects and interests of gender, race, sexual preference, and class. We must also build countercultural practices that do not reproduce privilege and that support an incorporative sense of the merging of individual with common interests in the group.

In effect our coalitions must forge a new counter-hegemonic collective identity for their members to redefine our interests as intertwined through the egalitarian and participatory political practices of our coalitions. At the same time it must acknowledge the right, for members whose social identities in the larger hegemonic culture subject them to oppression, to meet separately in order to articulate their ongoing concerns for the coalition based on their experiences of oppression. Indeed, it is likely that single-issue organizing around particular constituencies (e.g., labor union issues, reproductive rights, violence against women, racist incidents, etc.) will continue, with effective multi-issue coalitions forming occasionally for national demonstrations or around certain candidates for local and national elections.

. . .

A Transitional Morality for a Leftist Feminist Counterculture

One of the strengths of the U.S. women's movement of the 1960s and 1970s was its emphasis on examining the personal as a site of political power relations, thus resisting the neat dichotomy between public and private that is usually invoked to cut off discussion of sexism, racism, or homophobia. In the 1980s the feminist sex debate between those opposing pornography, S/M practices, and man–boy love and those supporting a pluralist right to choose has problematized the easy slogan "The personal is the political." After all, shouldn't we be able to make alliances with those whose adult consensual sexual choices don't agree with ours? And if so, don't we need to resurrect some distinction between those aspects of the personal that legitimately should be politicized (advocated or forbidden) and those that should be left to private preference?

Although it seems an obvious move to minimize our political disagreements over sexual differences by redrawing the line between the personal and the political, the question remains where and how to draw the line. In *Blood at the Root* (1989a) I suggested doing this by distinguishing between basic, risky, and forbidden practices from a feminist point of view, which assumes that it is a personal decision to engage in basic and risky practices but that forbidden practices should be politically challenged.

Just as we need to redraw the line between the personal and the political, I maintain that we need to redraw the line between the moral and the political. As a New Left coalition has to develop a counterhegemonic culture of participatory democracy to oppose the elitist values of our existing system, we need to engage the hope and imagination of masses of people by a new vision of an ideal society to strive for as well as a transitional morality of appropriate ways to live our lives in the process of struggling for a democratic socialism. . . . A set of such understood values as bottom-line ways of treating allies is central to the building of a populist antiracist, antisexist politics. Opportunistic strategies such as those commonly practiced in electoral politics are simply insufficient to galvanize individuals to the kind of self- and collective sacrifices needed for a total reconstruction of the values of dominant culture.

The transitional morality I advocate supports a cultural pluralism in sexual life-styles and personal life choices, as long as these life-styles don't substantially infringe on others' rights to respect and self-determination. *Respect, self-determination,* and *pluralism* are the three key values of a transitional morality for a coalition aiming at an overthrow of the existing capitalist, racist, and patriarchal structures.[1] Justice for various oppressed groups requires that each be able to develop its own voice, sense of self, and political agenda. The model for political interaction between dominants and (former) subordinates in the coalition should be a process in which the arbitrary one-way imposition of authority, the perpetuation of stereotypes, and the refusal of respect for diverse cultures are all constantly questioned (cf. Terry, 1972). Whites, men, and middle- and upper-class people must learn to see themselves as collaborators rather than bosses in this process. We must learn how to cede some of our structural and personal power in the service of a more egalitarian communication process.

The adoption of these general moral values and the use of more pluralist decisionmaking procedures (e.g., caucuses, rotating steering committees, etc.) does not mean that there will not be disagreements about the limits of cultural pluralism or the extent to which identity politics may be allowed to subvert the common agenda of the coalition. For example, the coalition may decide to defend the rights of consensual S/M practitioners but refuse to associate with public displays of S/M regalia (whips and chains, etc.) on the grounds that these symbols may be misunderstood by the general public. The coalition may agree on the right to self-determination in sexuality by teenagers but not on the rights of adults to consensual sex with youth where there is a wide age gap. The coalition may agree to give its support to a public "take back the night" march against violence against women but disagree whether men should also be allowed to march and whether the coalition should support the march if the issue of racist violence is not addressed as well.

The limits of identity politics are indicated in these political disagreements (cf. also Weeks, 1985). Radical pluralism as a politics for organizing the dispossessed into a populist coalition has three limits. First is the problem of priorities. All of the identities politicized in recent social movements, including women, blacks and other racial minorities, lesbians and gays, and people with AIDS, involve different contents and political priorities depending on the other contexts of domination in which they are engendered. Thus we may disagree about what issues to prioritize.

Second, identity politics spawns a pluralism of identities, not all of which are compatible with a leftist coalition politics. The obvious reactionary identity political tendencies, such as neo-Nazism based on a racist Aryan identity, and the New Right "total woman," clearly have no place in the coalition. But pedophiles and sex workers present an issue, as do those advocating polygamy in the black community to handle the problem of a shortage of black males for marriage partners. A transitional morality cannot give us the answers to all the particular questions that come up about which identity politics to support, which to relegate to the "private" (risky) sphere, and which to reject. At most, it suggests a process of making these decisions by a dialogue honoring respect, self-determination, and participatory democracy in the decisionmaking process in which such difficult questions are raised.

The third problematic aspect of identity politics is that it is easily co-optable in the United States, with its ideology of civil rights and autonomy for minority groups. Passage of a gay rights bill, for example, may suggest that gay liberation has been won, even though legislation doesn't deal with other institutional ways that compulsory heterosexuality persists. Furthermore, capitalist commodity fetishism, by encouraging the production of women's music, race records, sex toys, gay pornography and so on can persuade members of identity countercultural communities that they can succeed in validating their identities by separatist tactics.

Only a determined and sophisticated radical coalitionism can mitigate these negative tendencies of identity politics. We can't simply reject such politics out of hand, for racism, ethnicism, sexism, heterosexism, and sexual repression will continue to create personal identities that are liable to be either co-opted or radicalized, depending on the political context available to individuals. Separatist identity policies, then, will continue to exist and will often act as a necessary eye-opener to the repressive aspects of our society for those who may go on to become radical coalitionists later. A radical coalitionism must create a political context that respects the autonomy of groups organizing around identity politics and at the same time offers an alternative structure that allows a countercultural space to act as a corrective for the co-optive aspects of identity politics and a negotiating space for creating solidarity between different groups.

A New Left Agenda for the 1990s

Our capitalist, patriarchal, racist state is in crisis. The transition that it represents, from family-based patriarchy to public patriarchy, has focused public consciousness on those formerly controlled by the patriarchal family structure (women, youth, homosexuals) and on families that do not have a patriarchal structure, particularly families headed by black, single mothers. In the 1960s, to rebel against their marginalization in state decisionmaking, these groups formed student, women's, gay liberation, and welfare rights movements. We need to revitalize these movements. The demands of the civil rights and women's movements have forced some institutional concessions for women and minorities (affirmative action and entitlement programs). This disequilibrium in the status quo has spurred the New Right to try to institutionalize its own reactionary program, for example, to dismantle affirmative action programs, to reverse *Roe* v. *Wade* as a constitutional protection of the right to abortion, to pass the Hyde Amendment to deny federal funding for abortion, and to cut welfare and social services. Although the Right has won some victories, notably the recent Supreme Court rollbacks on abortion rights and affirmative action, there will continue to be a social crisis around these issues, for women and racial minorities are not likely to have rights taken away without ongoing resistance (cf. Winant, 1990).

The United States is also in continued crisis with respect to its foreign policy. We can no longer afford the costly defense and imperialist interventional foreign policy favored by our political elites as well as even the minimal services we have come to expect in the welfare state. Precisely because the established equilibrium of domination relations at home and abroad seems less steady now, there is a real possibility for the development of strong New Left, feminist, and antiracist coalitions.

. . . [O]ur present social formation is based on a political economy of racism and a symbolic code of sexual racism as well as a sexist political economy and a corresponding sex/affective symbolic code. Strategies for challenging the hegemony of both of these features must be developed. And of course the persistent class of hierarchies of U.S. capitalism, based on income, status, and degree of control over work, must be confronted by a democratic socialist vision and agenda that rejects inegalitarianism and the false meritocracy on which it rests. As all three of these "isms" are increasingly interconnected, agendas to challenge one will ameliorate one or more of the others.

Challenging Racism

The perpetuation of a black underclass must be halted by federally funded community action programs such as job training and job creation in black, Asian, Latino, and native American communities that give members some democratic input into program decisionmaking.

For example, are houses for the homeless being built? If so, are those who are given jobs to build them as much as possible those who will live in them? Are they given input into their design? Are job-training programs for unemployed minority youth set up? If so, do the programs allow the recruits themselves some say in the sort of jobs they want training for? Or do they simply funnel youth into dead-end, alienating jobs? Is new money being supplied to inner-city ghetto schools? If so, who controls how this money is spent? Is there a real possibility of minority community input into the educational content and priorities of their children's schooling?

Racism is a cross-class phenomenon. Thus it must continue to be challenged by effective affirmative action programs and strong initiatives in public education that regularly examine and critique racism, that supplement the regular teaching of U.S. history by attention to the contributions of Afro-Americans and minority Asian, Latino, and native American communities of color. Courses on popular culture should highlight the contributions of all racial minorities to music and dance.

Challenging the Class Hierarchies of Capitalism

The fact that women and children will constitute half of all poor families by the year 2000 shows the overlap of capitalism and patriarchy and the need of feminists to take democratic socialism seriously as a solution to the poverty of many women. In the short run, the feminization of poverty must be stopped by legislating better economic supports: federally funded childcare, health care, and reproductive options (abortion on demand, no forced sterilization), job training, and available jobs to allow single mothers to escape from poverty. Further, the stigma of undeserving single-mother welfare recipients must be overcome by a system of general family allowances for those in lower-income groups. There should be a guaranteed minimum family income, regardless of the family structure or wage-earning status of the parents. In this way, the line between deserving and undeserving poor could be bypassed.

Classism and sexism could be creatively challenged by the same means: a comprehensive program of comparable worth to revalue work of comparable skill and importance that is now paid less because it is considered manual as opposed to mental, black as opposed to white, or women's as opposed to men's work. Revaluing job categories will help to dismantle the sexual, racial, and class divisions of labor that unfairly limit status, social opportunities, and income to those in work socially defined as "inferior."

Challenging Sexism and Heterosexism

Socialist-feminists know that challenging public patriarchy means much more than passing the ERA and affirmative action legislation. It must also involve a whole revamping of the social structures and mores of sexuality and the family. Three central trends in our society that we must find symbolic ways to validate are:

1. The separation of sexuality from reproduction
2. The redefinition of kinship, which involves a reconceptualization of the family or household
3. The redefinition of the public versus private, individual versus social distinctions

All progressive groups should adopt a political agenda that highlights the defense of sexual freedoms in the broadest sense — reproductive rights for women, defense of lesbian/gay rights, defense of consensual sex for minors.[2] At the same time we must define a New Left family politics based on the somewhat contradictory implications of the family as the site not only of sexism and heterosexism but also of resistance to racism and classism. How can we dislodge the New Right from its symbolic position as the defender of good old American values while also avoiding the liberal tendency to validate the paternalistic role of the welfare state in reproducing public patriarchy?

With respect to family public policy, a key ingredient must be to refuse traditional definitions of the family that may reinstitute patriarchal, nuclear households. This means that extended- and single-family households must not be seen as "the problem" the state is trying to resolve by increasing job-training programs for black youths (Joseph, 1983). We should demand that the state create opportunities for couple co-parenting — mandatory flex-time jobs, a minimum family income to replace AFDC, maternity and paternity leaves, comparable worth, community-controlled childcare—but we also want to respect the right of noncouples—single parents, lesbian/gay parents, and communal households—to raise children. In short, we need to redefine the notion of "family" so that these alternative households and others, for example, two-household joint-custody parents, are socially acceptable.

Two public policy initiatives would be to legitimize gay and lesbian families and communal households. Moves like those of former Governor Michael Dukakis of Massachusetts to prevent foster parenting by gay parents must be strongly opposed. Another policy initiative would be to grant tax breaks for communal parenting: Anyone living in a communal household with children, whether biologically related or not, would be given tax incentives designed to recognize their input into household childcare and finances. Such a system could replace the punitive AFDC system, which penalizes single mothers who live with men assumed to be the fathers of their children. Finally, domestic partnership legislation is needed that allows nonmarried cohabitors of the same or opposite sex familial rights, for example, in health insurance coverage, income tax status, and joint property rights to eliminate the economic privileges of legal heterosexual marriage.

A feminist sexual and family political agenda is incomplete without economic measures to equalize gender, racial, and class inputs into housework and childcare. The feminization of poverty is a strong historical trend creating commonalities between white and black single mothers, increasingly subordinated to a public patriarchal system. Reversing this trend will require a turnaround in Republican cuts in social service programs and an economic conversion of military funds to peaceful uses. . . . [T]here will have to be massive government spending programs, such as in job training for young people of color, improvements in public schools, and affordable quality childcare and health care. But there will also have to be a radicalization of the welfare programs and the tax structure of this country. Instead of welfare benefits, there should be a guaranteed minimal family income for all, subsidized by federal tax credits to families, whether or not they are working in wage labor.

The negative sex/affective patterns and symbolic codes of single motherhood—isolated mothers caring for children with little help from fathers or other community members—must be altered. This should not be attempted by hierarchical sex education programs in which adults berate teenagers about the negative aspects of single mothering. Instead, a feminist safe-sex and parenting educational movement should organize separate as well as mixed peer support groups for teenage boys and girls. Those for girls should include both teenage mothers and others and could be facilitated by adult educators who emphasize the self-determination of the groups in discussions.

Sex and parenting support groups could explore the meaning of fatherhood; problems of single motherhood; contraception and safe sex; co-parenting; lesbian, gay, and bisexual sexuality; lesbian, gay, and communal family households; and domestic violence, rape, and incest, as well as traditional sex education. Alternatives to nuclear families for single parents, such as single-mother support groups and childcare swaps, single parents sharing a household, and so forth, could be discussed. Demystifying venereal diseases and AIDS and encouraging the overcoming of romantic and patriarchal barriers to the use of safe-sex techniques should be the job of the adult educators.

An import part of opposing the New Right and questioning the patriarchal racist symbolization of welfare as handouts to the undeserving, sexually promiscuous poor is the battle to fund AIDS research and to educate the public so as to encourage safe-sex practices. AIDS is presented in patriarchal and racist ideologies as a punishment for carnal sins, a symbolism doubly effective because its initial target populations have been gay men, HIV drug users, and nonwhite populations. The connection to HIV drug users has caused a higher incidence of AIDS in nonwhite than in white communities in the United States (Patton, 1985, 1990; Watney, 1987). Though initial homophobia, racism, and classism have made it difficult for these high-risk groups to develop effective coalition politics, there are increasing efforts to build such coalitions that now also include feminists.

A counterhegemonic popular culture to defy racism, classism, and sexism must have a social life based on an interracial and cross-class community. This is not to say that minority communities will not continue to require their own autonomous networks, just as trade unionists need autonomous groups to organize the working class and feminists need both autonomous networks and the right to separatist lesbian feminist communities. But the necessary trust to develop the kind of anti-oppression coalitions described here calls for the rejection of vanguardist politics. Thus, though "Black is beautiful" and "Lesbians are woman-loving women" should be accepted as necessary self-affirmations of Afro-American cultural nationalist and lesbian-feminist elements, respectively, coalitions must attack uses of separatist culture that condemn interracial liaisons and claim that straight women aren't true feminists. In other words, effective democratic socialist coalitions can support only nondivisive identity politics, which upholds the need for autonomous identity-group organizing but rejects the strategy of total separatism.

Conclusion

Feminists and leftists with a class and race consciousness must realize that challenging the present social order involves both effective coalition strategies for uniting women and men across race and class boundaries and an explicitly socialist-feminist agenda for reconstructing the welfare state. This will involve creating populist programs, that is, federal- and state-funded self-help programs for lower-income communities with democratic participation by their members. Because such programs threaten white male elites and destabilize capitalist markets that resist democratic input where profitability is not the bottom line, such an agenda will constantly be subject to reaction and backlash by right-wing forces. Only if and when a full democratic socialist economy is achieved, perhaps initially with market socialism and then with the council socialist model . . . could we expect to institutionalize an antisexist and antiracist state. And even then we should expect that remnants of the former white male elite will be working to undermine such a state. Nonetheless, feminists and progressives must find ways to make political and friendship bonds across gender, racial, and economic-class lines to unite in the long, complex struggle for such a socialist, feminist, and antiracist program.

. . . Little did I dream of the changes that the United States would witness from the 1960s to the 1980s; civil rights struggles, anti–Vietnam War demonstrations, a students' rights and hippie countercultural movement, the women's movement, the gay and lesbian liberation movement, the environmental movement, and the world peace movement to freeze the nuclear arms race, to name a few. Nor did I envision the changes I would undergo in response to the crises in U.S. society: In my life the theoretical and political have become the personal.

Younger generations and those from other races and class backgrounds have histories different from mine and thus may see the past and future possibilities otherwise. In spite of diversity, however, momentous changes in the recent past show that equally historic changes are possible in the future. Only if we empower ourselves by a political process of questioning given authorities who have a vested interest in misrepresenting reality (the government, mass media, corporations, schools, churches, the wealthy elite) will we be able to understand the actual workings of the social systems that shape our world. We must find a way to build a popular democracy, one that shakes us out of our passivity, complacency, and despair. In grassroots community organizing we can begin to build a base for trust that will allow us to debate and to fight for visions of a better future.

Popular liberation struggles all around the world, from Nicaragua and El Salvador to Eastern Europe, China, and South Africa, show both the promise and the difficulty of challenging a given power structure. There are bound to be disagreements and internecine battles. Nonetheless, to attempt nothing is to gain nothing. We have made important steps in human rights and social justice since the 1960s. We cannot afford to stand by and watch this progress be erased by the New Right, nor can we rest on our laurels and assume that the job is completed until there is full racial and gender equality and economic democracy. History has shown that this cannot occur in a capitalist system.

History is less clear about the solution to current social inequalities. But we have no alternative: Either we attempt to transform history or history will bury us. We cannot retire from the odyssey for democracy and social equality. For our children and future generations, we must continue to develop a practical vision of a socially egalitarian United States. I have argued that this will take a democratic socialism committed to fighting racism and sexism. May my daughter, my stepsons and foster son, my students, and all children, white and of color, straight or gay, rich or poor, experience a more just, more egalitarian, and less hypocritical United States. Long live the new American Revolution!

Notes

1. Robert Terry develops the ethic of respect, self-determination, and pluralism as an ethic of justice for "new whites" to adopt against conservative and liberal values that further dominate blacks or blame the victim by suggesting that black culture is to blame for racism (cf. Terry, 1972).

2. It is a hopeful sign of a coalescence of hitherto separate identity politics into more of a coalitionist approach that gay male rights advocates highlighted the importance of supporting the April 9, 1989, National Organization of Women's march on Washington to support the passage of the Equal Rights Amendment and to defend the constitutional right to abortion being challenged in the Supreme Court.

SOCIALIST FEMINISM
Our Bridge to Freedom

Nellie Wong

Nellie Wong defends socialist feminism, which she describes as a multi-issue feminism that can respond to the discrimination faced by workers, both as women and as women of color. She argues that neither feminism nor socialism can solve this discrimination by themselves, but that together they are a powerful force. (Source: From Third World Women and the Politics of Feminism, *ed. Chandra Talpade Mohanty, Ann Russo, and Lourdes Torres. Copyright © 1991 by University of Indiana Press. Reprinted by permission.)*

We work for enough to live each day,
    Without a day off, like the labor laws say.
The price of noodles, 12 hours' work don't pay,
    So, change our working conditions. Hey!

(Refrain)
Fellow workers, get it together,
    For prosperity in our land
Fellow workers, rise up together,
    To right things by our hand.

When we get our monthly paychecks,
    Our monthly worries merely grow,
Most of it goes for some rice and the rent —
    Our private debts we still owe.

Lifeless, as if they were poisoned,
    Are those fine young men,
Who once promised to work hard for us —
    Oh, revive your lost bravery again.

    Song of factory women, February 1973
    ("Change Our Working Conditions" 1982, 13)

This song illustrates only one of many working-class struggles being waged by women throughout the world. It shows that Korean women workers recognize their multi-issue oppression; their low wages won't pay for the price of noodles, their monthly paychecks do not alleviate their ongoing private debts, and they must take action into their own hands, independent from the men in their lives who act as if they were "poisoned" by their government's antilabor stance. South Korea's leading exports are textiles, shoes, and electronic goods — industries with a mostly female work force ("Change" 1982, 13). A primarily female work force has helped maintain Korea's economic growth. However, women workers are the lowest-paid and work under the bleakest conditions. Sister workers in the Philippines, Singapore, Japan, Hong Kong, and Taiwan also suffer long hours, unpaid overtime, and sexual harassment. The conditions of Korea's women workers are typical of the majority of Asia's industrial workers.

Women continue to be a part of the ongoing liberation movements throughout the world. In 1982, during International Women's Day, I spoke at a public forum sponsored by the Anti–Family Protection Act Coalition in Los Angeles, California, where I paid tribute to international working women:

Women workers started the Russian Revolution.

Women workers sparked the shipyard strikes in Poland.

Women workers and housewives marched by the thousands to protest the inhumane, antiwoman repression in Iran.

Women workers protested the sexist antiworker conditions in textile factories in Korea.

Women militants fought the Kisaeng tourism/prostitution in Korea.

Women workers formed a 100-year marriage resistance in Kwangtung, China.

Women fighters, young and old, fought in liberation struggles in Vietnam, Nicaragua, Cuba, El Salvador, South Africa, Lebanon.

Women workers are fighting to end nuclear testing in the Marshall Islands.

And in the United States, women continue to participate on all political fronts, from reproductive rights to union organizing, for social, economic, political, racial, and sexual equality.

Diné and Hopi women, mostly grandmothers and mothers, in 1986 were leading the resistance to the U.S. government's forced "relocation" from Big Mountain,

Arizona, of people from ancestral homelands in an area jointly held by the Navajo and Hopi nations. Giant energy corporations such as Peabody Coal, Kerr McGee, and Exxon want unhampered access to the estimated 44 billion tons of high-grade coal and deposits of oil, natural gas, and uranium found on and around Big Mountain (O'Gara and Hodderson, 1986).

The resistance of women is nothing new; however, it must be seen in the context of political, social, and economic conditions in which the total emancipation of women, as a sex, is hampered. The liberation of women cannot be relegated to simply overthrowing the patriarchy because male chauvinism is not eternal, any more than racism, anti-Semitism, or anti-gay bigotry is eternal. They are all products of the historical development of private property, where a few had everything, and most had virtually nothing (Hill 1984, 19). Resistance to the patriarchal institutions of private property has always existed. Opposition to the current epoch's's patriarchal institution—capitalism—is, by definition, socialist. Without overthrowing the economic system of capitalism, as socialists and communists organize to do, we cannot liberate women *and* everybody else who is also oppressed.

Socialist feminism is our bridge to freedom. By feminism, I mean the political analysis and practice to free *all* women. No woman, because of her race, class, sexuality, age, or disability, is left out. Feminism, the struggle for women's equal rights, is inseparable from socialism—but is not identical to socialism. Socialism is an economic system which reorganizes production, redistributes wealth, and redefines state power so that the exploiters are expropriated and workers gain hegemony. Feminism, like all struggles for liberation from a specific type of bondage, is a reason for socialism, a catalyst to organize for socialism, and a benefit of socialism. At the same time, feminism is decisive to socialism. Where male supremacy functions, socialism cannot, because true socialism, by definition, connotes a higher form of human relations that can't possibly exist under capitalism. Revolutionary Trotskyist feminism sees the most oppressed sections of the working class as decisive to revolution—working women and particularly working women of color. This is the theory which integrates socialism and feminism.

Socialist feminism is a radical, disciplined, and all-encompassing solution to the problems of race, sex,

sexuality, and class struggle. Socialist feminism lives in the battles of all people of color, in the lesbian and gay movement, and in the class struggle. Revolutionary feminism also happens to be an integral part, a cornerstone, of every movement. It objectively answers the ideological search of black women and men. It is the political foundation of the new revolutionary vanguard: socialist feminist people of color (Hill 1984, 19).

As a Chinese American working woman, I had been searching for many years to arrive at the heart and soul of my own liberation struggle. As a long-time office worker, I was laid off after eighteen and one-half years' service with Bethlehem Steel Corporation, the second-largest steelmaker in the United States. As a Chinese American, one of seven children of Cantonese immigrants, I questioned over and over why our lives were shaped by racism and sexism and our oppression as workers in this country. Historically, our lives as Chinese Americans are linked to those of other Asians, all people of color—of blacks who have been enslaved, and who are still fighting for their civil rights; of Japanese Americans who were incarcerated during World War II; and of other groups of workers who were brought in to build America.

I did not have the opportunity to attend college immediately a   I graduated from high school. Economics, and the ⌣onfucianist and feudal ideology pervasive in the Chinese American community, dictated my taking a secretarial job at the age of seventeen. As a young office worker, I learned that my secretarial career was supposed to be temporary—that if I met the "right" man, got married, and had children, I would become a "real" woman fulfilling what society ordained; and that in itself, life as a woman worker had no value, particularly when that woman worker took shorthand, typed, and filed for a living.

My feminist consciousness began to take hold when I got married and when I began college in my mid-thirties while still working full time. Silenced most of my life, I began to articulate my experiences through creative writing courses. My seemingly personal and private deprivation and angst as a Chinese American working woman began to express itself in a social milieu—with other women, other Asian Americans, other people of color, other feminists, and other workers. What I had thought was personal and private was truly political, social, and public. What a jolt it was to realize what I had learned from a capitalist bourgeois society—through the public school system and the workplace—that as a woman-of-color worker, I was simply an individual left to my own capacities and wiles! What a revelation, as long in coming as it was, to learn that workers everywhere were connected to one another—that it was our labor that provided wealth for a few, and that a class analysis of our lives was essential to find the root causes of our multifaceted oppression.

My development to integrate all parts of me—my gender, my ethnicity, my class, and my worker status—grew by leaps and bounds when I joined Radical Women and the Freedom Socialist party, two socialist feminist organizations which integrated the study of class, race, sex, and sexuality as interlocking roots of the capitalist system. Not only did we study, but we were consistently active in the democratic movements for radical social change.

To speak seriously as one who is committed to building a socialist feminist society at home and abroad takes real change; it takes examining one's attitudes which have been shaped by a powerful capitalist system through the institutions of the state, the schools, the media, the church, and monogamous marriage. I had absorbed "my place." I had kept silent because I was Asian and a woman, and I had been determined not to appear too smart because I wouldn't be able to attract and hold a man.

Attending college at night as an adult, being married, working full-time, and organizing and socializing with feminists and radicals brought me to socialist feminism: the belief that unless every woman, every lesbian and gay man, every worker, and every child is free, none of us is free. Such is the beauty and triumph of radical, social knowledge. Such is the basis upon which I have committed myself to working for a socialist feminist society. Such is the foundation upon which the leadership of all the oppressed is being built.

Socialist feminism is the viable alternative to capitalism and world imperialism, which use sexism, racism, colonialism, heterosexism, homophobia, and class oppression to keep us down. Although revolutions waged in Soviet Russia, Cuba, Vietnam, Nicaragua,

and China have brought about changes, oppression against women, sexual minorities, and workers still exists. While we can learn from the gains made by women in countries where revolutions have taken place, many inequalities still exist, and nowhere have women achieved total liberation. Gay oppression and racism still exist in these countries, and there are far too few democratic freedoms. For example, abortion rights are denied in Nicaragua, as the influence of the Catholic church dominates in Latin America. In China, feminism—at least officially—is deemed to be a product of decadent, bourgeois capitalist society.

While true socialism is to be strived for in each context, socialism cannot exist within a single country but must be a worldwide system, supplanting world capitalism. The nations of the world are wholly interdependent, and without an international system of socialism, countries can share only their poverty, rather than the world's wealth. Worldwide socialism will break the stranglehold of worldwide imperialism. It will end the exploitation of one country for the profit of another country's capitalist class. And that is why the U.S., as the most powerful capitalist country in the world, dominates the global market, and why there is a need for a socialist feminist revolution in the U.S. Socialism alone is not the answer. Feminism alone is not the answer. There won't be a socialist revolution in this country without socialist feminists in the lead, and there won't be true emancipation of women without a socialist overthrow of capitalism. Socialism without feminism is a contradiction in terms (Hill 1984, 21).

Our oppression as workers is rooted in the capitalist system. As women workers of color, we get the message, loud and clear, that if we only pull ourselves up by our own bootstraps, we will "succeed" as members of a capitalist society, and miraculously, our multi-issue oppressions as women and people of color will disappear. Within the women's movement, bourgeois feminist ideology teaches us that if we take the path of *partial* resistance, we might just make it to the executive boardroom. And if we do, we can become one of the bosses to stifle worker militance, and to uphold the profit-seeking status quo. Or radical feminist ideology teaches us that if we just overthrow the patriarchy, women will truly be free. Radical feminism does not take into account the oppression of gay men and men of color.

Multi-issue feminism is necessary to fight back and win against all forms of oppression. As my Asian American comrade Emily Woo Yamasaki says, "I cannot be an Asian American on Monday, a woman on Tuesday, a lesbian on Wednesday, a worker/student on Thursday, and a political radical on Friday. I am all these things every day." We are discriminated against as *workers* on the economic plane, as racial *minorities* on the economic and social planes, and as women on all three planes—economic, social, and domestic/family. We must cope with the world and with men as a unique category of people—women-of-color workers. We have been subjected to humiliations and brutalities unknown to most whites or even to men of color.

Feminism, in general, and socialist feminism, in particular, do have a vibrant history of militant struggle in this country. Today, increasing numbers of women of color and their allies are calling for an end to racism, sexism, and homophobia. Black women, Chicanas and Latinas, Native American women, and Asian/Pacific women have already demonstrated to the world their capacity for taking upon their shoulders the responsibility for social leadership. This talent and drive stem directly from the triple oppression unique to our position.

Women leaders have emerged from the radical movements of the 1950s, 1960s, and 1970s. In 1959, a black woman, Rosa Parks, refused to move to the back of the bus, inspiring the Montgomery Bus Boycott. In 1974, a Jewish woman, Clara Fraser, walked out on strike at Seattle City Light to protest unfair working conditions. Clara won a seven-year fight against the public utility based on a historic suit of political ideology and sex discrimination. Her fight and victory inspired a class-action suit against the utility by many more women workers who were fed up with sexism and racism on the job!

In 1982, a Chinese-Korean American lesbian, Merle Woo, was fired from her job as a lecturer in Asian American Studies at the University of California, Berkeley, for openly criticizing the right-wing moves of the Ethnic Studies Department. Merle was fired unfairly, though she received outstanding stu-

dent evaluations and had been promised Security of Employment when she was first hired. Her firing, based on the pretext of an arbitrary rule limiting lecturers' employment to four years, was imposed upon two thousand lecturers throughout the university system. Although the Public Employment Relations Board (PERB) had ruled that Merle and other affected lecturers were to be rehired with back pay, the university appealed the decision. Merle then filed a federal complaint charging discrimination based on race, sex, sexuality, and political ideology and abridgment of her First Amendment free-speech rights, which were the real reasons she was fired. In 1984, she was reinstated at the university. Merle fought back by organizing with the Merle Woo Defense Committee, composed of people of various communities who believed in the necessity of unifying around all of the issues.[1]

Henry Noble, a Jewish socialist feminist man, also fought an employment-rights case in Seattle. After several years with the Hutchinson Cancer Research Center, Henry's hours were reduced to 75 percent time. Why? Because he actively and successfully organized a union with his primarily female coworkers.

The workplace, where workers—people of color and white—often work side by side, offers a social arena in which the struggle against multi-issue oppressions can take place. Clearly, class analysis and action strike at the heart of capitalist exploitation of workers, whose rights are denied as workers, as women, and as people of color. The economy of capitalism could not have survived as long as it has if it did not depend on sexism and racism to split workers apart, and on the immense profits from paying people of color and women low, low wages. After all, combined, we represent the majority of workers, and that adds up to a lot of profits (Hill 1984, 19)!

Our politics and strategies must be forged through political action independent of the twin parties of capitalism, the Republicans and the Democrats. It was two Democratic presidents—Roosevelt and Truman—who signed Executive Order 9066 and dropped the first atomic bombs on the Japanese cities of Hiroshima and Nagasaki during World War II. Militarism engenders profits. Defense contracts and the manufacture of guns, airplanes, and bombs perpetuate the warmongering drive of the capitalists, both Republicans and Democrats. A labor party could further our multi-issue political struggle, and that labor party must be led by women of color, lesbians, and feminist men. Its program would express the interests and needs of workers and their allies. It would provide an effective alternative and challenge to the boss-party politics dominating the electoral arena. It would be democratic. Anyone could join who agreed with the program, and it would be ruled by the will of the majority, not the labor bureaucrats.

But whether the road taken is via a labor party or some other organization or a combination of strategies for struggle, solidarity and victory will be realized only through the understanding that in unity there is strength. There must be solidarity and mutual aid between all the oppressed for the genuine liberation of any one group. But that unity can come about only if it is based solidly on the demands of the most oppressed strata. We need the unity of blacks, Native Americans, Jews, Chicanos, Latinos, Asian Americans, Puerto Ricans, the working class, the elderly, youth, women, sexual minorities, the disabled—all of the oppressed groups—to win our liberation.

And it is women, especially women of color, who are equipped by our bottommost socioeconomic position to serve as the vanguard on the way to solidarity. We must because nobody needs revolutionary social change as much as we—working women of all races and orientations—need it to survive. We can honor and support the revolutionary and working-class struggles throughout the world by building a socialist feminist revolution here on the soil of the United States. The American revolution will be decisive to international socialism because when U.S. capitalism is dismantled, world capitalism will be dismantled, along with its tyrannical and oppressive forms of institutionalized racism, sexism, and homophobia, and its global greed for profits. While we fight for a socialist feminist society, however, we must, at the same time, fight for reforms under capitalism. Reforms alone, though, are not enough, for they provide only a band-aid solution to the tremendous political, social, and economic problems that we face.

Radical labor history and women's history have taught us that women workers/leaders of all races will lead the way for our total emancipation, as shown in this poem titled "A Woman":

> I am a woman
> and if I live
> I fight and
> if I fight
> I contribute to
> the liberation
> of all Women
> and so victory
> is born even in the darkest hours.
> ("Good News" 1980, 19)

A new song of factory women, under a vibrant socialist feminist society, might go like this:

> We work for enough to live each day.
> With three days off, like the labor laws say.
> The price of noodles, 15 minutes' work will pay.
> So, our working conditions are better. Hey!
>
> (Refrain)
> Fellow workers, get it together,
> For prosperity in our land
> Fellow workers, rise up together,
> We've made things right with our hand.
>
> When we get our monthly paychecks,
> Our monthly worries do not grow,
> Some of it goes for some rice and the rent—
> Our private debts are part of the old.
>
> Spirited as they smile and work with us
> Are those fine young men,
> Who promise to work and keep fighting back
> Oh, our bravery is revived again.
>
> Sisters, brothers, we now have time
> To write and paint and dance together
> Our backs no longer ache from working all day
> We love our children, with them we learn
> and play.

Notes

This essay was first presented as a speech at the conference "Common Differences: Third World Women and Feminist Perspectives," held at the University of Illinois, Urbana-Champaign, April 11–13, 1983. This version contains changes and updates since that presentation.

1. In June 1986, Merle Woo was terminated with no consideration for reappointment from her position as a visiting lecturer in the Graduate School of Education, University of California, Berkeley. Woo has filed a grievance with the American Federation of Teachers

(AFT) based on UC's violation of her settlement agreement and the Academic Personnel Manual.

References

"Change Our Working Conditions." 1982. *Connexions: An International Women's Quarterly,* no. 6 (Fall).

"Good News for Women." 1980. *Asian Women's Liberation,* no. 2 (April).

Hill, Monica. 1984. "Patriarchy, Class and the Left." (Speech) *Discussion Bulletin* (of Freedom Socialist party, Los Angeles, California) 1, no. 1 (February):19–21.

O'Gara, Debra, and Guerry Hoddersen. 1986. "Diné Elders Resist Eviction from Big Mountain." *The Freedom Socialist* 9, no. 3:2.

Radical Women. *Radical Women Manifesto.* Seattle, Wash.: Radical Women Publications.

COALITIONS BETWEEN NATIVES AND NON-NATIVES

Haunani-Kay Trask

This article was first written as a speech to be delivered at the second Women of Color and the Law conference hosted at the Stanford University Law School in 1990. I was not particularly interested in coalitions but when asked by the conference organizers to address this issue, I began to recall the many times I had participated in coalitions and how most of them were short-term, issue-focused, and rarely concerned with Native issues. These realities, by themselves, were worthy of discussion. The revised speech was finally accepted for publication as part of the *Stanford Law Review*, 1991, but only after heated and prolonged debate between Law Review members who thought the article anti-white and those who thought it reflected the truth of our experience as Hawaiians and as people of color.

Haunani-Kay Trask describes the cultural problems that arose in forming coalitions between Hawaiians and non-natives, even when both groups had some shared goals. She goes on to describe the kind of attitude required for successful coalitions: trust based on past history and the honest exploration of racism and the history of exploitation. (Source: From From a Native Daughter, Colonialism and Sovereignty in Hawai'i *by Haunani-Kay Trask. Copyright © 1993 by Haunani-Kay Trask. Published by Common Courage Press. Reprinted by permission of the author.)*

Given our plight as Native, colonized people — including our numerical minority in our homeland — the politics of coalitions in Hawai'i are very telling. They reveal the separateness of Native peoples' histories from settler histories, and the resulting conflicts that arise when Natives and non-Natives work together, especially in the area of Native claims, including cultural claims as the first people of the land.

The most illustrative examples revolve around land. Native Hawaiians, like most Native people, have a special relationship to our *one hānau* or birthsands. Land is our mother whom we must nurture and cultivate, and who in return will feed and protect us. This ancient and wise cultural value is called, in our Native language, *mālama 'āina* — to care for the land — and is enunciated not only in our many land and resource struggles but also in our drive for self-determination.[1]

Immigrants to Hawai'i, including both *haole* (white) and Asians, cannot truly understand this cultural value of *mālama 'āina* even when they feel some affection for Hawai'i. Two thousand years of practicing a careful husbandry of the land and regarding it as

a mother can never be and should never be claimed by recent arrivals to any Native shores. Such a claim amounts to an arrogation of Native status.

Beyond this, non-Natives who insist they too feel *mālama 'āina* reproduce American ideology and its racist insistence that all people within America's borders are the same. To such people, difference is a threat, especially when those who are different claim prior, historical residence as well as mistreatment which must be addressed by those currently enjoying the fruits of genocide and dispossession. Predictably, *haole* Americans are furious when faced with the anger of long-abused Native peoples: defenses are immediately employed which turn on lack of direct culpability; or arguments that injustice occurred during previous generations, thus relieving the current generations of any obligation to address the legacy of conquest. Indeed, *haole* have been consistent in their refusal to learn about Native peoples. Many *haole* also resent what they see as a Native claiming of priority of residence. Part of "American hegemony" means that Americans believe they have a "right" to settle anywhere within American boundaries (and often beyond) and assert themselves on an equal level with long-time residents, including Natives. Additionally, in Hawai'i, *haole* are often nervous about their numerical minority (about 21 percent of the population), especially recently-arrived *haole* who are accustomed to majority status on the American continent and who feel suddenly outnumbered by darker-skinned peoples.[2]

For nationalist Hawaiians, the constant refusal of many non-Natives to understand their place — that is, who and where they are—means their claims of equal status as Natives, or worse, superior status over us, are nothing but racist arrogance. The historical reality is that no non-Native culture can claim origins in Hawai'i. For example, only Hawaiians have a language whose words, *kaona* (multiple meanings), chants, prayers, and sounds relate directly to Hawai'i. We are the only people whose religion and hundreds of gods come from the place, Hawai'i. We are the only people whose material culture was based on the magnificent lands and waters of Hawai'i. And most crucial in today's destructive world, we are the only people who can claim a cultural way of living with the land that preserved it for millennia before contact with the West began to despoil our birthright. No settler culture can claim this.

Beyond our cultural difference, the legal history of Hawaiians places us in a separate category from that of immigrants to Hawai'i. Politically, Hawaiians are the only people who have legal and historical rights to lands in Hawai'i based on aboriginal occupation. Additionally, we have trust lands set aside by the American Congress for our use. Like some American Indian tribes, however, we do not control these lands or their revenues.[3]

Predictably, most non-Natives in Hawai'i are ignorant and resentful of this history and our indigenous status. Such resentments are always just below the emotional surface in group organizing where strategy and tactics are debated and criticized. *Haole* environmentalists, for example, tend to get nervous when Hawaiians begin talking about our indigenous claims, about the influx of *haole* and Asian settlers who demand more housing and land when our own people are homeless in our homeland. Often, when discussion turns toward Native land claims merging with environmental concerns, Hawaiians will be told to "stick to the issue." But for many of us, environmental destruction is directly traced to non-Native control. Therefore, one way to address preservation of Hawai'i's bounty is to frame the issue in Hawaiian cultural terms. It would seem that, far from avoiding the issue, such an approach is advancing it by merging two views into one political strategy.

Of course, fear of Native issues often masks fear of losing control over the coalition. This fear exacerbates

the already *haole* cultural trait of being aggressive and dominating in meetings. In turn, this familiar behavior angers Hawaiians, making us feel increasingly distant and sullen. As a Hawaiian brother once said, in a burst of frustration at *haole* paternalism, "why should we try to talk to these guys when they are so stupid they don't even know what they did to us?" (The reference here is to the genocidal impact of *haole* contact on Hawaiians.)

In general, Hawaiians need to be wary of "wannabe" *haole,* i.e., those *haole* who want to be Hawaiian because they can't stomach being identified as *haole.* Wannabes, like other aggressors, usually still want control. Their statements, then, can still signal impending *haole* takeover of the group, the swift backgrounding of Hawaiian ways of framing and arguing the issues at hand, and the foregrounding of *haole* leadership with a token Native for public relations purposes. Over time, Hawaiians drop out of the group, but not because they possess few organizing skills, or are unable to understand the issues. Rather, they leave because of the racism and individualism of *haole* members who presume their views and ideas must naturally take precedence over those of Hawaiians.

What should be a respectful *haole* attitude toward us, one based on the humility of a student rather than on the arrogance of a missionary, is thus transformed into a wedge which drives Hawaiians *from* the group. We know from long exposure to such attitudes that it is simply not worth our effort to try to change them. The larger struggle which first brought us together is pushed aside while we wrangle over *haole* behavior and attitude. Because so much time is wasted and emotional energies expended on trivia, it is better to organize another group without *haole* input.

Of course, long-time Hawaiian activists know the few *haole* exceptions to this rule. We trust these people implicitly because they have endured over the years in struggle after struggle. *Haole* who honestly support us, do so without loud pronouncements about how *they* feel what *we* feel or how they *know* just what we *mean.* Moreover, they readily acknowledge our leadership since they are present to support us, not to tell us what to do and how to do it. These *haole* are trusted by Hawaiian activists precisely because their behavior over the years speaks louder than any sympathetic public statements on their part ever could.

In environmental coalitions, *haole* members tend to be liberal and middle-class, which means they haven't examined their racism, their presence in Hawai'i, or anything else about their cultural behavior and historic role as settlers. In fact, they are incensed when the question of their presence in Hawai'i is raised, or when they are challenged about their role in Hawaiian organizations. They want to be both one of the group while also dominating the group. That is to say, *haole* tend to take command almost without thinking about whether they should, and they tend not to doubt their correctness when confronted by opposing cultural arguments which, in any event, they don't recognize as cultural behavior.

In this situation, Hawaiian members of the group tend to feel resentment but not to articulate it, and therefore fail to make clear why and how strategies, agendas, and especially leadership styles should be different from those suggested by the *haole*. A kind of unfocused fighting results from this cultural divide. Often, Hawaiians tend to be from the poorer strata of island society.[4] Class problems (e.g., *haole* assumptions that small change spent on projects must be reimbursed, *haole* styles of speech that tend to be formal rather than informal, local styles of speech including Hawai'i-based pidgin) then co-exist with cultural ones, creating a growing dislike between the *haole* and the Hawaiians.

Usually, the issue for Hawaiians is love of the land, which translates into anti-development postures. For the *haole*, the issue is environmental, which means preservation or conservation, but not an anger and attachment that comes from deep cultural wounding of our ancient love for our land. These differences result in different emotional levels at meetings where Hawaiians will speak in a manner that *haole* find irritating or childish. For example, Hawaiians (including myself) often depart from agendas to explain feelings by telling stories of our past, our family relationships to the land, sometimes our genealogical connections to it. Often, we express ourselves in tearful statements or angry outbursts, both of which are common to our cultural ways and are understood by other Hawaiians to be normal.

Haole, however, are obsessed with control of meetings and feel embarrassed and threatened by these Hawaiian behaviors.

To keep these difficulties at bay, *haole* often insist on tightly controlled meetings and agendas. They want orderly rules of procedure, including chairs, directors, minutes, and other structural impositions. Individuals may be more or less bureaucratic but their collective *haole* style is clear, and it is culturally derived.

Some examples. Ten years ago, I was involved in a coalition to prevent a hotel complex in an area called Queen's Beach. During the course of the struggle, I and others distributed over 5,000 flyers, organized community groups, spoke before various public audiences, and worked in a concerted effort over several years to prevent the resort.

Then, just prior to a public meeting which many *haole* were expected to attend, two white male organizers in the coalition asked me to withdraw from our presentation because they feared that as a Hawaiian nationalist I would be too "radical" for the audience. I argued that Hawaiians had first made the issue a public one and that if I wasn't too nationalist (whatever that means) to do basic organizing work, including the most repetitive and boring assignments, then I wasn't too nationalist to speak publicly. I won the day, but it was clear that as long as I didn't speak about Hawaiian rights issues I was on safe ground. As far as the *haole* were concerned, the coalition was to concentrate on non-Hawaiian issues.

In another case, a coalition formed specifically to unite Hawaiian land activists, *haole* environmentalists, and anti-resort community organizations began losing Hawaiian participation because several *haole* referred to Hawaiian groups as "less sophisticated" and in need of *haole* leadership and organizing skills. The anger and hostility generated by such comments and the general *haole* practice of patronizing Hawaiians was of such intensity that, at one flashpoint, people nearly came to blows.

These two small examples are representative of the cultural problems that arise during coalition formation. People don't behave differently in a coalition than they do in daily life. Racist beliefs continue to inform racist behavior: *haole* treat Hawaiians as childlike or threatening in their habitual, everyday interactions with us; in a coalition, *haole* continue to treat Hawaiians in a similar fashion.

Cultural humiliation or conflict is nigh impossible to resolve, especially when it is based on racist beliefs of Native inferiority and *haole* superiority. Hawaiians already feel bitterness and hurt because our lands have been taken, our nation crushed by the United States, our children forced out of Hawai'i by its high cost of living.[5] Those of us committed to recognition of our nationhood have evolved away from identification as Americans and, in many ways, despise all that is "American." When working with people who love American ways of life or have never questioned American culture, our underlying resentment of things American is bound to spill over into strategy discussions. This is especially true when the focus turns to subjects like "democracy" or "freedom," neither of which the American government, and most Americans, have ever allowed Natives.

The general ignorance on the part of *haole* about where they are geopolitically (i.e., on stolen Hawaiian land, not off the coast of Santa Barbara on a tiny vacation spot) and *who* they are (i.e., foreigners) creates deep-seated tensions in a coalition with Hawaiians. Thus our historic situation of oppression places us in a position where forming common ground with non-Natives, especially *haole,* means that we must suppress our true sentiments, that is, both our cultural and political nationalism, in order to make coalitions work. This is, for most of us, too high a price. Hawaiian nationalist participation dwindles or is maintained at a small level with the same people. *Real organizing of Hawaiians, then, takes place among Hawaiians, not in coalitions.*

For the last fifteen years, I have watched the coming together of community activists around land, including anti-nuclear issues, and independence movements. Each time, the same conflicts arise and each time, Hawaiians tend to leave the group. Hawaiian organizations form with Hawaiian leadership and Hawaiian values. These groups expand or decline based on Hawaiian strategies. But the most significant reality is that our organizing is around *our* issues, like sovereignty, control of *our* trust lands, and legal rights as Natives. It is a rare non-Native who wants to help *our* struggles in the way we decide he or she should help.

My personal participation has been in both kinds of groups, that is, in mixed and all-Hawaiian groups. I participate in coalitions but I do it rarely and only for struggles that I perceive to be of short duration. Most of my time and thinking goes towards my own people and organizing with and for them.

This brings me to some hard-won understanding. For Native peoples controlled by America, coalitions with non-Natives must be temporary and issue-oriented. We need to see such coalitions as immediate means to an immediate end, not as long-term answers to long-term goals. For example, sovereignty has always been and will always be the long-term goal of Native nations. Most settlers in Hawai'i, including Asians and *haole,* fear Hawaiian sovereignty since they see it as taking land and revenues for exclusive Hawaiian use. Hand-wringing about Hawaiian conditions is always preferable to repairing historical damage through the return of nationhood.

After two decades of protest and resistance in Hawaiian communities around the issue of self-determination and sovereignty, we have been able to force politicians and other political actors into a public discussion. Slowly and painfully and fearfully, some non-Natives have come out to support us. At this moment, there is an environmentalist/Hawaiian nationalist coalition that has taken a forceful stand on Hawaiian rights, including sovereignty. We will see how long this coalition lasts. Even now, Hawaiian membership in the coalition is dwindling.[6]

But in my view, this is not a bad state of affairs. Like Malcolm X, I believe white people should not join our cultural and political organizations. We must assert ourselves in our own way. *And this means organizational separatism.* The role of supportive white people — and this is almost a weary truism — is to convince other, non-supportive white people. In Malcolm's own words, "sincere white people" need to be "out on the battle lines of where America's racism really is — and that's in their own home communities; America's racism is among their own fellow whites. That's where the sincere whites who really mean to accomplish something have got to work."[7]

Unfortunately, very few white Americans take Malcolm's advice (perhaps because so many fear the truth of his analysis), but in parts of the Pacific, and in South Africa, whites have actually organized anti-racist, all-white groups to support Natives.[8] This kind of coalition is what *haole* need to form: a coalition of *haole* to support Native claims.

In this way, whites aren't present in Native groups; unease and resentment about their dominating style never arises. And Natives are free to speak bitterly or angrily or in any manner whatsoever without white constraints. More than this, Natives need political and organizational time to develop on their own path. This is a kind of self-determination that is practicable right now, in the present.

Finally, the historic role of white people and the global domination of their culture, including technology, popular culture, militarism and tourism tells us as Native people that we cannot trust the *haole*. For our own survival, we must take this as a general maxim to which only we can make exceptions. And these exceptions are to be decided *after* long experience and behavioral proof, not because some white people *tell* us they are sympathetic, or they have been involved in such-and-such a struggle with Indians, or they are one ten-thousandth Native Indian or Native Hawaiian.

And even when such proof is daily evident, we still need to operate on the principle that our organizations are to be led and staffed by us, to benefit us, and to reflect our cultural habits. In particular, Natives must beware of white liberals, particularly lawyers, anthropologists and archaeologists, and other scientists and technicians.[9] Always, we must trust our own cultural guides and ideas, particularly when we are told to discard them or to realign them with the *haole* world.

Unlike most *haole* Americans, I do not believe that cultural sameness is the best hope for human survival. Any kind of coalition-building that presumes this cannot be supported by Natives. In specific terms, this means coalitions must acknowledge not only difference but the necessity for struggle to *preserve that difference*. In Hawai'i, it would be unique to see non-Hawaiian groups joining Hawaiians in the effort to get State funding for Hawaiian language immersion schools, or to demand that we be given litigation rights in State courts regarding abuses of our trust lands, or that State and City agencies be required to hire Hawaiians (such as the University of Hawai'i whose

teaching staff is nearly 80 percent *haole*), or that the 20,000 Hawaiians on waiting lists for our reserve lands be given allotments and housing immediately.[10]

But we rarely see coalitions around these issues since they affect only Hawaiians. And yet, when non-Hawaiians want help to stop a freeway through their neighborhood, or to preserve a beautiful beach, or an area *they* regard as precious they expect, in fact, demand, Hawaiian support.

This is the situation I live in every day. A few coalitions respectful of things Hawaiian have been attempted. Some have succeeded, briefly. But, as I have already said, coalitions should be short-term and issue-oriented. For myself, as a Native nationalist, the only long-term coalition I could ever make would be with other Native people: first, my Polynesian relations, the Maori and Tahitians and Samoans; then other Native peoples like Indians and Aborigines; and then, Third World peoples.

If anything, this points up a truism: coalitions are made between groups that have some experience and some goals *in common*. I find, as many Natives have before me, that I have less and less in common with non-Natives. But if I work with my people and non-Natives work with theirs, it is not impossible for us to come together in certain instances. Both my sister and I, for example, joined the Rainbow Coalition. But our brief participation lasted only as long as Hawaiian issues were present.

In sum, I think coalitions need to be viewed by Native people in the context of immediate politics. To the extent that coalitions take us away from our people or divert our energies, they are a waste of effort and may actually be detrimental to us. At a certain early historical stage, coalitions with non-Natives may work. At later, perhaps more developed stages—when Natives are asserting their sovereignty, for example—coalitions don't usually work.

In Hawai'i, coalitions between Hawaiians and non-Hawaiians, especially *haole*, depend on a certain level of understanding of Hawaiian conditions and on a willingness to learn the oppressive role white cultural imperialism has played and continues to play in Hawai'i. But beyond an attitude based in such willingness, or respect, there is the larger question of political strategy. A violated Native people must always decide when, where, and even whether non-Natives can be trusted in any given political situation. The broader category of "coalition" does not address this issue which *always* needs addressing at many different points in any struggle. Supportive *haole* whose intention is to help Natives (rather than work out some personal/psychological problem, such as guilt, about being part of an oppressive white ruling class in a stolen Native country) generally understand the strategic necessity for constant evaluation of the role of *haole*. The decision, of course, must always rest with the Natives: *they* should decide the participation level of non-Natives. This is a lesson for organizing.

Let me end with another of Malcolm's insights that, like most of his wisdom, is both a warning and an invitation: "Work in conjunction with us — each of us working among our own kind."[11]

Notes

1. For a discussion of the traditional Hawaiian value of *mālama ʻāina*, see Lilikalā Kameʻeleihiwa, *Native Land and Foreign Desires,* (Honolulu: Bishop Museum Press, 1992).

2. See Nordyke, *The Peopling of Hawaiʻi,* op. cit., p. 105.

3. For a comparison of American Indian and Hawaiian land dispossession, including the conflict between cultural land values and American refusal to allow both Indians and Hawaiians to control their own land base, see Linda S. Parker, *Native American Estate: The Struggle over Indian and Hawaiian Lands,* (Honolulu: University of Hawaiʻi Press, 1989); also see Rex Weyler, *Blood of the Land: The Government and Corporate War against the American Indian Movement* (New York: Random House, 1984); Roxanne Dunbar Ortiz, *The Great Sioux Nation* (Cincinnati, OH: General Board of Global Ministries, The United Methodist Church, 1977).

4. *Native Hawaiians Study Commission Report,* op. cit., pp. 51–53.

5. As one example of this high cost, the Bank of Hawaiʻi reported that the median sales price for a single-family home on the most populated island of Oʻahu was $392,000 in August 1990. Condominium prices

were over $200,000 by the fall of 1990. See the Bank's *Hawaiʻi 1990: Annual Economic Report,* op. cit.

6. The name of this coalition is the Aloha ʻĀina Congress. Obviously, the title of the group is Hawaiian, but at this moment, most of the organizations affiliated with the coalition are non-Hawaiian.

7. *The Autobiography of Malcolm X* (New York: Ballantine, 1984), p. 376.

8. The support group called the Black Sash supported democracy in South Africa as an all-white organization. In New Zealand, the Maori sovereignty movement is supported by white groups and by other Pacific Islander groups who do not have Maori members but whose purpose is to organize to support the Maori among non-Maori groups.

9. Technicians, especially *haole,* must be directed by Natives or they will give technical advice that can be detrimental to Native goals. Archaeologists and anthropologists in particular can be dangerous since their professional training supports, for example, the exhumation of Native remains as well as other activities by museums, and colonialist kinds of institutions that view Natives as objects for inquiry rather than as human beings who deserve to control their own lives, communities, and ancestral places.

10. Hawaiians do not have standing to sue for breach of trust on their lands. This has caused much controversy over decades of political organizing in the Hawaiian communities. See the report of the *Federal-State Task Force on the Hawaiian Homes Commission Act,* op. cit., especially pp. 23–24. As of 1989, the University of Hawaiʻi faculty reported 13 tenured Hawaiian faculty, 659 tenured white faculty, 131 tenured Japanese faculty, 84 Korean/Chinese tenured faculty, 16 other, and 13 tenured Filipino faculty. Of the probationary faculty, Hawaiians made up 2% and *haole* made up 76% of the total. Figures are taken from the Biennial EE0-6 Reports of the University of Hawaiʻi administration. As of December 31, 1990, there are 20,807 pending applications for residential, agricultural, and pastoral Hawaiian Home Lands lots; see *Lease Activity and Application Status Report,* the Homestead Services Division, Department of Hawaiian Home Lands, State of Hawaiʻi.

11. *The Autobiography of Malcolm X,* op. cit., p. 377.